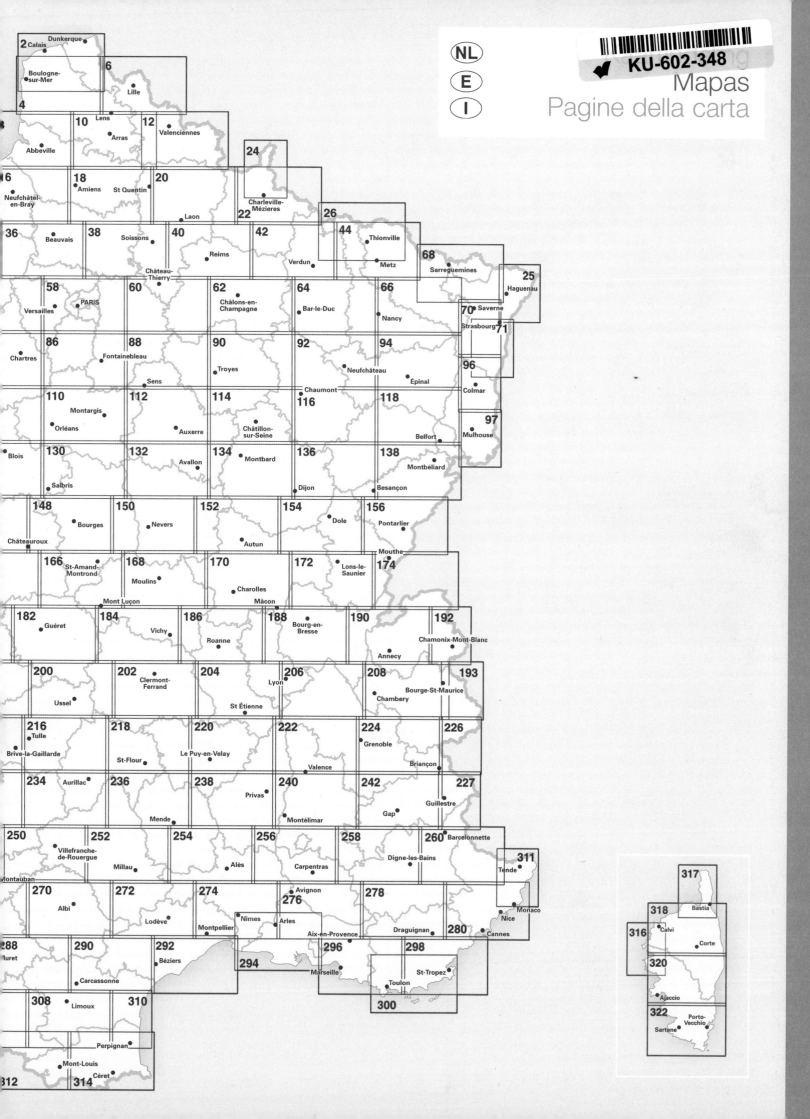

Mapas
Pagine della carta

Touring Atlas France

contents

Scale 1: 180,000
or 2.83 miles to 1 inch

Map pages	inside front cover
Route planner	II–V
Map symbols	VI–1
Road maps	**2–323**
Town plans	324–343
Paris	324–325
Key to town plans	326
Index to place names (Communes)	344–410
Département map	344
Distances and journey times	inside back cover

1st edition March 2001

© Automobile Association Developments Limited 2001

Maps © Institut Geographique National (France)

All rights reserved. No part of this publication may be reproduced, stored in a retrieval system, or transmitted in any form or by any means – electronic, mechanical, photocopying, recording or otherwise – unless the permission of the publisher has been given beforehand.

Published by AA Publishing (a trading name of Automobile Association Developments Limited, whose registered office is Norfolk House, Priestley Road, Basingstoke, Hampshire RG24 9NY. Registered number 1878835).

ISBN 0 7495 2575 4

ISBN 0 7495 2922 9

A CIP catalogue record for this book is available from The British Library.

Printed in Italy by Pizzi, Milan.

The contents of this atlas are believed to be correct at the time of the latest revision. However, the publishers cannot be held responsible for loss occasioned to any person acting or refraining from action as a result of any material in this atlas, nor for any errors, omissions or changes in such material.

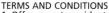

Route planner (GB)
Principaux axes routiers (F)
Übersichtskarte (D)

LA MANCHE

OCÉAN

ATLANTIQUE

LONDON
SOUTHAMPTON
PLYMOUTH
Exeter
Bath
BRISTOL
Newport
Reading
Portsmouth
Bournemouth
Brighton
Haverfordwest
Worcester
Warwick
Peterborough
Hereford
Northampton
Cheltenham
Gloucester
Oxford
Swindon
Cambridge
Ely
Thetfor
Bedford
Luton
Bury St Edmunds
St Albans
Ips
Colchester
Chelmsford
Windsor
Newbury
Basingstoke
Salisbury
Winchester
Guildford
Maidstone
Sheerness
Crawley
Tunbridge Wells
Canter
Dove
Folkest
Calai
Worthing
Newhaven
Eastbourne
super-Mare
Bude
Taunton
Launceston
Yeovil
Honiton
Newquay
Truro
Penzance
Falmouth
Torquay
Weymouth
Newport
Southend-o

Cherbourg
Valognes
Fécamp
Dieppe
Abbeville
Amie
LE HAVRE
Bayeux
Deauville
Yvetot
Rouen
St-Lô
Coutances
Caen
Beau
Granville
Lisieux
Avranches
Vire
Bernay
Evreux
Pontoise
Argentan
Mantes-la-Jolie
Roscoff
Lannion
Brest
Morlaix
Guingamp
St-Malo
Dinard
Dinan
Carhaix-Plouguer
St-Brieuc
Morgat
Quimper
Loudéac
Fougères
Mayenne
Alençon
Dreux
Versailles
Douarnenez
Pontivy
RENNES
Laval
Chartres
Nogent-le-Rotrou
Étampes
Concarneau
Lorient
Vannes
Redon
Châteaubriant
Le Mans
Châteaudun
Fontainebl
Pithivie
le Croisic
St-Nazaire
NANTES
Angers
La Flèche
Vendôme
Orléans
Noirmoutier-en-l'Ile
Saumur
Tours
Blois
Gien
Cholet
Selles-sur-Cher
La Roche-sur-Yon
Loches
Vierzon
Les Sables-d'Olonne
Fontenay-le-Comte
Parthenay
Châtellerault
Châteauroux
Bourge
St-Amar
Montror
La Rochelle
Niort
Poitiers
St-Denis-d'Oléron
Lussac-les-Châteaux
Rochefort
St-Jean-d'Angély
Bellac
Montluçon
Saintes
Guéret
Royan
le Verdon-sur-Mer
Cognac
Aubusson
Mou
Angoulême
Limoges
Barbezieux-St-Hilaire
Clermont-Ferrand

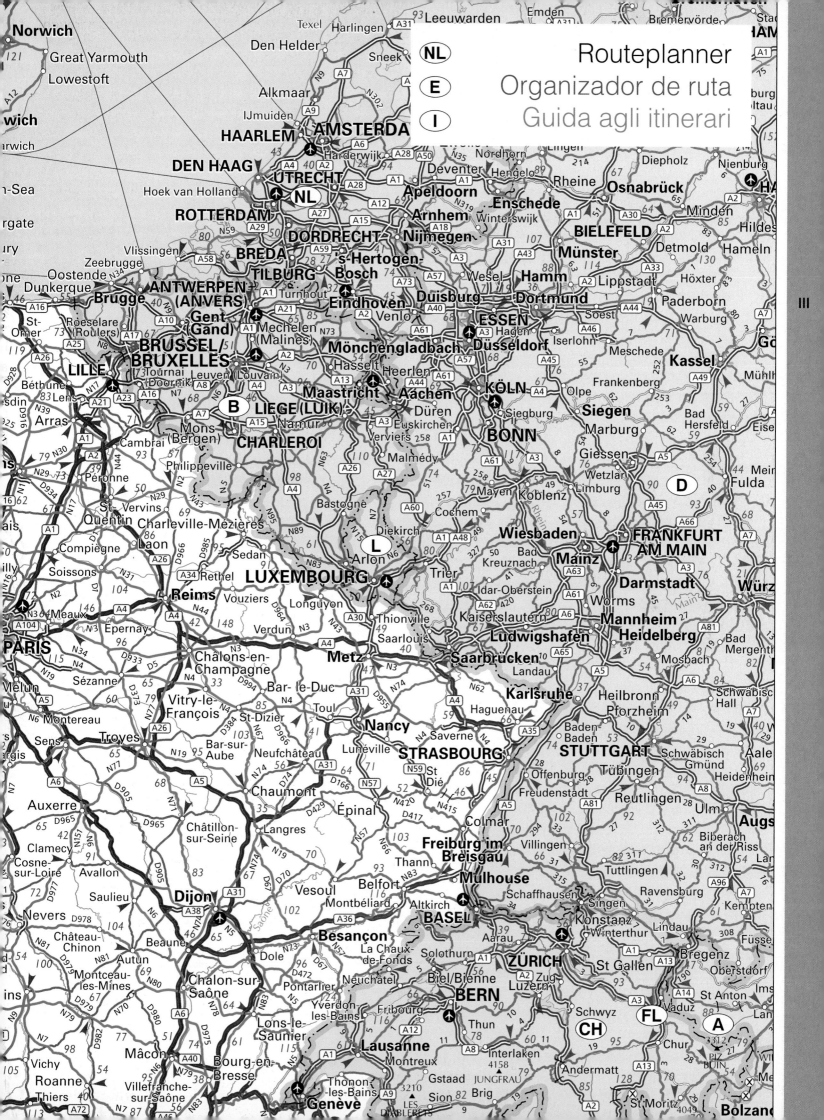

IV

OCÉAN
ATLANTIQUE
Golfe
MER
La Roche-sur-Yon
Les Sables-d'Olonne
Cholet
Selles-sur-Cher
Loches
Vierzon
Bourges
Fontenay-le-Comte
Parthenay
Châtellerault
Issoudun
Poitiers
Châteauroux
La Rochelle
Niort
Lussac-les-Châteaux
St-Denis-d'Oléron
Rochefort
St-Amand-Montrond
St-Jean-d'Angély
Bellac
Montluçon
Royan
Saintes
Cognac
Guéret
le Verdon-sur-Mer
Aubusson
Angoulême
Limoges
Barbezieux-St-Hilaire
Clermont-Ferrand
Ussel
Périgueux
Tulle
Arcachon
BORDEAUX
Sarlat-la-Canéda
Brive-la-Gaillarde
Mauriac
Bergerac
Dordogne
Langon
Souillac
Murat
Mimizan
Marmande
Aurillac
St-Flour
Figeac
Casteljaloux
Villeneuve-sur-Lot
Cahors
Villefranche-de-Rouergue
Sabres
Castets
Agen
Rodez
Castro Urdiales
Dax
Mont-de-Marsan
Condom
Bermeo
San Sebastián/Donostia
Biarritz
Aire-sur-l'Adour
Montauban
BILBO
Millau
Tolosa
St-Jean-Pied-de-Port
Lacq
Auch
Garonne
Albi
Vitoria/Gasteiz
Oloron-Ste-Marie
Pau
TOULOUSE
Castres
Lodève
Miranda de Ebro
Irurzun
Tarbes
Pamplona/Iruñea
Lourdes
Montpellier
Logroño
PYRÉNÉES
St-Gaudens
Carcassonne
Béziers
Tafalla
VIGNEMALE 3298
Bagnères-de-Luchon
St-Girons
Narbonne
3371
Foix
Benasque
Vielha
Quillan
PIRINEOS
Andorra la Vella
AND
E
Huesca
Perpignan
Benabarre
La Seu d'Urgell
Argelès-sur-Mer
Barbastro
Tremp
Berga
Ripoll
Sariñena
Ponts
Olot
Figueres
Balaguer
Vic
Tàrrega
Girona/Gerona
Lleida/Lérida
Manresa
Vilafranca del Penedès
Sant Feliu de Guixols
Alcañiz
Valls
Reus
BARCELONA
Gandesa
Tarragona
Tortosa
Vinaròs
Segorbe
Castellón de la Plana/Castelló de la Plana
Motorway, toll section
Autoroute, section à péage
Autobahn, gebührenpflichtiger Abschnitt
Snelweg, tol
Autopista de peaje
Autostrada, tratto a pedaggio
Motorway, free section
Autoroute, section libre
Autobahn, gebührenfreier Abschnitt
Snelweg, vrije sectie
Autovía en cada sentido
Autostrada, tratto senza pedaggio
Connecting road between main towns
Route appartenant au réseau
Verbindungsstraße zwischen wichtigen Städten
Verbindingsweg tussen grote steden
Carretera (comunicación entre dos ciudades importantes)
Collegamento stradale tra città principali
Trunk road
Autre route de liaison principale
Fernverkehrsstraße
Hoofdweg
Carretera nacional
Strada di grande comunicazione
Regional connecting road
Route de liaison régionale
Regionale Verbindungsstraße
Regionale verbindingsweg
Carretera regional
Strada di collegamento regionale
Distances in kilometres (km)
Distances kilométriques (km)
Entfernungen in Kilometern (km)
Afstanden in kilometers (km)
Distancias en kilómetros (km)
Distanze in chilometri (km)
72
0 kilometres 150
0 miles 100

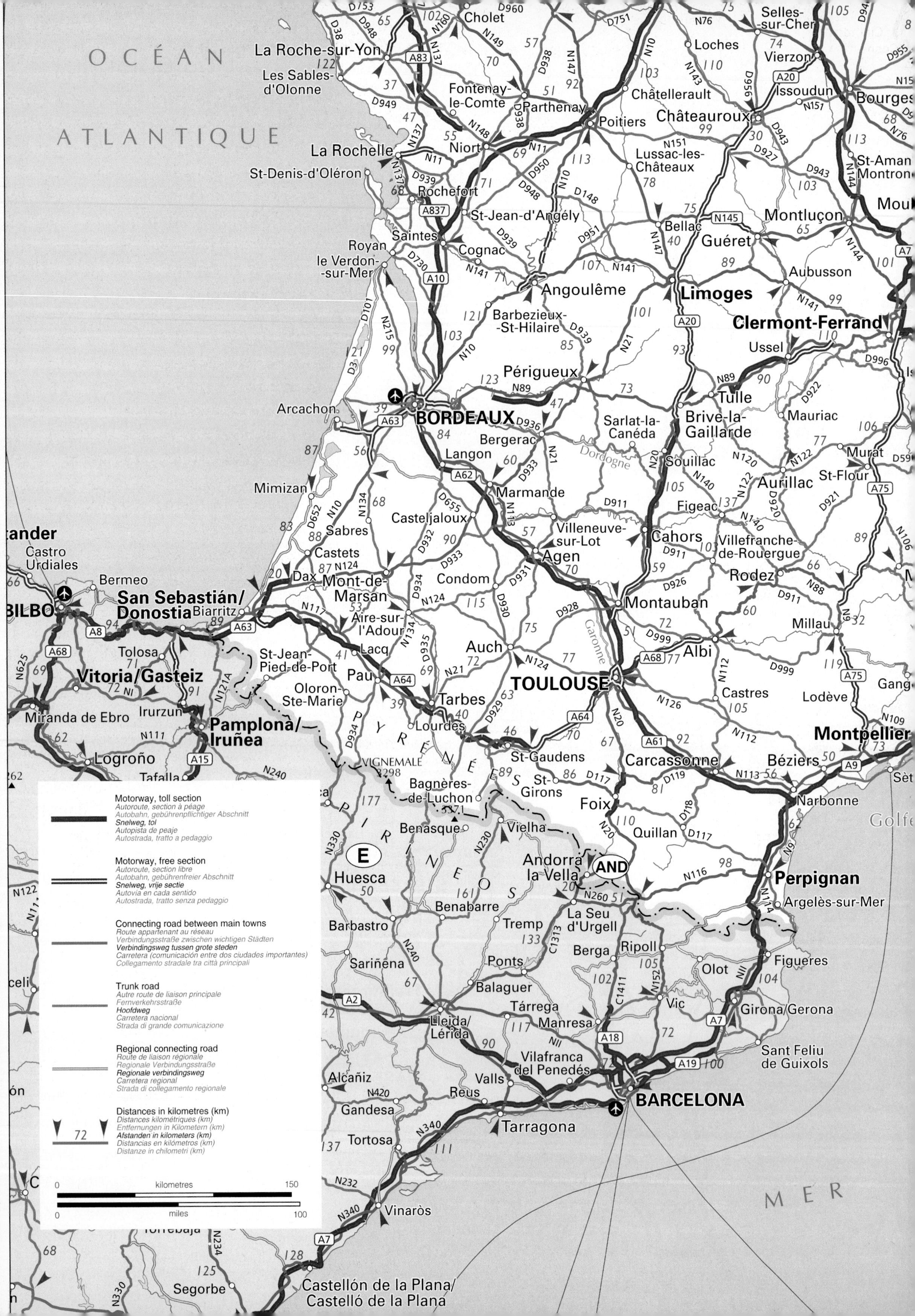

Châtillon-sur-Seine · Langres · Freiburg im Breisgau · Villingen · Biberach an der Riss
Clamecy · Avallon · Thann · Mulhouse · Tuttlingen · Ravensburg · Kempten
Cosne-sur-Loire · Saulieu · Vesoul · Belfort · Montbéliard · Altkirch · BASEL · Schaffhausen · Singen · Konstanz · Winterthur · Lindau · Füssen
Nevers · **Dijon** · Besançon · La Chaux-de-Fonds · Solothurn · Aarau · **ZÜRICH** · St Gallen · Bregenz · Oberstdorf
Château-Chinon · Beaune · Dole · Pontarlier · Neuchâtel · Biel/Bienne · **BERN** · Zug · Luzern · Schwyz · St Anton · Vaduz
Autun · Montceau-les-Mines · Chalon-sur-Saône · Lons-le-Saunier · Yverdon-les-Bains · Fribourg · Thun · Interlaken · Andermatt · Chur
Mâcon · Bourg-en-Bresse · **Lausanne** · Montreux · JUNGFRAU · Gstaad · Brig · Locarno · Bellinzona · **Bolzano**
Vichy · Roanne · Thiers · Villefranche-sur-Saône · **Genève** · Thonon-les-Bains · LES DIABLERETS · Sion · Martigny · Domodóssola · Lugano · Sondrio · Édolo
Feurs · Annecy · Cluses · MATTERHORN/MONTE CERVINO · Varese · Lecco · Como · **Bergamo**
LYON · Aix-les-Bains · Albertville · MONT BLANC · Aosta · Biella · Ivréa · **MILANO** · **BRÉSCIA** · **VERONA**
ST-ÉTIENNE · Vienne · Voiron · Val d'Isère · **Novara** · Vercelli · Vigévano · Lodi
Ambert · Grenoble · Modane · Susa · **TORINO** · Casale Monferrato · Pavia
Yssingeaux · Romans-sur-Isère · **Valence** · Briançon · Pinerolo · **Alessándria** · Asti · **Piacenza** · **Parma**
le Puy-en-Velay · Die · MT PELVOUX · Guillestre · Alba · Tortona · Bóbbio
Privas · Montélimar · Nyons · Gap · Barcelonnette · MT PELAT · **Cúneo** · **Réggio Nell'Emilia**
Alès · Orange · Sisteron · Digne-les-Bains · Tende · Savona · **GÉNOVA** · Rapallo · Berceto · **BOLOGNA**
Nîmes · Carpentras · Avignon · Apt · MT VENTOUX · **La Spézia** · Abetone
Arles · Salon-de-Provence · Aix-en-Provence · Draguignan · Grasse · **Nice** · Imperia · San Remo · Massa · Pistóia · Viaréggio · **Pisa** · Lucca
Martigues · **MARSEILLE** · Brignoles · Fréjus · Cannes · Monaco · **Livorno** · Volterra
La Ciotat · **Toulon** · Hyères · St-Tropez · Piombino · **Grosseto**
MÉDITERRANÉE
l'Île-Rousse · Calvi · Bastia · Ísola d'Elba
Porto · Corte · **Corse** · Vizzavona · Aléria
Cargèse · **Ajaccio** · Propriano · Sartène · Porto-Vecchio · Bonifacio
Santa Teresa Gallura · Golfo Aranci · Témpio Pausánia

GB Legend   Legenda NL
F Légende   Leyenda E
D Legende   Legenda I

Motorway, toll section Autoroute, section à péage Autobahn, gebührenpflichtiger Abschnitt		Snelweg, tol Autopista de peaje Autostrada, tratto a pedaggio
Motorway, free section, dual carriageway with motorway characteristics Autoroute, section libre, voie à caractère autoroutier Autobahn, gebührenfreier Abschnitt, Schnellverkehrsstraße		Snelweg, vrije sectie, vierbaansweg met snelweg karakteristieken Autovía con dos carriles en cada sentido Autostrada, tratto senza pedaggio, doppia carreggiata di tipo autostradale
Motorway under construction Autoroute en construction Autobahn im Bau		Snelweg onder constructie Autopista en construcción Autostrada in costruzione
Connecting road between main towns (green road sign) Route appartenant au réseau vert Verbindungsstraße zwischen wichtigen Städten (grüne Verkehrsschilder)		Verbindingsweg tussen grote steden (groene wegteken) Carretera verde (comunicación entre dos ciudades importantes) Collegamento stradale tra città principali (simbolo verde)
Trunk road Autre route de liaison principale Fernverkehrsstraße		Hoofdweg Carretera nacional Strada di grande comunicazione
Regional connecting road Route de liaison régionale Regionale Verbindungsstraße		Regionale verbindingsweg Carretera regional Strada di collegamento regionale
Other road Autre route Sonstige Straße		Andere weg Carretera local Altra strada
Prohibited road Route interdite Durchfahrt verboten		Geen doorgang Carretera prohibida o cortada Strada vietata
Dual carriageway with or without separator Route à deux chaussées séparées avec ou sans Zweibahnige Fernstraße mit oder ohne Mittelstreifen		Dubbele rijbaan met of zonder tussenberm Carretera de dos carriles con o sin mediana Doppia carreggiata con o senza spartitraffico
Road with two wide lanes or more Route à deux voies larges et plus Straße mit zwei breiten Fahrspuren und mehr		Weg met twee of meer brede rijstroken Carretera con dos o más carriles anchos Strada a due o più corsie ampie
Road with one lane or two lanes Route à une ou deux voies Ein- oder zweispurige Straße		Weg met één of twee rijstroken Carretera con uno o dos carriles Strada a corsia unica o doppia
Junction : complete (1), limited (2), number Échangeur : complet (1), partiel (2), numéro Vollanschlussstelle (1), beschränkte Anschlussstelle (2), Nummer	1 2	Knooppunt, compleet (1), beperkt (2), nummer Via de acceso (conexión): completa (1), parcial (2), número Svincolo: completo (1), parziale (2), numero
Toll gate (1), service area (2) Barrière de péage (1), aire de service (2) Mautstelle (1), Tankstelle (2)	1 2	Tol slagboom (1), benzinestation (2) Punto de peaje (1), estación de servicio (2) Barriera di pedaggio (1), area di servizio (2)
Road tunnel Tunnel routier Straßentunnel		Wegtunnel Túnel Galleria stradale
Distance in kilometres (km) Distances kilométriques (km) Entfernungen in Kilometern (km)	3	Afstanden in kilometers (km) Distancias en kilómetros (km) Distanze in chilometri (km)
Road numbering: Motorway Numération routière: Autoroute, type autoroutier Straßennumerierung : Autobahn	A57	Wegnummers: Snelweg Numeración de las carreteras: Autopista Numerazione stradale: Autostrada
Road numbering : National road, secondary road Numération routière: Route nationale, route secondaire Straßennumerierung : Nationalstraße, Nebenstraße	N171 D776	Wegnummers: Nationale weg, secundaire weg Numeración de las carreteras: Carretera nacional, provincial Numerazione stradale: strada nazionale, strada secondaria
Railway (1), station or stopping place open to passenger traffic (2) Chemin de fer (1), gare ou point d'arrêt ouvert au trafic voyageurs (2) Eisenbahn (1), Bahnhof oder Haltpunkt für Personenverkehr (2)	1 2	Spoorweg (1), station of stopplaats open voor passagiers (2) Ferrocarril (1), estación o parada abierta al tráfico de pasajeros (2) Ferrovia (1), stazione o fermata aperta al traffico passeggeri (2)
Ferry route Liaison par bac Fähre	Bastia	Veerdienst Ruta de transbordador (ferry) Traghetto
Airport Aéroport Flughafen	✈	Vliegveld Aeropuerto Aeroporto
Built-up area (1), industrial park (2) Zone bâtie (1), zone industrielle (2) Geschlossene Bebauung (1), Gewerbezone (2)	1 2	Bebouwde kom (1), industrie gebied (2) Zona edificada (1), polígono industrial (2) Area edificata (1), zona industriale (2)
Woods Bois Wald		Bos Bosque Boschi

GB Legend

Legenda NL

F Légende

Leyenda E

D Legende

Legenda I

Département boundary		Departementsgrens
Limite de département		Límite de departamento
Departementgrenze		Confine di dipartimento
Region boundary		Streekgrens
Limite de région		Límite regional
Regionsgrenze		Confine di regione
International boundary		Internationale grens
Frontière internationale		Frontera internacional
Internationalgrenze		Confine internazionale
Hamlet	la Californie	Gehucht
Hameau		Aldea, caserío
Weiler		Villaggio rurale
Chief town of commune	Biot	Gemeente hoofdstad
Chef-lieu de commune		Cabeza de término municipal
Gemeindehauptort		Capoluogo di comune
Chief town of canton	Cagnes-sur-Mer	Hoofdstad van het kanton
Chef-lieu de canton		Capital de cantón
Kantonhauptort		Capoluogo di cantone
Chief town of arrondissement	GRASSE	Hoofdstad van het arrondissement
Chef-lieu d'arrondissement		Capital de arrondissement
Arrondissementhauptort		Capoluogo di arrondissement
Chief town of département	NICE	Hoofdstad van het departement
Chef-lieu de département		Capital de departamento
Departementhauptort		Capoluogo di dipartimento
Marsh (1), salt pans (2)		Moeras (1), Zoutpan (2)
Marais (1), Marais salants (2)		Marisma, humedal (1), Salinas (2)
Sumpf (1), Salzteiche (2)		Palude (1), Saline (2)
Dry sand (1), wet sand (2)		Zandig gebied (1), Getijden gebied (2)
Région sableuse (1), Sable humide (2)		Zona arenosa (1), Banco de arena (2)
Sandgebiet (1), Gezeiten (2)		Area sabbiosa (1), Bassofondo sabbioso (2)
Cathedral (1), Abbey (2)		Kathedraal (1), Klooster (2)
Cathédrale (1), Abbaye (2)		Catedral (1), Abadía (2)
Dom (1), Abtei (2)		Cattedrale (1), Abbazia (2)
Castle		Kasteel
Château		Castillo
Schloss		Castello
Viewpoint		Uitzichtpunt
Panorama		Mirador
Aussichtspunkt		Panorama
Spa (1), Winter sports resort (2)		Kuuroord (1), Wintersportgebied (2)
Station thermale (1), Station ou centre de sports d'hiver (2)		Balneario (1), Estación de deportes de invierno (2)
Kurort (1), Wintersportort (2)		Stazione termale (1), Stazione di sport invernali (2)
Rampart		Borstwering
Remparts		Muralla
Wälle		Bastioni
Ancient remains (1), Interesting ruins (2), Memorial (3)		Historisch bouwwerk (1), Bezienswaardige ruïne (2), Gedenkteken (3)
Vestiges antiques (1), Ruines intéressantes (2), Monument commémoratif (3)		Restos antiguos (1), Ruinas interesantes (2), Monumento conmemorativo (3)
Zeugnisse des Altertums (1), Interessante Ruinen (2), Gedänkstätte (3)		Antiche rovine (1), Rovine interessanti (2), Monumento commemorativo (3)
Pilgrimage site		Bedevaartplaats
Pèlerinage		Peregrinaje
Wallfahrt		Luogo di pellegrinaggio
Military cemetery		Militaire begraafplaats
Cimetière militaire		Cementerio militar
Soldatenfriedhof		Cimitero militare
Cave		Grot
Grotte		Cueva
Höhle		Grotta
Town or place of interest	PARIS	Interessant Stad of plaats
Localité ou site remarquable	Baou-des-Blanc	Ciudad o lugar de interés
Sehenswerter Ortschaft oder Platz		Città o luogo d'interesse

1:180,000

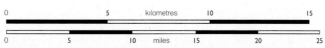

0	5	kilometres	10	15

0	5	10	miles	15	20	25

1

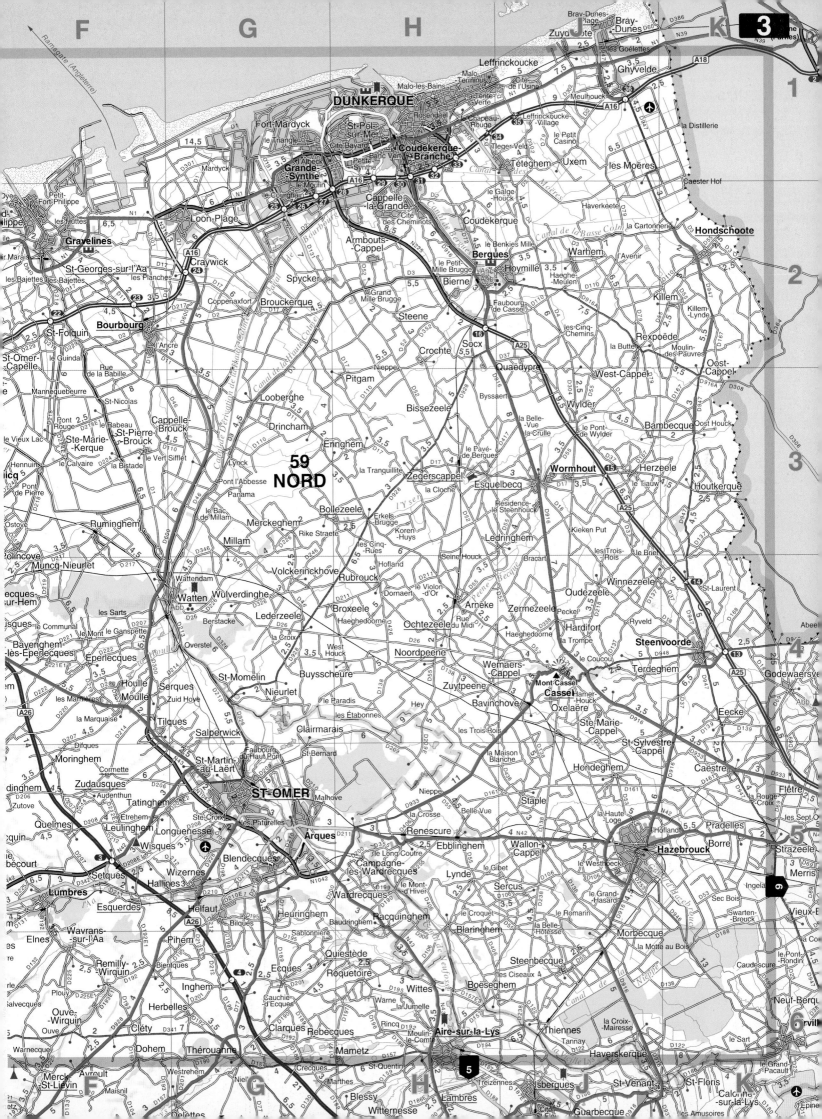

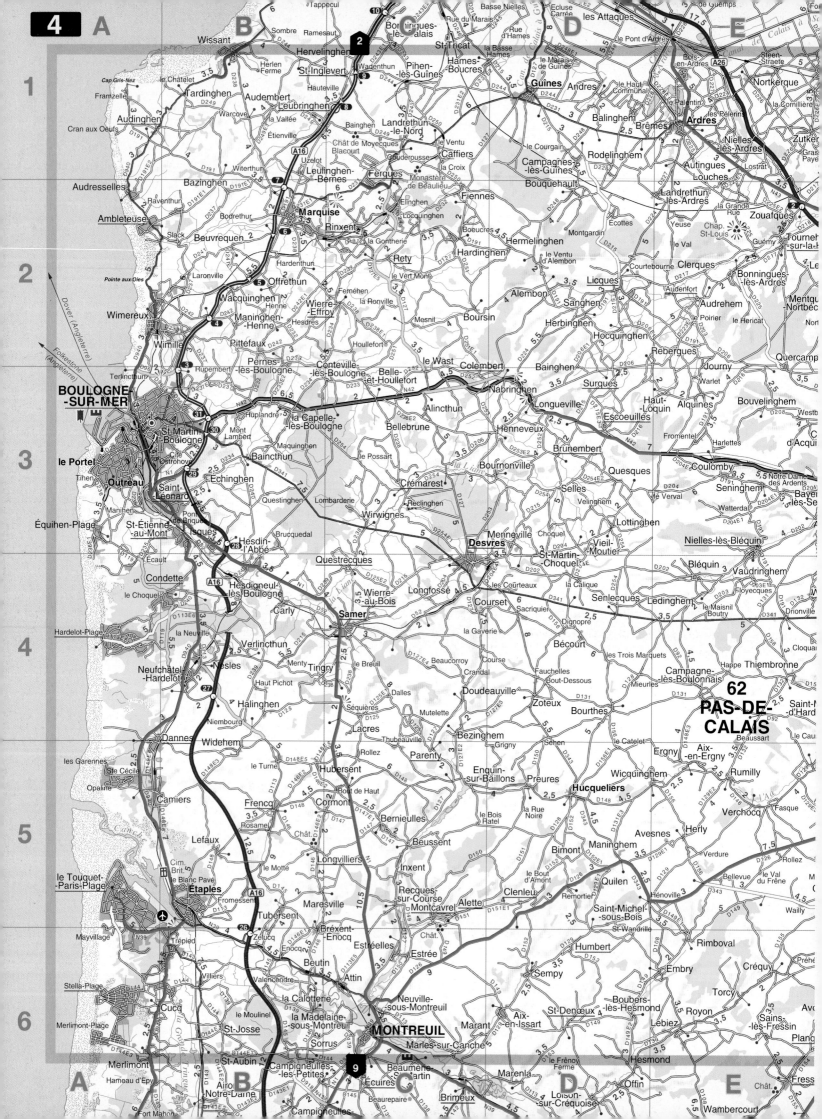

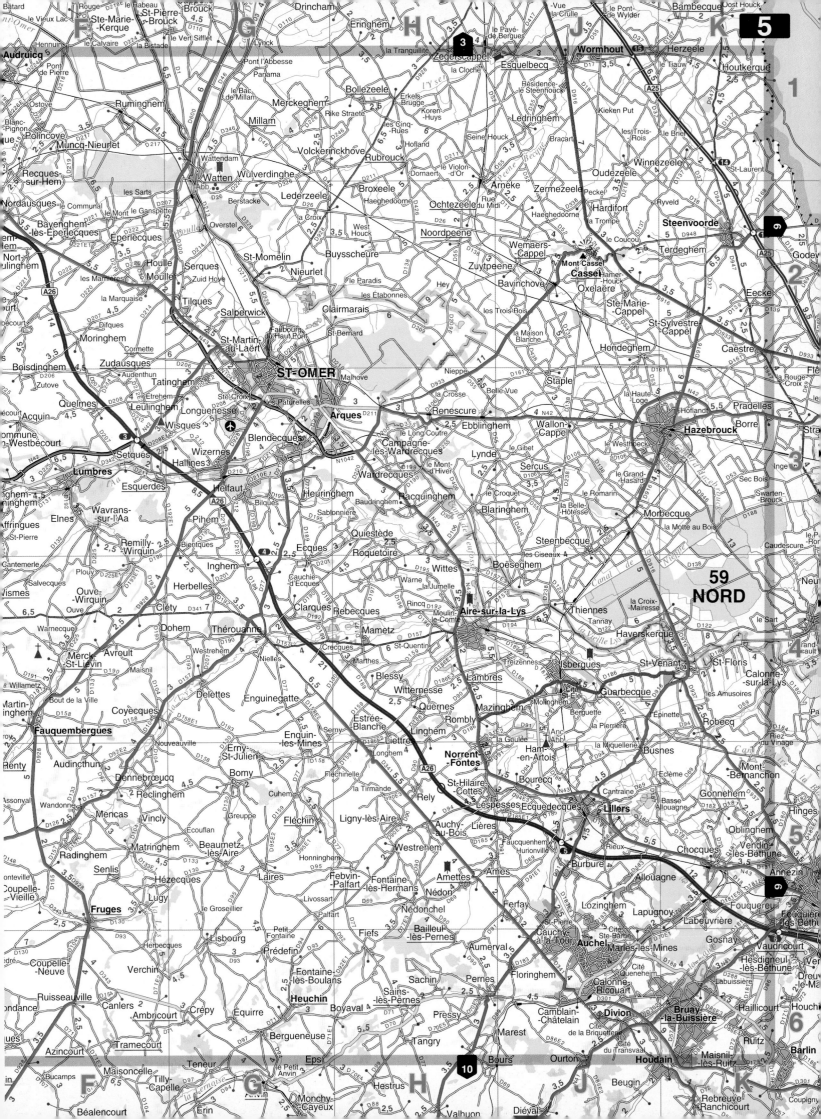

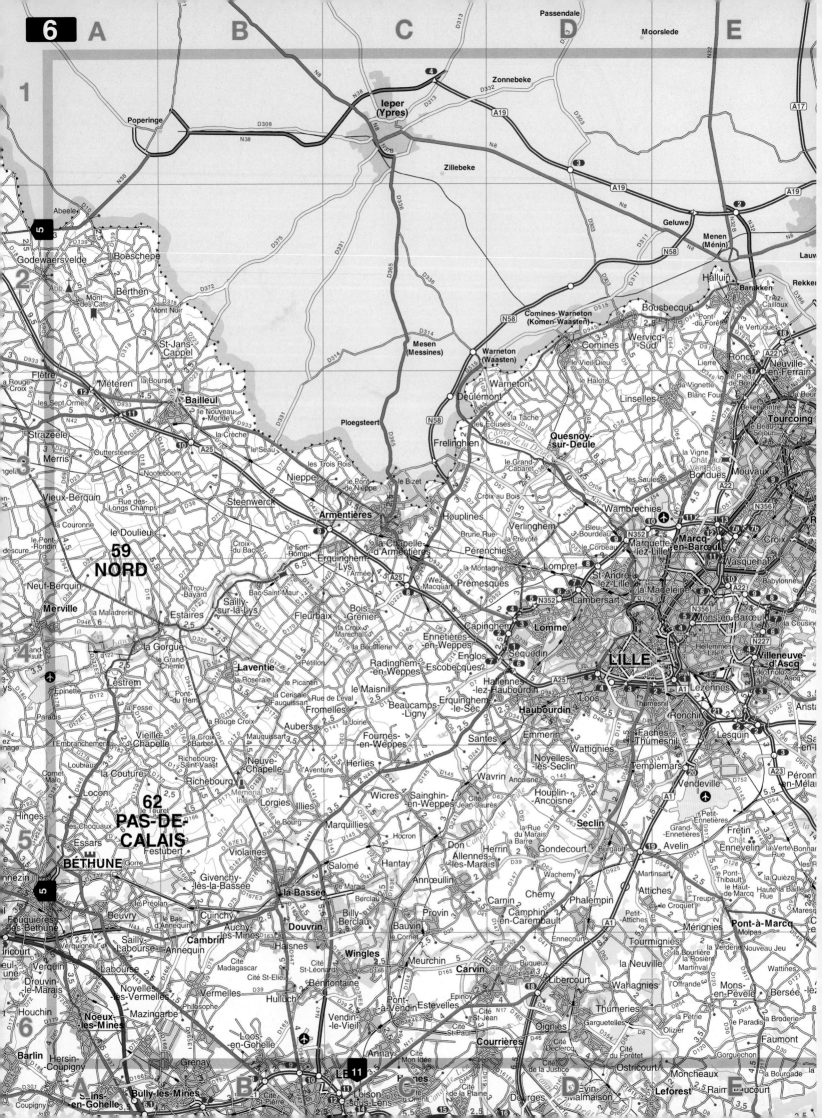

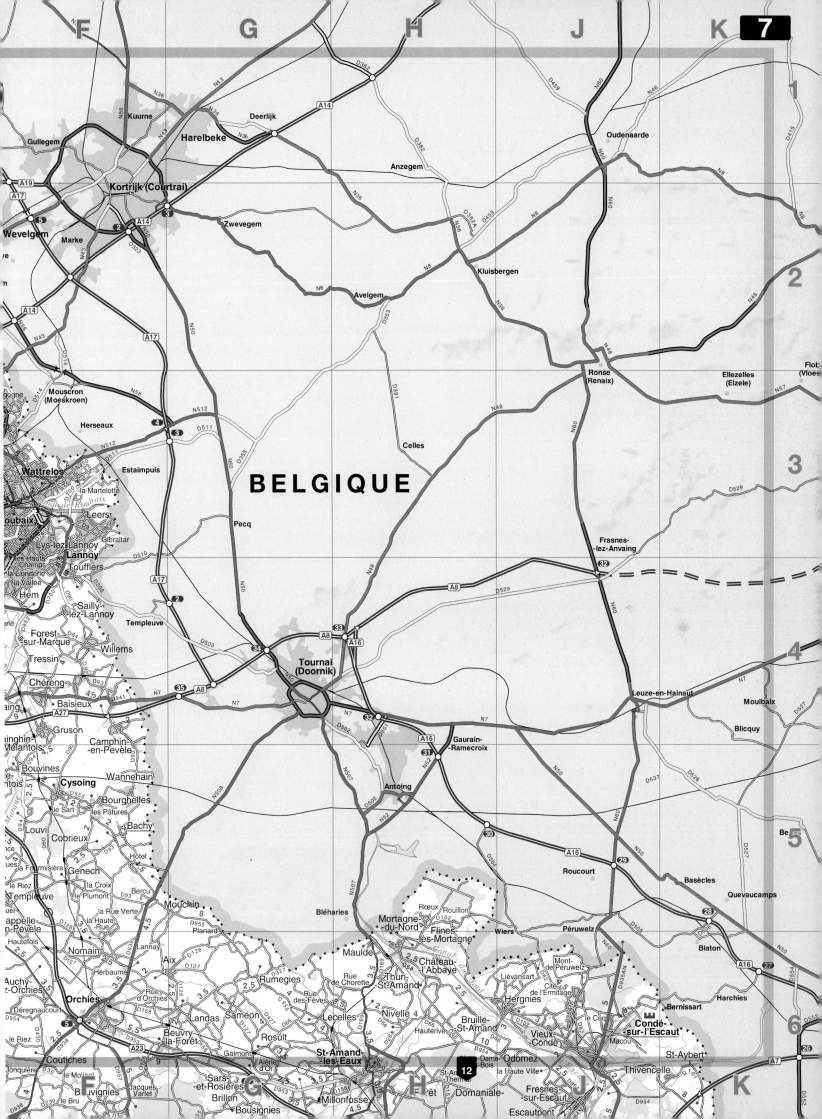

1

la Garenne
Orange
Rang-du-Fliers
Fort Mahon
Berck
Berck-Plage
Verton
Cité
du Phare
le Bahot
Groffliers
Ebruyères
Waben
Lépine
le Temple

Baie de l'Authie

Conchil-
le-Temple

2

le Vieux
Fort-Mahon
le Château
Neuf
Tigny-
Noyelle
Noyelle
Tigny
Fort-Mahon
-Plage
le Royon
le Muret
Colline-
Beaumont
Fresne
Quend-Plage
Routhiauville
Quend
Villers-
sur-Authie
la Dune Fleurie
Monchaux
Hère
Vercourt
Froise

3

St-Quentin-
en-Tourmont
Larronville
Flandre
Arry
le Bout
des Crocs
Rue
St-Firmin
Lannoy
la Bassée
Favières
le Marais
Forêt-
Monti

Baie de Somme

Quartier
de l'Aviation
le Hamelet
Ponthoile
le Crotoy
Morlay
Bon

le Hourdel
la Mollière
le Dien
Brighton
**St-Valéry-
sur-Somme**
Nolette
Cap Hornu
la Mollière
de Terre
la Ferté
Cim.
Chind

4

Cayeux-sur-Mer
Sallenelle
le Tivoli
le Soleil
Levant
Noyelle-
sur-M
Hurt
Wathiéhurt
Routhiauville
Pinchefalise
Pendé
Lanchères
Estréboeuf
Drancourt
Boismont
l'Alleu
Poutrincourt
Catigny
Mons
Saigneville
Brutelles
Tilloy
Hautebut
Élincourt
Arrest
Mons-
Boubert
Vaudricourt
Boubert
Offeux
St-Blimont
le Montant

5

Woignarue
Bourseville
Rimbehem
Ochancourt
Quesnoy-
le-Montant
Cal
Onival
Rimbehem
Franleu
Lamt
Belloy-
sur-Mer
Nibas
Campagne
Ault
Friaucourt
Fireuille
Bel-Air
Allenay
Tully
**Friville-
Escarbotin**
Valines
Mian
le Bois
de Cise
Friville
Saucourt
Frières
Moyen
la Croix
St-Quentin-la-Motte-
Croix-au-Bailly
Béthencourt-
sur-Mer
Woincourt
Acheux-
en-Vimeu
Toeufles

6

Mers-
les-Bains
Cité
Notre-Dame
Chépy
le Tréport
Gros-
Jacques
Yzengremer
Fressenneville
Feuquières-
en-Vimeu
le Tréport-Terrasse
la Chaussée
de Picardie
Méneslies
Houdent
Mesnil-Val-Plage
Mesnil-
Sorel
Ste-Croix
Eu
Ponts-
et-Marais
Dargnies
Tours-
en-Vimeu
Criel-Plage
Mancheville
Oust-Marest
Embreville
Aigneville
Ercourt
Mesnil-
Val
Flocques
Harancourt
Marest
Hocquélus
Corroy
Grebault-
Mesnil
Criel-sur-Mer
Étalondes
la Vierge
la Pipe
la Babeau
Bouvaincourt-
sur-Bresle
Courtieux
Hamicourt
Mesnil-
à-Caux
les
Quesnets
Chanteraine
Beauchamps
Buigny-
les-Gamaches
Maisnières
Vismes
Tocqueville-sur-Eu
Huppy
Boscrocourt
la
Bourdaine
St-Pierre-
en-Val
Monchelet
Harcelaines
le Plouy
Neuvillette
Ferme
Heudelimont
Sang-Roy
Godelmesnil
le Fresne
Incheville
Hélicourt
Onicourt

Biville-
sur-Mer
Assigny
Bourg-
l'Abbé
Baromesnil
St-Rémy-
Boscrocourt
St-Sulpice-
sur-Yères
Manchy-
-sur-Eu
la Cour
du Bosc
Gousseauville
Longroy
Gamaches
Tilloy-
Floriville
Wiammeville
Martainneville
Canehan
Litteville
Étocquigny
16
la Tuilerie
Maigneville
Morival
Biencourt
Bul

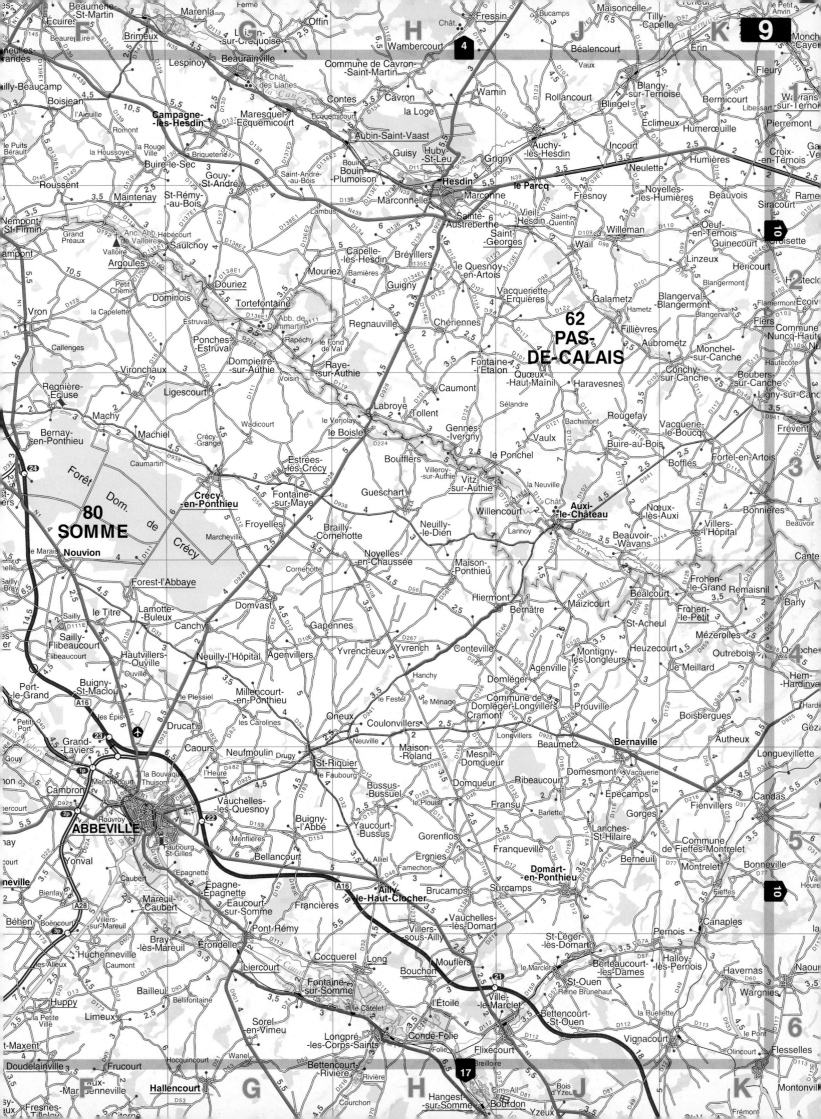

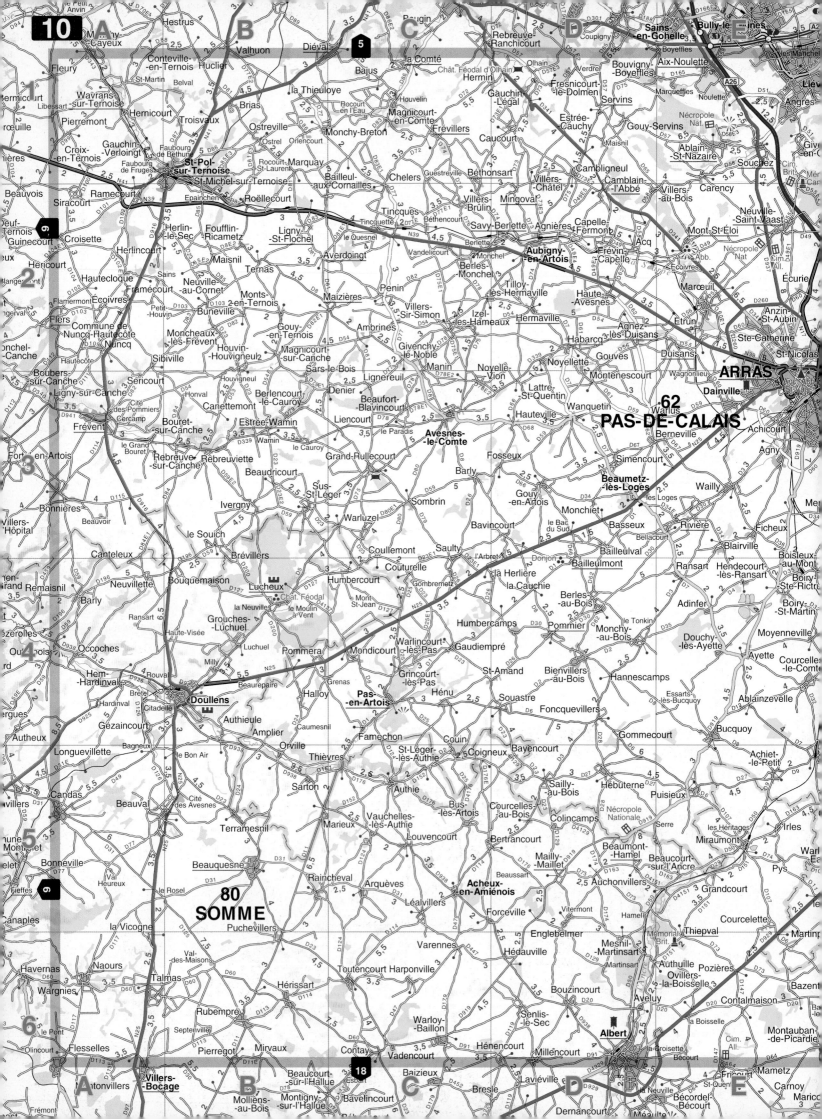

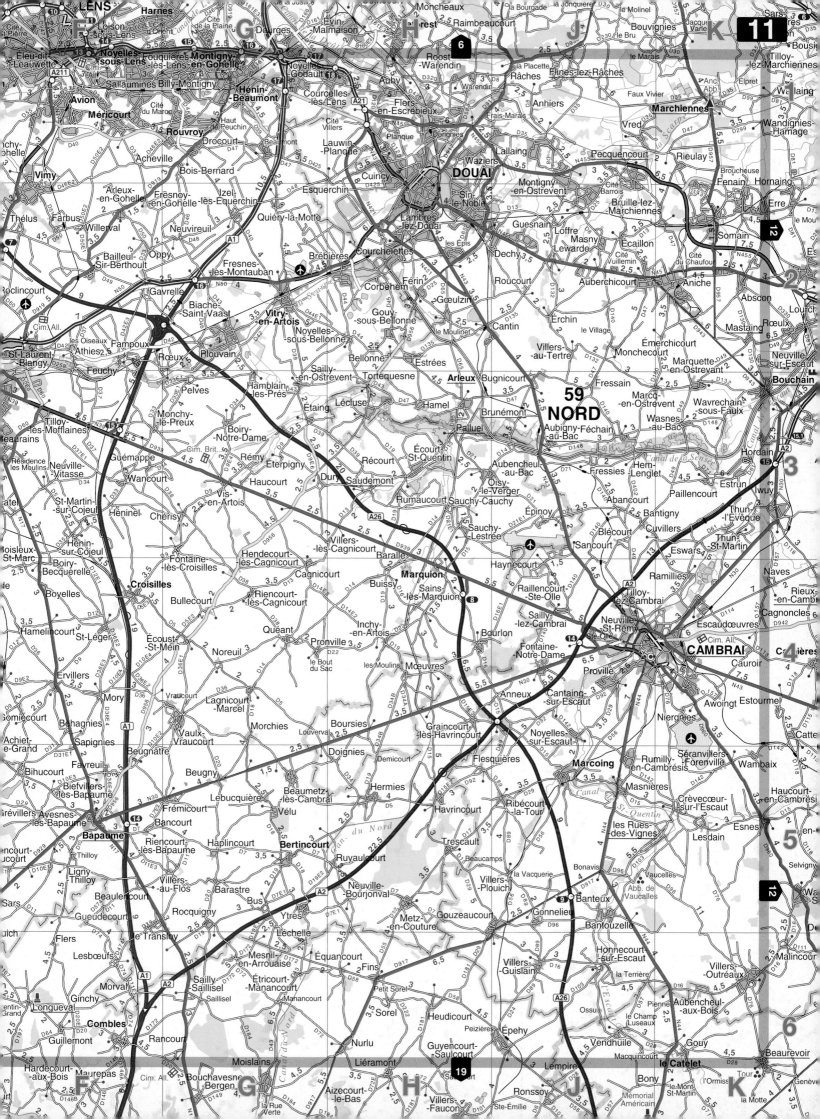

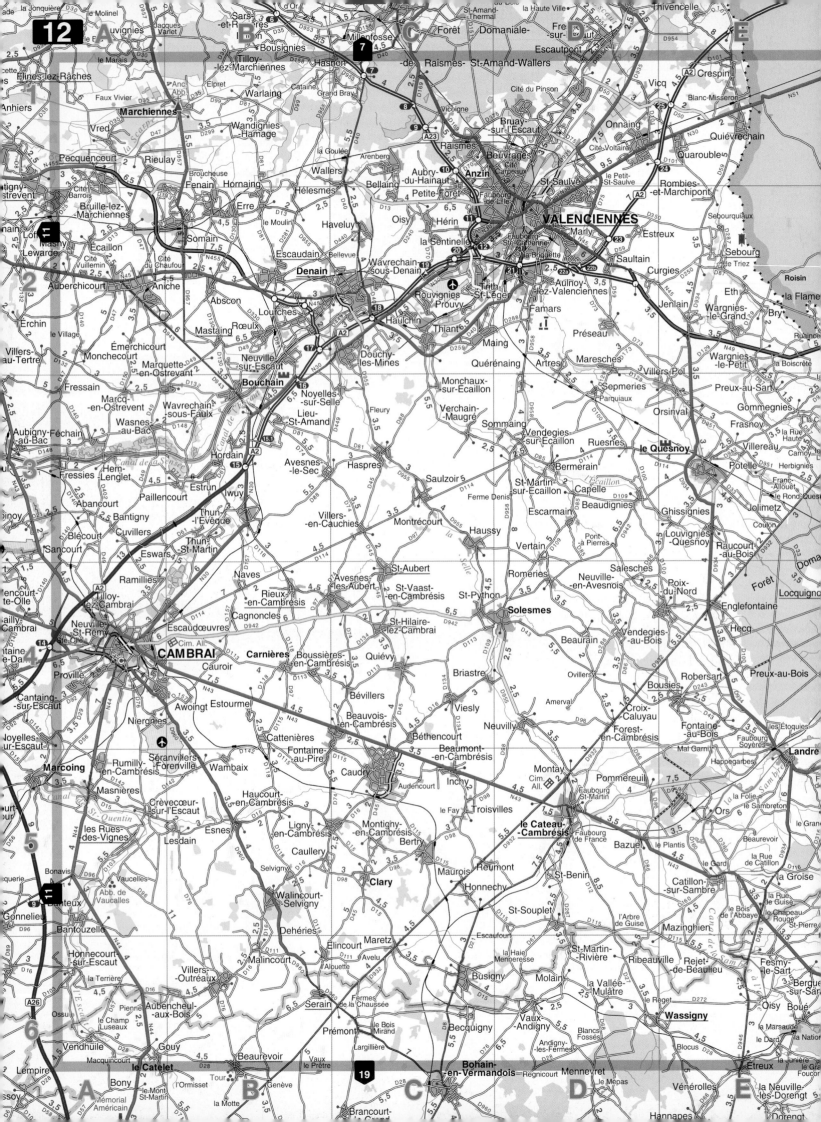

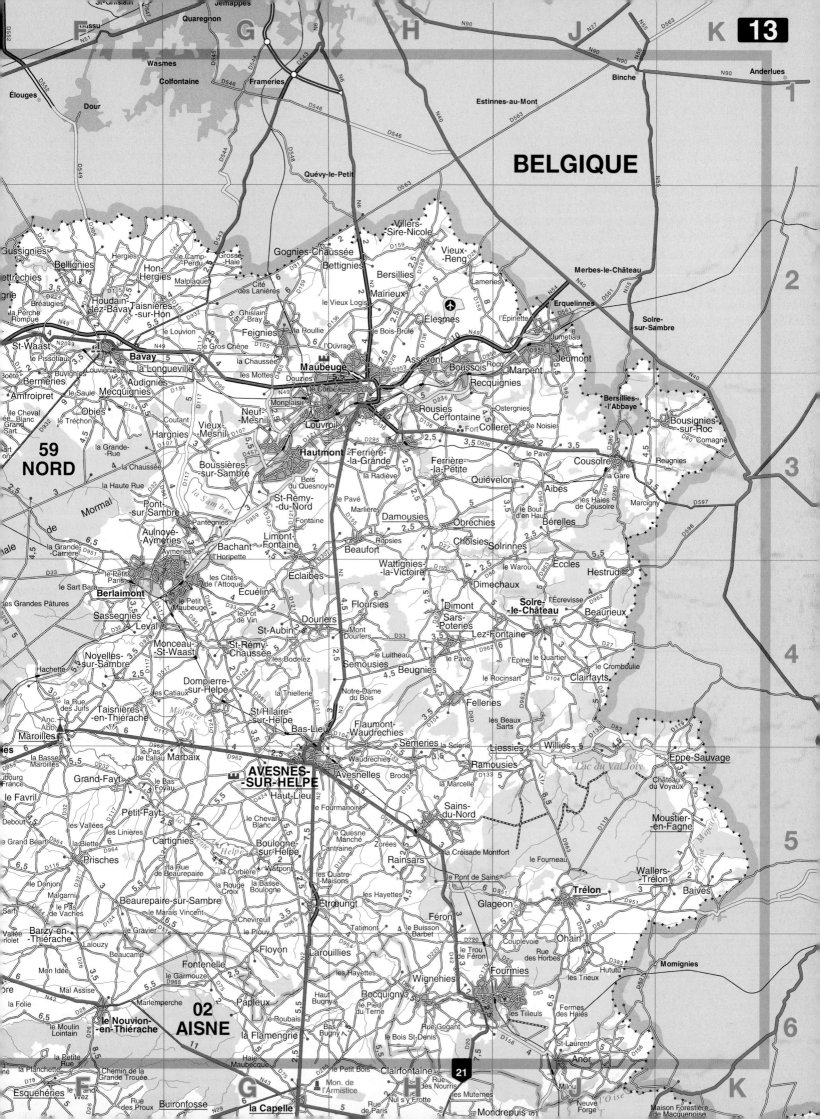

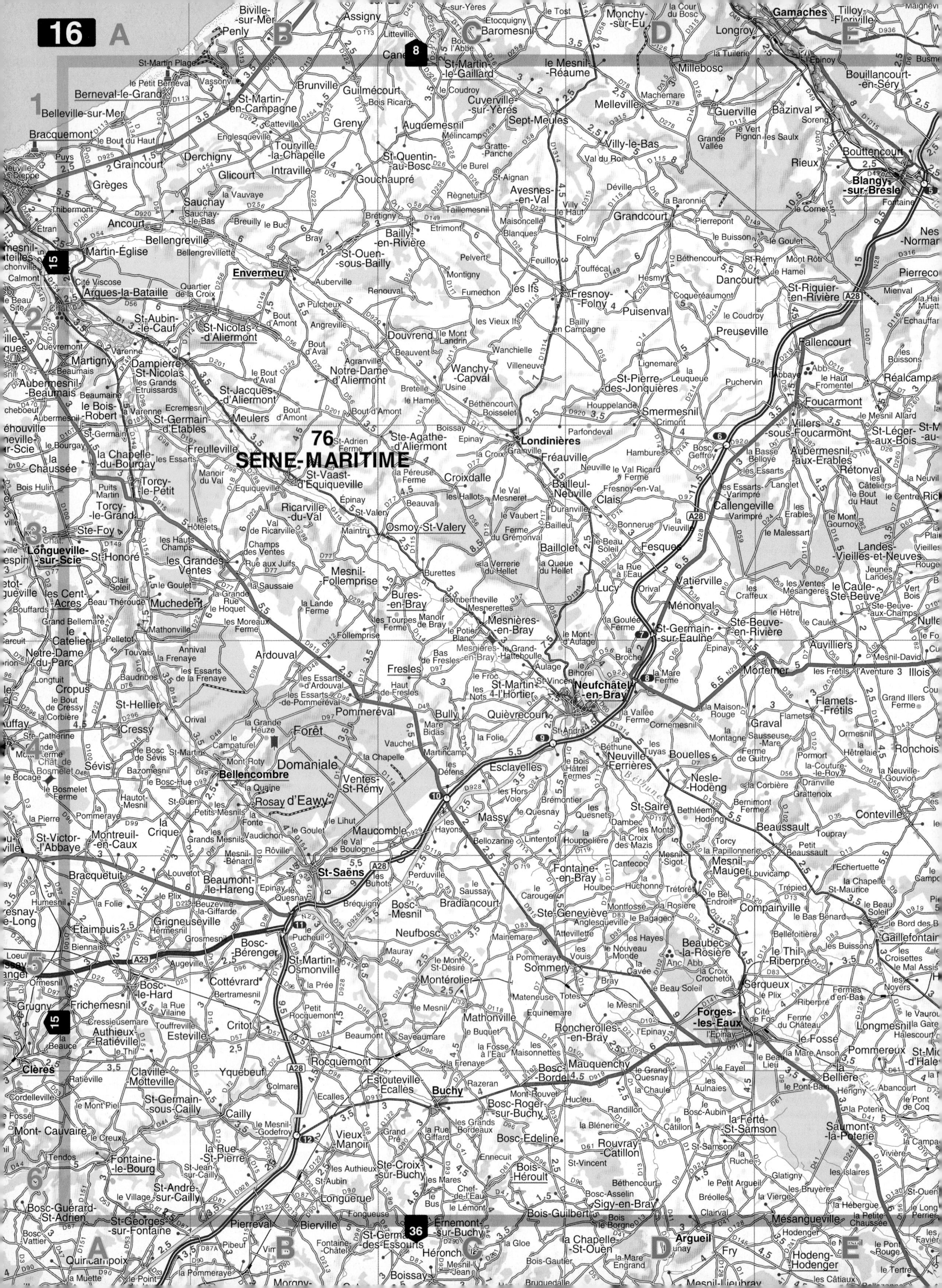
A
B
C
D
E
1
2
3
4
5
6
76
SEINE-MARITIME
Gamaches
Blangy-sur-Bresle
Envermeu
Arques-la-Bataille
St-Nicolas-d'Aliermont
Londinières
Neufchâtel-en-Bray
Longueville-sur-Scie
Bellencombre
St-Saëns
Forges-les-Eaux
Buchy
Clères
Argueil
Foucarmont
Aumale
Forêt Domaniale
Rosay d'Eawy
Berneval-le-Grand
Belleville-sur-Mer
Bracquemont
Martin-Église
Grandcourt
Smermesnil
Mesnières-en-Bray
Bures-en-Bray
Fresles
Massy
Sommery
Serqueux
Gaillefontaine
Saumont-la-Poterie
Mauquenchy
Sigy-en-Bray
Longuerue
Bosc-le-Hard
Cottévrard
Critot
Montérolier
Neufbosc
Bradiancourt
Beaussault
Compainville
Conteville
Londinières
Fréauville
Bailleul-Neuville
Fesques
Vatierville
Mortemer
Flamets-Frétils
Graval
Bouelles
Nesle-Hodeng
Esclavelles
Quièvrecourt
Bully
Pommeréval
Ardouval
Muchedent
Cropus
Cressy
St-Hellier
Sévis
Montreuil-en-Caux
St-Victor-l'Abbaye
Bracquetuit
Etaimpuis
Grigneuseville
Bosc-Bérenger
St-Martin-Osmonville
Yquebeuf
Cailly
Claville-Motteville
St-Germain-sous-Cailly
Fontaine-le-Bourg
St-André-sur-Cailly
Quincampoix
Pierreval
Bierville
Héronchelles
Boissay
Vieux-Manoir
Ste-Croix-sur-Buchy
Bois-Héroult
Bosc-Edeline
Rouvray-Catillon
la Ferté-St-Samson
Bois-Guilbert
A28
A29
N28
N29
8
15
36

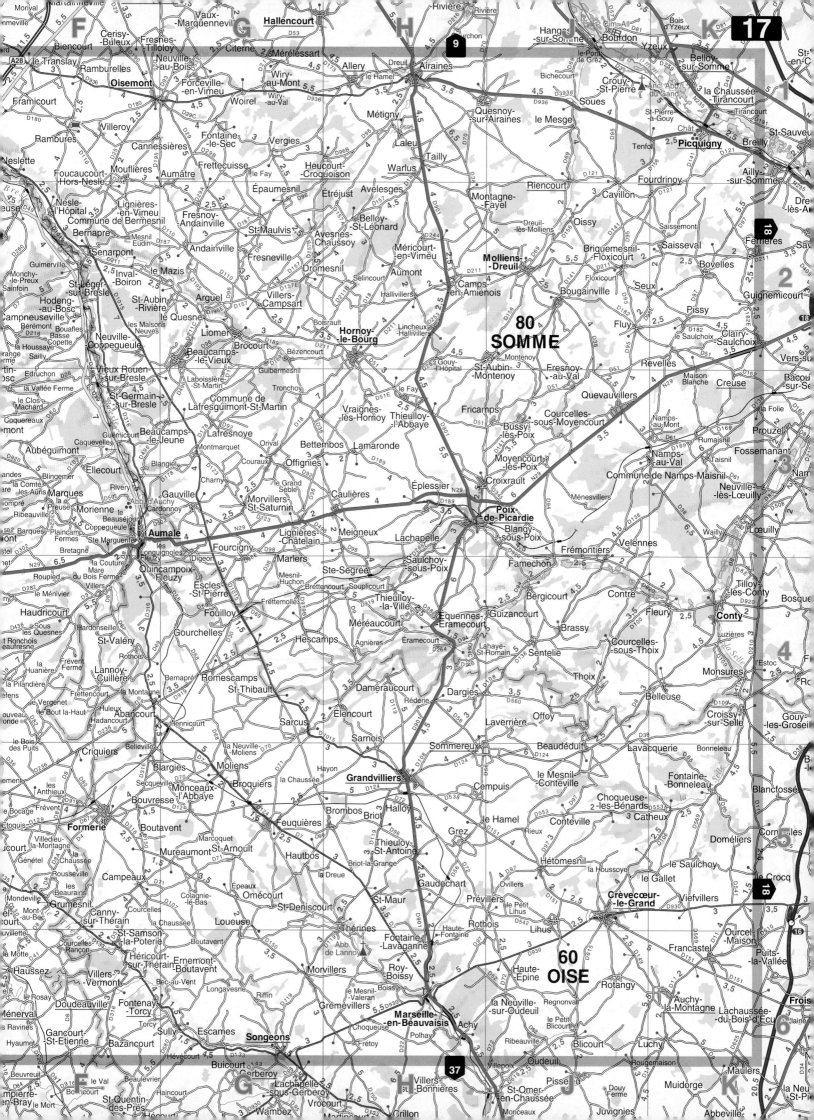

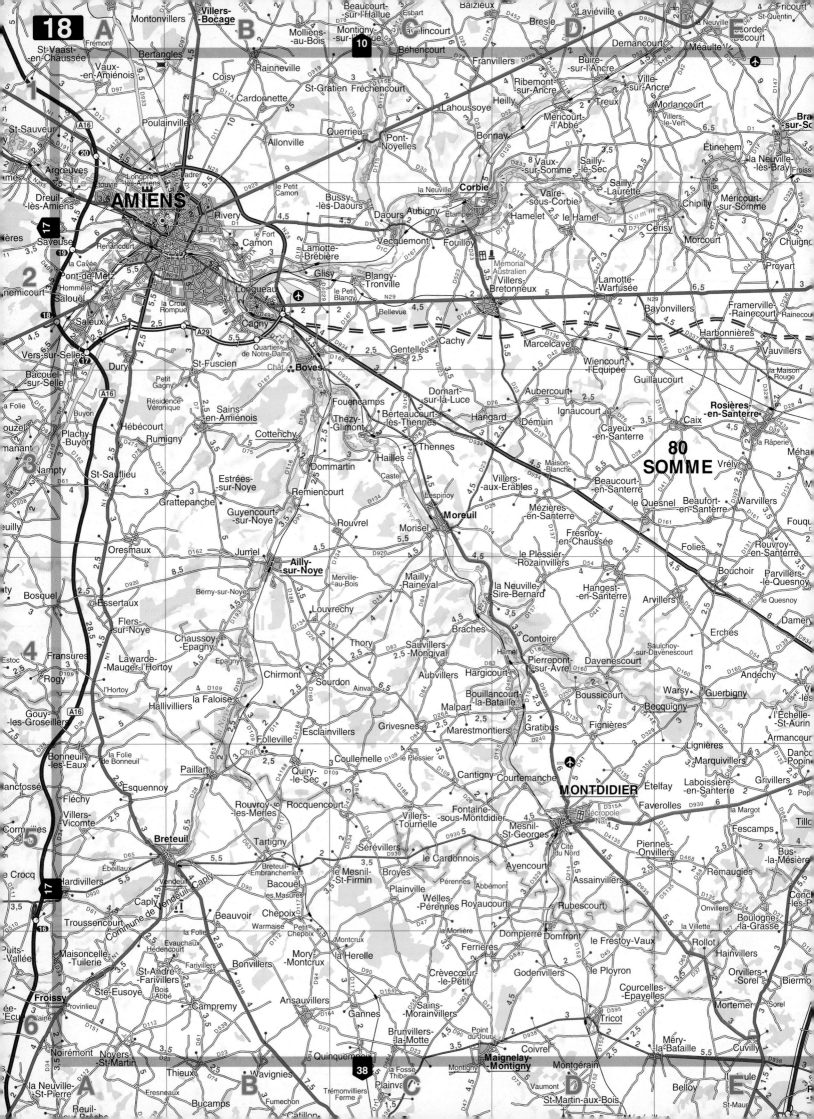

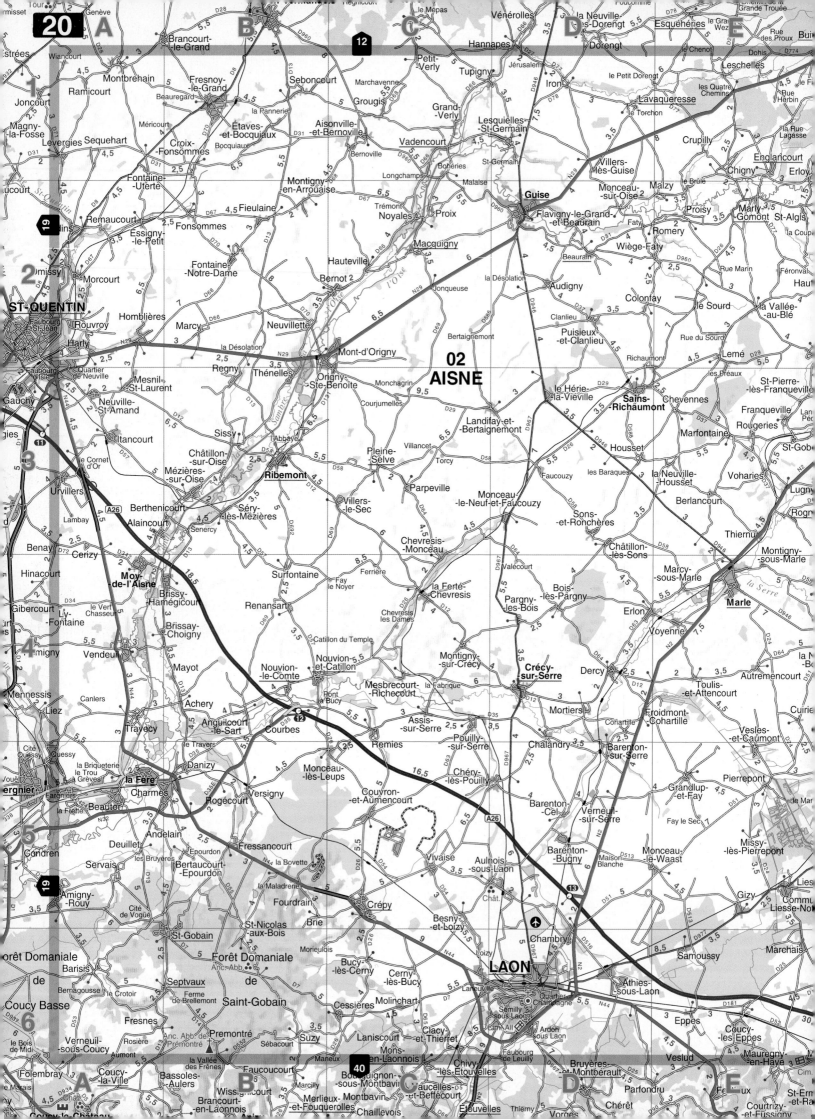

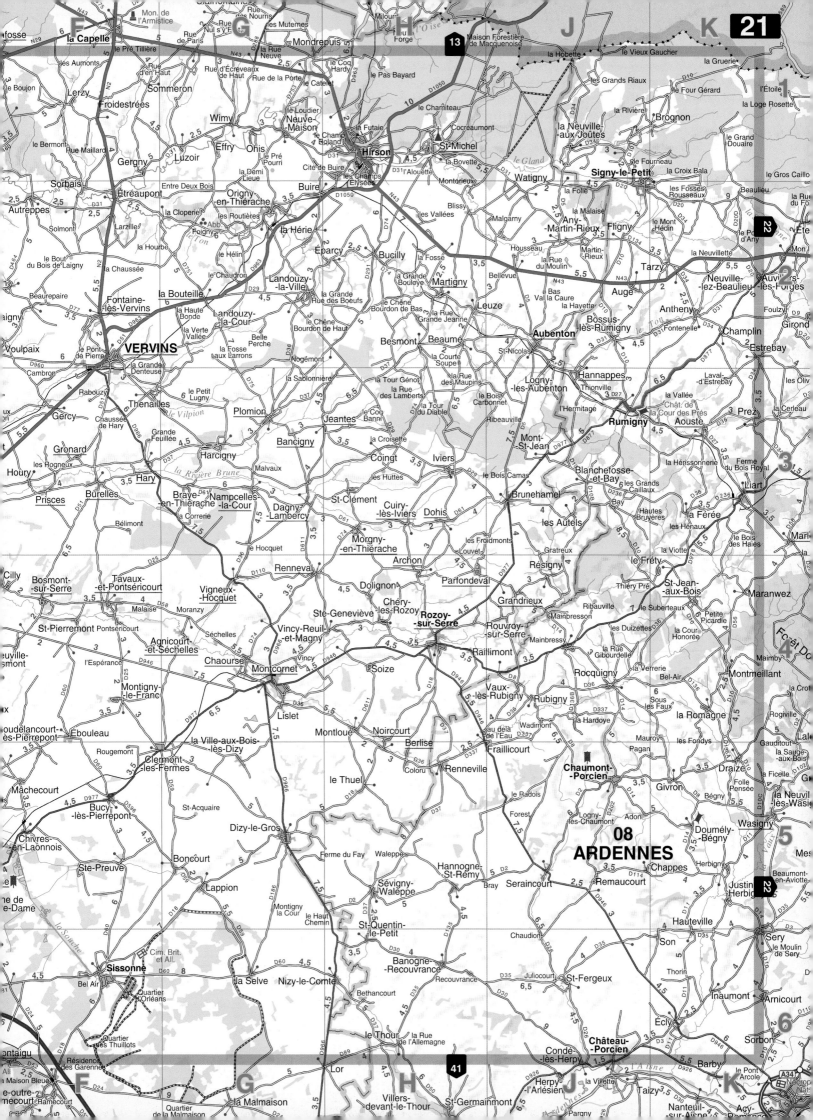

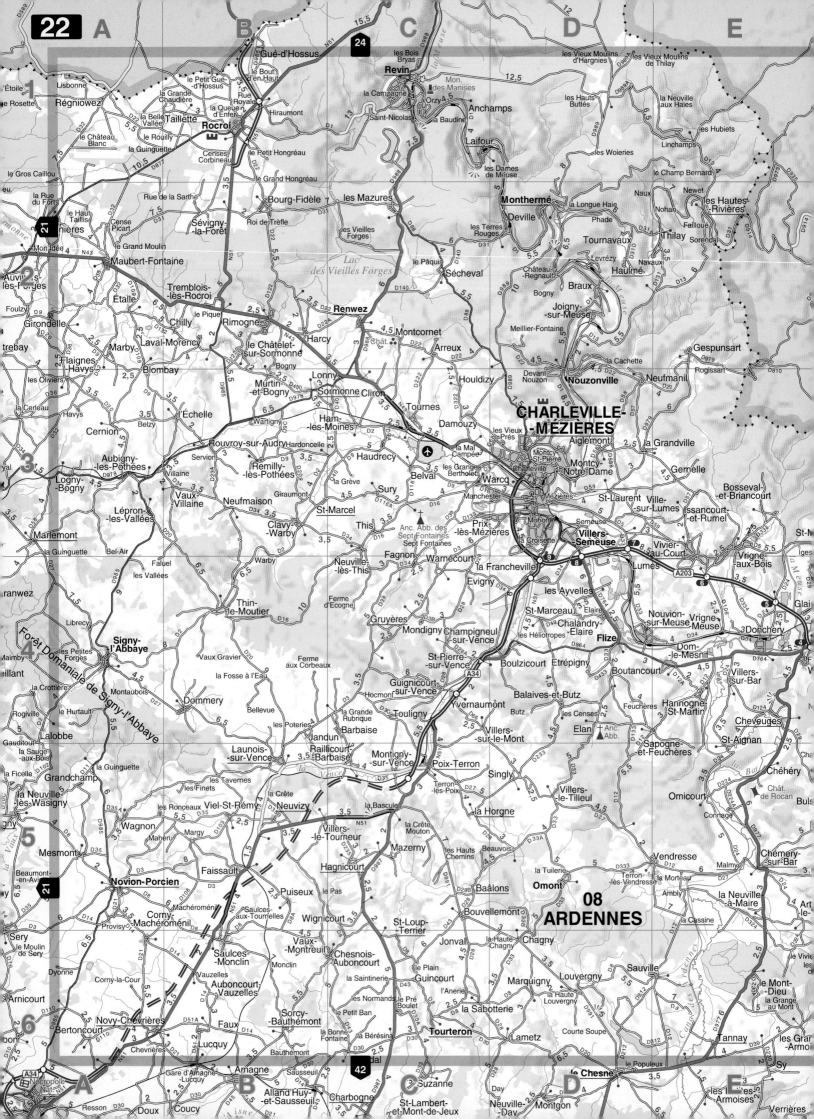

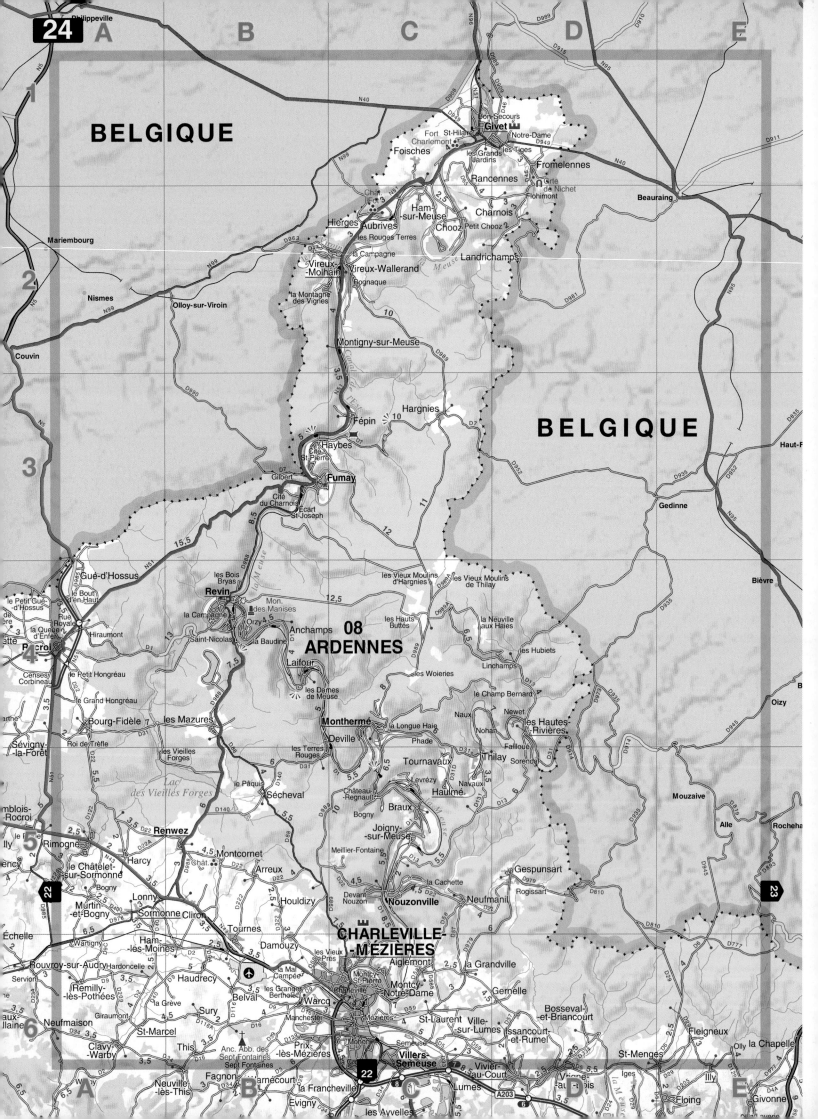

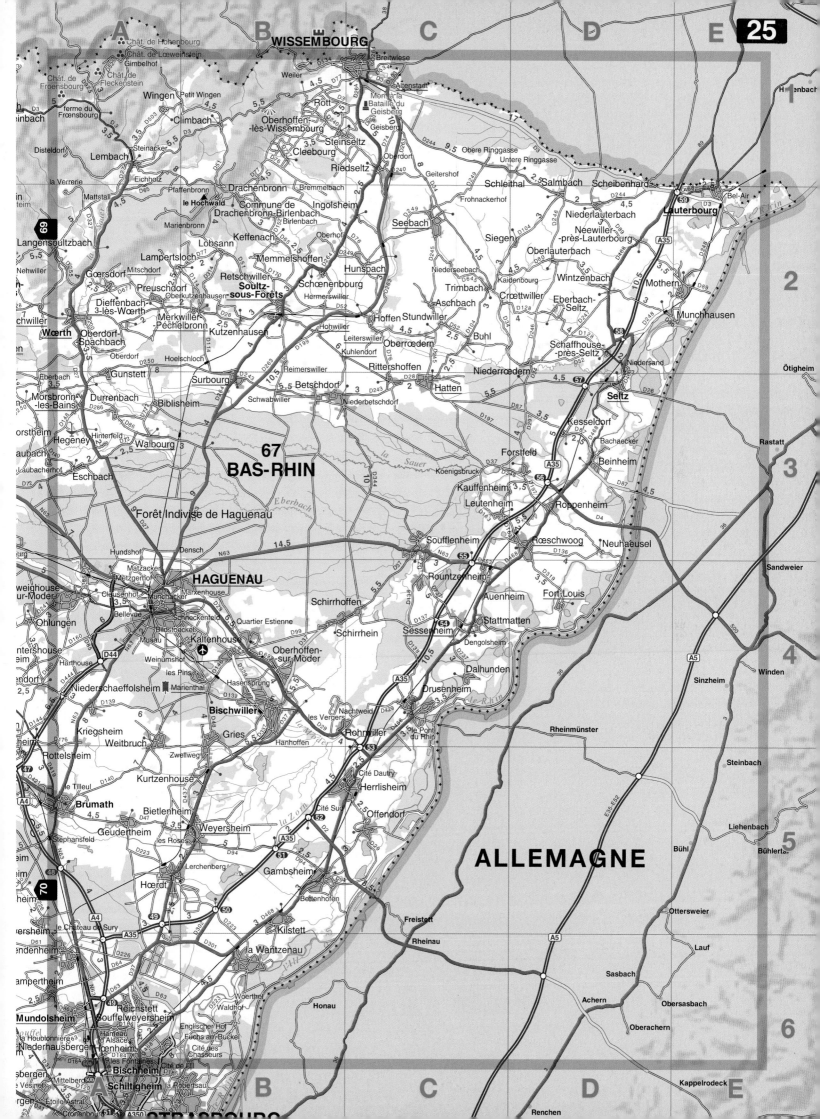

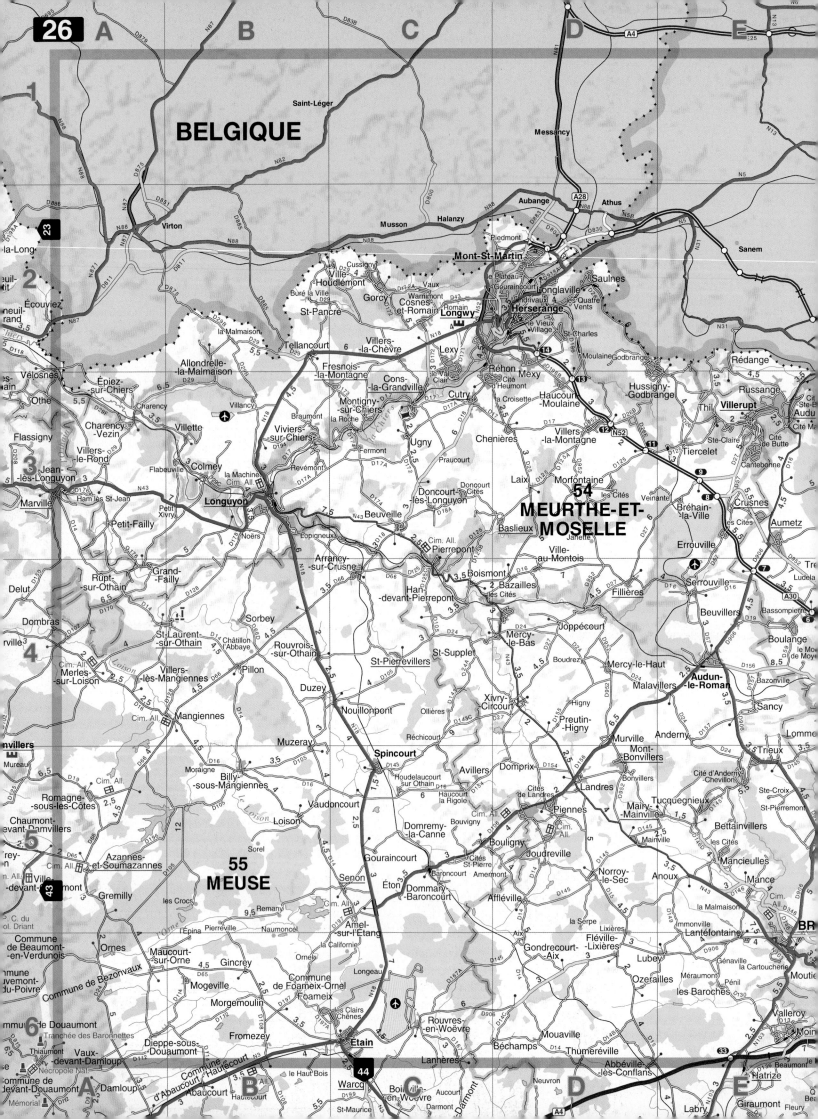

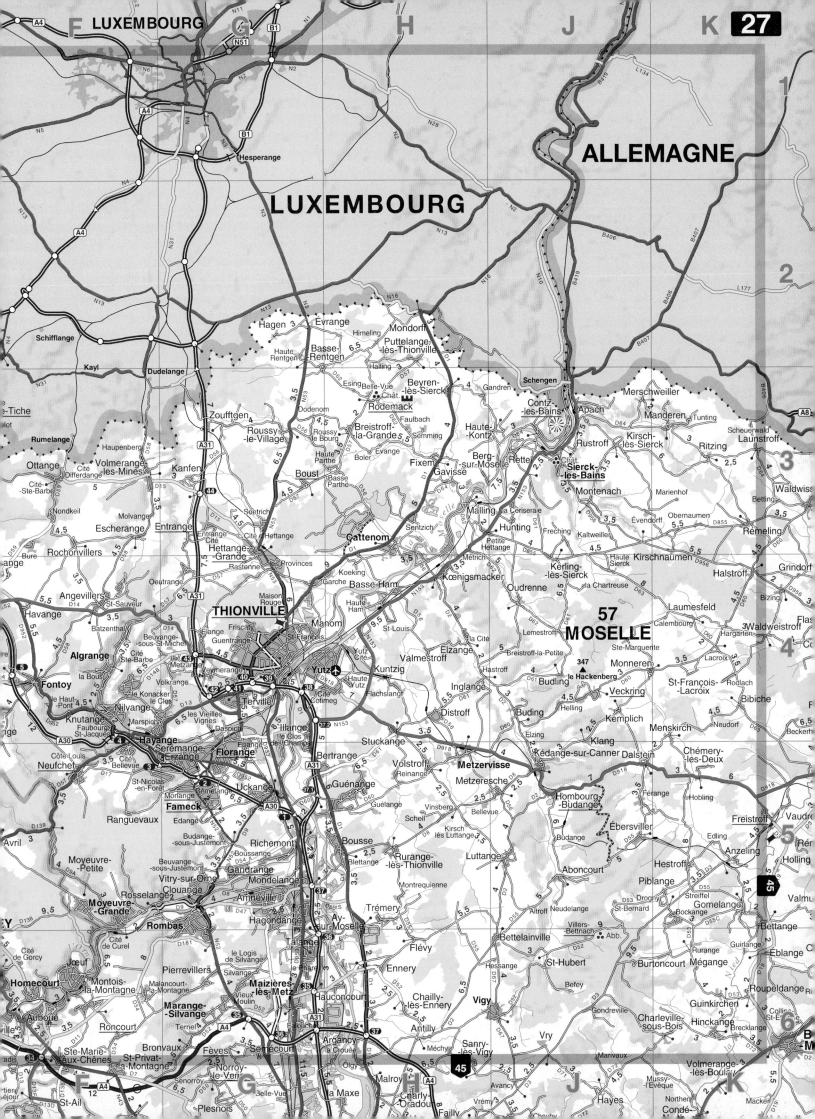

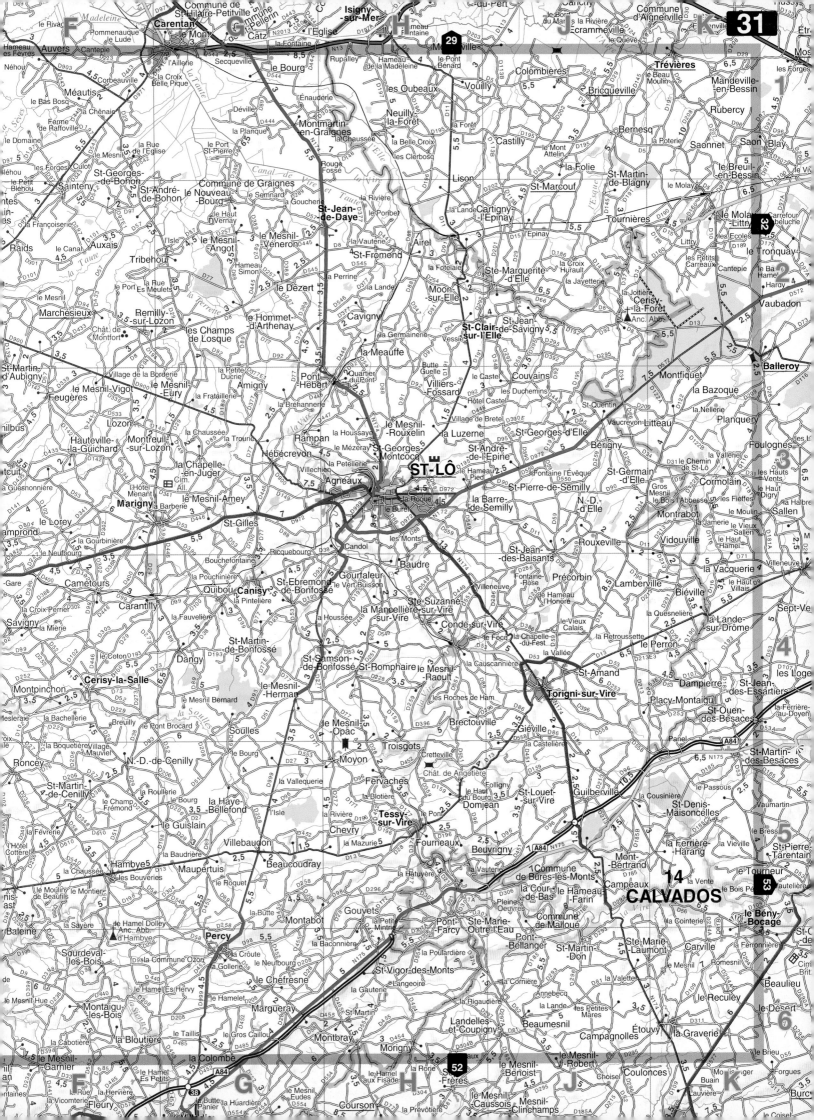

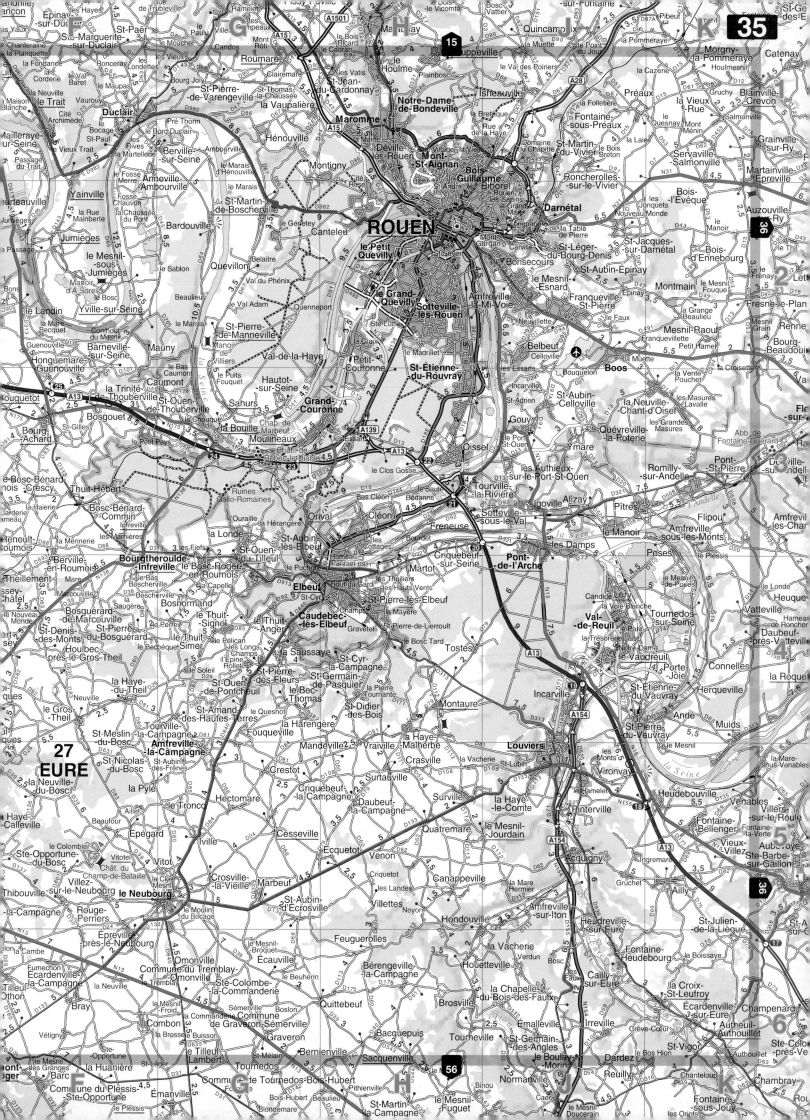

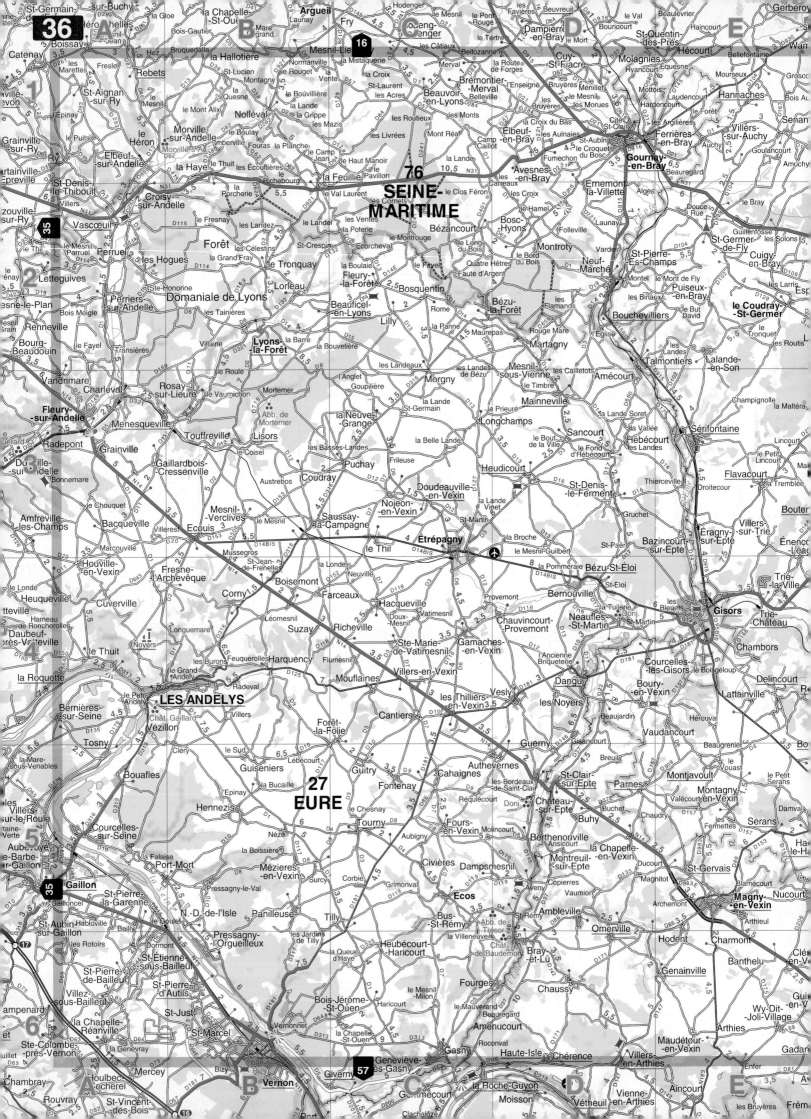

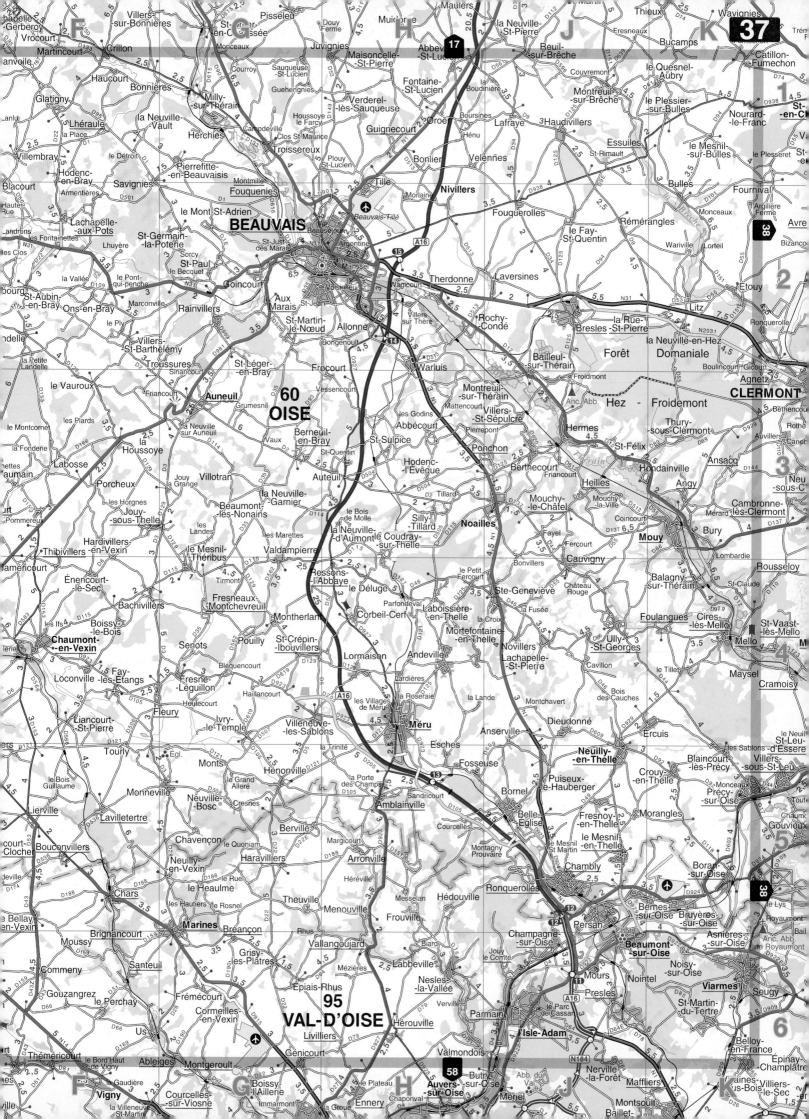

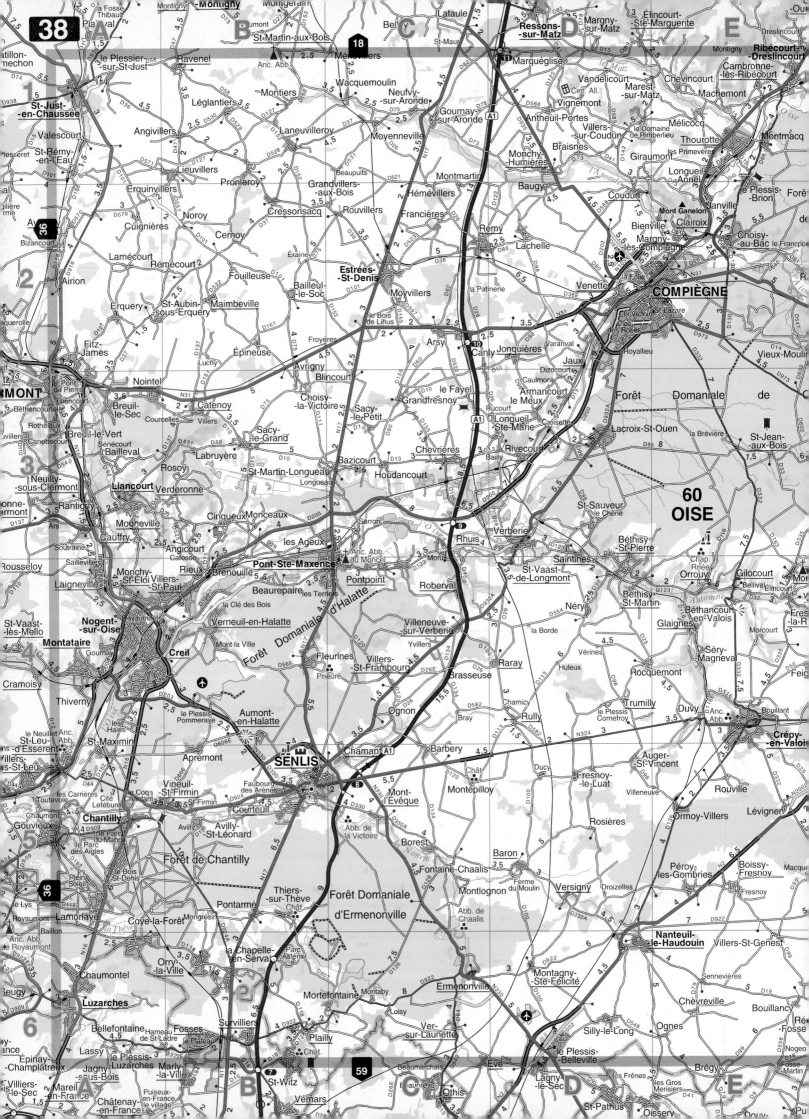

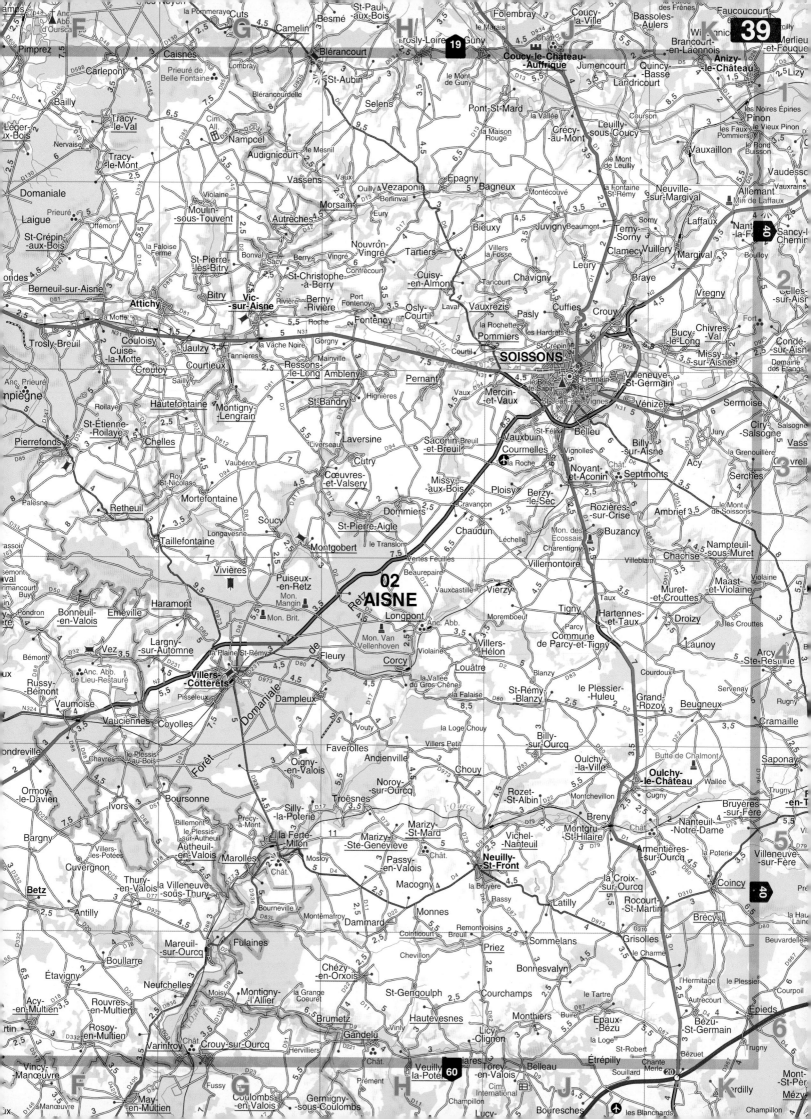

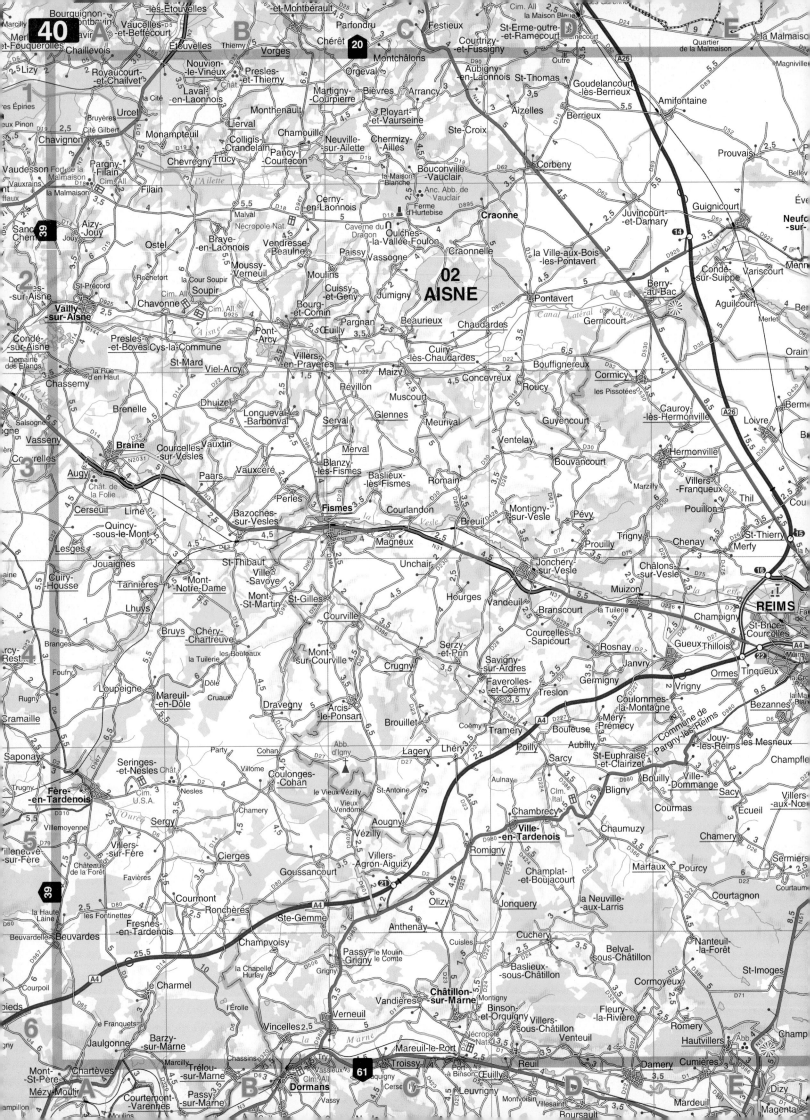

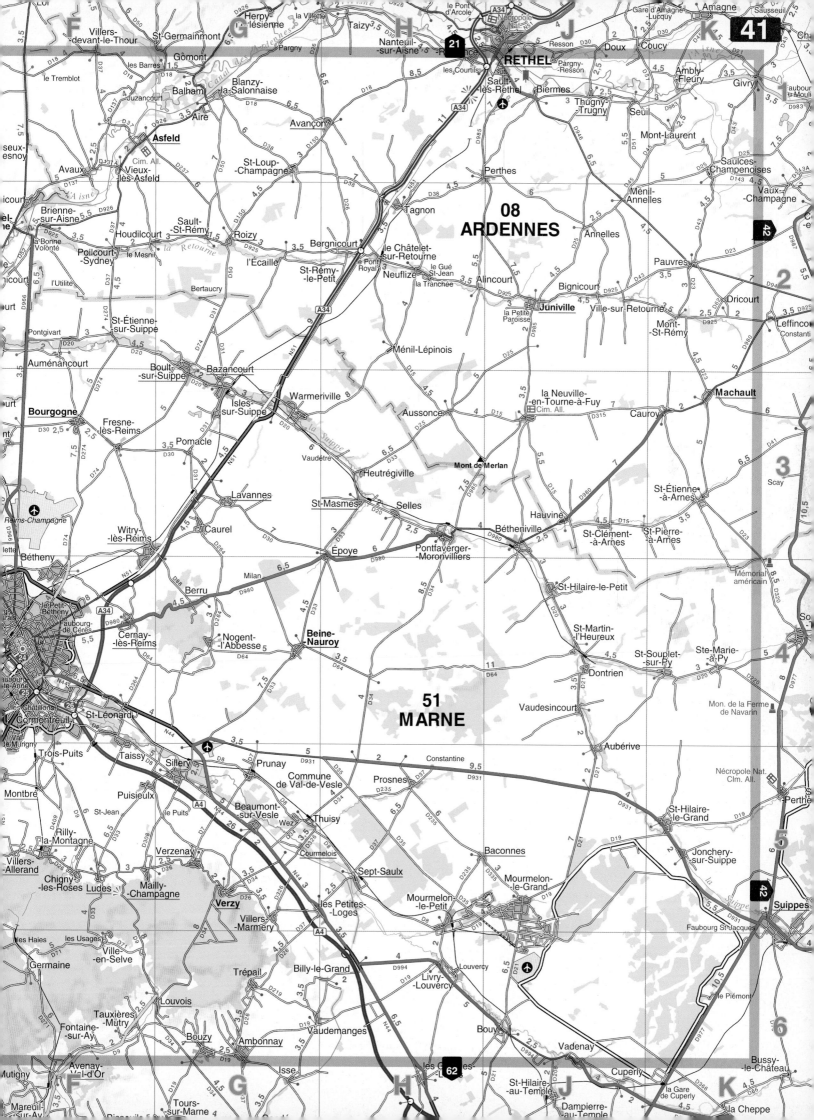

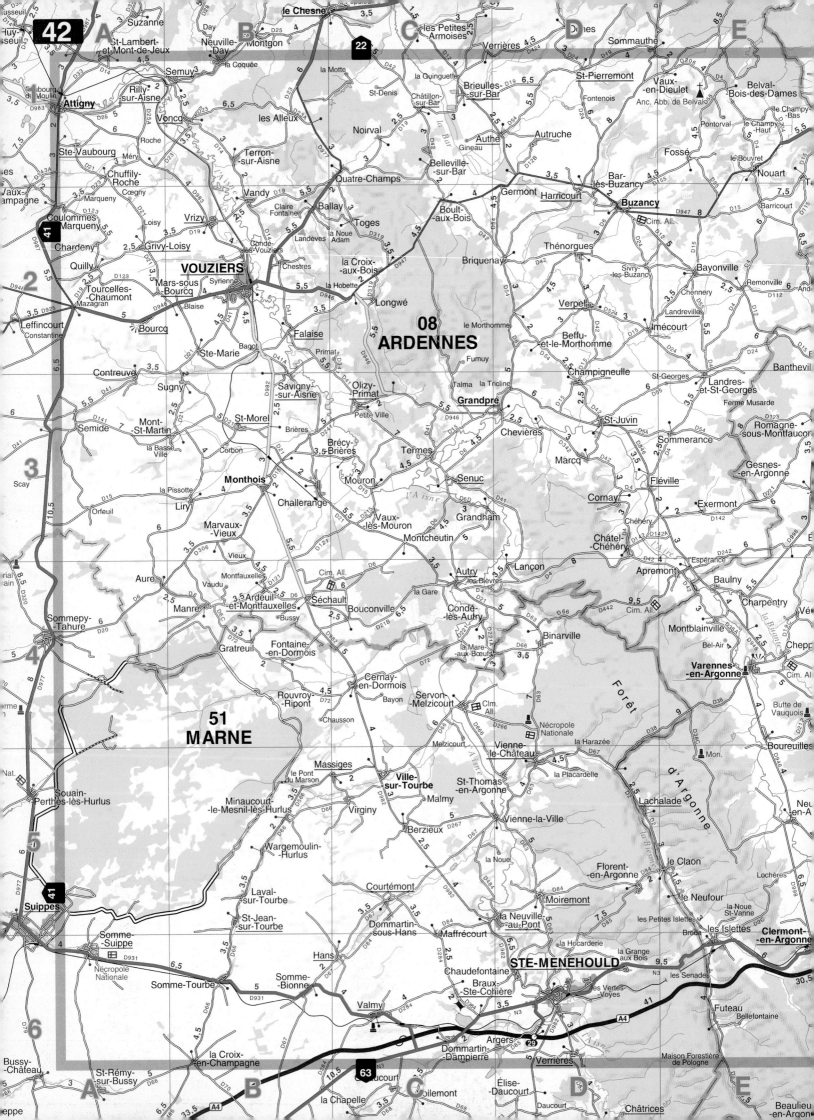

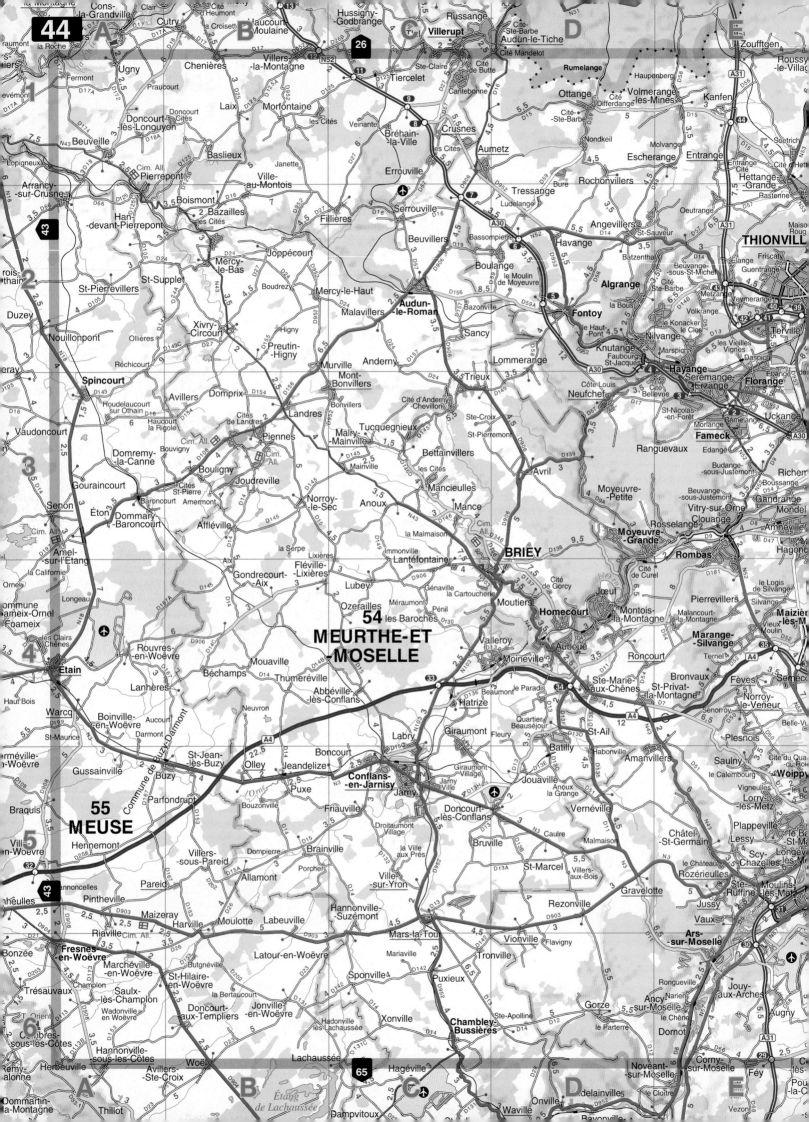

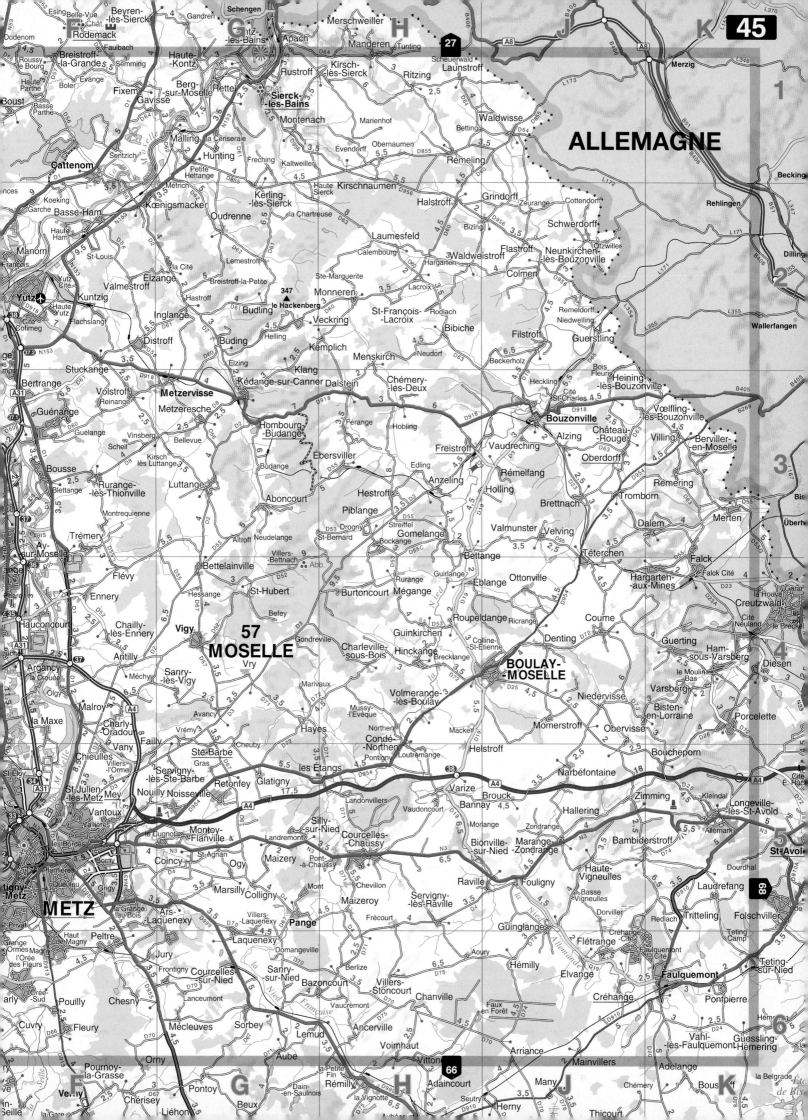

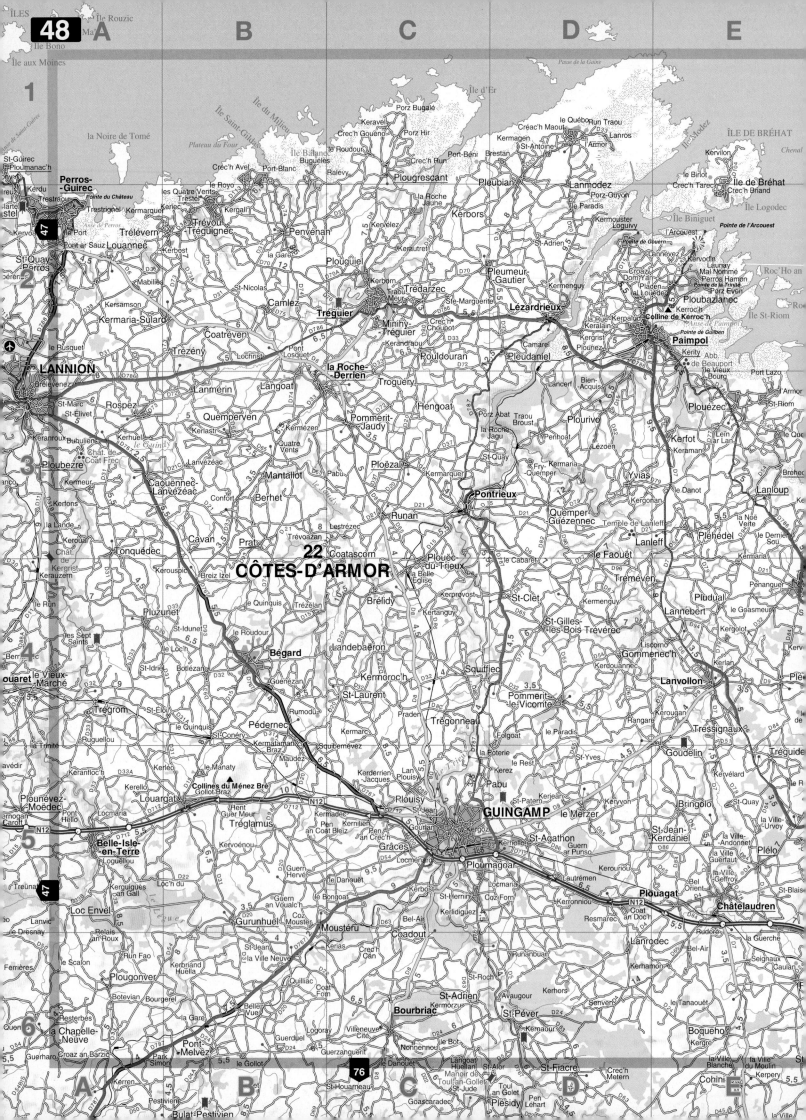

1

2

3

G O L F E   D E   S A I N T - M A L O

Trévos

Kerouziel

'louha

le Palus

Tréverneuc

Trélaouen

D 786

St-Quay

Bogouyen

ourdonnière

St-Barnabé

la Rue
Louais

St-Quay-Portrieux

Rade de Portrieux

le Point du Jour

Plourhan

Etables-sur-Mer

les Godelins

4

Chenal d'Erquy

Domaine
du Lanruen

la Moinerie

Pléhé
-Plage-Vieu

Beausoleil

Cap d'Erquy

Tu-Es-Roc

Sables
-d'Or-les-Pins

les Hôpitaux

Erquy

Bellevent

Plurien

Falaise de la Roche Jaune

Caroual

Langourian

N-D-
de la Cour

Lantic

la Ville
Jacob

la Ville Garnier

Binic

la Ville Berneuf

St-Pabu

la Ville
Evêque

le Bourgneuf

le Vaudic

la Ville
Louais

la Ville Rouault

la Ville Morel

Pointe de Pordic

Pléneuf-Val-André

le Val-André

la Ville
Bricault

la Couture

5

Trégomeur

Pordic

la Ville
au Guichou

la Ville
Guy

St-Éloy

les Rosaires

Dahouët

les Rues

Chât. de
Bien-Assis
l'Hôtel
des Landes

St-Laurent

la Chapelle
aux Comtes

St-Jean

50

Tréméloir

Pointe des Tablettes

Martin

le Port Morvan

le Puits
Merpault

la Bouillie

le Chemin
Chaussée

St-Samson

St-Nicolas

l'Arrivée

la Ville
Hervy

le Roselier

Pointe du Roselier

Treutran

St-Jacques

la Ville
Cochard

Hén

la Pougonnière

Ste-Anne

la Roche
Couverte

Kerpeux

N12

le Sepulcre

les Mines

liremuson

Plérin

le Légué

St-Laurent
-de la Mer

la Cotentin

le Poirier

l'Hôpital

St-Alban

les Rigaudais

Hénansal

D 712

St-Jouan

St-Michel

la Ville
Sous la Tour

Cesson

Lermot

Planguenoual

St-Gueltas

neuf
vara

St-Hervé

ST-BRIEUC

la Ville
Hello

Ginglin

St-Ilan

Carberon

le Crapont

la Grandville

Morieux

St-Denoual

St-Ignace

la Méaugon

le Plan

Ploufragan

Tréguoux

Languoux

D 700

le Rivage

les Quilles

Fortville

Licantois

les Ronts
Neufs

Quintenic

St-Aaron

la Doberie

6

les Croix

les Grèves

Licéllion

St-René

Coëtmieux

Andel

la Fontaine
aux Saules

Yffiniac

Carberon

Pommeret

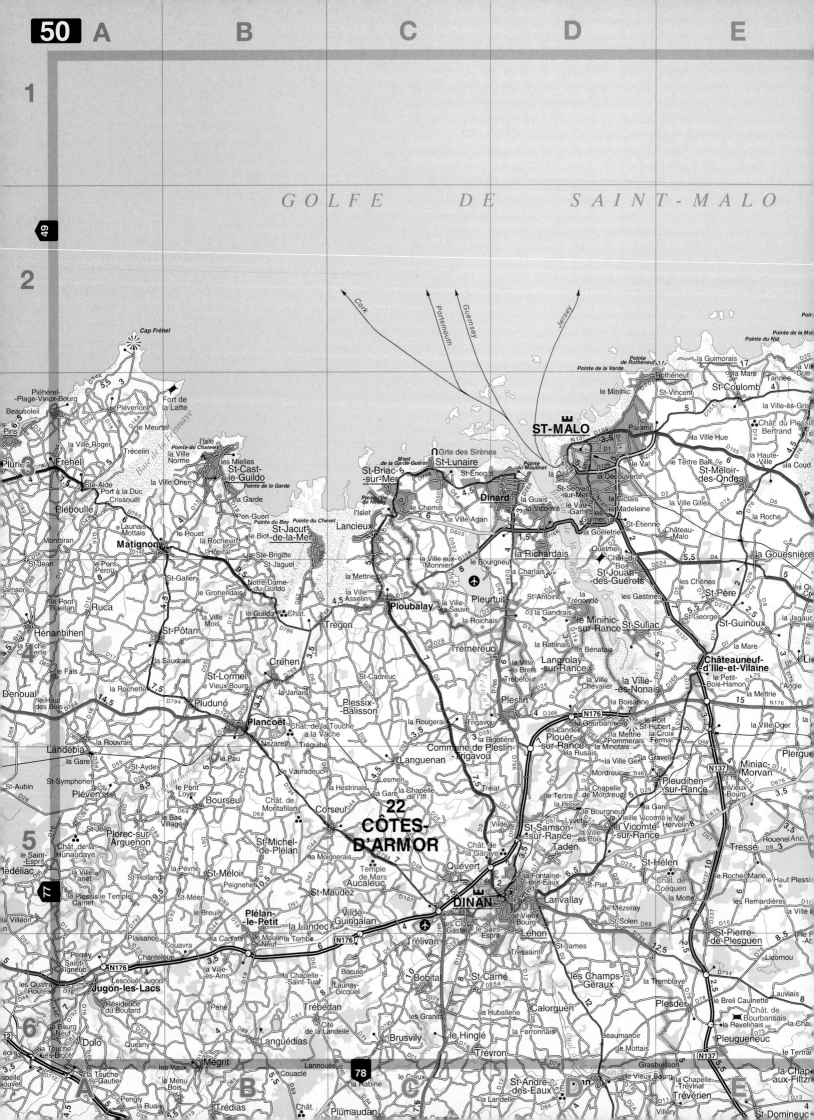

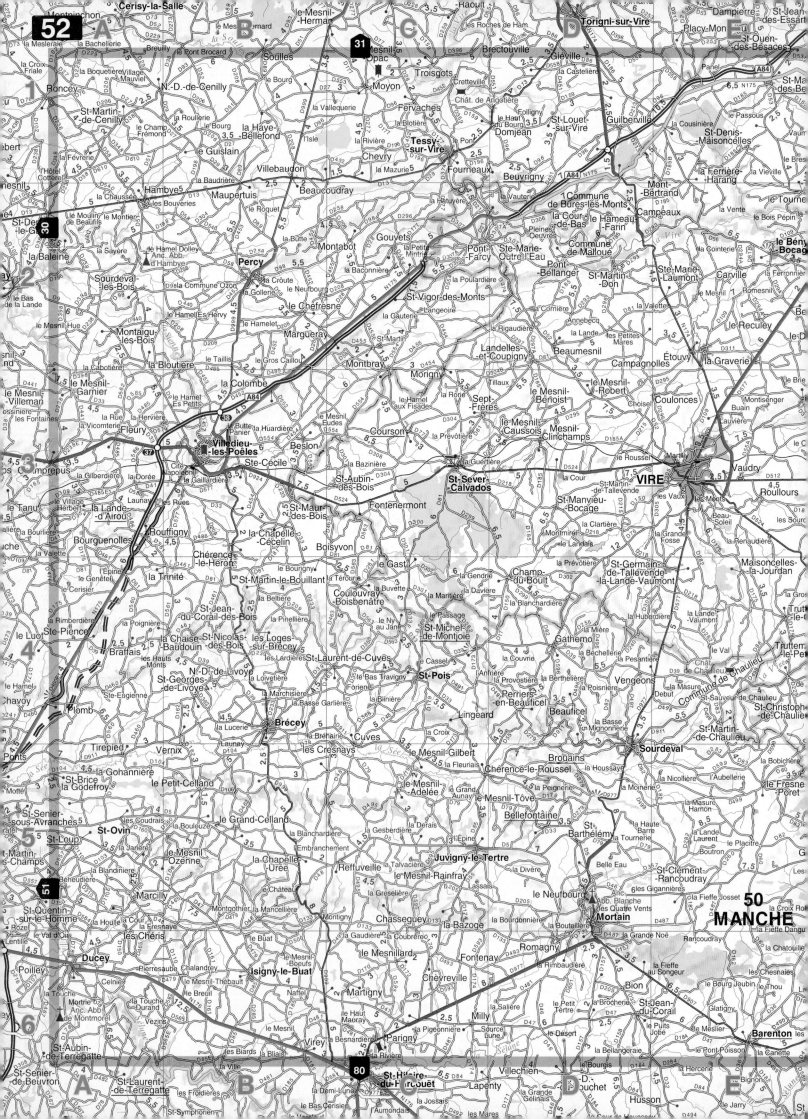

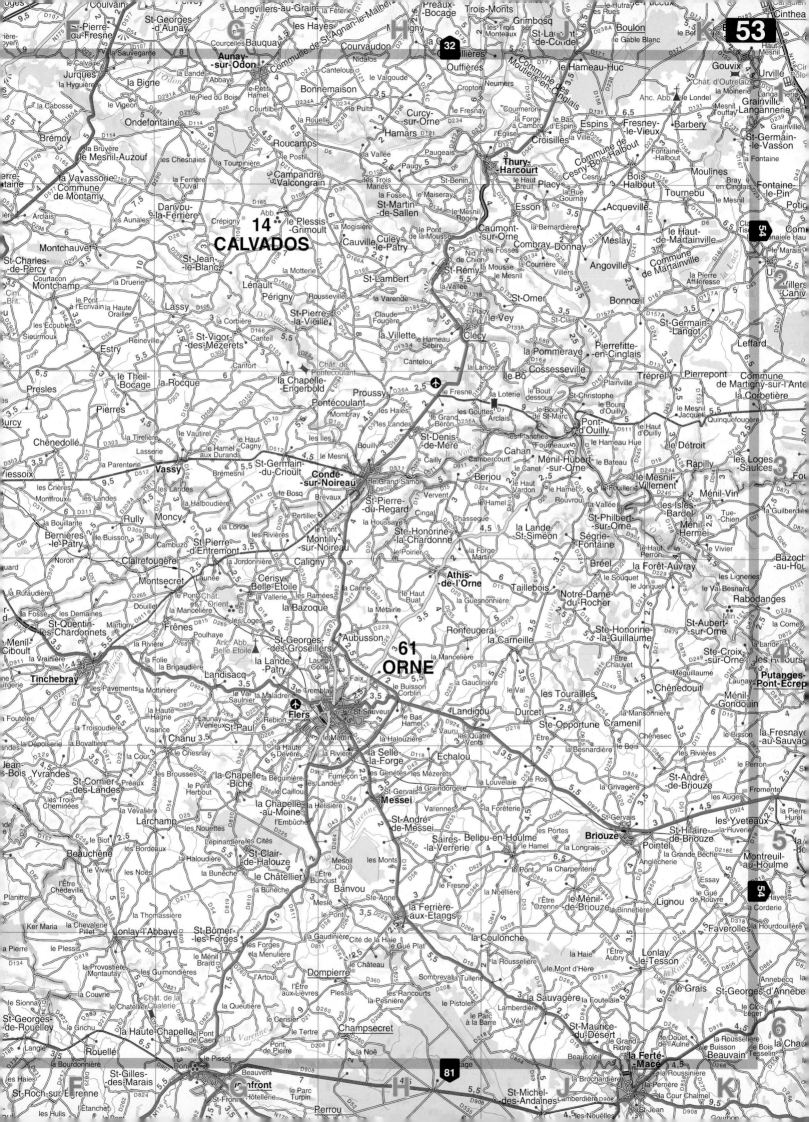

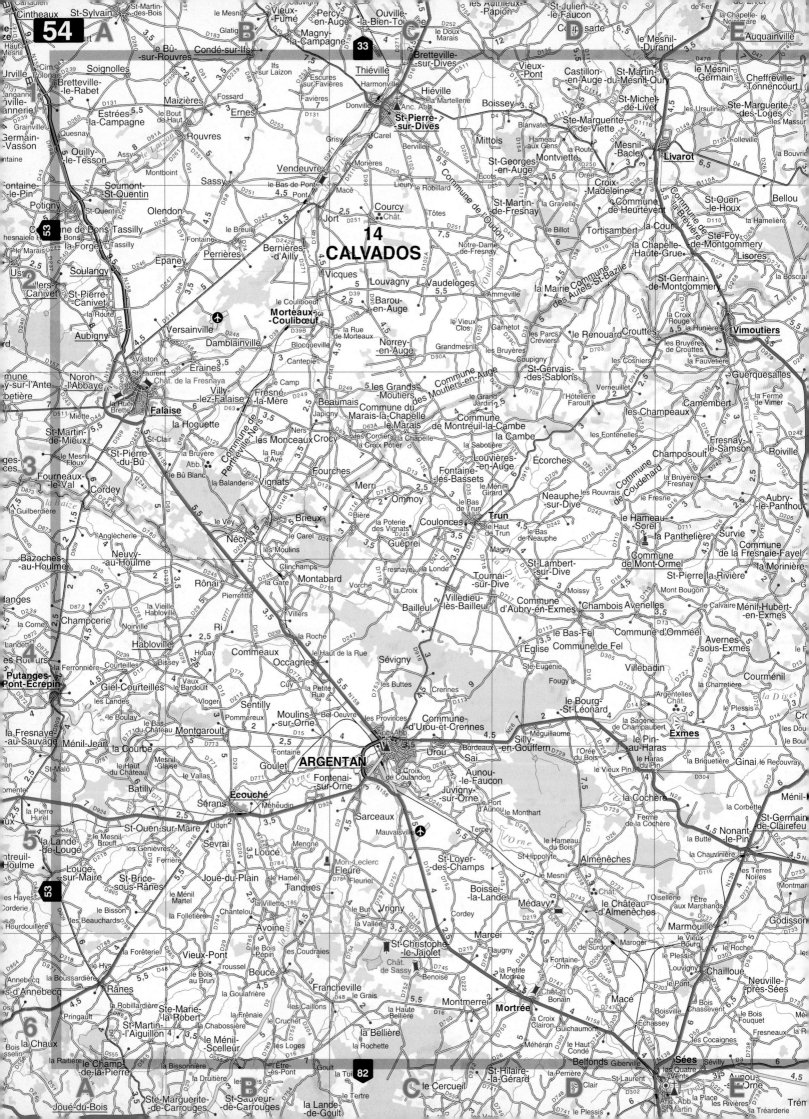

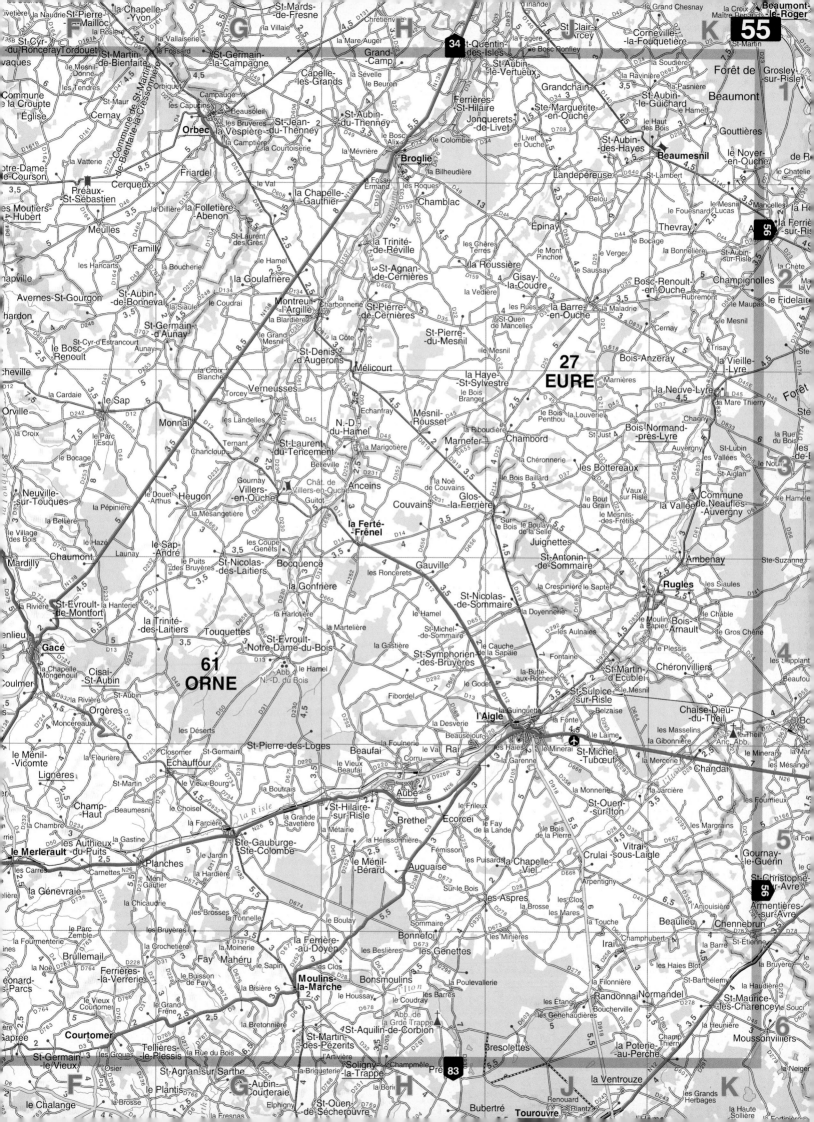

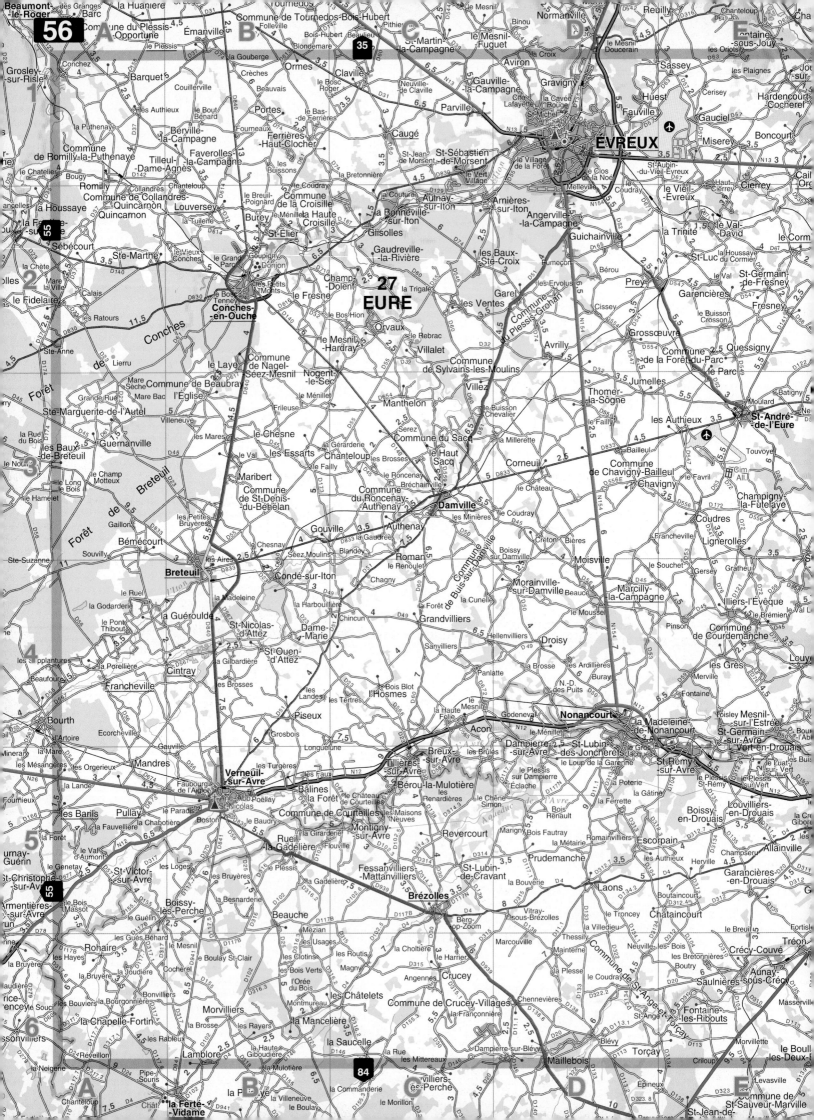

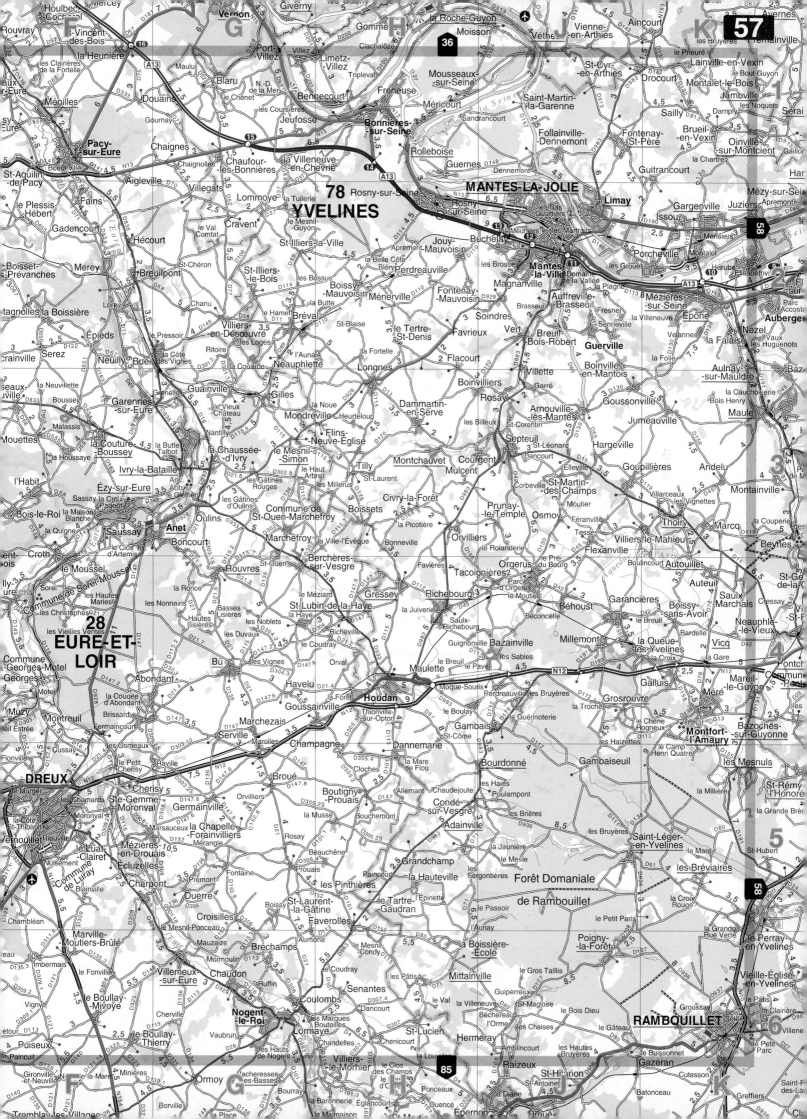

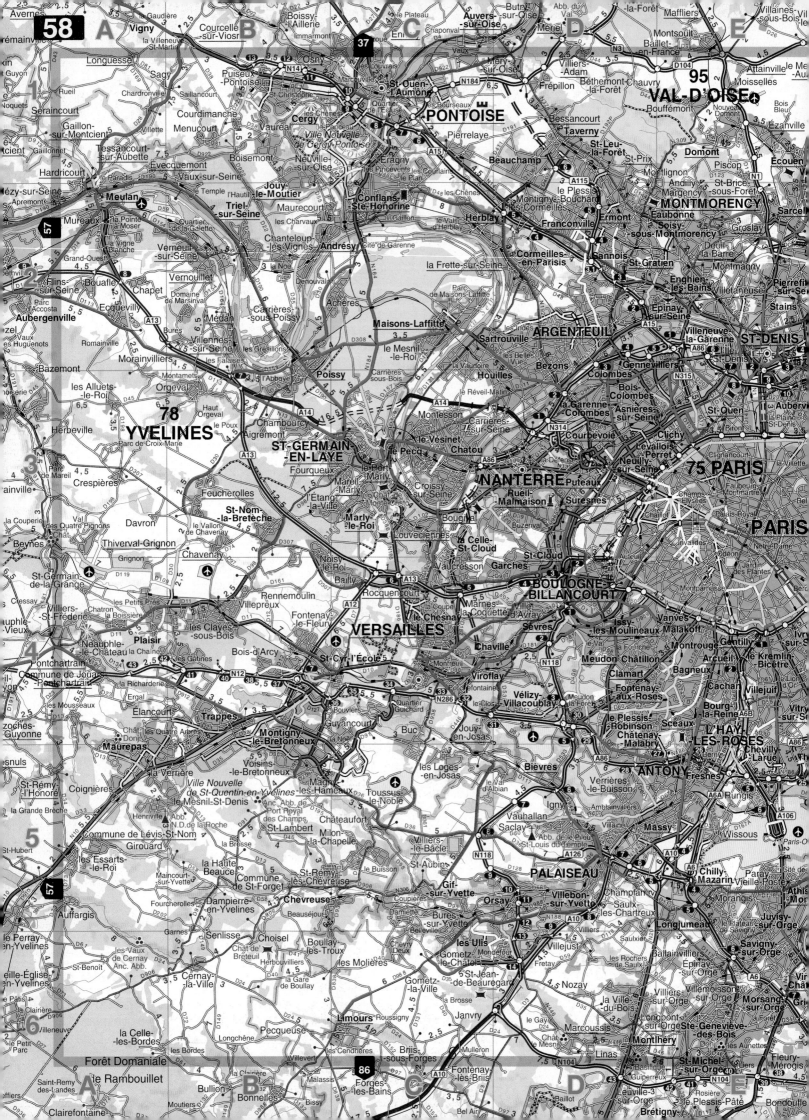

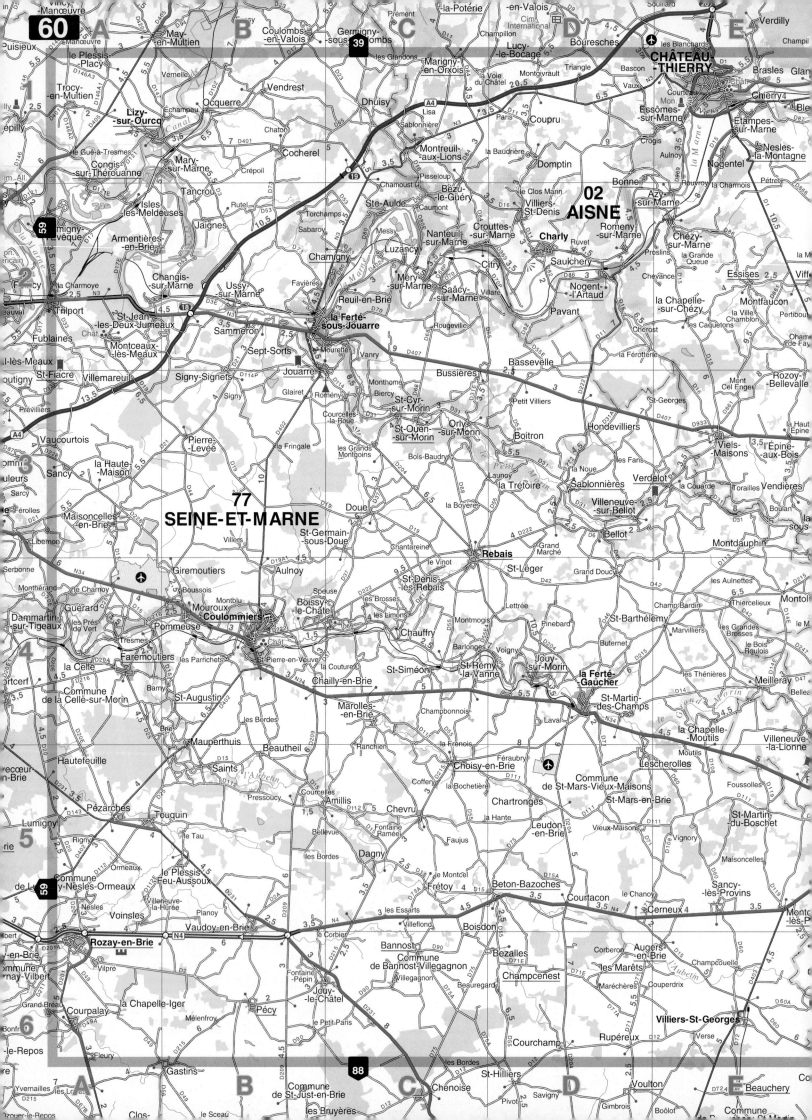

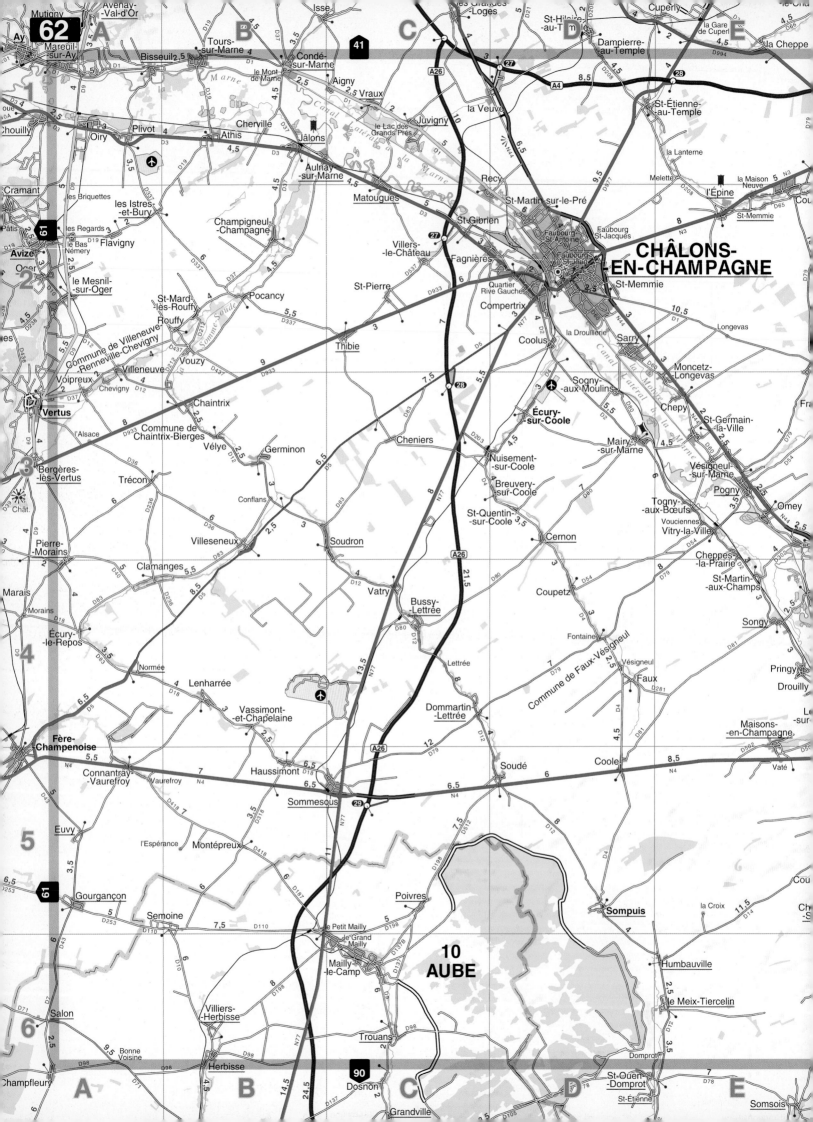

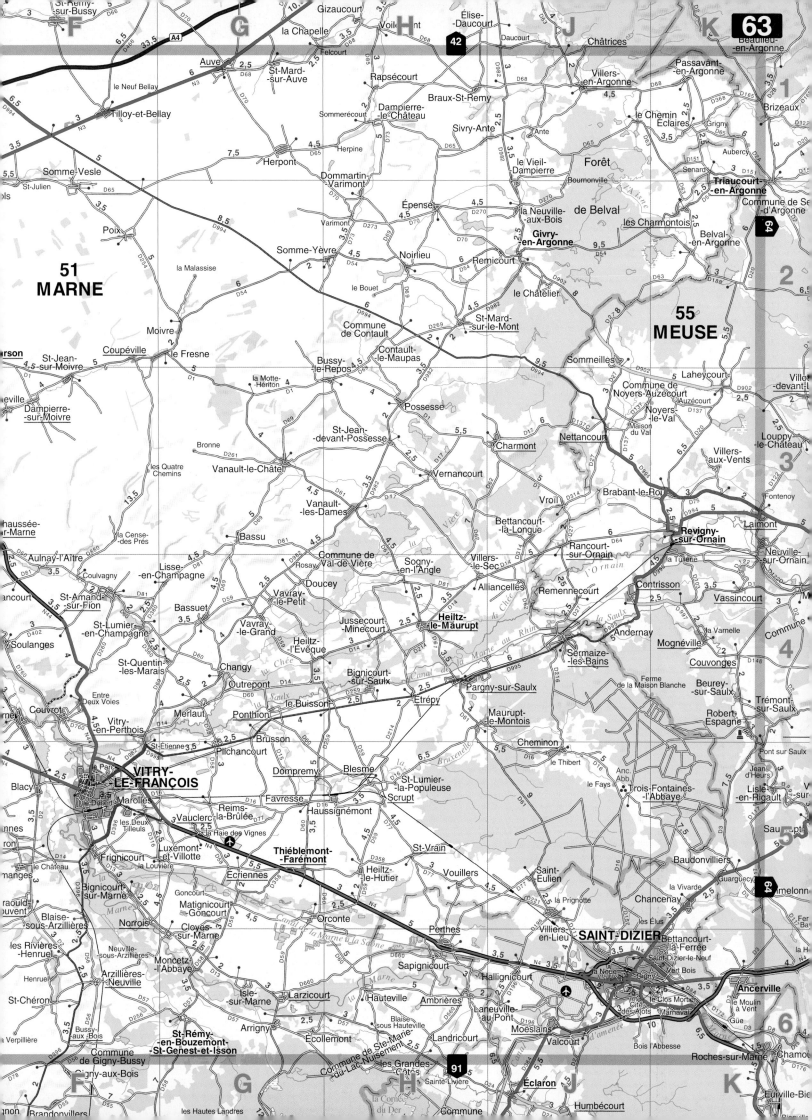

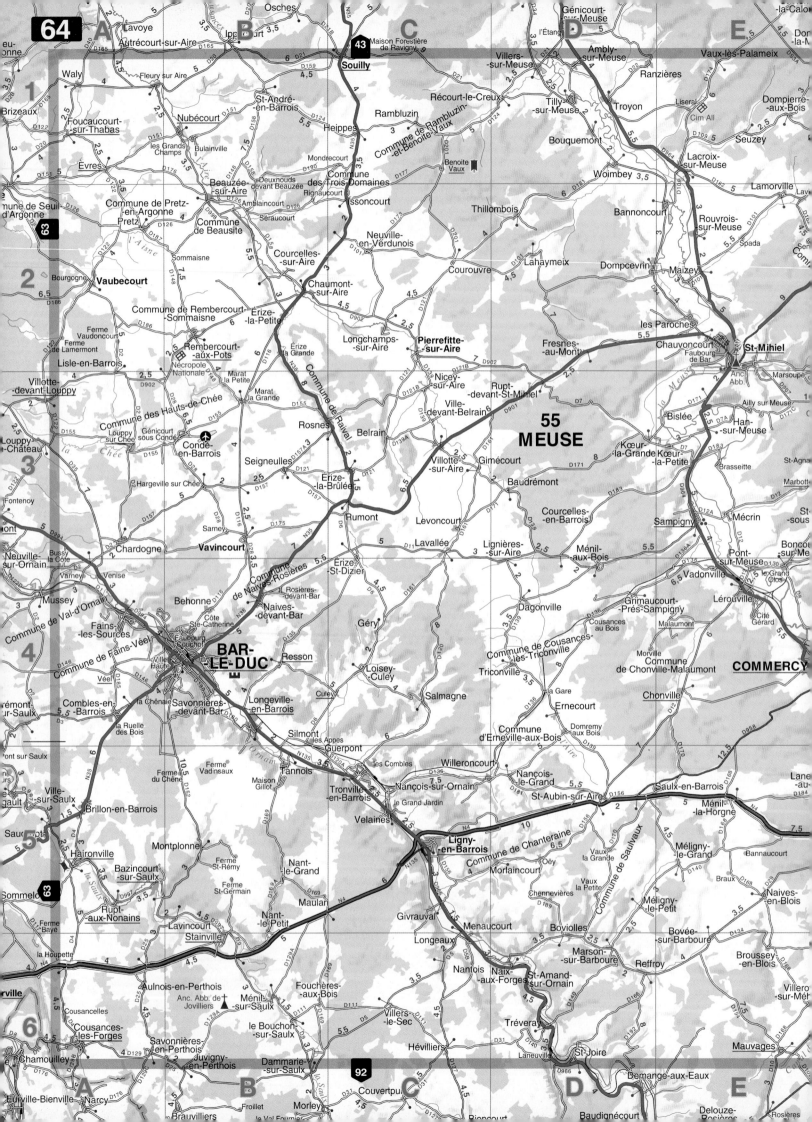

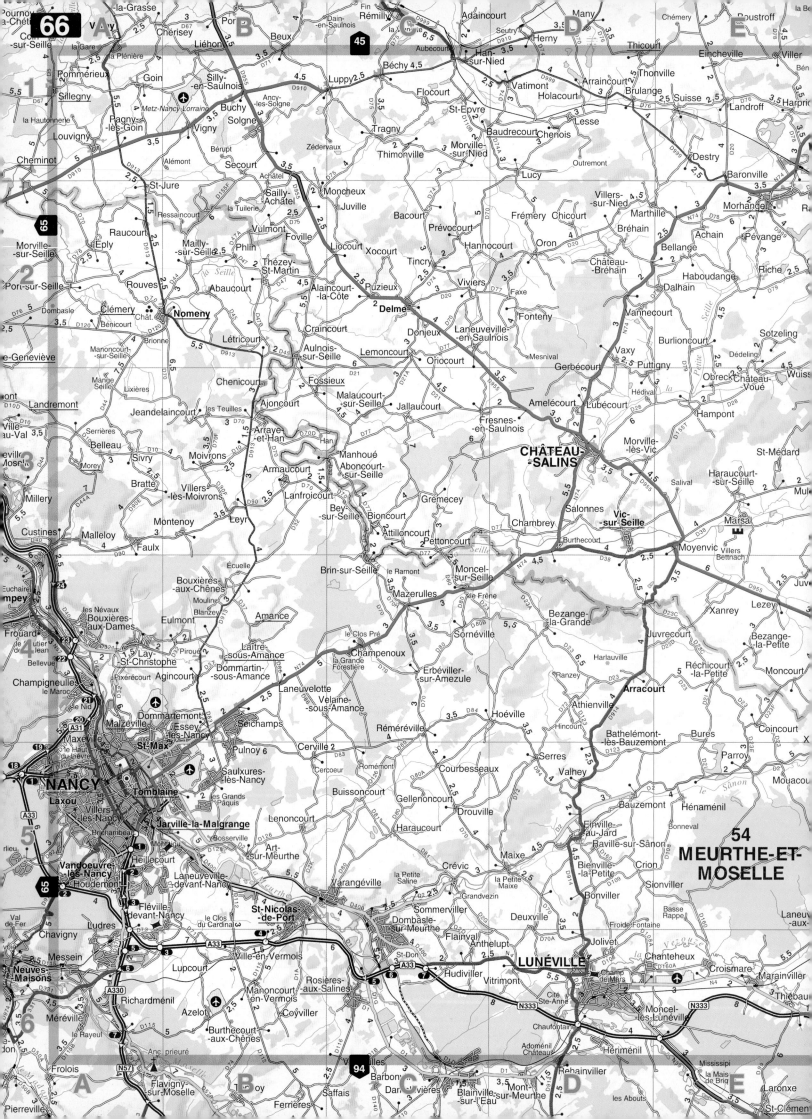

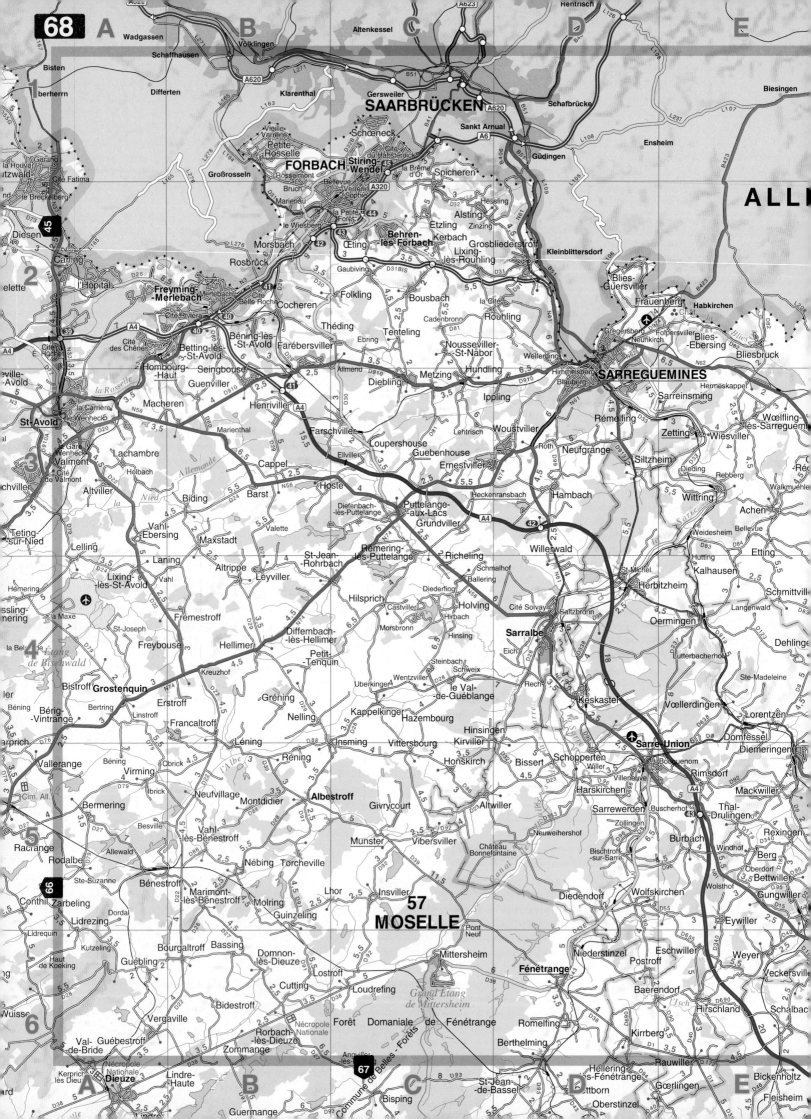

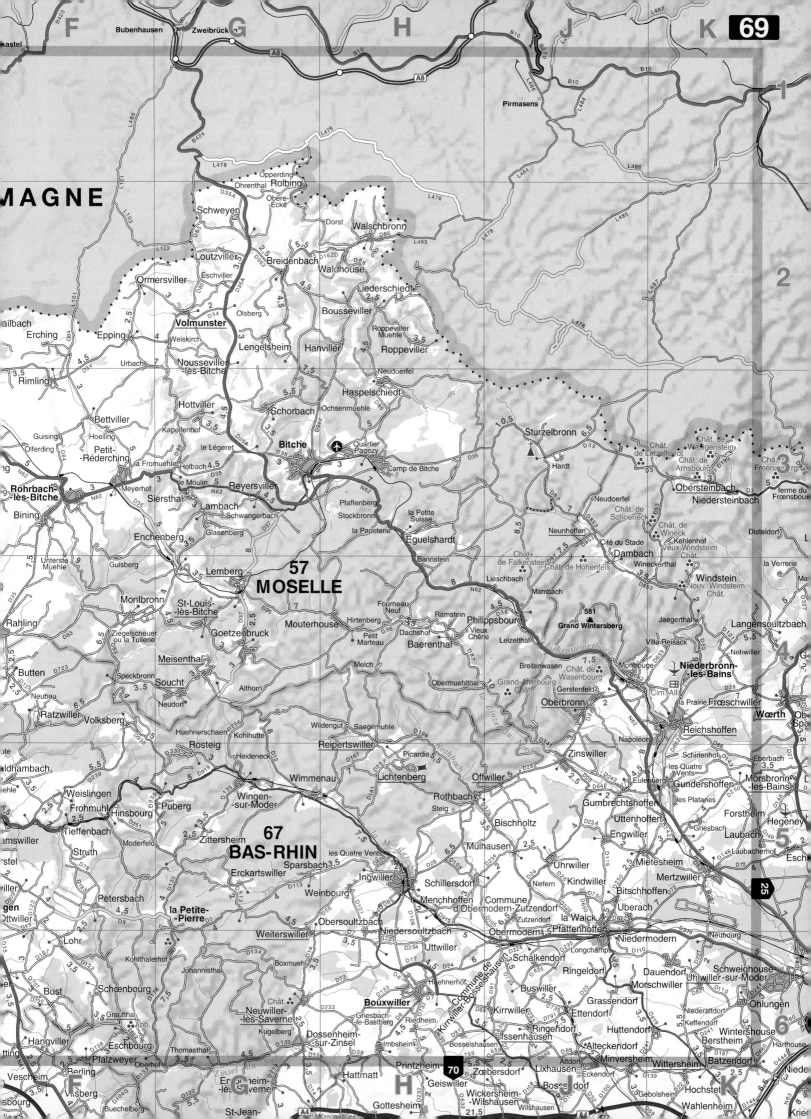

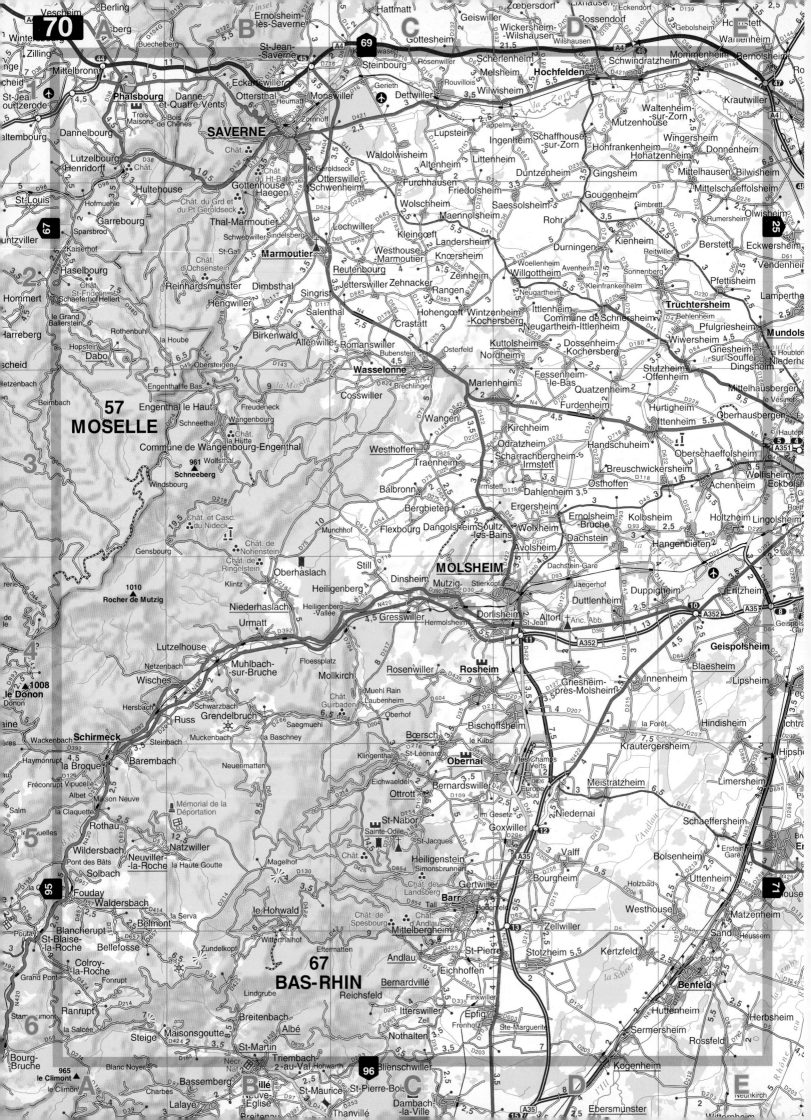

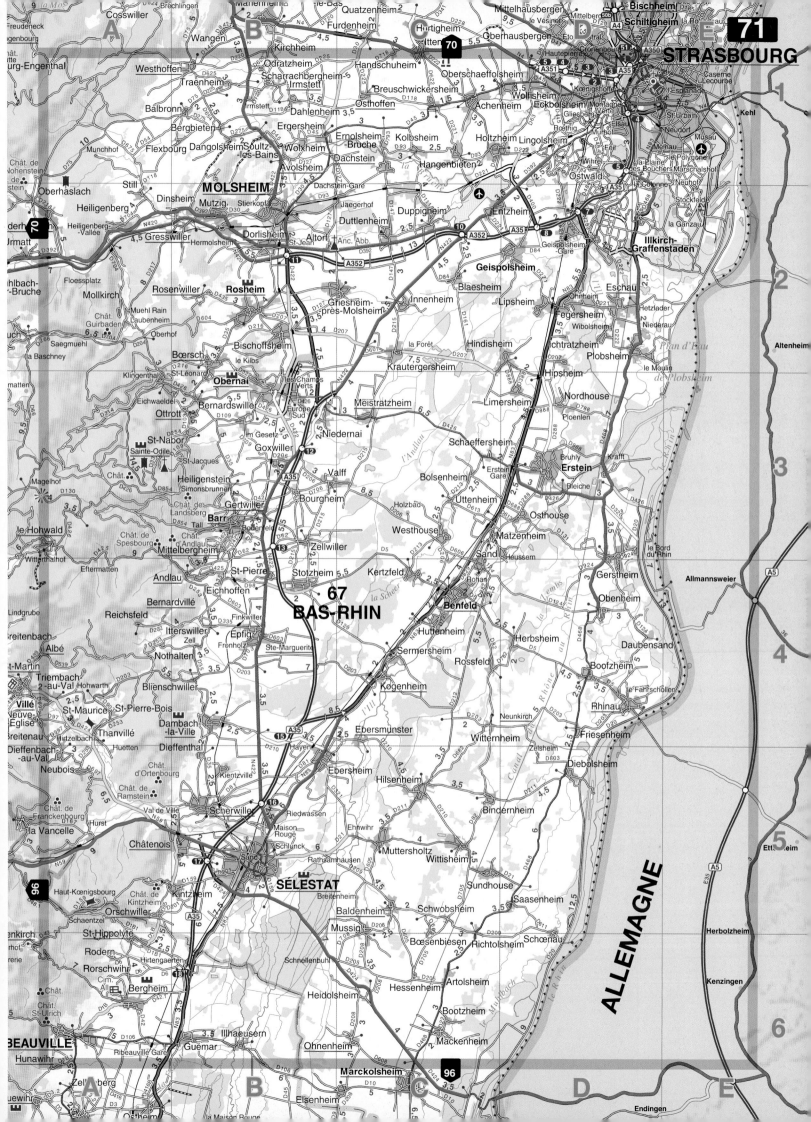

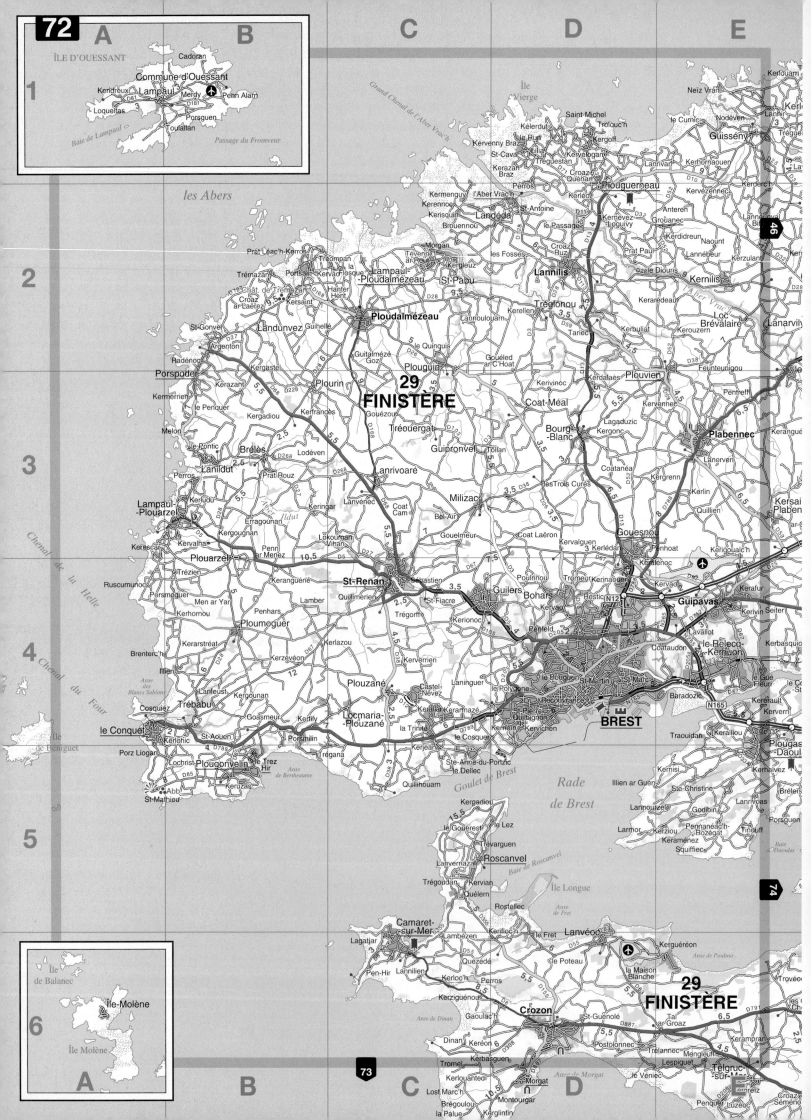

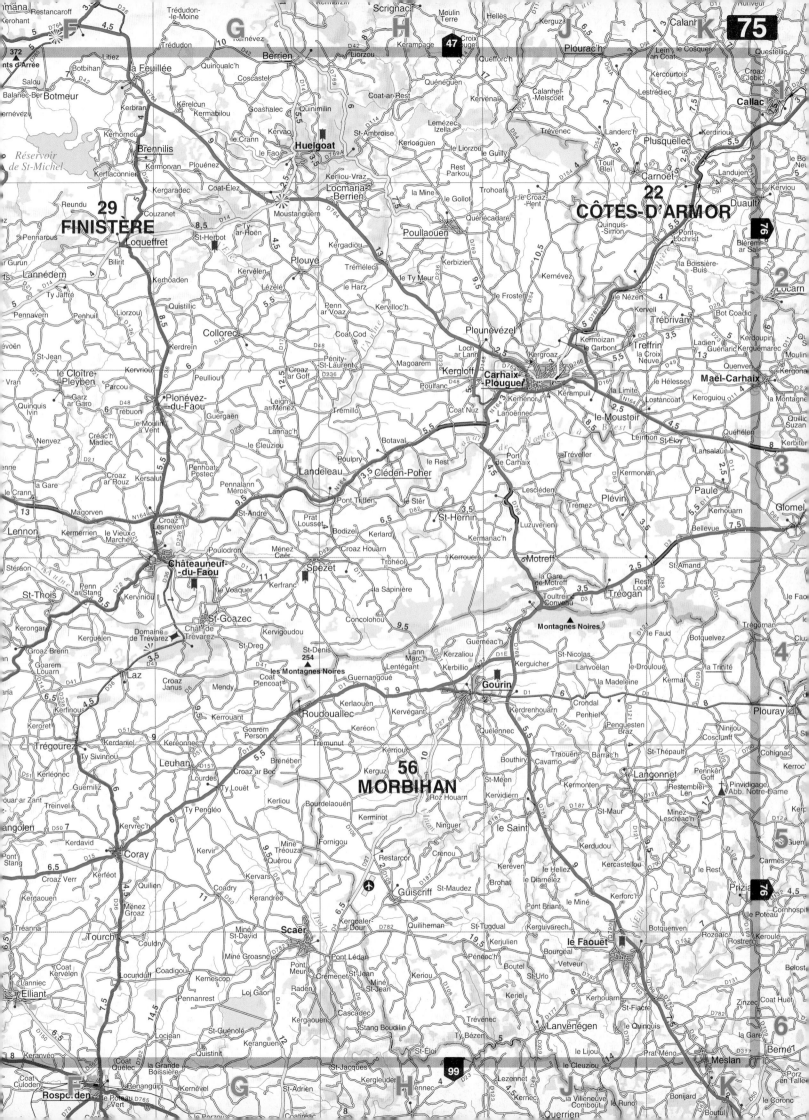

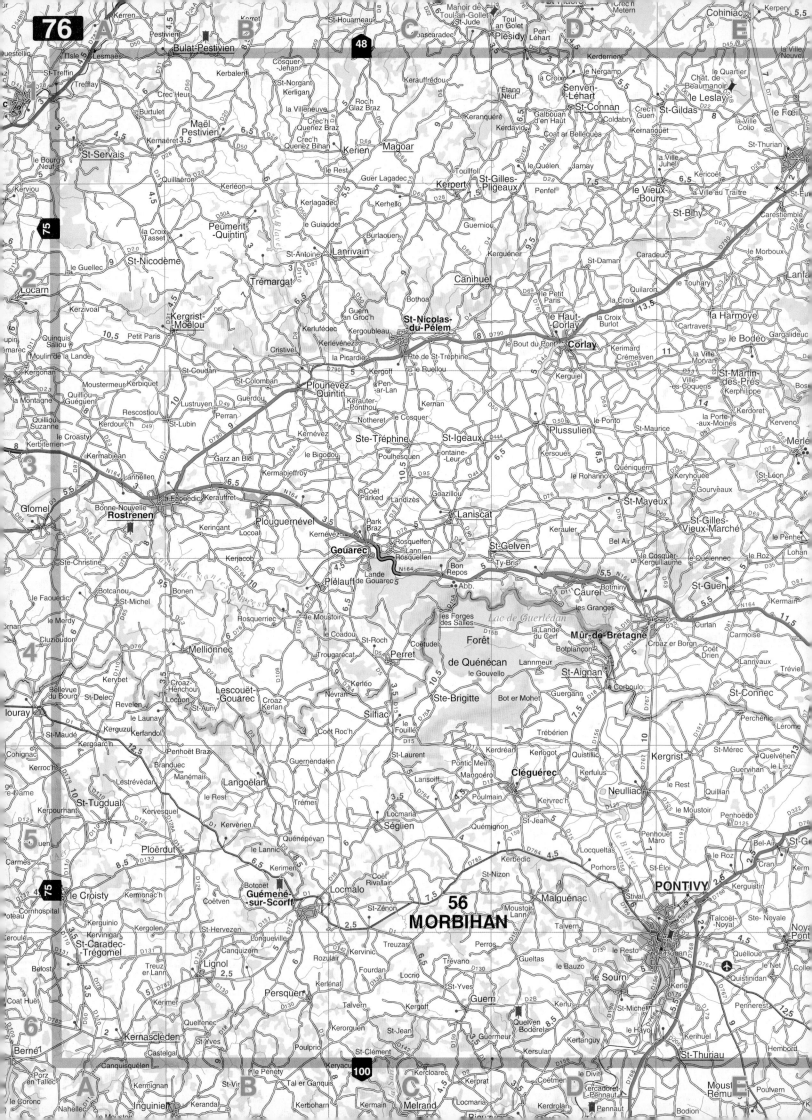

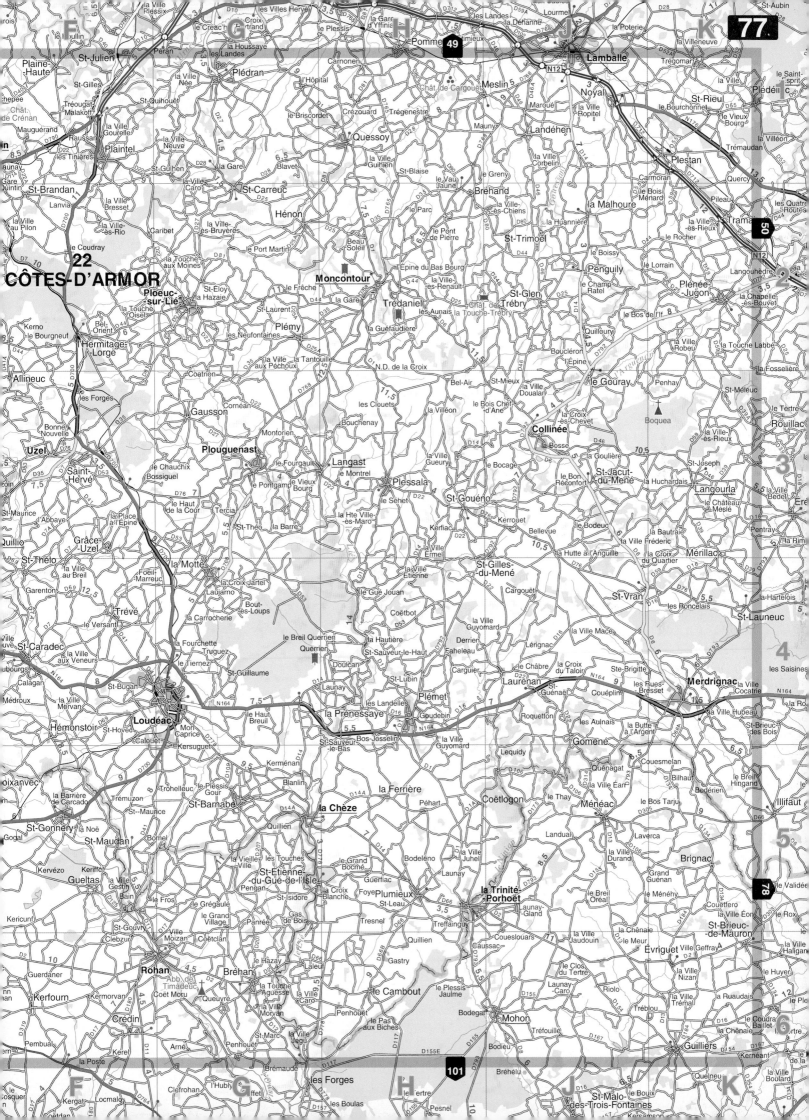

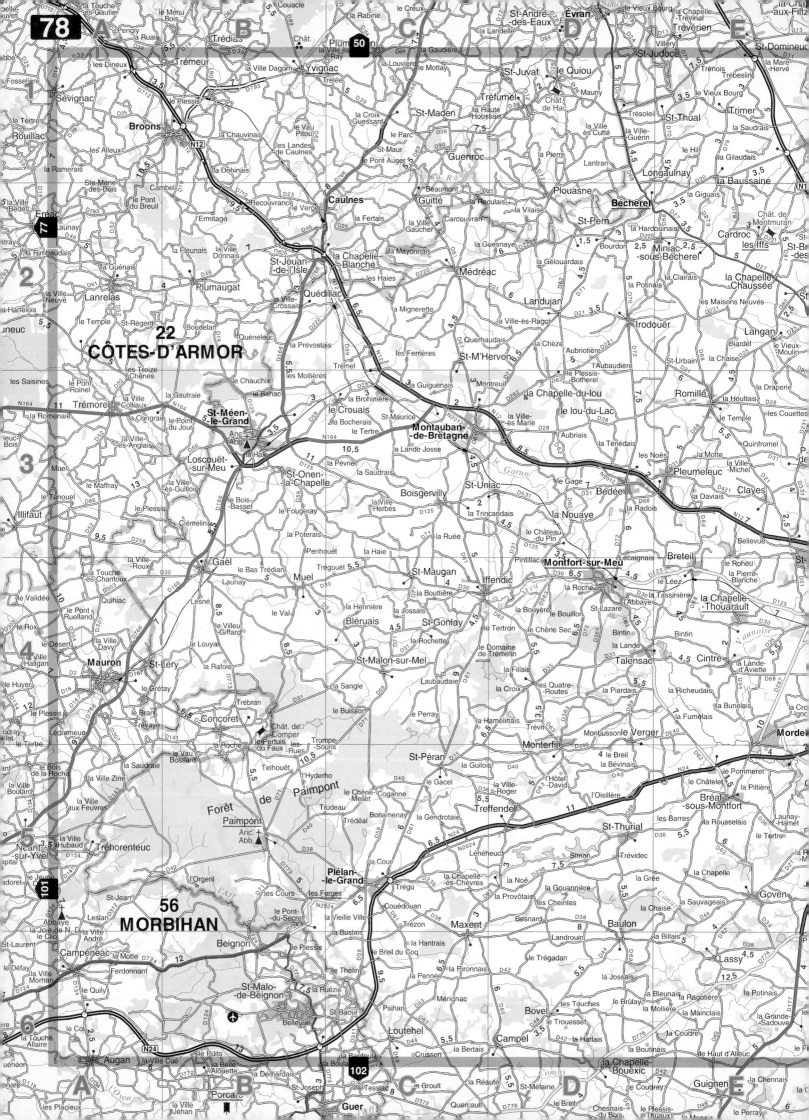

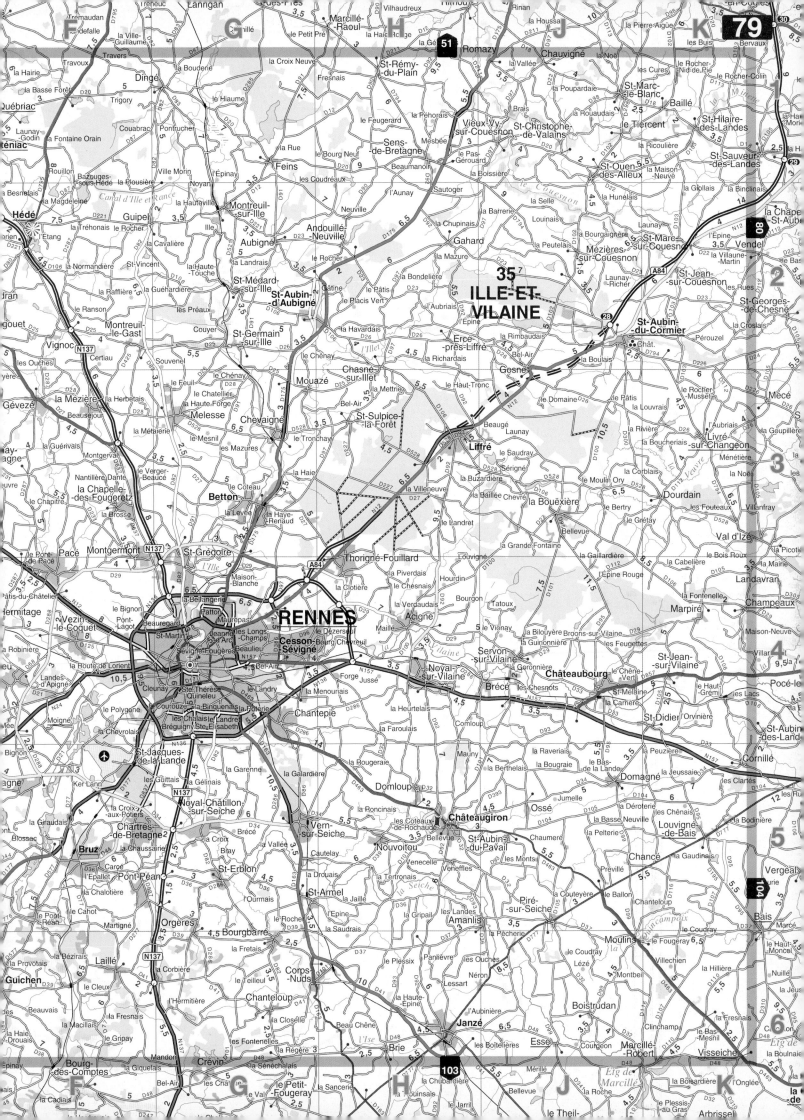

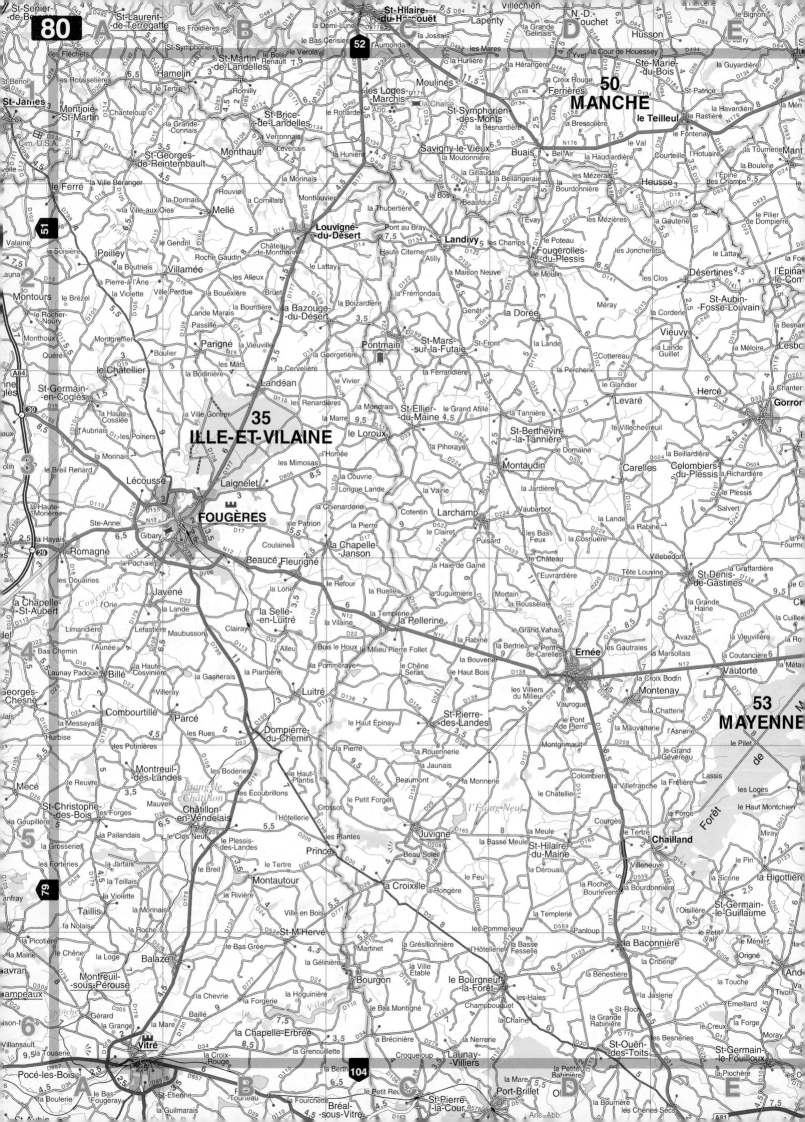

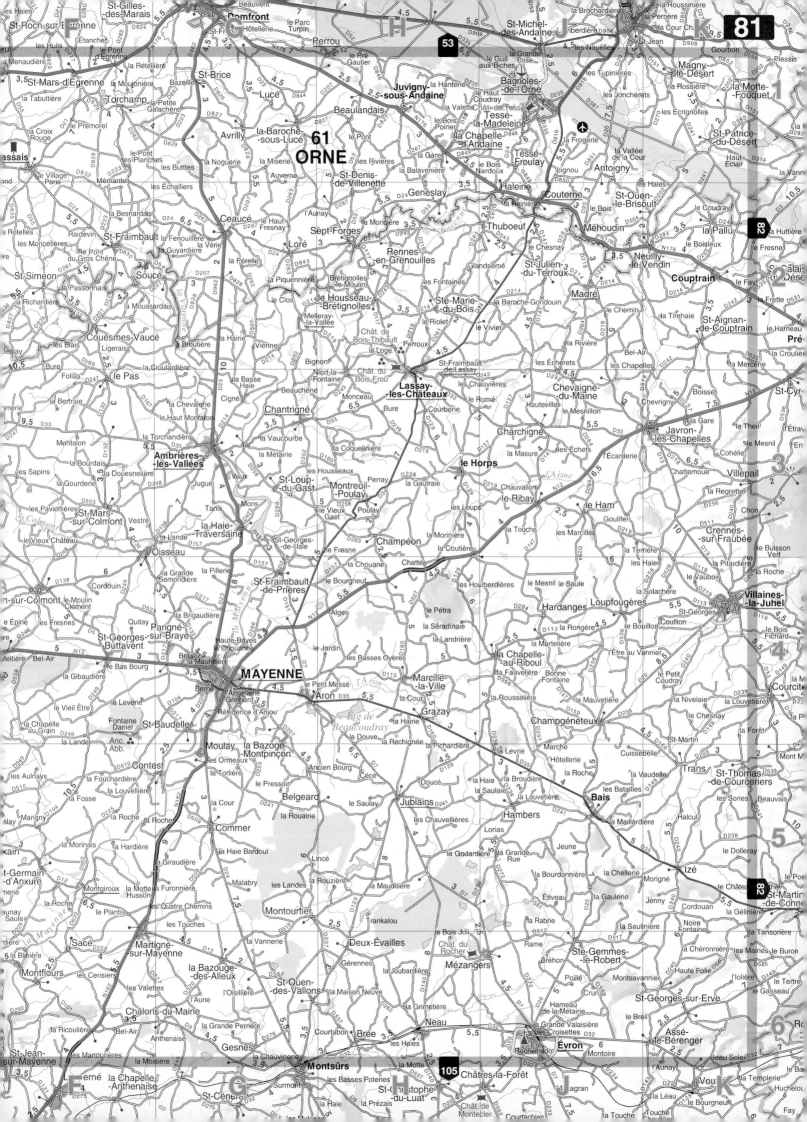

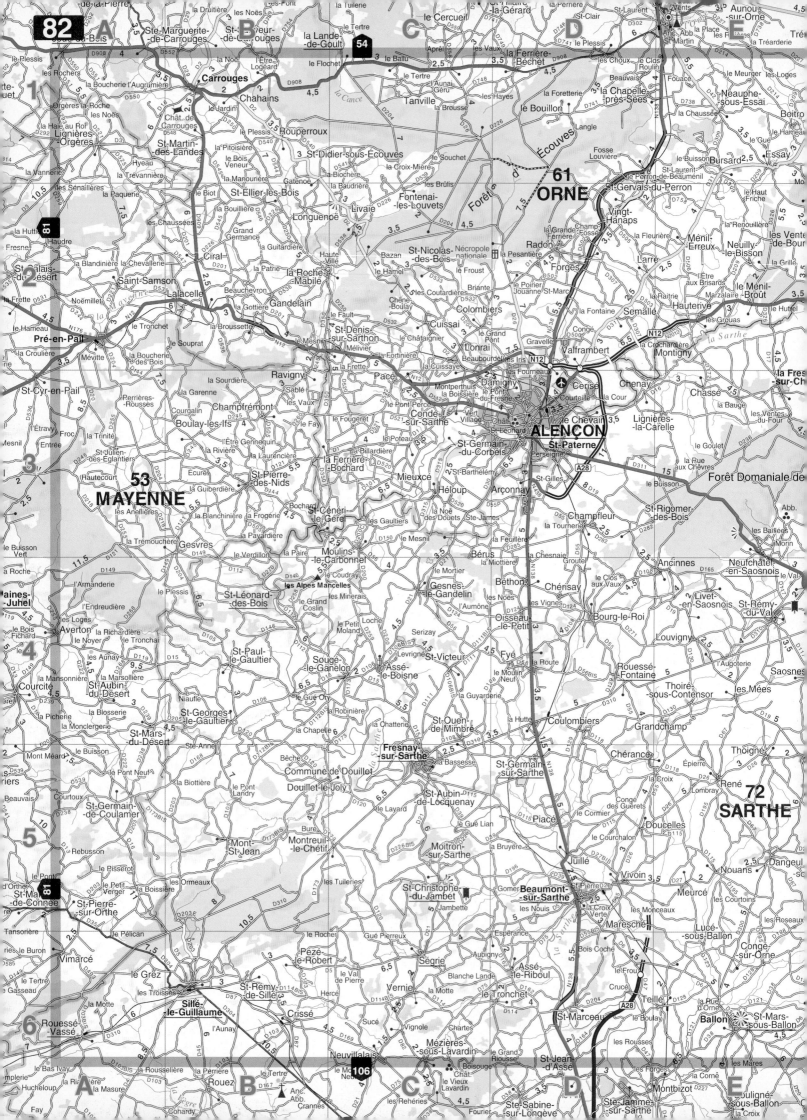

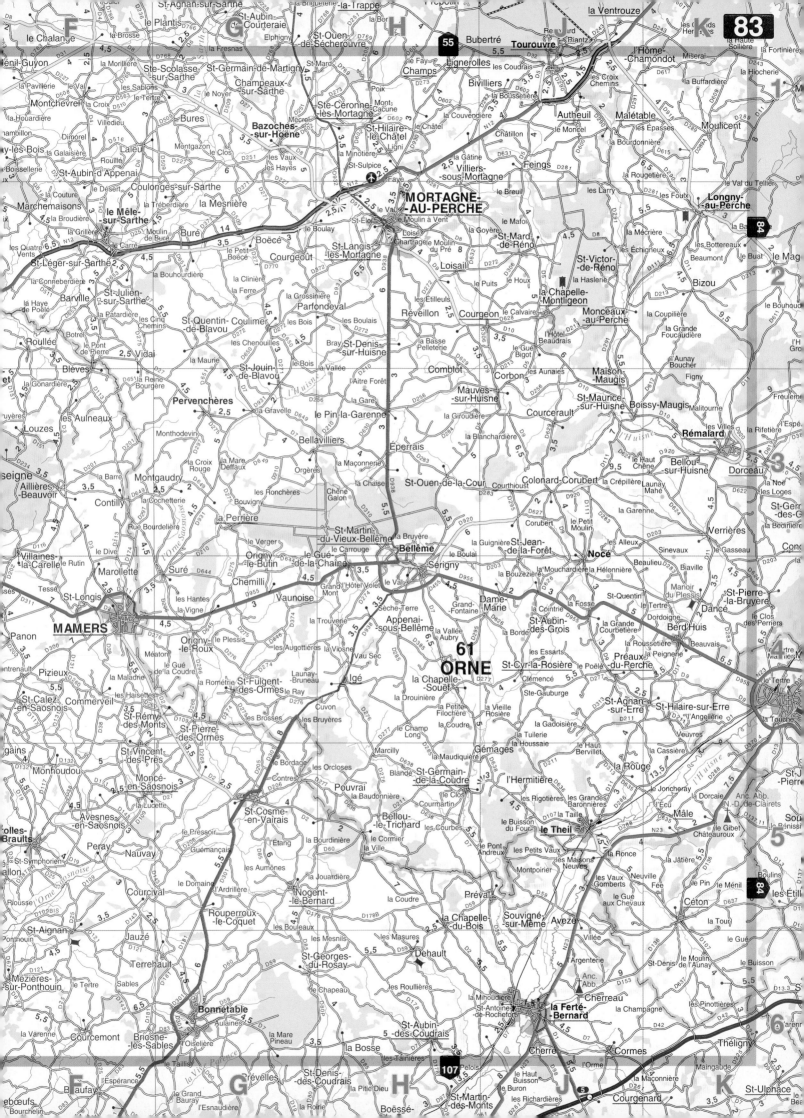

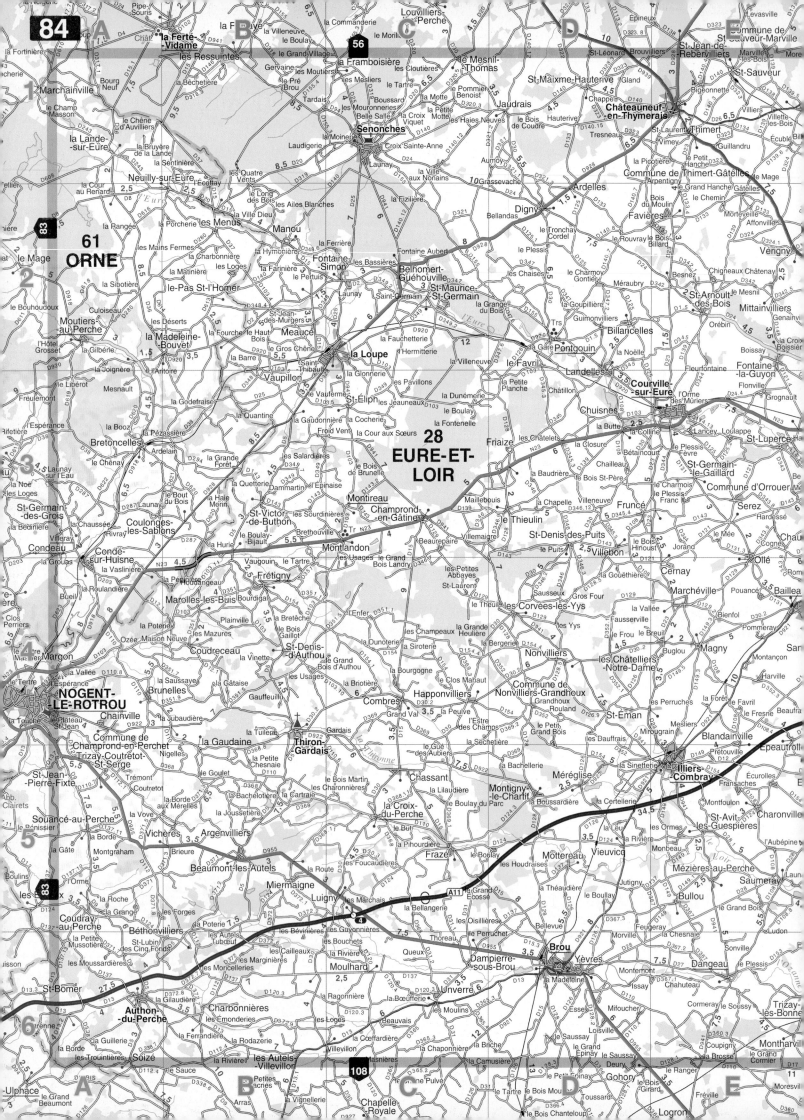

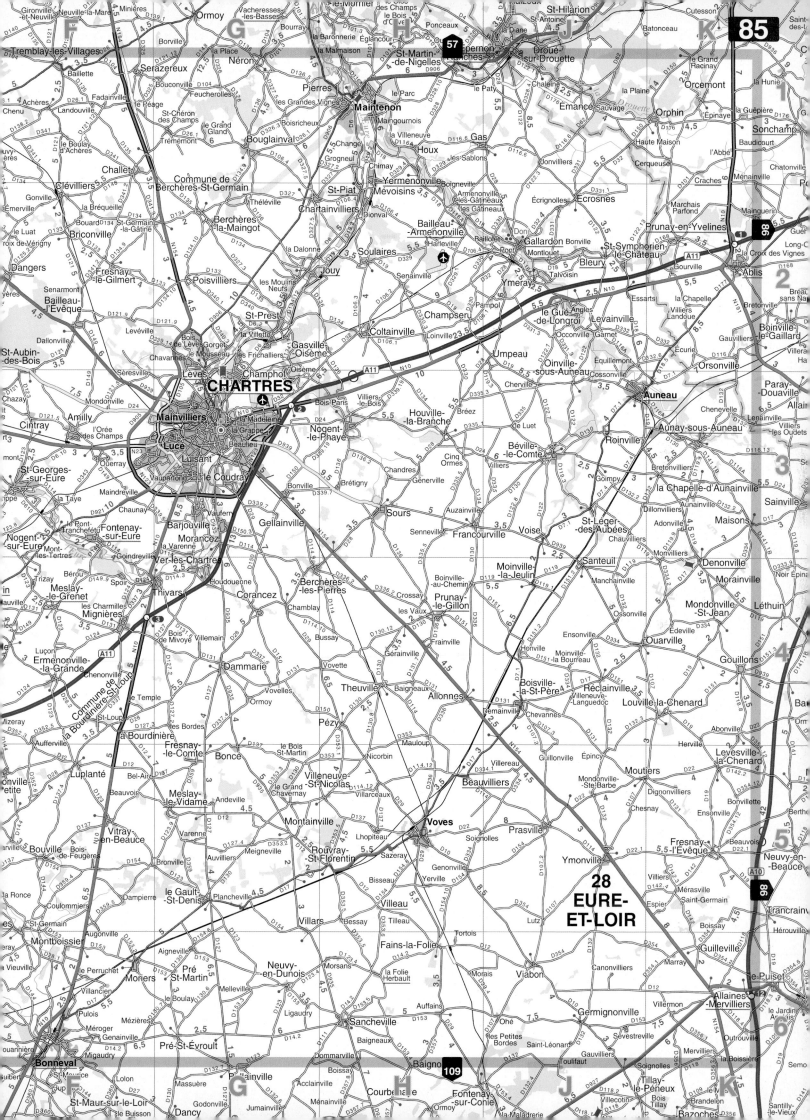

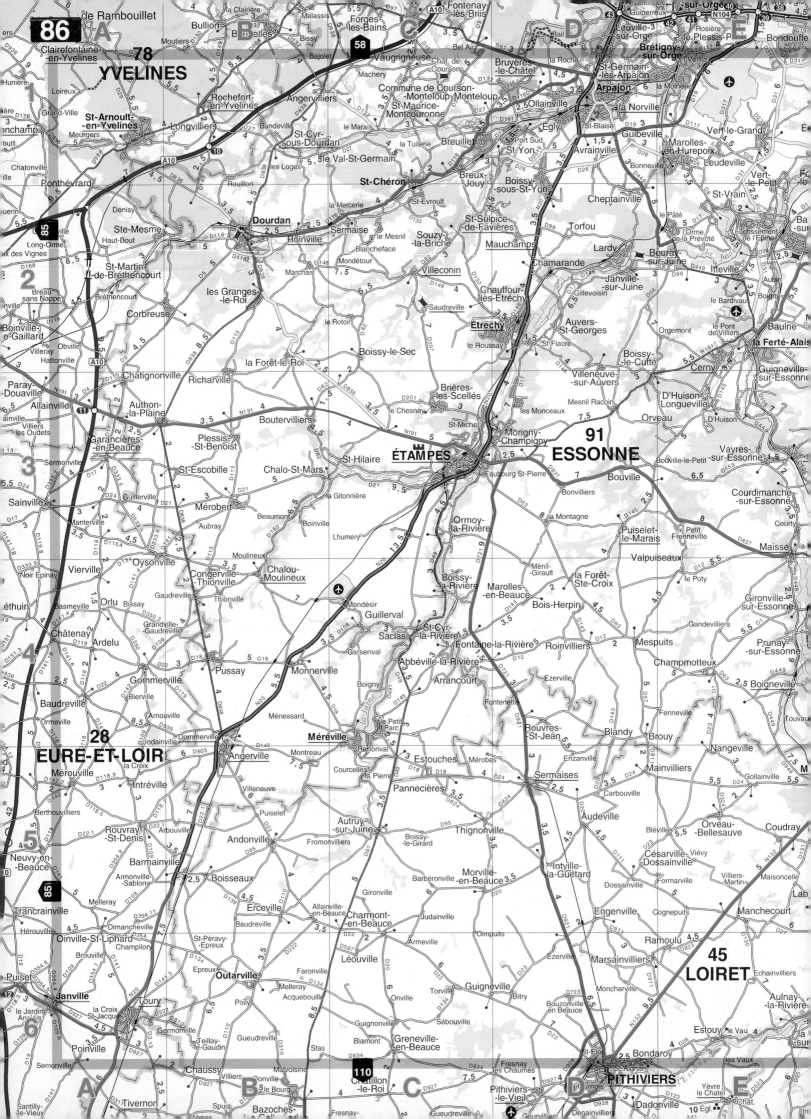

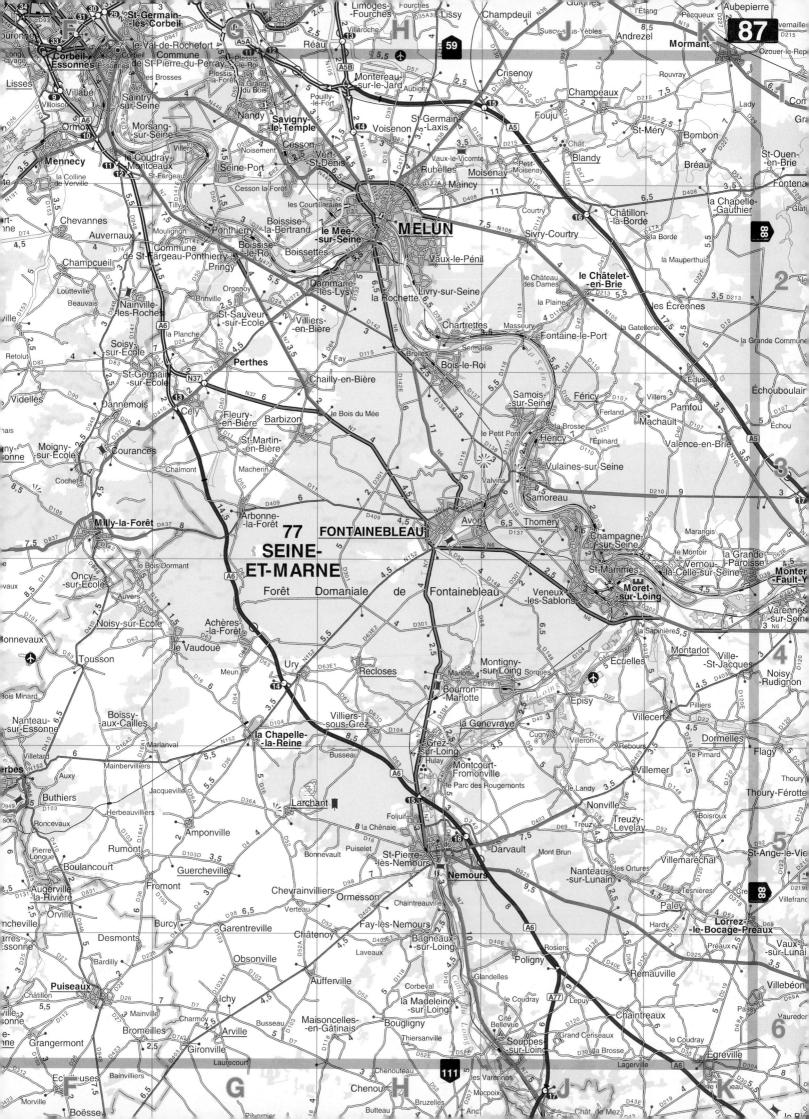

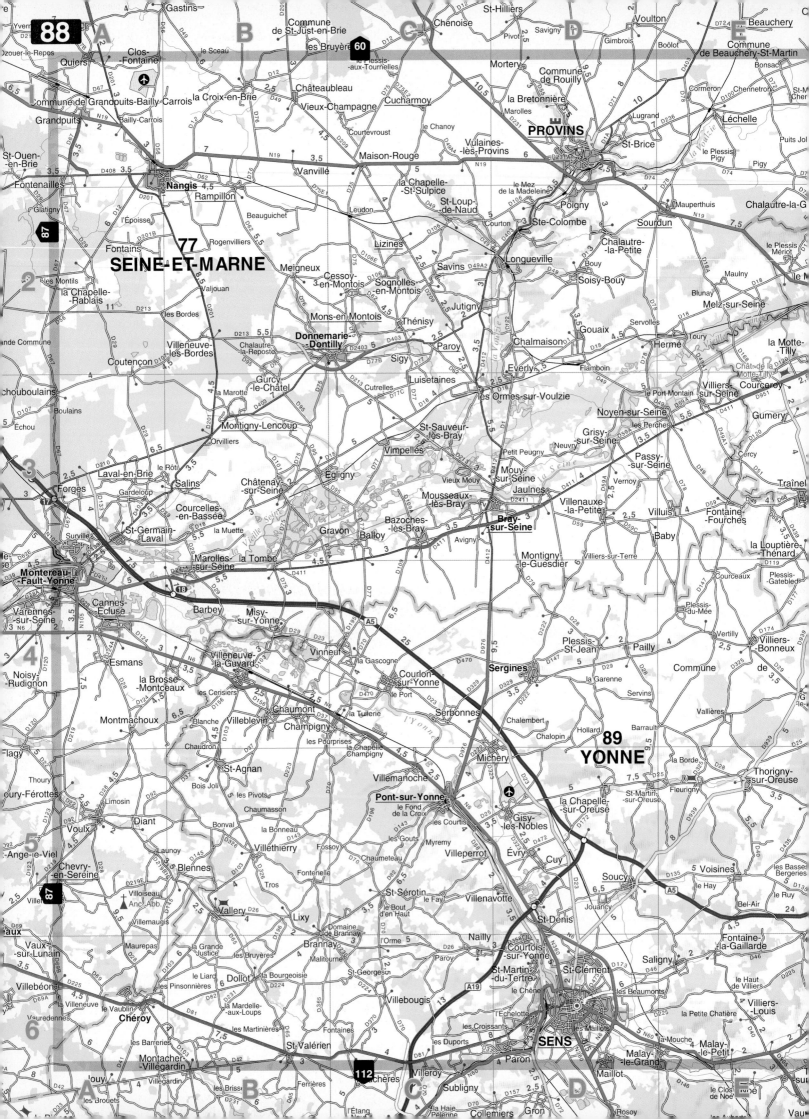

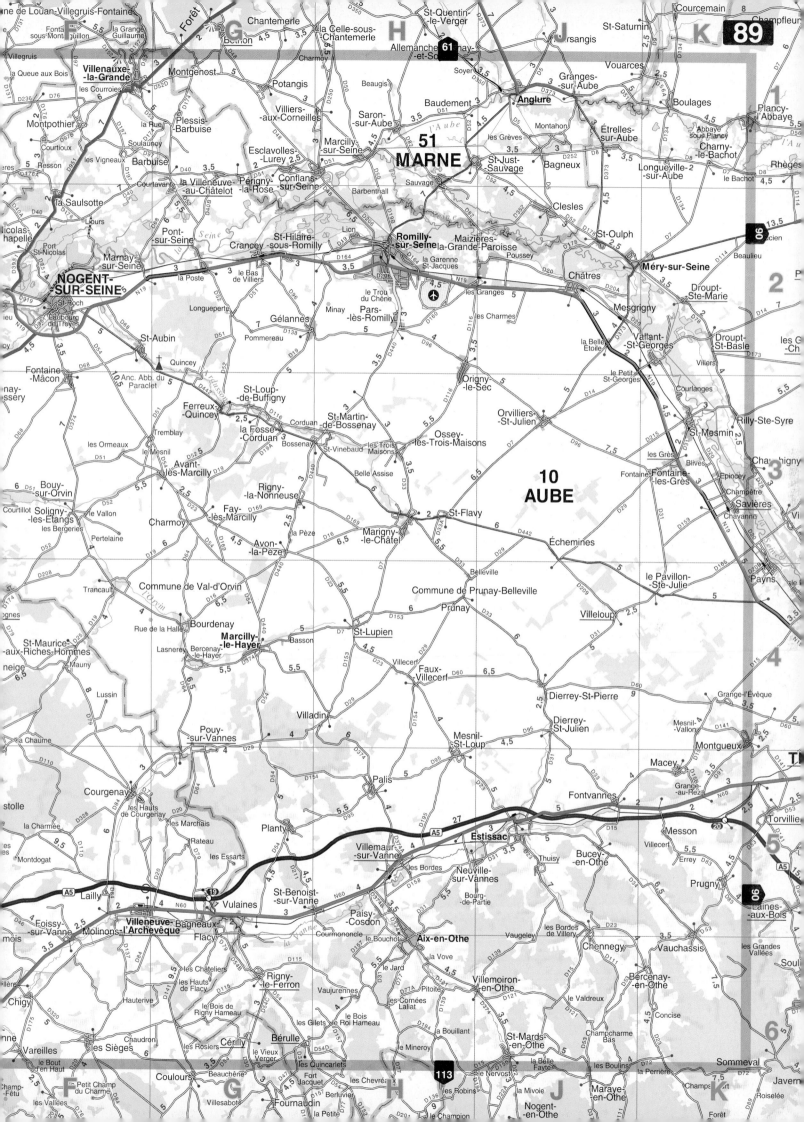

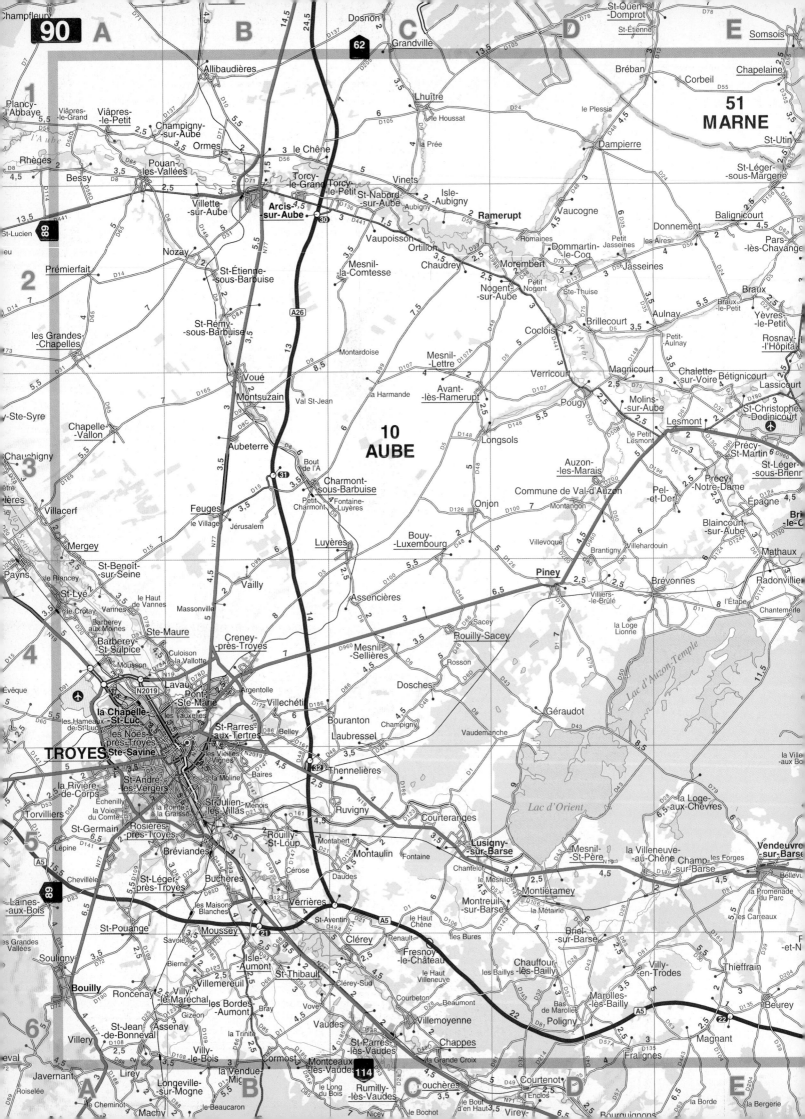

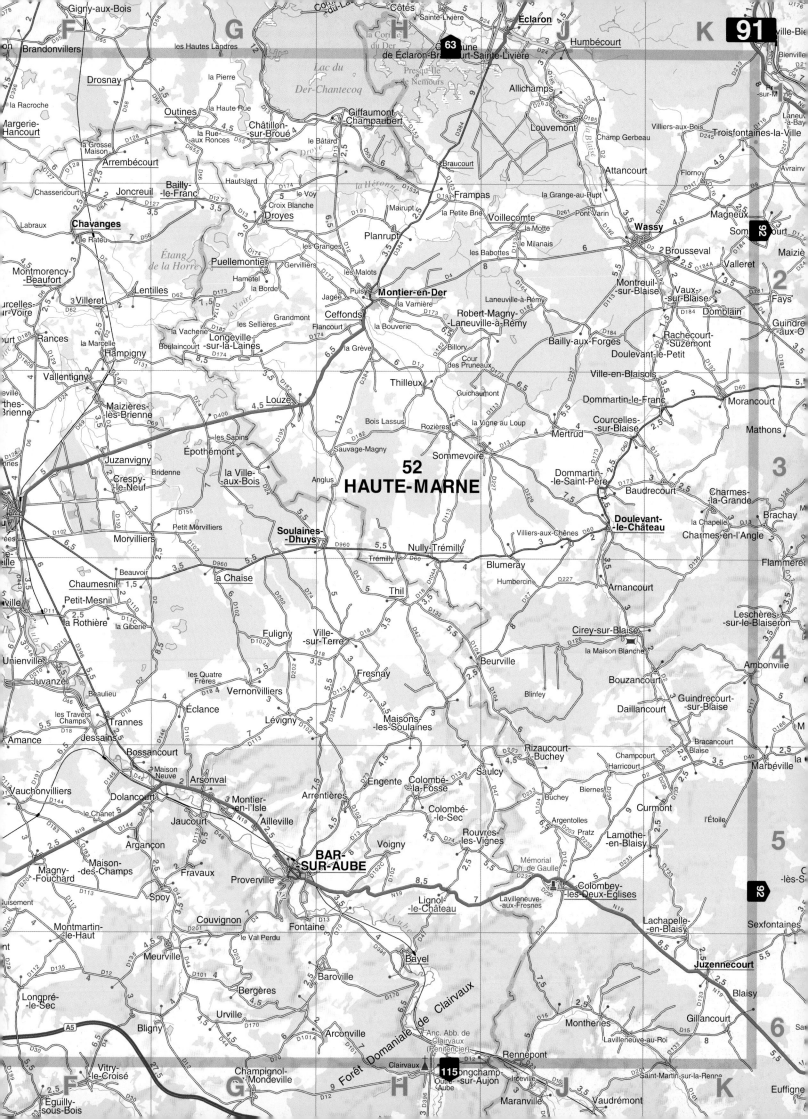

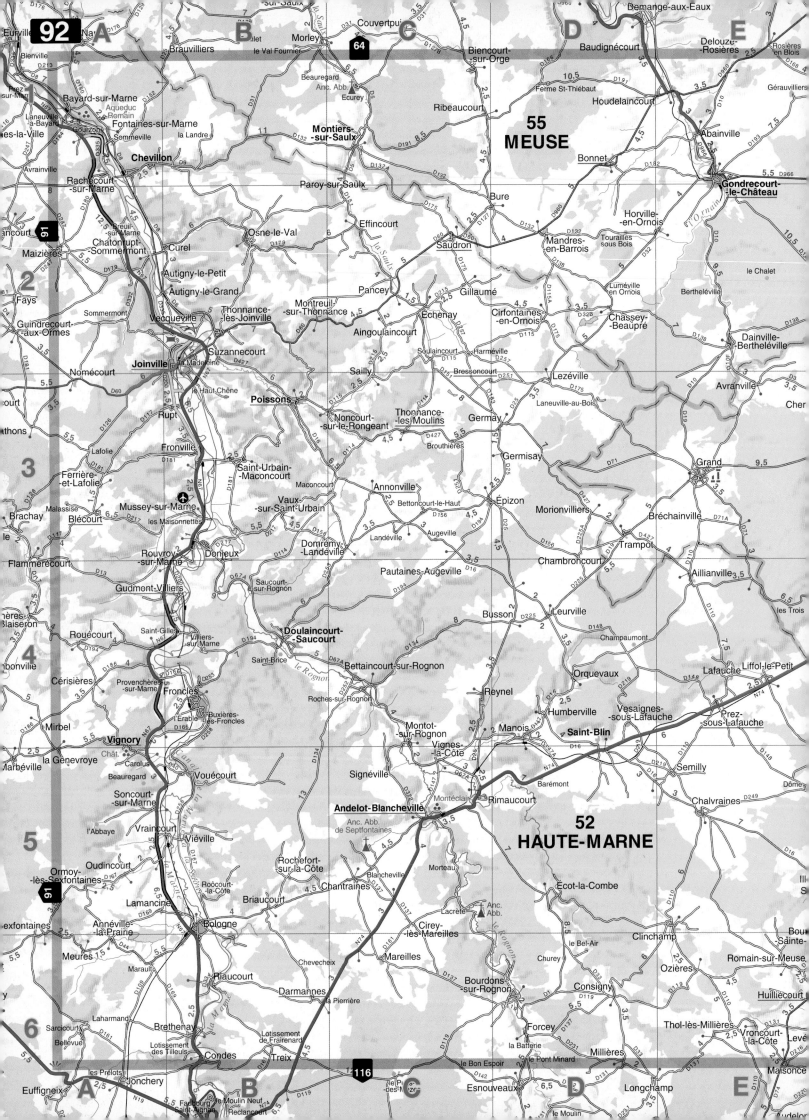

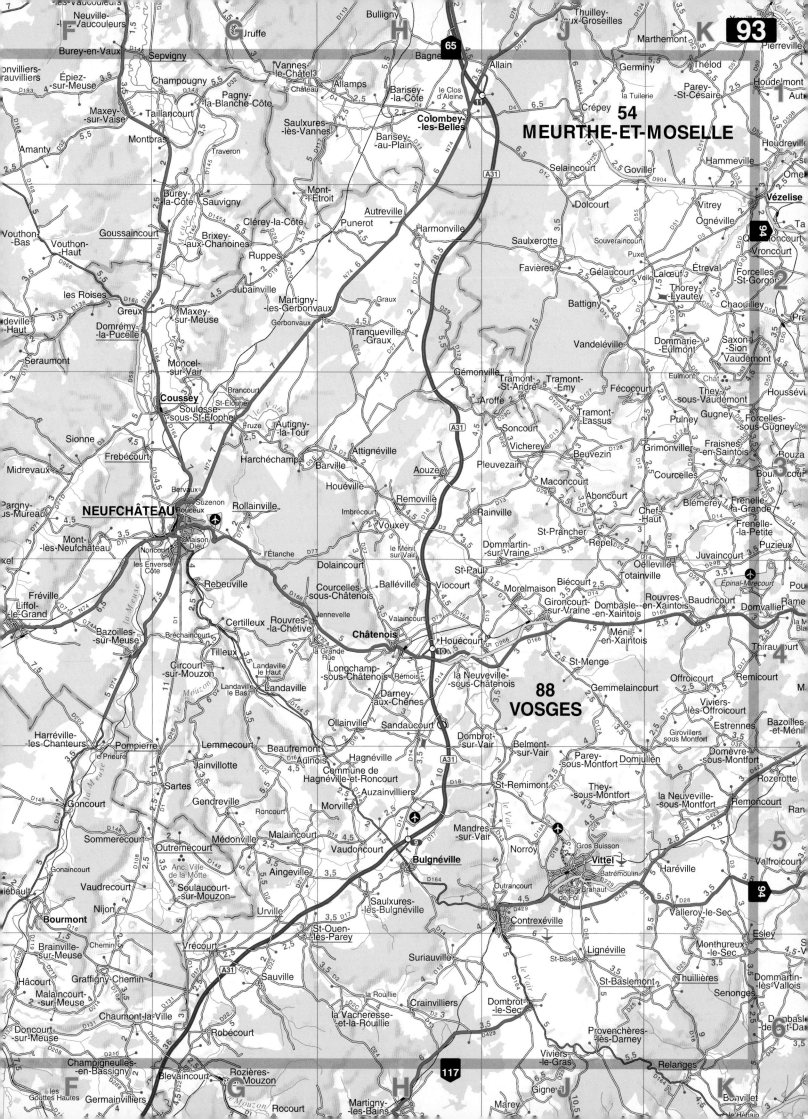

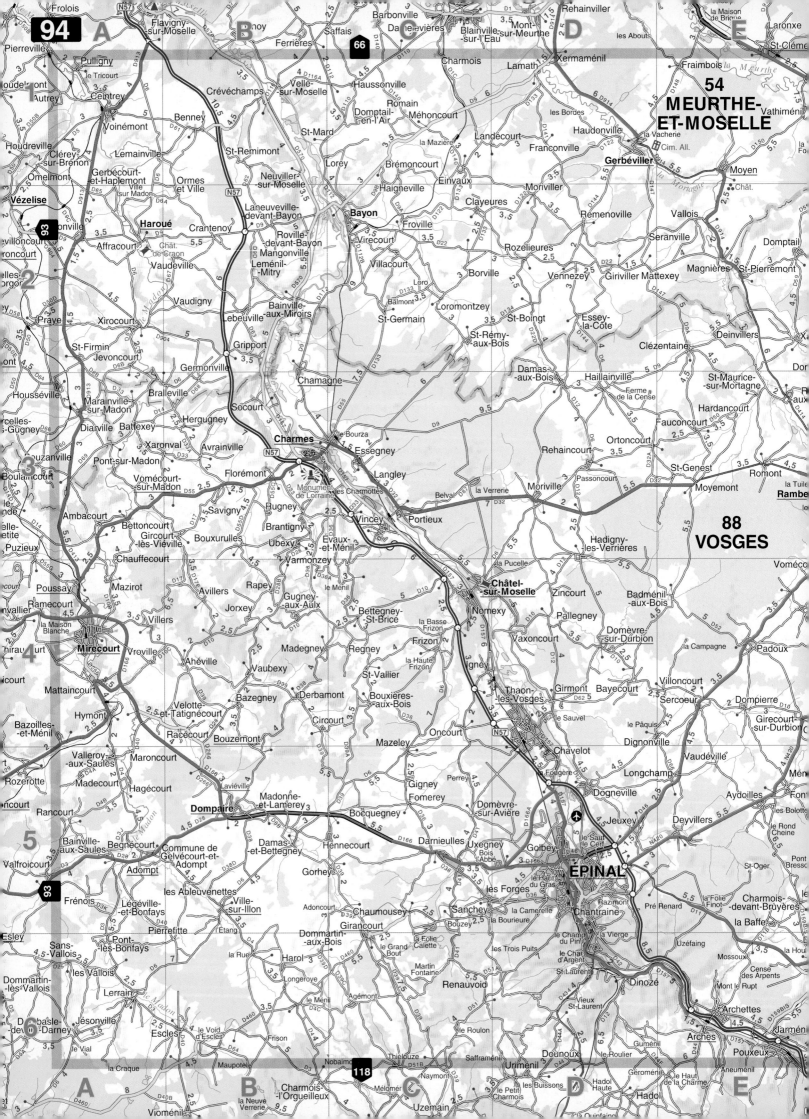

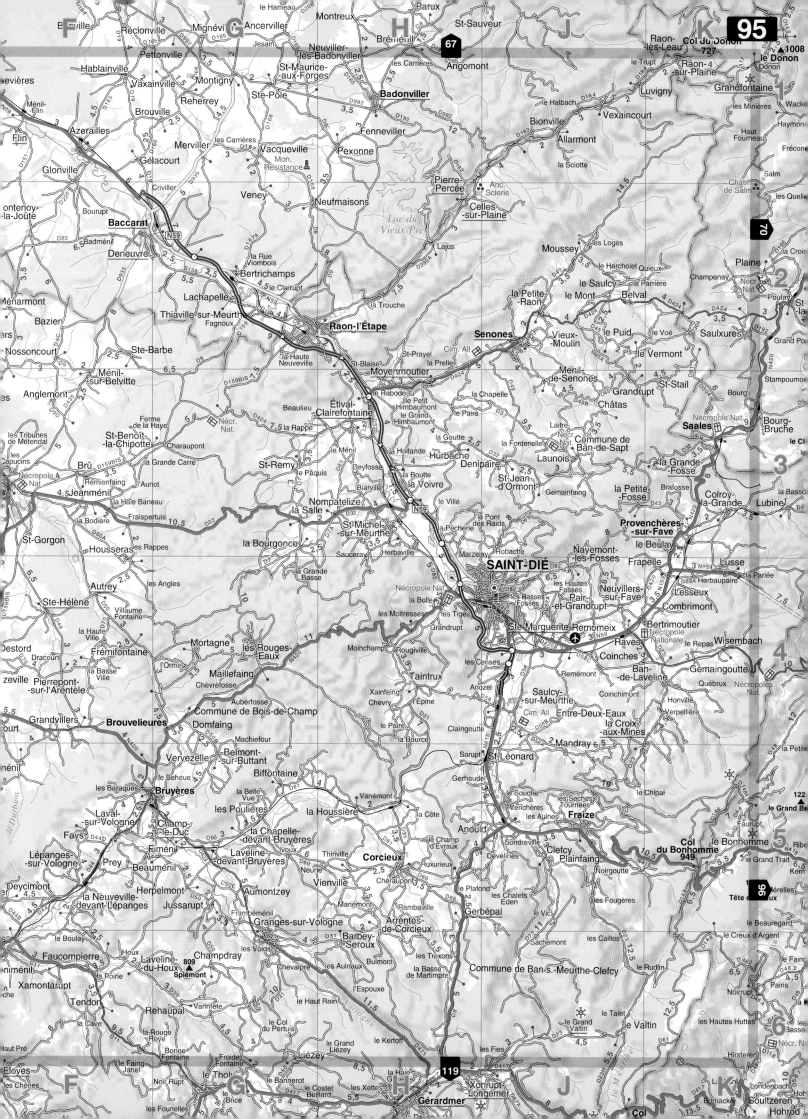

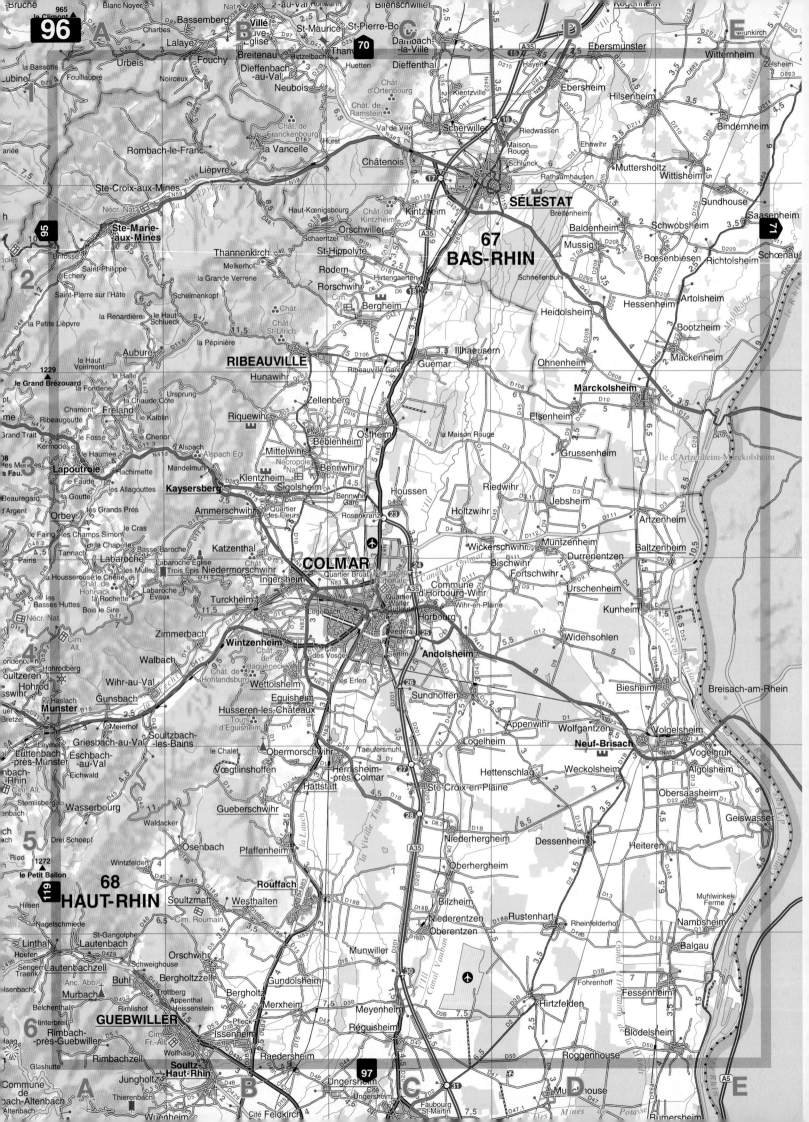

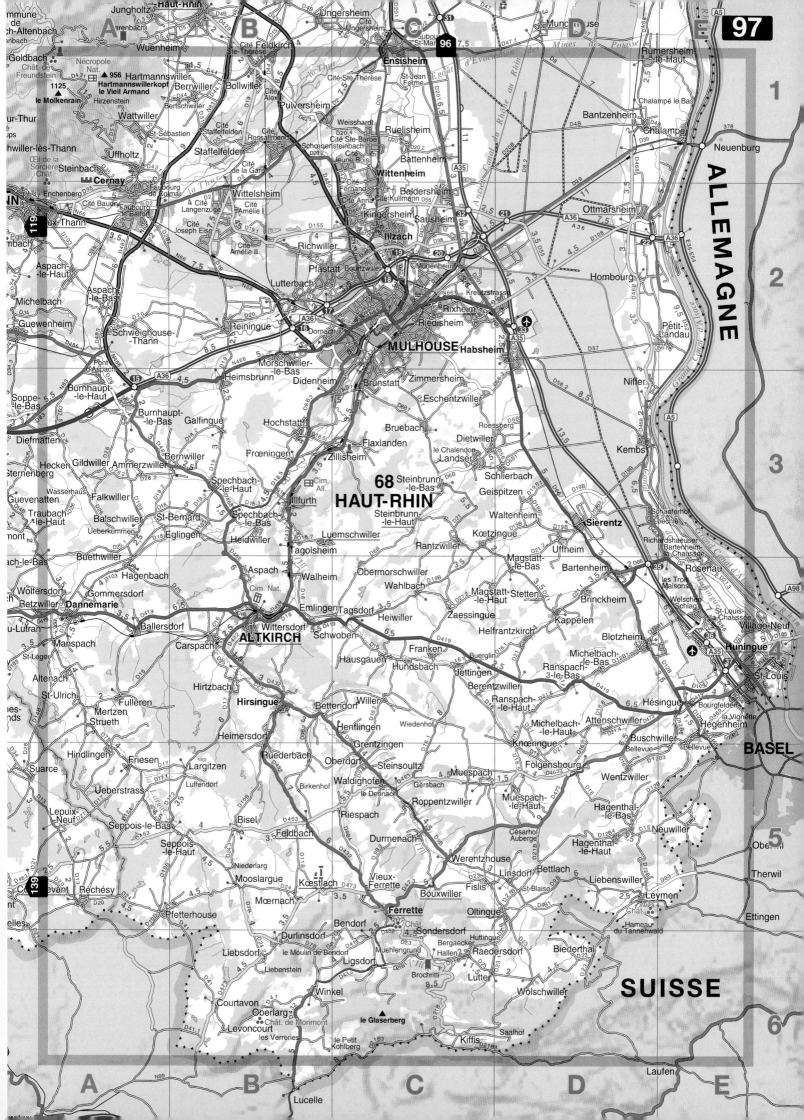

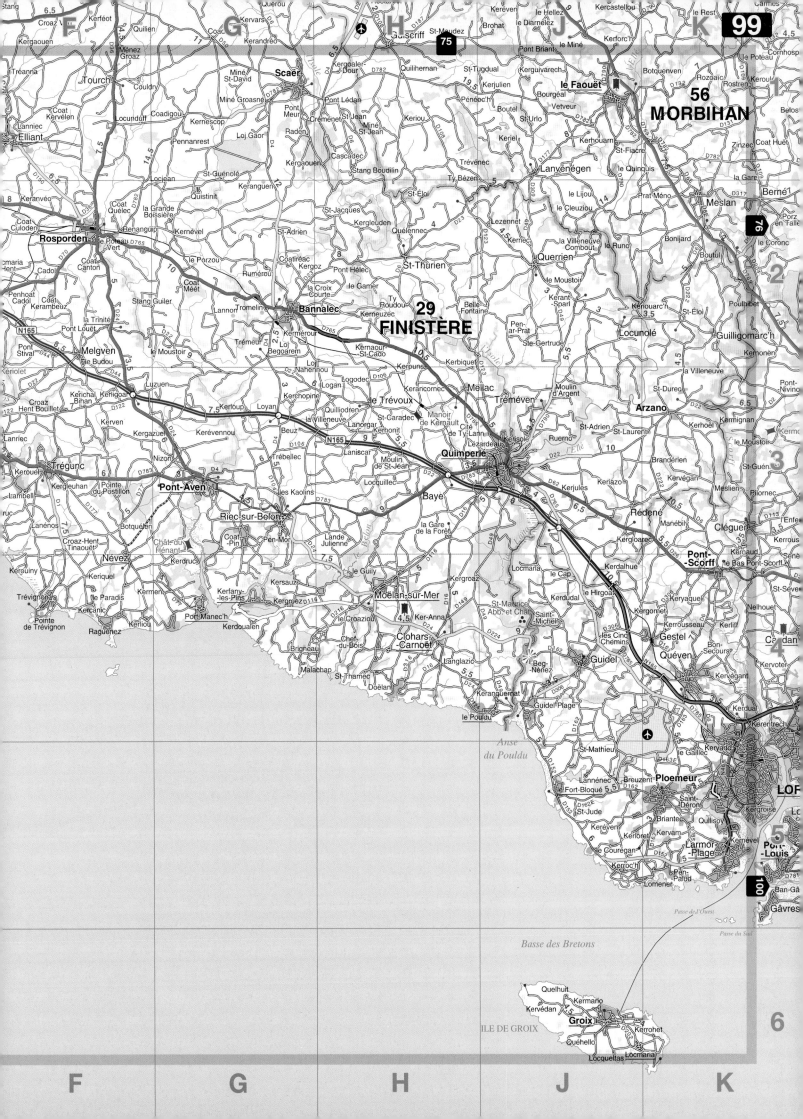

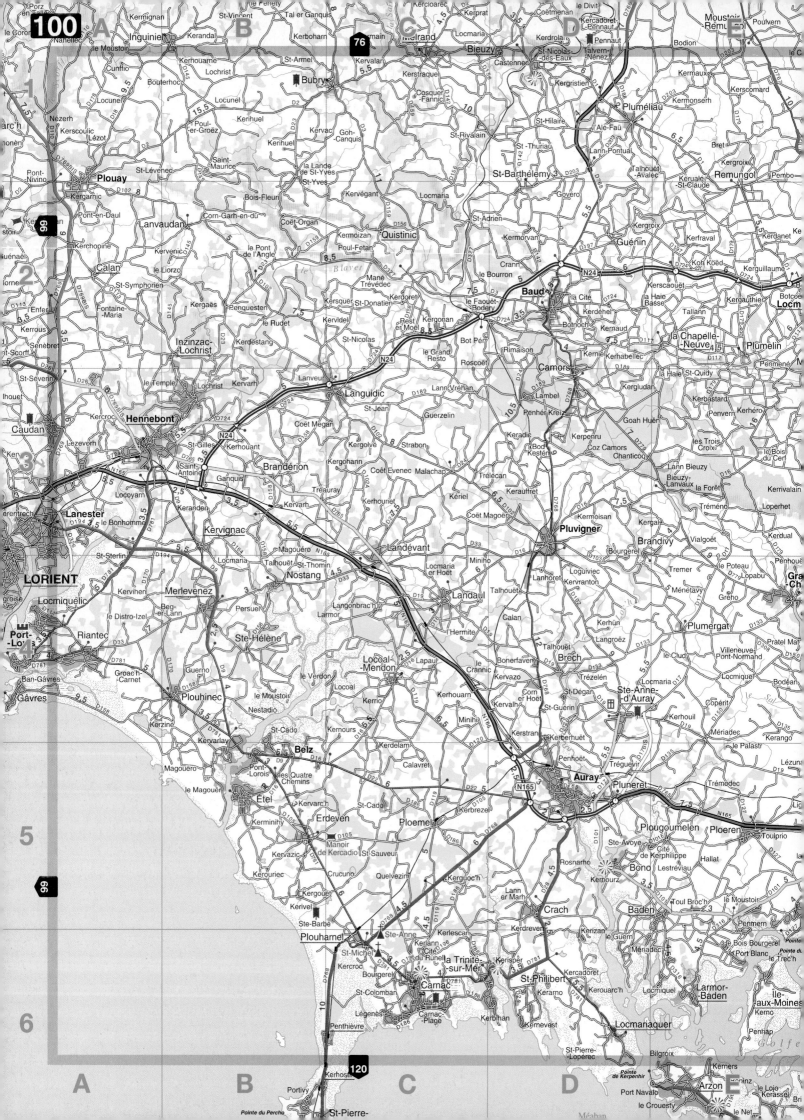

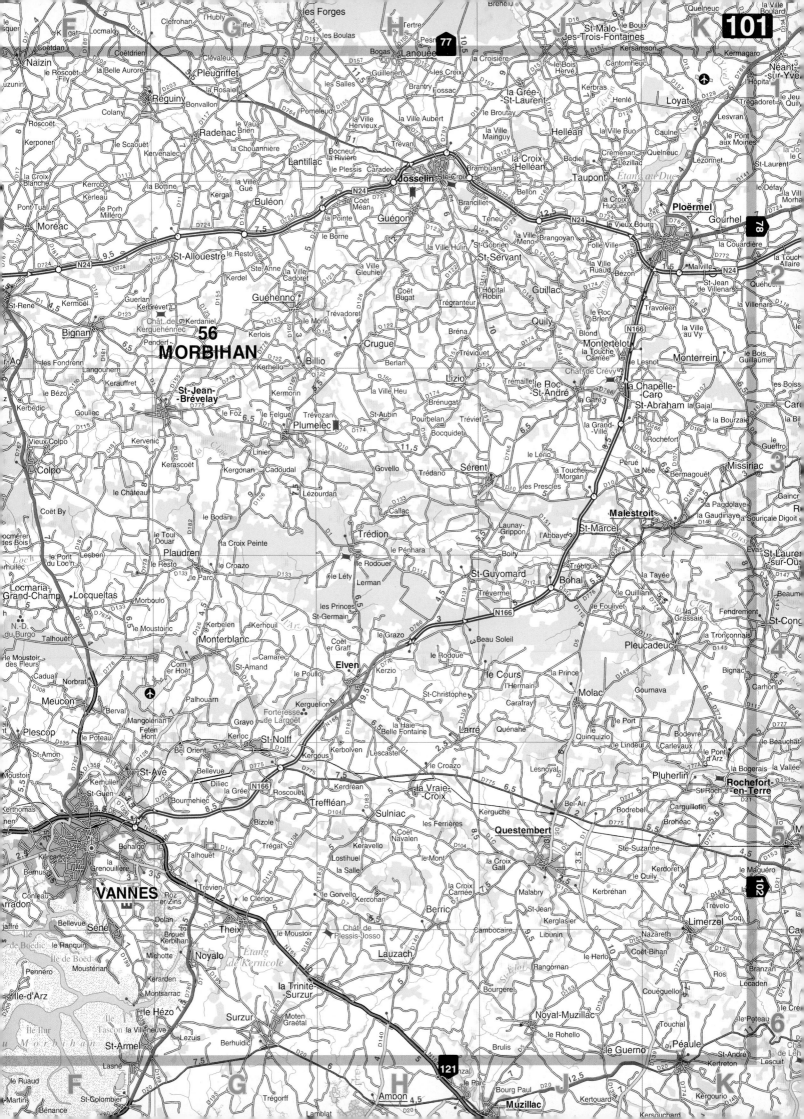

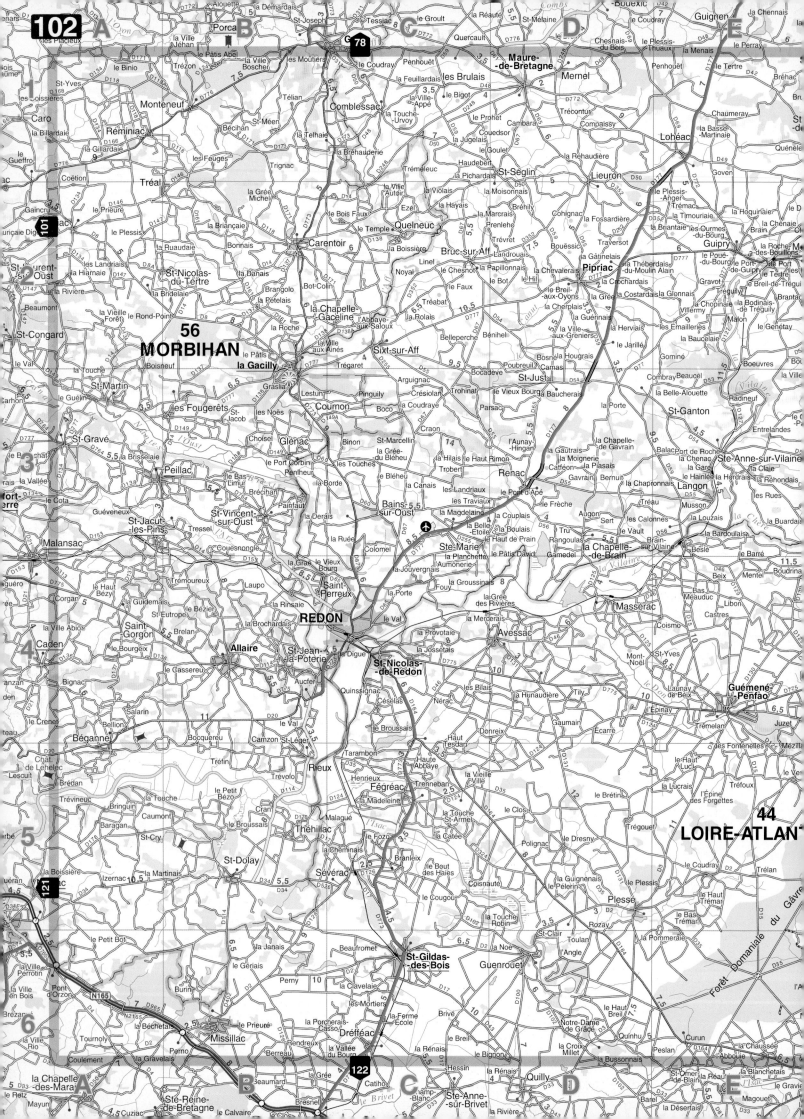

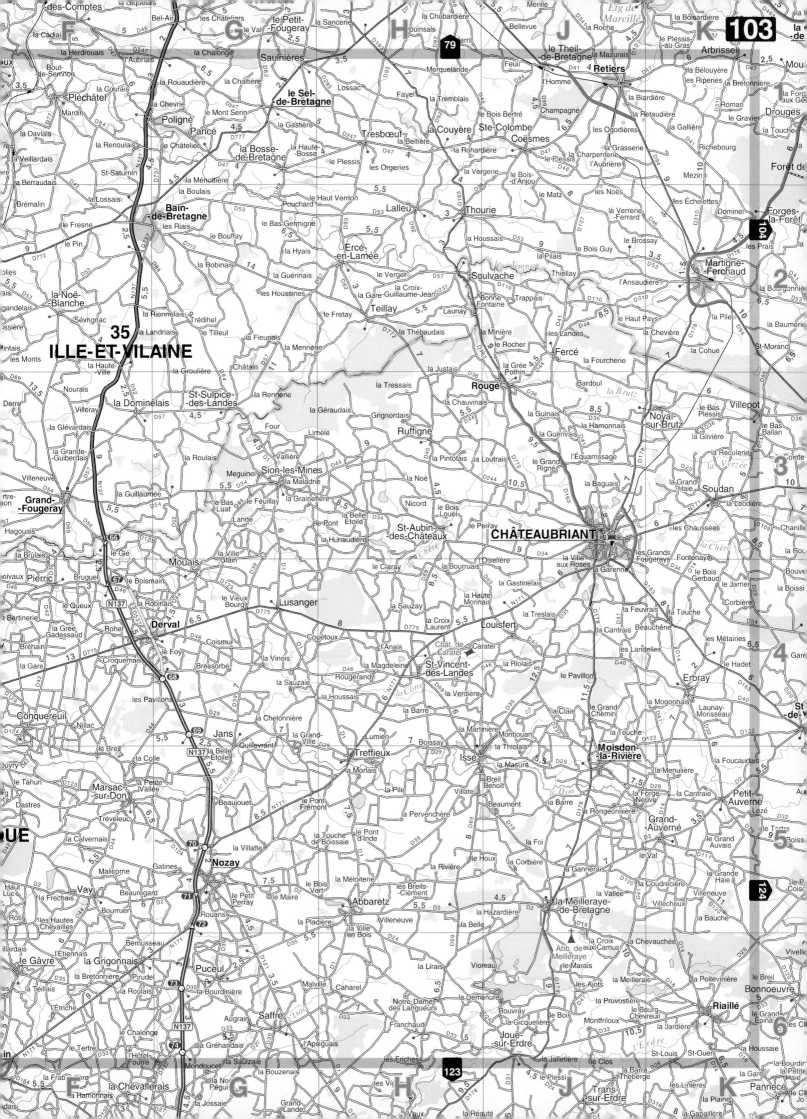

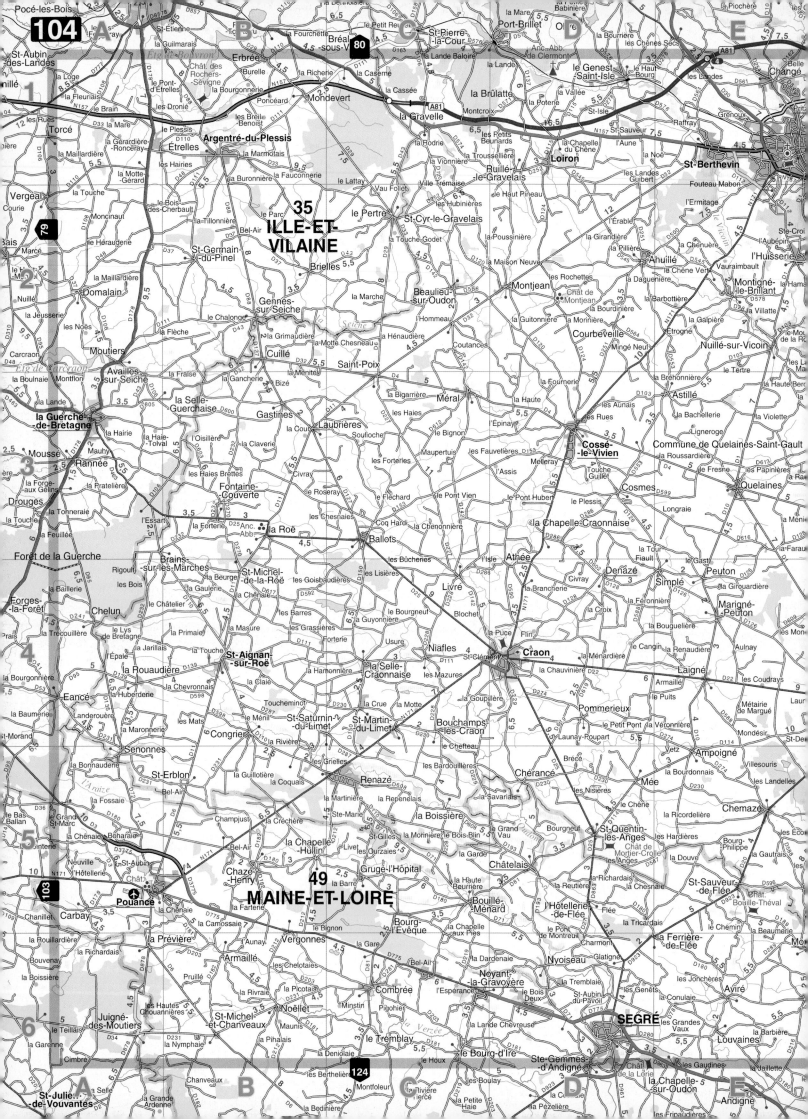

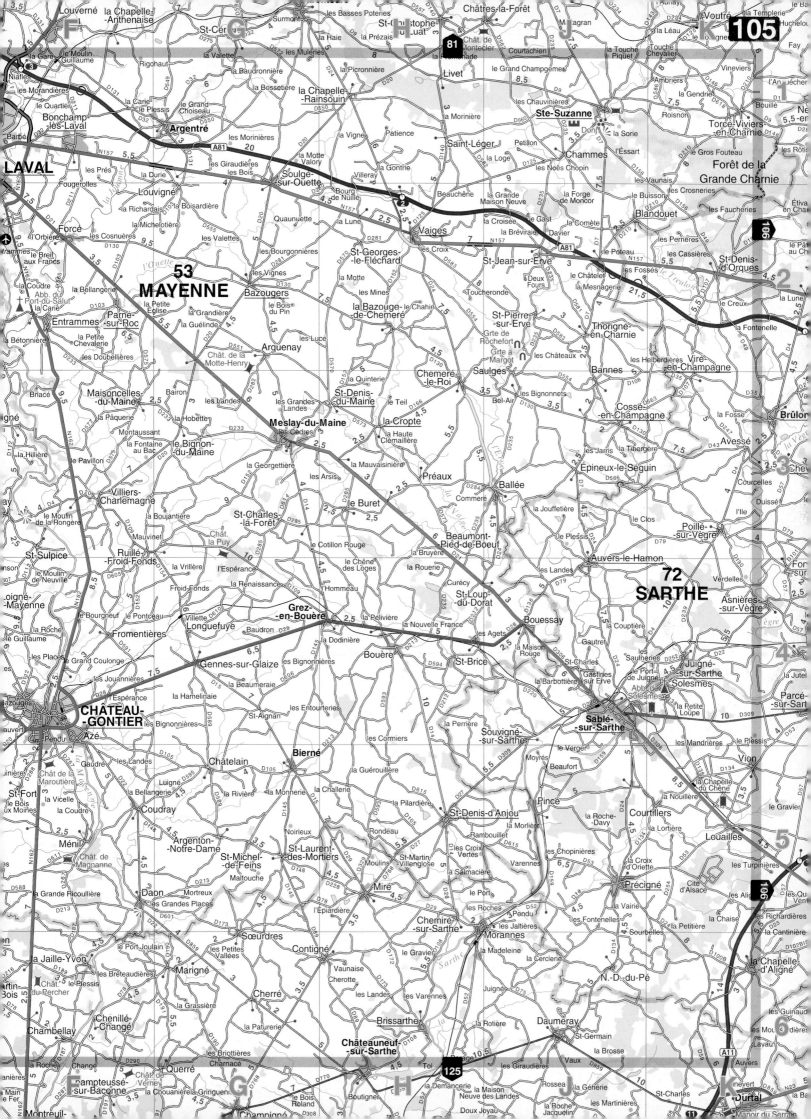

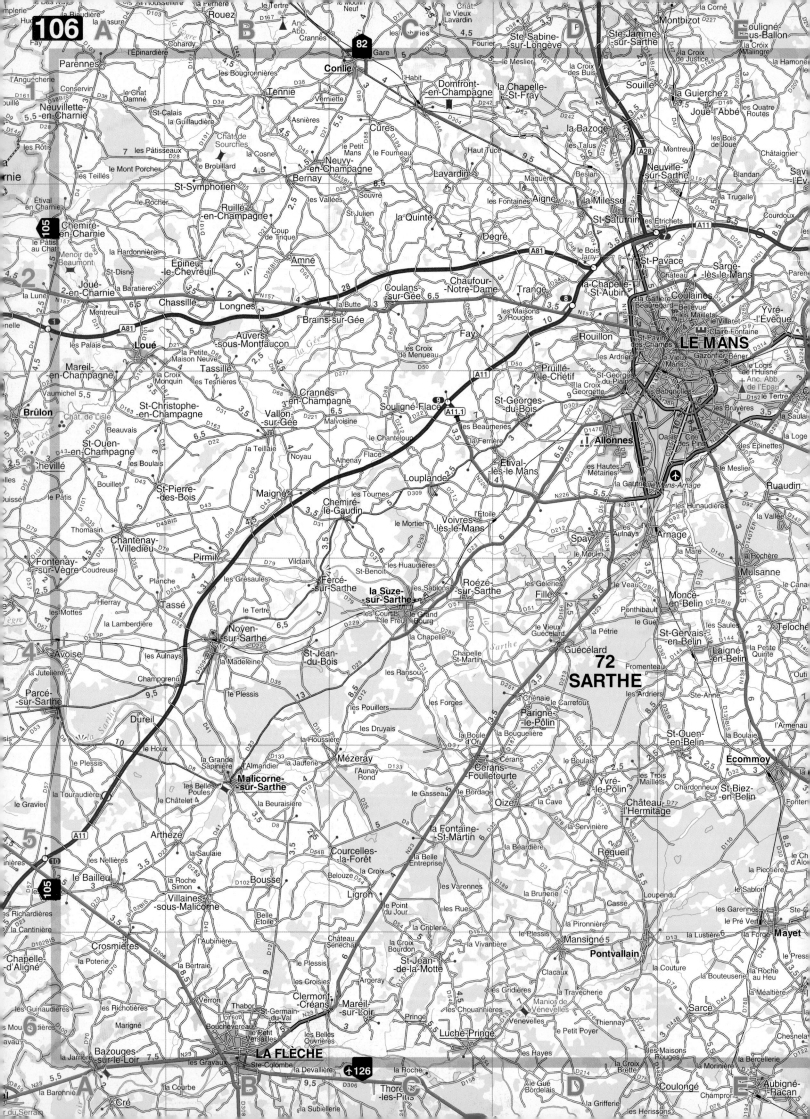

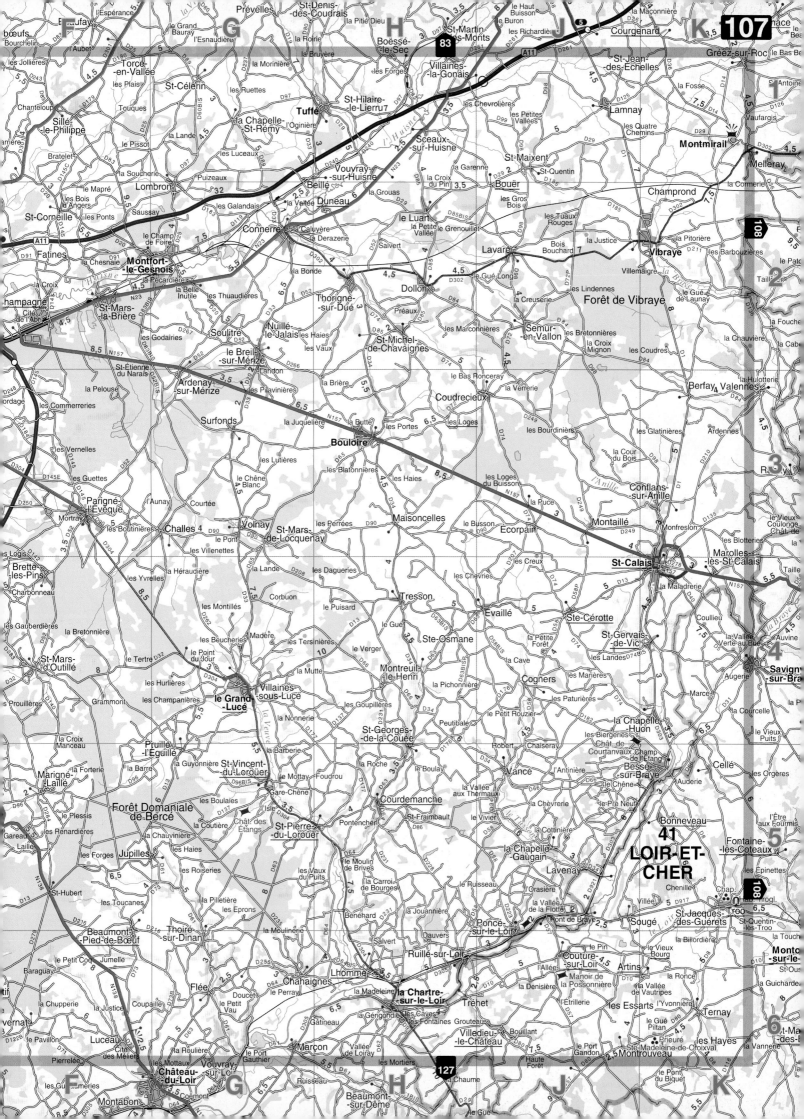

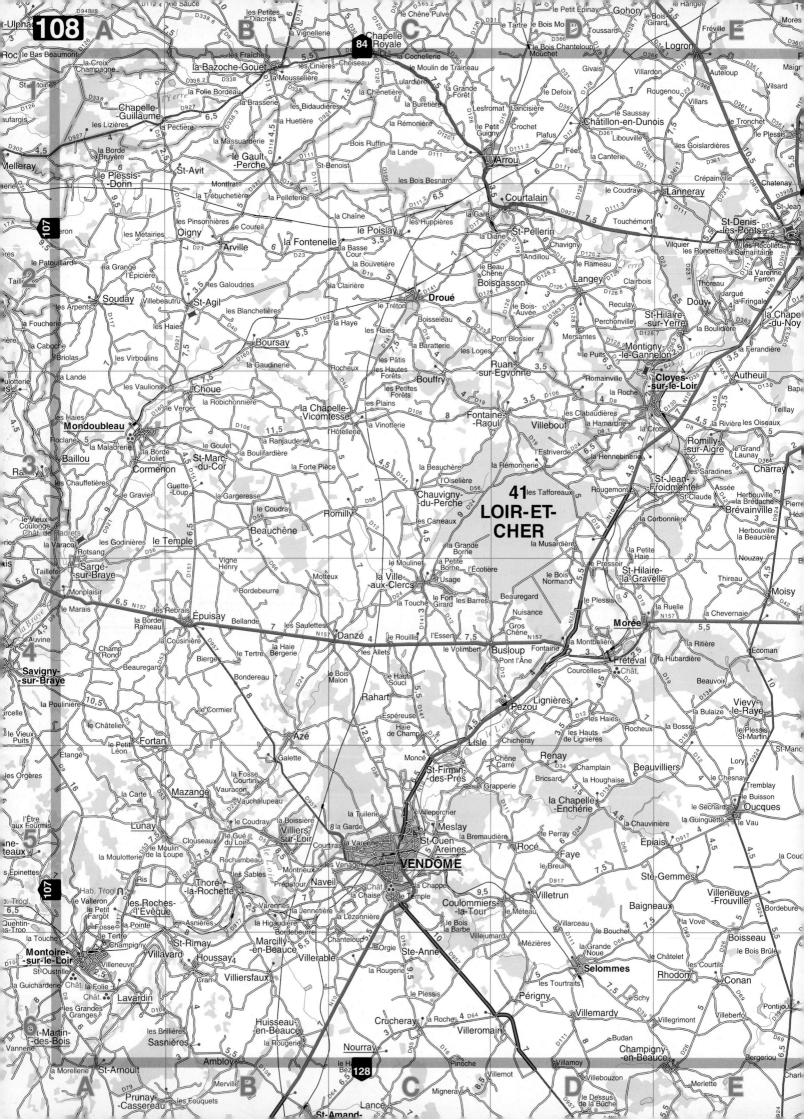

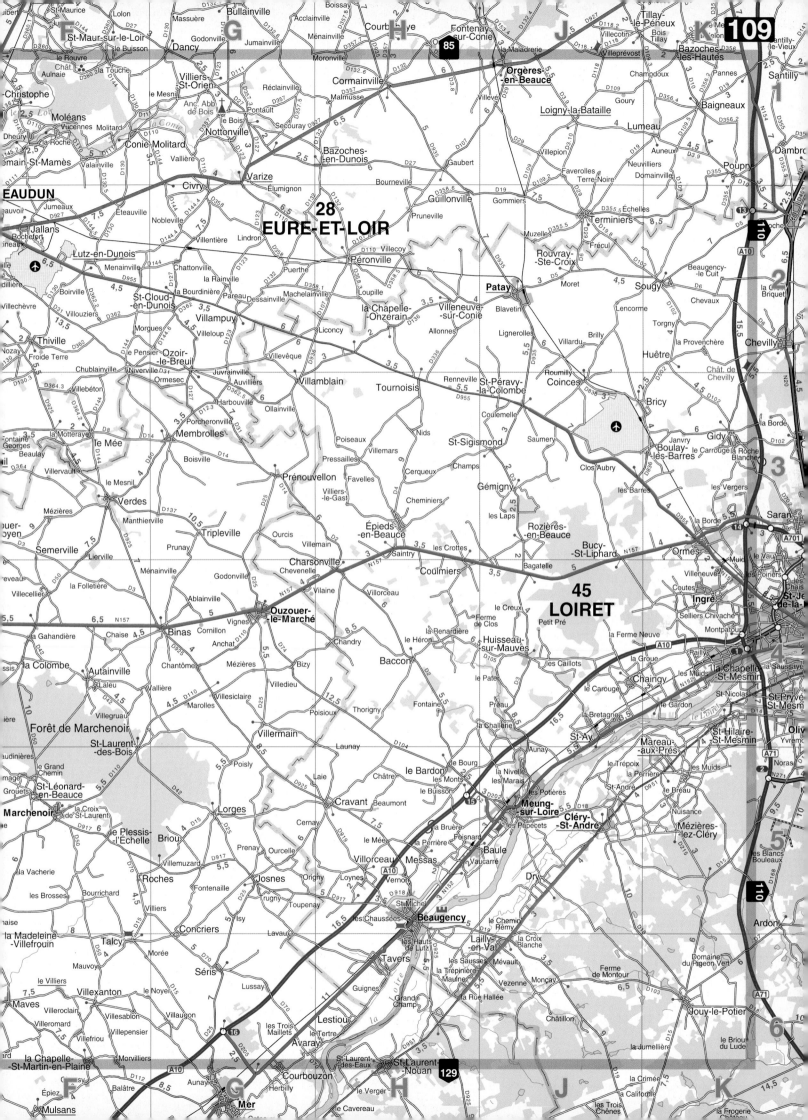

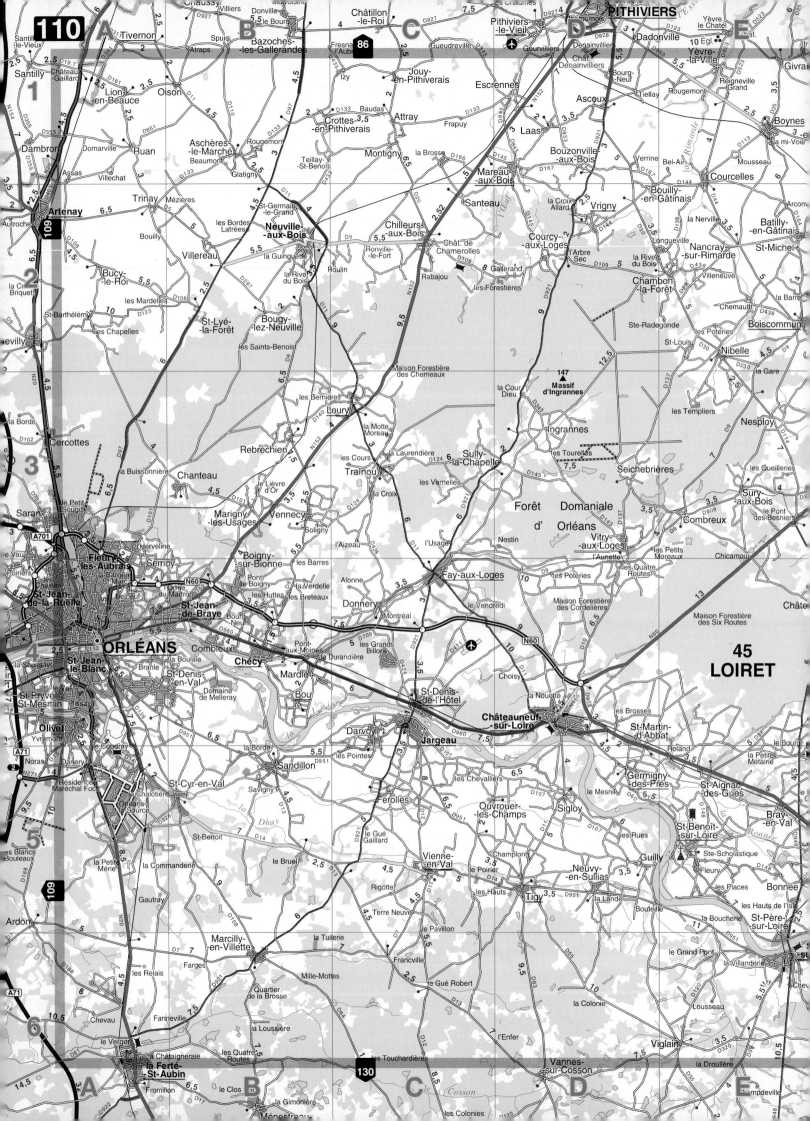

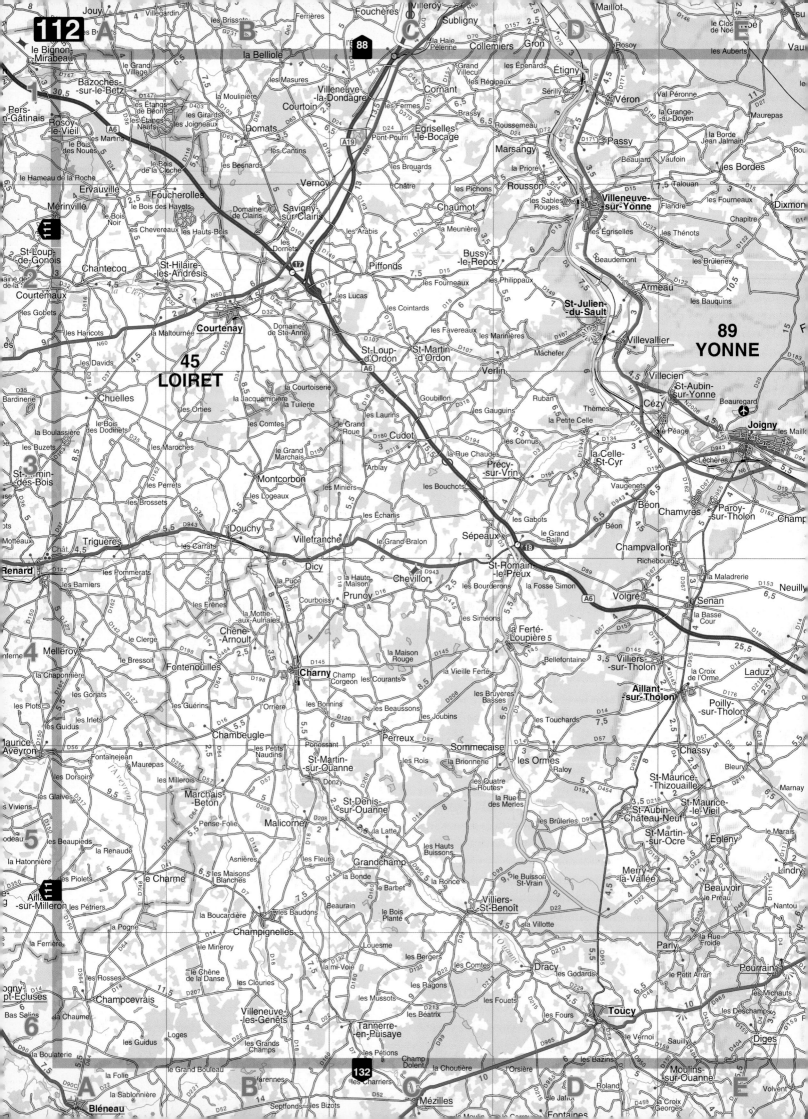

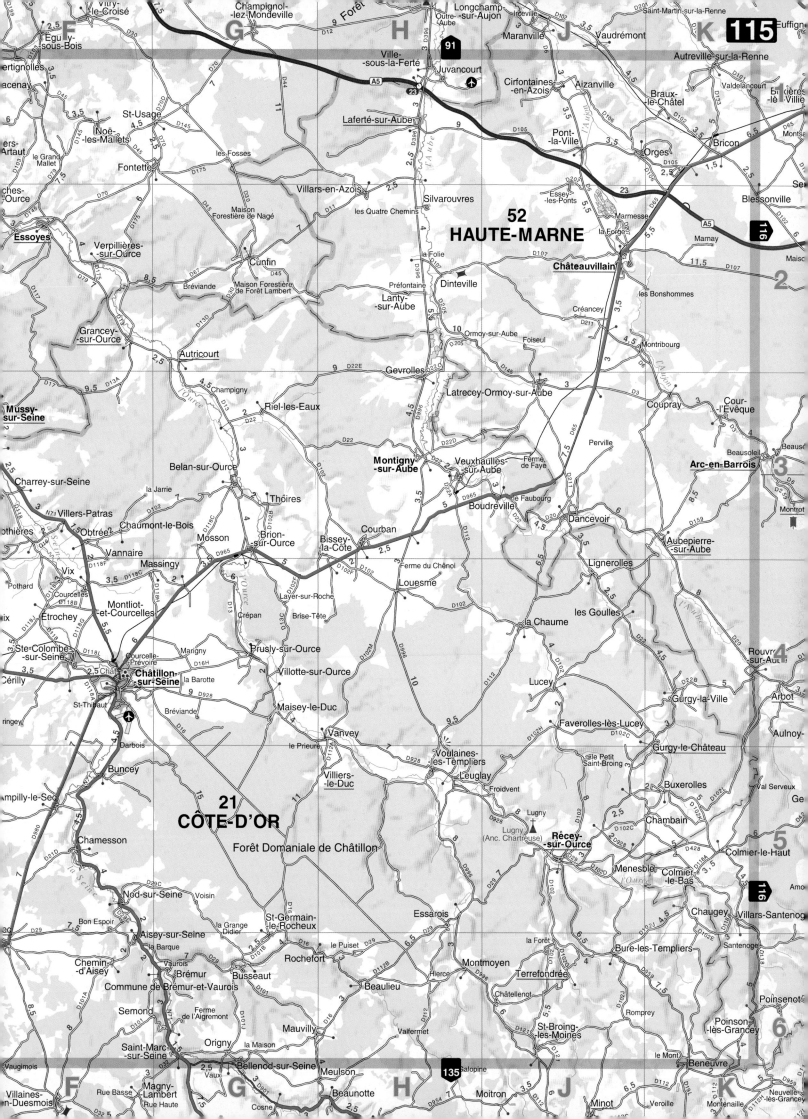

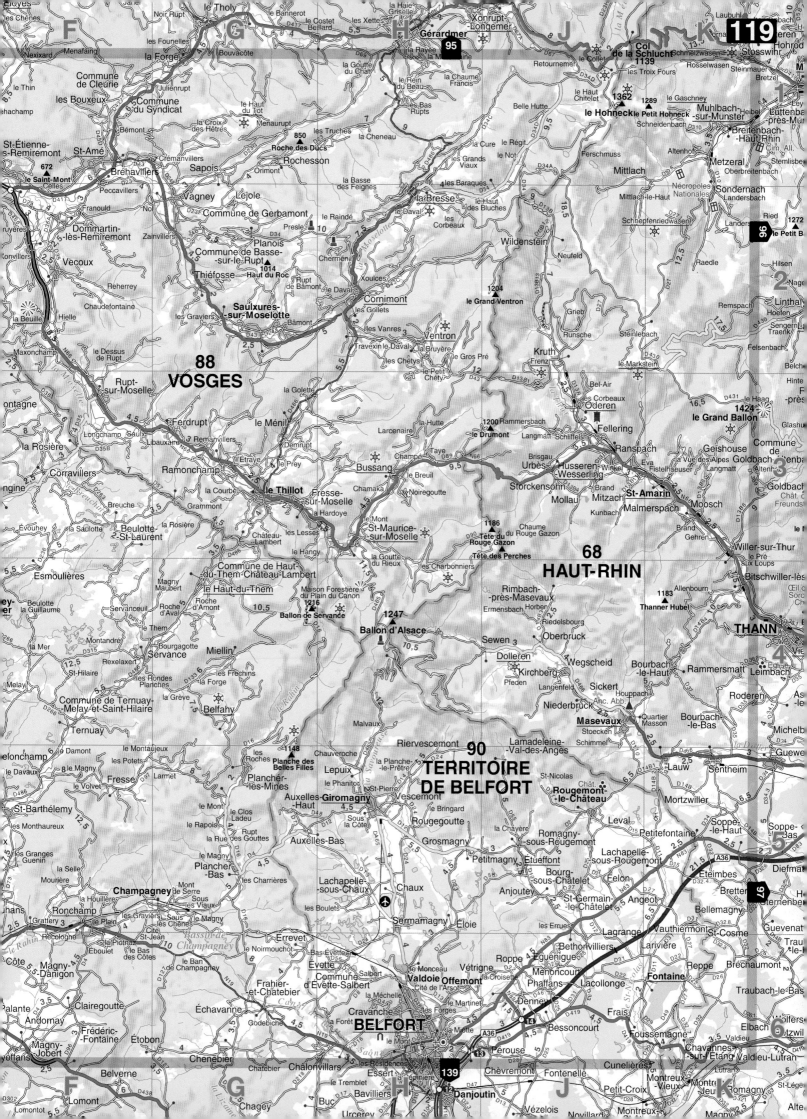

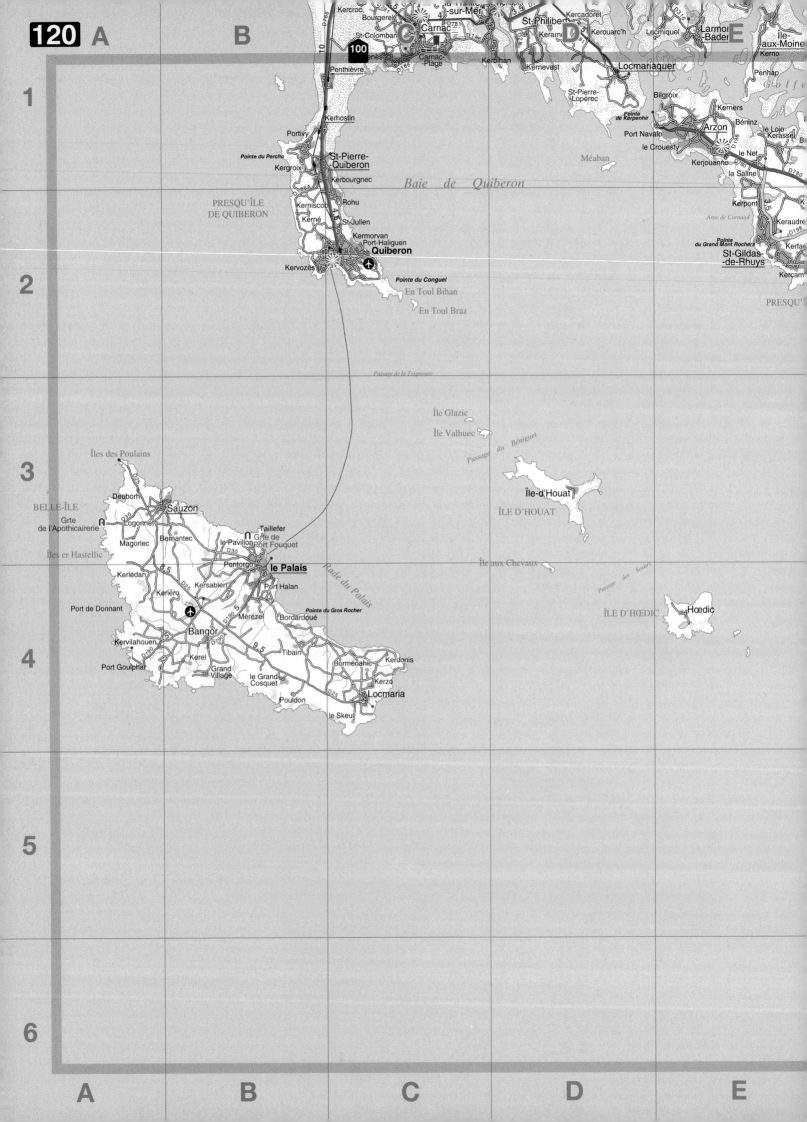

1

2

3

4

5

6

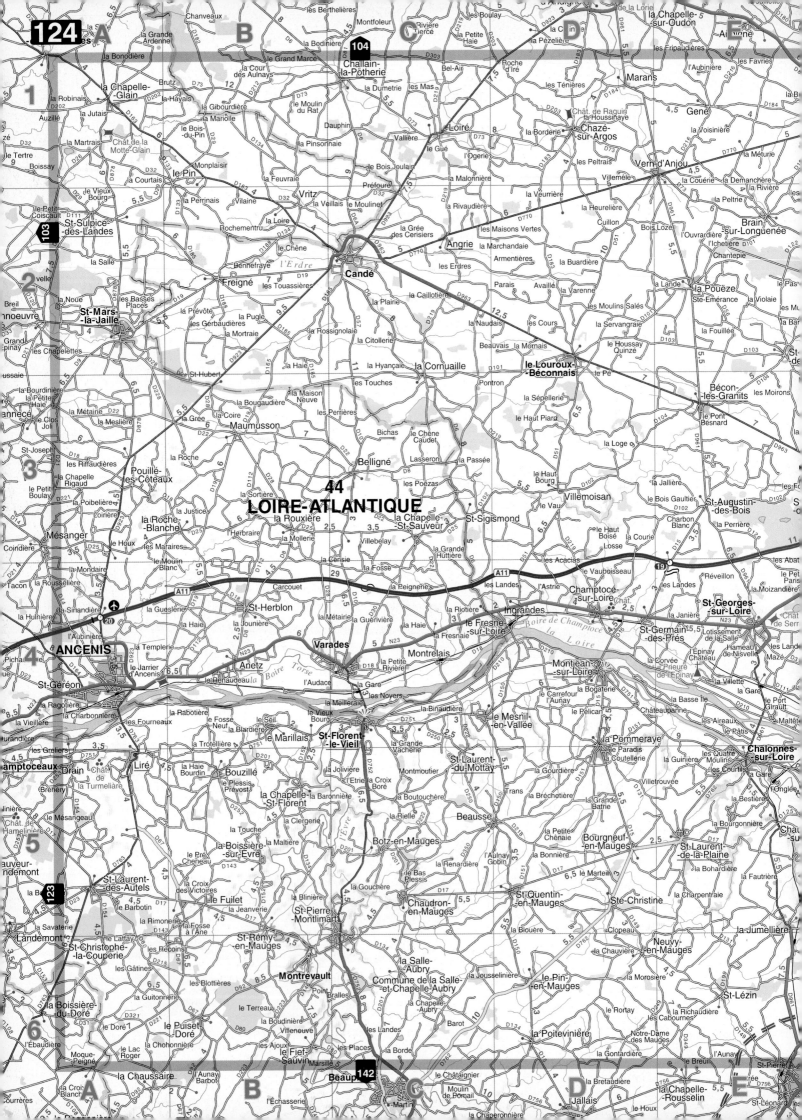

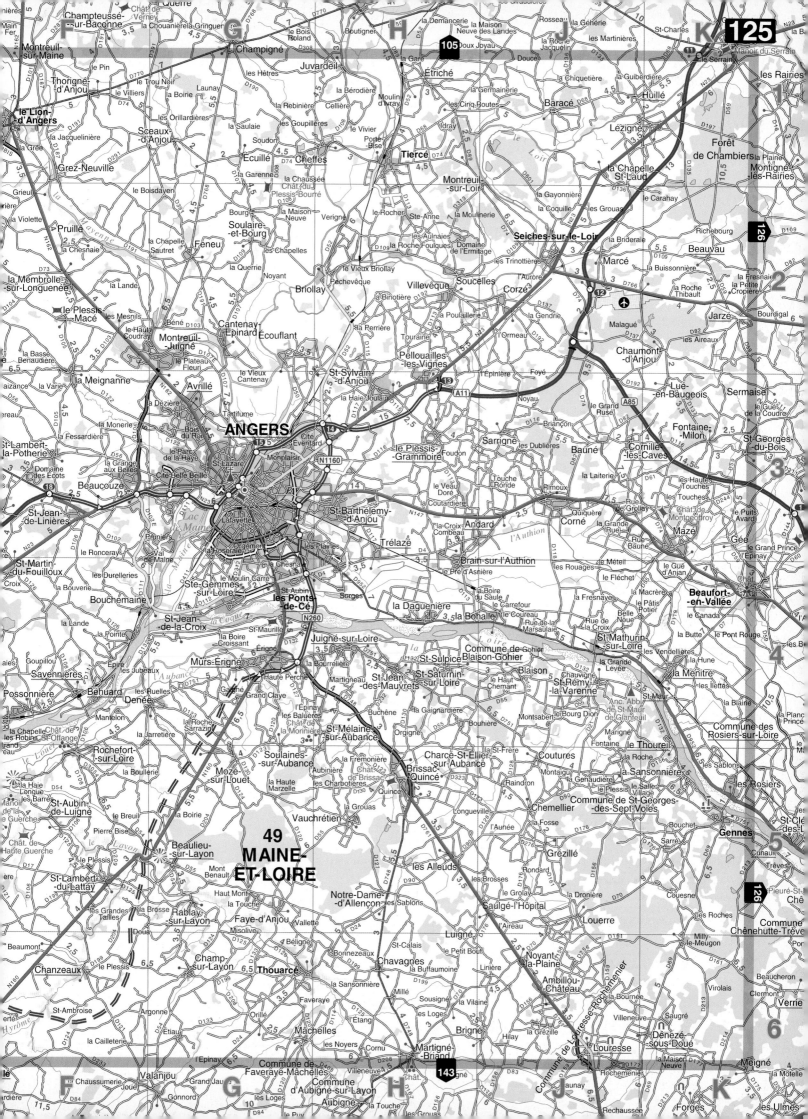

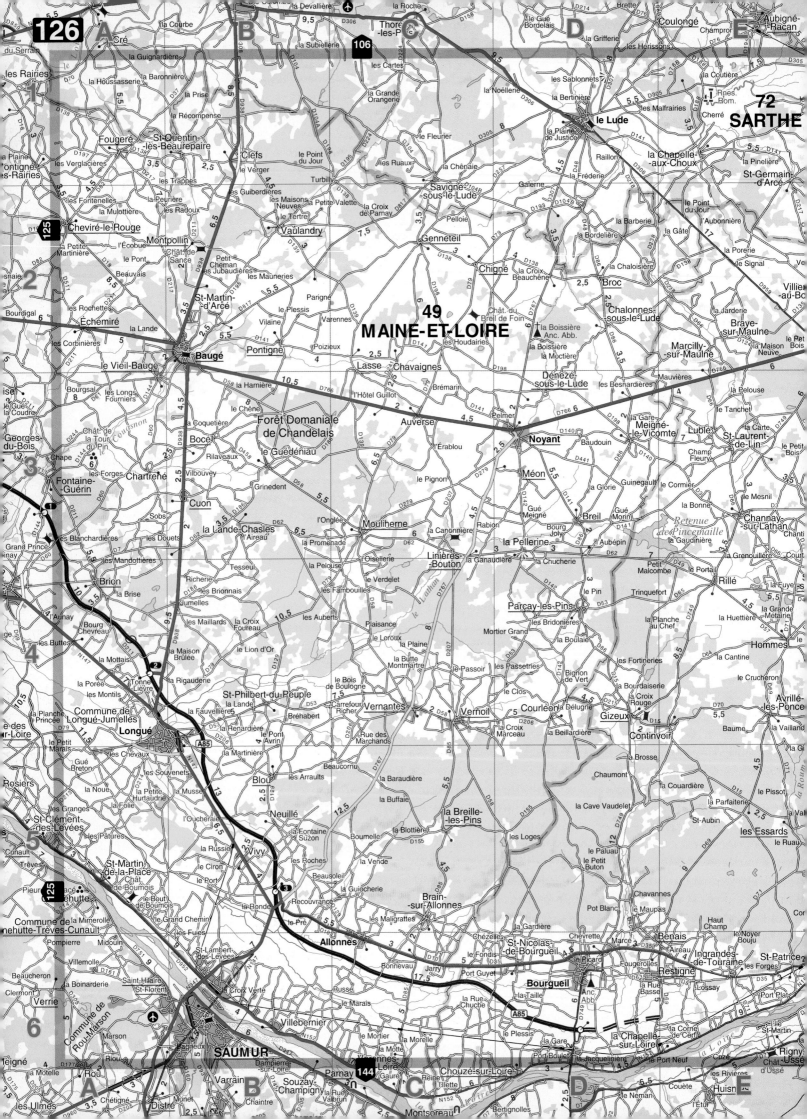

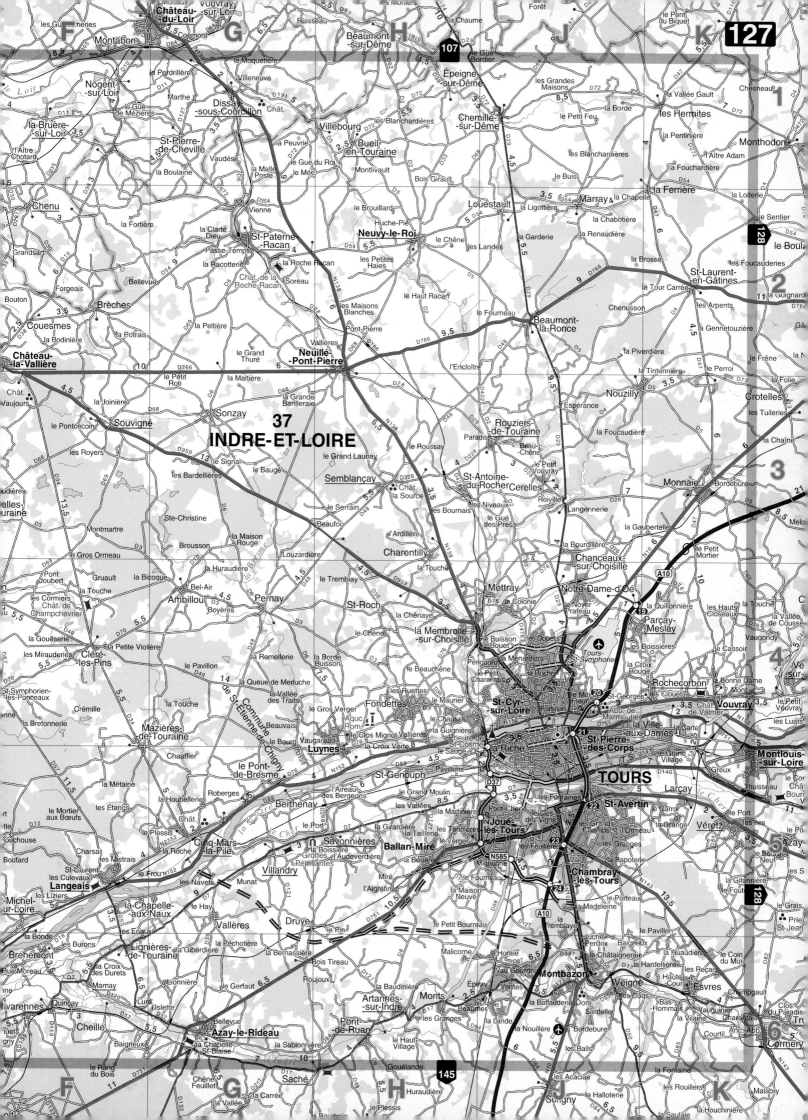

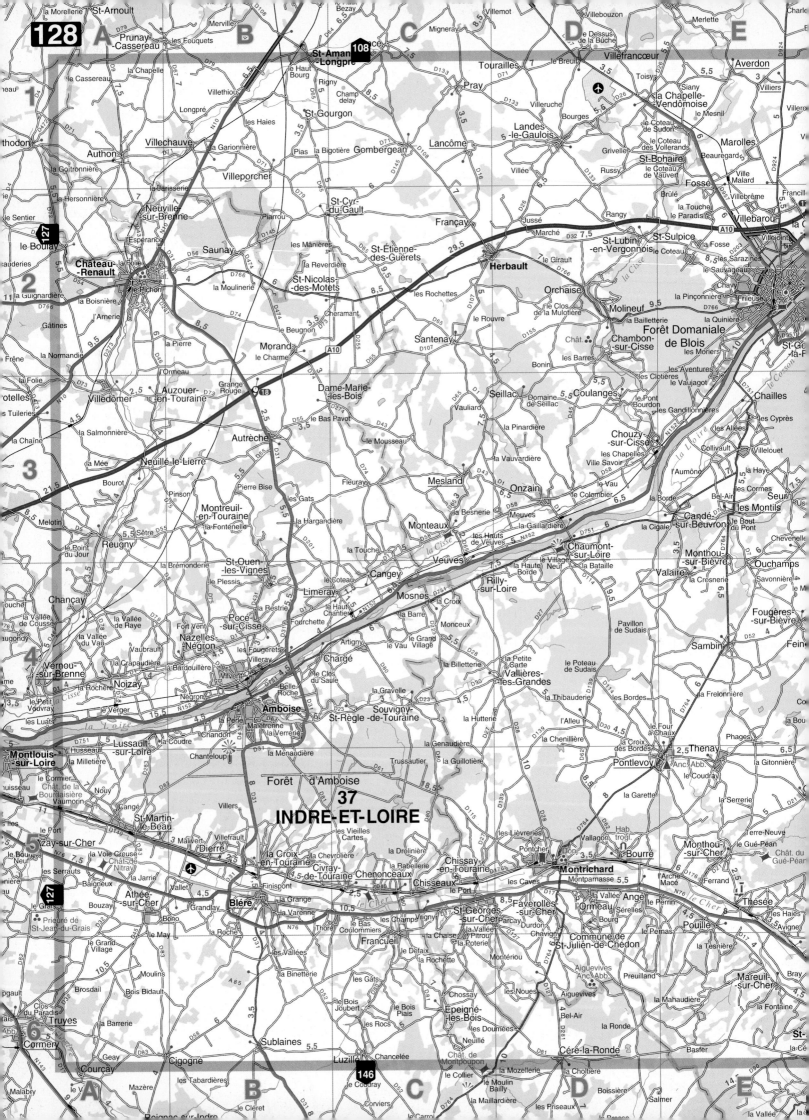

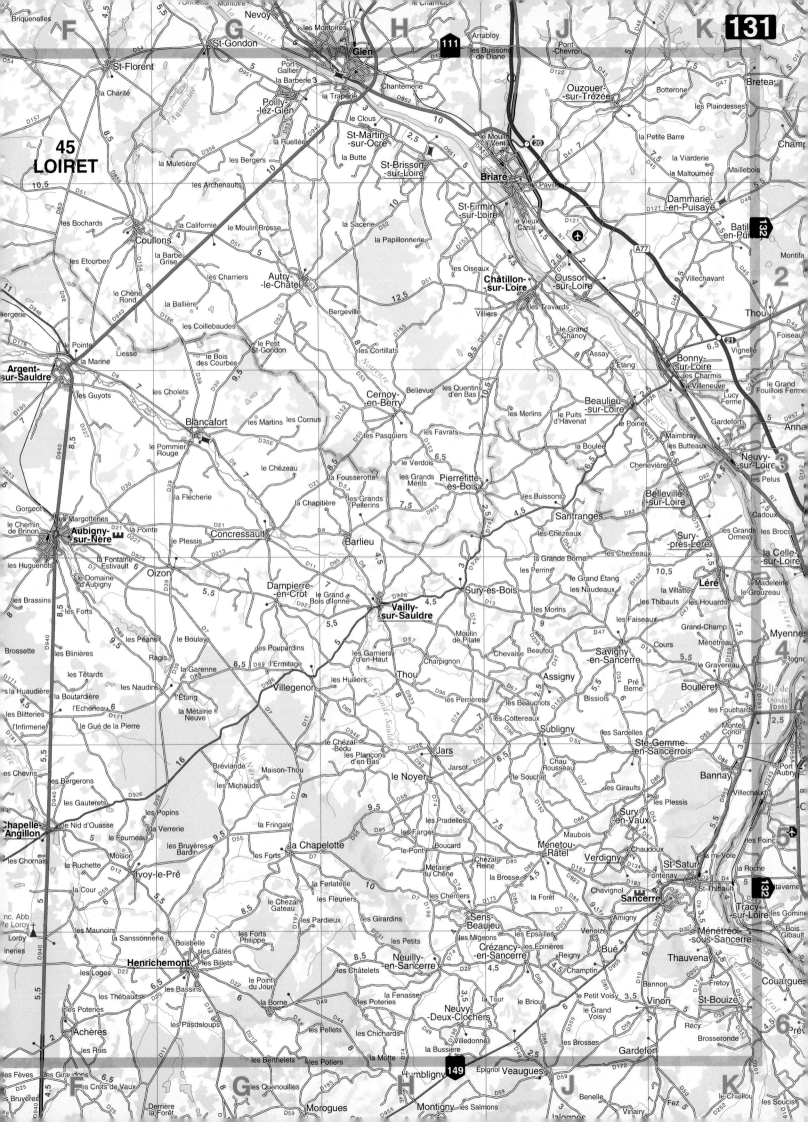

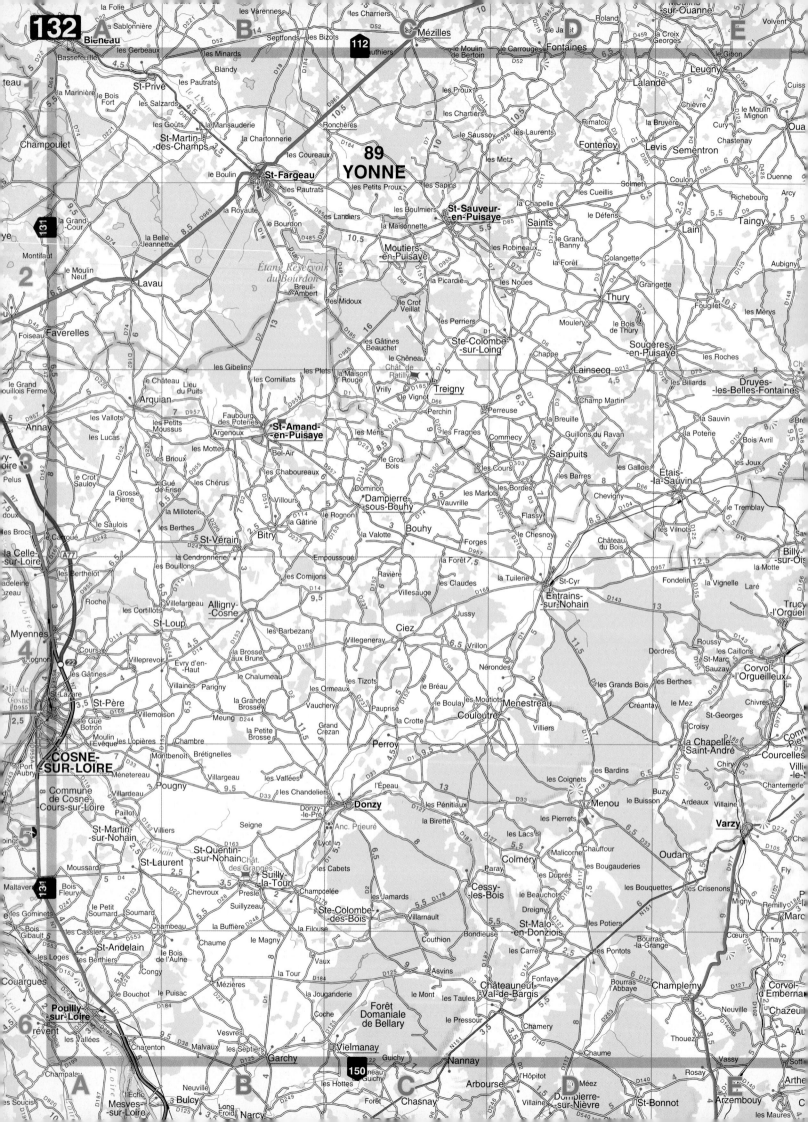

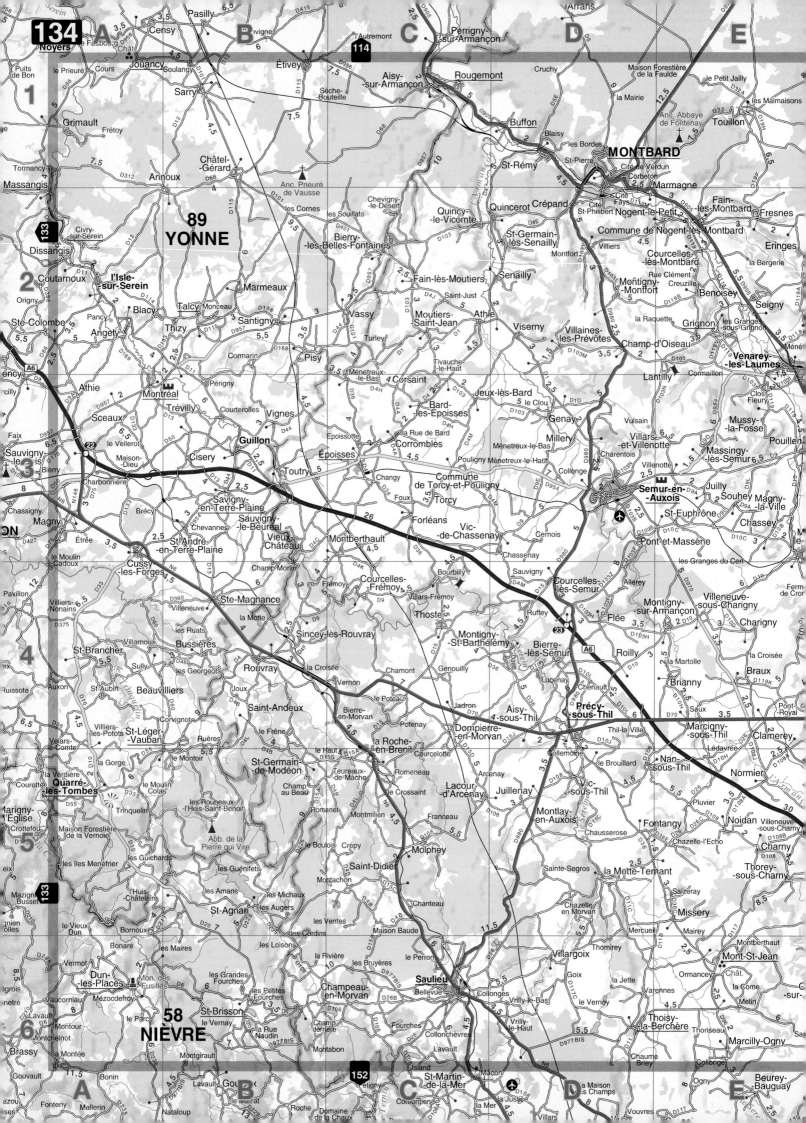

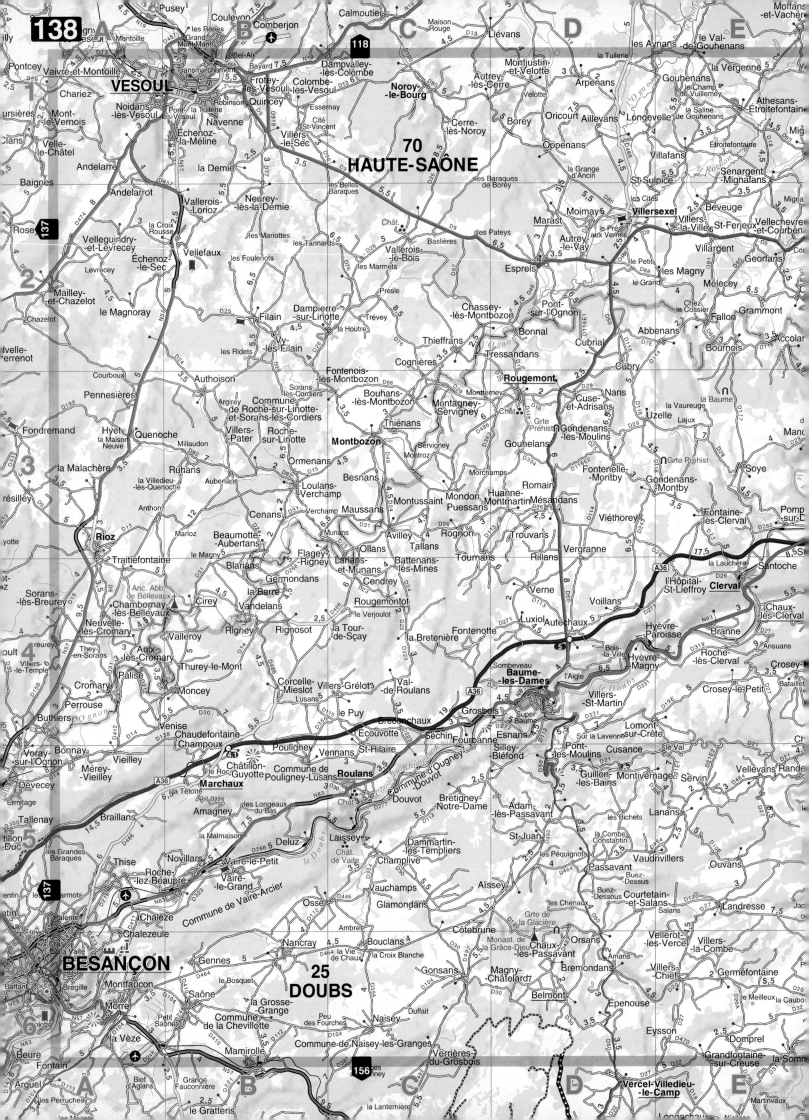

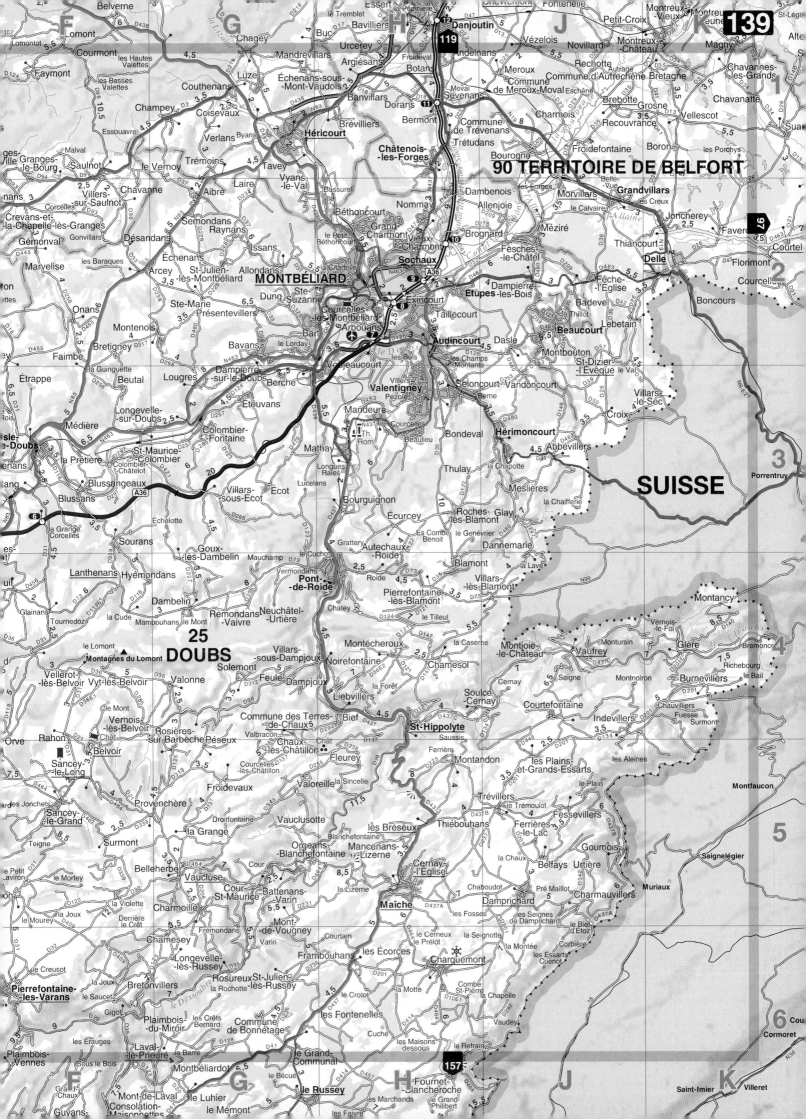

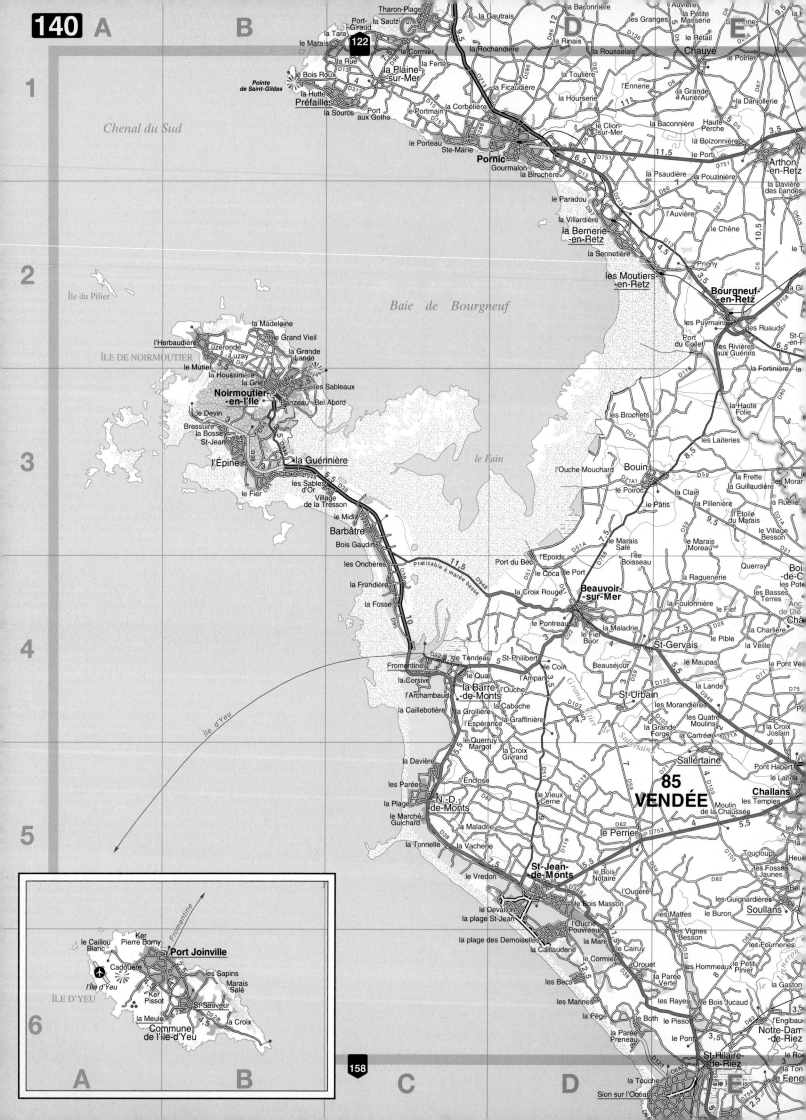

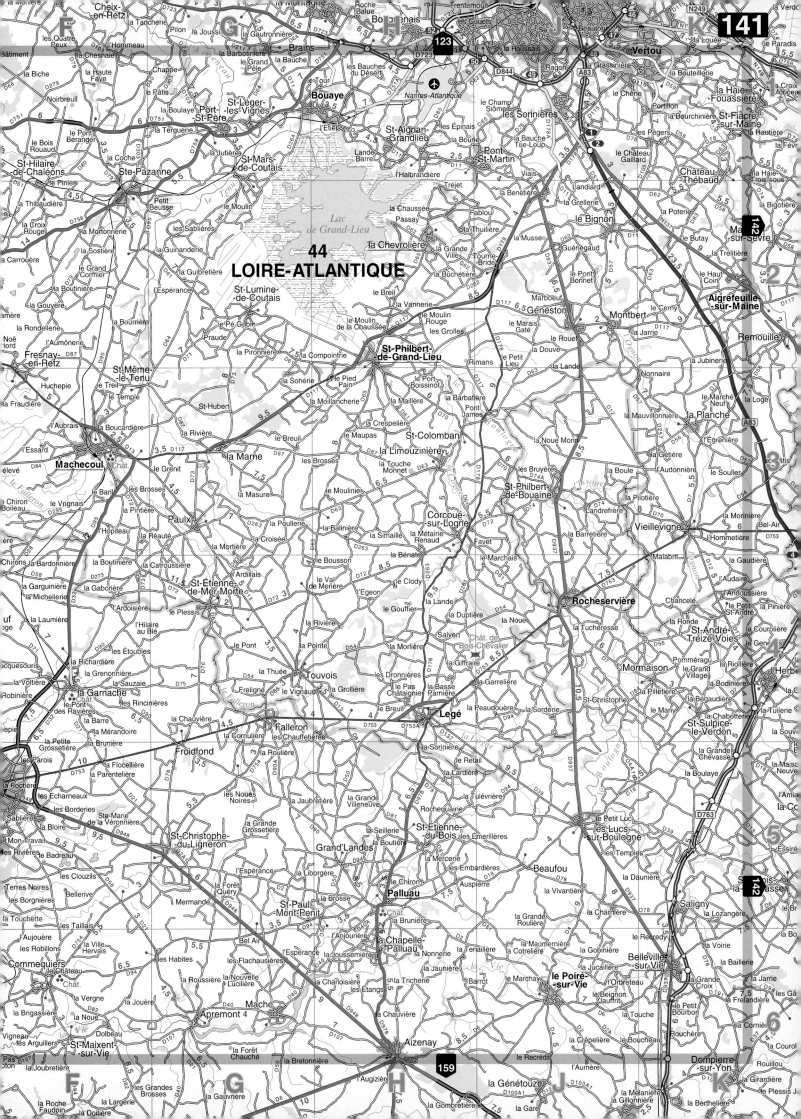

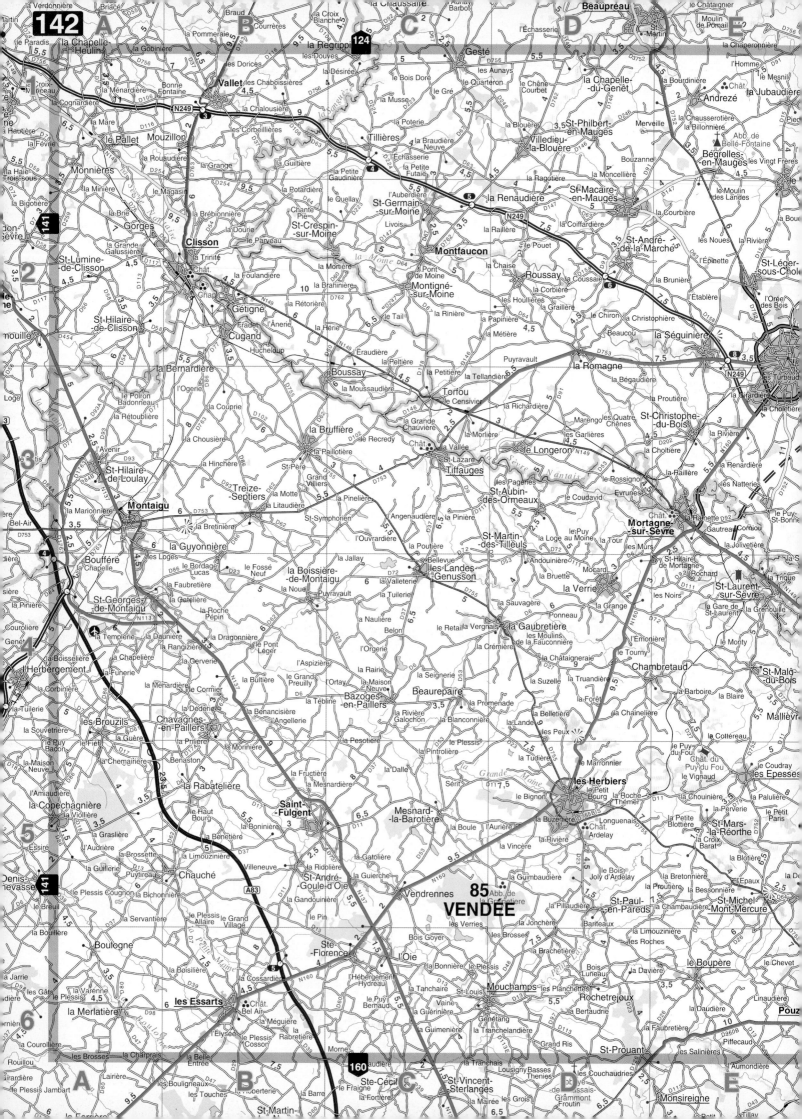

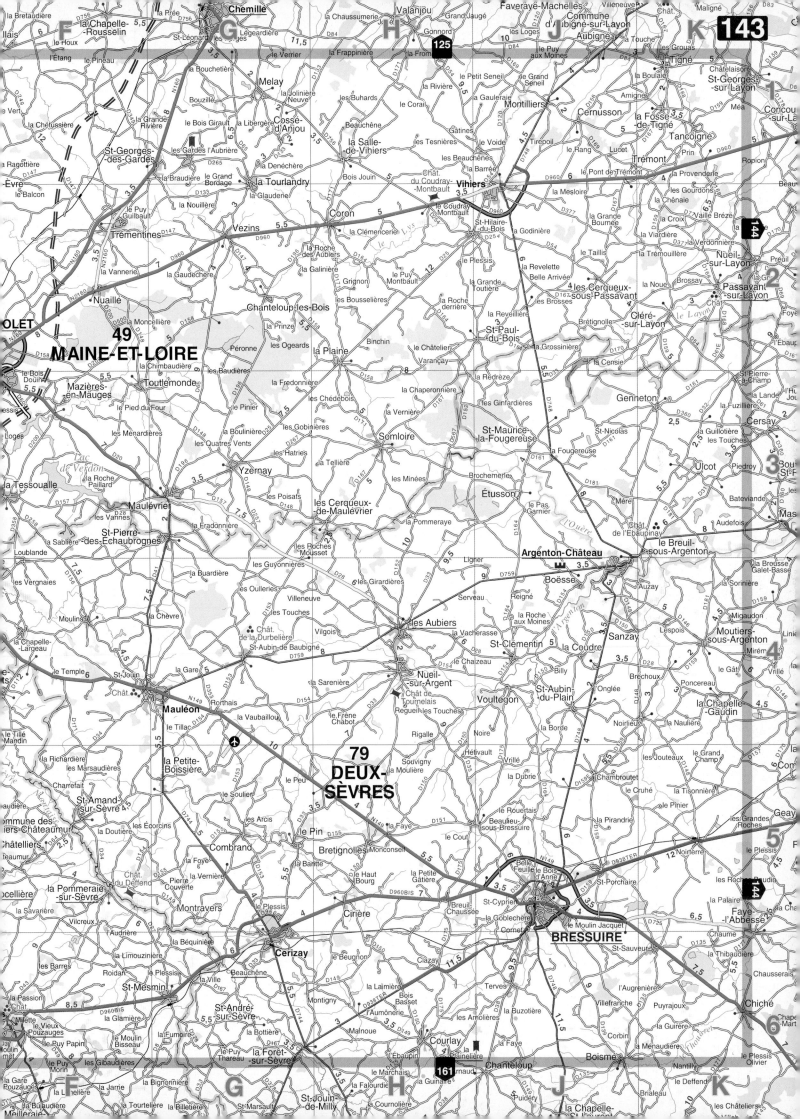

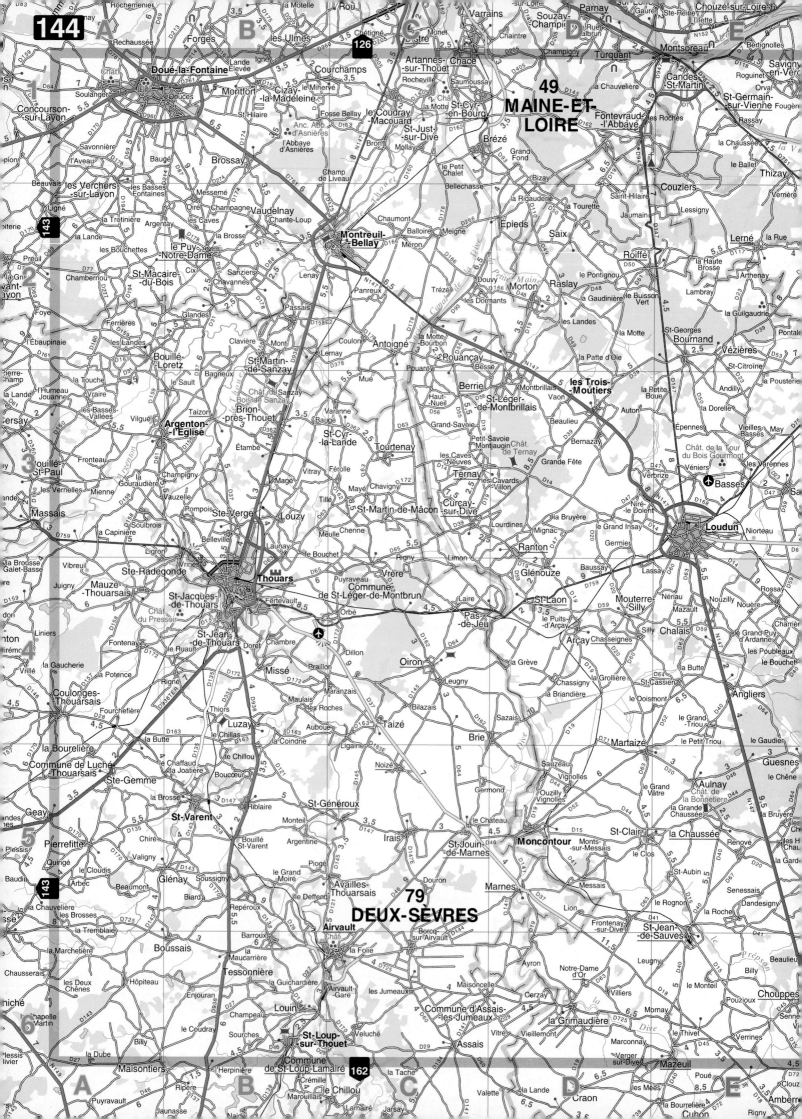

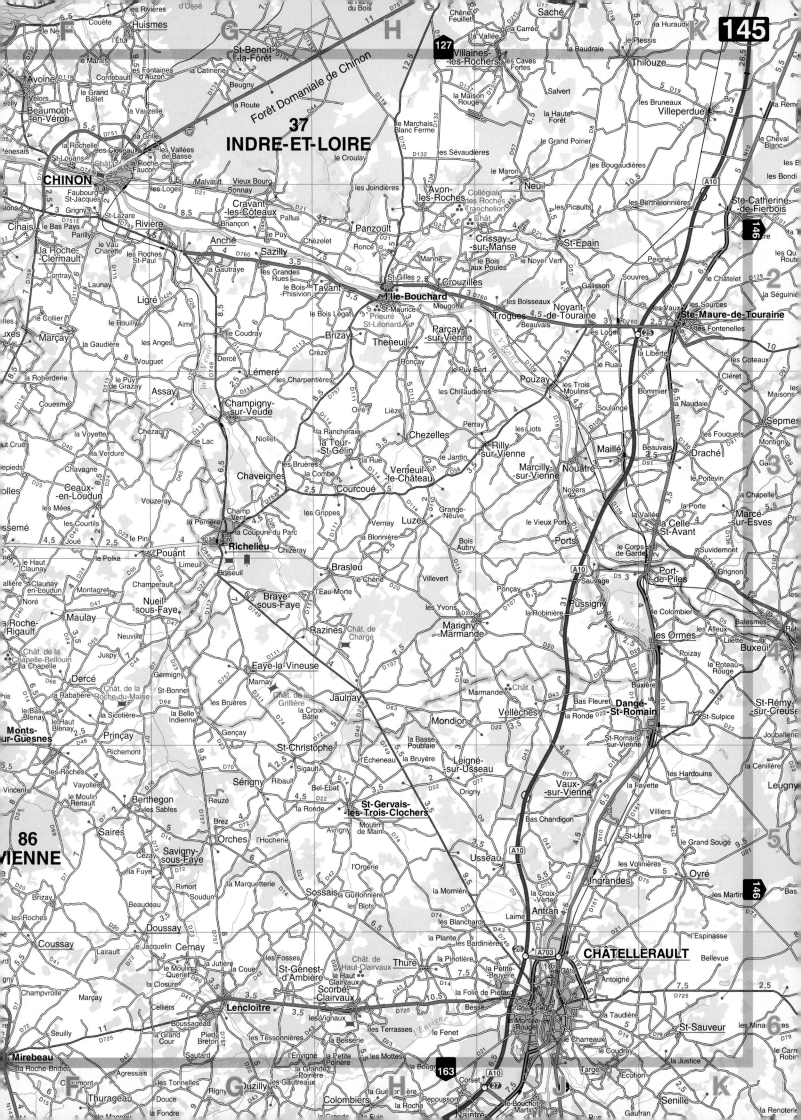

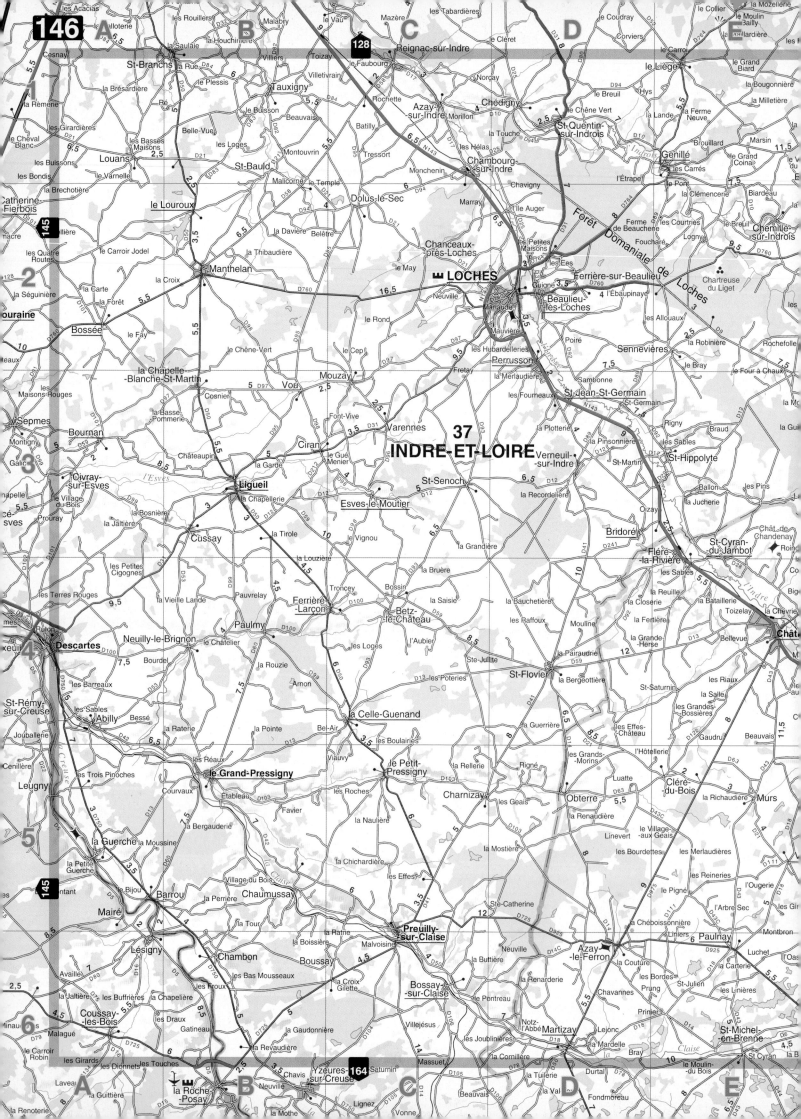

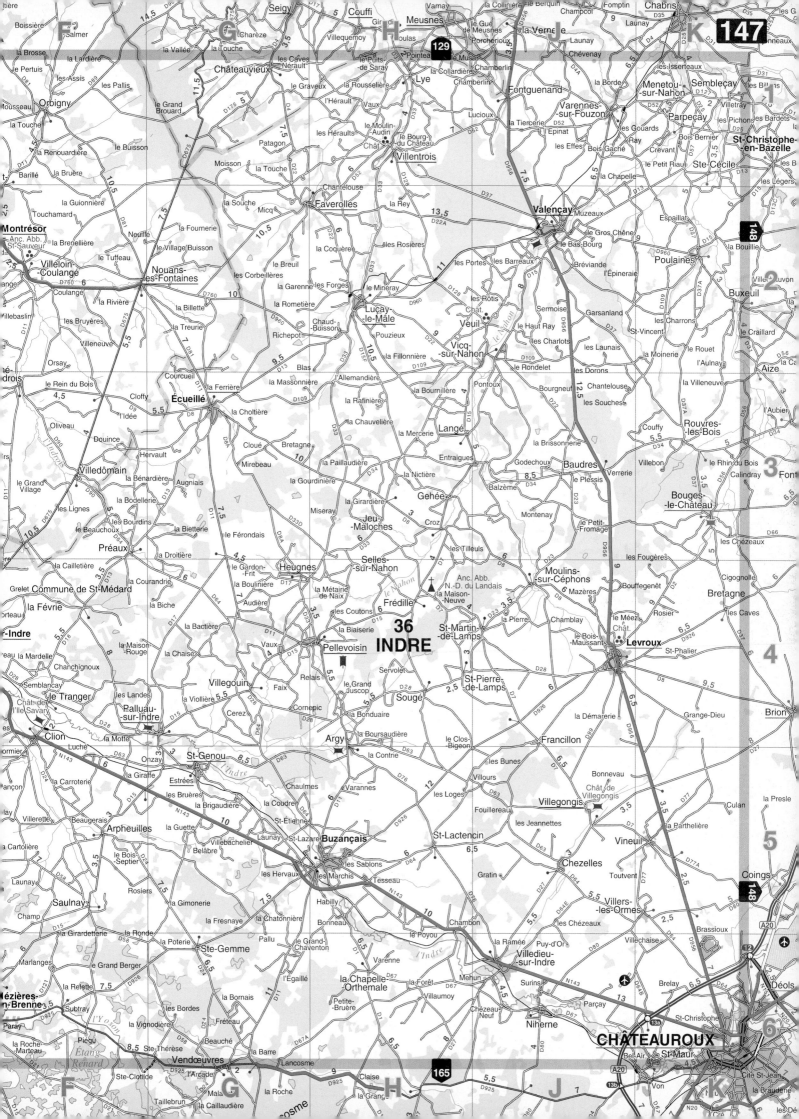

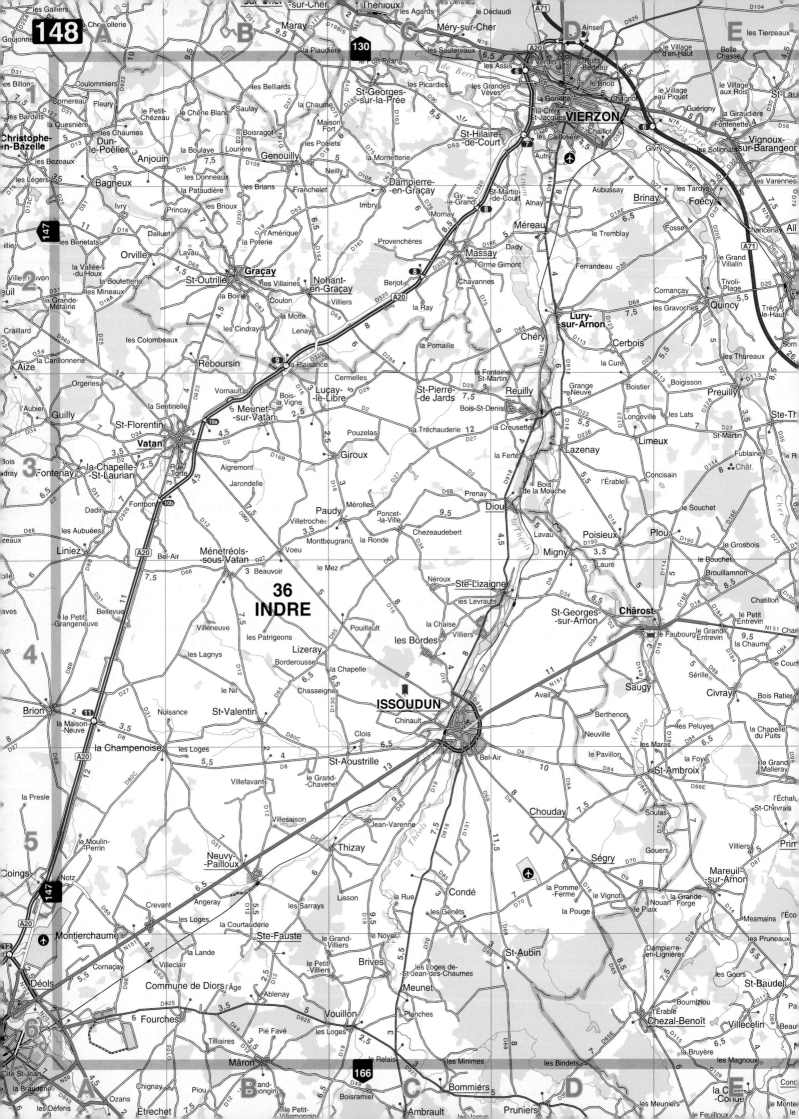

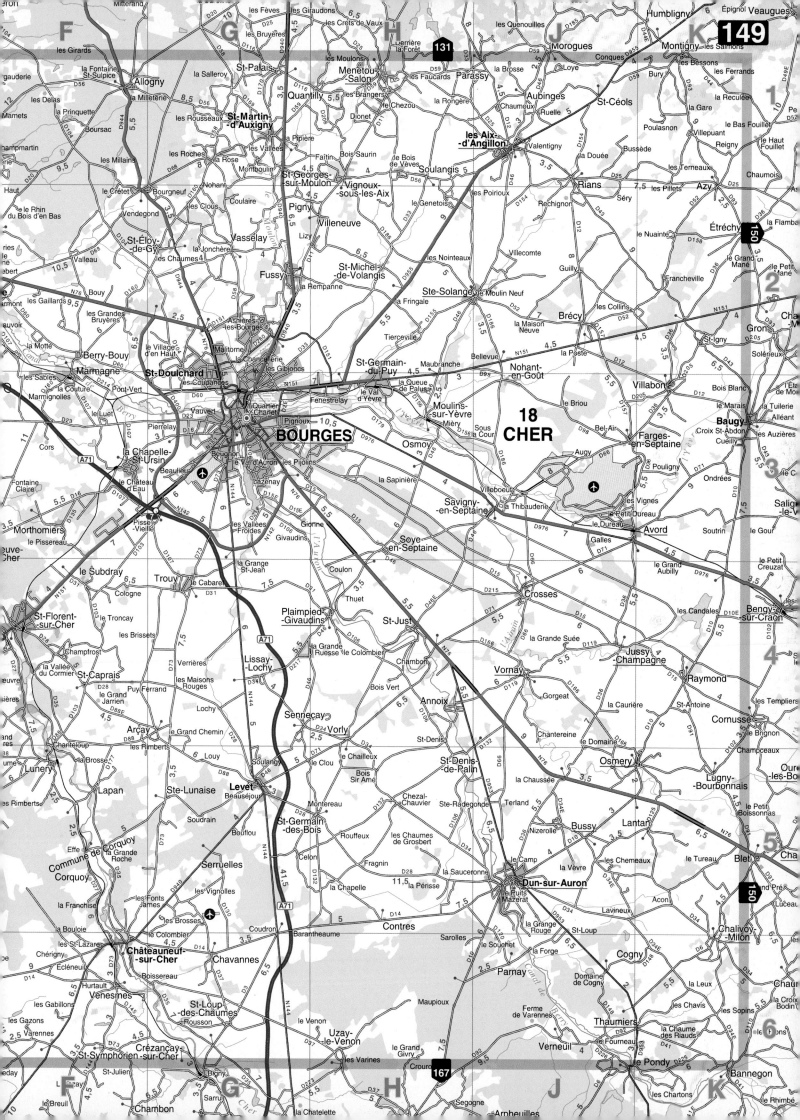

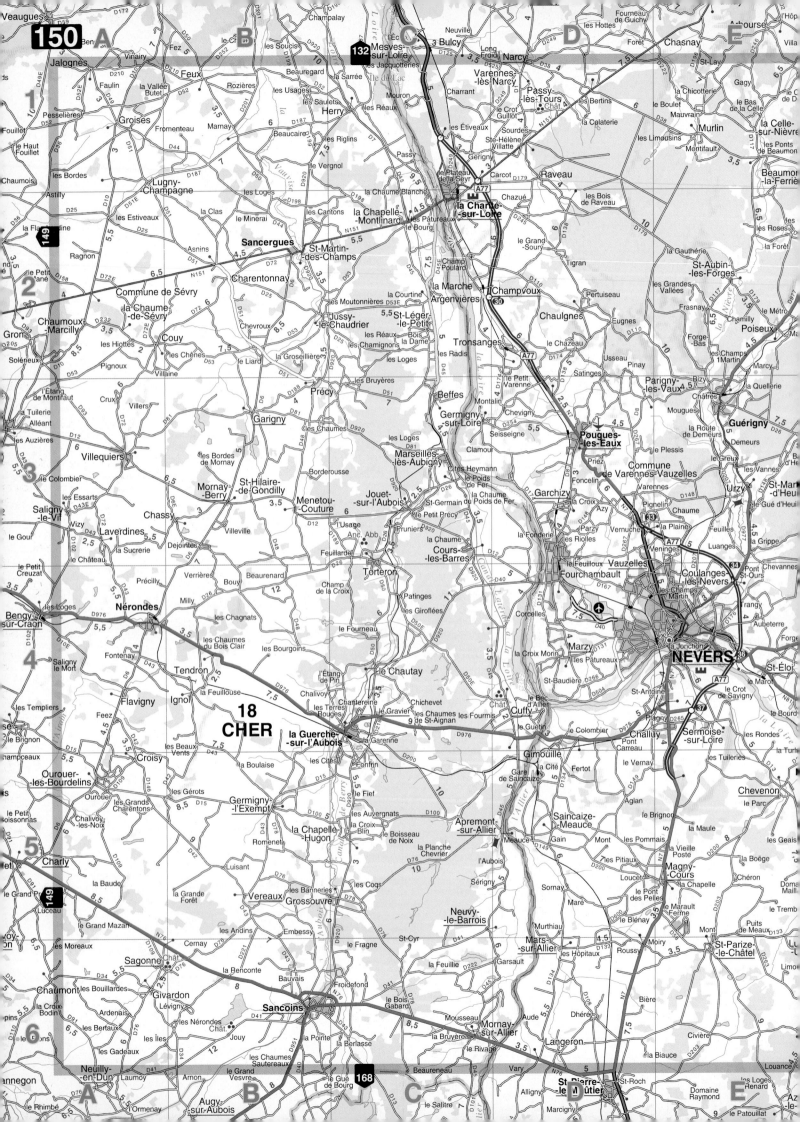

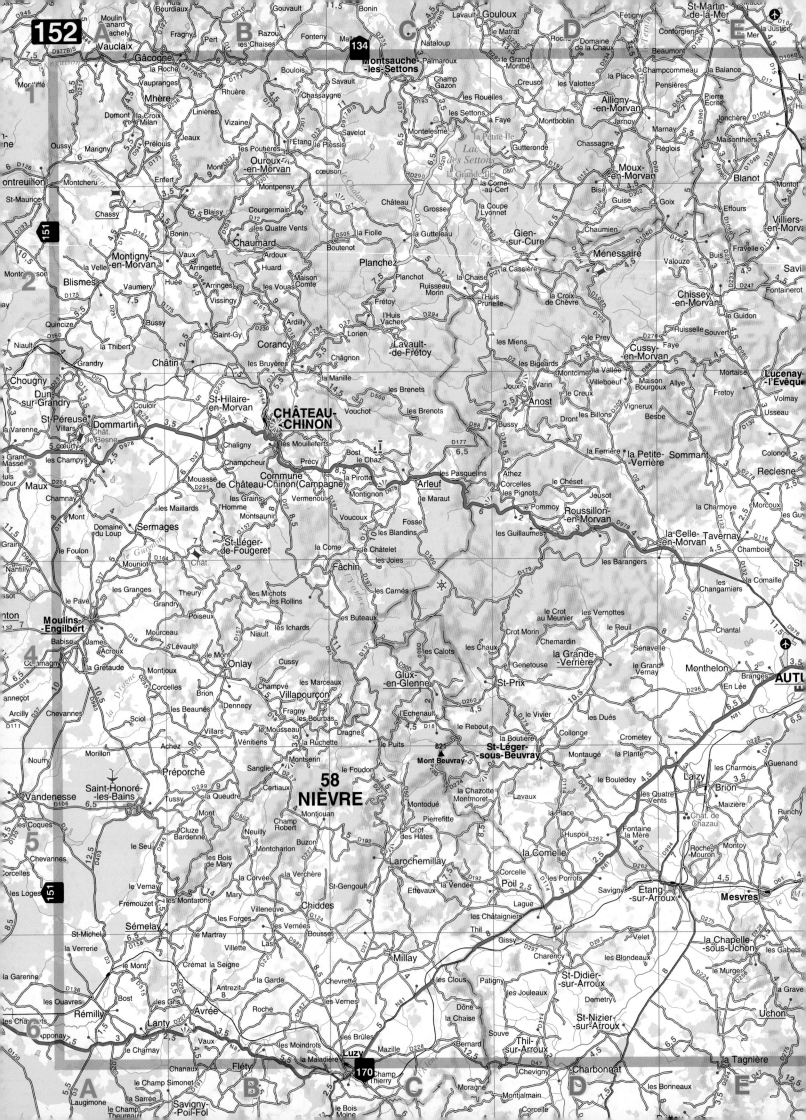

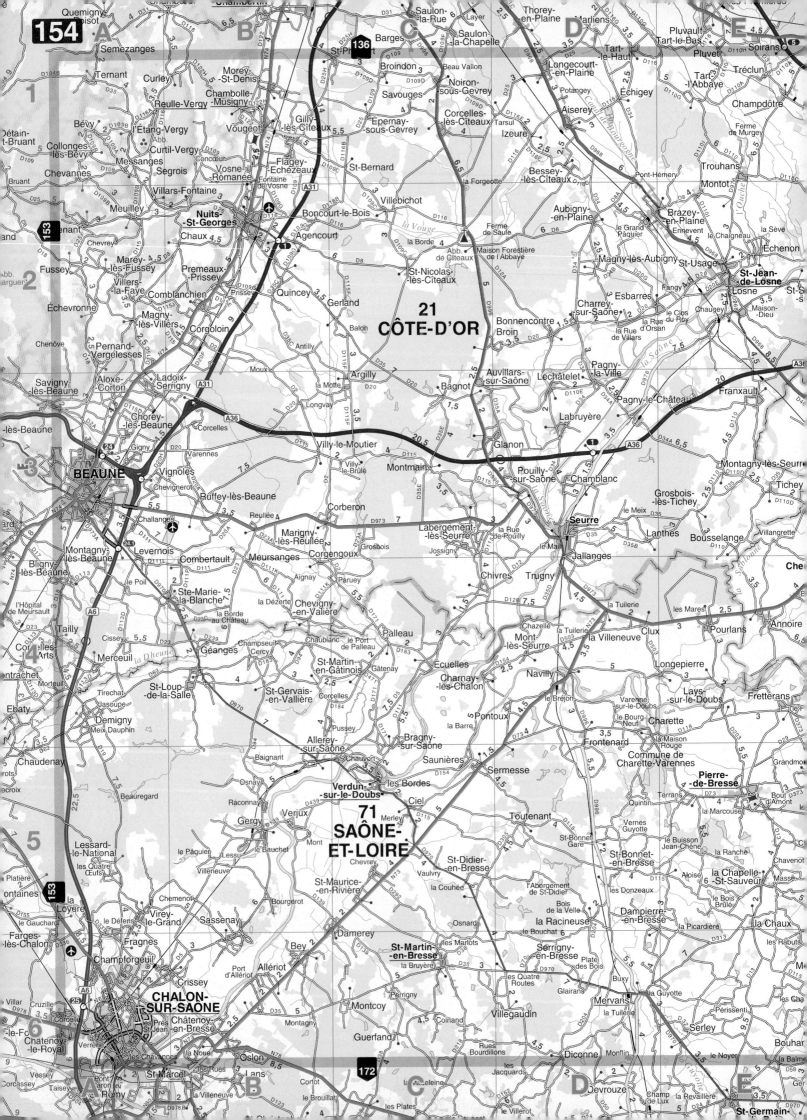

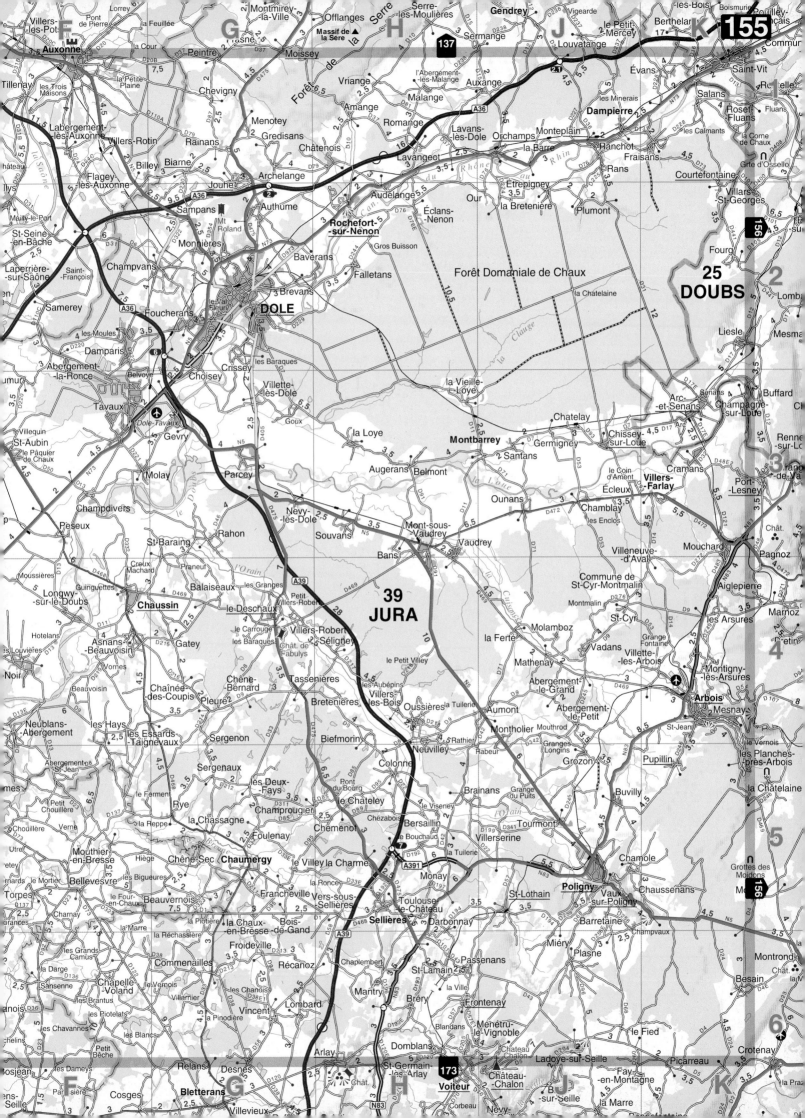

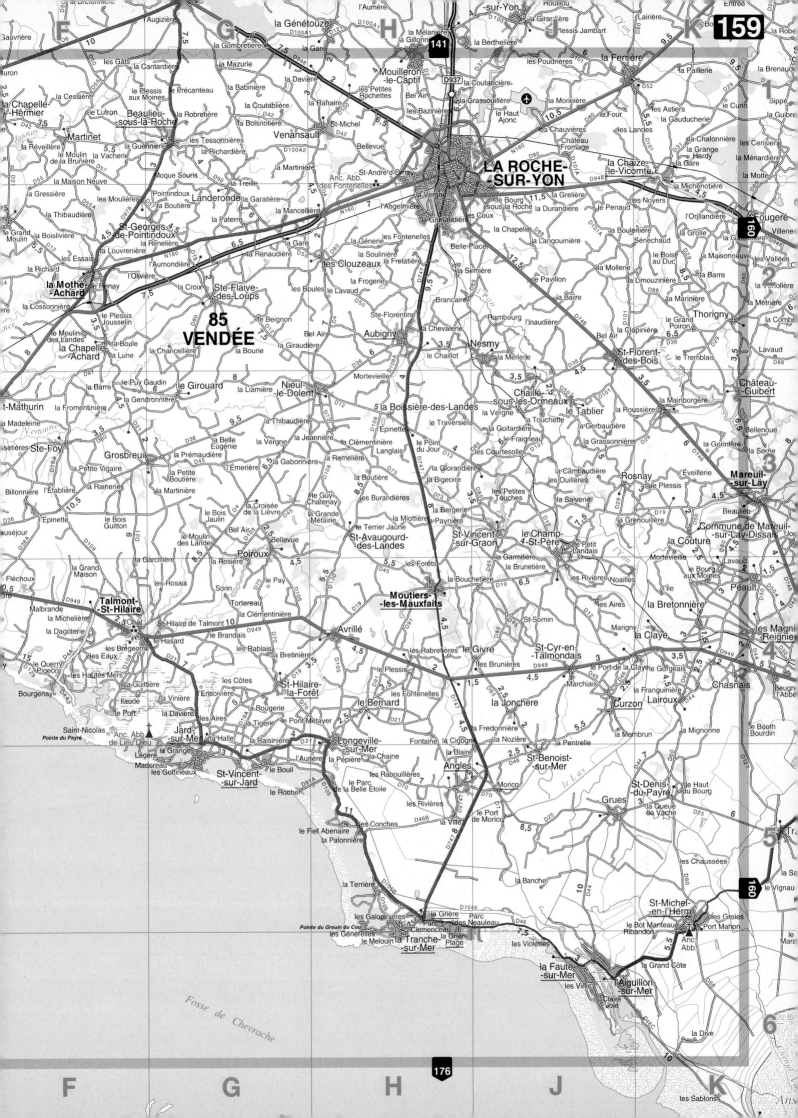

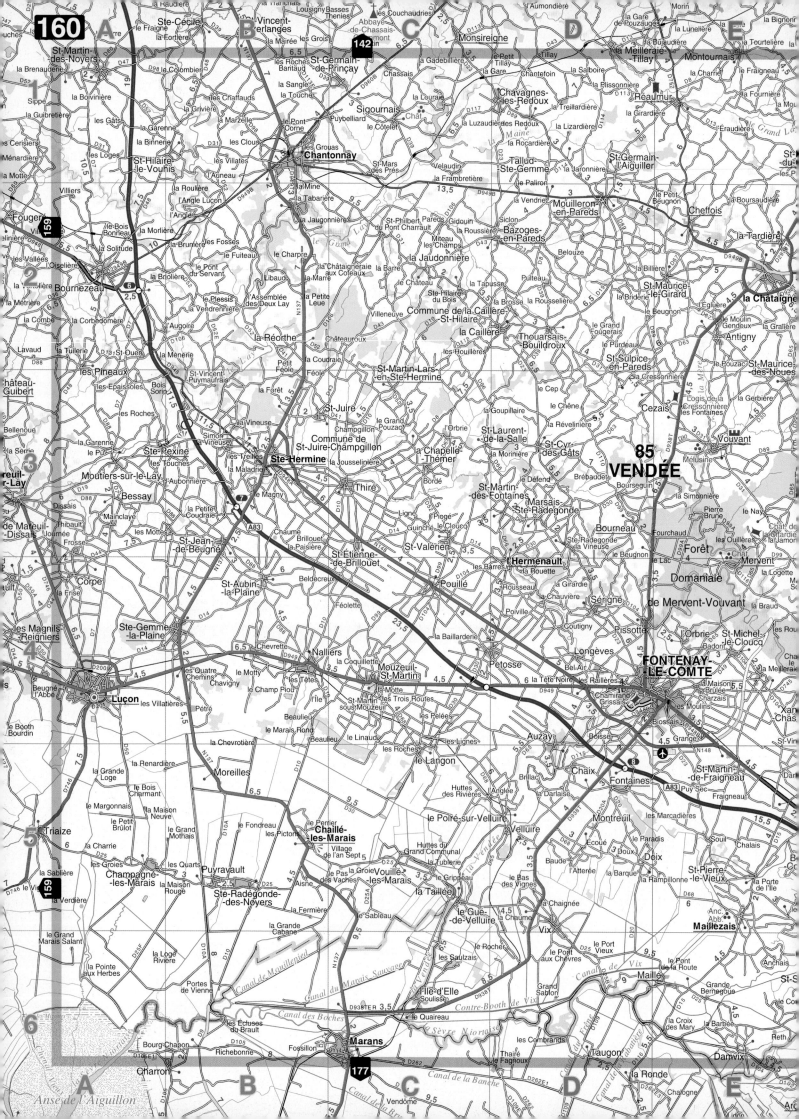

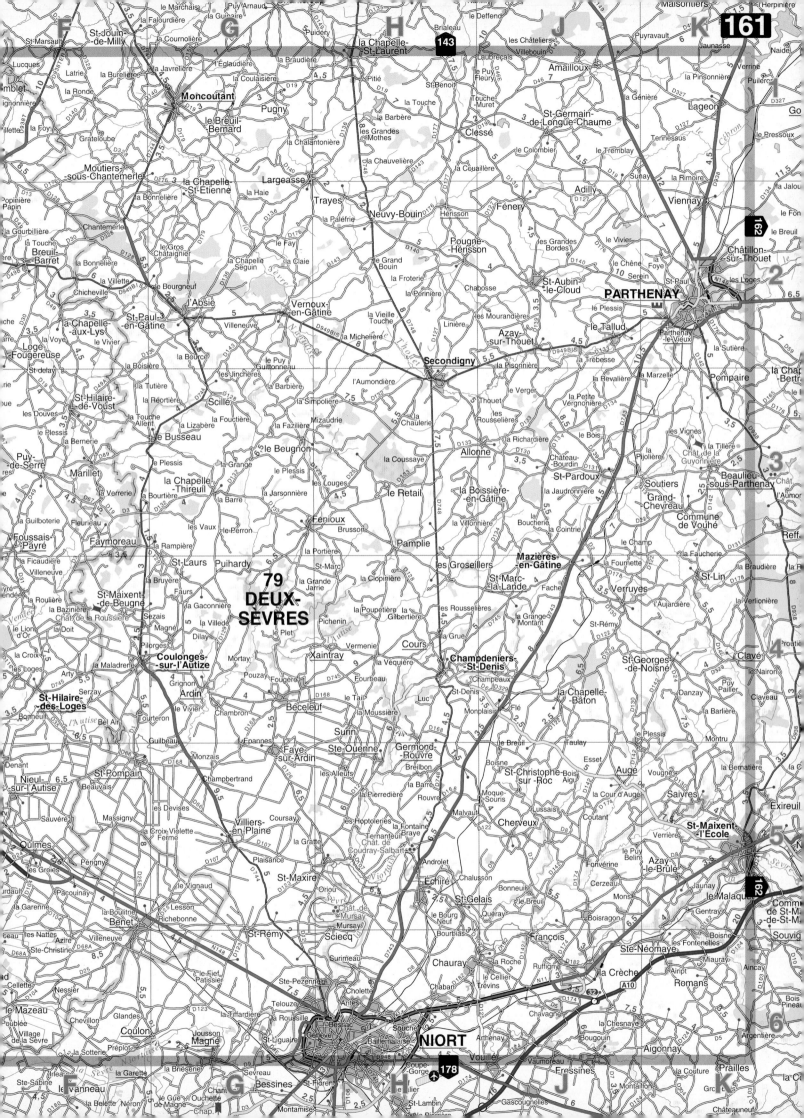

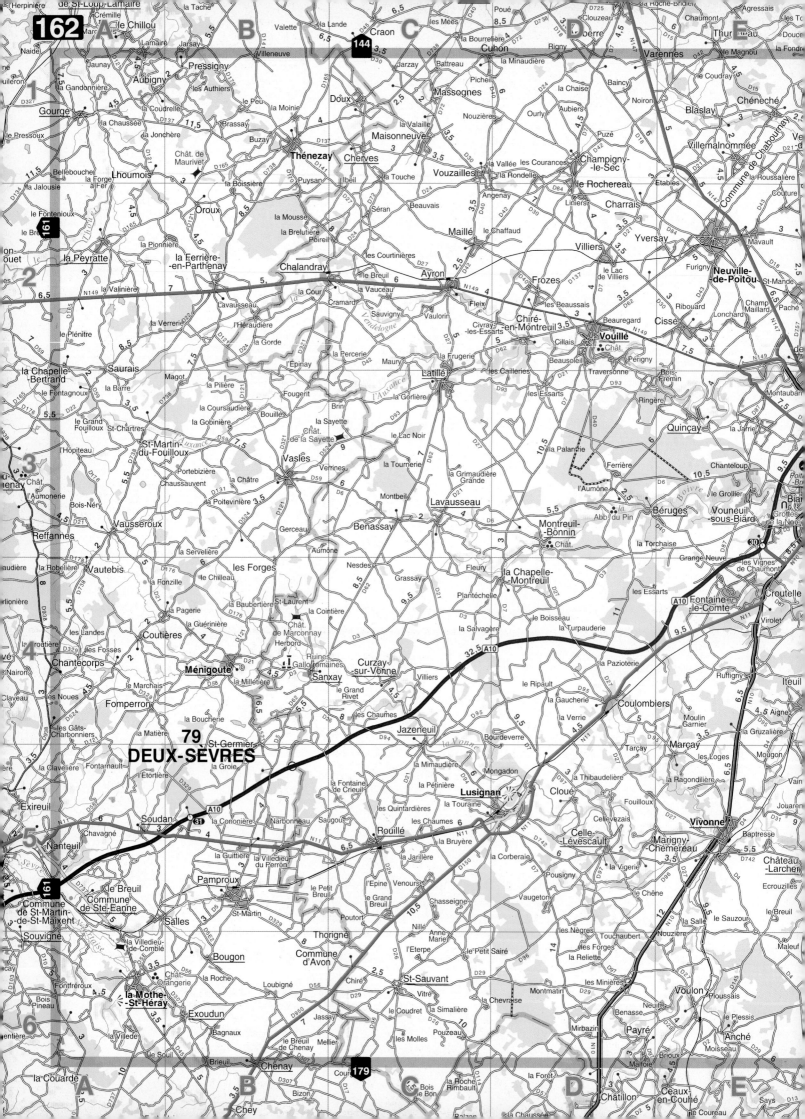

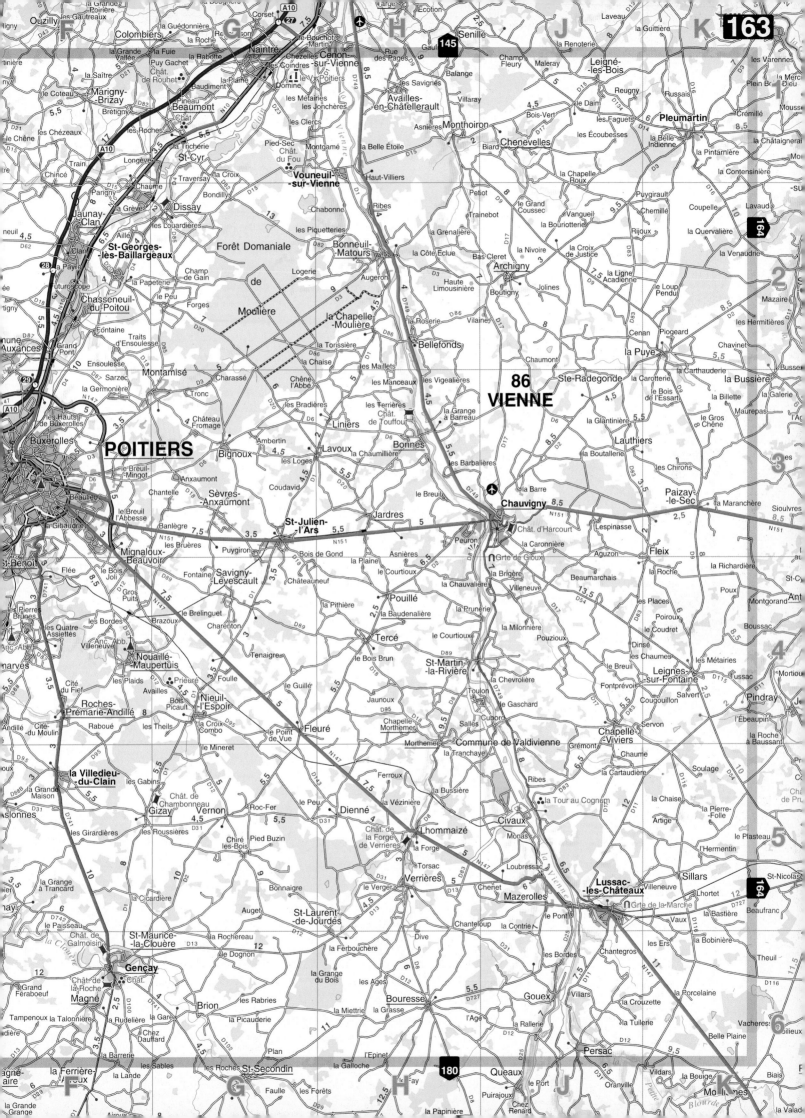

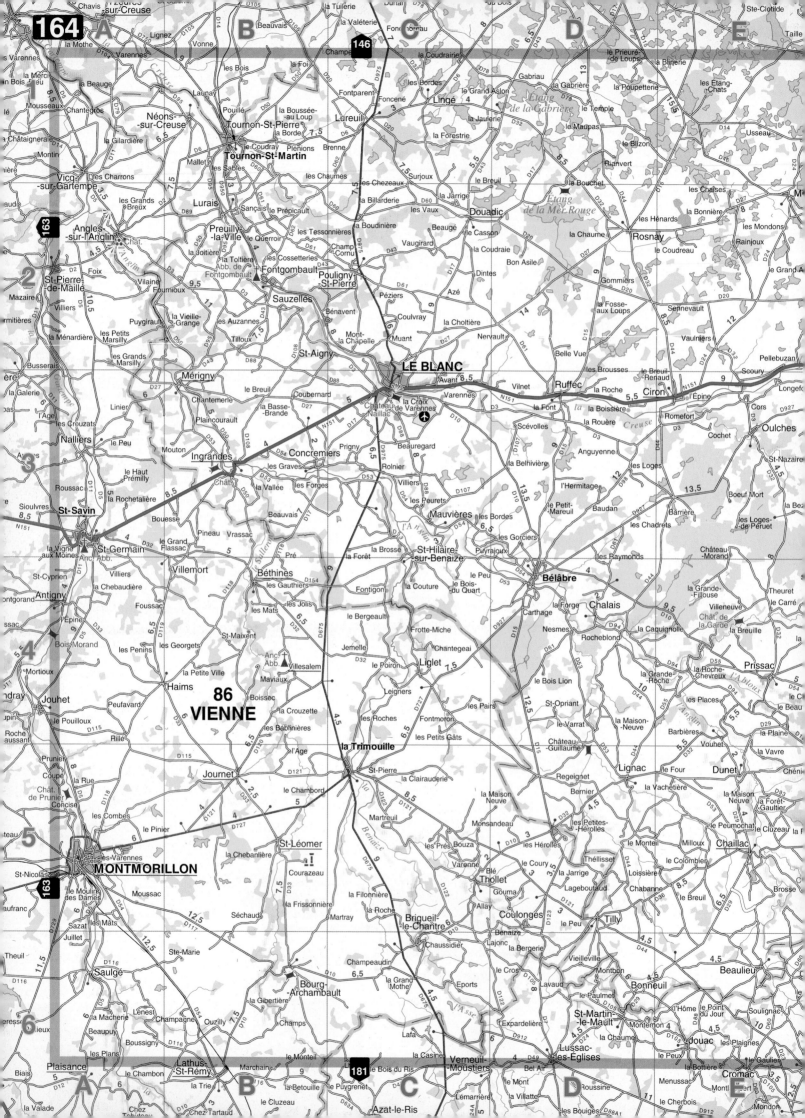

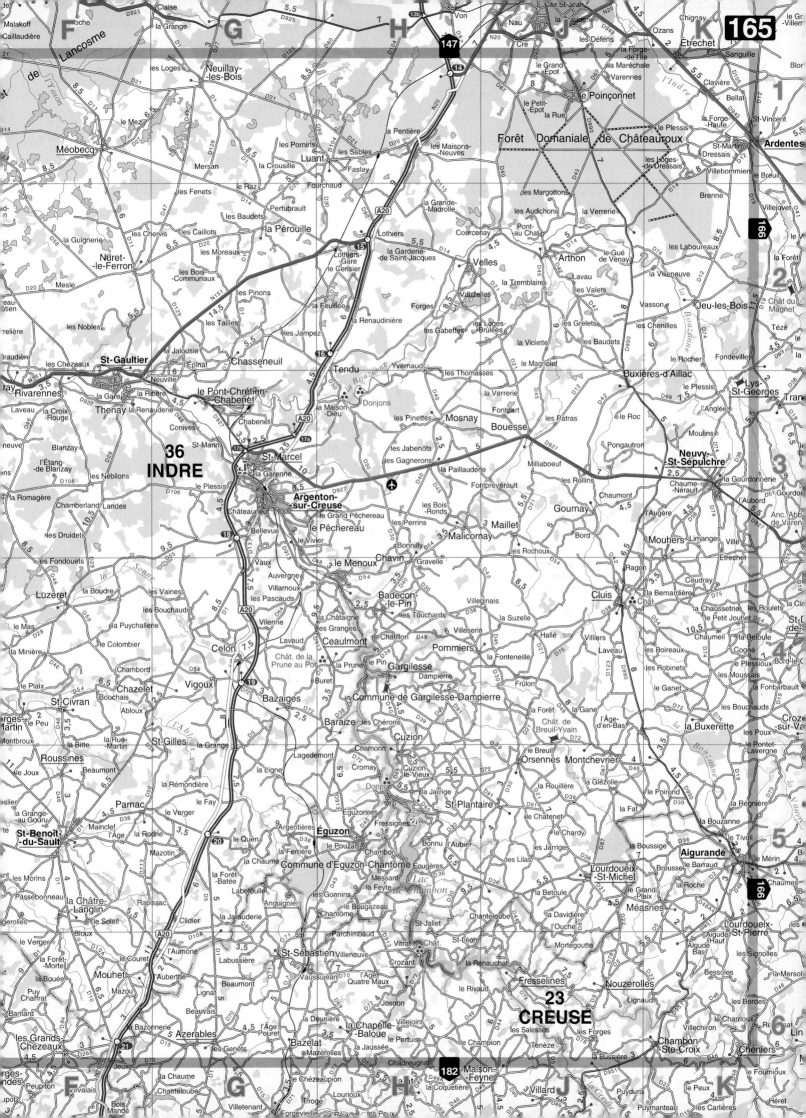

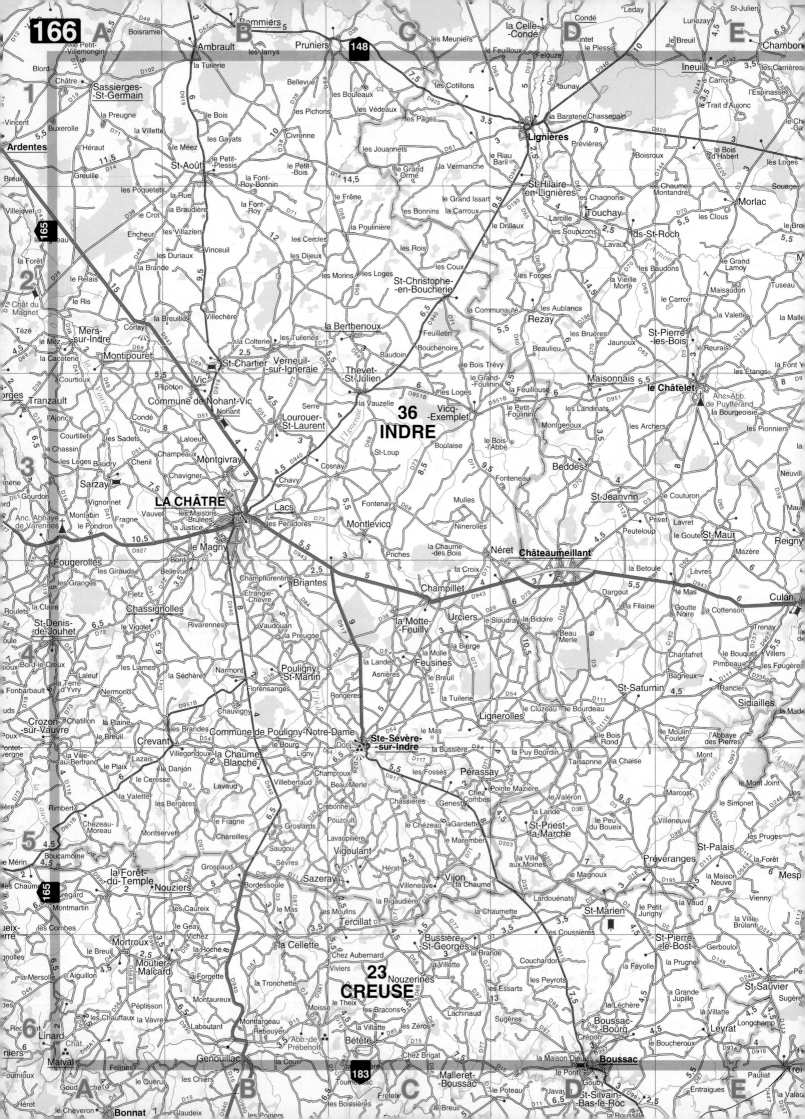

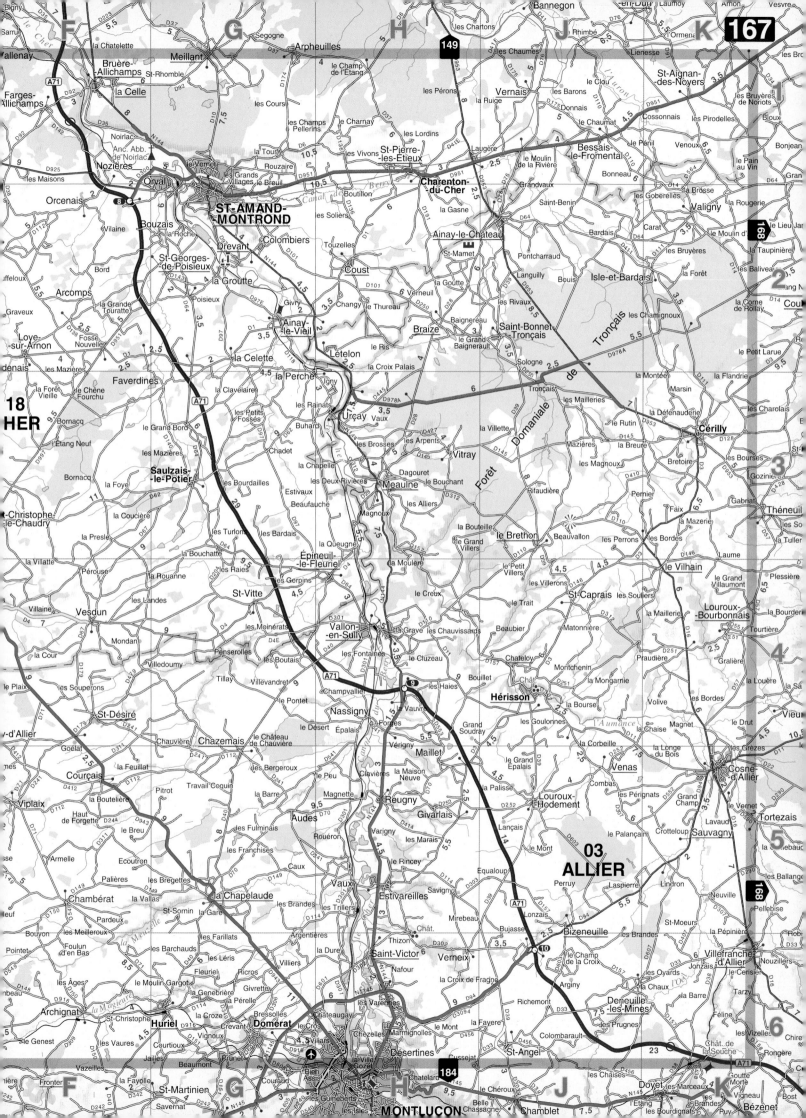

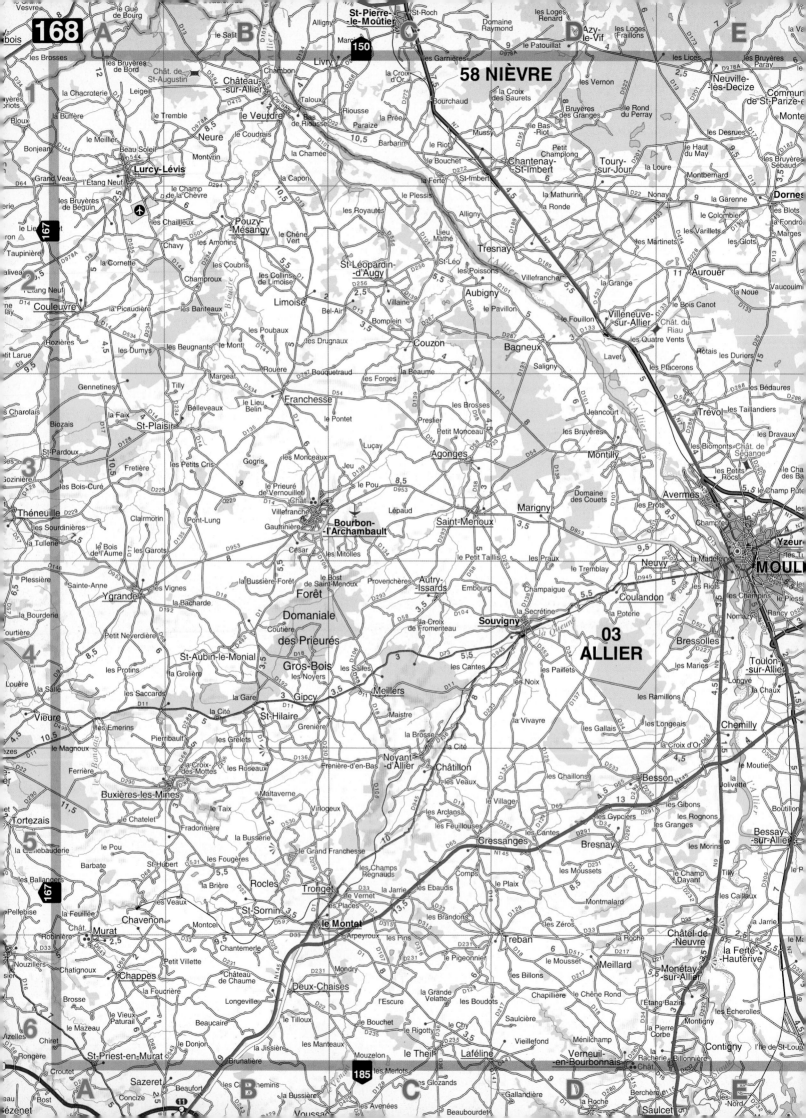

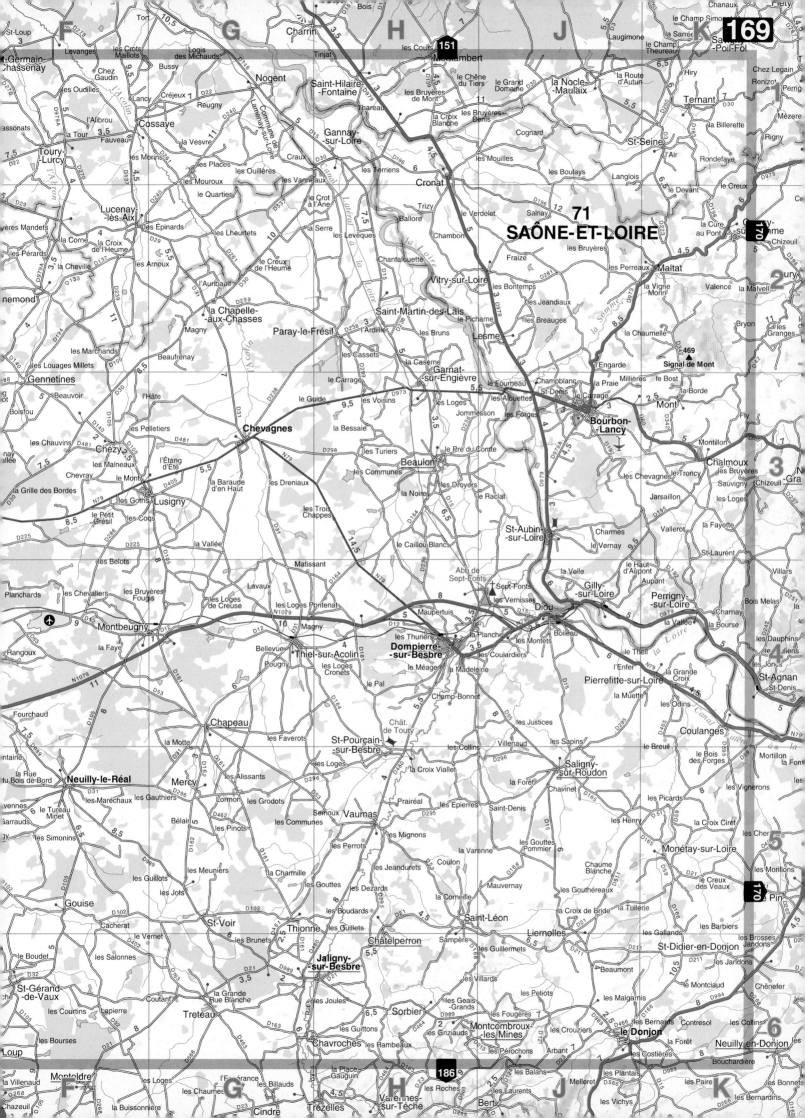

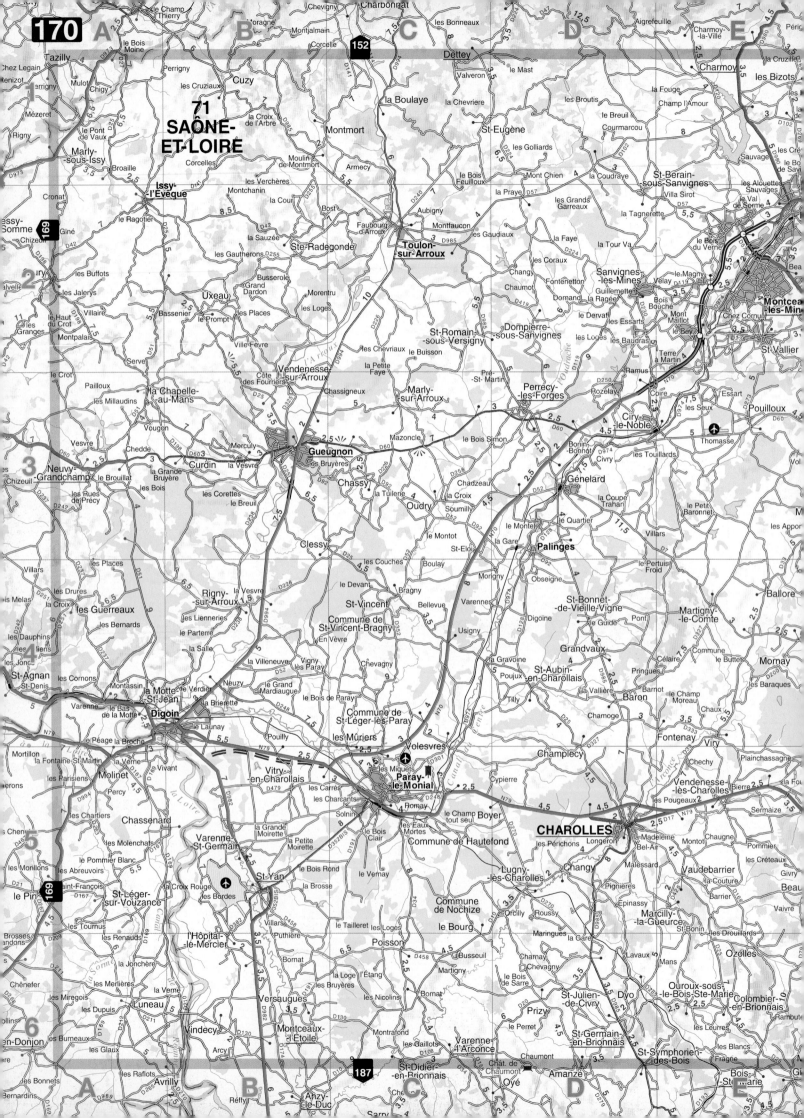

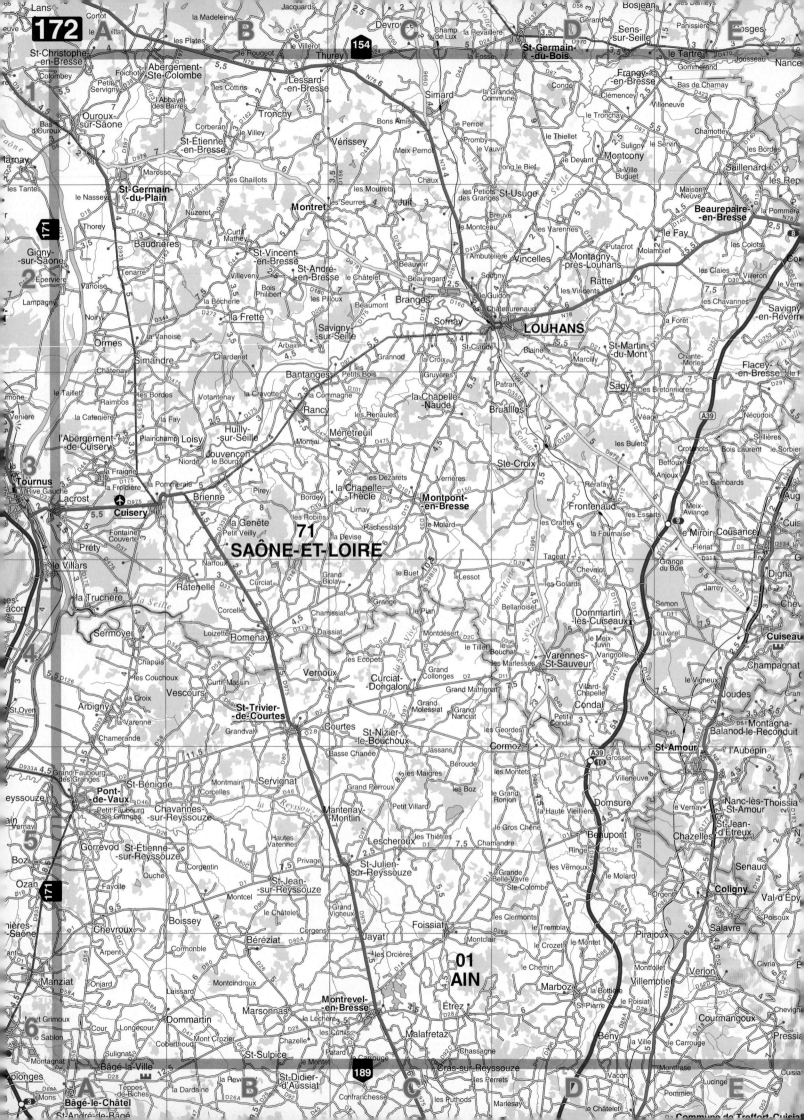

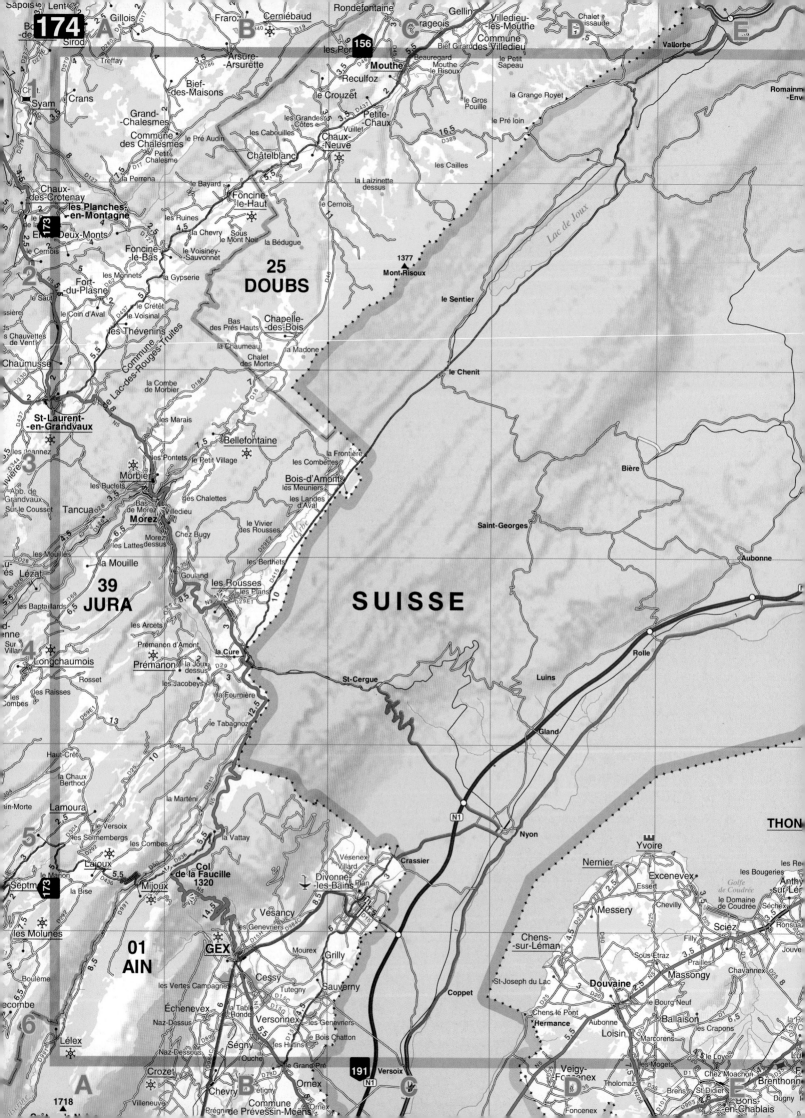

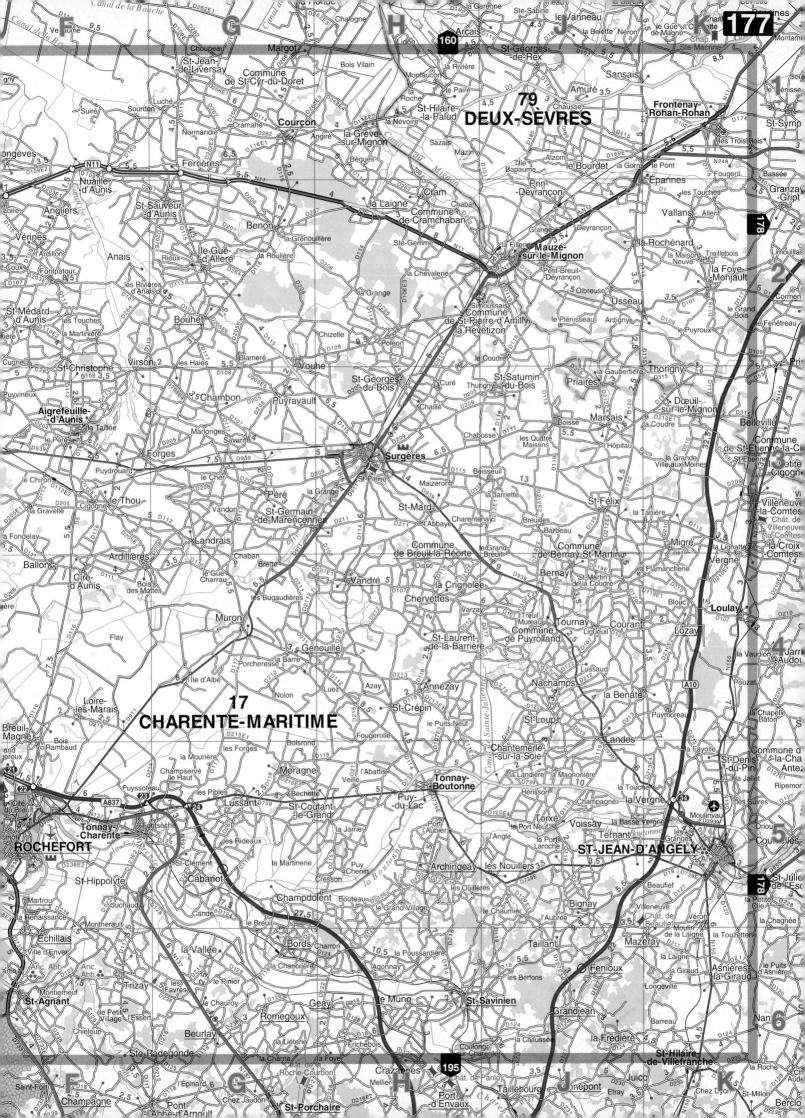

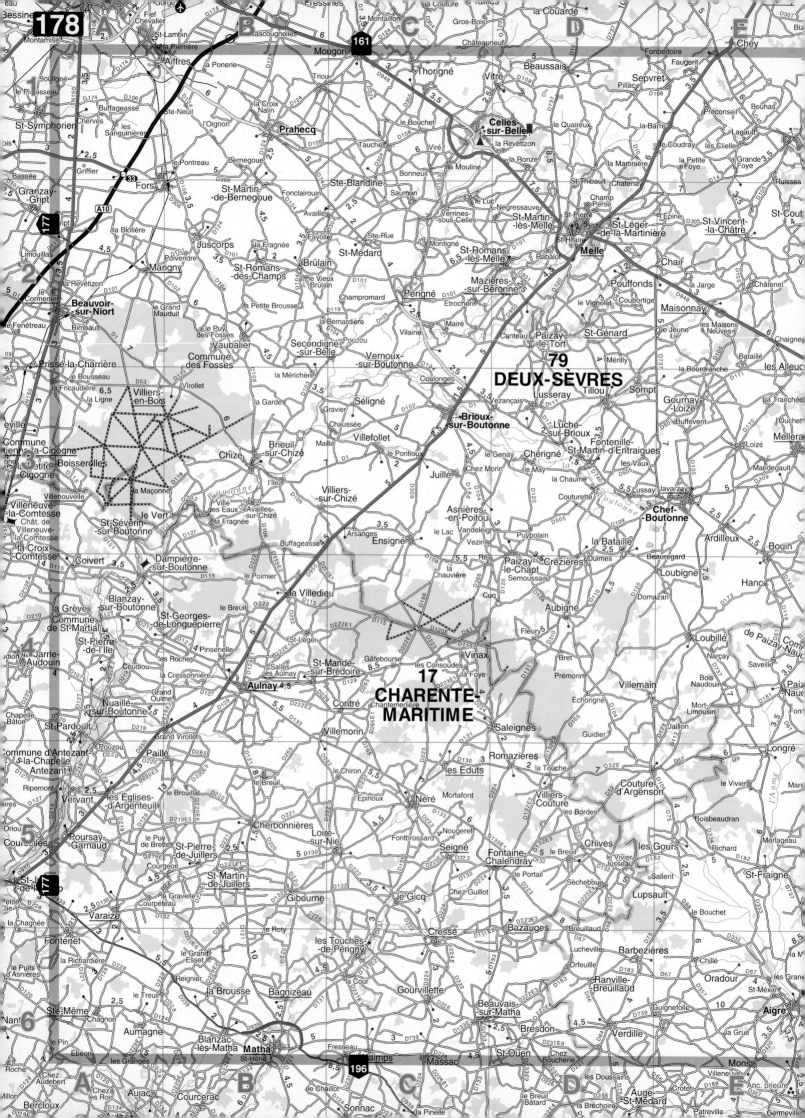

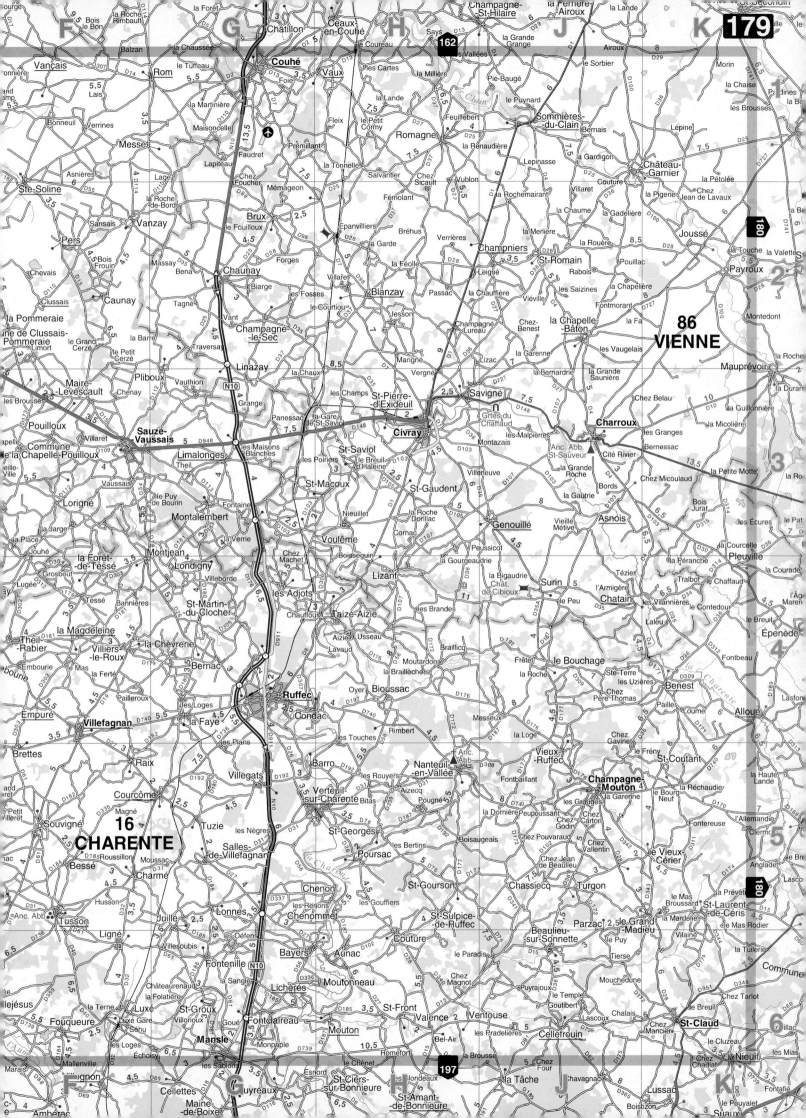

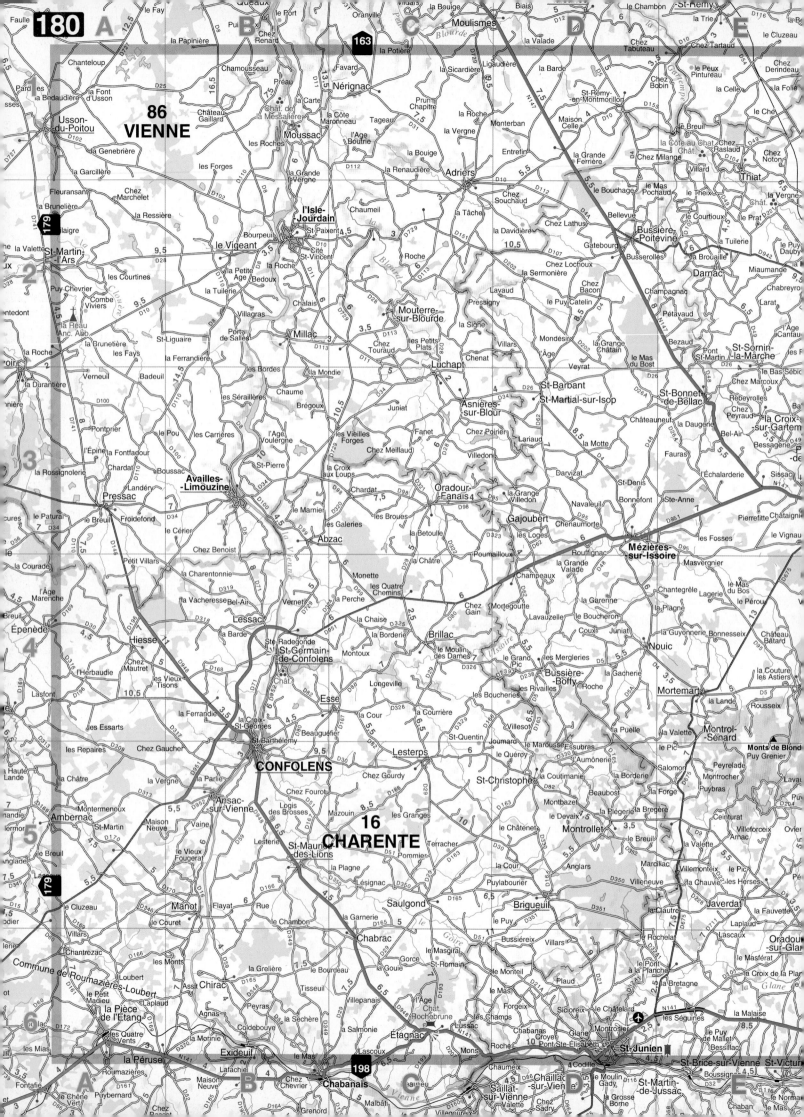

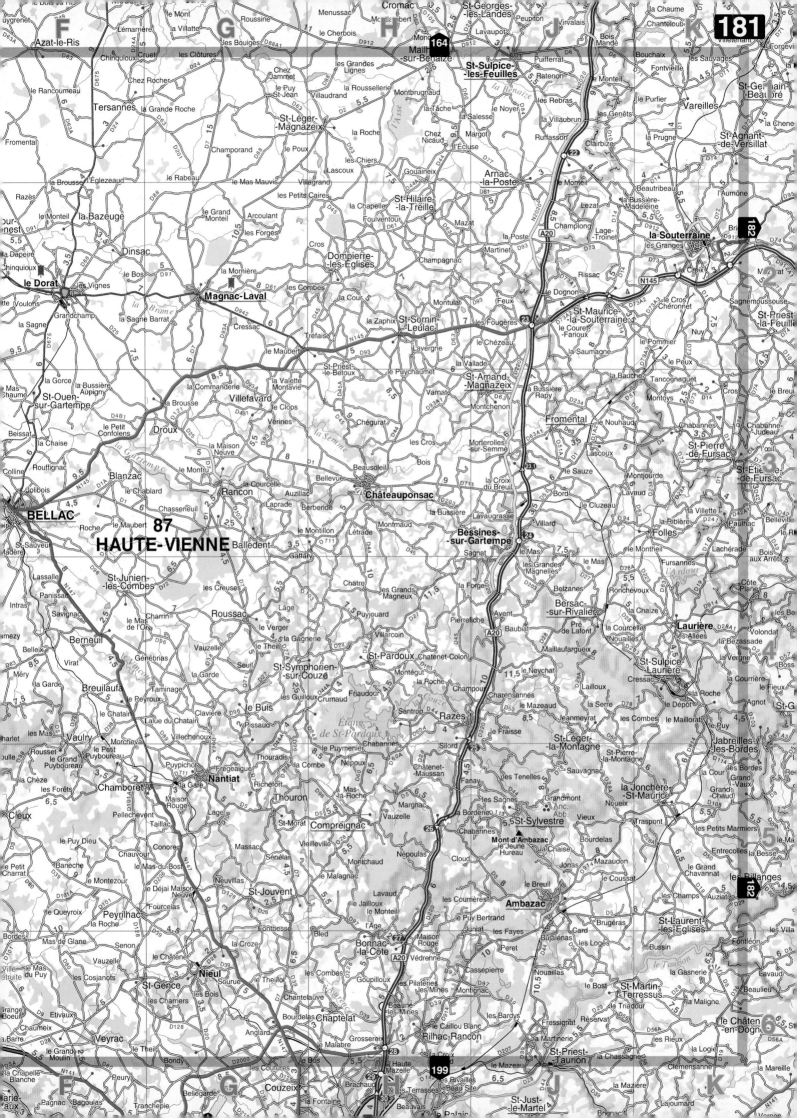

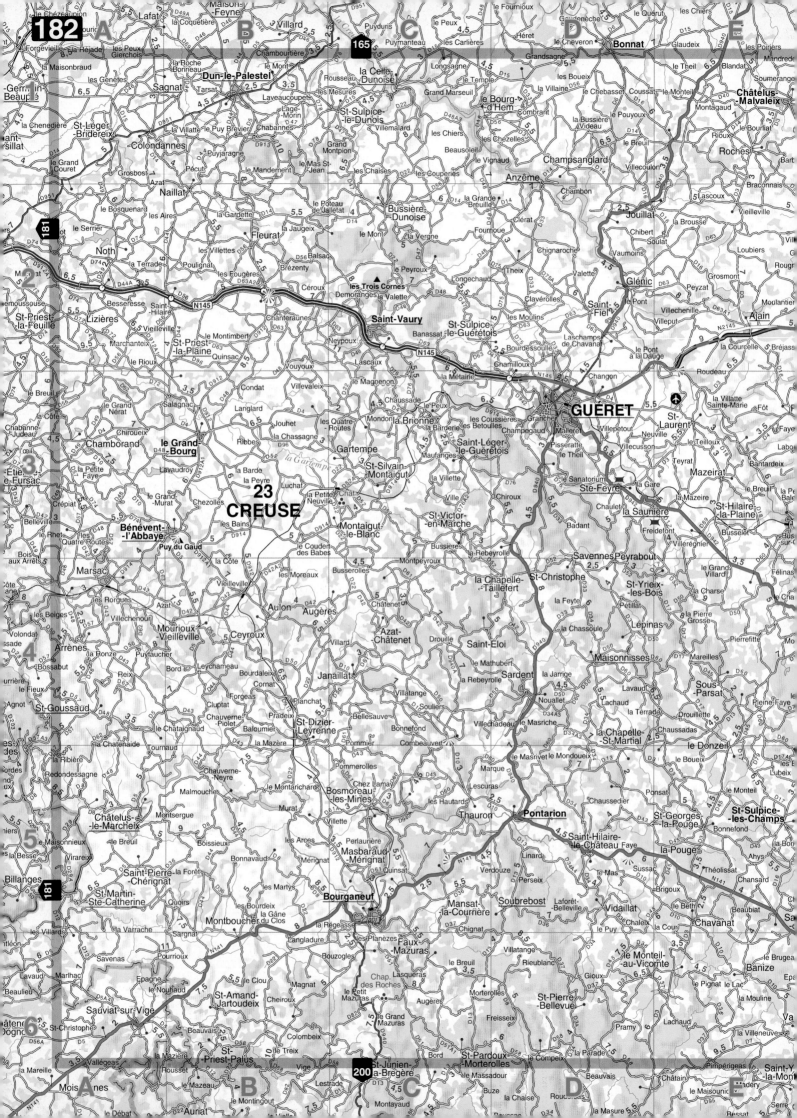

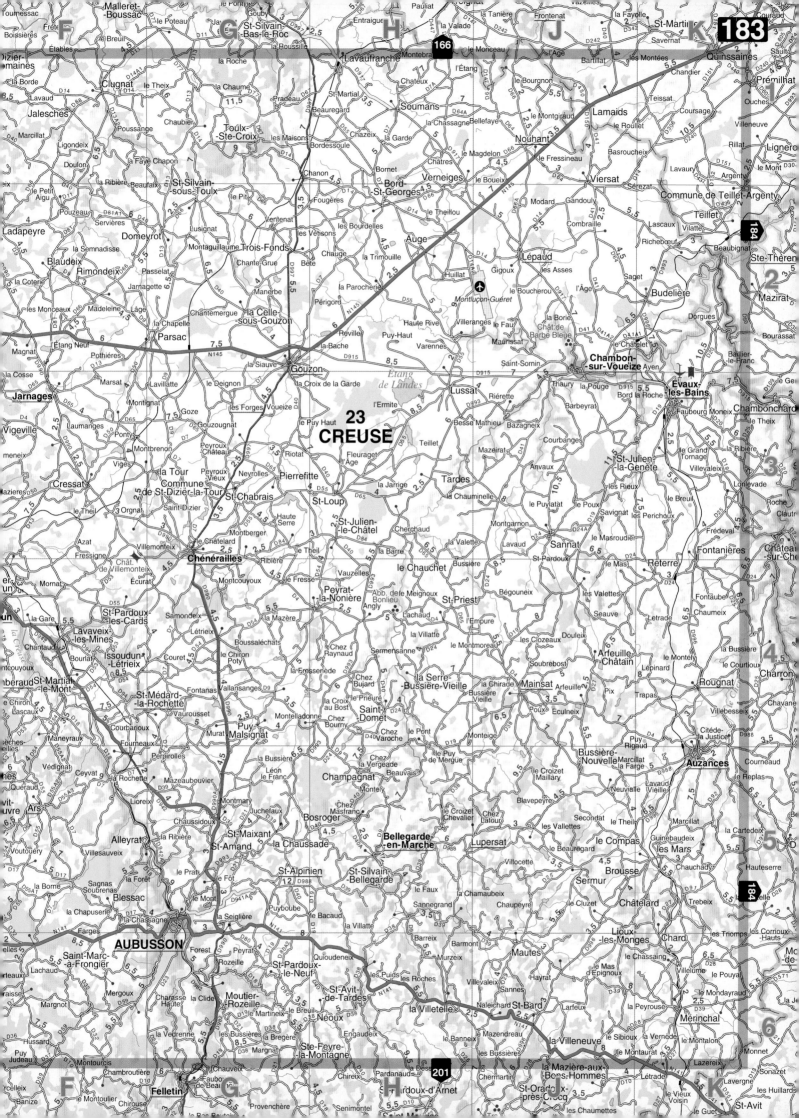

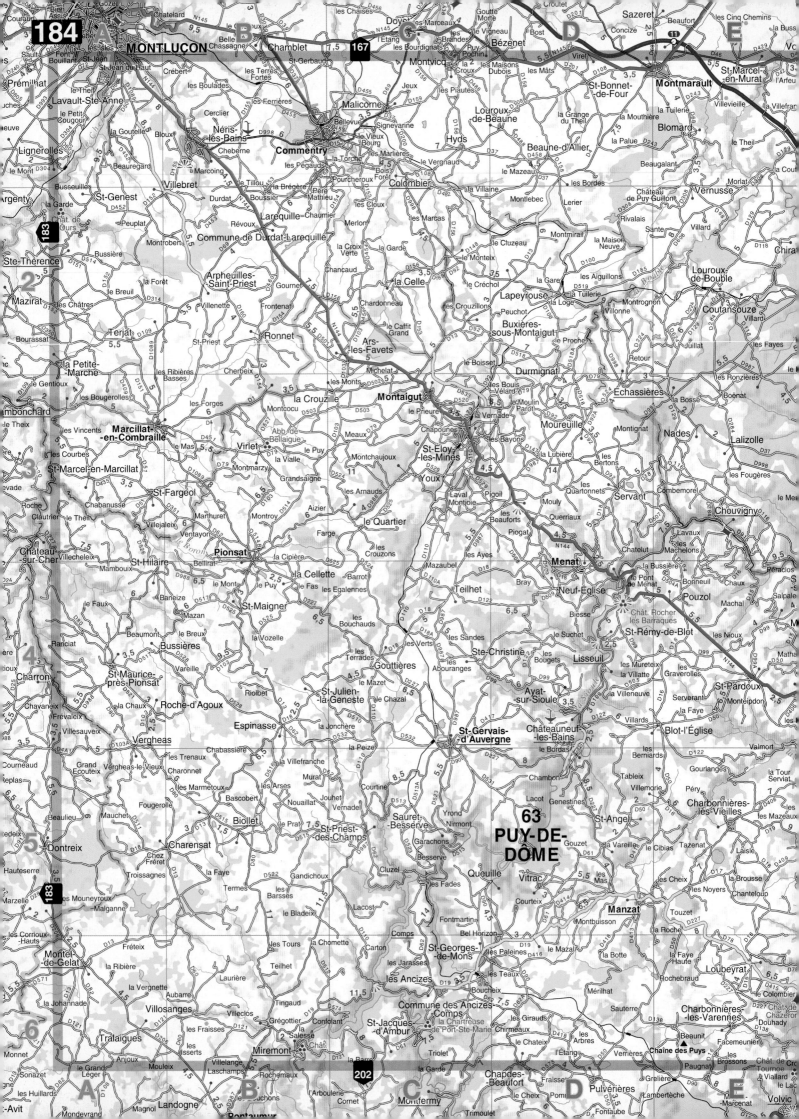

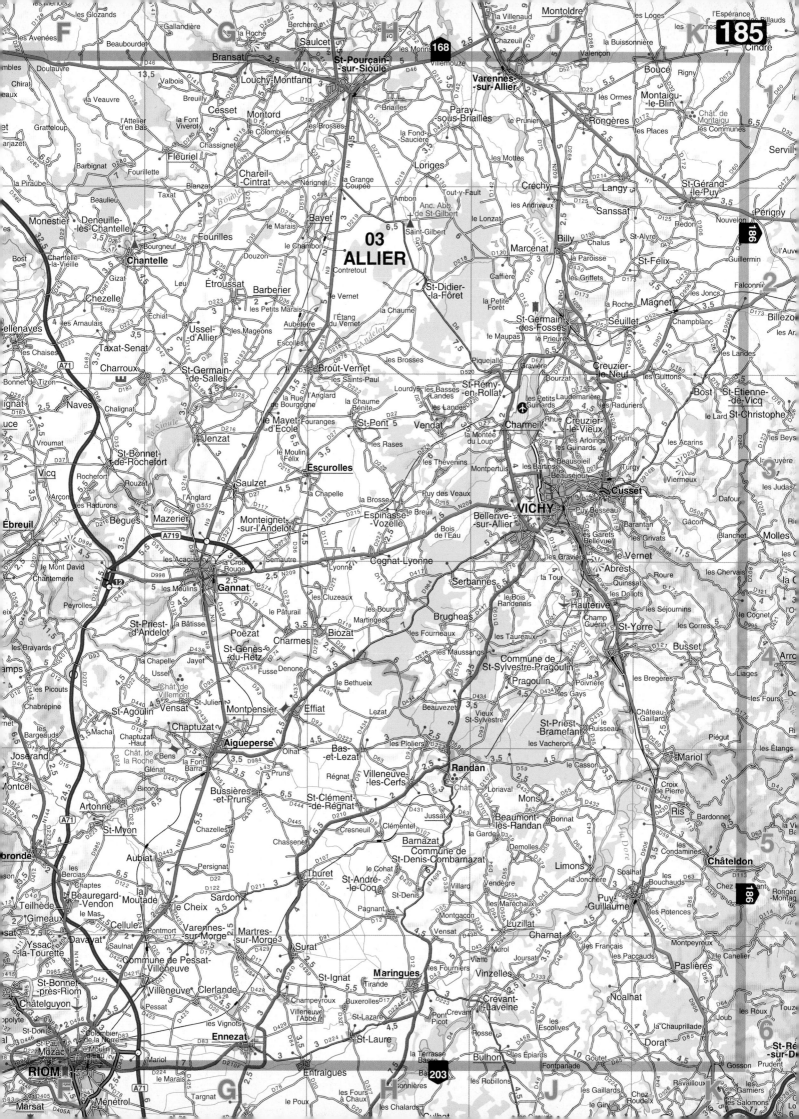

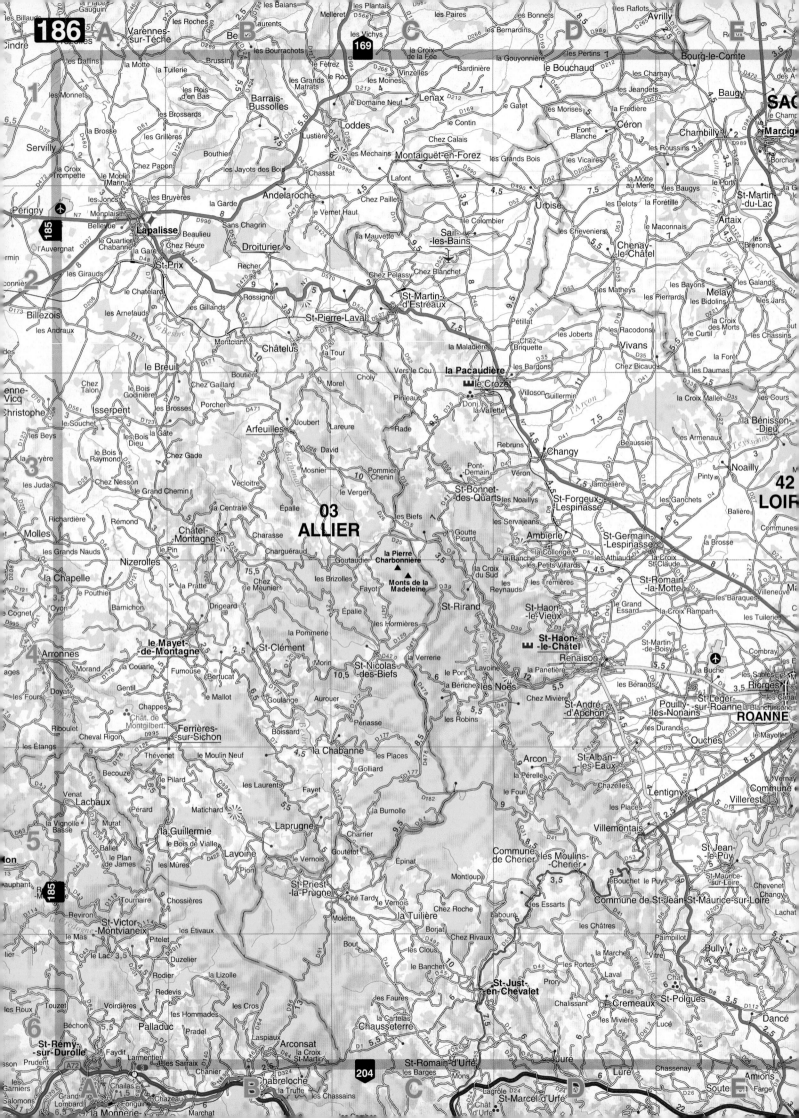

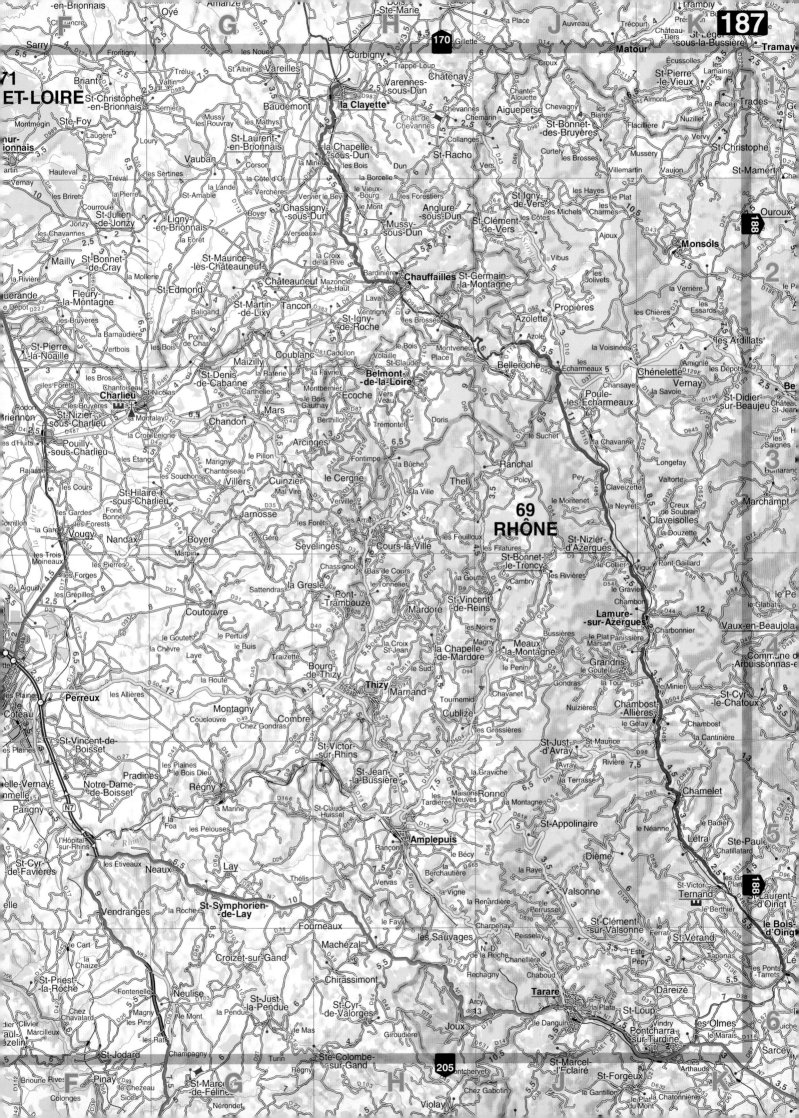

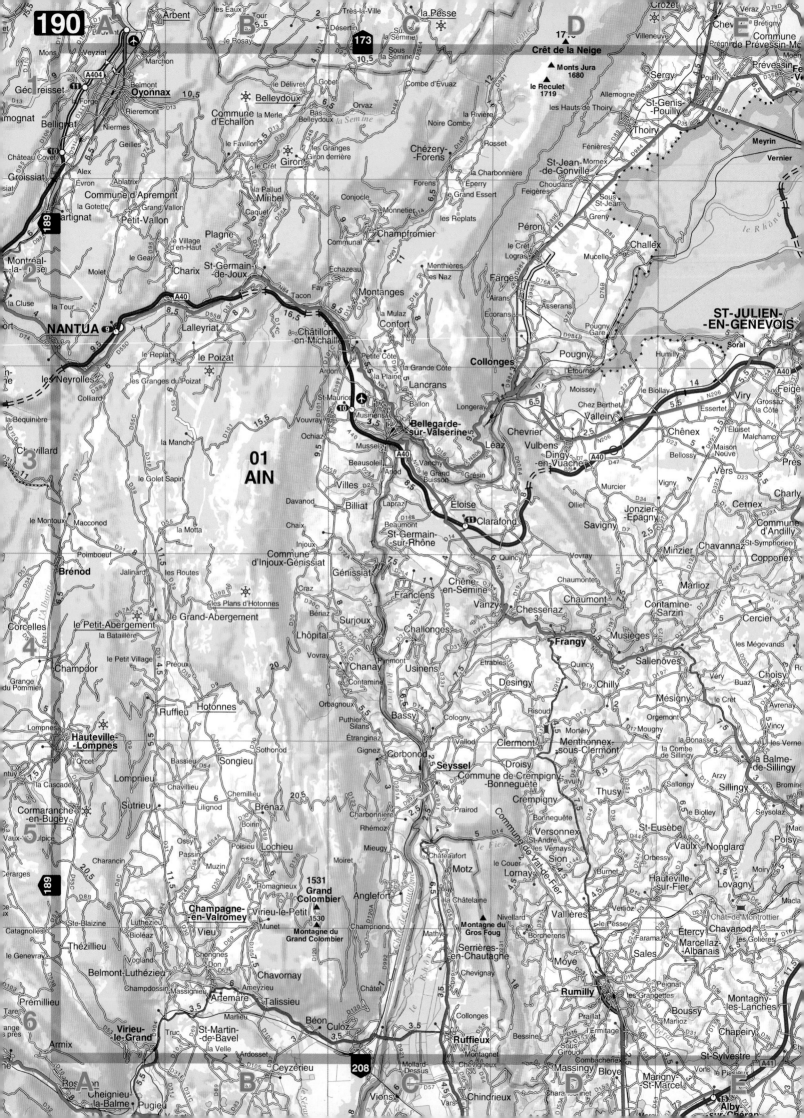

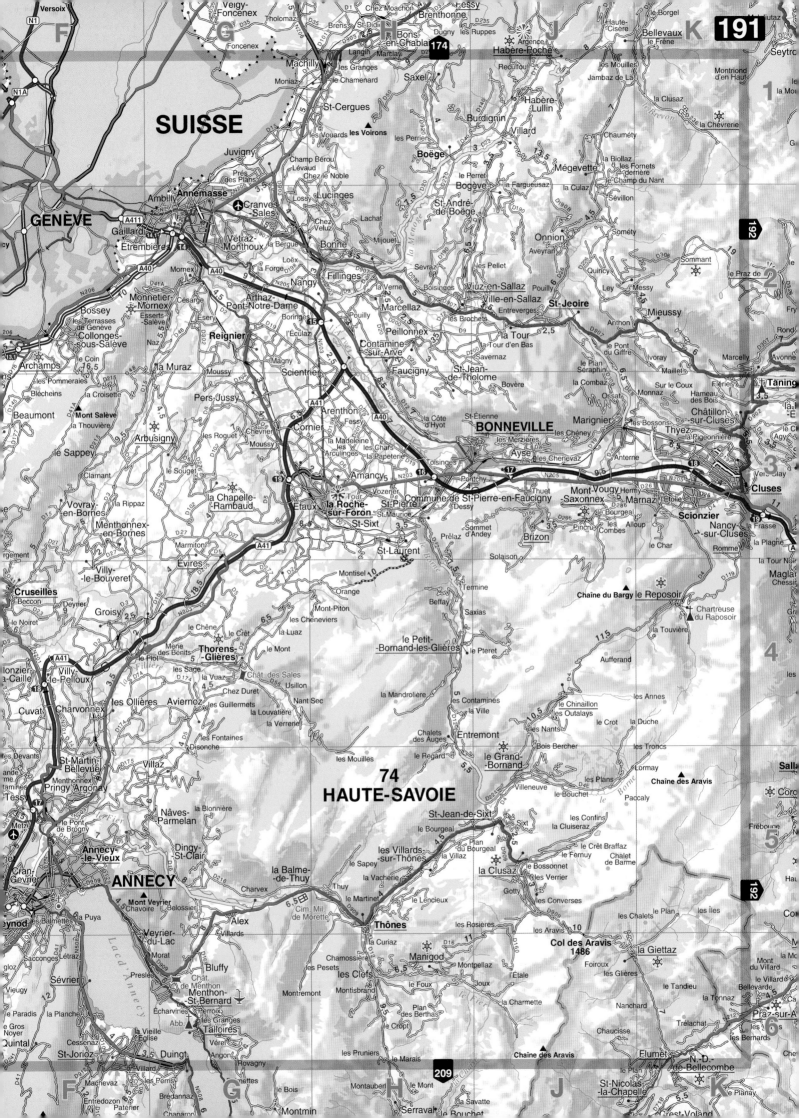

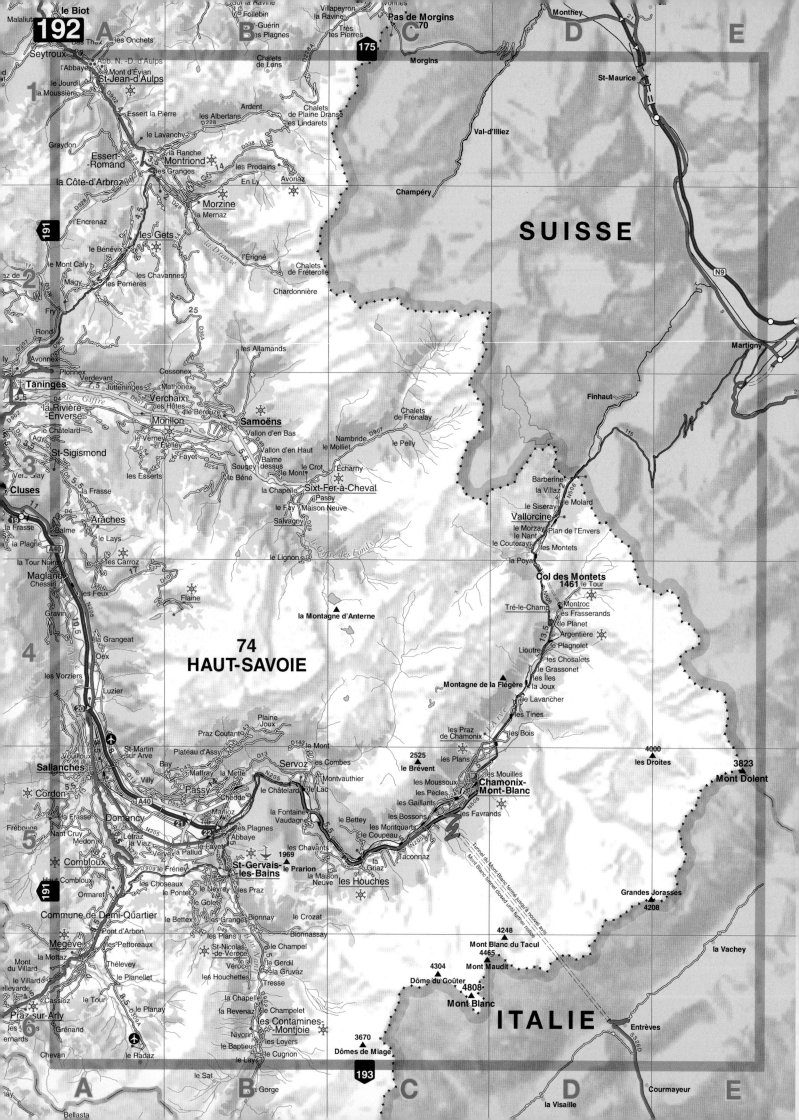

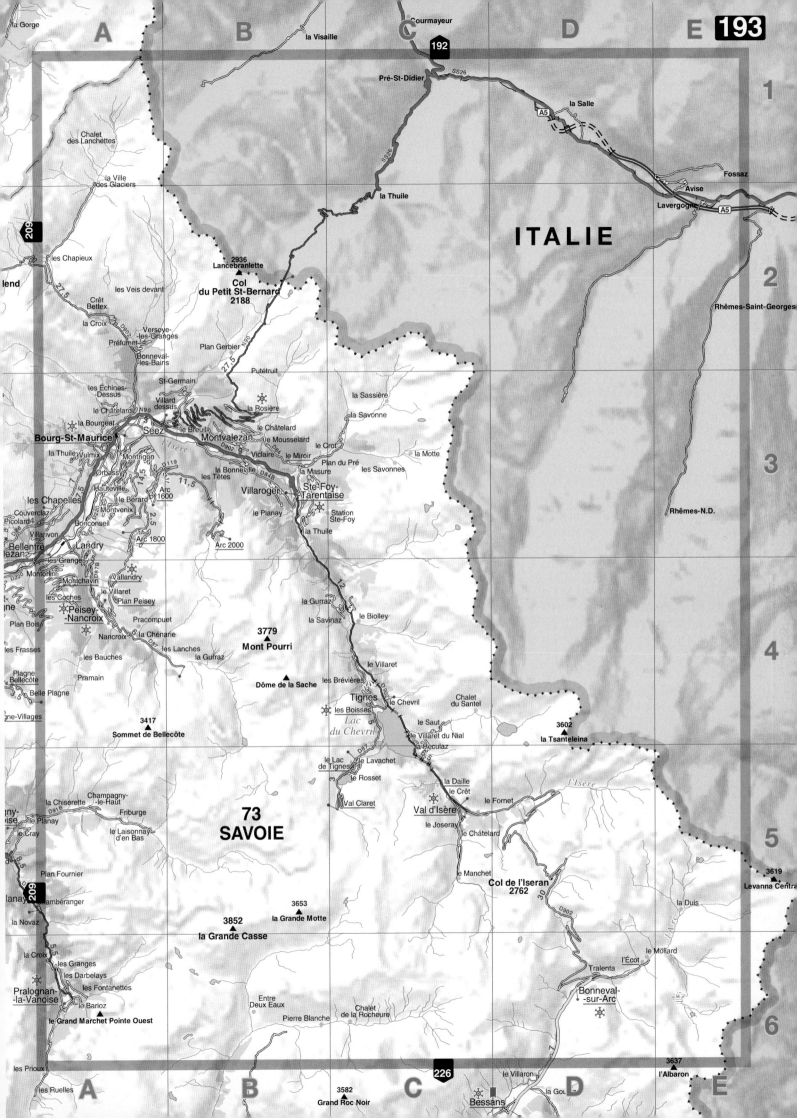

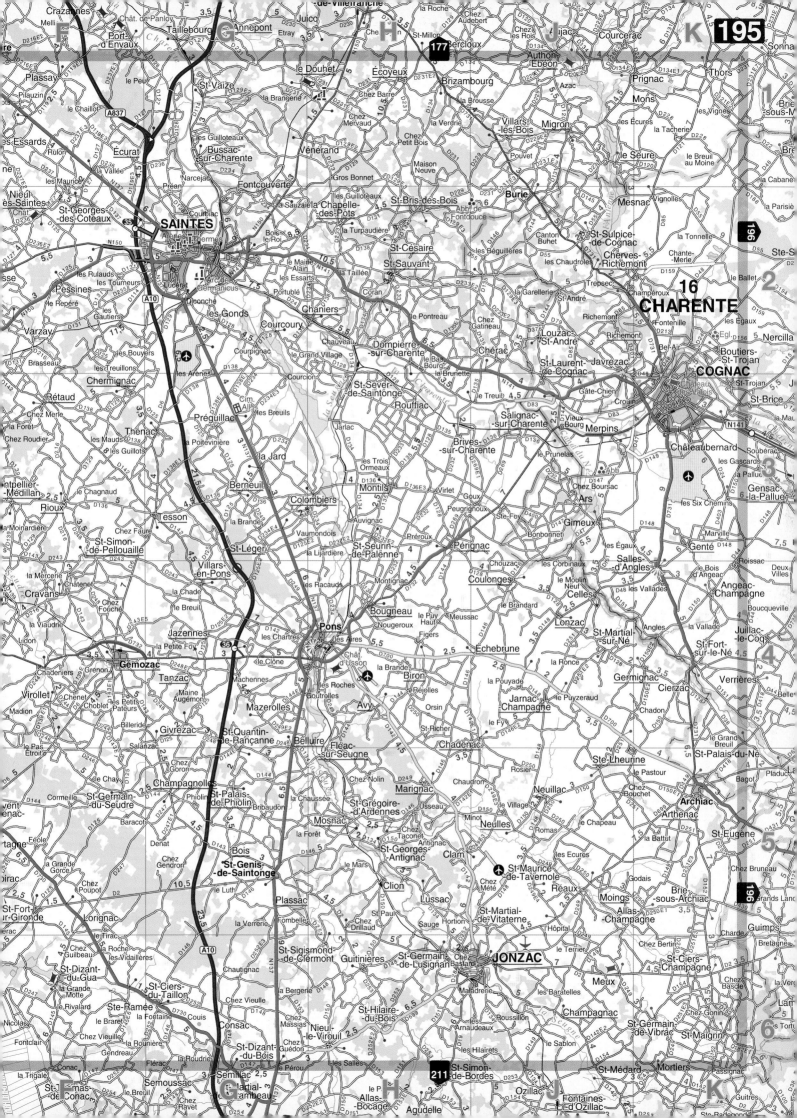

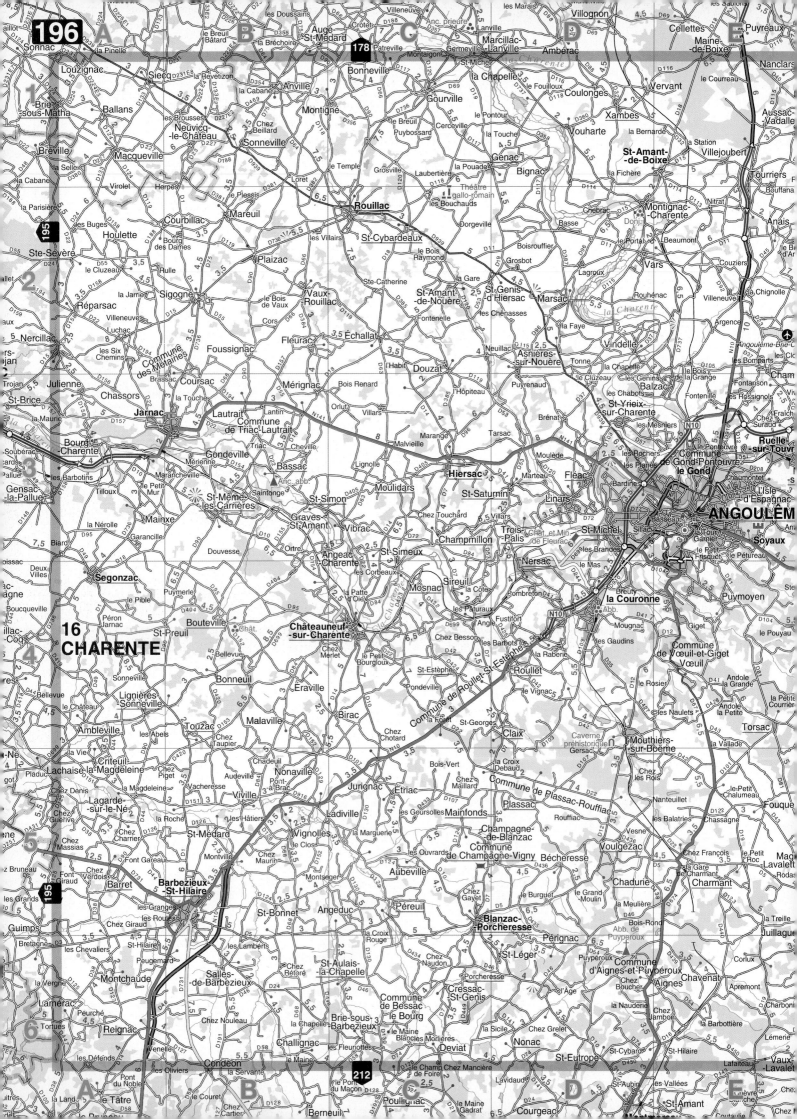

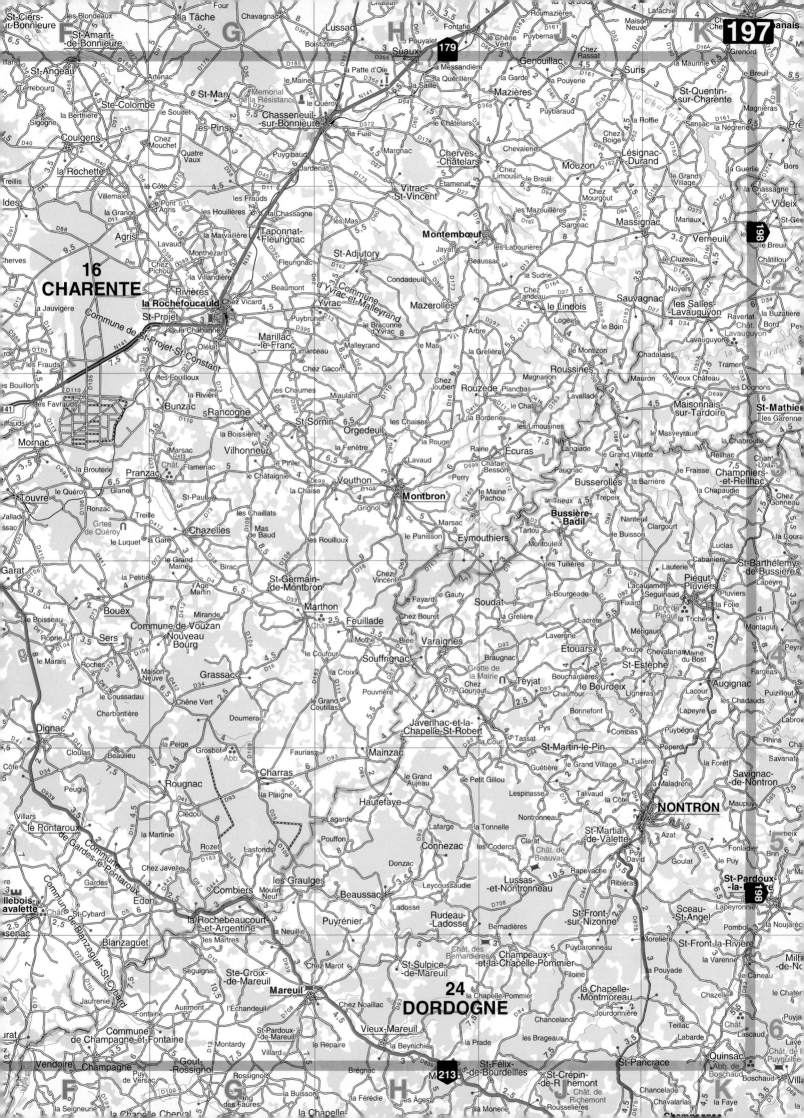

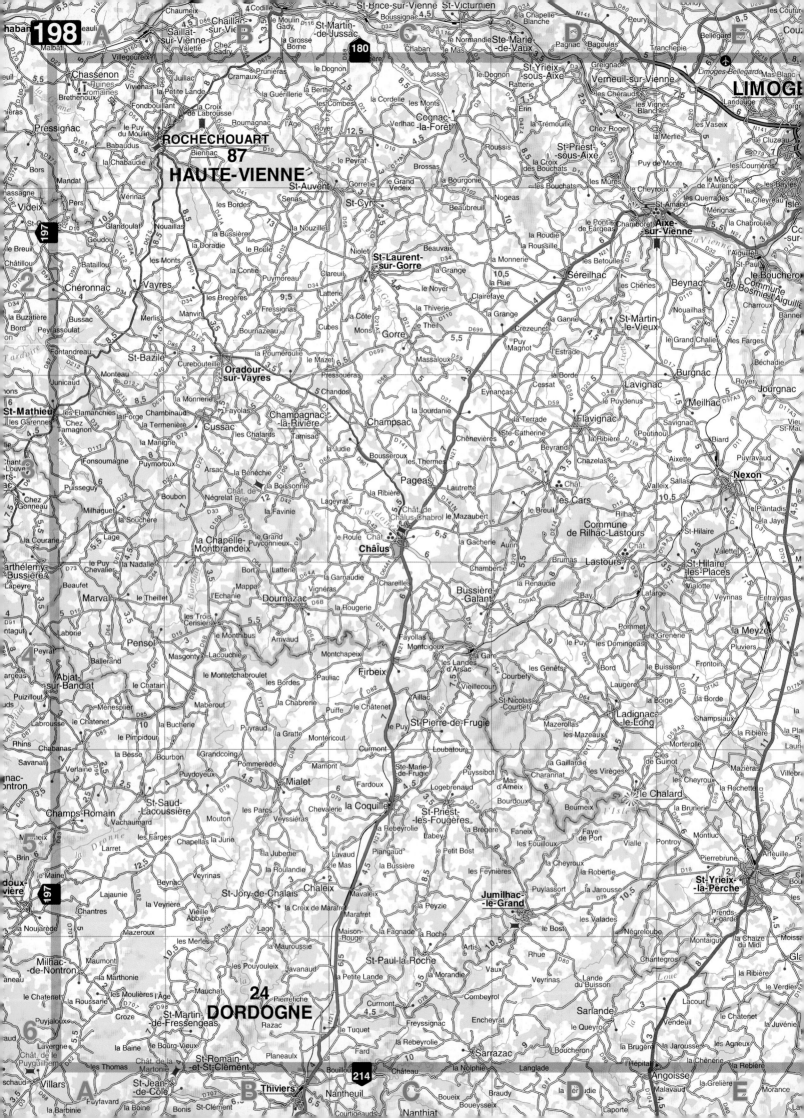

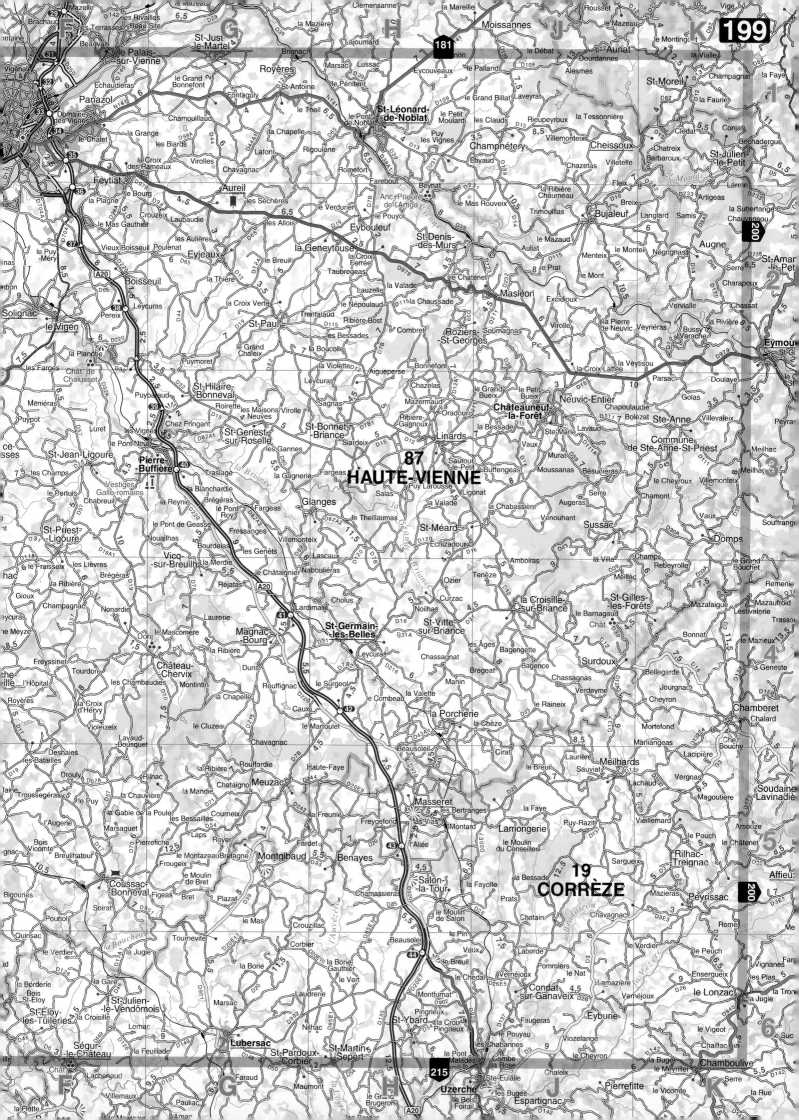

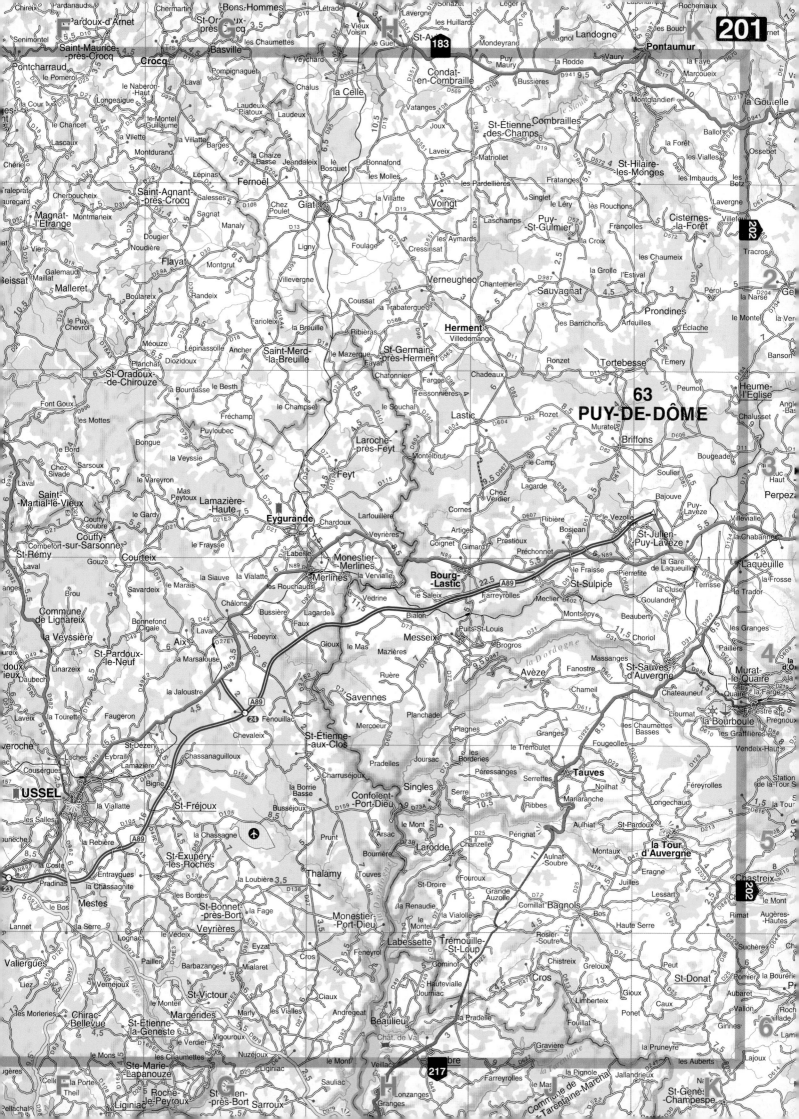

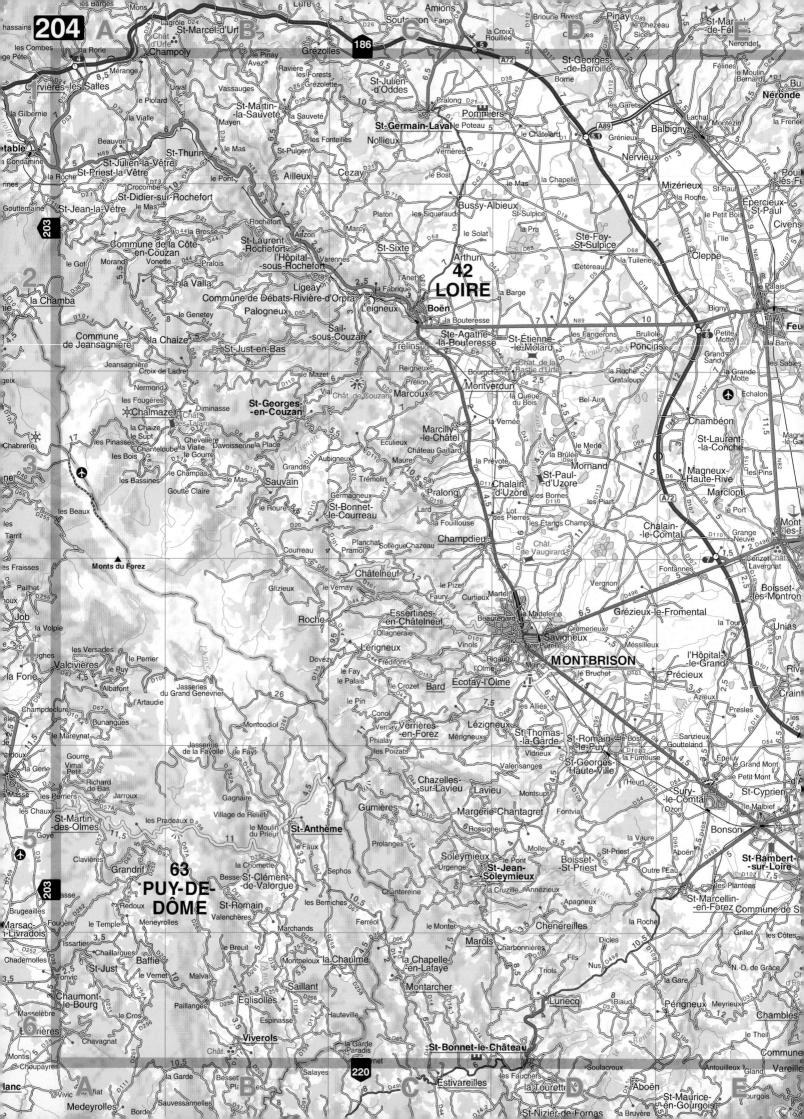

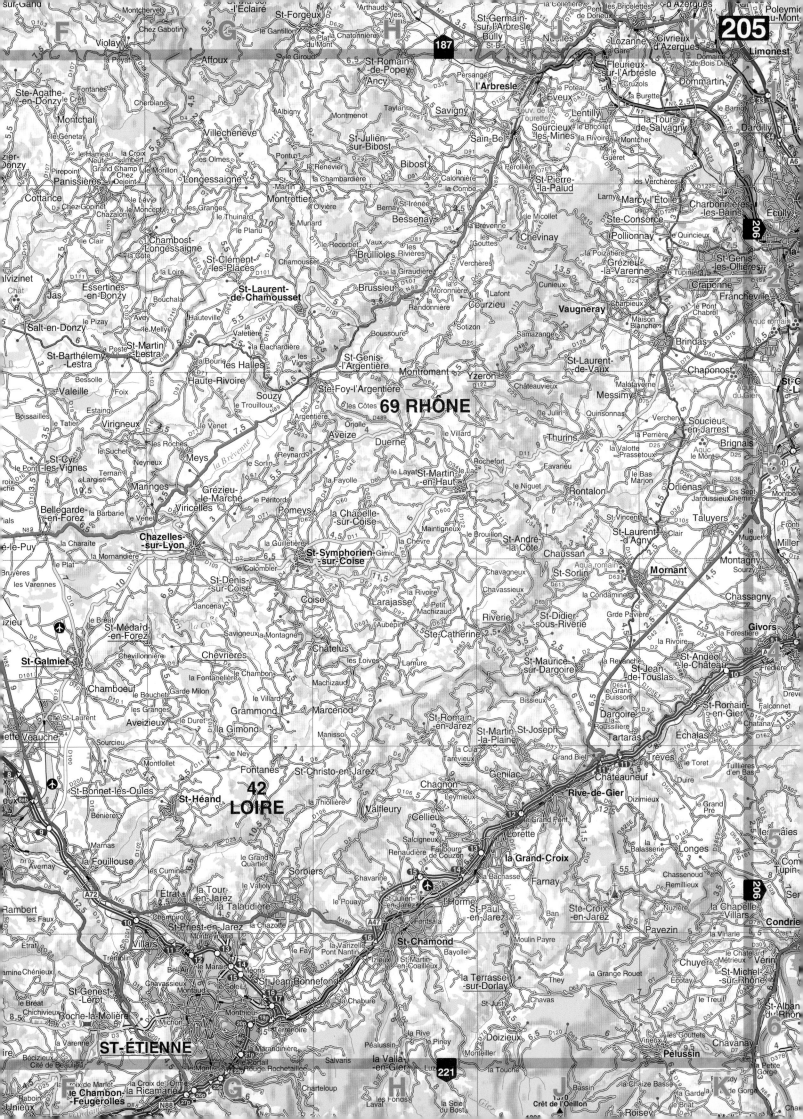

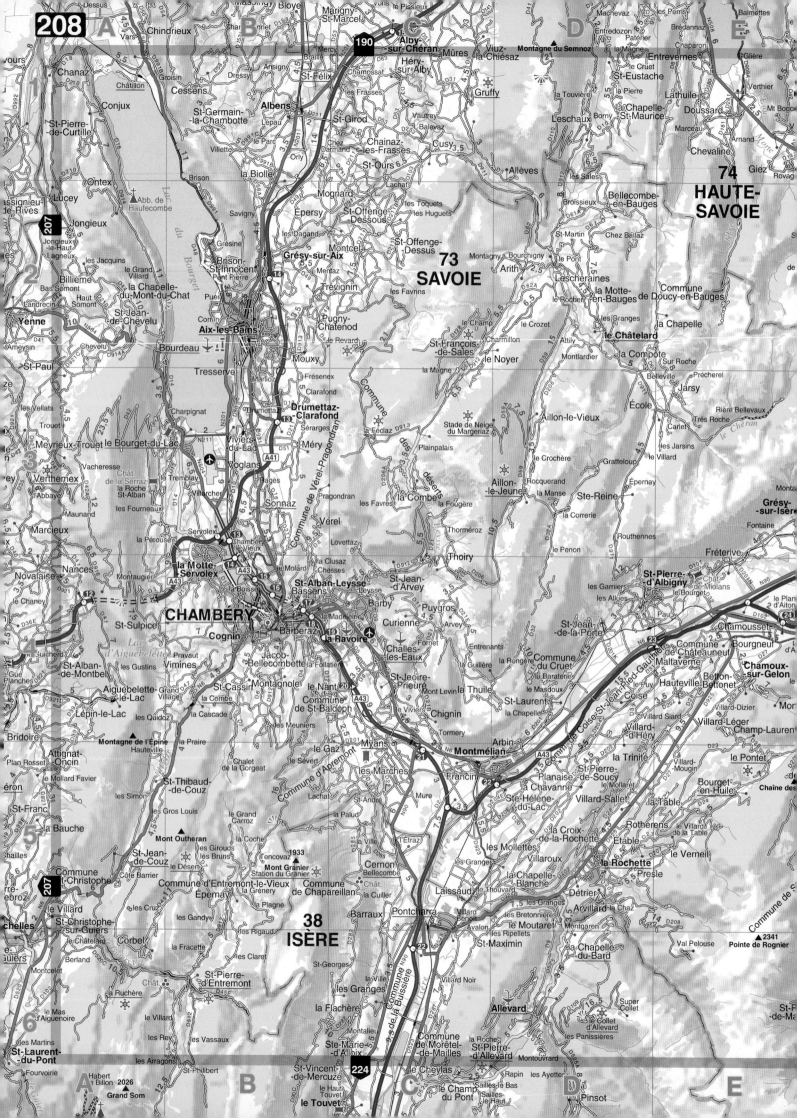

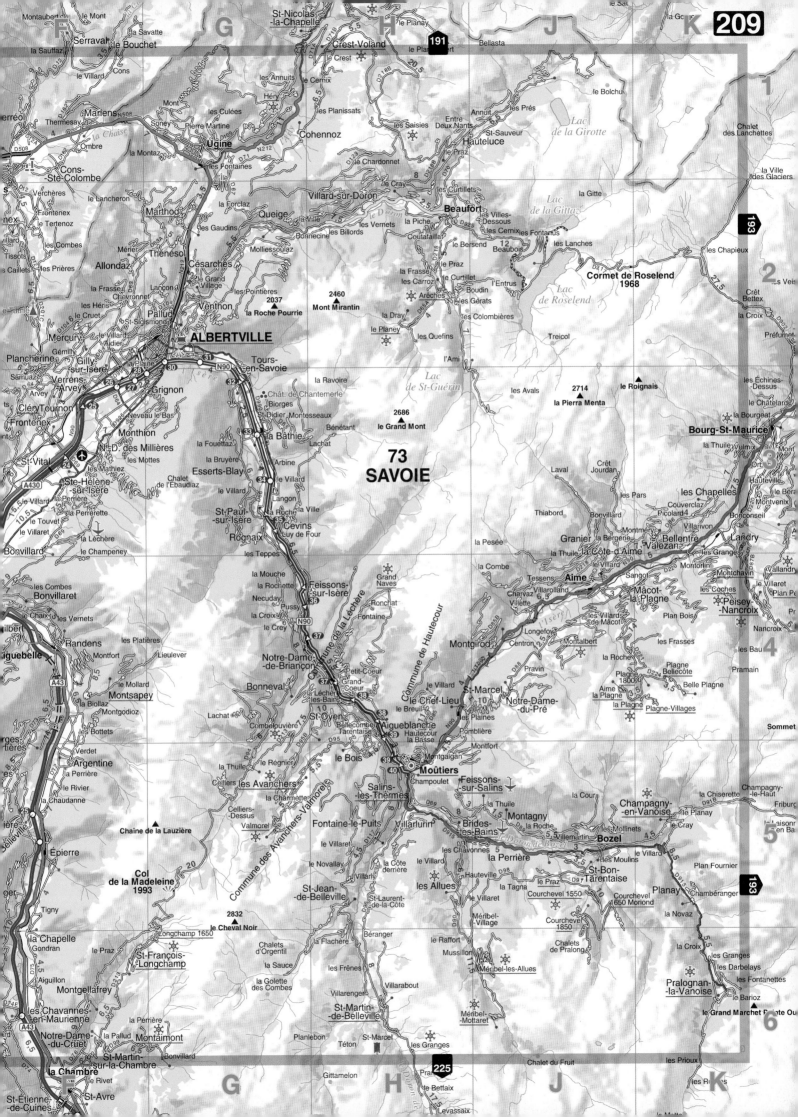

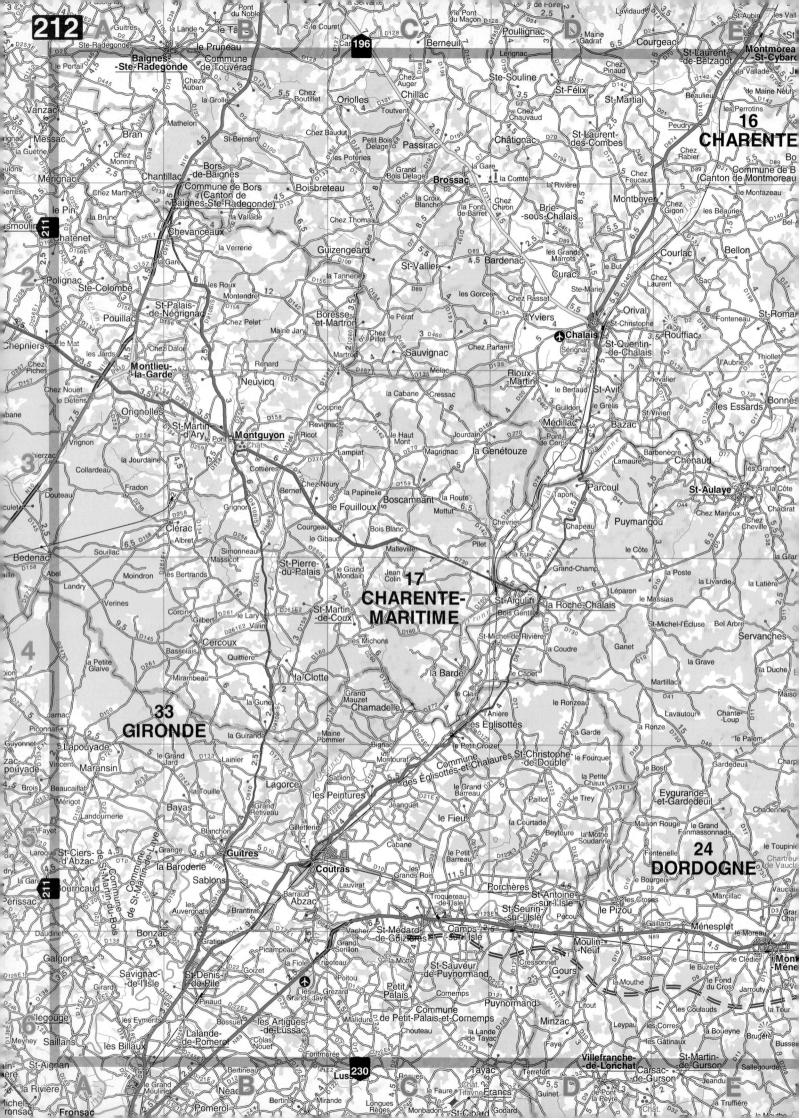

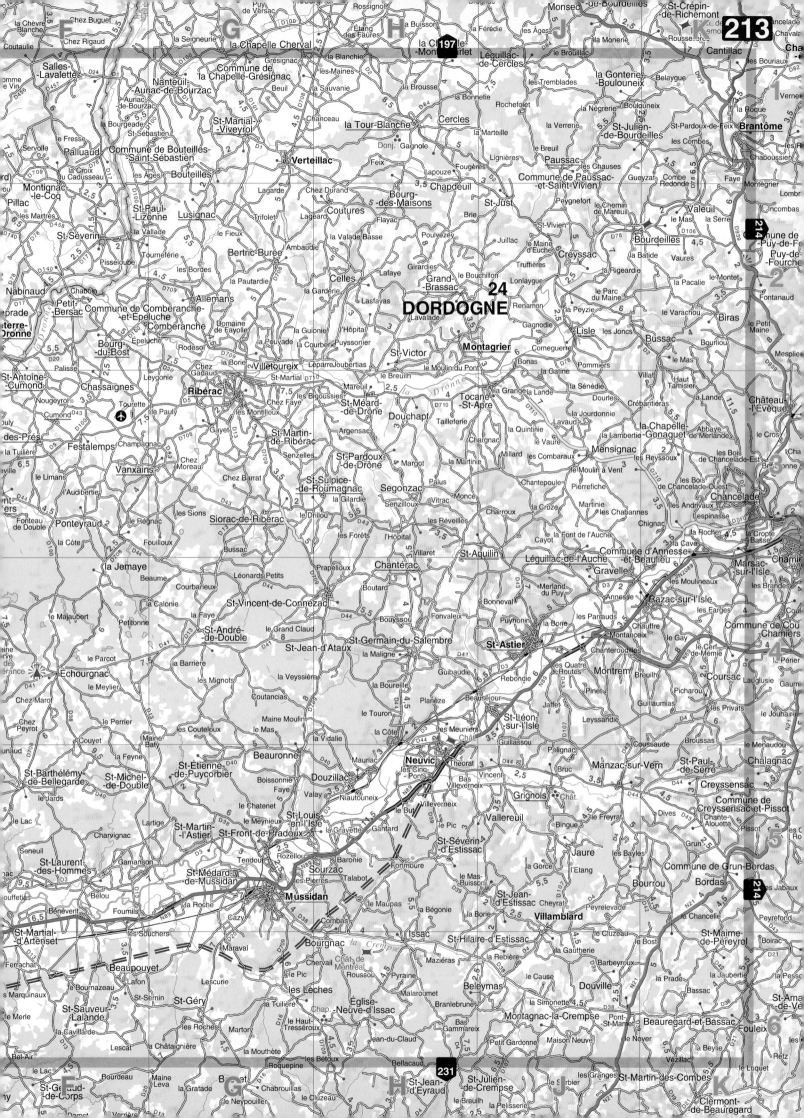

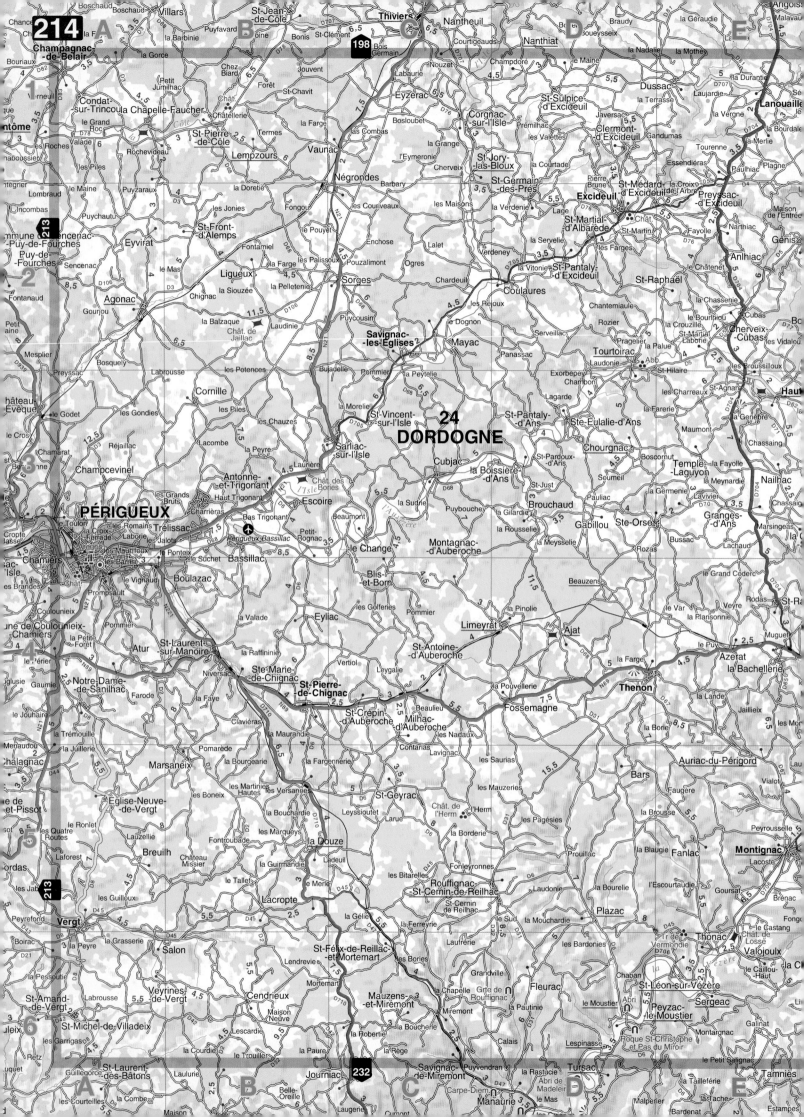

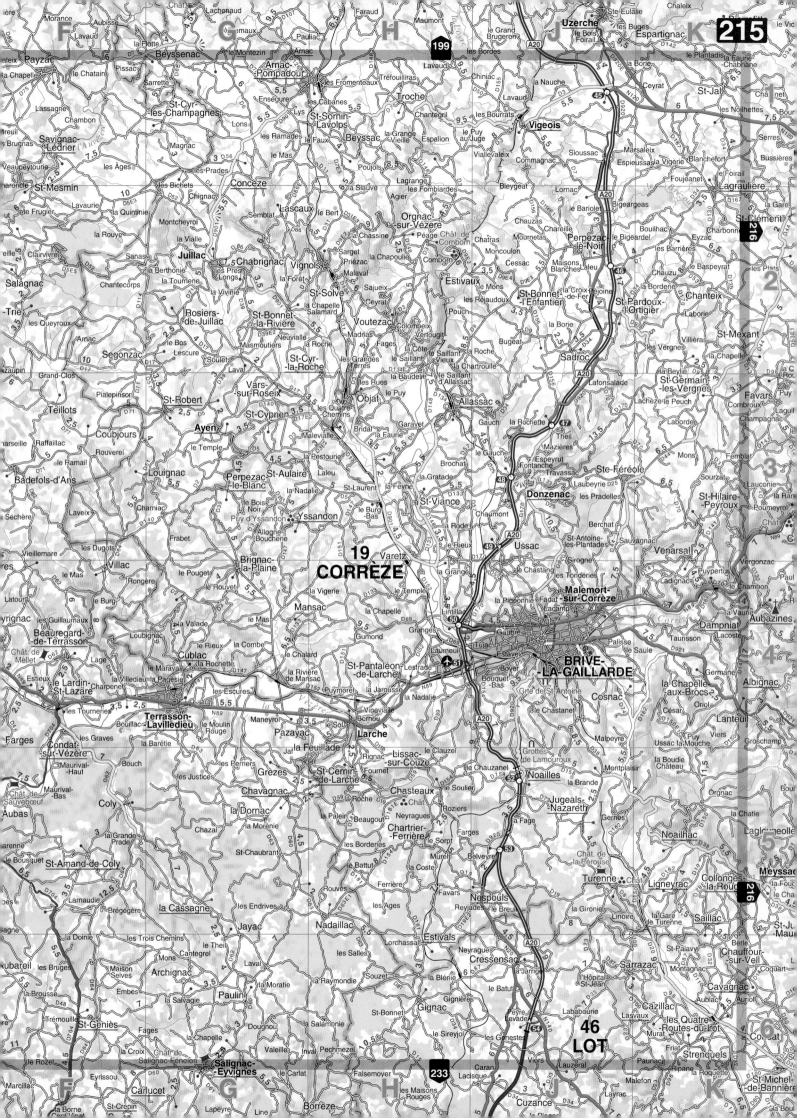

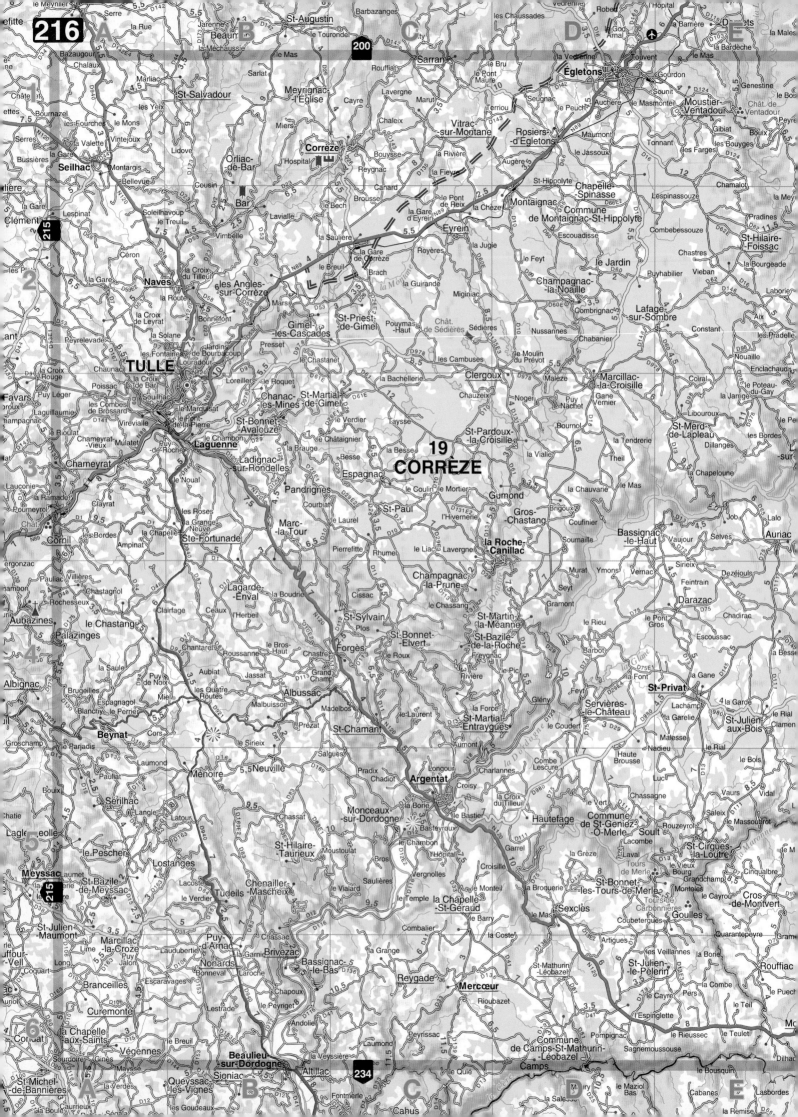

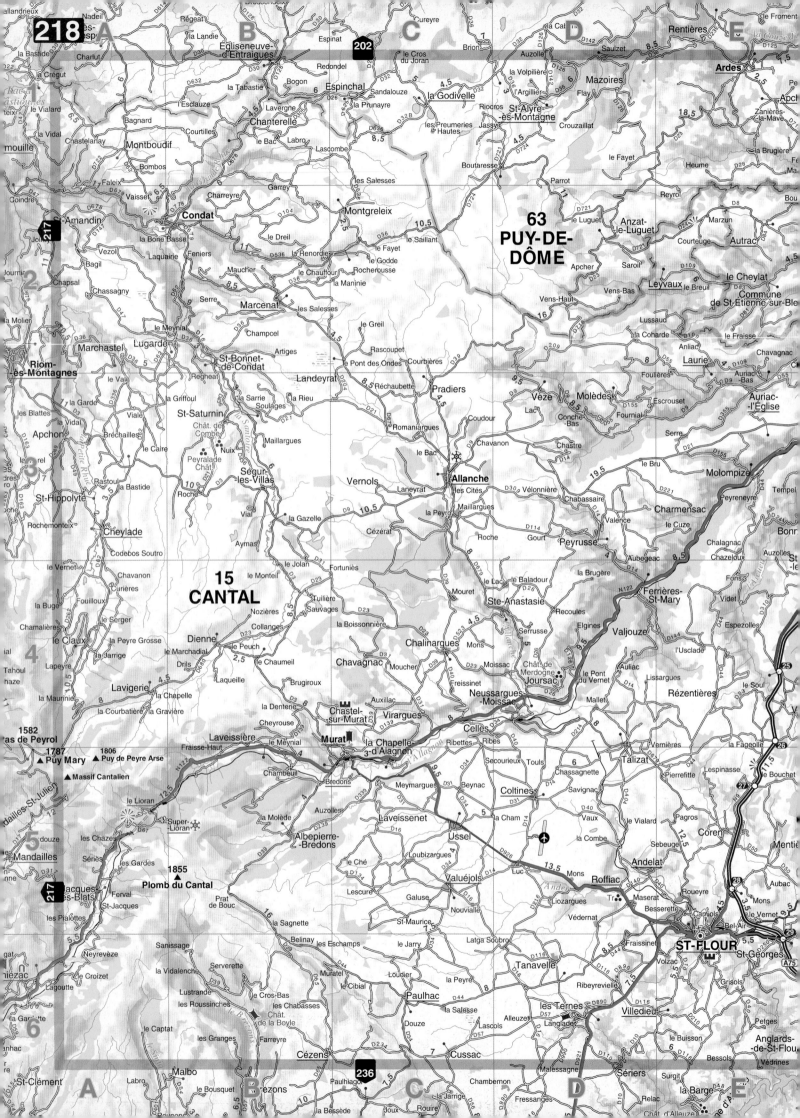

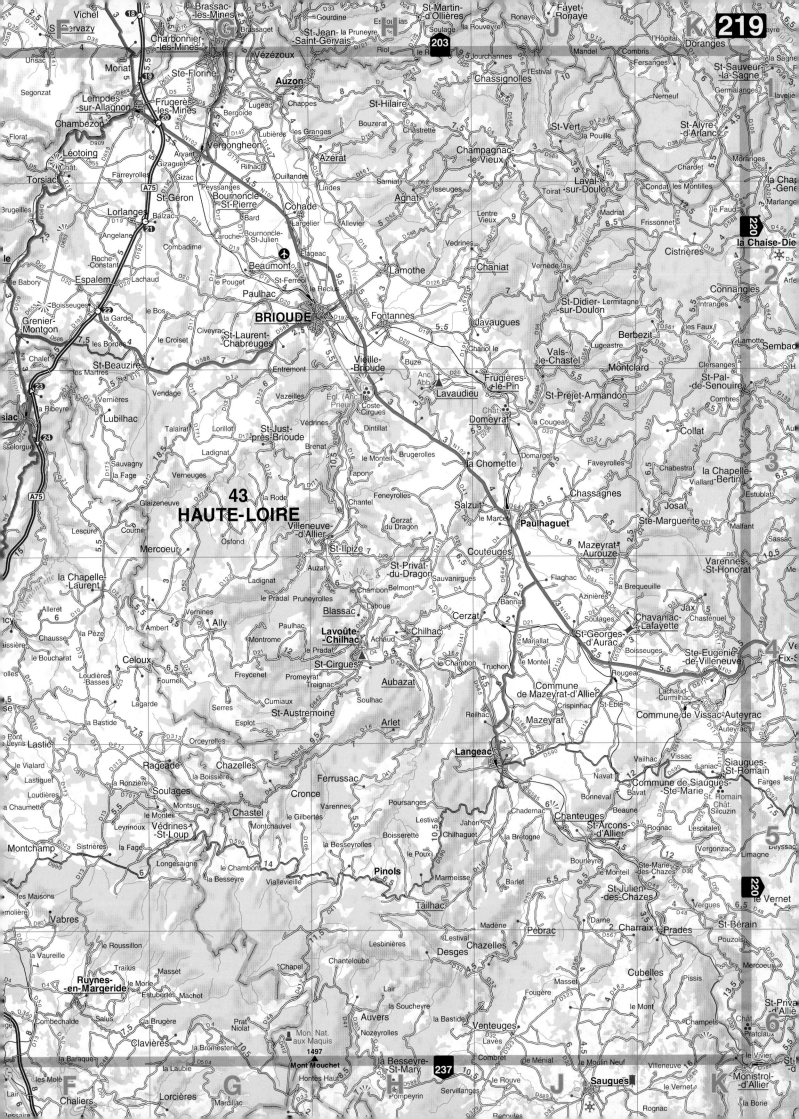

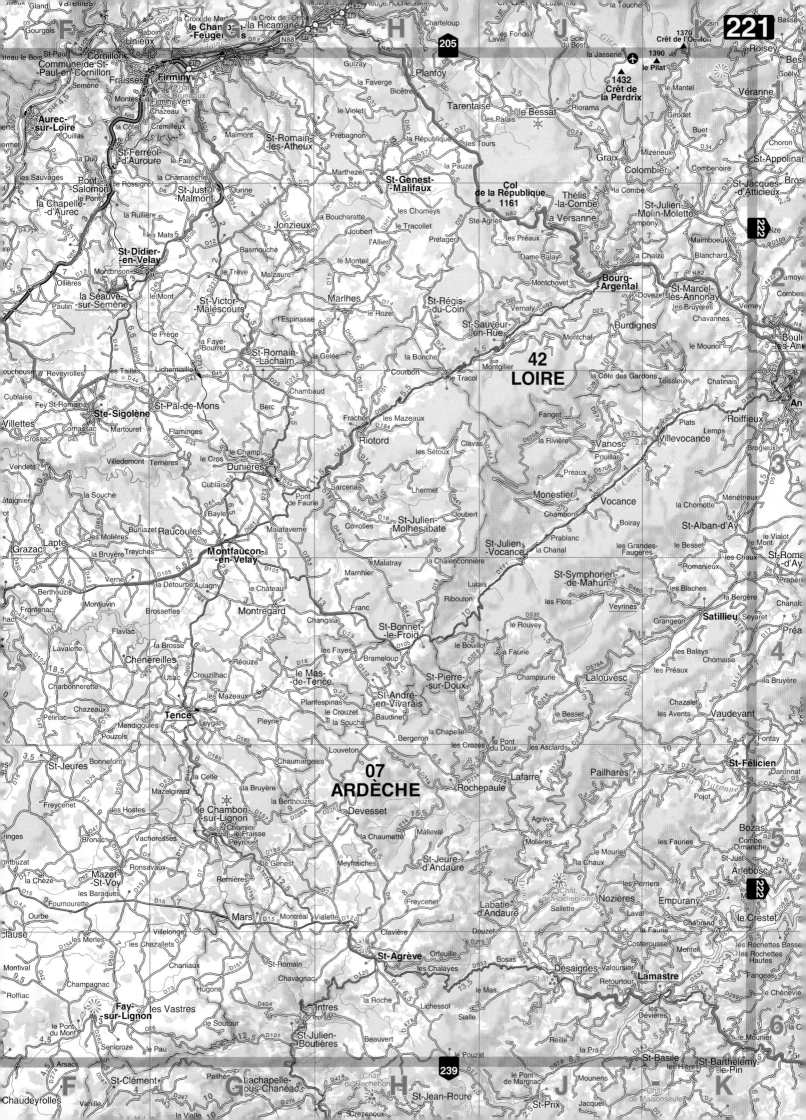

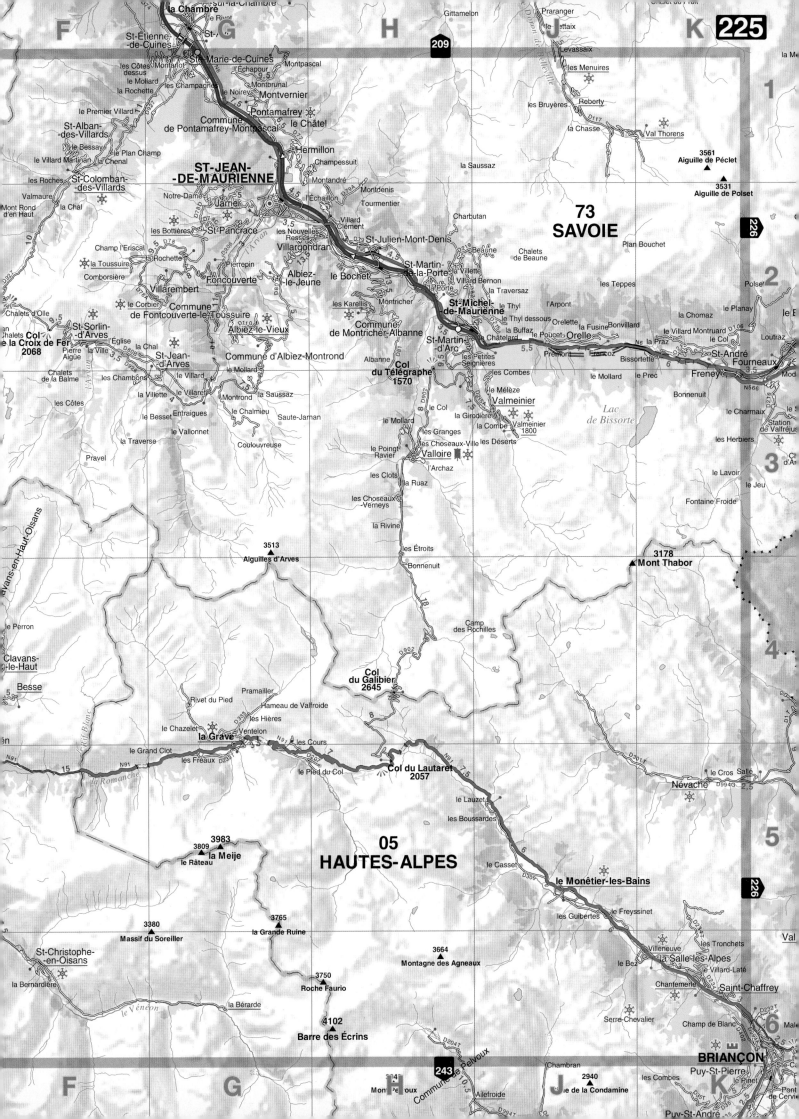

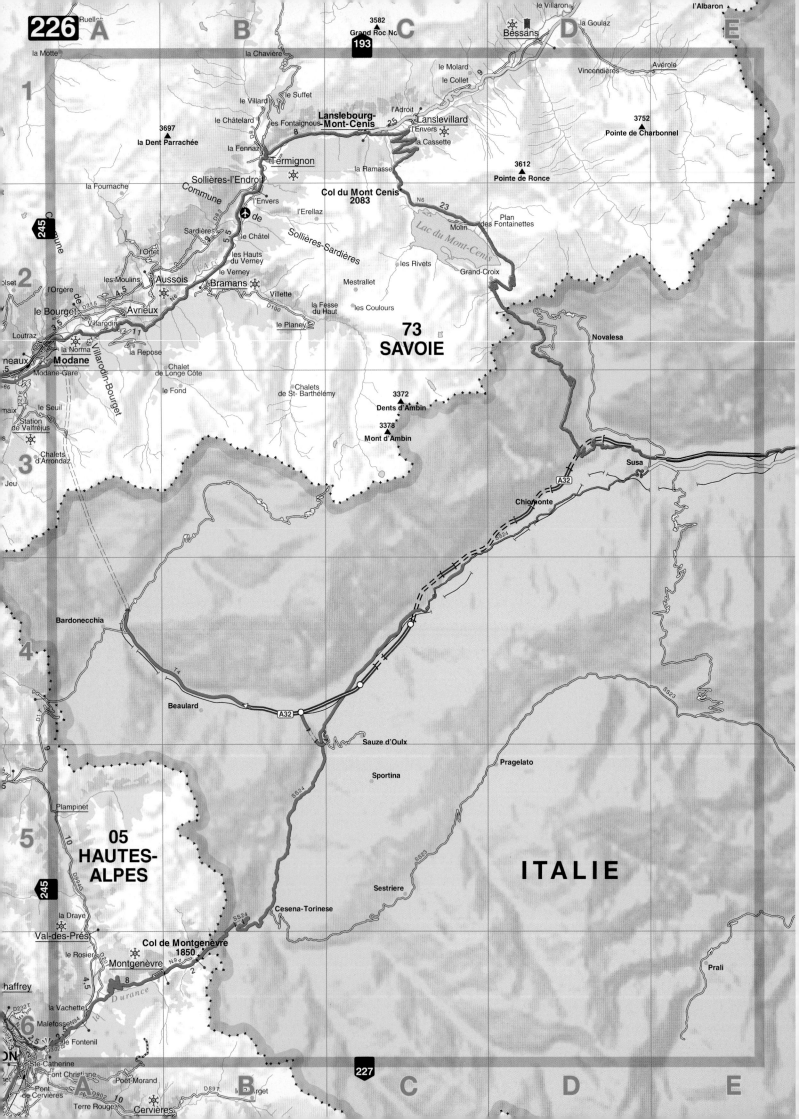

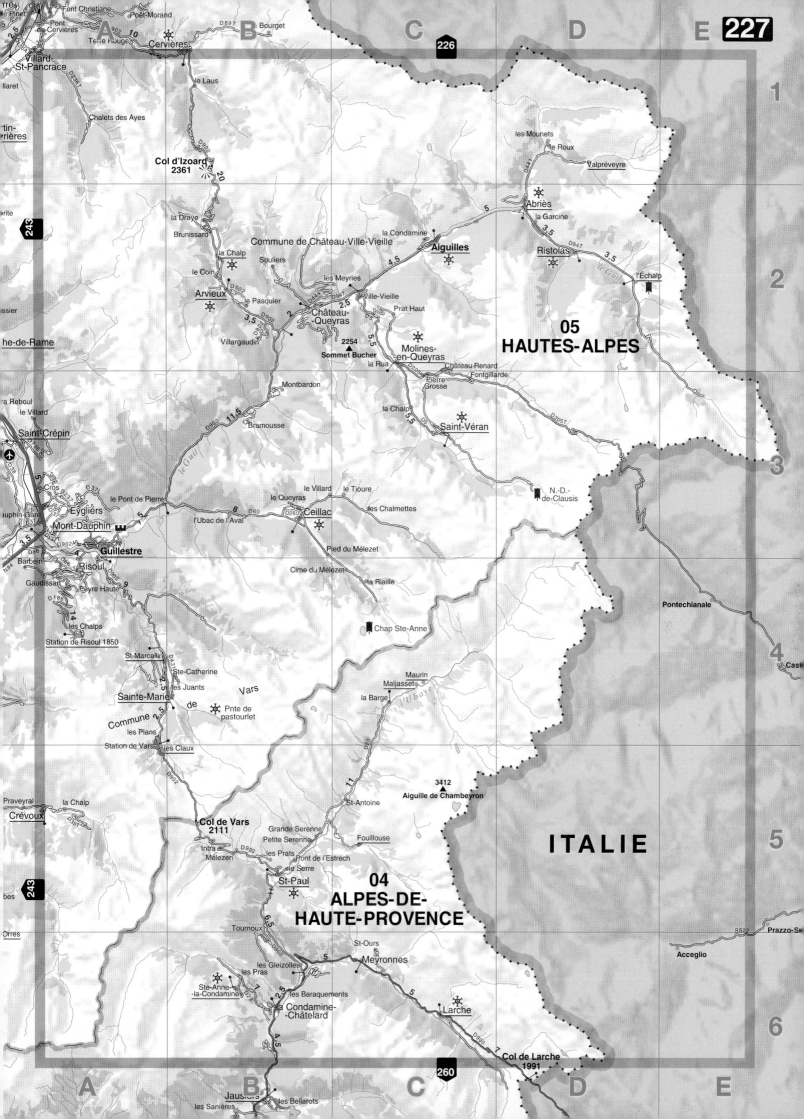

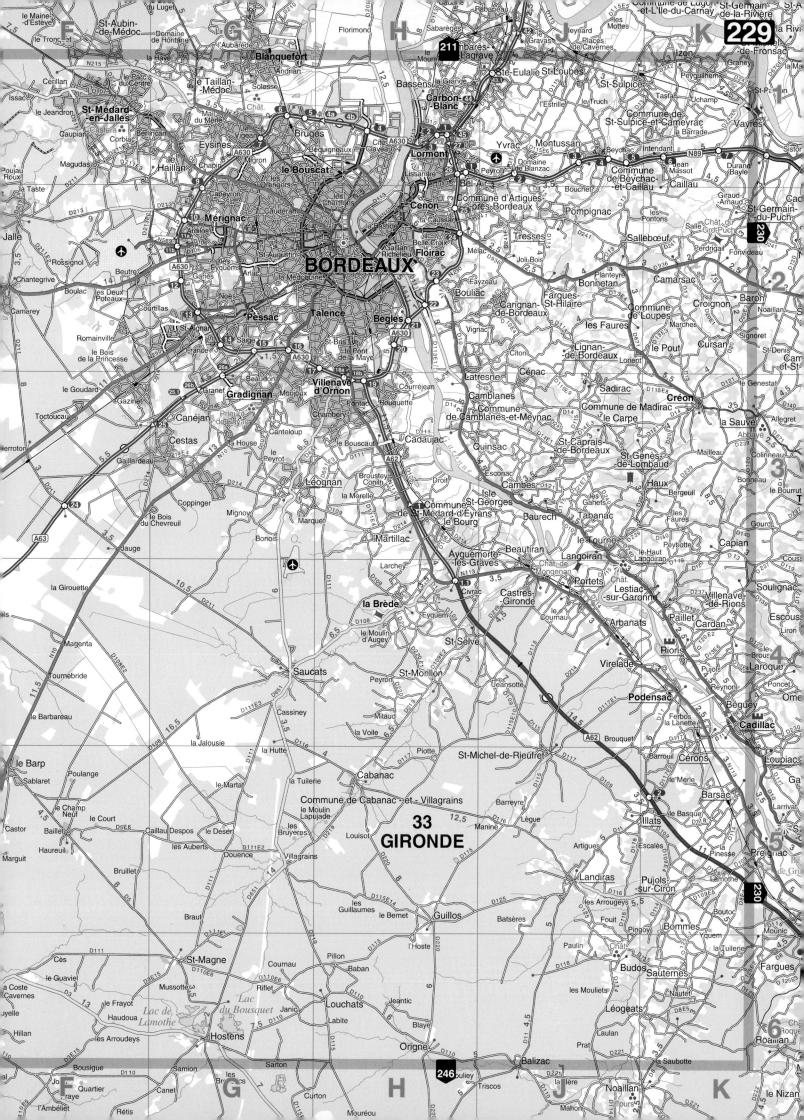

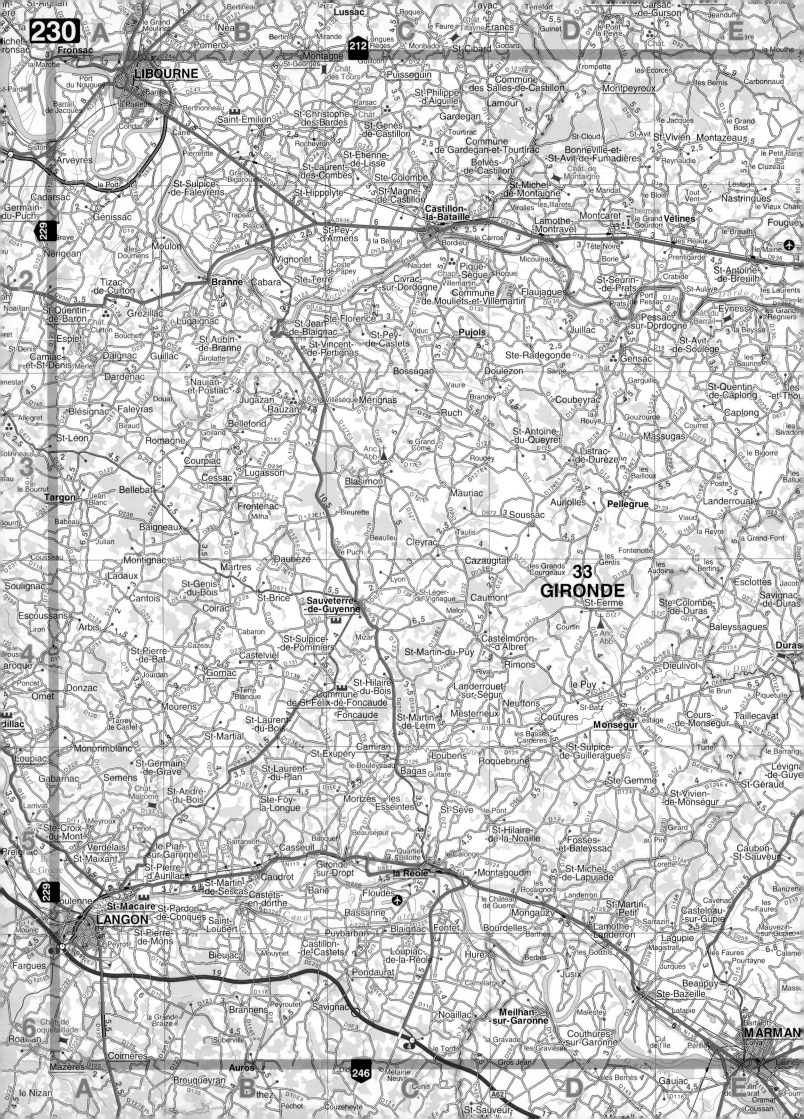

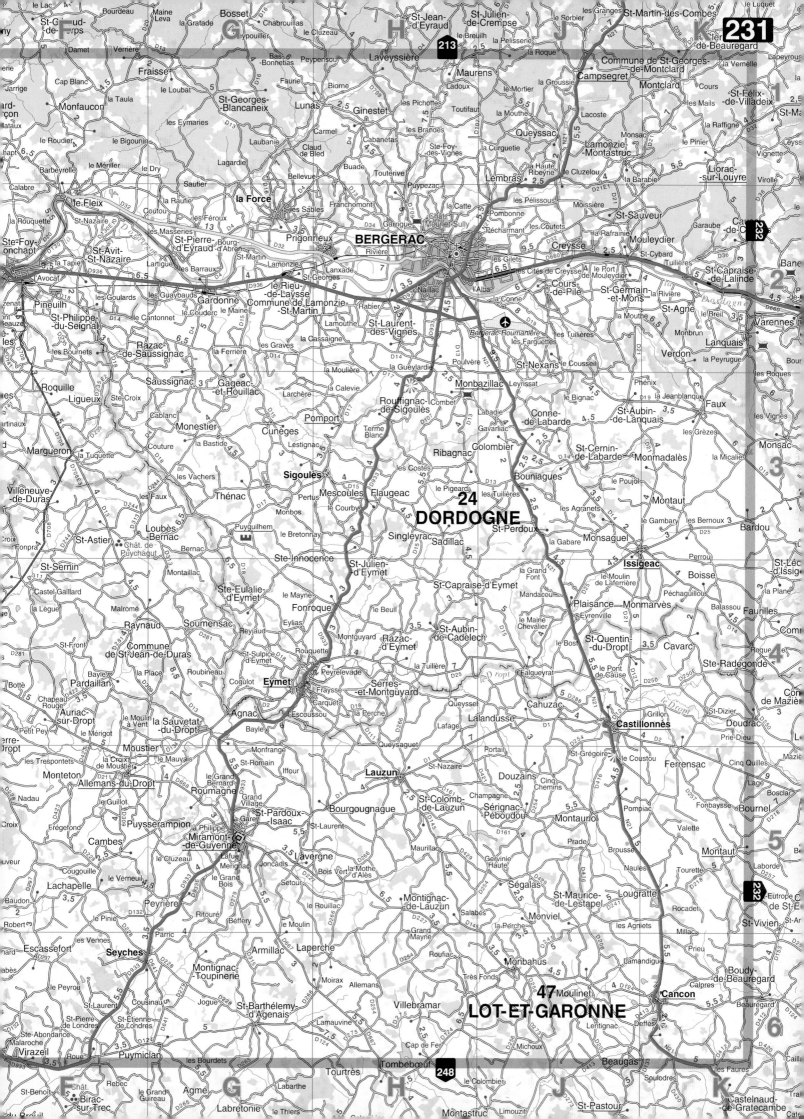

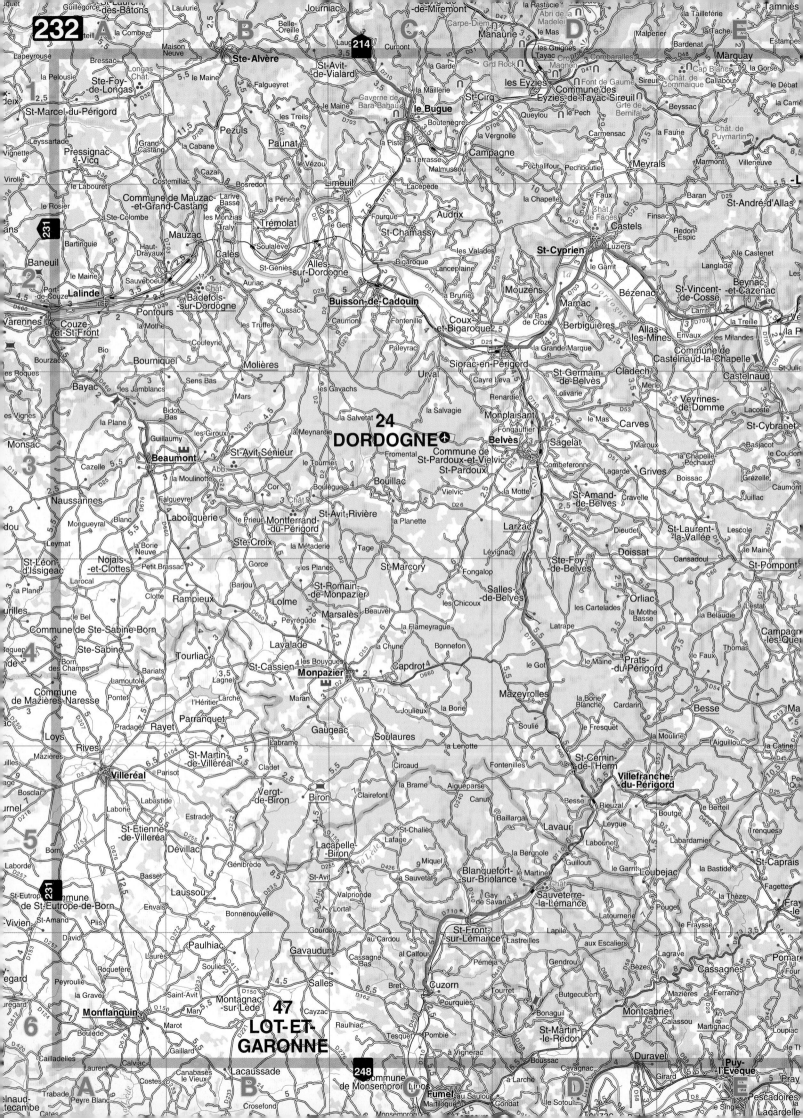

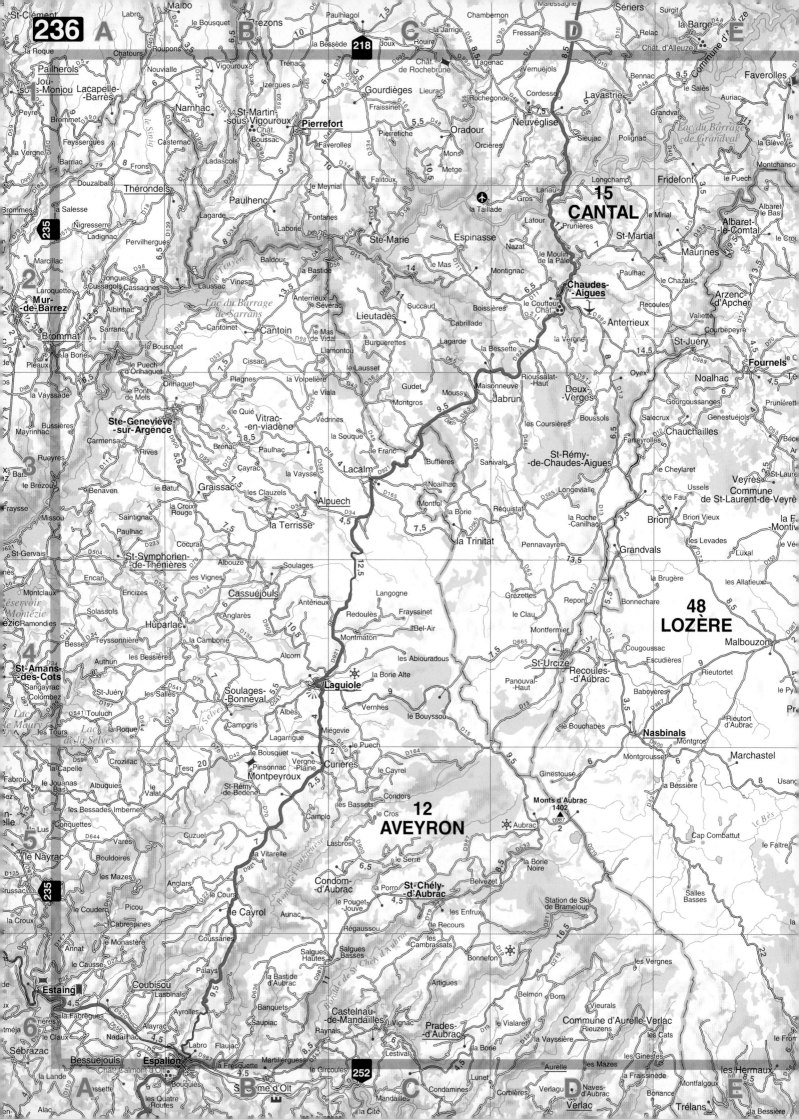

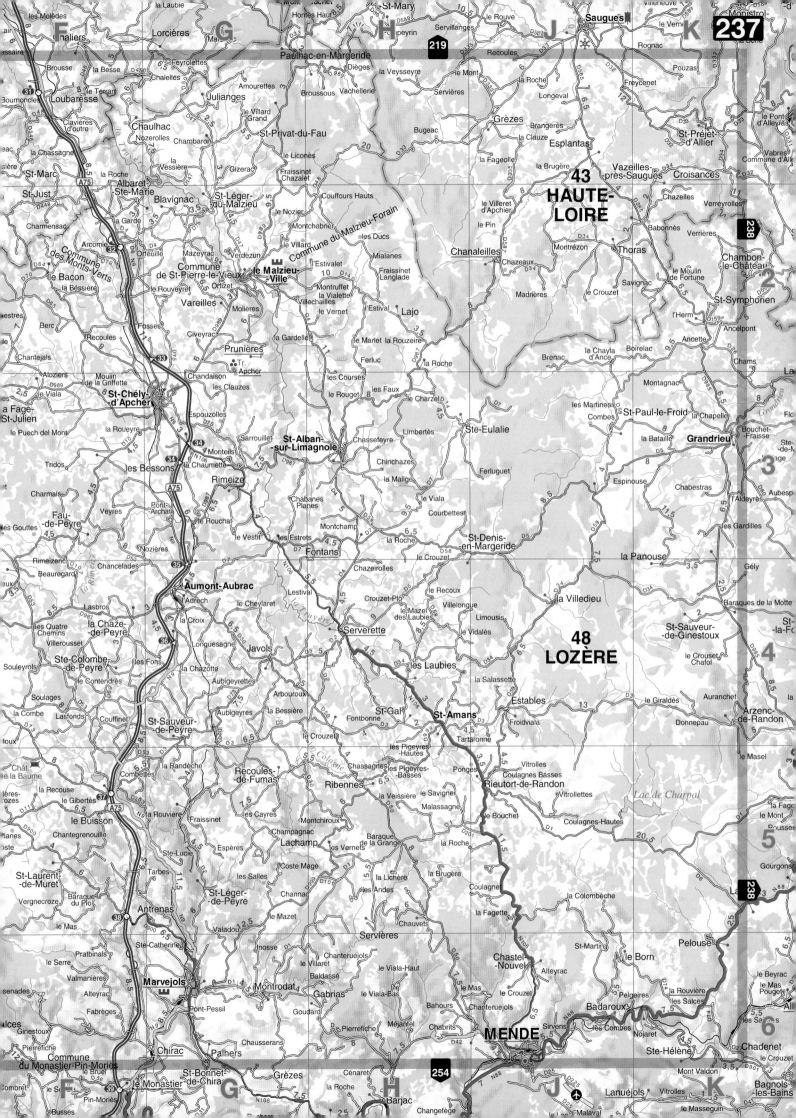

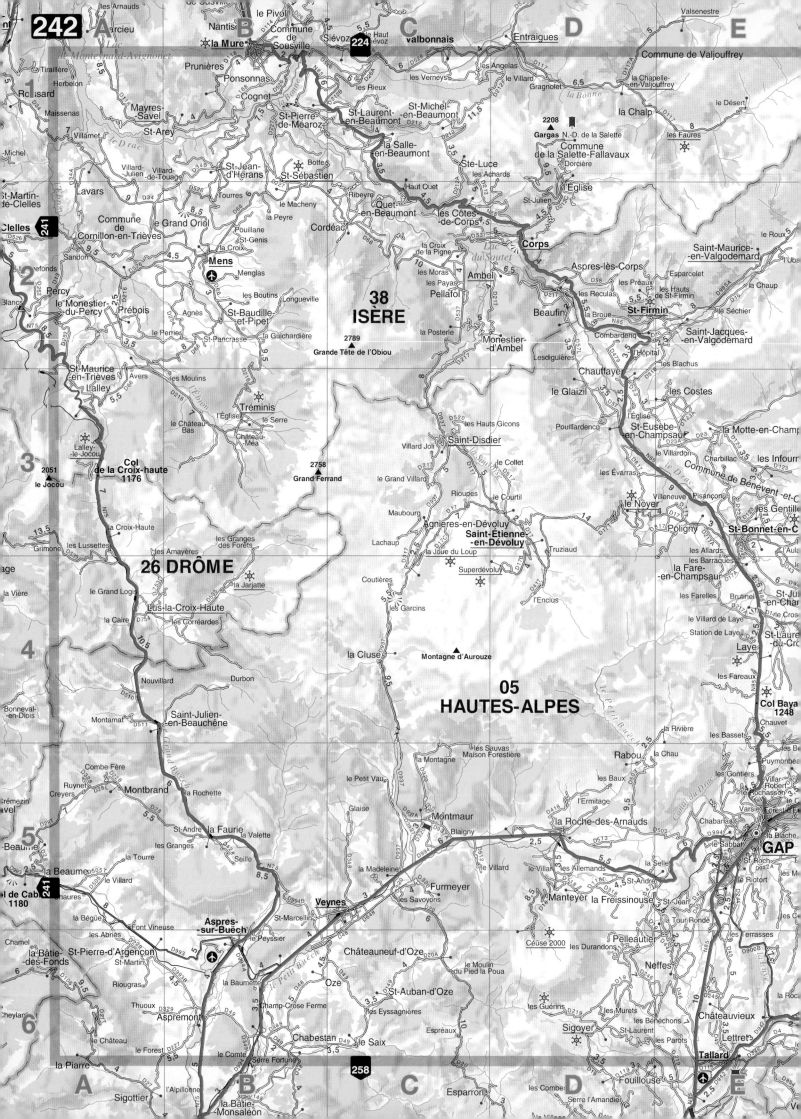

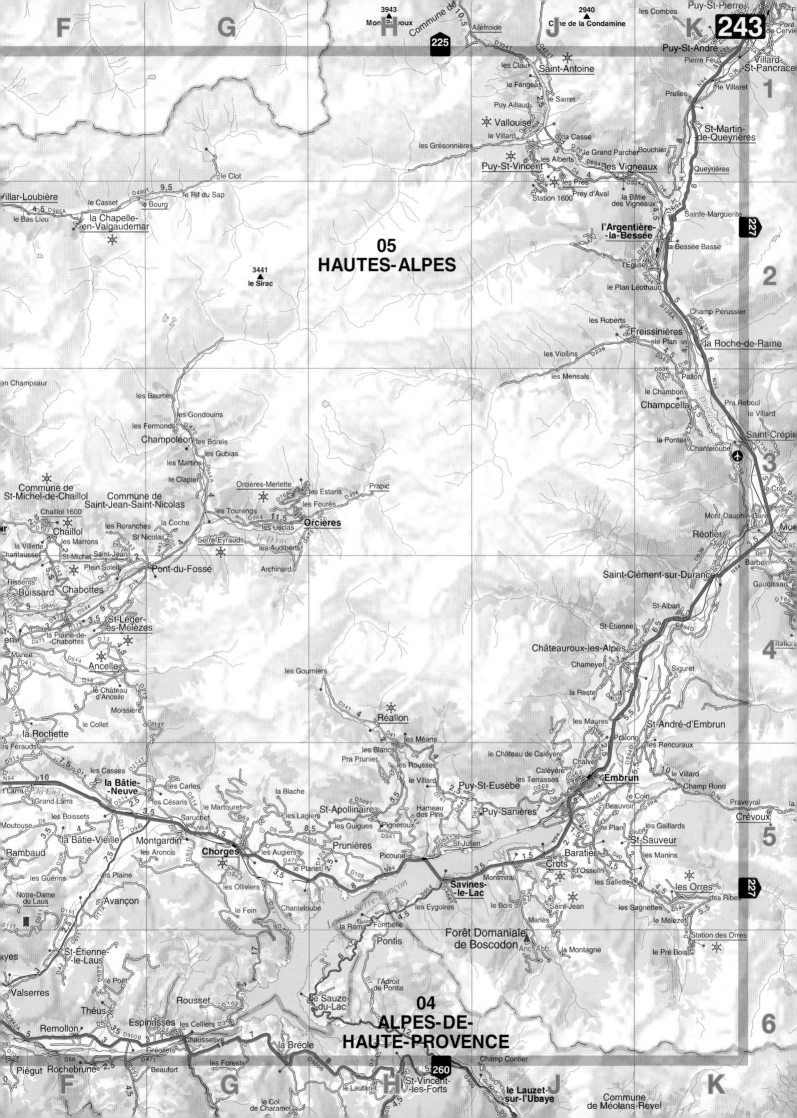

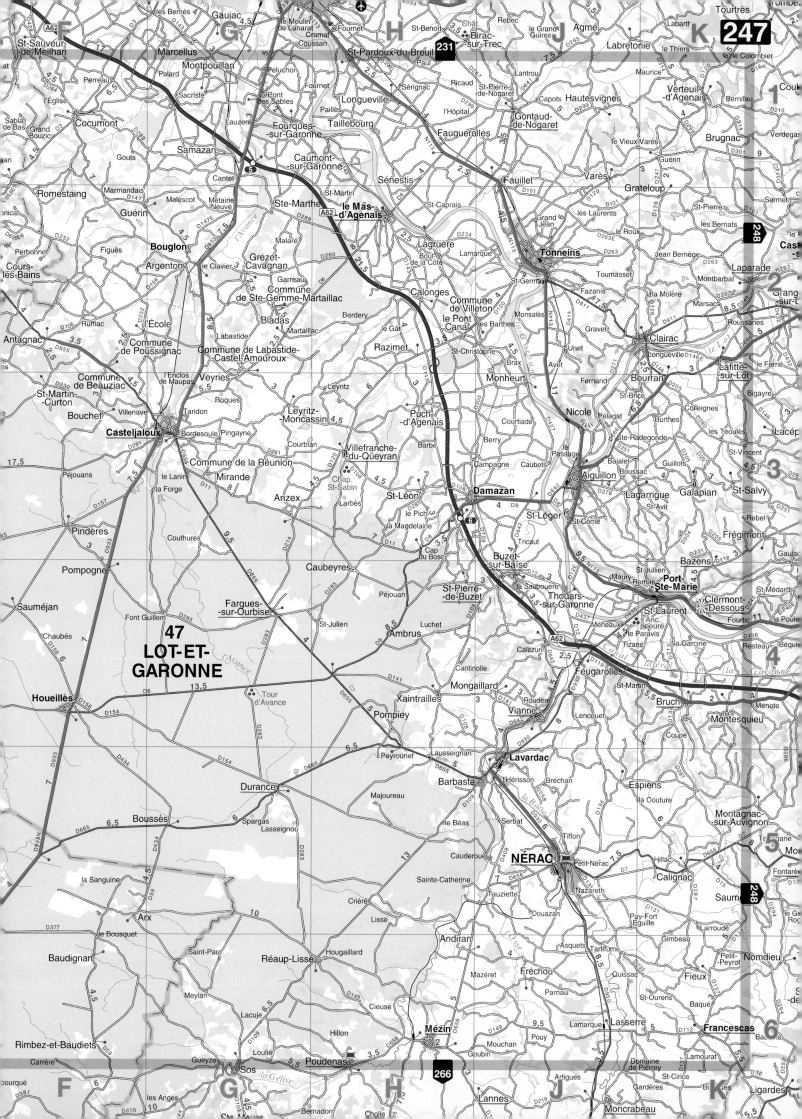

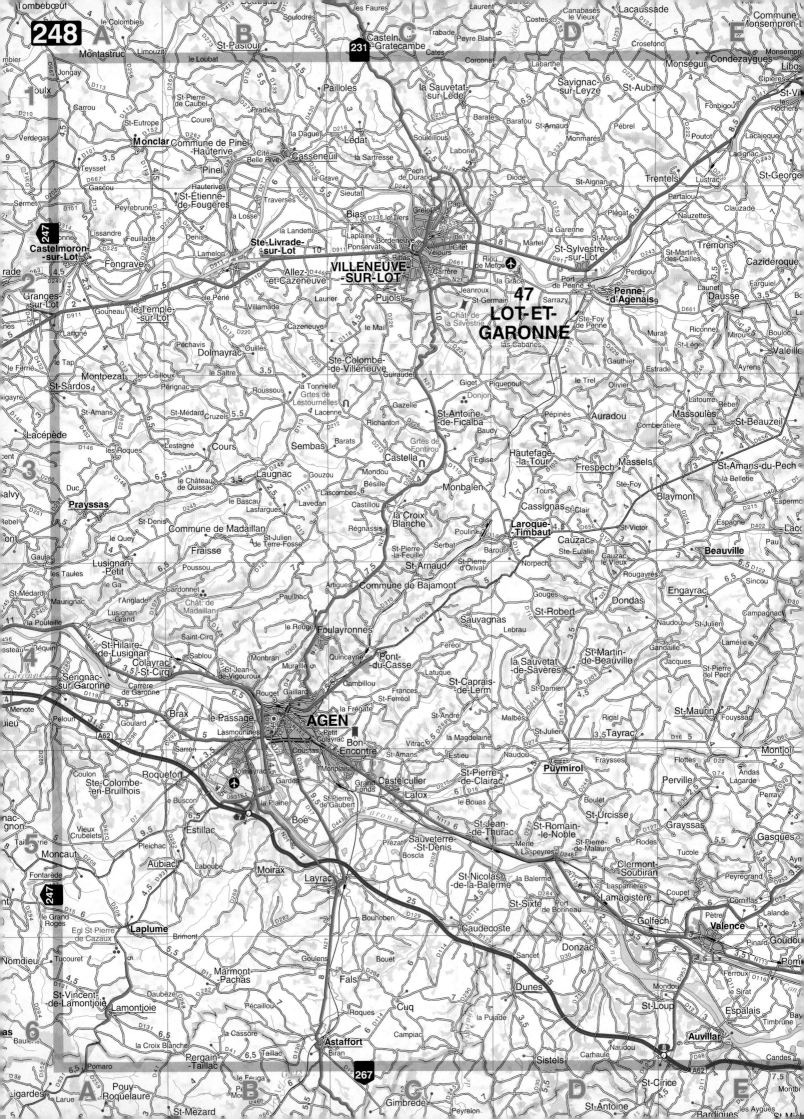

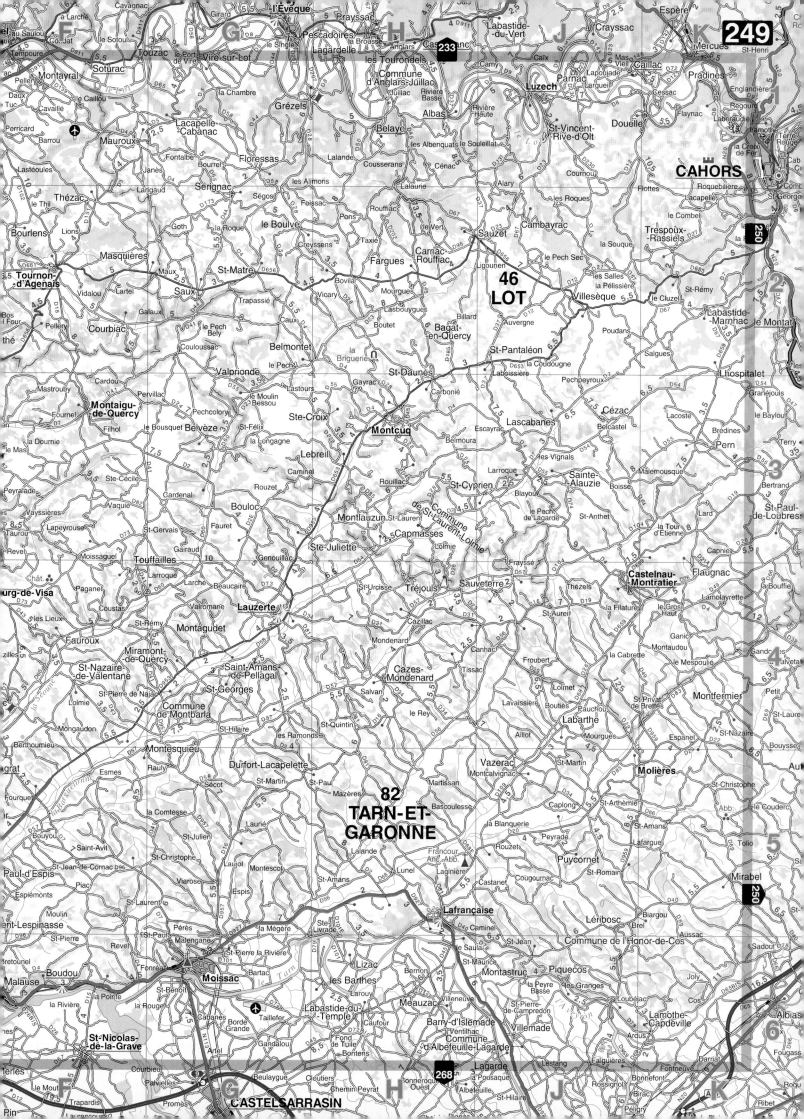

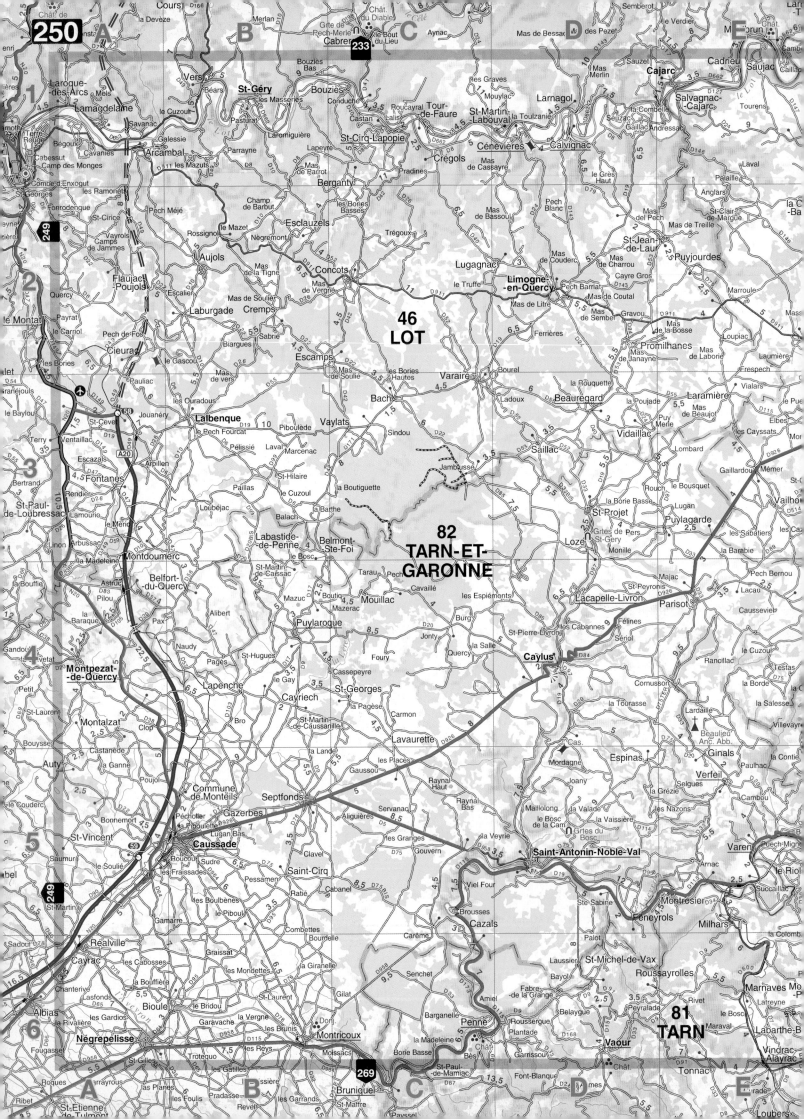

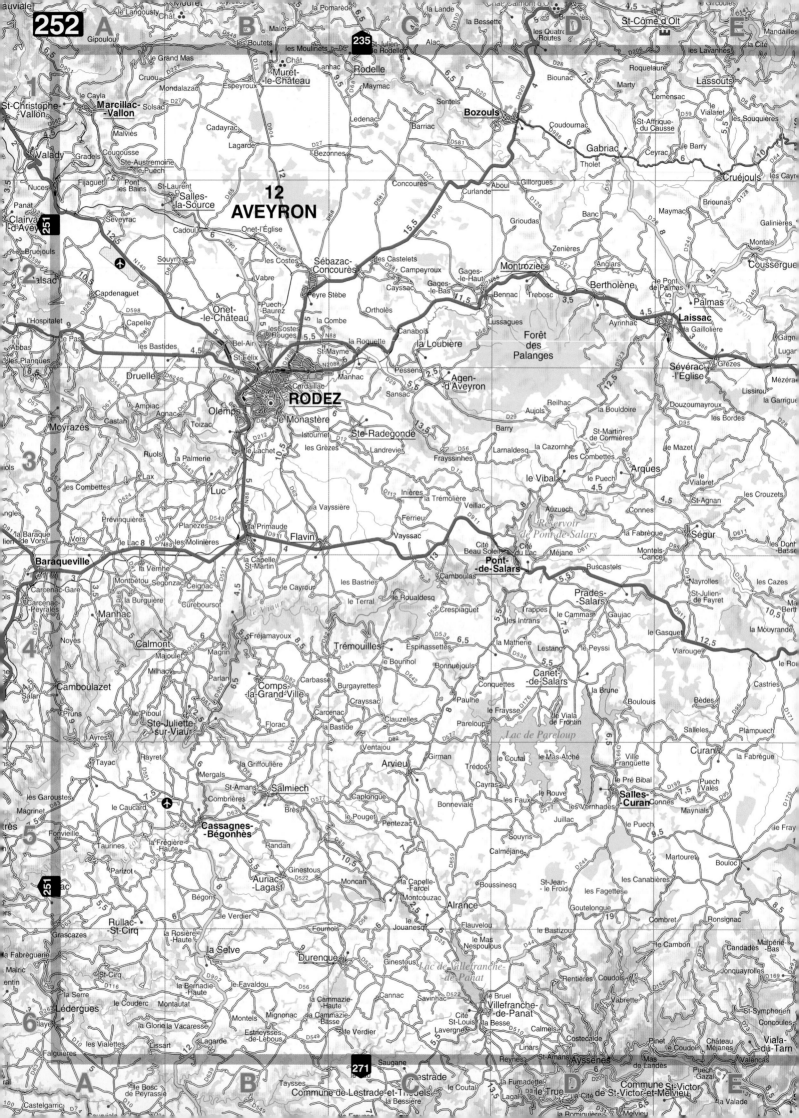

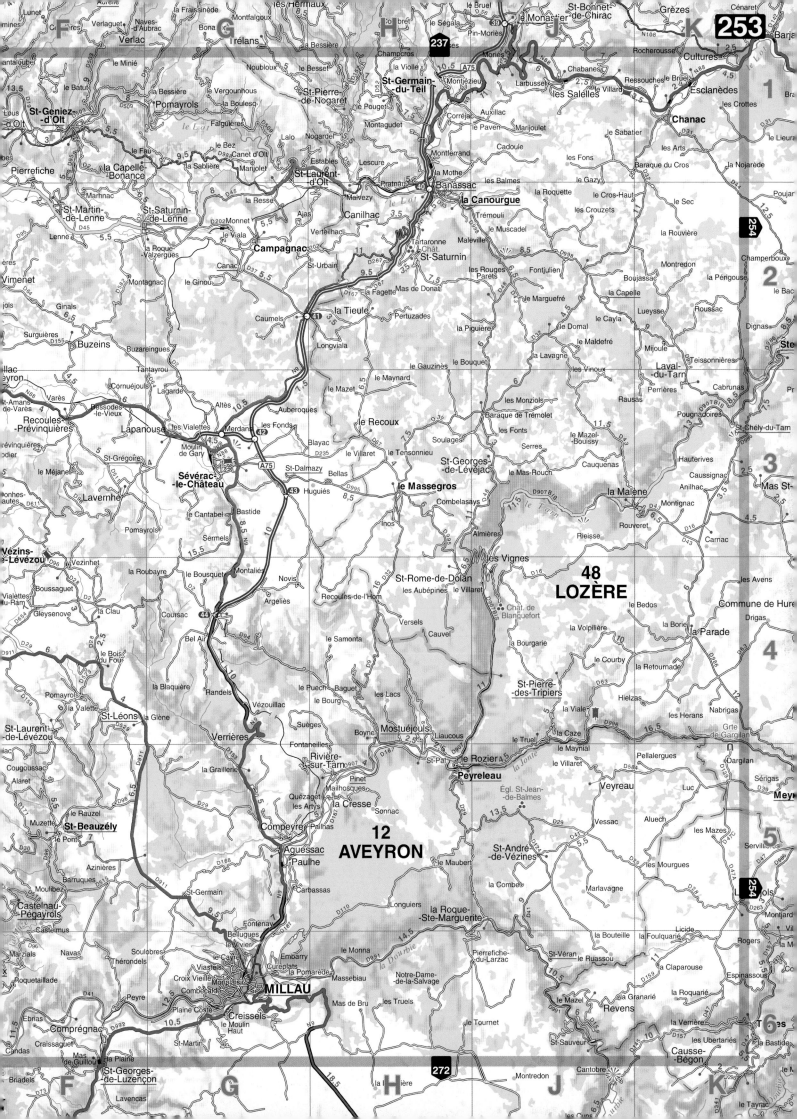

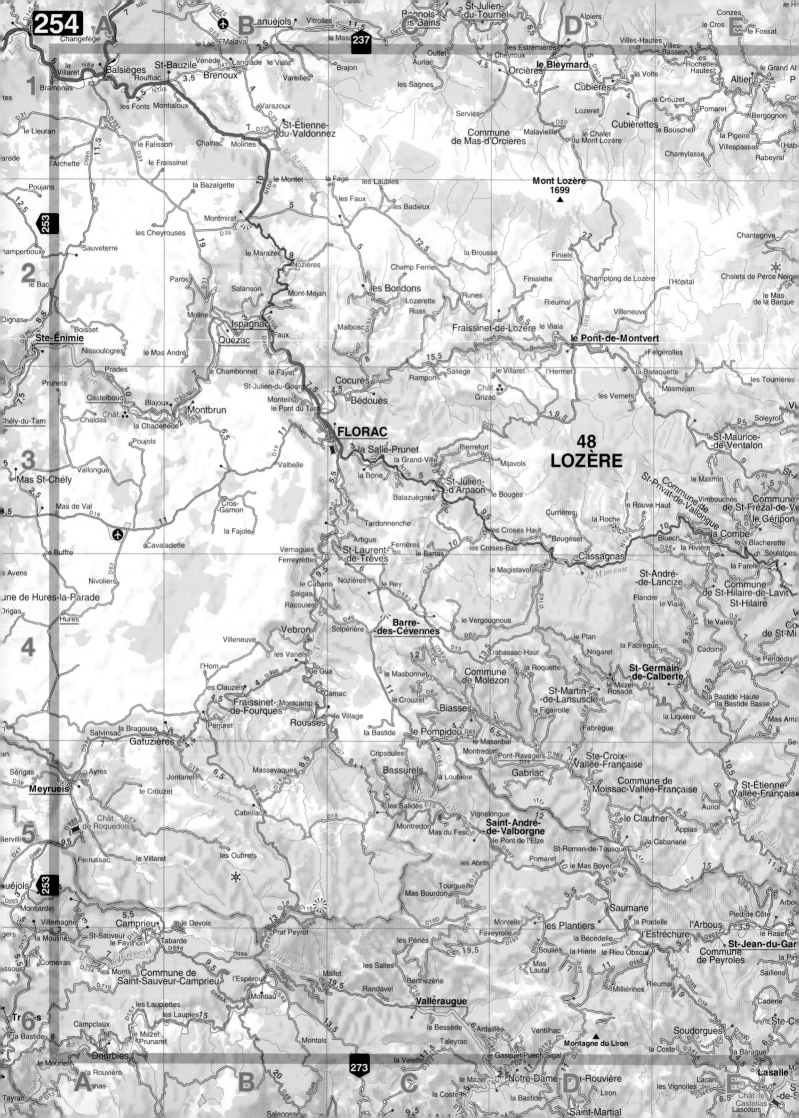

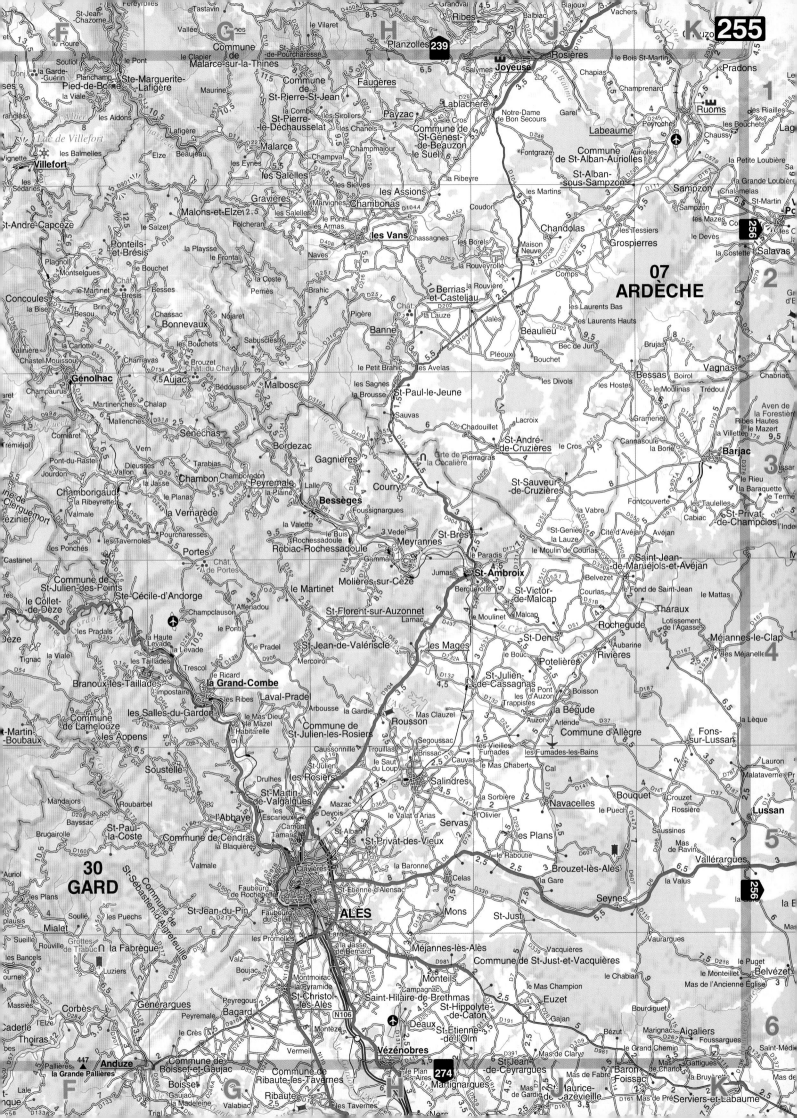

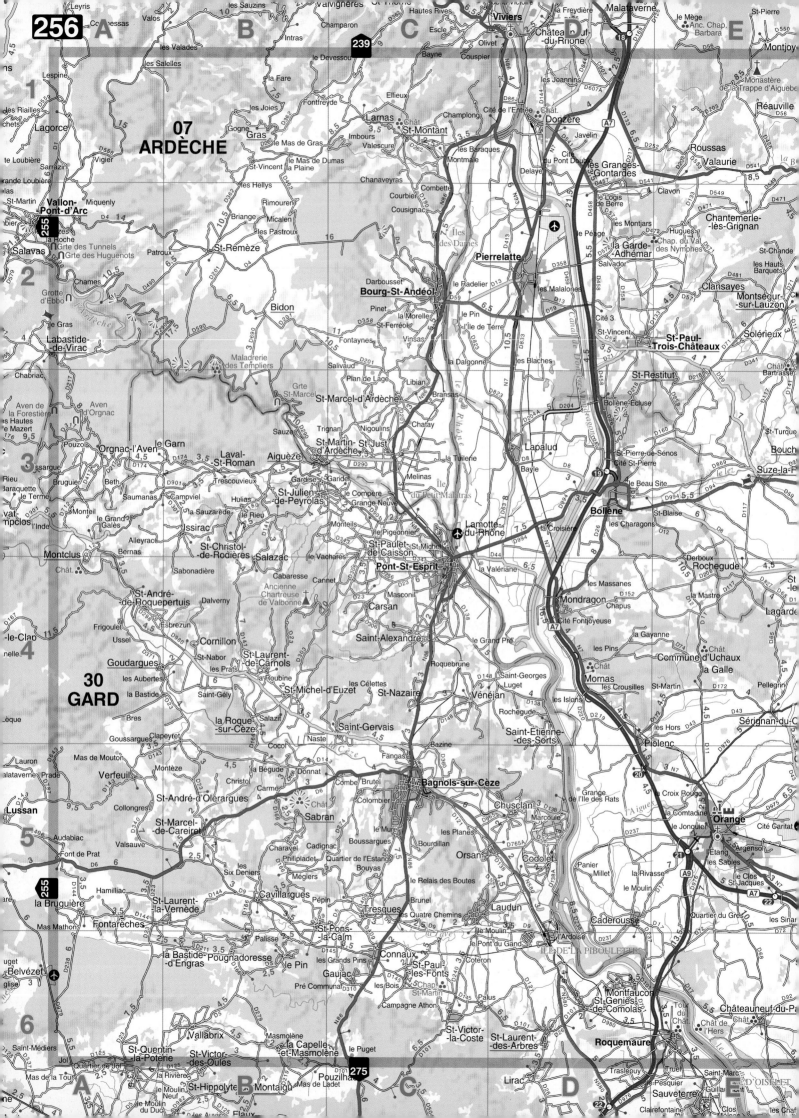

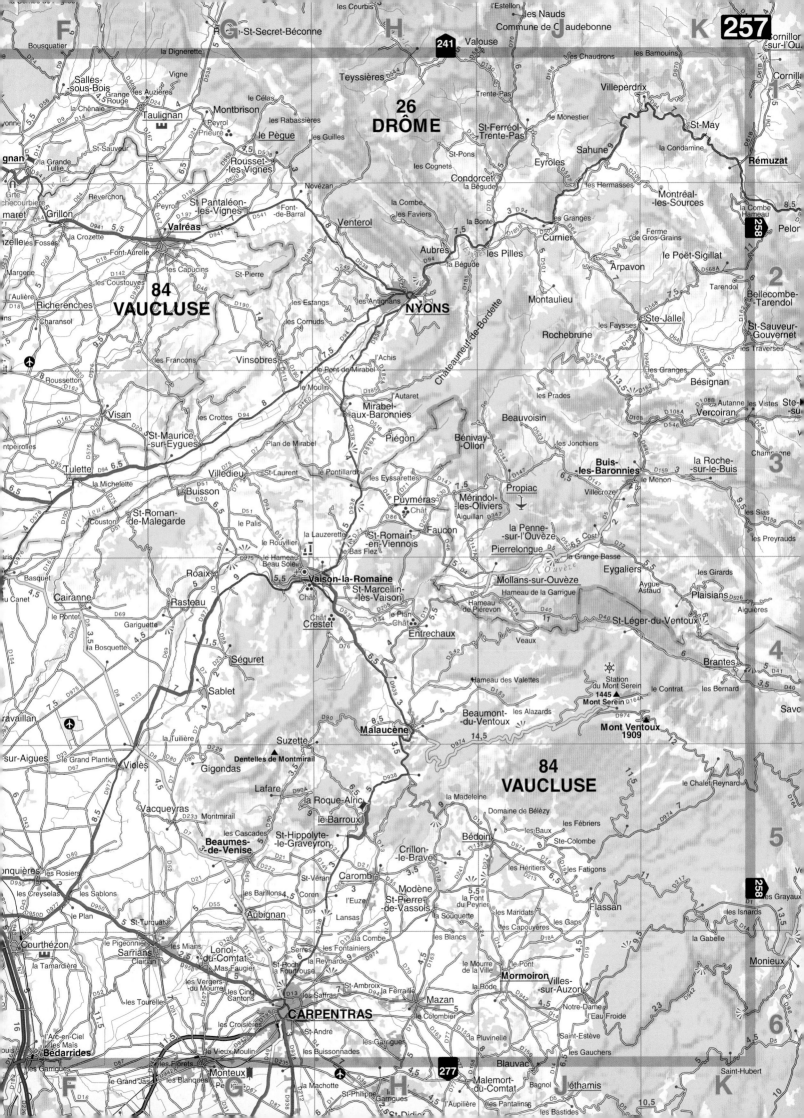

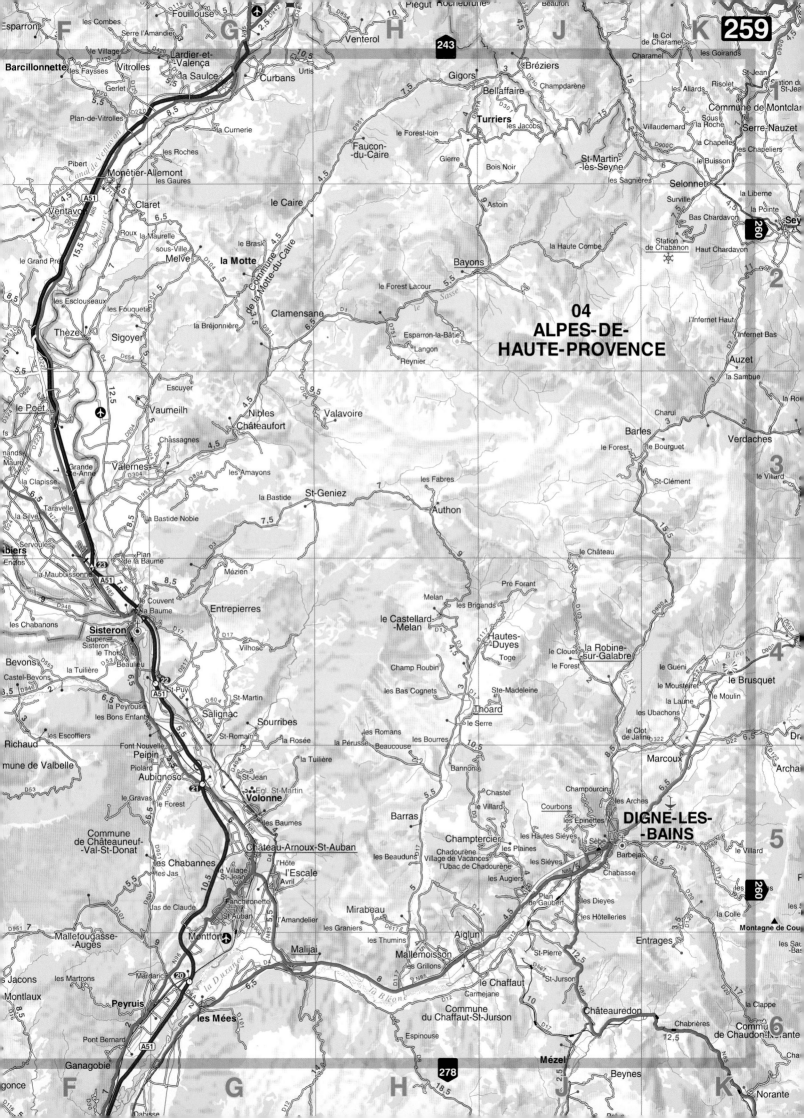

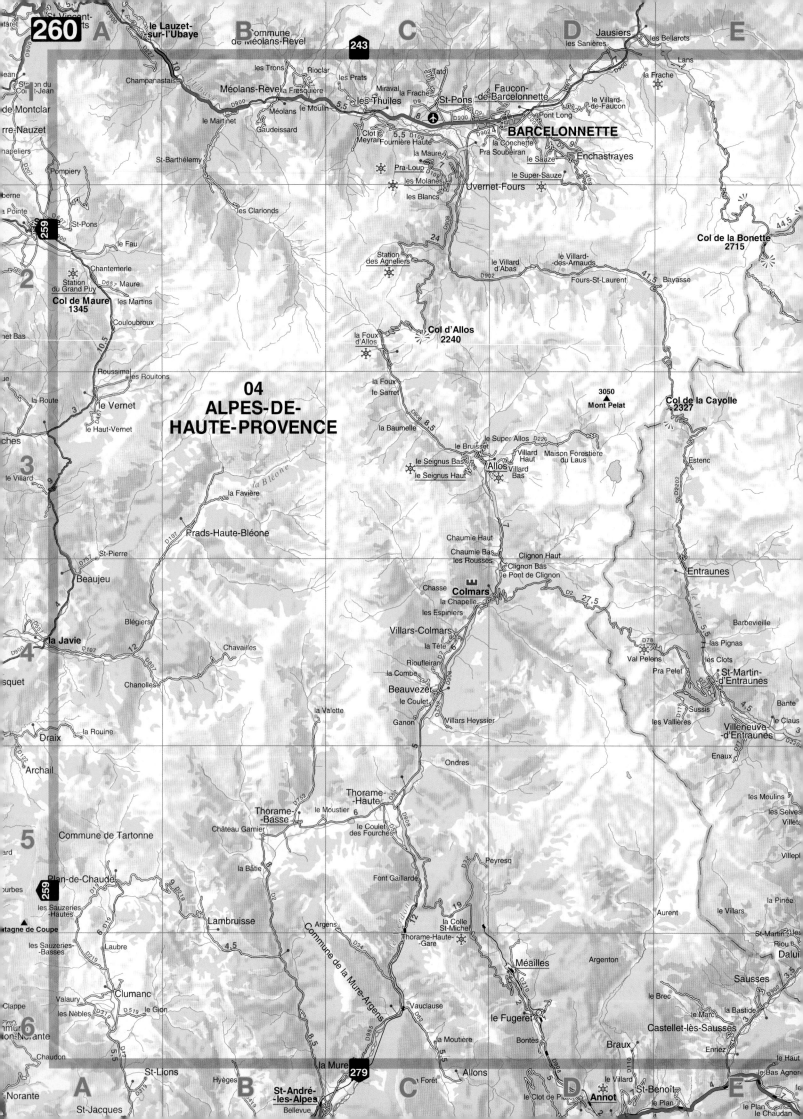

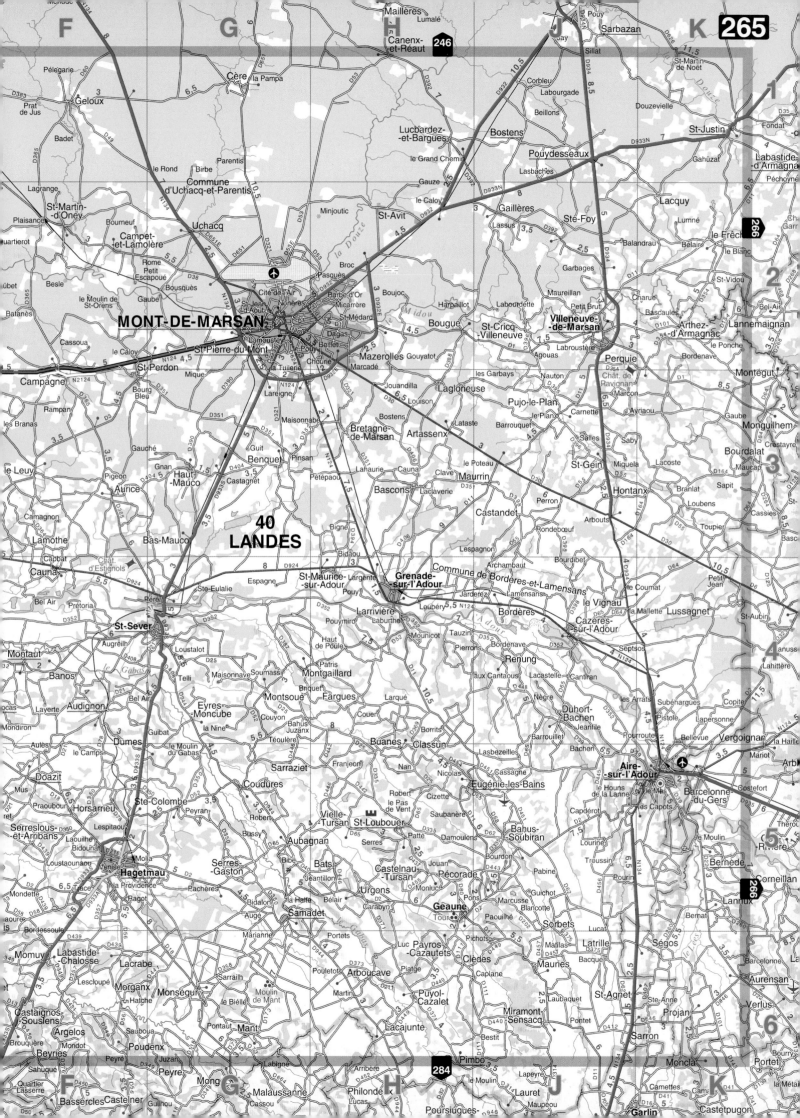

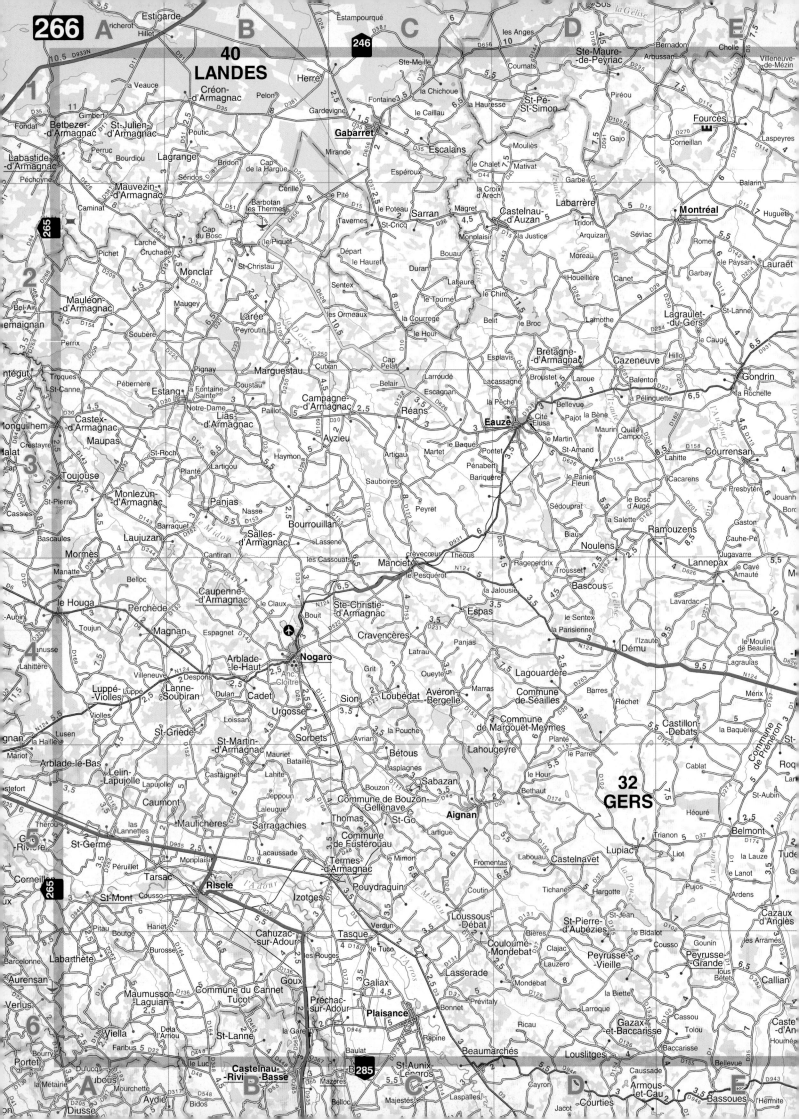

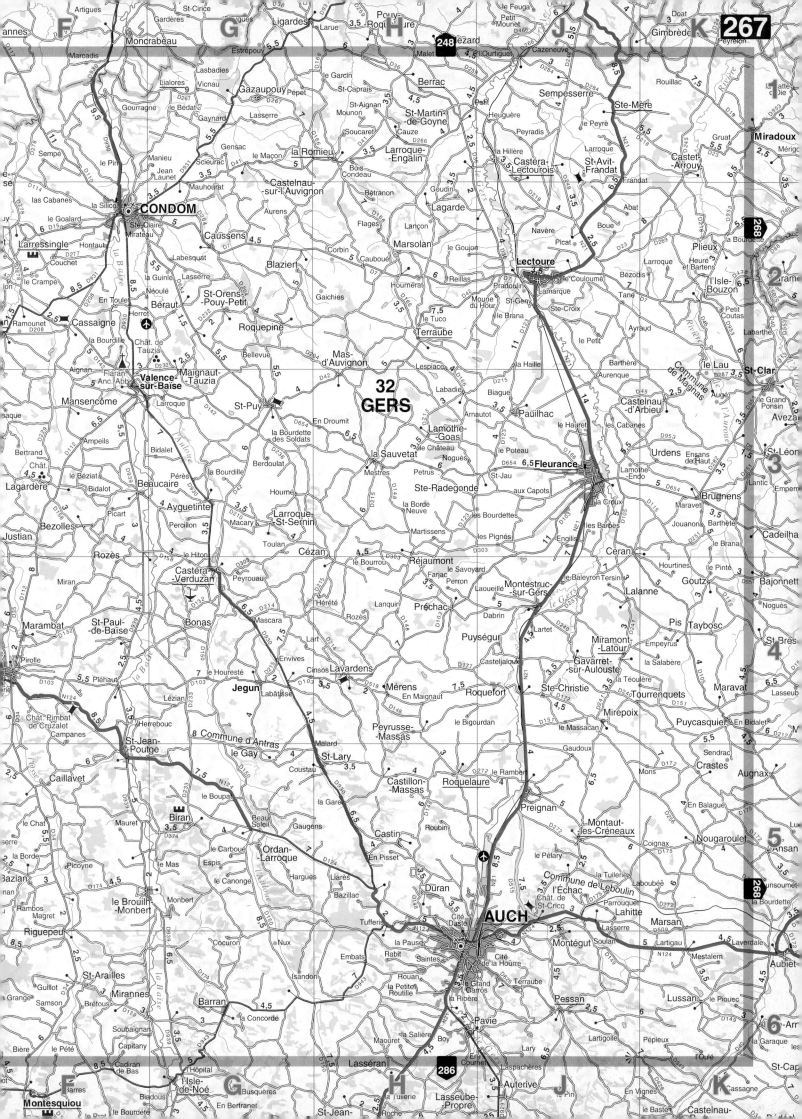

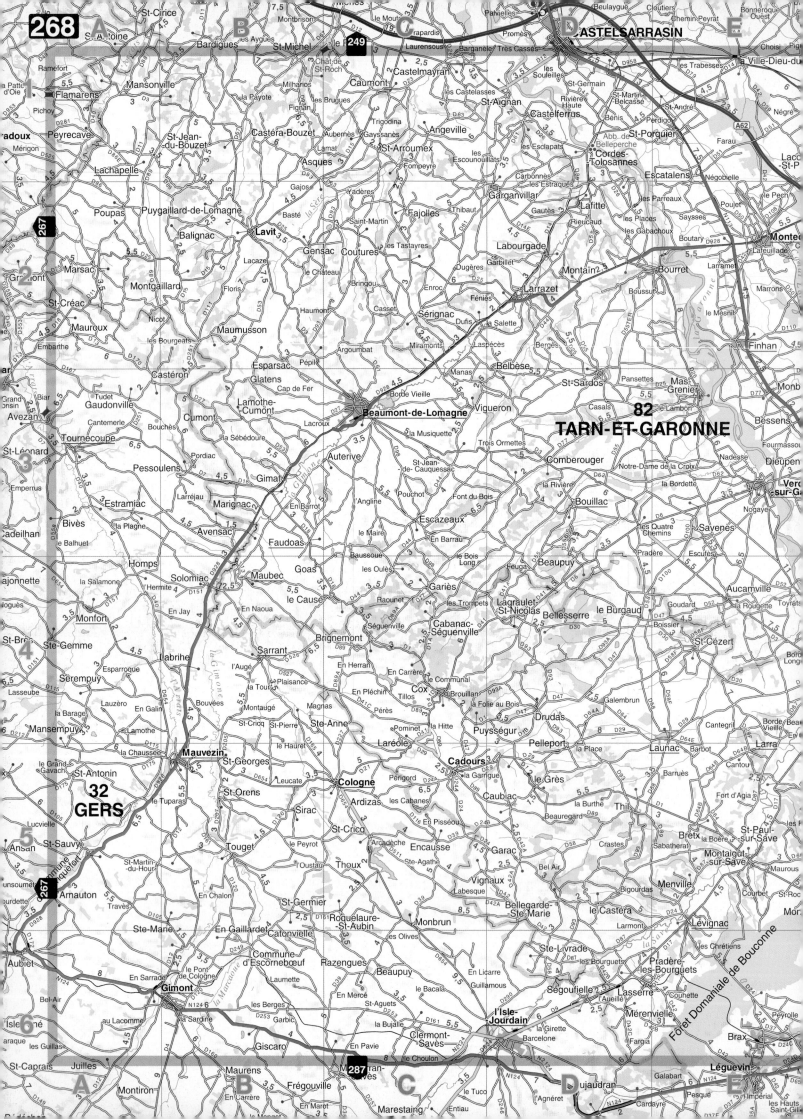

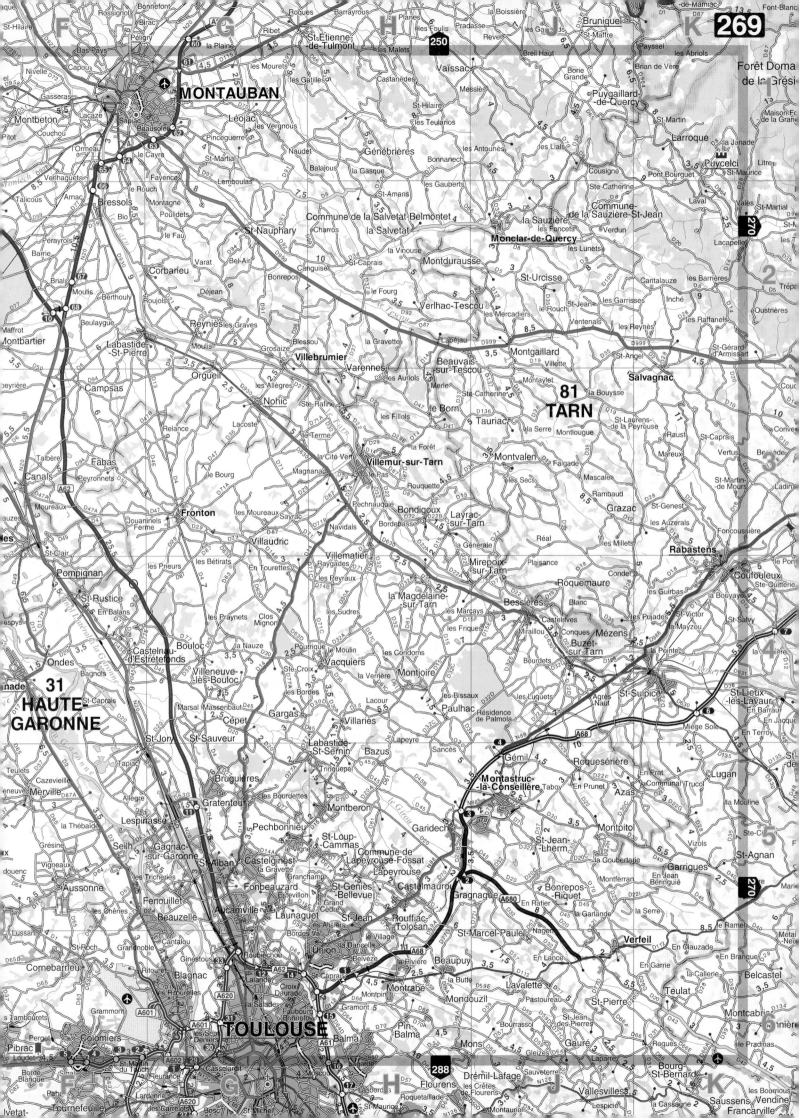

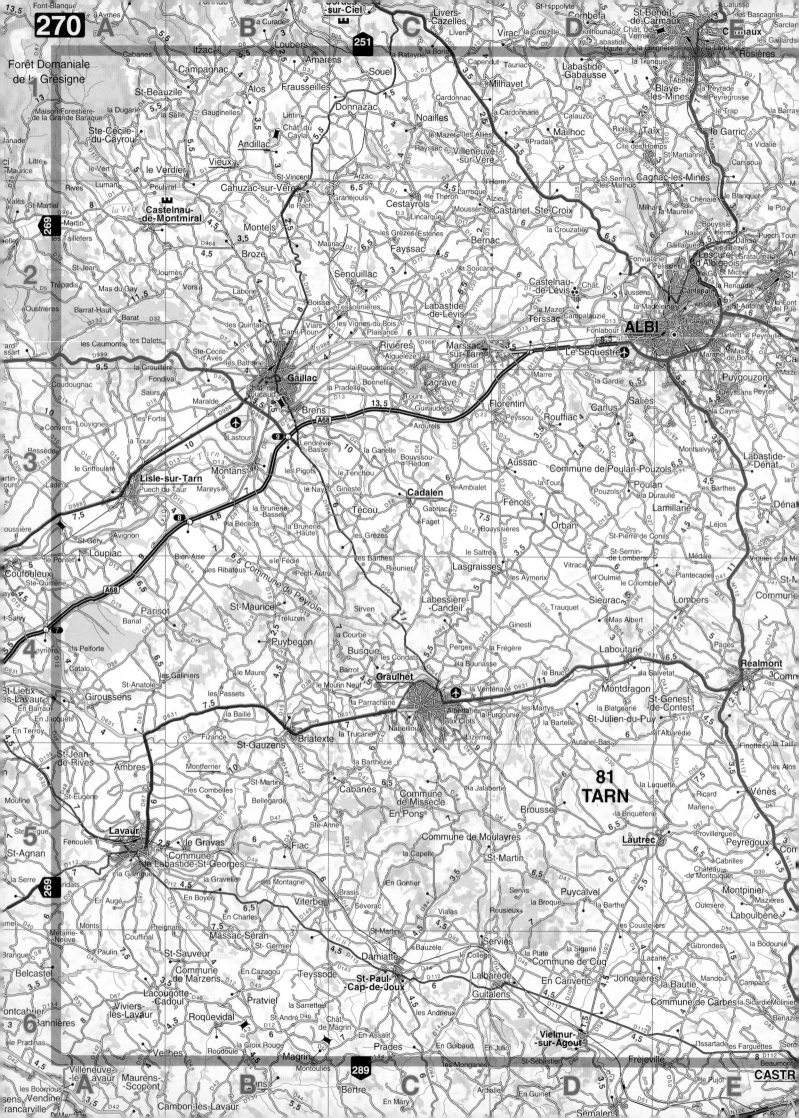

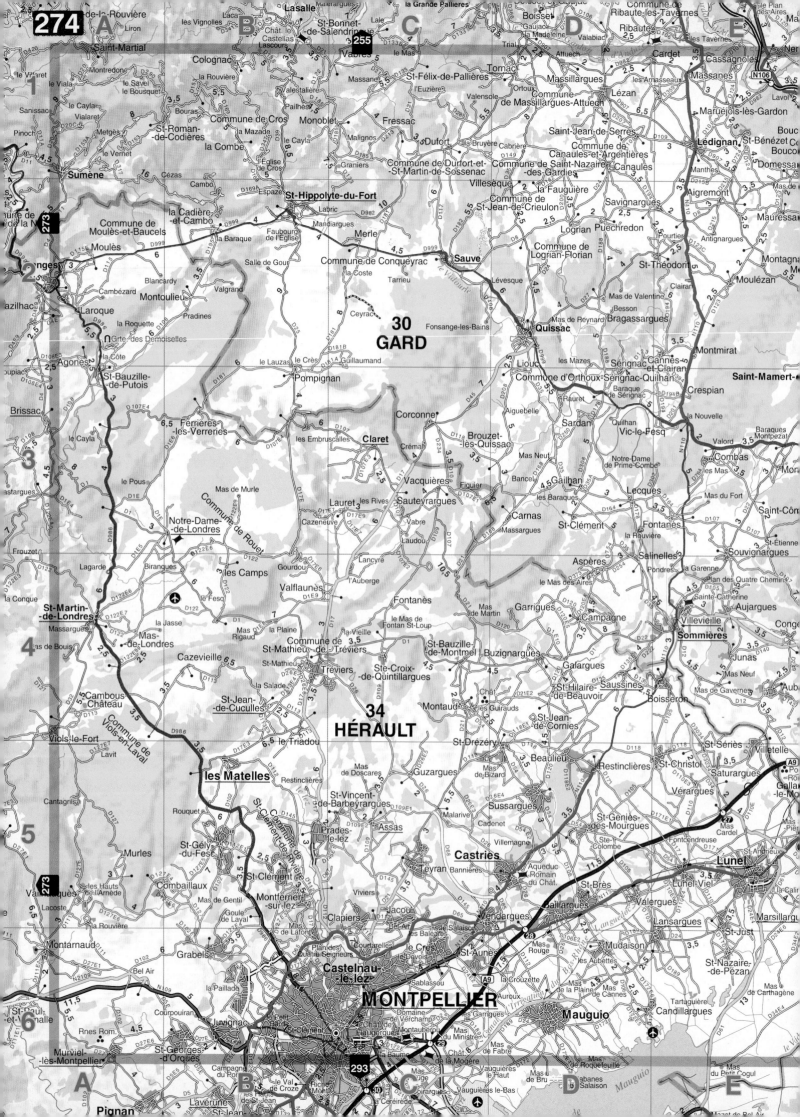

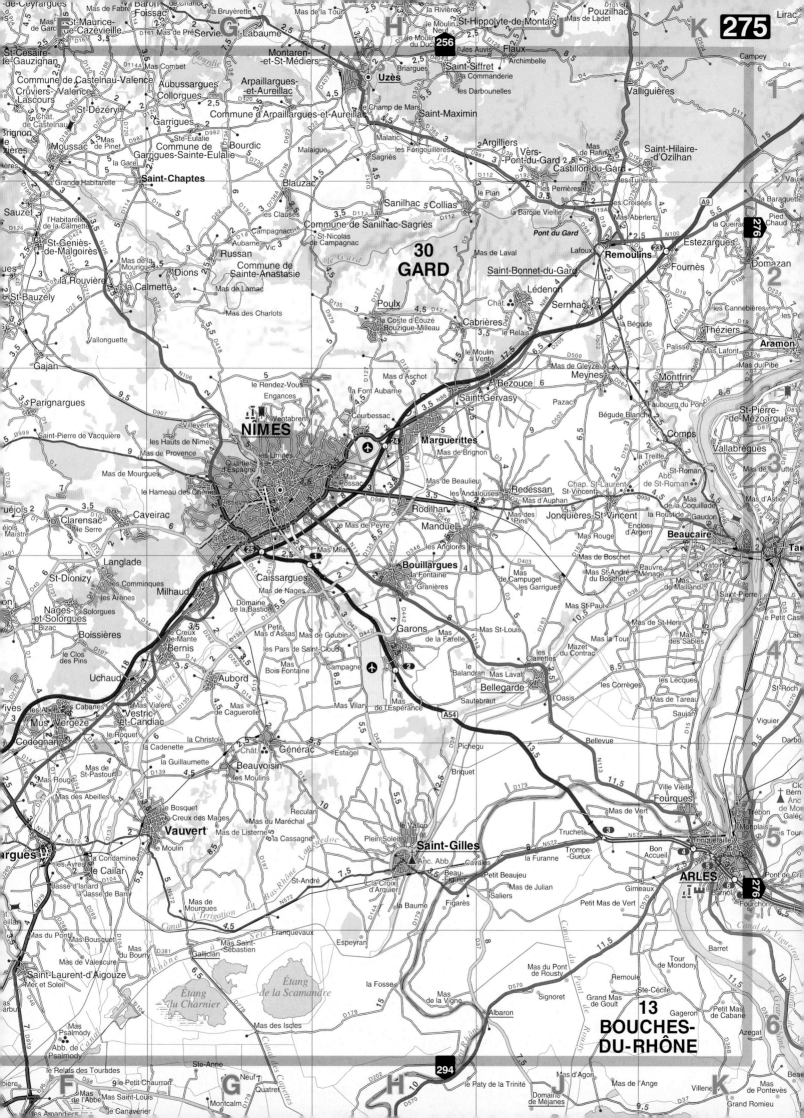

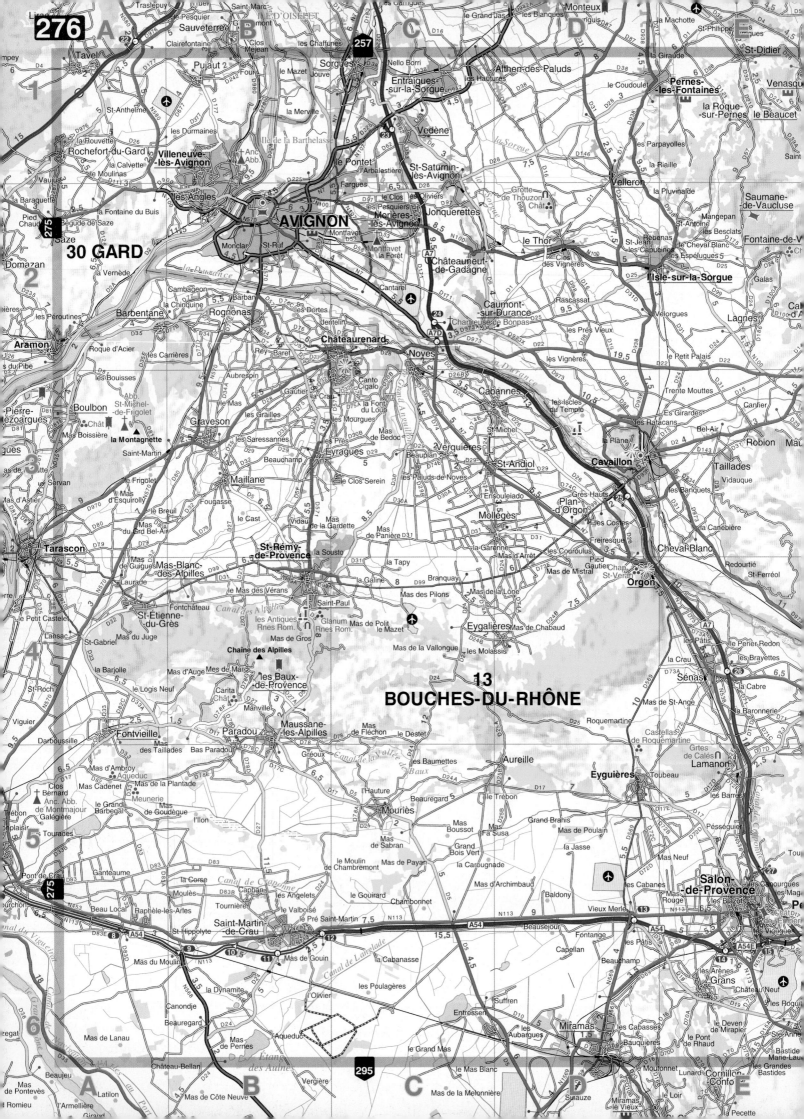

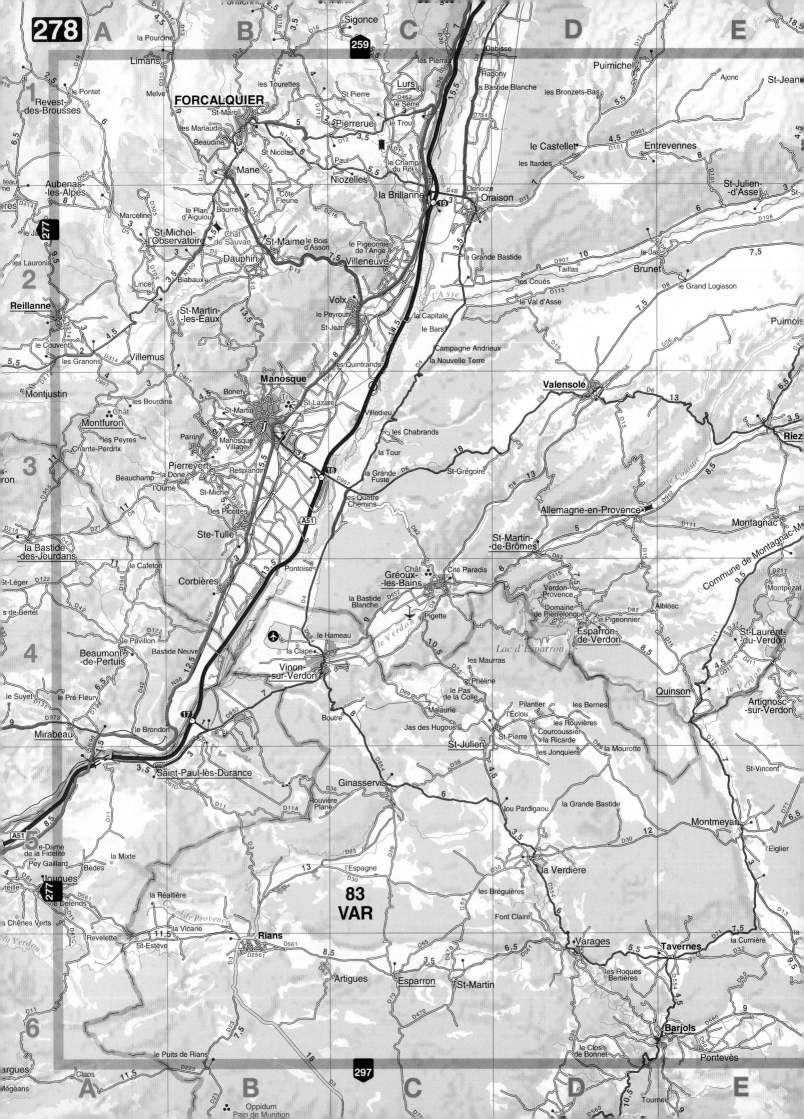

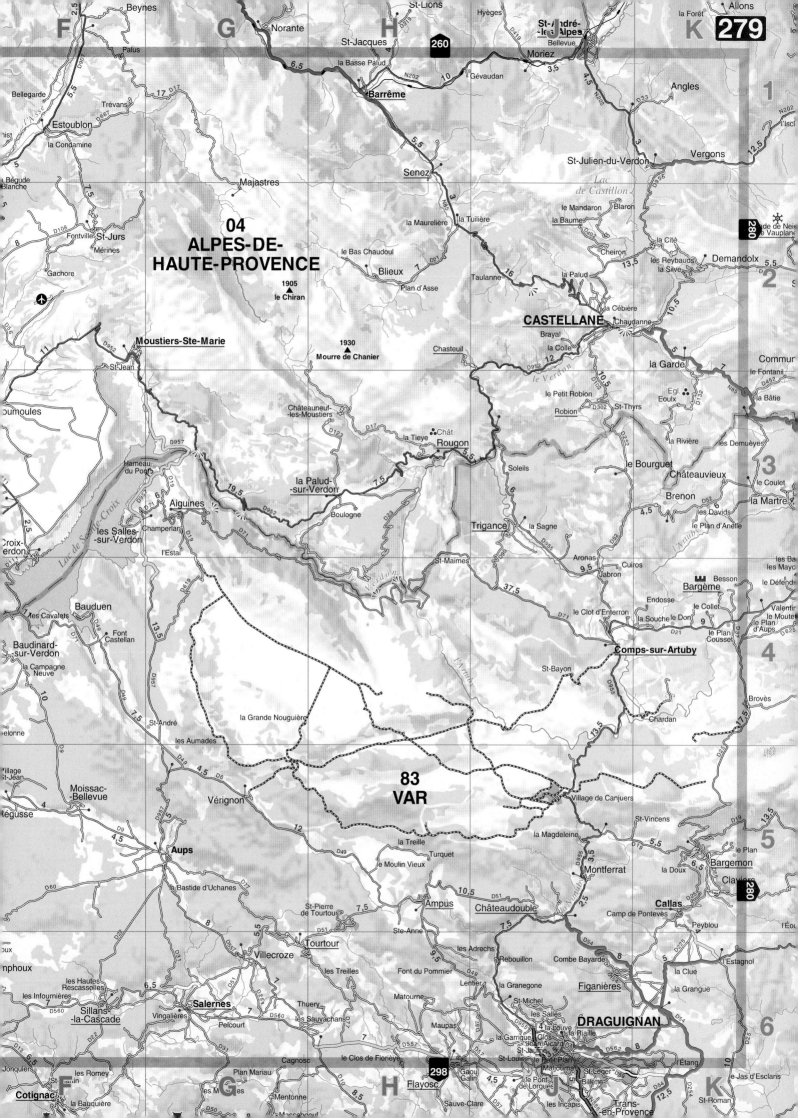

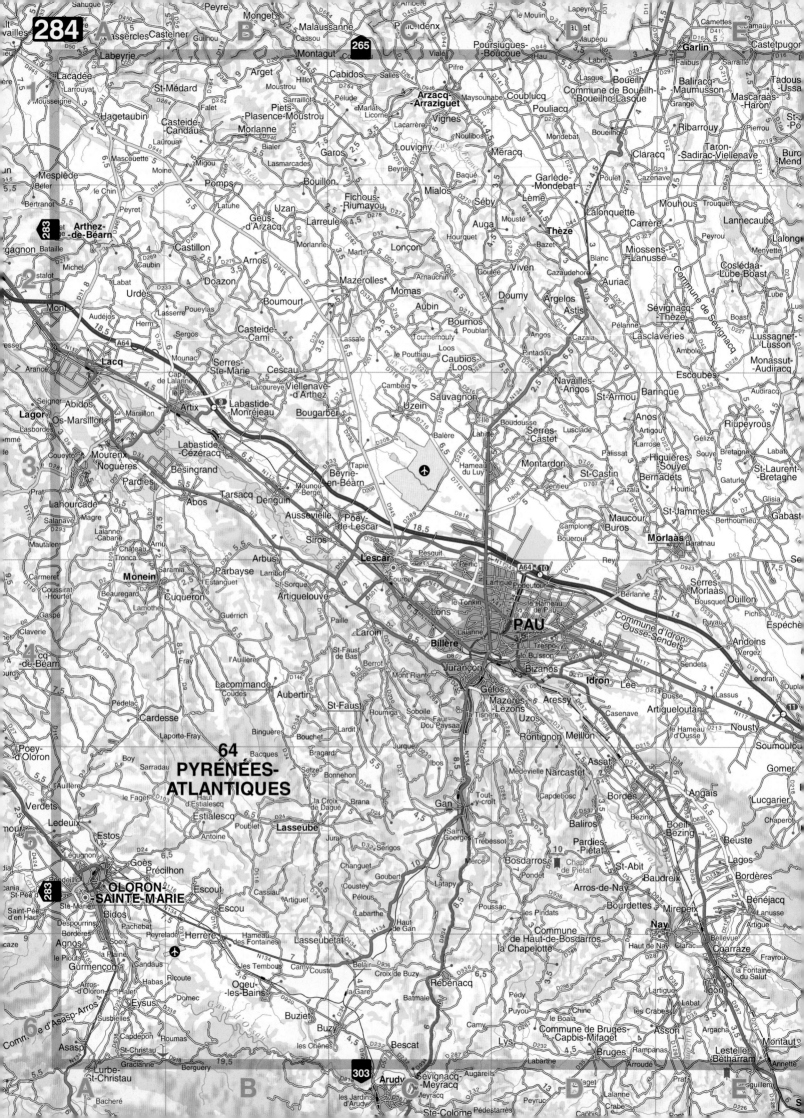

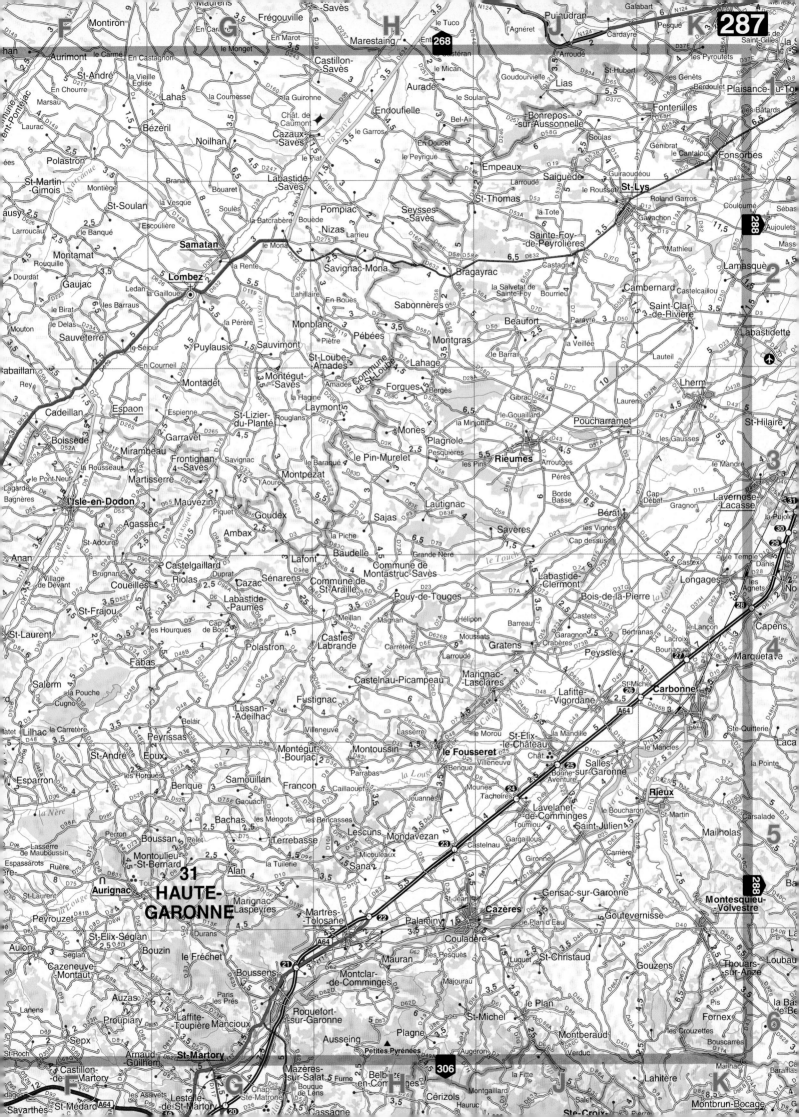

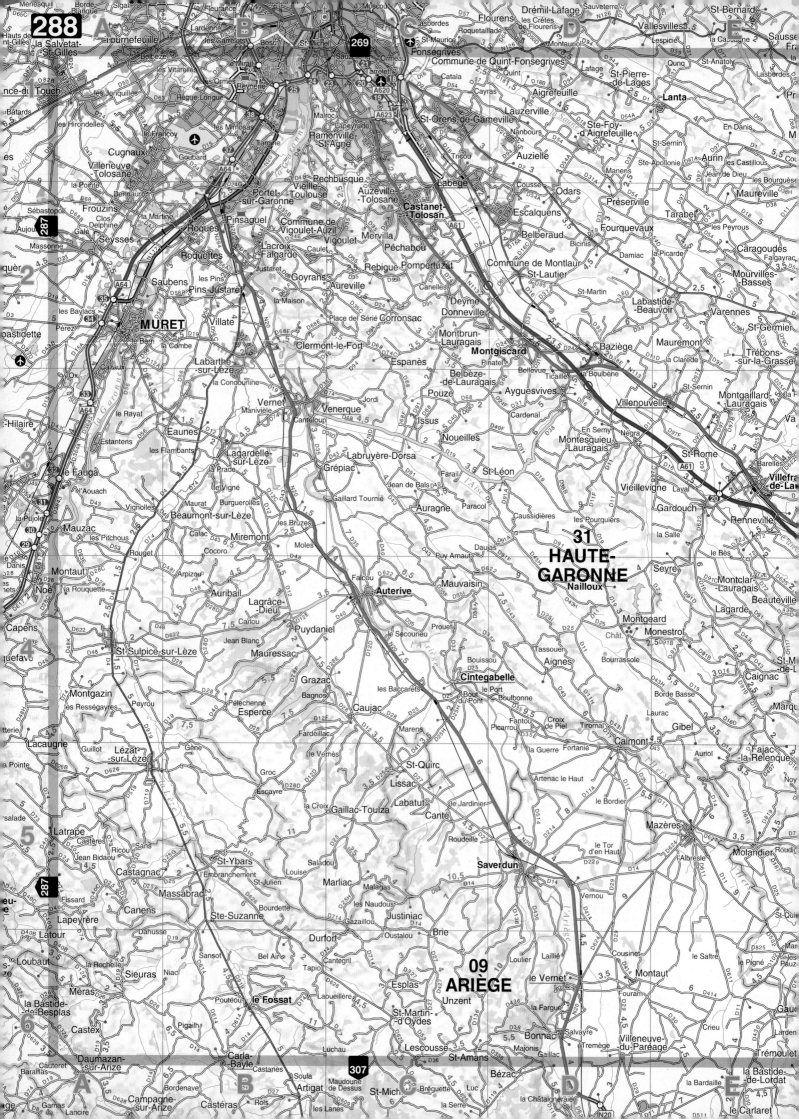

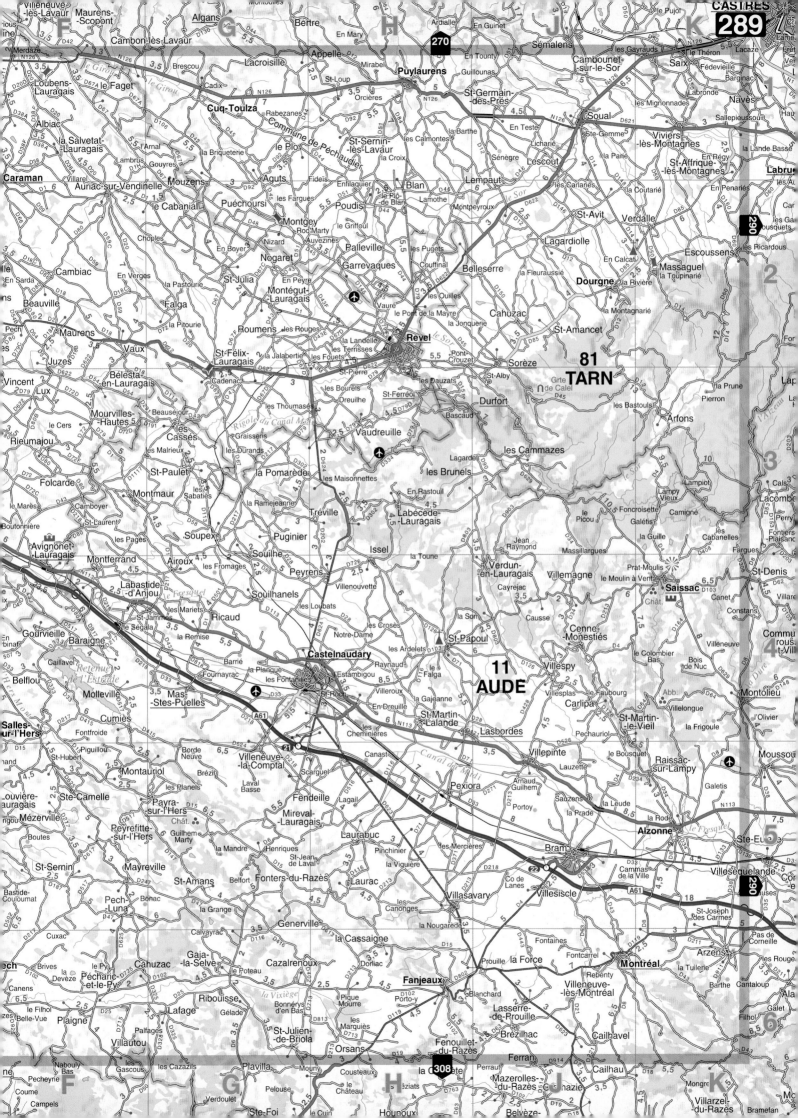

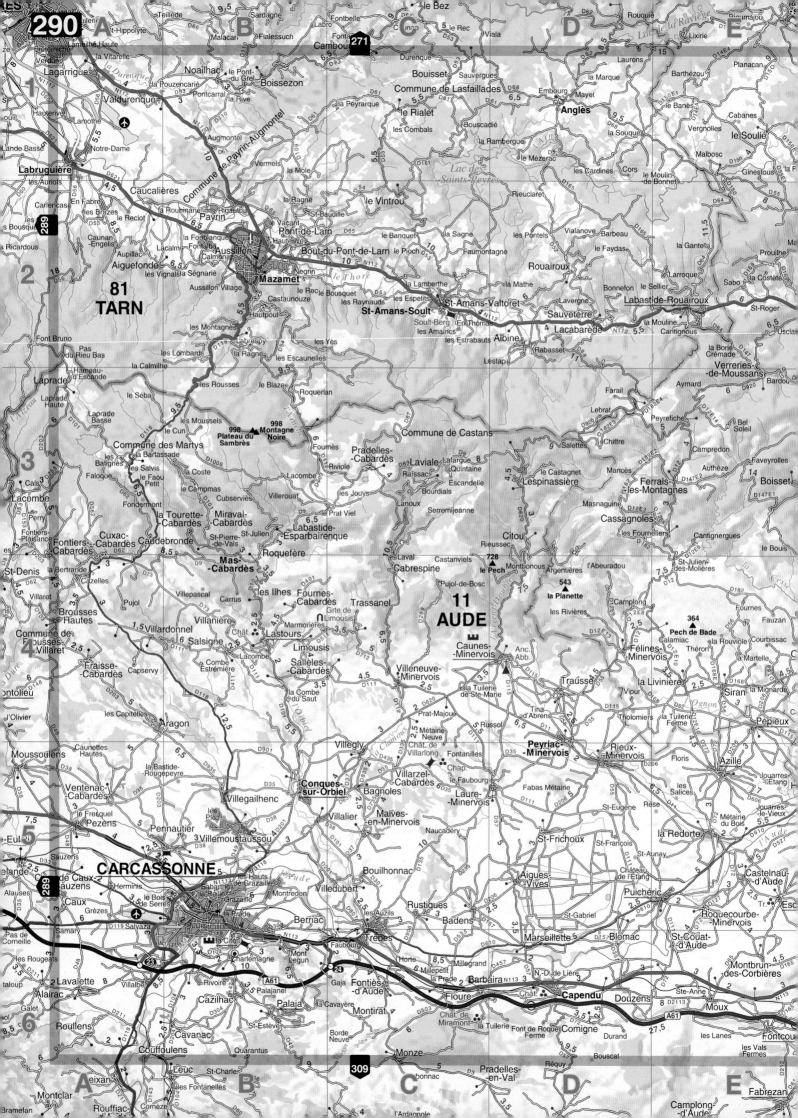

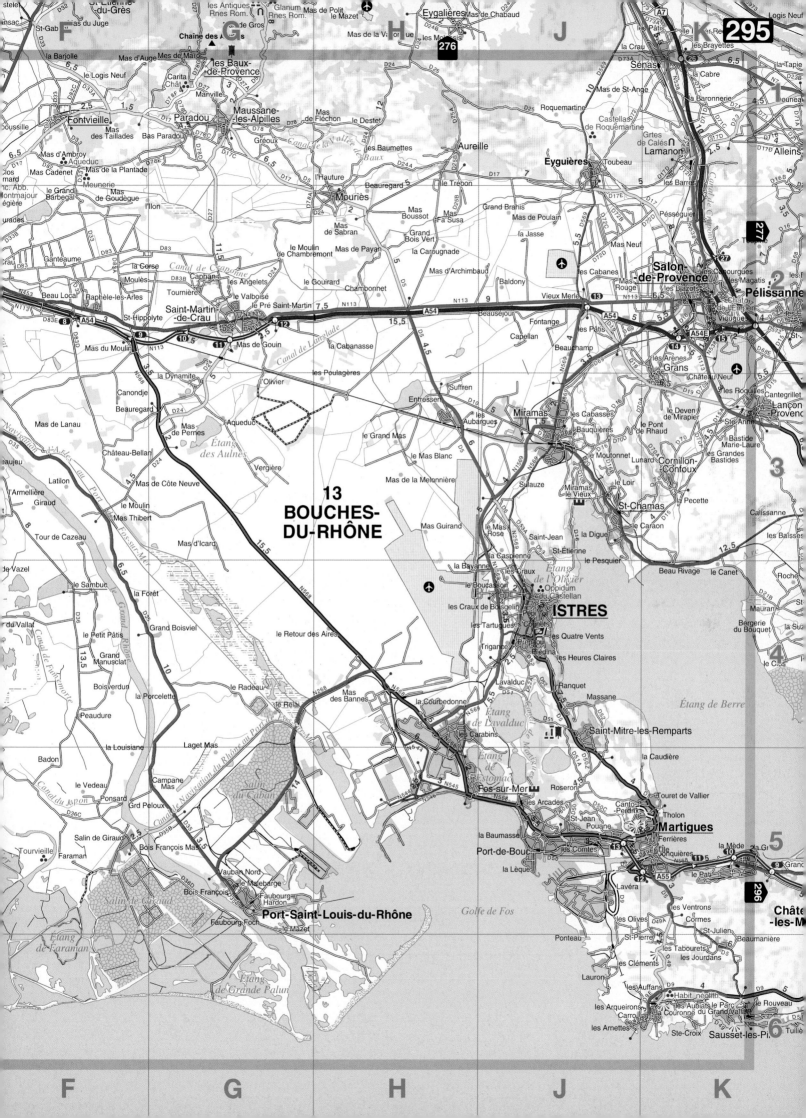

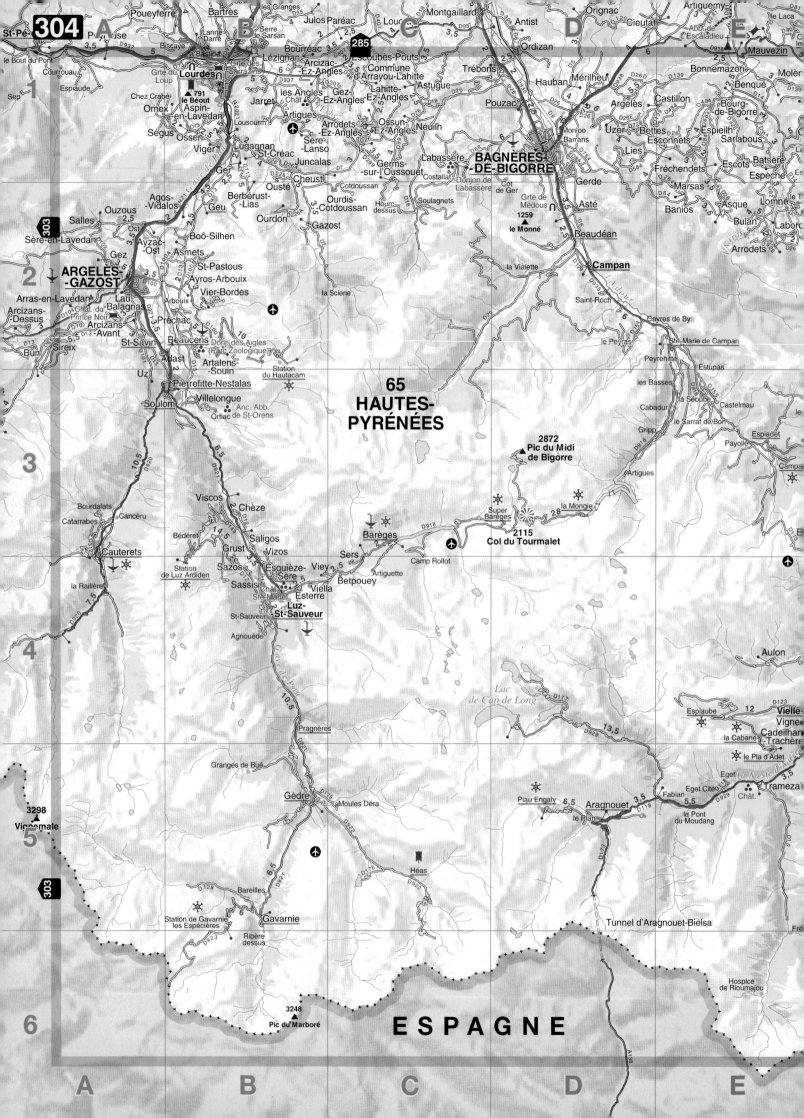

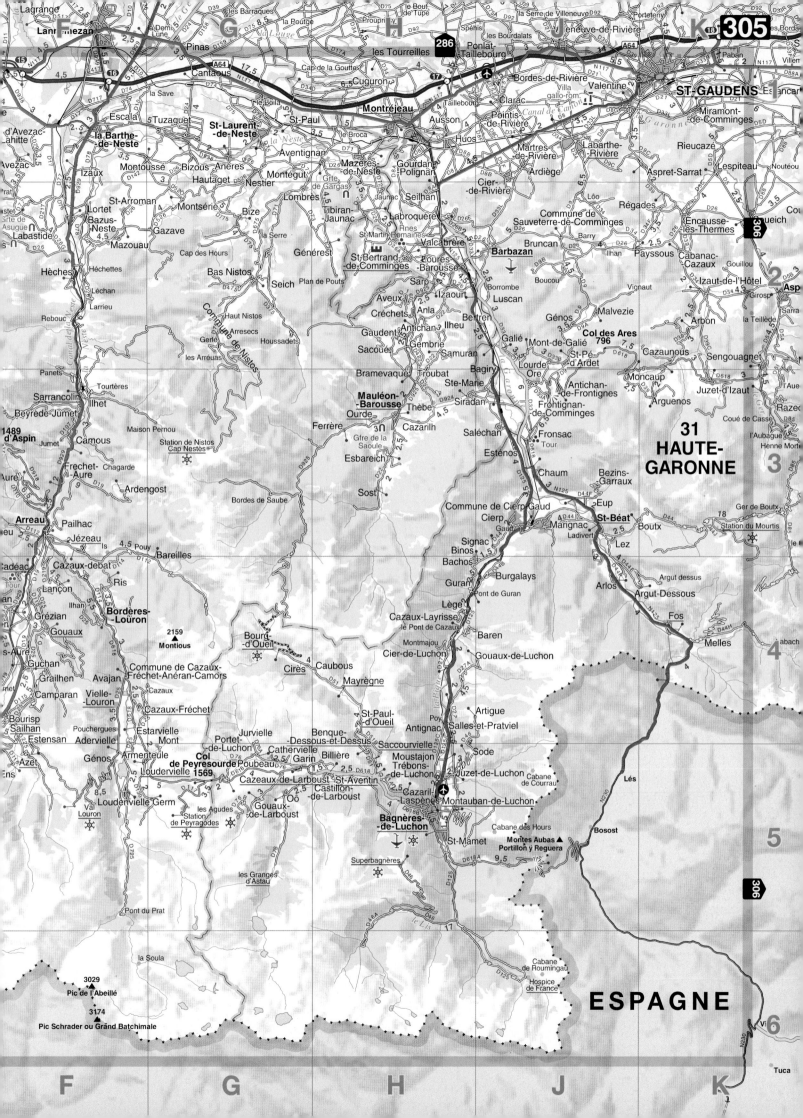

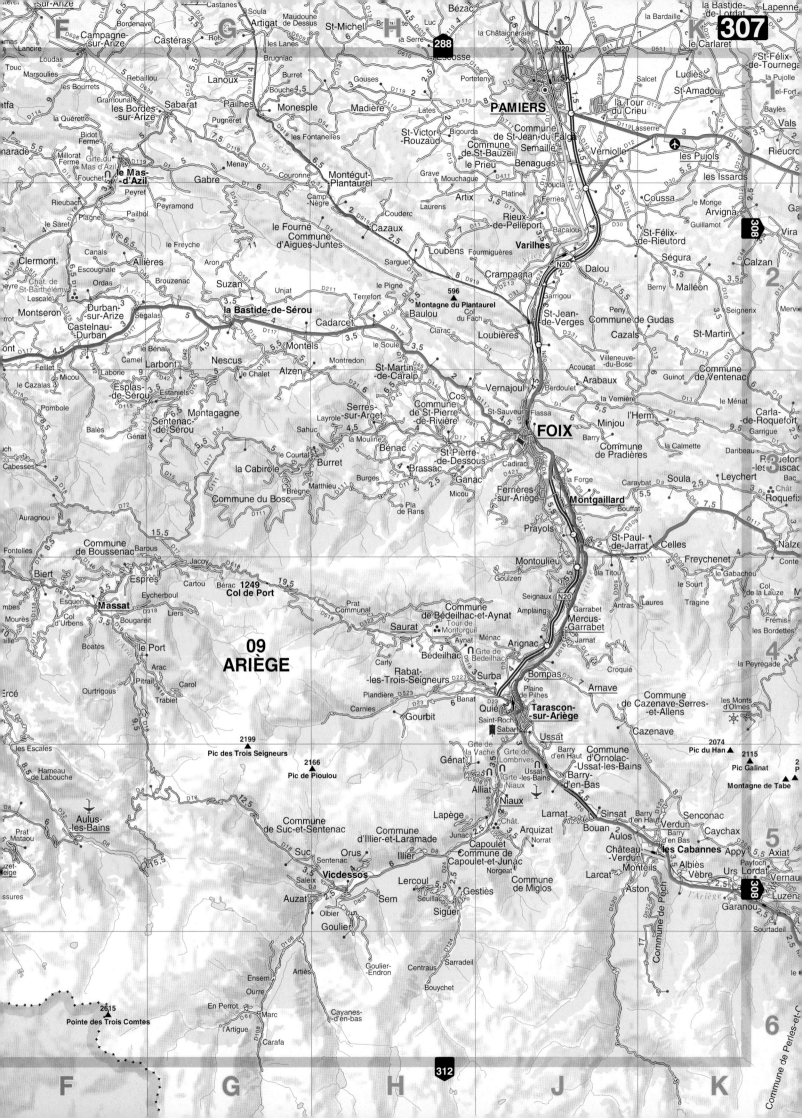

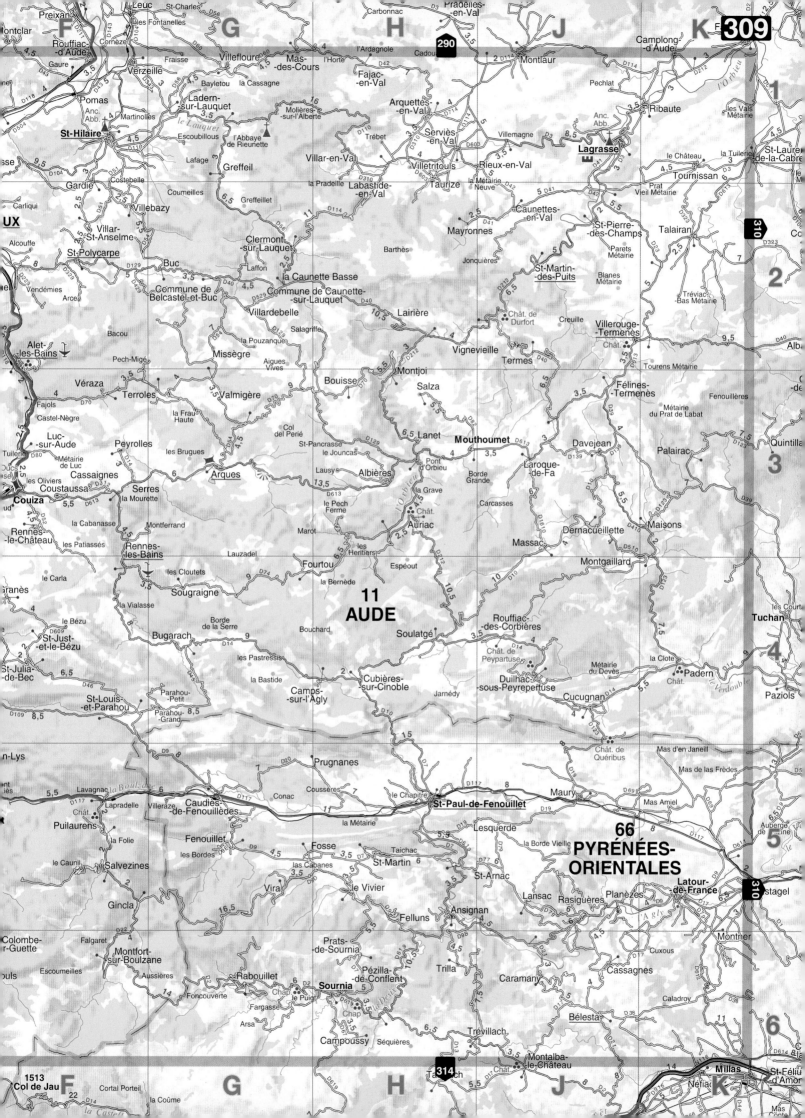

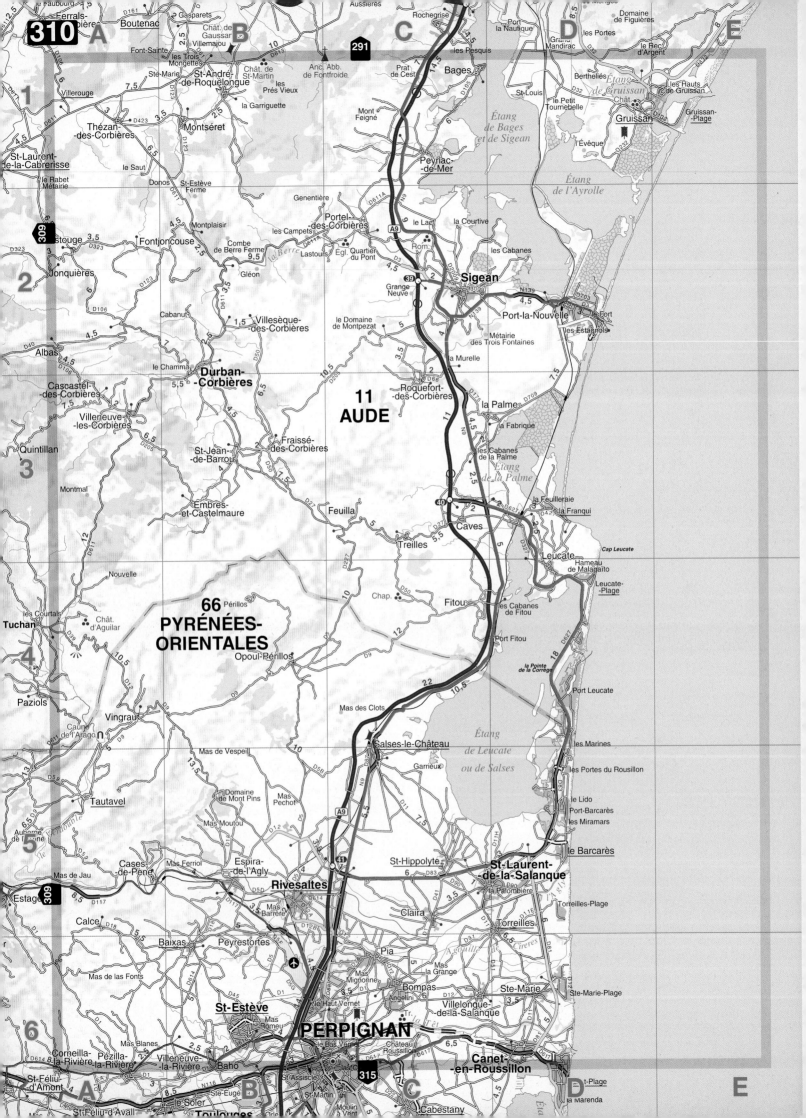

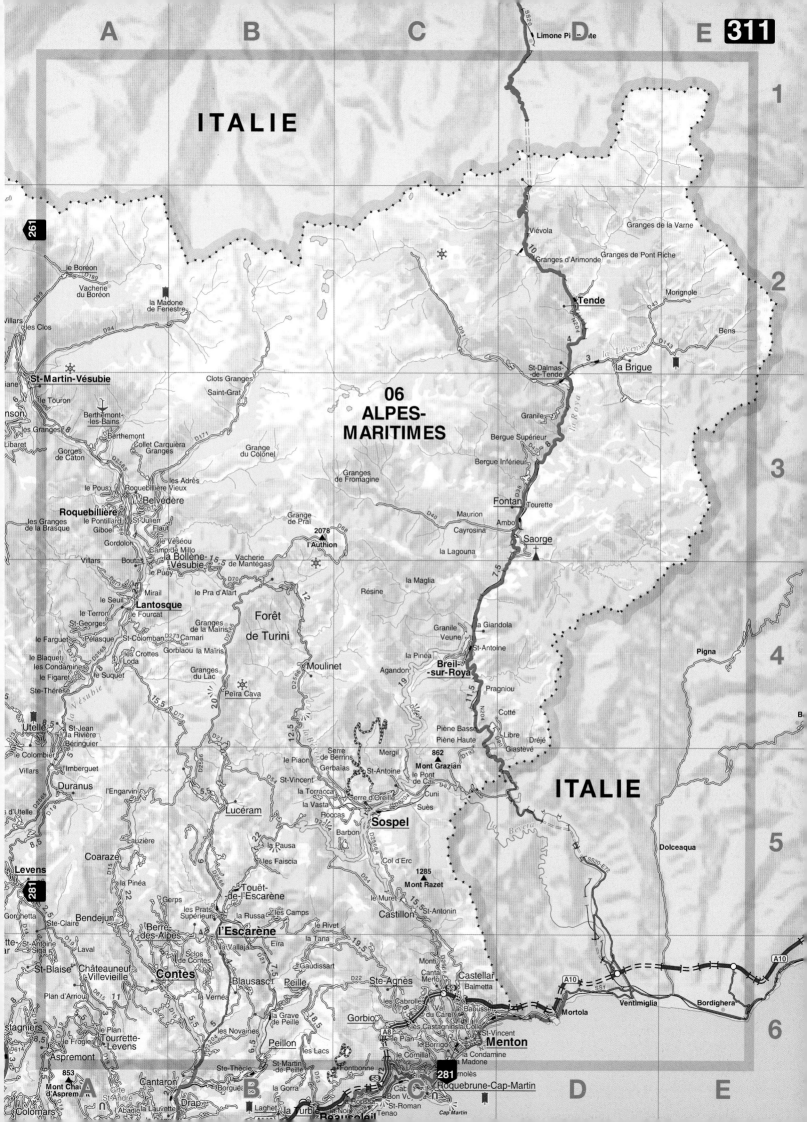

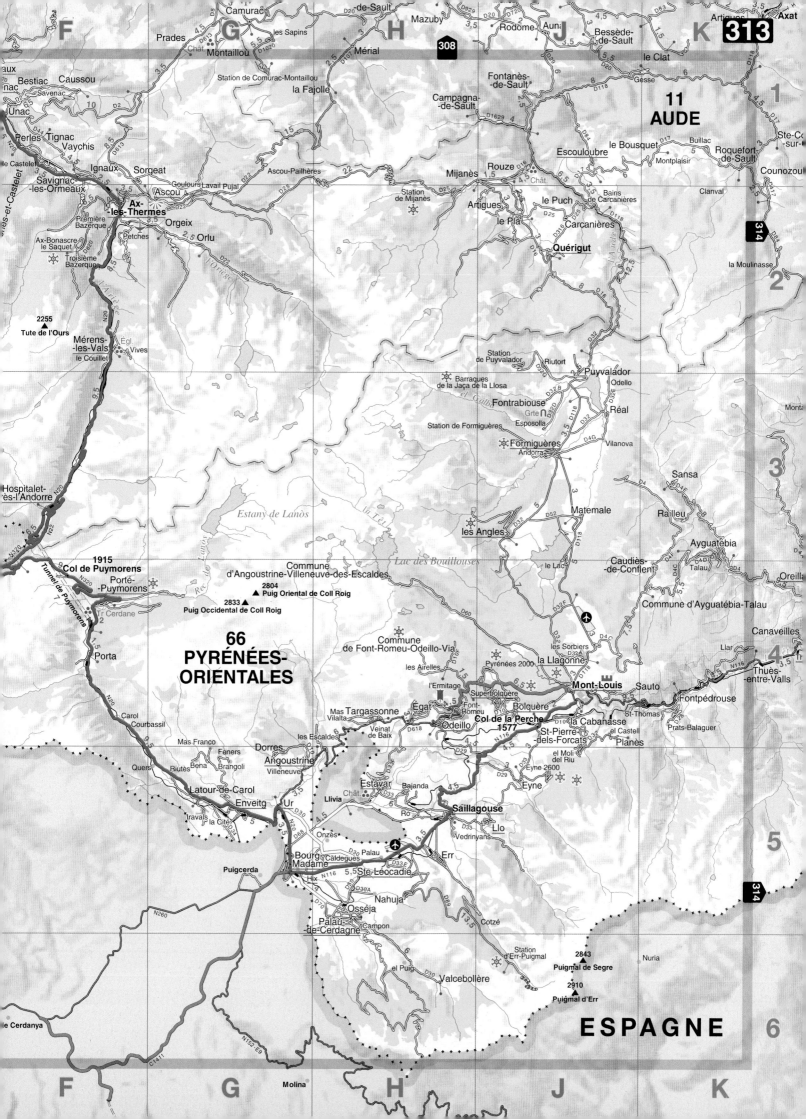

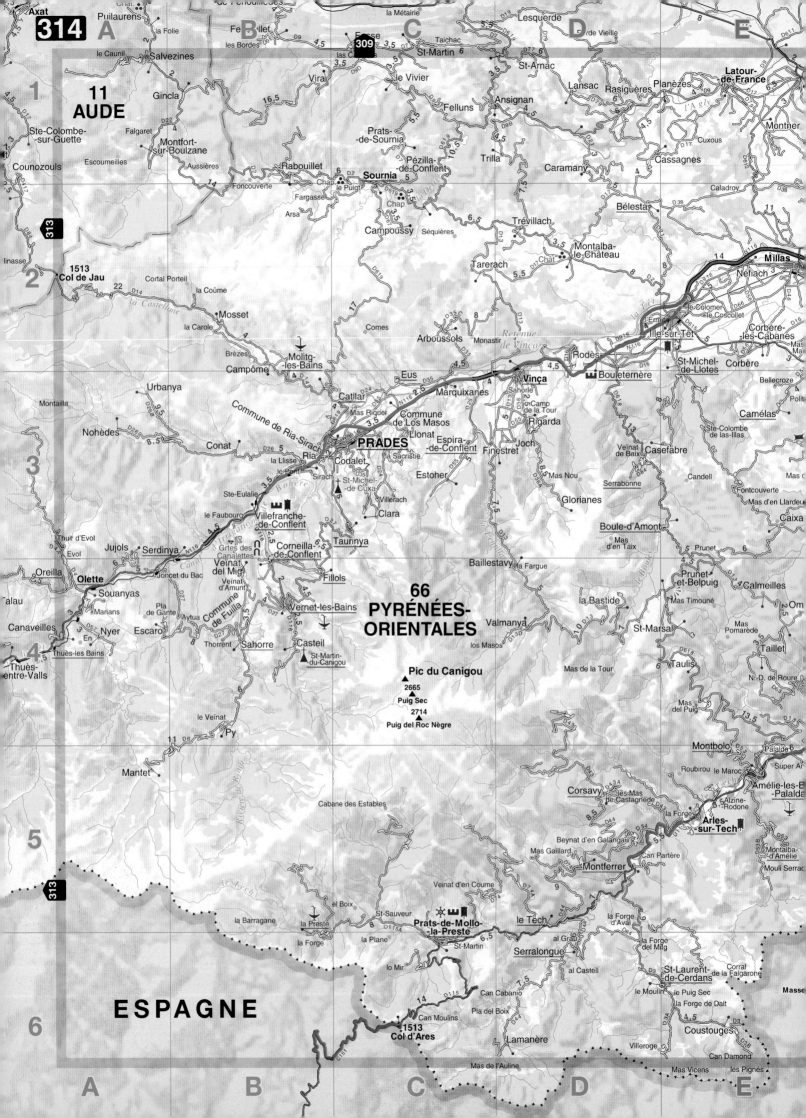

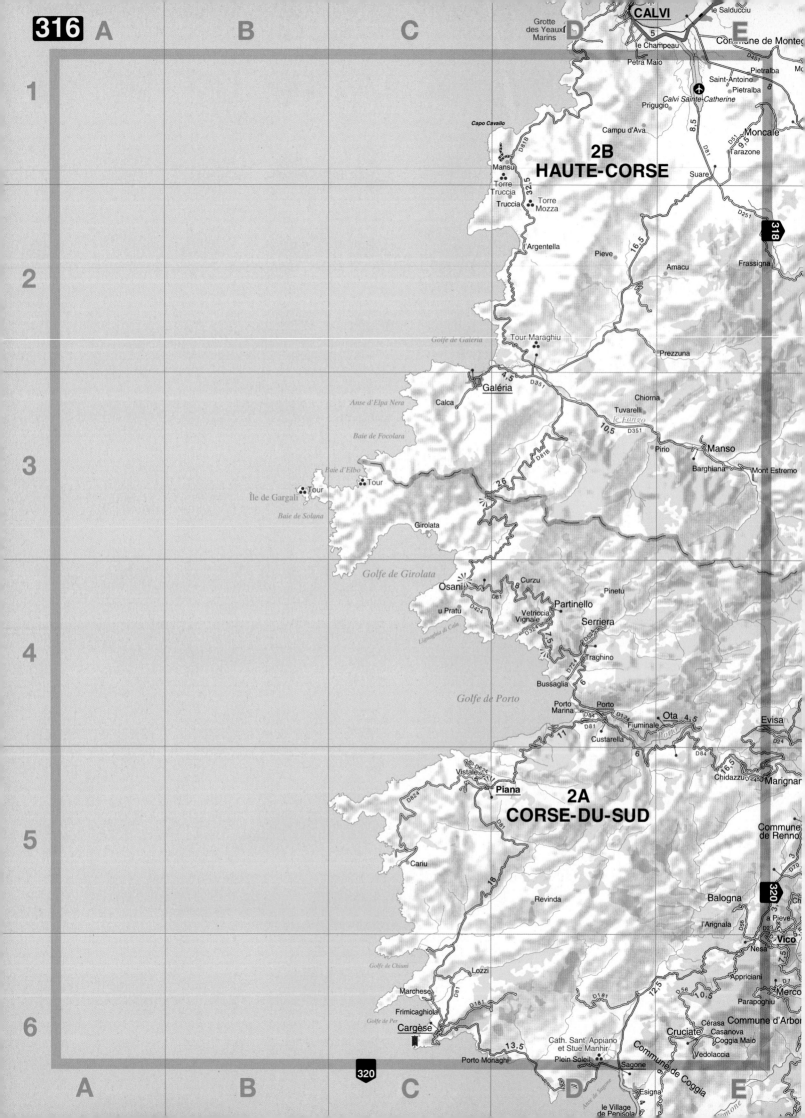

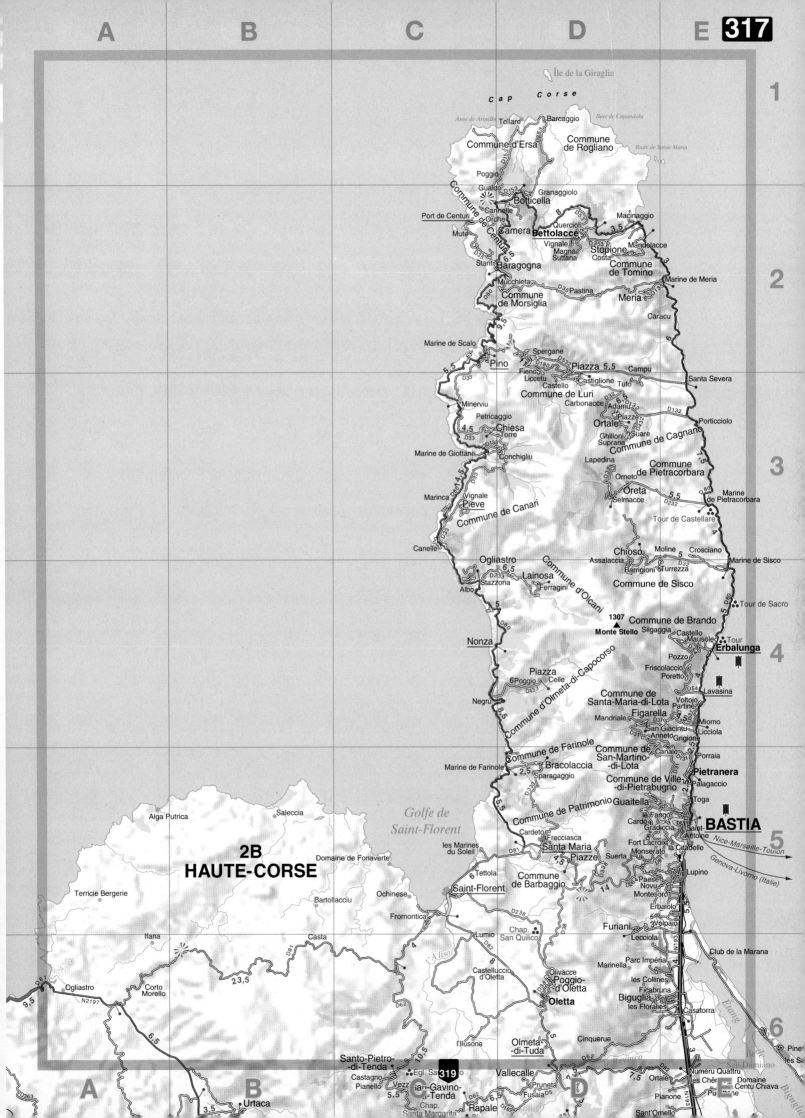

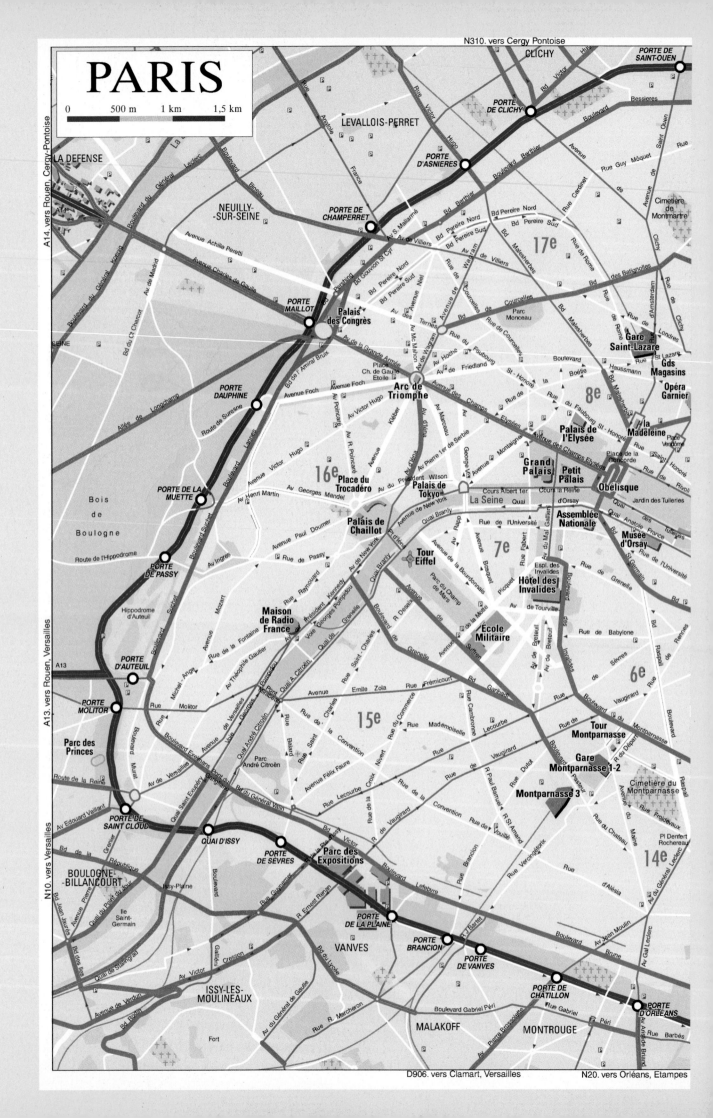

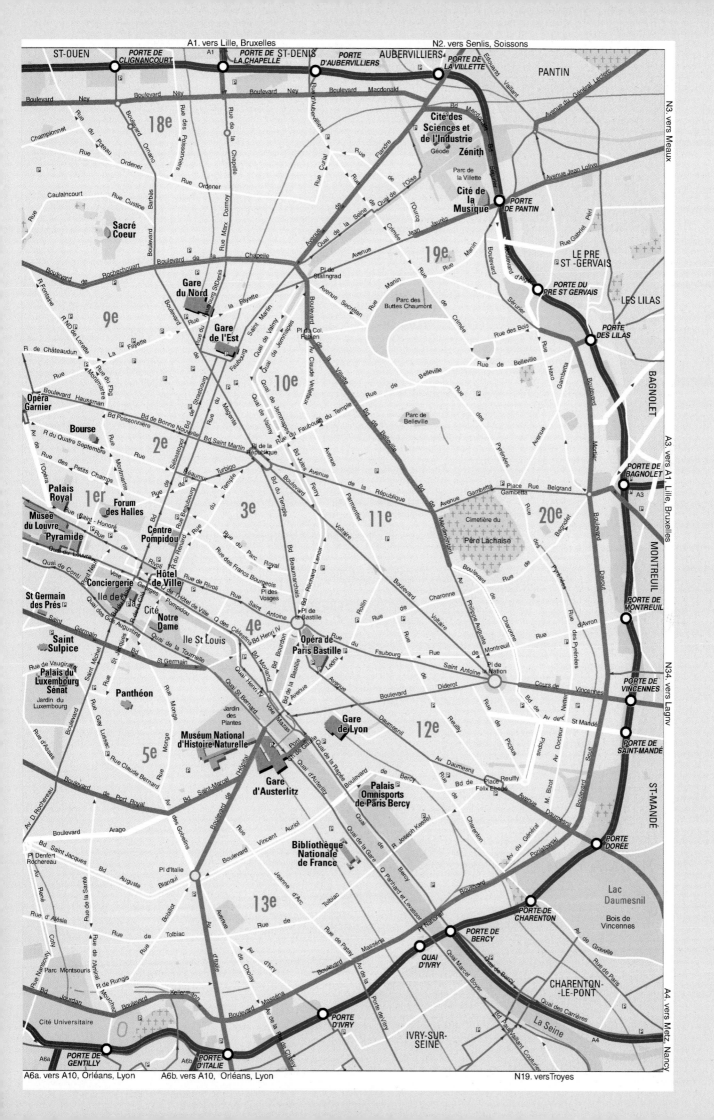

Town plan legend

Légende de plans de ville

Legende: Stadtpläne

 Legenda stadsplattegronden

Leyenda Plano de Ciudad

Legenda Pianta di Città

326

Motorway, toll section
Autoroute, section à péage
Autobahn, gebührenpflichtiger Abschnitt
Snelweg, tol
Autopista de peaje
Autostrada, tratto a pedaggio

Motorway, free section, dual carriageway with motorway characteristics
Autoroute, section libre, voie à caractère autoroutier
Autobahn, gebührenfreier Abschnitt, Schnellverkehrsstraße
Snelweg, vrije sectie, vier baansweg met snelweg karakteristieken
Autovía con dos carriles en cada sentido
Autostrada, tratto senza pedaggio, doppia carreggiata di tipo autostradale

Motorway under construction
Autoroute en construction
Autobahn im Bau
Snelweg onder constructie
Autopista en construcción
Autostrada in construzione

Junction : complete (1), limited (2), number
Échangeur : complet (1), partiel (2), numéro
Vollanschlußstelle (1), beschränkte Anschlußstelle (2), Nummer
Knooppunt, compleet (1), beperkt (2), nummer
Vía de acceso (conexión): completa (1), parcial (2), número
Svincolo: completo (1) parziale (2), numero

Toll gate (1), service area (2)
Barrière de péage (1), aire de service (2)
Mautstelle (1), Tankstelle (2)
Tol slagboom (1), benzinestation (2)
Punto de peaje (1), estación de servicio (2)
Barriera di pedaggio (1), area di servizio (2)

Trunk road
Autre route de liaison principale
Fernverkehrsstraße
Hoofdweg
Carretera nacional
Strada di grande comunicazione

Regional connecting road
Route de liaison régionale
Regionale Verbindungsstraße
Regional verbindingsweg
Carretera regional
Strada di collegamento regionale

Other road
Autre route
Sonstige Straße
Andere weg
Carretera local
Altra strada

Road tunnel
Tunnel
Straßentunnel
Tunnel
Túnel
Galleria

Administrative building (1), church, chapel (2), hospital (3)
Bâtiment administratif (1), église, chapelle (2), hôpital (3)
Verwaltungsgebäude (1); Kirche, Kapelle (2), Krankenhaus (3)
Administratief gebouw (1), kerk, kapel (2), ziekenhuis (3)
Edificio admiistrativo (1), iglesia, capilla (2), hospital (3)
Edificio pubblico (1), chiesa, cappella (2), ospedale (3)

Commune, canton boundary
Limite de commune, de canton
Gemeindegrenze, Kreisgrenze
Gemeente, provincie grens
Limite de municipio, limite de canton
Confine di comune, confine di cantone

Arrondissement, departement boundary
Limite d'arrondissement, de département
Bezirksgrenze, Departementsgrenze
Arrondissement, afdeling grens
Limite de arrondissement, limite de departamento
Confine di arrondissement, confine di dipartimento

Region, state boundary
Limite de région, d'État
Regiongrenze, Staatsgrenze
Streek, staatgrens
Limite de región, límite de estado
Confine di regione, confine di stato

Built-up area, more than 8 ha (1), less than 8 ha (2), industrial park (3)
Zone bâtie, superficie > 8 ha (1), < 8 ha (2), zone industrielle (3)
Geschlossene Bebauung, über 8 ha (1), unter 8 ha (2), Gewerbezone (3)
Bebouwde kom, groter dan 8 ha (1), kleiner dan 8 ha (2), industrie gebied (3)
Zona edificada: más de 8 ha (1), menos de 8 ha (2), polígono industrial (3)
Area edificata, più di 8 ha (1), meno di 8 ha (2), zona industriale (3)

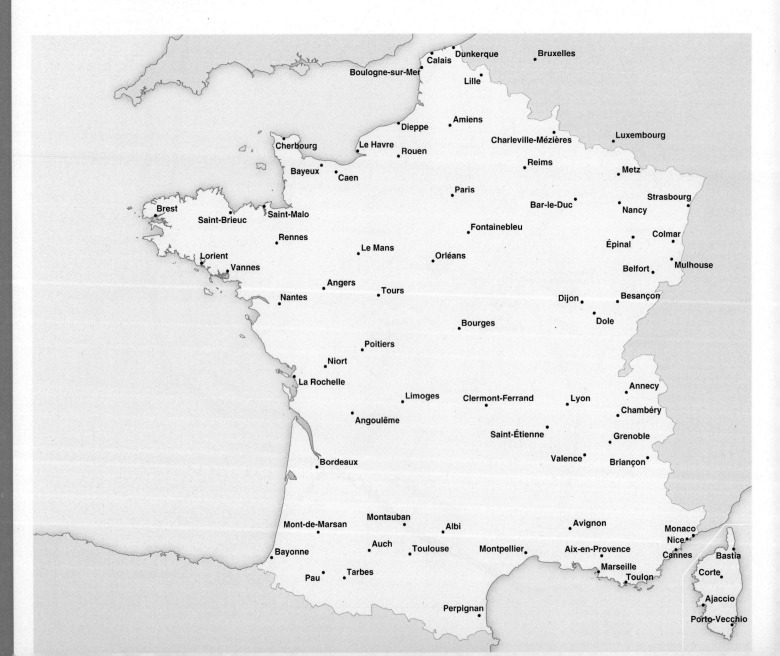

AIX-EN-PROVENCE

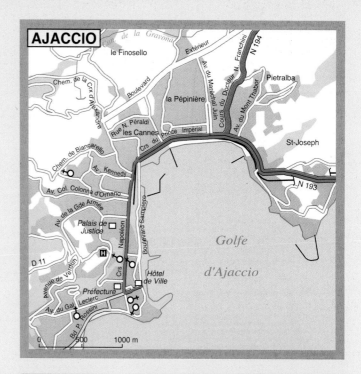

AJACCIO

327

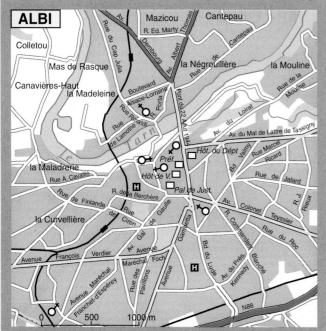

ALBI

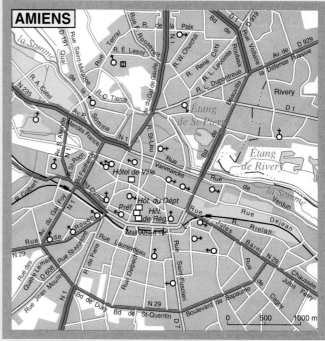

AMIENS

ANGERS

ANGOULÊME

ANNECY

les Carrés

Fier
Boulevard de la Rocade
Avenue du Stade
Avenue de Genève
Avenue de Novel
Avenue du Mont Blanc
Rue du Mont Blanc
Avenue des Carrés
Rue des Écoles
Rue des Mouettes
Av. de la Mavéria
Gambetta
Brogny
Plaine
Av. du Parmelan
Avenue de France
d'Albigny
Avenue de Cran
Bd du Lycée
Pal. de Just.
Préf.
Avenue des Hirondelles
Avenue Bouvard
Rue Carnot
Hôtel de Ville
Grande Rue d'Aléry
Avenue du Rhône
le Thiou
les Marquisats
Fbg des Balmettes
Rue des Marquisats
Av. de Loverchy
D 5
les Balmettes
Bd de la Corniche
N 201
N 508
les Alluèges
Lac d'Annecy

328

0   500   1000 m

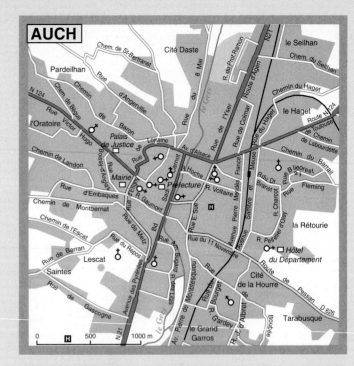

AUCH

le Seilhan
Cité Daste
Chem. de St-Bertraner
Chem. du Seilhan
Pardeilhan
Rue d'Angerville
R. du Prof. Ramon
N 21
Route d'Agen
Chemin du Haget
N 124
Chem. de Bigue
Rue de Baron
le Gers
le Haget
Route N 124
l'Oratoire
Rue Victor Hugo
Boissy d'Anglas
Palais de Justice
Lorraine
Av. d'Alsace
R. de Colmar
Chem. de Toulouse
Chem. de Labourdette
Chemin du Barrail
Chemin de Landon
Mairie
R. d'Etigny
Sadi Carnot
R. Hoche
R. Voltaire
Rue Pierre Mendès France
R. B. Prorest
Rue Fleming
d'Embaques
R. Gaumont
Rue E. Sue
Sambre et Meuse
Bd du Branet
R. Chardot
la Rétourie
Chemin de Montbernat
Rue de Metz
Bd
H
R. Pellieret d'Osby
Cité de la Hourre
Chemin de l'Escat
Rue du Repos
Rue du 11 Novembre
Hôtel du Département
Rue de Barran
Route de Pessan
D 626
Saintes
Lescat
Av. des Pyrénées
R. R. Gardev
Rue de Gascogne
Av. Pierre de Montesquiou
R. d'Albret
Tarabusque
le Gers
N 21
le Grand Garros
Bourdée

0   500   1000 m
H

AVIGNON

Jardin Neuf
N 7
Le Rhône
Pont d'Avignon
N 100
Bd du quai St-Lazare
St-Véran
la Croix Verte
Lyon
N 100
Mie
Rue Carreterie
Bd Limbert
Route de Lyon
Préf.
Avenue de la Folie
Clos de Saint-Jean
Bd St-Roch
Bd St-Michel Boulevard Limbert
Fontcouverte
Route de Montfavet
Saint-Roch
Av. St-Ruf
Avenue Pierre Sémard
les Rotondes
Cité Louis Gros
Avenue de Monclar
Bd de la 1ère DB
Av. de la Trillade
N 7
Monclar
St-Ruf
Av. de Tarascon
Rocade Charles de Gaulle
Rocade Charles de Gaulle
N 570
Clos Saint-Henri
Raymond

0   500   1000 m

BAR-LE-DUC

Côte Ste-Catherine
D 116
H
Rue du Barrois
Voie de Béhonne
N 35
Av. de la Libération
l'Ornain
Rue du Port
Bd des Flandres
Voie Sacrée
D 994
Rue des Fusillés
Bd des Vaux-de-Naves
Faubourg Couchot
St-Mihiel
R. des Foulans
Bd Poincaré
R. Allende
Faubourg Marbot
Chemin de Véel
Préfecture
Av. du Château
la Piscine
Ville Haute
Mairie
Rue
Chem. de Popey
Marne au Rhin
Rue de Véel
Tribunal
Av. du 94e
Ernest-Bradfer
Hinot
Avenue des Tilleuls
Hôtel du Département
R. de Savonnières
R. d'Aulnois
Rue de Phulaut
N 35
D 180
N 35
la Chênaie
Chem. du Fond du Loup
D 132

0   500   1000 m

BASTIA

Ruisseau de Toga
D 80
l'Annonciade
Toga
Route de Petrabugno
le Fango
Bd du Fango
Préfecture
Cardo
Hôtel de Ville
Gradiccia
Bd B. Danesi
Bd A. Gaudin
Fort Lacroix
Palais de Justice
la Citadelle
R. C. Vezzani
Monserato
D 81
N 193

0   500   1000 m

BAYEUX

l'Aure
D 104
D 516
Av. Jacques Prévert
Rue de Lubecke
Route de Vaux-sur-Aure
les Hauts Vents
Chemin de Beauvais
Rue d'Argouges
de la Cotardière
Hameau de la Rivière
Bd d'Eindhoven
N 13
Winston
Rue St-Patrice
Bd du Midi
St-Vigor-le-Grand
Route de Courseulles
D 12
Rue St-Malo
Av. G. Clemenceau
la Croix Rouge
Av. St-Julien
R. St-Loup
Croix Thuy
Churchill
Beau Site
Rue du 6 Juin
Avenue Conseil
R. de la
Hôtel de Ville
Sous-préfecture
St-Jean
R. St-Malo
Rue St-Jean
Rue Laitière
D 5
D 5A
Verdun
H
Bd Fabien Ware
R. St-Loup
Tardif
R. St-Exupère
Rue de Montgomery
D 126
D 96
Bellefontaine
D 36A
St-Loup Hors
Mal Leclerc
Sadi Carnot
Bd
Route de Caen
N 13
D 572
D 572B
Rue de la Résistance
Chemin de
Rue de Tilly
l'Aure
Crémel
D 948

0   500   1000 m

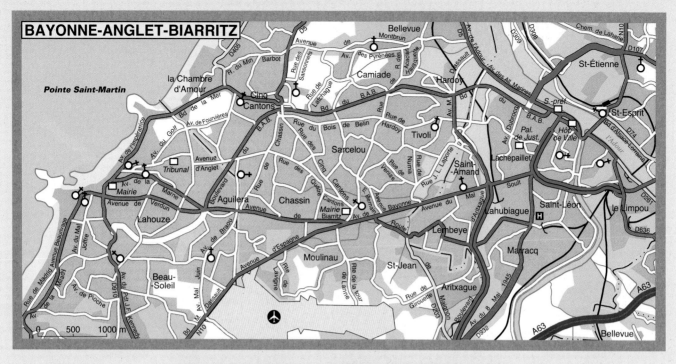

BAYONNE-ANGLET-BIARRITZ

Pointe Saint-Martin

la Chambre d'Amour

Cinq Cantons

Bellevue
Montbrun

Camiade

Hardoy

St-Étienne

S.-préf

St-Esprit

Pal. de Just.

Hôp. de Ville

Lachepaillet

Tribunal

Avenue d'Anglet

Mairie

Aguilera

Chassin

Sarcelou

Tivoli

Saint-Amand

Saint-Léon

le Limpou

Lahubiague

Mairie Biarritz

Lahouze

Lembeye

Matracq

Beau-Soleil

Moulinau

St-Jean

Aritxague

Bellevue

0   500   1000 m

329

Étang des Forges

les Forges

la Miotte

le Mont

Pal. de Just.

Préf.

Hôtel de Ville

Hôt. du Dépt

les Résidences

13

BELFORT

0   500   1000 m

BESANÇON

la Viotte

la Vaite

les Chaprais

Gare

Hôtel de Ville

Palais de Justice

Hôtel de Région
Préfecture

Hôtel du Département

Battant

Brégille

le Doubs

500   1000 m

BÉZIERS

la Croix de la Reille

Croix Poumeyrac

le Rouat

Sous-préfecture

Hôtel de Ville

Palais de Justice

Pech des Moulins

Pech de la Pomme

500   1000 m

BORDEAUX

BOULOGNE-SUR-MER

BRIANÇON

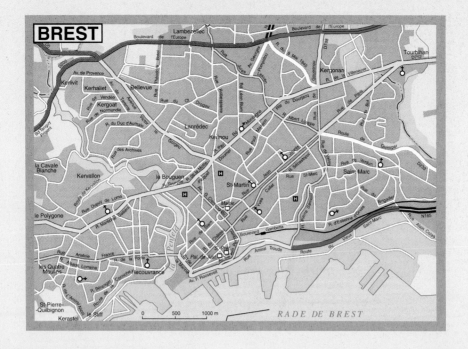

BREST

RADE DE BREST

0 500 1000 m

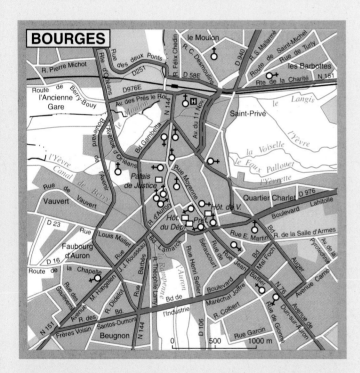

BOURGES

0 500 1000 m

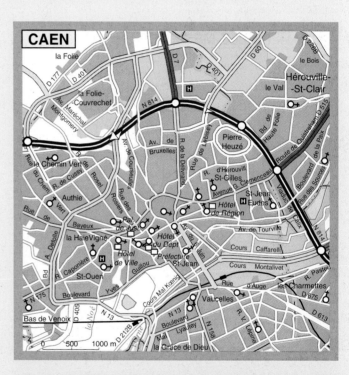

CAEN

0 500 1000 m

CALAIS

0 500 1000 m

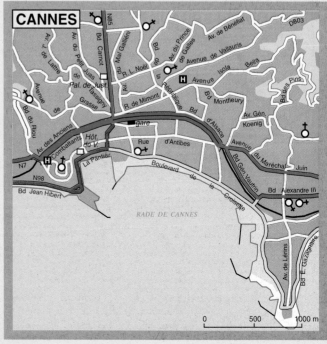

CANNES

RADE DE CANNES

0 500 1000 m

CHÂLONS-EN-CHAMPAGNE

D 1 · Av. Ampère · Av. du 106ème R.I. · Av. Lavoisier · Rue de Bouy · Cdt. Derrien · D 77 · N 44 · Fbg St-Jacques · Faubourg St. · R. C. Jacquiert · Rue du Général Sarrail · Rue du Camp d'Attila · Antoine · N 3 · Av. de Valmy · Avenue de Ste - Menehould · N 3 · Av. du Gal Patton · Cité St-Pierre · Av. de Metz · Palais de Justice · Hôtel de Ville · St-Memmie · Préfecture · Hôtel du Département · R. du Gd Mail · Hôtel de Région · Bd L. Blum · Rue J. Jaurès · Allées · P. Doumer · Avenue · Allées Voltaire · Ch. de Gaulle · Allées · A. Kahn · Allées de Forêts · Rue des Vieilles postes · Rue Jacques Simon · Avenue du Président Roosevelt · N 3 · 0 · 500 · 1000 m · D 77 · N 44

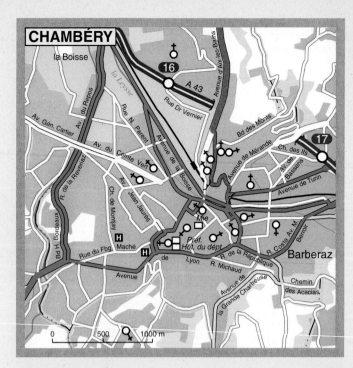

CHAMBÉRY

la Boisse · la Leysse · A 43 · 16 · 17 · Rue Dr Vernier · Avenue d'Aix-les-Bains · Bd des Monts · Av. Gén. Cartier · Av. du Comte Vert · R. N. Parent · Avenue de la Boisse · Avenue de Mérande · Ch. des Ifs · R. de la Revériaz · Av. Jean Jaurès · Av. de Bassens · Avenue de Turin · Ch. de Montjay · Mie · Bd H. Bordeaux · Rue du Fbg · Maché · Préf. · Hôt. du dépt · R. de la République · R. Costa · Av. M. Berloir · Barberaz · de · Lyon · R. Michaud · Avenue · Avenue de la Grande Chartreuse · Chemin des Acacias · 0 · 500 · 1000 m

CHARLEVILLE-MÉZIÈRES

Montcy-Notre-Dame · Avenue Charles Boutet · R. Castrice · Quai Jean Charcot · N 43 · R. de Montjoly · Bd Gambetta · Av. Forest · Rue Forest · Route de St-Laurent · Charles de Gaulle · J. Jaurès · Briand · Av. Cours A · la Meuse · Rue du Bois-en-Val · Avenue de l'Industrie · D 51 · Faubourg St-Julien · Av. Louis Tirman · Préfecture · Palais de Justice · Hôtel de Ville · la Citadelle · Chemin du Mémorial · Rue des Tambours · Rue de Berthaucourt · D 979 · le Theux · D 5 · Av. de St-Julien · Av. des Martyrs · de la Résistance · Rue du Theux · Rue Ambroise Croizat · Quai de l'Esplanade · R. St-Louis · la Meuse · Faubourg de Pierre · Route de Prix · Av. du Pdt V. · Auriol · Av. Carnot · R. du B. Forfant · les Granges Moulues · Mohon · R. Anatole France · les Ronces · N51 R. V. Hugo · N 43 · 0 · 500 · 1000 m

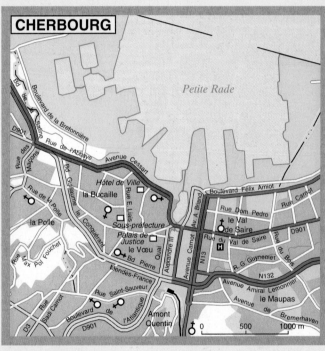

CHERBOURG

Petite Rade · Bd de la Bretonnière · Boulevard de la Bretonnière · Rue de l'Abbaye · Rue Saine · D901 · Avenue Cessart · Rue des Maçons · Rue de la Polle · Hôtel de Ville · la Bucaille · Rue E. Liais · Boulevard Félix Amiot · Rue Dom Pedro · Rue Carnot · Rue du Val de Saire · D901 · la Polle · Rue de la Polle · Rue Guillaume le Conquérant · Palais de Justice · le Vœu · Sous-préfecture · le Val de Saire · Bd Pierre · Alexandre III · R. du Val de Saire · R. G. Guynemer · du Bois · Rue Max Pol Fouchet · Mendès-France · Avenue Carnot · N13 · N132 · D3 · Rue Sadi Carnot · Boulevard de · l'Atlantique · Rue Saint-Sauveur · Avenue Amiral Lemonnier · Avenue de Bremerhaven · le Maupas · Amont Quentin · D901 · 0 · 500 · 1000 m

CLERMONT-FERRAND

Catarou · D 69 · Bd Gordon Ronnett · Rue du Clos Four · Av. Barbier Daubrée · Champfleuri · les Carmes · Avenue de la République · Rue du Ressort · Fontgiève · Bd Lavoisier · Bd J.B. · R. St-Alyre · de Blanzat · Rue · H. Barbusse · Rue Niel · Rue Auger · N 9 · Michelin · R. Fontgiève · R. Monier R. Montlosier · Avenue · Av. d'Italie · France Herbet · Trib. · Hôt. de Ville · Rue Guynemer · Rue de l'Union Soviétique · Anatole · Rue la Pradelle · R. Menat · Av. Carnot · Rue de la Cartoucherie · D 5 · R. Blatin · Hôt. du Dépt · Rue de la Pradelle · Av. Pasteur · Av. Julien · Préf. · Bd Lafayette · Rue Clovis Hugues · l'Oradou · A. Briand · R. Gilbert · Bd Pasteur · Bd Mitterrand · Neuf Soleil · Bd Lafayette · Rue de l'Oradou · R. André Theuriet · J. Jaurès · R. Marx Dormoy · Av. de la Libération · Bd Blum · N 389 · la Raye Dieu · les Ormeaux · R. de Bellevue · Rue des Liondards · R. Berthaud · Bd P. Pochet Lagaye · St-Jacques · N 9 · D 771 · 0 · 500 · 1000 m

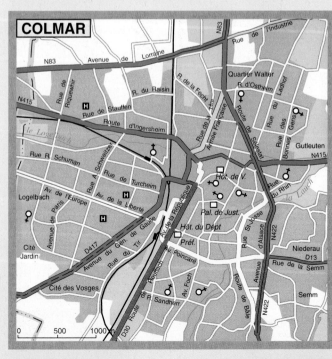

COLMAR

N83 · Rue de l'Industrie · N83 · Avenue de Lorraine · R. de la Fecht · Quartier Walter · R. d'Ostheim · N415 · R. du Raisin · Rue de Riquewihr · Rue de Stauffen · Route d'Ingersheim · Route de Sélestat · R. du Ladhof · le Logelbach · Rue R. Schuman · Rue des Gens · Gutleuten · N415 · Av. de l'Europe · Rue de Turcheim · Hôt. de V. · la Lauch · Logelbach · Av. de la Liberté · R. A. Schweitzer · Pal. de Just. · Cité Jardin · Av. de Paris · Av. du Gén. de Gaulle · Rue du Tir · Hôt. du Dépt · R. St-Josse · N422 · Niederau · D13 · Rue H. Poincaré · Préf. · Rue d'Alsace · Cité des Vosges · Av. de la République · R. de R. Sandherr · Av. Foch · Rue de la Semm · D30 · Route de Bâle · N422 · Semm · D17

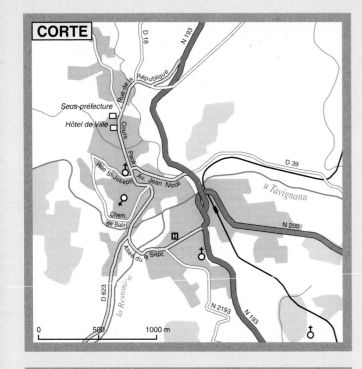

CORTE

Sous-préfecture
Hôtel de Ville

u Tavignanu

la Restonica

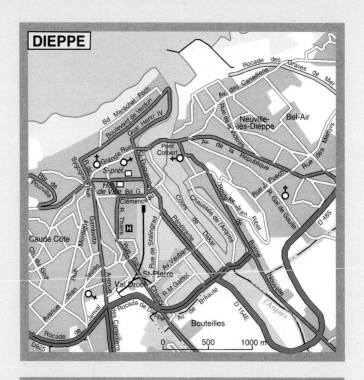

DIEPPE

Rocade des Graves de Mer
Av. des Canadiens
Neuville-lès-Dieppe
Bel-Air
Bd Maréchal Foch
Boulevard de Verdun
Quai Henri IV
Pont Colbert
Grande Rue
S-préf.
Hôtel de Ville
Clémence au
Caude Côte
St-Pierre
Val Druel
Bouteilles
Rocade de Dieppe
Rocade de
l'Arques

333

DIJON

les Génois
Bd Pascal
la Maladière
Bd des Allobroges
Montchapet
Clémenceau
les Perrières
Hôtel de Région
des Marmuzots
Préfecture
Hôtel de Ville
Tribunal
les Bouroches
R. du Transvaal
Fbg St-Pierre
Bd de Strasbourg
Rue de Mirande
Bd de l'Université
les Péjoces

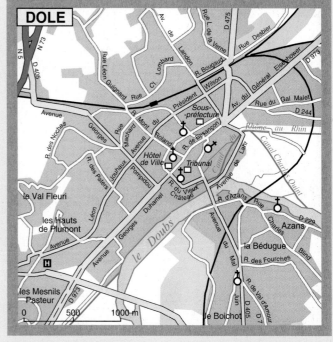

DOLE

Sous-préfecture
Rhône au Rhin
Hôtel de Ville
Tribunal
le Val Fleuri
les Hauts de Plumont
le Doubs
Azans
la Bédugue
les Mesnils Pasteur
le Boichot

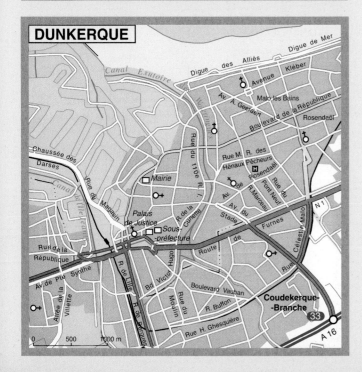

DUNKERQUE

Canal Exutoire
Digue de Mer
Digue des Alliés
Avenue Kléber
Malo-les-Bains
Boulevard de la République
Rosendaël
Chaussée des Darses
Rue M. R. des Hénaux Pêcheurs
Mairie
Palais de Justice
Sous-préfecture
Rue de la République
Coudekerque-Branche
Chantraine

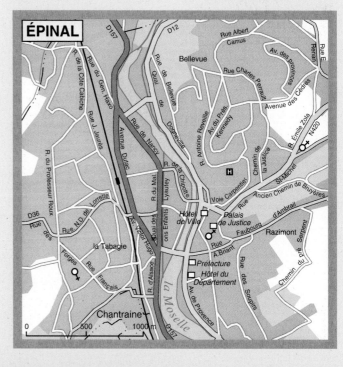

ÉPINAL

Bellevue
la Moselle
Hôtel de Ville
Palais de Justice
Razimont
la Tabagie
Préfecture
Hôtel du Département
Chantraine

FONTAINEBLEAU

N6 · Route de la Bonne Dame · D210 · Route Franklin Roosevelt · Avenue Franklin Roosevelt · Bd du Mal Foch · Boulevard Maréchal Joffre · Rte Louise · Rue Rémy Dumoncel · Viaduc · Avon · la Butte du Montceau · N7 · N6 · Palais de Justice · R. St-Merry · R. Grande · R. Aristide Briand · Hôtel de Ville · D409 · Rue de France · Sous-préfecture · Rue Royale · Bd Magenta · Rue de Constance · Château · Avenue du Rocher d'Avon · Rue Gambetta · D137 · Bd du Mal Juin · R. du Rocher d'Avon · N152 · Rte de Nemours · N7 · D58 · N6

0 · 500 · 1000 m

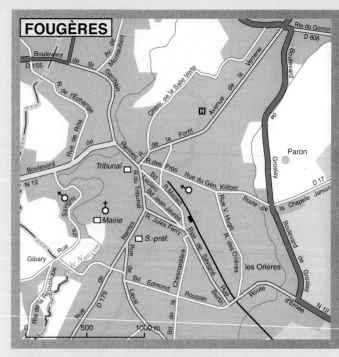

FOUGÈRES

Rte de Gorron · D 806 · Boulevard · de St · Av. de Montauban · Av. de la Verrerie · Boulevard · D 155 · R. de l'Échange · Germain · Chem. de la Salle Verte · Avenue · de la Forêt · 9p · Paron · Rue de Rillé · H · Rennes R. · R. de la Forêt · D 17 · Boulevard · Tribunal · R. des Prés · Rue du Gén. Kléber · Groslay · N 12 · Savigny · R. du Tribunal · Leclerc · R. Mahard · Route · de · la Chapelle Janson · Mairie · Bd Jean Jaurès · R. V. Hugo · R. des Orières · Boulevard · de · Groslay · Gibary · le Nançon · R. Jules Ferry · S.-préf. · Rue de Sévigné · Bertin · les Orières · Rue · de la République · Bd Edmond · Chesnardière · Rue · Rte · d'Ernée · D 179 · de Laval · Roussin · de la · Route · N 12 · Bd

0 · 500 · 1000 m

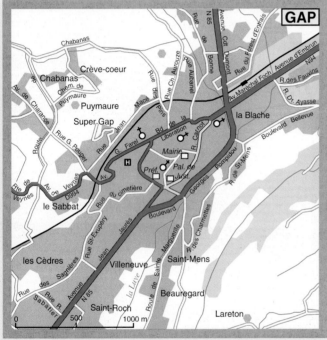

GAP

Chabanas · N 85 · Avenue Cdt Dumont · Rue du Forest d'Entrais · N94 · Avenue d'Embrun · Crève-coeur · de Bonne · Rue Ch. Arrouze · R. des Fauvins · Chabanas · Chem. de · Puymaure · Rue Aubanel · R. Dr. Ayasse · Av. de Charance · Mace · Bd de la · la Blache · Puymaure · Rue des Pins · Liberation · Super Gap · Rue Jean · G. Farel · R. Carnot · Boulevard Bellevue · Route · Rue G. Pouget · Mairie · Georges Pompidou · Rte de · Veynes · Av. de Veynes · Av. du cimetière · Préf. · Pal. de Just. · R. de St-Mens · D994 · Rue · St-Exupéry · Georges · R. des Charmettes · le Sabbat · Boulevard · R. des Charmettes · les Cèdres · Jean · Marguerite · Saint-Mens · Rue des Sagniéres · Villeneuve · la Luye · Route de Sainte · Avenue · Rue R. · N 85 · Beauregard · Saint-Roch · Rue R. Sabatier · Lareton

0 · 500 · 1000 m

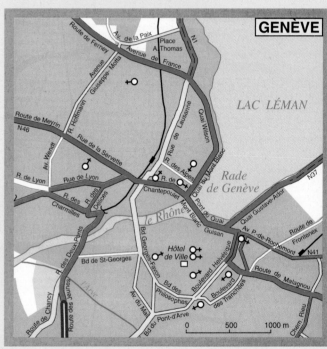

GENÈVE

Route de Ferney · Av. de la Paix · Place A. Thomas · N1 · Avenue de France · Avenue · R. Hoffmann · Giuseppe Motta · Route de Meyrin · Avenue · Quai Wilson · LAC LÉMAN · N46 · Rue de la Servette · Rue de Lausanne · Av. Wendt · R. des Alpes · Rade de Genève · R. de Lyon · Rue de Lyon · R. de · N37 · Chantepoulet · Quai du Mont-Blanc · R. des · Charmilles · Délices · Pont du Mont Blanc · Quai du · Pont de Quai · Quai Gustave-Ador · R. des Deux-Ponts · le Rhône · Guisan · Quai P.-de-Rochemont · Route de · Frontenex · Bd Georges-Favon · Hôtel de Ville · N41 · Bd de St-Georges · R. des Deux-Ponts · Boulevard Helvétique · Route de Malagnou · Route de Chancy · Av. du Mail · Boulevard des · Boulevard · Av. du Pont-d'Arve · Bd du Pont-d'Arve · Philosophes · des Tranchées · Chem. Rieu

0 · 500 · 1000 m

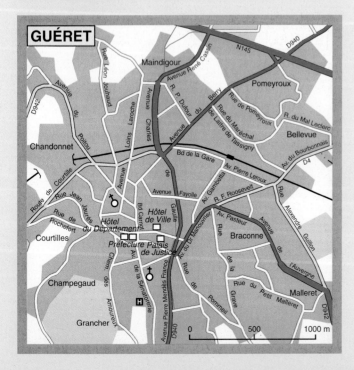

GUÉRET

D940 · Rue Léon Jouhaud · N145 · Maindigour · Avenue René Cassin · D942 · Avenue du Poitou · Avenue · Laroche · R. P. Dufour · Rue de Pomeyroux · Pomeyroux · Charles · Berry · Rue du Maréchal · R. du Mal Leclerc · Chandonnet · Loins · de Lattre de Tassigny · Bellevue · Av. du Bourbonnais · Bd de la Gare · D4 · Avenue Fayolle · Av. Pierre Leroux · Rue · Rue de Courtille · de · Avenue · R. F. Roosevelt · Rue Jean Jaurès · Bd Carnot · Hôtel de Ville · Av. Gambetta · Av. Pasteur · Alexandre Guillon · Route de Courtille · Gaulle · Rue · Braconne · Avenue de l'Auvergne · Courtilles · Hôtel du Département · Rue · Rue du Petit Malleret · Champegaud · Préfecture Palais de Justice · Chem. des · Rue Grand · Malleret · Av. de la Sénatorerie · Rue · Grancher · D940 · D942

0 · 500 · 1000 m

GUINGAMP

Runevarec · D 8 · Boulevard Mendès France · D 787 · le Croaz Hent · Penduo Braz · Av. Pierre Loti · Banval · St-Jean · Rue du Petit Lourdes · Rue de l'Armor · Chemin ar Vran · Goas ar Vran · Maudez · Rue de Saint-Jean · H · Kergoz · S.-Préf. · Av. du Président · Gourlan · Kennedy · Pal. de Just. · R. Pors an · D 9 · Rue du Mal Foch · Hôt. de V. · Quen · la Madeleine · Rue St-Nicolas · R. Saint-Martin · Kerholló · N 12 · Rue de la Madeleine · Bd de la · R. Jules Ferry · Marne · D 54 · Keribaut · Allée du Marquis · le Trieux · Rte de Callac · Croissant · D 767 · Ste-Croix · D 5 · D 712 · Locménard · Rue A. Mazier · D 8 · N 12 · Pont Glaz · D 787 · Ploumagoar · Runiou

0 · 500 · 1000 m

334

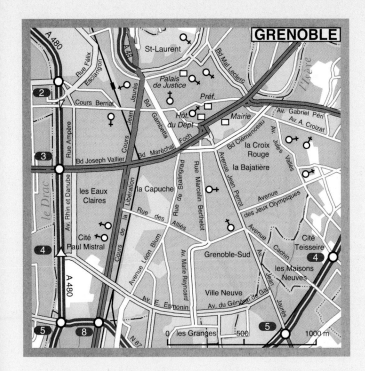

GRENOBLE

St-Laurent

A 480

Rue Félix

Esclangon

Palais de Justice

Bd Mal Leclerc

Cours Berriat

Préf.

Hôtel du Dépt

Mairie

Av. Gabriel Péri

Av. A. Croizat

Bd Clémenceau

la Croix Rouge

Bd Joseph Vallier

Bd Maréchal Foch

la Bajatière

Av. Rhin et Danube

les Eaux Claires

la Capuche

Avenue des Jeux Olympiques

Cité Paul Mistral

Cité Teisseire

Grenoble-Sud

les Maisons Neuves

Ville Neuve

Av. Marie Reynoard

Av. E. Esmonin

Av. du Général de Gaulle

A 480

le Drac

N 87

les Granges

0   500   1000 m

LE HAVRE

Forêt

Bléville

la Mare Rouge

de Montgeon

la Mare au Clerc

Sanvic

329 ème

Hôtel de Ville

S. préf.

Pal. de just.

Bd W. Churchill

N 15

Quai George V

Quai Colbert

l'Eure

Bd Amiral Mouchez

Avenue Lucien Corbeaux

R. Cuvier

0   500   1000 m

335

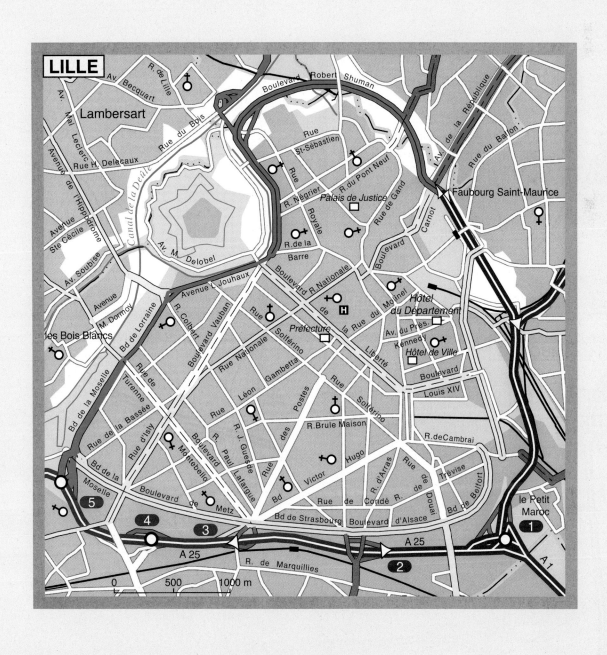

LILLE

Av. Becquart

R. de Lille

Boulevard   Robert Shuman

Lambersart

Rue du Bois

Rue

St-Sébastien

Mal Leclerc

Rue H. Delecaux

R. du Pont Neuf

Faubourg Saint-Maurice

Avenue de l'Hippodrome

R. Négrier

Palais de Justice

Rue de Gand

Canal de la Deûle

Royale

Av. Ste Cécile

R. de la Barre

Av. M. Delobel

Avenue L. Jouhaux

Av. Soubise

Boulevard R. Nationale

Avenue

M. Dormoy

R. Colbert

Rue

de

Hôtel du Département

les Bois Blancs

Bd de Lorraine

Boulevard Vauban

H

Préfecture

Hôtel de Ville

Bd de la Moselle

Rue Nationale

Soltérino

Av. du Prés. Kennedy

Louis XIV

Rue de

Turenne

Léon

Gambetta

Boulevard

Rue de la Bassée

Rue

Rue

des

Rue

Soltérino

R. de Cambrai

Rue d'Isly

Montebello

R. J. Guesde

R. Brule Maison

Boulevard

R. Paul Lafargue

postes

Victor

Hugo

Rue

de

Trévise

Moselle

Boulevard   de   Metz

Bd

R. d'Arras

Rue

de

Douai

Bd de Belfort

le Petit Maroc

Bd de Strasbourg   Boulevard   d'Alsace

A 25

R. de Marquillies

A 25

A 1

0   500   1000 m

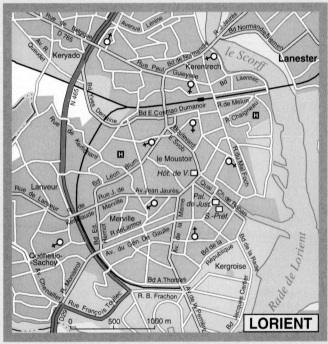

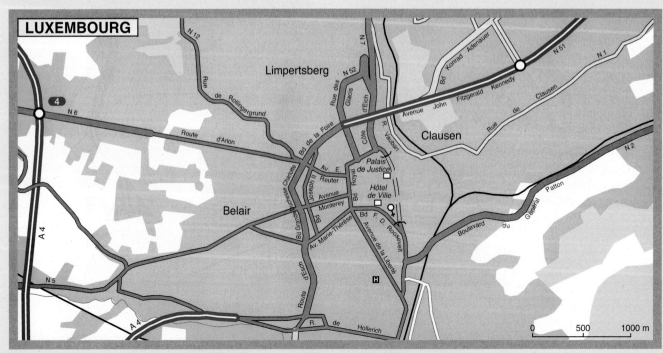

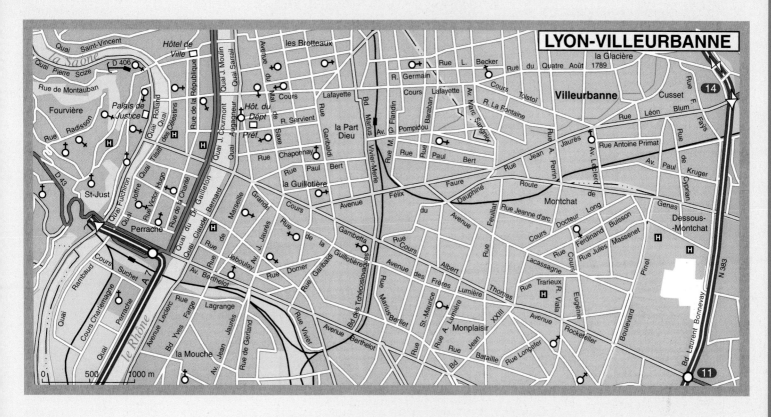

LYON-VILLEURBANNE

Quai Saint-Vincent
Quai Pierre Scize
la Saône
Hôtel de Ville
les Brotteaux
R. L. Becker
la Glacière
Cours du Quatre Août 1789
Villeurbanne
Cusset
14
D 406
Rue de Montauban
Fourvière
Palais de Justice
Rue Radisson
St-Just
D 43
Quai Fulchiron
Perrache
Quai Victor Hugo
Quai Joffre
Quai Tilsitt des Célestins
Rue de la République
Quai J. Courmont
Quai Augagneur
Hôt. du Dépt
Préf.
Cours
R. Servient
Rue de Saxe
Chaponnay
Rue Garibaldi
Lafayette
Bd Marius
la Part Dieu
Cours
Lafayette
Av. Marc Sangnier
R. Germain
Cours
Bd
R. La Fontaine
Av. G. Flandin
Av. Pompidou
Rue G. Flandin
Rue Bossuet
Rue Baraban
Cours Tolstoï
Rue Léon Blum
Jaurès
Av. Leclerc
Rue Antoine Primat
Av. Paul Kruger
Av. Cyprian
Genas
N 383
Bd Laurent Bonnevay
337

MARSEILLE
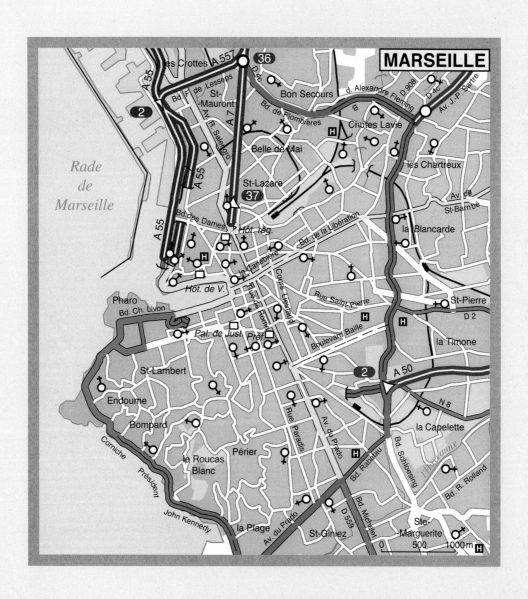

les Crottes
A 557
36
A 55
2
Bd F. de Lesseps
St-Mauront
A 7
Bon Secours
d. Alexandre Fleming
Av. J.-P. Sartre
Bd de Plombières
Chutes Lavie
Rade de Marseille
Av. R. Salengro
Belle de Mai
les Chartreux
A 55
St-Lazare
37
Av. de St-Barnbé
Bd des Dames
Hôt. rég.
la Blancarde
Hôt. de V.
La Canebière
Bd de la Libération
Cours Lieutaud
Pharo
Bd Ch. Livon
Pal. de Just.
Préf.
Rue Saint Pierre
St-Pierre
D 2
St-Lambert
Boulevard Baille
la Timone
Endoume
2
A 50
Bompard
N 8
la Capelette
Corniche
Périer
Rue Paradis
Av. du Prado
Bd Schloesing
le Roucas Blanc
Président
John Kennedy
la Plage
St-Giniez
Av. du Prado
D 55a
Bd Michelet
Bd R. Rolland
Ste-Marguerite

0   500   1000 m

MELUN

N6 · N105 · D414 · Av. Général Patton · Av. G. Pompidou · R. Pajot · R. E. Leclerc · R. J. Oudot · Av. du Gén. de Gaulle · Av. de Meaux · Rue des Trois Moulins · Trois Moulins · Av. de Corbeil · N6 · St-Barthélémy · Hôt. du Dépt · Préfecture · Palais de Justice · Hôtel de Ville · St-Liesne · R. de Vaux · D416 · Av. des Courtilleraies · Rue St-Liesne · D39 · les Fourneaux · la Seine · Quai H. Rossignol · Gabelle · R. de la Courtille · Promenade de Vaux · St Ambroise · Rue · Dajot · Quai Maréchal Joffre · Av. de la Libération · N6 · D39 · Rue Albert-Moreau · N372 · 0 500 1000 m

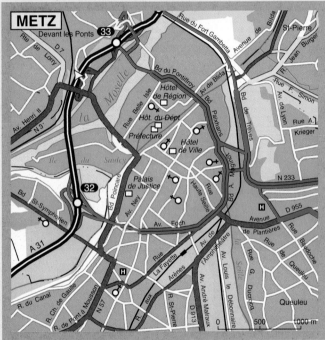

METZ

Rte de Lorry · D 7 · Devant les Ponts · **33** · Rue du Fort Gambetta · Avenue de Blida · St-Pierre · Rue Jean Burger · Av. Henri II · N 3 · Moselle · Bd du Pontiffroy · Av. de Blida · Bd · Bd de Trèves · Rue F. Simon · Hôtel de Région · R. Belle Isle · Rue Paixhans · Av. de Lyon · Rue A. · Hôt. du Dépt · Préfecture · Hôtel de Ville · Krieger · la · Ile du Saulcy · **32** · Palais de Justice · Bd Poincaré · Rue · Haute Seille · N 233 · Bd · St-Symphorien · Av. Ney · N 57 · R. du Pont à Mousson · Av. Foch · Avenue · D 955 · A 31 · R. du Canal · R. Ch. de Gaulle · N 57 · La Fayette · Arènes · de Plantières · Rue · Baldoche · Rue G. Ducrocq · Queuleu · R. aux Arènes · l'Amphithéâtre · Av. Louis le Débonnaire · Av. André Malraux · D 913 · R. St-Pierre · 0 500 1000 m

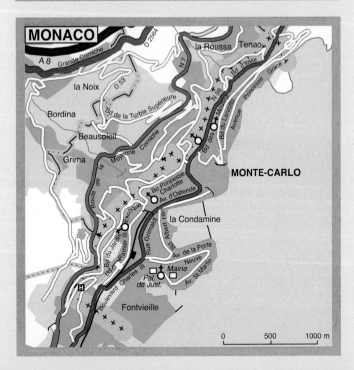

MONACO

A 8 · Grande Corniche · D 2564 · la Roussa · Tenao · N 7 · la Noix · D 53 · Bd de la Turbie Supérieure · Bd d'Italie · Grâce · Bordina · Moyenne Corniche · Bd de la · Beausoleil · Princesse Charlotte · Grima · Route de la · Bd du Jardin Exotique · Bd Princesse Charlotte · Av. d'Ostende · **MONTE-CARLO** · Rainier III · Bd Charles III · Mairie · Av. St. Martin · la Condamine · Pal. de Just. · Av. de la Porte Neuve · Albert 1er · Av. Grimaldi · Fontvieille · 0 500 1000 m

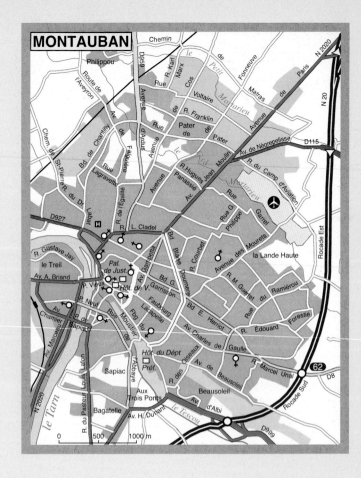

MONTAUBAN

Chemin · D959 · D 20 · le Petit · N 2020 · Philippou · Route de l'Aveyron · R. Marx · Cos · Voltaire · Montariou · Fonneuve · Matras · Paris · N 20 · Chem. de St-Pierre · R. du Dr. Lebat · Rue · Avenue · Voltaire · Rue · R. Franklin · Pater · de · Pater · Avenue · Av. de Négrepelisse · D115 · Chantilly · Bd · R. de l'Égalité · Rue · Lagravette · R. Hugues Jean · Rue · Rue G. · Philippe · Garrel · Av. de · Camp d'Aviation · D 927 · R. Gustave Jay · Pal. de Just. · R. L. Cladel · Bd Blaise Doumerc · Avenue des Mourets · la Lande Haute · Rocade Est · le Treil · Av. A. Briand · Hôt. de V. · Bd G. · R. M. Guétel · R. du Ramiérou · P. Vieux · Garrisson · Bd E. Herriol · R. Neuve · Faubourg Lacapelle · Av. Charles de · R. Édouard · Forestié · Chamier · R. de · Rue Moustier · Av. Charles de Gaulle · N 2020 · le Tarn · Hôt. du Dépt · Préf. · Av. des Oiseaux · Av. de Beausoleil · R. Marcel Unal · **62** · Sapiac · R. de l'Abbaye · D8 · Aux Trois Ponts · Beausoleil · D999 · Bagatelle · Av. H. Dunant · le Tescou · Av. d'Albi · Rocade Sud · R. du Pasteur Louis Laton · 0 500 1000 m

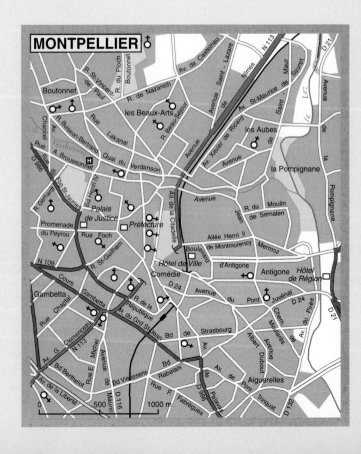

MONTPELLIER

N 113 · D 21 · Boutonnet · R. St-Vincent de Paul · R. du Ploch · Boutonnet · Av. de Castelnau · Nimes · St-Maure · Maur · Av. Saint Lazare · D 21 · R. de Nazareth · Rue · les Beaux-Arts · Av. St-Maurice · Av. Saint-Seriol · les Aubes · R. Buisson-Bertrand · Lakanal · R. Beau-Séjour · Chapel · A. Broussonnet · Quai du · Verdanson · Av. Xavier de Ricard · la Pompignane · Rue · R. de Bp St-Jaumes · Bd Henri · Palais de Justice · Préfecture · R. du Moulin de Semalen · Pompignane · Promenade du Peyrou · Rue Foch · Allée Henri II · N 109 · R. St-Guilhem · Boulevard de Montmorency · Mermoz · Hôtel de Ville · d'Antigone · Antigone · Hôtel de Région · Gambetta · Cours · Gambetta · R. de la · République · Comédie · D 24 · Avenue du Pont Juvénal · D 24 · N 113 · R. du Grd St-Jean · Bd de · Strasbourg · D 21 · Av. G. · Clemenceau · Rue Michel · Bd Rabelais · Av. Albert Dubout · Av. du Pirée · D 116 · Av. de la Liberté · Bd Berthelot · Rue F. Fabrèques · D 986 · D 132 · Aiguerelles · Trinquat · 0 500 1000 m

MONT-DE-MARSAN

la Sablière · D932 · Av. de Sabres · Av. du Colonel · KW Rozanoff · Avenue de Nonères · Nonères · Rue du Péglé · Av. Henri Farbos · Avenue du Maréchal Foch · Boulevard Saint-Médard · St-Jean d'Août · Pal. de Just. · Préf. · Avenue du · Av. P. de Coubertin · Chemin · de · Thore · Hôt. du Dépt · Avenue · Cronstadt · la Midouze · Hôt. de Ville · le Midou · Ducom · D1 · Quai · clauy · Éloi · d'Aingsès · Avenue · R. de la Croix Blanche · Av. des Martyrs de la Résistance · Bd de la République · R. P. Lisse · Av. G. Clémenceau · Boulevard · Bd de Majourau · Lamoustey · Bd Brémontier · Saint-Sever · Régiment d'Infanterie · Président · John Fitzgerald · Avenue du Houga · D30 · Biarnès · D933S · Avenue · Bd d'Aquitaine · D624 · Rue des Saules · le Pouy · Kennedy

0 · 500 · 1000 m

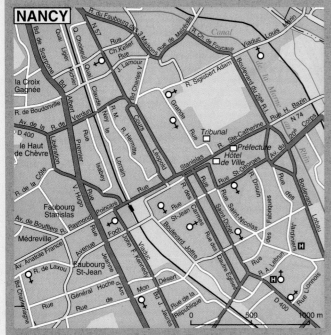

NANCY

R. du Faubourg des 3 Maisons · N 57 · R. Ch. de Foucault · Canal · Viaduc Louis · Marin · Bd de Scarpone · Quai Claude · O. Choiseul · Ch Keller · Rue · R. de Metz · R. Sigisbert Adam · Boulevard du 26e R.I. · la Croix Gagnée · Fichet · Albert · J. Lamour · Grande · Rue H. Bazin · N 74 · R. de Boudonville · Verdun · Claude · Ney · R. M. · Ste-Catherine · 20e Corps · Av. de la · R. de la Libération · Tribunal · D 400 · le Haut de Chèvre · R. Hermite · Léopold · Préfecture · Stanislas · Hôtel de Ville · Lorrain · Isabey · R. Doven · R. de la Côte · V. Hugo · Premier · Rue · R. des · Rue Saint-Georges · Boulevard Lobau · Faubourg Stanislas · Poincaré · Raymond · Rue St-Jean Carmes · Saint-Nicolas · Rue des Quatre Églises · Jardiniers · Av. de Boufflers · Foch · R. des · Médreville · John F. Kennedy · Viaduc · Mon · Désert · R. A. Lebrun · Av. Anatole France · Avenue · Jeanne d'Arc · Bd J. Jaurès · Rue Lionnois · Faubourg St-Jean · H · Bd Champagne · Général · Hoche · Rue de la · R. de Laxou · Rue · République · D 400

0 · 500 · 1000 m

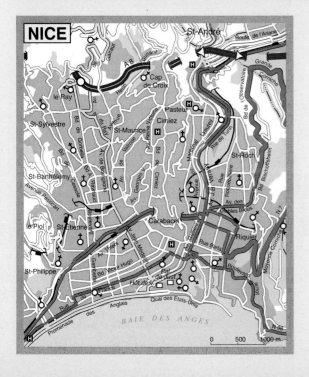

NICE

St-André · Route de l'Ariane · A 8 · Gairaut · Cap de Croix · Grande Corniche · le Ray · Pasteur · Bd de l'Observatoire · St-Sylvestre · Cimiez · St-Maurice · Rte de Turin · St-Roch · St-Barthélemy · Bd de Cimiez · Bd · Bischoffsheim · Av. des Diables Bleus · le Piol · Carabacel · N.7 · St-Étienne · Riquier · St-Philippe · Rue Barla · Pal. de Just. · Hôt. de Ville · Gambetta · Bd Victor Hugo · Moyenne Corniche · Promenade · des · Anglais · Quai des États-Unis · N 98 · BAIE DES ANGES

0 · 500 · 1000 m

MULHOUSE

A36 · Rue · D430 · D39 · Rue de Metzau · Colmar · Avenue · Rue Lefebvre · Katz · Av. A. Juin · Rue · Napoléon · N66 · Rue J. Hofer · D66 · Neppert · Rue Vauban · Rue · Lavoisier · Rue · Rue d'Illzach · Allée · Rue · de · Bâle · Rue Franklin · Rue · D56.5 · Rue de Rastatt · N66 · Franklin · S. Préf. · Kennedy · Rhône · Avenue de Riedisheim · Avenue A. · Bd de la · Mairie · Briand · Marne · Canal du Rhône · Bd A. Wallach · Bd de Zimmersheim · D56 · Bd Charles Stoessel · DB52 · R. Bd. de la Montagne · D432 · le Gambetta · Allée des Écureuils · D21 · H · Bd · de · la Montagne · D1

0 · 500 · 1000 m

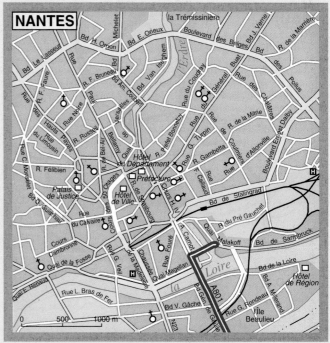

NANTES

la Trémissinière · Bd H. Orion · Michelet · Boulevard des Belges · Bd J. Verne · R. de la Matière · Bd E. Orieux · l'Erdre · Bd · Bd Le Lasseur · Rue · Van Iseghem · Rue · Poilus · Rue R. F. Bruneau · Paul · Rue du Coudrai · Rue · des Cadrates · Rue Nère · Bellamy · Rue du Général · Rue · d'Allonville · Hauts Pavés · R. Russeil · Rue · Rue G. Turpin · Rue P. Gambetta · Boulevard Ernest Dalby · du Limousin · Hôtel du Département · Rue · R. Félibien · Bd Bellamy · Préfecture · H · R. de la Mitrie · Palais de Justice · Hôtel de Ville · F. Cailaud · Bd de Stalingrad · Cours des Orages · Cours H. IV · R. du Pré Gauchet · Bd du Calvaire · Rue · Malakoff · Bd de Sarrebruck · Cours Cambronne · A801 · Quai de la Fosse · Rue Fouré · Quai Magellan · la Loire · Bd de la Loire · Quai E. Renard · Rue L. Bras de Fer · Quai de Gaulle · Hôtel de Région · Bd V. Gâche · Bd G. Hondeau · N23 · Ville Beaulieu

0 · 500 · 1000 m

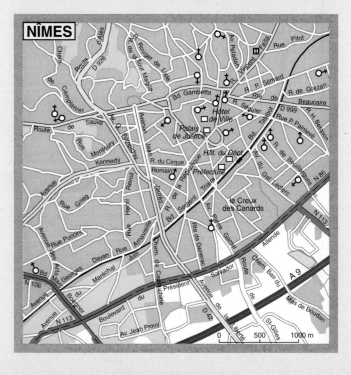

NÎMES

Allées · Av. Peladan · Rue Pitot · R. Rouget de l'Isle · Chem · D 926 · Route · Rue Sémard · R. de Grezan · Campanier · Bd Gambetta · Rté · Beaucaire · R. H. Bazan · Route · de Sauve · Hôtel de Ville · Rue Séguier · D 999 · Rue P. Painlevé · Palais de Justice · Monteury · Jean · Tala · bot · R. de Bouillargues · Av. du Gal Leclerc · R. du Cirque · N 86 · Kennedy · Romain · Hôt. du Dépt · Rue Grieg · Préfecture · le Creux des Canards · Avenue · Rue Puccini · Henri · Rté de Générac · Chem. Bas de Grézan · Rue · Revoil · N 106 · Bd · Mal. Georges · Maréchal · Président · Avenue · de · N 113 · Av. Jean Prouy · Boulevard · de · A 9 · Rue du Mas de Boudan · St-Gilles · D 42 · Allende

0 · 500 · 1000 m

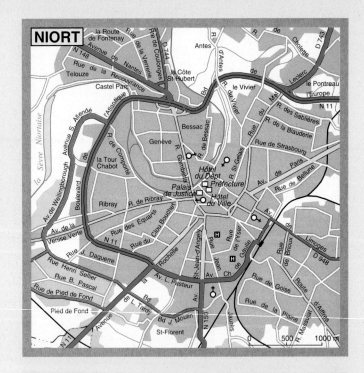

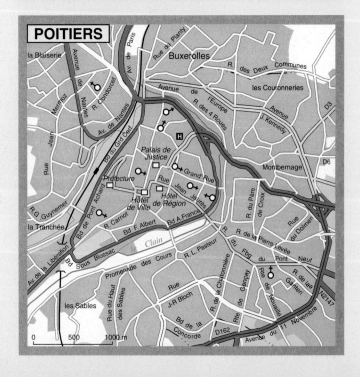

REIMS

R. St-Thierry · Av. de · R. É. Zola · D366 · N44 · L. Faucher · Rue · Rue de la Malatraie · R. de Sébastopol · N 51 · Gosset · R. de Châtel · Rue du Champ de Mars · Bd Janin · R. Jacquart · R. de Savoye · Jean · Jaurès · Bd · Dauphinot · Cernay · D 380 · Hôt. de V. · Rue Cérès · Bd Foch · Rue · Lundy · Bd Joffre · Bd Leclerc · S.-préf. · Rue · G. Laurent · Rue · de Venise · Av.G.Clémenceau · Av. de l'Iser · Pal. de Just. · 23 · R. d.uard · Rue de · R. du Barbâtre · Boulevard · R. Lanson · 24 · Bd du Ples Wilson · Fbg Ste-Anne · Diancourt · Av. du Gén. Giraud · Av. Henri Farman · N44 · 0 · 500 · 1000 m

RENNES

N137 · d'Armorique · Patton · Maurepas · Beauregard · Préfecture · Boulevard · Canal d'Ille et Rance · Av. du Gén. · Av. de Rochester · Saint-Martin · Avenue · d'Ile-de-France · Bd Volney · Bd de Metz · Av. de Fougères · Villejean · H · Rue · Rue de Verdun · Bd de la Duch · Anne · N 12 · Rue de Brest · Boulevard · Bd du Mal de Lattre de Tassigny · R. St-Martin d'Antrain · Sévigné-Fougères · J. Guéhenno · Sévigné · N 157 · la Vilaine · Rue Guilloux · Pal. de Just. · Hôt. de Rég. · Rue · de · Paris · Avenue · Aristide · Briand · N 112 · Avenue du Mail · Hôt. de V. · Avenue · Sergent · Maginot · la Vilaine · N24 · Quai · de la Prévalaye · Bd de la · Liberté · Rue · Saint-Hélier · Bd · Voltaire · Rue · de Redon · Bd du colombier · Bd Solférino · Bd · de Guines · Beaumont · Bd J. Cartier · D 463 · 0 · 500 · 1000 m · Sainte-Thérèse Quineleu · N 157 · D 163

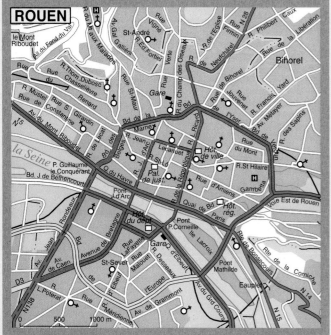

ROUEN

Av.Gal Galliéni · Rue Vigne · R. de l'Église · R. Philbert · R. de la Libération · Caux · le Mont Riboudet · Ald du Fond du Val · St-André · R. Ed Fortier · Firmin · N 28 · Gare · R. du Champ des Oiseaux · Verte · Rue de Bihorel · Bihorel · R. Thon. Dubosc · Chasselière · Rue St-Maur · R. de Neufchâtel · R. François · Yard · R. Muster · Rue du · Renard · Bd de la · Rue · Jouvenet · Av. Métayer · R. des Sapins · Rue S. Girardin · de l'Yser · Rue de Constantine · N 5 · Av. du Mont Riboudet · Bd de l'ecat · Marne · Hôt. de ville · Rue du Mont · la Seine · Borges · R. Jean · R. St-Lô · Ledanuet · R. St Hilaire · P. Guillaume le Conquérant · Pal. de just. · R. de la République · Rue d'Amiens · Gambetta · Bd. J de Béthencourt · Pont J. d'Arc · Q. du Havre · Hôt. rég. · Rondeaux · Pont P. Corneille · Île Lacroix · Voie Est de Rouen · Hôt. du dept · Quai de Paris · Av. Jean · Bd · Avenue de Bretagne · Gare d'Eibeuf · Pont Mathilde · Rue de Boiscours · Rte de la Corniche · Av. de Caen · Rue LaFayette · Matoure · Pont P. Desseaux · Eauplet · D3 · St-Sever · Fenbell · de · l'Europe · Av. du Grd Cours · N 14 · L. Polerat · Rue · R. Méridienne · Av. de Grammont · N 15 · N139 · 0 · 500 · 1000 m

SAINT-ÉTIENNE

le Marais · Bd G. Pompidou · Méons · 15 · Rue St-Simon · R. Bergson · le Soleil · A72 · Chavassieux · Montaud · J. Janin · R. de la Talaudière · le Monteil · Rue É. · Crêt de Roch · Rue du Montat · Zola · R. Palluat de Besset · Préf. · Hôt. de Ville · Rue de la · d'Espèrey · Pal. de Just. · St-François · R. de la Richelandière · Monthieu · Michon · Crs V. Hugo · la Dame Blanche · 20p · R. E. Deschanel · Villebœuf · Bd de la Palle · Rue · R. de Tardy · Rue de la Convention · R. A. Durafd · Rue de Boulingault · la Marandinière · le Devey · Florent · Montmartre · R. du 11 Novembre · 21p · Bd Dr Raoul Duval · la Cotonne · R. de Rochetaillée · R. Virgile · D201 · Rue · R. Buffon · le Portail Rouge · la Béraudière · le Mont · R. G. Péri · 23p · 0 · 500 · 1000 m

SAINT-BRIEUC

le Légué · St-Jouan · Bd Harel de la Noë · Bd de la Mer · Rue T. Ribot · Rue du Légué · St-Michel · Rue de la Corderie · Fres La G. · R. des · Bd Sévigné · N 12 · Ginglin · la Ville Hellio · Préf. · Hôt. de V. · Pal. de Just. · Rue Bagot · Bd de Brest · R. du 71ème · R. de la Gaudière · Bd Laennec · Quinté · R. Rég. d'Infant · Av. Corneille · Bd Charner · Bd · W. Rousseau · Rue A. France · Rue Luzel · Bd Carnot · J. Rue · Hoche · Rue Paul Bert · Rue Henri · Rue Marcel Planiol · D45 · le Carpont · les Villes Moisans · Rue des Villes Moisans · D 712 · Rue de Trégueux · Douvenant · D 700 · D 27 · D 1 · Tréfois · 0 · 500 · 1000 m · St-Rivily · Trégueux

SAINT-MALO

D 155 · Pasteur · Avenue · Chaussée du Sillon · Bd Th. Botrel · Av. du 47ème R.I. · Boulevard Gambetta · Hôt. de V. · Pal. de Just. · S.-Préf. · Avenue Louis Martin · Bd de la République · Av. de Moka · Avenue Aristide Briand · Quai St-Louis · Chaussée des Corsaires · Rue J.P. · Quai du Naye · Quai de Trichet · les Bas Sablons · Avenue de Marville · Avenue de Gaulle · Rue P. de Coubertin · Rive P. de Coubertin · N 137 · Rue de Triqueville · des Antilles · la Cité · Rue de la Cité · Rue Ville · Rue de la Motte · la Découverte · Saint-Servan-sur-Mer · Rue Jugan · Rue de la Nation · Bd Léonce · Demalivilain · Pointe des Corbières · Rue Jugan · Rue Pépin · les Corbières · la Giclais · Pointe de la Vicomté · 0 · 500 · 1000 m · le Rosais · N 137

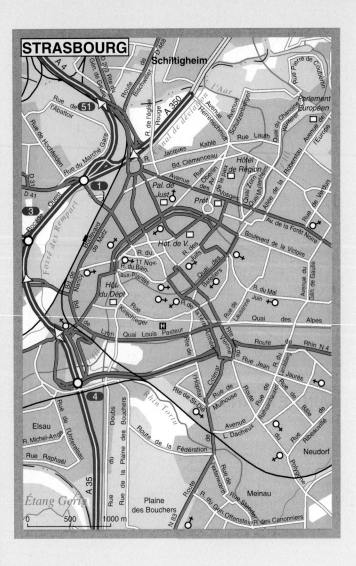

342

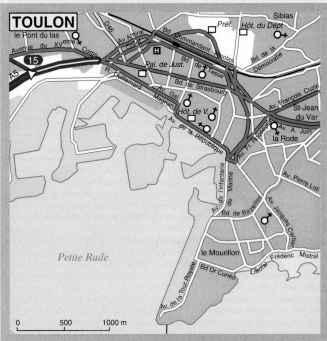

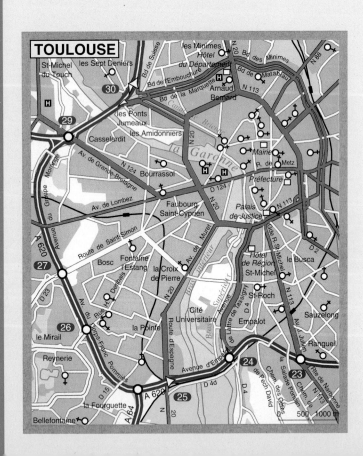

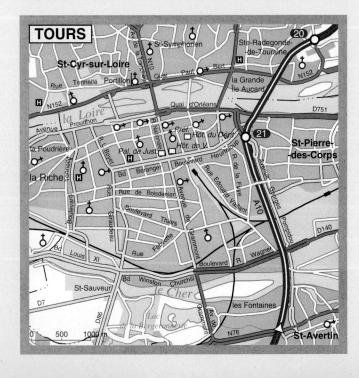

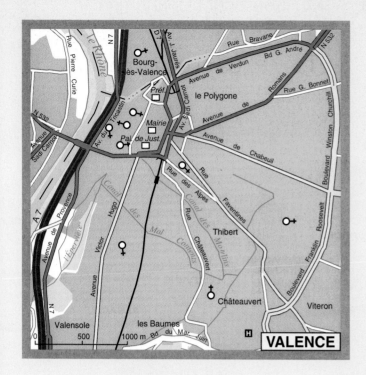

VALENCE

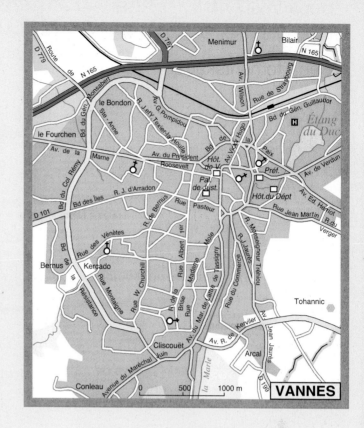

VANNES

343

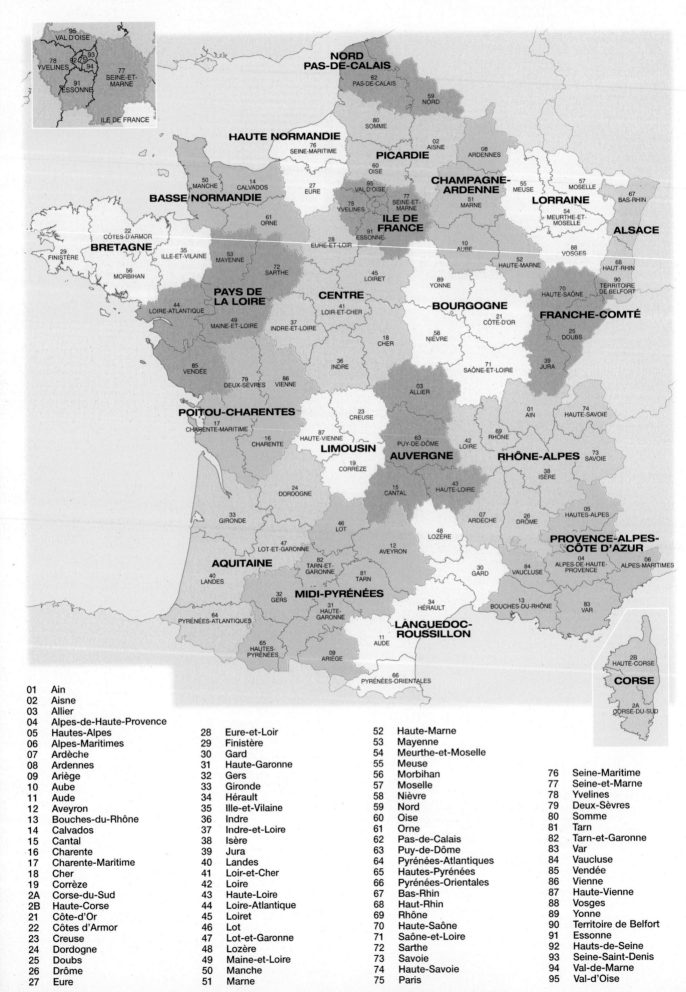

Department map GB

France administrative F

Departementskarte D

NL Overzicht Departementen

E Mapa departamental

I Carta dipartimentale

44

01	Ain
02	Aisne
03	Allier
04	Alpes-de-Haute-Provence
05	Hautes-Alpes
06	Alpes-Maritimes
07	Ardèche
08	Ardennes
09	Ariège
10	Aube
11	Aude
12	Aveyron
13	Bouches-du-Rhône
14	Calvados
15	Cantal
16	Charente
17	Charente-Maritime
18	Cher
19	Corrèze
2A	Corse-du-Sud
2B	Haute-Corse
21	Côte-d'Or
22	Côtes d'Armor
23	Creuse
24	Dordogne
25	Doubs
26	Drôme
27	Eure

28	Eure-et-Loir
29	Finistère
30	Gard
31	Haute-Garonne
32	Gers
33	Gironde
34	Hérault
35	Ille-et-Vilaine
36	Indre
37	Indre-et-Loire
38	Isère
39	Jura
40	Landes
41	Loir-et-Cher
42	Loire
43	Haute-Loire
44	Loire-Atlantique
45	Loiret
46	Lot
47	Lot-et-Garonne
48	Lozère
49	Maine-et-Loire
50	Manche
51	Marne

52	Haute-Marne
53	Mayenne
54	Meurthe-et-Moselle
55	Meuse
56	Morbihan
57	Moselle
58	Nièvre
59	Nord
60	Oise
61	Orne
62	Pas-de-Calais
63	Puy-de-Dôme
64	Pyrénées-Atlantiques
65	Hautes-Pyrénées
66	Pyrénées-Orientales
67	Bas-Rhin
68	Haut-Rhin
69	Rhône
70	Haute-Saône
71	Saône-et-Loire
72	Sarthe
73	Savoie
74	Haute-Savoie
75	Paris

76	Seine-Maritime
77	Seine-et-Marne
78	Yvelines
79	Deux-Sèvres
80	Somme
81	Tarn
82	Tarn-et-Garonne
83	Var
84	Vaucluse
85	Vendée
86	Vienne
87	Haute-Vienne
88	Vosges
89	Yonne
90	Territoire de Belfort
91	Essonne
92	Hauts-de-Seine
93	Seine-Saint-Denis
94	Val-de-Marne
95	Val-d'Oise

A

Aast (64) 285 F4
Abainville (55) 92 E1
Abancourt (59) 11 J3
Abancourt (60) 17 F4
Abaucourt (54) 66 B2
Abaucourt-Hautecourt (55) 26 B6
Abbans-Dessous (25) 156 A6
Abbans-Dessus (25) 156 A1
Abbaretz (44) 103 H5
Abbécourt (02) 19 J6
Abbecourt (60) 37 H3
Abbenans (25) 138 E2
Abbéville (80) 9 G5
Abbéville-la-Rivière (91) 86 C4
Abbéville-lès-Conflans (54) 26 D6
Abbeville-Saint-Lucien (60) 37 H1
Abbévillers (25) 139 J3
Abeilhan (34) 292 B2
Abelcourt (70) 118 C5
Abère (64) 285 F3
l'Abergement-Clémenciat (01) . . 188 D3
l'Abergement-de-Cuisery (71) . . 172 A3
l'Abergement-de-Varey (01) . . . 189 J4
Abergement-la-Ronce (39) 155 F2
Abergement-le-Grand (39) 155 H4
Abergement-le-Petit (39) 155 J4
Abergement-lès-Thésy (39) 156 B4
l'Abergement-Sainte-Colombe (71) 172 A1
Abidos (64) 284 A4
Abilly (37) 146 A4
Abitain (64) 283 G2
Abjat-sur-Bandiat (24) 198 A4
Ablain-Saint-Nazaire (62) 10 E1
Ablaincourt-Pressoir (80) 19 F2
Ablainzevelle (62) 10 E4
Ablancourt (51) 62 E1
Ableiges (95) 37 G6
les Ableuvenettes (88) 94 B5
Ablis (78) 85 K2
Ablon (14) 34 A2
Ablon-sur-Seine (94) 59 F5
Aboën (42) 204 D6
Aboncourt (54) 93 J3
Aboncourt (57) 27 J5
Aboncourt-Gesincourt (70) 117 K5
Aboncourt-sur-Seille (57) 66 C3
Abondance (74) 175 H6
Abondant (28) 57 H4
Abos (64) 284 B3
Abreschviller (57) 67 K5
Abrest (03) 185 J4
les Abrets (38) 207 J4
Abriès (05) 227 D2
Abscon (59) 11 K2
l'Absie (79) 161 G2
Abzac (16) 180 B3
Abzac (33) 212 B5
Accolans (25) 138 E2
Accolay (89) 133 H1
Accons (07) 239 H1
Accous (64) 303 F2
Achain (57) 66 E4
Achen (57) 68 E3
Achenheim (67) 70 C4
Achères (18) 131 F6
Achères (78) 58 C2
Achères-la-Forêt (77) 87 G4
Achery (02) 20 B4
Acheux-en-Amiénois (80) 10 C5
Acheux-en-Vimeu (80) 8 E6
Acheville (62) 11 F1
Achey (70) 137 F2
Achicourt (62) 10 E4
Achiet-le-Grand (62) 10 E5
Achiet-le-Petit (62) 10 E5
Achun (58) 151 J2
Achy (60) 17 H6
Acigné (35) 79 H4
Aclou (27) 34 E5
Acon (27) 56 C4
Acq (62) 10 D2
Acqueville (14) 53 J2
Acqueville (50) 28 B2
Acquigny (27) 35 J5
Acquin-Westbécourt (62) 2 E5
Acy (02) 39 K3
Acy-en-Multien (60) 39 F6
Acy-Romance (08) 41 J4
Adaincourt (57) 66 C1
Adainville (78) 57 H5
Adam-lès-Passavant (25) 138 D5
Adam-lès-Vercel (25) 157 F1
Adamswiller (67) 67 K2
Adast (65) 304 A2
Adé (65) 285 G6
Adelange (57) 45 K6
Adelans-et-le-Val-de-Bithaine (70) 118 D5
Adervielle-Pouchergues (65) . . 305 F4
Adilly (79) 161 J2
Adinfer (62) 10 E4
Adissan (34) 292 C1
les Adjots (16) 179 G4
Adon (45) 111 J6
les Adrets (38) 224 D2
Adriers (86) 180 C2
Afa (2A) 320 C4
Affieux (19) 200 A5
Affléville (54) 26 D5

Affoux (69) 205 G1
Affracourt (54) 94 A2
Affringues (62) 2 E6
Agassac (31) 287 F3
Agde (34) 292 C4
Agel (34) 291 G4
Agen (47) 248 B4
Agen-d'Aveyron (12) 252 C3
Agencourt (21) 154 B2
Agenville (80) 9 J4
Agenvillers (80) 9 H4
les Ageux (60) 38 B3
Ageville (52) 116 D1
Agey (21) 135 H6
Aghione (2B) 321 J2
Agincourt (54) 66 B4
Agme (47) 247 J1
Agnac (47) 231 G4
Agnat (43) 219 H2
Agneaux (50) 31 H3
Agnetz (60) 37 K3
Agnez-lès-Duisans (62) 10 D2
Agnicourt-et-Séchelles (02) . . . 21 G4
Agnières (62) 10 D2
Agnières-en-Dévoluy (05) 242 C3
Agnin (38) 222 B1
Agnos (64) 284 A6
Agny (62) 10 E3
Agon-Coutainville (50) 30 C4
Agonac (24) 214 A2
Agonès (34) 274 A2
Agonges (03) 168 C3
Agos-Vidalos (65) 304 D2
Agris (16) 197 F2
Agudelle (17) 211 J1
Aguessac (12) 253 G5
Aguilcourt (02) 40 E2
Aguts (81) 289 G1
Agy (14) 32 A4
Ahaxe-Alciette-Bascassan (64) 282 E6
Ahetze (64) 263 C1
Ahéville (88) 94 B4
Ahuillé (53) 104 D2
Ahun (23) 183 F4
Ahuy (21) 136 A4
Aibes (59) 13 J3
Aibre (25) 139 G2
Aïcirits-Camou-Suhast (64) . . . 283 G3
Aiffres (79) 178 A1
Aigaliers (30) 255 K6
l'Aigle (61) 55 J4
Aiglemont (08) 22 D3
Aiglepierre (39) 155 K4
Aigleville (27) 57 F1
Aiglun (04) 259 H6
Aiglun (06) 280 D2
Aignan (32) 266 C5
Aignay-le-Duc (21) 135 H1
Aigne (34) 291 F4
Aigné (72) 106 D2
Aignerville (14) 29 K6
Aignes (31) 288 D4
Aignes-et-Puypéroux (16) 196 D6
Aigneville (80) 8 E6
Aigny (51) 62 C1
Aigonnay (79) 161 K6
Aigre (16) 178 E6
Aigrefeuille (31) 288 D1
Aigrefeuille-d'Aunis (17) 177 F3
Aigrefeuille-sur-Maine (44) 123 J6
Aigremont (30) 274 E2
Aigremont (52) 117 G2
Aigremont (78) 58 B3
Aigremont (89) 113 K6
Aiguebelette-le-Lac (73) 208 A4
Aiguebelle (73) 209 F4
Aigueblanche (73) 209 H4
Aiguefonde (81) 290 A2
Aigueperse (63) 185 G5
Aigueperse (69) 187 J1
Aigues-Juntes (09) 307 G2
Aigues-Mortes (30) 294 A3
Aigues-Vives (09) 308 B2
Aigues-Vives (11) 290 D5
Aigues-Vives (30) 275 F4
Aigues-Vives (34) 291 G4
Aiguèze (30) 256 B3
Aiguilhe (43) 220 C5
Aiguilles (05) 227 C2
l'Aiguillon (09) 308 D3
Aiguillon (47) 247 J3
l'Aiguillon-sur-Mer (85) 159 J6
l'Aiguillon-sur-Vie (85) 158 E1
Aiguines (83) 279 G3
Aigurande (36) 165 K5
Ailhon (07) 239 G5
Aillant-sur-Milleron (45) 112 A5
Aillant-sur-Tholon (89) 112 E4
Aillas (33) 230 C5
Ailleux (42) 204 B1
Aillevans (70) 138 D1
Ailleville (10) 91 G5
Aillevillers-et-Lyaumont (70) . . 118 C3
Aillianville (52) 92 E4
Aillières-Beauvoir (72) 83 F3
Aillon-le-Jeune (73) 208 D3
Aillon-le-Vieux (73) 208 D3
Ailloncourt (70) 118 D5
Ailly (27) 35 K5
Ailly-le-Haut-Clocher (80) 9 H5
Ailly-sur-Noye (80) 18 B4
Ailly-sur-Somme (80) 17 K1

Aimargues (30) 275 F5
Aime (73) 209 J4
Ainay-le-Château (03) 167 J2
Ainay-le-Vieil (18) 167 G2
Aincille (64) 282 E6
Aincourt (95) 57 K1
Aincreville (55) 43 F2
Aingeray (54) 65 J4
Aingeville (88) 93 G5
Aingoulaincourt (52) 92 C2
Ainharp (64) 283 H4
Ainhice-Mongelos (64) 282 E5
Ainhoa (64) 263 D2
Ainvelle (70) 118 B4
Ainvelle (88) 117 H2
Airaines (80) 17 H1
Airan (14) 33 G6
Aire (08) 41 G1
Aire-sur-la-Lys (62) 3 H6
Aire-sur-l'Adour (40) 265 K4
Airel (50) 31 H2
les Aires (34) 291 J1
Airion (60) 38 A2
Airon-Notre-Dame (62) 8 E1
Airon-Saint-Vaast (62) 8 E1
Airoux (11) 289 G4
Airvault (79) 144 C6
Aiserey (21) 154 D1
Aisey-et-Richecourt (70) 117 J3
Aisey-sur-Seine (21) 115 F6
Aisonville-et-Bernoville (02) . . . 20 C1
Aïssey (25) 138 D5
Aisy-sous-Thil (21) 134 D4
Aisy-sur-Armançon (89) 134 C1
Aiti (2B) 319 G4
Aiton (73) 208 E4
Aix (19) 201 G4
Aix (59) 7 F6
les Aix-d'Angillon (18) 149 J1
Aix-en-Diois (26) 241 H3
Aix-en-Ergny (62) 4 E5
Aix-en-Issart (62) 4 D6
Aix-en-Othe (10) 89 H5
Aix-en-Provence (13) 296 D1
Aix-la-Fayette (63) 203 H5
Aix-les-Bains (73) 208 B2
Aix-Noulette (62) 10 E1
Aixe-sur-Vienne (87) 198 D2
Aizac (07) 239 G4
Aizanville (52) 115 J1
Aize (36) 147 K2
Aizecourt-le-Bas (80) 19 H1
Aizecourt-le-Haut (80) 19 H1
Aizelles (02) 40 D1
Aizenay (85) 141 H6
Aizier (27) 34 D2
Aizy-Jouy (02) 40 A2
Ajac (11) 308 E2
Ajaccio (2A) 320 B5
Ajain (23) 182 E3
Ajat (24) 214 D4
Ajoncourt (57) 66 B3
Ajou (27) 55 K2
Ajoux (07) 239 J3
Alaigne (11) 308 D1
Alaincourt (02) 20 A3
Alaincourt (70) 118 A3
Alaincourt-la-Côte (57) 66 C2
Alairac (11) 290 A6
Alan (31) 287 G5
Alando (2B) 319 G6
Alata (2A) 320 B4
Alba-la-Romaine (07) 239 K6
Alban (81) 271 H3
Albaret-le-Comtal (48) 236 E2
Albaret-Sainte-Marie (48) 237 F2
Albas (11) 310 A2
Albas (46) 249 H1
Albé (67) 70 B6
Albefeuille-Lagarde (82) 249 J6
l'Albenc (38) 223 H3
Albens (73) 208 B1
Albepierre-Bredons (15) 218 B5
l'Albère (66) 315 G5
Albert (80) 10 D6
Albertacce (2B) 318 D6
Albertville (73) 209 G2
Albestroff (57) 67 G1
Albi (81) 270 E2
Albiac (31) 289 F1
Albiac (46) 234 B3
Albias (82) 250 A6
Albières (11) 309 H3
Albiès (09) 307 K5
Albiez-le-Jeune (73) 225 G2
Albiez-Montrond (73) 225 G2
Albignac (19) 216 A4
Albigny-sur-Saône (69) 188 C6
Albine (81) 290 D2
Albitreccia (2A) 320 D6
Albon (07) 239 H2
Albon (26) 222 B3
Alboussière (07) 222 A6
les Albres (12) 234 E6
Albussac (19) 216 B4
Alby-sur-Chéran (74) 208 C1
Alçay-Alçabéhéty-Sunharette (64) 283 H6
Aldudes (64) 263 D5
Alembon (62) 2 D4
Alençon (61) 82 D3
Alénya (66) 315 H3
Aléria (2B) 321 K2

Alès (30) 255 G5
Alet-les-Bains (11) 309 F2
Alette (62) 4 C5
Aleu (09) 306 E4
Alex (74) 191 G5
Alexain (53) 80 E5
Aleyrac (26) 240 D6
Alfortville (94) 59 F4
Algajola (2B) 318 C2
Algans (81) 270 B6
Algolsheim (68) 96 E5
Algrange (57) 27 G4
Alièze (39) 173 G3
Alignan-du-Vent (34) 292 B2
Alincourt (08) 41 H2
Alincthun (62) 2 C5
Alise-Sainte-Reine (21) 135 F3
Alissas (07) 239 K4
Alix (69) 188 A6
Alixan (26) 222 D6
Alizay (27) 35 J3
Allain (54) 93 H1
Allaines (80) 19 G1
Allaines-Mervilliers (28) 85 K6
Allainville (28) 56 E5
Allainville (78) 86 A3
Allaire (56) 102 B4
Allamont (54) 44 B5
Allamps (54) 93 H1
Allan (26) 240 B6
Allanche (15) 218 C3
Alland'Huy-et-Sausseuil (08) . . 22 B6
Allarmont (88) 95 J1
Allas-Bocage (17) 211 J1
Allas-Champagne (17) 195 K5
Allas-les-Mines (24) 232 D2
Allassac (19) 215 H3
Allauch (13) 296 D3
Allègre (43) 220 A3
Allègre-les-Fumades (30) 255 J4
Alleins (13) 277 F5
Allemagne-en-Provence (04) . . 278 D3
Allemanche-Launay-et-Soyer (51) 89 H1
Allemans (24) 213 G2
Allemans-du-Dropt (47) 231 F5
Allemant (02) 39 K1
Allemant (51) 61 J4
Allemond (38) 224 D4
Allenay (80) 8 D5
Allenc (48) 238 A6
Allenjoie (25) 139 J2
Allennes-les-Marais (59) 6 C5
Allenwiller (67) 70 B2
Allerey (21) 153 G1
Allerey-sur-Saône (71) 154 B5
Allériot (71) 154 B6
Allery (80) 17 H1
Alles-sur-Dordogne (24) 232 B2
les Alleuds (49) 125 H5
les Alleuds (79) 178 E3
les Alleux (08) 42 B1
Alleuze (15) 236 E1
Allevard (38) 208 D6
Allèves (74) 208 D1
Allex (26) 240 C3
Alleyrac (43) 238 D1
Alleyras (43) 238 A1
Alleyrat (19) 200 E4
Alleyrat (23) 183 G5
Allez-et-Cazeneuve (47) 248 B2
Alliancelles (51) 63 J1
Alliat (09) 307 J5
Allibaudières (10) 90 B1
Allichamps (52) 91 J1
Allier (65) 285 H6
Allières (09) 307 F2
les Alliés (25) 157 F4
Alligny-Cosne (58) 132 B4
Alligny-en-Morvan (58) 152 D1
Allineuc (22) 77 F3
Allinges (74) 175 F5
Allogny (18) 149 F1
Allondans (25) 139 G2
Allondaz (73) 209 F2
Allonne (60) 37 H2
Allonne (79) 161 J3
Allonnes (28) 85 H4
Allonnes (49) 126 C6
Allonnes (72) 106 D3
Allons (04) 260 C6
Allons (47) 246 E4
Allonville (80) 18 B1
Allonzier-la-Caille (74) 191 F4
Allos (04) 260 D3
Allouagne (62) 5 J5
Alloue (16) 179 K4
Allouis (18) 148 E2
Allouville-Bellefosse (76) 15 H3
les Allues (73) 209 H5
les Alluets-le-Roi (78) 58 A3
Alluy (58) 151 J3
Alluyes (28) 85 F5
Ally (15) 217 G4
Ally (43) 219 G4
Almayrac (81) 251 H6
Almenêches (61) 54 D5
Almont-les-Junies (12) 235 G5
Alos (09) 306 D4
Alos (81) 270 B1
Alos-Sibas-Abense (64) 283 H6
Aloxe-Corton (21) 154 A3

Alpuech (12) 236 B3
Alquines (62) 2 E5
Alrance (12) 252 C5
Alsting (57) 68 C2
Altagène (2A) 323 F2
Alteckendorf (67) 69 J6
Altenach (68) 97 A4
Altenheim (67) 70 C1
Althen-des-Paluds (84) 276 C1
Altiani (2B) 321 G1
Altier (48) 254 E1
Altillac (19) 216 B6
Altkirch (68) 97 B4
Altorf (67) 70 C4
Altrippe (57) 68 B4
Altviller (57) 68 A3
Altwiller (67) 67 H1
Aluze (71) 153 J5
Alvignac (46) 234 A2
Alvimare (76) 15 F3
Alzen (09) 307 G3
Alzi (2B) 319 G6
Alzing (57) 45 J3
Alzon (30) 273 H2
Alzonne (11) 289 K5
Amage (70) 118 C4
Amagne (08) 22 B6
Amagney (25) 138 C5
Amailloux (79) 161 J1
Amance (10) 91 F4
Amance (54) 66 B4
Amance (70) 118 A4
Amancey (25) 156 C3
Amancy (74) 191 H3
Amange (39) 155 H1
Amanlis (35) 79 H5
Amanty (55) 93 F1
Amanvillers (57) 44 D4
Amanzé (71) 170 D6
Amarens (81) 270 E1
Amathay-Vésigneux (25) 156 D3
Amayé-sur-Orne (14) 32 D6
Amayé-sur-Seulles (14) 32 B6
Amazy (58) 133 G5
Ambacourt (88) 94 A3
Ambarès-et-Lagrave (33) 229 J1
Ambax (31) 287 G3
Ambazac (87) 181 J5
Ambel (38) 242 D2
Ambenay (27) 55 K4
Ambérac (16) 196 D1
Ambérieu-en-Bugey (01) 189 H5
Ambérieux (69) 188 B5
Ambérieux-en-Dombes (01) . . . 188 D5
Ambernac (16) 180 A5
Amberre (86) 162 D1
Ambert (63) 203 K5
Ambès (33) 211 H5
Ambeyrac (12) 251 F1
Ambialet (81) 271 G2
Ambiegna (2A) 320 C3
Ambierle (42) 186 B5
Ambiévillers (70) 118 B2
Ambillou (37) 127 G4
Ambillou-Château (49) 125 J6
Ambilly (74) 191 G2
Amblainville (60) 37 H5
Amblans-et-Velotte (70) 118 D6
Ambleny (02) 39 H3
Ambléon (01) 207 J2
Ambleteuse (62) 2 A4
Ambleville (16) 196 A4
Ambleville (95) 36 D5
Amblie (14) 32 D3
Amblimont (08) 23 G5
Ambloy (41) 108 B6
Ambly-Fleury (08) 41 K1
Ambly-sur-Meuse (55) 64 D1
Amboise (37) 128 B4
Ambon (56) 121 H1
Ambonil (26) 240 C2
Ambonnay (51) 41 G6
Ambonville (52) 91 K4
Ambrault (36) 166 B1
Ambres (81) 270 A4
Ambricourt (62) 5 F6
Ambrief (02) 39 K3
Ambrières (51) 63 H6
Ambrières-les-Vallées (53) 81 G3
Ambrines (62) 10 C2
Ambronay (01) 189 H4
Ambrugeat (19) 200 D5
Ambrumesnil (76) 15 J2
Ambrus (47) 247 H4
Ambutrix (01) 189 H5
Amécourt (27) 36 D3
Amel-sur-l'Étang (55) 26 C5
Amelécourt (57) 66 D3
Amélie-les-Bains-Palalda (66) . 314 E5
Amendeuix-Oneix (64) 283 F3
Amenoncourt (54) 67 G5
Amenucourt (95) 36 D6
Ames (62) 5 H5
Amettes (62) 5 H5
Ameugny (71) 171 H4
Ameuvelle (88) 117 J3
Amfreville (14) 33 F4
Amfreville (50) 28 E5
Amfreville-la-Campagne (27) . . 35 G5
Amfreville-la-Mi-Voie (76) 35 J2
Amfreville-les-Champs (27) . . . 35 K3
Amfreville-les-Champs (76) . . . 15 H4

346

Amfreville-sous-les-Monts (27) 35 K3
Amfreville-sur-Iton (27) 35 J5
Amfroipret (59) 13 F3
Amiens (80) 18 B2
Amifontaine (02) 40 E1
Amigny (50) 31 G3
Amigny-Rouy (02) 20 A5
Amillis (77) 60 B5
Amilly (28) 85 F3
Amilly (45) 111 J3
Amions (42) 186 E6
Amirat (06) 280 C2
Ammerschwihr (68) 96 B3
Ammerzwiller (68) 97 A3
Amné (72) 106 B2
Amnéville (57) 27 G5
Amoncourt (70) 118 A5
Amondans (25) 156 C2
Amont-et-Effreney (70) 118 E3
Amorots-Succos (64) 283 F3
Amou (40) 264 E6
Ampilly-le-Sec (21) 115 F5
Ampilly-les-Bordes (21) 135 G1
Amplepuis (69) 187 H5
Amplier (62) 10 B4
Ampoigné (53) 104 E5
Amponville (77) 87 G5
Ampriani (2B) 319 H6
Ampuis (69) 206 A5
Ampus (83) 279 H5
Amuré (79) 177 J1
Amy (60) 19 F5
Anais (16) 196 E2
Anais (17) 177 F2
Anan (31) 287 F4
Ance (64) 283 K6
Anceaumeville (76) 15 K6
Anceins (61) 55 H3
Ancelle (05) 243 F4
Ancemont (55) 43 H6
Ancenis (44) 124 A4
Ancerville (55) 63 K6
Ancerville (57) 45 H6
Ancerviller (54) 95 G1
Ancey (21) 135 J5
Anchamps (08) 22 C1
Anché (37) 145 G2
Anché (86) 162 E6
Anchenoncourt-et-Chazel (70) . . 118 A4
Ancienville (02) 39 H5
Ancier (70) 137 G3
Ancinnes (72) 82 E4
Ancizan (65) 305 F4
les Ancizes-Comps (63) 184 C6
Ancône (26) 240 B5
Ancourt (76) 16 A2
Ancourteville-sur-Héricourt (76) . . 15 F4
Ancretiéville-Saint-Victor (76) . . 15 J5
Ancretteville-sur-Mer (76) . . . 14 E3
Ancteville (50) 30 D3
Anctoville (14) 32 B6
Anctoville-sur-Boscq (50) . . . 51 J1
Ancy (69) 205 H1
Ancy-le-Franc (89) 114 C5
Ancy-le-Libre (89) 114 B5
Ancy-sur-Moselle (57) 44 E6
Andainville (80) 17 G2
Andance (07) 222 B3
Andancette (26) 222 B3
Andard (49) 125 J3
Andé (27) 35 K4
Andechy (80) 18 E4
Andel (22) 49 J6
Andelain (02) 20 A5
Andelaroche (03) 186 B2
Andelarre (70) 138 A1
Andelarrot (70) 138 A1
Andelat (15) 218 D5
Andelnans (90) 139 H1
Andelot-Blancheville (52) . . . 92 C5
Andelot-en-Montagne (39) . . . 156 B5
Andelot-Morval (39) 172 E5
Andelu (78) 57 K3
les Andelys (27) 36 A4
Andernay (55) 63 J4
Andernos-les-Bains (33) 228 C3
Anderny (54) 26 E4
Andert-et-Condon (01) 207 J1
Andeville (60) 37 H4
Andigné (49) 104 E6
Andillac (81) 270 B1
Andilly (17) 176 E1
Andilly (54) 65 H4
Andilly (74) 190 E4
Andilly (95) 58 E2
Andilly-en-Bassigny (52) 116 E3
Andiran (47) 247 H6
Andlau (67) 70 C6
Andoins (64) 284 E4
Andolsheim (68) 96 C4
Andon (06) 280 B3
Andonville (45) 86 B5
Andornay (70) 119 F6
Andouillé (53) 80 E6
Andouillé-Neuville (35) 79 H2
Andouque (81) 271 F1
Andrein (64) 283 H3
Andres (62) 2 D3
Andrest (65) 285 H4
Andrésy (78) 58 B2
Andrezé (49) 142 E1
Andrezel (77) 87 J1

Andrézieux-Bouthéon (42) 205 F5
Andryes (89) 133 F3
Anduze (30) 255 F6
Anères (65) 305 G1
Anet (28) 57 F3
Anetz (44) 124 B4
Angaïs (64) 284 E5
Angé (41) 128 D5
Angeac-Champagne (16) 195 K4
Angeac-Charente (16) 196 B3
Angecourt (08) 23 F5
Angeduc (16) 196 C5
Angely (89) 134 A2
Angeot (90) 119 K5
Angers (49) 125 G3
Angerville (14) 33 H4
Angerville (91) 86 B5
Angerville-Bailleul (76) 14 D4
Angerville-la-Campagne (27) . . 56 D2
Angerville-la-Martel (76) 14 E3
Angerville-l'Orcher (76) 14 C5
Angervilliers (91) 86 B1
Angeville (82) 268 C1
Angevillers (57) 27 F4
Angey (50) 51 J2
Angicourt (60) 38 B3
Angiens (76) 15 G3
Angirey (70) 137 H3
Angivillers (60) 38 B1
Anglade (33) 211 G3
Anglards-de-Saint-Flour (15) . . 218 E6
Anglards-de-Salers (15) 217 H3
Anglars (46) 234 C3
Anglars-Juillac (46) 249 H1
Anglars-Nozac (46) 233 J3
Anglars-Saint-Félix (12) 251 H2
Anglefort (01) 190 C5
Anglemont (88) 95 F3
Angles (04) 279 K1
les Angles (30) 276 B2
les Angles (65) 304 B1
les Angles (66) 313 J3
Anglès (81) 290 D1
Angles (85) 159 H5
les Angles-sur-Corrèze (19) . . 216 B2
Anglesqueville-la-Bras-Long . . 15 G3
Anglesqueville-l'Esneval (76) . . 14 B5
Anglet (64) 282 B1
Angliers (17) 177 F2
Angliers (86) 144 E4
Anglure (51) 89 J1
Anglure-sous-Dun (71) 187 H2
Angluzelles-et-Courcelles (51) . . 61 J6
Angoisse (24) 198 D6
Angomont (54) 95 H1
Angos (65) 285 J5
Angoulême (16) 196 E3
Angoulins (17) 176 D3
Angoumé (40) 262 E6
Angous (64) 283 J4
Angoustrine-Villeneuve-
  des-Escaldes (66) 313 G5
Angoville (14) 53 J2
Angoville-au-Plain (50) 29 G6
Angoville-sur-Ay (50) 30 D1
Angres (62) 10 E1
Angresse (40) 262 C5
Angrie (49) 124 C2
Anguerny (14) 32 E4
Anguilcourt-le-Sart (02) 20 B4
Angy (60) 37 K3
Anhaux (64) 282 D5
Anhiers (59) 11 J1
Aniane (34) 273 J5
Aniche (59) 11 K2
Anisy (14) 32 E4
Anizy-le-Château (02) 39 K1
Anjeux (70) 118 B3
Anjou (38) 222 C1
Anjouin (36) 148 B1
Anjoutey (90) 119 J5
Anla (65) 305 H2
Anlezy (58) 151 H4
Anlhiac (24) 214 E2
Annay (58) 132 A3
Annay (62) 6 C6
Annay-la-Côte (89) 133 K3
Annay-sur-Serein (89) 113 K6
Annebault (14) 33 J4
Annecy (74) 191 F5
Annecy-le-Vieux (74) 191 F5
Annelles (08) 41 J2
Annemasse (74) 191 G2
Annéot (89) 133 K3
Annepont (17) 177 J6
Annequin (62) 6 B6
Annesse-et-Beaulieu (24) . . . 213 J4
Annet-sur-Marne (77) 59 H3
Anneux (59) 11 J4
Anneville-Ambourville (76) . . . 35 F1
Anneville-en-Saire (50) 29 F2
Anneville-la-Prairie (52) 92 A6
Anneville-sur-Mer (50) 30 C3
Anneville-sur-Scie (76) 15 K3
Anneyron (26) 222 C2
Annezay (17) 177 H4
Annezin (62) 5 K5
Annoire (39) 154 E4
Annois (02) 19 J4
Annoisin-Chatelans (38) 207 F2
Annoix (18) 149 H4

Annonay (07) 222 A3
Annonville (52) 92 C3
Annot (04) 280 A1
Annouville-Vilmesnil (76) 14 D4
Annoux (89) 134 B2
Annoville (50) 30 D5
Annoeullin (59) 6 C5
Anor (59) 13 J6
Anos (64) 284 D3
Anost (71) 152 D3
Anould (88) 95 J3
Anoux (54) 26 E5
Anoye (64) 285 F3
Anquetierville (76) 15 F6
Anrosey (52) 117 G4
Ansac-sur-Vienne (16) 180 B5
Ansacq (60) 37 K3
Ansan (32) 267 K5
Ansauville (54) 65 H3
Ansauvillers (60) 18 B6
Anse (69) 188 B5
Anserville (60) 37 J4
Ansignan (66) 309 H1
Ansost (65) 285 H2
Ansouis (84) 277 J4
Anstaing (59) 7 F4
Antagnac (47) 247 F2
Anterrieux (15) 236 D2
Anteuil (25) 139 F4
Antezant-la-Chapelle (17) . . . 178 A5
Anthé (47) 249 F2
Anthelupt (54) 66 C6
Anthenay (51) 40 C5
Antheny (08) 21 K2
Antheuil (21) 153 K1
Antheuil-Portes (60) 38 D1
Anthien (58) 133 H3
Anthon (38) 206 E1
Anthy-sur-Léman (74) 174 E5
Antibes (06) 281 F5
Antichan (65) 305 H2
Antichan-de-Frontignes (31) . . 305 J3
Antignac (15) 217 J2
Antignac (31) 305 H4
Antigny (85) 160 E2
Antigny (86) 164 A4
Antigny-la-Ville (21) 153 H2
Antilly (57) 27 H6
Antilly (60) 39 F5
Antin (65) 285 K4
Antisanti (2B) 321 H2
Antist (65) 304 D1
Antogny le Tillac (37) 145 J4
Antoigné (49) 144 C2
Antoigny (61) 81 J1
Antoingt (63) 202 E5
Antonaves (05) 258 E4
Antonne-et-Trigonant (24) . . . 214 B3
Antony (92) 58 E5
Antraigues-sur-Volane (07) . . 239 H4
Antrain (35) 51 J5
Antran (86) 145 J5
Antras (09) 306 B4
Antras (32) 267 G5
Antrenas (48) 237 G5
Antugnac (11) 308 E3
Antully (71) 153 G5
Anvéville (76) 15 G4
Anville (16) 196 B1
Anvin (62) 5 G6
Any-Martin-Rieux (02) 21 J2
Anzat-le-Luguet (63) 218 D2
Anzeling (57) 27 K5
Anzême (23) 182 D2
Anzex (47) 247 G3
Anzin (59) 12 D1
Anzin-Saint-Aubin (62) 10 E2
Anzy-le-Duc (71) 186 E1
Aoste (38) 207 J4
Aougny (51) 40 C5
Aouste (08) 21 K3
Aouste-sur-Sye (26) 240 E3
Aouze (88) 93 H3
Apach (57) 27 J3
Apchat (63) 218 E1
Apchon (63) 218 A3
Apinac (42) 220 D1
Appelle (81) 289 H1
Appenai-sous-Bellême (61) . . 83 H4
Appenans (25) 139 F2
Appenwihr (68) 96 C4
Appeville (50) 29 F6
Appeville-Annebault (27) 34 D3
Appietto (2A) 320 B4
Appilly (60) 19 J6
Appoigny (89) 113 F4
Apprieu (38) 207 H6
Appy (09) 307 K5
Apremont (01) 190 A2
Apremont (08) 42 E4
Apremont (60) 38 B5
Apremont (70) 137 F4
Apremont (73) 208 C5
Apremont (85) 141 G6
Apremont-la-Forêt (55) 65 F3
Apremont-sur-Allier (18) 150 D5
Aprey (52) 116 C3
Apt (84) 277 H2
Arabaux (09) 307 J3
Arâches (74) 192 A3
Aragnouet (65) 304 E5
Aragon (11) 290 A4

Aramits (64) 283 K6
Aramon (30) 276 A2
Aranc (01) 189 K4
Arancou (64) 283 F2
Arandas (01) 189 J6
Arandon (38) 207 G2
Araujuzon (64) 283 J3
Araules (43) 221 F5
Araux (64) 283 J3
Arbanats (33) 229 J4
Arbas (31) 306 B2
Arbecey (70) 117 J5
Arbellara (2A) 322 E2
Arbent (01) 173 H6
Arbéost (65) 303 J2
Arbérats-Sillègue (64) 283 G3
Arbigny (01) 172 A4
Arbigny-sous-Varennes (52) . . 117 F4
Arbin (73) 208 D5
Arbis (33) 230 A4
Arblade-le-Bas (32) 266 A5
Arblade-le-Haut (32) 266 B4
Arbois (39) 155 K4
Arbon (31) 305 K2
Arbonne (64) 263 C1
Arbonne-la-Forêt (77) 87 G3
Arboras (34) 273 H5
Arbori (2A) 316 E6
Arbot (52) 115 K4
Arbouans (25) 139 H2
Arboucave (40) 265 H6
Arbouet-Sussaute (64) 283 G3
Arbourse (58) 132 D6
Arboussols (66) 314 C2
l'Arbresle (69) 205 J1
Arbrissel (35) 103 K1
Arbus (64) 284 B3
Arbusigny (74) 191 G3
Arc-en-Barrois (52) 115 K3
Arc-et-Senans (25) 155 K3
Arc-lès-Gray (70) 137 F3
Arc-sous-Cicon (25) 157 F2
Arc-sous-Montenot (25) 156 B4
Arc-sur-Tille (21) 136 C5
Arcachon (33) 228 B4
Arçais (79) 177 J1
Arcambal (46) 250 A1
Arcangues (64) 263 C1
Arçay (18) 149 G4
Arçay (86) 144 D4
Arceau (21) 136 C4
Arcenant (21) 154 A2
Arcens (07) 239 G1
Arces (17) 194 E4
Arces-Dilo (89) 113 G1
Arcey (21) 135 J6
Arcey (25) 139 F2
Archail (04) 259 K5
Archamps (74) 191 F3
Archelange (39) 155 G1
Arches (15) 217 G2
Arches (88) 94 E6
Archettes (88) 94 E6
Archiac (17) 195 K5
Archignac (24) 215 G6
Archignat (03) 167 F6
Archigny (86) 163 J2
Archingeay (17) 177 H5
Archon (02) 21 H4
Arcinges (42) 187 H3
Arcins (33) 211 F5
Arcis-le-Ponsart (51) 40 C4
Arcis-sur-Aube (10) 90 B2
Arcizac-Adour (65) 285 H6
Arcizac-ez-Angles (65) 304 B1
Arcizans-Avant (65) 304 A2
Arcizans-Dessus (65) 303 K2
Arcomps (18) 167 F5
Arçon (25) 157 F4
Arcon (42) 186 D5
Arconcey (21) 153 G1
Arçonnay (72) 82 D3
Arconsat (63) 186 B6
Arconville (10) 91 H6
les Arcs (83) 298 D1
Arcueil (94) 58 E4
Arcy-Sainte-Restitue (02) . . . 39 K4
Arcy-sur-Cure (89) 133 H2
Ardelles (28) 84 D2
Ardelu (28) 86 A4
Ardenais (18) 166 E2
Ardenay-sur-Mérize (72) 107 G3
Ardengost (65) 305 F3
Ardentes (36) 165 K1
Ardes (63) 218 E1
Ardeuil-et-Montfauxelles (08) . . 42 B4
Ardiège (31) 305 J1
les Ardillats (69) 187 K2
Ardilleux (79) 178 E3
Ardillières (17) 177 F4
Ardin (79) 161 G4
Ardizas (32) 268 A5
Ardoix (07) 222 A3
Ardon (39) 156 A4
Ardon (45) 109 K5
Ardouval (76) 16 B4
Ardres (62) 2 D3
Aregno (2B) 318 C2
Areines (41) 108 C3
Aren (64) 283 K4
Arengosse (40) 264 E1

Arenthon (74) 191 H3
Arès (33) 228 B2
Aresches (39) 156 A4
Aressy (64) 284 D4
Arette (64) 302 E1
Arfeuille-Châtain (23) 183 J4
Arfeuilles (03) 186 B3
Arfons (81) 289 K3
Argagnon (64) 283 K2
Arganchy (14) 32 A4
Argançon (10) 91 F5
Argancy (57) 27 H6
Argein (09) 306 C3
Argelès (65) 304 D1
Argelès-Gazost (65) 304 A2
Argelès-sur-Mer (66) 315 J4
Argeliers (11) 291 G4
Argelliers (34) 273 K5
Argelos (40) 265 F6
Argelos (64) 284 D2
Argelouse (40) 245 J2
Argences (14) 33 G5
Argens-Minervois (11) 291 F5
Argent-sur-Sauldre (18) 131 F3
Argentan (61) 54 C5
Argentat (19) 216 C5
Argentenay (89) 114 B5
Argenteuil (95) 58 D2
Argenteuil-sur-Armançon (89) . . 114 B6
l'Argentière-la-Bessée (05) . . . 243 K2
Argentières (77) 59 K6
Argentine (73) 209 F5
Argenton (47) 247 G2
Argenton-Château (79) 143 J4
Argenton-l'Église (79) 144 A3
Argenton-Notre-Dame (53) . . 105 G5
Argenton-sur-Creuse (36) . . . 165 G3
Argentré (53) 105 G1
Argentré-du-Plessis (35) 104 C1
Argenvières (18) 150 C2
Argenvilliers (28) 84 B5
Argers (51) 42 D6
Arget (64) 284 B1
Argiésans (90) 139 H1
Argillières (70) 117 G6
Argilliers (30) 275 J1
Argilly (21) 154 C3
Argis (01) 189 J5
Argiusta-Moriccio (2A) 320 E6
Argoeuves (80) 18 A1
Argol (29) 74 B2
Argonay (74) 191 F5
Argouges (50) 51 K5
Argoules (80) 9 G2
Argueil (76) 16 D6
Arguel (25) 137 K6
Arguel (80) 17 G2
Arguenos (31) 305 K3
Argut-Dessous (31) 305 J4
Argy (36) 147 H4
Arhansus (64) 283 F4
Aries-Espénan (65) 286 C4
Arifat (81) 271 G4
Arignac (09) 307 J4
Arinthod (39) 173 G5
Arith (73) 208 D2
Arjuzanx (40) 245 G6
Arlanc (63) 220 A1
Arlay (39) 155 H6
Arlebosc (07) 221 K5
Arlempdes (43) 238 C2
Arles (13) 275 K5
Arles-sur-Tech (66) 314 E5
Arlet (43) 219 H4
Arleuf (58) 152 C3
Arleux (59) 11 H3
Arleux-en-Gohelle (62) 11 F2
Arlos (31) 305 J4
Armaillé (49) 104 B6
Armancourt (60) 38 D3
Armancourt (80) 18 E5
Armaucourt (54) 66 B3
Armbouts-Cappel (59) 3 H2
Armeau (89) 112 D2
Armendarits (64) 282 E4
Armenteule (65) 305 F5
Armentières (59) 6 C3
Armentières-en-Brie (77) 60 A2
Armentières-sur-Avre (27) . . . 56 A5
Armentières-sur-Ourcq (02) . . 39 K5
Armentieux (32) 285 H1
Armes (58) 133 G4
Armillac (47) 231 G6
Armissan (11) 291 G5
Armix (01) 190 A6
Armous-et-Cau (32) 285 J1
Armoy (74) 175 F5
Arnac (15) 217 F5
Arnac-la-Poste (87) 181 J1
Arnac-Pompadour (19) 215 G1
Arnac-sur-Dourdou (12) 272 C5
Arnage (72) 106 D3
Arnancourt (52) 91 J4
Arnas (69) 188 B4
Arnaud-Guilhem (31) 287 G6
Arnave (09) 307 J4
Arnaville (54) 65 J1
Arnay-le-Duc (21) 153 G2
Arnay-sous-Vitteaux (21) 135 F4
Arnayon (26) 241 G6
Arné (65) 286 C6
Arnéguy (64) 282 D6

Arnèke (59) 3 H4
Arnicourt (08) 21 K6
Arnières-sur-Iton (27) 56 C2
Arnos (64) 284 B2
Arnouville-lès-Gonesse (95) 59 F2
Arnouville-lès-Mantes (78) 57 J2
Aroffe (88) 93 H3
Aromas (39) 189 J1
Aron (53) 81 G4
Aroue-Ithorots-Olhaïby (64) 283 H4
Aroz (70) 137 K1
Arpaillargues-et-Aureillac (30) . . . 275 G1
Arpajon (91) 86 D1
Arpajon-sur-Cère (15) 235 H1
Arpavon (26) 257 J2
Arpenans (70) 138 D1
Arpheuilles (18) 167 G1
Arpheuilles (36) 147 F5
Arpheuilles-Saint-Priest (03) . . . 184 B2
Arphy (30) 273 J1
Arquenay (53) 105 G2
Arques (11) 309 G3
Arques (12) 252 D3
les Arques (46) 233 F5
Arques (62) 3 G5
Arques-la-Bataille (76) 16 A2
Arquettes-en-Val (11) 309 H1
Arquèves (80) 10 C5
Arquian (58) 132 A3
Arracourt (54) 66 D4
Arradon (56) 100 E5
Arraincourt (57) 66 D1
Arrancourt (91) 86 C4
Arrancy (02) 40 C1
Arrancy-sur-Crusne (55) 26 C4
Arrans (21) 114 D6
Arras (62) 10 E3
Arras-en-Lavedan (65) 304 A2
Arras-sur-Rhône (07) 222 B4
Arrast-Larrebieu (64) 283 H4
Arraute-Charritte (64) 283 F2
Arraye-et-Han (54) 66 B3
Arrayou-Lahitte (65) 304 C1
Arre (30) 273 J2
Arreau (65) 305 F3
Arrelles (10) 114 C2
Arrembécourt (10) 91 F1
Arrènes (23) 182 A4
Arrens-Marsous (65) 303 K3
Arrentès-de-Corcieux (88) 95 H5
Arrentières (10) 91 H5
Arrest (80) 8 E5
Arreux (08) 22 C2
Arriance (57) 45 J6
Arricau-Bordes (64) 285 F2
Arrien (64) 285 F4
Arrien-en-Bethmale (09) 306 C4
Arrigas (30) 273 H1
Arrigny (51) 63 G6
Arro (2A) 320 C3
Arrodets (65) 304 E2
Arrodets-ez-Angles (65) 304 C1
Arromanches-les-Bains (14) 32 E4
Arronnes (03) 186 A4
Arronville (95) 37 H5
Arros-de-Nay (64) 284 D5
Arrosès (64) 285 F1
Arrou (28) 108 C1
Arrouède (32) 286 C3
Arrout (09) 306 C3
Arry (57) 65 K1
Arry (80) 9 F3
Ars (16) 195 H3
Ars (23) 183 F5
Ars-en-Ré (17) 158 B5
Ars-Laquenexy (57) 45 G5
Ars-les-Favets (63) 184 C2
Ars-sur-Formans (01) 188 C5
Ars-sur-Moselle (57) 44 E6
Arsac (33) 211 G5
Arsac-en-Velay (43) 220 C6
Arsague (40) 264 D6
Arsans (70) 137 G4
Arsonval (10) 91 G5
Arsure-Arsurette (39) 174 B1
les Arsures (39) 155 K4
Arsy (60) 38 C2
Art-sur-Meurthe (54) 66 B5
Artagnan (65) 285 H3
Artaise-le-Vivier (08) 22 E6
Artaix (71) 186 E2
Artalens-Souin (65) 304 B2
Artannes-sur-Indre (37) 127 H6
Artannes-sur-Thouet (49) 144 C1
Artas (38) 206 E5
Artassenx (40) 265 H3
Artemare (01) 190 B6
Artemps (02) 19 J3
Artenay (45) 110 A2
Arthaz-Pont-Notre-Dame (74) . . . 191 G2
Arthel (58) 151 G1
Arthémonay (26) 222 D4
Arthenac (17) 195 K5
Arthenas (39) 173 F3
Arthès (81) 270 E2
Arthez-d'Armagnac (40) 265 K2
Arthez-d'Asson (64) 303 J1
Arthez-de-Béarn (64) 284 A2
Arthezé (72) 106 B5
Arthies (95) 36 E6
Arthon (36) 165 J2
Arthon-en-Retz (44) 122 D5

Arthonnay (89) 114 C3
Arthun (42) 204 C2
Artigat (09) 307 G1
Artignosc-sur-Verdon (83) 278 E4
Artigue (31) 305 H4
Artigueloutan (64) 284 C4
Artiguelouve (64) 284 B4
Artiguemy (65) 285 K6
Artigues (09) 308 D6
Artigues (11) 308 E5
Artigues (65) 304 B1
Artigues (83) 278 C6
les Artigues-de-Lussac (33) 212 B6
Artigues-près-Bordeaux (33) 229 J2
Artins (41) 107 J6
Artix (09) 307 H2
Artix (64) 284 B3
Artolsheim (67) 71 C6
Artonges (02) 61 F2
Artonne (63) 185 F5
Artres (59) 12 D2
Arudy (64) 284 C6
Arue (40) 246 B6
Arvert (17) 194 B2
Arveyres (33) 230 A1
Arvieu (12) 252 C5
Arvieux (05) 227 B3
Arvigna (09) 307 K2
Arvillard (73) 208 D5
Arville (41) 108 B2
Arville (77) 87 G6
Arvillers (80) 18 E4
Arx (40) 247 F5
Arzacq-Arraziguet (64) 284 C1
Arzal (56) 121 J2
Arzano (29) 99 K3
Arzay (38) 206 E6
Arzembouy (58) 151 F1
Arzenc-d'Apcher (48) 236 E2
Arzenc-de-Randon (48) 237 K4
Arzens (11) 289 K6
Arzillières-Neuville (51) 63 F6
Arzon (56) 100 E4
Arzviller (57) 67 K4
Asasp-Arros (64) 284 A6
Ascain (64) 263 B2
Ascarat (64) 282 D5
Aschbach (67) 25 C2
Aschères-le-Marché (45) 110 B1
Asco (2B) 318 E4
Ascou (09) 308 B6
Ascoux (45) 110 D1
Ascros (06) 280 E1
Asfeld (08) 41 F1
Aslonnes (86) 163 F5
Asnan (58) 133 G6
Asnans-Beauvoisin (39) 155 F4
Asnelles (14) 32 C3
Asnières (27) 34 B5
Asnières-en-Bessin (14) 29 J6
Asnières-en-Montagne (21) 114 D6
Asnières-en-Poitou (79) 178 C3
Asnières-la-Giraud (17) 177 K6
Asnières-lès-Dijon (21) 136 A4
Asnières-sous-Bois (89) 133 G3
Asnières-sur-Blour (86) 180 C3
Asnières-sur-Nouère (16) 196 D2
Asnières-sur-Oise (95) 37 K6
Asnières-sur-Saône (01) 171 K5
Asnières-sur-Seine (92) 58 D3
Asnières-sur-Vègre (72) 105 K4
Asnois (58) 133 G4
Asnois (86) 179 J3
Aspach (57) 67 H5
Aspach (68) 97 A3
Aspach-le-Bas (68) 97 A2
Aspach-le-Haut (68) 97 A2
Aspères (30) 274 D4
Asperjoc (07) 239 H4
Aspet (31) 306 A2
Aspin-Aure (65) 305 F3
Aspin-en-Lavedan (65) 304 B1
Aspiran (34) 292 C1
Aspremont (05) 242 E6
Aspremont (06) 281 G3
les Aspres (61) 55 H5
Aspres-lès-Corps (05) 242 D2
Aspres-sur-Buëch (05) 242 B6
Aspret-Sarrat (31) 305 K1
Asprières (12) 234 E4
Asque (65) 304 E2
Asques (33) 211 J6
Asques (82) 268 B1
Asquins (89) 133 H3
Assac (81) 271 F2
Assainvillers (80) 18 D5
Assais-les-Jumeaux (79) 144 C6
Assas (34) 274 C5
Assat (64) 284 D5
Assay (37) 145 J2
Assé-le-Bérenger (53) 81 K5
Assé-le-Boisne (72) 82 C4
Assé-le-Riboul (72) 82 D6
Assenay (10) 90 A6
Assencières (10) 90 C4
Assenoncourt (57) 67 G3
Assérac (44) 121 J3
Assevent (59) 13 H2
Assevillers (80) 19 F2
Assier (46) 234 C1
Assieu (38) 206 B6

Assignan (34) 291 G3
Assigny (18) 131 J4
Assigny (76) 8 B6
les Assions (07) 255 H2
Assis-sur-Serre (02) 20 C4
Asson (64) 284 E6
Asswiller (67) 69 F5
Astaffort (47) 248 B6
Astaillac (19) 234 B1
Asté (65) 304 D2
Aste-Béon (64) 303 H2
Astet (07) 238 D4
Astillé (53) 104 E3
Astis (64) 284 D2
Aston (09) 307 J5
Astugue (65) 304 C1
Athée (21) 136 D6
Athée (53) 104 D4
Athée-sur-Cher (37) 128 A5
Athesans-Étroitefontaine (70) . . . 138 D1
Athie (21) 134 C2
Athie (89) 134 A3
Athienville (54) 66 D4
Athies (62) 11 F2
Athies (80) 19 H1
Athies-sous-Laon (02) 20 D6
Athis (51) 62 B1
Athis-de-l'Orne (61) 53 H4
Athis-Mons (91) 58 E5
Athos-Aspis (64) 283 G2
Athose (25) 156 E2
Attainville (95) 58 E1
Attancourt (52) 91 J1
les Attaques (62) 2 D3
Attenschwiller (68) 97 D4
Attiches (59) 6 D5
Attichy (60) 39 F2
Attignat (01) 189 F1
Attignat-Oncin (73) 208 A5
Attignéville (88) 93 H3
Attigny (08) 42 A1
Attigny (88) 117 K1
Attilloncourt (57) 66 C3
Attilly (02) 19 J2
Attin (62) 4 C5
Atton (54) 65 K2
Attray (45) 110 C1
Attricourt (70) 136 D3
Atur (24) 214 A4
Aubagnan (40) 265 G5
Aubagne (13) 296 E4
Aubaine (21) 153 J2
Aubais (30) 274 E4
Aubarède (65) 285 K4
Aubas (24) 215 F5
Aubazat (43) 219 H4
Aubazines (19) 215 K4
Aube (57) 45 G6
Aube (61) 55 H5
Aubéguimont (76) 17 F3
Aubenas (07) 239 H5
Aubenas-les-Alpes (04) 278 A2
Aubenasson (26) 241 H4
Aubencheul-au-Bac (59) 11 J3
Aubencheul-aux-Bois (02) 11 K6
Aubenton (02) 21 J2
Aubepierre-Ozouer-le-Repos (77) . . . 59 K6
Aubepierre-sur-Aube (52) 115 K3
l'Aubépin (39) 172 E5
Auberchicourt (59) 11 J2
Aubercourt (80) 18 D3
Aubergenville (78) 57 K2
Aubérive (51) 41 J5
Auberive (52) 116 A5
Auberives-en-Royans (38) 223 G5
Auberives-sur-Varèze (38) 206 A4
Aubermesnil-aux-Érables (76) . . . 16 E3
Aubermesnil-Beaumais (76) 16 A2
Aubers (59) 6 B4
Aubertin (64) 284 B4
Auberville (14) 33 H3
Auberville-la-Campagne (76) 15 F6
Auberville-la-Manuel (76) 15 F2
Auberville-la-Renault (76) 14 D4
Aubervilliers (93) 58 E3
Aubeterre (10) 90 B3
Aubeterre-sur-Dronne (16) 212 E2
Aubeville (16) 196 C5
Aubevoye (27) 36 A5
Aubiac (33) 246 C1
Aubiac (47) 248 B5
Aubiat (63) 185 G5
Aubie-et-Espessas (33) 211 J5
Aubière (63) 202 D2
les Aubiers (79) 143 H4
Aubiet (32) 268 A6
Aubignan (84) 257 G5
Aubignas (07) 239 K5
Aubigné (35) 79 H3
Aubigné (79) 178 D4
Aubigné-Racan (72) 106 E6
Aubigné-sur-Layon (49) 143 J1
Aubignosc (04) 259 G5
Aubigny (03) 168 C2
Aubigny (14) 54 A1
Aubigny (79) 162 A1
Aubigny (80) 18 C2
Aubigny (85) 159 H2
Aubigny-au-Bac (59) 11 J3
Aubigny-aux-Kaisnes (02) 19 J3
Aubigny-en-Artois (62) 10 D2
Aubigny-en-Laonnois (02) 40 C1

Aubigny-en-Plaine (21) 154 D2
Aubigny-la-Ronce (21) 153 J4
Aubigny-les-Pothées (08) 22 A3
Aubigny-lès-Sombernon (21) . . . 135 G5
Aubigny-sur-Nère (18) 131 F3
Aubilly (51) 40 D5
Aubin (12) 235 F6
Aubin (64) 284 C2
Aubin-Saint-Vaast (62) 9 H1
Aubinges (18) 149 J1
Auboncourt-Vauzelles (08) 22 B6
Aubonne (25) 156 E2
Aboué (54) 27 F6
Aubord (30) 275 G4
Aubous (64) 266 A6
Aubres (26) 257 H2
Aubréville (55) 43 F5
Aubrives (08) 24 C2
Aubrometz (62) 9 K2
Aubry-du-Hainaut (59) 12 C2
Aubry-en-Exmes (61) 54 D4
Aubry-le-Panthou (61) 54 E3
Aubure (68) 96 A2
Aubussargues (30) 275 G1
Aubusson (23) 183 G5
Aubusson (61) 53 H4
Aubusson-d'Auvergne (63) 203 J2
Aubvillers (80) 18 C4
Auby (59) 11 H1
Aucaleuc (22) 50 C5
Aucamville (31) 269 G5
Aucamville (82) 268 E4
Aucazein (09) 306 B3
Aucelon (26) 241 H4
Aucey-la-Plaine (50) 51 J5
Auch (32) 267 H6
Auchel (62) 5 J6
Auchonvillers (80) 10 D5
Auchy-au-Bois (62) 5 H5
Auchy-la-Montagne (60) 17 K6
Auchy-lès-Hesdin (62) 9 J1
Auchy-les-Mines (62) 6 B5
Auchy-lez-Orchies (59) 7 F6
Aucun (65) 303 K2
Audaux (64) 283 J3
Audelange (39) 155 H2
Audeloncourt (52) 116 E1
Audembert (62) 2 B3
Audenge (33) 228 C4
Auderville (50) 28 A1
Audes (03) 167 G5
Audeux (25) 137 J6
Audeville (45) 86 D5
Audierne (29) 73 C3
Audignicourt (02) 39 G1
Audignies (59) 13 F2
Audignon (40) 265 F4
Audigny (02) 20 D2
Audincourt (25) 139 H2
Audincthun (62) 5 F5
Audinghen (62) 2 A4
Audon (40) 264 D3
Audouville-la-Hubert (50) 29 G5
Audrehem (62) 2 E4
Audresein (09) 306 C3
Audresselles (62) 2 A4
Audrieu (14) 32 C4
Audrix (24) 232 C2
Audruicq (62) 2 E3
Audun-le-Roman (54) 26 E4
Audun-le-Tiche (57) 26 E3
Auenheim (67) 25 C4
Auffargis (78) 58 A5
Auffay (76) 15 K4
Aufferville (77) 87 G6
Auffreville-Brasseuil (78) 57 J2
Auflance (08) 23 J5
Auga (64) 284 C2
Augan (56) 78 A6
Auge (08) 21 J2
Auge (23) 183 H2
Augé (79) 161 J5
Auge-Saint-Médard (16) 196 B1
Augea (39) 172 E3
Auger-Saint-Vincent (60) 38 D5
Augerans (39) 155 H3
Augères (23) 182 C4
Augerolles (63) 203 J3
Augers-en-Brie (77) 60 E6
Augerville-la-Rivière (45) 87 F5
Augicourt (70) 117 K3
Augignac (24) 197 K4
Augirein (09) 306 B3
Augisey (39) 173 F3
Augnat (63) 219 F1
Augnax (32) 267 K5
Augne (87) 199 K2
Augny (57) 44 E6
Auguaise (61) 55 H5
Augy (02) 40 A3
Augy (89) 113 G6
Augy-sur-Aubois (18) 167 K1
Aujac (17) 195 J1
Aujac (30) 255 G3
Aujan-Mournède (32) 286 C3
Aujargues (30) 274 D4
Aujeurres (52) 116 B5
Aujols (46) 250 B2
Aulan (26) 258 A4
Aulas (30) 273 J1
Aulhat-Saint-Privat (63) 203 F4

Aulnat (63) 202 E2
Aulnay (10) 90 E2
Aulnay (17) 178 B4
Aulnay (86) 144 E5
Aulnay-la-Rivière (45) 86 E6
Aulnay-l'Aître (51) 63 F4
Aulnay-sous-Bois (93) 59 F2
Aulnay-sur-Iton (27) 56 C2
Aulnay-sur-Marne (51) 62 B1
Aulnay-sur-Mauldre (78) 57 K2
les Aulneaux (72) 83 F3
Aulnois (88) 93 H5
Aulnois-en-Perthois (55) 64 A6
Aulnois-sous-Laon (02) 20 D5
Aulnois-sur-Seille (57) 66 B2
Aulnoy (77) 60 B4
Aulnoy-lez-Valenciennes (59) . . . 12 D2
Aulnoy-sur-Aube (52) 116 A4
Aulnoye-Aymeries (59) 13 G2
Aulon (23) 182 B4
Aulon (31) 287 F6
Aulon (65) 304 E4
Aulos (09) 307 J5
Ault (80) 8 C5
Aulus-les-Bains (09) 307 F5
Aulx-lès-Cromary (70) 138 A4
Aumagne (17) 178 A6
Aumale (76) 17 F3
Aumâtre (80) 17 G1
Aumelas (34) 273 J6
Auménancourt (51) 41 F2
Aumerval (62) 5 H6
Aumes (34) 292 C2
Aumessas (30) 273 H1
Aumetz (57) 26 E3
Aumeville-Lestre (50) 29 F3
Aumont (39) 155 J4
Aumont (80) 17 H2
Aumont-Aubrac (48) 237 G4
Aumont-en-Halatte (60) 38 B4
Aumontzey (88) 95 G5
Aumur (39) 155 F3
Aunac (16) 179 H6
Aunat (11) 308 D5
Aunay-en-Bazois (58) 151 K2
Aunay-les-Bois (61) 83 F1
Aunay-sous-Auneau (28) 85 K3
Aunay-sous-Crécy (28) 56 E6
Aunay-sur-Odon (14) 53 G1
Auneau (28) 85 J3
Auneuil (60) 37 G3
Aunou-le-Faucon (61) 54 C5
Aunou-sur-Orne (61) 54 E6
Auppegard (76) 15 K3
Aups (83) 279 G5
Auquainville (14) 54 E1
Auquemesnil (76) 16 C1
Auradé (32) 287 H1
Auradou (47) 248 D3
Auragne (31) 288 C3
Auray (56) 100 D5
Aure (08) 42 A4
Aurec-sur-Loire (43) 221 F1
Aureil (87) 199 G2
Aureilhan (40) 244 C4
Aureilhan (65) 285 H5
Aureille (13) 276 D5
Aurel (26) 241 G4
Aurel (84) 258 A5
Aurelle-Verlac (12) 253 F1
Aurensan (32) 265 K6
Aurensan (65) 285 H4
Aureville (31) 288 C2
Auriac (11) 309 H3
Auriac (19) 216 E3
Auriac (64) 284 D2
Auriac-du-Périgord (24) 214 E5
Auriac-Lagast (12) 252 B5
Auriac-l'Église (15) 218 E3
Auriac-sur-Dropt (47) 231 F4
Auriac-sur-Vendinelle (31) 289 F2
Auriat (23) 199 J3
Auribail (31) 288 B4
Auribeau (84) 277 J3
Auribeau-sur-Siagne (06) 280 D5
Aurice (40) 265 F3
Auriébat (65) 285 H2
Aurières (63) 202 B3
Aurignac (31) 287 F5
Aurillac (15) 235 H1
Aurimont (32) 287 F1
Aurin (31) 288 E1
Auriol (13) 297 F3
Aurions-Idernes (64) 285 F1
Auris (38) 224 E5
Aurons (13) 277 F5
Auros (33) 230 B6
Auroux (03) 168 E2
Auroux (48) 238 A3
Aussac (81) 270 D3
Aussac-Vadalle (16) 196 E1
Ausseing (31) 287 H6
Aussevielle (64) 284 B3
Aussillon (81) 290 B2
Aussois (73) 226 A2
Ausson (31) 305 H1
Aussonce (08) 41 H3
Aussonne (31) 269 F5
Aussos (32) 286 D3
Aussurucq (64) 283 G6
Autainville (41) 109 F4

348

Autechaux (25). 138 D4
Autechaux-Roide (25) 139 H4
les Autels (02) 21 J3
les Autels-Saint-Bazile (14). . . 54 D2
les Autels-Villevillon (28). . . . 84 B6
Auterive (31) 288 C4
Auterive (32) 286 D1
Auterive (82) 268 C3
Auterrive (64) 283 G2
Autet (70) 137 G2
Auteuil (60) 37 H3
Auteuil (78) 57 K4
Autevielle-Saint-
  Martin-Bideren (64) 283 G3
Authe (08) 42 D1
Autheuil (28) 108 E3
Autheuil (61) 83 J1
Autheuil-Authouillet (27) . . . 35 K6
Autheuil-en-Valois (60) 39 G5
Autheux (80) 9 K4
Authevernes (27) 36 D5
Authezat (63) 202 E4
Authie (14) 32 D4
Authie (80) 10 C5
Authieule (80) 10 B4
les Authieux (27) 56 E3
les Authieux-du-Puits (61) . . . 55 F5
les Authieux-Papion (14) . . . 33 J6
Authieux-Ratiéville (76) . . . 16 A5
les Authieux-sur-Calonne (14) . . 34 A3
les Authieux-sur-le-
  Port-Saint-Ouen (76) . . . 35 J3
Authiou (58) 132 E6
Authoison (70) 138 B3
Authon (04) 259 H3
Authon (41) 128 A1
Authon-du-Perche (28) . . . 84 A6
Authon-Ébéon (17) 195 J1
Authon-la-Plaine (91) . . . 86 A3
Authou (27) 34 E4
Authuile (80) 10 D6
Authume (39) 155 G2
Authumes (71) 154 E5
Autichamp (26) 240 D4
Autignac (34) 291 K2
Autigny (76) 15 H3
Autigny-la-Tour (88) 93 G3
Autigny-le-Grand (52) . . . 92 A2
Autigny-le-Petit (52) . . . 92 A2
Autingues (62) 2 D4
Autoire (46) 234 B2
Autoreille (70) 137 H4
Autouillet (78) 57 K3
Autrac (43) 218 E2
Autrans (38) 223 J3
Autrêche (37) 128 B3
Autrechêne (90) 139 J1
Autrêches (60) 39 G2
Autrecourt-et-Pourron (08) . . 23 G5
Autrécourt-sur-Aire (55) . . 64 A1
Autremencourt (02) 20 E4
Autrepierre (54) 67 G5
Autreppes (02) 21 F2
Autretot (76) 15 G5
Autreville (02) 19 K6
Autreville (88) 93 H2
Autréville-Saint-Lambert (55) . . 23 G6
Autreville-sur-la-Renne (52) . . 115 K1
Autreville-sur-Moselle (54) . . 65 K3
Autrey (54) 94 A1
Autrey (88) 95 F4
Autrey-le-Vay (70) 138 D2
Autrey-lès-Cerre (70) 138 C1
Autrey-lès-Gray (70) 136 E3
Autricourt (21) 115 G2
Autruche (08) 42 D1
Autruy-sur-Juine (45) 86 C5
Autry (08) 42 C4
Autry-Issards (03) 168 C4
Autry-le-Châtel (45) 131 G2
Autun (71) 153 F4
Auty (82) 250 A5
Auvare (06) 261 F6
Auve (51) 63 G1
Auvernaux (91) 87 F2
Auvers (43) 219 H6
Auvers (50) 31 F1
Auvers-le-Hamon (72) . . . 105 J4
Auvers-Saint-Georges (91) . . 86 D2
Auvers-sous-Montfaucon (72) . . 106 B2
Auvers-sur-Oise (95) 58 C1
Auverse (49) 126 C3
Auvet-et-la-Chapelotte (70) . . 137 F3
Auvillar (82) 248 E6
Auvillars (14) 33 J5
Auvillars-sur-Saône (21) . . 154 C3
Auvilliers-les-Forges (08) . . 21 K2
Auvilliers (76) 16 E3
Auvilliers-en-Gâtinais (45) . . 111 F3
Aux-Aussat (32) 285 K2
Auxais (50) 31 F2
Auxange (39) 155 J1
Auxant (21) 153 J2
Auxelles-Bas (90) 119 G5
Auxelles-Haut (90) 119 G5
Auxerre (89) 113 G5
Auxey-Duresses (21) 153 K4
Auxi-le-Château (62) 9 J3
Aux Marais (60) 37 G2
Auxon (10) 113 K1
Auxon (70) 118 B6
Auxon-Dessous (25). 137 K5

Auxon-Dessus (25) 137 K5
Auxonne (21) 155 F1
Auxy (45) 111 F1
Auxy (71) 153 G4
Auzainvilliers (88) 93 H5
Auzances (23) 183 K5
Auzas (31) 287 F6
Auzat (09) 307 H5
Auzat-la-Combelle (63) . . . 203 F6
Auzay (85) 160 D4
Auzebosc (76) 15 G5
Auzelles (63) 203 H4
Auzers (15) 217 H3
Auzeville-Tolosane (31) . . . 288 C1
Auzielle (31) 288 D1
Auzits (12) 251 J1
Auzon (43) 219 G1
Auzouer-en-Touraine (37) . . 128 A3
Auzouville-Auberbosc (76) . . 14 E5
Auzouville-l'Esneval (76) . . 15 H5
Auzouville-sur-Ry (76) . . . 35 K2
Auzouville-sur-Saâne (76) . . 15 J4
Availles-en-Châtellerault (86) . . 163 H1
Availles-Limouzine (86) . . 180 B3
Availles-sur-Seiche (35) . . 104 A3
Availles-Thouarsais (79) . . 144 C5
Avajan (65) 305 F4
Avallon (89) 133 K3
les Avanchers-Valmorel (73) . . 209 G5
Avançon (05) 243 F5
Avançon (08) 41 H1
Avanne-Aveney (25) 137 K6
Avant-lès-Marcilly (10) . . . 89 G3
Avant-lès-Ramerupt (10) . . 90 C3
Avanton (86) 162 E2
Avapessa (2B) 318 C3
Avaray (41) 109 G6
Avaux (08) 41 F1
Aveize (69) 205 H3
Aveizieux (42) 205 G4
Avelanges (21) 136 A2
Avelesges (80) 17 H2
Avelin (59) 6 E5
Aveluy (80) 10 D6
Avenas (69) 188 A2
Avenay (14) 32 D6
Avenay-Val-d'Or (51) . . . 41 K6
Avène (34) 272 D4
les Avenières (38) 207 H3
Avensac (32) 268 A3
Avensan (33) 211 F5
Aventignan (65) 305 H1
Averan (65) 285 G6
Averdoingt (62) 10 B2
Averdon (41) 128 E1
Avermes (03) 168 E3
Avernes (95) 37 F6
Avernes-Saint-Gourgon (61) . . 55 F2
Avernes-sous-Exmes (61) . . 54 E4
Avéron-Bergelle (32) 266 C4
Averton (53) 82 A4
Avesnelles (59) 13 H5
Avesnes (62) 4 E5
Avesnes-Chaussoy (80) . . . 17 G2
Avesnes-en-Bray (76) 36 D1
Avesnes-en-Saosnois (72) . . 83 F5
Avesnes-en-Val (76) 16 C1
Avesnes-le-Comte (62) . . . 10 C3
Avesnes-le-Sec (59) 12 B3
Avesnes-les-Aubert (59) . . 12 C4
Avesnes-lès-Bapaume (62) . . 11 F5
Avesnes-sur-Helpe (59) . . . 13 G5
Avessac (44) 102 D4
Avessé (72) 105 K3
Aveux (65) 305 H2
Avezac-Prat-Lahitte (65) . . 305 F1
Avezan (32) 268 A3
Avèze (30) 273 J2
Avèze (63) 201 J4
Avezé (72) 83 J5
Aviernoz (74) 191 G4
Avignon (84) 276 B2
Avignon-lès-Saint-Claude (39) . . 173 K5
Avignonet (38) 224 A6
Avignonet-Lauragais (31) . . 289 F4
Avillers (54) 26 C5
Avillers (88) 94 B4
Avillers-Sainte-Croix (55) . . 44 A6
Avilley (25) 138 C3
Avilly-Saint-Léonard (60) . . 38 B5
Avion (62) 11 F1
Avioth (55) 23 K5
Aviré (49) 104 E6
Avirey-Lingey (10) 114 D2
Aviron (27) 56 D1
Avize (51) 62 A2
Avocourt (55) 43 F4
Avoine (37) 145 F1
Avoine (61) 54 B5
Avoise (72) 106 A4
Avolsheim (67) 70 D3
Avon (77) 87 H3
Avon (79) 162 C6
Avon-la-Pèze (10) 89 G3
Avon-les-Roches (37) 145 H2
Avondance (62) 5 F6
Avord (18) 149 J3
Avosnes (21) 135 G5
Avot (21) 136 A1
Avoudrey (25) 157 F1
Avrainville (54) 65 J4

Avrainville (88) 94 B3
Avrainville (91) 86 D3
Avranches (50) 51 K3
Avranville (88) 92 E3
Avrechy (60) 38 A2
Avrée (58) 152 B6
Avremesnil (76) 15 J2
Avressieux (73) 207 K4
Avreuil (10) 114 A2
Avricourt (54) 67 G5
Avricourt (57) 67 G5
Avricourt (60) 19 G5
Avrieux (73) 226 A2
Avrigney-Virey (70) 137 H5
Avrigny (60) 38 B3
Avril (54) 26 E5
Avril-sur-Loire (58) 151 F6
Avrillé (49) 125 G3
Avrillé (85) 159 H4
Avrillé-les-Ponceaux (37) . . 126 E4
Avrilly (03) 170 B6
Avrilly (27) 56 D2
Avrilly (61) 81 G1
Avroult (62) 3 F6
Avy (17) 195 H4
Awoingt (59) 11 K4
Ax-les-Thermes (09) 308 A6
Axat (11) 308 A5
Axiat (09) 307 K5
Ay (51) 61 K1
Ay-sur-Moselle (57) 27 H5
Ayat-sur-Sioule (63) 184 D4
Aydat (63) 202 C3
Aydie (64) 285 F1
Aydius (64) 303 F2
Aydoilles (88) 94 E5
Ayen (19) 215 G3
Ayencourt (80) 18 D5
Ayette (62) 10 E4
Ayguatébia-Talau (66) 313 K5
Ayguemorte-les-Graves (33) . . 229 H3
Ayguesvives (31) 288 D3
Ayguetinte (32) 267 G5
Ayherre (64) 282 D2
Ayn (73) 207 K4
Aynac (46) 234 B3
les Aynans (70) 138 D1
Ayrens (15) 217 G6
Ayron (86) 162 C2
Ayros-Arbouix (65) 304 B2
Ayse (74) 191 J3
Ayssènes (12) 252 D6
Aytré (17) 176 D3
les Ayvelles (08) 22 D4
Ayzac-Ost (65) 304 A2
Ayzieu (32) 266 B3
Azannes-et-Soumazannes (55) . . 26 A5
Azas (31) 269 K5
Azat-Châtenet (23) 182 C4
Azat-le-Ris (87) 181 F1
Azay-le-Brûlé (79) 161 J5
Azay-le-Ferron (36) 146 D6
Azay-le-Rideau (37) 127 G6
Azay-sur-Cher (37) 128 A5
Azay-sur-Indre (37) 146 C1
Azay-sur-Thouet (79) 161 J2
Azé (41) 108 B4
Azé (53) 105 F4
Azé (71) 171 J5
Azelot (54) 66 B6
Azerables (23) 165 G6
Azerailles (54) 95 F1
Azerat (24) 214 E4
Azérat (43) 219 H1
Azereix (65) 285 G5
Azet (65) 305 F5
Azeville (50) 29 F4
Azillanet (34) 291 F4
Azille (11) 290 E5
Azilone-Ampaza (2A) 320 E6
Azincourt (62) 5 F6
Azolette (69) 187 J2
Azoudange (57) 67 G4
Azur (40) 262 C3
Azy (18) 149 K1
Azy-le-Vif (58) 168 D1
Azy-sur-Marne (02) 60 E2
Azzana (2A) 320 D3

B

Baâlon (55) 43 G1
Baâlons (08) 22 C5
Babeau-Bouldoux (34) 291 G4
Baboeuf (60) 19 J6
Baby (77) 88 D3
Baccarat (54) 95 F2
Baccon (45) 109 H4
Bach (46) 250 D3
Bachant (59) 13 G3
Bachas (31) 287 G5
la Bachellerie (24) 214 E4
Bachivillers (60) 37 F4
Bachos (31) 305 H4
Bachy (59) 7 F3
Bacilly (50) 51 J3
Baconnes (51) 41 H5
la Baconnière (53) 80 D6
Bacouël (60) 18 B5
Bacouel-sur-Selle (80) 18 A3

Bacourt (57) 66 C2
Bacquepuis (27) 35 H6
Bacqueville (27) 36 A3
Bacqueville-en-Caux (76) . . 15 J3
Badailhac (15) 235 K1
Badaroux (48) 237 J6
Badecon-le-Pin (36) 165 H4
Badefols-d'Ans (24) 215 F3
Badefols-sur-Dordogne (24) . . 232 B2
Baden (56) 100 E5
Badens (11) 290 C5
Badevel (25) 139 J2
Badinières (38) 207 F5
Badménil-aux-Bois (88) . . . 94 E4
Badonviller (54) 95 H1
Badonvilliers-Gérauvilliers (55) . . 93 F1
Baerendorf (57) 67 J2
Baerenthal (57) 69 H4
la Baffe (88) 94 E5
Baffie (63) 204 A6
Bagard (30) 255 G6
Bagas (33) 230 C5
Bagat-en-Quercy (46) 249 H2
Bâgé-la-Ville (01) 172 A6
Bâgé-le-Châtel (01) 172 A6
Bagert (09) 306 D1
Bages (11) 310 C1
Bages (66) 315 G3
Bagiry (31) 305 J3
Bagnac-sur-Célé (46) 234 E4
Bagneaux (89) 89 G5
Bagneaux-sur-Loing (77) . . 87 H5
Bagnères-de-Bigorre (65) . . 304 D1
Bagnères-de-Luchon (31) . . 305 H5
Bagneux (02) 39 J2
Bagneux (03) 168 D2
Bagneux (36) 148 A1
Bagneux (51) 89 J2
Bagneux (54) 93 H1
Bagneux (92) 58 E4
Bagneux-la-Fosse (10) 114 D3
Bagnizeau (17) 178 B6
Bagnoles (11) 290 C5
Bagnoles-de-l'Orne (61) . . . 81 J1
Bagnolet (93) 59 F3
Bagnols (63) 201 J5
Bagnols (69) 188 A6
Bagnols-en-Forêt (83) 280 B6
Bagnols-les-Bains (48) . . . 238 A6
Bagnols-sur-Cèze (30) 256 C5
Bagnot (21) 154 C3
Baguer-Morvan (35) 51 F4
Baguer-Pican (35) 51 G4
Baho (66) 310 B6
Bahus-Soubiran (40) 265 J5
Baigneaux (28) 109 K1
Baigneaux (33) 230 B3
Baigneaux (41) 108 E5
Baignes (70) 138 A1
Baignes-Sainte-Radegonde (16) . . 212 B1
Baigneux-les-Juifs (21) . . . 135 G2
Baignolet (28) 85 H6
Baigts (40) 264 D5
Baigts-de-Béarn (64) 283 J1
Baillargues (34) 274 D5
Baillé (35) 79 K1
Bailleau-Armenonville (28) . . 85 H2
Bailleau-le-Pin (28) 84 E4
Bailleau-l'Évêque (28) 85 F2
Baillestavy (66) 314 D4
Baillet-en-France (95) 58 E1
Bailleul (59) 6 C2
Bailleul (61) 54 C4
le Bailleul (72) 106 A5
Bailleul (80) 9 G6
Bailleul-aux-Cornailles (62) . . 10 B2
Bailleul-la-Vallée (27) 34 B5
Bailleul-le-Soc (60) 38 B2
Bailleul-lès-Pernes (62) . . . 5 H6
Bailleul-Neuville (76) 16 C3
Bailleul-Sir-Berthoult (62) . . 11 F2
Bailleul-sur-Thérain (60) . . 37 J2
Bailleulmont (62) 10 D4
Bailleulval (62) 10 D3
Bailleval (62) 38 A3
Baillolet (76) 16 C3
Baillou (41) 108 A3
Bailly (60) 39 F1
Bailly (78) 58 C4
Bailly-aux-Forges (52) . . . 91 J2
Bailly-en-Rivière (76) 16 C2
Bailly-le-Franc (10) 91 G2
Bailly-Romainvilliers (77) . . 59 J3
Bain-de-Bretagne (35) 103 F2
Bainchun (62) 2 B5
Bainghen (62) 2 D5
Bains (43) 220 B6
Bains-les-Bains (88) 118 A6
Bains-sur-Oust (35) 102 D3
Bainville-aux-Miroirs (54) . . 94 A6
Bainville-aux-Saules (88) . . 94 A5
Bainville-sur-Madon (54) . . 65 K6
Bairols (06) 261 J6
Bais (35) 79 K5
Bais (53) 81 J5
Baisieux (59) 7 F4
Baissey (52) 116 C3
Baives (59) 13 K5
Baix (07) 240 B3
Baixas (66) 310 B6
Baizieux (80) 10 C6
le Baizil (51) 61 H2

Bajamont (47) 248 C4
Bajonnette (32) 267 K4
Bajus (62) 10 C1
Balacet (09) 306 B4
Baladou (46) 233 J1
Balagny-sur-Thérain (60) . . 37 K4
Balaguères (09) 306 C3
Balaguier-d'Olt (12) 234 C6
Balaguier-sur-Rance (12) . . 271 J3
Balaiseaux (39) 155 G4
Balaives-et-Butz (08) 22 C1
Balan (01) 206 D1
Balan (08) 23 F4
Balanod (39) 172 E4
Balansun (64) 283 K1
Balanzac (17) 194 E2
Balaruc-le-Vieux (34) 293 F2
Balaruc-les-Bains (34) . . . 292 E3
Balâtre (80) 19 G4
Balazé (35) 80 B6
Balazuc (07) 239 H6
Balbigny (42) 204 E3
Balbins (38) 206 E6
Balbronn (67) 70 C3
Baldenheim (67) 71 C5
Baldersheim (68) 97 C2
la Baleine (50) 31 F5
Baleix (64) 285 F3
Balesmes-sur-Marne (52) . . 116 D4
Balesta (31) 286 C5
Baleyssagues (47) 230 E4
Balgau (68) 96 E6
Balham (08) 41 G1
Balignac (82) 268 A2
Balignicourt (10) 90 E2
Bâlines (27) 56 B5
Balinghem (62) 2 D3
Baliracq-Maumusson (64) . . 284 E1
Baliros (64) 284 D5
Balizac (33) 229 J4
Ballainvilliers (91) 58 E6
Ballaison (74) 174 E6
Ballan-Miré (37) 127 H5
Ballancourt-sur-Essonne (91) . . 86 E2
Ballans (17) 196 A1
Ballay (08) 42 B2
Balledent (87) 181 G3
Ballée (53) 105 J2
Balleray (58) 151 F3
Balleroy (14) 31 K2
Ballersdorf (68) 97 A4
Balléville (88) 93 H4
Ballon (17) 177 F4
Ballon (72) 82 E6
Ballons (26) 258 C3
Ballore (71) 170 E4
Ballots (53) 104 C3
Balloy (77) 88 C3
Balma (31) 269 H6
la Balme (73) 207 K2
la Balme-de-Sillingy (74) . . 190 E5
la Balme-de-Thuy (74) . . . 191 F5
la Balme-d'Épy (39) 172 E5
la Balme-les-Grottes (38) . . 189 H6
Balnot-la-Grange (10) 114 C3
Balnot-sur-Laignes (10) . . . 114 D2
Balogna (2A) 316 E5
Balot (21) 114 E5
Balsac (12) 252 A2
Balschwiller (68) 97 A3
Balsièges (48) 254 A1
Baltzenheim (68) 96 E3
Balzac (16) 196 E3
Bambecque (59) 3 J4
Bambiderstroff (57) 45 J5
Ban-de-Laveline (88) 95 K4
Ban-de-Sapt (88) 95 J3
le Ban-Saint-Martin (57) . . 44 E5
Ban-sur-Meurthe-Clefcy (88) . . 95 J5
Banassac (48) 253 H6
Banca (64) 263 E5
Bancigny (02) 21 G3
Bancourt (62) 11 F5
Bandol (83) 297 G6
Baneins (01) 188 D3
Baneuil (24) 231 K2
Bangor (56) 120 B4
Banios (65) 304 E2
Banize (23) 182 E6
Bannalec (29) 99 G2
Bannans (25) 156 E3
Bannay (18) 131 K5
Bannay (51) 61 H3
Bannay (57) 45 H5
Banne (07) 255 H2
Bannegon (18) 149 K6
Bannes (46) 234 C3
Bannes (51) 61 K4
Bannes (52) 116 D3
Bannes (53) 105 J3
Banneville-la-Campagne (14) . . 33 F5
Banneville-sur-Ajon (14) . . 32 C6
Bannières (81) 270 A6
Bannoncourt (55) 64 E2
Bannost-Villegagnon (77) . . 60 C2
Banogne-Recouvrance (08) . . 21 H6
Banon (04) 258 C6
Banos (40) 265 F4
Bans (39) 155 H3
Bansat (63) 203 F6
Bantanges (71) 172 B3
Banteux (59) 11 J5

Banthelu (95) . . . 36 E6
Bantheville (55) . . . 42 E2
Bantigny (59) . . . 11 J3
Bantouzelle (59) . . . 11 J5
Bantzenheim (68) . . . 97 D1
Banvillars (90) . . . 139 H1
Banville (14) . . . 32 C3
Banvou (61) . . . 53 H5
Banyuls-dels-Aspres (66) . . . 315 G4
Banyuls-sur-Mer (66) . . . 315 G5
Baon (89) . . . 114 B4
Baons-le-Comte (76) . . . 15 G5
Bapaume (62) . . . 11 F5
Bar (19) . . . 216 B2
Bar-le-Duc (55) . . . 64 B4
Bar-lès-Buzancy (08) . . . 42 G2
Bar-sur-Aube (10) . . . 91 G5
le Bar-sur-Loup (06) . . . 280 E4
Bar-sur-Seine (10) . . . 114 A1
Baracé (49) . . . 125 J1
Baraigne (11) . . . 289 F4
Baraize (36) . . . 165 H4
Baralle (62) . . . 11 H4
Baraqueville (12) . . . 252 A4
Barastre (62) . . . 11 H5
Baratier (05) . . . 243 J5
Barbachen (65) . . . 285 J2
Barbaggio (2B) . . . 317 D5
Barbaira (11) . . . 290 C6
Barbaise (08) . . . 22 C4
Barbas (54) . . . 67 G6
Barbaste (47) . . . 247 J5
Barbâtre (85) . . . 140 C3
Barbazan (31) . . . 305 J2
Barbazan-Debat (65) . . . 285 H5
Barbazan-Dessus (65) . . . 285 J6
Barbechat (44) . . . 123 K3
la Barben (13) . . . 277 F5
Barbentane (13) . . . 276 A2
Barberaz (73) . . . 208 B4
Barberey-Saint-Sulpice (10) . . . 90 A4
Barberier (03) . . . 185 G2
Barbery (14) . . . 53 K1
Barbery (60) . . . 38 C5
Barbeville (14) . . . 32 A3
Barbey (77) . . . 88 B4
Barbey-Seroux (88) . . . 95 H6
Barbezières (16) . . . 178 D6
Barbezieux-Saint-Hilaire (16) . . . 196 B5
Barbières (26) . . . 222 E6
Barbirey-sur-Ouche (21) . . . 135 H6
Barbizon (77) . . . 87 G3
Barbonne-Fayel (51) . . . 61 H4
Barbonville (54) . . . 66 C6
le Barboux (25) . . . 157 J1
Barbuise (10) . . . 89 G1
Barby (08) . . . 21 K6
Barby (73) . . . 208 C4
Barc (27) . . . 35 F6
le Barcarès (66) . . . 310 D5
Barcelonne (26) . . . 240 E1
Barcelonne-du-Gers (32) . . . 265 K5
Barcelonnette (04) . . . 260 D1
Barchain (57) . . . 67 H4
Barcillonnette (05) . . . 259 F1
Barcugnan (32) . . . 286 B3
Barcus (64) . . . 283 J5
Barcy (77) . . . 59 K1
Bard (42) . . . 204 C4
Bard-le-Régulier (21) . . . 153 F2
Bard-lès-Époisses (21) . . . 134 C3
Bard-lès-Pesmes (70) . . . 137 G5
la Barde (17) . . . 212 C4
Bardenac (16) . . . 212 D2
Bardigues (82) . . . 268 B1
le Bardon (45) . . . 109 H5
Bardos (64) . . . 282 E1
Bardou (24) . . . 231 K3
Bardouville (76) . . . 35 G2
Barèges (65) . . . 304 C3
Bareilles (65) . . . 305 G4
Barembach (67) . . . 70 A5
Baren (31) . . . 305 H4
Barentin (76) . . . 15 J6
Barenton (50) . . . 52 E6
Barenton-Bugny (02) . . . 20 D5
Barenton-Cel (02) . . . 20 D5
Barenton-sur-Serre (02) . . . 20 D5
Barésia-sur-l'Ain (39) . . . 173 H3
Barfleur (50) . . . 29 G2
Bargème (83) . . . 279 K4
Bargemon (83) . . . 279 K5
Barges (21) . . . 154 C1
Barges (43) . . . 238 C2
Barges (70) . . . 117 H4
Bargny (60) . . . 39 F5
Barie (33) . . . 230 B5
les Barils (27) . . . 56 A5
Barinque (64) . . . 284 C3
Barisey-au-Plain (54) . . . 93 H1
Barisey-la-Côte (54) . . . 93 H1
Barisis (02) . . . 20 A5
Barizey (71) . . . 153 J6
Barjac (09) . . . 306 D2
Barjac (30) . . . 255 K3
Barjac (48) . . . 253 K1
Barjols (83) . . . 278 E6
Barjon (21) . . . 135 K1
Barjouville (28) . . . 85 G3
Barles (04) . . . 259 K3
Barlest (65) . . . 285 F6
Barleux (80) . . . 19 G2

Barlieu (18) . . . 131 H3
Barlin (62) . . . 5 K6
Barly (62) . . . 10 C3
Barly (80) . . . 10 A4
Barmainville (28) . . . 86 A5
Barnas (07) . . . 239 F4
Barnave (26) . . . 241 H4
Barnay (71) . . . 153 F2
Barneville-Carteret (50) . . . 28 B5
Barneville-la-Bertran (14) . . . 33 K2
Barneville-sur-Seine (27) . . . 35 H2
la Baroche-sous-Lucé (61) . . . 81 G1
les Baroches (54) . . . 26 A6
Baromesnil (76) . . . 8 C6
Baron (30) . . . 255 J6
Baron (33) . . . 229 K2
Baron (60) . . . 38 D5
Baron (71) . . . 170 D4
Baron-sur-Odon (14) . . . 32 D5
Baronville (57) . . . 66 E1
Barou-en-Auge (14) . . . 54 C2
Baroville (10) . . . 91 G6
le Barp (33) . . . 229 F5
Barquet (27) . . . 56 A1
Barr (67) . . . 70 C5
Barrais-Bussolles (03) . . . 186 B1
Barran (32) . . . 267 G6
Barrancoueu (65) . . . 305 F3
Barras (04) . . . 259 H5
Barraute-Camu (64) . . . 283 H3
Barraux (38) . . . 208 C5
la Barre (39) . . . 155 J1
la Barre (70) . . . 138 B4
Barre (81) . . . 272 B4
la Barre-de-Monts (85) . . . 140 C4
la Barre-de-Semilly (50) . . . 31 H3
Barre-des-Cévennes (48) . . . 254 C4
la Barre-en-Ouche (27) . . . 55 J2
Barrême (04) . . . 279 H1
Barret (16) . . . 196 A5
Barret-de-Lioure (26) . . . 258 B4
Barret-le-Bas (05) . . . 258 D3
Barretaine (39) . . . 155 J5
Barrettali (2B) . . . 317 C3
Barriac-les-Bosquets (15) . . . 217 F4
Barro (16) . . . 179 G5
Barrou (37) . . . 146 A5
le Barroux (84) . . . 257 H5
Barry (65) . . . 285 G6
Barry-d'Islemade (82) . . . 249 H6
Bars (24) . . . 214 D5
Bars (32) . . . 285 K1
Barsac (26) . . . 241 G3
Barsac (33) . . . 229 K5
Barst (57) . . . 68 B3
Bart (25) . . . 139 H2
Bartenheim (68) . . . 97 D4
Barthe (65) . . . 286 B4
la Barthe-de-Neste (65) . . . 305 F1
Barthelmont (55) . . . 92 D1
Bartherans (25) . . . 156 B3
Barville (27) . . . 34 C5
Barville (61) . . . 83 F2
Barville (88) . . . 93 G3
Barville-en-Gâtinais (45) . . . 111 F1
Barzan (17) . . . 194 E5
Barzun (64) . . . 285 F5
Barzy-en-Thiérache (02) . . . 13 F6
Barzy-sur-Marne (02) . . . 40 A6
Bas-en-Basset (43) . . . 220 E2
Bas-et-Lezat (63) . . . 185 H4
Bas-Lieu (59) . . . 13 G4
Bas-Mauco (40) . . . 265 G3
Bascons (40) . . . 265 H3
Bascous (32) . . . 266 D4
Baslieux (54) . . . 26 A3
Baslieux-lès-Fismes (51) . . . 40 C3
Baslieux-sous-Châtillon (51) . . . 40 D6
Basly (14) . . . 32 D3
Bassac (16) . . . 196 B3
Bassan (34) . . . 292 A3
Bassanne (33) . . . 230 C5
Basse-Goulaine (44) . . . 123 H4
Basse-Ham (57) . . . 27 H4
Basse-Rentgen (57) . . . 27 G3
Basse-sur-le-Rupt (88) . . . 119 G2
la Basse-Vaivre (70) . . . 117 K3
la Bassée (59) . . . 6 B5
Bassemberg (67) . . . 70 B6
Basseneville (14) . . . 33 G4
Bassens (33) . . . 229 H1
Bassens (73) . . . 208 B4
Bassercles (40) . . . 284 A1
Basses (86) . . . 144 E3
Basseux (62) . . . 10 D3
Bassevelle (77) . . . 60 D2
Bassignac (15) . . . 217 H2
Bassignac-le-Bas (19) . . . 216 B6
Bassignac-le-Haut (19) . . . 216 E3
Bassigney (70) . . . 118 B4
Bassilac (24) . . . 214 B3
Bassillon-Vauzé (64) . . . 285 G2
Bassing (57) . . . 67 G2
Bassoles-Aulers (02) . . . 39 J1
Bassoncourt (52) . . . 117 F1
Bassou (89) . . . 113 F4
Bassoues (32) . . . 266 E6
Bassu (51) . . . 63 G3
Bassuet (51) . . . 63 G4
Bassurels (48) . . . 254 C5
Bassussarry (64) . . . 263 D1

Bassy (74) . . . 190 C4
Bastanès (64) . . . 283 J3
Bastelica (2A) . . . 320 E4
Bastelicaccia (2A) . . . 320 C5
Bastennes (40) . . . 264 D5
Bastia (2B) . . . 317 E5
la Bastide (66) . . . 314 D4
la Bastide (83) . . . 280 A4
la Bastide-Clairence (64) . . . 282 D2
la Bastide-de-Besplas (09) . . . 288 A4
la Bastide-de-Bousignac (09) . . . 308 B2
la Bastide-de-Lordat (09) . . . 288 E6
la Bastide-de-Sérou (09) . . . 307 G2
la Bastide-d'Engras (30) . . . 256 B6
la Bastide-des-Jourdans (84) . . . 277 K3
la Bastide-l'Evêque (12) . . . 251 G3
la Bastide-Pradines (12) . . . 272 D1
la Bastide-Puylaurent (48) . . . 238 C5
la Bastide-Solages (12) . . . 271 H2
la Bastide-sur-l'Hers (09) . . . 308 B3
la Bastidonne (84) . . . 277 K4
le Bastit (46) . . . 233 K4
Basville (23) . . . 201 G1
la Bataille (79) . . . 178 D3
Bathelémont-lès-Bauzemont (54) . . . 66 D5
Bathernay (26) . . . 222 D3
la Bâthie (73) . . . 209 G3
la Bâtie-des-Fonds (26) . . . 242 A6
la Bâtie-Divisin (38) . . . 207 J3
la Bâtie-Montgascon (38) . . . 207 H4
la Bâtie-Montsaléon (05) . . . 258 D1
la Bâtie-Neuve (05) . . . 243 F5
la Bâtie-Rolland (26) . . . 240 C5
la Bâtie-Vieille (05) . . . 243 F5
les Bâties (70) . . . 137 J2
Batilly (54) . . . 44 D4
Batilly (61) . . . 54 A5
Batilly-en-Gâtinais (45) . . . 110 E2
Batilly-en-Puisaye (45) . . . 131 K2
Bats (40) . . . 265 H5
Batsère (65) . . . 304 E1
Battenans-les-Mines (25) . . . 138 C4
Battenans-Varin (25) . . . 139 G5
Battenheim (68) . . . 97 C1
Battexey (88) . . . 94 A3
Battigny (54) . . . 93 J2
Battrans (70) . . . 137 G4
Batz-sur-Mer (44) . . . 121 H5
Batzendorf (67) . . . 69 K6
Baubigny (21) . . . 153 J4
Baubigny (50) . . . 28 B5
la Bauche (73) . . . 208 A5
Baud (56) . . . 100 D2
Baudement (51) . . . 89 H1
Baudemont (71) . . . 187 H1
Baudignan (40) . . . 247 F6
Baudignécourt (55) . . . 92 D1
Baudinard-sur-Verdon (83) . . . 279 F4
Baudoncourt (70) . . . 118 C5
Baudonvilliers (55) . . . 63 K5
Baudre (50) . . . 31 H3
Baudrecourt (52) . . . 91 K3
Baudrecourt (57) . . . 66 C1
Baudreix (64) . . . 284 E5
Baudrémont (55) . . . 64 D1
Baudres (36) . . . 147 J3
Baudreville (28) . . . 86 A4
Baudreville (50) . . . 28 C6
Baudricourt (88) . . . 93 K4
Baudrières (71) . . . 172 B2
Bauduen (83) . . . 279 F4
Baugé (49) . . . 126 B2
Baugy (18) . . . 149 K3
Baugy (60) . . . 38 D2
Baugy (71) . . . 186 E1
Baulay (70) . . . 117 K5
Baule (45) . . . 109 H5
la Baule-Escoublac (44) . . . 121 J5
Baulme-la-Roche (21) . . . 135 J5
Baulne (91) . . . 86 E2
Baulne-en-Brie (02) . . . 61 G2
Baulny (55) . . . 42 E4
Baulon (35) . . . 78 D6
Baulou (09) . . . 307 H2
la Baume (74) . . . 175 G6
la Baume-Cornillane (26) . . . 240 D2
la Baume-de-Transit (26) . . . 256 E2
la Baume-d'Hostun (26) . . . 223 F5
Baume-les-Dames (25) . . . 138 D4
Baume-les-Messieurs (39) . . . 173 H1
Bauné (49) . . . 125 J3
Baupte (50) . . . 31 F1
Bauquay (14) . . . 53 G1
Baurech (33) . . . 229 J3
la Baussaine (35) . . . 78 E1
Bauvin (59) . . . 6 C5
les Baux-de-Breteuil (27) . . . 56 A3
les Baux-de-Provence (13) . . . 276 B4
les Baux-Sainte-Croix (27) . . . 56 C2
Bauzemont (54) . . . 66 D5
Bauzy (41) . . . 129 H3
Bavans (25) . . . 139 G2
Bavay (59) . . . 13 F2
Bavelincourt (80) . . . 18 C1
Bavent (14) . . . 33 H4
Baverans (39) . . . 155 H2
Bavilliers (90) . . . 139 H1
Bavinchove (59) . . . 3 J4
Bavincourt (62) . . . 10 D3
Bax (31) . . . 288 A5
Bay (70) . . . 137 H5

Bay-sur-Aube (52) . . . 116 A5
Bayac (24) . . . 232 A3
Bayard-sur-Marne (52) . . . 92 A1
Bayas (33) . . . 212 B5
Baye (29) . . . 99 H3
Baye (51) . . . 61 H3
Bayecourt (88) . . . 94 D4
Bayel (10) . . . 91 H4
Bayencourt (80) . . . 10 D5
Bayenghem-lès-Eperlecques (62) . . . 3 F4
Bayenghem-lès-Seninghem (62) . . . 2 E5
Bayers (16) . . . 179 G6
Bayet (03) . . . 185 H2
Bayeux (14) . . . 32 B3
Bayon (54) . . . 94 C2
Bayon-sur-Gironde (33) . . . 211 H5
Bayonne (64) . . . 282 B1
Bayons (04) . . . 259 H2
Bayonville (08) . . . 42 C2
Bayonville-sur-Mad (54) . . . 65 J1
Bayonvillers (80) . . . 18 D2
Bazac (16) . . . 212 D3
Bazaiges (36) . . . 165 G4
Bazailles (54) . . . 26 D4
Bazainville (78) . . . 57 J4
Bazancourt (51) . . . 41 G3
Bazancourt (60) . . . 17 F6
Bazarnes (89) . . . 133 H1
Bazas (33) . . . 246 D1
Bazauges (17) . . . 178 D6
Bazegney (88) . . . 94 B4
Bazeilles (08) . . . 23 F4
Bazeilles-sur-Othain (55) . . . 23 K6
Bazelat (23) . . . 165 G6
Bazemont (78) . . . 58 A2
Bazens (47) . . . 247 K4
Bazentin (80) . . . 10 E6
Bazenville (14) . . . 32 C3
la Bazeuge (87) . . . 181 F2
Bazian (32) . . . 267 F5
Bazicourt (60) . . . 38 C3
Baziège (31) . . . 288 D2
Bazien (88) . . . 95 F2
Bazillac (65) . . . 285 H3
Bazincourt-sur-Epte (27) . . . 36 E3
Bazincourt-sur-Saulx (55) . . . 64 A5
Bazinghen (62) . . . 2 B4
Bazinval (76) . . . 16 E1
la Bazoche-Gouet (28) . . . 108 B1
Bazoches (58) . . . 133 J5
Bazoches-au-Houlme (61) . . . 54 A4
Bazoches-en-Dunois (28) . . . 109 H1
Bazoches-lès-Bray (77) . . . 88 C3
Bazoches-les-Gallerandes (45) . . . 110 B1
Bazoches-les-Hautes (28) . . . 109 K1
Bazoches-sur-Guyonne (78) . . . 57 K4
Bazoches-sur-Hoëne (61) . . . 83 G1
Bazoches-sur-le-Betz (45) . . . 112 A1
Bazoches-sur-Vesles (02) . . . 40 B3
la Bazoge (50) . . . 52 C5
la Bazoge (72) . . . 106 D1
la Bazoge-Montpinçon (53) . . . 81 G6
Bazoges-en-Paillers (85) . . . 142 C4
Bazoges-en-Pareds (85) . . . 160 D2
Bazoilles-et-Ménil (88) . . . 94 A4
Bazoilles-sur-Meuse (88) . . . 93 F4
Bazolles (58) . . . 151 J2
Bazoncourt (57) . . . 45 G6
la Bazoque (14) . . . 31 K3
la Bazoque (61) . . . 53 G4
Bazoques (27) . . . 34 C5
Bazordan (65) . . . 286 C5
la Bazouge-de-Chemeré (53) . . . 105 H2
la Bazouge-des-Alleux (53) . . . 81 G6
la Bazouge-du-Désert (35) . . . 80 C2
Bazougers (53) . . . 105 G2
Bazouges-la-Pérouse (35) . . . 51 H6
Bazouges-sur-le-Loir (72) . . . 106 A6
Bazuel (59) . . . 12 D5
Bazugues (32) . . . 286 A2
Bazus (31) . . . 269 H5
Bazus-Aure (65) . . . 305 F2
Bazus-Neste (65) . . . 305 F2
le Béage (07) . . . 238 E2
Béalcourt (80) . . . 9 K4
Béalencourt (62) . . . 9 J1
Béard (58) . . . 151 F5
Beaubec-la-Rosière (76) . . . 16 D5
Beaubery (71) . . . 170 E5
Beaubray (27) . . . 56 B3
Beaucaire (30) . . . 275 K3
Beaucaire (32) . . . 267 F3
Beaucamps-le-Jeune (80) . . . 17 G3
Beaucamps-le-Vieux (80) . . . 17 G2
Beaucamps-Ligny (59) . . . 6 C4
Beaucé (35) . . . 80 B4
Beaucens (65) . . . 304 B2
le Beaucet (84) . . . 276 E1
Beauchalot (31) . . . 306 A1
Beauchamp (95) . . . 58 D1
Beauchamps (50) . . . 51 K1
Beauchamps (80) . . . 8 D6
Beauchamps-sur-Huillard (45) . . . 111 F3
Beauchastel (07) . . . 240 B2
Beauche (28) . . . 56 B5
Beauchemin (52) . . . 116 C3
Beauchêne (41) . . . 108 B3
Beauchêne (61) . . . 53 F5
Beauchery-Saint-Martin (77) . . . 60 E6
Beauclair (55) . . . 43 F1
Beaucoudray (50) . . . 31 G5

Beaucourt (90) . . . 139 J2
Beaucourt-en-Santerre (80) . . . 18 D3
Beaucourt-sur-l'Ancre (80) . . . 10 E5
Beaucourt-sur-l'Hallue (80) . . . 18 C1
Beaucouzé (49) . . . 125 F3
Beaucroissant (38) . . . 223 H1
Beaudéan (65) . . . 304 D2
Beaudéduit (60) . . . 17 J3
Beaudignies (59) . . . 12 D3
Beaudricourt (62) . . . 10 B3
Beaufai (61) . . . 55 H5
Beaufay (72) . . . 83 F6
Beauficel (50) . . . 52 D4
Beauficel-en-Lyons (27) . . . 36 B2
Beaufin (38) . . . 242 D2
Beaufort (31) . . . 287 J2
Beaufort (34) . . . 291 F4
Beaufort (38) . . . 222 E1
Beaufort (39) . . . 173 F3
Beaufort (59) . . . 13 H3
Beaufort (73) . . . 209 H2
Beaufort-Blavincourt (62) . . . 10 C3
Beaufort-en-Argonne (55) . . . 43 F1
Beaufort-en-Santerre (80) . . . 18 E3
Beaufort-en-Vallée (49) . . . 125 K4
Beaufort-sur-Gervanne (26) . . . 240 D2
Beaufou (85) . . . 141 J5
Beaufour-Druval (14) . . . 33 H4
Beaufremont (88) . . . 93 G5
Beaugas (47) . . . 231 K6
Beaugeay (17) . . . 176 E6
Beaugency (45) . . . 109 H5
Beaugies-sous-Bois (60) . . . 19 J5
Beaujeu (04) . . . 260 A4
Beaujeu (69) . . . 188 A3
Beaujeu-Saint-Vallier-
   Pierrejux-et-Quitteur (70) . . . 137 G3
Beaulandais (61) . . . 81 H1
Beaulencourt (62) . . . 11 F5
Beaulieu (07) . . . 255 J6
Beaulieu (14) . . . 31 K6
Beaulieu (15) . . . 201 H6
Beaulieu (21) . . . 115 H6
Beaulieu (34) . . . 274 D5
Beaulieu (36) . . . 164 E6
Beaulieu (38) . . . 223 H3
Beaulieu (43) . . . 220 C4
Beaulieu (58) . . . 133 F6
Beaulieu (61) . . . 55 K5
Beaulieu (63) . . . 203 F6
Beaulieu-en-Argonne (55) . . . 63 K1
Beaulieu-les-Fontaines (60) . . . 19 G5
Beaulieu-lès-Loches (37) . . . 146 D2
Beaulieu-sous-la-Roche (85) . . . 159 G1
Beaulieu-sous-Parthenay (79) . . . 161 K3
Beaulieu-sur-Dordogne (19) . . . 216 B6
Beaulieu-sur-Layon (49) . . . 125 G5
Beaulieu-sur-Loire (45) . . . 131 J3
Beaulieu-sur-Mer (06) . . . 281 H4
Beaulieu-sur-Oudon (53) . . . 104 C2
Beaulieu-sur-Sonnette (16) . . . 179 J6
Beaulon (03) . . . 169 H3
Beaumais (14) . . . 54 B3
Beaumarchés (32) . . . 266 C6
Beaumat (46) . . . 233 J4
Beaumé (02) . . . 21 H2
la Beaume (05) . . . 242 A5
Beauménil (88) . . . 95 G5
Beaumerie-Saint-Martin (62) . . . 4 C6
Beaumes-de-Venise (84) . . . 257 G5
Beaumesnil (14) . . . 31 J6
Beaumesnil (27) . . . 55 K1
Beaumettes (84) . . . 277 F3
Beaumetz (80) . . . 9 J4
Beaumetz-lès-Aire (62) . . . 5 G5
Beaumetz-lès-Cambrai (62) . . . 11 G5
Beaumetz-lès-Loges (62) . . . 10 D3
Beaumont (07) . . . 239 F6
Beaumont (19) . . . 216 B1
Beaumont (24) . . . 232 A3
Beaumont (32) . . . 266 E2
Beaumont (43) . . . 219 G2
Beaumont (54) . . . 65 G3
Beaumont (63) . . . 202 D2
Beaumont (74) . . . 191 F3
Beaumont (86) . . . 163 G1
Beaumont (89) . . . 113 G4
Beaumont-de-Lomagne (82) . . . 268 C3
Beaumont-de-Pertuis (84) . . . 278 A4
Beaumont-du-Gâtinais (77) . . . 111 F1
Beaumont-du-Lac (87) . . . 200 B2
Beaumont-du-Ventoux (84) . . . 257 H4
Beaumont-en-Argonne (08) . . . 23 G6
Beaumont-en-Auge (14) . . . 33 J4
Beaumont-en-Beine (02) . . . 19 J4
Beaumont-en-Cambrésis (59) . . . 12 C5
Beaumont-en-Diois (26) . . . 241 J5
Beaumont-en-Verdunois (55) . . . 43 H4
Beaumont-en-Véron (37) . . . 145 F1
Beaumont-Hague (50) . . . 28 B2
Beaumont-Hamel (80) . . . 10 D5
Beaumont-la-Ferrière (58) . . . 150 E1
Beaumont-la-Ronce (37) . . . 127 J2
Beaumont-le-Hareng (76) . . . 16 B5
Beaumont-le-Roger (27) . . . 34 E6
Beaumont-les-Autels (28) . . . 84 B5
Beaumont-les-Nonains (60) . . . 37 G3
Beaumont-lès-Randan (63) . . . 185 J5
Beaumont-lès-Valence (26) . . . 240 D2
Beaumont-Monteux (26) . . . 222 C5
Beaumont-Pied-de-Boeuf (53) . . . 105 H3
Beaumont-Pied-de-Boeuf (72) . . . 107 F5

Beaumont-Sardolles (58) 151 G5
Beaumont-sur-Dême (72) 107 H6
Beaumont-sur-Grosne (71) . . . 171 K2
Beaumont-sur-Lèze (31) 288 B3
Beaumont-sur-Oise (95) 37 J6
Beaumont-sur-Sarthe (72) . . . 82 D5
Beaumont-sur-Vesle (51) 41 G5
Beaumont-sur-Vingeanne (21) . 136 D3
Beaumont-Village (37) 147 F1
Beaumontel (27) 34 E6
Beaumotte-Aubertans (70) . . . 138 B3
Beaumotte-lès-Pin (70) 137 J5
Beaunay (51) 61 J3
Beaune (21) 154 A3
Beaune-d'Allier (03) 184 D1
Beaune-la-Rolande (45) 111 F2
Beaune-sur-Arzon (43) 220 B2
Beaunotte (21) 135 H1
Beaupont (01) 172 D5
Beaupouyet (24) 213 F6
Beaupréau (49) 142 D1
Beaupuy (31) 269 H6
Beaupuy (32) 268 C6
Beaupuy (47) 230 E6
Beaupuy (82) 268 D3
Beauquesne (80) 10 B5
Beaurain (59) 12 D4
Beaurains (62) 11 F3
Beaurains-lès-Noyon (60) . . . 19 H5
Beaurainville (62) 9 G1
Beaurecueil (13) 296 E1
Beauregard (01) 188 B5
Beauregard (46) 250 D3
Beauregard-Baret (26) 222 E5
Beauregard-de-Terrasson (24) . 215 F4
Beauregard-et-Bassac (24) . . . 213 K6
Beauregard-l'Évêque (63) . . . 203 F1
Beauregard-Vendon (63) 185 F5
Beaurepaire (38) 222 D1
Beaurepaire (60) 38 B4
Beaurepaire (76) 14 B4
Beaurepaire (85) 142 C4
Beaurepaire-en-Bresse (71) . . 172 E2
Beaurepaire-sur-Sambre (59) . 13 F5
Beaurevoir (02) 11 K6
Beaurières (26) 241 K5
Beaurieux (02) 40 C2
Beaurieux (59) 13 J4
Beauronne (24) 213 G5
Beausemblant (26) 222 B3
Beausite (55) 64 B2
Beausoleil (06) 281 J3
Beaussac (24) 197 H5
Beaussais (79) 178 D1
Beaussault (76) 16 E4
Beausse (49) 124 C5
le Beausset (83) 297 H5
Beauteville (31) 288 E4
Beautheil (77) 60 B5
Beautiran (33) 229 J3
Beautor (02) 20 A5
Beautot (76) 15 K5
Beauvain (61) 53 K6
Beauvais (60) 37 H2
Beauvais-sur-Matha (17) 178 C6
Beauvais-sur-Tescou (81) . . . 269 J2
Beauval (80) 10 A5
Beauval-en-Caux (76) 15 J4
Beauvallon (26) 240 C2
Beauvau (49) 125 K2
Beauvène (04) 239 J2
Beauvernois (71) 155 G5
Beauvezer (04) 260 C4
Beauville (31) 289 F2
Beauville (47) 248 E3
Beauvilliers (28) 85 H5
Beauvilliers (41) 108 E5
Beauvilliers (89) 134 A4
Beauvoir (50) 51 J4
Beauvoir (60) 18 B5
Beauvoir (77) 59 K6
Beauvoir (89) 112 E5
Beauvoir-de-Marc (38) 206 D5
Beauvoir-en-Lyons (76) 36 C1
Beauvoir-en-Royans (38) . . . 223 H4
Beauvoir-sur-Mer (85) 140 D4
Beauvoir-sur-Niort (79) 178 A2
Beauvoir-Wavans (62) 9 K3
Beauvois (62) 9 K2
Beauvois-en-Cambrésis (59) . . 12 C4
Beauvois-en-Vermandois (02) . 19 J2
Beauvoisin (26) 257 J3
Beauvoisin (30) 275 G5
Beaux (43) 220 E3
Beauzac (43) 220 E3
Beauzelle (31) 269 G5
Beauziac (47) 247 F3
Bébing (57) 67 J4
Beblenheim (68) 96 B3
Bec-de-Mortagne (76) 14 D2
le Bec-Hellouin (27) 34 E4
le Bec-Thomas (27) 35 G4
Beccas (32) 285 H4
Béceleuf (79) 161 G4
Béchamps (54) 26 C6
Bécherel (35) 78 D2
Bécheresse (16) 196 D5
Béchy (57) 66 C1
Bécon-les-Granits (49) 124 E3
Bécordel-Bécourt (80) 10 E6
Bécourt (62) 2 D6
Becquigny (02) 12 C6

Becquigny (80) 18 D4
Bédarieux (34) 272 E6
Bédarrides (84) 257 F6
Beddes (18) 166 D3
Bédéchan (32) 287 F1
Bédeille (09) 306 D1
Bédeille (64) 285 F3
Bedenac (17) 212 A3
Bédée (35) 78 D3
Bédoin (84) 257 J5
Bédouès (48) 254 C3
Bedous (64) 303 F2
Béduer (46) 234 C5
Beffes (18) 150 C3
Beffia (39) 173 G3
Beffu-et-le-Morthomme (08) . . 42 D1
Bégaar (40) 264 D3
Bégadan (33) 210 E1
Béganne (56) 102 A5
Bégard (22) 48 B4
Bègles (33) 229 H2
Begnécourt (88) 94 A5
Bégole (65) 286 A6
Bégrolles-en-Mauges (49) . . . 142 E1
la Bégude-de-Mazenc (26) . . . 240 D6
Bègues (03) 185 F3
Béguey (33) 229 K4
Béguios (64) 283 F3
Béhagnies (62) 11 F4
Béhasque-Lapiste (64) 283 G3
Béhen (80) 9 F5
Béhencourt (80) 18 C1
Béhéricourt (60) 19 H6
Behonne (55) 64 B4
Béhorléguy (64) 283 F6
Béhoust (78) 57 J4
Behren-lès-Forbach (57) 68 C2
Béhuard (49) 125 F4
Beignon (56) 78 B6
Beillé (72) 107 G1
Beine (89) 113 H5
Beine-Nauroy (51) 41 G4
Beinheim (67) 25 D3
Beire-le-Châtel (21) 136 C4
Beire-le-Fort (21) 136 C6
Beissat (23) 201 F2
Bélâbre (36) 164 D4
Belan-sur-Ource (21) 115 G3
Bélarga (34) 292 D1
Bélaye (46) 249 H1
Belberaud (31) 288 D2
Belbèse (82) 268 D2
Belbèze-de-Lauragais (31) . . . 288 D3
Belbèze-en-Comminges (31) . . 306 C1
Belcastel (12) 251 J2
Belcastel (81) 270 A6
Belcastel-et-Buc (11) 309 G2
Belcodène (13) 296 E2
Bélesta (09) 308 B4
Bélesta (66) 309 J6
Bélesta-en-Lauragais (31) . . . 289 F3
Beleymas (24) 213 J6
Belfahy (70) 119 G4
Belfays (25) 139 J5
Belflou (11) 289 F4
Belfonds (61) 54 D6
Belfort (90) 119 H6
Belfort-du-Quercy (46) 250 B4
Belfort-sur-Rebenty (11) 308 D5
Belgeard (53) 81 G5
Belgentier (83) 297 J4
Belgodère (2B) 318 D2
Belhade (40) 245 J3
Belhomert-Guéhouville (28) . . 84 C2
le Bélieu (25) 157 H1
Béligneux (01) 189 F6
Bélis (40) 246 A6
Bellac (87) 181 F3
Bellaffaire (04) 259 J1
Bellaing (59) 12 C2
Bellancourt (80) 9 G5
Bellange (57) 66 E2
Bellavilliers (61) 83 G3
le Bellay-en-Vexin (95) 37 F5
Belle-Église (60) 37 J5
Belle-et-Houllefort (62) 2 C5
Belle-Isle-en-Terre (22) 48 A5
Belleau (02) 39 J6
Belleau (54) 66 A3
Bellebat (33) 230 A3
Bellebrune (62) 2 C5
Bellechassagne (19) 200 E3
Bellechaume (89) 113 G2
Bellecombe (39) 173 K6
Bellecombe-en-Bauges (73) . . 208 D2
Bellecombe-Tarendol (26) . . . 257 K2
Bellefond (21) 136 A4
Bellefond (33) 230 B3
Bellefonds (86) 163 H2
Bellefontaine (39) 174 B3
Bellefontaine (50) 52 D5
Bellefontaine (88) 118 D2
Bellefontaine (95) 38 A6
Bellefosse (67) 70 A6
Bellegarde (30) 275 J4
Bellegarde (32) 286 D3
Bellegarde (45) 111 F3
Bellegarde (81) 271 F2

Bellegarde-du-Razès (11) . . . 308 D1
Bellegarde-en-Diois (26) . . . 241 H5
Bellegarde-en-Forez (42) . . . 205 F3
Bellegarde-en-Marche (23) . . 183 H5
Bellegarde-Poussieu (38) . . . 222 C1
Bellegarde-Sainte-Marie (31) . 268 D5
Belleherbe (25) 139 G5
Bellemagny (68) 119 K5
Bellême (61) 83 H4
Bellenaves (03) 185 F2
Bellencombre (76) 16 B4
Belleneuve (21) 136 C5
Bellenglise (02) 19 K1
Bellengreville (14) 33 F5
Bellengreville (76) 16 B2
Bellenod-sur-Seine (21) 115 G6
Bellenot-sous-Pouilly (21) . . . 135 F6
Bellentre (73) 193 A3
Belleray (55) 43 H5
Bellerive-sur-Allier (03) 185 J3
Belleroche (42) 187 J3
Belles-Forêts (57) 67 H3
Bellesserre (81) 289 J2
Bellesserre (31) 268 D4
Belleu (02) 39 J3
Belleuse (80) 17 K4
Belleville (54) 65 K3
Belleville (69) 188 B3
Belleville (79) 177 K3
Belleville-en-Caux (76) 15 J4
Belleville-et-Châtillon-sur-Bar (08) . . 42 C1
Belleville-sur-Loire (18) 131 K3
Belleville-sur-Mer (76) 16 A1
Belleville-sur-Meuse (55) . . . 43 H5
Belleville-sur-Vie (85) 141 K6
Bellevue-la-Montagne (43) . . 220 B3
Belley (01) 207 K2
Belleydoux (01) 190 B1
Bellicourt (02) 19 K1
la Bellière (61) 54 C6
la Bellière (76) 16 E5
Bellignat (01) 190 A1
Belligné (44) 124 C3
Bellignies (59) 13 F2
la Belliole (89) 112 B1
Belloc (09) 308 B2
Belloc-Saint-Clamens (32) . . . 286 B2
Bellocq (64) 283 H1
Bellon (16) 212 E2
Bellonne (62) 11 H2
Bellot (77) 60 D3
Bellou (14) 54 E2
Bellou-en-Houlme (61) 53 J5
Bellou-le-Trichard (61) 83 H5
Bellou-sur-Huisne (61) 83 K3
Belloy (18) 150 B6
Belloy-en-France (95) 37 K6
Belloy-Saint-Léonard (80) . . . 17 H1
Belloy-en-Santerre (80) 19 F2
Belluire (17) 195 G4
Belmesnil (76) 15 K3
Belmont (25) 138 D6
Belmont (32) 266 E5
Belmont (38) 207 G5
Belmont (39) 155 H3
Belmont (52) 117 F6
Belmont (67) 70 A6
Belmont (70) 118 E4
Belmont-Bretenoux (46) 234 C2
Belmont-d'Azergues (69) . . . 188 B6
Belmont-de-la-Loire (42) . . . 187 H3
Belmont-lès-Darney (88) . . . 117 K1
Belmont-Luthézieu (01) 190 A6
Belmont-Sainte-Foi (46) 250 C3
Belmont-sur-Buttant (88) . . . 95 G5
Belmont-sur-Rance (12) 272 A4
Belmont-sur-Vair (88) 93 J5
Belmont-Tramonet (73) 207 K4
Belmontet (46) 249 G2
Belonchamp (70) 119 F5
Belpech (11) 288 E6
Belrain (55) 64 C3
Belrupt (88) 118 A1
Belrupt-en-Verdunois (55) . . . 43 J5
Bélus (40) 264 A6
Belval (08) 22 C3
Belval (50) 30 E4
Belval (88) 95 J2
Belval-Bois-des-Dames (08) . . 42 E1
Belval-en-Argonne (51) 63 K2
Belval-sous-Châtillon (51) . . . 40 D6
Belvédère (06) 311 A3
Belvédère-Campomoro (2A) . . 322 C3
Belverne (70) 119 F6
Belvès (24) 232 D3
Belvès-de-Castillon (33) 230 C1
Belvèze (82) 249 G3
Belvèze-du-Razès (11) 308 D1
Belvézet (30) 255 K6
Belvezet (48) 238 B6
Belvianes-et-Cavirac (11) . . . 308 D4
Belvis (11) 308 D4
Belvoir (25) 139 F5
Belz (56) 100 B5
Bémécourt (27) 56 A3
Bénac (09) 307 H3
Bénac (65) 285 G6
Benagues (09) 307 J1

Benais (37) 126 D6
Bénaix (09) 308 B4
Bénaménil (54) 67 F6
Bénarville (76) 14 E4
Benassay (86) 162 C3
Benay (02) 20 A3
Benayes (19) 199 H5
Bendejun (06) 281 J3
Bendorf (68) 97 C5
Bénéjacq (64) 284 E5
Benerville-sur-Mer (14) 33 H4
Bénesse-lès-Dax (40) 264 B5
Bénesse-Maremne (40) 262 C5
Benest (16) 179 K4
Bénestroff (57) 67 G2
Bénesville (76) 15 H3
Benet (85) 161 G4
Beneuvre (21) 115 K6
Bengy-sur-Craon (18) 150 A4
Bénifontaine (62) 6 B6
Béning-lès-Saint-Avold (57) . . 68 B2
la Bénisson-Dieu (42) 186 E3
Bénivay-Ollon (26) 257 J3
Bennecourt (78) 57 H1
Bennetot (76) 14 E4
Benney (54) 94 B1
Bennwihr (68) 96 B3
Bénodet (29) 98 C3
Benoisey (21) 134 E2
Benoîtville (50) 28 B3
Benon (17) 177 G2
Bénonces (01) 207 G1
Bénouville (14) 33 F4
Bénouville (76) 14 C3
Benque (31) 287 G5
Benqué (65) 304 E1
Benque-Dessous-et-Dessus (31) . 305 H1
Benquet (40) 265 G3
Bentayou-Sérée (64) 285 G3
Bény (01) 172 D6
Bény-sur-Mer (14) 32 D3
Béon (01) 190 B6
Béon (89) 112 D3
Béost (64) 303 H2
Bérat (31) 287 J3
Béraut (32) 267 G3
Berbérust-Lias (65) 304 B2
Berbezit (43) 219 K2
Berbiguières (24) 232 D3
Bercenay-en-Othe (10) 89 K6
Berche (25) 139 G3
Berchères-les-Pierres (28) . . . 85 G4
Berchères-Saint-Germain (28) . 85 G3
Berchères-sur-Vesgre (28) . . . 57 G4
Berck (62) 8 E1
Bercloux (17) 195 H1
Berd'huis (61) 83 K4
Berdoues (32) 286 B2
Bérelles (59) 13 J3
Bérengeville-la-Campagne (27) . 35 H6
Berentzwiller (68) 97 C4
Bérenx (64) 283 H1
Béréziat (01) 172 B6
Berfay (72) 107 K3
Berg (67) 67 K2
Berg-sur-Moselle (57) 27 H3
Berganty (46) 250 C1
Bergbieten (67) 70 C3
Bergerac (24) 231 H2
Bergères (10) 91 G6
Bergères-lès-Vertus (51) . . . 62 A3
Bergères-sous-Montmirail (51) . 61 G3
Bergesserin (71) 171 H4
Bergheim (68) 71 A6
Bergholtz (68) 96 B5
Bergholtzzell (68) 96 B6
Bergicourt (80) 17 J4
Bergnicourt (08) 41 H2
Bergonne (63) 202 E5
Bergouey (40) 264 E5
Bergouey-Viellenave (64) . . . 283 F2
Bergueneuse (62) 5 G6
Bergues (59) 3 J2
Bergues-sur-Sambre (02) . . . 12 E6
Berhet (22) 48 B3
Bérig-Vintrange (57) 67 F1
Bérigny (50) 31 J3
Berjou (61) 53 H3
Berlaimont (59) 13 F4
Berlancourt (02) 20 E3
Berlancourt (60) 19 H5
Berlats (81) 271 J5
Berlencourt-le-Cauroy (62) . . 10 B3
Berles-au-Bois (62) 10 D4
Berles-Monchel (62) 10 C3
Berling (57) 69 F6
Berlise (02) 21 H5
Berlou (34) 291 H2
Bermerain (59) 12 D3
Berméricourt (51) 40 E3
Bermeries (59) 13 F3
Bermering (57) 67 F1
Bermesnil (80) 17 F2
Bermicourt (62) 9 K1
Bermont (90) 139 H1

Bermonville (76) 15 F5
Bernac (16) 179 K4
Bernac (81) 270 C2
Bernac-Debat (65) 285 H6
Bernac-Dessus (65) 285 H6
Bernadets (64) 284 D3
Bernadets-Debat (65) 286 A3
Bernadets-Dessus (65) 285 K5
le Bernard (85) 159 H4
la Bernardière (85) 123 K6
Bernardswiller (67) 70 C5
Bernardvillé (67) 70 C6
Bernâtre (80) 9 J4
Bernaville (80) 9 K5
Bernay (27) 34 D6
Bernay (72) 106 D1
Bernay-en-Ponthieu (80) . . . 9 F3
Bernay-Saint-Martin (17) . . . 177 J4
Bernay-Vilbert (77) 60 A2
Berné (56) 75 K6
Bernécourt (54) 65 H3
Bernède (32) 265 K5
la Bernerie-en-Retz (44) . . . 122 C5
Bernes (80) 19 J2
Bernes-sur-Oise (95) 37 J5
Bernesq (14) 31 J1
Berneuil (16) 212 C1
Berneuil (17) 195 G3
Berneuil (80) 9 K5
Berneuil (87) 181 F4
Berneuil-en-Bray (60) 37 G3
Berneuil-sur-Aisne (60) 39 F2
Berneval-le-Grand (76) 16 A1
Berneville (62) 10 D4
Bernex (74) 175 H5
Bernienville (27) 35 H4
Bernières (76) 14 E5
Bernières-d'Ailly (14) 54 B2
Bernières-le-Patry (14) 53 F3
Bernières-sur-Mer (14) 32 D3
Bernières-sur-Seine (27) . . . 36 A4
Bernieulles (62) 4 C5
Bernin (38) 224 C2
Bernis (30) 275 G4
Bernolsheim (67) 70 E1
Bernon (10) 114 A3
Bernos-Beaulac (33) 246 D3
Bernot (02) 20 C2
Bernouil (89) 113 K4
Bernouville (27) 36 D4
Bernwiller (68) 97 B3
Berny-en-Santerre (80) 19 F2
Berny-Rivière (02) 39 G2
Bérou-la-Mulotière (28) 56 C7
Berrac (32) 267 H1
Berre-les-Alpes (06) 281 H2
Berre-l'Étang (13) 296 A2
Berriac (11) 290 B5
Berrias-et-Casteljau (07) . . . 255 F1
Berric (56) 101 H5
Berrie (86) 144 C3
Berrien (29) 75 G1
Berrieux (02) 40 D1
Berrogain-Laruns (64) 283 H4
Berru (51) 41 G4
Berrwiller (68) 97 B1
Berry-au-Bac (02) 40 F2
Berry-Bouy (18) 149 F2
le Bersac (05) 258 D1
Bersac-sur-Rivalier (87) 181 J4
Bersaillin (39) 155 H5
Bersée (59) 6 E6
Bersillies (59) 13 H2
Berson (33) 211 H4
Berstett (67) 70 E2
Berstheim (67) 69 K6
Bert (03) 186 B1
Bertaucourt-Epourdon (02) . . 20 B5
Berteaucourt-les-Dames (80) . 9 K6
Berteaucourt-lès-Thennes (80) . 18 C3
Bertheauville (76) 15 F3
Berthecourt (60) 37 J3
Berthegon (86) 145 F5
Berthelange (25) 155 K1
Berthelming (57) 67 J3
Berthen (59) 6 A2
Berthenay (37) 127 G5
Berthenicourt (02) 20 B3
Berthenonville (27) 36 D5
la Berthenoux (36) 166 C3
Berthez (33) 230 B6
Bertholène (12) 252 D2
Berthouville (27) 34 D5
Bertignat (63) 203 K4
Bertignolles (10) 115 F1
Bertincourt (62) 11 G5
Bertoncourt (08) 22 A6
Bertrambois (54) 67 J5
Bertrancourt (80) 10 D5
Bertrange (57) 27 G5
Bertre (81) 270 C6
Bertren (65) 305 J2
Bertreville (76) 15 F3
Bertreville-Saint-Ouen (76) . . 15 K3
Bertric-Burée (24) 213 G2
Bertrichamps (54) 95 G2
Bertricourt (02) 40 E2
Bertrimont (76) 15 J5
Bertrimoutier (88) 95 J4
Bertry (59) 12 C5
Béru (89) 113 K5

Béruges (86) . . . 162 D3
Bérulle (10) . . . 89 G6
Bérus (72) . . . 82 C3
Berville (76) . . . 15 H4
Berville (95) . . . 37 G5
Berville-en-Roumois (27) . . . 35 F3
Berville-la-Campagne (27) . . . 56 B1
Berville-sur-Mer (27) . . . 34 B2
Berville-sur-Seine (76) . . . 35 G1
Berviller-en-Moselle (57) . . . 45 K3
Berzé-la-Ville (71) . . . 171 H6
Berzé-le-Châtel (71) . . . 171 H5
Berzème (07) . . . 239 K6
Berzieux (51) . . . 42 C5
Berzy-le-Sec (02) . . . 39 J3
la Besace (08) . . . 23 H6
Besain (39) . . . 155 K6
Besançon (25) . . . 138 A6
Bésayes (26) . . . 222 E6
Bescat (64) . . . 284 C4
Bésignan (26) . . . 257 K3
Bésingrand (64) . . . 284 B3
Beslon (50) . . . 52 B3
Besmé (02) . . . 19 J6
Besmont (02) . . . 21 H2
Besnans (70) . . . 138 C3
Besné (44) . . . 122 B1
Besneville (50) . . . 28 C6
Besny-et-Loizy (02) . . . 20 D5
Bessac (16) . . . 196 C6
Bessais-le-Fromental (18) . . . 167 J1
Bessamorel (43) . . . 220 E4
Bessan (34) . . . 292 C4
Bessancourt (95) . . . 58 D1
Bessans (73) . . . 226 D1
Bessas (07) . . . 255 J3
le Bessat (42) . . . 221 J1
Bessay (85) . . . 160 A3
Bessay-sur-Allier (03) . . . 168 E5
Besse (15) . . . 217 G5
Bessé (16) . . . 179 F5
Besse (24) . . . 232 E4
Besse (38) . . . 225 F4
Besse-et-Saint-Anastaise (63) . . . 202 B5
Bessé-sur-Braye (72) . . . 107 K5
Besse-sur-Issole (83) . . . 298 A3
Bessède-de-Sault (11) . . . 308 D5
Bessèges (30) . . . 255 H4
Bessenay (69) . . . 205 H2
Bessens (82) . . . 268 C3
Besset (09) . . . 308 A1
Bessey (42) . . . 222 A1
Bessey-en-Chaume (21) . . . 153 K2
Bessey-la-Cour (21) . . . 153 J2
Bessey-lès-Cîteaux (21) . . . 154 D1
la Besseyre-Saint-Mary (43) . . . 219 H6
Bessières (31) . . . 269 J4
Bessines (79) . . . 161 G6
Bessines-sur-Gartempe (87) . . . 181 J3
Bessins (38) . . . 223 F3
Besson (03) . . . 168 D5
Bessoncourt (90) . . . 119 J6
Bessonies (46) . . . 234 E3
les Bessons (48) . . . 237 F3
Bessuéjouls (12) . . . 236 A6
Bessy (10) . . . 90 A1
Bessy-sur-Cure (89) . . . 133 H2
Bestiac (09) . . . 308 A6
Bétaille (46) . . . 234 A1
Betaucourt (70) . . . 117 J4
Betbèze (65) . . . 286 C4
Betbezer-d'Armagnac (40) . . . 266 A1
Betcave-Aguin (32) . . . 286 E2
Betchat (09) . . . 306 C1
Bétête (23) . . . 166 C6
Béthancourt-en-Valois (60) . . . 38 E4
Béthancourt-en-Vaux (02) . . . 19 J5
Béthelainville (55) . . . 43 G5
Béthemont-la-Forêt (95) . . . 58 D1
Béthencourt (59) . . . 12 C4
Béthencourt-sur-Mer (80) . . . 8 D5
Béthencourt-sur-Somme (80) . . . 19 G3
Bétheniville (51) . . . 41 J3
Bétheny (51) . . . 41 F4
Béthincourt (55) . . . 43 G4
Béthines (86) . . . 164 B4
Béthisy-Saint-Martin (60) . . . 38 D4
Béthisy-Saint-Pierre (60) . . . 38 D4
Bethmale (09) . . . 306 C4
Bethon (51) . . . 89 G1
Béthon (72) . . . 82 D4
Bethoncourt (25) . . . 139 H2
Béthonsart (62) . . . 10 C1
Béthonvilliers (28) . . . 84 B6
Bethonvilliers (90) . . . 119 J6
Béthune (62) . . . 6 A5
Bétignicourt (10) . . . 90 E3
Beton-Bazoches (77) . . . 60 D5
Betoncourt-lès-Brotte (70) . . . 118 C5
Betoncourt-Saint-Pancras (70) . . . 118 B3
Betoncourt-sur-Mance (70) . . . 117 H4
Bétous (32) . . . 266 C5
Betplan (32) . . . 285 J3
Betpouey (65) . . . 304 C4
Betpouy (65) . . . 285 J5
Bétracq (64) . . . 285 G1
Betschdorf (67) . . . 25 B3
Bettainvillers (54) . . . 26 E5
Bettancourt-la-Ferrée (52) . . . 63 K6
Bettancourt-la-Longue (51) . . . 63 J3
Bettange (57) . . . 27 K5
Bettant (01) . . . 189 H5

Bettborn (57) . . . 67 J3
Bettegney-Saint-Brice (88) . . . 94 C4
Bettelainville (57) . . . 27 J6
Bettembos (80) . . . 17 G3
Bettencourt-Rivière (80) . . . 9 H6
Bettencourt-Saint-Ouen (80) . . . 9 J6
Bettendorf (68) . . . 97 B4
Bettes (65) . . . 304 D1
Betteville (76) . . . 15 G6
Bettignies (59) . . . 13 H2
Betting-lès-Saint-Avold (57) . . . 68 B2
Bettlach (68) . . . 97 D5
Betton (35) . . . 79 G3
Betton-Bettonet (73) . . . 208 E4
Bettoncourt (88) . . . 94 A3
Bettrechies (59) . . . 13 F2
Bettviller (57) . . . 69 F3
Bettwiller (67) . . . 67 K2
Betz (60) . . . 39 F5
Betz-le-Château (37) . . . 146 C4
Beugin (62) . . . 10 C1
Beugnâtre (62) . . . 11 F5
Beugneux (02) . . . 39 K4
Beugnies (59) . . . 13 H4
le Beugnon (79) . . . 161 G3
Beugnon (89) . . . 113 J2
Beugny (62) . . . 11 G5
Beuil (06) . . . 261 G5
le Beulay (88) . . . 95 K3
Beulotte-Saint-Laurent (70) . . . 119 F3
Beure (25) . . . 137 K6
Beurey (10) . . . 90 E6
Beurey-Bauguay (21) . . . 134 E6
Beurey-sur-Saulx (55) . . . 63 K4
Beurières (63) . . . 204 A6
Beurizot (21) . . . 135 F3
Beurlay (17) . . . 177 G6
Beurville (52) . . . 91 H4
Beussent (62) . . . 4 C5
Beuste (64) . . . 284 E5
Beutal (25) . . . 139 F3
Beutin (62) . . . 4 B5
Beuvardes (02) . . . 40 A5
Beuveille (54) . . . 26 C3
Beuvezin (54) . . . 93 J3
Beuvillers (14) . . . 33 K5
Beuvillers (54) . . . 26 E4
Beuvrages (59) . . . 12 D1
Beuvraignes (80) . . . 19 F5
Beuvrequen (62) . . . 2 B4
Beuvron (58) . . . 133 F5
Beuvron-en-Auge (14) . . . 33 H5
Beuvry (62) . . . 6 A5
Beuvry-la-Forêt (59) . . . 7 F6
Beux (57) . . . 66 B1
Beuxes (86) . . . 145 F2
Beuzec-Cap-Sizun (29) . . . 73 C2
Beuzeville (27) . . . 34 B3
Beuzeville-au-Plain (50) . . . 29 F5
Beuzeville-la-Bastille (50) . . . 29 F6
Beuzeville-la-Grenier (76) . . . 14 D5
Beuzeville-la-Guérard (76) . . . 15 F4
Beuzevillette (76) . . . 14 E6
Bévenais (38) . . . 207 G6
Beveuge (70) . . . 138 E2
Béville-le-Comte (28) . . . 85 J3
Bévillers (59) . . . 12 C4
Bevons (04) . . . 259 F4
Bévy (21) . . . 154 A1
Bey (01) . . . 188 C2
Bey (71) . . . 154 B6
Bey-sur-Seille (54) . . . 66 C3
Beychac-et-Caillau (33) . . . 229 K1
Beylongue (40) . . . 264 D2
Beynac (87) . . . 198 E2
Beynac-et-Cazenac (24) . . . 232 E2
Beynat (19) . . . 216 A4
Beynes (04) . . . 259 J6
Beynes (78) . . . 58 A3
Beynost (01) . . . 206 C1
Beyrède-Jumet (65) . . . 305 F3
Beyren-lès-Sierck (57) . . . 27 H3
Beyrie-en-Béarn (64) . . . 284 C3
Beyrie-sur-Joyeuse (64) . . . 283 F4
Beyries (40) . . . 265 F6
Beyssac (19) . . . 215 H1
Beyssenac (19) . . . 215 G1
le Bez (81) . . . 271 H6
Bez-et-Esparon (30) . . . 273 J2
Bézac (09) . . . 288 D6
Bézalles (77) . . . 60 D6
Bézancourt (76) . . . 36 C2
Bezange-la-Grande (54) . . . 66 D4
Bezange-la-Petite (57) . . . 66 E4
Bezannes (51) . . . 40 E4
Bézaudun-les-Alpes (06) . . . 280 E2
Bézaudun-sur-Bîne (26) . . . 241 F5
Bézaumont (54) . . . 65 K3
Bèze (21) . . . 136 C3
Bézenac (24) . . . 232 E2
Bézenet (03) . . . 184 C1
Bézéril (32) . . . 287 F1
Béziers (34) . . . 292 A4
Bezinghem (62) . . . 4 C5
Bezins-Garraux (31) . . . 305 J3
la Bezole (11) . . . 308 D2
Bezolles (32) . . . 267 F3
Bezons (95) . . . 58 D3
Bezonvaux (55) . . . 26 A6
Bezouce (30) . . . 275 J3
Bézouotte (21) . . . 136 D4

Bézu-la-Forêt (27) . . . 36 C2
Bézu-le-Guéry (02) . . . 60 C1
Bézu-Saint-Éloi (27) . . . 36 D1
Bézu-Saint-Germain (02) . . . 39 K6
Bézues-Bajon (32) . . . 286 D3
Biache-Saint-Vaast (62) . . . 11 F2
Biaches (80) . . . 19 G1
Biard (86) . . . 162 E1
Biarne (39) . . . 155 G1
Biarre (80) . . . 19 G4
Biarritz (64) . . . 282 A1
Biarrotte (40) . . . 262 D6
Biars-sur-Cère (46) . . . 234 B1
Bias (40) . . . 244 C4
Bias (47) . . . 248 C2
Biaudos (40) . . . 262 C6
Bibiche (57) . . . 27 K4
Biblisheim (67) . . . 25 A3
Bibost (69) . . . 205 H1
Bichancourt (02) . . . 19 K6
Biches (58) . . . 151 J4
Bickenholtz (57) . . . 67 K3
Bicqueley (54) . . . 65 H6
Bidache (64) . . . 283 F1
Bidarray (64) . . . 263 E3
Bidart (64) . . . 263 C1
Bidestroff (57) . . . 67 G2
Biding (57) . . . 68 B3
Bidon (07) . . . 256 B2
Bidos (64) . . . 284 A5
Biécourt (88) . . . 93 J4
Biederthal (68) . . . 97 D6
Bief (25) . . . 139 H4
Bief-des-Maisons (39) . . . 174 B1
Bief-du-Fourg (39) . . . 156 C5
Biefmorin (39) . . . 155 H4
Biefvillers-lès-Bapaume (62) . . . 11 F5
Bielle (64) . . . 303 H1
Biencourt (80) . . . 17 F3
Biencourt-sur-Orge (55) . . . 92 C1
Bienville (60) . . . 38 C2
Bienville-la-Petite (54) . . . 66 D5
Bienvillers-au-Bois (62) . . . 10 D4
Biermes (08) . . . 41 J1
Biermont (60) . . . 18 E5
Bierné (53) . . . 105 G5
Bierne (59) . . . 3 H2
Bierre-lès-Semur (21) . . . 134 D4
Bierry-les-Belles-Fontaines (89) . . . 134 C2
Biert (09) . . . 307 F4
Bierville (76) . . . 16 B1
Biesheim (68) . . . 96 E4
Biesles (52) . . . 116 C1
Bietlenheim (67) . . . 25 A5
Bieujac (33) . . . 230 B6
Bieuxy (02) . . . 39 H2
Bieuzy (56) . . . 100 D1
Biéville (50) . . . 31 K4
Biéville-Beuville (14) . . . 32 E4
Biéville-Quétiéville (14) . . . 33 H6
Bièvres (02) . . . 40 C1
Bièvres (08) . . . 23 J6
Bièvres (91) . . . 58 D5
Biffontaine (88) . . . 95 G5
Biganos (33) . . . 228 D3
Bignac (16) . . . 196 D2
Bignan (56) . . . 101 F2
Bignay (17) . . . 177 J5
le Bignon (44) . . . 123 H5
le Bignon-du-Maine (53) . . . 105 H4
le Bignon-Mirabeau (45) . . . 111 K1
Bignoux (86) . . . 163 G3
Bigorno (2B) . . . 319 G3
la Bigottière (53) . . . 80 E5
Bihorel (76) . . . 35 J2
Bihucourt (62) . . . 11 F5
Bilhères (64) . . . 303 G1
Bilia (2A) . . . 322 D3
Bilieu (38) . . . 207 H5
Billac (19) . . . 234 B1
Billancelles (28) . . . 84 D2
Billancourt (80) . . . 19 G4
les Billanges (87) . . . 181 K5
les Billaux (33) . . . 212 A6
Billé (35) . . . 80 A4
Billecul (39) . . . 156 C6
Billère (64) . . . 284 C4
Billey (21) . . . 155 F1
Billezois (03) . . . 186 A2
Billiat (01) . . . 190 D3
Billième (73) . . . 208 A2
Billière (31) . . . 305 H5
Billiers (56) . . . 121 K3
Billio (56) . . . 101 G2
Billom (63) . . . 203 F3
Billy (03) . . . 185 J2
Billy (14) . . . 33 F6
Billy (41) . . . 129 G6
Billy-Berclau (62) . . . 6 C5
Billy-Chevannes (58) . . . 151 G4
Billy-le-Grand (51) . . . 41 H6
Billy-lès-Chanceaux (21) . . . 135 H2
Billy-Montigny (62) . . . 11 G1
Billy-sous-Mangiennes (55) . . . 26 B5
Billy-sur-Aisne (02) . . . 39 K3
Billy-sur-Oisy (58) . . . 132 E3

Billy-sur-Ourcq (02) . . . 39 J5
Biltzheim (68) . . . 96 C5
Bilwisheim (67) . . . 70 E1
Bimont (62) . . . 4 D5
Binarville (51) . . . 42 D4
Binas (41) . . . 109 G4
Bindernheim (67) . . . 71 C5
Binges (21) . . . 136 C5
Binic (22) . . . 49 F5
Bining (57) . . . 69 F3
Biniville (50) . . . 28 E5
Binos (31) . . . 305 H3
Binson-et-Orquigny (51) . . . 40 D6
Bio (46) . . . 234 B3
Biol (38) . . . 207 G5
la Biolle (73) . . . 208 B1
Biollet (63) . . . 184 B5
Bion (50) . . . 52 D6
Bioncourt (57) . . . 66 C3
Bionville (54) . . . 95 J1
Bionville-sur-Nied (57) . . . 45 H5
Biot (06) . . . 281 F5
le Biot (74) . . . 175 G6
Bioule (82) . . . 250 B6
Bioussac (16) . . . 179 H4
Biozat (03) . . . 185 H4
Birac (16) . . . 196 C4
Birac (33) . . . 246 D1
Birac-sur-Trec (47) . . . 247 H1
Biran (32) . . . 267 G5
Biras (24) . . . 213 K2
Biriatou (64) . . . 263 A2
Birieux (01) . . . 188 E5
Birkenwald (67) . . . 70 B2
Biron (17) . . . 195 H4
Biron (24) . . . 232 B5
Biron (64) . . . 283 K2
Biscarrosse (40) . . . 244 D1
Bischheim (67) . . . 25 A6
Bischholtz (67) . . . 69 J5
Bischoffsheim (67) . . . 70 D4
Bischwihr (68) . . . 96 C4
Bischwiller (67) . . . 25 B4
Bisel (68) . . . 97 B5
Bisinchi (2B) . . . 319 G3
Bislée (55) . . . 64 E3
Bissert (67) . . . 67 J1
Bisseuil (51) . . . 62 A1
Bissey-la-Côte (21) . . . 115 H3
Bissey-la-Pierre (21) . . . 114 E4
Bissey-sous-Cruchaud (71) . . . 171 H1
Bissezeele (59) . . . 3 H3
Bissières (14) . . . 33 G6
Bissy-la-Mâconnaise (71) . . . 171 J4
Bissy-sous-Uxelles (71) . . . 171 H3
Bissy-sur-Fley (71) . . . 171 G2
Bisten-en-Lorraine (57) . . . 45 J4
Bistroff (57) . . . 67 F1
Bitche (57) . . . 69 G3
Bitry (58) . . . 132 B3
Bitry (60) . . . 39 G2
Bitschhoffen (67) . . . 69 J5
Bitschwiller-lès-Thann (68) . . . 119 K4
Bivès (32) . . . 268 A3
Biviers (38) . . . 224 B2
Biville (50) . . . 28 B2
Biville-la-Baignarde (76) . . . 15 K4
Biville-la-Rivière (76) . . . 15 K3
Biville-sur-Mer (76) . . . 16 B1
Bivilliers (61) . . . 83 J1
Bizanet (11) . . . 291 G6
Bizanos (64) . . . 284 D4
Bize (52) . . . 117 F4
Bize (65) . . . 305 G2
Bize-Minervois (11) . . . 291 G4
Bizeneuille (03) . . . 167 J5
Biziat (01) . . . 188 D2
Bizonnes (38) . . . 207 G5
le Bizot (25) . . . 157 H1
les Bizots (71) . . . 170 E1
Bizou (61) . . . 83 K2
Bizous (65) . . . 305 G1
Blacé (69) . . . 188 A4
Blacourt (60) . . . 36 E2
Blacqueville (76) . . . 15 H6
Blacy (51) . . . 63 F5
Blacy (89) . . . 134 A2
Blaesheim (67) . . . 70 E4
Blagnac (31) . . . 269 G6
Blagny (08) . . . 23 H5
Blagny-sur-Vingeanne (21) . . . 136 D4
Blaignac (33) . . . 230 C6
Blaignan (33) . . . 210 E1
Blain (44) . . . 102 E3
Blaincourt-lès-Précy (60) . . . 37 K5
Blaincourt-sur-Aube (10) . . . 90 E3
Blainville-Crevon (76) . . . 35 K1
Blainville-sur-l'Eau (54) . . . 66 C6
Blainville-sur-Mer (50) . . . 30 C4
Blainville-sur-Orne (14) . . . 32 E4
Blairville (62) . . . 10 E3
Blaise-sous-Arzillières (51) . . . 63 H5
Blaison-Gohier (49) . . . 125 J4
Blaisy (52) . . . 91 K6
Blaisy-Bas (21) . . . 135 H5
Blaisy-Haut (21) . . . 135 H5
Blajan (31) . . . 286 D5
Blamont (25) . . . 139 H4
Blâmont (54) . . . 67 G6
Blan (81) . . . 289 H2
le Blanc (36) . . . 164 C3
le Blanc-Mesnil (93) . . . 59 F2

Blancafort (18) . . . 131 G3
Blancey (21) . . . 134 E5
Blancfossé (60) . . . 17 K5
Blanche-Église (57) . . . 67 F3
Blanchefosse-et-Bay (08) . . . 21 J3
Blancherupt (67) . . . 70 A5
Blandainville (28) . . . 84 E4
Blandas (30) . . . 273 J2
Blandin (38) . . . 207 G5
Blandouet (53) . . . 105 J2
Blandy (77) . . . 87 J1
Blandy (91) . . . 86 D4
Blangerval-Blangermont (62) . . . 9 K2
Blangy-le-Château (14) . . . 34 A4
Blangy-sous-Poix (80) . . . 17 J3
Blangy-sur-Bresle (76) . . . 16 E1
Blangy-sur-Ternoise (62) . . . 9 K1
Blangy-Tronville (80) . . . 18 C2
Blannay (89) . . . 133 J3
Blanot (21) . . . 152 E1
Blanot (71) . . . 171 J4
Blanquefort (32) . . . 268 A5
Blanquefort (33) . . . 229 G1
Blanquefort-sur-Briolance (47) . . . 232 C5
Blanzac (43) . . . 220 B4
Blanzac (87) . . . 181 J5
Blanzac-lès-Matha (17) . . . 178 B6
Blanzac-Porcheresse (16) . . . 196 C5
Blanzaguet-Saint-Cybard (16) . . . 197 F6
Blanzat (63) . . . 202 D1
Blanzay (86) . . . 179 H2
Blanzay-sur-Boutonne (17) . . . 178 A4
Blanzée (55) . . . 43 K5
Blanzy (71) . . . 170 E2
Blanzy-la-Salonnaise (08) . . . 41 G1
Blanzy-lès-Fismes (02) . . . 40 B3
Blargies (60) . . . 17 F5
Blarians (25) . . . 138 B4
Blaringhem (59) . . . 3 H6
Blars (46) . . . 234 A6
Blaru (78) . . . 57 G1
Blasimon (33) . . . 230 C3
Blaslay (86) . . . 162 E1
Blassac (43) . . . 219 H4
Blaudeix (23) . . . 183 F2
Blausasc (06) . . . 281 H2
Blauvac (84) . . . 257 J6
Blauzac (30) . . . 275 G2
Blavignac (48) . . . 237 G2
Blavozy (43) . . . 220 D5
Blay (14) . . . 31 K1
Blaye (33) . . . 211 G4
Blaye-les-Mines (81) . . . 270 D1
Blaymont (47) . . . 248 E3
Blaziert (32) . . . 267 G2
Blécourt (52) . . . 92 A3
Blécourt (59) . . . 11 J3
Bleigny-le-Carreau (89) . . . 113 H5
Blémerey (54) . . . 67 F6
Blémerey (88) . . . 93 K3
Blendecques (62) . . . 3 G5
Bléneau (89) . . . 132 A1
Blennes (77) . . . 88 B5
Blénod-lès-Pont-à-Mousson (54) . . . 65 K2
Blénod-lès-Toul (54) . . . 65 H6
Bléquin (62) . . . 2 E6
Blérancourt (02) . . . 39 G1
Bléré (37) . . . 128 B5
Bléruais (35) . . . 78 C4
Blésignac (33) . . . 230 A3
Blesle (43) . . . 218 E2
Blesme (51) . . . 63 H5
Blesmes (02) . . . 60 E1
Blessac (23) . . . 183 F5
Blessey (21) . . . 135 G3
Blessonville (52) . . . 115 K2
Blessy (62) . . . 5 H4
Blet (18) . . . 149 K5
Bletterans (39) . . . 173 F1
Bleurville (88) . . . 117 J1
Bleury (28) . . . 85 J2
Blevaincourt (88) . . . 93 G6
Blèves (72) . . . 83 F2
le Bleymard (48) . . . 254 D1
Blicourt (60) . . . 17 J6
Blienschwiller (67) . . . 70 C6
Blies-Ebersing (57) . . . 68 E2
Blies-Guersviller (57) . . . 68 D2
Bliesbruck (57) . . . 68 E2
Blieux (04) . . . 279 H2
Blignicourt (10) . . . 91 F2
Bligny (10) . . . 91 G6
Bligny (51) . . . 40 D5
Bligny-le-Sec (21) . . . 135 H4
Bligny-lès-Beaune (21) . . . 154 A4
Bligny-sur-Ouche (21) . . . 153 J2
Blincourt (60) . . . 38 C3
Blingel (62) . . . 9 K1
Blis-et-Born (24) . . . 214 C4
Blismes (58) . . . 152 A2
Blodelsheim (68) . . . 96 E6
Blois (41) . . . 128 E2
Blois-sur-Seille (39) . . . 155 H6
Blomac (11) . . . 290 D6
Blomard (03) . . . 184 E1
Blombay (08) . . . 22 A2
Blond (87) . . . 180 E4
Blondefontaine (70) . . . 117 J4
Blonville-sur-Mer (14) . . . 33 H3
Blosseville (76) . . . 15 H2
Blosville (50) . . . 29 F6
Blot-l'Église (63) . . . 184 E4

Blotzheim (68) . . . 97 D4
Blou (49) . . . 126 B5
Blousson-Sérian (32) . . . 285 J2
la Bloutière (50) . . . 31 F6
Bloye (74) . . . 190 D6
Bluffy (74) . . . 191 G6
Blumeray (52) . . . 91 J3
Blussangeaux (25) . . . 139 F3
Blussans (25) . . . 139 F3
Blye (39) . . . 173 H2
Blyes (01) . . . 189 G6
le Bô (14) . . . 53 J2
Bobigny (93) . . . 59 F3
Bobital (22) . . . 50 C6
le Bocasse (76) . . . 15 K5
Bocé (49) . . . 126 B3
Bocognano (2A) . . . 320 E6
Bocquegney (88) . . . 94 C5
Bocquencé (61) . . . 55 G3
le Bodéo (22) . . . 76 E2
Bodilis (29) . . . 46 D5
Boé (47) . . . 248 B5
Boécé (61) . . . 83 G2
Boëge (74) . . . 191 H1
Boeil-Bezing (64) . . . 284 E5
Boën (42) . . . 204 C2
Boersch (67) . . . 70 C4
Boeschepe (59) . . . 6 A2
Boëseghem (59) . . . 3 H6
Boesenbiesen (67) . . . 71 C5
Boësse (45) . . . 111 F1
Boësse (79) . . . 143 J4
Boëssé-le-Sec (72) . . . 107 H1
Boeurs-en-Othe (89) . . . 113 H1
Boffles (62) . . . 9 K3
Boffres (07) . . . 240 A1
Bogève (74) . . . 191 J2
Bogny-sur-Meuse (08) . . . 22 D2
Bogy (07) . . . 222 B2
Bohain-en-Vermandois (02) . . . 12 C6
Bohal (56) . . . 101 J4
la Bohalle (49) . . . 125 J4
Bohars (29) . . . 72 D4
Bohas-Meyriat-Rignat (01) . . . 189 H3
Boigneville (91) . . . 86 E4
Boigny-sur-Bionne (45) . . . 110 B4
Boinville-en-Mantois (78) . . . 57 J2
Boinville-en-Woëvre (55) . . . 44 A4
Boinville-le-Gaillard (78) . . . 86 A2
Boinvilliers (78) . . . 57 H3
Boiry-Becquerelle (62) . . . 11 F4
Boiry-Notre-Dame (62) . . . 11 G3
Boiry-Saint-Martin (62) . . . 10 E4
Boiry-Sainte-Rictrude (62) . . . 10 E4
Bois (17) . . . 195 G5
le Bois (73) . . . 209 H5
Bois-Anzeray (27) . . . 55 J2
Bois-Arnault (27) . . . 55 K4
Bois-Bernard (62) . . . 11 G1
Bois-Colombes (92) . . . 58 D3
Bois-d'Amont (39) . . . 174 D3
Bois-d'Arcy (78) . . . 58 B4
Bois-d'Arcy (89) . . . 133 H3
Bois-de-Céné (85) . . . 141 F4
Bois-de-Champ (88) . . . 95 G4
Bois-de-Gand (39) . . . 155 G5
Bois-de-la-Pierre (31) . . . 287 J4
Bois-d'Ennebourg (76) . . . 35 K2
le Bois-d'Oingt (69) . . . 188 A6
Bois-Grenier (59) . . . 6 C4
Bois-Guilbert (76) . . . 16 C6
Bois-Guillaume (76) . . . 35 H1
le Bois-Hellain (27) . . . 34 B4
Bois-Héroult (76) . . . 16 C6
Bois-Herpin (91) . . . 86 D4
Bois-Himont (76) . . . 15 G6
Bois-Jérôme-Saint-Ouen (27) . . . 36 C6
Bois-le-Roi (27) . . . 57 F3
Bois-le-Roi (77) . . . 87 H2
Bois-lès-Pargny (02) . . . 20 D4
Bois-l'Évêque (76) . . . 35 K2
Bois-Normand-près-Lyre (27) . . . 55 J3
le Bois-Plage-en-Ré (17) . . . 176 B2
le Bois-Robert (76) . . . 16 A2
Bois-Sainte-Marie (71) . . . 170 E6
Boisbergues (80) . . . 9 K4
Boisbreteau (16) . . . 212 B2
Boiscommun (45) . . . 110 E2
Boisdinghem (62) . . . 2 E5
Boisdon (77) . . . 60 C6
Boisemont (27) . . . 36 B4
Boisemont (95) . . . 58 B1
Boisgasson (28) . . . 108 D2
Boisgervilly (35) . . . 78 C3
Boisjean (62) . . . 9 F1
le Boisle (80) . . . 9 H3
Boisleux-au-Mont (62) . . . 10 E4
Boisleux-Saint-Marc (62) . . . 11 F4
Boismé (79) . . . 143 J6
Boismont (54) . . . 26 C4
Boismont (80) . . . 8 E4
Boismorand (45) . . . 111 H5
Boisney (27) . . . 34 D5
Boisredon (17) . . . 211 H2
Boisroger (50) . . . 30 D3
Boissay (76) . . . 36 A1
la Boisse (01) . . . 206 C1
Boisse (24) . . . 231 K4
Boisse-Penchot (12) . . . 235 F5
Boisseau (41) . . . 108 E5
Boisseaux (45) . . . 86 B5
Boissède (31) . . . 287 F3

Boissei-la-Lande (61) . . . 54 D5
Boisserolles (79) . . . 178 A3
Boisseron (34) . . . 274 E4
Boisset (15) . . . 235 F3
Boisset (34) . . . 290 E3
Boisset (43) . . . 220 D2
Boisset-et-Gaujac (30) . . . 255 G6
Boisset-lès-Montrond (42) . . . 204 E4
Boisset-les-Prévanches (27) . . . 56 E2
Boisset-Saint-Priest (42) . . . 204 D5
Boissets (78) . . . 57 H3
Boissettes (77) . . . 87 G2
Boisseuil (87) . . . 199 F2
Boisseuilh (24) . . . 215 F2
Boissey (01) . . . 172 A5
Boissey (14) . . . 54 D1
Boissey-le-Châtel (27) . . . 34 E4
Boissezon (81) . . . 290 B1
Boissia (39) . . . 173 H3
la Boissière (14) . . . 33 J5
la Boissière (27) . . . 57 F2
la Boissière (34) . . . 273 K5
la Boissière (39) . . . 173 G5
la Boissière (53) . . . 104 C5
la Boissière-d'Ans (24) . . . 214 D3
la Boissière-de-Montaigu (85) . . . 142 B4
la Boissière-des-Landes (85) . . . 159 H3
la Boissière-du-Doré (44) . . . 124 A6
la Boissière-École (78) . . . 57 H6
la Boissière-en-Gâtine (79) . . . 161 J3
la Boissière-sur-Èvre (49) . . . 124 B5
Boissières (30) . . . 275 F4
Boissières (46) . . . 233 H6
Boissise-la-Bertrand (77) . . . 87 G2
Boissise-le-Roi (77) . . . 87 G2
Boissy-aux-Cailles (77) . . . 87 F4
Boissy-en-Drouais (28) . . . 56 E5
Boissy-Fresnoy (60) . . . 38 E5
Boissy-la-Rivière (91) . . . 86 C4
Boissy-l'Aillerie (95) . . . 37 G6
Boissy-Lamberville (27) . . . 34 D5
Boissy-le-Bois (60) . . . 37 F4
Boissy-le-Châtel (77) . . . 60 C4
Boissy-le-Cutté (91) . . . 86 D3
Boissy-le-Repos (51) . . . 61 G3
Boissy-le-Sec (91) . . . 86 C2
Boissy-lès-Perche (28) . . . 56 A5
Boissy-Maugis (61) . . . 83 J3
Boissy-Mauvoisin (78) . . . 57 H2
Boissy-Saint-Léger (94) . . . 59 G5
Boissy-sans-Avoir (78) . . . 57 K4
Boissy-sous-Saint-Yon (91) . . . 86 D1
Boistrudan (35) . . . 79 J6
Boisville-la-Saint-Père (28) . . . 85 J4
Boisyvon (50) . . . 52 C3
Boitron (61) . . . 82 E1
Boitron (77) . . . 60 D3
Bolandoz (25) . . . 156 C3
Bolazec (29) . . . 47 J6
Bolbec (76) . . . 14 E6
Bollène (84) . . . 256 D3
la Bollène-Vésubie (06) . . . 311 A3
Bolleville (50) . . . 30 D1
Bolleville (76) . . . 14 E5
Bollezeele (59) . . . 3 H3
Bollwiller (68) . . . 97 B1
Bologne (52) . . . 92 B5
Bolozon (01) . . . 189 J2
Bolquère (66) . . . 313 J4
Bolsenheim (67) . . . 70 E5
Bombon (77) . . . 87 K1
Bommes (33) . . . 229 K5
Bommiers (36) . . . 148 C6
Bompas (09) . . . 307 J4
Bompas (66) . . . 310 E5
Bomy (62) . . . 5 G5
Bon-Encontre (47) . . . 248 C5
Bona (58) . . . 151 G3
Bonac-Irazein (09) . . . 306 B4
Bonas (32) . . . 267 G4
Bonboillon (70) . . . 137 G3
Boncé (28) . . . 85 G5
Bonchamp-lès-Laval (53) . . . 105 F1
Boncourt (02) . . . 21 G5
Boncourt (27) . . . 56 E1
Boncourt (28) . . . 57 F5
Boncourt (54) . . . 44 G5
Boncourt-le-Bois (21) . . . 154 B2
Boncourt-sur-Meuse (55) . . . 64 B4
Bondaroy (45) . . . 86 D6
Bondeval (25) . . . 139 H3
Bondigoux (31) . . . 269 H3
les Bondons (48) . . . 254 C2
Bondoufle (91) . . . 86 E1
Bondues (59) . . . 6 E3
Bondy (93) . . . 59 F3
Bongheat (63) . . . 203 G3
le Bonhomme (68) . . . 95 K5
Bonifacio (2A) . . . 323 G6
Bonlier (60) . . . 37 H1
Bonlieu (39) . . . 173 K2
Bonlieu-sur-Roubion (26) . . . 240 C5
Bonloc (64) . . . 282 D3
Bonnac (09) . . . 288 D6
Bonnac (15) . . . 218 D3
Bonnac-la-Côte (87) . . . 181 H6
Bonnal (25) . . . 138 D2
Bonnard (89) . . . 113 F4
Bonnat (23) . . . 183 H2
Bonnaud (39) . . . 172 E2
Bonnay (25) . . . 138 A5
Bonnay (71) . . . 171 H3

Bonnay (80) . . . 18 C1
Bonne (74) . . . 191 H2
Bonnebosq (14) . . . 33 J4
Bonnecourt (52) . . . 116 E3
Bonnée (45) . . . 110 E5
Bonnefamille (38) . . . 206 D4
Bonnefoi (61) . . . 55 H6
Bonnefond (19) . . . 200 C5
Bonnefont (65) . . . 286 A5
Bonnefontaine (39) . . . 173 H1
Bonnegarde (40) . . . 264 E6
Bonneil (02) . . . 60 D1
Bonnelles (78) . . . 86 B1
Bonnemain (35) . . . 51 F5
Bonnemaison (14) . . . 53 H1
Bonnemazon (65) . . . 304 E1
Bonnencontre (21) . . . 154 D2
Bonnes (16) . . . 212 E3
Bonnes (86) . . . 163 H3
Bonnesvalyn (02) . . . 39 J4
Bonnet (55) . . . 92 D1
Bonnétable (72) . . . 83 G6
Bonnétage (25) . . . 139 G6
Bonnetan (33) . . . 229 J2
Bonneuil (16) . . . 196 B4
Bonneuil (36) . . . 164 D6
Bonneuil-en-France (95) . . . 59 F2
Bonneuil-en-Valois (60) . . . 39 F4
Bonneuil-les-Eaux (60) . . . 18 A5
Bonneuil-Matours (86) . . . 163 H2
Bonneuil-sur-Marne (94) . . . 59 F4
Bonneval (28) . . . 85 F6
Bonneval (43) . . . 220 A2
Bonneval (73) . . . 209 G4
Bonneval-sur-Arc (73) . . . 193 D6
Bonnevaux (25) . . . 156 D5
Bonnevaux (30) . . . 255 G2
Bonnevaux (74) . . . 175 H6
Bonnevaux-le-Prieuré (25) . . . 156 D1
Bonneveau (41) . . . 107 K5
Bonnevent-Velloreille (70) . . . 137 J4
Bonneville (16) . . . 196 C1
la Bonneville (50) . . . 28 C5
Bonneville (74) . . . 191 H3
Bonneville (80) . . . 10 A5
Bonneville-Aptot (27) . . . 34 E4
Bonneville-et-Saint-Avit-de-Fumadières (24) . . . 230 D1
Bonneville-la-Louvet (14) . . . 34 A4
la Bonneville-sur-Iton (27) . . . 56 C2
Bonneville-sur-Touques (14) . . . 33 J3
Bonnières (60) . . . 37 F1
Bonnières (62) . . . 10 A3
Bonnières-sur-Seine (78) . . . 57 F1
Bonnieux (84) . . . 277 G3
Bonningues-lès-Ardres (62) . . . 2 E4
Bonningues-lès-Calais (62) . . . 2 C3
Bonnoeil (14) . . . 53 J2
Bonnoeuvre (44) . . . 124 A2
Bonnut (64) . . . 283 J1
Bonny-sur-Loire (45) . . . 131 K2
Bono (56) . . . 100 D5
Bonrepos (65) . . . 286 A5
Bonrepos-Riquet (31) . . . 269 J5
Bonrepos-sur-Aussonnelle (31) . . . 287 J1
Bons-en-Chablais (74) . . . 191 H1
Bons-Tassilly (14) . . . 54 A2
Bonsecours (76) . . . 35 J2
Bonsmoulins (61) . . . 55 H6
Bonson (06) . . . 281 F2
Bonson (42) . . . 204 E5
Bonvillard (73) . . . 209 F3
Bonvillaret (73) . . . 209 F4
Bonviller (54) . . . 66 D5
Bonvillers (60) . . . 18 B6
Bonvillet (88) . . . 117 K1
Bony (02) . . . 11 J4
Bonzac (33) . . . 212 A5
Bonzée (55) . . . 43 K6
Boô-Silhen (65) . . . 304 B2
Boofzheim (67) . . . 71 D4
Boos (40) . . . 264 B2
Boos (76) . . . 35 J2
Bootzheim (67) . . . 71 C6
Boqueho (22) . . . 48 E6
Bor-et-Bar (12) . . . 251 G5
Boran-sur-Oise (60) . . . 37 K5
Borce (64) . . . 303 F3
Bord-Saint-Georges (23) . . . 183 H2
Bordeaux (33) . . . 229 H2
Bordeaux-en-Gâtinais (45) . . . 111 G3
Bordeaux-Saint-Clair (76) . . . 14 C4
Bordères (64) . . . 284 E5
Bordères-et-Lamensans (40) . . . 265 J4
Bordères-Louron (65) . . . 305 F4
Bordères-sur-l'Échez (65) . . . 285 H5
les Bordes (36) . . . 148 C4
les Bordes (45) . . . 111 F5
Bordes (64) . . . 284 D5
Bordes (65) . . . 285 J5
les Bordes (71) . . . 154 C5
les Bordes (89) . . . 112 E1
les Bordes-Aumont (10) . . . 90 B6
Bordes-de-Rivière (31) . . . 305 J1
les Bordes-sur-Arize (09) . . . 307 F1
les Bordes-sur-Lez (09) . . . 306 C4
Bordezac (30) . . . 255 G3
Bords (17) . . . 177 G6
Borée (07) . . . 239 F1
Boresse-et-Martron (17) . . . 212 C2
Borest (60) . . . 38 C5
Borey (70) . . . 138 D1

Borgo (2B) . . . 319 H2
Bormes-les-Mimosas (83) . . . 298 C5
le Born (31) . . . 269 H3
le Born (48) . . . 237 J6
Bornambusc (76) . . . 14 C5
Bornay (39) . . . 173 G2
Borne (07) . . . 238 D5
Borne (43) . . . 220 B5
Bornel (60) . . . 37 J5
Boron (90) . . . 139 K1
Borre (59) . . . 3 K5
Borrèze (24) . . . 233 G1
Bors(Canton de Baignes-SainteRadegonde) (16) . . . 212 B1
Bors(Canton de Montmoreau-Saint-Cybard) (16) . . . 212 E1
Bort-les-Orgues (19) . . . 217 J1
Bort-l'Étang (63) . . . 203 G3
Borville (54) . . . 94 C2
le Bosc (09) . . . 307 G3
le Bosc (34) . . . 273 G5
Bosc-Bénard-Commin (27) . . . 35 F3
Bosc-Bénard-Crescy (27) . . . 35 F3
Bosc-Bérenger (76) . . . 16 B5
Bosc-Bordel (76) . . . 16 C6
Bosc-Edeline (76) . . . 16 C6
Bosc-Guérard-Saint-Adrien (76) . . . 15 K6
Bosc-Hyons (76) . . . 36 D2
Bosc-le-Hard (76) . . . 16 A5
Bosc-Mesnil (76) . . . 16 C5
le Bosc-Renoult (61) . . . 55 F2
Bosc-Renoult-en-Ouche (27) . . . 55 K2
Bosc-Renoult-en-Roumois (27) . . . 34 E3
le Bosc-Roger-en-Roumois (27) . . . 35 G4
Bosc-Roger-sur-Buchy (76) . . . 16 C6
Boscamnant (17) . . . 212 C3
Bosdarros (64) . . . 284 D5
Bosgouet (27) . . . 35 F3
Bosguérard-de-Marcouville (27) . . . 35 F4
Bosjean (71) . . . 155 F6
Bosmie-l'Aiguille (87) . . . 198 F2
Bosmont-sur-Serre (02) . . . 21 F4
Bosmoreau-les-Mines (23) . . . 182 C5
Bosnormand (27) . . . 35 G4
Bosquel (80) . . . 18 A4
Bosquentin (27) . . . 36 C2
Bosrobert (27) . . . 34 E4
Bosroger (23) . . . 183 G5
Bossancourt (10) . . . 91 F5
Bossay-sur-Claise (37) . . . 146 C6
la Bosse (25) . . . 157 H1
la Bosse (72) . . . 83 H6
la Bosse-de-Bretagne (35) . . . 103 G1
Bossée (37) . . . 146 A2
Bossendorf (67) . . . 69 D1
Bosset (24) . . . 213 G6
Bosseval-et-Briancourt (08) . . . 22 E3
Bossey (74) . . . 191 F2
Bossieu (38) . . . 206 D6
Bossugan (33) . . . 230 C3
Bossus-lès-Rumigny (08) . . . 21 J2
Bost (03) . . . 185 K3
Bostens (40) . . . 265 J1
Bosville (76) . . . 15 F3
Botans (90) . . . 139 H1
Botmeur (29) . . . 75 F1
Botsorhel (29) . . . 47 H6
les Bottereaux (27) . . . 55 J3
Botz-en-Mauges (49) . . . 124 C5
Bou (45) . . . 110 B4
Bouafle (78) . . . 58 A4
Bouafles (27) . . . 36 A5
Bouan (09) . . . 307 J5
Bouaye (44) . . . 123 F5
Boubers-lès-Hesmond (62) . . . 4 D5
Boubers-sur-Canche (62) . . . 9 K3
Boubiers (60) . . . 37 F5
Bouc-Bel-Air (13) . . . 296 C4
Boucagnères (32) . . . 286 D1
Boucau (64) . . . 282 B1
Boucé (03) . . . 185 K1
Boucé (61) . . . 54 B6
le Bouchage (16) . . . 179 J4
le Bouchage (38) . . . 207 H3
Bouchain (59) . . . 11 K3
Bouchamps-lès-Craon (53) . . . 104 C4
le Bouchaud (03) . . . 186 D1
Bouchavesnes-Bergen (80) . . . 19 G1
Bouchemaine (49) . . . 125 G4
Boucheporn (57) . . . 45 K5
Bouchet (26) . . . 256 E3
le Bouchet (74) . . . 209 F1
le Bouchet-Saint-Nicolas (43) . . . 238 B1
Bouchevilliers (27) . . . 36 D2
Bouchoir (80) . . . 18 E4
le Bouchon-sur-Saulx (55) . . . 64 B6
les Bouchoux (39) . . . 173 J6
Bouchy-Saint-Genest (51) . . . 61 F6
Boucieu-le-Roi (07) . . . 222 A5
Bouclans (25) . . . 138 C3
Boucoiran-et-Nozières (30) . . . 275 F1
Bouconville (08) . . . 42 C4
Bouconville-sur-Madt (55) . . . 65 F3
Bouconville-Vauclair (02) . . . 40 C1
Bouconvillers (60) . . . 37 F5
Boucq (54) . . . 65 G3
Boudes (63) . . . 202 E6
Boudeville (76) . . . 15 H4
Boudou (82) . . . 249 F6
Boudrac (31) . . . 286 C6
Boudreville (21) . . . 115 J3

Boudy-de-Beauregard (47) . . . 231 K6
Boué (02) . . . 12 E6
Bouée (44) . . . 122 D2
Boueilh-Boueilho-Lasque (64) . . . 284 D1
Bouelles (76) . . . 16 D4
Bouër (72) . . . 107 J2
Bouère (53) . . . 105 H4
Bouessay (53) . . . 105 H4
Bouesse (36) . . . 165 J3
Bouëx (16) . . . 197 F4
la Bouëxière (35) . . . 79 J3
Bouffémont (95) . . . 58 E1
Boufféré (85) . . . 142 A4
Bouffignereux (02) . . . 40 D2
Boufflers (80) . . . 9 H3
Bouffry (41) . . . 108 C3
Bougainville (80) . . . 17 J2
Bougarber (64) . . . 284 C3
Bougé-Chambalud (38) . . . 222 C1
Bouges-le-Château (36) . . . 147 K3
Bougey (70) . . . 117 J5
Bougival (78) . . . 58 C4
Bouglainval (28) . . . 85 G1
Bougligny (77) . . . 87 H6
Bouglon (47) . . . 247 G2
Bougneau (17) . . . 195 H4
Bougnon (70) . . . 118 A6
Bougon (79) . . . 162 B6
Bougue (40) . . . 265 H2
Bougy (14) . . . 32 C5
Bougy-lez-Neuville (45) . . . 110 B2
Bouhans (71) . . . 154 E6
Bouhans-et-Feurg (70) . . . 136 E3
Bouhans-lès-Lure (70) . . . 118 D6
Bouhans-lès-Montbozon (70) . . . 138 C3
Bouhet (17) . . . 177 G2
Bouhey (21) . . . 153 J1
Bouhy (58) . . . 132 C3
Bouilh-Devant (65) . . . 285 K4
Bouilh-Péreuilh (65) . . . 285 J4
Bouilhonnac (11) . . . 290 C5
Bouillac (12) . . . 234 E6
Bouillac (24) . . . 232 C3
Bouillac (82) . . . 268 C3
la Bouilladisse (13) . . . 296 E3
Bouillancourt-en-Séry (80) . . . 16 E1
Bouillancourt-la-Bataille (80) . . . 18 D4
Bouillancy (60) . . . 38 E6
Bouilland (21) . . . 153 K2
Bouillargues (30) . . . 275 H4
la Bouille (76) . . . 35 G3
Bouillé-Courdault (85) . . . 161 F5
Bouillé-Loretz (79) . . . 144 A2
Bouillé-Ménard (49) . . . 104 C5
Bouillé-Saint-Paul (79) . . . 144 A3
la Bouillie (22) . . . 49 K5
le Bouillon (61) . . . 82 D1
Bouillon (64) . . . 284 B1
Bouillonville (54) . . . 65 H2
Bouilly (10) . . . 90 A6
Bouilly (51) . . . 40 D5
Bouilly-en-Gâtinais (45) . . . 110 D2
Bouin (79) . . . 178 E3
Bouin (85) . . . 140 D3
Bouin-Plumoison (62) . . . 9 H1
Bouisse (11) . . . 309 H3
Bouix (21) . . . 114 E4
Boujailles (25) . . . 156 C4
Boujan-sur-Libron (34) . . . 292 A3
Boulages (10) . . . 89 K1
Boulaincourt (88) . . . 93 H4
Boulancourt (77) . . . 87 F5
Boulange (57) . . . 26 E4
Boulaur (32) . . . 286 E1
le Boulay (37) . . . 128 A2
Boulay-les-Barres (45) . . . 109 K3
Boulay-les-Ifs (53) . . . 82 B3
le Boulay-Morin (27) . . . 35 J6
Boulay-Moselle (57) . . . 27 K6
la Boulaye (71) . . . 170 C1
Boulazac (24) . . . 214 B4
Boulbon (13) . . . 276 A3
Boulc (26) . . . 241 K4
Boule-d'Amont (66) . . . 314 D3
Bouleternère (66) . . . 314 D2
Bouleurs (77) . . . 59 K3
Bouleuse (51) . . . 40 D4
Bouliac (33) . . . 229 H2
Boulieu-lès-Annonay (07) . . . 221 K2
Bouligneux (01) . . . 188 E4
Bouligney (70) . . . 118 B3
Bouligny (55) . . . 26 C5
Boulin (65) . . . 285 J5
Boullarre (60) . . . 39 F6
le Boullay-les-Deux-Églises (28) . . . 56 E6
Boullay-les-Troux (91) . . . 58 B6
le Boullay-Mivoye (28) . . . 57 F6
le Boullay-Thierry (28) . . . 57 F6
Boulleret (18) . . . 131 K4
Boulleville (27) . . . 34 B3
Bouloc (31) . . . 269 G4
Bouloc (82) . . . 249 G3
Boulogne (85) . . . 142 A6
Boulogne-Billancourt (92) . . . 58 D4
Boulogne-la-Grasse (60) . . . 18 C5
Boulogne-sur-Gesse (31) . . . 286 D4
Boulogne-sur-Helpe (59) . . . 13 G5
Boulogne-sur-Mer (62) . . . 2 A4
Bouloire (72) . . . 107 H3
Boulon (14) . . . 32 D6
Boulot (70) . . . 137 K4

353

le Boulou (66) . . . 315 G4
Boult (70) . . . 137 K4
Boult-aux-Bois (08) . . . 42 C4
Boult-sur-Suippe (51) . . . 41 G2
le Boulvé (46) . . . 249 G2
Boulzicourt (08) . . . 22 D4
Boumourt (64) . . . 284 B2
Bouniagues (24) . . . 231 J3
le Boupère (85) . . . 142 E6
Bouquehault (62) . . . 2 E5
Bouquelon (27) . . . 34 C2
Bouquemaison (80) . . . 10 B4
Bouquemont (55) . . . 64 D1
Bouquet (30) . . . 255 J5
Bouquetot (27) . . . 34 E3
Bouqueval (95) . . . 59 F1
Bouranton (10) . . . 90 B4
Bouray-sur-Juine (91) . . . 86 E2
Bourbach-le-Bas (68) . . . 119 K4
Bourbach-le-Haut (68) . . . 119 K4
Bourberain (21) . . . 136 C3
Bourbévelle (70) . . . 117 J3
Bourbon-Lancy (71) . . . 169 J3
Bourbon-l'Archambault (03) . . . 168 B3
Bourbonne-les-Bains (52) . . . 117 J3
la Bourboule (63) . . . 201 K4
Bourbourg (59) . . . 3 F2
Bourbriac (22) . . . 48 C6
Bourcefranc-le-Chapus (17) . . . 176 D6
Bourcia (39) . . . 172 K6
Bourcq (08) . . . 42 A2
Bourdainville (76) . . . 15 J4
Bourdalat (40) . . . 265 K3
Bourdeau (73) . . . 208 A3
Bourdeaux (26) . . . 241 F5
Bourdeilles (24) . . . 213 J2
le Bourdeix (24) . . . 197 J4
Bourdelles (33) . . . 230 C6
le Bourdet (79) . . . 177 J1
Bourdettes (64) . . . 284 D5
Bourdic (30) . . . 275 G1
la Bourdinière-Saint-Loup (28) . . . 85 F4
Bourdon (80) . . . 17 J1
Bourdonnay (57) . . . 67 H4
Bourdonné (78) . . . 57 H5
Bourdons-sur-Rognon (52) . . . 92 D4
Bourecq (62) . . . 5 J5
Bouresches (02) . . . 60 D1
Bouresse (86) . . . 163 H6
Bouret-sur-Canche (62) . . . 10 A3
Boureuilles (55) . . . 42 E4
Bourg (33) . . . 211 H5
le Bourg (46) . . . 234 C4
Bourg (52) . . . 116 C5
Bourg-Achard (27) . . . 35 F3
Bourg-Archambault (86) . . . 164 B6
Bourg-Argental (42) . . . 221 J2
Bourg-Beaudouin (27) . . . 35 K2
Bourg-Blanc (29) . . . 72 D3
Bourg-Bruche (67) . . . 95 H3
Bourg-Charente (16) . . . 196 A3
Bourg-de-Bigorre (65) . . . 304 E1
Bourg-de-Péage (26) . . . 222 D5
Bourg-de-Sirod (39) . . . 174 A1
Bourg-de-Thizy (69) . . . 187 H4
Bourg-de-Visa (82) . . . 249 G6
Bourg-des-Comptes (35) . . . 79 F6
Bourg-des-Maisons (24) . . . 213 H2
le Bourg-d'Hem (23) . . . 182 C1
le Bourg-d'Iré (49) . . . 104 C6
le Bourg-d'Oisans (38) . . . 224 D4
Bourg-d'Oueil (31) . . . 305 G4
Bourg-du-Bost (24) . . . 213 F2
le Bourg-Dun (76) . . . 15 H3
Bourg-en-Bresse (01) . . . 189 G2
Bourg-et-Comin (02) . . . 40 B2
Bourg-Fidèle (08) . . . 22 B2
Bourg-la-Reine (92) . . . 58 E4
Bourg-Lastic (63) . . . 201 H4
Bourg-le-Comte (71) . . . 186 E1
Bourg-le-Roi (72) . . . 82 D4
Bourg-lès-Valence (26) . . . 222 C6
Bourg-l'Évêque (49) . . . 104 C6
Bourg-Madame (66) . . . 313 G5
Bourg-Saint-Andéol (07) . . . 256 C2
Bourg-Saint-Bernard (31) . . . 269 K6
Bourg-Saint-Christophe (01) . . . 189 F6
le Bourg-Saint-Léonard (61) . . . 54 D4
Bourg-Saint-Maurice (73) . . . 193 H2
Bourg-Sainte-Marie (52) . . . 93 F6
Bourg-sous-Châtelet (90) . . . 119 J5
Bourganeuf (23) . . . 182 C5
Bourgbarré (35) . . . 79 G5
Bourgeauville (14) . . . 33 J4
Bourges (18) . . . 149 G3
le Bourget (93) . . . 59 F2
le Bourget-du-Lac (73) . . . 208 B3
Bourget-en-Huile (73) . . . 208 C5
Bourgheim (67) . . . 70 D5
Bourghelles (59) . . . 7 F5
Bourgnac (24) . . . 213 H6
Bourgneuf (17) . . . 176 E2
Bourgneuf (73) . . . 208 E4
Bourgneuf-en-Mauges (49) . . . 124 D5
Bourgneuf-en-Retz (44) . . . 122 C4
le Bourgneuf-la-Forêt (53) . . . 80 D6
Bourgogne (51) . . . 41 F3
Bourgoin-Jallieu (38) . . . 207 F2
Bourgon (53) . . . 80 C6
la Bourgonce (88) . . . 95 G3
Bourgougnague (47) . . . 231 H5

Bourgtheroulde-Infreville (27) . . . 35 F3
Bourguébus (14) . . . 32 E5
Bourgueil (37) . . . 126 D6
Bourguenolles (50) . . . 52 A3
le Bourguet (83) . . . 279 J3
Bourguignon (25) . . . 139 H3
Bourguignon-lès-Conflans (70) . . . 118 B4
Bourguignon-lès-la-Charité (70) . . . 137 K2
Bourguignon-lès-Morey (70) . . . 117 G6
Bourguignon-sous-Coucy (02) . . . 19 J6
Bourguignon-sous-Montbavin (02). . . . 20 C6
Bourguignons (10) . . . 114 D1
Bourgvilain (71) . . . 171 H4
Bourideys (33) . . . 246 A2
Bouriège (11) . . . 308 E3
Bourigeole (11) . . . 308 D3
Bourisp (65) . . . 305 F4
Bourlens (47) . . . 249 F2
Bourlon (62) . . . 11 H4
Bourmont (52) . . . 93 F5
Bournainville-Faverolles (27) . . . 34 C6
Bournan (37) . . . 146 A3
Bournand (86) . . . 144 E2
Bournazel (12) . . . 251 J1
Bournazel (81) . . . 251 F6
Bourneau (85) . . . 160 D3
Bournel (47) . . . 231 K5
Bourneville (27) . . . 34 D2
Bournezeau (85) . . . 160 A4
Bourniquel (24) . . . 232 A2
Bournois (25) . . . 138 E2
Bournoncle-Saint-Pierre (43) . . . 219 G2
Bournonville (62) . . . 2 C5
Bournos (64) . . . 284 C2
Bourogne (90) . . . 139 J1
Bourran (47) . . . 247 K3
Bourré (41) . . . 128 D5
Bourréac (65) . . . 304 B1
Bourret (82) . . . 268 E2
Bourriot-Bergonce (40) . . . 246 C5
Bourron-Marlotte (77) . . . 87 H4
Bourrou (24) . . . 213 J3
Bourrouillan (32) . . . 266 B3
Bours (62) . . . 5 H6
Bours (65) . . . 285 H4
Boursault (51) . . . 61 J1
Boursay (41) . . . 108 B2
Bourscheid (57) . . . 67 K3
Bourseul (22) . . . 50 B5
Bourseville (80) . . . 8 D5
Boursières (70) . . . 137 K1
Boursies (59) . . . 11 H4
Boursin (62) . . . 2 C5
Boursonne (60) . . . 39 F5
Bourth (27) . . . 56 A4
Bourthes (62) . . . 4 E4
Bourville (76) . . . 15 H3
Boury-en-Vexin (60) . . . 36 D4
Bousbach (57) . . . 68 C2
Bousbecque (59) . . . 6 E2
le Bouscat (33) . . . 229 G1
Bousies (59) . . . 12 E4
Bousignies (59) . . . 12 B1
Bousignies-sur-Roc (59) . . . 13 K3
le Bousquet (11) . . . 308 E5
le Bousquet-d'Orb (34) . . . 272 E5
Boussac (12) . . . 251 K4
Boussac (23) . . . 166 B5
la Boussac (35) . . . 51 G5
Boussac (46) . . . 234 C5
Boussac-Bourg (23) . . . 166 D6
Boussais (79) . . . 144 B6
Boussan (31) . . . 287 F1
Boussay (37) . . . 146 C6
Boussay (44) . . . 142 B3
Bousse (57) . . . 27 H5
Bousse (72) . . . 106 D3
Bousselange (21) . . . 154 E3
Boussenac (09) . . . 307 F4
Boussenois (21) . . . 136 C1
Boussens (31) . . . 287 G6
Bousseraucourt (70) . . . 117 J2
Boussès (47) . . . 247 G5
Bousseviller (57) . . . 69 H2
Boussey (21) . . . 135 F5
Boussicourt (80) . . . 18 D4
Boussières (25) . . . 156 A1
Boussières-en-Cambrésis (59) . . . 12 B4
Boussières-sur-Sambre (59) . . . 13 G3
Boussois (59) . . . 13 H2
Boussy (74) . . . 190 E6
Boussy-Saint-Antoine (91) . . . 59 G5
Boust (57) . . . 27 G3
Boustroff (57) . . . 45 K6
Bout-du-Pont-de-Larn (81) . . . 290 B2
Boutancourt (08) . . . 22 D4
Boutavent (60) . . . 17 F5
la Bouteille (02) . . . 21 G2
Bouteilles-Saint-Sébastien (24) . . . 213 G1
Boutenac (11) . . . 291 F6
Boutenac-Touvent (17) . . . 194 E5
Boutencourt (60) . . . 36 E2
Boutervilliers (91) . . . 86 B3
Bouteville (16) . . . 196 B4
Boutiers-Saint-Trojan (16) . . . 195 K2
Boutigny (77) . . . 59 K3
Boutigny-Prouais (28) . . . 57 H5
Boutigny-sur-Essonne (91) . . . 86 E3
Bouttencourt (80) . . . 16 E1
Boutteville (50) . . . 29 G5
Boutx (31) . . . 305 J3
Bouvaincourt-sur-Bresle (80) . . . 8 D6

Bouvancourt (51) . . . 40 D3
Bouvante (26) . . . 223 G6
Bouvelinghem (62) . . . 2 E5
Bouvellemont (08) . . . 22 C5
Bouverans (25) . . . 156 D5
Bouvières (26) . . . 241 F6
Bouvignies (59) . . . 11 K1
Bouvigny-Boyeffles (62) . . . 10 D1
Bouville (28) . . . 85 F5
Bouville (76) . . . 15 H4
Bouville (91) . . . 86 D3
Bouvincourt-en-Vermandois (80) . . . 19 H2
Bouvines (59) . . . 7 F3
Bouvresse (60) . . . 17 F5
Bouvron (44) . . . 122 E1
Bouvron (54) . . . 65 H4
Boux-sous-Salmaise (21) . . . 135 G3
Bouxières-aux-Bois (88) . . . 94 C4
Bouxières-aux-Chênes (54) . . . 66 B4
Bouxières-aux-Dames (54) . . . 66 A4
Bouxières-sous-Froidmont (54) . . . 65 K1
Bouxurulles (88) . . . 94 B3
Bouxwiller (67) . . . 69 H6
Bouxwiller (68) . . . 97 C5
Bouy (51) . . . 41 J6
Bouy-Luxembourg (10) . . . 90 C3
Bouy-sur-Orvin (10) . . . 89 F3
Bouyon (06) . . . 281 F2
le Bouyssou (46) . . . 234 C4
Bouzais (18) . . . 167 G3
Bouzancourt (52) . . . 91 K4
Bouzanville (54) . . . 94 A3
Bouze-lès-Beaune (21) . . . 153 K3
Bouzel (63) . . . 203 F2
Bouzemont (88) . . . 94 B4
Bouzeron (71) . . . 153 K5
Bouzic (24) . . . 233 F4
Bouziès (46) . . . 250 C1
Bouzigues (34) . . . 292 E2
Bouzillé (49) . . . 124 B5
Bouzin (31) . . . 287 F6
Bouzincourt (80) . . . 10 D6
Bouzon-Gellenave (32) . . . 266 C5
Bouzonville (57) . . . 45 J3
Bouzonville-aux-Bois (45) . . . 110 D1
Bouzy (51) . . . 41 G6
Bouzy-la-Forêt (45) . . . 110 E5
Bovée-sur-Barboure (55) . . . 64 E6
Bovel (35) . . . 78 D6
Bovelles (80) . . . 17 K2
Boves (80) . . . 18 B2
Boviolles (55) . . . 64 D6
Boyaval (62) . . . 5 G6
Boyelles (62) . . . 11 F4
Boyer (42) . . . 187 G3
Boyer (71) . . . 171 K3
Boyeux-Saint-Jérôme (01) . . . 189 J4
Boynes (45) . . . 110 E1
Boz (01) . . . 171 K5
Bozas (07) . . . 221 K5
Bozel (73) . . . 209 J3
Bozouls (12) . . . 252 D1
Brabant-le-Roi (55) . . . 63 K3
Brabant-sur-Meuse (55) . . . 43 H3
Brach (33) . . . 210 D5
Brachay (52) . . . 91 K3
Braches (80) . . . 18 C4
Brachy (76) . . . 15 J3
Bracieux (41) . . . 129 G3
Bracon (39) . . . 156 A4
Bracquemont (76) . . . 16 A1
Bracquetuit (76) . . . 16 A5
Bradiancourt (76) . . . 16 C5
Braffais (50) . . . 52 A4
Bragassargues (30) . . . 274 D2
Bragayrac (31) . . . 287 H2
Brageac (15) . . . 217 G3
Bragelogne-Beauvoir (10) . . . 114 C3
Bragny-sur-Saône (71) . . . 154 C4
Braillans (25) . . . 138 A5
Brailly-Cornehotte (80) . . . 9 H3
Brain (21) . . . 135 F3
Brain-sur-Allonnes (49) . . . 126 C5
Brain-sur-l'Authion (49) . . . 125 H4
Brain-sur-Longuenée (49) . . . 124 E2
Brainans (39) . . . 155 H5
Braine (02) . . . 40 A3
Brains (44) . . . 123 F4
Brains-sur-Gée (72) . . . 106 C2
Brains-sur-les-Marches (53) . . . 104 A3
Brainville (50) . . . 30 D3
Brainville (54) . . . 44 B5
Brainville-sur-Meuse (52) . . . 93 F6
Braisnes (60) . . . 38 D1
Braize (03) . . . 167 H2
Bralleville (54) . . . 94 B3
Bram (11) . . . 289 J5
Bramans (73) . . . 226 B2
Brametot (76) . . . 15 H3
Bramevaque (65) . . . 305 H3
Bran (17) . . . 212 A1
Branceilles (19) . . . 216 A6
Branches (89) . . . 113 F4
Brancourt-en-Laonnois (02) . . . 39 K1
Brancourt-le-Grand (02) . . . 20 A1
Brandérion (56) . . . 100 B3
Brandeville (55) . . . 43 G2
Brandivy (56) . . . 100 D3
Brando (2B) . . . 317 E4
Brandon (71) . . . 171 G6
Brandonnet (12) . . . 251 G2

Brandonvillers (51) . . . 91 F1
Branges (71) . . . 172 C2
Brangues (38) . . . 207 H2
Brannay (89) . . . 88 B5
Branne (25) . . . 138 E4
Branne (33) . . . 230 B2
Brannens (33) . . . 230 B6
Branoux-les-Taillades (30) . . . 255 F5
Brans (39) . . . 137 F6
Bransat (03) . . . 185 G1
Branscourt (51) . . . 40 D4
Bransles (77) . . . 111 K1
Brantes (84) . . . 257 K4
Brantigny (88) . . . 94 B3
Brantôme (24) . . . 213 K1
Branville (14) . . . 33 H4
Branville-Hague (50) . . . 28 B2
Braquis (55) . . . 44 A5
Bras (83) . . . 297 J1
Bras-d'Asse (04) . . . 278 E1
Bras-sur-Meuse (55) . . . 43 H4
Brasc (12) . . . 271 J2
Brasles (02) . . . 60 E1
Braslou (37) . . . 145 H4
Brasparts (29) . . . 74 E2
Brassac (09) . . . 307 H3
Brassac (81) . . . 271 H6
Brassac (82) . . . 249 F4
Brassac-les-Mines (63) . . . 219 G1
Brassempouy (40) . . . 264 E5
Brasseuse (60) . . . 38 C4
Brassy (58) . . . 133 K6
Brassy (80) . . . 17 J4
Bratte (54) . . . 66 A3
Braud-et-Saint-Louis (33) . . . 211 G2
Brauvilliers (55) . . . 92 B1
Braux (04) . . . 260 D6
Braux (10) . . . 90 E2
Braux (21) . . . 134 E4
Braux-le-Châtel (52) . . . 115 K1
Braux-Saint-Remy (51) . . . 63 H1
Braux-Sainte-Cohière (51) . . . 42 C6
Brax (31) . . . 268 E6
Brax (47) . . . 248 A4
Bray (27) . . . 35 F6
Bray (71) . . . 171 J4
Bray-Dunes (59) . . . 3 J1
Bray-en-Val (45) . . . 110 E5
Bray-et-Lû (95) . . . 36 D6
Bray-lès-Mareuil (80) . . . 9 G6
Bray-Saint-Christophe (02) . . . 19 J3
Bray-sur-Seine (77) . . . 88 D3
Bray-sur-Somme (80) . . . 18 E1
Braye (27) . . . 39 J2
Braye-en-Laonnois (02) . . . 40 B2
Braye-et-Thiérache (02) . . . 21 G3
Braye-sous-Faye (37) . . . 145 G4
Braye-sur-Maulne (37) . . . 126 E2
Brazey-en-Morvan (21) . . . 152 E1
Brazey-en-Plaine (21) . . . 154 D2
Bréal-sous-Montfort (35) . . . 78 E5
Bréal-sous-Vitré (35) . . . 104 C1
Bréançon (95) . . . 37 G6
Bréau (77) . . . 87 K1
Bréau-et-Salagosse (30) . . . 273 J1
Bréauté (76) . . . 14 D5
Bréban (51) . . . 90 D1
Brebières (62) . . . 11 H2
Brebotte (90) . . . 139 J1
Brécé (35) . . . 79 J4
Brécé (53) . . . 80 E3
Brécey (50) . . . 52 B4
Brech (56) . . . 100 D4
Brechainville (88) . . . 92 E3
Bréchamps (28) . . . 57 G6
Bréchaumont (68) . . . 119 K6
Brèches (37) . . . 127 F2
Breconchaux (25) . . . 138 C4
Brectouville (50) . . . 31 H4
Brécy (02) . . . 39 K5
Brécy (18) . . . 149 J2
Brécy-Brières (08) . . . 42 C3
la Brède (33) . . . 229 H4
Brée (53) . . . 81 H6
la Brée-les-Bains (17) . . . 176 B4
Bréel (61) . . . 53 J4
Brégnier-Cordon (01) . . . 207 J3
Brégy (60) . . . 38 E6
Bréhain (57) . . . 66 D2
Bréhain-la-Ville (54) . . . 26 E3
Bréhal (50) . . . 30 D6
Bréhan (56) . . . 77 H6
Bréhand (22) . . . 77 H2
Bréhémont (37) . . . 127 F6
Bréhéville (55) . . . 43 H2
Breidenbach (57) . . . 69 G2
Breil (49) . . . 126 D3
le Breil-sur-Mérize (72) . . . 107 H2
Breil-sur-Roya (06) . . . 311 C4
la Breille-les-Pins (49) . . . 126 C5
Breilly (80) . . . 17 K1
Breistroff-la-Grande (57) . . . 27 H1
Breitenau (67) . . . 96 B1
Breitenbach (67) . . . 70 B6
Breitenbach-Haut-Rhin (68) . . . 119 K1
Brélès (29) . . . 72 B3
Brélidy (22) . . . 48 C4
Brem-sur-Mer (85) . . . 158 E2
Bréménil (54) . . . 95 H1
Brêmes (62) . . . 2 D4
Brémoncourt (54) . . . 94 C1
Bremondans (25) . . . 138 D6

Brémontier-Merval (76) . . . 36 C1
Brémoy (14) . . . 53 F1
Brémur-et-Vaurois (21) . . . 115 G6
Bren (26) . . . 222 C4
Brenac (11) . . . 308 E3
Brenas (34) . . . 273 F6
Brenat (63) . . . 203 F5
Brénaz (01) . . . 190 B5
Brenelle (02) . . . 40 A3
Brengues (46) . . . 234 B5
Brennes (52) . . . 116 C5
Brennilis (29) . . . 75 F1
Brénod (01) . . . 190 A4
Brenon (83) . . . 279 K3
Brenouille (60) . . . 38 B4
Brenoux (48) . . . 254 B1
Brens (01) . . . 207 K2
Brens (81) . . . 270 B3
Brenthonne (74) . . . 174 E6
Breny (02) . . . 39 J5
la Bréole (04) . . . 243 G6
Brères (25) . . . 156 A2
Bréry (39) . . . 155 H6
Bresdon (17) . . . 178 D6
les Bréseux (25) . . . 139 H5
Bressilly (70) . . . 137 G6
Bresle (80) . . . 18 D1
Bresles (60) . . . 37 J2
Bresnay (03) . . . 168 D5
Bresolettes (61) . . . 55 J6
la Bresse (88) . . . 119 H2
Bresse-sur-Grosne (71) . . . 171 J3
Bressey-sur-Tille (21) . . . 136 C5
Bressieux (38) . . . 223 G1
Bressolles (01) . . . 189 F6
Bressolles (03) . . . 168 E4
Bressols (82) . . . 269 F2
Bresson (38) . . . 224 B4
Bressuire (79) . . . 143 J5
Brest (29) . . . 72 D4
Brestot (27) . . . 34 E3
Bretagne (36) . . . 147 K4
Bretagne (90) . . . 139 K1
Bretagne-d'Armagnac (32) . . . 266 D2
Bretagne-de-Marsan (40) . . . 265 H3
Bretagnolles (27) . . . 57 F2
Breteau (45) . . . 131 K1
Breteil (35) . . . 78 E4
Bretenière (21) . . . 136 B6
la Bretenière (25) . . . 138 C4
la Bretenière (39) . . . 155 J2
Bretenières (39) . . . 155 H4
Bretenoux (46) . . . 234 B4
Breteuil (27) . . . 56 B4
Breteuil (60) . . . 18 A5
Brethel (61) . . . 55 H5
Brethenay (52) . . . 92 B6
le Brethon (03) . . . 167 J3
Bretigney (25) . . . 139 F2
Bretigney-Notre-Dame (25) . . . 138 C5
Bretignolles (79) . . . 143 H5
Bretignolles-sur-Mer (85) . . . 158 D2
Bretigny (21) . . . 136 B4
Brétigny (27) . . . 34 E4
Brétigny (60) . . . 19 J4
Brétigny-sur-Orge (91) . . . 86 E1
Bretoncelles (61) . . . 84 A3
la Bretonnière (85) . . . 159 K4
Bretonvillers (25) . . . 139 F6
Brette (26) . . . 241 G5
Brette-les-Pins (72) . . . 107 F4
Bretten (68) . . . 119 K5
Brettes (16) . . . 179 F5
Bretteville (50) . . . 28 D2
Bretteville-du-Grand-Caux (76) . . . 14 D4
Bretteville-le-Rabet (14) . . . 54 A1
Bretteville-l'Orgueilleuse (14) . . . 32 C4
Bretteville-Saint-Laurent (76) . . . 15 H3
Bretteville-sur-Ay (50) . . . 30 C1
Bretteville-sur-Dives (14) . . . 54 C1
Bretteville-sur-Laize (14) . . . 53 K1
Bretteville-sur-Odon (14) . . . 32 D5
Brettnach (57) . . . 45 J3
Bretx (31) . . . 268 E5
Breuches (70) . . . 118 C4
Breuchotte (70) . . . 118 D4
Breugnon (58) . . . 133 F4
le Breuil (03) . . . 186 B2
Breuil (51) . . . 40 C3
le Breuil (51) . . . 61 G2
le Breuil (69) . . . 188 A6
le Breuil (71) . . . 153 G6
Breuil (80) . . . 19 G4
Breuil-Barret (85) . . . 161 F2
le Breuil-Bernard (79) . . . 161 G1
le Breuil-en-Auge (14) . . . 33 K4
Breuil-en-Bessin (14) . . . 31 K2
Breuil-la-Réorte (17) . . . 177 H4
le Breuil-le-Sec (60) . . . 38 A3
Breuil-le-Vert (60) . . . 38 A3
le Breuil-Magné (17) . . . 177 F4
le Breuil-sous-Argenton (79) . . . 143 K3
le Breuil-sur-Couze (63) . . . 203 F6
Breuilaufa (87) . . . 181 F4
Breuilh (24) . . . 214 A5
Breuillet (17) . . . 194 C2
Breuillet (91) . . . 86 C1
Breuilpont (27) . . . 57 F2
Breurey-lès-Faverney (70) . . . 118 A5
Breuschwickersheim (67) . . . 70 E3
Breuvannes-en-Bassigny (52) . . . 117 F1

354

Breuvery-sur-Coole (51) . . . 62 D3
Breuville (50) . . . 28 C3
Breux (55) . . . 23 K5
Breux-Jouy (91) . . . 86 C1
Breux-sur-Avre (27) . . . 56 C4
Brévainville (41) . . . 108 E3
Bréval (78) . . . 57 G2
Brévands (50) . . . 29 G6
Brevans (39) . . . 155 G2
le Brévedent (14) . . . 34 A4
Brèves (58) . . . 133 G4
les Bréviaires (78) . . . 57 K5
Bréviandes (10) . . . 90 B5
la Brévière (14) . . . 54 E2
Bréville (14) . . . 33 F4
Bréville (16) . . . 196 A1
Bréville-sur-Mer (50) . . . 30 D4
Brévillers (62) . . . 9 H2
Brévillers (80) . . . 10 B4
Brevilliers (70) . . . 139 H1
Brévilly (08) . . . 23 G4
Brévonnes (10) . . . 90 D4
Bréxent-Enocq (62) . . . 4 B5
Brey-et-Maison-du-Bois (25) . . . 156 E6
Brézé (49) . . . 144 C1
Bréziers (05) . . . 259 J1
Brézilhac (11) . . . 289 J6
Brézins (38) . . . 223 G1
Brezolles (28) . . . 56 C5
Brezons (15) . . . 218 B6
Briançon (05) . . . 225 K6
Briançonnet (06) . . . 280 B2
Brianny (21) . . . 134 E4
Briant (71) . . . 187 F1
Briantes (36) . . . 166 B4
Briare (45) . . . 131 J2
Briarres-sur-Essonne (45) . . . 87 F6
Brias (62) . . . 10 B1
Briastre (59) . . . 12 C4
Briatexte (81) . . . 270 B4
Briaucourt (52) . . . 92 B5
Briaucourt (70) . . . 118 B4
Bricon (52) . . . 115 K1
Briconville (28) . . . 85 F2
Bricquebec (50) . . . 28 C4
Bricquebosq (50) . . . 28 C3
Bricqueville (14) . . . 31 J1
Bricqueville-la-Blouette (50) . . . 30 D4
Bricqueville-sur-Mer (50) . . . 30 D6
Bricy (45) . . . 109 J3
Brides-les-Bains (73) . . . 209 H5
la Bridoire (73) . . . 207 K4
Bridoré (37) . . . 146 D3
Brie (02) . . . 20 B5
Brie (09) . . . 288 C6
Brie (16) . . . 197 F2
Brie (35) . . . 79 H6
Brie (79) . . . 144 D4
Brie (80) . . . 19 G2
Brie-Comte-Robert (77) . . . 59 G5
Brié-et-Angonnes (38) . . . 224 B4
Brie-sous-Archiac (17) . . . 195 K5
Brie-sous-Barbezieux (16) . . . 196 C6
Brie-sous-Chalais (16) . . . 212 D2
Brie-sous-Matha (17) . . . 196 A1
Brie-sous-Mortagne (17) . . . 195 F5
Briec (29) . . . 74 E4
Briel-sur-Barse (10) . . . 90 D6
Brielles (35) . . . 104 B2
Brienne (71) . . . 172 B3
Brienne-la-Vieille (10) . . . 91 F3
Brienne-le-Château (10) . . . 91 H4
Brienne-sur-Aisne (08) . . . 41 F2
Briennon (42) . . . 187 F3
Brienon-sur-Armançon (89) . . . 113 G3
Brières-les-Scellés (91) . . . 86 C3
Brieuil-sur-Chizé (79) . . . 178 B3
Brieulles-sur-Bar (08) . . . 42 C1
Brieulles-sur-Meuse (55) . . . 43 F3
Brieux (61) . . . 54 B3
Briey (54) . . . 26 E6
Briffons (63) . . . 201 J3
Brignac (34) . . . 273 H6
Brignac (56) . . . 77 K5
Brignac-la-Plaine (19) . . . 215 G4
Brignais (69) . . . 205 K3
Brignancourt (95) . . . 37 F6
Brigné (49) . . . 125 J4
Brignemont (31) . . . 268 C4
Brignogan-Plage (29) . . . 46 B3
Brignoles (83) . . . 297 K2
Brignon (30) . . . 275 F1
le Brignon (43) . . . 238 C1
la Brigue (06) . . . 311 D2
Brigueil-le-Chantre (86) . . . 164 C6
Brigueuil (16) . . . 180 D5
Briis-sous-Forges (91) . . . 86 C6
Brillac (16) . . . 180 C4
la Brillanne (04) . . . 278 C2
Brillecourt (10) . . . 90 D2
Brillevast (50) . . . 28 E2
Brillon (59) . . . 11 K1
Brillon-en-Barrois (55) . . . 64 A5
Brimeux (62) . . . 4 C6
Brimont (51) . . . 41 F3
Brin-sur-Seille (54) . . . , 66 A3
Brinay (18) . . . 148 E2
Brinay (58) . . . 151 K4
Brinckheim (68) . . . 97 D4
Brindas (69) . . . 205 K2
Bringolo (22) . . . 48 E5
Brinon-sur-Beuvron (58) . . . 133 F6

Brinon-sur-Sauldre (18) . . . 130 D2
Briod (39) . . . 173 G2
Briollay (49) . . . 125 H2
Brion (01) . . . 189 K2
Brion (36) . . . 148 A4
Brion (38) . . . 223 G2
Brion (48) . . . 236 E3
Brion (71) . . . 152 E5
Brion (86) . . . 163 G6
Brion (89) . . . 113 F3
Brion-près-Thouet (79) . . . 144 B3
la Brionne (23) . . . 182 C3
Brionne (27) . . . 34 E5
Briord (01) . . . 207 G1
Briosne-lès-Sables (72) . . . 83 F6
Briot (60) . . . 17 H5
Briou (41) . . . 109 G5
Brioude (43) . . . 219 H2
Brioux-sur-Boutonne (79) . . . 178 C3
Briouze (61) . . . 53 J5
Briquemesnil-Floxicourt (80) . . . 17 J2
Briquenay (08) . . . 42 D2
Briscous (64) . . . 282 D2
Brison-Saint-Innocent (73) . . . 208 B2
Brissac (34) . . . 274 A3
Brissac-Quincé (49) . . . 125 H5
Brissarthe (49) . . . 105 H6
Brissay-Choigny (02) . . . 20 A4
Brissy-Hamégicourt (02) . . . 20 A4
Brive-la-Gaillarde (19) . . . 215 J4
Brives (36) . . . 148 C6
Brives-Charensac (43) . . . 220 C5
Brives-sur-Charente (17) . . . 195 H3
Brivezac (19) . . . 216 B6
Brix (50) . . . 28 D3
Brixey-aux-Chanoines (55) . . . 93 G2
Brizambourg (17) . . . 195 H1
Brizay (37) . . . 145 H2
Brizeaux (55) . . . 63 K1
Brizon (74) . . . 191 J3
le Broc (06) . . . 281 F2
le Broc (63) . . . 202 E5
Brocas (40) . . . 245 K6
Brochon (21) . . . 135 K6
Brocourt (80) . . . 17 G2
Broglie (27) . . . 55 H1
Brognard (25) . . . 139 H2
Brognon (08) . . . 21 K1
Brognon (21) . . . 136 B4
Broin (21) . . . 154 D2
Broindon (21) . . . 154 C1
Broissia (39) . . . 173 F6
Brombos (60) . . . 17 H5
Bromeilles (45) . . . 87 F6
Brommat (12) . . . 236 A2
Bromont-Lamothe (63) . . . 202 A1
Bron (69) . . . 206 B2
Bronvaux (57) . . . 27 G6
Broons (22) . . . 78 B1
la Broque (67) . . . 70 A5
Broquiers (60) . . . 17 G5
Broquiès (12) . . . 271 K1
Brossac (16) . . . 212 C1
Brossainc (07) . . . 222 A2
Brosses (89) . . . 133 H3
Brossville (27) . . . 35 H6
Brotte-lès-Luxeuil (70) . . . 118 C5
Brotte-lès-Ray (70) . . . 137 G1
Brou (28) . . . 84 D6
Brou-sur-Chantereine (77) . . . 59 H3
Brouains (50) . . . 52 D5
Broualan (35) . . . 51 K5
Brouay (14) . . . 32 C4
Brouchaud (24) . . . 214 D3
Brouchy (80) . . . 19 J4
Brouck (57) . . . 45 J5
Brouckerque (59) . . . 3 G2
Brouderdorff (57) . . . 67 K4
Broué (28) . . . 57 G5
Brouennes (55) . . . 23 J6
le Brouilh-Monbert (32) . . . 267 F5
Brouilla (66) . . . 315 G3
Brouillet (51) . . . 40 C4
Brouqueyran (33) . . . 230 B6
la Brousse (17) . . . 178 B6
Brousse (23) . . . 183 J5
Brousse (63) . . . 203 G4
Brousse (81) . . . 270 D5
Brousse-le-Château (12) . . . 271 J1
Brousses-et-Villaret (11) . . . 290 A4
Brousseval (52) . . . 91 K2
Broussey-en-Blois (55) . . . 64 E6
Broussey-Raulecourt (55) . . . 65 F3
Broussy-le-Grand (51) . . . 61 J4
Broussy-le-Petit (51) . . . 61 J4
Broût-Vernet (03) . . . 185 H2
Brouvelieures (88) . . . 95 G4
Brouville (54) . . . 95 G1
Brouviller (57) . . . 67 K3
Brouy (91) . . . 86 D4
Brouzet-lès-Alès (30) . . . 255 J5
Brouzet-lès-Quissac (30) . . . 274 D3
les Brouzils (85) . . . 142 A4
Broxeele (59) . . . 3 G4
Broye (71) . . . 153 F5
Broye-Aubigney-Montseugny (70) . . 137 F5
Broye-les-Loups-et-Verfontaine (70) . . 136 E3

Broyes (51) . . . 61 H5
Broyes (60) . . . 18 C5
Broze (81) . . . 270 B2
Brû (88) . . . 95 F3
Bruailles (71) . . . 172 D3
Bruay-la-Buissière (62) . . . 5 K6
Bruay-sur-l'Escaut (59) . . . 12 D1
Brucamps (80) . . . 9 J5
Bruch (47) . . . 247 K4
Brucheville (50) . . . 29 G6
Brucourt (14) . . . 33 G4
Brue-Auriac (83) . . . 297 J1
Bruebach (68) . . . 97 C3
Brueil-en-Vexin (78) . . . 57 K1
Bruère-Allichamps (18) . . . 167 F1
la Bruère-sur-Loir (72) . . . 127 F1
la Bruffière (85) . . . 142 B3
Brugairolles (11) . . . 308 C1
le Brugeron (63) . . . 203 K3
Bruges (33) . . . 229 G1
Bruges-Capbis-Mifaget (64) . . . 284 D6
Brugheas (03) . . . 185 H4
Brugnac (47) . . . 247 K1
Brugnens (32) . . . 267 K3
Brugny-Vaudancourt (51) . . . 61 J1
la Bruguière (30) . . . 256 A5
Bruguières (31) . . . 269 G5
Bruille-lez-Marchiennes (59) . . . 11 K2
Bruille-Saint-Amand (59) . . . 7 J6
Bruis (05) . . . 241 J6
Brûlain (79) . . . 178 B2
les Brulais (35) . . . 102 C1
Brulange (57) . . . 66 D1
la Brûlatte (53) . . . 104 D1
Bruley (54) . . . 65 H5
Brullemail (61) . . . 55 F6
Brulon (72) . . . 105 K3
Brumath (67) . . . 25 A5
Brumetz (02) . . . 39 H6
Brunehamel (02) . . . 21 J3
Brunelles (28) . . . 84 A4
les Brunels (11) . . . 289 H3
Brunémont (59) . . . 11 J3
Brunet (04) . . . 278 E2
Bruniquel (82) . . . 250 C6
Brunoy (91) . . . 59 F5
Brunstatt (68) . . . 97 C3
Brunville (76) . . . 16 B1
Brunvillers-la-Motte (60) . . . 18 C6
Brusque (12) . . . 272 C4
le Brusquet (04) . . . 259 K4
Brussey (70) . . . 137 H5
Brussieu (69) . . . 205 H2
Brusson (51) . . . 63 G4
Brusvily (22) . . . 50 C6
Brutelles (80) . . . 8 D4
Bruville (54) . . . 44 C5
Brux (86) . . . 179 G4
la Bruyère (70) . . . 118 E4
Bruyères (88) . . . 95 F5
Bruyères-et-Montbérault (02) . . . 40 B1
Bruyères-le-Châtel (91) . . . 86 D1
Bruyères-sur-Fère (02) . . . 39 K5
Bruyères-sur-Oise (95) . . . 37 K5
Bruys (02) . . . 40 A4
Bruz (35) . . . 79 F5
Bry (59) . . . 12 E2
Bry-sur-Marne (94) . . . 59 G4
Bû (28) . . . 57 G4
le Bû-sur-Rouvres (14) . . . 54 B1
Buais (50) . . . 80 D1
Buanes (40) . . . 265 H4
Bubertré (61) . . . 83 H1
Bubry (56) . . . 100 C1
Buc (78) . . . 58 C4
Buc (90) . . . 139 H1
Bucamps (60) . . . 37 K1
Bucéels (14) . . . 32 B4
Bucey-en-Othe (10) . . . 89 J5
Bucey-lès-Gy (70) . . . 137 J3
Bucey-lès-Traves (70) . . . 137 K1
Buchelay (78) . . . 57 J2
Buchères (10) . . . 90 B5
Buchy (57) . . . 66 B1
Buchy (76) . . . 16 C6
Bucilly (02) . . . 21 H2
Bucquoy (62) . . . 10 E4
Bucy-le-Long (02) . . . 39 K2
Bucy-le-Roi (45) . . . 110 A2
Bucy-lès-Cerny (02) . . . 20 C6
Bucy-lès-Pierrepont (02) . . . 21 F5
Bucy-Saint-Liphard (45) . . . 109 J3
Budelière (23) . . . 183 K2
Buding (57) . . . 27 J4
Budling (57) . . . 27 J4
Budos (33) . . . 229 J6
Bué (18) . . . 131 J4
Bueil (27) . . . 57 G2
Bueil-en-Touraine (37) . . . 127 H1
Buellas (01) . . . 189 F2
Buethwiller (68) . . . 97 A3
Buffard (25) . . . 155 K3
Buffières (71) . . . 171 G5
Buffignécourt (70) . . . 117 K4
Buffon (21) . . . 134 D1
Bugarach (11) . . . 309 G4
Bugard (65) . . . 286 A5
Bugeat (19) . . . 200 B4
Bugnein (64) . . . 283 J3

Bugnicourt (59) . . . 11 J3
Bugnières (52) . . . 116 A3
Bugny (25) . . . 157 F3
le Bugue (24) . . . 232 C1
Buhl (67) . . . 25 C2
Buhl (68) . . . 96 A6
Buhl-Lorraine (57) . . . 67 J4
Buhy (95) . . . 36 D5
Buicourt (60) . . . 17 G6
Buigny-l'Abbé (80) . . . 9 H5
Buigny-lès-Gamaches (80) . . . 8 D6
Buigny-Saint-Maclou (80) . . . 9 G5
Buire (02) . . . 21 G2
Buire-au-Bois (62) . . . 9 G1
Buire-Courcelles (80) . . . 19 H1
Buire-le-Sec (62) . . . 9 G1
Buire-sur-l'Ancre (80) . . . 18 D1
Buironfosse (02) . . . 20 E1
le Buis (87) . . . 181 G4
Buis-les-Baronnies (26) . . . 257 J3
Buis-sur-Damville (27) . . . 56 D4
Buissard (05) . . . 243 F4
la Buisse (38) . . . 223 K1
la Buissière (38) . . . 208 C6
le Buisson (48) . . . 237 F5
le Buisson (51) . . . 63 H4
le Buisson (84) . . . 257 G3
le Buisson-de-Cadouin (24) . . . 232 C2
Buissoncourt (54) . . . 66 C5
Buissy (62) . . . 11 H4
Bujaleuf (87) . . . 199 J2
Bulan (65) . . . 304 E2
Bulat-Pestivien (22) . . . 76 B1
Bulcy (58) . . . 150 C1
Buléon (56) . . . 101 G2
Bulgnéville (88) . . . 93 H5
Bulhon (63) . . . 185 J6
Bullainville (28) . . . 85 G6
Bulle (25) . . . 156 D2
Bullecourt (62) . . . 11 G4
Bulles (60) . . . 37 K2
Bulligny (54) . . . 65 H6
Bullion (78) . . . 58 B6
Bullou (28) . . . 84 E5
Bully (42) . . . 186 E6
Bully (69) . . . 205 J1
Bully (76) . . . 16 C4
Bully-les-Mines (62) . . . 10 E1
Bulson (08) . . . 23 F5
Bult (88) . . . 94 E4
Bun (65) . . . 304 A2
Buncey (21) . . . 115 F5
Buneville (62) . . . 10 B2
Bunus (64) . . . 283 F5
Bunzac (16) . . . 197 G3
Buoux (84) . . . 277 H3
Burbach (67) . . . 67 J2
la Burbanche (01) . . . 189 K6
Burcin (38) . . . 207 G6
Burcy (14) . . . 53 F3
Burcy (77) . . . 87 G5
Burdignes (42) . . . 221 J2
Burdignin (74) . . . 191 J1
Bure (55) . . . 92 C2
Buré (61) . . . 83 G2
Bure-les-Templiers (21) . . . 115 J6
Burelles (02) . . . 21 F3
Bures (54) . . . 66 E4
Bures (61) . . . 83 G1
Bures-en-Bray (76) . . . 16 C3
Bures-les-Monts (14) . . . 31 J5
Bures-sur-Yvette (91) . . . 58 C5
le Buret (53) . . . 105 H3
Burey (27) . . . 56 B2
Burey-en-Vaux (55) . . . 93 F1
Burey-la-Côte (55) . . . 93 G2
Burg (65) . . . 286 A6
Burgalays (31) . . . 305 J4
Burgaronne (64) . . . 283 H2
le Burgaud (31) . . . 268 D4
Burgille (25) . . . 137 H5
Burgnac (87) . . . 198 E2
Burgy (71) . . . 171 K4
Burie (17) . . . 195 J2
Buriville (54) . . . 95 F1
Burlats (81) . . . 271 F6
Burlioncourt (57) . . . 66 D2
Burnand (71) . . . 171 J4
Burnevillers (25) . . . 139 K4
Burnhaupt-le-Bas (68) . . . 97 A3
Burnhaupt-le-Haut (68) . . . 97 A3
Buros (64) . . . 284 D3
Burosse-Mendousse (64) . . . 284 E1
Burret (09) . . . 307 H3
Bursard (61) . . . 82 E1
Burthecourt-aux-Chênes (54) . . . 66 B6
Burtoncourt (57) . . . 27 K6
Bury (60) . . . 37 K3
Burzet (07) . . . 239 F2
Burzy (71) . . . 171 G3
Bus (62) . . . 11 G3
Bus-la-Mésière (80) . . . 18 E5
Bus-lès-Artois (80) . . . 10 C5
Bus-Saint-Rémy (27) . . . 36 C5
Busigny (59) . . . 12 C6
Busloup (41) . . . 108 E3
Busnes (62) . . . 5 J4
Busque (81) . . . 270 C4
Bussac (24) . . . 213 K2

Bussac-Forêt (17) . . . 211 K3
Bussac-sur-Charente (17) . . . 195 H3
Bussang (88) . . . 119 H3
le Busseau (79) . . . 161 G3
Busseaut (21) . . . 115 G6
Busséol (63) . . . 202 E3
Busserolles (24) . . . 197 J3
Busserotte-et-Montenaille (21) . . . 135 K1
Busset (03) . . . 185 K4
Bussiares (02) . . . 39 H6
la Bussière (45) . . . 111 J4
la Bussière (86) . . . 163 K3
Bussière-Badil (24) . . . 197 J3
Bussière-Boffy (87) . . . 180 D4
Bussière-Dunoise (23) . . . 182 C2
Bussière-Galant (87) . . . 198 C4
Bussière-Nouvelle (23) . . . 183 J5
Bussière-Poitevine (87) . . . 180 D2
Bussière-Saint-Georges (23) . . . 166 C6
la Bussière-sur-Ouche (21) . . . 153 J1
Bussières (21) . . . 135 K1
Bussières (42) . . . 205 F1
Bussières (63) . . . 184 A4
Bussières (70) . . . 137 K5
Bussières (71) . . . 171 H6
Bussières (77) . . . 60 C3
Bussières (89) . . . 134 B4
Bussières-et-Pruns (63) . . . 185 G5
Busson (52) . . . 92 D4
Bussu (80) . . . 19 H1
Bussunarits-Sarrasquette (64) . . . 282 E5
Bussus-Bussuel (80) . . . 9 H5
Bussy (18) . . . 149 J5
Bussy (60) . . . 19 H5
Bussy-Albieux (42) . . . 204 C2
Bussy-en-Othe (89) . . . 113 F2
Bussy-la-Pesle (21) . . . 135 H5
Bussy-la-Pesle (58) . . . 133 F6
Bussy-le-Château (51) . . . 42 A6
Bussy-le-Grand (21) . . . 135 F2
Bussy-le-Repos (51) . . . 63 H3
Bussy-le-Repos (89) . . . 112 D2
Bussy-lès-Daours (80) . . . 18 C2
Bussy-lès-Poix (80) . . . 17 J3
Bussy-Lettrée (51) . . . 62 C4
Bussy-Saint-Georges (77) . . . 59 H4
Bussy-Saint-Martin (77) . . . 59 H3
Bust (67) . . . 69 F6
Bustanico (2B) . . . 319 G5
Bustince-Iriberry (64) . . . 282 E5
Buswiller (67) . . . 69 H6
Busy (25) . . . 156 B1
Buthiers (70) . . . 138 A4
Buthiers (77) . . . 87 F5
Butot (76) . . . 15 K5
Butot-Vénesville (76) . . . 15 F3
Butteaux (89) . . . 113 J3
Butten (67) . . . 69 F4
Buverchy (80) . . . 19 H4
Buvilly (39) . . . 155 J5
la Buxerette (36) . . . 165 K4
Buxeuil (10) . . . 114 E2
Buxeuil (36) . . . 147 K2
Buxeuil (86) . . . 146 A4
Buxières-d'Aillac (36) . . . 165 J3
Buxières-les-Clefmont (52) . . . 116 E1
Buxières-les-Mines (03) . . . 168 A5
Buxières-lès-Villiers (52) . . . 116 A1
Buxières-sous-les-Côtes (55) . . . 65 F2
Buxières-sous-Montaigut (63) . . . 184 D2
Buxières-sur-Arce (10) . . . 114 E1
Buxy (71) . . . 171 H1
Buysscheure (59) . . . 3 H4
Buzan (09) . . . 306 D3
Buzançais (36) . . . 147 H5
Buzancy (02) . . . 39 J3
Buzancy (08) . . . 42 D2
Buzeins (12) . . . 253 F2
Buzet-sur-Baïse (47) . . . 247 J4
Buzet-sur-Tarn (31) . . . 269 J4
Buziet (64) . . . 284 B6
Buzignargues (34) . . . 274 D5
Buzon (65) . . . 285 J2
Buzy (64) . . . 284 C6
Buzy-Darmont (55) . . . 44 A5
By (25) . . . 156 A3
Byans-sur-Doubs (25) . . . 156 A2

C

Cabanac (65) . . . 285 K4
Cabanac-Cazaux (31) . . . 305 K2
Cabanac-et-Villagrains (33) . . . 229 H5
Cabanac-Séguenville (31) . . . 268 C4
la Cabanasse (66) . . . 313 J4
Cabanès (12) . . . 251 K5
Cabanès (81) . . . 270 C5
le Cabanial (31) . . . 289 G2
les Cabannes (09) . . . 307 K5
les Cabannes (13) . . . 276 A5
les Cabannes (81) . . . 251 F6
Cabara (33) . . . 230 B2
Cabariot (17) . . . 177 G5
Cabas-Loumassès (32) . . . 286 D4
Cabasse (83) . . . 298 D2
Cabestany (66) . . . 315 H2
Cabidos (64) . . . 284 C1

Cabourg (14) 33 G3
Cabrerets (46) 250 C1
Cabrerolles (34) 291 K1
Cabrespine (11) 290 C4
Cabrières (30) 275 H2
Cabrières (34) 292 B1
Cabrières-d'Aigues (84) 277 J3
Cabrières-d'Avignon (84) 276 E2
Cabriès (13) 296 C2
Cabris (06) 280 C4
Cachan (94) 58 E4
Cachen (40) 246 A6
Cachy (80) 18 C2
Cadalen (81) 270 C3
Cadarcet (09) 307 H2
Cadarsac (33) 230 A2
Cadaujac (33) 229 H3
Cadéac (65) 305 F4
Cadeilhan (32) 267 K3
Cadeilhan-Trachère (65) 304 D3
Cadeillan (32) 287 F3
Cademène (25) 156 B2
Caden (56) 102 A4
Cadenet (84) 277 H4
Caderousse (84) 256 D5
la Cadière-d'Azur (83) 297 G5
la Cadière-et-Cambo (30) 274 D2
Cadillac (33) 229 K4
Cadillac-en-Fronsadais (33) 211 K6
Cadillon (64) 285 F1
Cadix (81) 271 H2
Cadolive (13) 296 E3
Cadours (31) 268 C5
Cadrieu (46) 250 E1
Caen (14) 32 E5
Caëstre (59) 3 K5
Caffiers (62) 2 C4
Cagnac-les-Mines (81) 270 E2
Cagnano (2B) 317 D4
Cagnes-sur-Mer (06) 281 F4
Cagnicourt (62) 11 G4
Cagnoncles (59) 11 K4
Cagnotte (40) 264 B6
Cagny (14) 33 F5
Cagny (80) 18 B2
Cahagnes (14) 32 A6
Cahagnolles (14) 32 A5
Cahaignes (27) 36 C5
Cahan (61) 53 J3
Caharet (65) 286 A6
Cahon (80) 9 F5
Cahors (46) 249 K1
Cahus (46) 234 C1
Cahuzac (11) 289 F6
Cahuzac (47) 231 J4
Cahuzac (81) 289 J2
Cahuzac-sur-Adour (32) 266 B6
Cahuzac-sur-Vère (81) 270 B2
Caignac (31) 288 C4
le Cailar (30) 275 G4
Cailhau (11) 289 J6
Cailhavel (11) 289 H6
Cailla (11) 308 E5
Caillac (46) 249 J1
Caillavet (32) 267 F5
Caille (06) 280 B3
la Caillère-Saint-Hilaire (85) 160 D2
Cailleville (76) 15 G2
Caillouël-Crépigny (02) 19 J5
Caillouet-Orgeville (27) 56 E1
Cailloux-sur-Fontaines (69) 188 D6
Cailly (76) 16 B6
Cailly-sur-Eure (27) 35 J4
la Caine (14) 53 H1
Cairanne (84) 257 F4
le Caire (04) 259 G2
Cairon (14) 32 D4
Caisnes (60) 39 G1
Caissargues (30) 275 G4
Caix (80) 18 E3
Caixas (66) 314 E4
Caixon (65) 285 H3
Cajarc (46) 250 E1
Calacuccia (2B) 318 E5
Calais (62) 2 C2
Calamane (46) 233 G6
Calan (56) 100 A2
Calanhel (22) 47 K6
Calavanté (65) 285 J5
Calcatoggio (2A) 320 B4
Calce (66) 310 A5
Calenzana (2B) 318 C3
Calès (24) 232 E2
Calès (46) 233 J3
Calignac (47) 247 K5
Caligny (61) 53 G4
Callac (22) 75 K1
Callas (83) 279 K5
Callen (40) 246 A3
Callengeville (76) 16 D3
Calleville (27) 34 E5
Calleville-les-Deux-Églises (76) . . 15 J4
Callian (32) 266 E6
Callian (83) 280 B5
Calmeilles (66) 314 E4
Calmels-et-le-Viala (12) 272 A2
la Calmette (30) 275 F2
Calmont (12) 252 B4
Calmont (31) 288 D5
Calmoutier (70) 118 C6
Caloire (42) 204 E4
Calonges (47) 247 H2

Calonne-Ricouart (62) 5 J6
Calonne-sur-la-Lys (62) 5 K4
Calorguen (22) 50 D6
la Calotterie (62) 4 B6
Caluire-et-Cuire (69) 206 A1
Calvi (2B) 318 B3
Calviac (24) 234 D1
Calviac-en-Périgord (24) 233 G2
Calvignac (46) 250 D1
Calvinet (15) 235 G4
Calvisson (30) 275 F4
Calzan (09) 307 K2
Camalès (65) 285 H3
Camarade (09) 307 F1
Camarès (12) 272 B4
Camaret-sur-Aigues (84) 257 F5
Camaret-sur-Mer (29) 72 C6
Camarsac (33) 229 K2
Cambayrac (46) 249 J2
la Cambe (14) 29 J6
Cambernard (31) 287 J2
Cambernon (50) 30 E3
Cambes (33) 229 J3
Cambes (46) 234 C5
Cambes (47) 231 F5
Cambes-en-Plaine (14) 32 E4
Cambia (2B) 319 G6
Cambiac (31) 289 F2
Cambieure (11) 308 D1
Camblain-Châtelain (62) 5 J6
Camblain-l'Abbé (62) 10 D2
Camblanes-et-Meynac (33) 229 H3
Cambligneul (62) 10 D1
Cambo-les-Bains (64) 263 E2
Cambon (81) 270 E2
Cambon-et-Salvergues (34) 272 B6
Cambon-lès-Lavaur (81) 289 G1
Camboulazet (12) 252 A4
Camboulit (46) 234 C5
Cambounès (81) 290 C1
Cambounet-sur-le-Sor (81) 289 J1
le Cambout (22) 77 H6
Cambrai (59) 11 J4
Cambremer (14) 33 H5
Cambrin (62) 6 B5
Cambron (80) 9 F5
Cambronne-lès-Clermont (60) . . . 38 A3
Cambronne-lès-Ribécourt (60) . . . 38 E1
Camburat (46) 234 D5
Came (64) 283 F2
Camélas (66) 314 E2
Camelin (02) 39 G1
Camembert (61) 54 E3
Cametours (50) 31 F4
Camiac-et-Saint-Denis (33) 230 A2
Camiers (62) 4 A5
Camiran (33) 230 C5
Camjac (12) 251 K5
Camlez (22) 48 B2
les Cammazes (81) 289 J3
Camoël (56) 121 J2
Camon (09) 308 C2
Camon (80) 18 B2
Camors (56) 100 D3
Camou-Cihigue (64) 283 H6
Camous (65) 305 F3
Campagna-de-Sault (11) 308 D5
Campagnac (12) 253 G2
Campagnac (81) 270 B1
Campagnac-lès-Quercy (24) 232 E4
Campagnan (34) 292 D1
Campagne (24) 232 C1
Campagne (34) 274 D4
Campagne (40) 265 F3
Campagne (60) 19 G5
Campagne-d'Armagnac (32) 266 C4
Campagne-lès-Boulonnais (62) . . 4 E4
Campagne-lès-Guines (62) 2 D4
Campagne-lès-Hesdin (62) 9 G1
Campagne-lès-Wardrecques (62) . 3 H5
Campagne-sur-Arize (09) 307 F1
Campagne-sur-Aude (11) 308 D3
Campagnolles (14) 31 J6
Campan (65) 304 D2
Campana (2B) 319 H5
Campandré-Valcongrain (14) 53 H1
Camparan (65) 305 F4
Campbon (44) 122 D1
Campeaux (14) 31 J5
Campeaux (60) 17 F5
Campel (35) 78 D6
Campénéac (56) 78 A6
Campestre-et-Luc (30) 273 H2
Campet-et-Lamolère (40) 265 F2
Camphin-en-Carembault (59) . . . 6 D5
Camphin-en-Pévèle (59) 7 F4
Campi (2B) 319 J6
Campigneulles-les-Grandes (62) . 9 F1
Campigneulles-les-Petites (62) . . 4 A6
Campigny (14) 32 A4
Campigny (27) 34 C3
Campile (2B) 319 H3
Campistrous (65) 286 A6
Campitello (2B) 319 G3
Camplong (34) 272 E5
Camplong-d'Aude (11) 309 K1
Campneuseville (76) 17 F2
Campo (2A) 320 D5
Campôme (66) 314 B2
Campoussy (66) 309 H6
Campremy (60) 18 B6

Camprond (50) 31 F3
Camps-en-Amiénois (80) 17 H2
Camps-la-Source (83) 297 K2
Camps-Saint-Mathurin-
    Léobazel (19) 216 D6
Camps-sur-l'Agly (11) 309 G4
Camps-sur-l'Isle (33) 212 C5
Campsas (82) 269 F3
Campsegret (24) 231 J1
Campuac (12) 235 K6
Campugnan (33) 211 H3
Campuzan (65) 286 B5
Camurac (11) 308 B5
Canale-di-Verde (2B) 319 J6
Canals (82) 269 F3
Canaples (80) 9 K5
Canappeville (27) 35 H5
Canapville (14) 33 J3
Canapville (61) 55 F2
Canari (2B) 317 C3
Canaules-et-Argentières (30) 274 D1
Canavaggia (2B) 319 G3
Canaveilles (66) 314 A4
Cancale (35) 51 F3
Cancon (47) 231 K6
Candas (80) 10 A5
Candé (49) 124 C2
Candé-sur-Beuvron (41) 128 E3
Candes-Saint-Martin (37) 144 E1
Candillargues (34) 274 D6
Candor (60) 19 G5
Candresse (40) 264 B4
Canehan (76) 16 C1
Canéjan (33) 229 G3
Canens (31) 288 A5
Canenx-et-Réaut (40) 265 H1
Canet (11) 291 G5
Canet (34) 273 H6
Canet-de-Salars (12) 252 B4
Canet-en-Roussillon (66) 310 D6
Canettemont (62) 10 B3
Cangey (37) 128 C3
Caniac-du-Causse (46) 233 K5
Canihuel (22) 76 C2
Canilhac (48) 253 H1
Canisy (50) 31 G4
Canlers (62) 5 F6
Canly (60) 38 C2
Cannectancourt (60) 19 G6
Cannelle (2A) 320 C3
Cannes (06) 280 E6
Cannes-Écluse (77) 88 A4
Cannes-et-Clairan (30) 274 E2
Cannessières (80) 17 F1
le Cannet (06) 280 E5
Cannet (32) 266 B6
le Cannet-des-Maures (83) 298 C4
Canny-sur-Matz (60) 19 F5
Canny-sur-Thérain (60) 17 F5
Canohès (66) 315 G2
la Canourgue (48) 253 H2
Canouville (76) 15 F3
Cantaing-sur-Escaut (59) 11 J4
Cantaous (65) 305 G1
Cantaron (06) 281 H3
Canté (09) 288 C5
Canteleu (76) 35 H2
Canteloup (14) 33 G5
Canteloup (50) 29 F2
Cantenac (33) 211 G5
Cantenay-Épinard (49) 125 G2
Cantiers (27) 36 C4
Cantigny (80) 18 C5
Cantillac (24) 213 K1
Cantin (59) 11 H2
Cantoin (12) 236 B2
Cantois (33) 230 A4
Canville-la-Rocque (50) 28 C6
Canville-les-Deux-Églises (76) . . 15 H3
Cany-Barville (76) 15 F3
Caorches-Saint-Nicolas (27) 34 C6
Caouënnec-Lanvézéac (22) 48 A3
Caours (80) 9 G5
Cap-d'Ail (06) 281 J3
Capbreton (40) 262 B5
Capdenac (46) 234 D5
Capdenac-Gare (12) 234 E6
Capdrot (24) 232 E4
la Capelle (02) 21 F1
Capelle (59) 12 D3
la Capelle-Balaguier (12) 251 F4
la Capelle-Bleys (12) 251 H3
la Capelle-Bonance (12) 253 F1
la Capelle-et-Masmolène (30) . . . 256 B6
Capelle-Fermont (62) 10 D2
la Capelle-lès-Boulogne (62) 2 B5
Capelle-les-Grands (27) 55 G1
Capelle-lès-Hesdin (62) 9 H2
Capendu (11) 290 D6
Capens (31) 287 K4
Capestang (34) 291 H4
Capian (33) 229 K3
Capinghem (59) 6 D4
Caplong (33) 230 E3
Capoulet-et-Junac (09) 307 J5
Cappel (57) 68 B3
Cappelle-Brouck (59) 3 G3
Cappelle-en-Pévèle (59) 6 E5
Cappelle-la-Grande (59) 3 H2

Cappy (80) 19 F1
Captieux (33) 246 C3
Capvern (65) 305 F1
Caragoudes (31) 288 E2
Caraman (31) 289 F1
Caramany (66) 309 J6
Carantec (29) 47 F3
Carantilly (50) 31 F4
Carayac (46) 234 C6
Carbay (49) 104 A3
Carbes (81) 270 E6
Carbini (2A) 323 G2
Carbon-Blanc (33) 229 H1
Carbonne (31) 287 K4
Carbuccia (2A) 320 D3
Carcanières (09) 308 D6
Carcans (33) 210 C4
Carcarès-Sainte-Croix (40) 264 D3
Carcassonne (11) 290 B5
Carcen-Ponson (40) 264 D2
Carcès (83) 298 A1
Carcheto-Brustico (2B) 319 H5
Cardaillac (46) 234 D4
Cardan (33) 229 K4
Cardeilhac (31) 286 D5
Cardesse (64) 284 A4
Cardet (30) 274 D1
Cardo-Torgia (2A) 320 E6
Cardonnette (80) 18 B1
le Cardonnois (80) 18 C5
Cardonville (14) 29 H6
Cardroc (35) 78 E2
Carelles (53) 80 D3
Carency (62) 10 E1
Carennac (46) 234 A1
Carentan (50) 31 G1
Carentoir (56) 102 B2
Cargèse (2A) 316 C6
Cargiaca (2A) 323 F2
Carhaix-Plouguer (29) 75 J3
Carignan (08) 23 H5
Carignan-de-Bordeaux (33) 229 J2
Carisey (89) 113 J4
Carla-Bayle (09) 288 B6
Carla-de-Roquefort (09) 308 A3
le Carlaret (09) 288 E6
Carlat (15) 235 J2
Carlencas-et-Levas (34) 273 F6
Carlepont (60) 39 F1
Carling (57) 68 A2
Carlipa (11) 289 J4
Carlucet (46) 233 K4
Carlus (81) 270 D3
Carlux (24) 233 G2
Carmaux (81) 270 E1
Carnac (56) 100 C6
Carnac-Rouffiac (46) 249 H2
Carnas (30) 274 D3
la Carneille (61) 53 J4
Carnet (50) 51 K5
Carnetin (77) 59 H3
Carneville (50) 28 C2
Carnières (59) 12 B4
Carnin (59) 6 D5
Carnoët (22) 75 J1
Carnoules (83) 298 B3
Carnoux-en-Provence (13) 296 E4
Carnoy (80) 19 F1
Caro (56) 101 K3
Caro (64) 282 E6
Caromb (84) 257 H5
Carpentras (84) 257 G6
Carpineto (2B) 319 H5
Carpiquet (14) 32 D5
Carquebut (50) 29 F6
Carquefou (44) 123 H3
Carqueiranne (83) 297 K6
Carrépuis (80) 19 F4
Carrère (64) 284 E2
Carresse-Cassaber (64) 283 G2
Carrières-sous-Poissy (78) 58 B2
Carrières-sur-Seine (78) 58 D3
Carros (06) 281 F3
Carrouges (61) 82 B1
Carry-le-Rouet (13) 296 A4
Cars (33) 211 G4
les Cars (87) 198 D3
Carsac-Aillac (24) 233 F2
Carsac-de-Gurson (24) 212 E6
Carsan (30) 256 C4
Carsix (27) 34 D5
Carspach (68) 97 B4
Cartelègue (33) 211 H3
Carticasi (2B) 319 G5
Cartignies (59) 13 G5
Cartigny (80) 19 H2
Cartigny-l'Épinay (14) 31 J2
Carves (24) 232 D3
Carville (14) 31 K6
Carville-la-Folletière (76) 15 H4
Carville-Pot-de-Fer (76) 15 G4
Carvin (59) 6 D5
Casabianca (2B) 319 H4
Casaglione (2A) 320 C3
Casalabriva (2A) 322 D1
Casalta (2B) 319 H4
Casamaccioli (2B) 318 D6
Casanova (2B) 319 F6
Cascastel-des-Corbières (11) 310 A3
Casefabre (66) 314 E3

Caseneuve (84) 277 J2
Cases-de-Pène (66) 310 A5
Casevecchie (2B) 321 H2
Cassagnabère-Tournas (31) 286 E5
Cassagnas (48) 254 D4
Cassagne (31) 306 C1
Cassagnes (46) 232 E6
Cassagnes (66) 309 J6
Cassagnes-Bégonhès (12) 252 B5
Cassagnoles (30) 274 E1
Cassagnoles (34) 290 E3
la Cassaigne (11) 289 H6
Cassaigne (32) 267 F2
Cassaignes (11) 309 F3
Cassaniouze (15) 235 H4
Cassel (59) 3 J4
Cassen (40) 264 D4
Casseneuil (47) 248 B1
les Cassés (11) 289 G3
Casseuil (33) 230 B5
Cassignas (47) 248 B3
Cassis (13) 296 E5
Casson (44) 123 G2
Cassuéjouls (12) 236 B4
Cast (29) 74 D4
Castagnac (31) 288 A5
Castagnède (31) 306 B2
Castagnède (64) 283 G2
Castagniers (06) 281 G3
Castaignos-Souslens (40) 265 F6
Castandet (40) 265 J3
Castanet (12) 251 J4
Castanet (81) 270 C2
Castanet (82) 251 F4
Castanet-le-Haut (34) 272 C5
Castanet-Tolosan (31) 288 C2
Castans (11) 290 C3
Casteide-Cami (64) 284 B2
Casteide-Candau (64) 284 B1
Casteide-Doat (64) 285 G3
Casteil (66) 314 B4
Castel-Sarrazin (40) 264 D6
Castelbajac (65) 286 A6
Castelbiague (31) 306 B2
Castelculier (47) 248 C5
Castelferrus (82) 268 D1
Castelfranc (46) 249 H1
Castelgaillard (31) 287 G4
Castelginest (31) 269 G5
Casteljaloux (47) 247 G3
Castella (47) 248 C3
Castellane (04) 279 J2
Castellar (06) 281 J2
le Castellard-Melan (04) 259 H4
Castellare-di-Casinca (2B) 319 J3
Castellare-di-Mercurio (2B) 319 G6
le Castellet (04) 278 D1
le Castellet (83) 297 G5
Castellet (84) 277 J3
Castellet-lès-Sausses (04) 260 E6
Castello-di-Rostino (2B) 319 G4
Castelmary (12) 251 J5
Castelmaurou (31) 269 H5
Castelmayran (82) 268 C1
Castelmoron-d'Albret (33) 230 C4
Castelmoron-sur-Lot (47) 248 A2
Castelnau-Barbarens (32) 286 E1
Castelnau-Chalosse (40) 264 D5
Castelnau-d'Anglès (32) 266 E6
Castelnau-d'Arbieu (32) 267 K3
Castelnau-d'Aude (11) 290 E5
Castelnau-d'Auzan (32) 266 D2
Castelnau-de-Brassac (81) 271 H6
Castelnau-de-Guers (34) 292 C3
Castelnau-de-Lévis (81) 270 D2
Castelnau-de-Mandailles (12) . . . 236 C6
Castelnau-de-Médoc (33) 211 F5
Castelnau-de-Montmiral (81) 270 A2
Castelnau-d'Estrétefonds (31) . . . 269 F4
Castelnau-Durban (09) 307 F2
Castelnau-le-Lez (34) 274 C5
Castelnau-Magnoac (65) 286 C4
Castelnau-Montratier (46) 249 J4
Castelnau-Pégayrols (12) 253 F3
Castelnau-Picampeau (31) 287 H4
Castelnau-Rivière-Basse (65) . . . 266 B5
Castelnau-sur-Gupie (47) 230 E5
Castelnau-sur-l'Auvignon (32) . . . 267 G1
Castelnau-Tursan (40) 265 H5
Castelnau-Valence (30) 275 F1
Castelnaud-de-Gratecambe (47) . 248 C1
Castelnaud-la-Chapelle (24) 232 E3
Castelnaudary (11) 289 H4
Castelnavet (32) 266 D5
Castelner (40) 284 B1
Castelnou (66) 314 E3
Castelreng (11) 308 E2
Castels (24) 232 D2
Castelsagrat (82) 248 E5
Castelsarrasin (82) 268 D1
Castelvieilh (65) 285 J4
Castelviel (33) 230 B4
le Castéra (31) 268 D5
Castéra-Bouzet (82) 268 D1
Castéra-Lanusse (65) 285 K6
Castéra-Lectourois (32) 267 J1
Castéra-Lou (65) 285 J4
Castéra-Loubix (64) 285 G3
Castéra-Verduzan (32) 267 G4
Castéra-Vignoles (31) 286 E4
Castéras (09) 307 G1

356

Casterets (65) . . . 286 C4
Castéron (32) . . . 268 B3
Castet (64) . . . 303 H1
Castet-Arrouy (32) . . . 267 K1
Castetbon (64) . . . 283 J3
Castétis (64) . . . 283 K2
Castetnau-Camblong (64) . . . 283 J3
Castetner (64) . . . 283 J2
Castetpugon (64) . . . 284 E1
Castets (40) . . . 262 E2
Castets-en-Dorthe (33) . . . 230 B5
Castex (09) . . . 288 A6
Castex (32) . . . 286 A3
Castex-d'Armagnac (32) . . . 266 A3
Casties-Labrande (31) . . . 287 H4
Castifao (2B) . . . 318 E3
Castiglione (2B) . . . 319 F4
Castillon (06) . . . 281 J2
Castillon (14) . . . 32 A4
Castillon (65) . . . 304 D1
Castillon(Canton d'Arthez-de-Béarn) (64) . . . 284 B2
Castillon(Canton de Lembeye) (64) . . . 285 F2
Castillon-de-Castets (33) . . . 230 B6
Castillon-de-Larboust (31) . . . 305 H5
Castillon-de-Saint-Martory (31) . . . 287 F6
Castillon-Debats (32) . . . 266 E4
Castillon-du-Gard (30) . . . 275 J1
Castillon-en-Auge (14) . . . 54 D1
Castillon-en-Couserans (09) . . . 306 C1
Castillon-la-Bataille (33) . . . 230 C2
Castillon-Massas (32) . . . 267 H5
Castillon-Savès (32) . . . 287 H1
Castillonnès (47) . . . 231 J4
Castilly (14) . . . 31 J3
Castin (32) . . . 267 H5
Castineta (2B) . . . 319 G4
Castirla (2B) . . . 319 F5
Castres (02) . . . 19 K3
Castres (81) . . . 271 F6
Castres-Gironde (33) . . . 229 J4
Castries (34) . . . 274 D5
le Cateau-Cambrésis (59) . . . 12 D5
le Catelet (02) . . . 11 H4
le Catelier (76) . . . 16 A3
Catenay (76) . . . 36 A1
Catenoy (60) . . . 38 B3
Cateri (2B) . . . 318 C3
Cathervielle (31) . . . 305 G5
Catheux (60) . . . 17 K5
Catigny (60) . . . 19 G5
Catillon-Fumechon (60) . . . 37 K1
Catillon-sur-Sambre (59) . . . 12 E5
Catllar (66) . . . 314 C3
Catonvielle (32) . . . 268 B5
Cattenières (59) . . . 12 B4
Cattenom (57) . . . 27 H3
Catteville (50) . . . 28 D4
Catus (46) . . . 233 G6
Catz (50) . . . 31 G1
Caubeyres (47) . . . 247 H4
Caubiac (31) . . . 268 D5
Caubios-Loos (64) . . . 284 C2
Caubon-Saint-Sauveur (47) . . . 230 E5
Caubous (31) . . . 305 H4
Caubous (65) . . . 286 D5
Caucalières (81) . . . 290 A2
la Cauchie (62) . . . 10 D4
Cauchy-à-la-Tour (62) . . . 5 J4
Caucourt (62) . . . 10 D1
Caudan (56) . . . 100 A3
Caudebec-en-Caux (76) . . . 15 G6
Caudebec-lès-Elbeuf (76) . . . 35 H4
Caudebronde (11) . . . 290 A3
Caudecoste (47) . . . 248 C5
Caudeval (11) . . . 308 C1
Caudiès-de-Conflent (66) . . . 313 K3
Caudiès-de-Fenouillèdes (66) . . . 309 G1
Caudrot (33) . . . 230 B5
Caudry (59) . . . 12 C5
Cauffry (60) . . . 38 A3
Caugé (27) . . . 56 C1
Caujac (31) . . . 288 C4
Caulaincourt (02) . . . 19 J2
le Caule-Sainte-Beuve (76) . . . 16 E3
Caulières (80) . . . 17 H3
Caullery (59) . . . 12 B5
Caulnes (22) . . . 78 B2
Caumont (02) . . . 19 J5
Caumont (09) . . . 306 D2
Caumont (27) . . . 35 G3
Caumont (32) . . . 266 B5
Caumont (33) . . . 230 C4
Caumont (62) . . . 9 H3
Caumont (82) . . . 268 C1
Caumont-l'Éventé (14) . . . 32 A6
Caumont-sur-Durance (84) . . . 276 C2
Caumont-sur-Garonne (47) . . . 247 H1
Caumont-sur-Orne (14) . . . 53 H2
Cauna (40) . . . 265 F4
Caunay (79) . . . 179 F2
Cauneille (40) . . . 264 B6
Caunes-Minervois (11) . . . 290 D4
la Caunette (11) . . . 291 F4
Caunette-sur-Lauquet (11) . . . 309 G2
Caunettes-en-Val (11) . . . 309 J2
Caupenne (40) . . . 264 E5
Caupenne-d'Armagnac (32) . . . 266 B4
la Caure (51) . . . 61 H3
Caurel (22) . . . 76 D4
Caurel (51) . . . 41 G3

Cauro (2A) . . . 320 D5
Cauroir (59) . . . 11 K4
Cauroy (08) . . . 41 K3
Cauroy-lès-Hermonville (51) . . . 40 E3
le Causé (82) . . . 268 C4
Cause-de-Clérans (24) . . . 231 K2
Caussade (82) . . . 250 B5
Caussade-Rivière (65) . . . 285 H1
Causse-Bégon (30) . . . 253 K6
Causse-de-la-Selle (34) . . . 273 K4
Causse-et-Diège (12) . . . 234 D6
Caussens (32) . . . 267 G2
Causses-et-Veyran (34) . . . 291 J2
Caussiniojouls (34) . . . 291 K1
Caussols (06) . . . 280 D3
Caussou (09) . . . 308 A5
Cauterets (65) . . . 304 A3
Cauverville-en-Roumois (27) . . . 34 D3
Cauvicourt (14) . . . 54 A1
Cauvignac (33) . . . 246 E1
Cauvigny (60) . . . 37 J4
Cauville (14) . . . 53 H2
Cauville (76) . . . 14 A5
Caux (34) . . . 292 B2
Caux-et-Sauzens (11) . . . 290 A5
Cauzac (47) . . . 248 D3
Cavagnac (46) . . . 215 K6
Cavaillon (84) . . . 276 D3
Cavalaire-sur-Mer (83) . . . 298 E5
la Cavalerie (12) . . . 272 E1
Cavan (22) . . . 48 B3
Cavanac (11) . . . 290 B6
Cavarc (47) . . . 231 K4
Caveirac (30) . . . 275 F3
Caves (11) . . . 310 C3
Cavignac (33) . . . 211 K4
Cavigny (50) . . . 31 H2
Cavillargues (30) . . . 256 B5
Cavillon (80) . . . 17 J1
Cavron-Saint-Martin (62) . . . 9 H1
Caychax (09) . . . 307 K5
Cayeux-en-Santerre (80) . . . 18 D3
Cayeux-sur-Mer (80) . . . 8 D4
le Caylar (34) . . . 273 G3
Caylus (82) . . . 250 B4
Cayrac (82) . . . 250 A6
Cayres (43) . . . 238 B1
Cayriech (82) . . . 250 B4
le Cayrol (12) . . . 236 B5
Cayrols (15) . . . 235 F2
Cazac (31) . . . 287 G4
Cazalis (33) . . . 246 B2
Cazalis (40) . . . 265 F5
Cazalrenoux (11) . . . 289 G6
Cazals (46) . . . 233 F5
Cazals (82) . . . 250 C5
Cazals-des-Baylès (09) . . . 308 C1
Cazaril-Laspènes (31) . . . 305 H5
Cazaril-Tambourès (31) . . . 286 C6
Cazarilh (65) . . . 305 H3
Cazats (33) . . . 246 D1
Cazaubon (32) . . . 266 B2
Cazaugitat (33) . . . 230 D3
Cazaunous (31) . . . 305 K2
Cazaux (09) . . . 307 H2
Cazaux-d'Anglès (32) . . . 266 E5
Cazaux-Debat (65) . . . 305 F4
Cazaux-Fréchet-Anéran-Camors (65) . . . 305 F4
Cazaux-Layrisse (31) . . . 305 H4
Cazaux-Savès (32) . . . 287 G1
Cazaux-Villecomtal (32) . . . 285 J2
Cazavet (09) . . . 306 C2
Cazeaux-de-Larboust (31) . . . 305 H5
Cazedarnes (34) . . . 291 J3
Cazenave-Serres-et-Allens (09) . . . 307 J4
Cazeneuve (32) . . . 266 D2
Cazeneuve-Montaut (31) . . . 287 F6
Cazères (31) . . . 287 H5
Cazères-sur-l'Adour (40) . . . 265 J4
Cazes-Mondenard (82) . . . 249 H4
Cazevieille (34) . . . 274 B4
Cazideroque (47) . . . 248 E2
Cazilhac (11) . . . 290 B6
Cazilhac (34) . . . 274 A2
Cazillac (46) . . . 215 K6
Cazouls (24) . . . 233 H2
Cazouls-d'Hérault (34) . . . 292 C2
Cazouls-lès-Béziers (34) . . . 291 J3
Ceaucé (61) . . . 81 G2
Ceaulmont (36) . . . 165 G4
Céaux (50) . . . 51 K3
Céaux-d'Allègre (43) . . . 220 A4
Ceaux-en-Couhé (86) . . . 162 E6
Ceaux-en-Loudun (86) . . . 145 F3
Cébazan (34) . . . 291 H3
Cébazat (63) . . . 202 D1
Ceffonds (52) . . . 91 H2
Ceignes (39) . . . 189 J3
Ceilhes-et-Rocozels (34) . . . 272 E4
Ceillac (05) . . . 227 B3
Ceilloux (63) . . . 203 H3
Ceintrey (54) . . . 94 A1
la Celette (18) . . . 167 G2
la Celle (03) . . . 184 C2
la Celle (18) . . . 167 F1
Cellé (41) . . . 107 K5
la Celle (63) . . . 201 H1
la Celle (83) . . . 297 K2
la Celle-Condé (18) . . . 148 E6
la Celle-Dunoise (23) . . . 182 C1
la Celle-en-Morvan (71) . . . 152 E3

la Celle-Guenand (37) . . . 146 C4
la Celle-les-Bordes (78) . . . 58 A6
la Celle-Lévescault (86) . . . 162 D5
la Celle-Saint-Avant (37) . . . 145 K3
la Celle-Saint-Cloud (78) . . . 58 C3
la Celle-Saint-Cyr (89) . . . 112 D3
la Celle-sous-Chantemerle (51) . . . 61 G6
la Celle-sous-Gouzon (23) . . . 183 G2
la Celle-sous-Montmirail (02) . . . 61 F3
la Celle-sur-Loire (58) . . . 132 A4
la Celle-sur-Morin (77) . . . 60 A4
la Celle-sur-Nièvre (58) . . . 150 E1
Cellefrouin (16) . . . 179 J5
Celles (09) . . . 307 K3
Celles (15) . . . 218 C4
Celles (17) . . . 195 J4
Celles (24) . . . 213 H2
Celles (34) . . . 273 G6
Celles-en-Bassigny (52) . . . 117 F3
Celles-lès-Condé (02) . . . 61 F1
Celles-sur-Aisne (02) . . . 40 A2
Celles-sur-Belle (79) . . . 178 C1
Celles-sur-Durolle (63) . . . 203 J1
Celles-sur-Ource (10) . . . 114 E2
Celles-sur-Plaine (88) . . . 95 H2
la Cellette (23) . . . 166 B6
la Cellette (63) . . . 184 B4
Cellettes (16) . . . 179 G6
Cellettes (41) . . . 129 F3
le Cellier (44) . . . 123 J4
Cellier-du-Luc (07) . . . 238 C4
Cellieu (42) . . . 205 H5
Cellule (63) . . . 185 F5
Celon (36) . . . 165 G4
Celoux (15) . . . 219 F4
Celsoy (52) . . . 116 E4
Cély (77) . . . 87 G3
Cemboing (70) . . . 117 H4
Cempuis (60) . . . 17 H5
Cénac (33) . . . 229 J3
Cénac-et-Saint-Julien (24) . . . 233 F3
Cenans (70) . . . 138 B3
Cendras (30) . . . 255 G5
le Cendre (63) . . . 202 E3
Cendrecourt (70) . . . 117 J4
Cendrey (25) . . . 138 C4
Cendrieux (24) . . . 214 B6
Cénevières (46) . . . 250 D1
Cenne-Monestiés (11) . . . 289 J4
Cenon (33) . . . 229 H2
Cenon-sur-Vienne (86) . . . 163 H1
Censeau (39) . . . 156 C5
Censerey (21) . . . 153 F1
Censy (89) . . . 114 A6
les Cent-Acres (76) . . . 16 A3
Centrès (12) . . . 251 K5
Centuri (2B) . . . 317 D2
Cenves (69) . . . 188 A1
Cépet (31) . . . 269 G4
Cepoy (45) . . . 111 J2
Céran (32) . . . 267 J3
Cérans-Foulletourte (72) . . . 106 C5
Cerbère (66) . . . 315 K5
Cerbois (18) . . . 148 C2
Cercié (69) . . . 188 B3
Cercier (74) . . . 190 E4
Cercles (24) . . . 213 H1
Cercottes (45) . . . 110 A3
Cercoux (17) . . . 212 B4
le Cercueil (61) . . . 82 C1
Cercy-la-Tour (58) . . . 151 J5
Cerdon (01) . . . 189 J3
Cerdon (45) . . . 130 E2
Cère (40) . . . 265 G1
Céré-la-Ronde (37) . . . 128 D3
Cerelles (37) . . . 127 J3
Cérences (50) . . . 30 E6
Céreste (04) . . . 277 K3
Céret (66) . . . 315 F4
Cerfontaine (59) . . . 13 H3
le Cergne (42) . . . 187 H3
Cergy (95) . . . 58 B1
Cérilly (03) . . . 167 K3
Cérilly (21) . . . 115 F4
Cérilly (89) . . . 89 G6
Cerisé (61) . . . 82 D3
Cerisières (52) . . . 92 A4
Cerisiers (89) . . . 113 F1
Cerisy (80) . . . 18 E2
Cerisy-Belle-Étoile (61) . . . 53 G4
Cerisy-Buleux (80) . . . 17 F1
Cerisy-la-Forêt (50) . . . 31 J4
Cerisy-la-Salle (50) . . . 31 F4
Cerizay (79) . . . 143 G6
Cérizols (09) . . . 306 C1
Cerizy (02) . . . 20 A3
la Cerlangue (76) . . . 34 B1
Cernans (39) . . . 156 B4
Cernay (14) . . . 55 F1
Cernay (28) . . . 84 E4
Cernay (68) . . . 96 E1
Cernay (86) . . . 145 G6
Cernay-en-Dormois (51) . . . 42 C4
Cernay-la-Ville (78) . . . 58 B6
Cernay-l'Église (25) . . . 139 H5
Cernay-lès-Reims (51) . . . 41 F4
Cernex (77) . . . 60 D5
Cernex (74) . . . 190 E3
Cerniébaud (39) . . . 156 C6
Cernion (08) . . . 22 A3
Cernon (39) . . . 173 H5

Cernon (51) . . . 62 D3
Cernoy (60) . . . 38 D2
Cernoy-en-Berry (45) . . . 131 H3
Cernusson (49) . . . 143 J1
Cerny (91) . . . 86 E2
Cerny-en-Laonnois (02) . . . 40 E3
Cerny-lès-Bucy (02) . . . 20 C6
Céron (71) . . . 186 D1
Cérons (33) . . . 229 K4
Cerqueux (14) . . . 55 F1
les Cerqueux (49) . . . 143 H3
les Cerqueux-sous-Passavant (49) . . . 143 J2
Cerre-lès-Noroy (70) . . . 138 C1
Cers (34) . . . 292 B4
Cersay (79) . . . 143 K3
Cerseuil (02) . . . 40 A3
Cersot (71) . . . 171 H1
Certilleux (88) . . . 93 G4
Certines (01) . . . 189 G3
Cervens (74) . . . 175 F6
Cervières (05) . . . 227 B1
Cervières (42) . . . 204 A1
Cerville (54) . . . 66 B5
Cervione (2B) . . . 319 J5
Cervon (58) . . . 151 K1
Cerzat (43) . . . 219 H4
Cesancey (39) . . . 173 F2
Césarches (73) . . . 209 G2
Césarville-Dossainville (45) . . . 86 D5
Cescau (09) . . . 306 C3
Cescau (64) . . . 284 B3
Cesny-aux-Vignes-Ouézy (14) . . . 33 G6
Cesny-Bois-Halbout (14) . . . 53 J1
Cessac (33) . . . 230 B3
Cessales (31) . . . 288 E4
Cessens (73) . . . 208 B1
Cesseras (34) . . . 290 E4
Cesset (03) . . . 185 F5
Cesseville (27) . . . 35 G5
Cessey (21) . . . 156 A2
Cessey-sur-Tille (21) . . . 136 D2
Cessières (02) . . . 20 C6
Cessieu (38) . . . 207 G4
Cesson (77) . . . 87 G1
Cesson-Sévigné (35) . . . 79 G4
Cessoy-en-Montois (77) . . . 88 C2
Cessy (01) . . . 174 B6
Cessy-les-Bois (58) . . . 132 C5
Cestas (33) . . . 229 G3
Cestayrols (81) . . . 270 C3
Ceton (61) . . . 83 K5
Cette-Eygun (64) . . . 303 F3
Cevins (73) . . . 209 G4
Ceyras (34) . . . 273 H6
Ceyrat (63) . . . 202 D3
Ceyreste (13) . . . 297 F5
Ceyroux (23) . . . 182 B4
Ceyssac (43) . . . 220 B5
Ceyssat (63) . . . 202 B2
Ceyzériat (01) . . . 189 H2
Ceyzérieu (01) . . . 190 B3
Cézac (33) . . . 211 J4
Cézac (46) . . . 249 J3
Cezais (85) . . . 160 D3
Cézan (32) . . . 267 H3
Cezay (42) . . . 204 C1
Cézens (15) . . . 218 B6
Cézia (39) . . . 173 G5
Cézy (89) . . . 112 E3
Chabanais (16) . . . 180 B6
la Chabanne (03) . . . 186 C4
Chabestan (05) . . . 242 B6
Chabeuil (26) . . . 240 D1
Chablis (89) . . . 113 J5
Châbons (38) . . . 207 G2
Chabottes (05) . . . 243 F4
Chabournay (86) . . . 162 E1
Chabrac (16) . . . 180 C5
Chabreloche (63) . . . 186 B6
Chabrignac (19) . . . 215 G2
Chabrillan (26) . . . 240 D3
Chabris (36) . . . 129 H6
Chacé (49) . . . 144 C1
Chacenay (10) . . . 115 F1
Chacrise (02) . . . 39 K3
Chadeleuf (63) . . . 202 E4
Chadenac (17) . . . 195 J4
Chadenet (48) . . . 237 K6
Chadrac (43) . . . 220 C5
Chadron (43) . . . 220 C6
Chadurie (16) . . . 196 D5
le Chaffal (26) . . . 241 F1
le Chaffaut-Saint-Jurson (04) . . . 259 J6
Chagey (70) . . . 139 G1
Chagnon (42) . . . 205 H5
Chagny (08) . . . 22 D6
Chagny (71) . . . 153 K5
Chahaignes (72) . . . 107 G6
Chahains (61) . . . 82 B3
Chaignay (21) . . . 136 A3
Chaignes (27) . . . 57 G1
Chail (79) . . . 178 E2
Chaillac (36) . . . 164 E5
Chaillac-sur-Vienne (87) . . . 180 D6
Chailland (53) . . . 80 E5
Chaillé-les-Marais (85) . . . 160 B5
Chaillé-sous-les-Ormeaux (85) . . . 159 J3
Chailles (41) . . . 128 E3
Chaillevette (17) . . . 194 C2

Chaillevois (02) . . . 40 A1
Chailley (89) . . . 113 H2
Chaillon (55) . . . 65 H2
Chailloué (61) . . . 54 E6
Chailly-en-Bière (77) . . . 87 G3
Chailly-en-Brie (77) . . . 60 B4
Chailly-en-Gâtinais (45) . . . 111 G3
Chailly-lès-Ennery (57) . . . 27 H6
Chailly-sur-Armançon (21) . . . 135 F6
Chainaz-les-Frasses (74) . . . 208 C1
Chaînée-des-Coupis (39) . . . 155 G2
Chaingy (45) . . . 109 J4
Chaintré (71) . . . 188 B1
Chaintreaux (77) . . . 87 J6
Chaintrix-Bierges (51) . . . 62 B3
la Chaise (10) . . . 91 G4
la Chaise-Baudouin (50) . . . 52 B4
la Chaise-Dieu (43) . . . 220 A2
Chaise-Dieu-du-Theil (27) . . . 55 K1
Chaix (85) . . . 160 D5
la Chaize-Giraud (85) . . . 158 E2
la Chaize-le-Vicomte (85) . . . 159 K1
Chalabre (11) . . . 308 C3
Chalagnac (24) . . . 213 K5
Chalain-d'Uzore (42) . . . 204 D3
Chalain-le-Comtal (42) . . . 204 E3
Chalaines (55) . . . 65 F6
Chalais (16) . . . 212 D1
Chalais (36) . . . 164 D4
Chalais (86) . . . 144 E4
Chalamont (01) . . . 189 F4
Chalampé (68) . . . 97 E1
Chalancey (52) . . . 116 B6
Chalancon (26) . . . 241 H6
Chalandray (86) . . . 162 B2
Chalandry (02) . . . 20 D4
Chalandry-Elaire (08) . . . 22 D4
le Chalange (61) . . . 83 F1
le Chalard (87) . . . 198 C3
Chalautre-la-Grande (77) . . . 89 F2
Chalautre-la-Petite (77) . . . 88 D2
Chalaux (58) . . . 133 K5
Chaleins (01) . . . 188 C4
Chaleix (24) . . . 198 B5
Chalencon (07) . . . 239 K1
les Chalesmes (39) . . . 174 B1
Châlette-sur-Loing (45) . . . 111 J3
Chalette-sur-Voire (10) . . . 90 E3
Chaley (01) . . . 189 K5
Chalèze (25) . . . 138 A5
Chalezeule (25) . . . 138 A5
Chaliers (15) . . . 237 F1
Chalifert (77) . . . 59 J3
Chaligny (54) . . . 65 K6
Chalinargues (15) . . . 218 C4
Chalindrey (52) . . . 116 E5
Chalivoy-Milon (18) . . . 149 K6
Challain-la-Potherie (49) . . . 124 C1
Challans (85) . . . 141 F5
Challement (58) . . . 133 G2
Challerange (08) . . . 42 B3
Challes (01) . . . 189 J3
Challes (72) . . . 107 G3
Challes-les-Eaux (73) . . . 208 C4
Challet (28) . . . 85 F1
Challex (01) . . . 190 D2
Challignac (16) . . . 196 B6
Challonges (74) . . . 190 C4
Challuy (58) . . . 150 D4
Chalmaison (77) . . . 88 D2
Chalmazel (42) . . . 204 B3
Chalmoux (71) . . . 169 K3
Chalo-Saint-Mars (91) . . . 86 B3
le Chalon (26) . . . 222 F4
Chalon-sur-Saône (71) . . . 154 A6
Chalonnes-sous-le-Lude (49) . . . 126 D2
Chalonnes-sur-Loire (49) . . . 124 E5
Châlons (38) . . . 206 B6
Châlons-du-Maine (53) . . . 81 G6
Châlons-en-Champagne (51) . . . 62 B2
Châlons-sur-Vesle (51) . . . 40 E4
Châlonvillars (70) . . . 119 H6
Chalou-Moulineux (91) . . . 86 B3
Chaltrait (51) . . . 61 J2
Chalus (63) . . . 202 E6
Châlus (87) . . . 198 C3
Chalvignac (15) . . . 217 F3
Chalvraines (52) . . . 92 C5
Chamadelle (33) . . . 212 C4
Chamagne (88) . . . 94 B2
Chamagnieu (38) . . . 206 E3
Chamalières (63) . . . 202 D2
Chamalières-sur-Loire (43) . . . 220 D3
Chamaloc (26) . . . 241 H2
Chamant (60) . . . 38 C5
Chamarande (91) . . . 86 D2
Chamarandes-Choignes (52) . . . 116 B1
Chamaret (26) . . . 257 F2
la Chamba (42) . . . 203 K2
Chambain (21) . . . 115 K5
Chambeire (21) . . . 136 C5
Chambellay (49) . . . 105 F6
Chambéon (42) . . . 204 E4
Chambérat (03) . . . 167 F5
Chamberaud (23) . . . 182 E4
Chamberet (19) . . . 199 K4
Chambéria (39) . . . 173 G4
Chambéry (73) . . . 208 B4
Chambeugle (89) . . . 112 B4
Chambezon (43) . . . 219 F1
Chambilly (71) . . . 186 E1
Chamblac (27) . . . 55 H2

Chamblanc (21) 154 D3
Chamblay (39) 155 J3
Chambles (42) 204 E6
Chamblet (03) 184 B1
Chambley-Bussières (54) 44 C6
Chambly (60) 37 J5
Chamboeuf (21) 135 K6
Chamboeuf (42) 205 F4
Chambois (61) 54 D4
Chambolle-Musigny (21) 154 B1
le Chambon (07) 239 G2
Chambon (17) 177 G3
Chambon (18) 166 E1
Chambon (30) 255 G3
Chambon (37) 146 B6
le Chambon-Feugerolles (42) . . 221 F5
Chambon-la-Forêt (45) 110 E2
Chambon-le-Château (48) 237 K2
Chambon-Sainte-Croix (23) . . . 165 K6
Chambon-sur-Cisse (41) 128 D2
Chambon-sur-Dolore (63) 203 J5
Chambon-sur-Lac (63) 202 B4
le Chambon-sur-Lignon (43) . . 221 G5
Chambon-sur-Voueize (23) . . . 183 J2
Chambonas (07) 255 H2
Chambonchard (23) 183 K3
la Chambonie (42) 203 K2
Chamborand (23) 182 A3
Chambord (27) 55 J3
Chambord (41) 129 G2
Chamboret (87) 181 F5
Chamborigaud (30) 255 F3
Chambornay-lès-Bellevaux (70) . 138 A4
Chambornay-lès-Pin (70) 137 J5
Chambors (60) 36 E4
Chambost-Allières (69) 187 K4
Chambost-Longessaigne (69) . . 205 G2
Chamboulive (19) 199 K6
Chambourcy (78) 58 B3
Chambourg-sur-Indre (37) . . . 146 C1
Chambray (27) 35 K6
Chambray-lès-Tours (37) 127 J5
la Chambre (73) 209 F6
Chambrecy (51) 40 D5
les Chambres (50) 51 K2
Chambretaud (85) 142 D4
Chambrey (57) 66 D3
Chambroncourt (52) 92 D3
Chambry (02) 20 D6
Chambry (77) 59 K2
Chaméane (63) 203 G5
Chamelet (69) 187 K5
Chamery (51) 40 E5
Chamesey (25) 139 G6
Chamesol (25) 139 H4
Chamesson (21) 115 F5
Chameyrat (19) 216 A3
Chamigny (77) 60 C2
Chamilly (71) 153 J5
Chammes (53) 105 J1
Chamole (39) 155 J5
Chamonix-Mont-Blanc (74) . . . 192 C5
Chamouillac (17) 211 J2
Chamouille (02) 40 B1
Chamouilley (52) 63 K6
Chamousset (73) 208 E4
Chamoux (89) 133 H4
Chamoux-sur-Gelon (73) 208 E4
Chamoy (10) 113 K1
le Champ-de-la-Pierre (61) . . . 54 A6
Champ-d'Oiseau (21) 134 D2
Champ-Dolent (27) 56 C3
Champ-du-Boult (14) 52 D4
Champ-Haut (61) 55 F5
Champ-Laurent (73) 208 E4
Champ-le-Duc (88) 95 F5
le Champ-près-Froges (38) . . . 224 C2
le Champ-Saint-Père (85) 159 J3
Champ-sur-Barse (10) 90 E5
Champ-sur-Drac (38) 224 A4
Champ-sur-Layon (49) 125 G6
Champagnac (15) 217 H1
Champagnac (17) 195 J6
Champagnac-de-Belair (24) . . . 214 A1
Champagnac-la-Noaille (19) . . 216 D2
Champagnac-la-Prune (19) . . . 216 C4
Champagnac-la-Rivière (87) . . 198 B3
Champagnac-le-Vieux (43) . . . 219 J1
Champagnat (23) 183 H5
Champagnat (71) 172 E4
Champagnat-le-Jeune (63) . . . 203 G6
Champagne (07) 222 B2
Champagne (17) 194 D1
Champagne (28) 57 H5
Champagné (72) 107 F2
Champagne-au-Mont-d'Or (69) . 206 A1
Champagne-en-Valromey (01) . 190 B5
Champagne-et-Fontaine (24) . . 197 F6
Champagné-le-Sec (86) 179 G2
Champagné-les-Marais (85) . . . 160 A5
Champagne-Mouton (16) 179 J5
Champagné-Saint-Hilaire (86) . . 162 E4
Champagne-sur-Loue (39) 155 K3
Champagne-sur-Oise (95) 37 J6
Champagne-sur-Seine (77) . . . 87 J3
Champagne-sur-Vingeanne (21) . 136 D3
Champagne-Vigny (16) 196 C5
Champagneux (73) 207 J3
Champagney (25) 137 J6
Champagney (39) 137 F6
Champagney (70) 119 G3
Champagnier (38) 224 A4

Champagnole (39) 156 B6
Champagnolles (17) 195 G5
Champagny (21) 135 H3
Champagny-en-Vanoise (73) . . 209 K5
Champagny-sous-Uxelles (71) . 171 J3
Champallement (58) 151 H1
Champanges (74) 175 G5
Champaubert (51) 61 H3
Champcella (05) 243 K3
Champcenest (77) 60 D6
Champcerie (61) 54 A4
Champcervon (50) 51 K2
Champcevinel (24) 214 A3
Champcevrais (89) 112 A6
Champcey (50) 51 J2
Champclause (43) 221 F6
Champcueil (91) 87 F2
Champdeniers-Saint-Denis (79) . 161 H4
Champdeuil (77) 59 J4
Champdieu (42) 204 C3
Champdivers (39) 155 F3
Champdolent (17) 177 G5
Champdôtre (21) 154 E1
Champdor (01) 190 A4
Champdray (88) 95 G6
Champeau-en-Morvan (21) . . . 134 B6
Champeaux (35) 79 K4
Champeaux (50) 51 J2
les Champeaux (61) 54 D3
Champeaux (77) 87 J1
Champeaux-et-la-
  Chapelle-Pommier (24) 197 J6
Champeaux-sur-Sarthe (61) . . . 83 G1
Champeix (63) 202 D4
la Champenoise (36) 148 A5
Champenoux (54) 66 C4
Champéon (53) 81 H3
Champétières (63) 203 K5
Champey (70) 139 G1
Champey-sur-Moselle (54) . . . 65 K1
Champfleur (72) 82 D3
Champfleury (10) 62 A6
Champfleury (51) 41 F5
Champforgeuil (71) 154 A6
Champfrémont (53) 82 B3
Champfromier (01) 190 C2
Champgenéteux (53) 81 J4
Champguyon (51) 61 F4
Champhol (28) 85 G3
Champien (80) 19 G4
Champier (38) 207 F5
Champigné (49) 125 G1
Champignelles (89) 112 B5
Champigneul-Champagne (51) . 62 B2
Champigneul-sur-Vence (08) . . 22 C4
Champigneulle (08) 42 D3
Champigneulles (54) 66 A4
Champigneulles-en-Bassigny (52) . 93 F4
Champignol-lez-Mondeville (10) . 115 G1
Champignolles (21) 153 H3
Champignolles (27) 55 K2
Champigny (51) 40 E4
Champigny (89) 88 C4
Champigny-en-Beauce (41) . . . 108 E6
Champigny-la-Futelaye (27) . . . 56 E3
Champigny-le-Sec (86) 162 D1
Champigny-lès-Langres (52) . . 116 D4
Champigny-sous-Varennes (52) . 117 F4
Champigny-sur-Aube (10) 90 A1
Champigny-sur-Marne (94) . . . 59 G4
Champigny-sur-Veude (37) . . . 145 G3
Champillet (36) 166 C4
Champillon (51) 40 E6
Champis (07) 222 A6
Champlan (91) 58 D5
Champlat-et-Boujacourt (51) . . 40 D5
Champlay (89) 112 E3
Champlecy (71) 170 D4
Champlemy (58) 132 E6
Champlin (08) 21 K2
Champlin (58) 151 G1
Champlitte (70) 136 E1
Champlive (25) 138 C3
Champlost (89) 113 H2
Champmillon (16) 196 C3
Champmotteux (91) 86 E2
Champnétery (87) 199 J1
Champneuville (55) 43 H4
Champniers (16) 196 E2
Champniers (86) 179 J2
Champniers-et-Reilhac (24) . . . 197 K3
Champoléon (05) 243 G3
Champoly (42) 204 A1
Champosoult (61) 54 E3
Champougny (55) 93 G3
Champoulet (45) 132 A1
Champoux (25) 138 B5
Champrenault (21) 135 G4
Champrepus (50) 52 A3
Champrond (72) 107 K2
Champrond-en-Gâtine (28) . . . 84 C3
Champrond-en-Perchet (28) . . . 84 A4
Champrougier (39) 155 G5
Champs (02) 19 K6
Champs (61) 83 H1
Champs (63) 185 H4
les Champs-de-Losque (50) . . . 31 G2
les Champs-Géraux (22) 50 D6
Champs-Romain (24) 198 A5
Champs-sur-Marne (77) 59 G4
Champs-sur-Tarentaine-Marchal (15) . . 217 J1

Champs-sur-Yonne (89) 113 G6
Champsac (87) 198 C3
Champsanglard (23) 182 D1
Champsecret (61) 53 H6
Champseru (28) 85 H2
Champsevraine (52) 117 F5
Champtercier (04) 259 J5
Champteussé-sur-Baconne (49) . 125 F1
Champtocé-sur-Loire (49) 124 D4
Champtoceaux (49) 123 K4
Champtonnay (70) 137 G4
Champvallon (89) 112 E3
Champvans (39) 155 G2
Champvans (70) 137 F4
Champvans-les-Moulins (25) . . 137 J6
Champvert (58) 151 H6
Champvoisy (51) 40 B6
Champvoux (58) 150 D2
Chamrousse (38) 224 C4
Chamvres (89) 112 E3
Chanac (48) 253 K1
Chanac-les-Mines (19) 216 B3
Chanaleilles (43) 237 J2
Chanas (38) 222 B2
Chanat-la-Mouteyre (63) 202 C1
Chanay (01) 190 C4
Chanaz (73) 208 A1
Chançay (37) 128 A4
Chancé (35) 79 J5
Chanceaux (21) 135 H3
Chanceaux-près-Loches (37) . . 146 C2
Chanceaux-sur-Choisille (37) . . 127 J3
Chancelade (24) 213 K3
Chancenay (52) 63 K5
Chancey (70) 137 G5
Chancia (39) 173 H6
Chandai (61) 55 K5
Chandolas (07) 255 J2
Chandon (42) 187 G3
Chanéac (07) 239 G1
Chaneins (01) 188 C3
Chânes (71) 188 B1
le Change (24) 214 C3
Changé (53) 104 E1
Change (71) 153 J4
Changé (72) 106 E3
Changey (52) 116 D3
Changis-sur-Marne (77) 60 A2
Changy (42) 186 D3
Changy (51) 63 G4
Changy (71) 170 D5
Chaniat (43) 219 J2
Chaniers (17) 195 H2
Channay (21) 114 D4
Channay-sur-Lathan (37) 126 E3
Channes (10) 114 C3
Chanonat (63) 202 D3
Chanos-Curson (26) 222 C5
Chanousse (05) 258 C2
Chanoy (52) 116 D3
Chanoz-Châtenay (01) 188 E2
Chanteau (45) 110 B3
Chantecoq (45) 112 A2
Chantecorps (79) 162 A4
Chanteheux (54) 66 D4
Chanteix (19) 215 K2
Chantelle (03) 185 F2
Chanteloup (27) 56 C3
Chanteloup (35) 79 G6
Chanteloup (50) 30 D6
Chanteloup (79) 143 J6
Chanteloup-en-Brie (77) 59 J3
Chanteloup-les-Bois (49) 143 G2
Chanteloup-les-Vignes (78) . . . 58 B2
Chantelouve (38) 224 D5
Chantemerle (51) 89 G1
Chantemerle-les-Blés (26) 222 C4
Chantemerle-lès-Grignan (26) . 256 E2
Chantemerle-sur-la-Soie (17) . . 177 J5
Chantenay-Saint-Imbert (58) . . 168 D1
Chantenay-Villedieu (72) 106 A3
Chantepie (35) 79 G4
Chantérac (24) 213 H4
Chanteraine (55) 64 D5
Chanterelle (15) 218 B1
Chantes (70) 137 J1
Chantesse (38) 223 H2
Chanteuges (43) 219 J5
Chantillac (16) 212 A2
Chantilly (60) 38 A5
Chantonnay (85) 160 B1
Chantraine (88) 94 D5
Chantraines (52) 92 C5
Chantrans (25) 156 D2
Chantrigné (53) 81 G3
Chanu (61) 53 G5
Chanville (57) 45 H6
Chanzeaux (49) 125 F6
Chaon (41) 130 C2
Chaouilley (54) 93 K2
Chaource (10) 114 B2
Chaourse (02) 21 G4
Chapaize (71) 171 J3
Chapareillan (38) 208 C5
Chapdes-Beaufort (63) 184 D6
Chapdeuil (24) 213 H1
Chapeau (03) 169 G4
Chapeiry (74) 190 E6
Chapelaine (51) 90 E1
la Chapelaude (03) 167 G5
la Chapelle (03) 186 A4
la Chapelle (08) 23 F3

la Chapelle (16) 196 D1
la Chapelle (73) 209 F6
la Chapelle-Achard (85) 159 F2
la Chapelle-Agnon (63) 203 J4
la Chapelle-Anthenaise (53) . . 105 F1
la Chapelle-au-Mans (71) 170 A3
la Chapelle-au-Riboul (53) . . . 81 J4
la Chapelle-Aubareil (24) 215 F6
la Chapelle-Aubry (49) 124 D5
la Chapelle-aux-Bois (88) 118 C1
la Chapelle-aux-Brocs (19) . . . 215 K4
la Chapelle-aux-Chasses (03) . . 169 G2
la Chapelle-aux-Choux (72) . . . 126 E1
la Chapelle-aux-Filtzméens (35) . 51 F6
la Chapelle-aux-Lys (85) 161 F2
la Chapelle-aux-Naux (37) . . . 127 F5
la Chapelle-aux-Saints (19) . . . 216 A6
la Chapelle-Baloue (23) 165 H6
la Chapelle-Basse-Mer (44) . . . 123 J3
la Chapelle-Bâton (79) 161 J4
la Chapelle-Bâton (86) 179 J2
la Chapelle-Bayvel (27) 34 B4
la Chapelle-Bertin (43) 219 K3
la Chapelle-Bertrand (79) 162 A2
la Chapelle-Biche (61) 53 G5
la Chapelle-Blanche (22) 78 C2
la Chapelle-Blanche (73) 208 D5
la Chapelle-Blanche-
  Saint-Martin (37) 146 B3
la Chapelle-Bouëxic (35) 78 D6
la Chapelle-Caro (56) 101 J3
la Chapelle-Cécelin (50) 52 B3
la Chapelle-Chaussée (35) . . . 78 E2
la Chapelle-Craonnaise (53) . . 104 D3
la Chapelle-d'Abondance (74) . . 175 J6
la Chapelle-d'Alagnon (15) . . . 218 C5
la Chapelle-d'Aligné (72) 105 K6
la Chapelle-d'Andaine (61) . . . 81 H1
la Chapelle-d'Angillon (18) . . . 131 F5
la Chapelle-d'Armentières (59) . 6 C3
la Chapelle-d'Aunainville (28) . . 85 K3
la Chapelle-d'Aurec (43) 221 F2
la Chapelle-de-Bragny (71) . . . 171 J2
la Chapelle-de-Brain (35) 102 D3
la Chapelle-de-Guinchay (71) . 188 B2
la Chapelle-de-la-Tour (38) . . . 207 G4
la Chapelle-de-Mardore (69) . . 187 H4
la Chapelle-de-Surieu (38) . . . 222 C1
Chapelle-des-Bois (25) 174 B2
la Chapelle-des-Fougeretz (35) . 79 F3
la Chapelle-des-Marais (44) . . . 122 A1
la Chapelle-des-Pots (17) 195 H2
la Chapelle-devant-Bruyères (88) . 95 G5
Chapelle-d'Huin (25) 156 D4
la Chapelle-du-Bard (38) 208 D6
la Chapelle-du-Bois (72) 83 H5
la Chapelle-du-Bois-des-Faulx (27) . 35 J6
la Chapelle-du-Bourgay (76) . . 16 A3
la Chapelle-du-Châtelard (01) . . 188 E4
la Chapelle-du-Genêt (49) 142 D1
la Chapelle-du-Lou (35) 78 D3
la Chapelle-du-
  Mont-de-France (71) 171 G6
la Chapelle-du-Mont-du-Chat (73) . 208 A2
la Chapelle-du-Noyer (28) 108 E2
la Chapelle-en-Juger (50) 31 G3
la Chapelle-en-Lafaye (42) . . . 204 C6
la Chapelle-en-Serval (60) . . . 38 B6
la Chapelle-en-Valgaudémar (05) . 243 F2
la Chapelle-en-Vercors (26) . . . 223 H6
la Chapelle-en-Vexin (95) 36 E6
la Chapelle-Enchérie (41) 108 D5
la Chapelle-Engerbold (14) . . . 53 G3
la Chapelle-Erbrée (35) 80 B6
la Chapelle-Faucher (24) 214 A1
la Chapelle-Felcourt (51) 63 G1
la Chapelle-Forainvilliers (28) . . 57 G5
la Chapelle-Fortin (28) 56 A6
la Chapelle-Gaceline (56) 102 C2
la Chapelle-Gaudin (79) 143 K4
la Chapelle-Gaugain (72) 107 J5
la Chapelle-Gauthier (27) 55 G2
la Chapelle-Gauthier (77) 87 K2
la Chapelle-Geneste (43) 219 K1
la Chapelle-Glain (44) 124 A1
la Chapelle-Gonaguet (24) . . . 213 K3
la Chapelle-Grésignac (24) . . . 213 G1
Chapelle-Guillaume (28) 108 A1
la Chapelle-Hareng (27) 34 B6
la Chapelle-Haute-Grue (14) . . 54 D2
la Chapelle-Hermier (85) 159 F1
la Chapelle-Heulin (44) 123 J4
la Chapelle-Hugon (18) 150 C5
la Chapelle-Hullin (49) 104 B5
la Chapelle-Huon (72) 107 K4
la Chapelle-Iger (77) 60 A6
la Chapelle-Janson (35) 80 B3
la Chapelle-la-Reine (77) 87 G4
la Chapelle-Lasson (51) 61 J2
la Chapelle-Launay (44) 122 C2
la Chapelle-Laurent (15) 219 F4
la Chapelle-lès-Luxeuil (70) . . . 118 D5
la Chapelle-Marcousse (63) . . . 202 D6
la Chapelle-Montabourlet (24) . 213 H1
la Chapelle-Montbrandeix (87) . 198 B3
la Chapelle-Monthodon (02) . . 61 G1
la Chapelle-Montligeon (61) . . 83 J2
la Chapelle-Montlinard (18) . . . 150 C2
la Chapelle-Montmartin (41) . . 129 F6
la Chapelle-Montmoreau (24) . . 197 J6
la Chapelle-Montreuil (86) . . . 162 D2
la Chapelle-Moulière (86) 163 H2

la Chapelle-Moutils (77) 60 E4
la Chapelle-Naude (71) 172 C3
la Chapelle-Neuve (22) 48 A6
la Chapelle-Neuve (56) 100 E2
la Chapelle-Onzerain (45) 109 H2
la Chapelle-Orthemale (36) . . . 147 H6
la Chapelle-Palluau (85) 141 H6
la Chapelle-Pouilloux (79) 179 F3
la Chapelle-près-Sées (61) . . . 82 D1
la Chapelle-Rablais (77) 88 A2
la Chapelle-Rainsouin (53) . . . 105 H1
la Chapelle-Rambaud (74) . . . 191 G3
la Chapelle-Réanville (27) 36 A6
la Chapelle-Rousselin (49) . . . 124 E6
Chapelle-Royale (28) 108 C1
la Chapelle-Saint-André (58) . . 132 E5
la Chapelle-Saint-Aubert (35) . . 79 K2
la Chapelle-Saint-Aubin (72) . . 106 D2
la Chapelle-Saint-Étienne (79) . 161 G2
la Chapelle-Saint-Florent (49) . 124 B5
la Chapelle-Saint-Fray (72) . . . 106 D1
la Chapelle-Saint-Géraud (19) . 216 C5
la Chapelle-Saint-Jean (24) . . . 214 E3
la Chapelle-Saint-Laurent (79) . 161 H1
la Chapelle-Saint-Laurian (36) . 148 A3
la Chapelle-Saint-Luc (10) . . . 90 A4
la Chapelle-Saint-Martial (23) . 182 D5
la Chapelle-Saint-Martin (73) . . 207 K3
la Chapelle-Saint-Martin-
  en-Plaine (41) 109 F6
la Chapelle-Saint-Maurice (74) . 208 D1
la Chapelle-Saint-Mesmin (45) . 109 K4
la Chapelle-Saint-Ouen (76) . . 16 C6
la Chapelle-Saint-Quillain (70) . 137 H3
la Chapelle-Saint-Rémy (72) . . 107 G1
la Chapelle-Saint-Sauveur (44) . 124 C3
la Chapelle-Saint-Sauveur (71) . 154 E5
la Chapelle-Saint-Sépulcre (45) . 111 K2
la Chapelle-Saint-Sulpice (77) . 88 C1
la Chapelle-Saint-Ursin (18) . . 149 F3
la Chapelle-Souëf (61) 83 H4
la Chapelle-sous-Brancion (71) . 171 J3
la Chapelle-sous-Dun (71) . . . 187 H1
la Chapelle-sous-Orbais (51) . . 61 H3
la Chapelle-sous-Uchon (71) . . 152 E6
Chapelle-Spinasse (19) 216 D1
la Chapelle-sur-Aveyron (45) . . 111 K4
la Chapelle-sur-Chézy (02) . . . 60 E2
la Chapelle-sur-Coise (69) . . . 205 H3
la Chapelle-sur-Dun (76) 15 H2
la Chapelle-sur-Erdre (44) . . . 123 G3
la Chapelle-sur-Furieuse (39) . . 156 A3
la Chapelle-sur-Loire (37) 126 E6
la Chapelle-sur-Oreuse (89) . . 88 D5
la Chapelle-sur-Oudon (49) . . . 104 E6
la Chapelle-sur-Usson (63) . . . 203 G6
la Chapelle-Taillefert (23) 182 D4
la Chapelle-Thècle (71) 172 C3
la Chapelle-Thémer (85) 160 C3
la Chapelle-Thireuil (79) 161 G3
la Chapelle-Thouarault (35) . . . 78 E4
la Chapelle-Urée (50) 52 B5
Chapelle-Vallon (10) 90 A3
la Chapelle-Vaupelteigne (89) . 113 H5
la Chapelle-Vendômoise (41) . . 128 D1
la Chapelle-Vicomtesse (41) . . 108 C3
la Chapelle-Viel (61) 55 J5
la Chapelle-Villars (42) 205 K5
Chapelle-Viviers (86) 163 H4
la Chapelle-Voland (39) 155 F6
la Chapelle-Yvon (14) 34 A6
les Chapelles (73) 193 H3
les Chapelles-Bourbon (77) . . . 59 K5
Chapelon (45) 111 G2
la Chapelotte (18) 131 F5
Chapet (78) 58 A2
Chapois (39) 156 B5
Chaponnay (69) 206 B3
Chaponost (69) 205 K2
Chappes (03) 168 A6
Chappes (08) 21 J5
Chappes (10) 90 C6
Chappes (63) 202 E1
Chaptelat (87) 181 H6
Chaptuzat (63) 185 G4
Charancieu (38) 207 J3
Charantonnay (38) 206 D5
Charavines (38) 207 H6
Charbogne (08) 42 A1
Charbonnat (71) 152 D6
Charbonnier-les-Mines (63) . . . 219 G1
Charbonnières (28) 84 B6
Charbonnières (71) 171 K5
Charbonnières-les-Bains (69) . . 205 K2
Charbonnières-les-Sapins (25) . 156 D3
Charbonnières-les-Varennes (63) . 184 E6
Charbonnières-les-Vieilles (63) . 184 E5
Charbuy (89) 113 F5
la Charce (26) 241 J6
Charcé-Saint-Ellier-
  sur-Aubance (49) 125 H5
Charcenne (70) 137 H4
Charchigné (53) 81 J3
Charchilla (39) 173 H4
Charcier (39) 173 J2
Chard (23) 183 K6
Chardeny (08) 42 A2
Chardogne (55) 64 A3
Chardonnay (71) 171 K4
Chareil-Cintrat (03) 185 G1
Charencey (21) 135 G4

357

Charency (39) 156 B6
Charency-Vezin (54) 26 A3
Charens (26) 241 J5
Charentay (69) 188 B3
Charensat (63) 184 A5
Charentenay (89) 133 F1
Charentilly (37) 127 H3
Charenton-du-Cher (18) 167 H1
Charenton-le-Pont (94) 59 F4
Charentonnay (18) 150 B2
Charette (38) 207 F1
Charette-Varennes (71) 154 D4
Charey (54) 65 H1
Charézier (39) 173 H2
Chargé (37) 128 B4
Chargey-lès-Gray (70) 137 F3
Chargey-lès-Port (70) 117 K5
Chariez (70) 138 A1
Charigny (21) 134 E4
la Charité-sur-Loire (58) 150 C2
Charix (01) 190 B2
Charlas (31) 286 E5
Charleval (13) 277 F4
Charleval (27) 36 A3
Charleville (51) 61 G4
Charleville-Mézières (08) 22 D3
Charleville-sous-Bois (57) 27 K6
Charlieu (42) 187 F3
Charly (02) 60 D2
Charly (18) 150 A5
Charly (69) 206 A3
Charly-Oradour (57) 27 H6
Charmant (16) 196 E5
Charmauvillers (25) 139 J5
Charmé (16) 179 F5
la Charme (39) 155 H5
le Charme (45) 112 A5
la Charmée (71) 171 J1
Charmeil (03) 185 J3
le Charmel (02) 40 A6
Charmensac (15) 218 E3
Charmentray (77) 59 J2
Charmes (02) 20 B5
Charmes (03) 185 G4
Charmes (21) 136 D4
Charmes (52) 116 D3
Charmes (88) 94 B3
Charmes-en-l'Angle (52) 91 K3
Charmes-la-Côte (54) 65 H6
Charmes-la-Grande (52) 91 K3
Charmes-Saint-Valbert (70) . . . 117 G5
Charmes-sur-l'Herbasse (26) . . 222 D4
Charmes-sur-Rhône (07) 240 B2
Charmoille (25) 139 G5
Charmoille (70) 118 A6
Charmois (54) 94 C1
Charmois (90) 139 J1
Charmois-devant-Bruyères (88) . 94 E5
Charmois-l'Orgueilleux (88) . . . 94 B6
Charmont (51) 63 J3
Charmont (95) 36 E6
Charmont-en-Beauce (45) 86 C5
Charmont-sous-Barbuise (10) . . 90 B3
les Charmontois (51) 63 K2
Charmoy (10) 89 G3
Charmoy (71) 170 E1
Charmoy (89) 113 F3
Charnas (07) 222 A1
Charnat (63) 185 J5
Charnay (25) 156 B1
Charnay (69) 188 B6
Charnay-lès-Chalon (71) 154 C4
Charnay-lès-Mâcon (71) 188 C1
Charnècles (38) 223 J1
Charnizay (37) 146 C4
Charnod (39) 173 H6
Charnois (08) 24 C2
Charnoz-sur-Ain (01) 189 G6
Charny (21) 134 E5
Charny (77) 59 J2
Charny (89) 112 B4
Charny-le-Bachot (10) 89 K1
Charny-sur-Meuse (55) 43 H4
Charolles (71) 170 D5
Charols (26) 240 D5
Charonville (28) 84 E5
Chârost (18) 148 D4
Charpentry (55) 42 E4
Charpey (26) 222 E6
Charpont (28) 57 F5
Charquemont (25) 139 H6
Charrais (86) 162 E2
Charraix (43) 219 J6
Charras (16) 197 G5
Charray (28) 108 E3
Charre (64) 283 H4
Charrecey (71) 153 J5
Charrey-sur-Saône (21) 154 D2
Charrey-sur-Seine (21) 115 F3
Charrin (58) 151 J6
Charritte-de-Bas (64) 283 H4
Charron (17) 160 B6
Charron (23) 184 A4
Charroux (03) 185 F3
Charroux (86) 179 J3
Chars (95) 37 F5
Charsonville (45) 109 H4
Chartainvilliers (28) 85 G2
Chartèves (02) 40 A6
la Chartre-sur-le-Loir (72) 107 H6
Chartrené (49) 126 A3
Chartres (28) 85 G3

Chartres-de-Bretagne (35) 79 F5
Chartrettes (77) 87 H2
Chartrier-Ferrière (19) 215 H5
Chartronges (77) 60 D5
Chartuzac (17) 211 J1
Charvieu-Chavagneux (38) 206 D2
Charvonnex (74) 191 F4
Chas (63) 203 F2
Chaserey (10) 114 B3
Chasnais (85) 159 K4
Chasnans (25) 156 E2
Chasnay (58) 150 E1
Chasné-sur-Illet (35) 79 H2
Chaspinhac (43) 220 C5
Chaspuzac (43) 220 A5
la Chassagne (39) 155 G5
Chassagne (63) 202 D5
Chassagne-Montrachet (21) . . . 153 K4
Chassagne-Saint-Denis (25) . . . 156 C2
Chassagnes (43) 219 J3
Chassagny (69) 205 K4
Chassaignes (24) 213 F3
Chassal (39) 173 J5
Chassant (28) 84 C5
Chassé (72) 82 E3
Chasse-sur-Rhône (38) 206 A4
Chasseguey (50) 52 C5
Chasselas (71) 188 B1
Chasselay (38) 223 G2
Chasselay (69) 188 C6
Chassemy (02) 40 A2
Chassenard (03) 170 B5
Chasseneuil (36) 165 G2
Chasseneuil-du-Poitou (86) . . . 163 F2
Chasseneuil-sur-Bonnieure (16) . 197 H1
Chassenon (16) 198 A1
Chasseradès (48) 238 B6
Chassey (21) 134 E3
Chassey-Beaupré (55) 92 D2
Chassey-le-Camp (71) 153 J5
Chassey-lès-Montbozon (70) . . 138 C2
Chassey-lès-Scey (70) 137 K1
Chassiecq (16) 179 J5
Chassiers (07) 239 G6
Chassieu (69) 206 C2
Chassignelles (89) 114 C6
Chassignieu (38) 207 H5
Chassignolles (36) 166 A4
Chassignolles (43) 219 J1
Chassigny (52) 116 D6
Chassigny-sous-Dun (71) 187 H2
Chassillé (72) 106 B2
Chassors (16) 196 A2
Chassy (18) 150 B3
Chassy (71) 170 C3
Chassy (89) 112 E4
le Chastang (19) 216 A4
Chastanier (48) 238 B4
Chasteaux (19) 215 H5
Chastel (43) 219 G5
Chastel-Arnaud (26) 241 F4
Chastel-Nouvel (48) 237 J6
Chastel-sur-Murat (15) 218 B4
Chastellux-sur-Cure (89) 133 K5
Chastreix (63) 201 K5
la Châtaigneraie (85) 160 E2
Chatain (86) 179 J4
Châtaincourt (28) 56 E5
Châtas (88) 95 J3
Château (71) 171 G5
Château-Arnoux-Saint-Auban (04) . 259 G5
Château-Bernard (38) 223 K6
Château-Bréhain (57) 66 D2
Château-Chalon (39) 155 J6
Château-Chervix (87) 199 G4
Château-Chinon(Campagne) (58) . 152 B3
Château-Chinon(Ville) (58) 152 B3
le Château-d'Almenêches (61) . 54 D5
le Château-des-Prés (39) 173 K4
le Château-d'Oléron (17) 176 C6
Château-d'Olonne (85) 158 E3
Château-du-Loir (72) 107 G6
Château-Gaillard (01) 189 H5
Château-Garnier (86) 179 J1
Château-Gontier (53) 105 F4
Château-Guibert (85) 159 K3
Château-la-Vallière (37) 127 F2
Château-l'Abbaye (59) 7 H4
Château-Landon (77) 111 H1
Château-Larcher (86) 162 E5
Château-l'Évêque (24) 214 A3
Château-l'Hermitage (72) 106 D5
Château-Porcien (08) 21 J7
Château-Renard (45) 112 A4
Château-Renault (37) 128 A2
Château-Rouge (57) 45 J3
Château-Salins (57) 66 D3
Château-sur-Allier (03) 168 B1
Château-sur-Cher (63) 184 A3
Château-sur-Epte (27) 36 D5
Château-Thébaud (44) 123 H5
Château-Thierry (02) 60 E1
Château-Verdun (09) 307 K5
Château-Ville-Vieille (05) 227 B2
Château-Voué (57) 66 E3
Châteaubernard (16) 195 K3
Châteaubleau (77) 88 B1
Châteaubourg (07) 222 B6
Châteaubourg (35) 79 J4
Châteaubriant (44) 103 J3
Châteaudouble (26) 240 E1
Châteaudouble (83) 279 J5

Châteaudun (28) 108 E2
Châteaufort (04) 259 G3
Châteaufort (78) 58 C5
Châteaugay (63) 202 D1
Châteaugiron (35) 79 H5
Châteaulin (29) 74 D3
Châteaumeillant (18) 166 D4
Châteauneuf (21) 153 J1
Châteauneuf (42) 205 J5
Châteauneuf (71) 187 G2
Châteauneuf (73) 208 E4
Châteauneuf (85) 140 E4
Châteauneuf-de-Bordette (26) . 257 H2
Châteauneuf-de-Chabre (05) . . 258 E3
Châteauneuf-de-Gadagne (84) . 276 C2
Châteauneuf-de-Galaure (26) . . 222 C3
Châteauneuf-de-Randon (48) . . 238 A5
Châteauneuf-de-Vernoux (07) . 239 K1
Châteauneuf-d'Entraunes (06) . 261 F4
Châteauneuf-d'Ille-et-Vilaine (35) . 50 E4
Châteauneuf-d'Oze (05) 242 C6
Châteauneuf-du-Faou (29) 75 G4
Châteauneuf-du-Pape (84) 256 E6
Châteauneuf-du-Rhône (26) . . . 240 A6
Châteauneuf-en-Thymerais (28) . 84 E1
Châteauneuf-Grasse (06) 280 C5
Châteauneuf-la-Forêt (87) 199 J3
Châteauneuf-le-Rouge (13) . . . 296 E1
Châteauneuf-les-Bains (63) . . . 184 D4
Châteauneuf-les-Martigues (13) . 296 A3
Châteauneuf-Miravail (04) 258 D4
Châteauneuf-sur-Charente (16) . 196 C4
Châteauneuf-sur-Cher (18) 149 F6
Châteauneuf-sur-Isère (26) . . . 222 C5
Châteauneuf-sur-Loire (45) . . . 110 D4
Châteauneuf-sur-Sarthe (49) . . 105 H6
Châteauneuf-Val-de-Bargis (58) . 132 D6
Châteauneuf-Val-Saint-Donat (04) . 259 G5
Châteauneuf-Villevieille (06) . . . 281 G2
Châteauponsac (87) 181 H3
Châteauredon (04) 259 J6
Châteaurenard (13) 276 C2
Châteauroux (36) 147 K6
Châteauroux-les-Alpes (05) . . . 243 J4
Châteauvert (83) 297 K1
Châteauvieux (05) 242 E6
Châteauvieux (41) 147 G1
Châteauvieux (83) 279 K3
Châteauvieux-les-Fossés (25) . . 156 D2
Châteauvilain (38) 207 F5
Châteauvillain (52) 115 J2
le Châtel (73) 225 G1
Châtel (74) 175 J6
Châtel-Censoir (89) 133 G3
Châtel-Chéhéry (08) 42 D3
Châtel-de-Joux (39) 173 J3
Châtel-de-Neuvre (03) 168 E5
Châtel-Gérard (89) 134 B1
Châtel-Montagne (03) 186 B3
Châtel-Moron (71) 153 J6
Châtel-Saint-Germain (57) 44 E5
Châtel-sur-Moselle (88) 94 C4
Châtelaillon-Plage (17) 176 E3
Châtelain (53) 105 G5
la Châtelaine (39) 155 K5
Châtelais (49) 104 D5
Châtelard (23) 183 K5
le Châtelard (73) 208 D2
Châtelaudren (22) 48 E5
Chatelay (39) 155 J3
Châtelblanc (25) 174 B1
Châteldon (63) 185 K5
le Châtelet (18) 166 E3
le Châtelet-en-Brie (77) 87 J2
le Châtelet-sur-Meuse (52) 117 F2
le Châtelet-sur-Retourne (08) . . 41 H4
le Châtelet-sur-Sormonne (08) . 22 B2
les Châtelets (28) 56 C6
le Châteley (39) 155 H5
Châtelguyon (63) 185 F6
le Châtelier (51) 63 J2
Châtellenot (21) 135 F6
Châtellerault (86) 145 J6
le Châtellier (35) 80 A3
le Châtellier (61) 53 G5
les Châtelliers-Châteaumur (85) . 143 F5
les Châtelliers-Notre-Dame (28) . 84 D4
Châtelneuf (39) 173 K1
Châtelneuf (42) 204 D4
Châtelperron (03) 169 H5
Châtelraould-Saint-Louvent (51) . 63 F5
Châtelus (03) 186 B2
Châtelus (38) 223 H5
Châtelus (42) 205 G4
Châtelus-le-Marcheix (23) 182 A5
Châtelus-Malvaleix (23) 182 E1
Châtenay (01) 189 G2
Châtenay (28) 86 A4
Châtenay (38) 223 F1
Châtenay (71) 187 H1
Châtenay-en-France (95) 59 F1
Châtenay-Mâcheron (52) 116 D2
Châtenay-Malabry (92) 58 D5
Châtenay-sur-Seine (77) 88 B3
Chatenay-Vaudin (52) 116 E4
Chatenet (17) 212 A2
le Châtenet-en-Dognon (87) . . 181 K6
Châteney (70) 118 C6
Châtenois (39) 155 H1
Châtenois (67) 71 B5
Châtenois (70) 118 C6
Châtenois (88) 93 H4

Châtenois-les-Forges (90) 139 H1
Châtenoy (45) 110 E4
Châtenoy (77) 87 H5
Châtenoy-en-Bresse (71) 154 B6
Châtenoy-le-Royal (71) 154 A6
Châtignac (16) 212 D1
Chatignonville (91) 86 A3
Châtillon (03) 168 C5
Châtillon (39) 173 H2
Châtillon (69) 188 A6
Châtillon (86) 162 D6
Châtillon (92) 58 E4
Châtillon-Coligny (45) 111 K5
Châtillon-en-Bazois (58) 151 J3
Châtillon-en-Diois (26) 241 J3
Châtillon-en-Dunois (28) 108 D1
Châtillon-en-Michaille (01) 190 B5
Châtillon-en-Vendelais (35) . . . 80 B5
Châtillon-Guyotte (25) 138 B5
Châtillon-la-Borde (77) 87 J2
Châtillon-la-Palud (01) 189 G5
Châtillon-le-Duc (25) 137 K5
Châtillon-le-Roi (45) 86 C6
Châtillon-lès-Sons (02) 20 D3
Châtillon-Saint-Jean (26) 222 E4
Châtillon-sous-les-Côtes (55) . . 43 K5
Châtillon-sur-Broué (51) 91 G1
Châtillon-sur-Chalaronne (01) . . 188 D3
Châtillon-sur-Cher (41) 129 G6
Châtillon-sur-Cluses (74) 191 K3
Châtillon-sur-Colmont (53) 81 F4
Châtillon-sur-Indre (36) 146 E4
Châtillon-sur-Lison (25) 156 B2
Châtillon-sur-Loire (45) 131 J2
Châtillon-sur-Marne (51) 40 C6
Châtillon-sur-Morin (51) 61 G5
Châtillon-sur-Oise (02) 20 B3
Châtillon-sur-Saône (88) 117 J3
Châtillon-sur-Seine (21) 115 F4
Châtillon-sur-Thouet (79) 161 K2
Châtin (58) 152 B2
Châtonnay (38) 206 E5
Chatonnay (39) 173 G5
Chatonrupt-Sommermont (52) . 92 A2
Chatou (78) 58 C3
la Châtre (36) 166 B3
la Châtre-Langlin (36) 165 F5
Châtres (10) 89 J2
Châtres (24) 215 F4
Châtres (77) 59 J5
Châtres-la-Forêt (53) 81 J6
Châtres-sur-Cher (41) 130 A6
Châtrices (51) 63 J1
Chattancourt (55) 43 G4
Chatte (38) 223 G4
Chatuzange-le-Goubet (26) . . . 222 E5
Chaucenne (70) 137 J5
Chauchailles (48) 236 E3
Chauché (85) 142 B5
le Chauchet (23) 183 H4
Chauchigny (10) 89 K3
Chauconin-Neufmontiers (77) . . 59 J2
Chaudardes (02) 40 C2
Chaudebonne (26) 241 F6
Chaudefonds-sur-Layon (49) . . 125 F5
Chaudefontaine (25) 138 B4
Chaudefontaine (51) 42 D6
Chaudenay (52) 116 E4
Chaudenay (71) 153 K5
Chaudenay-la-Ville (21) 153 J1
Chaudenay-le-Château (21) . . . 153 J1
Chaudeney-sur-Moselle (54) . . . 65 H6
Chaudes-Aigues (15) 236 D2
Chaudeyrac (48) 238 B4
Chaudeyrolles (43) 239 F1
la Chaudière (26) 241 F4
Chaudon (28) 57 G6
Chaudon-Norante (04) 279 G1
Chaudrey (10) 90 C2
Chaudron-en-Mauges (49) 124 C5
Chaudun (02) 39 H3
Chauffailles (71) 187 H2
Chauffayer (05) 242 E3
Chauffecourt (88) 94 A3
Chauffour-lès-Bailly (10) 90 D6
Chauffour-lès-Étréchy (91) 86 C2
Chauffour-sur-Vell (19) 215 K6
Chauffours (28) 85 F3
Chauffourt (52) 116 D2
Chauffry (77) 60 C4
Chaufour-lès-Bonnières (78) . . . 57 G1
Chaufour-Notre-Dame (72) . . . 106 C2
Chaugey (21) 115 K5
Chaulgnes (58) 150 D2
Chaulhac (48) 237 F1
Chaulieu (50) 52 E4
la Chaulme (63) 204 C6
Chaulnes (80) 19 F3
Chaum (31) 305 J3
Chaumard (58) 152 B2
la Chaume (21) 115 J4
Chaume-et-Courchamp (21) . . . 136 D2
Chaume-lès-Baigneux (21) 135 F1
Chaumeil (19) 200 B6
Chaumercenne (70) 137 G5
Chaumergy (39) 155 G5
Chaumes-en-Brie (77) 59 K6
Chaumesnil (10) 91 H4
Châtenois (39) 155 H1
Chaumont (18) 150 A6
Chaumont (52) 116 B1
Chaumont (61) 55 F3
Chaumont (74) 190 D4

Chaumont (89) 88 B4
Chaumont-d'Anjou (49) 125 K3
Chaumont-devant-Damvillers (55) . 43 J3
Chaumont-en-Vexin (60) 37 F4
Chaumont-la-Ville (52) 93 F6
Chaumont-le-Bois (21) 115 F3
Chaumont-le-Bourg (63) 204 A6
Chaumont-Porcien (08) 21 J5
Chaumont-sur-Aire (55) 64 B2
Chaumont-sur-Loire (41) 128 D3
Chaumont-sur-Tharonne (41) . . 130 A2
Chaumontel (95) 38 A6
Chaumot (58) 133 H6
Chaumot (89) 112 C2
Chaumousey (88) 94 C5
Chaumoux-Marcilly (18) 150 A2
Chaumussay (37) 146 B5
la Chaumusse (39) 173 K3
Chaumuzy (51) 40 C5
Chaunac (17) 211 K1
Chaunay (86) 179 G2
Chauny (02) 19 K5
Chauray (79) 161 H6
Chauriat (63) 203 F2
la Chaussade (23) 183 G5
la Chaussaire (49) 124 A6
Chaussan (69) 205 J3
la Chaussée (76) 16 A3
la Chaussée (86) 144 E5
la Chaussée-d'Ivry (28) 57 G3
la Chaussée-Saint-Victor (41) . . 129 F2
la Chaussée-sur-Marne (51) . . . 62 E3
la Chaussée-Tirancourt (80) . . . 17 K1
Chaussenac (15) 217 G4
Chaussenans (39) 155 J5
Chausseterre (42) 186 C6
Chaussin (39) 155 F4
Chaussoy-Epagny (80) 18 B4
Chaussy (45) 86 B6
Chaussy (95) 36 D6
le Chautay (18) 150 C4
Chauvac (26) 258 C2
Chauvé (44) 122 C4
Chauvency-le-Château (55) . . . 23 J6
Chauvency-Saint-Hubert (55) . . 23 J6
Chauvigné (35) 79 J1
Chauvigny (86) 163 J3
Chauvigny-du-Perche (41) 108 C3
Chauvincourt-Provemont (27) . 36 D4
Chauvirey-le-Châtel (70) 117 H5
Chauvirey-le-Vieil (70) 117 H5
Chauvoncourt (55) 64 E2
Chauvry (95) 58 D1
Chaux (21) 154 B2
la Chaux (25) 157 F3
la Chaux (61) 53 K6
la Chaux (71) 154 E5
Chaux (90) 119 H5
Chaux-Champagny (39) 156 A4
Chaux-des-Crotenay (39) 174 A2
Chaux-des-Prés (39) 173 K4
la Chaux-du-Dombief (39) 173 K2
la Chaux-en-Bresse (39) 155 G5
Chaux-la-Lotière (70) 137 K4
Chaux-lès-Clerval (25) 138 E4
Chaux-lès-Passavant (25) 138 D6
Chaux-lès-Port (70) 117 K6
Chaux-Neuve (25) 174 B1
Chauzon (07) 255 K1
Chavagnac (15) 218 C4
Chavagnac (24) 215 G5
Chavagne (35) 79 F5
Chavagnes (49) 125 H6
Chavagnes-en-Paillers (85) . . . 142 B4
Chavagnes-les-Redoux (85) . . . 160 D1
Chavaignes (49) 126 C2
Chavanac (19) 200 D4
Chavanat (23) 182 E5
Chavanatte (90) 139 K1
Chavanay (42) 205 K6
Chavanges (10) 91 F2
Chavaniac-Lafayette (43) 219 J4
Chavannaz (74) 190 E3
Chavanne (70) 139 F2
la Chavanne (73) 208 D3
Chavannes (18) 149 G6
Chavannes (26) 222 C4
les Chavannes-en-Maurienne (73) . 209 F6
Chavannes-les-Grands (90) . . . 139 K1
Chavannes-sur-l'Étang (68) . . . 119 K6
Chavannes-sur-Reyssouze (01) . 172 A5
Chavannes-sur-Suran (01) 189 J3
Chavanod (74) 190 E5
Chavanoz (38) 206 E1
Chavaroux (63) 203 F1
la Chavatte (80) 19 F3
Chaveignes (37) 145 G3
Chavelot (88) 94 D5
Chavenat (16) 196 E6
Chavenay (78) 58 B3
Chavençon (60) 37 G5
Chavenon (03) 168 A5
Chavéria (39) 173 G4
Chaveroche (19) 201 F4
Chaveyriat (01) 188 E2
Chavignon (02) 40 A1
Chavigny (02) 39 J2
Chavigny (54) 66 A5
Chavigny-Bailleul (27) 56 D3
Chaville (92) 58 D4
Chavin (36) 165 H4
Chavonne (02) 40 B2

Chavornay (01) . . . 190 B6
Chavot-Courcourt (51) . . . 61 K1
Chavoy (50) . . . 51 K2
Chavroches (03) . . . 169 G6
le Chay (17) . . . 194 D3
Chay (25) . . . 156 A3
Chazay-d'Azergues (69) . . . 188 B6
la Chaze-de-Peyre (48) . . . 237 F4
Chazé-Henry (49) . . . 104 B5
Chazé-sur-Argos (49) . . . 124 D1
Chazeaux (07) . . . 239 G5
Chazelet (36) . . . 165 F4
Chazelles (15) . . . 219 G5
Chazelles (16) . . . 197 G3
Chazelles (39) . . . 172 E5
Chazelles (43) . . . 219 G6
Chazelles-sur-Albe (54) . . . 67 G6
Chazelles-sur-Lavieu (42) . . . 204 C5
Chazelles-sur-Lyon (42) . . . 205 G3
Chazemais (03) . . . 167 G5
Chazeuil (21) . . . 136 C2
Chazeuil (58) . . . 132 E6
Chazey-Bons (01) . . . 207 J1
Chazey-sur-Ain (01) . . . 189 G6
Chazilly (21) . . . 153 H1
Chazot (25) . . . 139 F4
Chécy (45) . . . 110 B4
Chédigny (37) . . . 146 D1
Chef-Boutonne (79) . . . 178 E3
Chef-du-Pont (50) . . . 29 F5
Chef-Haut (88) . . . 93 K3
Cheffes (49) . . . 125 H1
Cheffois (85) . . . 160 E2
Cheffreville-Tonnencourt (14) . . . 54 E1
le Chefresne (50) . . . 31 G6
Chéhéry (08) . . . 22 E5
Cheillé (37) . . . 127 G6
Cheilly-lès-Maranges (71) . . . 153 J5
Chein-Dessus (31) . . . 306 B2
Cheissoux (87) . . . 199 J1
le Cheix (63) . . . 185 G5
Cheix-en-Retz (44) . . . 122 E4
Chélan (32) . . . 286 C1
Chelers (62) . . . 10 C1
Chélieu (38) . . . 207 H5
Chelle-Debat (65) . . . 285 K4
Chelle-Spou (65) . . . 285 K6
Chelles (60) . . . 39 F3
Chelles (77) . . . 59 G3
Chelun (35) . . . 104 A4
Chemaudin (25) . . . 137 J6
Chemazé (53) . . . 104 E5
Chemellier (49) . . . 125 J5
Chemenot (39) . . . 155 H5
Chéméré (44) . . . 122 D5
Chéméré-le-Roi (53) . . . 105 H3
Chémery (41) . . . 129 G5
Chémery-les-Deux (57) . . . 27 K5
Chémery-sur-Bar (08) . . . 22 E5
Chemilla (39) . . . 173 G6
Chemillé (49) . . . 124 E2
Chemillé-sur-Dême (37) . . . 127 J1
Chemillé-sur-Indrois (37) . . . 146 E2
Chemilli (61) . . . 83 G4
Chemilly (03) . . . 168 E4
Chemilly (70) . . . 137 K1
Chemilly-sur-Serein (89) . . . 113 J5
Chemilly-sur-Yonne (89) . . . 113 G4
Chemin (39) . . . 154 E4
le Chemin (51) . . . 63 J1
Chemin-d'Aisey (21) . . . 115 F6
Cheminas (07) . . . 222 B4
Cheminon (51) . . . 63 J5
Cheminot (57) . . . 66 A2
Chemiré-en-Charnie (72) . . . 106 A2
Chemiré-le-Gaudin (72) . . . 106 C3
Chemiré-sur-Sarthe (49) . . . 105 H5
Chemy (59) . . . 6 D1
Chenac-Saint-Seurin-d'Uzet (17) . . . 194 E5
Chenailler-Mascheix (19) . . . 216 B5
la Chenalotte (25) . . . 157 J1
Chénas (69) . . . 188 B2
Chenaud (24) . . . 212 E3
Chenay (51) . . . 40 E3
Chenay (72) . . . 82 D3
Chenay (79) . . . 162 B6
Chenay-le-Châtel (71) . . . 186 D2
le Chêne (10) . . . 90 B1
Chêne-Arnoult (89) . . . 112 B4
Chêne-Bernard (39) . . . 155 G4
Chêne-en-Semine (74) . . . 190 C4
Chêne-Sec (39) . . . 155 G5
Chenebier (70) . . . 119 G6
Chenecey-Buillon (25) . . . 156 B1
Cheneché (86) . . . 162 E1
Chênedollé (14) . . . 53 F3
Chênedouit (61) . . . 53 K4
Chênehutte-Trèves-Cunault (49) . . . 126 A5
Chénelette (69) . . . 187 K2
Chénérailles (23) . . . 183 G3
Chenereilles (42) . . . 204 D5
Chenereilles (43) . . . 221 F4
Chenevelles (86) . . . 163 J1
Chenevières (54) . . . 94 E1
Chenevrey-et-Morogne (70) . . . 137 H5
Chênex (74) . . . 190 E3
Cheney (89) . . . 113 K4
Chenicourt (54) . . . 66 B3
Chenières (54) . . . 26 B4
Chéniers (23) . . . 165 K6
Cheniers (51) . . . 62 C3

Chenillé-Changé (49) . . . 105 F6
Cheniménil (88) . . . 94 E6
Chennebrun (27) . . . 55 K5
Chennegy (10) . . . 89 J5
Chennevières-lès-Louvres (95) . . . 59 G1
Chennevières-sur-Marne (94) . . . 59 G4
Chenois (57) . . . 66 D1
Chenoise (77) . . . 88 C1
Chenommet (16) . . . 179 H5
Chenon (16) . . . 179 H5
Chenonceaux (37) . . . 128 C5
Chenou (77) . . . 87 H6
Chenôve (21) . . . 136 A5
Chenôves (71) . . . 171 H2
Chenu (72) . . . 127 F2
Chepniers (17) . . . 212 A2
Chepoix (60) . . . 18 B5
la Cheppe (51) . . . 62 E1
Cheppes-la-Prairie (51) . . . 62 E3
Cheppy (55) . . . 42 A4
Cheptainville (91) . . . 86 D2
Chepy (51) . . . 62 E3
Chépy (80) . . . 8 E5
Chérac (17) . . . 195 J2
Chérancé (53) . . . 104 D5
Chérancé (72) . . . 82 D5
Chéraute (64) . . . 283 H5
Cherbonnières (17) . . . 178 D5
Cherbourg (50) . . . 28 D2
Chérence (95) . . . 36 D6
Chérencé-le-Héron (50) . . . 52 B3
Chérencé-le-Roussel (50) . . . 52 C5
Chéreng (59) . . . 7 F4
les Chères (69) . . . 188 B6
Chérêt (02) . . . 40 C1
Chériennes (62) . . . 9 J2
Cherier (42) . . . 186 D5
Chérigné (79) . . . 178 D3
les Chéris (50) . . . 52 A5
Chérisay (72) . . . 82 D4
Chérisey (57) . . . 45 F6
Cherisy (28) . . . 57 F5
Chérisy (62) . . . 11 G3
Chérizet (71) . . . 171 G4
Chermignac (17) . . . 195 F3
Chermisey (88) . . . 92 E3
Chermizy-Ailles (02) . . . 40 C1
Chéronnac (87) . . . 198 A2
Chéronvilliers (27) . . . 55 K4
Chéroy (89) . . . 88 A6
Cherré (49) . . . 105 G6
Cherré (72) . . . 83 J6
Cherreau (72) . . . 83 J6
Cherrueix (35) . . . 51 G4
Cherval (24) . . . 213 G1
Cherveix-Cubas (24) . . . 214 E2
Cherves (17) . . . 162 C1
Cherves-Châtelars (16) . . . 197 H1
Cherves-Richemont (16) . . . 195 J2
Chervettes (17) . . . 177 H4
Cherveux (79) . . . 161 J5
Chervey (10) . . . 114 E1
Cherville (51) . . . 62 B1
Chéry (18) . . . 148 D2
Chéry-Chartreuve (02) . . . 40 B4
Chéry-lès-Pouilly (02) . . . 20 D5
Chéry-lès-Rozoy (02) . . . 21 H4
Chesley (10) . . . 114 B3
le Chesnay (78) . . . 58 C4
le Chesne (08) . . . 22 D6
le Chesne (27) . . . 56 B3
Chesnois-Auboncourt (08) . . . 22 B6
Chesny (57) . . . 45 F6
Chessenaz (74) . . . 190 D4
Chessy (69) . . . 188 A6
Chessy (77) . . . 59 J3
Chessy-les-Prés (10) . . . 113 K2
Chéu (89) . . . 113 H3
Cheuge (21) . . . 136 D4
Cheust (65) . . . 304 B1
Cheux (14) . . . 32 C5
Chevagnes (03) . . . 169 G3
Chevagny-les-Chevrières (71) . . . 171 J4
Chevagny-sur-Guye (71) . . . 171 F4
Chevaigné (35) . . . 79 G3
Chevaigné-du-Maine (53) . . . 81 J3
le Chevain (72) . . . 82 D3
Cheval-Blanc (84) . . . 276 E3
Chevaline (74) . . . 208 E1
la Chevallerais (44) . . . 123 F1
Chevanceaux (17) . . . 212 B3
Chevannay (21) . . . 135 G4
Chevannes (21) . . . 154 A1
Chevannes (45) . . . 111 K1
Chevannes (89) . . . 113 F6
Chevannes (91) . . . 87 F2
Chevannes-Changy (58) . . . 133 F6
Chevennes (02) . . . 20 E3
Chevenon (58) . . . 150 E5
Chevenoz (74) . . . 175 G5
Cheverny (41) . . . 129 F3
Cheveuges (08) . . . 22 E4
Chevières (08) . . . 42 D1
Chevigney (70) . . . 137 F5
Chevigney-lès-Vercel (25) . . . 157 F1
Chevigney-sur-l'Ognon (25) . . . 137 J5
Chevigny (39) . . . 155 G1
Chevigny-en-Valière (21) . . . 154 B4
Chevigny-Saint-Sauveur (21) . . . 136 B5
Chevillard (01) . . . 189 K3

Chevillé (72) . . . 106 A3
Chevillon (52) . . . 92 A1
Chevillon (89) . . . 112 C4
Chevillon-sur-Huillard (45) . . . 111 H3
la Chevillotte (25) . . . 138 B6
Chevilly (45) . . . 110 A2
Chevilly-Larue (94) . . . 58 E5
Chevinay (69) . . . 205 J2
Chevincourt (60) . . . 38 E1
Cheviré-le-Rouge (49) . . . 126 A2
Chevrainvilliers (77) . . . 87 G5
Chevreaux (39) . . . 172 E4
Chevregny (02) . . . 40 D1
Chèvremont (90) . . . 119 J6
la Chèvrerie (16) . . . 179 G4
Chevresis-Monceau (02) . . . 20 C3
Chevreuse (78) . . . 58 B5
Chèvreville (50) . . . 52 C6
Chèvreville (60) . . . 38 E6
Chevrier (74) . . . 190 D3
Chevrières (38) . . . 223 G3
Chevrières (42) . . . 205 G4
Chevrières (60) . . . 38 C3
Chevroches (58) . . . 133 G4
la Chevrolière (44) . . . 123 G5
Chevrotaine (39) . . . 173 J2
Chevroux (01) . . . 172 A5
Chevroz (25) . . . 137 K5
Chevru (77) . . . 60 C5
Chevry (01) . . . 174 B6
Chevry (50) . . . 31 H5
Chevry-Cossigny (77) . . . 59 H5
Chevry-en-Sereine (77) . . . 88 A5
Chevry-sous-le-Bignon (45) . . . 111 K1
Chey (79) . . . 178 E1
Cheylade (15) . . . 218 A3
le Cheylard (07) . . . 239 H1
Cheylard-l'Évêque (48) . . . 238 B5
le Cheylas (38) . . . 208 C6
Cheyssieu (38) . . . 206 B6
Chezal-Benoît (18) . . . 148 D6
la Chèze (22) . . . 77 G5
Chèze (65) . . . 304 B3
Chezelle (03) . . . 185 F2
Chezelles (36) . . . 147 J5
Chezelles (37) . . . 145 H3
Chèzeneuve (38) . . . 206 E4
Chézery-Forens (01) . . . 190 C1
Chézy (03) . . . 169 F3
Chézy-en-Orxois (02) . . . 39 H6
Chézy-sur-Marne (02) . . . 60 E2
Chiatra (2B) . . . 319 J6
Chiché (79) . . . 143 K6
Chicheboville (14) . . . 33 F6
Chichée (89) . . . 113 J5
Chichery (89) . . . 113 F4
Chichey (51) . . . 61 H5
Chichilianne (38) . . . 241 K2
Chicourt (57) . . . 66 D2
Chiddes (58) . . . 152 B5
Chiddes (71) . . . 171 G5
Chidrac (63) . . . 202 D5
Chierry (02) . . . 60 E1
Chieulles (57) . . . 45 F5
Chignin (73) . . . 208 C4
Chigny (02) . . . 20 E1
Chigny-les-Roses (51) . . . 41 F5
Chigy (89) . . . 89 F6
Chilhac (43) . . . 219 H4
Chille (39) . . . 173 G1
Chillac (16) . . . 212 C1
Chilleurs-aux-Bois (45) . . . 110 C2
le Chillou (79) . . . 162 A1
Chilly (08) . . . 22 B2
Chilly (74) . . . 190 D4
Chilly (80) . . . 19 F3
Chilly-le-Vignoble (39) . . . 173 F2
Chilly-Mazarin (91) . . . 58 E5
Chilly-sur-Salins (39) . . . 156 A4
Chimilin (38) . . . 207 J4
Chindrieux (73) . . . 208 A1
Chinon (37) . . . 145 F1
Chipilly (80) . . . 18 E2
Chirac (16) . . . 180 B6
Chirac (48) . . . 237 G4
Chirac-Bellevue (19) . . . 201 F6
Chirassimont (42) . . . 187 H6
Chirat-l'Église (03) . . . 184 E2
Chiré-en-Montreuil (86) . . . 162 D3
Chirens (38) . . . 207 H6
Chirmont (80) . . . 18 B4
Chirols (07) . . . 239 G4
Chiroubles (69) . . . 188 A2
Chiry-Ourscamps (60) . . . 19 G6
Chis (65) . . . 285 H4
Chisa (2B) . . . 321 H5
Chissay-en-Touraine (41) . . . 128 C5
Chisseaux (37) . . . 128 C5
Chisséria (39) . . . 173 G5
Chissey-en-Morvan (71) . . . 152 E2
Chissey-lès-Mâcon (71) . . . 171 J4
Chissey-sur-Loue (39) . . . 155 J3
Chitenay (41) . . . 129 F3
Chitray (36) . . . 165 F3
Chitry (89) . . . 113 H6
Chitry-les-Mines (58) . . . 133 H6
Chives (17) . . . 178 D3
Chivres (21) . . . 154 C4
Chivres-en-Laonnois (02) . . . 21 F5
Chivres-Val (02) . . . 39 K2
Chivy-lès-Étouvelles (02) . . . 20 C6

Chizé (79) . . . 178 B3
Chocques (62) . . . 5 K5
Choilley-Dardenay (52) . . . 136 D1
Choisel (78) . . . 58 B6
Choiseul (52) . . . 117 F1
Choisies (39) . . . 155 G2
Choisies (59) . . . 13 H3
Choisy (74) . . . 190 E4
Choisy-au-Bac (60) . . . 38 E2
Choisy-en-Brie (77) . . . 60 C5
Choisy-la-Victoire (60) . . . 38 B3
Choisy-le-Roi (94) . . . 59 F5
Cholet (49) . . . 142 E2
Cholonge (38) . . . 224 B5
Choloy-Ménillot (54) . . . 65 H5
la Chomette (43) . . . 219 H3
Chonas-l'Amballan (38) . . . 206 A6
Chonville-Malaumont (55) . . . 64 E4
Chooz (08) . . . 24 C2
Choqueuse-les-Bénards (60) . . . 17 J5
Choranche (38) . . . 223 H5
Chorey-les-Beaune (21) . . . 154 A3
Chorges (05) . . . 243 G5
Chouain (14) . . . 32 B4
Chouday (36) . . . 148 D5
Choue (41) . . . 108 B3
Chougny (58) . . . 151 K3
Chouilly (51) . . . 62 A1
Chouppes (86) . . . 144 E6
Chourgnac (24) . . . 214 D3
Choussy (41) . . . 128 E5
Chouvigny (03) . . . 184 E3
Choux (39) . . . 173 J6
les Choux (45) . . . 111 H5
Chouy (02) . . . 39 H5
Chouzé-sur-Loire (37) . . . 126 D6
Chouzelot (25) . . . 156 A2
Chouzy-sur-Cisse (41) . . . 128 D3
Choye (70) . . . 137 H4
Chozeau (38) . . . 206 E2
Chuelles (45) . . . 112 A3
Chuffilly-Roche (08) . . . 42 A1
Chuignes (80) . . . 19 F2
Chuignolles (80) . . . 18 E2
Chuisnes (28) . . . 84 D3
Chusclan (30) . . . 256 D5
Chuyer (42) . . . 205 K6
Chuzelles (38) . . . 206 B4
Ciadoux (31) . . . 286 E5
Ciamannacce (2A) . . . 321 F4
Ciboure (64) . . . 263 B1
Cideville (76) . . . 15 H5
Ciel (71) . . . 154 C5
Cier-de-Luchon (31) . . . 305 H4
Cier-de-Rivière (31) . . . 305 J1
Cierges (02) . . . 40 B5
Cierges-sous-Montfaucon (55) . . . 43 F3
Cierp-Gaud (31) . . . 305 J3
Cierrey (27) . . . 56 E1
Cierzac (17) . . . 195 K4
Cieurac (46) . . . 250 A2
Cieutat (65) . . . 285 J6
Cieux (87) . . . 181 F5
Ciez (58) . . . 132 C4
Cigogné (37) . . . 128 A6
Cilly (02) . . . 21 F4
Cinais (37) . . . 145 F2
Cindré (03) . . . 185 K1
Cinq-Mars-la-Pile (37) . . . 127 G5
Cinqueux (60) . . . 38 B3
Cintegabelle (31) . . . 288 C4
Cintheaux (14) . . . 32 E6
Cintray (27) . . . 56 A4
Cintray (28) . . . 85 F3
Cintré (35) . . . 78 E4
Cintrey (70) . . . 117 H5
la Ciotat (13) . . . 297 F5
Cipières (06) . . . 280 C3
Ciral (61) . . . 82 B2
Ciran (37) . . . 146 B3
Circourt (88) . . . 94 B4
Circourt-sur-Mouzon (88) . . . 93 G4
Ciré-d'Aunis (17) . . . 177 F4
Cirès (31) . . . 305 G4
Cires-lès-Mello (60) . . . 37 K4
Cirey (70) . . . 138 D2
Cirey-lès-Mareilles (52) . . . 92 C5
Cirey-lès-Pontailler (21) . . . 136 D5
Cirey-sur-Blaise (52) . . . 91 J4
Cirey-sur-Vezouze (54) . . . 67 H6
Cirfontaines-en-Azois (52) . . . 115 J1
Cirfontaines-en-Ornois (52) . . . 92 D2
Cirière (79) . . . 143 H5
Ciron (36) . . . 164 E3
Ciry-le-Noble (71) . . . 170 D3
Ciry-Salsogne (02) . . . 39 K3
Cisai-Saint-Aubin (61) . . . 55 F4
Cisery (89) . . . 134 B3
Cissac-Médoc (33) . . . 210 E3
Cissé (86) . . . 162 E2
Cisternes-la-Forêt (63) . . . 201 K2
Cistrières (43) . . . 219 K2
Citerne (80) . . . 17 G1
Citers (70) . . . 118 D3
Citey (70) . . . 137 H3
Citou (11) . . . 290 D1
Citry (77) . . . 60 D2
Civaux (86) . . . 163 J5
Civens (42) . . . 204 E2
Civières (27) . . . 36 C5

Civrac-de-Blaye (33) . . . 211 J4
Civrac-en-Médoc (33) . . . 210 E1
Civrac-sur-Dordogne (33) . . . 230 C2
Civray (18) . . . 148 K4
Civray (86) . . . 179 H3
Civray-de-Touraine (37) . . . 128 C5
Civray-sur-Esves (37) . . . 146 A3
Civrieux (01) . . . 188 D5
Civrieux-d'Azergues (69) . . . 188 B6
Civry (89) . . . 109 G2
Civry-en-Montagne (21) . . . 135 G6
Civry-la-Forêt (78) . . . 57 H3
Cizancourt (80) . . . 19 G2
Cizay-la-Madeleine (49) . . . 144 B1
Cize (01) . . . 189 J2
Cize (39) . . . 173 K1
Cizos (65) . . . 286 B5
Clacy-et-Thierret (02) . . . 20 C6
Cladech (24) . . . 232 D2
Claira (66) . . . 310 C5
Clairac (47) . . . 247 J2
Clairavaux (23) . . . 200 E2
Clairefontaine-en-Yvelines (78) . . . 86 A1
Clairefougère (61) . . . 53 F4
Clairegoutte (70) . . . 119 F6
Clairfayts (59) . . . 13 J4
Clairfontaine (02) . . . 13 H6
Clairmarais (62) . . . 3 G5
Clairoix (60) . . . 38 E2
Clairvaux-d'Aveyron (12) . . . 251 K2
Clairvaux-les-Lacs (39) . . . 173 J3
Clairy-Saulchoix (80) . . . 17 K2
Clais (76) . . . 16 D3
Claix (16) . . . 196 D4
Claix (38) . . . 224 A4
Clam (17) . . . 195 H5
Clamanges (51) . . . 62 A4
Clamart (92) . . . 58 D4
Clamecy (02) . . . 39 J2
Clamecy (58) . . . 133 F4
Clamensane (04) . . . 259 H2
Clamerey (21) . . . 134 E4
Clans (06) . . . 261 J6
Clans (70) . . . 137 K1
Clansayes (26) . . . 256 E5
le Claon (55) . . . 42 E5
le Clapier (12) . . . 272 E3
Clapiers (34) . . . 274 C5
Clara (66) . . . 314 C3
Clarac (31) . . . 305 J1
Clarac (65) . . . 285 K5
Claracq (64) . . . 284 D1
Clarafond (74) . . . 190 D3
Clarbec (14) . . . 33 J4
Clarens (65) . . . 286 B6
Clarensac (30) . . . 275 F3
Claret (04) . . . 259 F2
Claret (34) . . . 274 C3
Clarques (62) . . . 3 G6
Clary (59) . . . 12 C5
Classun (40) . . . 265 H5
Clastres (02) . . . 19 K4
Clasville (76) . . . 15 F3
le Clat (11) . . . 308 E5
Claudon (88) . . . 117 K2
le Claux (15) . . . 218 A4
Clavans-en-Haut-Oisans (38) . . . 225 F4
Clavé (79) . . . 161 K4
Claveisolles (69) . . . 187 K3
Clavette (17) . . . 176 E2
Claveyson (26) . . . 222 C3
Clavières (15) . . . 219 G6
Claviers (83) . . . 279 K5
Claville (27) . . . 56 C1
Claville-Motteville (76) . . . 16 A5
Clavy-Warby (08) . . . 22 B3
la Claye (85) . . . 159 K4
Claye-Souilly (77) . . . 59 H2
Clayes (35) . . . 78 E3
les Clayes-sous-Bois (78) . . . 58 B4
la Clayette (71) . . . 187 H1
Clayeures (54) . . . 94 C2
Clécy (14) . . . 53 H2
Cléden-Cap-Sizun (29) . . . 73 B3
Cléden-Poher (29) . . . 75 H3
Cléder (29) . . . 46 D3
Clèdes (40) . . . 265 H6
Cleebourg (67) . . . 25 B1
Clefmont (52) . . . 116 E1
Clefs (49) . . . 126 B1
les Clefs (74) . . . 191 H6
Cléguer (56) . . . 99 K3
Cléguérec (56) . . . 76 D5
Clelles (38) . . . 241 K2
Clémencey (21) . . . 135 J6
Clémensat (63) . . . 202 D5
Clémery (54) . . . 66 A2
Clémont (18) . . . 130 E2
Clénay (21) . . . 136 B4
Clenleu (62) . . . 4 D5
Cléon (76) . . . 35 H3
Cléon-d'Andran (26) . . . 240 D5
Cleppé (42) . . . 204 E2
Clérac (17) . . . 212 B3
Cléré-du-Bois (36) . . . 146 E5
Cléré-les-Pins (37) . . . 127 F4
Cléré-sur-Layon (49) . . . 143 K2
Clères (76) . . . 15 K5
Clérey (10) . . . 90 C6
Clérey-la-Côte (88) . . . 93 G2
Clérey-sur-Brenon (54) . . . 94 A1

360

Clergoux (19)	216 D2	Cognat-Lyonne (03)	185 H3
Clérieux (26)	222 D5	Cogners (72)	107 J4
les Clérimois (89)	88 E5	Cognet (38)	242 B1
le Clerjus (88)	118 C2	Cognières (70)	138 C3
Clerlande (63)	185 G6	Cognin (73)	208 B4
Clermain (71)	171 G6	Cognin-les-Gorges (38)	223 H3
Clermont (09)	307 F2	Cognocoli-Monticchi (2A)	320 D6
Clermont (40)	264 C5	Cogny (18)	149 K6
Clermont (60)	38 A3	Cogny (69)	188 A5
Clermont (74)	190 D5	Cogolin (83)	298 E4
Clermont-Créans (72)	106 B6	Cohade (43)	219 G2
Clermont-de-Beauregard (24)	231 K1	Cohennoz (73)	209 G1
Clermont-Dessous (47)	247 K4	Cohiniac (22)	48 E6
Clermont-d'Excideuil (24)	214 D1	Cohons (52)	116 D5
Clermont-en-Argonne (55)	42 E6	Coiffy-le-Bas (52)	117 G3
Clermont-Ferrand (63)	202 D2	Coiffy-le-Haut (52)	117 G3
Clermont-le-Fort (31)	288 B2	Coigneux (80)	10 C5
Clermont-les-Fermes (02)	21 G5	Coignières (78)	58 A5
Clermont-l'Hérault (34)	273 H6	Coigny (50)	28 E6
Clermont-Pouyguillès (32)	286 C2	Coimères (33)	230 A6
Clermont-Savès (32)	268 C6	Coin-lès-Cuvry (57)	45 F6
Clermont-Soubiran (47)	248 D5	Coin-sur-Seille (57)	66 A1
Clermont-sur-Lauquet (11)	309 G2	Coinces (45)	109 J3
Cléron (25)	156 C2	Coinches (88)	95 J4
Clerques (62)	2 E4	Coincourt (54)	66 E4
Clerval (25)	138 E4	Coincy (02)	39 K5
Cléry (21)	136 E5	Coincy (57)	45 G5
Cléry (73)	209 F3	Coings (36)	148 A5
Cléry-en-Vexin (95)	36 E6	Coirac (33)	230 B4
Cléry-Grand (55)	43 F2	Coise (69)	205 H4
Cléry-Petit (55)	43 F2	Coise-Saint-Jean-	
Cléry-Saint-André (45)	109 J5	Pied-Gauthier (73)	208 D4
Cléry-sur-Somme (80)	19 G1	Coiserette (39)	173 J6
Clesles (51)	89 J2	Coisevaux (70)	139 G1
Clessé (71)	171 J5	Coisia (39)	173 G6
Clessé (79)	161 H1	Coisy (80)	18 B1
Clessy (71)	170 B3	Coivert (17)	178 A4
Cléty (62)	3 F6	Coivrel (60)	18 D6
Cleurie (88)	119 F1	Coizard-Joches (51)	61 J4
Cleuville (76)	15 F4	Colayrac-Saint-Cirq (47)	248 B4
Cléville (14)	33 G5	Colembert (62)	2 C5
Cléville (76)	15 F5	Coligny (01)	172 E5
Clévilliers (28)	85 F2	Colincamps (80)	10 D5
Cleyrac (33)	230 C3	la Collancelle (58)	151 J2
Cleyzieu (01)	189 J5	Collandres (15)	217 K3
Clézentaine (88)	94 E2	Collandres-Quincarnon (27)	56 A2
Clichy (92)	58 E4	Collanges (63)	202 E6
Clichy-sous-Bois (93)	59 G3	Collat (43)	219 K3
Climbach (67)	25 B1	la Colle-sur-Loup (06)	281 F4
Clinchamp (52)	92 E5	Collégien (77)	59 H4
Clinchamps-sur-Orne (14)	32 D6	Collemiers (89)	112 D1
Clion (17)	195 H5	Colleret (59)	13 J3
Clion (36)	147 F4	Colleville (76)	14 D3
Cliousclat (26)	240 C3	Colleville-Montgomery (14)	32 E4
Cliponville (76)	15 F4	Colleville-sur-Mer (14)	29 K6
Cliron (08)	22 C3	Collias (30)	275 H2
la Clisse (17)	195 F2	Colligis-Crandelain (02)	40 B1
Clisson (44)	123 K6	Colligny (57)	45 G5
Clitourps (50)	29 F2	Colline-Beaumont (62)	8 E2
Clohars-Carnoët (29)	99 H4	Collinée (22)	77 J3
Clohars-Fouesnant (29)	98 D2	Collioure (66)	315 J4
le Cloître-Pleyben (29)	75 F3	Collobrières (83)	298 C4
le Cloître-Saint-Thégonnec (29)	47 G6	Collonge-en-Charollais (71)	171 G2
Clomot (21)	153 G1	Collonge-la-Madeleine (71)	153 H4
Clonas-sur-Varèze (38)	206 A6	Collonges (01)	190 D2
Clos-Fontaine (77)	88 A1	Collonges-au-Mont-d'Or (69)	206 A1
la Clotte (17)	212 B4	Collonges-la-Rouge (19)	215 K5
Clouange (57)	27 G5	Collonges-lès-Bévy (21)	154 A1
Cloué (86)	162 D5	Collonges-lès-Premières (21)	136 C5
les Clouzeaux (85)	159 H2	Collonges-sous-Salève (74)	191 F2
Cloyes-sur-le-Loir (28)	108 D3	Collongues (06)	280 C2
Cloyes-sur-Marne (51)	63 G6	Collongues (65)	285 J4
Clucy (39)	156 A4	Collorec (29)	75 G2
Clugnat (23)	183 F1	Collorgues (30)	275 G1
Cluis (36)	165 J4	Colmar (68)	96 C4
Clumanc (04)	260 A6	Colmars (04)	260 C4
Cluny (71)	171 H5	Colmen (57)	45 J2
la Clusaz (74)	191 J5	Colméry (58)	132 D5
la Cluse (05)	242 C4	Colmesnil-Manneville (76)	15 K2
la Cluse-et-Mijoux (25)	157 F4	Colmey (54)	26 B3
les Cluses (66)	315 G4	Colmier-le-Bas (52)	115 K5
Cluses (74)	191 K3	Colmier-le-Haut (52)	115 K5
Clussais-la-Pommeraie (79)	179 F2	Colognac (30)	274 B1
Clux (71)	154 D4	Cologne (32)	268 C5
Coadout (22)	48 C5	Colomars (06)	281 G3
Coaraze (06)	281 G2	Colombe (38)	207 G6
Coarraze (64)	284 E6	la Colombe (41)	109 F4
Coat-Méal (29)	72 D3	la Colombe (50)	31 G6
Coatascorn (22)	48 C3	Colombé-la-Fosse (10)	91 H5
Coatréven (22)	48 B2	Colombé-le-Sec (10)	91 H5
Cobonne (26)	240 E3	Colombelles (14)	32 E4
Cobrieux (59)	7 F5	Colombes (92)	58 D3
la Cochère (61)	54 D5	Colombey-les-Belles (54)	93 H1
Cocherel (77)	60 B1	Colombey-les-Deux-Églises (52)	91 J3
Cocheren (57)	68 B2	Colombier (03)	184 C1
Coclois (10)	90 D2	Colombier (21)	153 J1
Cocquerel (80)	9 H6	Colombier (24)	231 J3
Cocumont (47)	247 F1	Colombier (42)	221 K1
Cocurès (48)	254 C3	Colombier (70)	118 B6
Codalet (66)	314 B3	Colombier-en-Brionnais (71)	170 E6
Codognan (30)	275 F4	Colombier-Fontaine (25)	139 F3
Codolet (30)	256 D5	Colombier-le-Cardinal (07)	222 A2
Coësmes (35)	103 J1	Colombier-le-Jeune (07)	222 A5
Coëtlogon (22)	77 H5	Colombier-le-Vieux (07)	222 A5
Coëtmieux (22)	49 H6	Colombier-Saugnieu (69)	206 D2
Coeuvres-et-Valsery (02)	39 G3	Colombières (14)	31 J1
Coëx (85)	158 E1	Colombières-sur-Orb (34)	291 H1
Coggia (2A)	316 D5	
Coglès (35)	51 K6	
Cogna (39)	173 J3	
Cognac (16)	195 K3	
Cognac-la-Forêt (87)	198 C1	

Colombiers (17)	195 H3	Conchy-les-Pots (60)	18 E5
Colombiers (18)	167 G2	Conchy-sur-Canche (62)	9 K2
Colombiers (34)	291 K4	Concorès (46)	233 H4
Colombiers (61)	82 C2	Concoret (56)	78 B4
Colombiers (86)	163 G1	Concots (46)	250 C2
Colombiers-du-Plessis (53)	80 E3	Concourson-sur-Layon (49)	144 A1
Colombiers-sur-Seulles (14)	32 D3	Concremiers (36)	164 B3
Colombiès (12)	251 J2	Concressault (18)	131 G3
Colombotte (70)	118 C6	Conciers (41)	109 G6
Colomby (50)	28 D4	Condac (16)	179 G4
Colomby-sur-Thaon (14)	32 D4	Condal (71)	172 D4
Colomiers (31)	269 F6	Condamine (01)	189 K3
Colomieu (01)	207 J2	Condamine (39)	173 F2
Colonard-Corubert (61)	83 J3	la Condamine-Châtelard (04)	227 B6
Colondannes (23)	182 A1	Condat (15)	218 A2
Colonfay (02)	20 D2	Condat (46)	215 K6
Colonne (39)	155 H5	Condat-en-Combraille (63)	201 J1
Colonzelle (26)	257 F2	Condat-lès-Montboissier (63)	203 J1
Colpo (56)	101 F3	Condat-sur-Ganaveix (19)	199 J6
Colroy-la-Grande (88)	95 K3	Condat-sur-Trincou (24)	214 A1
Colroy-la-Roche (67)	70 A6	Condat-sur-Vézère (24)	215 F4
Coltainville (28)	85 H2	Condat-sur-Vienne (87)	198 E2
Coltines (15)	218 D5	Condé (36)	148 C5
Coly (24)	215 F5	Condé-en-Brie (02)	61 F1
Combaillaux (34)	274 A5	Condé-Folie (80)	9 H6
Combas (30)	274 E3	Condé-lès-Autry (08)	42 C4
la Combe-de-Lancey (38)	224 C2	Condé-lès-Herpy (08)	21 J6
Combeaufontaine (70)	117 J6	Condé-Northen (57)	45 H4
Combefa (81)	251 G6	Condé-Sainte-Libiaire (77)	59 J3
Comberanche-et-Épeluche (24)	213 F2	Condé-sur-Aisne (02)	39 K2
Comberjon (70)	118 B6	Condé-sur-Huisne (61)	84 A4
Comberouger (82)	268 D3	Condé-sur-Ifs (14)	54 B1
Combertault (21)	154 B4	Condé-sur-Iton (27)	56 B2
les Combes (25)	157 G2	Condé-sur-l'Escaut (59)	7 J2
Combès (34)	272 D6	Condé-sur-Marne (51)	62 B1
Combiers (16)	197 G5	Condé-sur-Noireau (14)	53 H3
Comblanchien (21)	154 B2	Condé-sur-Risle (27)	34 D3
Combles (80)	11 F6	Condé-sur-Sarthe (61)	82 C3
Combles-en-Barrois (55)	64 A4	Condé-sur-Seulles (14)	32 C4
Comblessac (35)	102 C1	Condé-sur-Suippe (02)	40 E2
Combleux (45)	110 B4	Condé-sur-Vesgre (78)	57 H5
Comblot (61)	83 H2	Condé-sur-Vire (50)	31 H4
Combloux (74)	192 A5	Condeau (61)	84 A3
Combon (27)	35 F6	Condécourt (95)	58 A1
Combourg (35)	51 F6	Condéon (16)	196 B6
Combourtillé (35)	80 A4	Condes (39)	173 G6
Combovin (26)	240 E1	Condes (52)	92 B6
Combrailles (63)	201 J1	Condette (62)	2 A6
Combrand (79)	143 G5	Condezaygues (47)	248 E1
Combray (14)	53 J2	Condillac (26)	240 B4
Combre (42)	187 G4	Condom (32)	267 F2
Combrée (49)	104 C6	Condom-d'Aubrac (12)	236 C5
Combres (28)	84 C4	Condorcet (26)	257 J1
Combres-sous-les-Côtes (55)	44 A6	Condren (02)	19 K5
Combressol (19)	200 E6	Condrieu (69)	206 A6
Combret (12)	271 K3	Conflandey (70)	117 K5
Combreux (45)	110 E3	Conflans-en-Jarnisy (54)	44 C5
Combrimont (88)	95 K4	Conflans-Sainte-Honorine (78)	58 C2
Combrit (29)	98 C2	Conflans-sur-Anille (72)	107 K3
Combronde (63)	185 F5	Conflans-sur-Lanterne (70)	118 B4
Combs-la-Ville (77)	59 G6	Conflans-sur-Loing (45)	111 J2
la Comelle (71)	152 D5	Conflans-sur-Seine (51)	89 H1
Comiac (46)	234 D1	Confolens (16)	180 B5
Comigne (11)	290 D6	Confolent-Port-Dieu (19)	201 H5
Comines (59)	6 D2	Confort (01)	190 C2
Commana (29)	46 E6	Confracourt (70)	117 J6
Commarin (21)	135 G2	Confrançon (01)	188 E1
Commeaux (61)	54 B4	Congé-sur-Orne (72)	82 E6
Commelle (38)	206 E6	Congénies (30)	274 E4
Commelle-Vernay (42)	187 F5	Congerville-Thionville (91)	86 B4
Commenailles (39)	155 G6	Congis-sur-Thérouanne (77)	60 A1
Commenchon (02)	19 J5	Congrier (53)	104 B4
Commensacq (40)	245 G4	Congy (51)	61 J3
Commentry (03)	184 B1	Conie-Molitard (28)	109 F1
Commeny (95)	37 F6	Conilhac-Corbières (11)	290 E6
Commequiers (85)	141 F6	Conilhac-de-la-Montagne (11)	308 E3
Commer (53)	81 G5	Conjux (73)	208 A1
Commercy (55)	64 E4	Connac (12)	271 J1
Commerveil (72)	83 F4	Connangles (43)	219 K2
Commes (14)	32 B3	Connantray-Vaurefroy (51)	62 A5
Communailles-en-Montagne (39)	156 C6	Connantre (51)	61 K5
Communay (69)	206 A4	Connaux (30)	256 C6
Compains (63)	202 B6	Conne-de-Labarde (24)	231 J3
Compainville (76)	16 E5	Connelles (27)	35 K4
Compans (77)	59 H2	Connerré (72)	107 G2
le Compas (23)	183 J5	Connezac (24)	197 H5
Compertrix (51)	62 D2	Connigis (02)	61 F1
Compeyre (12)	253 G5	Conquereuil (44)	103 F4
Compiègne (60)	38 D2	Conques (12)	235 H5
Compigny (89)	88 D4	Conques-sur-Orbiel (11)	290 B5
Complibat (12)	251 H2	le Conquet (29)	72 A4
la Compôte (73)	208 D2	Conqueyrac (30)	274 C2
Comprégnac (12)	253 F6	Cons-la-Grandville (54)	26 C3
Compreignac (87)	181 H5	Cons-Sainte-Colombe (74)	209 F1
Comps (26)	240 E5	Consac (17)	195 G6
Comps (30)	275 K3	Conségudes (06)	280 E2
Comps (33)	211 H5	Consenvoye (55)	43 G3
Comps-la-Grand-Ville (12)	252 B4	Consigny (52)	117 F4
Comps-sur-Artuby (83)	279 J4	Consolation-Maisonnettes (25)	157 H1
la Comté (62)	10 C1	Contalmaison (80)	10 E6
Comus (11)	308 B5	Contamine-Sarzin (74)	191 F2
Conan (41)	108 E4	Contamine-sur-Arve (74)	191 H2
Conand (01)	189 J6	les Contamines-Montjoie (74)	192 B6
Conat (66)	314 B3	Contault (51)	63 H3
Conca (2A)	323 J1	Contay (80)	10 C6
Concarneau (29)	98 E3	Conte (39)	156 B6
Concevreux (02)	40 C2	Contes (06)	281 H2
Concèze (19)	215 G1	Contes (62)	9 H1
Conches-en-Ouche (27)	56 B2		
Conches-sur-Gondoire (77)	59 H3		
Conchez-de-Béarn (64)	285 F1		
Conchil-le-Temple (62)	8 E2		

Contescourt (02)	19 K3	Corme-Écluse (17)	194 E3
Contest (53)	81 G5	Corme-Royal (17)	194 E2
Conteville (14)	33 F6	Cormeilles (27)	34 B4
Conteville (27)	34 B2	Cormeilles (60)	17 K5
Conteville (60)	17 J5	Cormeilles-en-Parisis (95)	58 D2
Conteville (76)	16 E4	Cormeilles-en-Vexin (95)	37 G6
Conteville (80)	9 J4	Cormelles-le-Royal (14)	32 E5
Conteville-en-Ternois (62)	10 A1	Cormenon (41)	108 A3
Conteville-lès-Boulogne (62)	2 B5	Cormeray (41)	129 F3
Conthil (57)	66 E2	Cormery (37)	127 K6
Contigné (49)	105 H6	Cormes (72)	83 J6
Contigny (03)	168 E6	
Contilly (72)	83 F3	
Continvoir (37)	126 E4	
Contoire (80)	18 D4	
Contrazy (09)	306 C2	
Contré (17)	178 C4	
Contre (80)	17 J4	
Contréglise (70)	117 K4	
Contremoulins (76)	14 D4	
Contres (18)	149 H5	
Contres (41)	129 F4	
Contreuve (08)	42 A3	
Contrevoz (01)	207 J1	
Contrexéville (88)	93 J5	
Contrières (50)	30 E5	
Contrisson (55)	63 J4	
Conty (80)	17 K4	
Contz-les-Bains (57)	27 J3	
Conzieu (01)	207 J2	
Coole (51)	62 D5	
Coolus (51)	62 D2	
la Copechagnière (85)	142 A5	
Copponex (74)	190 E3	
Coquainvilliers (14)	33 K5	
Coquelles (62)	2 C3	
la Coquille (24)	198 C5	
Corancez (28)	85 G4	
Corancy (58)	152 B2	
Coray (29)	75 F5	
Corbara (2B)	318 C2	
Corbarieu (82)	269 G2	
Corbas (69)	206 B3	
Corbehem (62)	11 H2	
Corbeil (51)	90 E1	
Corbeil-Cerf (60)	37 H4	
Corbeil-Essonnes (91)	87 F1	
Corbeilles (45)	111 G2	
Corbel (73)	208 A6	
Corbelin (38)	207 H3	
Corbenay (70)	118 C3	
Corbeny (02)	40 D1	
Corbère (66)	314 E2	
Corbère-Abères (64)	285 F2	
Corbère-les-Cabanes (66)	314 E2	
Corberon (21)	154 B3	
Corbès (30)	255 F6	
Corbie (80)	18 C2	
la Corbière (70)	118 E4	
Corbières (04)	278 B4	
Corbières (11)	308 C2	
Corbigny (58)	133 H6	
Corbon (14)	33 H5	
Corbon (61)	83 J3	
Corbonod (01)	190 C5	
Corbreuse (91)	86 B2	
Corcelle-Mieslot (25)	138 B4	
Corcelles (01)	189 K4	
Corcelles-en-Beaujolais (69)	188 B3	
Corcelles-Ferrières (25)	137 H6	
Corcelles-les-Arts (21)	153 K4	
Corcelles-lès-Cîteaux (21)	154 C1	
Corcelles-les-Monts (21)	135 K5	
Corcieux (88)	95 H5	
Corcondray (25)	137 J6	
Corconne (30)	274 C3	
Corcoué-sur-Logne (44)	141 H3	
Corcy (02)	39 H4	
Cordéac (38)	242 C2	
Cordebugle (14)	34 B6	
Cordelle (42)	186 E5	
Cordemais (44)	122 E3	
Cordes-sur-Ciel (81)	251 F6	
Cordes-Tolosannes (82)	268 D1	
Cordesse (71)	153 F3	
Cordey (14)	54 A3	
Cordon (74)	192 A5	
Cordonnet (70)	137 K4	
Coren (15)	218 E5	
Corenc (38)	224 B3	
Corent (63)	202 E3	
Corfélix (51)	61 H4	
Corgengoux (21)	154 B4	
Corgnac-sur-l'Isle (24)	214 C1	
Corgoloin (21)	154 B2	
Corignac (17)	211 K2	
Corlay (22)	76 D2	
Corlier (01)	189 K4	
Cormainville (28)	109 H1	
Cormaranche-en-Bugey (01)	190 A5	
Cormatin (71)	171 H3	

Cormicy (51) . . . 40 D3
le Cormier (27) . . . 56 E2
Cormolain (14) . . . 31 K3
Cormont (62) . . . 4 C5
Cormontreuil (51) . . . 41 F4
Cormoranche-sur-Saône (01) . . . 188 C2
Cormost (10) . . . 90 B6
Cormot-le-Grand (21) . . . 153 J4
Cormoyeux (51) . . . 40 E6
Cormoz (01) . . . 172 D4
Corn (46) . . . 234 D3
Cornac (46) . . . 234 C1
Cornant (89) . . . 112 C1
Cornas (07) . . . 222 C6
Cornay (08) . . . 42 D3
Corné (49) . . . 125 D3
Cornebarrieu (31) . . . 269 F6
Corneilhan (34) . . . 291 K3
Corneilla-de-Conflent (66) . . . 314 B4
Corneilla-del-Vercol (66) . . . 315 H3
Corneilla-la-Rivière (66) . . . 310 A6
Corneillan (32) . . . 266 A5
Corneuil (27) . . . 56 D3
Corneville-la-Fouquetière (27) . . . 34 E6
Corneville-sur-Risle (27) . . . 34 D3
Cornier (74) . . . 191 G3
Cornil (19) . . . 216 A3
Cornillac (26) . . . 258 A1
Cornille (24) . . . 214 B3
Cornillé (35) . . . 79 K5
Cornillé-les-Caves (49) . . . 125 J3
Cornillon (30) . . . 256 B4
Cornillon-Confoux (13) . . . 295 K3
Cornillon-en-Trièves (38) . . . 242 A2
Cornillon-sur-l'Oule (26) . . . 257 K1
Cornimont (88) . . . 119 J2
Cornod (39) . . . 173 G6
Cornot (70) . . . 117 H6
la Cornuaille (49) . . . 124 C3
Cornus (12) . . . 272 E3
Cornusse (18) . . . 149 K4
Corny (27) . . . 36 B4
Corny-Machéroménil (08) . . . 22 A6
Corny-sur-Moselle (57) . . . 44 E6
Coron (49) . . . 143 H2
Corpe (85) . . . 160 A4
Corpeau (21) . . . 153 K4
Corpoyer-la-Chapelle (21) . . . 135 G2
Corps (38) . . . 242 D2
Corps-Nuds (35) . . . 79 G6
Corquilleroy (45) . . . 111 H2
Corquoy (18) . . . 149 F5
Corrano (2A) . . . 321 F5
Corravillers (70) . . . 119 F3
Corre (70) . . . 117 K3
Corrençon-en-Vercors (38) . . . 223 J4
Correns (83) . . . 297 K1
Corrèze (19) . . . 216 C1
Corribert (51) . . . 61 H2
Corrobert (51) . . . 61 G2
Corrombles (21) . . . 134 C3
Corronsac (31) . . . 288 C2
Corroy (51) . . . 61 K5
Corsaint (21) . . . 134 C3
Corsavy (66) . . . 314 C5
Corsept (44) . . . 122 C3
Corseul (22) . . . 50 B5
Cortambert (71) . . . 171 H4
Corte (2B) . . . 319 F6
Cortevaix (71) . . . 171 H4
Cortrat (45) . . . 111 J4
les Corvées-les-Yys (28) . . . 84 D4
Corveissiat (01) . . . 189 J1
Corvol-d'Embernard (58) . . . 132 E6
Corvol-l'Orgueilleux (58) . . . 132 E4
Corzé (49) . . . 125 J2
Cos (09) . . . 307 H3
Cosges (39) . . . 172 E1
Coslédaà-Lube-Boast (64) . . . 284 E1
Cosmes (53) . . . 104 D3
Cosnac (19) . . . 215 J4
Cosne-Cours-sur-Loire (58) . . . 132 A4
Cosne-d'Allier (03) . . . 167 K5
Cosnes-et-Romain (54) . . . 26 C2
Cosqueville (50) . . . 28 E2
Cossaye (58) . . . 169 F1
Cossé-d'Anjou (49) . . . 143 G1
Cossé-en-Champagne (53) . . . 105 J3
Cossé-le-Vivien (53) . . . 104 D3
Cossesseville (14) . . . 53 J3
Cosswiller (67) . . . 70 C3
Costa (2B) . . . 318 D2
Costaros (43) . . . 238 C1
les Costes (05) . . . 242 E4
les Costes-Gozon (12) . . . 272 A1
la Côte (70) . . . 119 F6
la Côte-d'Aime (73) . . . 209 J4
la Côte-d'Arbroz (74) . . . 192 A4
la Côte-en-Couzan (42) . . . 204 A4
la Côte-Saint-André (38) . . . 207 F6
le Coteau (42) . . . 187 F4
Côtebrune (25) . . . 138 C5
les Côtes-d'Arey (38) . . . 206 B6
les Côtes-de-Corps (38) . . . 242 C2
Coti-Chiavari (2A) . . . 322 C1
Cotignac (83) . . . 298 A1
Cottance (42) . . . 205 F2
Cottenchy (80) . . . 18 B3
Cottévrard (76) . . . 16 B5
Cottun (14) . . . 32 H3
la Couarde (79) . . . 162 A6

la Couarde-sur-Mer (17) . . . 176 A2
Couargues (18) . . . 132 A6
Coubert (77) . . . 59 H6
Coubeyrac (33) . . . 230 D3
Coubisou (12) . . . 236 A6
Coubjours (24) . . . 215 F3
Coublanc (52) . . . 116 E6
Coublanc (71) . . . 187 G2
Coublevie (38) . . . 223 K1
Coublucq (64) . . . 284 C1
Coubon (43) . . . 220 C6
Coubron (93) . . . 59 G3
Couches (71) . . . 153 H5
Couchey (21) . . . 135 K6
la Coucourde (26) . . . 240 B4
Coucouron (07) . . . 238 D3
Coucy (08) . . . 41 J1
Coucy-la-Ville (02) . . . 20 A6
Coucy-le-Château-Auffrique (02) . . . 39 J1
Coucy-lès-Eppes (02) . . . 20 E6
Couddes (41) . . . 129 F5
Coudehard (61) . . . 54 D3
Coudekerque (59) . . . 3 H2
Coudekerque-Branche (59) . . . 3 H1
Coudes (63) . . . 202 E4
Coudeville-sur-Mer (50) . . . 30 D6
Coudons (11) . . . 308 D4
Coudoux (13) . . . 296 B1
Coudray (27) . . . 36 B3
le Coudray (28) . . . 85 G3
Coudray (45) . . . 86 E5
Coudray (53) . . . 105 F5
Coudray-au-Perche (28) . . . 84 A5
le Coudray-Macouard (49) . . . 144 C1
le Coudray-Montceaux (91) . . . 87 F1
Coudray-Rabut (14) . . . 33 K3
le Coudray-Saint-Germer (60) . . . 36 E2
le Coudray-sur-Thelle (60) . . . 37 H3
Coudreceau (28) . . . 84 B4
Coudrecieux (72) . . . 107 J3
Coudres (27) . . . 56 E3
Coudroy (45) . . . 111 F4
Coudun (60) . . . 38 D2
Coudures (40) . . . 265 G5
Coueilles (31) . . . 287 F4
Couëron (44) . . . 123 F4
Couesmes (37) . . . 127 F2
Couesmes-Vaucé (53) . . . 81 F2
Couffé (44) . . . 123 K2
Couffoulens (11) . . . 290 A6
Couffy (41) . . . 129 F6
Couffy-sur-Sarsonne (19) . . . 201 F3
Couflens (09) . . . 306 E5
Coufouleux (81) . . . 269 K4
Couhé (86) . . . 179 G1
Couilly-Pont-aux-Dames (77) . . . 59 K3
Couin (62) . . . 10 C5
Couiza (11) . . . 309 F3
Couladère (31) . . . 287 H6
Coulaines (72) . . . 106 E2
Coulandon (89) . . . 168 D4
Coulangeron (89) . . . 133 F1
Coulanges (03) . . . 169 K4
Coulanges (41) . . . 128 D3
Coulanges-la-Vineuse (89) . . . 113 G6
Coulanges-lès-Nevers (58) . . . 150 E4
Coulanges-sur-Yonne (89) . . . 133 F3
Coulans-sur-Gée (72) . . . 106 C2
Coulaures (24) . . . 214 D2
Couleuvre (03) . . . 168 A2
Coulevon (70) . . . 118 B6
Coulgens (16) . . . 197 F1
Coulimer (61) . . . 83 G2
Coullemelle (80) . . . 18 C5
Coullemont (62) . . . 10 C4
Coullons (45) . . . 131 F2
Coulmer (61) . . . 55 F4
Coulmier-le-Sec (21) . . . 115 F6
Coulmiers (45) . . . 109 H4
Coulobres (34) . . . 292 A2
Coulogne (62) . . . 2 D3
Couloisy (60) . . . 39 F2
Coulombiers (72) . . . 82 D4
Coulombiers (86) . . . 162 D4
Coulombs (14) . . . 32 C4
Coulombs (28) . . . 57 G6
Coulombs-en-Valois (77) . . . 60 B1
Coulomby (62) . . . 2 E5
Coulommes (51) . . . 59 K3
Coulommes-et-Marqueny (08) . . . 42 A2
Coulommes-la-Montagne (51) . . . 40 E4
Coulommiers (77) . . . 60 B4
Coulommiers-la-Tour (41) . . . 108 D5
Coulon (79) . . . 161 F6
Coulonces (14) . . . 31 J4
Coulonces (61) . . . 54 C3
la Coulonche (61) . . . 53 J6
Coulongé (72) . . . 106 D6
Coulonges (16) . . . 196 D1
Coulonges (17) . . . 195 J4
Coulonges (86) . . . 164 D5
Coulonges-Cohan (02) . . . 40 B5
Coulonges-les-Sablons (61) . . . 84 A3
Coulonges-sur-l'Autize (79) . . . 161 F4
Coulonges-sur-Sarthe (61) . . . 83 G2
Coulonges-Thouarsais (79) . . . 144 A4
Coulonvillers (80) . . . 9 H4
Couloumé-Mondebat (32) . . . 266 C6
Couloumieix-Chamiers (24) . . . 214 A3
Coulours (89) . . . 89 G6
Couloutre (58) . . . 132 D4

Coulouvray-Boisbenâtre (50) . . . 52 C4
Coulvain (14) . . . 32 A4
Coulx (47) . . . 248 A1
Coume (57) . . . 45 J4
Counozouls (11) . . . 308 E6
Coupelle-Neuve (62) . . . 5 F6
Coupelle-Vieille (62) . . . 5 F6
Coupesarte (14) . . . 33 J6
Coupetz (51) . . . 62 D4
Coupéville (51) . . . 63 F2
Coupiac (12) . . . 271 J2
Coupray (52) . . . 115 K3
Coupru (02) . . . 60 D1
Couptrain (53) . . . 81 J2
Coupvray (77) . . . 59 J3
Couquèques (33) . . . 210 E1
Cour-Cheverny (41) . . . 129 F3
Cour-et-Buis (38) . . . 206 C6
Cour-l'Évêque (52) . . . 115 K3
la Cour-Marigny (45) . . . 111 G4
Cour-Saint-Maurice (25) . . . 139 G5
Cour-sur-Loire (41) . . . 129 F1
Courances (91) . . . 87 F2
Courant (17) . . . 177 J4
Courban (21) . . . 115 H3
la Courbe (61) . . . 54 A4
Courbehaye (28) . . . 109 H1
Courbépine (27) . . . 34 E5
Courbes (02) . . . 20 B4
Courbesseaux (54) . . . 66 C5
Courbette (39) . . . 173 G3
Courbeveille (53) . . . 104 D2
Courbevoie (92) . . . 58 D3
Courbiac (47) . . . 249 F2
Courbillac (16) . . . 196 A2
Courboin (02) . . . 61 F2
Courbouzon (39) . . . 173 F2
Courbouzon (41) . . . 109 G6
Courçais (03) . . . 167 F5
Courçay (37) . . . 128 A6
Courceboeufs (72) . . . 106 E1
Courcelette (80) . . . 10 E5
Courcelles (17) . . . 178 A5
Courcelles (25) . . . 156 B2
Courcelles (45) . . . 110 E1
Courcelles (54) . . . 93 K3
Courcelles (58) . . . 132 E4
Courcelles (90) . . . 97 A5
Courcelles-au-Bois (80) . . . 10 D5
Courcelles-Chaussy (57) . . . 45 H5
Courcelles-de-Touraine (37) . . . 126 E3
Courcelles-en-Barrois (55) . . . 64 D3
Courcelles-en-Bassée (77) . . . 88 B3
Courcelles-en-Montagne (52) . . . 116 C4
Courcelles-Epayelles (60) . . . 18 D6
Courcelles-Frémoy (21) . . . 134 C4
Courcelles-la-Forêt (72) . . . 106 C4
Courcelles-le-Comte (62) . . . 10 E4
Courcelles-lès-Gisors (60) . . . 36 D4
Courcelles-lès-Lens (62) . . . 11 H1
Courcelles-lès-Montbard (21) . . . 134 E2
Courcelles-lès-Montbéliard (25) . . . 139 H2
Courcelles-lès-Semur (21) . . . 134 D4
Courcelles-Sapicourt (51) . . . 40 D4
Courcelles-sous-Châtenois (88) . . . 93 H4
Courcelles-sous-Moyencourt (80) . . . 17 J3
Courcelles-sous-Thoix (80) . . . 17 J4
Courcelles-sur-Aire (55) . . . 64 B2
Courcelles-sur-Blaise (52) . . . 91 J3
Courcelles-sur-Nied (57) . . . 45 G6
Courcelles-sur-Seine (27) . . . 36 A5
Courcelles-sur-Vesles (02) . . . 40 B3
Courcelles-sur-Viosne (95) . . . 37 G6
Courcelles-sur-Voire (10) . . . 91 F2
Courcemain (51) . . . 61 K6
Courcemont (72) . . . 82 F6
Courcerac (17) . . . 195 J1
Courcerault (61) . . . 83 J3
Courceroy (10) . . . 88 E3
Courchamp (77) . . . 60 D6
Courchamps (02) . . . 39 H6
Courchamps (49) . . . 144 C1
Courchapon (25) . . . 137 H2
Courchaton (70) . . . 138 E2
Courchelettes (59) . . . 11 H2
Courcité (53) . . . 81 K4
Courcival (72) . . . 83 F5
Courcôme (16) . . . 179 G5
Courçon (17) . . . 177 G1
Courcoué (37) . . . 145 H3
Courcouronnes (91) . . . 87 F1
Courcoury (17) . . . 195 G2
Courcuire (70) . . . 137 H5
Courcy (14) . . . 54 C4
Courcy (50) . . . 30 E4
Courcy (51) . . . 40 E3
Courcy-aux-Loges (45) . . . 110 D2
Courdemanche (27) . . . 56 E4
Courdemanche (72) . . . 107 H5
Courdemanges (51) . . . 63 F3
Courdimanche (95) . . . 58 B1
Courdimanche-sur-Essonne (91) . . . 86 E3
Couret (31) . . . 306 C1
Courgains (72) . . . 82 E5
Courgeac (16) . . . 212 E1
Courgenard (72) . . . 107 K1
Courgenay (89) . . . 89 F3
Courgent (78) . . . 57 H3
Courgeon (61) . . . 83 J2
Courgeoût (61) . . . 83 H2
Courgis (89) . . . 113 H5
Courgivaux (51) . . . 61 F5

Courgoul (63) . . . 202 C5
Courjeonnet (51) . . . 61 J4
Courlac (16) . . . 212 E2
Courlandon (51) . . . 40 C3
Courlans (39) . . . 173 F2
Courlaoux (39) . . . 173 F2
Courlay (79) . . . 143 H6
Courléon (49) . . . 126 D4
Courlon (21) . . . 136 A1
Courlon-sur-Yonne (89) . . . 88 C4
Courmangoux (01) . . . 172 E6
Courmas (51) . . . 40 E5
Courmelles (02) . . . 39 J3
Courmemin (41) . . . 129 H4
Courménil (61) . . . 54 E4
Courmes (06) . . . 280 E3
Courmont (02) . . . 40 B5
Courmont (70) . . . 139 F1
Cournanel (11) . . . 308 C2
Courniou (34) . . . 290 E4
Cournols (63) . . . 202 C4
Cournon (56) . . . 102 C3
Cournon-d'Auvergne (63) . . . 202 E3
Cournonsec (34) . . . 293 F1
Cournonterral (34) . . . 293 F1
la Couronne (16) . . . 196 D4
Courouvre (55) . . . 64 C2
Courpalay (77) . . . 60 A6
Courpiac (33) . . . 230 B3
Courpière (63) . . . 203 H2
Courpignac (17) . . . 211 J1
Courquetaine (77) . . . 59 J6
Courrensan (32) . . . 266 E3
Courrières (62) . . . 6 C6
Courris (81) . . . 271 G2
Courry (30) . . . 255 H3
Cours (46) . . . 233 J6
Cours (47) . . . 248 B3
le Cours (56) . . . 101 J4
Cours (79) . . . 161 H4
Cours-de-Monségur (33) . . . 230 E4
Cours-de-Pile (24) . . . 231 J2
Cours-la-Ville (69) . . . 187 H3
Cours-les-Bains (33) . . . 247 F2
Cours-les-Barres (18) . . . 150 C3
Coursac (24) . . . 213 K4
Coursan (11) . . . 291 J5
Coursan-en-Othe (10) . . . 113 J2
Coursegoules (06) . . . 280 E3
Courset (62) . . . 2 C6
Courseulles-sur-Mer (14) . . . 32 D3
Courson (14) . . . 52 C3
Courson-les-Carrières (89) . . . 133 F2
Courson-Monteloup (91) . . . 86 C1
Courtacon (77) . . . 60 D5
Courtagnon (51) . . . 40 E5
Courtalain (28) . . . 108 D2
Courtaoult (10) . . . 113 J2
Courtauly (11) . . . 308 D2
Courtavon (68) . . . 97 B6
Courtefontaine (25) . . . 139 J4
Courtefontaine (39) . . . 155 K2
Courteilles (27) . . . 56 B5
Courteix (19) . . . 201 F4
Courtelevant (90) . . . 97 A5
Courtemanche (80) . . . 18 D5
Courtemaux (45) . . . 112 A2
Courtémont (51) . . . 42 D5
Courtemont-Varennes (02) . . . 40 A6
Courtempierre (45) . . . 111 G1
Courtenay (38) . . . 207 G2
Courtenay (45) . . . 112 B2
Courtenot (10) . . . 90 D6
Courteranges (10) . . . 90 C5
Courteron (10) . . . 114 C2
Courtes (01) . . . 172 B4
Courtesoult-et-Gatey (70) . . . 137 F1
Courtétain-et-Salans (25) . . . 138 D5
la Courtète (11) . . . 289 H6
Courteuil (60) . . . 38 B5
Courthézon (84) . . . 257 F6
Courthiézy (51) . . . 61 G1
Courties (32) . . . 285 J1
Courtieux (60) . . . 39 G2
Courtillers (72) . . . 105 K5
Courtils (50) . . . 51 K3
la Courtine (23) . . . 201 F3
Courtisols (51) . . . 62 E2
Courtivron (21) . . . 135 K2
Courtoin (89) . . . 112 B1
Courtois-sur-Yonne (89) . . . 88 D6
Courtomer (61) . . . 55 F6
Courtomer (77) . . . 59 K6
Courtonne-la-Meurdrac (14) . . . 34 A6
Courtonne-les-Deux-Églises (14) . . . 34 B6
Courtrizy-et-Fussigny (02) . . . 40 C1
Courtry (77) . . . 59 G3
Courvaudon (14) . . . 53 H1
Courvières (25) . . . 156 C2
Courville (51) . . . 40 C4
Courville-sur-Eure (28) . . . 84 E3
Courzieu (69) . . . 205 H2
Cousance (39) . . . 172 E3
Cousances-les-Forges (55) . . . 64 A3
Cousances-lès-Triconville (55) . . . 64 D4
Cousolre (59) . . . 13 J3
Coussa (09) . . . 307 K2
Coussac-Bonneval (87) . . . 199 F5
Coussan (65) . . . 285 J5
Coussay (86) . . . 145 F6
Coussay-les-Bois (86) . . . 146 A3

Coussegrey (10) . . . 114 A3
Coussergues (12) . . . 252 E2
Coussey (88) . . . 93 G3
Coust (18) . . . 167 H2
Coustaussa (11) . . . 309 F3
Coustouge (11) . . . 310 A2
Coustouges (66) . . . 314 C6
Coutances (50) . . . 30 E4
Coutansouze (03) . . . 184 E2
Coutarnoux (89) . . . 134 A2
Coutençon (77) . . . 88 A2
Coutens (09) . . . 308 A1
Couterne (61) . . . 81 J2
Couternon (21) . . . 136 B5
Couteuges (43) . . . 219 J4
Coutevroult (77) . . . 59 K3
Couthenans (70) . . . 139 G1
Couthures-sur-Garonne (47) . . . 230 D6
Coutiches (59) . . . 7 F6
Coutières (79) . . . 162 A4
Coutouvre (42) . . . 187 G4
Coutras (33) . . . 212 B5
Couture (16) . . . 179 H6
la Couture (62) . . . 6 A5
la Couture (85) . . . 159 K3
la Couture-Boussey (27) . . . 57 F3
Couture-d'Argenson (79) . . . 178 D5
Couture-sur-Loir (41) . . . 107 K3
Couturelle (62) . . . 10 C4
Coutures (24) . . . 213 H4
Coutures (33) . . . 230 D4
Coutures (49) . . . 125 J5
Coutures (82) . . . 268 C2
Couvains (50) . . . 31 J3
Couvains (61) . . . 55 H3
la Couvertoirade (12) . . . 273 G2
Couvertpuis (55) . . . 92 C1
Couvignon (10) . . . 91 G6
Couville (50) . . . 28 C3
Couvonges (55) . . . 63 K4
Couvrelles (02) . . . 40 A3
Couvron-et-Aumencourt (02) . . . 20 C5
Couvrot (51) . . . 63 F4
Coux (07) . . . 239 K3
Coux (17) . . . 211 K2
Coux-et-Bigaroque (24) . . . 232 C2
Couy (18) . . . 150 A2
la Couyère (35) . . . 103 H1
Couze-et-Saint-Front (24) . . . 232 A4
Couzeix (87) . . . 181 G6
Couziers (37) . . . 144 E2
Couzon (03) . . . 168 C2
Couzon-au-Mont-d'Or (69) . . . 206 A1
Couzou (46) . . . 233 K3
Cox (31) . . . 268 C4
Coye-la-Forêt (60) . . . 38 A4
Coyecques (62) . . . 5 F4
Coyolles (02) . . . 39 F4
Coyrière (39) . . . 173 K6
Coyron (39) . . . 173 H4
Coyviller (54) . . . 66 B6
Cozes (17) . . . 194 E4
Cozzano (2A) . . . 321 F5
Crach (56) . . . 100 D5
Crachier (38) . . . 206 E4
Crain (89) . . . 133 G3
Craincourt (57) . . . 66 B2
Craintilleux (42) . . . 204 E4
Crainvilliers (88) . . . 93 H6
Cramaille (02) . . . 39 K4
Cramans (39) . . . 155 K3
Cramant (51) . . . 61 K2
Cramchaban (17) . . . 177 H2
Craménil (61) . . . 53 J4
Cramoisy (60) . . . 38 A4
Cramont (80) . . . 9 J4
Crampagna (09) . . . 307 J2
Cran-Gevrier (74) . . . 191 F5
Crancey (10) . . . 89 G2
Crançot (39) . . . 173 H1
Crandelles (15) . . . 235 G1
Crannes-en-Champagne (72) . . . 106 B3
Crans (01) . . . 189 G5
Crans (39) . . . 174 A1
Cransac (12) . . . 235 G6
Crantenoy (54) . . . 94 B2
Cranves-Sales (74) . . . 191 G2
Craon (53) . . . 104 D4
Craon (86) . . . 144 D6
Craonne (02) . . . 40 C2
Craonnelle (02) . . . 40 C2
Crapeaumesnil (60) . . . 19 F5
Craponne (69) . . . 205 K2
Craponne-sur-Arzon (43) . . . 220 B2
Cras (38) . . . 223 H2
Cras (46) . . . 233 J6
Cras-sur-Reyssouze (01) . . . 172 C6
Crastatt (67) . . . 70 C2
Crastes (32) . . . 267 K5
Crasville (27) . . . 35 H5
Crasville (50) . . . 29 F3
Crasville-la-Mallet (76) . . . 15 H3
Crasville-la-Rocquefort (76) . . . 15 H3
la Crau (83) . . . 297 K5
Cravanche (90) . . . 119 H6
Cravans (17) . . . 195 F4
Cravant (45) . . . 109 H5
Cravant (89) . . . 133 H4
Cravant-les-Côteaux (37) . . . 145 G2
Cravencères (32) . . . 266 C4
Cravent (78) . . . 57 H2
Crayssac (46) . . . 233 G6

Craywick (59)	3	G2
Crazannes (17)	177	H6
Cré (72)	126	A1
Créances (50)	30	D2
Créancey (21)	135	G6
Crécey-sur-Tille (21)	136	B2
la Crèche (79)	161	J4
Crêches-sur-Saône (71)	188	C1
Créchets (65)	305	H2
Créchy (03)	185	J4
Crécy-au-Mont (02)	39	J1
Crécy-Couvé (28)	56	E6
Crécy-en-Ponthieu (80)	9	G3
Crécy-la-Chapelle (77)	59	K3
Crécy-sur-Serre (02)	20	D4
Crédin (56)	77	F6
Crégols (46)	250	C1
Crégy-lès-Meaux (77)	59	K2
Créhange (57)	45	J6
Créhen (22)	50	B4
Creil (60)	38	A4
Creissan (34)	291	H4
Creissels (12)	253	G6
Crémarest (62)	2	C6
Cremeaux (42)	186	D6
Crémery (80)	19	F4
Crémieu (38)	206	E2
Crempigny-Bonneguête (74)	190	D5
Cremps (46)	250	B2
Crenans (39)	173	H4
Creney-près-Troyes (10)	90	B4
Crennes-sur-Fraubée (53)	81	K3
Créon (33)	229	K3
Créon-d'Armagnac (40)	266	B1
Créot (71)	153	J5
Crépand (21)	134	D2
Crépey (54)	93	J1
Crépol (26)	222	E3
Crépon (14)	32	C3
Crépy (02)	20	C5
Crépy (62)	5	G6
Crépy-en-Valois (60)	38	E4
Créquy (62)	4	E6
le Crès (34)	274	C6
Cresancey (70)	137	G4
Crésantignes (10)	114	A1
les Cresnays (50)	52	C4
Crespian (30)	274	E3
Crespières (78)	58	A3
Crespin (12)	251	J5
Crespin (59)	12	E1
Crespin (81)	271	F1
Crespinet (81)	271	F2
Crespy-le-Neuf (10)	91	H3
Cressac-Saint-Genis (16)	196	C6
Cressanges (03)	168	C5
Cressat (23)	183	F3
la Cresse (12)	253	H5
Cressé (17)	178	C6
Cressensac (46)	215	J6
Cresserons (14)	32	E3
Cresseveuille (14)	33	H4
Cressia (39)	173	F3
Cressin-Rochefort (01)	207	K1
Cressonsacq (60)	38	B2
Cressy (76)	16	A4
Cressy-Omencourt (80)	19	G4
Cressy-sur-Somme (71)	169	K2
Crest (26)	240	D3
le Crest (63)	202	D3
Crest-Voland (73)	209	H1
Creste (63)	202	C5
le Crestet (07)	221	K6
Crestet (84)	257	H4
Crestot (27)	35	G5
Créteil (94)	59	F4
Cretteville (50)	28	E6
Creully (14)	32	C3
la Creuse (70)	118	C6
Creuse (80)	17	K3
le Creusot (71)	153	G6
Creutzwald (57)	68	A1
Creuzier-le-Neuf (03)	185	J3
Creuzier-le-Vieux (03)	185	J3
Crevans-et-la-Chapelle-lès-Granges (70)	139	F2
Crevant (36)	166	B4
Crevant-Laveine (63)	185	J6
Crévéchamps (54)	94	B1
Crèvecoeur-en-Auge (14)	33	H6
Crèvecoeur-en-Brie (77)	59	K5
Crèvecoeur-le-Grand (60)	17	J5
Crèvecoeur-le-Petit (60)	18	C6
Crèvecoeur-sur-l'Escaut (59)	11	K5
Creveney (70)	118	C6
Crévic (54)	66	C5
Crévin (35)	79	G6
Crévoux (05)	227	A5
Creys-Mépieu (38)	207	H2
Creyssac (24)	213	J2
Creysse (24)	231	J2
Creysse (46)	233	K2
Creysseilles (07)	239	J3
Creyssensac-et-Pissot (24)	213	K5
Crézançay-sur-Cher (18)	149	G6
Crézancy (02)	61	F1
Crézancy-en-Sancerre (18)	131	J6
Crézières (79)	178	D3
Crézilles (54)	65	H6
Cricquebœuf (14)	33	J2
Cricqueville-en-Auge (14)	33	H4
Cricqueville-en-Bessin (14)	29	J6
Criel-sur-Mer (76)	8	B6
Crillon (60)	37	F1
Crillon-le-Brave (84)	257	H5
Crimolois (21)	136	B6
Crion (54)	66	D3
la Crique (76)	16	A4
Criquebeuf-en-Caux (76)	14	C4
Criquebeuf-la-Campagne (27)	35	G5
Criquebeuf-sur-Seine (27)	35	H3
Criquetot-le-Mauconduit (76)	14	C3
Criquetot-l'Esneval (76)	14	C5
Criquetot-sur-Longueville (76)	15	K3
Criquetot-sur-Ouville (76)	15	H4
Criquiers (76)	17	F5
Crisenoy (77)	87	J1
Crisolles (60)	19	H5
Crissay-sur-Manse (37)	145	J2
Crissé (72)	82	B6
Crissey (39)	155	G2
Crissey (71)	154	A6
Cristinacce (2A)	320	C1
Cristot (14)	32	C4
Criteuil-la-Magdeleine (16)	196	A5
Critot (76)	16	B5
Croce (2B)	319	H4
Crochte (59)	3	H3
Crocicchia (2B)	319	H4
Crocq (23)	201	G1
le Crocq (60)	17	K5
Crocy (14)	54	C3
Croettwiller (67)	25	C2
Croignon (33)	229	K2
Croisances (43)	237	K1
Croisette (62)	10	A2
le Croisic (44)	121	H5
la Croisille (87)	56	B2
la Croisille-sur-Briance (87)	199	J4
Croisilles (14)	53	J1
Croisilles (28)	57	G5
Croisilles (61)	54	E4
Croisilles (62)	11	F4
Croismare (54)	66	E4
Croissanville (14)	33	G5
Croissy-Beaubourg (77)	59	H4
Croissy-sur-Celle (60)	17	K4
Croissy-sur-Seine (78)	58	C3
le Croisty (56)	76	A5
Croisy (18)	150	A5
Croisy-sur-Andelle (76)	36	A2
Croisy-sur-Eure (27)	57	F1
Croix (59)	6	E3
Croix (90)	139	J3
la Croix-aux-Bois (08)	42	C4
la Croix-aux-Mines (88)	95	J4
la Croix-Avranchin (50)	51	K4
la Croix-Blanche (47)	248	C3
Croix-Caluyau (59)	12	D4
Croix-Chapeau (17)	176	E3
la Croix-Comtesse (17)	177	K3
la Croix-de-la-Rochette (73)	208	D5
la Croix-du-Perche (28)	84	C5
la Croix-en-Brie (77)	88	B1
la Croix-en-Champagne (51)	42	B6
Croix-en-Ternois (62)	10	A1
la Croix-en-Touraine (37)	128	B5
Croix-Fonsommes (02)	20	B1
la Croix-Helléan (56)	101	J1
Croix-Mare (76)	15	H5
Croix-Moligneaux (80)	19	H3
la Croix-Saint-Leufroy (27)	35	K6
la Croix-sur-Gartempe (87)	180	E3
la Croix-sur-Ourcq (02)	39	J5
la Croix-sur-Roudoule (06)	261	F6
la Croix-Valmer (83)	299	F4
Croixanvec (56)	76	E5
Croixdalle (76)	16	C3
la Croixille (53)	80	C5
Croixrault (80)	17	H3
Croizet-sur-Gand (42)	187	G6
Crolles (38)	224	C2
Crollon (50)	51	K4
Cromac (87)	164	E6
Cromary (70)	138	A4
Cronat (71)	169	H1
Cronce (43)	219	G5
la Crope (53)	105	H3
Cropus (76)	16	A4
Cros (30)	274	B1
le Cros (34)	273	G3
Cros (63)	201	J6
Cros-de-Géorand (07)	238	E3
Cros-de-Montvert (15)	216	E5
Cros-de-Ronesque (15)	235	K2
Crosey-le-Grand (25)	138	E4
Crosey-le-Petit (25)	138	E4
Crosmières (72)	106	A6
Crosne (91)	59	F5
Crossac (44)	122	B1
Crosses (18)	149	J4
Crosville-la-Vieille (27)	35	G5
Crosville-sur-Douve (50)	28	E5
Crosville-sur-Scie (76)	15	K3
Crotelles (37)	128	A3
Crotenay (39)	155	K6
Croth (27)	57	F3
le Crotoy (80)	8	D5
Crots (05)	243	J5
Crottes-en-Pithiverais (45)	110	B1
Crottet (01)	188	D1
le Crouais (35)	78	C3
Crouay (14)	32	A3
la Croupte (14)	55	F1
Crouseilles (64)	285	F1
Croutelle (86)	162	E4
les Croûtes (10)	113	J3
Croutoy (60)	39	F2
Crouttes (61)	54	D2
Crouttes-sur-Marne (02)	60	C2
Crouy (02)	39	J2
Crouy-en-Thelle (60)	37	K5
Crouy-Saint-Pierre (80)	17	J1
Crouy-sur-Cosson (41)	129	H1
Crouy-sur-Ourcq (77)	39	G6
le Crouzet (25)	174	B1
Crouzet-Migette (25)	156	B4
la Crouzille (63)	184	C3
Crouzilles (37)	145	H2
Crozant (23)	165	H5
Croze (23)	200	E1
Crozes-Hermitage (26)	222	B4
Crozet (01)	174	B6
le Crozet (42)	186	C3
les Crozets (39)	173	J4
Crozon (29)	72	D6
Crozon-sur-Vauvre (36)	166	A4
Cruas (07)	240	B4
Crucey-Villages (28)	56	C6
Crucheray (41)	108	C6
Cruéjouls (12)	252	E1
Cruet (73)	208	D2
Crugey (21)	153	J1
Crugny (51)	40	C4
Cruguel (56)	101	H2
Cruis (04)	258	E6
Crupies (26)	241	F5
Crupilly (02)	20	E1
Cruscades (11)	291	G6
Cruseilles (74)	191	F4
Crusnes (54)	26	E3
Cruviers-Lascours (30)	275	F1
Crux-la-Ville (58)	151	H2
Cruzille (71)	171	J4
Cruzilles-lès-Mépillat (01)	188	D2
Cruzy (34)	291	H4
Cruzy-le-Châtel (89)	114	C4
Cry (89)	114	C6
Cubelles (43)	219	J6
Cubières (48)	254	D1
Cubières-sur-Cinoble (11)	309	H4
Cubiérettes (48)	254	D1
Cubjac (24)	214	C3
Cublac (19)	215	G4
Cublize (69)	187	H4
Cubnezais (33)	211	J5
Cubrial (25)	138	D2
Cubry (25)	138	D2
Cubry-lès-Faverney (70)	118	A4
Cubzac-les-Ponts (33)	211	J6
Cucharmoy (77)	88	C1
Cuchery (51)	40	D6
Cucq (62)	4	A6
Cucugnan (11)	309	J4
Cucuron (84)	277	H4
Cudos (33)	246	D2
Cudot (89)	112	C3
Cuébris (06)	280	E1
Cuélas (32)	286	B4
Cuers (83)	297	K4
Cuffies (02)	39	J2
Cuffy (18)	150	D4
Cugand (85)	123	K6
Cuges-les-Pins (13)	297	F4
Cugnaux (31)	288	A1
Cugney (70)	137	G4
Cugny (02)	19	J4
Cuguen (35)	51	G6
Cuguron (31)	305	H1
Cuhon (86)	162	C1
Cuignières (60)	38	A2
Cuigy-en-Bray (60)	36	E2
Cuillé (53)	104	B2
Cuinchy (62)	6	B5
le Cuing (31)	286	D6
Cuinzier (42)	187	G3
Cuirieux (02)	20	E4
Cuiry-Housse (02)	40	A4
Cuiry-lès-Chaudardes (02)	40	C2
Cuiry-lès-Iviers (02)	21	H3
Cuis (51)	61	K2
Cuise-la-Motte (60)	39	F2
Cuiseaux (71)	172	E4
Cuiserey (21)	136	D4
Cuisery (71)	172	A3
Cuisia (39)	172	E3
Cuissai (61)	82	C2
Cuissy-et-Geny (02)	40	C2
Cuisy (55)	43	F4
Cuisy (77)	59	J1
Cuisy-en-Almont (02)	39	H2
Culan (18)	166	E4
Culètre (21)	153	H2
Culey-le-Patry (14)	53	H2
Culhat (63)	203	F1
Culin (38)	206	E5
Culles-les-Roches (71)	171	H2
Cully (14)	32	C4
Culmont (52)	116	E4
Culoz (01)	190	C6
Cult (70)	137	H5
Cultures (48)	253	K1
Cumières (51)	40	E6
Cumières-le-Mort-Homme (55)	43	G4
Cumiès (11)	289	F4
Cumont (82)	268	B3
Cunac (81)	270	E2
Cuncy-lès-Varzy (58)	133	F5
Cunèges (24)	231	G3
Cunel (55)	43	F3
Cunelières (90)	119	J6
Cunfin (10)	115	G2
Cunlhat (63)	203	H4
Cuon (49)	126	B3
Cuperly (51)	41	J6
Cuq (47)	248	C6
Cuq (81)	270	D6
Cuq-Toulza (81)	289	G1
Cuqueron (64)	284	B4
Curac (16)	212	D2
Curan (12)	252	E5
Curbans (04)	259	G1
Curbigny (71)	187	H1
Curçay-sur-Dive (86)	144	C2
Curchy (80)	19	G3
Curciat-Dongalon (01)	172	C4
Curcy-sur-Orne (14)	53	H1
Curdin (71)	170	B3
Curel (04)	258	D4
Curel (52)	92	A2
Curemonte (19)	216	A6
Cures (72)	106	C1
Curgies (59)	12	D2
Curgy (71)	153	F4
Curienne (73)	208	C4
Curières (12)	236	C5
Curis-au-Mont-d'Or (69)	188	C6
Curley (21)	154	B1
Curlu (80)	19	F1
Curmont (52)	91	K5
Curnier (26)	257	J2
Cursan (33)	229	K2
Curtafond (01)	188	E1
Curtil-Saint-Seine (21)	135	K3
Curtil-sous-Buffières (71)	171	G5
Curtil-sous-Burnand (71)	171	H3
Curtil-Vergy (21)	154	A1
Curvalle (81)	271	H2
Curzay-sur-Vonne (86)	162	C4
Curzon (85)	159	J4
Cusance (25)	138	E5
Cuse-et-Adrisans (25)	138	D3
Cusey (70)	136	D1
Cussac (15)	218	C6
Cussac (87)	198	B3
Cussac-Fort-Médoc (33)	211	F4
Cussac-sur-Loire (43)	220	C6
Cussangy (10)	114	B2
Cussay (37)	146	B3
Cusset (03)	185	J3
Cussey-les-Forges (21)	136	A1
Cussey-sur-Lison (25)	156	B2
Cussey-sur-l'Ognon (25)	137	K5
Cussy (14)	32	A3
Cussy-en-Morvan (71)	152	D2
Cussy-la-Colonne (21)	153	J3
Cussy-le-Châtel (21)	153	H1
Cussy-les-Forges (89)	134	A3
Custines (54)	66	A3
Cusy (74)	208	C1
Cutry (02)	39	H3
Cutry (54)	26	C3
Cuts (60)	19	J6
Cutting (57)	67	G2
Cuttoli-Corticchiato (2A)	320	D4
Cuttura (39)	173	J5
Cuvat (74)	191	F4
Cuve (70)	118	B3
Cuvergnon (60)	39	F5
Cuverville (14)	33	F5
Cuverville (27)	36	A4
Cuverville (76)	14	C4
Cuverville-sur-Yères (76)	16	C1
Cuves (50)	52	C4
Cuves (52)	116	D1
Cuvier (39)	156	C5
Cuvillers (59)	11	J3
Cuvilly (60)	18	E6
Cuvry (57)	45	F6
Cuxac-Cabardès (11)	290	C4
Cuxac-d'Aude (11)	291	H5
Cuy (60)	19	G6
Cuy (89)	88	D5
Cuy-Saint-Fiacre (76)	36	D1
Cuzac (46)	234	E5
Cuzance (46)	233	J1
Cuzieu (01)	207	J1
Cuzieu (42)	205	F4
Cuzion (36)	165	H5
Cuzorn (47)	232	C6
Cuzy (71)	170	B1
Cys-la-Commune (02)	40	B2
Cysoing (59)	7	F5

D

Dabo (57)	70	A2
Dachstein (67)	70	D3
Dadonville (45)	110	D1
Daglan (24)	233	F3
Dagneux (01)	188	E6
Dagny (77)	60	D2
Dagny-Lambercy (02)	21	G3
Dagonville (55)	64	D4
la Daguenière (49)	125	H4
Dahlenheim (67)	70	D3
Daignac (33)	230	A2
Daigny (08)	23	F4
Daillancourt (52)	91	K4
Daillecourt (52)	116	E1
Dainville (62)	10	E3
Dainville-Bertheléville (55)	92	E2
Daix (21)	136	A5
Dalem (57)	45	K3
Dalhain (57)	66	E2
Dalhunden (67)	25	C4
Dallet (63)	202	E2
Dallon (02)	19	K3
Dalou (09)	307	J2
Dalstein (57)	27	J4
Daluis (06)	260	E6
Damas-aux-Bois (88)	94	D3
Damas-et-Bettegney (88)	94	B5
Damazan (47)	247	H3
Dambach (67)	69	J4
Dambach-la-Ville (67)	71	B4
Dambelin (25)	139	G4
Dambenois (25)	139	H2
Dambenoît-lès-Colombe (70)	118	D5
Damblain (88)	117	F1
Damblainville (14)	54	B2
Dambron (28)	109	K1
Dame-Marie (27)	56	B4
Dame-Marie (61)	83	J4
Dame-Marie-les-Bois (37)	128	B3
Dameleviéres (54)	66	C6
Daméraucourt (60)	17	H4
Damerey (71)	154	C5
Damery (51)	40	D6
Damery (80)	18	E4
Damgan (56)	121	H2
Damiatte (81)	270	C6
Damigny (61)	82	D3
Damloup (55)	26	A6
Dammard (02)	39	H5
Dammarie (28)	85	G4
Dammarie-en-Puisaye (45)	131	K2
Dammarie-les-Lys (77)	87	H2
Dammarie-sur-Loing (45)	111	K5
Dammarie-sur-Saulx (55)	64	B6
Dammartin-en-Goële (77)	59	H1
Dammartin-en-Serve (78)	57	H3
Dammartin-les-Templiers (25)	138	C5
Dammartin-Marpain (39)	137	F6
Dammartin-sur-Meuse (52)	117	F2
Dammartin-sur-Tigeaux (77)	59	K4
Damousies (59)	13	H4
Damouzy (08)	22	C3
Damparis (39)	155	F2
Dampierre (10)	90	D1
Dampierre (14)	31	K4
Dampierre (39)	155	J1
Dampierre (52)	116	D3
Dampierre-au-Temple (51)	62	D1
Dampierre-en-Bray (76)	16	E6
Dampierre-en-Bresse (71)	154	D5
Dampierre-en-Burly (45)	111	G6
Dampierre-en-Crot (18)	131	G4
Dampierre-en-Graçay (18)	148	C2
Dampierre-en-Montagne (21)	135	F4
Dampierre-en-Yvelines (78)	58	B5
Dampierre-et-Flée (21)	136	D3
Dampierre-le-Château (51)	63	H1
Dampierre-les-Bois (25)	139	J2
Dampierre-lès-Conflans (70)	118	B4
Dampierre-Saint-Nicolas (76)	16	A2
Dampierre-sous-Bouhy (58)	132	C3
Dampierre-sous-Brou (28)	84	C6
Dampierre-sur-Avre (28)	56	D4
Dampierre-sur-Boutonne (17)	178	A4
Dampierre-sur-le-Doubs (25)	139	G3
Dampierre-sur-Linotte (70)	138	B2
Dampierre-sur-Moivre (51)	63	F3
Dampierre-sur-Salon (70)	137	G2
Dampjoux (25)	139	G4
Dampleux (02)	39	G4
Dampmart (77)	59	J3
Dampniat (19)	215	K4
Damprichard (25)	139	J3
les Damps (27)	35	J3
Dampsmesnil (27)	36	C5
Dampvalley-lès-Colombe (70)	138	C1
Dampvalley-Saint-Pancras (70)	118	B3
Dampvitoux (54)	65	H1
Damrémont (52)	117	F3
Damville (27)	56	C3
Damvillers (55)	43	H3
Damvix (85)	160	E6
Dancé (42)	186	E6
Dancé (61)	83	K4
Dancevoir (52)	115	J3
Dancourt (76)	16	E2
Dancourt-Popincourt (80)	18	E5
Dancy (28)	109	G1
Danestal (14)	33	H4
Dangé-Saint-Romain (86)	145	K4
Dangeau (28)	84	E6
Dangers (28)	85	F2
Dangeul (72)	82	E5
Dangolsheim (67)	70	C3
Dangu (27)	36	D4
Dangy (50)	31	K4
Danizy (02)	20	B5
Danjoutin (90)	139	H1
Danne-et-Quatre-Vents (57)	70	B1
Dannelbourg (57)	70	A1

Dannemarie (25) 139 J3
Dannemarie (68) 97 A4
Dannemarie (78) 57 H5
Dannemarie-sur-Crète (25) 137 J6
Dannemoine (89) 113 K4
Dannemois (91) 87 F3
Dannes (62) 4 A4
Dannevoux (55) 43 G3
Danvou-la-Ferrière (14) 53 G2
Danzé (41) 108 C4
Daon (53) 105 F5
Daoulas (29) 74 C1
Daours (80) 18 C2
Darazac (19) 216 E4
Darbonnay (39) 155 H5
Darbres (07) 239 J4
Darcey (21) 135 F2
Dardenac (33) 230 A3
Dardez (27) 35 J6
Dardilly (69) 205 K1
Dareizé (69) 187 K6
Dargies (60) 17 H4
Dargnies (80) 8 D6
Dargoire (42) 205 J4
Darmannes (52) 92 B6
Darnac (87) 180 E2
Darnétal (76) 35 J2
Darnets (19) 200 D6
Darney (88) 117 K1
Darney-aux-Chênes (88) 93 H4
Darnieulles (88) 94 C5
Darois (21) 135 K4
Darvault (77) 87 J3
Darvoy (45) 110 C4
Dasle (25) 139 J2
Daubensand (67) 71 D4
Daubeuf-la-Campagne (27) 35 H5
Daubeuf-près-Vatteville (27) 35 K4
Daubeuf-Serville (76) 14 E4
Daubèze (33) 230 B3
Dauendorf (67) 69 K6
Daumazan-sur-Arize (09) 288 A6
Daumeray (49) 105 J6
Dauphin (04) 278 B2
Dausse (47) 248 E2
Daux (31) 269 F5
Dauzat-sur-Vodable (63) 202 D6
Davayat (63) 185 F5
Davayé (71) 188 B1
Davejean (11) 309 H1
Davenescourt (80) 18 D4
Davézieux (07) 222 A2
Davignac (19) 200 D6
Davrey (10) 113 K2
Davron (78) 58 A3
Dax (40) 264 B4
Deauville (14) 33 J3
Deaux (30) 255 H6
Débats-Rivière-d'Orpra (42) 204 B2
Decazeville (12) 235 F6
Dechy (59) 11 J2
Décines-Charpieu (69) 206 C2
Decize (58) 151 G6
Dégagnac (46) 233 G4
Degré (72) 106 C2
Dehault (72) 83 H6
Déhéries (59) 12 B5
Dehlingen (67) 68 E4
Deinvillers (88) 94 E2
Delain (70) 137 G2
Delettes (62) 5 G4
Delincourt (60) 36 E4
Delle (90) 139 K2
Delme (57) 66 C2
Delouze-Rosières (55) 92 E1
le Déluge (60) 37 H4
Delut (55) 43 J2
Deluz (25) 138 B5
Demandolx (04) 279 K2
Demange-aux-Eaux (55) 64 D6
Demangevelle (70) 117 K3
Demi-Quartier (74) 192 A4
la Demie (70) 138 B1
Demigny (71) 154 A4
Démouville (14) 33 F5
Dému (32) 266 D4
Démuin (80) 18 D3
Denain (59) 12 C2
Dénat (81) 270 E3
Denazé (53) 104 D4
Denée (49) 125 G4
Dénestanville (76) 15 K3
Deneuille-lès-Chantelle (03) 185 F2
Deneuille-les-Mines (03) 167 J6
Deneuvre (54) 95 F2
Denèvre (70) 137 G2
Dénezé-sous-Doué (49) 125 K6
Dénezé-sous-le-Lude (49) 126 D3
Denezières (39) 173 J2
Denguin (64) 284 B3
Denicé (69) 188 A5
Denier (62) 10 B3
Denipaire (88) 95 J3
Dennebrœucq (62) 5 F5
Denneville (50) 28 C6
Dennevy (71) 153 J5
Denney (90) 119 J6
Denonville (28) 85 K3
Denting (57) 45 J4
Déols (36) 147 K6
Derbamont (88) 94 B4
Dercé (86) 145 F4

Derchigny (76) 16 A1
Dercy (02) 20 D4
Dernacueillette (11) 309 J3
Dernancourt (80) 18 D1
Derval (44) 103 F4
Désaignes (07) 221 J6
Désandans (25) 139 G2
Descartes (37) 146 A4
le Deschaux (39) 155 G4
le Désert (14) 31 K4
Désertines (03) 167 H6
Désertines (53) 80 E2
les Déserts (73) 208 C3
Déservillers (25) 156 C3
Desges (43) 219 H6
Desingy (74) 190 D4
Desmonts (45) 87 F6
Desnes (39) 155 G6
Desseling (57) 67 G3
Dessenheim (68) 96 D5
Dessia (39) 173 F5
Destord (88) 95 F4
la Destrousse (13) 296 E3
Destry (57) 66 E1
Desvres (62) 2 C6
Détain-et-Bruant (21) 153 K1
Détrier (73) 208 B5
le Détroit (14) 53 K3
Dettey (71) 170 C1
Dettwiller (67) 70 C1
Deuil-la-Barre (95) 58 E2
Deuillet (02) 20 A5
Deûlémont (59) 6 C3
Deux-Chaises (03) 168 B6
Deux-Évailles (53) 81 H6
les Deux-Fays (39) 155 G5
Deux-Jumeaux (14) 29 J6
Deux-Verges (15) 236 D3
les Deux-Villes (08) 23 H4
Deuxville (54) 66 D5
Devay (58) 151 H6
Devecey (25) 137 K5
Devesset (07) 221 J4
Devèze (65) 286 C5
Deviat (16) 196 C6
Dévillac (47) 232 B5
Deville (08) 22 D2
Déville-lès-Rouen (76) 35 H1
Devise (80) 19 H2
Devrouze (71) 154 D6
Deycimont (88) 95 F5
Deyme (31) 288 C2
Deyvillers (88) 94 E5
le Dézert (50) 31 G2
Dezize-lès-Maranges (71) 153 J5
D'Huison-Longueville (91) 86 E3
Dhuisy (77) 60 C1
Dhuizel (02) 40 B3
Dhuizon (41) 129 H2
Diancey (21) 153 F1
Diane-Capelle (57) 67 H4
Diant (77) 88 A5
Diarville (54) 94 A3
Diconne (71) 154 D6
Dicy (89) 112 B3
Didenheim (68) 97 C3
Die (26) 241 H3
Diebling (57) 68 C3
Diebolsheim (67) 71 D5
Diedendorf (67) 67 J2
Dieffenbach-au-Val (67) 71 A5
Dieffenbach-lès-Woerth (67) 25 A2
Dieffenthal (67) 71 B5
Dieffmatten (68) 97 A3
Dième (69) 187 J5
Diemeringen (67) 67 K1
Diémoz (38) 206 D4
Diénay (21) 136 A3
Dienne (15) 218 B4
Dienné (86) 163 H5
Diennes-Aubigny (58) 151 J5
Dienville (10) 91 F4
Dieppe (76) 15 K1
Dieppe-sous-Douaumont (55) 26 A6
Dierre (37) 128 B5
Dierrey-Saint-Julien (10) 89 J4
Dierrey-Saint-Pierre (10) 89 J4
Diesen (57) 45 K4
Dietwiller (68) 97 C3
Dieudonné (60) 37 J4
Dieue-sur-Meuse (55) 43 J6
Dieulefit (26) 240 E6
Dieulivol (33) 230 E4
Dieulouard (54) 65 K3
Dieupentale (82) 269 F3
Dieuze (57) 67 F3
Diéval (62) 10 C1
Diffembach-lès-Hellimer (57) 68 B4
Diges (89) 112 E6
Digna (39) 172 E4
Dignac (16) 197 F4
la Digne-d'Amont (11) 308 E2
la Digne-d'Aval (11) 308 E2
Digne-les-Bains (04) 259 J5
Dignonville (88) 94 D1
Digny (28) 84 D2
Digoin (71) 170 A4
Digosville (50) 28 D2
Diguilleville (50) 28 A1
Dijon (21) 136 A5
Dimancheville (45) 87 F5
Dimbsthal (67) 70 B2

Dimechaux (59) 13 H4
Dimont (59) 13 H4
Dinan (22) 50 D5
Dinard (35) 50 D3
Dinéault (29) 74 C3
Dingé (35) 79 G1
Dingsheim (67) 70 E2
Dingy-en-Vuache (74) 190 D3
Dingy-Saint-Clair (74) 191 G5
Dinozé (88) 94 D6
Dinsac (87) 181 F2
Dinsheim (67) 70 C4
Dinteville (52) 115 H2
Dio-et-Valquières (34) 273 F5
Dionay (38) 223 F3
Dions (30) 275 G2
Diors (36) 148 B6
Diou (03) 169 J4
Diou (36) 148 D3
Dirac (16) 197 F4
Dirinon (29) 46 C6
Dirol (58) 133 H5
Dissangis (89) 134 A2
Dissay (86) 163 G2
Dissay-sous-Courcillon (72) 127 G1
Dissé-sous-Ballon (72) 83 F5
Dissé-sous-le-Lude (72) 126 D2
Distré (49) 144 C1
Distroff (57) 27 H4
Diusse (64) 285 F1
Divajeu (26) 240 D4
Dives (60) 19 G6
Dives-sur-Mer (14) 33 G3
Divion (62) 5 J6
Divonne-les-Bains (01) 174 C5
Dixmont (89) 112 E2
Dizimieu (38) 207 F2
Dizy (51) 40 E6
Dizy-le-Gros (02) 21 G5
Doazit (40) 265 F5
Doazon (64) 284 B2
Docelles (88) 95 F6
Doeuil-sur-le-Mignon (17) 177 K3
Dognen (64) 283 J4
Dogneville (88) 94 D5
Dohem (62) 3 F6
Dohis (02) 21 H3
Doignies (59) 11 H5
Doingt (80) 19 G1
Doissat (24) 232 D4
Doissin (38) 207 G5
Doix (85) 160 D5
Doizieux (42) 205 J6
Dol-de-Bretagne (35) 51 F4
Dolaincourt (88) 93 H4
Dolancourt (10) 91 G5
Dolcourt (54) 93 J2
Dole (39) 155 G2
Dolignon (02) 21 H4
Dolleren (68) 119 J4
Dollon (72) 107 H2
Dollot (89) 88 B6
Dolmayrac (47) 248 B2
Dolo (22) 50 A6
Dolomieu (38) 207 H3
Dolus-d'Oléron (17) 176 C5
Dolus-le-Sec (37) 146 C2
Dolving (57) 67 J3
Dom-le-Mesnil (08) 22 E4
Domagné (35) 79 J5
Domaize (63) 203 H3
Domalain (35) 104 A2
Domancy (74) 192 A5
Domarin (38) 206 E4
Domart-en-Ponthieu (80) 9 J5
Domart-sur-la-Luce (80) 18 C3
Domats (89) 112 B1
Domazan (30) 275 K2
Dombasle-devant-Darney (88) 93 K6
Dombasle-en-Argonne (55) 43 G5
Dombasle-en-Xaintois (88) 93 J4
Dombasle-sur-Meurthe (54) 66 C5
Domblain (52) 91 K2
Domblans (39) 155 H6
Dombras (55) 26 A4
Dombrot-le-Sec (88) 93 J6
Dombrot-sur-Vair (88) 93 H4
Domecy-sur-Cure (89) 133 J4
Domecy-sur-le-Vault (89) 133 J3
Doméliers (60) 17 K5
Domène (38) 224 B3
Domérat (03) 167 G6
Domesmont (80) 9 K5
Domessargues (30) 274 E1
Domessin (73) 207 K4
Domèvre-en-Haye (54) 65 J3
Domèvre-sous-Montfort (88) 93 K5
Domèvre-sur-Avière (88) 94 C5
Domèvre-sur-Durbion (88) 94 D4
Domèvre-sur-Vezouze (54) 67 G6
Domeyrat (43) 219 J3
Domeyrot (23) 183 G2
Domezain-Berraute (64) 283 G3
Domfaing (88) 95 G4
Domfessel (67) 67 K1
Domfront (60) 18 D5
Domfront (61) 53 G6
Domfront-en-Champagne (72) 106 C1
Domgermain (54) 65 H5
la Dominelais (35) 103 F3
Dominois (80) 9 G2
Domjean (50) 31 H4

Domjevin (54) 67 F6
Domjulien (88) 93 J5
Domléger-Longvillers (80) 9 J4
Domloup (35) 79 H5
Dommarie-Eulmont (54) 93 K2
Dommarien (52) 116 D6
Dommartemont (54) 66 B4
Dommartin (01) 172 A6
Dommartin (25) 156 E4
Dommartin (58) 152 A3
Dommartin (69) 205 K1
Dommartin (80) 18 B3
Dommartin-aux-Bois (88) 94 B6
Dommartin-Dampierre (51) 42 C6
Dommartin-la-Chaussée (54) 65 H1
Dommartin-la-Montagne (55) 43 H6
Dommartin-le-Coq (10) 90 D2
Dommartin-le-Franc (52) 91 K3
Dommartin-le-Saint-Père (52) 91 J3
Dommartin-lès-Cuiseaux (71) 172 D4
Dommartin-lès-Remiremont (88) . . . 119 F2
Dommartin-lès-Toul (54) 65 H5
Dommartin-lès-Vallois (88) 94 A6
Dommartin-Lettrée (51) 62 C4
Dommartin-sous-Amance (54) 66 B4
Dommartin-sous-Hans (51) 42 C5
Dommartin-sur-Vraine (88) 93 J4
Dommartin-Varimont (51) 63 H2
Dommary-Baroncourt (55) 26 C5
Domme (24) 233 F3
Dommery (08) 22 B4
Dommiers (02) 39 H3
Domnon-lès-Dieuze (57) 67 G2
Domont (95) 58 E1
Dompaire (88) 94 B5
Dompcevrin (55) 64 D2
Dompierre (60) 18 D6
Dompierre (61) 53 H6
Dompierre (88) 94 E4
Dompierre-aux-Bois (55) 64 E1
Dompierre-Becquincourt (80) 19 F2
Dompierre-du-Chemin (35) 80 B4
Dompierre-les-Églises (87) 181 H2
Dompierre-les-Ormes (71) 171 F6
Dompierre-les-Tilleuls (25) 156 D5
Dompierre-sous-Sanvignes (71) . . . 170 D2
Dompierre-sur-Authie (80) 9 J3
Dompierre-sur-Besbre (03) 169 H4
Dompierre-sur-Chalaronne (01) . . . 188 D3
Dompierre-sur-Charente (17) 195 H2
Dompierre-sur-Helpe (59) 13 G4
Dompierre-sur-Héry (58) 133 G6
Dompierre-sur-Mer (17) 176 E2
Dompierre-sur-Mont (39) 173 G3
Dompierre-sur-Nièvre (58) 150 E1
Dompierre-sur-Veyle (01) 189 G4
Dompierre-sur-Yon (85) 141 K6
Dompnac (07) 238 E6
Domprel (25) 138 E6
Dompremy (51) 63 G5
Domprix (54) 26 C5
Domps (87) 199 K3
Domptail (88) 94 E2
Domptail-en-l'Air (54) 94 C1
Domptin (02) 60 D1
Domqueur (80) 9 J5
Domremy-la-Canne (55) 26 C5
Domrémy-la-Pucelle (88) 93 F2
Domremy-Landéville (52) 92 C3
Domsure (01) 172 D5
Domvallier (88) 93 K4
Domvast (80) 9 H4
Don (59) 6 C5
Donazac (11) 308 D1
Donchery (08) 22 E4
Doncières (88) 95 F2
Doncourt-aux-Templiers (55) 44 B6
Doncourt-lès-Conflans (54) 44 B5
Doncourt-lès-Longuyon (54) 26 C3
Doncourt-sur-Meuse (52) 93 F6
Dondas (47) 248 D4
Donges (44) 122 B2
Donjeux (52) 92 B3
Donjeux (57) 66 C2
le Donjon (03) 169 J6
Donnay (14) 53 J2
Donnazac (81) 270 C1
Donnelay (57) 67 F4
Donnemain-Saint-Mamès (28) . . . 109 F1
Donnemarie-Dontilly (77) 88 C2
Donnement (10) 90 E2
Donnenheim (67) 70 E1
Donnery (45) 110 C4
Donneville (31) 288 C2
Donnezac (33) 211 J2
Dontreix (23) 184 A5
Dontrien (51) 41 J4
Donville-les-Bains (50) 30 C6
Donzac (33) 230 A4
Donzac (82) 248 D6
Donzacq (40) 264 D5
le Donzeil (23) 182 E5
Donzenac (19) 215 J3
Donzère (26) 256 D1
Donzy (58) 132 C5
Donzy-le-National (71) 171 G5
Donzy-le-Pertuis (71) 171 J5
Doranges (63) 219 K1
Dorans (90) 139 H1
Dorat (63) 185 K6
le Dorat (87) 181 F2

Dorceau (61) 83 K3
Dordives (45) 111 J1
Dore-l'Église (63) 220 A1
la Dorée (53) 80 D2
Dorengt (02) 20 D1
Dorlisheim (67) 70 D4
Dormans (51) 40 E6
Dormelles (77) 87 K4
la Dornac (24) 215 G5
Dornas (07) 239 G2
Dornecy (58) 133 G4
Dornes (58) 168 E2
Dornot (57) 44 E6
Dorres (66) 313 G5
Dortan (01) 173 H6
Dosches (10) 90 C4
Dosnon (10) 62 C6
Dossenheim-Kochersberg (67) 70 D2
Dossenheim-sur-Zinsel (67) 69 G6
Douadic (36) 164 C2
Douai (59) 11 H2
Douains (27) 57 F1
Douarnenez (29) 73 K4
Douaumont (55) 26 A6
Doubs (25) 157 F4
Doucelles (72) 82 D5
Douchapt (24) 213 H3
Douchy (02) 19 J3
Douchy (45) 112 B3
Douchy-lès-Ayette (62) 10 E4
Douchy-les-Mines (59) 12 C2
Doucier (39) 173 J2
Doucy-en-Bauges (73) 208 D2
Doudeauville (62) 4 C4
Doudeauville (76) 17 F6
Doudeauville-en-Vexin (27) 36 C3
Doudelainville (80) 9 F6
Doudeville (76) 15 G4
Doudrac (47) 231 K4
Doue (77) 60 C3
Doué-la-Fontaine (49) 144 A1
le Douhet (17) 195 G1
Douillet (72) 82 B5
Douilly (80) 19 H3
Doulaincourt-Saucourt (52) 92 B4
Doulcon (55) 43 F2
Doulevant-le-Château (52) 91 J3
Doulevant-le-Petit (52) 91 K2
Doulezon (33) 230 D3
le Doulieu (59) 6 A3
Doullens (80) 10 B4
Doumely-Bégny (08) 21 K5
Doumy (64) 284 D2
Dounoux (88) 94 D6
Dourbies (30) 254 A6
Dourdain (35) 79 K3
Dourdan (91) 86 B2
Dourges (62) 11 G1
Dourgne (81) 289 J2
Douriez (62) 9 G2
le Dourn (81) 271 H1
Dournazac (87) 198 B4
Dournon (39) 156 B4
Dours (65) 285 J4
Doussard (74) 208 E1
Doussay (86) 145 F5
Douvaine (74) 174 D6
Douville (24) 213 J6
Douville-en-Auge (14) 33 H4
Douville-sur-Andelle (27) 35 K3
Douvrend (76) 16 C2
Douvres (01) 189 H4
Douvres-la-Délivrande (14) 32 E3
Douvrin (62) 6 B6
Doux (08) 41 J1
Doux (79) 162 C1
Douy (28) 108 E2
Douy-la-Ramée (77) 59 K1
Douzains (47) 231 J5
Douzat (16) 196 C2
la Douze (24) 214 B5
Douzens (11) 290 D6
Douzillac (24) 213 H5
Douzy (08) 23 G4
Doville (50) 28 D6
Doye (39) 156 C6
Doyet (03) 184 C1
Dozulé (14) 33 H4
Dracé (69) 188 B3
Draché (37) 145 K3
Drachenbronn-Birlenbach (67) 25 B2
Dracy (89) 112 D6
Dracy-le-Fort (71) 153 K6
Dracy-lès-Couches (71) 153 H5
Dracy-Saint-Loup (71) 153 F3
Dragey-Ronthon (50) 51 J2
Draguignan (83) 279 J6
Drain (49) 124 A5
Draix (04) 260 A4
Draize (08) 21 K5
Drambon (21) 136 D5
Dramelay (39) 173 G5
Drancy (93) 59 F3
Drap (06) 281 H3
Dravegny (02) 40 B4
Draveil (91) 59 F4
Drée (21) 135 H5
Dréfféac (44) 102 C6
Drémil-Lafage (31) 269 J6
le Drennec (29) 46 B4

Dreuil-lès-Amiens (80) . . . 18 A2
Dreuilhe (09) . . . 308 B3
Dreux (28) . . . 57 F5
Drevant (18) . . . 167 G2
Dricourt (08) . . . 41 K2
Driencourt (80) . . . 19 H1
Drincham (59) . . . 3 G3
Drocourt (62) . . . 11 G1
Drocourt (78) . . . 57 J1
Droisy (27) . . . 56 D4
Droisy (74) . . . 190 D5
Droiturier (03) . . . 186 B5
Droizy (02) . . . 39 K4
Drom (01) . . . 189 H2
Dromesnil (80) . . . 17 G2
Drosay (76) . . . 15 G3
Drosnay (51) . . . 91 F1
Droué (41) . . . 108 C2
Droue-sur-Drouette (28) . . . 85 J1
Drouges (35) . . . 104 A3
Drouilly (51) . . . 62 E4
Droupt-Saint-Basle (10) . . . 89 K2
Droupt-Sainte-Marie (10) . . . 89 K2
Drouville (54) . . . 66 C5
Drouvin-le-Marais (62) . . . 6 A6
Droux (87) . . . 181 H1
Droyes (52) . . . 91 G2
Drubec (14) . . . 33 J4
Drucat (80) . . . 9 G4
Drucourt (27) . . . 34 C6
Drudas (31) . . . 268 C4
Druelle (12) . . . 252 A3
Drugeac (15) . . . 217 H4
Druillat (01) . . . 189 H4
Drulhe (12) . . . 251 G1
Drulingen (67) . . . 67 K2
Drumettaz-Clarafond (73) . . . 208 B3
Drusenheim (67) . . . 25 C4
Druy-Parigny (58) . . . 151 G5
Druye (37) . . . 127 G5
Druyes-les-Belles-
  Fontaines (89) . . . 132 E3
Dry (45) . . . 109 J5
Duault (22) . . . 75 K2
Ducey (50) . . . 52 A6
Duclair (76) . . . 35 F1
Ducy-Sainte-Marguerite (14) . . . 32 C4
Duerne (69) . . . 205 H3
Duesme (21) . . . 135 G1
Duffort (32) . . . 286 B4
Dugny (93) . . . 59 F2
Dugny-sur-Meuse (55) . . . 43 H6
Duhort-Bachen (40) . . . 265 J4
Duilhac-sous-Peyrepertuse (11) . . . 309 H4
Duingt (74) . . . 191 H6
Duisans (62) . . . 10 E2
Dullin (73) . . . 207 K4
Dumes (40) . . . 265 F5
Dun (09) . . . 308 A2
Dun-le-Palestel (23) . . . 182 B1
Dun-le-Poëlier (36) . . . 148 A1
Dun-les-Places (58) . . . 134 A6
Dun-sur-Auron (18) . . . 149 J5
Dun-sur-Grandry (58) . . . 152 A3
Dun-sur-Meuse (55) . . . 43 F2
Duneau (72) . . . 107 H2
Dunes (82) . . . 248 D6
Dunet (36) . . . 164 E5
Dung (25) . . . 139 G2
Dunières (43) . . . 221 G3
Dunières-sur-Eyrieux (07) . . . 240 A2
Dunkerque (59) . . . 3 H1
Duntzenheim (67) . . . 70 D2
Duppigheim (67) . . . 70 E4
Duran (32) . . . 267 H5
Durance (47) . . . 247 G5
Duranus (06) . . . 281 G1
Duranville (27) . . . 34 C5
Duras (47) . . . 230 E4
Duravel (46) . . . 232 D6
Durban (32) . . . 286 C4
Durban-Corbières (11) . . . 310 B2
Durban-sur-Arize (09) . . . 307 F2
Durbans (46) . . . 234 B4
Durcet (61) . . . 53 J4
Durdat-Larequille (03) . . . 184 B2
Dureil (72) . . . 106 A4
Durenque (12) . . . 252 C6
Durfort (09) . . . 288 C5
Durfort (81) . . . 289 J3
Durfort-et-Saint-Martin-
  de-Sossenac (30) . . . 274 C1
Durfort-Lacapelette (82) . . . 249 G5
Durlinsdorf (68) . . . 97 B6
Durmenach (68) . . . 97 C5
Durmignat (63) . . . 184 D3
Durnes (25) . . . 156 D2
Durningen (67) . . . 70 D2
Durrenbach (67) . . . 25 A3
Durrenentzen (68) . . . 96 D4
Durstel (67) . . . 67 K2
Durtal (49) . . . 125 K1
Durtol (63) . . . 202 D2
Dury (02) . . . 19 J4
Dury (62) . . . 11 G3
Dury (80) . . . 18 A2
Dussac (24) . . . 214 E1
Duttlenheim (67) . . . 70 D4
Duvy (60) . . . 38 E4
Duzey (55) . . . 26 B4
Dyé (89) . . . 113 J4
Dyo (71) . . . 170 D6

E

Eancé (35) . . . 104 A4
Eaubonne (95) . . . 58 E2
Eaucourt-sur-Somme (80) . . . 9 G5
Eaunes (31) . . . 288 B3
Eaux-Bonnes (64) . . . 303 G1
Eaux-Puiseaux (10) . . . 113 K1
Eauze (32) . . . 266 D3
Ebaty (21) . . . 153 K4
Ebblinghem (59) . . . 3 H5
Eberbach-Seltz (67) . . . 25 D2
Ebersheim (67) . . . 71 B5
Ebersmunster (67) . . . 71 C4
Ébersviller (57) . . . 27 J5
Éblange (57) . . . 27 K6
Ébouleau (02) . . . 21 F4
Ebréon (16) . . . 179 F5
Ébreuil (03) . . . 185 F3
l'Écaille (08) . . . 41 G2
Écaillon (59) . . . 11 J2
Écalles-Alix (76) . . . 15 H5
Écaquelon (27) . . . 34 E4
Écardenville-la-Campagne (27) . . . 35 F6
Écardenville-sur-Eure (27) . . . 35 K6
Écausseville (50) . . . 29 F4
Écauville (27) . . . 35 G6
Eccica-Suarella (2A) . . . 320 D5
Eccles (59) . . . 13 J3
Échalas (69) . . . 205 K4
Échallat (16) . . . 196 C2
Échallon (01) . . . 190 B2
Échalot (21) . . . 135 J2
Échalou (61) . . . 53 H5
Échandelys (63) . . . 203 H5
Échannay (21) . . . 135 G4
Écharcon (91) . . . 87 F1
Échassières (03) . . . 184 D3
Échauffour (61) . . . 55 G5
Échavanne (70) . . . 119 G6
Échay (25) . . . 156 B3
Echebrune (17) . . . 195 H4
l'Échelle (08) . . . 22 B3
l'Échelle-Saint-Aurin (80) . . . 18 E4
les Échelles (73) . . . 207 K6
Échemines (10) . . . 89 J3
Échemiré (49) . . . 126 A2
Échenans (25) . . . 139 G2
Échenans-sous-Mont-Vaudois (70) . . . 139 G1
Échenay (52) . . . 92 C2
Échenevex (01) . . . 174 B6
Échenon (21) . . . 154 E2
Échenoz-la-Méline (70) . . . 138 B1
Échenoz-le-Sec (70) . . . 138 A2
Échevannes (21) . . . 136 B2
Échevannes (25) . . . 156 D2
Échevis (26) . . . 223 H5
Échevronne (21) . . . 154 A2
Échigey (21) . . . 154 D1
Échillais (17) . . . 177 F6
Échilleuses (45) . . . 87 F6
Echinghen (62) . . . 2 B5
Échiré (79) . . . 161 H5
Échirolles (38) . . . 224 A4
Échouboulains (77) . . . 88 A3
Échourgnac (24) . . . 213 F4
Eckartswiller (67) . . . 70 B1
Eckbolsheim (67) . . . 71 D1
Eckwersheim (67) . . . 25 A5
Éclaibes (59) . . . 13 G4
Éclaires (51) . . . 63 K1
Éclance (10) . . . 91 G4
Éclans-Nenon (39) . . . 155 H2
Eclaron-Braucourt-
  Sainte-Livière (52) . . . 91 J1
Eclassan (07) . . . 222 B4
Écleux (39) . . . 155 J3
Éclimeux (62) . . . 9 K1
Eclose (38) . . . 207 F5
Éclusier-Vaux (80) . . . 19 F1
Écluzelles (28) . . . 57 F5
Écly (08) . . . 21 K6
Écoche (42) . . . 187 H3
Écoivres (62) . . . 10 A2
École (73) . . . 208 E3
École-Valentin (25) . . . 137 K5
Écollemont (51) . . . 63 G6
Écommoy (72) . . . 106 E5
Écoquenéauville (50) . . . 29 F5
Écorcei (61) . . . 55 H5
les Écorces (25) . . . 139 H6
Écorches (61) . . . 54 D3
Écordal (08) . . . 22 C6
Écorpain (72) . . . 107 J3
Écos (27) . . . 36 C5
Écot (25) . . . 139 G3
Écot-la-Combe (52) . . . 92 D5
Écotay-l'Olme (42) . . . 204 C4
Écouché (61) . . . 54 B5
Écouen (95) . . . 58 E1
Écouflant (49) . . . 125 G2
Écouis (27) . . . 36 B3
Écourt-Saint-Quentin (62) . . . 11 H3
Écoust-Saint-Mein (62) . . . 11 G4
Écouviez (55) . . . 26 A2
l'Écouvotte (25) . . . 138 C4
Écoyeux (17) . . . 195 H1
Ecquedecques (62) . . . 5 J5
Ecques (62) . . . 3 G6
Ecquetot (27) . . . 35 H5
Ecquevilly (78) . . . 58 A2

Écrainville (76) . . . 14 C5
Écrammeville (14) . . . 29 J6
les Écrennes (77) . . . 87 K2
Écretteville-lès-Baons (76) . . . 15 F5
Écretteville-sur-Mer (76) . . . 14 E3
Écriennes (51) . . . 63 G5
Écrille (39) . . . 173 G4
Écromagny (70) . . . 118 E4
Écrosnes (28) . . . 85 J2
Écrouves (54) . . . 65 H5
Ectot-l'Auber (76) . . . 15 H5
Ectot-lès-Baons (76) . . . 15 H5
Écueil (51) . . . 40 E5
Écueillé (36) . . . 147 G3
Écuélin (59) . . . 13 G4
Écuelle (70) . . . 137 F2
Écuelles (71) . . . 154 C4
Écuelles (77) . . . 87 J4
Écuillé (49) . . . 125 G1
Écuires (62) . . . 4 C5
Écuisses (71) . . . 171 G1
Éculleville (50) . . . 28 B1
Écully (69) . . . 206 A2
Écuras (16) . . . 197 J3
Écurat (17) . . . 195 F1
Écurcey (25) . . . 139 H3
Écurey-en-Verdunois (55) . . . 43 H2
Écurie (62) . . . 10 E2
Écury-le-Repos (51) . . . 62 A4
Écury-sur-Coole (51) . . . 62 D3
Écutigny (21) . . . 153 J2
Écuvilly (60) . . . 19 G5
Edern (29) . . . 74 E4
Edon (16) . . . 197 G5
les Éduts (17) . . . 178 C5
Eecke (59) . . . 3 K5
Effiat (63) . . . 185 G4
Effincourt (52) . . . 92 C2
Effry (02) . . . 21 G1
Égat (66) . . . 313 H4
Égleny (89) . . . 112 E5
Égletons (19) . . . 216 D1
Égligny (77) . . . 88 B3
Eglingen (68) . . . 97 A3
l'Église-aux-Bois (19) . . . 200 A4
Église-Neuve-de-Vergt (24) . . . 214 A5
Église-Neuve-d'Issac (24) . . . 213 H6
Égliseneuve-d'Entraigues (63) . . . 218 D1
Égliseneuve-des-Liards (63) . . . 203 G4
Égliseneuve-près-Billom (63) . . . 203 G3
les Églises-d'Argenteuil (17) . . . 178 A5
Églisolles (63) . . . 204 B6
les Églisottes-et-Chalaures (33) . . . 212 C4
Égly (91) . . . 86 D1
Egreville (77) . . . 87 K6
Égriselles-le-Bocage (89) . . . 112 C1
Egry (45) . . . 111 F1
Éguelshardt (57) . . . 69 H3
Eguenigue (90) . . . 119 J6
l'Éguille (17) . . . 194 C2
Éguilles (13) . . . 277 H6
Éguilly (21) . . . 135 F5
Éguilly-sous-Bois (10) . . . 115 F1
Éguisheim (68) . . . 96 B4
Éguzon-Chantôme (36) . . . 165 H5
Éhuns (70) . . . 118 C5
Eichhoffen (67) . . . 70 C6
Eincheville (57) . . . 66 E1
Einvaux (54) . . . 94 C1
Einville-au-Jard (54) . . . 66 D5
Élan (08) . . . 22 D4
Élancourt (78) . . . 58 B4
Elbach (68) . . . 119 K6
Elbeuf (76) . . . 35 H4
Elbeuf-en-Bray (76) . . . 36 D1
Elbeuf-sur-Andelle (76) . . . 36 A1
Élencourt (60) . . . 17 H4
Élesmes (59) . . . 13 H2
Életot (76) . . . 14 D3
Éleu-dit-Leauwette (62) . . . 11 F1
Élincourt (59) . . . 12 B6
Élincourt-Sainte-Marguerite (60) . . . 38 D1
Élise-Daucourt (51) . . . 63 H1
Ellecourt (76) . . . 17 F3
Elliant (29) . . . 75 F6
Ellon (14) . . . 32 B4
Elne (66) . . . 315 H3
Elnes (62) . . . 3 F6
Éloie (90) . . . 119 H5
Éloise (74) . . . 190 C3
Éloyes (88) . . . 95 F6
Elsenheim (67) . . . 71 C6
Elvange (57) . . . 45 J6
Elven (56) . . . 101 H4
Elzange (57) . . . 27 H4
Émagny (25) . . . 137 J5
Émalleville (27) . . . 35 J6
Émancé (78) . . . 85 J1
Émanville (27) . . . 56 B1
Émanville (76) . . . 15 J5
Emberménil (54) . . . 67 F5
Embres-et-Castelmaure (11) . . . 310 D3
Embreville (80) . . . 8 D6
Embrun (05) . . . 243 J5
Embry (62) . . . 4 E6
Émerainville (77) . . . 59 H4
Émerchicourt (59) . . . 11 K2
Émeringes (69) . . . 188 B2
Émeville (60) . . . 39 F4
Émiéville (14) . . . 33 F5
Emlingen (68) . . . 97 B4

Emmerin (59) . . . 6 D4
Émondeville (50) . . . 29 F4
Empeaux (31) . . . 287 J1
Empurany (07) . . . 221 K5
Empuré (16) . . . 179 F4
Empury (58) . . . 133 J5
Encausse (32) . . . 268 C5
Encausse-les-Thermes (31) . . . 305 K2
Enchastrayes (04) . . . 260 D1
Enchenberg (57) . . . 69 G4
Encourtiech (09) . . . 306 E3
Endoufielle (32) . . . 287 H1
Énencourt-le-Sec (60) . . . 37 F4
Énencourt-Léage (60) . . . 36 E3
Enfonvelle (52) . . . 117 H3
Engayrac (47) . . . 248 E4
Engente (10) . . . 91 H5
Engenville (45) . . . 86 D5
Enghien-les-Bains (95) . . . 58 E2
Engins (38) . . . 223 K3
Englancourt (02) . . . 20 E1
Englebelmer (80) . . . 10 D5
Englefontaine (59) . . . 12 E4
Englesqueville-en-Auge (14) . . . 33 J4
Englesqueville-la-Percée (14) . . . 29 J6
Englos (59) . . . 6 D4
Engomer (09) . . . 306 C3
Enguinegatte (62) . . . 5 G4
Engwiller (67) . . . 69 G5
Ennemain (80) . . . 19 G2
Ennery (57) . . . 27 H6
Ennery (95) . . . 58 C2
Ennetières-en-Weppes (59) . . . 6 C4
Ennevelin (59) . . . 6 E5
Ennezat (63) . . . 185 G5
Ennordres (18) . . . 130 E4
Enquin-les-Mines (62) . . . 5 G5
Enquin-sur-Baillons (62) . . . 4 C5
Ens (65) . . . 305 F5
Ensignè (79) . . . 178 C3
Ensuès-la-Redonne (13) . . . 296 A5
Entrages (04) . . . 259 K6
Entraigues (38) . . . 242 D1
Entraigues (63) . . . 185 G6
Entraigues-sur-la-Sorgue (84) . . . 276 C1
Entrains-sur-Nohain (58) . . . 132 C4
Entrammes (53) . . . 105 F2
Entrange (57) . . . 27 G3
Entraunes (06) . . . 260 E4
Entraygues-sur-Truyère (12) . . . 235 J3
Entre-deux-Eaux (88) . . . 95 J4
Entre-deux-Guiers (38) . . . 207 K6
Entre-deux-Monts (39) . . . 174 A2
Entrecasteaux (83) . . . 298 D3
Entrechaux (84) . . . 257 H4
Entremont (74) . . . 191 H4
Éntremont-le-Vieux (73) . . . 208 B5
Entrepierres (04) . . . 259 G4
Entrevaux (04) . . . 280 C1
Entrevennes (04) . . . 278 A2
Entrevernes (74) . . . 208 E1
Entzheim (67) . . . 70 E4
Enval (63) . . . 184 E6
Enveitg (66) . . . 313 G5
Envermeu (76) . . . 16 B2
Environville (76) . . . 15 F5
Éourres (05) . . . 258 D4
Eoux (31) . . . 287 F2
Épagne (10) . . . 90 E3
Épagne-Epagnette (80) . . . 9 G5
Épagny (21) . . . 136 A3
Épagny (74) . . . 191 F5
Épaignes (27) . . . 34 B4
Épaney (14) . . . 54 B2
Épannes (79) . . . 177 J2
Éparcy (02) . . . 21 H2
les Éparges (55) . . . 43 K6
Épargnes (17) . . . 194 E4
les Éparres (38) . . . 207 F4
Épaumesnil (80) . . . 17 G2
Épaux-Bézu (02) . . . 39 J6
Épeautrolles (28) . . . 84 E4
Épécamps (80) . . . 9 K5
Épégard (27) . . . 35 F5
Épehy (80) . . . 11 J6
Épeigné-les-Bois (37) . . . 128 C6
Épeigné-sur-Dême (37) . . . 127 H1
Épénancourt (80) . . . 19 G2
Épenède (16) . . . 180 A4
Épenouse (25) . . . 138 D6
Épenoy (25) . . . 157 F1
Épense (51) . . . 63 H2
Épercieux-Saint-Paul (42) . . . 204 E2
Éperlecques (62) . . . 3 F4
Épernay (51) . . . 61 K1
Épernay-sous-Gevrey (21) . . . 154 B2
Épernon (28) . . . 85 J1
Éperrais (61) . . . 83 H3
Épersy (73) . . . 208 B2
Épertully (71) . . . 153 J4
Épervans (71) . . . 171 K1
les Epesses (85) . . . 142 E5
Épeugney (25) . . . 156 B2
Épfig (67) . . . 70 C6
Épiais (41) . . . 108 E3
Épiais-lès-Louvres (95) . . . 59 G1
Épiais-Rhus (95) . . . 37 K5
Épieds (02) . . . 39 K6
Épieds (27) . . . 57 F2
Épieds (49) . . . 144 D2

Épieds-en-Beauce (45) . . . 109 H3
Épierre (73) . . . 209 H5
Épiez-sur-Chiers (54) . . . 26 A3
Épiez-sur-Meuse (55) . . . 93 F1
Épinac (71) . . . 153 H4
Épinal (88) . . . 94 D5
Épinay (27) . . . 55 J3
Épinay-Champlâtreux (95) . . . 38 A5
l'Épinay-le-Comte (61) . . . 80 E2
Épinay-sous-Sénart (91) . . . 59 G5
Épinay-sur-Duclair (76) . . . 15 H6
Épinay-sur-Odon (14) . . . 32 B6
Épinay-sur-Orge (91) . . . 58 E6
Épinay-sur-Seine (93) . . . 58 E2
l'Épine (05) . . . 258 C1
l'Épine (51) . . . 62 E2
l'Épine (85) . . . 140 B3
l'Épine-aux-Bois (02) . . . 60 E1
Epineu-les-Voves (89) . . . 113 F3
Épineu-le-Chevreuil (72) . . . 106 B2
Épineuil (89) . . . 114 A4
Épineuil-le-Fleuriel (18) . . . 167 H4
Épineuse (60) . . . 38 B2
Épineux-le-Seguin (53) . . . 105 J3
Épiniac (35) . . . 51 G5
Épinonville (55) . . . 42 E3
Épinouze (26) . . . 222 C2
Épinoy (62) . . . 11 J3
Épiry (58) . . . 151 K1
Épisy (77) . . . 87 J4
Épizon (52) . . . 92 C3
Éplessier (80) . . . 17 H3
Éply (54) . . . 66 A2
Époisses (21) . . . 134 C3
Épône (78) . . . 57 K2
Épothémont (10) . . . 91 G3
Épouville (76) . . . 14 B6
Époye (51) . . . 41 H3
Eppe-Sauvage (59) . . . 13 K5
Eppes (02) . . . 20 E5
Eppeville (80) . . . 19 H4
Epping (57) . . . 69 F2
Épretot (76) . . . 14 C6
Épreville (76) . . . 14 D4
Épreville-en-Lieuvin (27) . . . 34 C5
Épreville-en-Roumois (27) . . . 34 E4
Épreville-près-le-Neubourg (27) . . . 35 F5
Épron (14) . . . 32 E4
Eps (62) . . . 5 G6
Épuisay (41) . . . 108 B4
Équancourt (80) . . . 11 H6
Équemauville (14) . . . 33 K2
Équennes-Eramecourt (80) . . . 17 H4
Équeurdreville-Hainneville (50) . . . 28 C2
Équevillon (39) . . . 156 B6
Équevilley (70) . . . 118 B5
Équihen-Plage (62) . . . 2 A6
Équilly (50) . . . 51 K1
Équirre (62) . . . 5 G6
Éragny (95) . . . 58 C1
Éragny-sur-Epte (60) . . . 36 E3
Eraines (14) . . . 54 B2
Éraville (16) . . . 196 B4
Erbajolo (2B) . . . 319 G6
Erbéviller-sur-Amezule (54) . . . 66 C4
Erbray (44) . . . 103 K4
Erbrée (35) . . . 104 B1
Ercé (09) . . . 307 F4
Ercé-en-Lamée (35) . . . 103 H4
Ercé-près-Liffré (35) . . . 79 H2
Erceville (45) . . . 86 B5
Erches (80) . . . 18 E4
Ercheu (80) . . . 19 G4
Erchin (59) . . . 11 J2
Erching (57) . . . 69 F2
Erckartswiller (67) . . . 69 G5
Ercourt (80) . . . 9 F4
Ercuis (60) . . . 37 K4
Erdeven (56) . . . 100 B5
Éréac (22) . . . 78 A2
Ergersheim (67) . . . 70 D3
Ergnies (80) . . . 9 J5
Ergny (62) . . . 4 E5
Ergué-Gabéric (29) . . . 74 D6
Érin (62) . . . 9 K1
Eringes (21) . . . 134 E2
Eringhem (59) . . . 3 H3
Érize-la-Brûlée (55) . . . 64 C3
Érize-la-Petite (55) . . . 64 B2
Érize-Saint-Dizier (55) . . . 64 C3
Erlon (02) . . . 20 D4
Erloy (02) . . . 20 E1
Ermenonville (60) . . . 38 C6
Ermenonville-la-Grande (28) . . . 85 F4
Ermenonville-la-Petite (28) . . . 85 F5
Ermenouville (76) . . . 15 G3
Ermont (95) . . . 58 D2
Ernée (53) . . . 80 D4
Ernemont-Boutavent (60) . . . 17 G4
Ernemont-la-Villette (76) . . . 36 D2
Ernemont-sur-Buchy (76) . . . 16 C6
Ernes (14) . . . 54 B1
Ernestviller (57) . . . 68 C3
Erneville-aux-Bois (55) . . . 64 D4
Ernolsheim-Bruche (67) . . . 70 D4
Ernolsheim-lès-Saverne (67) . . . 69 G4
Erny-Saint-Julien (62) . . . 5 G5
Érôme (26) . . . 222 B4
Erone (2B) . . . 319 G5
Érondelle (80) . . . 9 G4
Éroudeville (50) . . . 28 E4
Erp (09) . . . 306 E3

Erquery (60). 38 A2
Erquinghem-le-Sec (59) 6 C4
Erquinghem-Lys (59) 6 C3
Erquinvillers (60) 38 A2
Erquy (22) 49 K4
Err (66) 313 H5
Erre (59) 11 K2
Errevet (70) 119 G6
Errouville (54) 26 E3
Ersa (2B) 317 D2
Erstein (67) 71 D3
Erstroff (57) 67 F1
Ervauville (45) 112 A2
Ervillers (62) 11 F4
Ervy-le-Châtel (10) 113 J5
Esbareich (65) 305 H3
Esbarres (21) 154 D2
Esboz-Brest (70) 118 D4
Escala (65) 305 F1
Escalans (40) 266 C1
l'Escale (04) 259 G6
Escales (11) 290 E5
Escalles (62) 2 B3
Escalquens (31) 288 C2
Escames (60) 17 G6
Escamps (46) 250 C2
Escamps (89) 113 F6
Escandolières (12) 251 J1
Escanecrabe (31) 286 E5
Escardes (51) 61 F5
l'Escarène (06) 281 H2
Escarmain (59) 12 D3
Escaro (66) 314 A4
Escassefort (47) 231 F6
Escatalens (82) 268 E1
Escaudain (59) 12 B2
Escaudes (33) 246 D3
Escaudoeuvres (59) 11 K4
Escaunets (65) 285 F3
Escautpont (59) 12 D1
Escazeaux (82) 268 C4
Eschau (67) 71 D2
Eschbach (67) 25 A3
Eschbach-au-Val (68) 96 A4
Eschbourg (67) 69 F6
Eschentzwiller (68) 97 C3
Escherange (57) 27 F3
Esches (60) 37 H5
Eschwiller (67) 67 K2
Esclagne (09) 308 B3
Esclainvillers (80) 18 B4
Esclanèdes (48) 253 K1
Esclassan-Labastide (32) 286 C2
Esclauzels (46) 250 B2
Esclavelles (76) 16 C4
Esclavolles-Lurey (51) 89 G1
Escles (88) 94 B6
Escles-Saint-Pierre (60) 17 G4
Esclottes (47) 230 E4
Escobecques (59) 6 C4
Escoeuilles (62) 2 D5
Escoire (24) 214 B3
Escolives-Sainte-Camille (89) 113 G6
Escombres-et-le-Chesnois (08) 23 G4
Escondeaux (65) 285 J4
Esconnets (65) 304 E1
Escorailles (15) 217 G4
Escorneboeuf (32) 268 B6
Escorpain (28) 56 D5
Escos (64) 283 G2
Escosse (09) 307 H1
Escot (64) 303 F1
Escots (65) 304 E1
Escou (64) 284 B5
Escoubès (64) 284 E3
Escoubès-Pouts (65) 304 C1
Escoulis (31) 306 C1
Escouloubre (11) 308 D6
Escource (40) 244 E4
Escoussans (33) 230 A4
Escoussens (81) 289 K2
Escout (64) 284 B5
Escoutoux (63) 203 H1
Escoville (14) 33 F4
Escragnolles (06) 280 B4
Escrennes (45) 110 D1
Escrignelles (45) 111 J6
Escroux (81) 271 J4
Escueillens-et-Saint-Just-
de-Bélengard (11) 308 C1
Escurès (64) 285 F2
Escurolles (03) 185 G3
Eslettes (76) 15 K6
Esley (88) 93 K6
Eslourenties-Daban (64) 285 F4
Esmans (77) 88 A4
Esmery-Hallon (80) 19 H4
Esmoulières (70) 119 H4
Esmoulins (70) 137 F4
Esnandes (17) 176 D1
Esnans (25) 138 C4
Esnes (59) 11 K5
Esnes-en-Argonne (55) 43 G4
Esnon (89) 113 G3
Esnouveaux (52) 92 D6
Espagnac (19) 216 C3
Espagnac-Sainte-Eulalie (46) 234 B5
Espalais (82) 248 E6
Espalem (43) 219 F2
Espalion (12) 236 B6
Espaly-Saint-Marcel (43) 220 C5

Espanès (31) 288 C2
Espaon (32) 287 F3
Esparron (05) 242 C6
Esparron (31) 287 F5
Esparron (83) 278 C6
Esparron-de-Verdon (04) 278 D4
Esparros (65) 305 F2
Esparsac (82) 268 B2
Espartignac (19) 215 K1
Espas (32) 266 C4
Espaubourg (60) 37 F2
Espèche (65) 304 E1
Espéchède (64) 284 E4
Espédaillac (46) 234 B5
Espelette (64) 263 D2
Espeluche (26) 240 B6
Espenel (26) 241 F4
Espérausses (81) 271 H5
Espéraza (11) 308 D3
Esperce (31) 288 B4
Espère (46) 233 G6
Espès-Undurein (64) 283 H4
Espeyrac (12) 235 J5
Espeyroux (46) 234 C3
Espezel (11) 308 C5
Espieilh (65) 304 E1
Espiens (47) 247 J5
Espiet (33) 230 A2
Espinas (82) 250 D5
Espinasse (15) 236 C3
Espinasse (63) 184 B4
Espinasse-Vozelle (03) 185 H3
Espinasses (05) 243 G5
Espinchal (63) 218 C1
Espins (14) 53 J1
Espira-de-Conflent (66) 314 C3
Espira-de-l'Agly (66) 310 B5
Espirat (63) 203 F2
Espiute (64) 283 H1
Esplantas (43) 237 J1
Esplas (09) 288 C6
Esplas-de-Sérou (09) 307 F3
Espoey (64) 285 F5
Espondeilhan (34) 292 A3
Esprels (70) 138 D2
Esquay-Notre-Dame (14) 32 D5
Esquay-sur-Seulles (14) 32 C3
Esquéhéries (02) 13 H4
Esquelbecq (59) 3 H3
Esquennoy (60) 18 A5
Esquerchin (59) 11 G1
Esquerdes (62) 3 F5
Esquibien (29) 73 C3
Esquièze-Sère (65) 304 E4
Esquiule (64) 283 K5
les Essards (16) 212 E3
les Essards (17) 195 F1
les Essards (37) 126 E5
les Essards-Taignevaux (39) 155 F4
Essarois (21) 115 H5
les Essarts (27) 56 B3
les Essarts (41) 107 J6
les Essarts (85) 142 B6
les Essarts-le-Roi (78) 58 A5
les Essarts-le-Vicomte (51) 61 F6
les Essarts-lès-Sézanne (51) 61 G5
Essay (61) 82 E1
Esse (16) 180 C4
Essé (35) 79 J6
Essegney (88) 94 C3
les Esseintes (33) 230 C5
Essert (90) 119 H6
Essert-Romand (74) 192 A1
Essertaux (80) 18 A4
Essertenne (71) 153 H6
Essertenne-et-Cecey (70) 136 E4
Essertines-en-Châtelneuf (42) 204 C4
Essertines-en-Donzy (42) 205 F2
Esserts-Blay (73) 209 G3
Esserval-Combe (39) 156 C6
Esserval-Tartre (39) 156 C5
Essey (21) 153 H1
Essey-et-Maizerais (54) 65 G2
Essey-la-Côte (54) 94 D2
Essey-lès-Nancy (54) 66 B4
Essia (39) 173 G3
Essigny-le-Grand (02) 19 K3
Essigny-le-Petit (02) 20 A2
Essises (02) 60 E2
Essômes-sur-Marne (02) 60 E1
Esson (14) 53 J2
Essoyes (10) 115 F2
Essuiles (60) 37 J1
les Estables (43) 238 E1
Estables (48) 237 J4
Establet (26) 241 H6
Estadens (31) 306 A2
Estagel (66) 309 K5
Estaing (12) 236 A6
Estaing (65) 303 K3
Estaires (59) 6 A4
Estal (46) 234 C1
Estampes (32) 285 K3
Estampures (65) 285 K3
Estancarbon (31) 305 K1
Estandeuil (63) 203 G3
Estang (32) 266 B3
Estarvielle (65) 305 F4
Estavar (66) 313 H5
Esteil (63) 203 G6
Esténos (31) 305 J3

Estensan (65) 305 F4
Estérençuby (64) 282 E6
Esternay (51) 61 F5
Esterre (65) 304 B4
Estevelles (62) 6 C6
Esteville (76) 16 B5
Estézargues (30) 275 K2
Estialescq (64) 284 B5
Estibeaux (40) 264 C6
Estigarde (40) 246 E6
Estillac (47) 248 B5
Estipouy (32) 286 A1
Estirac (65) 285 H2
Estissac (10) 89 J5
Estivals (19) 215 H6
Estivareilles (03) 167 H5
Estivareilles (42) 204 C6
Estivaux (19) 215 H2
Estouy (45) 86 E6
Estoher (66) 314 C3
Estos (64) 284 A5
Estoublon (04) 279 F1
Estouches (91) 86 C5
Estourmel (59) 11 K4
Estouteville-Écalles (76) 16 B6
Estouy (45) 86 E6
Estrablin (38) 206 C3
Estramiac (32) 268 A3
Estrebay (08) 21 K2
Estréboeuf (80) 8 E4
l'Estréchure (30) 254 D6
Estrée (62) 4 C6
Estrée-Blanche (62) 5 H4
Estrée-Cauchy (62) 10 D1
Estrée-Wamin (62) 10 B3
Estréelles (62) 4 C6
Estrées (02) 19 K1
Estrées (59) 11 H4
Estrées-Deniécourt (80) 19 F2
Estrées-la-Campagne (14) 54 A1
Estrées-lès-Crécy (80) 9 G4
Estrées-Mons (80) 19 H2
Estrées-Saint-Denis (60) 38 C2
Estrées-sur-Noye (80) 18 B3
Estrennes (88) 93 K4
Estreux (59) 12 D2
Estrun (59) 11 K3
Estry (14) 53 F2
Esves-le-Moutier (37) 146 D3
Esvres (37) 127 K6
Eswars (59) 11 K3
Étable (73) 208 D5
Étables (07) 222 A4
Étables-sur-Mer (22) 49 F4
Étagnac (16) 180 C5
Étaimpuis (76) 16 A5
Étain (55) 26 C4
Étaing (62) 11 G3
Étainhus (76) 14 C6
Étais (21) 114 E6
Étais-la-Sauvin (89) 132 C3
Étalans (25) 156 E1
Étalante (21) 135 H1
Étalle (08) 22 A2
Étalleville (76) 15 H4
Étalon (80) 19 G3
Étalondes (76) 8 C6
Étampes (91) 86 C3
Étampes-sur-Marne (02) 60 E1
l'Étang-Bertrand (50) 28 D4
l'Étang-la-Ville (78) 58 C3
l'Étang-Vergy (21) 154 A1
les Étangs (57) 45 H5
Étaples (62) 4 B5
Étaule (89) 133 K3
Étaules (17) 194 B2
Étaules (21) 135 K4
Étauliers (33) 211 H3
Étaux (74) 191 G3
Étaves-et-Bocquiaux (02) 20 B1
Étavigny (60) 39 F6
Éteignières (08) 22 A2
Éteimbes (68) 119 K5
Étel (56) 100 B5
Ételfay (80) 18 D5
Étercy (74) 190 E5
Éternoz (25) 156 C2
Éterpigny (62) 11 G3
Éterpigny (80) 19 G2
Éterville (14) 32 D5
Étevaux (21) 136 D5
Eth (59) 12 E2
Étienville (50) 28 E5
Étigny (89) 112 D1
les Étilleux (28) 84 A5
Étinehem (80) 18 E1
Étiolles (91) 59 F6
Étival (39) 173 J4
Étival-Clairefontaine (88) 95 H3
Étival-lès-le-Mans (72) 106 D3
Étivey (89) 134 B1
Étobon (70) 119 G6
Étoges (51) 61 J3
l'Étoile (39) 173 F1
l'Étoile (80) 9 J6
Étoile-Saint-Cyrice (05) 258 C2
Étoile-sur-Rhône (26) 240 C2
Éton (55) 26 C5
Étormay (21) 135 F2
Étouars (24) 197 J4

Étourvy (10) 114 B3
Étoutteville (76) 15 G4
Étouvans (25) 139 G3
Étouvelles (02) 40 B1
Étouvy (14) 31 K6
Étouy (60) 37 K2
Étrabonne (25) 137 H6
Étrappe (25) 139 F3
l'État (42) 205 G5
Étray (25) 156 E1
Étraye (55) 43 H3
Étréaupont (02) 21 F2
Étrechet (36) 165 K1
Étréchy (18) 149 K2
Étréchy (51) 61 K3
Étréchy (91) 86 D2
Étréham (14) 32 A3
Étreillers (02) 19 J3
Étréjust (80) 17 H2
Étrelles (35) 104 A1
Étrelles-et-la-Montbleuse (70) 137 J3
Étrelles-sur-Aube (10) 89 J1
Étrembières (74) 191 G2
Étrépagny (27) 36 C3
Étrepigney (39) 155 J2
Étrépigny (08) 22 D4
Étrépilly (02) 39 J6
Étrépilly (77) 59 H1
Étrepy (51) 63 H4
Étretat (76) 14 B4
Étreux (02) 12 E6
Étreval (54) 93 K2
Étréville (27) 34 D3
Étrez (01) 172 C6
Étriac (16) 196 C5
Étriché (49) 306 D1
Étricourt-Manancourt (80) 11 G6
Étrigny (71) 171 J3
Étrochey (21) 115 F4
Étroeungt (59) 13 G5
Étroussat (03) 185 G2
Étrun (62) 10 E2
Etsaut (64) 303 F3
Ettendorf (67) 69 J6
Etting (57) 68 E3
Étueffont (90) 119 J5
Étupes (25) 139 H2
Éturqueraye (27) 34 D3
Étusson (79) 143 J3
Étuz (70) 137 K4
Etzling (57) 68 C2
Eu (76) 8 C6
Euffigneix (52) 116 A1
Eugénie-les-Bains (40) 265 H5
Euilly-et-Lombut (08) 23 G5
Eulmont (54) 66 B4
Eup (31) 305 J3
Eurre (26) 240 D3
Eurville-Bienville (52) 91 K1
Eus (66) 314 C3
Euvezin (54) 65 H2
Euville (55) 65 F4
Euvy (51) 62 A5
Euzet (30) 255 J6
Évans (39) 155 K1
Évaux-et-Ménil (88) 94 C4
Évaux-les-Bains (23) 183 K3
Ève (60) 38 C6
Évecquemont (78) 58 A1
Évenos (83) 297 H5
Évergnicourt (02) 41 F2
Everly (77) 88 D3
Évette-Salbert (90) 119 H6
Éveux (69) 205 J1
Évian-les-Bains (74) 175 G5
Évigny (08) 22 C4
Évillers (25) 156 D3
Évin-Malmaison (62) 11 H1
Évires (74) 191 G4
Évisa (2A) 316 E4
Évran (22) 50 D6
Évrange (57) 27 G2
Évrecy (14) 32 C6
Èvres (55) 64 A1
Évreux (27) 56 D1
Évricourt (60) 19 G6
Évriguet (56) 77 K6
Évron (53) 81 J6
Évry (89) 88 D3
Évry (91) 59 F6
Evry-Grégy-sur-Yerre (77) 59 H6
Excenevex (74) 174 E5
Excideuil (24) 214 D2
Exermont (08) 42 E3
Exideuil (16) 180 B6
Exincourt (25) 139 H2
Exireuil (79) 161 K5
Exmes (61) 54 E4
Exoudun (79) 162 B6
Eybens (38) 224 B3
Eybouleuf (87) 199 H2
Eyburie (19) 199 J6
Eycheil (09) 306 D3
Eydoche (38) 207 F6
Eygalayes (26) 258 C3
Eygalières (13) 276 D4
Eygaliers (26) 257 J4
Eygliers (05) 227 A3
Eygluy-Escoulin (26) 241 F2

Eyguians (05) 258 E2
Eyguières (13) 276 D5
Eygurande (19) 201 G3
Eygurande-et-Gardedeuil (24) 212 E5
Eyjeaux (87) 199 G2
Eyliac (24) 214 B4
Eymet (24) 231 G4
Eymeux (26) 223 F5
Eymouthiers (16) 197 H3
Eymoutiers (87) 199 K2
Eyne (66) 313 J5
Eynesse (33) 230 E2
Eyragues (13) 276 B3
Eyrans (33) 211 G3
Eyrein (19) 216 C2
Eyres-Moncube (40) 265 G4
Eyroles (26) 257 J1
Eysines (33) 229 G1
Eysson (25) 138 E6
Eysus (64) 284 A6
Eyvirat (24) 214 A2
Eywiller (67) 67 K2
Eyzahut (26) 240 D5
Eyzerac (24) 214 C1
les Eyzies-de-Tayac-Sireuil (24) 232 D1
Eyzin-Pinet (38) 206 C5
Ézanville (95) 58 E1
Èze (06) 281 H3
Ézy-sur-Eure (27) 57 F3

365

F

Fa (11) 308 E3
Faÿ-lès-Nemours (77) 87 H5
Fabas (09) 306 D1
Fabas (31) 287 G4
Fabas (82) 269 F3
Fabras (07) 239 G4
Fabrègues (34) 293 F1
Fabrezan (11) 309 K1
Faches-Thumesnil (59) 6 E4
Fâchin (58) 152 C4
la Fage-Montivernoux (48) 236 E3
la Fage-Saint-Julien (48) 237 F3
le Faget (31) 289 F1
Faget-Abbatial (32) 286 E2
Fagnières (51) 62 D2
Fagnon (08) 22 C4
Fahy-lès-Autrey (70) 136 E3
Failly (57) 45 F5
Faimbe (25) 139 F2
Fain-lès-Montbard (21) 134 E2
Fain-lès-Moutiers (21) 134 C2
Fains (27) 57 F2
Fains-la-Folie (28) 85 H6
Fains-Véel (55) 64 A4
Faissault (08) 22 B5
Fajac-en-Val (11) 309 H1
Fajac-la-Relenque (11) 288 E5
Fajoles (46) 233 H3
la Fajolle (11) 308 C5
Fajolles (82) 268 C2
Falaise (08) 42 B2
Falaise (14) 54 A3
la Falaise (78) 57 K2
Falck (57) 45 K4
Faleyras (33) 230 A3
Falga (31) 289 G2
le Falgoux (15) 217 K4
Falicon (06) 281 G3
Falkwiller (68) 97 A3
Fallencourt (76) 16 E2
Fallerans (25) 156 E1
Falleron (85) 141 G4
Falletans (39) 155 H2
Fallon (70) 138 C2
la Faloise (80) 18 B4
Fals (47) 248 C6
Falvy (80) 19 G3
Famars (59) 12 D2
Famechon (62) 10 C4
Famechon (80) 17 J3
Fameck (57) 27 G5
Familly (14) 55 F2
Fampoux (62) 11 F2
Fanjeaux (11) 289 H6
Fanlac (24) 214 C5
le Faou (29) 74 C2
le Faouët (22) 48 D3
le Faouët (56) 75 J4
Faramans (01) 189 F6
Faramans (38) 206 E6
Farbus (62) 11 F2
Farceaux (27) 36 B4
la Fare-en-Champsaur (05) 242 E4
la Fare-les-Oliviers (13) 296 A1
Farébersviller (57) 68 B3
Fareins (01) 188 B4
Faremoutiers (77) 60 A4
Farges (01) 190 D2
les Farges (24) 215 F4
Farges-Allichamps (18) 167 F1
Farges-en-Septaine (18) 149 J3
Farges-lès-Chalon (71) 154 A3
Farges-lès-Mâcon (71) 171 K4
Fargues (33) 229 K6
Fargues (40) 265 H4
Fargues (46) 249 H2
Fargues-Saint-Hilaire (33) 229 J2
Fargues-sur-Ourbise (47) 247 G4

Farincourt (52) . . . 117 G6
Farinole (2B) . . . 317 D5
la Farlède (83) . . . 297 K5
Farnay (42) . . . 205 J5
Farschviller (57) . . . 68 C3
Fatines (72) . . . 107 F2
Fatouville-Grestain (27) . . . 34 A2
le Fau (15) . . . 217 J3
Fau-de-Peyre (48) . . . 237 F3
Fauch (81) . . . 271 F3
Faucigny (74) . . . 191 H2
Faucompierre (88) . . . 95 F6
Faucon (84) . . . 257 H3
Faucon-de-Barcelonnette (04) . . . 260 D1
Faucon-du-Caire (04) . . . 259 H1
Faucoucourt (02) . . . 20 B6
Faudoas (82) . . . 268 B3
le Fauga (31) . . . 288 A3
Faugères (07) . . . 255 H1
Faugères (34) . . . 291 K1
Fauguernon (14) . . . 34 A5
Fauguerolles (47) . . . 247 H1
Fauillet (47) . . . 247 J1
le Faulq (14) . . . 34 A4
Faulquemont (57) . . . 45 K6
Faulx (54) . . . 66 A3
Faumont (59) . . . 6 E6
Fauquembergues (62) . . . 5 F4
la Faurie (05) . . . 242 B5
Faurilles (24) . . . 231 K4
Fauroux (82) . . . 249 F4
Faussergues (81) . . . 271 H1
la Faute-sur-Mer (85) . . . 159 J6
Fauverney (21) . . . 136 B6
Fauville (27) . . . 56 D1
Fauville-en-Caux (76) . . . 15 F5
Faux (08) . . . 22 B6
Faux (24) . . . 231 K3
Faux-Fresnay (51) . . . 61 K6
Faux-la-Montagne (23) . . . 200 B2
Faux-Mazuras (23) . . . 182 C6
Faux-Vésigneul (51) . . . 62 D4
Faux-Villecerf (10) . . . 89 H4
Favalello (2B) . . . 319 G6
Favars (19) . . . 216 A3
Faveraye-Mâchelles (49) . . . 125 G6
Faverdines (18) . . . 167 G3
Faverelles (45) . . . 132 A2
Faverges (74) . . . 209 F1
Faverges-de-la-Tour (38) . . . 207 H4
Faverney (70) . . . 118 A5
Faverois (90) . . . 139 K2
Faverolles (02) . . . 39 H4
Faverolles (15) . . . 236 E1
Faverolles (28) . . . 57 H5
Faverolles (36) . . . 147 H2
Faverolles (52) . . . 116 B3
Faverolles (61) . . . 53 K5
Faverolles (80) . . . 18 D5
Faverolles-et-Coëmy (51) . . . 40 D4
Faverolles-la-Campagne (27) . . . 56 B1
Faverolles-lès-Lucey (21) . . . 115 J4
Faverolles-sur-Cher (41) . . . 128 D5
la Favière (39) . . . 156 C6
Favières (28) . . . 84 D2
Favières (54) . . . 93 J2
Favières (77) . . . 59 J5
Favières (80) . . . 8 E3
Favresse (51) . . . 63 G5
Favreuil (62) . . . 11 F5
Favrieux (78) . . . 57 H2
le Favril (27) . . . 34 C5
le Favril (28) . . . 84 H4
le Favril (59) . . . 13 F5
le Fay (61) . . . 55 G6
le Fay (71) . . . 172 E2
Fay (72) . . . 106 C2
Fay (80) . . . 19 F2
Fay-aux-Loges (45) . . . 110 C4
Fay-de-Bretagne (44) . . . 122 E1
Fay-en-Montagne (39) . . . 155 J6
Fay-le-Clos (26) . . . 222 C3
Fay-les-Étangs (60) . . . 37 F4
Fay-lès-Marcilly (10) . . . 89 G3
le Fay-Saint-Quentin (60) . . . 37 J2
Fay-sur-Lignon (43) . . . 221 F6
Faycelles (46) . . . 234 D6
la Faye (16) . . . 179 G4
Faye (41) . . . 108 D5
Faye-d'Anjou (49) . . . 125 G6
Faye-la-Vineuse (37) . . . 145 G4
Faye-l'Abbesse (79) . . . 143 K6
Faye-sur-Ardin (79) . . . 161 G5
le Fayel (60) . . . 38 C3
Fayence (83) . . . 280 B5
Fayet (02) . . . 19 K2
Fayet (12) . . . 272 C4
Fayet-le-Château (63) . . . 203 G3
Fayet-Ronaye (63) . . . 203 H6
Fayl-la-Forêt (52) . . . 117 F5
Faymont (70) . . . 139 F1
Faymoreau (85) . . . 161 F3
Fays (52) . . . 91 K2
Fays (88) . . . 95 F5
Fays-la-Chapelle (10) . . . 114 A1
Fayssac (81) . . . 270 C2
Féas (64) . . . 283 K6
Febvin-Palfart (62) . . . 5 H5
Fécamp (76) . . . 14 D3
Féchain (59) . . . 11 J3

Fêche-l'Église (90) . . . 139 J2
Fécocourt (54) . . . 93 K3
Fédry (70) . . . 137 J1
Fegersheim (67) . . . 71 D2
Fégréac (44) . . . 102 C5
Feigères (74) . . . 190 E3
Feignies (59) . . . 13 G2
Feigneux (60) . . . 38 E4
Feillens (01) . . . 171 K6
Feings (41) . . . 128 E3
Feings (61) . . . 83 J1
Feins (35) . . . 79 G1
Feins-en-Gâtinais (45) . . . 111 K6
Feissons-sur-Isère (73) . . . 209 G4
Feissons-sur-Salins (73) . . . 209 H5
le Fel (12) . . . 235 J3
Felce (2B) . . . 319 J5
Feldbach (68) . . . 97 B5
Feldkirch (68) . . . 97 B1
Feliceto (2B) . . . 318 C3
Félines (07) . . . 222 A1
Félines (43) . . . 220 A2
Félines-Minervois (34) . . . 290 D4
Félines-sur-Rimandoule (26) . . . 240 E5
Félines-Termenès (11) . . . 309 J3
Felleries (59) . . . 13 H4
Fellering (68) . . . 119 J3
Felletin (23) . . . 183 G6
Felluns (66) . . . 309 H5
Felon (90) . . . 119 J5
Felzins (46) . . . 234 E5
Fenain (59) . . . 11 K2
Fénay (21) . . . 136 A6
Fendeille (11) . . . 289 G5
Fénery (79) . . . 161 J2
Fénétrange (57) . . . 67 J2
Feneu (49) . . . 125 G2
Féneyrols (82) . . . 250 D5
Féniers (23) . . . 200 D2
Fenioux (17) . . . 177 J6
Fenioux (79) . . . 161 J3
Fenneviller (54) . . . 95 H1
Fénols (81) . . . 270 D3
le Fenouiller (85) . . . 140 E6
Fenouillet (31) . . . 269 G5
Fenouillet (66) . . . 309 G5
Fenouillet-du-Razès (11) . . . 289 H6
Fépin (08) . . . 24 C3
Fercé (44) . . . 103 J2
Fercé-sur-Sarthe (72) . . . 106 B4
Ferdrupt (88) . . . 119 J3
la Fère (02) . . . 20 A5
Fère-Champenoise (51) . . . 61 K5
Fère-en-Tardenois (02) . . . 40 A4
Fèrebrianges (51) . . . 61 J3
la Férée (08) . . . 21 K3
Férel (56) . . . 121 K2
Ferfay (62) . . . 5 J5
Féricy (77) . . . 87 J3
Férin (59) . . . 11 H2
Fermanville (50) . . . 28 C2
la Fermeté (58) . . . 151 F4
Ferney-Voltaire (01) . . . 191 F1
Fernoël (63) . . . 201 G2
Férolles (45) . . . 110 C5
Férolles-Attilly (77) . . . 59 H5
Féron (59) . . . 13 H5
Ferques (62) . . . 2 C4
Ferrals-les-Corbières (11) . . . 291 F6
Ferrals-les-Montagnes (34) . . . 290 E3
Ferran (11) . . . 289 J6
Ferrassières (26) . . . 258 B5
le Ferré (35) . . . 80 A2
Ferrensac (47) . . . 231 K5
Ferrère (65) . . . 305 H3
les Ferres (06) . . . 280 E2
Ferrette (68) . . . 97 C5
Ferreux-Quincey (10) . . . 89 G3
Ferrière (62) . . . 10 E2
la Ferrière (22) . . . 77 H5
la Ferrière (37) . . . 127 K1
la Ferrière (38) . . . 224 E1
la Ferrière (85) . . . 159 J1
la Ferrière-Airoux (86) . . . 163 F6
la Ferrière-au-Doyen (61) . . . 55 H6
la Ferrière-aux-Étangs (61) . . . 53 H5
la Ferrière-Béchet (61) . . . 82 D1
la Ferrière-Bochard (61) . . . 82 C3
la Ferrière-de-Flée (49) . . . 104 D6
la Ferrière-en-Parthenay (79) . . . 162 B2
Ferrière-et-Lafolie (52) . . . 92 A3
la Ferrière-Harang (14) . . . 31 K5
Ferrière-la-Grande (59) . . . 13 H3
Ferrière-la-Petite (59) . . . 13 H3
Ferrière-Larçon (37) . . . 146 C4
Ferrière-sur-Beaulieu (37) . . . 146 D2
la Ferrière-sur-Risle (27) . . . 55 K2
Ferrières (17) . . . 177 G1
Ferrières (45) . . . 111 J2
Ferrières (50) . . . 80 D1
Ferrières (54) . . . 66 B6
Ferrières (60) . . . 18 D6
Ferrières (65) . . . 303 J2
Ferrières (80) . . . 17 K2
Ferrières (81) . . . 271 H6
Ferrières-en-Bray (76) . . . 36 D1
Ferrières-en-Brie (77) . . . 59 H4
Ferrières-Haut-Clocher (27) . . . 56 B1
la Ferrière-la-Verrerie (61) . . . 55 F6
Ferrières-le-Lac (25) . . . 139 J5
Ferrières-les-Bois (25) . . . 137 H6
Ferrières-lès-Ray (70) . . . 137 H2

Ferrières-lès-Scey (70) . . . 117 K6
Ferrières-les-Verreries (34) . . . 274 B3
Ferrières-Poussarou (34) . . . 291 G2
Ferrières-Saint-Hilaire (27) . . . 55 H1
Ferrières-Saint-Mary (15) . . . 218 D4
Ferrières-sur-Ariège (09) . . . 307 J3
Ferrières-sur-Sichon (03) . . . 186 B4
Ferrussac (43) . . . 219 H5
Fertans (25) . . . 156 C2
la Ferté (39) . . . 155 J4
la Ferté-Alais (91) . . . 86 E2
la Ferté-Beauharnais (41) . . . 129 K3
la Ferté-Bernard (72) . . . 83 J6
la Ferté-Chevresis (02) . . . 20 C4
la Ferté-Frênel (61) . . . 55 H3
la Ferté-Gaucher (77) . . . 60 D4
la Ferté-Hauterive (03) . . . 168 E6
la Ferté-Imbault (41) . . . 130 A5
la Ferté-Loupière (89) . . . 112 D4
la Ferté-Macé (61) . . . 53 J6
la Ferté-Milon (02) . . . 39 G5
la Ferté-Saint-Aubin (45) . . . 110 A6
la Ferté-Saint-Cyr (41) . . . 129 H1
la Ferté-Saint-Samson (76) . . . 16 D6
la Ferté-sous-Jouarre (77) . . . 60 B2
la Ferté-sur-Chiers (08) . . . 23 J5
la Ferté-Vidame (28) . . . 56 B6
la Ferté-Villeneuil (28) . . . 108 E3
Fertrève (58) . . . 151 J4
Fervaches (50) . . . 31 H5
Fervaques (14) . . . 54 C1
Fescamps (80) . . . 18 E5
Fesches-le-Châtel (25) . . . 139 J2
Fesmy-le-Sart (02) . . . 12 A6
Fesques (76) . . . 16 D3
Fessanvilliers-Mattanvilliers (28) . . . 56 C5
Fessenheim (68) . . . 96 E6
Fessenheim-le-Bas (67) . . . 70 D2
Fessevillers (25) . . . 139 J5
les Fessey (70) . . . 118 E4
Fessy (74) . . . 174 E6
Festalemps (24) . . . 213 F3
Festes-et-Saint-André (11) . . . 308 E3
Festieux (02) . . . 40 C1
Festigny (51) . . . 61 H1
Festigny (89) . . . 133 F2
Festubert (62) . . . 6 B5
le Fête (21) . . . 153 H1
Féternes (74) . . . 175 G5
Fétigny (39) . . . 173 G4
Feucherolles (78) . . . 58 B3
Feuchy (62) . . . 11 F3
Feugarolles (47) . . . 247 J4
Feugères (50) . . . 31 F3
Feuges (10) . . . 90 B3
Feuguerolles (27) . . . 35 H6
Feuguerolles-Bully (14) . . . 32 D5
Feuilla (11) . . . 310 C3
Feuillade (16) . . . 197 H4
la Feuillade (24) . . . 215 H4
la Feuillée (29) . . . 75 F1
Feuillères (80) . . . 19 F1
la Feuillie (50) . . . 30 D2
la Feuillie (76) . . . 36 B1
Feule (58) . . . 139 G4
Feuquières (60) . . . 17 G5
Feuquières-en-Vimeu (80) . . . 8 E5
Feurs (42) . . . 204 E2
Feusines (36) . . . 166 C4
Feux (18) . . . 150 B1
Fèves (57) . . . 27 G6
Féy (57) . . . 44 E6
Fey-en-Haye (54) . . . 65 J2
Feyt (19) . . . 201 H3
Feytiat (87) . . . 199 F1
Feyzin (69) . . . 206 B3
Fiac (81) . . . 270 B5
Ficaja (2B) . . . 319 H4
Ficheux (62) . . . 10 E3
Fichous-Riumayou (64) . . . 284 C2
le Fidelaire (27) . . . 56 A2
le Fied (39) . . . 155 J6
le Fief-Sauvin (49) . . . 124 B6
Fieffes-Montrelet (80) . . . 9 K5
Fiefs (62) . . . 5 H6
Fiennes (62) . . . 2 C4
Fienvillers (80) . . . 9 K5
Fierville-Bray (14) . . . 33 F6
Fierville-les-Mines (50) . . . 28 C5
Fierville-les-Parcs (14) . . . 33 K4
Fieulaine (02) . . . 20 B2
Fieux (47) . . . 247 K6
Figanières (83) . . . 279 J6
Figari (2A) . . . 323 G5
Figarol (31) . . . 306 B1
Figeac (46) . . . 234 D5
Fignévelle (88) . . . 117 J2
Fignières (80) . . . 18 D4
Filain (02) . . . 40 A1
Filain (70) . . . 138 B2
Fillé (72) . . . 106 D4
Fillières (54) . . . 26 D4
Fillièvres (62) . . . 9 K2
Fillinges (74) . . . 191 H2
Fillols (66) . . . 314 B4
Filstroff (57) . . . 45 J2
Fiménil (88) . . . 95 F5
Finestret (66) . . . 314 C3
Finhan (82) . . . 268 E2
les Fins (25) . . . 157 H2
Fins (80) . . . 11 H6

Fiquefleur-Equainville (27) . . . 34 A2
Firbeix (24) . . . 198 C4
Firfol (14) . . . 34 A5
Firmi (12) . . . 235 G6
Firminy (42) . . . 221 G1
Fislis (68) . . . 97 C5
Fismes (51) . . . 40 C3
Fitilieu (38) . . . 207 H4
Fitou (11) . . . 310 C4
Fitz-James (60) . . . 38 A2
Fix-Saint-Geneys (43) . . . 219 K4
Fixem (57) . . . 27 H3
Fixin (21) . . . 135 K6
Flacey (21) . . . 136 B4
Flacey (28) . . . 109 F1
Flacey-en-Bresse (71) . . . 172 E3
la Flachère (38) . . . 208 C6
Flachères (38) . . . 207 F5
Flacourt (78) . . . 57 H2
Flacy (89) . . . 89 G5
Flagey (25) . . . 156 C3
Flagey (52) . . . 116 C5
Flagey-Echézeaux (21) . . . 154 B1
Flagey-lès-Auxonne (21) . . . 155 F1
Flagey-Rigney (25) . . . 138 B3
Flagnac (12) . . . 235 F5
Flagy (70) . . . 118 B6
Flagy (71) . . . 171 H4
Flagy (77) . . . 87 K4
Flaignes-Havys (08) . . . 22 A3
Flainval (54) . . . 66 C5
Flamanville (50) . . . 28 A3
Flamanville (76) . . . 15 H5
Flamarens (32) . . . 268 A1
la Flamengrie (02) . . . 13 F4
la Flamengrie (59) . . . 12 E5
Flamets-Frétils (76) . . . 16 E4
Flammerans (21) . . . 136 E6
Flammerécourt (52) . . . 92 A3
Flancourt-Catelon (27) . . . 34 E3
Flangebouche (25) . . . 157 G1
Flassan (84) . . . 257 J5
Flassans-sur-Issole (83) . . . 298 B3
Flassigny (55) . . . 26 A3
Flastroff (57) . . . 45 J2
Flat (63) . . . 203 F4
Flaucourt (80) . . . 19 G2
Flaugeac (24) . . . 231 H3
Flaujac-Gare (46) . . . 234 B4
Flaujac-Poujols (46) . . . 250 A2
Flaujagues (33) . . . 230 D2
Flaumont-Waudrechies (59) . . . 13 H4
Flaux (30) . . . 275 J1
Flavacourt (60) . . . 36 E3
Flaviac (07) . . . 240 A3
Flavignac (87) . . . 198 D3
Flavignerot (21) . . . 135 K6
Flavigny (18) . . . 150 A4
Flavigny (51) . . . 62 A2
Flavigny-le-Grand-et-Beaurain (02) . . . 20 D2
Flavigny-sur-Moselle (54) . . . 66 A6
Flavigny-sur-Ozerain (21) . . . 135 F3
Flavin (12) . . . 252 B3
Flavy-le-Martel (02) . . . 19 K4
Flavy-le-Meldeux (60) . . . 19 H4
Flaxieu (01) . . . 207 K1
Flaxlanden (68) . . . 97 C3
Flayat (23) . . . 201 G2
Flayosc (83) . . . 279 H6
Fléac (17) . . . 196 D3
Fléac-sur-Seugne (17) . . . 195 H5
la Flèche (72) . . . 106 B6
Fléchin (62) . . . 5 G5
Fléchy (60) . . . 18 A5
Flée (21) . . . 134 D4
Flée (72) . . . 107 G6
Fleigneux (08) . . . 23 H1
Fleisheim (57) . . . 67 K3
le Fleix (24) . . . 231 F2
Fleix (86) . . . 163 K3
Fléré-la-Rivière (36) . . . 146 E3
Flers (61) . . . 53 H4
Flers (62) . . . 10 A2
Flers (80) . . . 11 F6
Flers-en-Escrebieux (59) . . . 11 H1
Flers-sur-Noye (80) . . . 18 A4
Flesquières (59) . . . 11 H5
Flesselles (80) . . . 10 A4
Flétrange (57) . . . 45 J6
Flêtre (59) . . . 3 K5
Fléty (58) . . . 152 B6
Fleurac (16) . . . 196 B2
Fleurac (24) . . . 214 D6
Fleurance (32) . . . 267 G3
Fleurat (23) . . . 182 B2
Fleurbaix (62) . . . 6 B2
Fleuré (61) . . . 54 C5
Fleuré (86) . . . 163 G4
Fleurey (25) . . . 139 H5
Fleurey-lès-Faverney (70) . . . 118 A5
Fleurey-lès-Lavoncourt (70) . . . 117 H6
Fleurey-lès-Saint-Loup (70) . . . 118 C3
Fleurey-sur-Ouche (21) . . . 135 J5
Fleurie (69) . . . 188 B2
Fleuriel (03) . . . 185 G1
Fleurieu-sur-Saône (69) . . . 188 C6
Fleurieux-sur-l'Arbresle (69) . . . 205 J1
Fleurigné (35) . . . 80 A4
Fleurines (60) . . . 38 B4
Fleurville (71) . . . 171 K5
Fleury (02) . . . 39 G4

Fleury (11) . . . 291 K5
Fleury (50) . . . 52 A3
Fleury (57) . . . 45 F6
Fleury (60) . . . 37 F3
Fleury (62) . . . 10 A3
Fleury (80) . . . 17 K4
Fleury-devant-Douaumont (55) . . . 43 J4
Fleury-en-Bière (77) . . . 87 G3
Fleury-la-Forêt (27) . . . 36 C2
Fleury-la-Montagne (71) . . . 187 F2
Fleury-la-Rivière (51) . . . 40 D6
Fleury-la-Vallée (89) . . . 113 F4
Fleury-les-Aubrais (45) . . . 110 A4
Fleury-Mérogis (91) . . . 58 E6
Fleury-sur-Andelle (27) . . . 36 A3
Fleury-sur-Loire (58) . . . 151 F6
Fleury-sur-Orne (14) . . . 32 E5
Fléville (08) . . . 42 D3
Fléville-devant-Nancy (54) . . . 66 A5
Fléville-Lixières (54) . . . 26 E4
Flévy (57) . . . 27 H6
Flexanville (78) . . . 57 J3
Flexbourg (67) . . . 70 C3
Fley (71) . . . 171 H2
Fleys (89) . . . 113 J5
Flez-Cuzy (58) . . . 133 G5
Fligny (08) . . . 21 J2
Flin (54) . . . 95 F1
Flines-lès-Mortagne (59) . . . 7 H5
Flines-lez-Raches (59) . . . 11 J1
Flins-Neuve-Église (78) . . . 57 H3
Flins-sur-Seine (78) . . . 58 A2
Flipou (27) . . . 35 K3
Flirey (54) . . . 65 H3
Flixecourt (80) . . . 9 J6
Flize (08) . . . 22 D4
la Flocellière (85) . . . 142 E5
Flocourt (57) . . . 66 C1
Flocques (76) . . . 8 C6
Flogny-la-Chapelle (89) . . . 113 J3
Floing (08) . . . 23 F4
Floirac (17) . . . 195 F5
Floirac (33) . . . 229 H4
Floirac (46) . . . 233 K1
Florac (48) . . . 254 B3
Florange (57) . . . 27 G5
Florémont (88) . . . 94 B3
Florensac (34) . . . 292 C3
Florent-en-Argonne (51) . . . 42 D5
Florentia (39) . . . 173 F5
Florentin (81) . . . 270 D3
Florentin-la-Capelle (12) . . . 235 K5
Floressas (46) . . . 249 G1
Florimont (90) . . . 139 K2
Florimont-Gaumier (24) . . . 233 F4
Floringhem (62) . . . 5 J6
la Flotte (17) . . . 176 B2
Flottemanville (50) . . . 28 E4
Flottemanville-Hague (50) . . . 28 C2
Floudès (33) . . . 230 C5
Floure (11) . . . 290 C6
Flourens (31) . . . 269 H6
Floursies (59) . . . 13 G6
Floyon (59) . . . 13 G6
Flumet (73) . . . 191 K6
Fluquières (02) . . . 19 J3
Fluy (80) . . . 17 J2
Foameix-Ornel (55) . . . 26 B6
Foce (2A) . . . 323 F3
Focicchia (2B) . . . 319 G6
Foëcy (18) . . . 148 E2
le Foeil (22) . . . 76 E1
Foisches (08) . . . 24 C1
Foissac (12) . . . 234 D6
Foissac (30) . . . 255 K6
Foissiat (01) . . . 172 C5
Foissy (21) . . . 153 H2
Foissy-lès-Vézelay (89) . . . 133 J4
Foissy-sur-Vanne (89) . . . 89 F6
Foix (09) . . . 307 J3
Folcarde (31) . . . 289 F3
Folembray (02) . . . 20 A6
Folgensbourg (68) . . . 97 D5
le Folgoët (29) . . . 46 B4
la Folie (14) . . . 31 J1
Folies (80) . . . 18 E3
Folkling (57) . . . 68 C2
Follainville-Dennemont (78) . . . 57 H1
Folles (87) . . . 181 K3
la Folletière (76) . . . 15 G6
la Folletière-Abenon (14) . . . 55 G2
Folleville (27) . . . 34 C5
Folleville (80) . . . 18 B5
Folligny (50) . . . 51 K1
Folschviller (57) . . . 68 A3
Fomerey (88) . . . 94 C5
Fomperron (79) . . . 162 A4
Fonbeauzard (31) . . . 269 G5
Foncegrive (21) . . . 136 B1
Fonches-Fonchette (80) . . . 19 F3
Foncine-le-Bas (39) . . . 174 A2
Foncine-le-Haut (39) . . . 174 B2
Foncquevillers (62) . . . 10 D5
Fondamente (12) . . . 272 E3
Fondettes (37) . . . 127 H4
Fondremand (70) . . . 137 K3
Fongrave (47) . . . 248 A2
Fongueusemare (76) . . . 14 C4
Fonroque (24) . . . 231 H4
Fons (07) . . . 239 G5
Fons (30) . . . 275 F2
Fons (46) . . . 234 C4

Fons-sur-Lussan (30) 255 K4
Fonsommes (02) 20 B2
Fonsorbes (31) 287 K1
Font-Romeu-Odeillo-Via (66) . 313 H4
Fontain (25) 138 A6
Fontaine (10) 91 G5
Fontaine (38) 224 A3
Fontaine (90) 119 J6
Fontaine-au-Bois (59) 12 E4
Fontaine-au-Pire (59) 12 B5
Fontaine-Bellenger (27) . . . 35 K5
Fontaine-Bonneleau (60) . . . 17 K5
Fontaine-Chaalis (60) 38 C5
Fontaine-Chalendray (17) . . 178 D5
Fontaine-Couverte (53) . . . 104 B3
Fontaine-de-Vaucluse (84) . . 276 E2
Fontaine-Denis-Nuisy (51) . . 61 H6
Fontaine-en-Bray (76) 16 C5
Fontaine-en-Dormois (51) . . 42 B4
Fontaine-Étoupefour (14) . . . 32 D5
Fontaine-Fourches (77) 88 E3
Fontaine-Française (21) . . . 136 D2
Fontaine-Guérin (49) 126 A3
Fontaine-Henry (14) 32 D4
Fontaine-Heudebourg (27) . . 35 J6
Fontaine-la-Gaillarde (89) . . 88 E6
Fontaine-la-Guyon (28) 84 E2
Fontaine-la-Louvet (27) . . . 34 B5
Fontaine-la-Mallet (76) 14 B6
Fontaine-la-Rivière (91) . . . 86 C4
Fontaine-la-Soret (27) 34 E5
Fontaine-l'Abbé (27) 34 E6
Fontaine-Lavaganne (60) . . . 17 H6
Fontaine-le-Bourg (76) 16 A6
Fontaine-le-Comte (86) . . . 162 E4
Fontaine-le-Dun (76) 15 H3
Fontaine-le-Pin (14) 53 E4
Fontaine-le-Port (77) 87 J2
Fontaine-le-Puits (73) 209 H5
Fontaine-le-Sec (80) 17 G1
Fontaine-les-Bassets (61) . . 54 C3
Fontaine-lès-Boulans (62) . . 5 G6
Fontaine-lès-Cappy (80) . . . 19 F2
Fontaine-lès-Clercs (02) . . . 19 K3
Fontaine-lès-Clerval (25) . . 138 E3
Fontaine-les-Coteaux (41) . . 107 K5
Fontaine-lès-Croisilles (62) . . 11 G5
Fontaine-lès-Dijon (21) . . . 136 A5
Fontaine-lès-Grès (10) 89 K3
Fontaine-lès-Hermans (62) . . 5 H5
Fontaine-lès-Luxeuil (70) . . 118 C4
Fontaine-lès-Ribouts (28) . . 56 E6
Fontaine-lès-Vervins (02) . . . 21 F2
Fontaine-l'Étalon (62) 9 J2
Fontaine-Mâcon (10) 89 F3
Fontaine-Milon (49) 125 K3
Fontaine-Notre-Dame (02) . . 20 B2
Fontaine-Notre-Dame (59) . . 11 J4
Fontaine-Raoul (41) 108 D3
Fontaine-Saint-Lucien (60) . . 37 H1
la Fontaine-Saint-Martin (72) . 106 C5
Fontaine-Simon (28) 84 C2
Fontaine-sous-Jouy (27) . . . 56 E1
Fontaine-sous-Montdidier (80) . 18 D5
Fontaine-sous-Préaux (76) . . 35 J1
Fontaine-sur-Ay (51) 41 F6
Fontaine-sur-Maye (80) 9 H3
Fontaine-sur-Somme (80) . . . 9 H6
Fontaine-Uterte (02) 20 A1
Fontainebleau (77) 87 H3
Fontainebrux (39) 172 E1
Fontaines (71) 153 K5
Fontaines (85) 160 D5
Fontaines (89) 132 D1
Fontaines-d'Ozillac (17) . . . 211 K1
Fontaines-en-Duesmois (21) . 135 F1
Fontaines-en-Sologne (41) . . 129 G3
Fontaines-les-Sèches (21) . . 114 D5
Fontaines-Saint-Clair (55) . . 43 G2
Fontaines-Saint-Martin (69) . 206 A1
Fontaines-sur-Marne (52) . . 92 A4
Fontaines-sur-Saône (69) . . 206 A1
Fontains (77) 88 A2
Fontan (06) 311 D3
Fontanès (30) 274 D2
Fontanès (34) 274 C4
Fontanes (42) 205 G5
Fontanes (46) 250 A3
Fontanes (48) 238 B3
Fontanès-de-Sault (11) . . . 308 D5
Fontanes-du-Causse (46) . . 233 K4
Fontanges (15) 217 J5
Fontangy (21) 134 D5
Fontanières (23) 183 K3
Fontanil-Cornillon (38) . . . 223 K2
Fontannes (43) 219 H2
Fontans (48) 237 H3
Fontarèches (30) 256 A5
Fontclaireau (16) 179 G6
Fontcouverte (11) 290 E6
Fontcouverte (17) 195 G2
Fontcouverte-la-Toussuire (73) . 225 G2
la Fontelaye (76) 15 J4
Fontenai-les-Louvets (61) . . 82 C2
Fontenai-sur-Orne (61) 54 D5
Fontenailles (77) 88 A1
Fontenailles (89) 133 F2
Fontenay (27) 36 C5
Fontenay (36) 148 A3
Fontenay (50) 52 C6
Fontenay (71) 170 E2
Fontenay (76) 14 B6

Fontenay (88) 94 E5
Fontenay-aux-Roses (92) . . . 58 D4
Fontenay-de-Bossery (10) . . 89 F3
Fontenay-en-Parisis (95) . . . 59 F1
Fontenay-le-Comte (85) . . . 160 D4
Fontenay-le-Fleury (78) . . . 58 B4
Fontenay-le-Marmion (14) . . 32 E4
Fontenay-le-Pesnel (14) . . . 32 C5
Fontenay-le-Vicomte (91) . . . 87 F2
Fontenay-Mauvoisin (78) . . . 57 H2
Fontenay-près-Chablis (89) . . 113 J4
Fontenay-près-Vézelay (89) . . 133 J4
Fontenay-Saint-Père (78) . . . 57 J1
Fontenay-sous-Bois (94) . . . 59 F3
Fontenay-sous-Fouronnes (89) . 133 G2
Fontenay-sur-Conie (28) . . . 85 H6
Fontenay-sur-Eure (28) . . . 85 F3
Fontenay-sur-Loing (45) . . . 111 J1
Fontenay-sur-Mer (50) 29 F4
Fontenay-sur-Vègre (72) . . . 106 A4
Fontenay-Torcy (60) 17 F6
Fontenay-Trésigny (77) 59 K5
Fontenelle (02) 13 G6
Fontenelle (21) 136 D3
la Fontenelle (35) 51 J5
la Fontenelle (41) 108 C2
Fontenelle (90) 119 J6
Fontenelle-en-Brie (02) . . . 61 F3
Fontenelle-Montby (25) . . . 138 D3
les Fontenelles (25) 139 G6
Fontenermont (14) 52 C3
Fontenet (17) 178 A6
Fontenille (16) 179 G6
Fontenille-Saint-
  Martin-d'Entraigues (79) . 178 D3
Fontenilles (31) 287 K1
Fontenois-la-Ville (70) 118 B3
Fontenois-lès-Montbozon (70) . 138 C3
Fontenotte (25) 138 C4
Fontenouilles (89) 112 B4
Fontenoy (02) 39 H2
Fontenoy (89) 132 D1
Fontenoy-la-Joûte (54) 95 F2
Fontenoy-le-Château (88) . . 118 B2
Fontenoy-sur-Moselle (54) . . 65 J5
Fontenu (39) 173 J2
Fonteny (57) 66 D2
Fonters-du-Razès (11) 289 G5
Fontès (34) 292 A4
Fontet (33) 230 C5
Fontette (10) 115 G1
Fontevraud-l'Abbaye (49) . . 144 D1
Fontgombault (36) 164 B2
Fontguenand (36) 147 J1
Fontienne (04) 258 E6
Fontiers-Cabardès (11) . . . 290 A4
Fontiès-d'Aude (11) 290 C6
Fontjoncouse (11) 310 A2
Fontoy (57) 27 F4
Fontpédrouse (66) 313 K4
Fontrabiouse (66) 313 J3
Fontrailles (65) 286 A4
Fontvannes (10) 89 J5
Fontvieille (13) 276 A4
Forbach (57) 68 C2
Forcalqueiret (83) 297 K3
Forcalquier (04) 278 B1
la Force (11) 289 J6
la Force (24) 231 G2
Forcé (53) 105 F2
Forcelles-Saint-Gorgon (54) . 93 K2
Forcelles-sous-Gugney (54) . 93 K3
Forceville (80) 10 C5
Forceville-en-Vimeu (80) . . . 17 G1
Forcey (52) 92 D5
Forciolo (2A) 320 E6
la Forclaz (74) 175 G6
Forest-en-Cambrésis (59) . . 12 D4
Forest-l'Abbaye (80) 9 G4
la Forest-Landerneau (29) . . 46 B6
Forest-Montiers (80) 9 F3
Forest-Saint-Julien (05) . . . 243 F4
Forest-sur-Marque (59) . . . 7 F4
Foreste (80) 19 J3
la Forestière (51) 61 G6
la Forêt-Auvray (61) 53 K4
la Forêt-de-Tessé (16) 179 F4
la Forêt-du-Parc (27) 56 E3
la Forêt-du-Temple (23) . . . 166 A3
la Forêt-Fouesnant (29) . . . 98 E2
Forêt-la-Folie (27) 36 C4
la Forêt-le-Roi (91) 86 B2
la Forêt-Sainte-Croix (91) . . 86 D4
la Forêt-sur-Sèvre (79) . . . 143 G6
Forfry (77) 59 H1
la Forge (88) 119 G1
Forges (17) 177 F3
Forgès (19) 216 C4
Forges (49) 144 B1
les Forges (56) 77 G6
Forges (61) 82 D2
Forges (77) 88 A3
les Forges (79) 162 B4
les Forges (88) 94 D5
Forges-la-Forêt (35) 103 K2
Forges-les-Bains (91) 58 C6
Forges-les-Eaux (76) 16 D5
Forges-sur-Meuse (55) 43 G4
Forgues (31) 287 H3
la Forie (63) 204 A4
Forléans (21) 134 C3

Formentin (14) 33 J5
Formerie (60) 17 F5
Formigny (14) 29 K6
Formiguères (66) 313 J3
Fornex (09) 287 K6
Fors (79) 178 A1
Forstfeld (67) 25 D3
Forstheim (67) 69 K5
Fort-du-Plasne (39) 174 A2
Fort-Louis (67) 25 D4
Fort-Mahon-Plage (80) 8 D2
Fort-Mardyck (59) 3 G1
Fort-Moville (27) 34 B3
Fortan (41) 108 A5
Fortel-en-Artois (62) 9 K3
la Forteresse (38) 223 H4
Fortschwihr (68) 96 D4
Fos (31) 305 K4
Fos (34) 292 A1
Fos-sur-Mer (13) 295 H5
le Fossat (09) 288 B2
Fossé (08) 42 E1
Fossé (41) 128 E2
Fosse (66) 309 G5
le Fossé (76) 16 E5
la Fosse-Corduan (10) 89 G3
la Fosse-de-Tigné (49) 143 K1
Fossemagne (24) 214 D4
Fossemanant (80) 17 K3
les Fosses (79) 178 B2
Fosses (95) 38 B6
Fossés-et-Baleyssac (33) . . . 230 D5
Fosseuse (60) 37 H5
Fosseux (62) 10 D3
Fossieux (57) 66 B3
Fossoy (02) 61 F1
Foucarmont (76) 16 E4
Foucart (76) 15 F5
Foucarville (50) 29 G5
Foucaucourt-en-Santerre (80) . 19 F2
Foucaucourt-Hors-Nesle (80) . 17 F7
Foucaucourt-sur-Thabas (55) . 64 A1
Fouchécourt (70) 117 K5
Fouchécourt (88) 117 H2
Foucherans (25) 156 C1
Foucherans (39) 155 G2
Fouchères (10) 90 C6
Fouchères (89) 88 C6
Fouchères-aux-Bois (55) . . . 64 B6
Foucherolles (45) 112 A2
Fouchy (67) 96 B1
Foucrainville (27) 56 E2
Fouday (67) 70 A5
Fouencamps (80) 18 C3
Fouesnant (29) 98 D2
Foufflin-Ricametz (62) 10 C1
Foug (54) 65 G5
Fougaron (31) 306 B2
Fougax-et-Barrineuf (09) . . . 308 B4
Fougeré (49) 126 A1
Fougeré (85) 159 K2
Fougères (35) 80 B3
Fougères-sur-Bièvre (41) . . . 128 E4
les Fougerêts (56) 102 B3
Fougerolles (36) 166 A4
Fougerolles (70) 118 D3
Fougerolles-du-Plessis (53) . . 80 D2
Fougueyrolles (24) 230 E2
la Fouillade (12) 251 G4
Fouilleuse (60) 38 B2
la Fouillouse (05) 242 D6
la Fouillouse (42) 205 F5
le Fouilloux (17) 212 C4
Fouilloy (60) 17 G4
Fouilloy (80) 18 C2
Fouju (77) 87 J1
Foulain (52) 116 B2
Foulangues (60) 37 K4
Foulayronnes (47) 248 B4
Foulbec (27) 34 B2
Foulcrey (57) 67 G4
Fouleix (24) 213 K6
Foulenay (39) 155 G5
Fouligny (57) 45 J5
Foulognes (14) 32 A5
Fouquebrune (16) 196 E5
Fouquenies (60) 37 G1
Fouquereuil (62) 5 K5
Fouquerolles (60) 37 J2
Fouquescourt (80) 19 F3
Fouqueure (16) 179 F6
Fouqueville (27) 35 G4
Fouquières-lès-Béthune (62) . 5 K5
Fouquières-lès-Lens (62) . . . 11 G1
Four (38) 206 E4
Fouras (17) 176 E4
Fourbanne (25) 138 C4
Fourcatier-et-Maison-Neuve (25) . 156 E6
Fourcès (32) 266 E1
Fourchambault (58) 150 D4
Fourches (14) 54 B3
Fourcigny (80) 17 G3
Fourdrain (02) 20 B5
Fourdrinoy (80) 17 J2
Fourg (25) 155 K2
Fourges (27) 36 D6
les Fourgs (25) 157 F5
Fourilles (03) 185 G2
Fourmagnac (46) 234 D4
Fourmetot (27) 34 D2
Fourmies (59) 13 J6
Fournaudin (89) 113 G2

Fourneaux (42) 187 G5
Fourneaux (50) 31 H5
Fourneaux (73) 225 K3
Fourneaux-le-Val (14) 54 A3
Fournels (48) 236 E2
Fournès (30) 275 K2
Fournes-Cabardès (11) . . . 290 B4
Fournes-en-Weppes (59) . . . 6 C5
le Fournet (14) 33 J5
Fournet-Blancheroche (25) . . 139 H6
Fournets-Luisans (25) 157 G1
Fourneville (14) 33 K3
Fournival (60) 37 K1
Fournols (63) 203 J5
Fouronnes (89) 133 G2
Fourques (30) 275 K5
Fourques (66) 315 F3
Fourques-sur-Garonne (47) . 247 G1
Fourqueux (78) 58 B3
Fourquevaux (31) 288 C2
Fours (33) 211 G3
Fours (58) 151 K6
Fours-en-Vexin (27) 36 C5
Fourtou (11) 309 G4
Foussais-Payré (85) 161 F3
Foussemagne (90) 119 K6
le Fousseret (31) 287 H5
Foussignac (16) 196 B2
Fouvent-Saint-Andoche (70) . 137 G1
Fouzilhon (34) 292 A2
Fox-Amphoux (83) 278 E6
la Foye-Monjault (79) 177 K2
Fozières (34) 273 G4
Fozzano (2A) 322 E2
Fragnes (71) 154 A6
Frahier-et-Chatebier (70) . . 119 G6
Fraignot-et-Vesvrotte (21) . . 135 K1
Fraillicourt (08) 21 J4
Fraimbois (54) 94 E1
Frain (88) 117 J1
Frais (90) 119 J6
Fraisans (39) 155 K1
Fraisnes-en-Saintois (54) . . 93 K3
Fraisse (24) 231 G1
Fraisse-Cabardès (11) 290 A4
Fraissé-des-Corbières (11) . . 310 B3
Fraisse-sur-Agout (34) 272 A6
Fraisses (42) 221 F1
Fraissines (81) 271 H2
Fraissinet-de-Fourques (48) . 254 B4
Fraissinet-de-Lozère (48) . . 254 D2
Fraize (88) 95 J5
Fralignes (10) 90 D6
la Framboisière (28) 84 C1
Frambouhans (25) 139 H6
Framecourt (62) 10 A2
Framerville-Rainecourt (80) . . 18 E2
Framicourt (80) 17 F1
Framont (70) 137 F2
Frampas (52) 91 H2
Francalmont (70) 118 C4
Francaltroff (57) 67 G1
Francarville (31) 288 E1
Francastel (60) 17 K6
Françay (41) 128 C2
Francazal (31) 306 C2
Francescas (47) 247 K6
Franchesse (03) 168 B3
Francheval (08) 23 G4
Franchevelle (70) 118 D5
la Francheville (08) 22 D4
Francheville (21) 135 J3
Francheville (27) 56 A4
Francheville (39) 155 G5
Francheville (51) 63 F3
Francheville (54) 65 J4
Francheville (61) 54 B6
Francheville (69) 205 K2
Francières (60) 38 C2
Francières (80) 9 H5
Francillon (36) 147 J4
Francillon-sur-Roubion (26) . . 240 E5
Francilly-Selency (02) 19 K2
Francin (73) 208 D5
Franclens (74) 190 C4
François (79) 161 J5
Francon (31) 287 G5
Franconville (54) 94 D1
Franconville (95) 58 D2
Françoulès (46) 233 H6
Francourt (70) 137 H1
Francourville (28) 85 H2
Francs (33) 212 D6
Francueil (37) 128 C5
Franey (25) 137 H6
Frangy (74) 190 D4
Frangy-en-Bresse (71) 172 E1
Franken (68) 97 C4
Franleu (80) 8 E5
Franois (25) 137 J6
Franquevielle (31) 286 C6
Franqueville (02) 20 E3
Franqueville (27) 34 E5
Franqueville (80) 9 H5
Franqueville-Saint-Pierre (76) . 35 J2
Frans (01) 188 C5
Fransart (80) 19 F3
Fransèches (23) 183 F5
Fransu (80) 9 J5

Fransures (80) 18 A4
Franvillers (80) 18 C1
Franxault (21) 154 E3
Frapelle (88) 95 K4
Fraquelfing (57) 67 J5
Fraroz (39) 156 C6
Frasnay-Reugny (58) 151 H4
Frasne (25) 156 D5
Frasne (39) 155 G1
Frasne-le-Château (70) . . . 137 J3
la Frasnée (39) 173 J3
le Frasnois (39) 173 K2
Frasnoy (59) 12 E3
Frasseto (2A) 320 E5
Frauenberg (57) 68 E2
Frausseilles (81) 270 B1
Fravaux (10) 91 G5
le Fraysse (81) 271 G3
Frayssinet (46) 233 H4
Frayssinet-le-Gélat (46) . . . 232 E5
Frayssinhes (46) 234 C2
Frazé (28) 84 C5
Fréauville (76) 16 C3
Frebécourt (88) 93 F3
Frébuans (39) 173 F2
le Frêche (40) 265 K2
Fréchède (65) 285 K3
Fréchencourt (80) 18 C1
Fréchendets (65) 304 E1
le Fréchet (31) 287 G6
Fréchet-Aure (65) 305 F3
Fréchou (47) 247 J6
Fréchou-Fréchet (65) 285 J6
Frécourt (52) 116 E3
Frédéric-Fontaine (70) 119 F6
la Frédière (17) 177 J6
Frédille (36) 147 H4
Frégimont (47) 247 K3
Frégouville (32) 287 G1
Fréhel (22) 50 A3
Freigné (49) 124 B2
Freissinières (05) 243 J2
la Freissinouse (05) 242 D5
Freistroff (57) 27 K5
Freix-Anglards (15) 217 H6
Fréjairolles (81) 270 E3
Fréjeville (81) 270 E6
Fréjus (83) 299 G2
Fréland (68) 96 A3
Frelinghien (59) 6 C3
Frémainville (95) 58 A1
Frémécourt (95) 37 G6
Fréménil (54) 67 F6
Frémeréville-sous-les-Côtes (55) . 65 F4
Frémery (57) 66 D2
Frémestroff (57) 68 B4
Frémicourt (62) 11 G5
Fremifontaine (88) 95 F4
Frémontiers (80) 17 J4
Frémonville (54) 67 H6
la Frénaye (76) 14 E6
Frencq (62) 4 B5
Frenelle-la-Grande (88) . . . 93 K3
Frenelle-la-Petite (88) 93 K3
Frênes (61) 53 G4
Freneuse (76) 35 H3
Freneuse (78) 57 H1
Freneuse-sur-Risle (27) . . . 34 D4
Freney (73) 225 K2
le Freney-d'Oisans (38) . . . 224 E5
Fréniches (60) 19 H5
Frénois (21) 135 J3
Frénois (88) 94 A5
Frénouville (14) 33 F5
Frépillon (95) 58 D1
Fresles (76) 16 C4
la Fresnaie-Fayel (61) 54 E4
la Fresnais (35) 51 J4
Fresnay (10) 91 H4
Fresnay-en-Retz (44) 122 D6
Fresnay-le-Comte (28) 85 G5
Fresnay-le-Gilmert (28) . . . 85 F2
Fresnay-le-Long (76) 15 K5
Fresnay-le-Samson (61) . . . 54 E3
Fresnay-l'Évêque (28) 85 K5
Fresnay-sur-Sarthe (72) . . . 82 C5
la Fresnaye-au-Sauvage (61) . 54 A5
la Fresnaye-sur-Chédouet (72) . 82 E3
le Fresne (27) 56 B2
le Fresne (51) 63 F2
le Fresne-Camilly (14) 32 D4
Fresné-la-Mère (14) 54 B3
Fresne-l'Archevêque (27) . . 36 A4
Fresne-le-Plan (76) 35 K2
Fresne-Léguillon (60) 37 G4
Fresne-lès-Reims (51) 41 F3
le Fresne-Poret (50) 52 E5
Fresne-Saint-Mamès (70) . . 137 J2
le Fresne-sur-Loire (44) . . . 124 D4
Fresneaux-Montchevreuil (60) . 37 G4
Fresnes (02) 20 A6
Fresnes (21) 134 E3
Fresnes (41) 129 F4
Fresnes (89) 114 A6
Fresnes (94) 58 E5
Fresnes-au-Mont (55) 64 C3
Fresnes-en-Saulnois (57) . . 66 C3
Fresnes-en-Tardenois (02) . . 40 A5
Fresnes-en-Woëvre (55) . . . 44 A6
Fresnes-lès-Montauban (62) . 11 G2
Fresnes-Mazancourt (80) . . 19 G2

Fresnes-sur-Apance (52) 117 H3
Fresnes-sur-Escaut (59) 12 D1
Fresnes-sur-Marne (77) 59 J2
Fresnes-Tilloloy (80) 17 F1
Fresneville (80) 17 G2
Fresney (27) 56 E2
Fresney-le-Puceux (14) 32 K6
Fresney-le-Vieux (14) 53 J1
Fresnicourt-le-Dolmen (62) 10 D1
Fresnières (60) 19 F5
Fresnois-la-Montagne (54) . . . 26 B3
Fresnoy (62) 9 J2
Fresnoy-Andainville (80) 17 G2
Fresnoy-au-Val (80) 17 J3
Fresnoy-en-Chaussée (80) 18 D3
Fresnoy-en-Gohelle (62) 11 F2
Fresnoy-en-Thelle (60) 37 J5
Fresnoy-Folny (76) 16 C2
Fresnoy-la-Rivière (60) 38 E4
Fresnoy-le-Château (10) 90 C6
Fresnoy-le-Grand (02) 20 B1
Fresnoy-le-Luat (60) 38 D5
Fresnoy-lès-Roye (80) 19 F4
Frespech (47) 248 E3
Fresquiennes (76) 15 J6
Fressac (30) 274 C1
Fressain (59) 11 J3
Fressancourt (02) 20 B5
Fresse (70) 119 F5
Fresse-sur-Moselle (88) 119 G3
Fresselines (23) 165 H3
Fressenneville (80) 8 D5
Fressies (59) 11 J3
Fressin (62) 4 E6
Fressines (79) 161 J6
le Frestoy-Vaux (60) 18 D6
Fresville (50) 29 F3
Fréterive (73) 208 E4
Fréteval (41) 108 D3
Fréthun (62) 2 C3
Fretigney-et-Velloreille (70) . . 137 K3
Frétigny (28) 84 B4
Fretin (59) 6 E5
Frétoy (77) 60 C5
Frétoy-le-Château (60) 19 H5
la Frette (38) 207 G6
la Frette (71) 172 B2
la Frette-sur-Seine (95) 58 D2
Frettecuisse (80) 17 G1
Frettemeule (80) 8 E6
Fretterans (71) 154 E4
le Fréty (08) 21 K4
Freulleville (76) 16 B3
Frévent (62) 10 A3
Fréville (76) 15 H6
Fréville (88) 93 F4
Fréville-du-Gâtinais (45) 111 F2
Frévillers (62) 10 C1
Frévin-Capelle (62) 10 C2
Freybouse (57) 68 B4
Freycenet-la-Cuche (43) 238 E1
Freycenet-la-Tour (43) 238 E1
Freychenet (09) 307 K4
Freyming-Merlebach (57) . . . 68 B2
Freyssenet (07) 239 J4
Friaize (28) 84 D3
Friardel (14) 55 G1
Friaucourt (80) 8 D5
Friauville (54) 44 C5
Fribourg (57) 67 G3
Fricamps (80) 17 J3
Frichemesnil (76) 16 A5
Fricourt (80) 10 E6
Fridefont (15) 236 E1
Friedolsheim (67) 70 C2
Frières-Faillouël (02) 19 K4
Friesen (68) 97 A5
Friesenheim (67) 71 D4
Frignicourt (51) 63 F5
Frise (80) 19 F4
Friville-Escarbotin (80) 8 D5
Frizon (88) 94 C4
Froberville (76) 14 C4
Frocourt (60) 37 H3
Froeningen (68) 97 B3
Froeschwiller (67) 69 K4
Froges (38) 224 C2
Frohen-le-Grand (80) 9 K4
Frohen-le-Petit (80) 9 K4
Frohmuhl (67) 69 F5
Froideconche (70) 118 D4
Froidefontaine (90) 139 J1
Froidestrées (02) 21 F1
Froideterre (70) 118 E5
Froidevaux (25) 139 G5
Froideville (39) 155 G6
Froidfond (85) 141 G4
Froidmont-Cohartille (02) . . . 20 D4
Froidos (55) 43 F6
Froissy (60) 18 A6
Frôlois (21) 135 G3
Frolois (54) 66 A6
Fromelennes (08) 24 D1
Fromelles (59) 6 C4
Fromental (87) 181 J3
Fromentières (51) 61 H3
Fromentières (53) 105 F4
Fromeréville-les-Vallons (55) . . 43 G5
Fromezey (55) 26 B6
Fromont (77) 87 F5
Fromy (08) 23 J3
Froncles (52) 92 B4

G

Gaas (40) 264 B5
Gabarnac (33) 230 A5
Gabarret (40) 266 C1
Gabaston (64) 284 E3
Gabat (64) 283 G3
Gabian (34) 292 A2
Gabillou (24) 214 D3
Gabre (09) 307 G1
Gabriac (12) 252 D1
Gabriac (48) 254 D5
Gabrias (48) 237 H6
Gacé (61) 55 F4
la Gacilly (56) 102 B2
Gâcogne (58) 152 B1
Gadancourt (95) 36 E6
Gadencourt (27) 57 F2
Gaël (35) 78 B4
Gageac-et-Rouillac (24) 231 G3
Gagnac-sur-Cère (46) 234 C1
Gagnac-sur-Garonne (31) . . . 269 G5
Gagnières (30) 255 H3
Gagny (93) 59 G4
Gahard (35) 79 H2
Gailhan (30) 274 D3
Gaillac (81) 270 B3
Gaillac-d'Aveyron (12) 253 F3
Gaillac-Toulza (31) 288 C5
Gaillagos (65) 303 K2
Gaillan-en-Médoc (33) 210 D1
Gaillard (74) 191 G2
Gaillardbois-Cressenville (27) . . 36 A3
la Gaillarde (76) 15 H4
Gaillefontaine (76) 16 E5
Gaillères (40) 265 J2
Gaillon (27) 36 A5
Gaillon-sur-Montcient (78) . . . 58 A1
Gainneville (76) 14 C6
Gaja-et-Villedieu (11) 308 E1
Gaja-la-Selve (11) 289 G6
Gajac (33) 246 E1
Gajan (09) 306 D2
Gajan (30) 275 F2
Gajoubert (87) 180 D3
Galametz (62) 9 J2
Galan (65) 286 B5
Galapian (47) 247 K3
Galargues (34) 274 D4
Galéria (2B) 316 C3
Galey (09) 306 B3
Galez (65) 286 B6
Galfingue (68) 97 B3
Galgan (12) 251 H1

Galgon (33) 212 A6
Galiax (32) 266 C6
Galié (31) 305 J2
Galinagues (11) 308 D5
Gallardon (28) 85 J2
le Gallet (60) 17 K5
Galluis (78) 57 K4
Gamaches (80) 8 D6
Gamaches-en-Vexin (27) . . . 36 C4
Gamarde-les-Bains (40) 264 D4
Gamarthe (64) 282 E5
Gambais (78) 57 J4
Gambaiseuil (78) 57 J5
Gambsheim (67) 25 B5
Gan (64) 284 C5
Ganac (09) 307 H3
Ganagobie (04) 259 F6
Gancourt-Saint-Etienne (76) . . 17 F6
Gandelain (61) 82 B2
Gandelu (02) 39 H6
Gandrange (57) 27 G5
Ganges (34) 274 A2
Gannat (03) 185 G4
Gannay-sur-Loire (03) 169 H1
Gannes (60) 18 C6
Gans (33) 246 D1
Ganties (31) 306 A1
Ganzeville (76) 14 D4
Gap (05) 242 E5
Gapennes (80) 9 H4
Gâprée (61) 55 F6
Garac (31) 268 D5
Garancières (78) 57 J4
Garancières-en-Beauce (28) . . 86 A3
Garancières-en-Drouais (28) . . 56 E5
Garanou (09) 307 K5
Garat (16) 197 F4
Garcelles-Secqueville (14) . . . 32 K6
Garches (92) 58 D4
Garchizy (58) 150 D3
Garchy (58) 132 B6
Gardanne (13) 296 D2
la Garde (38) 224 D4
la Garde (83) 297 K6
la Garde-Adhémar (26) 256 D2
la Garde-Freinet (83) 298 D3
Gardefort (18) 131 K6
Gardegan-et-Tourtirac (33) . . . 230 C1
Gardères (65) 285 F4
Gardes-le-Pontaroux (16) . . . 197 F5
Gardie (11) 309 F1
Gardonne (24) 231 G2
Gardouch (31) 288 E3
Garein (40) 245 J6
Garencières (27) 56 E2
la Garenne-Colombes (92) . . . 58 D3
Garennes-sur-Eure (27) 57 F3
Garentreville (77) 87 G5
Garéoult (83) 297 K3
Garganvillar (82) 268 D2
Gargas (31) 269 H4
Gargas (84) 277 H2
Gargenville (78) 57 K2
Garges-lès-Gonesse (95) . . . 59 F2
Gargilesse-Dampierre (36) . . . 165 H4
Garidech (31) 269 H5
Gariès (82) 268 C4
Garigny (18) 150 B3
Garin (31) 305 G5
Garindein (64) 283 H5
Garlan (29) 47 G4
Garlède-Mondebat (64) 284 D1
Garlin (64) 284 E1
le Garn (30) 256 D3
la Garnache (85) 141 F4
Garnat-sur-Engièvre (03) . . . 169 H3
Garnay (28) 57 F5
Garnerans (01) 188 C2
Garons (30) 275 H4
Garos (64) 284 C1
Garravet (32) 287 G3
Garrebourg (57) 70 A2
Garrevaques (81) 289 H2
Garrey (40) 264 C5
le Garric (81) 270 E1
Garrigues (34) 274 D4
Garrigues (81) 269 K5
Garrigues-Sainte-Eulalie (30) . . 275 G1
Garris (64) 283 F3
Garrosse (40) 245 F6
Gars (06) 280 C2
Gartempe (23) 182 C3
Gas (28) 85 J1
Gasny (27) 36 C6
Gasques (82) 248 E5
Gassin (83) 299 F4
le Gast (14) 52 C4
Gastes (40) 244 D2
Gastines (53) 104 B3
Gastins (77) 60 A6
Gasville-Oisème (28) 85 G3
Gatey (39) 155 G4
Gathemo (50) 52 D4
Gatteville-le-Phare (50) 29 G2
Gattières (06) 281 F3
Gatuzières (48) 254 B4
Gaubertin (45) 111 F1
la Gaubretière (85) 142 D4
Gauchin-Légal (62) 10 D1
Gauchin-Verloingt (62) 10 A1

Gauchy (02) 19 K3
Gauciel (27) 56 E1
la Gaudaine (28) 84 B5
la Gaude (06) 281 F3
Gaudechart (60) 17 H5
Gaudent (65) 305 H2
Gaudiempré (62) 10 C2
Gaudiès (09) 288 E6
Gaudonville (32) 268 A3
Gaudreville-la-Rivière (27) . . . 56 C2
Gaugeac (24) 232 B4
Gaujac (30) 256 C6
Gaujac (32) 287 G1
Gaujac (47) 230 E6
Gaujacq (40) 264 E5
Gaujan (32) 286 E2
le Gault-Perche (41) 108 B1
le Gault-Saint-Denis (28) 85 G5
le Gault-Soigny (51) 61 G4
Gauré (31) 269 J6
Gauriac (33) 211 G5
Gauriaguet (33) 211 K5
Gaussan (65) 286 B5
Gausson (22) 77 G3
Gauville (61) 55 H4
Gauville (80) 17 G3
Gauville-la-Campagne (27) . . . 56 C1
Gavarnie (65) 304 B5
Gavarret-sur-Aulouste (32) . . . 267 J4
Gavaudun (47) 232 C6
Gavignano (2B) 319 G4
Gavisse (57) 27 H3
Gavray (50) 30 E6
Gavrelle (62) 11 F2
Gâvres (56) 99 K5
Gavrus (14) 32 C5
Gayan (65) 285 H4
Gaye (51) 61 J5
Gayon (64) 285 F2
Gazaupouy (32) 267 G1
Gazave (65) 305 G2
Gazax-et-Baccarisse (32) . . . 266 D6
Gazeran (78) 57 J6
Gazost (65) 304 B2
Géanges (71) 154 B4
Geaune (40) 265 H5
Geay (17) 177 H6
Geay (79) 144 A5
Gèdre (65) 304 B5
Gée (49) 125 K3
Gée-Rivière (32) 266 A5
Geffosses (50) 30 D3
Géfosse-Fontenay (14) 29 H4
Gehée (36) 147 H3
Geishouse (68) 119 K3
Geispitzen (68) 97 D3
Geispolsheim (67) 70 E4
Geiswasser (68) 96 E5
Geiswiller (67) 69 H6
Gélacourt (54) 95 F1
Gélannes (10) 89 G2
Gélaucourt (54) 93 J2
Gellainville (28) 85 G3
Gellenoncourt (54) 66 C5
Gelles (63) 202 A2
Gellin (25) 156 E6
Gelos (64) 284 D4
Geloux (40) 265 F1
Gelucourt (57) 67 F4
Gelvécourt-et-Adompt (88) . . . 94 A5
Gémages (61) 83 J5
Gemaingoutte (88) 95 K4
Gembrie (65) 305 H2
Gemeaux (21) 136 B3
Gémenos (13) 297 F4
Gémigny (45) 109 J3
Gémil (31) 269 J5
Gemmelaincourt (88) 93 J4
Gémonval (25) 139 F2
Gémonville (54) 93 H3
Gémozac (17) 195 F4
Genac (16) 196 C1
Genainville (95) 36 E6
Genas (69) 206 C2
Génat (09) 307 H5
Genay (21) 135 J6
Genay (69) 188 C6
Gençay (86) 163 H6
Gendreville (88) 93 G5
Gendrey (39) 137 G6
Gené (49) 124 E1
Génébrières (82) 269 H1
Genech (59) 7 F5
Génelard (71) 170 D3
Générac (30) 275 G4
Générac (33) 211 H3
Générargues (30) 255 F6
Générest (65) 305 H2
Generville (11) 289 G6
Geneslay (61) 81 H2
le Genest-Saint-Isle (53) 104 D1
Genestelle (07) 239 H4
Geneston (44) 123 H6
la Genête (71) 172 B3
la Genétouze (17) 212 C3
la Genétouze (85) 159 H1
Genêts (50) 51 J3
les Genettes (61) 55 H6
Geneuille (25) 137 K5
la Genevraie (61) 55 F5
la Genevraye (77) 87 J4

Genevreuille (70) 118 D6
Genevrey (70) 118 C5
Genevrières (52) 117 C5
la Genevroye (52) 92 A5
Geney (25) 139 F2
Génicourt (95) 37 G6
Génicourt-sur-Meuse (55) . . . 64 D1
Genilac (42) 205 J5
Genillé (37) 146 E1
Génis (24) 214 E2
Génissac (33) 230 A2
Génissieux (26) 222 E4
Genlis (21) 136 C6
Gennes (25) 138 B6
Gennes (49) 125 K5
Gennes-Ivergny (62) 9 J3
Gennes-sur-Glaize (53) 105 G4
Gennes-sur-Seiche (35) 104 B2
Genneteil (49) 126 C2
Gennetines (03) 169 F3
Genneton (79) 143 K3
Genneville (14) 34 A2
Gennevilliers (92) 58 E2
Genod (39) 173 G6
Génolhac (30) 255 F3
Génos (31) 305 J2
Génos (65) 305 F5
Genouillac (16) 197 J1
Genouillac (23) 166 B6
Genouillé (17) 177 G4
Genouillé (86) 179 J3
Genouilleux (01) 188 C3
Genouilly (18) 148 B1
Genouilly (71) 171 G2
Gensac (33) 230 D2
Gensac (65) 285 H2
Gensac (82) 268 B2
Gensac-de-Boulogne (31) . . . 286 C5
Gensac-la-Pallue (16) 196 A3
Gensac-sur-Garonne (31) . . . 287 J5
Genté (16) 195 K3
Gentelles (80) 18 C2
Gentilly (94) 58 E4
Gentioux-Pigerolles (23) 200 C2
Genvry (60) 19 H5
Georfans (70) 138 C2
Géovreisset (01) 190 A1
Géovreissiat (01) 189 K2
Ger (50) 53 F5
Ger (64) 285 G5
Ger (65) 304 B1
Geraise (39) 156 B4
Gérardmer (88) 119 H1
Géraudot (10) 90 D4
Gerbaix (73) 207 K3
Gerbamont (88) 119 G2
Gerbécourt (57) 66 D3
Gerbécourt-et-Haplemont (54) . . 94 A2
Gerbépal (88) 95 H5
Gerberoy (60) 17 G6
Gerbéviller (54) 94 D1
Gercourt-et-Drillancourt (55) . . 43 G3
Gercy (02) 21 F3
Gerde (65) 304 D1
Gerderest (64) 285 F3
Gère-Bélesten (64) 303 H2
Gergny (02) 21 F1
Gergueil (21) 135 J6
Gergy (71) 154 B5
Gerland (21) 154 C2
Germ (65) 305 G5
Germagnat (01) 173 F6
Germagny (71) 171 G2
Germaine (02) 19 J3
Germaine (51) 41 F6
Germaines (52) 116 A5
Germainville (28) 57 G5
Germainvilliers (52) 117 F1
Germay (52) 92 D3
Germéfontaine (25) 138 E6
Germenay (58) 133 G6
Germignac (17) 195 K4
Germigney (39) 155 J3
Germigney (70) 137 F4
Germignonville (28) 85 J6
Germigny (51) 40 D4
Germigny (89) 113 J3
Germigny-des-Prés (45) 110 D5
Germigny-l'Évêque (77) 60 A2
Germigny-l'Exempt (18) 150 B3
Germigny-sous-Coulombs (77) . . 60 C1
Germigny-sur-Loire (58) 150 C3
Germinon (51) 62 B3
Germiny (54) 93 J1
Germisay (52) 92 D3
Germolles-sur-Grosne (71) . . . 188 A1
Germond-Rouvre (79) 161 H4
Germondans (25) 138 B4
Germont (08) 42 D2
Germonville (54) 94 B3
Gerns-sur-l'Oussouet (65) . . . 304 C1
Gernelle (08) 22 E3
Gernicourt (02) 40 D2
Géronce (64) 283 K5
Gerponville (76) 14 E3
Gerrots (14) 33 H5
Gerstheim (67) 71 D3
Gertwiller (67) 70 C5
Geruge (39) 173 F2
Gervans (26) 222 B4
Gerville (76) 14 C4

Commune	Page	Grid
Géry (55)	64	C4
Gerzat (63)	202	D1
Gesnes (53)	81	G6
Gesnes-en-Argonne (55)	42	E3
Gesnes-le-Gandelin (72)	82	C4
Gespunsart (08)	22	E2
Gestas (64)	283	H3
Gesté (49)	142	C1
Gestel (56)	99	K4
Gestiès (09)	307	H5
Gesvres (53)	82	B3
Gesvres-le-Chapitre (77)	59	K1
Gétigné (44)	123	K6
les Gets (74)	192	A2
Geu (65)	304	B2
Geudertheim (67)	25	A5
Géus-d'Arzacq (64)	284	B2
Géüs-d'Oloron (64)	283	K4
Gévezé (35)	79	F3
Gevigney-et-Mercey (70)	117	J5
Geville (55)	65	K4
Gevingey (39)	173	F2
Gevresin (25)	156	C3
Gevrey-Chambertin (21)	135	K6
Gevrolles (21)	115	H3
Gevry (39)	155	H3
Gex (01)	174	B6
Geyssans (26)	222	E4
Gez (65)	304	A2
Gez-ez-Angles (65)	304	C1
Gézaincourt (80)	10	A4
Gézier-et-Fontenelay (70)	137	J4
Gézoncourt (54)	65	J3
Ghisonaccia (2B)	321	J3
Ghisoni (2B)	321	G2
Ghissignies (59)	12	E4
Ghyvelde (59)	3	J1
Giat (63)	201	H2
Gibeaumeix (54)	65	G6
Gibel (31)	288	E4
Gibercourt (02)	19	K4
Giberville (14)	33	F5
Gibles (71)	170	E6
Gibourne (17)	178	B5
Gibret (40)	264	D5
le Gicq (17)	178	C5
Gidy (45)	109	K3
Giel-Courteilles (61)	54	A4
Gien (45)	131	H1
Gien-sur-Cure (58)	152	D2
Gières (38)	224	B3
la Giettaz (73)	191	J6
Giéville (50)	31	J4
Gièvres (41)	129	H6
Giey-sur-Aujon (52)	116	A3
Giez (74)	208	E1
Gif-sur-Yvette (91)	58	C5
Giffaumont-Champaubert (51)	91	H1
Gigean (34)	293	F2
Gignac (34)	273	J6
Gignac (46)	215	H6
Gignac (84)	277	J2
Gignac-la-Nerthe (13)	296	B3
Gignat (63)	202	E6
Gignéville (88)	117	J1
Gigney (88)	94	C5
Gigny (39)	173	F4
Gigny (89)	114	D5
Gigny-Bussy (51)	63	F6
Gigny-sur-Saône (71)	172	A2
Gigondas (84)	257	G5
Gigors (04)	259	H1
Gigors-et-Lozeron (26)	240	E2
Gigouzac (46)	233	H5
Gijounet (81)	271	J5
Gildwiller (68)	97	A3
Gilette (06)	281	F2
Gilhac-et-Bruzac (07)	240	A2
Gilhoc-sur-Ormèze (07)	222	A6
Gillancourt (52)	91	K6
Gillaumé (52)	92	C2
Gilles (28)	57	G3
Gilley (25)	157	G2
Gilley (52)	117	G6
Gillois (39)	174	A1
Gillonnay (38)	207	F6
Gilly-lès-Cîteaux (21)	154	E1
Gilly-sur-Isère (73)	209	F3
Gilly-sur-Loire (71)	169	J4
Gilocourt (60)	38	E4
Gimat (82)	268	B3
Gimbrède (32)	267	K1
Gimeaux (63)	185	F5
Gimécourt (55)	64	C3
Gimel-les-Cascades (19)	216	B2
Gimeux (16)	195	J3
la Gimond (42)	205	G4
Gimont (32)	268	B6
Gimouille (58)	150	D4
Ginai (61)	54	E5
Ginals (82)	250	E5
Ginasservis (83)	278	C5
Ginchy (80)	11	F6
Gincla (11)	309	H5
Gincrey (55)	26	B6
Gindou (46)	233	F5
Ginestas (11)	291	G5
Ginestet (24)	231	H1
Gingsheim (67)	70	D1
Ginoles (11)	308	E4
Ginouillac (46)	233	J4
Gintrac (46)	234	A2
Giocatojo (2B)	319	H4
Gionges (51)	61	K2
Giou-de-Mamou (15)	235	J1
Gioux (23)	200	D2
Gipcy (03)	168	B4
Girac (46)	234	B1
Girancourt (88)	94	C5
Giraumont (54)	44	C4
Giraumont (60)	38	D1
Girauvoisin (55)	65	F3
Gircourt-lès-Viéville (88)	94	B3
Girecourt-sur-Durbion (88)	94	E4
Girefontaine (70)	118	B3
Giremoutiers (77)	60	B4
Girgols (15)	217	H5
Girmont (88)	94	D4
Girmont-Val-d'Ajol (88)	118	C2
Girolles (45)	111	H2
Girolles (89)	133	J3
Giromagny (90)	119	H5
Giron (01)	190	B1
Gironcourt-sur-Vraine (88)	93	J4
Gironde-sur-Dropt (33)	230	C5
Girondelle (08)	22	A2
Gironville (77)	87	G6
Gironville-sur-Essonne (91)	86	E4
le Girouard (85)	159	G3
Giroussens (81)	270	A4
Giroux (36)	148	C3
Gisay-la-Coudre (27)	55	J2
Giscaro (32)	268	A4
Giscos (33)	246	D3
Gisors (27)	36	E4
Gissey-le-Vieil (21)	135	F5
Gissey-sous-Flavigny (21)	135	G3
Gissey-sur-Ouche (21)	135	H6
Gisy-les-Nobles (89)	88	D5
Giuncaggio (2B)	321	H1
Giuncheto (2A)	322	E3
Givardon (18)	150	A6
Givarlais (03)	167	H5
Givenchy-en-Gohelle (62)	10	E1
Givenchy-le-Noble (62)	10	C2
Givenchy-lès-la-Bassée (62)	6	B5
Giverny (27)	36	B6
Giverville (27)	34	D5
Givet (08)	24	C1
Givonne (08)	23	F4
Givors (69)	206	A4
Givraines (45)	110	E1
Givrand (85)	158	D1
Givrauval (55)	64	C5
le Givre (85)	159	J4
Givrezac (17)	195	G4
Givron (08)	21	K5
Givry (08)	41	K1
Givry (71)	153	K6
Givry (89)	133	J3
Givry-en-Argonne (51)	63	J2
Givry-lès-Loisy (51)	61	K3
Givrycourt (57)	67	H1
Gizaucourt (51)	42	C6
Gizay (86)	163	F5
Gizeux (37)	126	D4
Gizia (39)	172	E3
Gizy (02)	20	E5
la Glacerie (50)	28	D2
Glageon (59)	13	J5
Glaignes (60)	38	E4
Glaine-Montaigut (63)	203	D3
Glaire (08)	23	F4
le Glaizil (05)	242	D3
Glamondans (25)	138	C5
Gland (02)	60	E1
Gland (89)	114	C5
Glandage (26)	241	K4
Glandon (87)	198	E6
Glanes (46)	234	C1
Glanges (87)	199	G3
Glannes (51)	63	F5
Glanon (21)	154	D3
Glanville (14)	33	J3
Glatens (82)	268	B3
Glatigny (50)	30	C1
Glatigny (57)	45	G5
Glatigny (60)	37	F1
Glay (25)	139	J3
Gleizé (69)	188	B5
Glénac (56)	102	B3
Glénat (15)	235	F1
Glénay (79)	144	B3
Glénic (23)	182	D2
Glennes (02)	40	C3
Glénouze (86)	144	D3
Glère (25)	139	K4
Glicourt (76)	16	B1
Glisolles (27)	56	C2
Glisy (80)	18	B2
Glomel (22)	76	A3
Glonville (54)	95	F1
Glorianes (66)	314	D3
Glos (14)	34	A6
Glos-la-Ferrière (61)	55	J3
Glos-sur-Risle (27)	34	E4
Gluiras (07)	239	K5
Glun (07)	222	B5
Glux-en-Glenne (58)	152	C4
Goas (82)	268	C4
la Godefroy (50)	52	A5
Godenvillers (60)	18	D6
Goderville (76)	14	D5
Godewaersvelde (59)	3	K4
Godisson (61)	54	E5
la Godivelle (63)	218	C1
Godoncourt (88)	117	J2
Goès (64)	284	A5
Goetzenbruck (57)	69	G4
Goeulzin (59)	11	H3
Gogney (54)	67	G5
Gognies-Chaussée (59)	13	G2
la Gohannière (50)	52	A5
Gohory (28)	84	D6
Goin (57)	66	A1
Goincourt (60)	37	H3
Golancourt (60)	19	H4
Golbey (88)	94	D5
Goldbach-Altenbach (68)	119	K3
Golfech (82)	248	E5
Golinhac (12)	235	J5
Golleville (50)	28	D5
Gombergean (41)	128	C1
Gomelange (57)	27	K5
Gomené (22)	77	J4
Gomer (64)	284	E5
Gometz-la-Ville (91)	58	C6
Gometz-le-Châtel (91)	58	C6
Gomiécourt (62)	11	F4
Gommecourt (62)	10	D4
Gommecourt (78)	36	C6
Gommegnies (59)	12	E3
Gommenec'h (22)	48	C3
Gommersdorf (68)	97	A4
Gommerville (28)	86	A4
Gommerville (76)	14	D6
Gomméville (21)	115	F3
Gomont (08)	41	G1
Goncelin (38)	224	D1
Goncourt (52)	93	F5
Gond-Pontouvre (16)	196	E3
Gondecourt (59)	6	D5
Gondenans-les-Moulins (25)	138	D3
Gondenans-Montby (25)	138	E3
Gondeville (16)	196	B3
Gondrecourt-Aix (54)	26	D6
Gondrecourt-le-Château (55)	92	E1
Gondreville (45)	111	H2
Gondreville (54)	65	J5
Gondreville (60)	39	F5
Gondrexange (57)	67	H4
Gondrexon (54)	67	G5
Gondrin (32)	266	E3
les Gonds (17)	195	G2
Gonesse (95)	59	F2
Gonez (65)	285	J5
Gonfaron (83)	298	C3
Gonfreville (50)	30	E2
Gonfreville-Caillot (76)	14	D5
Gonfreville-l'Orcher (76)	33	K1
la Gonfrière (61)	55	G4
Gonnehem (62)	5	K5
Gonnelieu (59)	11	J5
Gonnetot (76)	15	H3
Gonneville (50)	28	E4
Gonneville-en-Auge (14)	33	F4
Gonneville-la-Mallet (76)	14	B5
Gonneville-sur-Honfleur (14)	34	A4
Gonneville-sur-Mer (14)	33	H3
Gonneville-sur-Scie (76)	15	K3
Gonsans (25)	138	C5
Gontaud-de-Nogaret (47)	247	J1
la Gonterie-Boulouneix (24)	213	K1
Gonzeville (76)	15	H3
Goos (40)	264	C4
Gorbio (06)	281	J2
Gorcy (54)	26	C2
Gordes (84)	277	F2
Gorenflos (80)	9	J5
Gorges (44)	123	K5
Gorges (50)	30	E1
Gorges (80)	9	K5
la Gorgue (59)	6	A4
Gorhey (88)	94	B5
Gornac (33)	230	B4
Gorniès (34)	273	K5
Gorre (87)	198	C2
Gorrevod (01)	172	A3
Gorron (53)	80	E3
Gorses (46)	234	D3
Gorze (57)	44	D6
Gosnay (62)	5	K6
Gosné (35)	79	J2
Gosselming (57)	67	J3
Gotein-Libarrenx (64)	283	H5
Gottenhouse (67)	70	B1
Gottesheim (67)	70	C1
Gouaix (77)	88	D2
Goualade (33)	246	D3
Gouarec (22)	76	C3
Gouaux (65)	305	F4
Gouaux-de-Larboust (31)	305	G5
Gouaux-de-Luchon (31)	305	H4
Gouberville (50)	29	F2
Gouchaupre (76)	16	B1
Goudargues (30)	256	A4
Goudelancourt-lès-Berrieux (02)	40	D1
Goudelancourt-lès-Pierrepont (02)	21	F5
Goudelin (22)	48	E5
Goudet (43)	238	C1
Goudex (31)	287	J5
Goudon (65)	285	K5
Goudourville (82)	248	E5
Gouesnach (29)	98	C2
la Gouesnière (35)	50	E4
Gouesnou (29)	46	A5
Gouex (86)	163	J6
Gouézec (29)	74	E4
Gougenheim (67)	70	D2
Gouhelans (25)	138	D3
Gouhenans (70)	138	C1
Gouillons (28)	85	K4
Gouise (03)	169	F5
Goujounac (46)	233	F5
la Goulafrière (27)	55	G2
Goulet (61)	54	B5
Goulien (29)	73	C3
Goulier (09)	307	H5
Goulles (19)	216	E5
les Goulles (21)	115	J4
Gouloux (58)	134	B6
Goult (84)	277	F3
Goulven (29)	46	C3
Goumois (25)	139	J5
Goupillières (14)	53	J1
Goupillières (27)	34	E6
Goupillières (76)	15	J6
Goupillières (78)	57	J3
Gouraincourt (55)	26	C5
Gourbera (40)	264	B3
Gourbesville (50)	28	E5
Gourbit (09)	307	H4
Gourchelles (60)	17	G4
Gourdan-Polignan (31)	305	H1
Gourdièges (15)	236	C1
Gourdon (06)	280	D4
Gourdon (07)	239	H3
Gourdon (46)	233	G3
Gourdon (71)	171	F2
Gourdon-Murat (19)	200	B5
Gourfaleur (50)	31	H4
Gourgançon (51)	62	A5
Gourgé (79)	162	A1
Gourgeon (70)	117	H6
Gourgue (65)	285	K6
Gourhel (56)	101	K2
Gourin (56)	75	H4
Gourlizon (29)	74	B5
Gournay (36)	165	J3
Gournay-en-Bray (76)	36	D1
Gournay-le-Guérin (27)	55	K5
Gournay-Loizé (79)	178	E3
Gournay-sur-Aronde (60)	38	C1
Gournay-sur-Marne (93)	59	G3
les Gours (16)	178	E5
Gours (33)	212	D6
Gourvieille (11)	289	F4
Gourville (16)	196	C1
Gourvillette (17)	178	C6
Goussaincourt (55)	93	G2
Goussainville (28)	57	H4
Goussainville (95)	59	F1
Goussancourt (02)	40	B5
Gousse (40)	264	C4
Goussonville (78)	57	J3
Goustranville (14)	33	G4
Gout-Rossignol (24)	197	G6
la Goutelle (63)	202	A1
Goutevernisse (31)	287	J5
Goutrens (12)	251	K1
Gouts (40)	264	D3
Gouttières (27)	55	K1
Gouttières (63)	184	C4
Goutz (32)	267	K4
Gouvernes (77)	59	H3
Gouves (62)	10	D2
Gouvets (50)	31	H5
Gouvieux (60)	38	A5
Gouville (27)	56	B3
Gouville-sur-Mer (50)	30	C3
Gouvix (14)	53	K1
Goux (32)	266	B6
Goux-lès-Dambelin (25)	139	G4
Goux-les-Usiers (25)	156	E3
Goux-sous-Landet (25)	156	B2
Gouy (02)	11	K6
Gouy (76)	35	J3
Gouy-en-Artois (62)	10	D3
Gouy-en-Ternois (62)	10	B2
Gouy-les-Groseillers (60)	18	A4
Gouy-Saint-André (62)	9	G2
Gouy-Servins (62)	10	D1
Gouy-sous-Bellonne (62)	11	H2
Gouzangrez (95)	37	F6
Gouzeaucourt (59)	11	J5
Gouzens (31)	287	J6
Gouzon (23)	183	G2
Goven (35)	78	E5
Goviller (54)	93	J1
Goxwiller (67)	70	D5
Goyencourt (80)	19	F4
Goyrans (31)	288	B2
Grabels (34)	274	B6
Graçay (18)	148	B2
Grâce-Uzel (22)	77	F3
Grâces (22)	48	C5
Graffigny-Chemin (52)	93	F6
Gragnague (31)	269	J5
Graignes (50)	31	G2
Grailhen (65)	305	F4
Graimbouville (76)	14	C6
Graincourt-lès-Havrincourt (62)	11	H4
Grainville (27)	36	A3
Grainville-la-Teinturière (76)	15	F4
Grainville-Langannerie (14)	54	A1
Grainville-sur-Odon (14)	32	C5
Grainville-sur-Ry (76)	35	K1
Grainville-Ymauville (76)	14	D5
le Grais (61)	53	K6
Graissac (12)	236	B3
Graissessac (34)	272	D5
Graix (42)	221	J1
Gramat (46)	234	A3
Gramazie (11)	308	D1
Grambois (84)	277	K4
Grammond (42)	205	G4
Grammont (70)	138	C1
Gramond (12)	251	K4
Gramont (82)	267	K2
Granace (2A)	322	E3
Grancey-le-Château-Neuvelle (21)	136	A1
Grancey-sur-Ource (21)	115	F2
Grand (88)	92	E3
le Grand-Abergement (01)	190	B4
Grand-Auverné (44)	103	K5
le Grand-Bornand (74)	191	J5
le Grand-Bourg (23)	182	B3
Grand-Brassac (24)	213	H2
Grand-Camp (27)	55	H1
Grand-Camp (76)	15	F6
le Grand-Celland (50)	52	B5
Grand-Champ (56)	100	E4
Grand-Charmont (25)	139	H2
la Grand-Combe (30)	255	G4
Grand-Corent (01)	189	G4
Grand-Couronne (76)	35	H3
la Grand-Croix (42)	205	J5
Grand-Failly (54)	26	A4
Grand-Fayt (59)	13	F5
Grand-Fort-Philippe (59)	3	F2
Grand-Fougeray (35)	103	F3
Grand-Laviers (80)	9	F5
le Grand-Lemps (38)	207	G6
le Grand-Lucé (72)	107	G4
le Grand-Madieu (16)	179	K5
le Grand-Pressigny (37)	146	C4
le Grand-Quevilly (76)	35	H2
Grand-Rozoy (02)	39	K4
Grand-Rullecourt (62)	10	C3
le Grand-Serre (26)	222	E2
Grand-Vabre (12)	235	G5
Grand-Verly (02)	20	C1
le Grand-Village-Plage (17)	176	C6
Grandcamp-Maisy (14)	29	H5
Grandchain (27)	55	J1
Grandchamp (08)	22	A5
Grandchamp (52)	116	E5
Grandchamp (72)	82	E4
Grandchamp (78)	57	H5
Grandchamp (89)	112	C5
Grandchamp-le-Château (14)	33	J6
Grandchamps-des-Fontaines (44)	123	G2
Grand'Combe-Châteleu (25)	157	H2
Grand'Combe-des-Bois (25)	157	K1
Grandcourt (76)	16	D2
Grandcourt (80)	10	E5
la Grande-Fosse (88)	95	K3
la Grande-Motte (34)	293	J1
la Grande-Paroisse (77)	87	K4
la Grande-Résie (70)	137	F5
Grande-Rivière (39)	173	K3
Grande-Synthe (59)	3	G2
la Grande-Verrière (71)	152	D4
Grandecourt (70)	137	J1
les Grandes-Armoises (08)	22	E6
les Grandes-Chapelles (10)	90	A2
les Grandes-Loges (51)	41	H6
les Grandes-Ventes (76)	16	B3
Grandeyrolles (63)	202	D4
Grandfontaine (25)	137	J6
Grandfontaine (67)	95	K1
Grandfontaine-sur-Creuse (25)	138	C6
Grandfresnoy (60)	38	C3
Grandham (08)	42	C3
Grandjean (17)	177	J6
Grand'Landes (85)	141	H5
Grandlup-et-Fay (02)	20	E5
Grandpré (08)	42	D3
Grandpuits-Bailly-Carrois (77)	88	A1
Grandrieu (48)	237	K3
Grandrieux (02)	21	J4
Grandrif (63)	204	A5
Grandris (69)	187	J4
Grandrû (60)	19	J5
Grandrupt (88)	95	J3
Grandrupt-de-Bains (88)	118	B1
les Grands-Chézeaux (87)	165	F5
Grandsaigne (19)	200	B6
Grandval (63)	203	J4
Grandvals (48)	236	D4
Grandvaux (71)	170	D4
Grandvelle-et-le-Perrenot (70)	137	J2
Grandvillars (90)	139	J2
la Grandville (08)	22	D3
Grandville (10)	90	C1
Grandvillers (88)	95	F4
Grandvillers-aux-Bois (60)	38	C2
Grandvilliers (27)	56	C4
Grandvilliers (60)	17	H5
Grane (26)	240	C3
Granès (11)	309	F4
la Grange (25)	139	G5
Grange-de-Vaivre (39)	156	A3

Grangermont (45) . . . 87 F6
les Granges (10) . . . 114 A2
Granges (71) . . . 171 J1
Granges-d'Ans (24) . . . 214 E3
les Granges-Gontardes (26) . . . 256 D1
Granges-la-Ville (70) . . . 139 E4
Granges-le-Bourg (70) . . . 139 F1
les Granges-le-Roi (91) . . . 86 B2
Granges-les-Beaumont (26) . . . 222 D5
Granges-Narboz (25) . . . 156 E4
Granges-sur-Aube (51) . . . 89 J1
Granges-sur-Baume (39) . . . 173 G1
Granges-sur-Lot (47) . . . 248 A2
Granges-sur-Vologne (88) . . . 95 G6
les Grangettes (25) . . . 156 E5
Grangues (14) . . . 33 H4
Granier (73) . . . 209 J3
Granieu (38) . . . 207 J4
Grans (13) . . . 276 E6
Granville (50) . . . 51 H1
Granzay-Gript (79) . . . 178 A2
Gras (07) . . . 256 B1
les Gras (25) . . . 157 G3
Grassac (16) . . . 197 G4
Grasse (06) . . . 280 D4
Grassendorf (67) . . . 69 J6
Grateloup (47) . . . 247 K2
Gratens (31) . . . 287 J4
Gratentour (31) . . . 269 G5
Gratibus (80) . . . 18 D4
Gratot (50) . . . 30 D4
Gratreuil (51) . . . 42 B4
Grattepanche (80) . . . 18 A3
le Gratteris (25) . . . 156 C1
Grattery (70) . . . 118 A6
le Grau-du-Roi (30) . . . 293 K1
les Graulges (24) . . . 197 G3
Graulhet (81) . . . 270 C4
Grauves (51) . . . 61 K2
Graval (76) . . . 16 D4
la Grave (05) . . . 225 G4
Gravelines (59) . . . 3 F2
la Gravelle (53) . . . 104 C1
Gravelotte (57) . . . 44 D5
la Graverie (14) . . . 31 K6
Graveron-Sémerville (27) . . . 35 G6
Graves-Saint-Amant (16) . . . 196 B3
Graveson (13) . . . 276 B3
Gravières (07) . . . 255 G2
Gravigny (27) . . . 56 D1
Gravon (77) . . . 88 D3
Gray (70) . . . 137 F3
Gray-la-Ville (70) . . . 137 F3
Grayan-et-l'Hôpital (33) . . . 194 B5
Graye-et-Charnay (39) . . . 173 F4
Graye-sur-Mer (14) . . . 32 D3
Grayssas (47) . . . 248 C5
Grazac (31) . . . 288 C4
Grazac (43) . . . 221 F3
Grazac (81) . . . 269 C5
Grazay (53) . . . 81 H4
Gréalou (46) . . . 234 C6
Gréasque (13) . . . 296 E2
Grébault-Mesnil (80) . . . 9 F6
Grécourt (80) . . . 19 H4
Gredisans (39) . . . 155 G1
la Grée-Saint-Laurent (56) . . . 101 J1
Gréez-sur-Roc (72) . . . 107 K1
Greffeil (11) . . . 309 G1
Grèges (76) . . . 16 A1
Grémecey (57) . . . 66 C3
Grémévillers (60) . . . 17 H6
Gremilly (55) . . . 26 A5
Grémonville (76) . . . 15 H4
Grenade (31) . . . 269 F4
Grenade-sur-l'Adour (40) . . . 265 H4
Grenand-lès-Sombernon (21) . . . 135 H6
Grenant (52) . . . 116 E6
Grenay (38) . . . 206 D3
Grenay (62) . . . 6 B6
Grendelbruch (67) . . . 70 B4
Greneville-en-Beauce (45) . . . 86 C6
Grenier-Montgon (43) . . . 219 F2
Gréning (57) . . . 67 G1
Grenoble (38) . . . 224 A3
Grenois (58) . . . 133 F5
Grentheville (14) . . . 32 E5
Grentzingen (68) . . . 97 C5
Greny (76) . . . 16 B1
Gréolières (06) . . . 280 D3
Gréoux-les-Bains (04) . . . 278 C4
Grépiac (31) . . . 288 B3
le Grès (68) . . . 268 D5
Grésigny-Sainte-Reine (21) . . . 135 F2
Gresin (73) . . . 207 K3
la Gresle (42) . . . 187 H4
Gresse-en-Vercors (38) . . . 241 K1
Gressey (78) . . . 57 H4
Gresswiller (67) . . . 70 C4
Gressy (77) . . . 59 H2
Grésy-sur-Aix (73) . . . 208 B2
Grésy-sur-Isère (73) . . . 208 E3
Gretz-Armainvilliers (77) . . . 59 J5
Greucourt (70) . . . 137 J2
Greuville (76) . . . 15 H3
Greux (88) . . . 93 F2
la Grève-sur-Mignon (17) . . . 177 H1
Gréville-Hague (50) . . . 28 B2
Grévillers (62) . . . 11 F5
Grevilly (71) . . . 171 J4
Grez (60) . . . 17 H5
le Grez (72) . . . 82 A6

Grez-en-Bouère (53) . . . 105 H4
Grez-Neuville (49) . . . 125 F1
Grez-sur-Loing (77) . . . 87 H4
Grézac (17) . . . 194 E4
Grézels (46) . . . 249 G1
Grèzes (24) . . . 215 G5
Grèzes (43) . . . 237 J1
Grèzes (46) . . . 234 B5
Grèzes (48) . . . 237 G6
Grézet-Cavagnan (47) . . . 247 G2
Grézian (65) . . . 305 F4
Grézieu-la-Varenne (69) . . . 205 K2
Grézieu-le-Marché (69) . . . 205 G3
Grézieux-le-Fromental (42) . . . 204 D4
Grézillac (33) . . . 230 A2
Grézillé (49) . . . 125 J5
Grézolles (42) . . . 204 B1
Gricourt (02) . . . 19 K2
Grièges (01) . . . 188 C1
Griesbach-au-Val (68) . . . 96 A4
Griesheim-près-Molsheim (67) . . . 70 D4
Griesheim-sur-Souffel (67) . . . 70 E2
Grignan (26) . . . 257 F1
Grigneuseville (76) . . . 16 A5
Grignols (24) . . . 213 J5
Grignols (33) . . . 246 E2
Grignon (21) . . . 134 E2
Grignon (73) . . . 209 G3
Grignoncourt (88) . . . 117 J3
Grigny (62) . . . 9 J1
Grigny (69) . . . 206 A4
Grigny (91) . . . 58 E6
la Grigonnais (44) . . . 103 F6
Grillon (84) . . . 257 F2
Grilly (01) . . . 174 B6
Grimaucourt-en-Woëvre (55) . . . 43 K5
Grimaucourt-près-Sampigny (55) . . . 64 D4
Grimaud (83) . . . 298 C4
la Grimaudière (86) . . . 144 D6
Grimault (89) . . . 134 A1
Grimbosq (14) . . . 32 D6
Grimesnil (50) . . . 30 E5
Grimonviller (54) . . . 93 K3
Grincourt-lès-Pas (62) . . . 10 C4
Grindorff (57) . . . 45 J2
la Gripperie-Saint-
    Symphorien (17) . . . 194 D1
Gripport (54) . . . 94 B2
Griscourt (54) . . . 65 J3
Griselles (21) . . . 114 D4
Griselles (45) . . . 111 J2
Grisolles (02) . . . 39 J3
Grisolles (82) . . . 269 F3
Grisy-les-Plâtres (95) . . . 37 G6
Grisy-Suisnes (77) . . . 59 H6
Grisy-sur-Seine (77) . . . 88 D3
Grives (24) . . . 232 D3
Grivesnes (80) . . . 18 C4
Grivillers (80) . . . 18 E5
Grivy-Loisy (08) . . . 42 A2
Groisy (74) . . . 191 F4
Groix (56) . . . 99 J6
Groléjac (24) . . . 233 G2
Gron (18) . . . 149 K2
Gron (89) . . . 112 D1
Gronard (02) . . . 21 F3
Gros-Chastang (19) . . . 216 D3
Gros-Réderching (57) . . . 68 E3
le Gros-Theil (27) . . . 35 F4
Grosbliederstroff (57) . . . 68 D2
Grosbois (25) . . . 138 C4
Grosbois-en-Montagne (21) . . . 135 G5
Grosbois-lès-Tichey (21) . . . 154 E3
Grosbreuil (85) . . . 159 F3
les Groseillers (79) . . . 161 H4
Groslay (95) . . . 58 E2
Groslée (01) . . . 207 H2
Grosley-sur-Risle (27) . . . 56 A1
Grosmagny (90) . . . 119 H5
Grosne (90) . . . 139 K1
Grospierres (07) . . . 255 J2
Grosrouvre (78) . . . 57 J4
Grosrouvres (54) . . . 65 H3
Grossa (2A) . . . 322 D3
Grosseto-Prugna (2A) . . . 320 E6
Grossœuvre (27) . . . 56 D2
Grossouvre (18) . . . 150 C5
Grostenquin (57) . . . 67 F1
Grosville (50) . . . 28 B4
Grouches-Luchuel (80) . . . 10 B4
Grougis (02) . . . 20 C1
la Groutte (18) . . . 167 G2
Grozon (39) . . . 155 J5
Gruchet-le-Valasse (76) . . . 14 E6
Gruchet-Saint-Siméon (76) . . . 15 H3
Grues (85) . . . 159 J5
Gruey-lès-Surance (88) . . . 117 H1
Gruffy (74) . . . 208 C1
Grugé-l'Hôpital (49) . . . 104 C5
Grugies (02) . . . 19 K3
Grugny (76) . . . 15 K5
Gruissan (11) . . . 310 D1
Grumesnil (76) . . . 17 F5
Grun-Bordas (24) . . . 213 K5
Grundviller (57) . . . 68 C3
Gruny (80) . . . 19 F4
Grury (71) . . . 170 A2

Gruson (59) . . . 7 F4
Grusse (39) . . . 173 F3
Grussenheim (68) . . . 96 D3
Grust (65) . . . 304 B3
Gruyères (08) . . . 22 C4
le Gua (17) . . . 194 D2
le Gua (38) . . . 223 K6
Guagno (2A) . . . 320 D2
Guainville (28) . . . 57 G3
Guarbecque (62) . . . 5 J4
Guargualé (2A) . . . 320 D6
Guchan (65) . . . 305 F4
Guchen (65) . . . 305 F4
Gudas (09) . . . 307 K2
Gudmont-Villiers (52) . . . 92 B4
le Gué-d'Alleré (17) . . . 177 G2
le Gué-de-la-Chaîne (61) . . . 83 H4
le Gué-de-Longroi (28) . . . 85 J2
le Gué-de-Velluire (85) . . . 160 C5
Gué-d'Hossus (08) . . . 22 B1
Guébenhouse (57) . . . 68 C3
Gueberschwihr (68) . . . 96 B5
Guébestroff (57) . . . 67 F3
Guéblange-lès-Dieuze (57) . . . 67 F3
Guébling (57) . . . 67 F2
Guebwiller (68) . . . 96 B6
Guécélard (72) . . . 106 D4
le Guédéniau (49) . . . 126 B3
Guégon (56) . . . 101 H2
Guéhébert (50) . . . 30 E5
Guéhenno (56) . . . 101 G2
Gueltas (56) . . . 77 F5
Guémappe (62) . . . 11 F3
Guémar (68) . . . 71 B6
Guémené-Penfao (44) . . . 102 E4
Guémené-sur-Scorff (56) . . . 76 B3
Guemps (62) . . . 2 E3
Guénange (57) . . . 27 H5
Guengat (29) . . . 74 C5
Guénin (56) . . . 100 D2
Guenroc (22) . . . 78 C1
Guenrouet (44) . . . 102 D4
Guenviller (57) . . . 68 B3
Guêprei (61) . . . 54 C3
Guer (56) . . . 102 B1
Guérande (44) . . . 121 J4
Guérard (77) . . . 60 A4
Guerbigny (80) . . . 18 E4
la Guerche (37) . . . 146 A5
la Guerche-de-Bretagne (35) . . . 104 A3
la Guerche-sur-l'Aubois (18) . . . 150 C4
Guercheville (77) . . . 87 G5
Guerchy (89) . . . 112 E4
Guéreins (01) . . . 188 C3
Guéret (23) . . . 182 D3
Guerfand (71) . . . 154 C6
Guérigny (58) . . . 150 E3
Guérin (47) . . . 247 F2
la Guérinière (85) . . . 140 B3
Guerlesquin (29) . . . 47 J5
Guermange (57) . . . 67 G3
Guermantes (77) . . . 59 H3
Guern (56) . . . 76 C6
Guernanville (27) . . . 56 A3
Guernes (78) . . . 57 H1
le Guerno (56) . . . 101 J6
Guerny (27) . . . 36 D5
Guéron (14) . . . 32 A4
la Guéroulde (27) . . . 56 A4
Guerpont (55) . . . 64 B5
Guerquesalles (61) . . . 54 E3
les Guerreaux (71) . . . 170 A4
Guerstling (57) . . . 45 J2
Guerting (57) . . . 45 K4
Guerville (76) . . . 16 D1
Guerville (78) . . . 57 J2
Gueschart (80) . . . 9 H3
Guesnain (59) . . . 11 J2
Guesnes (86) . . . 144 E5
Guessling-Hémering (57) . . . 45 K6
Guéthary (64) . . . 263 C1
Gueudecourt (80) . . . 11 F5
Gueugnon (71) . . . 170 B3
Gueures (76) . . . 15 J2
Gueutteville (76) . . . 15 J5
Gueutteville-les-Grès (76) . . . 15 G2
Gueux (51) . . . 40 E4
Guevenatten (68) . . . 119 K5
Guewenheim (68) . . . 119 K5
Gueytes-et-Labastide (11) . . . 308 C2
Gugnécourt (88) . . . 95 F4
Gugney (54) . . . 93 K3
Gugney-aux-Aulx (88) . . . 94 B4
Guibeville (91) . . . 86 D1
Guichainville (27) . . . 56 D2
Guiche (64) . . . 282 E1
la Guiche (71) . . . 171 F4
Guichen (35) . . . 79 F6
Guiclan (29) . . . 47 F5
Guidel (56) . . . 99 J4
la Guierche (72) . . . 106 E1
Guignecourt (60) . . . 37 H1
Guignemicourt (80) . . . 17 K2
Guignen (35) . . . 102 E1
Guigneville (45) . . . 86 C6
Guigneville-sur-Essonne (91) . . . 86 E2
Guignicourt (02) . . . 40 E2
Guignicourt-sur-Vence (08) . . . 22 C4
Guigny (62) . . . 9 H2
Guilberville (50) . . . 31 J5
Guiler-sur-Goyen (29) . . . 73 E3

Guilers (29) . . . 72 C4
Guilherand-Granges (07) . . . 240 C1
Guillac (33) . . . 230 A2
Guillac (56) . . . 101 J2
Guillaucourt (80) . . . 18 D2
Guillaumes (06) . . . 261 F5
Guillemont (80) . . . 11 F6
la Guillermie (03) . . . 186 A5
Guillerval (91) . . . 86 C4
Guillestre (05) . . . 227 A3
Guilleville (28) . . . 85 K6
Guilliers (56) . . . 77 K6
Guilligomarc'h (29) . . . 99 K2
Guillon (89) . . . 134 B3
Guillon-les-Bains (25) . . . 138 D5
Guillonville (28) . . . 109 H2
Guillos (33) . . . 229 H5
Guilly (36) . . . 148 A3
Guilly (45) . . . 110 D5
Guilmécourt (76) . . . 16 B1
Guilvinec (29) . . . 73 E6
Guimaëc (29) . . . 47 H3
Guimiliau (29) . . . 46 E5
Guimps (16) . . . 196 A5
Guinarthe-Parenties (64) . . . 283 G3
Guincourt (08) . . . 22 C6
Guindrecourt-aux-Ormes (52) . . . 91 K2
Guindrecourt-sur-Blaise (52) . . . 91 K4
Guinecourt (62) . . . 9 K2
Guînes (62) . . . 2 D3
Guingamp (22) . . . 48 C5
Guinglange (57) . . . 45 J5
Guinkirchen (57) . . . 27 K6
Guinzeling (57) . . . 67 G2
Guipavas (29) . . . 46 A6
Guipel (35) . . . 79 F2
Guipronvel (29) . . . 72 C3
Guipry (35) . . . 102 E2
Guipy (58) . . . 151 H1
Guiry-en-Vexin (95) . . . 36 E6
Guiscard (60) . . . 19 H5
Guiscriff (56) . . . 75 H5
Guise (02) . . . 20 D2
Guiseniers (27) . . . 36 B5
le Guislain (50) . . . 31 G5
Guissény (29) . . . 46 B3
Guisy (62) . . . 9 H1
Guitalens (81) . . . 270 D6
Guitera-les-Bains (2A) . . . 321 F5
Guitinières (17) . . . 195 H6
Guitrancourt (78) . . . 57 K1
Guîtres (33) . . . 212 B5
Guitry (27) . . . 36 C5
Guitté (22) . . . 78 C2
Guivry (02) . . . 19 J5
Guizancourt (80) . . . 17 H4
Guizengeard (16) . . . 212 C2
Guizerix (65) . . . 286 B4
Gujan-Mestras (33) . . . 228 C4
Gumbrechtshoffen (67) . . . 69 J5
Gumery (10) . . . 88 E3
Gumiane (26) . . . 241 G6
Gumières (42) . . . 204 C5
Gumond (19) . . . 216 D3
Gundershoffen (67) . . . 69 K5
Gundolsheim (68) . . . 96 B5
Gungwiller (67) . . . 67 K2
Gunsbach (68) . . . 96 A4
Gunstett (67) . . . 25 A2
Guntzviller (57) . . . 67 K4
Guny (02) . . . 39 H1
Guran (31) . . . 305 H4
Gurat (16) . . . 197 F6
Gurcy-le-Châtel (77) . . . 88 B2
Gurgy (89) . . . 113 G4
Gurgy-la-Ville (21) . . . 115 K4
Gurgy-le-Château (21) . . . 115 K4
Gurmençon (64) . . . 284 A6
Gurs (64) . . . 283 J4
Gurunhuel (22) . . . 48 B5
Gury (60) . . . 19 F6
Gussainville (55) . . . 44 A5
Gussignies (59) . . . 13 F2
Guyancourt (78) . . . 58 C4
Guyans-Durnes (25) . . . 156 D1
Guyans-Vennes (25) . . . 157 F2
Guyencourt (02) . . . 40 D3
Guyencourt-Saulcourt (80) . . . 11 H6
Guyencourt-sur-Noye (80) . . . 18 B3
la Guyonnière (85) . . . 142 B4
Guyonvelle (52) . . . 117 G4
Guzargues (34) . . . 274 C5
Gy (70) . . . 137 H4
Gy-en-Sologne (41) . . . 129 H5
Gy-les-Nonains (45) . . . 111 K3
Gy-l'Évêque (89) . . . 113 G6
Gye (54) . . . 65 H3
Gyé-sur-Seine (10) . . . 114 E2

H

l'Haÿ-les-Roses (94) . . . 58 E4
Habarcq (62) . . . 10 D2
Habas (40) . . . 264 C6
Habère-Lullin (74) . . . 191 J1
Habère-Poche (74) . . . 191 J1
l'Habit (27) . . . 57 F3
Hablainville (54) . . . 95 F1
Habloville (61) . . . 54 B4
Haboudange (57) . . . 66 E2

Habsheim (68) . . . 97 D2
Hachan (65) . . . 286 B4
Hâcourt (52) . . . 93 F6
Hacqueville (27) . . . 36 C4
Hadancourt-le-Haut-Clocher (60) . . . 36 E5
Hadigny-les-Verrières (88) . . . 94 D3
Hadol (88) . . . 94 D6
Haegen (67) . . . 70 B2
Hagécourt (88) . . . 94 A5
Hagedet (65) . . . 285 G1
Hagen (57) . . . 27 G2
Hagenbach (68) . . . 97 A4
Hagenthal-le-Bas (68) . . . 97 D5
Hagenthal-le-Haut (68) . . . 97 D5
Haget (32) . . . 285 J3
Hagetaubin (64) . . . 284 A1
Hagetmau (40) . . . 265 F5
Hagéville (54) . . . 44 C6
Hagnéville-et-Roncourt (88) . . . 93 H5
Hagnicourt (08) . . . 22 C5
Hagondange (57) . . . 27 G5
Haguenau (67) . . . 25 A4
la Haie-Fouassière (44) . . . 123 J5
la Haie-Traversaine (53) . . . 81 G3
les Haies (69) . . . 205 K5
Haigneville (54) . . . 94 C1
Haillainville (88) . . . 94 D3
le Haillan (33) . . . 229 G1
Hailles (80) . . . 18 C3
Haillicourt (62) . . . 5 K6
Haimps (17) . . . 178 C4
Haims (86) . . . 164 A4
Hainvillers (60) . . . 18 E6
Haironville (55) . . . 64 A5
Haisnes (62) . . . 6 B6
Haleine (61) . . . 81 J2
Halinghen (62) . . . 4 B4
Hallencourt (80) . . . 9 G6
Hallennes-lez-Haubourdin (59) . . . 6 D4
Hallering (57) . . . 45 J5
les Halles (69) . . . 205 G2
Halles-sous-les-Côtes (55) . . . 43 F1
Hallignicourt (52) . . . 63 J6
Hallines (62) . . . 3 F5
Hallivillers (80) . . . 18 A4
la Hallotière (76) . . . 36 B1
Halloville (54) . . . 67 H6
Halloy (60) . . . 17 H6
Halloy (62) . . . 10 B4
Halloy-lès-Pernois (80) . . . 9 K6
Hallu (80) . . . 19 F3
Halluin (59) . . . 6 E2
Halsou (64) . . . 263 D2
Halstroff (57) . . . 27 K4
le Ham (50) . . . 28 E5
le Ham (53) . . . 81 J4
Ham (80) . . . 19 H4
Ham-en-Artois (62) . . . 5 J5
Ham-les-Moines (08) . . . 22 C3
Ham-sous-Varsberg (57) . . . 45 K4
Ham-sur-Meuse (08) . . . 24 C2
Hamars (14) . . . 53 H1
Hambach (57) . . . 68 D3
Hambers (53) . . . 81 J5
Hamblain-les-Prés (62) . . . 11 G3
Hambye (50) . . . 31 F5
Hamel (59) . . . 11 H3
le Hamel (60) . . . 17 H5
le Hamel (80) . . . 18 D2
Hamelet (80) . . . 18 D2
Hamelin (50) . . . 80 B1
Hamelincourt (62) . . . 11 F4
Hames-Boucres (62) . . . 2 C3
Hammeville (54) . . . 93 K1
Hamonville (54) . . . 65 G3
Hampigny (10) . . . 91 F2
Hampont (57) . . . 66 E3
Han-devant-Pierrepont (54) . . . 26 C4
Han-lès-Juvigny (55) . . . 43 H1
Han-sur-Meuse (55) . . . 64 E3
Han-sur-Nied (57) . . . 66 C1
Hanc (79) . . . 178 E4
Hanches (28) . . . 85 H1
Hancourt (80) . . . 19 H2
Handschuheim (67) . . . 70 D3
Hangard (80) . . . 18 C3
Hangenbieten (67) . . . 70 E3
Hangest-en-Santerre (80) . . . 18 D4
Hangest-sur-Somme (80) . . . 17 J1
Hangviller (57) . . . 69 F6
Hannaches (60) . . . 36 E1
Hannapes (02) . . . 20 D1
Hannappes (08) . . . 21 J3
Hannescamps (62) . . . 10 D4
Hannocourt (57) . . . 66 C2
Hannogne-Saint-Martin (08) . . . 22 C4
Hannogne-Saint-Rémy (08) . . . 21 H5
Hannonville-sous-les-Côtes (55) . . . 44 A6
Hannonville-Suzémont (54) . . . 44 C5
le Hanouard (76) . . . 15 F4
Hans (51) . . . 42 C6
Hantay (59) . . . 6 C5
Hanvec (29) . . . 74 D2
Hanviller (57) . . . 69 H2
Hanvoile (60) . . . 37 F1
Haplincourt (62) . . . 11 G5
Happencourt (02) . . . 19 J3
Happonvilliers (28) . . . 84 C4
Haramont (02) . . . 39 G4
Haraucourt (08) . . . 23 F5
Haraucourt (54) . . . 66 C5
Haraucourt-sur-Seille (57) . . . 66 E3

Haravesnes (62) 9 J3
Haravilliers (95) 37 G5
Harbonnières (80) 18 E2
Harbouey (54) 67 H6
Harcanville (76) 15 G4
Harchéchamp (88) 93 G3
Harcigny (02) 21 G3
Harcourt (27) 34 E5
Harcy (08) 22 B2
Hardancourt (88) 94 E3
Hardanges (53) 81 J4
Hardecourt-aux-Bois (80) 11 F6
Hardencourt-Cocherel (27) 56 E1
Hardifort (59) 3 J4
Hardinghen (62) 2 C4
Hardinvast (50) 28 C3
Hardivillers (60) 18 A5
Hardivillers-en-Vexin (60) 37 F3
Hardricourt (78) 58 A1
la Harengère (27) 35 G4
Haréville (88) 93 K5
Harfleur (76) 33 K1
Hargarten-aux-Mines (57) 45 K4
Hargeville (78) 57 J3
Hargicourt (02) 19 J1
Hargicourt (80) 18 D4
Hargnies (08) 24 C3
Hargnies (59) 13 G3
Harly (02) 20 A2
Harmonville (88) 93 H2
la Harmoye (22) 76 E2
Harnes (62) 6 C6
Harol (88) 94 B6
Haroué (54) 94 A2
Harponville (80) 10 C6
Harprich (57) 66 E1
Harquency (27) 36 B4
Harreberg (57) 67 K5
Harréville-les-Chanteurs (52) 93 H5
Harricourt (08) 42 D2
Harsault (88) 118 B1
Harskirchen (67) 67 J1
Hartennes-et-Taux (02). 39 J4
Hartmannswiller (68) 97 B1
Hartzviller (57) 67 J5
Harville (55) 44 B5
Hary (02) 21 F3
Haselbourg (57) 70 A2
Hasnon (59) 12 C1
Hasparren (64) 282 D3
Haspelschiedt (57) 69 H3
Haspres (59) 12 C3
Hastingues (40) 283 F1
Hatrize (54) 26 E6
Hatten (67) 25 C3
Hattencourt (80) 19 F3
Hattenville (76) 14 E5
Hattigny (57) 67 H5
Hattmatt (67) 69 H4
Hattstatt (68) 96 B5
Hauban (65) 304 D1
Haubourdin (59) 6 D4
Hauconcourt (57) 27 H6
Haucourt (60) 37 F1
Haucourt (62) 11 G3
Haucourt (76) 17 F5
Haucourt-en-Cambrésis (59) 12 B5
Haucourt-Moulaine (54) 26 D3
Haudainville (55) 43 J5
Haudiomont (55) 44 K5
Haudivillers (60) 37 J1
Haudonville (54) 94 D1
Haudrecy (08) 22 C2
Haudricourt (76) 17 F4
Haulchin (59) 12 C2
Haulies (32) 286 E2
Haulmé (08) 22 D2
Haumont-près-Samogneux (55) 43 H3
Hauriet (40) 264 E4
Hausgauen (68) 97 C4
Haussez (76) 17 F6
Haussignémont (51) 63 H5
Haussimont (51) 62 B5
Haussonville (54) 94 C1
Haussy (59) 12 C3
Haut-Clocher (57) 67 J3
le Haut-Corlay (22) 76 D2
Haut-de-Bosdarros (64) 284 D6
Haut-du-Them-Château-
    Lambert (70) 119 G2
Haut-Lieu (59) 13 G5
Haut-Loquin (62) 2 D5
Haut-Mauco (40) 265 H4
Hautaget (65) 305 G2
Hautbos (60) 17 G5
Haute-Amance (52) 117 F4
Haute-Avesnes (62) 10 D2
la Haute-Beaume (05) 242 A5
la Haute-Chapelle (61) 53 G6
Haute-Épine (60) 17 J6
Haute-Goulaine (44). 123 H4
Haute-Isle (95) 36 D6
Haute-Kontz (57) 27 J3
la Haute-Maison (77) 60 A3
Haute-Rivoire (69) 205 G2
Haute-Vigneulles (57) 45 J5
Hautecloque (62) 10 A2
Hautecour (39) 173 J3
Hautecour (73) 209 H4
Hautecourt-Romanèche (01) 189 J2
Hautefage (19) 216 D5
Hautefage-la-Tour (47) 248 D3

Hautefaye (24) 197 H5
Hautefeuille (77) 60 A5
Hautefond (71) 170 D5
Hautefontaine (60) 39 G3
Hautefort (24) 214 E3
Hauteluce (73) 209 H1
Hautepierre-le-Châtelet (25) 156 E2
Hauterive (03) 185 J4
Hauterive (61) 82 E4
Hauterive (89) 113 G4
Hauterive-la-Fresse (25) 157 F3
Hauterives (26) 222 D2
Hauteroche (21) 135 F3
Hautes-Duyes (04) 259 J4
les Hautes-Rivières (08) 22 E2
Hautesvignes (47) 247 J1
Hautevelle (70) 118 C4
Hautevesnes (02) 39 H6
Hauteville (02) 20 C2
Hauteville (08) 21 K6
Hauteville (51) 63 H6
Hauteville (62) 10 D6
Hauteville (73) 208 E4
la Hauteville (78) 57 H5
Hauteville-la-Guichard (50) 31 F3
Hauteville-lès-Dijon (21) 136 A5
Hauteville-Lompnes (01) 190 B4
Hauteville-sur-Fier (74) 190 D5
Hauteville-sur-Mer (50) 30 D5
Haution (02) 21 F2
Hautmont (59) 13 G3
Hautmougey (88) 118 B2
Hautot-l'Auvray (76) 15 G3
Hautot-le-Vatois (76) 15 G5
Hautot-Saint-Sulpice (76) 15 G4
Hautot-sur-Mer (76) 15 K2
Hautot-sur-Seine (76) 35 G3
les Hauts-de-Chée (55) 64 B3
Hautteville-Bocage (50) 28 C5
Hautvillers (51) 40 E6
Hautvillers-Ouville (80) 9 G4
Hauville (27) 34 E2
Hauviné (08) 41 J3
Haux (33) 229 K3
Haux (64) 302 C5
Havange (57) 27 F4
Havelu (28) 57 G4
Haveluy (59) 12 C2
Havernas (80) 9 K6
Haverskerque (59) 3 J6
le Havre (76) 33 J1
Havrincourt (62) 11 H5
Hayange (57) 27 F4
Haybes (08) 24 B3
la Haye (76) 36 B1
la Haye (88) 118 H1
la Haye-Aubrée (27) 34 E2
la Haye-Bellefond (50) 31 G5
la Haye-de-Calleville (27) 34 E5
la Haye-de-Routot (27) 34 E2
la Haye-d'Ectot (50) 28 B5
la Haye-du-Puits (50) 30 D1
la Haye-du-Theil (27) 35 F4
la Haye-le-Comte (27) 35 J5
la Haye-Malherbe (27) 35 H4
la Haye-Pesnel (50) 51 K1
la Haye-Saint-Sylvestre (27) 55 J3
les Hayes (41) 107 K6
Hayes (57) 45 G4
Haynecourt (59) 11 J4
les Hays (39) 155 F4
Hazebrouck (59) 3 J5
Hazembourg (57) 67 H1
le Heaulme (95) 37 G5
Héauville (50) 28 B3
Hébécourt (27) 36 D3
Hébécourt (80) 18 A3
Hébécrevon (50) 31 G3
Héberville (76) 15 H3
Hébuterne (62) 10 D5
Hèches (65) 305 F2
Hecken (68) 97 A3
Hecmanville (27) 34 D5
Hécourt (27) 57 F2
Hécourt (60) 36 E1
Hecq (59) 12 E4
Hectomare (27) 35 G5
Hédauville (80) 10 D6
Hédé (35). 79 F2
Hédouville (95) 37 H5
Hegeney (67) 25 A3
Hégenheim (68) 97 E4
Heidolsheim (67) 71 C6
Heidwiller (68) 97 B3
Heiligenberg (67) 70 C4
Heiligenstein (67) 70 C5
Heillecourt (54) 66 A5
Heilles (60) 37 J3
Heilly (80) 18 D1
Heiltz-le-Hutier (51) 63 H5
Heiltz-le-Maurupt (51) 63 H4
Heiltz-l'Évêque (51) 63 G4
Heimersdorf (68) 97 B4
Heimsbrunn (68) 97 B3
Heining-lès-Bouzonville (57) 45 J2
Heippes (55) 64 C1
Heiteren (68) 96 E5
Heiwiller (68) 97 C4
Hélesmes (59) 12 B2
Hélette (64) 282 D4
Helfaut (62) 3 G6
Helfrantzkirch (68) 97 D4

Helléan (56) 101 J1
Hellering-lès-Fénétrange (57) 67 J3
Helleville (50) 28 B3
Hellimer (57) 68 B4
Héloup (61) 82 C3
Helstroff (57) 45 H4
Hem (59) 7 F4
Hem-Hardinval (80) 10 A4
Hem-Lenglet (59) 11 J3
Hem-Monacu (80) 19 F1
Hémevez (50) 28 C4
Hémévillers (60) 38 C2
Hémilly (57) 45 J6
Héming (57) 67 H4
Hémonstoir (22) 77 F4
Hénaménil (54) 66 E5
Hénanbihen (22) 50 A4
Hénansal (22) 49 K6
Hendecourt-lès-Cagnicourt (62) ... 11 G4
Hendecourt-lès-Ransart (62) 10 E4
Hénencourt (80) 10 D6
Henflingen (68) 97 C5
Hengoat (22) 48 C3
Hengwiller (67) 70 B2
Hénin-Beaumont (62) 11 G1
Hénin-sur-Cojeul (62) 11 F3
Héninel (62) 11 F3
Hennebont (56) 100 A3
Hennecourt (88) 94 C5
Hennemont (55) 44 A5
Henneveux (62) 2 C5
Hennezel (88) 118 A1
Hennezis (27) 36 B5
Hénon (22). 77 G2
Hénonville (60) 37 G5
Hénouville (76) 35 G1
Henrichemont (18) 131 G6
Henridorff (57) 70 A1
Henriville (57) 68 B3
Hénu (62) 10 C4
Henvic (29) 47 F4
Hérange (57) 67 K3
Herbault (41) 128 C2
Herbécourt (80) 19 F1
Herbelles (62) 3 G6
l'Herbergement (85) 141 K4
Herbeuval (08) 23 J4
Herbeuville (55) 44 A6
Herbeville (78) 58 A3
Herbéviller (54) 67 G6
Herbeys (38) 224 B4
les Herbiers (85) 142 D5
Herbignac (44) 121 K3
Herbinghen (62) 2 D5
Herbisse (10) 62 B6
Herbitzheim (67) 68 D4
Herblay (95) 58 C2
Herbsheim (67) 70 E6
Hercé (53) 80 E3
Herchies (60) 37 G1
la Hérelle (60) 18 C6
Hérenguerville (50) 30 D5
Hérépian (34) 291 J1
Hères (65) 285 G1
Hergnies (59) 7 J6
Hergugney (88) 94 B3
Héric (44) 123 F1
Héricourt (62) 10 A2
Héricourt (70) 139 G1
Héricourt-en-Caux (76) 15 G4
Héricourt-sur-Thérain (60) 17 F6
Héricy (77) 87 J3
la Hérie (02) 21 G2
le Hérie-la-Viéville (02) 20 D3
Hériménil (54) 66 D6
Hérimoncourt (25) 139 J3
Hérin (59) 12 C2
Hérissart (80) 10 B6
Hérisson (03) 167 J4
Herleville (80) 19 F2
la Herlière (62) 10 C5
Herlies (59) 6 C5
Herlin-le-Sec (62) 10 A2
Herlincourt (62) 10 A2
Herly (62) 4 E5
Herly (80) 19 G4
l'Herm (09) 307 K3
Herm (40) 262 E3
Hermanville (76) 15 J3
Hermanville-sur-Mer (14) 32 E3
les Hermaux (48) 236 E6
Hermaville (62) 10 D2
Hermé (77) 88 D2
Hermelange (57) 67 J4
Hermelinghen (62) 2 C4
l'Hermenault (85) 160 D3
Herment (63) 201 J2
Hermeray (78) 57 J6
Hermes (60) 37 J3
Herméville (76) 14 C5
Hermeville-en-Woëvre (55). 45 K5
Hermies (62) 11 H5
Hermillon (73) 225 G1
Hermin (62) 10 C1
l'Hermitage (35) 78 E4
l'Hermitage-Lorge (22) 77 F2
les Hermites (37) 127 K1
l'Hermitière (61) 83 J5
Hermival-les-Vaux (14) 34 A5
Hermonville (51) 40 E3
Hernicourt (62) 10 A1

Herny (57) 66 D1
le Héron (76) 36 A1
Héronchelles (76) 16 C6
Hérouville (95) 37 H6
Hérouville-Saint-Clair (14) 32 E4
Hérouvillette (14) 33 F4
Herpelmont (88) 95 G5
Herpont (51) 63 G1
Herpy-l'Arlésienne (08) 21 J6
Herqueville (27) 35 K4
Herqueville (50) 28 A2
Herran (31) 306 B3
Herré (40) 266 B1
Herrère (64) 284 B6
Herrin (59) 6 D5
Herrlisheim (67) 25 C5
Herrlisheim-près-Colmar (68) 96 C5
Herry (18) 150 C1
Herserange (54) 26 D2
Hersin-Coupigny (62) 6 A6
Hertzing (57) 67 H4
Hervelinghen (62) 2 B3
Hervilly (80) 19 J1
Héry (58) 133 G6
Héry (89) 113 G4
Héry-sur-Alby (74) 208 C1
Herzeele (59) 3 J3
Hesbécourt (80) 19 J1
Hescamps (80) 17 G4
Hesdigneul-lès-Béthune (62) 5 K6
Hesdigneul-lès-Boulogne (62) 2 B6
Hesdin (62) 9 J2
Hesdin-l'Abbé (62) 2 B6
Hésingue (68) 97 E4
Hesmond (62) 4 D6
Hesse (57) 67 J4
Hessenheim (67) 71 C6
Hestroff (57) 27 K5
Hestrud (59) 13 J4
Hestrus (62) 5 H6
Hétomesnil (60) 17 J5
Hettange-Grande (57) 27 G3
Hettenschlag (68) 96 D5
Heubécourt-Haricourt (27) 36 C6
Heuchin (62) 5 G6
Heucourt-Croquoison (80) 17 H1
Heudebouville (27) 35 K5
Heudicourt (27) 36 B6
Heudicourt (80) 11 H6
Heudicourt-sous-les-Côtes (55) ... 65 F2
Heudreville-en-Lieuvin (27) 34 C5
Heudreville-sur-Eure (27) 35 J5
Heugas (40) 264 A5
Heugleville-sur-Scie (76) 15 K4
Heugnes (36) 147 G4
Heugon (61) 55 G3
Heugueville-sur-Sienne (50) 30 D4
Heuilley-Cotton (52) 116 D5
Heuilley-le-Grand (52) 116 D5
Heuilley-sur-Saône (21) 136 E5
Heuland (14) 33 H4
Heuqueville (27) 36 A4
Heuqueville (76) 14 B5
Heuringhem (62) 3 G6
Heurteauville (76) 35 F2
Heurtevent (14) 54 K2
Heussé (50) 80 D2
Heutrégiville (51) 41 H3
Heuzecourt (80) 9 K4
Hévilliers (55) 64 C6
Heyrieux (38) 206 D3
Hézecques (62) 5 F5
le Hézo (56) 101 G6
Hibarette (65) 285 H6
Hières-sur-Amby (38) 207 F1
Hierges (08) 24 C2
Hiermont (80) 9 J4
Hiers-Brouage (17) 176 E6
Hiersac (16) 196 C3
Hiesse (16) 180 A4
Hiesville (50) 29 F6
Hiéville (14) 54 C1
Higuères-Souye (64) 284 E3
Hiis (65) 285 H6
Hilbesheim (57) 67 J3
Hillion (22) 49 H6
Hilsenheim (67) 71 C5
Hilsprich (57) 68 C4
Hinacourt (02) 20 A4
Hinckange (57) 27 K6
Hindisheim (67) 70 E4
Hindlingen (68) 97 A5
Hinges (62) 5 K5
le Hinglé (22) 50 D6
Hinsbourg (67) 69 F5
Hinsingen (67) 67 H1
Hinx (40) 264 C4
Hipsheim (67) 71 D2
Hirel (35) 51 F4
Hirschland (67) 67 K2
Hirsingue (68) 97 B5
Hirson (02) 21 H1
Hirtzbach (68) 97 B4
Hirtzfelden (68) 96 D6
His (31) 306 B3
Hitte (65) 285 J6
Hochfelden (67) 70 D1
Hochstatt (68) 97 B3
Hochstett (67) 69 K6
Hocquigny (50). 51 K1

Hocquinghen (62). 2 D5
Hodenc-en-Bray (60) 37 F1
Hodenc-l'Évêque (60) 37 H3
Hodeng-au-Bosc (76) 17 F2
Hodeng-Hodenger (76) 36 C1
Hodent (95) 36 E5
Hoedic (56) 120 E4
Hoenheim (67) 25 A6
Hoerdt (67) 25 A5
Hoéville (54) 66 D4
Hoffen (67) 25 C5
les Hogues (27) 36 A2
la Hoguette (14) 54 B3
Hohatzenheim (67) 70 E1
Hohengoeft (67) 70 C2
Hohfrankenheim (67) 70 D1
Hohrod (67) 119 K1
le Hohwald (67) 70 B5
Holacourt (57) 66 D1
Holling (57) 27 K5
Holnon (02) 19 K2
Holque (59) 3 F4
Holtzheim (67) 70 E3
Holtzwihr (68) 96 C3
Holving (57) 68 C4
Hombleux (80) 19 H4
Homblières (02) 20 A2
Hombourg (68) 97 D3
Hombourg-Budange (57) 27 J5
Hombourg-Haut (57) 68 A2
l'Hôme-Chamondot (61) 83 K1
Homécourt (54) 27 F6
Hommarting (57) 67 K4
Hommert (57) 67 K4
Hommes (37) 126 E4
le Hommet-d'Arthenay (50). 31 G2
Homps (11) 291 F5
Homps (32) 268 A4
Hon-Hergies (59) 13 F2
Hondainville (60) 37 J3
Hondeghem (59) 3 J5
Hondevilliers (77) 60 D3
Hondouville (27) 35 H5
Hondschoote (59) 3 K2
Honfleur (14) 33 K2
Honguemare-Guenouville (27) 35 F3
Honnechy (59) 12 C5
Honnecourt-sur-Escaut (59) 11 J6
l'Honor-de-Cos (82) 249 J5
Honskirch (57) 67 H1
Hontanx (40) 265 K3
l'Hôpital (57) 68 A2
l'Hôpital-Camfrout (29). 74 C1
l'Hôpital-d'Orion (64) 283 H2
l'Hôpital-du-Grosbois (25) 156 D1
l'Hôpital-le-Grand (42) 204 E4
l'Hôpital-le-Mercier (71) 170 B6
l'Hôpital-Saint-Blaise (64) 283 J4
l'Hôpital-Saint-Lieffroy (25) 138 E4
l'Hôpital-sous-Rochefort (42) 204 B2
les Hôpitaux-Neufs (25) 157 F6
les Hôpitaux-Vieux (25) 157 F6
Horbourg-Wihr (68) 96 C4
Hordain (59) 11 K3
la Horgne (08) 22 C5
Horgues (65) 285 H5
l'Horme (42) 205 H5
Hornaing (59) 11 K2
Hornoy-le-Bourg (80) 17 H2
le Horps (53) 81 H3
Horsarrieu (40) 265 F5
Horville-en-Ornois (55) 92 E2
l'Hosmes (27) 56 C4
l'Hospitalet (04) 258 D5
l'Hospitalet-du-Larzac (12) 272 E2
l'Hospitalet-près-l'Andorre (09) ... 313 F3
Hosta (64) 283 F5
Hoste (57) 68 B3
Hostens (33) 229 G6
Hostias (01) 189 K6
Hostun (26) 223 F5
l'Hôtellerie (14) 34 B5
l'Hôtellerie-de-Flée (49) 104 D5
Hotonnes (01) 190 B4
Hotot-en-Auge (14) 33 H5
Hottot-les-Bagues (14) 32 B5
Hottviller (57) 69 G3
la Houblonnière (14) 33 J5
les Houches (74) 192 C5
Houchin (62) 5 K6
Houdain (62) 5 K6
Houdain-lez-Bavay (59) 13 F2
Houdan (78) 57 H4
Houdancourt (60) 38 C3
Houdelaincourt (55) 92 E1
Houdemont (54) 93 K1
Houdemont (54) 66 A5
Houdetot (76) 15 H3
Houdilcourt (08) 41 F2
Houdreville (54) 93 K1
Houécourt (88) 93 J4
Houeillès (47) 247 F4
Houesville (50) 29 F6
Houetteville (27) 35 H6
Houéville (88) 93 H3
Houeydets (65) 286 A6
le Houga (32) 266 A4
Houilles (78) 58 D3
Houlbec-Cocherel (27) 36 A6
Houlbec-près-le-Gros-Theil (27) ... 35 F4
Houldizy (08) 22 C3
Houlette (16) 196 A2

Houlgate (14) 33 G3
Houlle (62) 3 F4
le Houlme (76) 35 H1
l'Houmeau (17) 176 D2
Hounoux (11) 308 C1
Houplin-Ancoisne (59) 6 D5
Houplines (59) 6 C3
Houppeville (76) 35 H1
Houquetot (76) 14 D5
Hourc (65) 285 J5
Hourges (51) 40 C4
Hours (64) 285 F5
Hourtin (33) 210 C3
Houry (02) 21 F3
Houssay (41) 108 B6
Houssay (53) 105 F3
la Houssaye (27) 56 A2
la Houssaye-Béranger (76) 15 K5
la Houssaye-en-Brie (77) 59 K5
le Houssau-Brétignolles (53) . . . 81 H4
Houssen (68) 96 C3
Housseras (88) 95 F3
Housset (27) 20 D3
Housséville (54) 94 A3
la Houssière (88) 95 H5
la Houssoye (60) 37 F3
Houtaud (25) 156 E4
Houtkerque (59) 3 K3
Houtteville (50) 29 F6
Houville-en-Vexin (27) 36 A4
Houville-la-Branche (28) 85 H3
Houvin-Houvigneul (62) 10 B2
Houx (28) 85 H1
Hoymille (59) 3 J2
Huanne-Montmartin (25) 138 D3
Hubersent (62) 4 B5
Hubert-Folie (14) 32 E5
Huberville (50) 28 E4
Huby-Saint-Leu (62) 9 J1
Huchenneville (80) 9 F6
Huclier (62) 10 B1
Hucqueliers (62) 4 D5
Hudimesnil (50) 30 D6
Hudiviller (54) 66 C6
Huelgoat (29) 75 G1
Huest (27) 56 D1
Huêtre (45) 109 K2
Huez (38) 224 E4
Hugier (70) 137 G5
Hugleville-en-Caux (76) 15 J5
Huillé (49) 125 J1
Huilliécourt (52) 92 E6
Huilly-sur-Seille (71) 172 B3
Huiron (51) 63 F5
Huismes (37) 126 E6
Huisnes-sur-Mer (50) 51 J4
Huisseau-en-Beauce (41) 108 B6
Huisseau-sur-Cosson (41) . . . 129 F2
Huisseau-sur-Mauves (45) . . . 109 J4
l'Huisserie (53) 104 E2
Hulluch (62) 6 B6
Hultehouse (57) 70 A2
Humbauville (51) 62 E6
Humbécourt (52) 91 J1
Humbercamps (62) 10 D4
Humbercourt (80) 10 C4
Humbert (62) 4 D6
Humberville (52) 92 D4
Humbligny (18) 131 H6
Humeroeuille (62) 9 K1
Humes-Jorquenay (52) 116 C1
Humières (62) 9 K1
Hunawihr (68) 71 A6
Hundling (57) 68 C3
Hundsbach (68) 97 C4
Huningue (68) 97 E4
Hunspach (67) 25 C2
Hunting (57) 27 J3
Huos (31) 305 H1
Huparlac (12) 236 B4
Huppy (80) 9 F6
Hure (33) 230 C6
Hurecourt (70) 118 A3
Hures-la-Parade (48) 253 K4
Huriel (03) 167 G6
Hurigny (71) 171 J6
Hurtières (38) 224 D2
Hurtigheim (67) 70 D3
Husseren-les-Châteaux (68) . . . 96 B4
Husseren-Wesserling (68) . . . 119 A3
Hussigny-Godbrange (54) 26 E3
Husson (50) 80 E1
Huttendorf (67) 69 K6
Huttenheim (67) 70 E6
Hyds (03) 184 C1
Hyémondans (25) 139 F4
Hyencourt-le-Grand (80) 19 G3
Hyenville (50) 30 D5
Hyères (83) 298 A6
Hyet (70) 138 D2
Hyèvre-Magny (25) 138 D4
Hyèvre-Paroisse (25) 138 D4
Hymont (88) 94 A4

I

Ibarrolle (64) 283 F5
Ibigny (57) 67 H5
Ibos (65) 285 G5

Ichtratzheim (67) 71 D2
Ichy (77) 87 G6
Idaux-Mendy (64) 283 H5
Idrac-Respaillès (32) 286 B1
Idron-Ousse-Sendets (64) . . . 284 D4
Ids-Saint-Roch (18) 166 D2
Iffendic (35) 78 C4
les Iffs (35) 78 E2
Ifs (14) 32 E5
les Ifs (76) 16 C2
Igé (61) 83 H4
Igé (71) 171 J5
Ignaucourt (80) 18 D3
Ignaux (09) 308 A6
Igney (54) 67 G5
Igney (88) 94 C4
Ignol (18) 150 B4
Igny (70) 137 H3
Igny (91) 58 D5
Igny-Comblizy (51) 61 H1
Igon (64) 284 E6
Igornay (71) 153 F3
Igoville (27) 35 J3
Iguerande (71) 187 F2
Iholdy (64) 282 E4
Île-aux-Moines (56) 100 E6
l'Île-Bouchard (37) 145 H2
Île-d'Aix (17) 176 D4
Île-d'Arz (56) 101 F6
Île-de-Batz (29) 46 E2
Île-de-Bréhat (22) 48 E1
Île-de-Sein (29) 73 A6
l'Île-d'Elle (85) 160 C6
Île-d'Houat (56) 120 D3
l'Île-d'Olonne (85) 158 E4
l'Île-d'Yeu (85) 140 B6
Île-Molène (29) 72 A6
l'Île-Rousse (2B) 318 C2
l'Île-Saint-Denis (93) 58 E2
Île-Tudy (29) 98 C3
Ilharre (64) 283 G3
Ilhat (09) 308 A3
les Ilhes (11) 290 B4
Ilhet (65) 305 F3
Ilheu (65) 305 H2
Illange (57) 27 G4
Illartein (09) 306 B3
Illats (33) 229 K5
Ille-sur-Têt (66) 314 E2
Illeville-sur-Montfort (27) 34 E3
Illfurth (68) 97 B3
Illhaeusern (68) 71 B6
Illiat (01) 188 D2
Illier-et-Laramade (09) 307 H5
Illiers-Combray (28) 84 E5
Illiers-l'Évêque (27) 56 E4
Illies (59) 6 B5
Illifaut (22) 77 K5
Illkirch-Graffenstaden (67) . . . 71 D4
Illois (76) 16 E4
Illoud (52) 93 F5
Illy (08) 23 F3
Illzach (68) 97 C2
Ilonse (06) 261 H5
Imbleville (76) 15 J4
Imécourt (08) 42 D2
Imling (57) 67 J4
Imphy (58) 151 F5
Inaumont (08) 21 K6
Incarville (27) 35 J3
Incheville (76) 8 D6
Inchy (59) 12 C5
Inchy-en-Artois (62) 11 H4
Incourt (62) 9 K1
Indevillers (25) 139 J4
Indre (44) 123 F4
Ineuil (18) 166 E1
les Infournas (05) 242 E3
Ingenheim (67) 70 D1
Ingersheim (68) 96 B4
Inghem (62) 3 G6
Inglange (57) 27 H4
Ingolsheim (67) 25 C2
Ingouville (76) 15 G2
Ingrandes (36) 164 B3
Ingrandes (49) 124 D4
Ingrandes (86) 145 J5
Ingrandes-de-Touraine (37) . . 126 E6
Ingrannes (45) 110 D3
Ingré (45) 109 K4
Inguiniel (56) 100 B1
Inguiller (67) 69 H5
Injoux-Génissiat (01) 190 C4
Innenheim (67) 70 D4
Innimond (01) 207 H1
Inor (55) 23 H6
Insming (57) 67 G1
Insviller (57) 67 H2
Intraville (76) 16 B1
Intres (07) 221 G6
Intréville (28) 86 A5
Intville-la-Guétard (45) 86 D5
Inval-Boiron (80) 17 F2
Inxent (62) 4 C5
Inzinzac-Lochrist (56) 100 B2
Ippécourt (55) 64 D1
Ippling (57) 68 D3
Irai (61) 55 J6
Irais (79) 144 C5
Irancy (89) 113 H6
Iré-le-Sec (55) 43 H1
Irigny (69) 206 A3

Irissarry (64) 282 E4
Irles (80) 10 E5
Irodouër (35) 78 D2
Iron (02) 20 D1
Irouléguy (64) 282 D5
Irreville (27) 35 J6
Irvillac (29) 74 C1
Is-en-Bassigny (52) 116 E2
Is-sur-Tille (21) 136 B3
Isbergues (62) 5 J4
Isches (88) 117 H2
Isdes (45) 130 D1
Isenay (58) 151 K5
Isigny-le-Buat (50) 52 B6
Isigny-sur-Mer (14) 29 H6
Island (89) 133 J3
l'Isle-Adam (95) 37 J6
l'Isle-Arné (32) 267 K6
Isle-Aubigny (10) 90 C2
Isle-Aumont (10) 90 B6
l'Isle-Bouzon (32) 267 K2
l'Isle-d'Abeau (38) 206 E3
l'Isle-de-Noé (32) 267 G6
l'Isle-d'Espagnac (16) 196 B3
l'Isle-en-Dodon (31) 287 F3
Isle-et-Bardais (03) 167 K2
l'Isle-Jourdain (32) 268 D6
l'Isle-Jourdain (86) 180 B2
Isle-Saint-Georges (33) 229 J3
Isle-sur-la-Sorgue (84) 276 D2
Isle-sur-Marne (51) 63 G6
Isle-sur-Serein (89) 134 A2
les Isles-Bardel (14) 53 K3
Isles-les-Meldeuses (77) 60 A2
Isles-lès-Villenoy (77) 59 J3
Isles-sur-Suippe (51) 41 G3
les Islettes (55) 42 E6
Isneauville (76) 35 J1
Isola (06) 261 H3
Isolaccio-di-Fiumorbo (2B) . . 321 H4
Isômes (52) 136 C1
Ispagnac (48) 254 B2
Ispoure (64) 282 D5
Isques (62) 2 B6
Issac (24) 213 H6
Issamoulenc (07) 239 J3
Issancourt-et-Rumel (08) 22 E3
Issanlas (07) 238 D3
Issans (25) 139 G2
les Issards (09) 307 K1
Issarlès (07) 238 D2
Issé (44) 103 H5
Isse (51) 41 G6
Issel (11) 289 H4
Issendolus (46) 234 B3
Issenhausen (67) 69 J6
Issenheim (68) 96 B6
Issepts (46) 234 C4
Isserpent (03) 186 A3
Isserteaux (63) 203 G3
Issigeac (24) 231 J3
Issirac (30) 256 B3
Issoire (63) 202 E5
Issor (64) 283 K6
Issou (78) 57 K2
Issoudun (36) 148 C4
Issoudun-Létrieix (23) 183 F4
Issus (31) 288 C3
Issy-les-Moulineaux (92) 58 D4
Issy-l'Évêque (71) 170 A2
Istres (13) 295 J4
les Istres-et-Bury (51) 62 A2
Isturits (64) 282 E3
Itancourt (02) 20 A3
Iteuil (86) 162 E4
Ittenheim (67) 70 D3
Itterswiller (67) 70 C6
Itxassou (64) 263 D2
Itzac (81) 270 B1
Ivergny (62) 10 B3
Iverny (77) 59 J2
Iviers (02) 21 H3
Iville (27) 35 G5
Ivors (60) 39 F5
Ivory (39) 156 A4
Ivoy-le-Pré (18) 131 F5
Ivrey (39) 156 A3
Ivry-en-Montagne (21) 153 J3
Ivry-la-Bataille (27) 57 G3
Ivry-le-Temple (60) 37 G4
Ivry-sur-Seine (94) 58 E4
Iwuy (59) 11 K3
Izaourt (65) 305 H2
Izaut-de-l'Hôtel (31) 305 K2
Izaux (65) 305 F1
Izé (53) 81 K5
Izeaux (38) 223 H1
Izel-lès-Équerchin (62) 11 G2
Izel-les-Hameaux (62) 10 C2
Izenave (01) 189 K4
Izernore (01) 189 K2
Izeron (38) 223 H4
Izeure (21) 154 D1
Izier (21) 136 C6
Izieu (01) 207 J3
Izon (33) 229 K1
Izon-la-Bruisse (26) 258 C3
Izotges (32) 266 B5

J

Jablines (77) 59 J3
Jabreilles-les-Bordes (87) . . . 181 K5
Jabrun (15) 236 D3
Jacob-Bellecombette (73) . . . 208 B4
Jacou (34) 274 C5
Jacque (65) 285 J5
Jagny-sous-Bois (95) 38 A6
Jaignes (77) 60 B2
Jaillans (26) 223 F5
la Jaille-Yvon (49) 105 F6
Jaillon (54) 65 J4
Jailly (58) 151 H3
Jailly-les-Moulins (21) 135 G3
Jainvillotte (88) 93 G5
Jalesches (23) 183 F1
Jaleyrac (15) 217 G3
Jaligny-sur-Besbre (03) 169 H6
Jallais (49) 143 F1
Jallanges (21) 154 C3
Jallans (28) 109 F2
Jallaucourt (57) 66 C3
Jallerange (25) 137 H6
Jalogny (71) 171 J5
Jâlons (51) 62 B1
Jambles (71) 153 J6
Jambville (78) 57 K1
Jaméricourt (60) 37 F3
Jametz (55) 43 H1
Janailhac (87) 198 E4
Janaillat (23) 182 C4
Jancigny (21) 136 E4
Jandun (08) 22 B4
Janneyrias (38) 206 D2
Jans (44) 103 G5
Janville (14) 33 G5
Janville (28) 86 A6
Janville (60) 38 E2
Janville-sur-Juine (91) 86 D2
Janvilliers (51) 61 G3
Janvry (51) 40 D4
Janvry (91) 58 C6
Janzé (35) 79 H6
Jarcieu (38) 222 C1
la Jard (17) 195 G3
Jard-sur-Mer (85) 159 G4
le Jardin (19) 216 D2
Jardin (38) 206 B5
Jardres (86) 163 H3
Jargeau (45) 110 C4
Jarjayes (05) 242 E6
Jarménil (88) 94 E6
Jarnac (16) 196 A3
Jarnac-Champagne (17) 195 J4
Jarnages (23) 183 F3
la Jarne (17) 176 E3
Jarnioux (69) 188 A5
Jarnosse (42) 187 G3
Jarny (54) 44 C5
Jarret (65) 304 B1
la Jarrie (17) 176 E3
Jarrie (38) 224 B4
la Jarrie-Audouin (17) 177 K4
Jarrier (73) 225 G2
Jars (18) 131 H5
Jarsy (73) 208 E3
Jarville-la-Malgrange (54) 66 A5
Jarzé (49) 125 K2
Jas (42) 205 F2
Jasney (70) 118 B4
Jassans-Riottier (01) 188 B5
Jasseines (10) 90 D2
Jasseron (01) 189 H2
Jasses (64) 283 J4
Jatxou (64) 263 D2
Jau-Dignac-et-Loirac (33) . . . 194 C6
Jaucourt (10) 91 G5
la Jaudonnière (85) 160 C2
Jaudrais (28) 84 D1
Jaujac (07) 239 G5
Jauldes (16) 197 F2
Jaulges (89) 113 J3
Jaulgonne (02) 40 A6
Jaulnay (37) 145 H4
Jaulnes (77) 88 D3
Jaulny (54) 65 H1
Jaulzy (60) 39 G2
Jaunac (07) 239 H1
Jaunay-Clan (86) 163 F2
Jaure (24) 213 J5
Jausiers (04) 260 D1
Jaux (60) 38 D2
Jauze (72) 83 F6
Javaugues (43) 219 H2
Javené (35) 80 A4
Javerdat (87) 180 E5
Javerlhac-et-la-Chapelle-
   Saint-Robert (24) 197 J4
Javernant (10) 90 A6
la Javie (04) 260 A4
Javols (48) 237 G2
Javrezac (16) 195 J2
Javron-les-Chapelles (53) . . . 81 K3
Jax (43) 219 K4
Jaxu (64) 282 E5
Jayac (24) 215 G3
Jayat (01) 172 C6
Jazeneuil (86) 162 C4
Jazennes (17) 195 G4

Jeancourt (02) 19 J1
Jeandelaincourt (54) 66 B3
Jeandelize (54) 44 B5
Jeanménil (88) 95 F3
Jeansagnière (42) 204 A2
Jeantes (02) 21 H3
Jebsheim (68) 96 D3
Jegun (32) 267 G4
la Jemaye (24) 213 F4
Jenlain (59) 12 E2
Jenzat (03) 185 G3
Jésonville (88) 94 A6
Jessains (10) 91 F4
Jetterswiller (67) 70 C2
Jettingen (68) 97 C4
Jeu-les-Bois (36) 165 K2
Jeu-Maloches (36) 147 H5
Jeufosse (78) 57 G1
Jeugny (10) 114 A1
Jeumont (59) 13 J2
Jeurre (39) 173 H5
Jeux-lès-Bard (21) 134 C3
Jeuxey (88) 94 D5
Jevoncourt (54) 94 A2
Jezainville (54) 65 K2
Jézeau (65) 305 F3
Joannas (07) 239 G5
Job (63) 203 K4
Jobourg (50) 28 A1
Joch (66) 314 D3
Joeuf (54) 27 F6
Joganville (50) 29 F4
Joigny (89) 112 E3
Joigny-sur-Meuse (08) 22 D2
Joinville (52) 92 B2
Joinville-le-Pont (94) 59 F4
Joiselle (51) 61 F4
Jolimetz (59) 12 E3
Jolivet (54) 66 D6
Jonage (69) 206 C1
la Jonchère (85) 159 J4
la Jonchère-Saint-Maurice (87) . 181 K5
Jonchères (26) 241 H5
Joncherey (90) 139 K2
Jonchery (52) 92 A6
Jonchery-sur-Suippe (51) 41 K5
Jonchery-sur-Vesle (51) 40 D4
Joncourt (02) 20 A1
Joncreuil (10) 91 F2
Joncy (71) 171 G3
Jongieux (73) 208 A2
Jonquerets-de-Livet (27) 55 J1
Jonquerettes (84) 276 C2
Jonquery (51) 40 D5
Jonquières (11) 310 A2
Jonquières (34) 273 H5
Jonquières (60) 38 D2
Jonquières (81) 270 D6
Jonquières (84) 257 F5
Jonquières-Saint-Vincent (30) . 275 J3
Jons (69) 206 D1
Jonval (08) 22 C6
Jonvelle (70) 117 J3
Jonville-en-Woëvre (55) 44 B6
Jonzac (17) 195 J6
Jonzier-Épagny (74) 190 E3
Jonzieux (42) 221 G2
Joppécourt (54) 26 D4
Jort (14) 54 B2
Jorxey (88) 94 B4
Josat (43) 219 K3
Joserand (63) 185 F5
Josnes (41) 109 G5
Josse (40) 262 D5
Josselin (56) 101 H1
Jossigny (77) 59 J4
Jou-sous-Monjou (15) 235 K1
Jouac (87) 164 E6
Jouaignes (02) 40 A3
Jouancy (89) 134 A1
Jouars-Pontchartrain (78) 58 A4
Jouaville (54) 44 D5
Joucas (84) 277 F2
Joucou (11) 308 D5
Joudes (71) 172 E4
Joudreville (54) 26 D5
Joué-du-Bois (61) 82 A1
Joué-du-Plain (61) 54 B5
Joué-en-Charnie (72) 106 A2
Joué-l'Abbé (72) 106 E1
Joué-lès-Tours (37) 127 J5
Joué-sur-Erdre (44) 103 J6
Jouet-sur-l'Aubois (18) 150 C3
Jouey (21) 153 G2
Jougne (25) 157 F6
Jouhe (39) 155 G1
Jouhet (86) 164 A4
Jouillat (23) 182 D2
Jouques (13) 278 A5
Jouqueviel (81) 251 G5
Jourgnac (87) 198 D4
Journans (01) 189 H3
Journet (86) 164 B5
Journiac (24) 214 C6
Journy (62) 2 E5
Jours-en-Vaux (21) 153 H3
Jours-lès-Baigneux (21) 135 G1
Joursac (15) 218 D4
Joussé (86) 179 K2
Jouvençon (71) 172 B3

Joux (69) . . . 187 H6
Joux-la-Ville (89) . . . 133 J2
Jouy (28) . . . 85 G2
Jouy (89) . . . 88 A4
Jouy-aux-Arches (57) . . . 44 E6
Jouy-en-Argonne (55) . . . 43 G5
Jouy-en-Josas (78) . . . 58 C4
Jouy-en-Pithiverais (45) . . . 110 C1
Jouy-le-Châtel (77) . . . 60 B6
Jouy-le-Moutier (95) . . . 58 B1
Jouy-le-Potier (45) . . . 109 K6
Jouy-lès-Reims (51) . . . 40 E4
Jouy-Mauvoisin (78) . . . 57 H2
Jouy-sous-Thelle (60) . . . 37 F3
Jouy-sur-Eure (27) . . . 56 E1
Jouy-sur-Morin (77) . . . 60 D4
Joyeuse (07) . . . 255 J1
Joyeux (01) . . . 189 F5
Joze (63) . . . 203 F1
Jû-Belloc (32) . . . 266 C6
Juaye-Mondaye (14) . . . 32 B4
Jubainville (88) . . . 93 G2
la Jubaudière (49) . . . 142 E1
Jublains (53) . . . 81 H5
le Juch (29) . . . 74 B5
Jugazan (33) . . . 230 B3
Jugeals-Nazareth (19) . . . 215 J3
Jugon-les-Lacs (22) . . . 50 A6
Jugy (71) . . . 171 K3
Juicq (17) . . . 177 K6
Juif (71) . . . 172 C2
Juignac (16) . . . 212 E1
Juigné-des-Moutiers (44) . . . 104 A6
Juigné-sur-Loire (49) . . . 125 H4
Juigné-sur-Sarthe (72) . . . 105 K4
Juignettes (27) . . . 55 J3
Juillac (19) . . . 215 G2
Juillac (32) . . . 285 J1
Juillac (33) . . . 230 D2
Juillac-le-Coq (16) . . . 195 K4
Juillaguet (16) . . . 196 E5
Juillan (65) . . . 285 G5
Juillé (16) . . . 179 G5
Juillé (72) . . . 82 D5
Juillé (79) . . . 178 C3
Juillenay (21) . . . 134 D5
Juilles (32) . . . 268 A6
Juilley (50) . . . 51 K4
Juilly (21) . . . 134 E3
Juilly (77) . . . 59 H1
Jujols (66) . . . 314 B6
Jujurieux (01) . . . 189 J4
Julianges (48) . . . 237 G1
Juliénas (69) . . . 188 B2
Julienne (16) . . . 196 A3
Jullianges (43) . . . 220 B2
Jullié (69) . . . 188 B2
Jullouville (50) . . . 51 H2
Jully (89) . . . 114 D5
Jully-lès-Buxy (71) . . . 171 K3
Jully-sur-Sarce (10) . . . 114 D1
Julos (65) . . . 285 G6
Julvécourt (55) . . . 43 G6
Jumeauville (78) . . . 57 K3
Jumeaux (63) . . . 203 F6
Jumel (80) . . . 18 B6
Jumelles (27) . . . 56 D3
la Jumellière (49) . . . 124 E5
Jumencourt (02) . . . 39 J1
Jumièges (76) . . . 35 F2
Jumigny (02) . . . 40 C2
Jumilhac-le-Grand (24) . . . 198 D5
Junas (30) . . . 274 E4
Junay (89) . . . 113 K4
Juncalas (65) . . . 304 B1
Jungholtz (68) . . . 96 A6
Junhac (15) . . . 235 H4
les Junies (46) . . . 233 F6
Juniville (08) . . . 41 J2
Jupilles (72) . . . 107 F5
Jurançon (64) . . . 284 C4
Juranville (45) . . . 111 F2
Juré (42) . . . 186 D6
Jurignac (16) . . . 196 C5
Jurques (14) . . . 53 F1
Jurvielle (31) . . . 305 G5
Jury (57) . . . 45 F6
Juscorps (79) . . . 178 B2
Jusix (47) . . . 230 D6
Jussac (15) . . . 217 H6
Jussarupt (88) . . . 95 G5
Jussas (17) . . . 211 K2
Jussecourt-Minecourt (51) . . . 63 H4
Jussey (70) . . . 117 J4
Jussy (02) . . . 19 K4
Jussy (57) . . . 44 E5
Jussy (89) . . . 113 G6
Jussy-Champagne (18) . . . 149 J4
Jussy-le-Chaudrier (18) . . . 150 B2
Justian (32) . . . 267 F3
Justine-Herbigny (08) . . . 21 K5
Justiniac (09) . . . 288 C3
Jutigny (77) . . . 88 C2
Juvaincourt (88) . . . 93 K4
Juvancourt (10) . . . 115 H1
Juvanzé (10) . . . 91 F4
Juvardeil (49) . . . 125 H1
Juvelize (57) . . . 66 E4
Juvignac (34) . . . 274 B6
Juigné (53) . . . 80 C5
Juvignies (60) . . . 37 H1
Juvigny (02) . . . 39 J2

Juvigny (51) . . . 62 C1
Juvigny (74) . . . 191 G1
Juvigny-en-Perthois (55) . . . 64 B6
Juvigny-le-Tertre (50) . . . 52 C5
Juvigny-sous-Andaine (61) . . . 81 H1
Juvigny-sur-Loison (55) . . . 43 H1
Juvigny-sur-Orne (61) . . . 54 C5
Juvigny-sur-Seulles (14) . . . 32 C5
Juville (57) . . . 66 C2
Juvinas (07) . . . 239 G4
Juvincourt-et-Damary (02) . . . 40 D2
Juvisy-sur-Orge (91) . . . 58 E5
Juvrecourt (54) . . . 66 C4
Juxue (64) . . . 283 F5
Juzanvigny (10) . . . 91 F3
Juzennecourt (52) . . . 91 K6
Juzes (31) . . . 289 F2
Juzet-de-Luchon (31) . . . 305 H5
Juzet-d'Izaut (31) . . . 305 K3
Juziers (78) . . . 57 K2

K

Kalhausen (57) . . . 68 E4
Kaltenhouse (67) . . . 25 B4
Kanfen (57) . . . 27 G3
Kappelen (68) . . . 97 D4
Kappelkinger (57) . . . 67 H1
Katzenthal (68) . . . 96 B3
Kauffenheim (67) . . . 25 C3
Kaysersberg (68) . . . 96 B3
Kédange-sur-Canner (57) . . . 27 J5
Keffenach (67) . . . 25 B2
Kembs (68) . . . 97 D3
Kemplich (57) . . . 27 J4
Kerbach (57) . . . 68 C2
Kerbors (22) . . . 48 C2
Kerfot (22) . . . 48 E3
Kerfourn (56) . . . 77 F6
Kergloff (29) . . . 75 H3
Kergrist (56) . . . 76 E5
Kergrist-Moëlou (22) . . . 76 B2
Kerien (22) . . . 76 C1
Kerlaz (29) . . . 74 B4
Kerling-lès-Sierck (57) . . . 27 J4
Kerlouan (29) . . . 46 B3
Kermaria-Sulard (22) . . . 48 B2
Kermoroc'h (22) . . . 48 C4
Kernascléden (56) . . . 76 A4
Kernilis (29) . . . 46 A4
Kernouës (29) . . . 46 B4
Kerpert (22) . . . 76 C2
Kerprich-aux-Bois (57) . . . 67 H4
Kersaint-Plabennec (29) . . . 46 B5
Kertzfeld (67) . . . 70 D6
Kervignac (56) . . . 100 B3
Keskastel (67) . . . 67 J1
Kesseldorf (67) . . . 25 D3
Kienheim (67) . . . 70 D2
Kientzheim (68) . . . 96 B3
Kiffis (68) . . . 97 C6
Killem (59) . . . 3 K2
Kilstett (67) . . . 25 B5
Kindwiller (67) . . . 69 J5
Kingersheim (68) . . . 97 C2
Kintzheim (67) . . . 71 A5
Kirchberg (68) . . . 119 J4
Kirchheim (67) . . . 70 D3
Kirrberg (67) . . . 67 J3
Kirrwiller-Bosselshausen (67) . . . 69 J6
Kirsch-lès-Sierck (57) . . . 27 J3
Kirschnaumen (57) . . . 27 K3
Kirviller (57) . . . 67 H1
Klang (57) . . . 27 J4
Kleingoeft (67) . . . 70 C2
Knoeringue (68) . . . 97 D4
Knoersheim (67) . . . 70 C2
Knutange (57) . . . 27 F4
Koenigsmacker (57) . . . 27 H4
Koestlach (68) . . . 97 B5
Koetzingue (68) . . . 97 C3
Koeur-la-Grande (55) . . . 64 D3
Koeur-la-Petite (55) . . . 64 E3
Kogenheim (67) . . . 70 D6
Kolbsheim (67) . . . 70 D3
Krautergersheim (67) . . . 70 D4
Krautwiller (67) . . . 70 E1
le Kremlin-Bicêtre (94) . . . 58 E4
Kriegsheim (67) . . . 70 D2
Kruth (68) . . . 119 J2
Kunheim (68) . . . 96 D4
Kuntzig (57) . . . 27 H4
Kurtzenhouse (67) . . . 25 B5
Kuttolsheim (67) . . . 70 D2
Kutzenhausen (67) . . . 25 B2

L

Laà-Mondrans (64) . . . 283 J2
Laas (32) . . . 286 A2
Laas (45) . . . 110 D1
Laàs (64) . . . 283 H3
Labalme (01) . . . 189 J3
Labarde (33) . . . 211 G5
Labarrère (32) . . . 266 D2
Labarthe (32) . . . 286 C2
Labarthe (82) . . . 249 J4
Labarthe-Bleys (81) . . . 250 E6

Labarthe-Inard (31) . . . 306 A1
Labarthe-Rivière (31) . . . 305 J1
Labarthe-sur-Lèze (31) . . . 288 B2
Labarthète (32) . . . 266 A6
Labassère (65) . . . 304 C1
Labastide (65) . . . 305 F2
Labastide-Beauvoir (31) . . . 288 C2
Labastide-Castel-Amouroux (47) . . . 247 G3
Labastide-Cézéracq (64) . . . 284 B3
Labastide-Chalosse (40) . . . 265 H6
Labastide-Clermont (31) . . . 287 J4
Labastide-d'Anjou (11) . . . 289 F4
Labastide-d'Armagnac (40) . . . 266 A1
Labastide-de-Lévis (81) . . . 270 C2
Labastide-de-Penne (82) . . . 250 B3
Labastide-de-Virac (07) . . . 256 A2
Labastide-Dénat (81) . . . 270 E3
Labastide-du-Haut-Mont (46) . . . 234 E2
Labastide-du-Temple (82) . . . 249 H6
Labastide-du-Vert (46) . . . 233 F6
Labastide-en-Val (11) . . . 309 H1
Labastide-Esparbairenque (11) . . . 290 B3
Labastide-Gabausse (81) . . . 270 D1
Labastide-Marnhac (46) . . . 249 K2
Labastide-Monréjeau (64) . . . 284 B3
Labastide-Murat (46) . . . 233 J5
Labastide-Paumès (31) . . . 287 G4
Labastide-Rouairoux (81) . . . 290 E2
Labastide-Saint-Georges (81) . . . 270 B5
Labastide-Saint-Pierre (82) . . . 269 G2
Labastide-Saint-Sernin (31) . . . 269 H5
Labastide-Savès (32) . . . 287 G2
Labastide-sur-Bésorgues (07) . . . 239 G3
Labastide-Villefranche (64) . . . 283 G2
Labastidette (31) . . . 287 K2
Labathude (46) . . . 234 D4
Labatie-d'Andaure (07) . . . 221 J5
Labatmale (64) . . . 285 F5
Labatut (09) . . . 288 C5
Labatut (40) . . . 264 B6
Labatut (64) . . . 285 G3
Labatut-Rivière (65) . . . 285 H1
Labbeville (95) . . . 37 H6
Labeaume (07) . . . 255 J1
Labécède-Lauragais (11) . . . 289 H3
Labège (31) . . . 288 C1
Labégude (07) . . . 239 H4
Labéjan (32) . . . 286 C1
Labenne (40) . . . 262 B6
Labergement-du-Navois (25) . . . 156 C3
Labergement-Foigney (21) . . . 136 C6
Labergement-lès-Auxonne (21) . . . 155 F1
Labergement-lès-Seurre (21) . . . 154 C3
Labergement-Sainte-Marie (25) . . . 156 E6
Laberlière (60) . . . 19 F6
Labescau (33) . . . 246 E1
Labesserette (15) . . . 235 H3
Labessette (63) . . . 201 H6
Labessière-Candeil (81) . . . 270 C4
Labets-Biscay (64) . . . 283 F3
Labeuville (55) . . . 44 B5
Labeuvrière (62) . . . 5 H5
Labeyrie (64) . . . 284 A1
Lablachère (07) . . . 255 J1
Laboissière-en-Santerre (80) . . . 18 E5
Laboissière-en-Thelle (60) . . . 37 H4
Laborde (65) . . . 304 E2
Laborel (26) . . . 258 C3
Labosse (60) . . . 37 F3
Labouheyre (40) . . . 245 F4
Laboulbène (81) . . . 270 E5
Laboule (07) . . . 239 F5
Labouquerie (24) . . . 232 B3
Labourgade (82) . . . 268 D2
Labourse (62) . . . 6 A6
Laboutarie (81) . . . 270 D4
Labretonie (47) . . . 247 J1
Labrihe (32) . . . 268 B4
Labrit (40) . . . 245 K5
Labroquère (31) . . . 305 H2
Labrosse (45) . . . 86 E5
Labrousse (15) . . . 235 J2
Labroye (62) . . . 9 H3
Labruguière (81) . . . 290 A1
Labruyère (21) . . . 154 D3
Labruyère (60) . . . 38 B1
Labruyère-Dorsa (31) . . . 288 C3
Labry (54) . . . 44 C4
Laburgade (46) . . . 250 B2
Lac-des-Rouges-Truites (39) . . . 174 A2
le Lac-d'Issarlès (07) . . . 238 E2
Lacabarède (81) . . . 290 D2
Lacadée (64) . . . 284 A1
Lacajunte (40) . . . 265 H6
Lacalm (12) . . . 236 C3
Lacam-d'Ourcet (46) . . . 234 D2
Lacanau (33) . . . 210 C6
Lacanche (21) . . . 153 H3
Lacapelle-Barrès (15) . . . 236 A1
Lacapelle-Biron (47) . . . 232 C5
Lacapelle-Cabanac (46) . . . 249 G1
Lacapelle-del-Fraisse (15) . . . 235 H3
Lacapelle-Livron (82) . . . 250 D4
Lacapelle-Marival (46) . . . 234 C4
Lacapelle-Pinet (81) . . . 251 J6
Lacapelle-Ségalar (81) . . . 251 F6
Lacapelle-Viescamp (15) . . . 235 F1
Lacarre (64) . . . 282 E5
Lacarry-Arhan-Charritte-
   de-Haut (64) . . . 302 C1
Lacassagne (65) . . . 285 J3
Lacaugne (31) . . . 287 K4

Lacaune (81) . . . 271 K5
Lacaussade (47) . . . 232 B6
Lacave (09) . . . 306 C2
Lacave (46) . . . 233 J2
Lacaze (81) . . . 271 H5
Lacelle (19) . . . 200 A4
Lacenas (69) . . . 188 A5
Lacépède (47) . . . 247 K3
Lachaise (16) . . . 196 A5
Lachalade (55) . . . 42 D5
Lachambre (57) . . . 68 A3
Lachamp (48) . . . 237 H5
Lachamp-Raphaël (07) . . . 239 G2
Lachapelle (47) . . . 231 F5
Lachapelle (54) . . . 95 G2
Lachapelle (80) . . . 17 H3
Lachapelle (82) . . . 268 A1
Lachapelle-aux-Pots (60) . . . 37 F2
Lachapelle-Auzac (46) . . . 233 H1
Lachapelle-en-Blaisy (52) . . . 91 K6
Lachapelle-Graillouse (07) . . . 238 D2
Lachapelle-Saint-Pierre (60) . . . 37 J4
Lachapelle-sous-Aubenas (07) . . . 239 H5
Lachapelle-sous-Chanéac (07) . . . 239 G1
Lachapelle-sous-Chaux (90) . . . 119 H5
Lachapelle-sous-Gerberoy (60) . . . 17 G6
Lachapelle-sous-Rougemont (90) . . . 119 K5
Lachassagne (69) . . . 188 B5
Lachau (26) . . . 258 C4
Lachaussée (55) . . . 44 C6
Lachaussée-du-Bois-d'Écu (60) . . . 17 K6
Lachaux (63) . . . 186 A5
Lachelle (60) . . . 38 C2
Lachy (51) . . . 61 H4
Lacollonge (90) . . . 119 J6
Lacombe (11) . . . 289 K3
Lacommande (64) . . . 284 B3
Lacoste (34) . . . 273 H6
Lacoste (84) . . . 277 G3
Lacougotte-Cadoul (81) . . . 270 A6
Lacour (82) . . . 248 B3
Lacour-d'Arcenay (21) . . . 134 C5
Lacourt (09) . . . 306 D3
Lacourt-Saint-Pierre (82) . . . 269 F1
Lacq (64) . . . 284 A2
Lacquy (40) . . . 265 K2
Lacrabe (40) . . . 265 F6
Lacres (62) . . . 4 C4
Lacroisille (81) . . . 289 G1
Lacroix-Barrez (12) . . . 235 K3
Lacroix-Falgarde (31) . . . 288 B2
Lacroix-Saint-Ouen (60) . . . 38 D3
Lacroix-sur-Meuse (55) . . . 64 C1
Lacropte (24) . . . 214 B5
Lacrost (71) . . . 172 A3
Lacrouzette (81) . . . 271 G6
Lacs (36) . . . 166 B3
Ladapeyre (23) . . . 183 F2
Ladaux (33) . . . 230 A4
Ladern-sur-Lauquet (11) . . . 309 G1
Ladevèze-Rivière (32) . . . 285 H1
Ladevèze-Ville (32) . . . 285 H1
Ladignac-le-Long (87) . . . 198 D4
Ladignac-sur-Rondelles (19) . . . 216 B3
Ladinhac (15) . . . 235 J3
Ladirat (46) . . . 234 C3
Ladiville (16) . . . 196 B5
Ladoix-Serrigny (21) . . . 154 A3
Ladon (45) . . . 111 G3
Lados (33) . . . 246 D1
Ladoye-sur-Seille (39) . . . 155 J6
Laduz (89) . . . 112 E4
Lafage (11) . . . 289 G6
Lafage-sur-Sombre (19) . . . 216 E2
Lafare (84) . . . 257 G5
Lafarre (07) . . . 221 J6
Lafarre (43) . . . 238 D2
Lafat (23) . . . 182 A1
Lafauche (52) . . . 92 C4
Laféline (03) . . . 168 C6
Laferté-sur-Amance (52) . . . 117 G2
Laferté-sur-Aube (52) . . . 115 H1
Lafeuillade-en-Vézie (15) . . . 235 H3
Laffaux (02) . . . 39 K2
Laffite-Toupière (31) . . . 287 G6
Laffrey (38) . . . 224 B5
Lafitole (65) . . . 285 H2
Lafitte (82) . . . 268 D2
Lafitte-sur-Lot (47) . . . 247 K2
Lafitte-Vigordane (31) . . . 287 J4
Lafox (47) . . . 248 C5
Lafrançaise (82) . . . 249 H5
Lafraye (60) . . . 37 J1
Lafresguimont-Saint-Martin (80) . . . 17 G3
Lafrimbolle (57) . . . 67 J6
Lagamas (34) . . . 273 J5
Lagarde (09) . . . 308 D2
Lagarde (31) . . . 288 E4
Lagarde (32) . . . 267 H2
Lagarde (57) . . . 67 F4
Lagarde (65) . . . 285 H4
Lagarde-d'Apt (84) . . . 277 J1
Lagarde-Enval (19) . . . 216 B4
Lagarde-Hachan (32) . . . 286 C2
Lagarde-Pareol (84) . . . 256 E4
Lagarde-sur-le-Né (16) . . . 196 A5
Lagardelle (46) . . . 249 H1
Lagardelle-sur-Lèze (31) . . . 288 B3
Lagardère (32) . . . 267 F2
Lagardiolle (81) . . . 289 J2
Lagarrigue (47) . . . 247 J3
Lagarrigue (81) . . . 290 A1

Lageon (79) . . . 161 K1
Lagery (51) . . . 40 C5
Lagesse (10) . . . 114 B2
Lagleygeolle (19) . . . 216 A5
Laglorieuse (40) . . . 265 H3
Lagnes (84) . . . 276 E3
Lagney (54) . . . 65 H4
Lagnicourt-Marcel (62) . . . 11 G2
Lagnieu (01) . . . 189 H6
Lagny (60) . . . 19 G5
Lagny-le-Sec (60) . . . 38 D6
Lagny-sur-Marne (77) . . . 59 H3
Lagor (64) . . . 284 A3
Lagorce (07) . . . 256 A1
Lagorce (33) . . . 212 B5
Lagord (17) . . . 176 D2
Lagos (64) . . . 284 D5
Lagrâce-Dieu (31) . . . 288 A4
Lagrand (05) . . . 258 D2
Lagrange (40) . . . 266 B1
Lagrange (65) . . . 286 A6
Lagrange (90) . . . 119 J6
Lagrasse (11) . . . 309 J1
Lagraulet-du-Gers (32) . . . 266 E2
Lagraulet-Saint-Nicolas (31) . . . 268 D4
Lagraulière (19) . . . 215 K2
Lagrave (81) . . . 270 C3
Lagruère (47) . . . 247 H2
Laguenne (19) . . . 216 B3
Laguépie (82) . . . 251 F5
Laguian-Mazous (32) . . . 285 K3
Laguinge-Restoue (64) . . . 302 C1
Laguiole (12) . . . 236 B4
Lagupie (47) . . . 230 E4
Lahage (31) . . . 287 H3
Lahas (32) . . . 287 G1
Lahaymeix (55) . . . 64 B2
Lahayville (55) . . . 65 G2
Laheycourt (55) . . . 63 K3
Lahitère (31) . . . 287 K6
Lahitte (32) . . . 267 J5
Lahitte-Toupière (65) . . . 285 G2
Lahonce (64) . . . 282 C1
Lahontan (64) . . . 283 G1
Lahosse (40) . . . 264 D4
Lahourcade (64) . . . 284 A3
Lahoussoye (80) . . . 18 C1
Laifour (08) . . . 22 C1
la Laigne (17) . . . 177 H2
Laigné (53) . . . 104 E4
Laigné-en-Belin (72) . . . 106 E4
Laignelet (35) . . . 80 B3
Laignes (21) . . . 114 D4
Laigneville (60) . . . 38 A4
Laigny (02) . . . 21 F2
Laillé (35) . . . 79 F6
Lailly (89) . . . 89 F5
Lailly-en-Val (45) . . . 109 J6
Laimont (55) . . . 63 K3
Lain (89) . . . 132 E2
Laines-aux-Bois (10) . . . 90 A5
Lains (39) . . . 173 F5
Lainsecq (89) . . . 132 D3
Lainville-en-Vexin (78) . . . 57 K1
Laire (25) . . . 139 G2
Laires (62) . . . 5 G5
Lairière (11) . . . 309 H2
Lairoux (85) . . . 159 K4
Laissac (12) . . . 252 E2
Laissaud (73) . . . 208 C5
Laissey (25) . . . 138 C5
Laître-sous-Amance (54) . . . 66 B4
Laives (71) . . . 171 K2
Laix (54) . . . 26 D3
Laiz (01) . . . 188 D1
Laizé (71) . . . 171 J5
Laize-la-Ville (14) . . . 32 E6
Laizy (71) . . . 152 E5
Lajo (48) . . . 237 H2
Lajoux (39) . . . 174 A5
Lalacelle (61) . . . 82 B2
Lalande (89) . . . 132 D1
Lalande-de-Pomerol (33) . . . 212 B6
Lalande-en-Son (60) . . . 36 E2
Lalandelle (60) . . . 37 F2
Lalandusse (47) . . . 231 J4
Lalanne (32) . . . 267 J4
Lalanne (65) . . . 286 C5
Lalanne-Arqué (32) . . . 286 D4
Lalanne-Trie (65) . . . 286 A4
Lalaye (67) . . . 96 B1
Lalbarède (81) . . . 270 D6
Lalbenque (46) . . . 250 B3
Laleu (61) . . . 83 F1
Laleu (80) . . . 17 H1
Lalevade-d'Ardèche (07) . . . 239 G4
Lalheue (71) . . . 171 J2
Lalinde (24) . . . 232 A2
Lalizolle (03) . . . 184 E3
Lallaing (59) . . . 11 J1
Lalleu (35) . . . 103 H2
Lalley (38) . . . 242 A3
Lalleyriat (01) . . . 190 B2
Lalobbe (08) . . . 22 A4
Laloeuf (54) . . . 93 K2
Lalongue (64) . . . 284 D2
Lalonquette (64) . . . 284 D2
Laloubère (65) . . . 285 H5
Lalouret-Laffiteau (31) . . . 286 E6
Lalouvesc (07) . . . 221 J4
Laluque (40) . . . 264 B3
Lama (2B) . . . 319 F2

Lamadeleine-Val-des-Anges (90) . . 119 J5
Lamagdelaine (46) 250 A1
Lamagistère (82) 248 D5
Lamaguère (32) 286 D2
Lamaids (03) 183 J1
Lamalou-les-Bains (34) 272 D6
Lamancine (52) 92 A5
Lamanère (66) 314 D6
Lamanon (13) 276 E5
Lamarche (88) 117 H1
Lamarche-sur-Saône (21) 136 D6
Lamargelle (21) 135 J2
Lamaronde (80) 17 H3
Lamarque (33) 211 H4
Lamarque-Pontacq (65) 285 F6
Lamarque-Rustaing (65) 285 K4
Lamasquère (31) 287 K2
Lamastre (07) 221 K6
Lamath (54) 94 D1
Lamativie (46) 234 D1
Lamayou (64) 285 G3
Lamazère (32) 286 B1
Lamazière-Basse (19) 216 E1
Lamazière-Haute (19) 201 G3
Lambach (57) 69 G3
Lamballe (22) 77 J1
Lambersart (59) 6 D4
Lamberville (50) 31 K4
Lamberville (76) 15 J3
Lambesc (13) 277 G5
Lamblore (28) 56 B6
Lambres (62) 5 H4
Lambres-lez-Douai (59) 11 H2
Lambrey (70) 117 J5
Lambruisse (04) 260 B5
Laméac (65) 285 K4
Lamécourt (60) 38 A2
Lamelouze (30) 255 F4
Lamenay-sur-Loire (58) 169 G1
Lamérac (16) 196 A4
Lametz (08) 22 D6
Lamillarié (81) 270 E3
Lammerville (76) 15 J3
Lamnay (72) 107 J1
Lamongerie (19) 199 J5
Lamontélarié (81) 271 J6
Lamontgie (63) 203 F6
Lamontjoie (47) 248 A4
Lamonzie-Montastruc (24) 231 J1
Lamonzie-Saint-Martin (24) . . . 231 G2
Lamorlaye (60) 38 A5
Lamorville (55) 64 E2
Lamothe (40) 265 F3
Lamothe (43) 219 H2
Lamothe-Capdeville (82) 249 K6
Lamothe-Cassel (46) 233 J5
Lamothe-Cumont (82) 268 B3
Lamothe-en-Blaisy (52) 91 K5
Lamothe-Fénelon (46) 233 H2
Lamothe-Goas (32) 267 H3
Lamothe-Landerron (33) 230 D5
Lamothe-Montravel (24) 230 D2
Lamotte-Beuvron (41) 130 B2
Lamotte-Brebière (80) 18 B2
Lamotte-Buleux (80) 9 G4
Lamotte-du-Rhône (84) 256 D3
Lamotte-Warfusée (80) 18 D2
Lamouilly (55) 23 H6
Lamoura (39) 174 A5
Lampaul-Guimiliau (29) 46 E5
Lampaul-Plouarzel (29) 72 B3
Lampaul-Ploudalmézeau (29) . . 72 C2
Lampertheim (67) 25 A6
Lampertsloch (67) 25 A2
Lamure-sur-Azergues (69) . . . 187 K4
Lanans (25) 138 E5
Lanarce (07) 238 D3
Lanarvily (29) 46 B4
Lanas (07) 239 H6
Lancé (41) 128 C1
Lanchères (80) 8 D4
Lanches-Saint-Hilaire (80) 9 J5
Lanchy (02) 19 H3
Lancié (69) 188 B2
Lancieux (22) 50 C3
Lancôme (41) 128 C1
Lançon (08) 42 E4
Lançon (65) 305 G4
Lançon-Provence (13) 276 E6
Lancrans (01) 190 C3
Landange (57) 67 H5
Landas (59) 7 G6
Landaul (56) 100 C4
Landaville (88) 93 G4
Landavran (35) 79 K4
la Lande-Chasles (49) 126 B3
la Lande-d'Airou (50) 52 A3
la Lande-de-Fronsac (33) 211 K6
la Lande-de-Goult (61) 82 C1
la Lande-de-Lougé (61) 54 A5
la Lande-Patry (61) 53 G4
la Lande-Saint-Léger (27) 34 B3
la Lande-Saint-Siméon (61) . . . 53 J3
la Lande-sur-Drôme (14) 31 K4
la Lande-sur-Eure (61) 84 A1
Landéan (35) 80 B3
Landebaëron (22) 48 C4
Landébia (22) 50 A4
la Landec (22) 50 B5
Landécourt (54) 94 C1
Landéda (29) 72 D2
Landéhen (22) 77 J1

Landeleau (29) 75 G3
Landelles (28) 84 D2
Landelles-et-Coupigny (14) . . . 31 J6
Landemont (49) 123 K3
Landepéreuse (27) 55 J1
Landerneau (29) 46 C6
Landeronde (85) 159 G2
Landerrouat (33) 230 E3
Landerrouet-sur-Ségur (33) . . . 230 C4
Landersheim (67) 70 C2
Landes (17) 177 J4
les Landes-Genusson (85) 142 C4
Landes-le-Gaulois (41) 128 D1
Landes-sur-Ajon (14) 32 C6
Landes-Vieilles-et-Neuves (76) . . 16 E3
Landévant (56) 100 C3
Landévennec (29) 74 C2
Landevieille (85) 158 E2
Landeyrat (15) 218 C3
Landifay-et-Bertaignemont (02) . . 20 D3
Landigou (61) 53 H4
le Landin (27) 35 F2
Landiras (33) 229 J5
Landisacq (61) 53 G4
Landivisiau (29) 46 K5
Landivy (53) 80 C2
Landogne (63) 201 J1
Landorthe (31) 286 G1
Landos (43) 238 B2
Landouzy-la-Cour (02) 21 G2
Landouzy-la-Ville (02) 21 G2
Landrais (17) 177 G3
le Landreau (44) 123 K4
Landrecies (59) 12 E5
Landrecourt-Lempire (55) 43 H6
Landremont (54) 66 A3
Landres (54) 26 B6
Landres-et-Saint-Georges (08) . . 42 E3
Landresse (25) 138 E5
Landrethun-le-Nord (62) 2 C4
Landrethun-lès-Ardres (62) . . . 2 D4
Landrévarzec (29) 74 D5
Landreville (10) 114 E2
Landrichamps (08) 24 D2
Landricourt (02) 39 J1
Landricourt (51) 63 H6
Landroff (57) 66 E1
Landry (73) 193 H4
Landser (68) 97 C3
Landudal (29) 74 E5
Landudec (29) 73 E3
Landujan (35) 78 D2
Landunvez (29) 72 B2
Lanespède (65) 285 K6
Lanester (56) 100 A3
Lanet (11) 309 H3
Laneuvelle (52) 117 G3
Laneuvelotte (54) 66 B4
Laneuveville-aux-Bois (54) 67 F5
Laneuveville-derrière-Foug (54) . . 65 G5
Laneuveville-devant-Bayon (54) . . 94 B2
Laneuveville-devant-Nancy (54) . . 66 B5
Laneuveville-en-Saulnois (57) . . 66 C2
Laneuveville-lès-Lorquin (57) . . . 67 J5
Laneuville-au-Pont (52) 63 J2
Laneuville-au-Rupt (55) 64 E5
Laneuville-sur-Meuse (55) 43 F1
Lanfains (22) 76 E2
Lanfroicourt (54) 66 B3
Langan (35) 78 E2
Langast (22) 77 G3
Langatte (57) 67 H4
Langé (36) 147 H3
Langeac (43) 219 J5
Langeais (37) 127 F5
Langensoultzbach (67) 25 A2
Langeron (58) 150 D6
Langesse (45) 111 H5
Langey (28) 108 D2
Langlade (30) 275 F4
Langley (88) 94 C3
Langoat (22) 48 B3
Langoëlan (56) 76 B5
Langogne (48) 238 C2
Langoiran (33) 229 J3
Langolen (29) 74 E5
Langon (33) 230 A5
Langon (35) 102 E3
Langon (41) 129 K6
le Langon (85) 160 C5
Langonnet (56) 75 J5
Langouet (35) 78 E2
Langourla (22) 77 K3
Langres (52) 116 D4
Langrolay-sur-Rance (22) 50 D4
Langrune-sur-Mer (14) 32 K3
Languédias (22) 50 B6
Languenan (22) 50 C5
Langueux (22) 49 G6
Languevoisin-Quiquery (80) . . . 19 G4
Languidic (56) 100 C3
Languimberg (57) 67 G4
Langy (03) 185 J1
Lanhélin (35) 51 F5
Lanhères (54) 26 C4
Lanhouarneau (29) 46 C4
Lanildut (29) 72 B3
Laning (57) 68 B4
Laniscat (22) 76 C3
Laniscourt (02) 20 C6
Lanleff (22) 48 D3

Lanloup (22) 48 E3
Lanmérin (22) 48 B3
Lanmeur (29) 47 H4
Lanmodez (22) 48 D1
Lanne (65) 285 G6
Lanne-en-Barétous (64) 283 J6
Lanne-Soubiran (32) 266 A4
Lannéanou (29) 47 H6
Lannebert (22) 48 E4
Lannecaube (64) 284 E2
Lannédern (29) 75 F2
Lannemaignan (32) 265 K2
Lannemezan (65) 305 F1
Lannepax (32) 266 E4
Lanneplaà (64) 283 J2
Lanneray (28) 108 E2
Lannes (47) 247 J6
Lanneuffret (29) 46 C5
Lannilis (29) 72 D2
Lannion (22) 48 A3
Lannoy (59) 7 F4
Lannoy-Cuillère (60) 17 F4
Lannux (32) 265 K5
Lano (2B) 319 G5
Lanobre (15) 201 H6
Lanouaille (24) 214 E1
Lanouée (56) 101 H1
Lanoux (09) 307 G1
Lanquais (24) 231 K2
Lanques-sur-Rognon (52) 116 D1
Lanquetot (76) 14 E2
Lanrelas (22) 78 A2
Lanrigan (35) 51 G6
Lanrivain (22) 76 C2
Lanrivoaré (29) 72 C3
Lanrodec (22) 48 D6
Lans (71) 154 B6
Lans-en-Vercors (38) 223 K4
Lansac (33) 211 H5
Lansac (65) 285 J5
Lansac (66) 309 J5
Lansargues (34) 274 D6
Lanslebourg-Mont-Cenis (73) . . 226 C1
Lanslevillard (73) 226 C1
Lanta (31) 288 E1
Lantabat (64) 283 F4
Lantages (10) 114 C2
Lantan (18) 149 K5
Lantéfontaine (54) 26 E6
Lantenay (01) 189 K4
Lantenay (21) 135 J3
Lantenne-Vertière (25) 137 H6
Lantenot (70) 118 E5
la Lanterne-et-les-Armonts (70) . . 118 E4
Lanteuil (19) 215 K4
Lanthenans (25) 139 F4
Lanthes (21) 154 D3
Lantheuil (14) 32 C4
Lantic (22) 49 F5
Lantignié (69) 188 A3
Lantillac (56) 101 G1
Lantilly (21) 134 E2
Lanton (33) 228 C3
Lantosque (06) 311 A4
Lantriac (43) 220 D6
Lanty (58) 152 A6
Lanty-sur-Aube (52) 115 H2
Lanuéjols (30) 253 K5
Lanuéjols (48) 254 B1
Lanuéjouls (12) 251 H2
Lanvallay (22) 50 D5
Lanvaudan (56) 100 B2
Lanvellec (22) 47 K4
Lanvénégen (56) 75 J3
Lanvéoc (29) 72 D6
Lanvollon (22) 48 E4
Lanzac (46) 233 H2
Laon (02) 20 D6
Laons (28) 56 D5
Lapalisse (03) 186 A2
Lapalud (84) 256 D3
Lapan (18) 149 F5
Lapanouse (12) 253 G3
Lapanouse-de-Cernon (12) . . . 272 D1
Laparade (47) 247 K2
Laparrouquial (81) 251 F6
Lapège (09) 307 H5
Lapenche (82) 250 B4
Lapenne (09) 288 E6
Lapenty (50) 52 C6
Laperche (47) 231 H6
Laperrière-sur-Saône (21) 155 F2
Lapeyre (65) 286 A4
Lapeyrère (31) 288 A4
Lapeyrouse (01) 188 E5
Lapeyrouse (63) 184 D2
Lapeyrouse-Fossat (31) 269 H5
Lapeyrouse-Mornay (26) 222 D2
Lapeyrugue (15) 235 J4
Lapleau (19) 216 B2
Laplume (47) 248 A5
Lapoutroie (68) 96 A3
Lapouyade (33) 212 A4
Lappion (02) 21 G5
Laprade (11) 290 A3
Laprade (16) 213 F4
Laprugne (03) 186 B5
Laps (63) 203 F3
Lapte (43) 221 F3
Lapugnoy (62) 5 K5
Laquenexy (57) 45 G6
Laqueuille (63) 201 K4

Laragne-Montéglin (05) 258 E2
Larajasse (69) 205 H4
Laramière (46) 250 E3
Laran (65) 286 B5
Larbey (40) 264 E4
Larbont (09) 307 G2
Larbroye (60) 19 G6
Larcan (31) 286 E6
Larcat (09) 307 J5
Larçay (37) 127 K5
Larceveau-Arros-Cibits (64) . . . 283 F5
Larchamp (53) 80 C3
Larchamp (61) 53 F5
Larchant (77) 87 G5
Larche (04) 227 C6
Larche (19) 215 H4
le Larderet (39) 156 B5
Lardier-et-Valença (05) 259 G1
Lardiers (04) 258 D6
le Lardin-Saint-Lazare (24) . . . 215 F4
Lardy (91) 86 D2
Larée (32) 266 B2
Laréole (31) 268 C5
Largeasse (79) 161 G1
Largentière (07) 239 G6
Largillay-Marsonnay (39) 173 H3
Largitzen (68) 97 B5
Largny-sur-Automne (02) 39 F4
Larians-et-Munans (70) 138 C3
Larivière (90) 119 J6
Larivière-Arnoncourt (52) 117 G2
Larmor-Baden (56) 100 E4
Larmor-Plage (56) 99 K5
Larnage (26) 222 C4
Larnagol (46) 250 D1
Larnas (07) 256 C1
Larnat (09) 307 J5
Larnaud (39) 173 F1
Larnod (25) 156 B1
Laroche-près-Feyt (19) 201 H3
Laroche-Saint-Cydroine (89) . . 113 F3
Larochemillay (58) 152 C5
Larodde (63) 201 H5
Laroin (64) 284 C4
Laronxe (54) 94 C1
Laroque (33) 229 K4
Laroque (34) 274 A2
Laroque-de-Fa (11) 309 J3
Laroque-des-Albères (66) 315 H6
Laroque-des-Arcs (46) 250 A1
Laroque-d'Olmes (09) 308 B3
Laroque-Timbaut (47) 248 D3
Laroquebrou (15) 217 F6
Laroquevieille (15) 217 J6
Larouillies (59) 13 G6
Larra (31) 268 E5
Larrau (64) 302 B2
Larrazet (82) 268 C3
Larré (56) 101 H4
Larré (61) 82 D2
Larressingle (32) 267 F2
Larressore (64) 263 D2
Larret (70) 137 F1
Larreule (64) 284 C2
Larreule (65) 285 G2
Larrey (21) 114 E4
Larribar-Sorhapuru (64) 283 G4
Larringes (74) 175 G5
Larrivière (40) 265 H4
Larrivoire (39) 173 J6
Larroque (31) 286 D6
Larroque (65) 286 B4
Larroque (81) 269 K1
Larroque-Engalin (32) 267 H1
Larroque-Saint-Sernin (32) . . . 267 G3
Larroque-sur-l'Osse (32) 266 E1
Larroque-Toirac (46) 234 C6
Lartigue (33) 286 E1
Lartigue (33) 246 E4
Laruns (64) 303 H2
Laruscade (33) 211 K4
Larzac (24) 232 B3
Larzicourt (51) 63 G6
Lasalle (30) 254 E6
Lasbordes (11) 289 H4
Lascabanes (46) 249 J3
Lascaux (19) 215 G2
Lascazères (65) 285 G1
Lascelle (15) 217 J6
Lasclaveries (64) 284 D2
Lasfaillades (81) 290 C1
Lasgraisses (81) 270 C4
Laslades (65) 285 J5
Lassales (65) 286 B5
Lassay-les-Châteaux (53) 81 H3
Lassay-sur-Croisne (41) 129 H5
Lasse (49) 126 C2
Lasse (64) 282 D5
Lasserade (32) 266 C6
Lasséran (32) 267 H6
Lasserre (09) 306 D1
Lasserre (31) 268 C5
Lasserre (47) 247 K6
Lasserre (64) 285 F1
Lasserre-de-Prouille (11) 289 J6
Lasseube (64) 284 B5
Lasseube-Propre (32) 286 C1
Lasseubetat (64) 284 C6
Lassicourt (10) 90 E3
Lassigny (60) 19 F6
Lasson (14) 32 D4
Lasson (89) 113 J2

Lassouts (12) 252 E1
Lassur (09) 307 K5
Lassy (14) 53 G2
Lassy (35) 78 E6
Lassy (95) 38 A6
Lastic (15) 219 F4
Lastic (63) 201 J3
Lastours (11) 290 B4
Lataule (60) 18 E6
le Latet (39) 156 B6
la Latette (39) 156 C6
Lathuile (74) 208 E1
Lathus-Saint-Rémy (86) 164 B6
Latillé (86) 162 C3
Latilly (02) 39 J5
Latoue (31) 286 E6
Latouille-Lentillac (46) 234 C2
Latour (31) 288 A6
Latour-Bas-Elne (66) 315 H3
Latour-de-Carol (66) 313 G5
Latour-de-France (66) 309 K5
Latour-en-Woëvre (55) 44 B6
Latrape (31) 288 A5
Latrecey-Ormoy-sur-Aube (52) . . 115 J3
Latresne (33) 229 H2
Latrille (40) 265 J6
Latronche (19) 217 F2
Latronquière (46) 234 E3
Lattainville (60) 36 E4
Lattes (34) 293 H1
Lattre-Saint-Quentin (62) 10 E3
Lau-Balagnas (65) 304 A2
Laubach (67) 25 A3
Laubert (48) 237 K5
les Laubies (48) 237 H5
Laubressel (10) 90 C4
Laubrières (53) 104 B3
Laucourt (80) 19 F5
Laudrefang (57) 45 K5
Laudun (30) 256 C5
Laugnac (47) 248 B3
Laujuzan (32) 266 A3
Laulne (50) 30 E1
Laumesfeld (57) 27 K4
Launac (31) 268 E4
Launaguet (31) 269 G5
Launay (27) 34 E6
Launay-Villiers (53) 80 C6
Launois-sur-Vence (08) 22 B5
Launoy (02) 39 K4
Launstroff (57) 27 K3
la Laupie (26) 240 C5
Laurabuc (11) 289 H5
Laurac (11) 289 H5
Laurac-en-Vivarais (07) 239 G6
Lauraët (32) 266 E2
Lauraguel (11) 308 E1
Laure-Minervois (11) 290 D5
Laurède (40) 264 D4
Laurenan (22) 77 J4
Laurens (34) 291 K2
Lauresses (46) 234 E3
Lauret (34) 274 C3
Lauret (40) 284 D1
Laurie (15) 218 E2
Laurière (87) 181 K4
Lauris (84) 277 G4
Lauroux (34) 273 F4
Laussonne (43) 220 D6
Laussou (47) 232 B5
Lautenbach (68) 96 A6
Lautenbachzell (68) 96 A6
Lauterbourg (67) 25 E2
Lauthiers (86) 163 J3
Lautignac (31) 287 H3
Lautrec (81) 270 E5
Lauw (68) 119 K5
Lauwin-Planque (59) 11 H1
Laux-Montaux (26) 258 B2
Lauzach (56) 101 H4
Lauzerte (82) 249 G4
Lauzerville (31) 288 D1
Lauzès (46) 233 J6
le Lauzet-Ubaye (04) 260 A1
Lauzun (47) 231 H5
Lavacquerie (60) 17 J4
Laval (38) 224 C2
Laval (53) 104 E1
Laval-Atger (48) 238 A3
Laval-d'Aix (26) 241 H3
Laval-d'Aurelle (07) 238 D6
Laval-de-Cère (46) 234 C1
Laval-du-Tarn (48) 253 K3
Laval-en-Laonnois (02) 40 B1
Laval-le-Prieuré (25) 139 F6
Laval-Morency (08) 22 B2
Laval-Pradel (30) 255 G4
Laval-Roquecezière (12) 271 K4
Laval-Saint-Roman (30) 256 B3
Laval-sur-Doulon (43) 219 J1
Laval-sur-Luzège (19) 216 B3
Laval-sur-Tourbe (51) 42 B5
Laval-sur-Vologne (88) 95 F5
Lavalade (24) 232 B4
Lavaldens (38) 224 C5
Lavalette (11) 290 A6
Lavalette (31) 269 J6
Lavalette (34) 273 F5
Lavallée (55) 64 C3
Lavancia-Épercy (39) 173 H6
le Lavandou (83) 298 D5

Lavangeot (39) . . . 155 H1
Lavannes (51) . . . 41 G3
Lavans-lès-Dole (39) . . . 155 H1
Lavans-lès-Saint-Claude (39) . . . 173 J5
Lavans-Quingey (25) . . . 156 A2
Lavans-sur-Valouse (39) . . . 173 G6
Lavans-Vuillafans (25) . . . 156 D2
Lavaqueresse (02) . . . 20 D1
Lavardac (47) . . . 247 J5
Lavardens (32) . . . 267 H4
Lavardin (41) . . . 108 A6
Lavardin (72) . . . 106 C1
Lavaré (72) . . . 107 J2
Lavars (38) . . . 242 A1
Lavastrie (15) . . . 236 D1
Lavatoggio (2B) . . . 318 C3
Lavau (10) . . . 90 B4
Lavau (89) . . . 132 A2
Lavau-sur-Loire (44) . . . 122 C3
Lavaudieu (43) . . . 219 H3
Lavaufranche (23) . . . 183 H1
Lavault-de-Frétoy (58) . . . 152 C2
Lavault-Sainte-Anne (03) . . . 184 A1
Lavaur (24) . . . 232 D5
Lavaur (81) . . . 270 A4
Lavaurette (82) . . . 250 C4
Lavausseau (86) . . . 162 C3
Lavaveix-les-Mines (23) . . . 183 F4
Lavazan (33) . . . 246 E2
Laveissenet (15) . . . 218 C5
Laveissière (15) . . . 218 B4
Lavelanet (09) . . . 308 B3
Lavelanet-de-Comminges (31) . . . 287 J5
Laveline-devant-Bruyères (88) . . . 95 G5
Laveline-du-Houx (88) . . . 95 F6
Lavenay (72) . . . 107 J5
Laventie (62) . . . 6 B4
Laveraët (32) . . . 285 J1
Lavercantière (46) . . . 233 G5
Laverdines (18) . . . 150 A3
Lavergne (46) . . . 234 A3
Lavergne (47) . . . 231 G5
Lavernat (72) . . . 107 F6
Lavernay (25) . . . 137 H6
Lavernhe (12) . . . 253 F3
Lavernose-Lacasse (31) . . . 287 K3
Lavernoy (52) . . . 117 F3
Laverrière (60) . . . 17 J4
Laversine (02) . . . 39 H3
Laversines (60) . . . 37 J2
Lavérune (34) . . . 293 G1
Laveyron (26) . . . 222 B3
Laveyrune (07) . . . 238 C5
Laveyssière (24) . . . 231 H1
Lavieu (42) . . . 204 C4
Laviéville (80) . . . 10 D6
Lavigerie (15) . . . 218 A4
Lavignac (87) . . . 198 D3
Lavigney (70) . . . 117 H6
Lavigny (39) . . . 173 G1
Lavillatte (07) . . . 238 D3
Laville-aux-Bois (52) . . . 116 C1
Lavilledieu (07) . . . 239 J5
Lavilleneuve (52) . . . 116 E2
Lavilletertre (60) . . . 37 F5
Lavincourt (55) . . . 64 B5
Laviolle (07) . . . 239 G3
Laviron (25) . . . 139 F5
Lavit (82) . . . 268 B2
Lavoine (03) . . . 186 B5
Lavoncourt (70) . . . 137 H1
Lavours (01) . . . 207 K1
Lavoûte-Chilhac (43) . . . 219 H4
Lavoûte-sur-Loire (43) . . . 220 C4
Lavoux (86) . . . 163 G3
Lavoye (55) . . . 43 F6
Lawarde-Mauger-l'Hortoy (80) . . . 18 A4
Laxou (54) . . . 66 A5
Lay (42) . . . 187 G5
Lay-Lamidou (64) . . . 283 K4
Lay-Saint-Christophe (54) . . . 66 A4
Lay-Saint-Remy (54) . . . 65 G5
Laye (05) . . . 242 E4
Laymont (32) . . . 287 G2
Layrac (47) . . . 248 C6
Layrac-sur-Tarn (31) . . . 269 H3
Layrisse (65) . . . 285 H6
Lays-sur-le-Doubs (71) . . . 154 E4
Laz (29) . . . 75 F4
Lazenay (18) . . . 148 D3
Lazer (05) . . . 258 E2
Léalvillers (80) . . . 10 C5
Léaupartie (14) . . . 33 H5
Léaz (01) . . . 190 D3
Lebetain (90) . . . 139 J2
Lebeuville (54) . . . 94 B2
Lebiez (62) . . . 4 E6
Leboulin (32) . . . 267 H4
Lebreil (46) . . . 249 H3
Lebucquière (62) . . . 11 G5
Lécaude (14) . . . 33 H6
Lecci (2A) . . . 323 H2
Lecelles (59) . . . 7 G3
Lecey (52) . . . 116 E4
Lechâtelet (21) . . . 154 D3
Léchelle (62) . . . 11 G5
Léchelle (77) . . . 88 E1
la Léchère (73) . . . 209 H4
les Lèches (24) . . . 213 G6
Lécluse (59) . . . 11 H3
Lécousse (35) . . . 80 A3
Lecques (30) . . . 274 D3

Lect (39) . . . 173 H5
Lectoure (32) . . . 267 J2
Lecumberry (64) . . . 282 E6
Lécussan (31) . . . 286 C6
Lédas-et-Penthiès (81) . . . 251 K6
Lédat (47) . . . 248 C1
Lédenon (30) . . . 275 J2
Lédergues (12) . . . 252 A6
Lederzeele (59) . . . 3 G4
Ledeuix (64) . . . 284 A5
Lédignan (30) . . . 274 E1
Ledinghem (62) . . . 2 E6
Ledringhem (59) . . . 3 J4
Lée (64) . . . 284 D4
Leers (59) . . . 7 F3
Lées-Athas (64) . . . 303 F2
Lefaux (62) . . . 4 B5
Leffard (14) . . . 53 K2
Leffincourt (08) . . . 41 K2
Leffonds (52) . . . 116 B3
Leffrinckoucke (59) . . . 3 H1
Leforest (62) . . . 11 H1
Lège (31) . . . 305 H4
Legé (44) . . . 141 H4
Lège-Cap-Ferret (33) . . . 228 B2
Légéville-et-Bonfays (88) . . . 94 A5
Léglantiers (60) . . . 38 B1
Légna (39) . . . 173 G5
Légny (69) . . . 188 A6
Léguevin (31) . . . 268 E6
Léguillac-de-Cercles (24) . . . 213 J1
Léguillac-de-l'Auche (24) . . . 213 J3
Lehaucourt (02) . . . 19 K1
Léhon (22) . . . 50 D5
Leigné-les-Bois (86) . . . 163 J1
Leigné-sur-Usseau (86) . . . 145 H5
Leignes-sur-Fontaine (86) . . . 163 K4
Leigneux (42) . . . 204 C2
Leimbach (68) . . . 119 K4
Leintrey (54) . . . 67 F5
Lélex (01) . . . 174 A6
Lelin-Lapujolle (32) . . . 266 A5
Lelling (57) . . . 68 A4
Lemainville (54) . . . 94 B1
Lembach (67) . . . 25 A1
Lemberg (57) . . . 69 G4
Lembeye (64) . . . 285 F2
Lembras (24) . . . 231 J1
Lemé (02) . . . 20 E2
Lème (64) . . . 284 D2
Leménil-Mitry (54) . . . 94 B2
Lémeré (37) . . . 145 G3
Lemmecourt (88) . . . 93 G5
Lemmes (55) . . . 43 G6
Lemoncourt (57) . . . 66 C2
Lempaut (81) . . . 289 J2
Lempdes (63) . . . 202 E2
Lempdes-sur-Allagnon (43) . . . 219 F1
Lempire (02) . . . 11 J6
Lemps (07) . . . 222 B4
Lemps (26) . . . 258 A2
Lempty (50) . . . 203 F1
Lempzours (24) . . . 214 B1
Lemud (57) . . . 45 G6
Lemuy (39) . . . 156 B4
Lénault (14) . . . 53 G2
Lenax (03) . . . 186 C1
Lencloître (86) . . . 145 G6
Lencouacq (40) . . . 246 B5
Lengelsheim (57) . . . 69 G2
Lengronne (50) . . . 30 E5
Lenharrée (51) . . . 62 B4
Léning (57) . . . 67 G1
Lennon (29) . . . 75 F3
Lenoncourt (54) . . . 66 B5
Lens (62) . . . 11 F1
Lens-Lestang (26) . . . 222 D2
Lent (01) . . . 189 G5
Lent (39) . . . 156 B6
Lentigny (42) . . . 186 E5
Lentillac-du-Causse (46) . . . 233 K6
Lentillac-Saint-Blaise (46) . . . 234 E5
Lentillères (07) . . . 239 G5
Lentilles (10) . . . 91 F2
Lentilly (69) . . . 205 J1
Lentiol (38) . . . 222 E2
Lento (2B) . . . 319 G3
Léobard (46) . . . 233 G4
Léogeats (33) . . . 229 K6
Léognan (33) . . . 229 G3
Léojac (82) . . . 269 G1
Léon (40) . . . 262 D2
Léoncel (26) . . . 241 F1
Léotoing (43) . . . 219 F1
Léouville (45) . . . 86 C6
Léoville (17) . . . 211 K1
Lépanges-sur-Vologne (88) . . . 95 F5
Lépaud (23) . . . 183 J2
Lépin-le-Lac (73) . . . 208 A4
Lépinas (23) . . . 182 D4
Lépine (62) . . . 9 F1
Lépron-les-Vallées (08) . . . 22 A3
Lepuix (90) . . . 119 H5
Lepuix-Neuf (90) . . . 97 A5
Léran (09) . . . 308 B3
Lercoul (09) . . . 307 H5
Léré (18) . . . 131 K4
Lérigneux (42) . . . 204 C4
Lerm-et-Musset (33) . . . 246 D3
Lerné (37) . . . 144 E2
Lérouville (55) . . . 64 E4

Lerrain (88) . . . 94 A6
Léry (21) . . . 135 J2
Léry (27) . . . 35 J4
Lerzy (02) . . . 21 F1
Les Adrets-de-l'Estérel (83) . . . 280 C6
Lesboeufs (80) . . . 11 F6
Lesbois (53) . . . 80 E2
Lescar (64) . . . 284 C4
Leschaux (74) . . . 208 D1
Leschelles (02) . . . 20 E1
Lescheraines (73) . . . 208 D2
Leschères (39) . . . 173 H5
Leschères-sur-le-Blaiseron (52) . . . 92 A4
Lescherolles (77) . . . 60 D5
Lescheroux (01) . . . 172 C5
Lesches (77) . . . 59 J3
Lesches-en-Diois (26) . . . 241 J5
Lescouët-Gouarec (22) . . . 76 B4
Lescousse (09) . . . 288 C6
Lescout (81) . . . 289 J1
Lescun (64) . . . 303 F3
Lescuns (31) . . . 287 F4
Lescure (09) . . . 306 D2
Lescure-d'Albigeois (81) . . . 270 E2
Lescure-Jaoul (12) . . . 251 J4
Lescurry (65) . . . 285 J4
Lesdain (59) . . . 11 K5
Lesdins (02) . . . 20 A2
Lesges (02) . . . 40 A3
Lesgor (40) . . . 264 C3
Lésignac-Durand (16) . . . 197 J1
Lésigny (77) . . . 59 G5
Lésigny (86) . . . 146 A6
le Leslay (22) . . . 76 E1
Lesme (71) . . . 169 J2
Lesménils (54) . . . 65 K2
Lesmont (10) . . . 90 E3
Lesneven (29) . . . 46 B4
Lesparre-Médoc (33) . . . 210 D2
Lesparrou (09) . . . 308 A3
Lespéron (07) . . . 238 C3
Lesperon (40) . . . 264 B1
Lespesses (62) . . . 5 J5
Lespielle (64) . . . 285 F2
Lespignan (34) . . . 291 K5
Lespinasse (31) . . . 269 G5
Lespinassière (11) . . . 290 D3
Lespinoy (62) . . . 9 G1
Lespiteau (31) . . . 305 K1
Lespouey (65) . . . 285 J5
Lespourcy (64) . . . 285 F3
Lespugue (31) . . . 286 D5
Lesquerde (66) . . . 309 H5
Lesquielles-Saint-Germain (02) . . . 20 D1
Lesquin (59) . . . 6 E4
Lessac (16) . . . 180 B4
Lessard-en-Bresse (71) . . . 172 B1
Lessard-et-le-Chêne (14) . . . 33 J6
Lessard-le-National (71) . . . 154 A5
Lessay (50) . . . 30 C2
Lesse (57) . . . 66 D1
Lesseux (88) . . . 95 K4
Lessy (57) . . . 44 E5
Lestanville (76) . . . 15 J4
Lestards (19) . . . 200 B5
Lestelle-Bétharram (64) . . . 284 E6
Lestelle-de-Saint-Martory (31) . . . 306 B1
Lesterps (16) . . . 180 C5
Lestiac-sur-Garonne (33) . . . 229 K4
Lestiou (41) . . . 109 H6
Lestrade-et-Thouels (12) . . . 252 C6
Lestre (50) . . . 29 F4
Lestrem (62) . . . 6 A4
Létanne (08) . . . 23 G5
Lételon (03) . . . 167 H2
Léthuin (28) . . . 85 K4
Letia (2A) . . . 320 C2
Létra (69) . . . 187 K5
Létricourt (54) . . . 66 B2
Letteguives (27) . . . 36 A2
Lettret (05) . . . 242 E6
Leubringhen (62) . . . 2 B4
Leuc (11) . . . 290 B6
Leucamp (15) . . . 235 G3
Leucate (11) . . . 310 D4
Leuchey (52) . . . 116 C6
Leudeville (91) . . . 86 E1
Leudon-en-Brie (77) . . . 60 D5
Leuglay (21) . . . 115 H5
Leugny (86) . . . 146 A5
Leugny (89) . . . 132 E1
Leuhan (29) . . . 75 G5
Leuilly-sous-Coucy (02) . . . 39 J1
Leulinghem (62) . . . 3 F5
Leulinghen-Bernes (62) . . . 2 B4
Leurville (52) . . . 92 D4
Leury (02) . . . 39 J2
Leutenheim (67) . . . 25 C3
Leuville-sur-Orge (91) . . . 86 D1
Leuvrigny (51) . . . 40 C6
le Leuy (40) . . . 265 F3
Leuze (02) . . . 21 H2
Levainville (28) . . . 85 J2
Leval (59) . . . 13 F4
Leval (90) . . . 119 J5
Levallois-Perret (92) . . . 58 E3
Levaré (53) . . . 80 D3
Lévécourt (52) . . . 93 G4
Levens (06) . . . 281 G2
Levergies (02) . . . 20 A1
Levernois (21) . . . 154 A3
Lèves (28) . . . 85 G2

les Lèves-et-Thoumeyragues (33) . . . 230 E3
Levesville-la-Chenard (28) . . . 85 K5
Levet (18) . . . 149 G5
Levie (2A) . . . 323 F2
Levier (25) . . . 156 C4
Lévignac (31) . . . 268 E5
Lévignac-de-Guyenne (47) . . . 230 E5
Lévignacq (40) . . . 244 B6
Lévignen (60) . . . 38 E5
Lévigny (10) . . . 91 G4
Levis (39) . . . 132 D1
Lévis-Saint-Nom (78) . . . 58 A5
Levoncourt (55) . . . 64 C3
Levoncourt (68) . . . 97 B6
Levroux (36) . . . 147 J4
Lewarde (59) . . . 11 J2
Lexy (54) . . . 26 C2
Ley (57) . . . 67 F4
Leychert (09) . . . 307 K3
Leyme (46) . . . 234 C3
Leymen (68) . . . 97 D5
Leyment (01) . . . 189 H5
Leynes (71) . . . 188 B1
Leynhac (15) . . . 235 G3
Leyr (54) . . . 66 B3
Leyrat (23) . . . 166 E6
Leyrieu (38) . . . 206 E2
Leyritz-Moncassin (47) . . . 247 G3
Leyssard (01) . . . 189 J2
Leyvaux (15) . . . 218 E2
Leyviller (57) . . . 68 A4
Lez (31) . . . 305 J3
Lez-Fontaine (59) . . . 13 J4
Lézan (30) . . . 274 D1
Lézardrieux (22) . . . 48 D2
Lézat (39) . . . 174 A4
Lézat-sur-Lèze (09) . . . 288 A5
Lezay (79) . . . 178 E1
Lezennes (59) . . . 6 E4
Lezéville (52) . . . 92 D3
Lezey (57) . . . 66 E4
Lézignan (65) . . . 304 B1
Lézignan-Corbières (11) . . . 291 F6
Lézignan-la-Cèbe (34) . . . 292 C2
Lézigné (49) . . . 125 K1
Lézigneux (42) . . . 204 D4
Lézinnes (89) . . . 114 B5
Lezoux (63) . . . 203 G1
Lhéraule (60) . . . 37 F1
Lherm (31) . . . 287 K3
Lherm (46) . . . 233 F6
Lhéry (51) . . . 40 C5
Lhez (65) . . . 285 J5
Lhommaizé (86) . . . 163 H5
Lhomme (72) . . . 107 H6
Lhôpital (01) . . . 190 C4
Lhor (57) . . . 67 G2
Lhospitalet (46) . . . 249 K2
Lhoumois (79) . . . 162 A1
Lhuis (01) . . . 207 H2
Lhuître (10) . . . 90 C1
Lhuys (02) . . . 40 A4
Liac (65) . . . 285 H3
Liancourt (60) . . . 38 A3
Liancourt-Fosse (80) . . . 19 F4
Liancourt-Saint-Pierre (60) . . . 37 F4
Liart (08) . . . 21 K3
Lias (31) . . . 287 J1
Lias-d'Armagnac (32) . . . 266 A3
Liausson (34) . . . 273 G6
Libaros (65) . . . 286 A5
Libercourt (62) . . . 6 D6
Libermont (60) . . . 19 H4
Libourne (33) . . . 230 A1
Licey-sur-Vingeanne (21) . . . 136 D3
Lichans-Sunhar (64) . . . 302 C1
Lichères (16) . . . 179 G6
Lichères-près-Aigremont (89) . . . 113 J6
Lichères-sur-Yonne (89) . . . 133 G3
Lichos (64) . . . 283 H4
Lichtenberg (67) . . . 69 H5
Licourt (80) . . . 19 G3
Licq-Athérey (64) . . . 302 C1
Licques (62) . . . 2 D4
Licy-Clignon (02) . . . 39 J5
Lidrezing (57) . . . 67 F2
Liebenswiller (68) . . . 97 D5
Liebsdorf (68) . . . 97 B6
Liebvillers (25) . . . 139 H4
Liederschiedt (57) . . . 69 H2
Lieffrans (70) . . . 137 K2
le Liège (37) . . . 146 E1
Liéhon (57) . . . 66 B1
Liencourt (62) . . . 10 C3
Lièpvre (68) . . . 96 B1
Liéramont (80) . . . 11 H6
Liercourt (80) . . . 9 G6
Lières (62) . . . 5 H5
Liergues (69) . . . 188 B5
Liernais (21) . . . 152 E1
Liernolles (03) . . . 169 J6
Lierval (02) . . . 40 B1
Lierville (60) . . . 37 F5
Lies (65) . . . 304 D1
Liesle (25) . . . 155 K2
Liesse-Notre-Dame (02) . . . 20 C5
Liessies (59) . . . 13 J5
Liesville-sur-Douve (50) . . . 29 F6
Liettres (62) . . . 5 H4
Lieu-Saint-Amand (59) . . . 12 B3
Lieuche (06) . . . 261 G6
Lieucourt (70) . . . 137 G3

Lieudieu (38) . . . 206 E5
Lieuran-Cabrières (34) . . . 292 C1
Lieuran-lès-Béziers (34) . . . 292 C3
Lieurey (27) . . . 34 C4
Lieuron (35) . . . 102 C1
Lieusaint (50) . . . 28 E4
Lieusaint (77) . . . 59 G6
Lieutadès (15) . . . 236 C2
Lieuvillers (60) . . . 38 B1
Liévans (70) . . . 138 C1
Liévin (62) . . . 10 E1
Liez (02) . . . 20 A4
Liez (85) . . . 160 E5
Liézey (88) . . . 95 G6
Liffol-le-Grand (88) . . . 93 F4
Liffol-le-Petit (52) . . . 92 E4
Liffré (35) . . . 79 H3
Ligardes (32) . . . 248 A6
Ligescourt (80) . . . 9 G3
Liginiac (19) . . . 217 G1
Liglet (86) . . . 164 C4
Lignac (36) . . . 164 D5
Lignairolles (11) . . . 308 C4
Lignan-de-Bazas (33) . . . 246 C1
Lignan-de-Bordeaux (33) . . . 229 G2
Lignan-sur-Orb (34) . . . 291 K3
Lignareix (19) . . . 201 F4
Ligné (16) . . . 179 F6
Ligné (44) . . . 123 J2
Lignères (61) . . . 55 F5
Lignereuil (62) . . . 10 C3
Lignerolles (03) . . . 184 A1
Lignerolles (21) . . . 115 J4
Lignerolles (27) . . . 56 E3
Lignerolles (36) . . . 166 C4
Lignerolles (61) . . . 83 H1
Lignéville (88) . . . 93 J6
Lignéyrac (19) . . . 215 K5
Lignières (10) . . . 113 K3
Lignières (18) . . . 166 D1
Lignières (41) . . . 108 D4
Lignières (80) . . . 18 E5
Lignières-Châtelain (80) . . . 17 G3
Lignières-de-Touraine (37) . . . 127 F6
Lignières-en-Vimeu (80) . . . 17 F2
Lignières-la-Carelle (72) . . . 82 E3
Lignières-Orgères (53) . . . 82 A1
Lignières-Sonneville (16) . . . 196 A4
Lignières-sur-Aire (55) . . . 64 D4
Lignol (56) . . . 76 B6
Lignol-le-Château (10) . . . 91 H5
Lignon (51) . . . 91 F1
Lignorelles (89) . . . 113 H4
Lignou (61) . . . 53 K5
Ligny-en-Barrois (55) . . . 64 C5
Ligny-en-Brionnais (71) . . . 187 G2
Ligny-en-Cambrésis (59) . . . 12 C5
Ligny-le-Châtel (89) . . . 113 H4
Ligny-le-Ribault (45) . . . 129 J1
Ligny-lès-Aire (62) . . . 5 H5
Ligny-Saint-Flochel (62) . . . 10 B2
Ligny-sur-Canche (62) . . . 10 A3
Ligny-Thilloy (62) . . . 11 F5
Ligré (37) . . . 145 G2
Ligron (72) . . . 106 C5
Ligsdorf (68) . . . 97 C6
Ligueil (37) . . . 146 B3
Ligueux (24) . . . 214 B2
Ligueux (33) . . . 231 F3
Ligugé (86) . . . 163 F4
Lihons (80) . . . 19 F3
Lihus (60) . . . 17 J5
les Lilas (93) . . . 59 F3
Lilhac (31) . . . 287 F4
Lille (59) . . . 6 D4
Lillebonne (76) . . . 14 E6
Lillemer (35) . . . 50 E4
Lillers (62) . . . 5 J5
Lilly (27) . . . 36 C2
Limalonges (79) . . . 179 G3
Limans (04) . . . 278 A1
Limanton (58) . . . 151 K4
Limas (69) . . . 188 B5
Limay (78) . . . 57 J2
Limbrassac (09) . . . 308 B2
Limé (02) . . . 40 A3
Limeil-Brévannes (94) . . . 59 F5
Limendous (64) . . . 284 E4
Limeray (37) . . . 128 C4
Limersheim (67) . . . 70 E5
Limerzel (56) . . . 101 K6
Limésy (76) . . . 15 J5
Limetz-Villez (78) . . . 57 G1
Limeuil (24) . . . 232 C2
Limeux (18) . . . 148 D3
Limeux (80) . . . 9 G6
Limey-Remenauville (54) . . . 65 H2
Limeyrat (24) . . . 214 D4
Limoges (87) . . . 199 F1
Limoges-Fourches (77) . . . 59 H6
Limogne-en-Quercy (46) . . . 250 D2
Limoise (03) . . . 168 B2
Limon (58) . . . 151 G4
Limonest (69) . . . 206 A1
Limons (63) . . . 185 J5
Limont-Fontaine (59) . . . 13 G3
Limony (07) . . . 222 A1
Limours (91) . . . 58 C6
Limousis (11) . . . 290 B4
Limoux (11) . . . 308 E2
la Limouzinière (44) . . . 141 H3

Limpiville (76)...... 14 E4
Linac (46)...... 234 E4
Linard (23)...... 166 A6
Linards (87)...... 199 H3
Linars (16)...... 196 D3
Linas (91)...... 58 D6
Linay (08)...... 23 H5
Linazay (86)...... 179 G3
Lindebeuf (76)...... 15 H4
le Lindois (16)...... 197 J2
Lindre-Basse (57)...... 67 F3
Lindre-Haute (57)...... 67 F3
Lindry (89)...... 112 E5
Linexert (70)...... 118 E5
Lingé (36)...... 164 C1
Lingeard (50)...... 52 C4
Lingèvres (14)...... 32 B5
Linghem (62)...... 5 H4
Lingolsheim (67)...... 71 D1
Lingreville (50)...... 30 D5
Linguizzetta (2B)...... 319 J6
Linières-Bouton (49)...... 126 C3
Liniers (86)...... 163 H3
Liniez (36)...... 148 A3
Linsdorf (68)...... 97 D5
Linselles (59)...... 6 B3
Linthal (68)...... 96 A6
Linthelles (51)...... 61 J5
Linthes (51)...... 61 J5
Lintot (76)...... 14 E6
Lintot-les-Bois (76)...... 15 K3
Linxe (40)...... 262 D2
Liny-devant-Dun (55)...... 43 F2
Linzeux (62)...... 9 K2
Liocourt (57)...... 66 C2
Liomer (80)...... 17 G2
le Lion-d'Angers (49)...... 125 F1
Lion-devant-Dun (55)...... 43 G2
Lion-en-Beauce (45)...... 110 A1
Lion-en-Sullias (45)...... 111 F6
Lion-sur-Mer (14)...... 32 E3
Liorac-sur-Louyre (24)...... 231 K1
Liouc (30)...... 274 D2
Liourdres (19)...... 234 B1
Lioux (84)...... 277 G1
Lioux-les-Monges (23)...... 183 J5
Liposthey (40)...... 245 G2
Lipsheim (67)...... 70 E4
Lirac (30)...... 256 D6
Liré (49)...... 124 A5
Lirey (10)...... 90 A6
Lironcourt (88)...... 117 J2
Lironville (54)...... 65 H3
Liry (08)...... 42 B3
Lisbourg (62)...... 5 G6
Lisieux (14)...... 33 H5
Lisle (24)...... 213 J2
Lisle (41)...... 108 C4
Lisle-en-Barrois (55)...... 64 A2
Lisle-en-Rigault (55)...... 63 K5
Lisle-sur-Tarn (81)...... 270 A3
Lislet (02)...... 21 G4
Lison (14)...... 31 H2
Lisores (14)...... 54 E2
Lisors (27)...... 36 B3
Lissac (09)...... 288 C5
Lissac (43)...... 220 B4
Lissac-et-Mouret (46)...... 234 D5
Lissac-sur-Couze (19)...... 215 H5
Lissay-Lochy (18)...... 149 G4
Lisse-en-Champagne (51)...... 63 G4
Lisses (91)...... 87 F1
Lisseuil (63)...... 184 D4
Lissey (55)...... 43 H2
Lissieu (69)...... 188 B6
Lissy (77)...... 59 H6
Listrac-de-Durèze (33)...... 230 D3
Listrac-Médoc (33)...... 211 H4
Lit-et-Mixe (40)...... 244 C6
Lithaire (50)...... 30 D1
Litteau (50)...... 31 K3
Littenheim (67)...... 70 C1
Litz (60)...... 37 K2
Livaie (61)...... 82 C2
Livarot (14)...... 54 E1
Liverdun (54)...... 65 K4
Liverdy-en-Brie (77)...... 59 J5
Livernon (46)...... 234 B5
Livers-Cazelles (81)...... 270 C1
Livet (53)...... 105 H1
Livet-en-Saosnois (72)...... 82 H4
Livet-et-Gavet (38)...... 224 C4
Livet-sur-Authou (27)...... 34 D4
Livilliers (95)...... 37 H6
Livinhac-le-Haut (12)...... 235 F5
la Livinière (34)...... 290 E4
Livré (53)...... 104 C4
Livré-sur-Changeon (35)...... 79 K3
Livron (64)...... 285 F5
Livron-sur-Drôme (26)...... 240 C3
Livry (14)...... 32 A5
Livry (58)...... 168 C1
Livry-Gargan (93)...... 59 G3
Livry-Louvercy (51)...... 41 H6
Livry-sur-Seine (77)...... 87 H2
Lixhausen (67)...... 69 J6
Lixheim (57)...... 67 K3
Lixing-lès-Rouhling (57)...... 68 C2
Lixing-lès-Saint-Avold (57)...... 68 A4
Lixy (89)...... 88 B5
Lizac (82)...... 249 H6
Lizant (86)...... 179 H4

Lizeray (36)...... 148 B4
Lizières (23)...... 182 A2
Lizine (25)...... 156 B2
Lizines (77)...... 88 C2
Lizio (56)...... 101 H3
Lizos (65)...... 285 J5
Lizy (02)...... 40 A1
Lizy-sur-Ourcq (77)...... 60 A1
la Llagonne (66)...... 313 J6
Llauro (66)...... 315 F4
Llo (66)...... 313 J5
Llupia (66)...... 315 F3
Lobsann (67)...... 25 B2
Loc-Brévalaire (29)...... 46 B4
Loc-Eguiner (29)...... 46 D5
Loc-Eguiner-Saint-Thégonnec (29)... 46 E6
Loc-Envel (22)...... 48 A5
Locarn (22)...... 75 K2
Loché-sur-Indrois (37)...... 147 F3
Loches (37)...... 146 D2
Loches-sur-Ource (10)...... 115 F2
le Locheur (14)...... 32 C6
Lochieu (01)...... 190 B5
Lochwiller (67)...... 70 C2
Locmalo (56)...... 76 B5
Locmaria (56)...... 120 C4
Locmaria-Berrien (29)...... 75 H2
Locmaria-Grand-Champ (56)...... 101 F4
Locmaria-Plouzané (29)...... 72 C4
Locmariaquer (56)...... 100 D6
Locmélar (29)...... 46 E6
Locminé (56)...... 101 F2
Locmiquélic (56)...... 100 A4
Locoal-Mendon (56)...... 100 C4
Locon (62)...... 6 A5
Loconville (60)...... 37 H4
Locqueltas (56)...... 101 F4
Locquénolé (29)...... 47 G4
Locquignol (59)...... 12 E4
Locquirec (29)...... 47 J3
Locronan (29)...... 74 C4
Loctudy (29)...... 98 C3
Locunolé (29)...... 99 J2
Loddes (03)...... 186 C1
Lodes (31)...... 286 D6
Lodève (34)...... 273 G5
Lods (25)...... 156 E2
Loeuilley (70)...... 136 D3
Loeuilly (80)...... 17 K3
Loffre (59)...... 11 J2
la Loge (62)...... 9 J1
la Loge-aux-Chèvres (10)...... 90 E5
Loge-Fougereuse (85)...... 161 F2
la Loge-Pomblin (10)...... 114 A2
Logelheim (68)...... 96 C4
les Loges (14)...... 32 A6
les Loges (52)...... 116 E5
les Loges (76)...... 14 C4
les Loges-en-Josas (78)...... 58 C5
les Loges-Marchis (50)...... 80 C1
les Loges-Margueron (10)...... 114 B1
les Loges-Saulces (14)...... 53 K3
les Loges-sur-Brécey (50)...... 52 B4
Lognes (77)...... 59 H4
Logny-Bogny (08)...... 22 A3
Logny-lès-Aubenton (02)...... 21 J2
Logonna-Daoulas (29)...... 74 B2
Lograin-Florian (30)...... 274 D2
Logron (28)...... 108 E1
Loguivy-Plougras (22)...... 47 K5
Lohéac (35)...... 102 E1
Lohitzun-Oyhercq (64)...... 283 G4
Lohr (67)...... 69 F6
Lohuec (22)...... 47 J6
Loigné-sur-Mayenne (53)...... 104 E4
Loigny-la-Bataille (28)...... 109 J1
Loiré (49)...... 124 C1
Loire-les-Marais (17)...... 177 F4
Loiré-sur-Nie (17)...... 178 C5
Loire-sur-Rhône (69)...... 206 A4
Loiron (53)...... 104 D1
Loisail (61)...... 83 H2
Loisey-Culey (55)...... 64 C4
Loisia (39)...... 173 F4
Loisieux (73)...... 207 K3
Loisin (74)...... 174 D6
Loison (55)...... 26 B5
Loison-sous-Lens (62)...... 11 F1
Loison-sur-Créquoise (62)...... 9 H1
Loisy (54)...... 65 K3
Loisy (71)...... 172 B3
Loisy-en-Brie (51)...... 61 J3
Loisy-sur-Marne (51)...... 63 F4
Loivre (51)...... 40 E3
Loix (17)...... 176 A1
Lolif (50)...... 51 K2
Lolme (24)...... 232 B4
Lombard (25)...... 156 A2
Lombard (39)...... 155 G6
Lombers (81)...... 270 E4
Lombez (32)...... 287 G2
Lombia (64)...... 285 F4
Lombrès (65)...... 305 G2
Lombreuil (45)...... 111 H3
Lombron (72)...... 107 G2
Lomme (59)...... 6 D4
Lommerange (57)...... 26 E4
Lommoye (78)...... 57 G2
Lomné (65)...... 304 E2
Lomont (70)...... 139 F1
Lomont-sur-Crête (25)...... 138 D4
Lompnas (01)...... 207 H1

Lompnieu (01)...... 190 A5
Lompret (59)...... 6 D4
Lonçon (64)...... 284 C2
la Londe (76)...... 35 G3
la Londe-les-Maures (83)...... 298 B6
Londigny (16)...... 179 G4
Londinières (76)...... 16 C3
Long (80)...... 9 H6
Longages (31)...... 287 K4
Longaulnay (35)...... 78 D1
Longavesnes (80)...... 19 H1
Longchamp (21)...... 136 D6
Longchamp (52)...... 92 D6
Longchamp (88)...... 94 E5
Longchamp-sous-Châtenois (88).. 93 H4
Longchamp-sur-Aujon (10)...... 91 J6
Longchamps (27)...... 36 C3
Longchamps-sur-Aire (55)...... 64 C2
Longchaumois (39)...... 174 A4
Longcochon (39)...... 156 C6
Longeau-Percey (52)...... 116 C5
Longeault (21)...... 136 C6
Longeaux (55)...... 64 C6
Longechaux (25)...... 157 F1
Longechenal (38)...... 207 F6
Longecourt-en-Plaine (21)...... 154 D1
Longecourt-lès-Culêtre (21)...... 153 H2
Longemaison (25)...... 157 F2
Longemer (71)...... 154 E4
le Longeron (49)...... 142 D3
Longes (69)...... 205 K5
Longessaigne (69)...... 205 G2
Longevelle (70)...... 138 D1
Longevelle-lès-Russey (25)...... 139 G6
Longevelle-sur-Doubs (25)...... 139 F3
Longèves (17)...... 177 F1
Longèves (85)...... 160 D4
la Longeville (25)...... 157 G3
Longeville (25)...... 156 D3
Longeville-en-Barrois (55)...... 64 B4
Longeville-lès-Metz (57)...... 44 E5
Longeville-lès-Saint-Avold (57)... 45 K5
Longeville-sur-la-Laines (52)...... 91 G2
Longeville-sur-Mer (85)...... 159 H4
Longeville-sur-Mogne (10)...... 114 A1
Longevilles-Mont-d'Or (25)...... 156 E6
Longfossé (62)...... 2 C6
la Longine (70)...... 119 F3
Longjumeau (91)...... 58 E5
Longlaville (54)...... 26 D2
Longmesnil (76)...... 16 E5
Longnes (72)...... 106 B2
Longnes (78)...... 57 H3
Longny-au-Perche (61)...... 83 K2
Longperrier (77)...... 59 H1
Longpont (02)...... 39 H4
Longpont-sur-Orge (91)...... 58 E4
Longpré-le-Sec (10)...... 91 F6
Longpré-les-Corps-Saints (80)...... 9 H6
Longraye (14)...... 32 B5
Longré (16)...... 178 E5
Longroy (76)...... 8 D6
Longsols (10)...... 90 C3
Longué-Jumelles (49)...... 126 A4
Longueau (80)...... 18 B2
Longuefuye (53)...... 105 G4
Longueil (76)...... 15 J2
Longueil-Annel (60)...... 38 E1
Longueil-Sainte-Marie (60)...... 38 D3
Longuenesse (62)...... 3 G5
Longuenoë (61)...... 82 B2
Longueron (14)...... 29 J6
Longueville (14)...... 29 J6
Longueville (47)...... 247 H1
Longueville (50)...... 30 D6
la Longueville (59)...... 13 G2
Longueville (62)...... 2 D5
Longueville (77)...... 88 D2
Longueville-sur-Aube (10)...... 89 K1
Longueville-sur-Scie (76)...... 15 K3
Longuevillette (80)...... 10 A5
Longuyon (54)...... 26 B3
Longvic (21)...... 136 A5
Longvillers (14)...... 32 B6
Longvilliers (62)...... 4 B5
Longvilliers (78)...... 86 B1
Longwé (08)...... 42 C2
Longwy (54)...... 26 D2
Longwy-sur-le-Doubs (39)...... 155 F4
Lonlay-l'Abbaye (61)...... 53 F6
Lonlay-le-Tesson (61)...... 53 J6
Lonnes (16)...... 179 G5
Lonny (08)...... 22 C3
Lonrai (61)...... 82 C2
Lons (64)...... 284 C4
Lons-le-Saunier (39)...... 173 G2
Lonzac (17)...... 195 J4
le Lonzac (19)...... 199 K6
Looberghe (59)...... 3 H3
Loon-Plage (59)...... 3 G2
Loos (59)...... 6 D4
Loos-en-Gohelle (62)...... 6 B6
Looze (89)...... 112 E3
Lopérec (29)...... 74 D2
Loperhet (29)...... 74 B1
Lopigna (2A)...... 320 C3
Loqueffret (29)...... 75 F2
Lor (02)...... 21 H6

Loray (25)...... 157 G1
Lorcières (15)...... 237 G1
Lorcy (45)...... 111 G2
Lordat (09)...... 307 K5
Loré (61)...... 81 G2
Lorentzen (67)...... 67 K1
Loreto-di-Casinca (2B)...... 319 J3
Loreto-di-Tallano (2A)...... 322 E2
Lorette (42)...... 205 J5
le Loreur (50)...... 30 E6
Loreux (41)...... 129 K4
le Lorey (50)...... 31 F2
Lorey (54)...... 94 B1
Lorges (41)...... 109 G5
Lorgies (62)...... 6 B5
Lorgues (83)...... 298 C1
Lorient (56)...... 99 K5
Loriges (03)...... 185 H1
Lorignac (17)...... 195 F5
Lorigné (79)...... 179 F3
Loriol-du-Comtat (84)...... 257 G6
Loriol-sur-Drôme (26)...... 240 B3
Lorlanges (43)...... 219 F2
Lorleau (27)...... 36 B2
Lormaison (60)...... 37 H4
Lormaye (28)...... 57 G6
Lormes (58)...... 133 J6
Lormont (33)...... 229 H1
Lornay (74)...... 190 D5
Loromontzey (54)...... 94 C2
le Loroux (35)...... 80 C3
le Loroux-Bottereau (44)...... 123 J4
Lorp-Sentaraille (09)...... 306 D2
Lorquin (57)...... 67 J5
Lorrez-le-Bocage-Préaux (77)...... 87 K5
Lorris (45)...... 111 G4
Lorry-lès-Metz (57)...... 44 E6
Lorry-Mardigny (57)...... 65 K1
Lortet (65)...... 305 F2
Loscouët-sur-Meu (22)...... 78 B3
Losne (21)...... 154 E2
Losse (40)...... 246 E5
Lostanges (19)...... 216 A5
Lostroff (57)...... 67 G2
Lothey (29)...... 74 E3
Lottinghen (62)...... 2 D6
le Lou-du-Lac (35)...... 78 D3
Louailles (72)...... 105 K5
Louan-Villegruis-Fontaine (77)... 61 F6
Louannec (22)...... 48 A2
Louans (37)...... 146 A1
Louargat (22)...... 48 B5
Louâtre (02)...... 39 H4
Loubajac (65)...... 285 F6
Loubaresse (07)...... 238 E5
Loubaresse (15)...... 237 F1
Loubaut (09)...... 288 A6
Loubédat (32)...... 266 C4
Loubejac (24)...... 232 D5
Loubens (09)...... 307 H2
Loubens (33)...... 230 C3
Loubens-Lauragais (31)...... 289 F1
Loubers (81)...... 270 B1
Loubersan (32)...... 286 C2
Loubès-Bernac (47)...... 231 F3
Loubeyrat (63)...... 184 E6
Loubieng (64)...... 283 J2
la Loubière (12)...... 252 C2
Loubières (09)...... 307 J2
Loubigné (79)...... 178 D4
Loubillé (79)...... 178 E4
Loubressac (46)...... 234 B1
Loucé (61)...... 54 B5
Loucelles (14)...... 32 C4
Louchats (33)...... 229 H6
Louches (62)...... 2 E4
Louchy-Montfand (03)...... 185 G1
Loucrup (65)...... 285 H6
Loudéac (22)...... 77 G4
Loudenvielle (65)...... 305 F5
Loudervielle (65)...... 305 F5
Loudes (43)...... 220 A5
Loudet (31)...... 286 C6
Loudrefing (57)...... 67 G2
Loudun (86)...... 144 E3
Loué (72)...... 106 A2
Louer (40)...... 264 C4
Louerre (49)...... 125 J5
Louesme (21)...... 115 H4
Louestault (37)...... 127 J2
Loueuse (60)...... 17 G5
Louey (65)...... 285 G6
Lougé-sur-Maire (61)...... 54 A5
Lougratte (47)...... 231 K5
Lougres (25)...... 139 G3
Louhans (71)...... 172 D2
Louhossoa (64)...... 263 E2
Louignac (19)...... 215 F3
Louin (79)...... 144 B6
Louisfert (44)...... 103 H4
Louit (65)...... 285 J4
Loulans-Verchamp (70)...... 138 B3
Loulay (17)...... 177 K4
Loulle (39)...... 173 K1
la Loupe (28)...... 84 C2
Loupeigne (02)...... 40 A4
Loupershouse (57)...... 68 C3
Loupes (33)...... 229 J2
Loupfougères (53)...... 81 H4
Loupia (11)...... 308 D2
Loupiac (33)...... 229 K5

Loupiac (46)...... 233 H2
Loupiac (81)...... 270 A3
Loupiac-de-la-Réole (33)...... 230 C6
Loupian (34)...... 292 E2
Louplande (72)...... 106 C3
Loupmont (55)...... 65 F3
Louppy-le-Château (55)...... 64 A3
Louppy-sur-Loison (55)...... 43 H1
la Louptière-Thénard (10)...... 88 E3
Lourches (59)...... 12 B2
Lourde (31)...... 305 J2
Lourdes (65)...... 304 B1
Lourdios-Ichère (64)...... 302 E1
Lourdoueix-Saint-Michel (36)...... 165 J5
Lourdoueix-Saint-Pierre (23)...... 165 K5
Lourenties (64)...... 285 F4
Loures-Barousse (65)...... 305 H2
Louresse-Rochemenier (49)...... 125 J6
Lourmais (35)...... 51 G6
Lourmarin (84)...... 277 H4
Lournand (71)...... 171 H5
Lourouer-Saint-Laurent (36)...... 166 B3
le Louroux (37)...... 146 B2
le Louroux-Béconnais (49)...... 124 D2
Louroux-Bourbonnais (03)...... 167 K4
Louroux-de-Beaune (03)...... 184 D1
Louroux-de-Bouble (03)...... 184 E2
Louroux-Hodement (03)...... 167 J5
Lourquen (40)...... 264 D4
Lourties-Monbrun (32)...... 286 C2
Loury (45)...... 110 C3
Louslitges (32)...... 266 D6
Loussous-Débat (32)...... 266 C5
Loutehel (35)...... 78 C6
Loutzviller (57)...... 69 G2
Louvagny (14)...... 54 C2
Louvaines (49)...... 104 E6
Louvatange (39)...... 155 J1
Louveciennes (78)...... 58 C3
Louvemont (52)...... 91 J1
Louvemont-Côte-du-Poivre (55)... 43 H4
Louvencourt (80)...... 10 C5
Louvenne (39)...... 173 F5
Louvergny (08)...... 22 D6
Louverné (53)...... 105 F1
le Louverot (39)...... 173 G1
Louversey (27)...... 56 B2
Louvetot (76)...... 15 G6
Louvie-Juzon (64)...... 303 H1
Louvie-Soubiron (64)...... 303 H2
la Louvière-Lauragais (11)...... 288 E5
Louvières (14)...... 29 K6
Louvières (52)...... 116 C2
Louvières-en-Auge (61)...... 54 C3
Louviers (27)...... 35 J5
Louvigné (53)...... 105 G2
Louvigné-de-Bais (35)...... 79 K5
Louvigné-du-Désert (35)...... 80 B2
Louvignies-Quesnoy (59)...... 12 E3
Louvigny (14)...... 32 E5
Louvigny (57)...... 66 A1
Louvigny (64)...... 284 C1
Louvigny (72)...... 82 E3
Louvil (59)...... 7 F5
Louville-la-Chenard (28)...... 85 K4
Louvilliers-en-Drouais (28)...... 56 E5
Louvilliers-lès-Perche (28)...... 56 C6
Louvois (51)...... 41 F6
Louvrechy (80)...... 18 B4
Louvres (95)...... 59 F1
Louvroil (59)...... 13 H3
Louye (27)...... 56 E4
Louzac-Saint-André (16)...... 195 J2
Louze (52)...... 91 G3
Louzes (72)...... 83 F3
Louzignac (17)...... 196 A1
Louzouer (45)...... 111 K2
Louzy (79)...... 144 B3
Lovagny (74)...... 190 E5
Loyat (56)...... 101 K2
la Loye (39)...... 155 H3
Loye-sur-Arnon (18)...... 167 F2
la Loyère (71)...... 154 A5
Loyettes (01)...... 206 E2
Lozanne (69)...... 188 B6
Lozay (17)...... 177 K4
Loze (82)...... 250 D3
Lozinghem (62)...... 5 J5
Lozon (50)...... 31 F3
Lozzi (2B)...... 318 D5
Luant (36)...... 165 H1
le Luart (72)...... 107 H2
Lubbon (40)...... 246 E5
Lubécourt (57)...... 66 D2
Lubersac (19)...... 199 G6
Lubey (54)...... 26 E6
Lubilhac (43)...... 219 F3
Lubine (88)...... 96 A1
Lublé (37)...... 126 E3
Lubret-Saint-Luc (65)...... 285 K4
Luby-Betmont (65)...... 285 K4
Luc (12)...... 252 B3
Luc (48)...... 238 C4
Luc (65)...... 285 J6
le Luc (83)...... 298 C2
Luc-Armau (64)...... 285 G3
Luc-en-Diois (26)...... 241 J4
Luc-sur-Aude (11)...... 309 F3
Luc-sur-Mer (14)...... 32 E3
Luc-sur-Orbieu (11)...... 291 F6
Lucarré (64)...... 285 F3
Luçay-le-Libre (36)...... 148 B3

Luçay-le-Mâle (36) 147 H2
Lucbardez-et-Bargues (40) 265 H1
Lucciana (2B) 319 H3
Lucé (28) 85 G3
Lucé (61) 81 G1
Lucé-sous-Ballon (72) 82 E6
Luceau (72) 107 F6
Lucelle (68) 97 B6
Lucenay (69) 188 B6
Lucenay-le-Duc (21) 135 F2
Lucenay-lès-Aix (58) 169 F2
Lucenay-l'Évêque (71) 152 E3
Lucéram (06) 281 H1
la Lucerne-d'Outremer (50) 51 J1
Lucey (21) 115 J4
Lucey (54) 65 H1
Lucey (73) 208 A2
Lucgarier (64) 284 E5
Luchapt (86) 180 C3
Luchat (17) 195 F2
Luché-Pringé (72) 106 C6
Luché-sur-Brioux (79) 178 D3
Luché-Thouarsais (79) 144 A5
Lucheux (80) 10 B4
Luchy (60) 17 K6
Lucinges (74) 191 H2
Lucmau (33) 246 C2
Luçon (85) 160 A4
Lucq-de-Béarn (64) 283 K4
Lucquy (08) 22 B6
les Lucs-sur-Boulogne (85) 141 J5
Lucy (57) 66 D1
Lucy (76) 16 D3
Lucy-le-Bocage (02) 60 D1
Lucy-le-Bois (89) 133 K2
Lucy-sur-Cure (89) 133 H2
Lucy-sur-Yonne (89) 133 G3
le Lude (72) 126 D1
Ludes (51) 41 F5
Ludesse (63) 202 D4
Ludiès (09) 307 K1
Ludon-Médoc (33) 211 G6
Ludres (54) 66 A6
Lüe (40) 245 F4
Lué-en-Baugeois (49) 125 K3
Luemschwiller (68) 97 B3
Lugagnac (46) 250 D2
Lugagnan (65) 304 B1
Lugaignac (33) 230 B2
Lugan (12) 251 J1
Lugan (81) 269 K5
Lugarde (15) 218 C4
Lugasson (33) 230 B3
Luglon (40) 245 H5
Lugny (02) 20 E3
Lugny (71) 171 J4
Lugny-Bourbonnais (18) 149 K5
Lugny-Champagne (18) 150 A1
Lugny-lès-Charolles (71) 170 D5
Lugo-di-Nazza (2B) 321 H3
Lugon-et-l'Île-du-Carnay (33) . . . 211 K6
Lugos (33) 228 D6
Lugrin (74) 175 H5
Lugy (62) 5 F5
le Luhier (25) 157 H1
Luigné (49) 125 H6
Luigny (28) 84 C5
Luisant (28) 85 G3
Luisetaines (77) 88 C3
Luitré (35) 80 B4
Lullin (74) 175 F6
Lully (74) 174 E6
Lumbin (38) 224 C1
Lumbres (62) 3 F5
Lumeau (28) 109 K1
Lumes (08) 22 D4
Lumigny-Nesles-Ormeaux (77) . . . 60 A5
Lumio (2B) 318 B2
Lunac (12) 251 G4
Lunan (46) 234 E5
Lunas (24) 231 H1
Lunas (34) 272 E5
Lunax (31) 286 D4
Lunay (41) 108 A5
Luneau (03) 170 A6
Lunegarde (46) 234 A3
Lunel (34) 274 E5
Lunel-Viel (34) 274 E6
Luneray (76) 15 J3
Lunery (18) 149 F5
Lunéville (54) 66 D6
le Luot (50) 52 A4
Lupcourt (54) 66 B6
Lupé (42) 222 A1
Lupersat (23) 183 H5
Lupiac (32) 266 D5
Luplanté (28) 85 F5
Luppé-Violles (32) 266 A4
Luppy (57) 66 C1
Lupsault (16) 178 E5
Lupstein (67) 70 C1
Luquet (65) 285 F4
Lurais (36) 164 B2
Luray (28) 57 F5
Lurbe-Saint-Christau (64) 284 A6
Lurcy (01) 188 C4
Lurcy-le-Bourg (58) 151 G2
Lurcy-Lévis (03) 168 A1
Luré (42) 186 D6
Lure (70) 118 E6
Lureuil (36) 164 C1
Luri (2B) 317 D3

Luriecq (42) 204 D6
Lurs (04) 278 C1
Lury-sur-Arnon (18) 148 D2
Lus-la-Croix-Haute (26) 242 A4
Lusanger (44) 103 G3
Luscan (31) 305 J2
Lusignac (24) 213 G2
Lusignan (86) 162 D5
Lusignan-Petit (47) 248 A3
Lusigny (03) 169 G3
Lusigny-sur-Barse (10) 90 C5
Lusigny-sur-Ouche (21) 153 J2
Lussac (16) 197 H1
Lussac (17) 195 H5
Lussac (33) 212 C6
Lussac-les-Châteaux (86) 163 J5
Lussac-les-Églises (87) 164 D5
Lussagnet (40) 265 K4
Lussagnet-Lusson (64) 284 E2
Lussan (30) 255 K5
Lussan (32) 267 K6
Lussan-Adeilhac (31) 287 G4
Lussant (17) 177 G5
Lussas (07) 239 J5
Lussas-et-Nontronneau (24) 197 J5
Lussat (23) 183 H3
Lussat (63) 202 E1
Lussault-sur-Loire (37) 128 A4
Lusse (88) 95 K4
Lusseray (79) 178 D3
Lustar (65) 286 A5
Luthenay-Uxeloup (58) 151 F6
Lutilhous (65) 286 A6
Luttange (57) 27 J5
Luttenbach-près-Munster (68) . . . 119 K1
Lutter (68) 97 C6
Lutterbach (68) 97 B2
Lutz-en-Dunois (28) 109 F2
Lutzelbourg (57) 70 A1
Lutzelhouse (67) 70 B4
Luvigny (88) 95 J1
Lux (21) 136 C3
Lux (31) 289 F3
Lux (71) 171 K1
Luxé (16) 179 F6
Luxe-Sumberraute (64) 283 F3
Luxémont-et-Villotte (51) 63 F5
Luxeuil-les-Bains (70) 118 D4
Luxey (40) 245 K3
Luxiol (25) 138 D4
Luyères (10) 90 C3
Luynes (37) 127 H5
Luz-Saint-Sauveur (65) 304 B4
Luzancy (77) 60 C2
Luzarches (95) 38 A6
Luzay (79) 144 B4
Luzé (37) 145 H3
Luze (70) 139 G1
Luzech (46) 249 J1
Luzenac (09) 308 A5
Luzeret (36) 165 F4
la Luzerne (50) 31 H4
Luzillat (63) 185 J5
Luzillé (37) 128 C6
Luzinay (38) 206 C4
Luzoir (02) 21 G1
Luzy (58) 152 C6
Luzy-Saint-Martin (55) 23 H6
Luzy-sur-Marne (52) 116 B2
Ly-Fontaine (02) 20 A4
Lyas (07) 239 K3
Lyaud (74) 175 F5
Lye (36) 147 H1
Lynde (59) 3 H5
Lyoffans (70) 119 F6
Lyon (69) 206 A2
Lyons-la-Forêt (27) 36 B2
Lys (58) 133 G5
Lys (64) 284 D6
Lys-lez-Lannoy (59) 7 J2
Lys-Saint-Georges (36) 165 K3

M

Maast-et-Violaine (02) 39 K4
Maâtz (52) 116 E6
Mably (42) 186 E4
Macau (33) 211 G5
Macaye (64) 282 D3
Macé (61) 54 D6
Macey (10) 89 K5
Macey (50) 51 J4
Machault (08) 41 K3
Machault (77) 87 J3
Maché (85) 141 G6
Machecoul (44) 141 F3
Mâchecourt (02) 21 F5
Machemont (60) 38 E1
Machéménil (57) 68 A3
Machézal (42) 187 H6
Machiel (80) 9 G3
Machilly (74) 191 H1
la Machine (58) 151 G5
Machy (10) 114 A1
Machy (80) 9 F3
Mackenheim (67) 71 C6
Mackwiller (67) 67 K1
Maclas (42) 222 A1
Macogny (02) 39 H5
Mâcon (71) 188 C1

Maconcourt (88) 93 J3
Maconge (21) 153 H1
Macornay (39) 173 G2
Mâcot-la-Plagne (73) 209 J4
Macqueville (17) 196 A1
Macquigny (02) 20 C2
Madaillan (47) 248 B3
Madecourt (88) 94 A5
Madegney (88) 94 B4
Madirac (33) 229 J3
Madiran (65) 285 G1
Madonne-et-Lamerey (88) 94 B5
Madranges (19) 200 A6
Madré (53) 81 J2
Madriat (63) 202 E6
Maël-Carhaix (22) 75 K3
Maël-Pestivien (22) 76 B1
Maennolsheim (67) 70 C2
Maffliers (95) 37 K6
Maffrécourt (51) 42 C6
Magalas (34) 292 A2
la Magdelaine-sur-Tarn (31) 269 H4
la Magdeleine (16) 179 F4
le Mage (61) 83 K2
Magenta (51) 61 K1
les Mages (30) 255 H4
Magescq (40) 262 D6
Magland (74) 192 A4
Magnac-Bourg (87) 199 G4
Magnac-Laval (87) 181 G2
Magnac-Lavalette-Villars (16) . . . 197 F5
Magnac-sur-Touvre (16) 196 E3
Magnan (32) 266 A3
Magnant (10) 90 E6
Magnanville (78) 57 J2
Magnas (32) 267 K2
Magnat-l'Étrange (23) 201 F2
Magné (79) 161 G6
Magné (86) 163 F6
Magnet (03) 185 K2
Magneux (51) 40 C3
Magneux (52) 91 K2
Magneux-Haute-Rive (42) 204 E3
Magneville (50) 28 D5
Magnicourt (10) 90 D3
Magnicourt-en-Comte (62) 10 C1
Magnicourt-sur-Canche (62) 10 B2
Magnien (21) 153 G2
Magnières (54) 94 E2
Magnieu (01) 207 K1
les Magnils-Reigniers (85) 159 K4
Magnivray (70) 118 E5
Magnoncourt (70) 118 C3
le Magnoray (70) 138 A2
Magny (28) 84 E4
le Magny (36) 166 B3
Magny (68) 139 K1
les Magny (70) 138 E2
le Magny (88) 118 B2
Magny (89) 134 A3
Magny-Châtelard (25) 138 D6
Magny-Cours (58) 150 E5
Magny-Danigon (70) 119 F6
Magny-en-Bessin (14) 32 B3
Magny-en-Vexin (95) 36 E5
Magny-Fouchard (10) 91 F5
Magny-Jobert (70) 119 F6
Magny-la-Campagne (14) 54 B1
Magny-la-Fosse (02) 19 K1
Magny-la-Ville (21) 134 E3
Magny-Lambert (21) 135 F1
Magny-le-Désert (61) 81 K1
Magny-le-Freule (14) 33 G6
Magny-le-Hongre (77) 59 J3
Magny-lès-Aubigny (21) 154 D2
Magny-les-Hameaux (78) 58 B5
Magny-lès-Jussey (70) 117 K4
Magny-lès-Villers (21) 154 A2
Magny-Lormes (58) 133 J6
Magny-Montarlot (21) 136 D6
Magny-Saint-Médard (21) 136 C4
Magny-sur-Tille (21) 136 B6
Magny-Vernois (70) 118 E6
Magoar (22) 76 C1
Magrie (11) 308 E2
Magrin (81) 270 B6
Magstatt-le-Bas (68) 97 C4
Magstatt-le-Haut (68) 97 C4
Mahalon (29) 73 D3
Mahéru (61) 55 G6
Maîche (25) 139 H5
Maidières (54) 65 J4
Maignaut-Tauzia (32) 267 G2
Maigné (72) 106 B3
Maignelay-Montigny (60) 18 D6
Mailhac (11) 291 G4
Mailhac-sur-Benaize (87) 181 H1
Mailhoc (81) 270 D1
Mailholas (31) 287 K5
Maillane (13) 276 B3
Maillas (40) 246 D4
Maillat (01) 189 K3
Maillé (37) 145 J3
Maillé (85) 160 E6

Maillé (86) 162 C2
Maillebois (28) 56 D6
la Mailleraye-sur-Seine (76) 34 E1
Maillères (40) 246 A6
Mailleroncourt-Charette (70) . . . 118 C5
Mailleroncourt-Saint-Pancras (70) . 118 A3
Maillet (03) 167 H5
Maillet (36) 165 J3
Mailley-et-Chazelot (70) 138 A2
Maillezais (85) 160 E5
Mailly (71) 187 F2
Mailly-Champagne (51) 41 F5
Mailly-la-Ville (89) 133 H2
Mailly-le-Camp (10) 62 C6
Mailly-le-Château (89) 133 G2
Mailly-Maillet (80) 10 D5
Mailly-Raineval (80) 18 C4
Mailly-sur-Seille (54) 66 B2
les Maillys (21) 155 F2
Maimbeville (60) 38 B2
Maincy (77) 87 H2
Maine-de-Boixe (16) 196 E1
Mainfonds (16) 196 C5
Maing (59) 12 C2
Mainneville (27) 36 D3
Mainsat (23) 183 J4
Maintenay (62) 9 F2
Maintenon (28) 85 H1
Mainvillers (57) 45 J6
Mainvilliers (28) 85 G3
Mainvilliers (45) 86 D5
Mainxe (16) 196 A3
Mainzac (16) 197 H5
Mairé (86) 146 A5
Mairé-Levescault (79) 179 F3
Mairieux (59) 13 H2
Mairy (08) 23 G5
Mairy-Mainville (54) 26 E5
Mairy-sur-Marne (51) 62 D3
Maisdon-sur-Sèvre (44) 123 J5
Maisey-le-Duc (21) 115 G4
Maisnières (80) 8 E6
le Maisnil (59) 6 C4
Maisnil (62) 10 B2
Maisnil-lès-Ruitz (62) 5 K6
Maisod (39) 173 H4
Maison-des-Champs (10) 91 F5
la Maison-Dieu (58) 133 G4
Maison-Feyne (23) 165 J6
Maison-Maugis (61) 83 J3
Maison-Ponthieu (80) 9 J4
Maison-Roland (80) 9 H5
Maison-Rouge (77) 88 C1
Maisoncelle (62) 5 F6
Maisoncelle-et-Villers (08) 23 F5
Maisoncelle-Saint-Pierre (60) . . . 37 H1
Maisoncelle-Tuilerie (60) 18 A6
Maisoncelles (52) 92 E6
Maisoncelles (72) 107 H3
Maisoncelles-du-Maine (53) 105 F3
Maisoncelles-en-Brie (77) 60 A3
Maisoncelles-en-Gâtinais (77) . . . 87 H6
Maisoncelles-la-Jourdan (14) 52 E4
Maisoncelles-Pelvey (14) 32 B6
Maisoncelles-sur-Ajon (14) 32 C6
Maisonnais (18) 166 D3
Maisonnais-sur-Tardoire (87) . . . 197 K3
Maisonnay (79) 178 E2
Maisonneuve (86) 162 C1
Maisonnisses (23) 182 D4
Maisons (11) 309 K3
Maisons (14) 32 A3
Maisons (28) 85 K3
Maisons-Alfort (94) 59 F4
Maisons-du-Bois-Lièvremont (25) . 157 F3
Maisons-en-Champagne (51) 62 E4
Maisons-Laffitte (78) 58 C2
Maisons-lès-Chaource (10) 114 B2
Maisons-lès-Soulaines (10) 91 H4
Maisonsgoutte (67) 70 B6
Maisontiers (79) 144 A6
Maisse (91) 86 E3
Maissemy (02) 19 J2
Maixe (54) 66 D5
Maizeray (55) 44 A5
Maizeroy (57) 45 H5
Maizery (57) 45 G5
Maizet (14) 32 D6
Maizey (55) 64 E2
Maizicourt (80) 9 J4
Maizières (14) 54 B1
Maizières (52) 92 A2
Maizières (54) 66 C2
Maizières (62) 10 C2
Maizières (70) 137 K3
Maizières-la-Grande-Paroisse (10) . 89 J2
Maizières-lès-Brienne (10) 91 F3
Maizières-lès-Metz (57) 27 G6
Maizières-lès-Vic (57) 67 G4
Maizières-sur-Amance (52) 117 F4
Maizilly (42) 187 G2
Maizy (02) 40 C2
Majastres (04) 279 G2
Malabat (32) 285 J2
la Malachère (70) 138 B3
Malafretaz (01) 172 C4
Mâlain (21) 135 J5
Malakoff (92) 58 E4
Malancourt (55) 43 F4

Malandry (08) 23 H5
Malange (39) 155 H1
Malans (25) 156 B2
Malans (70) 137 F6
Malansac (56) 102 A3
Malarce-sur-la-Thines (07) 255 G1
Malataverne (26) 240 B6
Malaucène (84) 257 H4
Malaucourt-sur-Seille (57) 66 C3
Malaunay (76) 15 K6
Malause (82) 249 F6
Malaussanne (64) 284 C1
Malaussène (06) 281 F1
Malauzat (63) 202 D1
Malaville (16) 196 B5
Malavillers (54) 26 E4
Malay (71) 171 H3
Malay-le-Grand (89) 88 E6
Malay-le-Petit (89) 88 E6
Malbo (15) 218 A6
Malbosc (07) 255 G3
Malbouhans (70) 119 F5
Malbouzon (48) 236 E4
Malbrans (25) 156 C2
Malbuisson (25) 156 E5
Mâle (61) 83 K5
Malegoude (09) 308 C1
Malemort-du-Comtat (84) 257 H6
Malemort-sur-Corrèze (19) 215 J4
la Malène (48) 253 J3
Malesherbes (45) 87 F5
Malestroit (56) 101 K3
Malétable (61) 83 J1
Maleville (12) 251 G2
Malguénac (56) 76 D5
la Malhoure (22) 77 J2
Malicornay (36) 165 H3
Malicorne (03) 184 C1
Malicorne (89) 112 B5
Malicorne-sur-Sarthe (72) 106 B3
Maligny (21) 153 H2
Maligny (89) 113 H4
Malijai (04) 259 G6
Malincourt (59) 11 K6
Malintrat (63) 202 E1
Malissard (26) 240 D1
Mallefougasse-Augès (04) 259 F5
Malleloy (54) 66 A3
Mallemoisson (04) 259 H6
Mallemort (13) 277 F4
Malléon (09) 307 K2
Malleret (23) 201 F2
Malleret-Boussac (23) 166 C6
Mallerey (39) 173 F2
Malleval (38) 223 H4
Malleval (42) 222 A1
Malleville-les-Grès (76) 15 F2
Malleville-sur-le-Bec (27) 34 E4
Mallièvre (85) 142 E4
Malling (57) 27 H3
Malloué (14) 31 J5
la Malmaison (02) 40 E1
Malmerspach (68) 119 K3
Malmy (51) 42 C5
Malons-et-Elze (30) 255 G2
Malouy (27) 34 C6
Malpart (80) 18 C4
Malpas (25) 156 E5
Malras (11) 308 C2
Malrevers (43) 220 D5
Malroy (57) 27 H6
Maltat (71) 169 K2
Maltot (14) 32 D5
Malval (23) 166 A6
Malvalette (43) 220 E1
Malves-en-Minervois (11) 290 C5
Malvezie (31) 305 J2
Malvières (43) 220 A2
Malviès (11) 308 E1
Malville (44) 122 D2
Malvillers (70) 117 H5
Malzéville (54) 66 A4
le Malzieu-Forain (48) 237 G2
le Malzieu-Ville (48) 237 G2
Malzy (02) 20 E2
Mamers (72) 83 F4
Mametz (62) 3 H6
Mametz (80) 10 E6
Mamey (54) 65 J2
Mamirolle (25) 138 B6
Manas (32) 240 D5
Manas-Bastanous (32) 286 A3
Manaurie (24) 214 D6
Mance (54) 26 E5
la Mancellière (28) 56 B6
la Mancellière-sur-Vire (50) 31 H4
Mancenans (25) 138 E3
Mancenans-Lizerne (25) 139 H5
Mancey (71) 171 K3
Manchecourt (45) 86 E5
Manciet (32) 266 C4
Mancieulles (54) 26 E5
Mancioux (31) 287 G3
Mancy (51) 61 K2
Mandagout (30) 273 K1
Mandailles-Saint-Julien (15) 217 K5
Mandelieu-la-Napoule (06) 280 D6
Manderen (57) 27 K3
Mandeure (25) 139 H3
Mandeville (27) 35 H4
Mandeville-en-Bessin (14) 31 K1
Mandray (88) 95 J5

Mandres (27) 56 A5
Mandres-aux-Quatre-Tours (54) . . 65 G3
Mandres-en-Barrois (55) 92 D2
Mandres-la-Côte (52) 116 D1
Mandres-les-Roses (94) 59 G5
Mandres-sur-Vair (88) 93 J5
Mandrevillars (70) 139 G1
Manduel (30) 275 H3
Mane (04) 278 B1
Mane (31) 306 B1
Manéglise (76) 14 C6
Manéhouville (76) 15 K2
Manent-Montané (32) 286 D4
Manerbe (14) 33 K5
Mangiennes (55) 26 B4
Manglieu (63) 203 F4
Mangonville (54) 94 B2
Manhac (12) 252 A4
Manheulles (55) 43 K5
Manhoué (57) 66 C3
Manicamp (02) 19 J6
Manigod (74) 191 H6
Manin (62) 10 C2
Maninghem (62) 4 D5
Maninghen-Henne (62) 2 B5
Maniquerville (76) 14 C4
Manlay (21) 153 F2
Manneville-ès-Plains (76) 15 G2
Manneville-la-Goupil (76) 14 C5
Manneville-la-Pipard (14) 33 K4
Manneville-la-Raoult (27) 34 A2
Manneville-sur-Risle (27) 34 C3
Mannevillette (76) 14 B5
Mano (40) 245 J1
le Manoir (14) 32 C3
le Manoir (27) 35 J3
Manois (52) 92 D4
Manom (57) 27 G4
Manoncourt-en-Vermois (54) . . . 66 B6
Manoncourt-en-Woëvre (54) . . . 65 J4
Manonville (54) 65 H3
Manonviller (54) 67 F6
Manosque (04) 278 B3
Manot (16) 180 B5
Manou (28) 84 B2
Manre (08) 42 B4
le Mans (72) 106 E2
Mansac (19) 215 G4
Mansan (65) 285 J4
Mansat-la-Courrière (23) 182 C5
Mansempuy (32) 268 A4
Mansencôme (32) 267 F3
Manses (09) 308 A1
Mansigné (72) 106 D6
Mansle (16) 179 G6
Manso (2B) 316 E3
Mansonville (82) 268 A1
Manspach (68) 97 A4
Mant (40) 265 G6
Mantaillot (21) 48 B3
Mantenay-Montlin (01) 172 B5
Mantes-la-Jolie (78) 57 J2
Mantes-la-Ville (78) 57 J2
Mantet (66) 314 A5
Manteyer (05) 242 D5
Manthelan (37) 146 B2
Manthelon (27) 56 C3
Manthes (26) 222 D2
Mantilly (61) 80 E1
Mantoche (70) 137 F4
Mantry (39) 155 H6
Manvieux (14) 32 B4
Many (57) 66 D1
Manzac-sur-Vern (24) 213 J5
Manzat (63) 184 D5
Manziat (01) 172 A6
Marac (52) 116 B3
Marainville-sur-Madon (88) 94 A3
Marainviller (54) 66 E6
le Marais-la-Chapelle (14) 54 C3
Marais-Vernier (27) 34 C2
Marambat (32) 267 F4
Marandeuil (21) 136 D5
Marange-Silvange (57) 27 G6
Marange-Zondrange (57) 45 J5
Marans (17) 160 C6
Marans (49) 124 D1
Maransin (33) 212 A5
Marant (62) 4 C6
Maranville (52) 115 J1
Maranwez (08) 21 K4
Marast (70) 138 D2
Marat (63) 203 K3
Maraussan (34) 291 K4
Maravat (32) 267 K4
Maray (41) 148 B1
Maraye-en-Othe (10) 89 J6
Marbache (54) 65 K3
Marbaix (59) 13 G4
Marbeuf (27) 35 G5
Marbéville (52) 91 K5
Marboué (28) 108 E1
Marboz (01) 172 D6
Marby (08) 22 A2
Marc-la-Tour (19) 216 B3
Marçais (18) 167 F2
Marçay (37) 145 F2
Marçay (86) 162 E5
Marcé (49) 125 J2
Marcé-sur-Esves (37) 145 K3
Marcei (61) 54 C6
Marcelcave (80) 18 D2

Marcellaz (74) 191 H2
Marcellaz-Albanais (74) 190 E6
Marcellois (21) 135 G5
Marcellus (47) 247 G1
Marcenais (33) 211 K5
Marcenat (03) 185 J2
Marcenat (15) 218 B2
Marcenay (21) 114 E4
Marcenod (42) 205 H4
Marcey-les-Grèves (50) 51 K3
Marchainville (61) 84 A1
Marchais (02) 20 E6
Marchais-Beton (89) 112 B5
Marchais-en-Brie (02) 61 J3
Marchamp (01) 207 H1
Marchampt (69) 187 K3
Marchastel (15) 218 A2
Marchastel (48) 236 E5
Marchaux (25) 138 B5
la Marche (58) 150 C2
Marché-Allouarde (80) 19 G4
Marchélepot (80) 19 G3
Marchemaisons (61) 83 F2
Marchémoret (77) 59 J1
Marchenoir (41) 109 F5
Marcheprime (33) 228 E4
Marches (26) 222 E6
les Marches (73) 208 C5
Marcheseuil (21) 153 F2
Marchésieux (50) 31 F2
Marchéville (28) 84 E4
Marchéville-en-Woëvre (55) 44 A6
Marchezais (28) 57 G4
Marchiennes (59) 11 K1
Marciac (32) 285 H1
Marcieu (38) 242 A1
Marcieux (73) 207 K3
Marcigny (71) 186 E1
Marcigny-sous-Thil (21) 134 E4
Marcilhac-sur-Célé (46) 234 B6
Marcillac (33) 211 H2
Marcillac-la-Croisille (19) 216 D3
Marcillac-la-Croze (19) 216 A5
Marcillac-Lanville (16) 196 C1
Marcillac-Saint-Quentin (24) . . . 233 F1
Marcillac-Vallon (12) 252 A1
Marcillat (63) 184 E4
Marcillat-en-Combraille (03) . . . 184 A3
Marcillé-la-Ville (53) 81 H4
Marcillé-Raoul (35) 79 H1
Marcillé-Robert (35) 79 K6
Marcilloles (38) 223 F1
Marcilly (50) 52 A5
Marcilly (77) 59 K1
Marcilly-d'Azergues (69) 188 B6
Marcilly-en-Bassigny (52) 116 E3
Marcilly-en-Beauce (41) 108 B6
Marcilly-en-Gault (41) 129 K4
Marcilly-en-Villette (45) 110 B6
Marcilly-la-Campagne (27) 56 D4
Marcilly-la-Gueurce (71) 170 E5
Marcilly-le-Châtel (42) 204 C3
Marcilly-le-Hayer (10) 89 G4
Marcilly-lès-Buxy (71) 171 G1
Marcilly-lès-Vitteaux (21) 135 F4
Marcilly-Ogny (21) 134 E6
Marcilly-sur-Eure (27) 57 F4
Marcilly-sur-Maulne (37) 126 E2
Marcilly-sur-Seine (51) 89 H1
Marcilly-sur-Tille (21) 136 B3
Marcilly-sur-Vienne (37) 145 J3
Marck (62) 2 D2
Marckolsheim (67) 71 C6
Marclopt (42) 204 E3
Marcoing (59) 11 J5
Marcolès (15) 235 G3
Marcollin (38) 222 E2
Marcols-les-Eaux (07) 239 H2
Marçon (72) 107 G6
Marconne (62) 9 J2
Marconnelle (62) 9 H2
Marcorignan (11) 291 H5
Marcoussis (91) 58 D6
Marcoux (04) 259 K5
Marcoux (42) 204 C3
Marcq (08) 42 D1
Marcq (78) 57 K3
Marcq-en-Barœul (59) 6 E3
Marcq-en-Ostrevent (59) 11 K3
Marcy (02) 20 B2
Marcy (58) 132 E5
Marcy (69) 188 B6
Marcy-l'Étoile (69) 205 K2
Marcy-sous-Marle (02) 20 E4
Mardeuil (51) 61 K1
Mardié (45) 110 B4
Mardilly (61) 55 F3
Mardor (52) 116 B4
Mardore (69) 187 H4
Mareau-aux-Bois (45) 110 D1
Mareau-aux-Prés (45) 109 K5
Mareil-en-Champagne (72) 106 A3
Mareil-en-France (95) 59 F1
Mareil-le-Guyon (78) 57 K4
Mareil-Marly (78) 58 C3
Mareil-sur-Loir (72) 106 C6
Mareil-sur-Mauldre (78) 58 A3
Mareilles (52) 92 C6
Marenla (62) 4 D6
Marennes (17) 194 B1
Marennes (69) 206 B4
Mareschés (72) 82 D5

Maresches (59) 12 D2
Maresquel-Ecquemicourt (62). . . 9 H1
Marest (62) 5 H6
Marest-Dampcourt (02) 19 J5
Marest-sur-Matz (60) 38 D1
Marestaing (32) 287 H1
Marestmontiers (80) 18 D4
Maresville (62) 4 B5
les Marêts (77) 60 D6
Maretz (59) 12 C6
Mareugheol (63) 202 E6
Mareuil (16) 196 B2
Mareuil (24) 197 G6
Mareuil-Caubert (80) 9 G5
Mareuil-en-Brie (51) 61 H2
Mareuil-en-Dôle (02) 40 A4
Mareuil-la-Motte (60) 19 F6
Mareuil-le-Port (51) 40 C6
Mareuil-lès-Meaux (77) 59 K2
Mareuil-sur-Arnon (18) 148 E5
Mareuil-sur-Ay (51) 62 A1
Mareuil-sur-Cher (41) 128 E6
Mareuil-sur-Lay-Dissais (85) . . . 159 K3
Mareuil-sur-Ourcq (60) 39 G6
Marey (88) 117 J1
Marey-lès-Fussey (21) 154 A2
Marey-sur-Tille (21) 136 A2
Marfaux (51) 40 D5
Marfontaine (02) 20 E3
Margaux (33) 211 G5
Margencel (74) 174 E5
Margency (95) 58 E2
Margerides (19) 201 G6
Margerie-Chantagret (42) 204 D5
Margerie-Hancourt (51) 91 F1
Margès (26) 222 D4
Margival (02) 39 K2
le Margnès (81) 271 J6
Margny (08) 23 J5
Margny (51) 61 G2
Margny-aux-Cerises (60) 19 G5
Margny-lès-Compiègne (60) . . . 38 D2
Margny-sur-Matz (60) 38 D1
Margon (28) 84 A4
Margon (34) 292 B2
Margouët-Meymes (32) 266 D3
Margueray (50) 31 G6
Marguerittes (30) 275 H3
Margueron (33) 231 F3
Marguestau (32) 266 B2
Margut (08) 23 J5
Mariac (07) 239 H1
Maricourt (80) 19 F1
Marie (06) 261 J5
Marieulles (57) 65 K1
Marieux (80) 10 B5
Marigna-sur-Valouse (39) 173 G4
Marignac (17) 195 H5
Marignac (31) 305 J3
Marignac (82) 268 B3
Marignac-en-Diois (26) 241 G2
Marignac-Lasclares (31) 287 J4
Marignac-Laspeyres (31) 287 G5
Marignana (2A) 316 E5
Marignane (13) 296 A2
Marigné (49) 105 G6
Marigné-Laillé (72) 107 F5
Marigné-Peuton (53) 104 E4
Marignier (74) 191 J3
Marignieu (01) 207 K1
Marigny (03) 168 D3
Marigny (39) 173 J1
Marigny (50) 31 G3
Marigny (51) 61 J6
Marigny (71) 171 G2
Marigny (79) 178 A2
Marigny-Brizay (86) 163 F1
Marigny-Chémereau (86) 162 D5
Marigny-en-Orxois (02) 60 C1
Marigny-le-Cahouët (21) 134 E3
Marigny-le-Châtel (10) 89 H3
Marigny-l'Église (58) 133 K5
Marigny-lès-Reullée (21) 154 B3
Marigny-les-Usages (45) 110 B3
Marigny-Marmande (37) 145 J4
Marigny-Saint-Marcel (74) 190 E6
Marigny-sur-Yonne (58) 133 H6
Marillac-le-Franc (16) 197 G2
le Marillais (49) 124 B4
Marillet (85) 161 F3
Marimbault (33) 246 C2
Marimont-lès-Bénestroff (57) . . 67 G2
Marin (74) 175 F5
Marines (95) 37 G5
Maringes (42) 205 F3
Maringues (63) 185 H6
Mariol (03) 185 K5
Marions (33) 246 E2
Marizy (71) 171 F3
Marizy-Saint-Mard (02) 39 H5
Marizy-Sainte-Geneviève (02) . . 39 H5
Marle (02) 20 E4
Marlemont (08) 22 A3
Marlenheim (67) 70 D4
Marlens (74) 209 F1
Marlers (80) 17 G3
Marles-en-Brie (77) 59 K5
Marles-les-Mines (62) 5 J6
Marles-sur-Canche (62) 4 C5
Marlhes (42) 221 H2
Marliac (31) 288 C5
Marliens (21) 154 D1

Marlieux (01) 188 E4
Marlioz (74) 190 E4
Marly (57) 45 F6
Marly (59) 12 D2
Marly-Gomont (02) 20 E2
Marly-la-Ville (95) 38 B6
Marly-le-Roi (78) 58 C3
Marly-sous-Issy (71) 170 A1
Marly-sur-Arroux (71) 170 A3
Marmagne (18) 149 F3
Marmagne (21) 134 D1
Marmagne (71) 153 F6
Marmande (47) 230 E6
Marmanhac (15) 217 H6
Marmeaux (89) 134 B2
Marminiac (46) 233 F4
Marmont-Pachas (47) 248 B6
Marmouillé (61) 54 E5
Marmoutier (67) 70 B2
Marnac (24) 232 D2
Marnand (69) 187 H4
Marnans (38) 223 F2
Marnaves (81) 250 E6
Marnay (70) 137 H5
Marnay (71) 172 A1
Marnay (86) 163 F5
Marnay-sur-Marne (52) 116 C2
Marnay-sur-Seine (10) 89 F2
Marnaz (74) 191 K3
la Marne (44) 141 G3
Marnefer (61) 55 H3
Marnes (79) 144 D5
Marnes-la-Coquette (92) 58 C4
Marnézia (39) 173 H3
Marnhagues-et-Latour (12) 272 D3
Marnoz (39) 156 A3
Maroeuil (62) 10 C2
Maroilles (59) 13 F4
la Marolle-en-Sologne (41) 129 J2
Marolles (14) 34 B5
Marolles (41) 128 E1
Marolles (51) 63 F5
Marolles (60) 39 G5
Marolles-en-Beauce (91) 86 D4
Marolles-en-Brie (77) 60 C4
Marolles-en-Brie (94) 59 G5
Marolles-en-Hurepoix (91) 86 E4
Marolles-lès-Bailly (10) 90 D6
Marolles-les-Braults (72) 83 F5
Marolles-les-Buis (28) 84 B4
Marolles-lès-Saint-Calais (72) . . 107 K2
Marolles-sous-Lignières (10) . . . 113 K3
Marolles-sur-Seine (77) 88 B4
Marollette (72) 83 F4
Marols (42) 204 C6
Maromme (76) 35 H1
Mâron (36) 148 B6
Maron (54) 65 K5
Maroncourt (88) 94 A5
Marpaps (40) 264 E6
Marpent (59) 13 J2
Marpiré (35) 79 K4
Marquaix (80) 19 H1
Marquay (24) 232 E1
Marquay (62) 10 B1
Marquefave (31) 287 K4
Marquéglise (60) 38 D1
Marquein (11) 288 E4
Marquerie (65) 285 J5
Marques (76) 17 F3
Marquette-en-Ostrevant (59) . . . 11 K3
Marquette-lez-Lille (59) 6 D3
Marquigny (08) 22 D6
Marquillies (59) 6 C5
Marquion (62) 11 H4
Marquise (62) 2 B4
Marquivillers (80) 18 E5
Marquixanes (66) 314 C3
Marray (37) 127 J2
la Marre (39) 173 H1
Marre (55) 43 G4
Mars (07) 221 G5
les Mars (23) 183 K5
Mars (30) 273 J1
Mars (42) 187 G3
Mars-la-Tour (54) 44 C5
Mars-sous-Bourcq (08) 42 A2
Mars-sur-Allier (58) 150 D6
Marsa (11) 308 E5
Marsac (16) 196 D2
Marsac (23) 182 A4
Marsac (65) 285 H4
Marsac (82) 268 A2
Marsac-en-Livradois (63) 203 K6
Marsac-sur-Don (44) 103 J3
Marsac-sur-l'Isle (24) 213 J5
Marsainvilliers (45) 86 D6
Marsais (17) 177 J3
Marsais-Sainte-Radégonde (85) . 160 D3
Marsal (57) 66 E3
Marsal (81) 271 F2
Marsalès (24) 232 C4
Marsan (32) 267 K5
Marsaneix (24) 214 B5
Marsangis (51) 89 J1
Marsangy (89) 112 D1
Marsannay-la-Côte (21) 136 A6
Marsannay-le-Bois (21) 136 A4
Marsanne (26) 240 C4
Marsas (33) 211 K5
Marsas (65) 304 E2
Marsat (63) 202 D3

Marsaz (26) 222 C4
Marseillan (32) 286 D4
Marseillan (34) 292 D4
Marseillan (65) 285 J4
Marseille (13) 296 C4
Marseille-en-Beauvaisis (60) . . . 17 H6
Marseilles-lès-Aubigny (18) . . . 150 C3
Marseillette (11) 290 C5
Marsillargues (34) 275 F5
Marsilly (17) 176 D1
Marsilly (57) 45 G5
Marsolan (32) 267 H2
Marson (51) 62 E2
Marson-sur-Barboure (55) 64 D5
Marsonnas (01) 172 B6
Marsoulas (31) 306 C1
Marssac-sur-Tarn (81) 270 C2
Martagny (27) 36 D2
Martailly-lès-Brancion (71) 171 J3
Martainneville (80) 9 F6
Martainville (14) 53 K2
Martainville (27) 34 B3
Martainville-Épreville (76) 35 K1
Martaizé (86) 144 D5
Martel (46) 233 K1
Marthemont (54) 93 K1
Marthille (57) 66 D2
Marthod (73) 209 G2
Marthon (16) 197 G4
Martiel (12) 250 E2
Martigna (39) 173 H5
Martignargues (30) 255 H6
Martignas-sur-Jalle (33) 229 F2
Martignat (01) 190 A2
Martigné-Briand (49) 125 H6
Martigné-Ferchaud (35) 103 K2
Martigné-sur-Mayenne (53) . . . 81 H5
Martigny (02) 21 H2
Martigny (50) 52 D5
Martigny (76) 16 A2
Martigny-Courpierre (02) 40 B1
Martigny-le-Comte (71) 170 E4
Martigny-les-Bains (88) 117 H1
Martigny-les-Gerbonvaux (88) . . 93 H2
Martigny-sur-l'Ante (14) 53 K2
Martigues (13) 295 J5
Martillac (33) 229 H3
Martin-Église (76) 16 A2
Martincourt (54) 65 J3
Martincourt (60) 37 F1
Martincourt-sur-Meuse (55) . . . 23 H6
le Martinet (30) 255 G4
Martinet (85) 159 F1
Martinpuich (62) 10 E6
Martinvast (50) 28 C3
Martinvelle (88) 117 K2
Martisserre (31) 287 F3
Martizay (36) 146 D6
Martot (27) 35 H4
Martragny (14) 32 C4
la Martre (83) 279 K3
Martres (33) 230 B4
les Martres-d'Artière (63) 203 F1
Martres-de-Rivière (31) 305 J1
les Martres-de-Veyre (63) 202 E3
Martres-sur-Morge (63) 185 G6
Martres-Tolosane (31) 287 H6
Martrin (12) 271 J2
Martrois (21) 135 F5
la Martyre (29) 46 D6
les Martys (11) 290 A4
Maruéjols-lès-Gardon (30) 274 E1
Marval (87) 198 A4
Marvaux-Vieux (08) 42 B3
Marvejols (48) 237 G6
Marvelise (25) 139 F2
Marville-Moutiers-Brûlé (28) . . . 57 F6
Mary (71) 171 F3
Mary-sur-Marne (77) 60 B1
Marzan (56) 121 K2
Marzens (81) 270 B6
Marzy (58) 150 D4
le Mas (06) 280 C2
Mas-Blanc-des-Alpilles (13) . . . 276 B4
Mas-Cabardès (11) 290 B3
le Mas-d'Agenais (47) 247 H2
le Mas-d'Artige (23) 200 E2
Mas-d'Auvignon (32) 267 H2
le Mas-d'Azil (09) 307 F1
Mas-de-Londres (34) 274 A4
le Mas-de-Tence (43) 221 H2
Mas-des-Cours (11) 309 G1
Mas-d'Orcières (48) 254 D1
Mas-Grenier (82) 268 E3
Mas-Saint-Chély (48) 253 K3
Mas-Saintes-Puelles (11) 289 G4
Masbaraud-Mérignat (23) 182 C5
Mascaràs-Haron (64) 284 E1
Mascaras (32) 285 K1
Mascaras (65) 285 J5
Mascarville (31) 289 C1
Masclat (46) 233 H2
Masevaux (68) 119 A4
Maslacq (64) 283 K2
Masléon (87) 199 J2
Maslives (41) 129 G2
le Masnau-Massuguiès (81) . . . 271 H4
Masnières (59) 11 J5
Masny (59) 11 J2
Masparraute (64) 283 F3
Maspie-Lalonquère-Juillacq (64) . . . 285 F2

378

Masquières (47) . . . 249 F2
Massabrac (31) . . . 288 B5
Massac (11) . . . 309 J3
Massac (17) . . . 178 C6
Massac-Séran (81) . . . 270 B6
Massaguel (81) . . . 289 K2
Massais (79) . . . 144 A3
Massals (81) . . . 271 H3
Massanes (30) . . . 274 E1
Massangis (89) . . . 134 A2
Massat (09) . . . 307 F4
Massay (18) . . . 148 C2
le Massegros (48) . . . 253 H6
Masseilles (33) . . . 246 E2
Massels (47) . . . 248 D3
Massérac (44) . . . 102 A4
Masseret (19) . . . 199 H5
Masseube (32) . . . 286 C3
Massiac (15) . . . 219 F3
Massieu (38) . . . 207 J6
Massieux (01) . . . 188 C6
Massiges (51) . . . 42 C5
Massignac (16) . . . 197 K2
Massignieu-de-Rives (01) . . . 207 K2
Massillargues-Attuech (30) . . . 274 D1
Massilly (71) . . . 171 H4
Massingy (21) . . . 115 G4
Massingy (74) . . . 190 D6
Massingy-lès-Semur (21) . . . 134 E3
Massingy-lès-Vitteaux (21) . . . 135 G4
Massognes (86) . . . 162 C1
Massoins (06) . . . 281 F1
Massongy (74) . . . 174 E6
Massoulès (47) . . . 248 D3
Massugas (33) . . . 230 D3
Massy (71) . . . 171 G4
Massy (76) . . . 16 C4
Massy (91) . . . 58 D5
Mastaing (59) . . . 11 K2
Matafelon-Granges (01) . . . 189 K1
les Matelles (34) . . . 274 B5
Matemale (66) . . . 313 H6
Matha (17) . . . 178 B6
Mathaux (10) . . . 90 E4
Mathay (25) . . . 139 H3
Mathenay (39) . . . 155 H4
les Mathes (17) . . . 194 B2
Mathieu (14) . . . 32 E4
Mathons (52) . . . 92 A3
Mathonville (76) . . . 16 C5
Matignicourt-Goncourt (51) . . . 63 G5
Matignon (22) . . . 50 A3
Matigny (80) . . . 19 H3
Matougues (51) . . . 62 C1
Matour (71) . . . 187 J1
Matra (2B) . . . 319 H6
Matringhem (62) . . . 5 F5
Mattaincourt (88) . . . 94 A4
Mattexey (54) . . . 94 D2
Matton-et-Clémency (08) . . . 23 H4
Matzenheim (67) . . . 70 E5
Maubec (38) . . . 207 H4
Maubec (82) . . . 268 B4
Maubec (84) . . . 276 E3
Maubert-Fontaine (08) . . . 22 A2
Maubeuge (59) . . . 13 H3
Maubourguet (65) . . . 285 H2
Mauchamps (91) . . . 86 D2
Maucomble (76) . . . 16 C4
Maucor (64) . . . 284 D1
Maucourt (60) . . . 19 H5
Maucourt (80) . . . 19 F3
Maucourt-sur-Orne (55) . . . 26 A4
Maudétour-en-Vexin (95) . . . 36 E6
Mauguio (34) . . . 274 D6
Maulan (55) . . . 64 B5
Maulay (86) . . . 145 F4
Maulde (59) . . . 7 H6
Maule (78) . . . 57 H3
Mauléon (79) . . . 143 G4
Mauléon-Barousse (65) . . . 305 H3
Mauléon-d'Armagnac (32) . . . 266 A2
Mauléon-Licharre (64) . . . 283 H5
Maulers (60) . . . 17 K6
Maulette (78) . . . 57 H4
Maulévrier (49) . . . 143 G3
Maulévrier-Sainte-Gertrude (76) . . . 15 G6
Maulichères (32) . . . 266 B5
Maumusson (44) . . . 124 B3
Maumusson (82) . . . 268 B2
Maumusson-Laguian (32) . . . 266 B6
Mauny (76) . . . 35 F2
Maupas (10) . . . 114 A1
Maupas (32) . . . 266 A3
Mauperthuis (77) . . . 60 B4
Maupertuis (50) . . . 31 G5
Maupertus-sur-Mer (50) . . . 28 E2
Mauprévoir (86) . . . 179 K3
Mauquenchy (76) . . . 16 D5
Mauran (31) . . . 287 H6
Maure (64) . . . 285 G3
Maure-de-Bretagne (35) . . . 102 D1
Maurecourt (78) . . . 58 B2
Mauregard (77) . . . 59 G1
Mauregny-en-Haye (02) . . . 20 D4
Maureilhan (34) . . . 291 K4
Maureillas-las-Illas (66) . . . 315 G4
Mauremont (31) . . . 288 E2
Maurens (24) . . . 231 H1
Maurens (31) . . . 289 F2
Maurens (32) . . . 268 B6
Maurens-Scopont (81) . . . 289 F1

Maurepas (78) . . . 58 A5
Maurepas (80) . . . 11 F6
Mauressac (31) . . . 288 B4
Mauressargues (30) . . . 274 E2
Maureville (31) . . . 288 E2
Mauriac (15) . . . 217 G3
Mauriac (33) . . . 230 C3
Mauries (40) . . . 265 J6
Maurines (15) . . . 236 E2
Maurois (59) . . . 12 C5
Mauron (56) . . . 78 A4
Mauroux (32) . . . 268 A2
Mauroux (46) . . . 249 F1
Maurrin (40) . . . 265 J3
Maurs (15) . . . 235 F4
Maurupt-le-Montois (51) . . . 63 H4
Maury (66) . . . 309 J5
Mausoléo (2B) . . . 318 D3
Maussac (19) . . . 200 D6
Maussane-les-Alpilles (13) . . . 276 B4
Maussans (70) . . . 138 C3
Mautes (23) . . . 183 J6
Mauvages (55) . . . 64 E6
Mauvaisin (31) . . . 288 C4
Mauves (07) . . . 222 B5
Mauves-sur-Huisne (61) . . . 83 J3
Mauves-sur-Loire (44) . . . 123 J3
Mauvezin (31) . . . 287 G2
Mauvezin (32) . . . 268 B5
Mauvezin (65) . . . 304 E1
Mauvezin-d'Armagnac (40) . . . 266 A2
Mauvezin-de-Prat (09) . . . 306 C2
Mauvezin-de-Sainte-Croix (09) . . . 306 E1
Mauvières (36) . . . 164 C3
Mauvilly (21) . . . 115 G6
Maux (58) . . . 152 A3
Mauzac (31) . . . 288 A3
Mauzac-et-Grand-Castang (24) . . . 232 B2
Mauzé-sur-le-Mignon (79) . . . 177 J2
Mauzé-Thouarsais (79) . . . 144 A4
Mauzens-et-Miremont (24) . . . 214 C6
Mauzun (63) . . . 203 G3
Maves (41) . . . 109 F6
Mavilly-Mandelot (21) . . . 153 K3
la Maxe (57) . . . 45 F4
Maxent (35) . . . 78 C6
Maxéville (54) . . . 66 A4
Maxey-sur-Meuse (88) . . . 93 G2
Maxey-sur-Vaise (55) . . . 93 F1
Maxilly-sur-Léman (74) . . . 175 G5
Maxilly-sur-Saône (21) . . . 136 E5
Maxou (46) . . . 233 H6
Maxstadt (57) . . . 68 B3
May-en-Multien (77) . . . 60 A1
le May-sur-Èvre (49) . . . 142 E2
May-sur-Orne (14) . . . 32 E6
Mayac (24) . . . 214 C2
Mayenne (53) . . . 81 G4
Mayet (72) . . . 106 C5
le Mayet-de-Montagne (03) . . . 186 B4
le Mayet-d'École (03) . . . 185 G3
Maylis (40) . . . 264 E5
Maynal (39) . . . 172 E2
les Mayons (83) . . . 298 C3
Mayot (02) . . . 20 B4
Mayrac (46) . . . 233 J1
Mayran (12) . . . 251 K2
Mayrègne (31) . . . 305 H4
Mayres (07) . . . 238 E3
Mayres (63) . . . 220 A1
Mayres-Savel (38) . . . 242 A1
Mayreville (11) . . . 289 F5
Mayrinhac-Lentour (46) . . . 234 B3
Mayronnes (11) . . . 309 H2
Maysel (60) . . . 37 K4
Mazamet (81) . . . 290 B2
Mazan (84) . . . 257 H6
Mazan-l'Abbaye (07) . . . 238 E3
Mazangé (41) . . . 108 B3
Mazaugues (83) . . . 297 J3
Mazaye (63) . . . 202 B2
Mazé (49) . . . 125 K3
le Mazeau (85) . . . 161 F6
Mazeirat (23) . . . 182 E3
Mazeley (88) . . . 94 C5
Mazerat-Aurouze (43) . . . 219 J4
Mazeray (17) . . . 177 K6
Mazères (09) . . . 288 E5
Mazères (33) . . . 230 A6
Mazères-de-Neste (65) . . . 305 H1
Mazères-Lezons (64) . . . 284 C4
Mazères-sur-Salat (31) . . . 287 G6
Mazerier (03) . . . 185 G3
Mazerny (08) . . . 22 C5
Mazerolles (16) . . . 197 H2
Mazerolles (17) . . . 195 G4
Mazerolles (40) . . . 265 H2
Mazerolles (64) . . . 284 C2
Mazerolles (65) . . . 285 K3
Mazerolles (86) . . . 163 J5
Mazerolles-du-Razès (11) . . . 308 D1
Mazerolles-le-Salin (25) . . . 137 J6
Mazerulles (54) . . . 66 C4
Mazet-Saint-Voy (43) . . . 221 F5
Mazeuil (86) . . . 144 E6
Mazeyrat-d'Allier (43) . . . 219 J4
Mazeyrolles (24) . . . 232 D4
la Mazière-aux-Bons-
   Hommes (23) . . . 183 J6
Mazières (16) . . . 197 J1
Mazières-de-Touraine (37) . . . 127 F4
Mazières-en-Gâtine (79) . . . 161 J4

Mazières-en-Mauges (49) . . . 143 F3
Mazières-Naresse (47) . . . 232 A4
Mazières-sur-Béronne (79) . . . 178 D2
Mazille (71) . . . 171 G5
Mazingarbe (62) . . . 6 A6
Mazinghem (62) . . . 5 H4
Mazinghien (59) . . . 12 E5
Mazion (33) . . . 211 G3
Mazirat (03) . . . 183 K2
Mazirot (88) . . . 94 A5
le Mazis (80) . . . 17 G2
Mazoires (63) . . . 218 D1
Mazouau (65) . . . 305 F2
Mazuby (11) . . . 308 C5
les Mazures (08) . . . 22 C2
Mazzola (2B) . . . 319 H6
Méailles (04) . . . 260 D6
Méallet (15) . . . 217 H3
Méasnes (23) . . . 165 K5
Meaucé (28) . . . 84 B2
Méaudre (38) . . . 223 J4
la Meauffe (50) . . . 31 H2
la Méaugon (22) . . . 49 F6
Meaulne (03) . . . 167 H3
Méaulte (80) . . . 18 E1
Méautis (50) . . . 31 F1
Meaux (77) . . . 59 K2
Meaux-la-Montagne (69) . . . 187 J4
Meauzac (82) . . . 249 H6
Mecé (35) . . . 79 K3
Mechmont (46) . . . 233 H5
Mécleuves (57) . . . 45 G6
Mecquignies (59) . . . 13 F3
Mécrin (55) . . . 64 E3
Mécringes (51) . . . 61 F2
Médan (78) . . . 58 B2
Médavy (61) . . . 54 D5
Medeyrolles (63) . . . 220 B1
Médière (25) . . . 139 F3
Médillac (16) . . . 212 D3
Médis (17) . . . 194 D3
Médonville (88) . . . 93 G5
Médréac (35) . . . 78 C2
le Mée (28) . . . 109 F3
Mée (53) . . . 104 D5
le Mée-sur-Seine (77) . . . 87 H2
les Mées (04) . . . 259 G6
Mées (40) . . . 264 A4
les Mées (72) . . . 82 E4
Mégange (57) . . . 27 K6
Megève (74) . . . 192 A6
Mégevette (74) . . . 191 J1
Mégrit (22) . . . 50 B6
Méharicourt (80) . . . 18 E3
Méharin (64) . . . 282 E3
Méhers (41) . . . 129 F5
Méhoncourt (54) . . . 94 C1
Méhoudin (61) . . . 81 J2
Mehun-sur-Yèvre (18) . . . 148 C2
la Meignanne (49) . . . 125 F3
Meigné (49) . . . 125 K6
Meigné-le-Vicomte (49) . . . 126 D3
Meigneux (77) . . . 88 B2
Meigneux (80) . . . 17 H3
Meilars (29) . . . 73 D3
Meilhac (87) . . . 198 E3
Meilhan (32) . . . 286 C4
Meilhan (40) . . . 264 E2
Meilhan-sur-Garonne (47) . . . 230 D6
Meilhards (19) . . . 199 J5
Meilhaud (63) . . . 202 E5
Meillac (35) . . . 51 F6
Meillant (18) . . . 167 G1
le Meillard (80) . . . 9 K4
la Meilleraie-Tillay (85) . . . 160 D1
Meilleray (77) . . . 60 E4
la Meilleraye-de-Bretagne (44) . . . 103 J5
Meillerie (74) . . . 175 H4
Meillers (03) . . . 168 C4
Meillon (64) . . . 284 D4
Meillonnas (01) . . . 189 H1
Meilly-sur-Rouvres (21) . . . 153 H1
Meisenthal (57) . . . 69 G4
Meistratzheim (67) . . . 70 D5
le Meix (21) . . . 135 K2
le Meix-Saint-Epoing (51) . . . 61 G5
le Meix-Tiercelin (51) . . . 62 E6
Méjannes-le-Clap (30) . . . 255 K4
Méjannes-lès-Alès (30) . . . 255 H6
Mela (2A) . . . 323 F2
Mélagues (12) . . . 272 D5
Mélamare (76) . . . 14 D6
Melay (49) . . . 143 G1
Melay (52) . . . 117 H3
Melay (71) . . . 186 E2
le Mêle-sur-Sarthe (61) . . . 83 F2
Mélecey (70) . . . 138 C3
Melesse (35) . . . 79 G2
Melgven (29) . . . 99 F2
Mélicocq (60) . . . 38 E1
Mélicourt (27) . . . 55 H2
Méligny-le-Grand (55) . . . 64 E5
Méligny-le-Petit (55) . . . 64 D5
Melin (70) . . . 117 H5
Melincourt (70) . . . 118 A3
Mélisey (70) . . . 119 F5
Mélisey (89) . . . 114 D1
Meljac (12) . . . 252 A5
Mellac (29) . . . 99 H3
Mellé (35) . . . 80 B2
Melle (79) . . . 178 D2

Mellecey (71) . . . 153 K6
Melleran (79) . . . 178 E3
Melleray (72) . . . 107 K1
Melleroy (45) . . . 112 A4
Melles (31) . . . 305 K4
Melleville (76) . . . 16 D1
Mellionnec (22) . . . 76 B4
Mello (60) . . . 37 K4
Méon (49) . . . 126 D3
Méolans-Revel (04) . . . 260 B1
Méobecq (36) . . . 165 F1
Meloisey (21) . . . 153 K3
Melrand (56) . . . 100 C1
Melsheim (67) . . . 70 D1
Melun (77) . . . 87 H2
Melz-sur-Seine (77) . . . 88 E2
Membrey (70) . . . 137 H1
la Membrolle-sur-Choisille (37) . . . 127 H4
la Membrolle-sur-Longuenée (49) . . . 125 F2
Membrolles (41) . . . 109 G3
Méménil (88) . . . 94 C5
le Mémont (25) . . . 157 J1
Menades (89) . . . 133 J4
Ménarmont (88) . . . 95 F2
Menars (41) . . . 129 F1
Menat (63) . . . 184 D4
Menaucourt (55) . . . 64 C5
Mencas (62) . . . 5 F5
Menchhoffen (67) . . . 69 H5
Mende (48) . . . 237 J6
Mendionde (64) . . . 282 D3
Menditte (64) . . . 283 H5
Mendive (64) . . . 282 E6
Ménéac (56) . . . 77 J5
Ménerbes (84) . . . 277 F3
Ménerval (76) . . . 16 E6
Ménerville (78) . . . 57 H2
Menesble (21) . . . 115 J5
Méneslies (80) . . . 8 D5
Ménesplet (24) . . . 212 E5
Ménesqueville (27) . . . 36 A3
Ménessaire (21) . . . 152 D2
Menestreau (58) . . . 132 D4
Ménestreau-en-Villette (45) . . . 130 B1
Menet (15) . . . 217 J2
Menetou-Couture (18) . . . 150 B3
Menetou-Râtel (18) . . . 131 J5
Menetou-Salon (18) . . . 149 H1
Menetou-sur-Nahon (36) . . . 147 K1
Ménétréol-sous-Sancerre (18) . . . 131 K5
Ménétréol-sur-Sauldre (18) . . . 130 E4
Ménétréols-sous-Vatan (36) . . . 148 B4
Ménétreuil (71) . . . 172 C3
Ménétreux-le-Pitois (21) . . . 134 E2
Ménétrol (63) . . . 202 D1
Menetru-le-Vignoble (39) . . . 155 H6
Menetrux-en-Joux (39) . . . 173 J2
Ménévillers (60) . . . 38 C1
Menglon (26) . . . 241 J4
Ménigoute (79) . . . 162 B4
Ménil (53) . . . 105 F5
le Ménil (88) . . . 119 G3
Ménil-Annelles (08) . . . 41 J2
Ménil-aux-Bois (55) . . . 64 D4
le Ménil-Bérard (61) . . . 55 H5
le Ménil-Broût (61) . . . 82 E2
le Ménil-Ciboult (61) . . . 53 F4
le Ménil-de-Briouze (61) . . . 53 J5
Ménil-de-Senones (88) . . . 95 J3
Ménil-en-Xaintois (88) . . . 93 J4
Ménil-Erreux (61) . . . 82 E2
Ménil-Froger (61) . . . 55 F5
Ménil-Gondouin (61) . . . 53 K4
le Ménil-Guyon (61) . . . 83 F1
Ménil-Hermei (61) . . . 53 K3
Ménil-Hubert-en-Exmes (61) . . . 54 E4
Ménil-Hubert-sur-Orne (61) . . . 53 J3
Ménil-Jean (61) . . . 54 A5
Ménil-la-Horgne (55) . . . 64 E5
Ménil-la-Tour (54) . . . 65 H4
Ménil-Lépinois (08) . . . 41 H2
le Ménil-Scelleur (61) . . . 54 B6
Ménil-sur-Belvitte (88) . . . 95 F3
Ménil-sur-Saulx (55) . . . 64 B6
le Ménil-Vicomte (61) . . . 55 F5
le Ménil-Vin (61) . . . 53 K3
Ménilles (27) . . . 57 F1
la Ménitré (49) . . . 125 K3
Mennecy (91) . . . 87 F1
Mennessis (02) . . . 19 K4
Mennetou-sur-Cher (41) . . . 129 K6
Menneval (27) . . . 34 D2
Menneville (02) . . . 40 E2
Menneville (62) . . . 2 D6
Mennevret (02) . . . 12 D6
Mennouveaux (52) . . . 116 D1
Ménoire (19) . . . 216 B5
Menomblet (85) . . . 160 E1
Menoncourt (90) . . . 119 J6
Menotey (39) . . . 155 G1
Menou (58) . . . 132 D5
Menoux (70) . . . 118 A4
Mens (38) . . . 242 B2
Mensignac (24) . . . 213 J3
Menskirch (57) . . . 27 K4
Menthon-Saint-Bernard (74) . . . 191 G6
Menthonnex-en-Bornes (74) . . . 191 F3
Menthonnex-sous-Clermont (74) . . . 190 D5
Mentières (15) . . . 218 E5

Menton (06) . . . 281 K3
Mentque-Nortbécourt (62) . . . 2 E4
Menucourt (95) . . . 58 B1
les Menus (61) . . . 84 B2
Menville (31) . . . 268 D3
Méolans-Revel (04) . . . 260 B1
Méon (49) . . . 126 D3
Méounes-lès-Montrieux (83) . . . 297 J4
Mer (41) . . . 129 G1
Méracq (64) . . . 284 C1
Méral (53) . . . 104 C3
Méras (09) . . . 288 A6
Mercatel (62) . . . 11 F3
Mercenac (09) . . . 306 C2
Merceuil (21) . . . 154 A3
Mercey (27) . . . 36 A6
Mercey-le-Grand (25) . . . 137 H6
Mercey-sur-Saône (70) . . . 137 G2
Mercin-et-Vaux (02) . . . 39 J3
Merck-Saint-Liévin (62) . . . 5 F4
Merckeghem (59) . . . 3 G3
Mercœur (19) . . . 216 C6
Mercœur (43) . . . 219 G3
Mercuer (07) . . . 239 H5
Mercuès (46) . . . 249 K1
Mercurey (71) . . . 153 K5
Mercurol (26) . . . 222 C5
Mercury (73) . . . 209 F2
Mercus-Garrabet (09) . . . 307 J4
Mercy (03) . . . 169 G5
Mercy (89) . . . 113 G2
Mercy-le-Bas (54) . . . 26 D4
Mercy-le-Haut (54) . . . 26 D4
Merdrignac (22) . . . 77 K4
Méré (78) . . . 57 K4
Méré (89) . . . 113 J4
Méreau (18) . . . 148 D2
Méréaucourt (80) . . . 17 H4
Méréglise (28) . . . 84 D5
Mérélessart (80) . . . 17 G1
Mérens (32) . . . 267 H4
Mérens-les-Vals (09) . . . 313 H2
Mérenvielle (31) . . . 268 D6
Méreuil (05) . . . 258 D2
Méréville (54) . . . 66 A6
Méréville (91) . . . 86 C4
Merey (27) . . . 57 F2
Mérey-sous-Montrond (25) . . . 156 C1
Mérey-Vieilley (25) . . . 138 A5
Merfy (51) . . . 40 E3
Mergey (10) . . . 90 A3
Meria (2B) . . . 317 D2
Mérial (11) . . . 308 C5
Méricourt (62) . . . 11 F1
Méricourt (78) . . . 57 H1
Méricourt-en-Vimeu (80) . . . 17 H2
Méricourt-l'Abbé (80) . . . 18 D1
Méricourt-sur-Somme (80) . . . 18 E2
Mériel (95) . . . 37 J6
Mérifons (34) . . . 273 F6
Mérignac (16) . . . 196 B3
Mérignac (17) . . . 212 A2
Mérignac (33) . . . 229 G2
Mérignas (33) . . . 230 C3
Mérignat (01) . . . 189 J3
Mérignies (59) . . . 6 E6
Mérigny (36) . . . 164 B3
Mérigon (09) . . . 306 E1
Mérilheu (65) . . . 304 D1
Mérillac (22) . . . 77 K3
Mérinchal (23) . . . 183 K6
Mérindol (84) . . . 277 F4
Mérindol-les-Oliviers (26) . . . 257 H3
Mérinville (45) . . . 112 A2
le Mériot (10) . . . 88 E2
Méritein (64) . . . 283 J3
Merkwiller-Pechelbronn (67) . . . 25 B2
Merlas (38) . . . 207 J5
la Merlatière (85) . . . 142 A6
Merlaut (51) . . . 63 G4
Merle-Leignec (42) . . . 220 D1
Merléac (22) . . . 76 E3
le Merlerault (61) . . . 55 F5
Merles (82) . . . 249 F6
Merles-sur-Loison (55) . . . 26 A4
Merlevenez (56) . . . 100 B4
Merlieux-et-Fouquerolles (02) . . . 40 A1
Merlimont (62) . . . 4 A6
Merlines (19) . . . 201 H4
Mernel (56) . . . 102 D1
Mérobert (91) . . . 86 B3
Mérona (39) . . . 173 G3
Mérouville (28) . . . 86 A5
Meroux (90) . . . 139 J1
Merpins (16) . . . 195 J3
Merrey (52) . . . 117 F1
Merrey-sur-Arce (10) . . . 114 E1
Merri (61) . . . 54 C3
Merris (59) . . . 6 A3
Merry-la-Vallée (89) . . . 112 D5
Merry-Sec (89) . . . 133 F1
Merry-sur-Yonne (89) . . . 133 G2
Mers-les-Bains (80) . . . 8 C5
Mers-sur-Indre (36) . . . 166 A2
Merschweiller (57) . . . 27 J3
Mersuay (70) . . . 118 A5
Merten (57) . . . 45 K3
Mertrud (52) . . . 91 J3
Mertzen (68) . . . 97 A4
Mertzwiller (67) . . . 69 K5
Méru (60) . . . 37 H4

Merval (02) 40 C3
Mervans (71) 154 D6
Mervent (85) 160 E4
Mervilla (31) 288 C2
Merville (31) 269 F5
Merville (59) 3 K6
Merville-Franceville-Plage (14) 33 F3
Merviller (54) 95 G1
Merxheim (68) 96 B6
Méry (73) 208 B3
Méry-Corbon (14) 33 G5
Méry-ès-Bois (18) 130 E6
Méry-la-Bataille (60) 18 D6
Méry-Prémecy (51) 40 D4
Méry-sur-Cher (18) 148 C1
Méry-sur-Marne (77) 60 C2
Méry-sur-Oise (95) 58 D1
Méry-sur-Seine (10) 89 J2
le Merzer (22) 48 D5
Mésandans (25) 138 D3
Mésanger (44) 124 A3
Mésangueville (76) 16 E6
Mesbrecourt-Richecourt (02) 20 C4
Meschers-sur-Gironde (17) 194 D4
Mescoules (24) 231 H3
le Mesge (80) 17 J1
Mesgrigny (10) 89 J2
Mésigny (74) 190 E4
Meslan (56) 75 K6
Mesland (41) 128 C3
Meslay (14) 53 J2
Meslay (41) 108 C5
Meslay-du-Maine (53) 105 G3
Meslay-le-Grenet (28) 85 F4
Meslay-le-Vidame (28) 85 G5
Meslières (25) 139 J3
Meslin (22) 77 H1
Mesmay (25) 156 A2
Mesmont (08) 22 A5
Mesmont (21) 135 H5
Mesnac (16) 195 K2
Mesnard-la-Barotière (85) 142 C5
Mesnay (39) 155 K4
les Mesneux (51) 40 E4
la Mesnière (61) 83 G2
Mesnières-en-Bray (76) 16 C3
le Mesnil (50) 28 C5
le Mesnil-Adelée (50) 52 C5
le Mesnil-Amand (50) 30 E6
le Mesnil-Amelot (77) 59 G1
le Mesnil-Amey (50) 31 G3
le Mesnil-Angot (50) 31 G2
le Mesnil-au-Grain (14) 32 C6
le Mesnil-au-Val (50) 28 D3
le Mesnil-Aubert (50) 30 E5
le Mesnil-Aubry (95) 59 F1
le Mesnil-Auzouf (14) 53 F1
le Mesnil-Bacley (14) 54 D1
le Mesnil-Benoist (14) 31 J6
Mesnil-Bruntel (80) 19 G2
le Mesnil-Caussois (14) 52 D3
le Mesnil-Clinchamps (14) 52 D3
le Mesnil-Conteville (60) 17 J5
Mesnil-Domqueur (80) 9 J4
le Mesnil-Durand (14) 54 D1
le Mesnil-Durdent (76) 15 G3
Mesnil-en-Arrouaise (80) 11 G6
le Mesnil-en-Thelle (60) 37 J5
le Mesnil-en-Vallée (49) 124 C4
le Mesnil-Esnard (76) 35 J2
le Mesnil-Eudes (14) 33 K6
le Mesnil-Eury (50) 31 G3
Mesnil-Follemprise (76) 16 B3
le Mesnil-Fuguet (27) 35 H6
le Mesnil-Garnier (50) 31 F6
le Mesnil-Germain (14) 54 E1
le Mesnil-Gilbert (50) 52 C5
le Mesnil-Guillaume (14) 34 A6
le Mesnil-Hardray (27) 56 B2
le Mesnil-Herman (50) 31 G4
le Mesnil-Jourdain (27) 35 H5
Mesnil-la-Comtesse (10) 90 C2
le Mesnil-le-Roi (78) 58 C2
Mesnil-Lettre (10) 90 C3
le Mesnil-Lieubray (76) 36 B1
Mesnil-Martinsart (80) 10 D6
le Mesnil-Mauger (14) 33 H6
Mesnil-Mauger (76) 16 D5
le Mesnil-Opac (50) 31 H4
le Mesnil-Ozenne (50) 52 B5
Mesnil-Panneville (76) 15 H6
le Mesnil-Patry (14) 32 C4
le Mesnil-Rainfray (50) 52 C5
Mesnil-Raoul (76) 35 K2
le Mesnil-Raoult (50) 31 H4
le Mesnil-Réaume (76) 16 D1
le Mesnil-Robert (14) 31 J6
le Mesnil-Rogues (50) 30 E6
Mesnil-Rousset (27) 55 H3
le Mesnil-Rouxelin (50) 31 H3
le Mesnil-Saint-Denis (78) 58 B5
le Mesnil-Saint-Firmin (60) 18 C5
Mesnil-Saint-Georges (80) 18 D5
Mesnil-Saint-Laurent (02) 20 A3
Mesnil-Saint-Loup (10) 89 H5
Mesnil-Saint-Nicaise (80) 19 G3
Mesnil-Saint-Père (10) 90 D5
Mesnil-Sellières (10) 90 C4
le Mesnil-Simon (14) 33 J6
le Mesnil-Simon (28) 57 G3
le Mesnil-sous-Jumièges (76) 35 F2
Mesnil-sous-Vienne (27) 36 D2

le Mesnil-sur-Blangy (14) 34 A4
le Mesnil-sur-Bulles (60) 37 K1
Mesnil-sur-l'Estrée (27) 56 E4
le Mesnil-sur-Oger (51) 62 A2
le Mesnil-Théribus (60) 37 G4
le Mesnil-Thomas (28) 84 C1
le Mesnil-Tôve (50) 52 C5
le Mesnil-Véneron (50) 31 G2
Mesnil-Verclives (27) 36 B3
le Mesnil-Vigot (50) 31 F3
le Mesnil-Villeman (50) 31 F6
le Mesnil-Villement (14) 53 J3
le Mesnilbus (50) 31 F3
le Mesnillard (50) 52 C6
Mesnois (39) 173 H2
les Mesnuls (78) 57 K5
Mespaul (29) 46 E4
Mesplède (64) 284 A1
Mesples (03) 166 E5
Mespuits (91) 86 D4
Mesquer (44) 121 J3
Messac (17) 212 A1
Messac (35) 102 E2
Messanges (21) 154 A1
Messanges (40) 262 C3
Messas (45) 109 H5
Messé (79) 179 F1
Messei (61) 53 H5
Messein (54) 66 A6
Messeix (63) 201 H4
Messemé (86) 145 F3
Messery (74) 174 D5
Messey-sur-Grosne (71) 171 J2
Messia-sur-Sorne (39) 173 F2
Messigny-et-Vantoux (21) 136 A4
Messimy (69) 205 J3
Messimy-sur-Saône (01) 188 B4
Messincourt (08) 23 H4
Messon (10) 89 K5
Messy (77) 59 H2
Mesterrieux (33) 230 C4
Mestes (19) 201 F5
Mesves-sur-Loire (58) 150 C1
Mesvres (71) 152 C5
Métabief (25) 157 F6
les Métairies (16) 196 B2
Métairies-Saint-Quirin (57) 67 J5
Méteren (59) 6 A3
Méthamis (84) 277 F1
Métigny (80) 17 H1
Metting (57) 69 F6
Mettray (37) 127 J4
Metz (57) 45 H1
Metz-en-Couture (62) 11 H5
Metz-le-Comte (58) 133 G5
Metz-Robert (10) 114 B2
Metz-Tessy (74) 191 F5
Metzeral (68) 119 K1
Metzeresche (57) 27 J5
Metzervisse (57) 27 H5
Metzing (57) 68 C3
Meucon (56) 101 F4
Meudon (92) 58 D4
Meuilley (21) 154 A2
Meulan (78) 58 A2
Meulers (76) 16 B2
Meulles (14) 55 F2
Meulson (21) 115 G2
Meung-sur-Loire (45) 109 J5
Meurcé (72) 82 E5
Meurchin (62) 6 C6
Meurcourt (70) 118 D5
la Meurdraquière (50) 51 K1
Meures (52) 92 A6
Meurival (02) 40 C3
Meursac (17) 194 E3
Meursanges (21) 154 B4
Meursault (21) 153 K4
Meurville (10) 91 G6
Meusnes (41) 129 G6
Meussia (39) 173 H4
Meuvaines (14) 32 C3
Meux (17) 195 J6
le Meux (60) 38 D3
Meuzac (87) 199 G5
Mévoisins (28) 85 H1
Mévouillon (26) 258 B3
Meximieux (01) 189 G6
Mexy (54) 26 D2
Mey (57) 45 H5
Meyenheim (68) 96 C6
Meylan (38) 224 B3
Meymac (19) 200 D5
Meynes (30) 275 J3
Meyrals (24) 232 D1
Meyrannes (30) 255 H3
Meyrargues (13) 277 J5
Meyras (07) 239 G4
Meyreuil (13) 296 D1
Meyrié (38) 207 F4
Meyrieu-les-Étangs (38) 206 E5
Meyrieux-Trouet (73) 208 A3
Meyrignac-l'Église (19) 216 B1
Meyronne (46) 233 J2
Meyronnes (04) 227 C6
Meyrueis (48) 254 C4
Meys (69) 205 G3
Meyssac (19) 215 K5
Meysse (07) 240 A5
Meyssiès (38) 206 D5

Meythet (74) 191 F5
la Meyze (87) 198 E4
Meyzieu (69) 206 C2
Mézangers (53) 81 J6
Mézel (04) 259 J6
Mezel (63) 202 E2
Mézens (81) 269 K4
Mézeray (72) 106 C3
Mézères (43) 220 D4
Mézériat (01) 188 C2
Mézerolles (80) 9 K4
Mézerville (11) 289 F5
Mézidon-Canon (14) 33 G6
la Mézière (35) 79 F3
Mézières-au-Perche (28) 84 E5
Mézières-en-Brenne (36) 147 F6
Mézières-en-Drouais (28) 57 F5
Mézières-en-Gâtinais (45) 111 F2
Mézières-en-Santerre (80) 18 D3
Mézières-en-Vexin (27) 36 B5
Mézières-lez-Cléry (45) 109 K5
Mézières-sous-Lavardin (72) 82 C6
Mézières-sur-Couesnon (35) 79 J2
Mézières-sur-Issoire (87) 180 D3
Mézières-sur-Oise (02) 20 B3
Mézières-sur-Ponthouin (72) 83 F6
Mézières-sur-Seine (78) 57 K2
Mézilhac (07) 239 G2
Mézilles (89) 132 C1
Mézin (47) 247 H5
Méziré (90) 139 J2
Mézos (40) 244 D5
Mézy-Moulins (02) 61 F1
Mézy-sur-Seine (78) 58 A2
Mhère (58) 152 A1
Mialet (24) 198 D5
Mialet (30) 255 F5
Mialos (64) 284 C2
Miannay (80) 9 F5
Michaugues (58) 133 F6
Michelbach (68) 97 A2
Michelbach-le-Bas (68) 97 D4
Michelbach-le-Haut (68) 97 D4
Michery (89) 88 D4
Midrevaux (88) 93 F3
Mièges (39) 156 C6
Miélan (32) 286 A3
Miellin (70) 119 G4
Miermaigne (28) 84 B5
Miers (46) 234 A2
Miéry (39) 155 J6
Mietesheim (67) 69 J5
Mieussy (74) 191 K3
Mieuxcé (61) 82 C3
Migé (89) 133 F1
Migennes (89) 113 F3
Miglos (09) 307 J5
Mignaloux-Beauvoir (86) 163 F4
Mignavillers (70) 138 E1
Migné (36) 164 E2
Migné-Auxances (86) 162 E3
Mignères (45) 111 H2
Mignerette (45) 111 G2
Mignéville (54) 95 G1
Mignières (28) 85 F4
Mignovillard (39) 156 D6
Migny (36) 148 D3
Migré (17) 177 K3
Migron (17) 195 J1
Mijanès (09) 308 D4
Mijoux (01) 174 A5
la Milesse (72) 106 D2
Milhac (46) 233 G3
Milhac-d'Auberoche (24) 214 C4
Milhac-de-Nontron (24) 198 A6
Milhars (81) 250 E5
Milhas (31) 306 A2
Milhaud (30) 275 G4
Milhavet (81) 270 C1
Milizac (29) 72 C3
Millac (86) 180 B2
Millam (59) 3 H3
Millançay (41) 129 J4
Millas (66) 309 K6
Millau (12) 253 G6
Millay (58) 152 C6
Millebosc (76) 16 D1
Millemont (78) 57 J4
Millencourt (80) 10 D6
Millencourt-en-Ponthieu (80) 9 G4
Millery (21) 134 D3
Millery (54) 66 A3
Millery (69) 206 A3
Millevaches (19) 200 D4
Milly (50) 52 C6
Milly-la-Forêt (91) 87 F3
Milly-Lamartine (71) 171 H6
Milly-sur-Bradon (55) 43 G2
Milly-sur-Thérain (60) 37 G1
Milon-la-Chapelle (78) 58 B5
Mimbaste (40) 264 C5
Mimet (13) 296 D2
Mimeure (21) 153 G2
Mimizan (40) 244 C4
Minaucourt-le-Mesnil-
  lès-Hurlus (51) 42 B5
Minerve (34) 291 F4
Mingot (65) 285 J3

Mingoval (62) 10 D2
Miniac-Morvan (35) 50 E5
Miniac-sous-Bécherel (35) 78 E2
le Minihic-sur-Rance (35) 50 D4
Minihy-Tréguier (22) 48 C2
Minorville (54) 65 H3
Minot (21) 135 J1
Minversheim (67) 69 J4
Minzac (24) 212 D6
Minzier (74) 190 E3
Miolles (81) 271 J3
Mionnay (01) 188 D6
Mions (69) 206 B3
Mios (33) 228 D5
Miossens-Lanusse (64) 284 D2
Mirabeau (04) 259 H5
Mirabeau (84) 278 A4
Mirabel (07) 239 J5
Mirabel (82) 249 K5
Mirabel-aux-Baronnies (26) 257 H3
Mirabel-et-Blacons (26) 240 E3
Miradoux (32) 267 K1
Miramas (13) 276 D6
Mirambeau (17) 211 H1
Mirambeau (31) 287 F3
Miramont-d'Astarac (32) 286 B1
Miramont-de-Comminges (31) 305 K1
Miramont-de-Guyenne (47) 231 G5
Miramont-de-Quercy (82) 249 G4
Miramont-Latour (32) 267 J4
Miramont-Sensacq (40) 265 J6
Mirande (32) 286 B1
Mirandol-Bourgnounac (81) 251 H5
Mirannes (32) 267 F6
Miraumont (80) 10 E5
Miraval-Cabardès (11) 290 B3
Mirbel (52) 92 A4
Miré (49) 105 H5
Mirebeau (86) 145 F6
Mirebeau-sur-Bèze (21) 136 D3
Mirebel (39) 173 H1
Mirecourt (88) 94 A4
Mirefleurs (63) 202 E3
Miremont (31) 288 B3
Miremont (63) 184 B6
Mirepeisset (11) 291 G5
Mirepeix (64) 284 E5
Mirepoix (09) 308 B1
Mirepoix (32) 267 J4
Mirepoix-sur-Tarn (31) 269 G4
Mireval (34) 293 G2
Mireval-Lauragais (11) 289 H5
Miribel (01) 206 B1
Miribel (26) 222 E4
Miribel-Lanchâtre (38) 223 K6
Miribel-les-Échelles (38) 207 K6
Mirmande (26) 240 C4
le Miroir (71) 172 E3
Mirvaux (80) 10 B6
Mirville (76) 14 D5
Miscon (26) 241 J4
Miserey (27) 56 E1
Miserey-Salines (25) 137 K5
Misérieux (01) 188 C6
Misery (80) 19 G2
Mison (04) 259 F3
Missé (79) 144 B4
Missècle (81) 270 C5
Missègre (11) 309 G2
Missery (21) 134 E5
Missillac (44) 102 B6
Missiriac (56) 101 K3
Misson (40) 264 C6
Missy (14) 32 C5
Missy-aux-Bois (02) 39 H3
Missy-lès-Pierrepont (02) 20 E5
Missy-sur-Aisne (02) 39 K2
Misy-sur-Yonne (77) 88 B4
Mitry-Mory (77) 59 G2
Mittainville (78) 57 H6
Mittainvilliers (28) 84 E2
Mittelbergheim (67) 70 C5
Mittelbronn (57) 70 A1
Mittelhausbergen (67) 25 A6
Mittelhausen (67) 70 E1
Mittelschaeffolsheim (67) 70 E2
Mittelwihr (68) 96 B3
Mittersheim (57) 67 H2
Mittlach (68) 119 J1
Mittois (14) 54 C1
Mitzach (68) 119 J3
Mizérieux (42) 204 E2
Mizoën (38) 224 E4
Moÿ-de-l'Aisne (02) 20 A4
Mobecq (50) 30 D1
Moca-Croce (2A) 320 E6
Modane (73) 226 A2
Modène (84) 257 H5
Moëlan-sur-Mer (29) 99 H4
les Moëres (59) 3 J2
Moernach (68) 97 C6
Moëslains (52) 63 J6
Moeurs-Verdey (51) 61 G5
Moeuvres (59) 11 H4
Moëze (17) 176 E5
Moffans-et-Vacheresse (70) 138 E1
Mogeville (55) 26 E6
Mognard (73) 208 B2
Mogneneins (01) 188 C3
Mognéville (55) 63 K4
Mogneville (60) 38 A3
Mogues (08) 23 J4

Mohon (56) 77 J6
Moidieu-Détourbe (38) 206 C5
Moigny-sur-École (91) 87 F3
Moimay (70) 138 D2
Moineville (54) 26 E6
Moings (17) 195 J5
Moinville-la-Jeulin (28) 85 J4
Moirans (38) 223 J4
Moirans-en-Montagne (39) 173 H5
Moirax (47) 248 B5
Moiré (69) 188 A5
Moiremont (51) 42 D5
Moirey-Flabas-Crépion (55) 43 H3
Moiron (39) 173 G2
Moiry (08) 23 J4
Moisdon-la-Rivière (44) 103 J5
Moisenay (77) 87 J3
Moislains (80) 11 G6
Moissac (82) 249 G6
Moissac-Bellevue (83) 279 F5
Moissac-Vallée-Française (48) 254 D5
Moissannes (87) 199 J1
Moissat (63) 203 F2
Moisselles (95) 58 E1
Moissey (39) 155 G1
Moissieu-sur-Dolon (38) 222 D1
Moisson (78) 57 J1
Moissy-Cramayel (77) 59 G3
Moissy-Moulinot (58) 133 H5
Moisville (27) 56 D4
Moisy (41) 108 E4
Moïta (2B) 319 J6
les Moitiers-d'Allonne (50) 28 B5
les Moitiers-en-Bauptois (50) 28 C6
Moitron (21) 135 J1
Moitron-sur-Sarthe (72) 82 C5
Moivre (51) 63 G2
Moivrons (54) 66 B3
Molac (56) 101 J4
Molagnies (76) 36 D1
Molain (02) 12 D6
Molain (39) 155 K5
Molamboz (39) 155 J4
Molandier (11) 288 E5
Molas (31) 286 E3
Molay (39) 155 F3
Molay (70) 117 G5
Môlay (89) 113 K6
le Molay-Littry (14) 31 K2
la Môle (83) 298 D5
Moléans (28) 109 F1
Molèdes (15) 218 D4
Molère (65) 304 E1
Molesme (21) 114 D3
Molesmes (89) 133 F2
Molezon (48) 254 C4
Moliens (60) 17 G5
Molières (24) 232 B2
Molières (46) 234 C3
Molières (82) 249 G5
les Molières (91) 58 C6
Molières-Cavaillac (30) 273 J2
Molières-Glandaz (26) 241 H3
Molières-sur-Cèze (30) 255 H4
Moliets-et-Maa (40) 262 C2
Molinchart (02) 20 C6
Molines-en-Queyras (05) 227 C2
Molinet (03) 170 A5
Molineuf (41) 128 D2
Molinges (39) 173 J5
Molinons (89) 89 F5
Molinot (21) 153 H3
Molins-sur-Aube (10) 90 D3
Molitg-les-Bains (66) 314 B2
Mollans (70) 118 D6
Mollans-sur-Ouvèze (26) 257 J4
Mollau (68) 119 J3
Mollégès (13) 276 C3
Molles (03) 185 K3
les Mollettes (73) 208 B5
Molleville (11) 289 F4
Molliens-au-Bois (80) 10 B6
Molliens-Dreuil (80) 17 J2
Mollkirch (67) 70 C4
Molompize (15) 218 E3
Molosmes (89) 114 A4
Moloy (21) 135 K2
Molphey (21) 134 C5
Molpré (39) 156 C6
Molring (57) 67 G2
Molsheim (67) 70 D4
Moltifao (2B) 318 E3
les Molunes (39) 173 K6
Momas (64) 284 C2
Mombrier (33) 211 H4
Momères (65) 285 H6
Momerstroff (57) 45 J4
Mommenheim (67) 70 E1
Momuy (40) 265 F6
Momy (64) 285 F3
Monacia-d'Aullène (2A) 322 E4
Monacia-d'Orezza (2B) 319 H5
Monampteuil (02) 40 B1
Monassut-Audiracq (64) 284 C3
le Monastère (12) 252 C4
le Monastier-Pin-Moriès (48) 237 F6
le Monastier-sur-Gazeille (43) 238 D1
Monay (39) 155 H5
Monbahus (47) 231 H4
Monbalen (47) 248 C3
Monbardon (32) 286 E3
Monbazillac (24) 231 H3

Monbéqui (82) . . . 268 E3
Monblanc (32) . . . 287 H2
Monbrun (32) . . . 268 C5
Moncale (2B) . . . 316 E1
Moncassin (32) . . . 286 B2
Moncaup (31) . . . 305 J3
Moncaup (64) . . . 285 G2
Moncaut (47) . . . 248 A5
Moncayolle-Larrory-Mendibieu (64) . . . 283 H4
Moncé-en-Belin (72) . . . 106 E4
Moncé-en-Saosnois (72) . . . 83 F5
Monceau-le-Neuf-et-Faucouzy (02) . . . 20 D3
Monceau-le-Waast (02) . . . 20 E5
Monceau-lès-Leups (02) . . . 20 C5
Monceau-Saint-Waast (59) . . . 13 G4
Monceau-sur-Oise (02) . . . 20 D2
les Monceaux (14) . . . 33 J6
Monceaux (60) . . . 38 B3
Monceaux-au-Perche (61) . . . 83 J2
Monceaux-en-Bessin (14) . . . 32 B4
Monceaux-l'Abbaye (60) . . . 17 G5
Monceaux-le-Comte (58) . . . 133 H5
Monceaux-sur-Dordogne (19) . . . 216 C5
Moncel-lès-Lunéville (54) . . . 66 D6
Moncel-sur-Seille (54) . . . 66 C4
Moncel-sur-Vair (88) . . . 93 G3
la Moncelle (08) . . . 23 F4
Moncetz-l'Abbaye (51) . . . 63 G6
Moncetz-Longevas (51) . . . 62 E3
Moncey (25) . . . 138 B4
Monchaux-Soreng (76) . . . 16 E1
Monchaux-sur-Écaillon (59) . . . 12 C3
Moncheaux (59) . . . 6 E6
Moncheaux-lès-Frévent (62) . . . 10 B2
Monchecourt (59) . . . 11 J2
Monchel-sur-Canche (62) . . . 9 K2
Moncheux (57) . . . 66 B2
Monchiet (62) . . . 10 D3
Monchy-au-Bois (62) . . . 10 D4
Monchy-Breton (62) . . . 10 B1
Monchy-Cayeux (62) . . . 10 A1
Monchy-Humières (60) . . . 38 D1
Monchy-Lagache (80) . . . 19 H2
Monchy-le-Preux (62) . . . 11 F3
Monchy-Saint-Éloi (60) . . . 38 A4
Monchy-sur-Eu (76) . . . 8 C6
Moncla (64) . . . 265 K6
Monclar (32) . . . 266 C2
Monclar (47) . . . 248 A1
Monclar-de-Quercy (82) . . . 269 J2
Monclar-sur-Losse (32) . . . 286 A1
Moncley (25) . . . 137 J5
Moncontour (22) . . . 77 H2
Moncontour (86) . . . 144 D5
Moncorneil-Grazan (32) . . . 286 D2
Moncourt (57) . . . 66 E4
Moncoutant (79) . . . 161 G2
Moncrabeau (47) . . . 267 F1
Moncy (61) . . . 53 G3
Mondavezan (31) . . . 287 H5
Mondelange (57) . . . 27 J4
Mondement-Montgivroux (51) . . . 61 H2
Mondescourt (60) . . . 19 J5
Mondevert (35) . . . 104 B1
Mondeville (14) . . . 32 E5
Mondeville (91) . . . 87 F2
Mondicourt (62) . . . 10 C4
Mondigny (08) . . . 22 C4
Mondilhan (31) . . . 286 E4
Mondion (86) . . . 145 H4
Mondon (25) . . . 138 C3
Mondonville (31) . . . 269 F5
Mondonville-Saint-Jean (28) . . . 85 K4
Mondorff (57) . . . 27 H2
Mondoubleau (41) . . . 108 A3
Mondouzil (31) . . . 269 H6
Mondragon (84) . . . 256 D3
Mondrainville (14) . . . 32 C5
Mondrepuis (02) . . . 21 G1
Mondreville (77) . . . 111 G3
Mondreville (78) . . . 57 H3
Monein (64) . . . 284 A4
Monès (31) . . . 287 H3
Monesple (09) . . . 307 G1
Monestier (03) . . . 185 G2
Monestier (07) . . . 221 J3
Monestier (24) . . . 231 G3
le Monestier (63) . . . 203 J6
Monestier-d'Ambel (38) . . . 242 C2
Monestier-de-Clermont (38) . . . 241 K1
le Monestier-du-Percy (38) . . . 242 A2
Monestier-Merlines (19) . . . 201 H3
Monestier-Port-Dieu (19) . . . 201 H5
Monestiés (81) . . . 251 G6
Monestrol (31) . . . 288 E4
Monétay-sur-Allier (03) . . . 168 C4
Monétay-sur-Loire (03) . . . 169 K5
Monéteau (89) . . . 113 G4
Monétier-Allemont (05) . . . 259 G4
le Monétier-les-Bains (05) . . . 225 J3
Monfaucon (24) . . . 231 F1
Monfaucon (65) . . . 285 H2
Monferran-Plavès (32) . . . 286 D2
Monferran-Savès (32) . . . 268 C6
Monflanquin (47) . . . 232 A4
Monfort (32) . . . 268 A4
Monfréville (14) . . . 31 H1
Mongaillard (47) . . . 247 J4
Mongausy (32) . . . 287 F2
Mongauzy (33) . . . 230 D5
Monget (40) . . . 265 G6
Monguilhem (32) . . . 266 A3

Monheurt (47) . . . 247 J3
Monhoudou (72) . . . 83 F5
Monieux (84) . . . 258 A6
Monistrol-d'Allier (43) . . . 219 K6
Monistrol-sur-Loire (43) . . . 221 F2
Monlaur-Bernet (32) . . . 286 C4
Monléon-Magnoac (65) . . . 286 C5
Monlet (43) . . . 220 A3
Monlezun (32) . . . 285 J2
Monlezun-d'Armagnac (32) . . . 266 A3
Monlong (65) . . . 286 B5
Monmadalès (24) . . . 231 K3
Monmarvès (24) . . . 231 K4
Monnai (61) . . . 55 G3
Monnaie (37) . . . 127 K3
Monneren (57) . . . 27 J4
la Monnerie-le-Montel (63) . . . 203 J1
Monnerville (91) . . . 86 B4
Monnes (02) . . . 39 H5
Monnet-la-Ville (39) . . . 173 J1
Monnetay (39) . . . 173 F4
Monnetier-Mornex (74) . . . 191 G2
Monneville (60) . . . 37 G5
Monnières (39) . . . 155 G2
Monnières (44) . . . 123 J4
Monoblet (30) . . . 274 C1
Monpardiac (32) . . . 285 K2
Monpazier (24) . . . 232 C4
Monpezat (64) . . . 285 G2
Monplaisant (24) . . . 232 D3
Monprimblanc (33) . . . 230 A4
Mons (16) . . . 178 E6
Mons (17) . . . 195 K1
Mons (30) . . . 255 H5
Mons (31) . . . 269 J6
Mons (34) . . . 291 H1
Mons (63) . . . 185 J5
Mons (83) . . . 280 B4
Mons-Boubert (80) . . . 8 E5
Mons-en-Baroeul (59) . . . 6 E4
Mons-en-Laonnois (02) . . . 20 C6
Mons-en-Montois (77) . . . 88 C2
Mons-en-Pévèle (59) . . . 6 E6
Monsac (24) . . . 232 A3
Monsaguel (24) . . . 231 J3
Monsec (24) . . . 197 H6
Monségur (33) . . . 230 D4
Monségur (40) . . . 265 G6
Monségur (47) . . . 248 E1
Monségur (64) . . . 285 G2
la Monselie (15) . . . 217 J2
Monsempron-Libos (47) . . . 248 E1
Monsireigne (85) . . . 160 C1
Monsols (69) . . . 187 K2
Monsteroux-Milieu (38) . . . 206 B6
Monsures (80) . . . 17 K4
Monswiller (67) . . . 70 B1
Mont (64) . . . 284 A2
Mont (65) . . . 305 G5
Mont (71) . . . 169 K3
le Mont (88) . . . 95 J2
Mont-Bernanchon (62) . . . 5 K5
Mont-Bertrand (14) . . . 31 J5
Mont-Bonvillers (54) . . . 26 D5
Mont-Cauvaire (76) . . . 15 K6
Mont-d'Astarac (32) . . . 286 C4
Mont-Dauphin (05) . . . 227 A3
Mont-de-Galié (31) . . . 305 J2
Mont-de-Lans (38) . . . 224 E5
Mont-de-Laval (25) . . . 157 H1
Mont-de-l'If (76) . . . 15 H6
Mont-de-Marrast (32) . . . 286 A4
Mont-de-Marsan (40) . . . 265 G2
Mont-de-Vougney (25) . . . 139 G5
Mont-devant-Sassey (55) . . . 43 F2
le Mont-Dieu (08) . . . 22 E6
Mont-Disse (64) . . . 285 F1
Mont-Dol (35) . . . 51 F4
Mont-Dore (63) . . . 202 A4
Mont-d'Origny (02) . . . 20 C2
Mont-et-Marré (58) . . . 151 J3
Mont-Laurent (08) . . . 41 K1
Mont-le-Vernois (70) . . . 138 A1
Mont-le-Vignoble (54) . . . 65 H6
Mont-lès-Lamarche (88) . . . 117 H2
Mont-lès-Neufchâteau (88) . . . 93 F2
Mont-lès-Seurre (71) . . . 154 D4
Mont-l'Étroit (54) . . . 93 G2
Mont-l'Évêque (60) . . . 38 C5
Mont-Louis (66) . . . 313 J4
Mont-Notre-Dame (02) . . . 40 B4
Mont-Ormel (61) . . . 54 E3
Mont-près-Chambord (41) . . . 129 F2
Mont-Roc (81) . . . 271 G4
le Mont-Saint-Adrien (60) . . . 37 G2
Mont-Saint-Aignan (76) . . . 35 H2
Mont-Saint-Éloi (62) . . . 10 E2
Mont-Saint-Jean (02) . . . 21 J3
Mont-Saint-Jean (21) . . . 134 E6
Mont-Saint-Jean (72) . . . 82 B5
Mont-Saint-Léger (70) . . . 137 H1
Mont-Saint-Martin (02) . . . 40 B4
Mont-Saint-Martin (08) . . . 42 B3
Mont-Saint-Martin (38) . . . 224 A2
Mont-Saint-Martin (54) . . . 26 D2
le Mont-Saint-Michel (50) . . . 51 J3
Mont-Saint-Père (02) . . . 40 A6
Mont-Saint-Remy (08) . . . 41 K2
Mont-Saint-Sulpice (89) . . . 113 G3
Mont-Saint-Vincent (71) . . . 171 F2
Mont-Saxonnex (74) . . . 191 H3
Mont-sous-Vaudrey (39) . . . 155 H3

Mont-sur-Courville (51) . . . 40 C4
Mont-sur-Meurthe (54) . . . 66 D6
Mont-sur-Monnet (39) . . . 173 J1
Montabard (61) . . . 54 B4
Montabon (72) . . . 127 F1
Montabot (50) . . . 31 G5
Montacher-Villegardin (89) . . . 88 B6
Montadet (32) . . . 287 G3
Montady (34) . . . 291 K4
Montagagne (09) . . . 307 G3
Montagna-le-Reconduit (39) . . . 172 E4
Montagna-le-Templier (39) . . . 173 F6
Montagnac (30) . . . 274 E2
Montagnac (34) . . . 292 C2
Montagnac-d'Auberoche (24) . . . 214 C4
Montagnac-la-Crempse (24) . . . 213 J6
Montagnac-Montpezat (04) . . . 278 E3
Montagnac-sur-Auvignon (47) . . . 247 K5
Montagnac-sur-Lède (47) . . . 232 B6
Montagnat (01) . . . 189 G2
Montagne (33) . . . 230 B1
Montagne (38) . . . 223 F4
la Montagne (44) . . . 123 F4
la Montagne (70) . . . 119 F3
Montagne-Fayel (80) . . . 17 H2
Montagney (70) . . . 137 G5
Montagney-Servigney (25) . . . 138 C3
Montagnieu (01) . . . 207 J3
Montagnieu (38) . . . 207 G5
Montagnol (12) . . . 272 D3
Montagnole (73) . . . 208 B4
Montagny (42) . . . 187 G4
Montagny (69) . . . 205 K3
Montagny (73) . . . 209 J5
Montagny-en-Vexin (60) . . . 36 E5
Montagny-lès-Beaune (21) . . . 154 A4
Montagny-lès-Buxy (71) . . . 171 H1
Montagny-les-Lanches (74) . . . 190 E6
Montagny-lès-Seurre (21) . . . 154 E3
Montagny-près-Louhans (71) . . . 172 D2
Montagny-Sainte-Félicité (60) . . . 38 D6
Montagny-sur-Grosne (71) . . . 171 G6
Montagoudin (33) . . . 230 C5
Montagrier (24) . . . 213 H2
Montagudet (82) . . . 249 G4
Montagut (64) . . . 284 B1
Montaignac-Saint-Hippolyte (19) . . . 216 D2
Montaigu (02) . . . 21 F6
Montaigu (39) . . . 173 G2
Montaigu (85) . . . 142 A3
Montaigu-de-Quercy (82) . . . 249 F3
Montaigu-la-Brisette (50) . . . 28 E3
Montaigu-le-Blin (03) . . . 185 K1
Montaigu-les-Bois (50) . . . 31 F6
Montaiguët-en-Forez (03) . . . 186 C1
Montaigut (63) . . . 184 C3
Montaigut-le-Blanc (23) . . . 182 C3
Montaigut-le-Blanc (63) . . . 202 D4
Montaigut-sur-Save (31) . . . 268 E5
Montaillé (72) . . . 107 J3
Montailleur (73) . . . 209 F3
Montaillou (09) . . . 308 K5
Montaimont (73) . . . 209 F6
Montain (39) . . . 173 G1
Montaïn (82) . . . 268 D2
Montainville (28) . . . 85 G5
Montainville (78) . . . 57 K3
Montalba-le-Château (66) . . . 309 J6
Montalembert (79) . . . 179 J3
Montalet-le-Bois (78) . . . 57 K1
Montalieu-Vercieu (38) . . . 207 G1
Montalzat (82) . . . 250 A4
Montamat (32) . . . 287 F2
Montambert (58) . . . 169 H5
Montamel (46) . . . 233 H5
Montamisé (86) . . . 163 F3
Montamy (14) . . . 53 F1
Montanay (69) . . . 188 D6
Montancy (25) . . . 139 K4
Montandon (25) . . . 139 H5
Montanel (50) . . . 51 J5
Montaner (64) . . . 285 G3
Montanges (01) . . . 190 C2
Montans (81) . . . 270 B3
Montapas (58) . . . 151 J3
Montarcher (42) . . . 204 C6
Montardit (09) . . . 306 E1
Montardon (64) . . . 284 D3
Montaren-et-Saint-Médiers (30) . . . 275 G1
Montargis (45) . . . 111 J3
Montarlot (77) . . . 87 K4
Montarlot-lès-Rioz (70) . . . 137 K4
Montarnaud (34) . . . 274 A6
Montaron (58) . . . 169 K5
Montastruc (47) . . . 248 A1
Montastruc (65) . . . 286 A5
Montastruc (82) . . . 249 J6
Montastruc-de-Salies (31) . . . 306 B2
Montastruc-la-Conseillère (31) . . . 269 J5
Montastruc-Savès (31) . . . 287 H4
le Montat (46) . . . 250 A2
Montataire (60) . . . 38 A4
Montauban (82) . . . 269 F1
Montauban-de-Bretagne (35) . . . 78 C3
Montauban-de-Luchon (31) . . . 305 H5
Montauban-de-Picardie (80) . . . 10 E6
Montauban-sur-l'Ouvèze (26) . . . 258 B3
Montaud (34) . . . 274 C4
Montaud (38) . . . 223 J2
Montaudin (53) . . . 80 D3
Montaulieu (26) . . . 257 J2
Montaulin (10) . . . 90 C5

Montaure (27) . . . 35 H4
Montauriol (11) . . . 289 F5
Montauriol (47) . . . 231 J5
Montauriol (66) . . . 315 F3
Montauriol (81) . . . 251 J6
Montauroux (83) . . . 280 B5
Montaut (09) . . . 288 D6
Montaut (24) . . . 231 K3
Montaut (31) . . . 288 A4
Montaut (32) . . . 286 B3
Montaut (40) . . . 265 F4
Montaut (47) . . . 231 K5
Montaut (64) . . . 284 E6
Montaut-les-Créneaux (32) . . . 267 J5
Montautour (35) . . . 80 B5
Montauville (54) . . . 65 J2
Montay (59) . . . 12 D5
Montayral (47) . . . 249 F1
Montazeau (24) . . . 230 E1
Montazels (11) . . . 309 F3
Montbard (21) . . . 134 D1
Montbarla (82) . . . 249 G4
Montbarrey (39) . . . 155 J3
Montbarrois (45) . . . 111 F2
Montbartier (82) . . . 269 F2
Montbavin (02) . . . 40 A1
Montbazens (12) . . . 251 H1
Montbazin (34) . . . 293 F2
Montbazon (37) . . . 127 J6
Montbel (09) . . . 308 C3
Montbel (48) . . . 238 C3
Montbéliard (25) . . . 139 H2
Montbéliardot (25) . . . 139 G6
Montbellet (71) . . . 171 K4
Montbenoît (25) . . . 157 K3
Montberaud (31) . . . 287 J6
Montbernard (31) . . . 286 E4
Montberon (31) . . . 269 H5
Montbert (44) . . . 123 H6
Montberthault (21) . . . 134 C3
Montbeton (82) . . . 269 F1
Montbeugny (03) . . . 169 F4
Montbizot (72) . . . 82 D6
Montblainville (55) . . . 42 E4
Montblanc (34) . . . 292 B3
Montboillon (70) . . . 137 J4
Montboissier (28) . . . 85 F6
Montbolo (66) . . . 314 E5
Montbonnot-Saint-Martin (38) . . . 224 B2
Montboucher (23) . . . 182 B5
Montboucher-sur-Jabron (26) . . . 240 B5
Montboudif (15) . . . 218 A1
Montbouton (90) . . . 139 J2
Montbouy (45) . . . 111 J4
Montboyer (16) . . . 212 E2
Montbozon (70) . . . 138 C3
Montbrand (05) . . . 242 A6
Montbras (55) . . . 93 G1
Montbray (50) . . . 31 H6
Montbré (51) . . . 41 F5
Montbrehain (02) . . . 20 A1
Montbrison (26) . . . 257 G1
Montbrison (42) . . . 204 D4
Montbron (16) . . . 197 H3
Montbronn (57) . . . 69 F4
Montbrun (46) . . . 250 E1
Montbrun (48) . . . 254 B3
Montbrun-Bocage (31) . . . 306 E1
Montbrun-des-Corbières (11) . . . 290 E6
Montbrun-Lauragais (31) . . . 288 C2
Montbrun-les-Bains (26) . . . 258 A4
Montcabrier (46) . . . 232 D6
Montcabrier (81) . . . 269 K6
Montcaret (24) . . . 230 D2
Montcarra (38) . . . 207 G3
Montcavrel (62) . . . 4 C5
Montceau-et-Écharnant (21) . . . 153 J3
Montceau-les-Mines (71) . . . 170 E2
Montceaux (01) . . . 188 C3
Montceaux-lès-Meaux (77) . . . 60 A2
Montceaux-lès-Provins (77) . . . 60 E5
Montceaux-lès-Vaudes (10) . . . 90 B6
Montceaux-l'Étoile (71) . . . 170 B6
Montceaux-Ragny (71) . . . 171 K2
Montcel (63) . . . 185 F5
Montcel (73) . . . 208 C2
Montcenis (71) . . . 153 G6
Montcet (01) . . . 189 F2
Montcey (70) . . . 118 B6
Montchaboud (38) . . . 224 B4
Montchal (42) . . . 205 F1
Montchâlons (02) . . . 40 C1
Montchamp (14) . . . 53 F2
Montchamp (15) . . . 219 F5
Montchanin (71) . . . 171 F1
Montcharvot (52) . . . 117 G3
Montchaton (50) . . . 30 D4
Montchaude (16) . . . 196 A6
Montchauvet (14) . . . 53 F1
Montchauvet (78) . . . 57 H3
Montchenu (26) . . . 222 D3
Montcheutin (08) . . . 42 C1
Montchevrel (61) . . . 83 F1
Montchevrier (36) . . . 165 J5
Montclar (04) . . . 259 K1
Montclar (11) . . . 309 F1
Montclar (12) . . . 271 K2
Montclar-de-Comminges (31) . . . 287 H6
Montclar-Lauragais (31) . . . 288 E4
Montclar-sur-Gervanne (26) . . . 241 F3
Montclard (43) . . . 219 J3
Montcléra (46) . . . 233 F5

Montclus (05) . . . 258 D1
Montclus (30) . . . 256 A4
Montcombroux-les-Mines (03) . . . 169 H6
Montcony (71) . . . 172 D1
Montcorbon (45) . . . 112 B3
Montcornet (02) . . . 21 G4
Montcornet (08) . . . 22 C2
Montcourt (70) . . . 117 J2
Montcourt-Fromonville (77) . . . 87 H5
Montcoy (71) . . . 154 C6
Montcresson (45) . . . 111 J4
Montcuit (50) . . . 31 F3
Montcuq (46) . . . 249 H3
Montcusel (39) . . . 173 H6
Montcy-Notre-Dame (08) . . . 22 D3
Montdardier (30) . . . 273 J2
Montdauphin (77) . . . 60 E3
Montdidier (57) . . . 67 G1
Montdidier (80) . . . 18 D5
Montdoré (70) . . . 118 A3
Montdoumerc (46) . . . 250 A3
Montdragon (81) . . . 270 D4
Montdurausse (81) . . . 269 J2
Monte (2B) . . . 319 H3
Monteaux (41) . . . 128 C3
Montebourg (50) . . . 29 F4
Montech (82) . . . 268 E2
Montécheroux (25) . . . 139 H4
Montegrosso (2B) . . . 318 C3
Montégut (32) . . . 267 J6
Montégut (40) . . . 265 K3
Montégut (65) . . . 305 G1
Montégut-Arros (32) . . . 285 J3
Montégut-Bourjac (31) . . . 287 G4
Montégut-en-Couserans (09) . . . 306 D3
Montégut-Lauragais (31) . . . 289 G2
Montégut-Plantaurel (09) . . . 307 H2
Montégut-Savès (32) . . . 287 G2
Monteignet-sur-l'Andelot (03) . . . 185 G3
le Monteil (15) . . . 217 J2
le Monteil (43) . . . 220 C5
le Monteil-au-Vicomte (23) . . . 182 D6
Monteille (14) . . . 33 H6
Monteils (12) . . . 251 F4
Monteils (30) . . . 255 H6
Monteils (82) . . . 250 B5
Montel-de-Gelat (63) . . . 184 A6
Montéléger (26) . . . 240 C2
Montélier (26) . . . 222 D6
Montélimar (26) . . . 240 B5
le Montellier (01) . . . 188 E5
Montels (09) . . . 307 G2
Montels (34) . . . 291 J4
Montels (81) . . . 270 B2
Montemboeuf (16) . . . 197 J2
Montenach (57) . . . 27 J3
Montenay (53) . . . 80 D4
Montendre (17) . . . 211 J2
Montendry (73) . . . 208 E4
Montenescourt (62) . . . 10 D3
Monteneuf (56) . . . 102 B1
Montenils (77) . . . 61 F4
Montenois (25) . . . 139 G2
Montenoison (58) . . . 151 G1
Montenoy (54) . . . 66 B3
Montépilloy (60) . . . 38 C5
Monteplain (39) . . . 155 J1
Montépreux (51) . . . 62 B5
Monterblanc (56) . . . 101 K2
Montereau (45) . . . 111 G4
Montereau-Fault-Yonne (77) . . . 88 A4
Montereau-sur-le-Jard (77) . . . 87 H1
Monterfil (35) . . . 78 D4
Montérolier (76) . . . 16 C5
Monterrein (56) . . . 101 K2
Montertelot (56) . . . 101 J2
Montescot (66) . . . 315 H3
Montescourt-Lizerolles (02) . . . 19 K4
Montespan (31) . . . 306 A1
Montesquieu (34) . . . 292 A1
Montesquieu (47) . . . 247 K4
Montesquieu (82) . . . 249 G5
Montesquieu-Avantès (09) . . . 306 E2
Montesquieu-des-Albères (66) . . . 315 G4
Montesquieu-Guittaut (31) . . . 286 E4
Montesquieu-Lauragais (31) . . . 288 D3
Montesquieu-Volvestre (31) . . . 287 K5
Montesquiou (32) . . . 286 A1
Montessaux (70) . . . 118 E5
Montesson (78) . . . 58 C3
Montestruc-sur-Gers (32) . . . 267 J4
le Montet (03) . . . 168 B5
Montet-et-Bouxal (46) . . . 234 D3
Monteton (47) . . . 231 F5
Monteux (84) . . . 257 G6
Montévrain (77) . . . 59 J3
Monteynard (38) . . . 224 A6
Montézic (12) . . . 235 K4
Montfa (09) . . . 307 F1
Montfa (81) . . . 271 F5
Montfalcon (38) . . . 223 F4
Montfarville (50) . . . 29 G2
Montfaucon (02) . . . 60 E2
Montfaucon (25) . . . 138 A6
Montfaucon (30) . . . 256 D6
Montfaucon (46) . . . 233 J4
Montfaucon (49) . . . 142 C2
Montfaucon-d'Argonne (55) . . . 43 F4
Montfaucon-en-Velay (43) . . . 221 G3
Montfermeil (93) . . . 59 G3
Montfermier (82) . . . 249 K4
Montfermy (63) . . . 184 C6

Montferrand (11). . . .	289	F4
Montferrand-du-Périgord (24) . .	232	B3
Montferrand-la-Fare (26) . .	258	A2
Montferrand-le-Château (25) . .	156	A1
Montferrat (38) . .	207	J5
Montferrat (83) . .	279	J5
Montferrer (66) . .	314	D5
Montferrier (09) . .	308	A4
Montferrier-sur-Lez (34) . .	274	B5
Montfey (10) . .	113	J2
Montfiquet (14) . .	31	K3
Montfleur (39) . .	173	F6
Montflours (53) . .	81	F6
Montflovin (25) . .	157	F3
Montfort (04) . .	259	G5
Montfort (25) . .	156	A2
Montfort (49) . .	144	B1
Montfort (64) . .	283	H3
Montfort-en-Chalosse (40) . .	264	D4
Montfort-l'Amaury (78) . .	57	K4
Montfort-le-Gesnois (72) . .	107	F2
Montfort-sur-Argens (83) . .	298	A1
Montfort-sur-Boulzane (11) . .	309	F6
Montfort-sur-Meu (35) . .	78	D4
Montfort-sur-Risle (27) . .	34	D3
Montfranc (12) . .	271	J3
Montfroc (26) . .	258	C4
Montfuron (04) . .	278	A3
Montgaillard (09) . .	307	J3
Montgaillard (11) . .	309	J4
Montgaillard (40) . .	265	G4
Montgaillard (65) . .	285	H6
Montgaillard (81) . .	269	J2
Montgaillard (82) . .	268	B2
Montgaillard-de-Salies (31) . .	306	B2
Montgaillard-Lauragais (31) . .	288	C3
Montgaillard-sur-Save (31) . .	286	E5
Montgardin (05) . .	243	G5
Montgardon (50) . .	30	D1
Montgaroult (61) . .	54	B4
Montgauch (09) . .	306	C2
Montgaudry (61) . .	83	G3
Montgazin (31) . .	288	A4
Montgé-en-Goële (77) . .	59	J1
Montgeard (31) . .	288	D4
Montgellafrey (73) . .	209	F6
Montgenèvre (05) . .	226	A6
Montgenost (51) . .	89	G1
Montgérain (60) . .	18	D6
Montgermont (35) . .	79	F3
Montgeron (91) . .	59	F5
Montgeroult (95) . .	37	G6
Montgesoye (25) . .	156	D2
Montgesty (46) . .	233	G5
Montgey (81) . .	289	G2
Montgibaud (19) . .	199	G5
Montgilbert (73) . .	209	F4
Montgirod (73) . .	209	J4
Montgiscard (31) . .	288	D2
Montgivray (36) . .	166	B3
Montgobert (02) . .	39	G3
Montgon (08) . .	42	B1
Montgradail (11) . .	308	C1
Montgras (31) . .	287	H2
Montgreleix (15) . .	218	C2
Montgru-Saint-Hilaire (02) . .	39	J5
Montguers (26) . .	258	B3
Montgueux (10) . .	89	K4
Montguillon (49) . .	104	E6
Montguyon (17) . .	212	B3
les Monthairons (55) . .	43	J6
Montharville (28) . .	84	E6
Monthault (35) . .	80	B1
Monthaut (11) . .	308	D1
Monthelie (21) . .	153	K4
Monthelon (51) . .	61	K2
Monthelon (71) . .	152	E4
Monthenault (02) . .	40	B1
Montheries (52) . .	91	J6
Montherlant (60) . .	37	G4
Monthermé (08) . .	22	D2
Monthiers (02) . .	39	J6
Monthieux (01) . .	188	D5
Monthion (73) . .	209	F3
Monthodon (37) . .	128	A1
Monthoiron (86) . .	163	H1
Monthois (08) . .	42	B3
Montholier (39) . .	155	J4
Monthou-sur-Bièvre (41) . .	128	E3
Monthou-sur-Cher (41) . .	128	E5
Monthuchon (50) . .	30	E3
Monthurel (02) . .	61	F1
Monthureux-le-Sec (88) . .	93	K6
Monthureux-sur-Saône (88) . .	117	J2
Monthyon (77) . .	59	J1
Monticello (2B) . .	318	D2
Montier-en-Der (52) . .	91	H2
Montier-en-l'Isle (10) . .	91	G5
Montiéramey (10) . .	90	D5
Montierchaume (36) . .	148	A5
Montiers (60) . .	38	B1
Montiers-sur-Saulx (55) . .	92	C1
Monties (32) . .	286	D3
Montignac (24) . .	214	E5
Montignac (33) . .	230	A3
Montignac (65) . .	285	J6
Montignac-Charente (16) . .	196	D2
Montignac-de-Lauzun (47) . .	231	H5
Montignac-le-Coq (16) . .	213	F1
Montignac-Toupinerie (47) . .	231	G6
Montignargues (30) . .	275	F2
Montigné (16) . .	196	B1
Montigné-le-Brillant (53) . .	104	E2
Montigné-lès-Rairies (49) . .	126	A1
Montigné-sur-Moine (49) . .	142	C2
Montigny (14) . .	32	C6
Montigny (18) . .	149	K1
Montigny (45) . .	110	C1
Montigny (54) . .	95	G1
Montigny (72) . .	82	E2
Montigny (76) . .	35	G1
Montigny-aux-Amognes (58) . .	151	F3
Montigny-devant-Sassey (55) . .	43	F1
Montigny-en-Arrouaise (02) . .	20	B2
Montigny-en-Cambrésis (59) . .	12	C5
Montigny-en-Gohelle (62) . .	11	G1
Montigny-en-Morvan (58) . .	152	A2
Montigny-en-Ostrevent (59) . .	11	J2
Montigny-la-Resle (89) . .	113	H4
Montigny-l'Allier (02) . .	39	G6
Montigny-le-Bretonneux (78) . .	58	B4
Montigny-le-Chartif (28) . .	84	D5
Montigny-le-Franc (02) . .	21	F4
Montigny-le-Gannelon (28) . .	108	D2
Montigny-le-Guesdier (77) . .	88	D4
Montigny-Lencoup (77) . .	88	B3
Montigny-Lengrain (02) . .	39	G3
Montigny-lès-Arsures (39) . .	155	K4
Montigny-lès-Cherlieu (70) . .	117	H5
Montigny-lès-Condé (02) . .	61	F2
Montigny-lès-Cormeilles (95) . .	58	D2
Montigny-lès-Jongleurs (80) . .	9	J4
Montigny-lès-Metz (57) . .	45	F5
Montigny-lès-Monts (10) . .	113	K1
Montigny-lès-Vaucouleurs (55) . .	65	F6
Montigny-Montfort (21) . .	134	D2
Montigny-Mornay-Villeneuve-sur-Vingeanne (21) . .	136	E2
Montigny-Saint-Barthélemy (21) . .	134	D4
Montigny-sous-Marle (02) . .	20	E4
Montigny-sur-Armançon (21) . .	134	E4
Montigny-sur-Aube (21) . .	115	H3
Montigny-sur-Avre (28) . .	56	C5
Montigny-sur-Canne (58) . .	151	J5
Montigny-sur-Chiers (54) . .	26	C3
Montigny-sur-Crécy (02) . .	20	C4
Montigny-sur-l'Ain (39) . .	173	J1
Montigny-sur-l'Hallue (80) . .	18	C1
Montigny-sur-Loing (77) . .	87	J4
Montigny-sur-Meuse (08) . .	24	C2
Montigny-sur-Vence (08) . .	22	C5
Montigny-sur-Vesle (51) . .	40	D3
Montilliers (49) . .	143	J1
Montillot (89) . .	133	H3
Montilly (03) . .	168	B2
Montilly-sur-Noireau (61) . .	53	H3
Montils (17) . .	195	H3
les Montils (41) . .	128	E3
Montipouret (36) . .	166	A2
Montirat (11) . .	290	C6
Montirat (81) . .	251	G5
Montireau (28) . .	84	C3
Montiron (32) . .	287	F1
Montivernage (25) . .	138	D5
Montivilliers (76) . .	14	B6
Montjardin (11) . .	308	C3
Montjaux (12) . .	252	E6
Montjavoult (60) . .	36	E5
Montjay (05) . .	258	C6
Montjay (71) . .	155	F6
Montjean (16) . .	179	F3
Montjean (53) . .	104	D2
Montjean-sur-Loire (49) . .	124	D4
Montjoi (11) . .	309	H3
Montjoi (82) . .	248	E4
Montjoie-en-Couserans (09) . .	306	D2
Montjoie-le-Château (25) . .	139	J4
Montjoie-Saint-Martin (50) . .	80	A1
Montjoire (31) . .	269	H4
Montjoux (26) . .	240	E6
Montjoyer (26) . .	256	E1
Montjustin (04) . .	277	K3
Montjustin-et-Velotte (70) . .	138	D1
Montlandon (28) . .	84	C3
Montlaur (11) . .	309	H1
Montlaur (12) . .	272	B3
Montlaur (31) . .	288	D2
Montlaur-en-Diois (26) . .	241	H4
Montlaux (04) . .	259	F6
Montlauzun (46) . .	249	H3
Montlay-en-Auxois (21) . .	134	D5
Montlebon (25) . .	157	H2
Montlevicq (36) . .	166	C3
Montlevon (02) . .	61	F2
Montlhéry (91) . .	58	D6
Montliard (45) . .	111	F2
Montlieu-la-Garde (17) . .	212	A3
Montlignon (95) . .	58	D1
Montliot-et-Courcelles (21) . .	115	F4
Montlivault (41) . .	129	F1
Montlognon (60) . .	38	C5
Montloué (02) . .	21	H4
Montlouis (18) . .	149	F6
Montlouis-sur-Loire (37) . .	127	K5
Montluçon (03) . .	167	H6
Montluel (01) . .	188	B6
Montmachoux (77) . .	88	A4
Montmacq (60) . .	38	E1
Montmagny (95) . .	58	E2
Montmahoux (25) . .	156	C3
Montmain (21) . .	154	C3
Montmain (76) . .	35	K2
Montmançon (21) . .	136	D5
Montmarault (03) . .	184	E1
Montmarlon (39) . .	156	B5
Montmartin (60) . .	38	C1
Montmartin-en-Graignes (50) . .	31	G1
Montmartin-le-Haut (10) . .	91	F6
Montmartin-sur-Mer (50) . .	30	D5
Montmaur (05) . .	242	C5
Montmaur (11) . .	289	F3
Montmaur-en-Diois (26) . .	241	H4
Montmaurin (31) . .	286	D5
Montmédy (55) . .	23	K6
Montmeillant (08) . .	21	K4
Montmelard (71) . .	171	H6
Montmelas-Saint-Sorlin (69) . .	188	A4
Montmélian (73) . .	208	D5
Montmerle-sur-Saône (01) . .	188	B4
Montmerrei (61) . .	54	C6
Montmeyan (83) . .	278	E5
Montmeyran (26) . .	240	D2
Montmin (74) . .	208	E1
Montmirail (51) . .	61	F3
Montmirail (72) . .	107	K1
Montmiral (26) . .	222	E4
Montmirat (30) . .	274	E2
Montmirey-la-Ville (39) . .	137	F6
Montmirey-le-Château (39) . .	137	F6
Montmoreau-Saint-Cybard (16) . .	212	E1
Montmorency (95) . .	58	E2
Montmorency-Beaufort (10) . .	91	F2
Montmorillon (86) . .	164	A5
Montmorin (05) . .	258	B1
Montmorin (63) . .	203	F3
Montmorot (39) . .	173	F2
Montmort (71) . .	170	B1
Montmort-Lucy (51) . .	61	J2
Montmotier (88) . .	118	B2
Montmoyen (21) . .	115	H6
Montmurat (15) . .	235	F5
Montner (66) . .	309	K6
Montoillot (21) . .	135	G6
Montoir-de-Bretagne (44) . .	122	B2
Montoire-sur-le-Loir (41) . .	108	A6
Montois-la-Montagne (57) . .	27	F6
Montoison (26) . .	240	D2
Montoldre (03) . .	169	F4
Montolieu (11) . .	289	K4
Montolivet (77) . .	60	E4
Montonvillers (80) . .	10	A6
Montord (03) . .	185	G1
Montory (64) . .	283	J4
Montot (21) . .	154	E2
Montot (70) . .	137	F2
Montot-sur-Rognon (52) . .	92	C4
Montouliers (34) . .	291	G1
Montoulieu (09) . .	307	J4
Montoulieu (34) . .	274	B2
Montoulieu-Saint-Bernard (31) . .	287	G5
Montournais (85) . .	160	E1
Montours (35) . .	51	K6
Montourtier (53) . .	81	G5
Montoussé (65) . .	305	F1
Montoussin (31) . .	287	H5
Montoy-Flanville (57) . .	45	G5
Montpellier (34) . .	274	C6
Montpellier-de-Médillan (17) . .	195	F3
Montpensier (63) . .	185	G4
Montperreux (25) . .	157	F5
Montpeyroux (12) . .	236	B5
Montpeyroux (24) . .	230	D1
Montpeyroux (34) . .	273	K5
Montpeyroux (63) . .	202	E4
Montpezat (30) . .	274	E3
Montpézat (32) . .	287	G3
Montpezat (47) . .	248	A3
Montpezat-de-Quercy (82) . .	250	A4
Montpezat-sous-Bauzon (07) . .	239	F4
Montpinchon (50) . .	31	F4
Montpinier (81) . .	270	E5
Montpitol (31) . .	269	J5
Montplonne (55) . .	64	B5
Montpollin (49) . .	126	B2
Montpon-Ménestérol (24) . .	212	E6
Montpont-en-Bresse (71) . .	172	C3
Montpothier (10) . .	89	F1
Montpouillan (47) . .	247	G1
Montrabé (31) . .	269	H6
Montrabot (50) . .	31	K3
Montracol (01) . .	189	F2
Montravers (79) . .	143	G5
Montréal (07) . .	239	G6
Montréal (11) . .	289	J6
Montréal (32) . .	266	E2
Montréal (89) . .	134	A3
Montréal-la-Cluse (01) . .	189	K2
Montréal-les-Sources (26) . .	257	K2
Montrécourt (59) . .	12	C3
Montredon (46) . .	235	F5
Montredon-des-Corbières (11) . .	291	H6
Montredon-Labessonnié (81) . .	271	F5
Montregard (43) . .	221	G4
Montréjeau (31) . .	305	H1
Montrelais (44) . .	124	C4
Montrem (24) . .	213	J4
Montrésor (37) . .	147	F2
Montret (71) . .	172	B2
Montreuil (28) . .	57	F4
Montreuil (62) . .	4	C6
Montreuil (85) . .	160	D5
Montreuil (93) . .	59	F3
Montreuil-au-Houlme (61) . .	53	K5
Montreuil-aux-Lions (02) . .	60	C1
Montreuil-Bellay (49) . .	144	C2
Montreuil-Bonnin (86) . .	162	D3
Montreuil-des-Landes (35) . .	80	A5
Montreuil-en-Auge (14) . .	33	J5
Montreuil-en-Caux (76) . .	16	A4
Montreuil-en-Touraine (37) . .	128	B3
Montreuil-Juigné (49) . .	125	G2
Montreuil-la-Cambe (61) . .	54	D3
Montreuil-l'Argillé (27) . .	55	G2
Montreuil-le-Chétif (72) . .	82	C5
Montreuil-le-Gast (35) . .	79	F2
Montreuil-le-Henri (72) . .	107	H4
Montreuil-Poulay (53) . .	81	H3
Montreuil-sur-Barse (10) . .	90	D5
Montreuil-sur-Blaise (52) . .	91	K2
Montreuil-sur-Brêche (60) . .	37	J1
Montreuil-sur-Epte (95) . .	36	D5
Montreuil-sur-Ille (35) . .	79	G2
Montreuil-sur-Loir (49) . .	125	J1
Montreuil-sur-Lozon (50) . .	31	G3
Montreuil-sur-Maine (49) . .	125	F1
Montreuil-sur-Thérain (60) . .	37	H3
Montreuil-sur-Thonnance (52) . .	92	B2
Montreuillon (58) . .	152	A1
Montreux (54) . .	67	H6
Montreux-Château (90) . .	139	K1
Montreux-Jeune (68) . .	139	K1
Montreux-Vieux (68) . .	119	K6
Montrevault (49) . .	124	B6
Montrevel (38) . .	207	G5
Montrevel (39) . .	173	F5
Montrevel-en-Bresse (01) . .	172	C6
Montrichard (41) . .	128	D5
Montricher-Albanne (73) . .	225	H2
Montricoux (82) . .	250	B6
Montrieux-en-Sologne (41) . .	129	J3
Montrigaud (26) . .	222	E3
Montriond (74) . .	192	A1
Montrodat (48) . .	237	G6
Montrol-Sénard (87) . .	180	E4
Montrollet (16) . .	180	D5
Montromant (69) . .	205	H3
Montrond (05) . .	258	D2
Montrond (39) . .	156	A6
Montrond-le-Château (25) . .	156	C1
Montrond-les-Bains (42) . .	204	E3
Montrosier (81) . .	250	E5
Montrottier (69) . .	205	G2
Montroty (76) . .	36	D2
Montrouge (92) . .	58	E4
Montrouveau (41) . .	107	J6
Montroy (17) . .	176	E2
Montrozier (12) . .	252	C2
Montry (77) . .	59	J3
Monts (37) . .	127	H6
Monts (60) . .	37	G5
Monts-en-Bessin (14) . .	32	C5
Monts-en-Ternois (62) . .	10	B2
Monts-sur-Guesnes (86) . .	145	F5
les Monts-Verts (48) . .	237	F2
Montsalès (12) . .	251	F1
Montsalier (04) . .	258	C6
Montsalvy (15) . .	235	J4
Montsapey (73) . .	209	F4
Montsauche-les-Settons (58) . .	152	C1
Montsaugeon (52) . .	136	C1
Montsaunès (31) . .	306	B1
Montsec (55) . .	65	G2
Montsecret (61) . .	53	G4
Montségur (09) . .	308	A4
Montségur-sur-Lauzon (26) . .	256	E2
Montselgues (07) . .	238	D6
Montséret (11) . .	310	B1
Montsérié (65) . .	305	G2
Montseron (09) . .	307	F2
Montseveroux (38) . .	206	C6
Montsoreau (49) . .	144	E1
Montsoué (40) . .	265	G6
Montsoult (95) . .	58	E1
Montsûrs (53) . .	81	G6
Montsurvent (50) . .	30	D3
Montsuzain (10) . .	90	B3
Montureux-et-Prantigny (70) . .	137	G3
Montureux-lès-Baulay (70) . .	117	K4
Montusclat (43) . .	220	E6
Montussaint (25) . .	138	C3
Montussan (33) . .	229	J1
Montvalen (81) . .	269	J3
Montvalent (46) . .	233	K2
Montvalezan (73) . .	193	B3
Montvendre (26) . .	240	D1
Montverdun (42) . .	204	D3
Montvernier (73) . .	225	G1
Montvert (15) . .	216	E6
Montviette (14) . .	54	D1
Montville (76) . .	15	K6
Montviron (50) . .	51	J2
Montzéville (55) . .	43	G4
Monviel (47) . .	231	J5
Monze (11) . .	290	C6
Moon-sur-Elle (50) . .	31	H2
Moosch (68) . .	119	K3
Mooslargue (68) . .	97	B5
Moraches (58) . .	133	G6
Moragne (17) . .	177	G5
Morainville (28) . .	85	K4
Morainville-Jouveaux (27) . .	34	B4
Morainvilliers (78) . .	58	A2
Morancé (69) . .	188	B6
Morancez (28) . .	85	G3
Morancourt (52) . .	91	K3
Morand (37) . .	128	B2
Morangis (51) . .	61	K2
Morangis (91) . .	58	E5
Morangles (60) . .	37	J5
Morannes (49) . .	105	H5
Moranville (55) . .	43	K5
Moras (38) . .	206	D3
Moras-en-Valloire (26) . .	222	D2
Morbecque (59) . .	3	J6
Morbier (39) . .	174	A3
Morcenx (40) . .	245	F6
Morchain (80) . .	19	G3
Morchies (62) . .	11	G4
Morcourt (02) . .	20	A2
Morcourt (80) . .	18	E2
Mordelles (35) . .	78	E4
Moréac (56) . .	101	F2
Morée (41) . .	108	D4
Moreilles (85) . .	160	B5
Morelmaison (88) . .	93	J4
Morembert (10) . .	90	D2
Morestel (38) . .	207	G3
Moret-sur-Loing (77) . .	87	J4
Morétel-de-Mailles (38) . .	208	C4
Morette (38) . .	223	H2
Moreuil (80) . .	18	C3
Morey (71) . .	153	J6
Morey-Saint-Denis (21) . .	154	B1
Morez (39) . .	174	A3
Morfontaine (54) . .	26	D3
Morganx (40) . .	265	G6
Morgemoulin (55) . .	26	B6
Morgny (27) . .	36	C2
Morgny-en-Thiérache (02) . .	21	H3
Morgny-la-Pommeraye (76) . .	35	K1
Morhange (57) . .	66	E2
Moriat (63) . .	219	F1
Morienne (59) . .	17	F3
Morienval (60) . .	38	E4
Morières-lès-Avignon (84) . .	276	C2
Moriers (28) . .	85	F6
Morieux (22) . .	49	H6
Moriez (04) . .	279	J1
Morigny (50) . .	31	H6
Morigny-Champigny (91) . .	86	D3
Morillon (74) . .	192	A3
Morionvilliers (52) . .	92	D3
Morisel (80) . .	18	C3
Moriville (88) . .	94	D3
Moriviller (54) . .	94	D2
Morizécourt (88) . .	117	H1
Morizès (33) . .	230	C5
Morlaàs (64) . .	284	C3
Morlac (18) . .	166	E2
Morlaix (29) . .	47	G4
Morlancourt (80) . .	18	D1
Morlanne (64) . .	284	B1
Morlet (71) . .	153	H4
Morley (55) . .	92	B1
Morlhon-le-Haut (12) . .	251	H3
Morlincourt (60) . .	19	H6
Mormaison (85) . .	141	K4
Mormant (77) . .	87	K1
Mormant-sur-Vernisson (45) . .	111	J3
Mormès (32) . .	266	A3
Mormoiron (84) . .	257	J5
Mornac (16) . .	197	F3
Mornac-sur-Seudre (17) . .	194	C2
Mornand (42) . .	204	D3
Mornans (26) . .	240	E5
Mornant (69) . .	205	J4
Mornas (84) . .	256	E4
Mornay (71) . .	170	E4
Mornay-Berry (18) . .	150	B3
Mornay-sur-Allier (18) . .	150	C6
Moroges (71) . .	171	H1
Morogues (18) . .	149	J2
Morosaglia (2B) . .	319	G4
Morre (25) . .	138	A6
Morsain (02) . .	39	H2
Morsains (51) . .	61	F4
Morsalines (50) . .	29	F3
Morsan (27) . .	34	D5
Morsang-sur-Orge (91) . .	58	E6
Morsang-sur-Seine (91) . .	87	F1
Morsbach (57) . .	68	B2
Morsbronn-les-Bains (67) . .	25	A3
Morschwiller (67) . .	69	J6
Morschwiller-le-Bas (68) . .	97	B2
Morsiglia (2B) . .	317	C2
Mortagne (88) . .	95	G4
Mortagne-au-Perche (61) . .	83	H2
Mortagne-du-Nord (59) . .	7	H6
Mortagne-sur-Gironde (17) . .	194	E5
Mortagne-sur-Sèvre (85) . .	142	E3
Mortain (50) . .	52	D5
Mortcerf (77) . .	59	K4
la Morte (38) . .	224	C5
Morteau (25) . .	157	H2
Morteaux-Coulibœuf (14) . .	54	D2
Mortefontaine (02) . .	39	G3
Mortefontaine (60) . .	38	B6
Mortefontaine-en-Thelle (60) . .	37	H4
Mortemart (87) . .	180	E4
Mortemer (60) . .	18	E6
Mortemer (76) . .	16	E4
Mortery (77) . .	88	D1
Morthomiers (18) . .	149	F3
Mortiers (02) . .	20	D4
Mortiers (17) . .	195	K6

Morton (86) 144 D2
Mortrée (61) 54 D6
Mortroux (23) 166 A6
Mortzwiller (68) 119 K5
Morval (62) 11 F6
Morvillars (90) 139 J2
Morville (50) 28 D4
Morville (88) 93 H5
Morville-en-Beauce (45) 86 C5
Morville-lès-Vic (57) 66 D3
Morville-sur-Andelle (76) 36 B1
Morville-sur-Nied (57) 66 C1
Morville-sur-Seille (54) 66 A2
Morvillers (60) 17 G6
Morvillers-Saint-Saturnin (80) 17 G3
Morvilliers (10) 91 F3
Morvilliers (28) 56 B6
Mory (62) 11 F4
Mory-Montcrux (60) 18 B6
Morzine (74) 192 B2
Mosles (14) 32 A3
Moslins (51) 61 K5
Mosnac (16) 196 C4
Mosnac (17) 195 H5
Mosnay (36) 165 H3
Mosnes (37) 128 C4
Mosset (66) 314 B2
Mosson (21) 115 G3
Mostuéjouls (12) 253 H4
Motey-Besuche (70) 137 G5
Motey-sur-Saône (70) 137 H2
la Mothe-Achard (85) 159 F2
la Mothe-Saint-Héray (79) 162 A6
Mothern (67) 25 E2
Motreff (29) 75 J3
la Motte (22) 77 K4
la Motte (83) 298 E1
la Motte-Chalancon (26) 241 H6
la Motte-d'Aigues (84) 277 J4
la Motte-d'Aveillans (38) 224 B6
la Motte-de-Galaure (26) 222 C3
la Motte-du-Caire (04) 259 G2
la Motte-en-Bauges (73) 208 D2
la Motte-en-Champsaur (05) . . . 242 E6
la Motte-Fanjas (26) 223 G5
la Motte-Feuilly (36) 166 C4
la Motte-Fouquet (61) 81 K1
la Motte-Saint-Jean (71) 170 A4
la Motte-Saint-Martin (38) 224 A6
la Motte-Servolex (73) 208 B3
la Motte-Ternant (21) 134 C6
la Motte-Tilly (10) 88 E2
Mottereau (28) 84 D5
Motteville (76) 15 H5
Mottier (38) 207 F6
Motz (73) 190 C5
Mouacourt (54) 66 E5
Mouais (44) 103 G4
Mouans-Sartoux (06) 280 D5
Mouaville (54) 26 D6
Mouazé (35) 79 G3
Mouchamps (85) 142 C6
Mouchan (32) 267 F2
Mouchard (39) 155 K3
la Mouche (50) 51 K1
Mouchès (32) 286 B1
Mouchin (59) 7 F5
Mouchy-le-Châtel (60) 37 J3
Moudeyres (43) 220 E6
Mouen (14) 32 D5
Mouettes (27) 57 F3
Mouffy (89) 133 F1
Mouflaines (27) 36 C4
Mouflers (80) 9 J6
Mouflières (80) 17 F1
Mougins (06) 280 E5
Mougon (79) 178 C1
Mouguerre (64) 282 C1
Mouhers (36) 165 K3
Mouhet (36) 165 F6
Mouhous (64) 284 E2
Mouillac (33) 211 K5
Mouillac (82) 250 D3
la Mouille (39) 174 A4
Mouilleron (52) 116 B6
Mouilleron-en-Pareds (85) . . . 160 D2
Mouilleron-le-Captif (85) 159 H1
Mouilly (55) 43 K6
Moulainville (55) 43 J5
Moularès (81) 251 J6
Moulay (53) 81 G3
Moulayrès (81) 270 C5
Moulédous (65) 285 K5
Moulès-et-Baucels (34) 274 A2
Mouleydier (24) 231 J2
Moulézan (30) 274 E2
Moulhard (28) 84 C6
Moulicent (61) 83 K1
Moulidars (16) 196 C3
Mouliets-et-Villemartin (33) . . . 230 C2
Mouliherne (49) 126 C3
Moulin-Mage (81) 272 D6
Moulin-Neuf (09) 308 C1
Moulin-Neuf (24) 212 D6
Moulin-sous-Touvent (60) 39 G2
Moulineaux (76) 35 G3
Moulines (14) 53 K1
Moulines (50) 80 C1
Moulinet (06) 311 B4
Moulinet (47) 231 J6
le Moulinet-sur-Solin (45) 111 H5
Moulins (02) 40 C2

Moulins (03) 168 E3
Moulins (35) 79 J6
Moulins-en-Tonnerrois (89) . . . 114 A6
Moulins-Engilbert (58) 152 A4
Moulins-la-Marche (61) 55 G6
Moulins-le-Carbonnel (72) 82 C3
Moulins-lès-Metz (57) 44 E5
Moulins-Saint-Hubert (55) . . . 23 G5
Moulins-sur-Céphons (36) 147 J4
Moulins-sur-Orne (61) 54 A4
Moulins-sur-Ouanne (89) 112 E6
Moulins-sur-Yèvre (18) 149 H3
Moulis (09) 306 D3
Moulis-en-Médoc (33) 211 F5
Moulismes (86) 163 K6
Moulle (62) 3 F4
Moulon (33) 230 A2
Moulon (45) 111 G2
Moulotte (55) 44 B5
Moult (14) 33 G6
Moumoulous (65) 285 K3
Moumour (64) 283 K5
Mounes-Prohencoux (12) 272 B4
Mourède (32) 267 F4
Mourens (33) 230 A4
Mourenx (64) 284 A3
Mouret (12) 235 J6
Moureuille (63) 184 D3
Mourèze (34) 273 G6
Mouriès (13) 276 C5
Mouriez (62) 9 H2
Mourioux-Vieilleville (23) 182 B4
Mourjou (15) 235 G4
Mourmelon-le-Grand (51) 41 J5
Mourmelon-le-Petit (51) 41 H5
Mournans-Charbonny (39) . . . 156 B6
Mouron (08) 42 C3
Mouron-sur-Yonne (58) 151 K1
Mouroux (77) 60 B4
Mours (95) 37 J6
Mours-Saint-Eusèbe (26) 222 D5
Mourvilles-Basses (31) 288 C4
Mourvilles-Hautes (31) 289 F3
Mouscardès (40) 264 C6
Moussac (30) 275 F1
Moussac (86) 180 B1
Moussages (15) 217 H3
Moussan (11) 291 H5
Moussé (35) 104 A3
Mousseaux-lès-Bray (77) 88 C3
Mousseaux-Neuville (27) 57 F3
Mousseaux-sur-Seine (78) . . . 57 H1
Moussey (10) 90 B6
Moussey (57) 67 G5
Moussey (88) 95 J2
les Moussières (39) 173 K6
Mousson (54) 65 K2
Moussonvilliers (61) 55 K6
Moussoulens (11) 289 K5
Moussy (51) 61 K1
Moussy (58) 151 G1
Moussy (95) 37 F6
Moussy-le-Neuf (77) 59 G1
Moussy-le-Vieux (77) 59 H1
Moussy-Verneuil (02) 40 B2
Moustajon (31) 305 H5
Moustéru (22) 48 B5
Moustey (40) 245 H2
Moustier (47) 231 F5
Moustier-en-Fagne (59) 13 K5
Moustier-Ventadour (19) 216 E1
Moustiers-Sainte-Marie (04) . . . 279 F2
le Moustoir (22) 75 J3
Moustoir-Ac (56) 101 F3
Moustoir-Remungol (56) 100 E1
la Moutade (63) 185 G5
le Moutaret (38) 208 D5
Mouterhouse (57) 69 H4
Mouterre-Silly (86) 144 D4
Mouterre-sur-Blourde (86) . . . 180 C2
Mouthe (25) 174 C1
le Moutherot (39) 137 H6
Mouthier-en-Bresse (71) 155 F5
Mouthier-Haute-Pierre (25) . . . 156 E2
Mouthiers-sur-Boëme (16) . . . 196 D4
Mouthoumet (11) 309 H3
Moutier-d'Ahun (23) 183 F4
Moutier-Malcard (23) 166 B6
Moutier-Rozeille (23) 183 G6
Moutiers (28) 85 J5
Moutiers (35) 104 A2
Moutiers (54) 27 F6
Moûtiers (73) 209 H5
Moutiers-au-Perche (61) 84 A2
les Moutiers-en-Auge (14) . . . 54 C3
les Moutiers-en-Cinglais (14) . . . 53 J1
Moutiers-en-Puisaye (89) 132 C2
les Moutiers-en-Retz (44) 122 C6
les Moutiers-Hubert (14) 55 F2
Moutiers-les-Mauxfaits (85) . . . 159 H4
Moutiers-Saint-Jean (21) 134 C2
Moutiers-sous-Argenton (79) . . . 143 K4
Moutiers-sous-Chantemerle (79) . . . 161 F1
Moutiers-sur-le-Lay (85) 160 A3
Mouton (16) 179 H6
Moutonne (39) 173 G3
Moutonneau (16) 179 H6
Moutoux (39) 156 B6
Moutrot (54) 65 H6
Mouvaux (59) 6 E3
Moux (11) 290 E6
Moux-en-Morvan (58) 152 D1

Mouxy (73) 208 B2
Mouy (60) 37 K3
Mouy-sur-Seine (77) 88 D3
Mouzay (37) 146 C3
Mouzay (55) 43 G1
Mouzeil (44) 123 J1
Mouzens (24) 232 D2
Mouzens (81) 289 G1
Mouzeuil-Saint-Martin (85) . . . 160 C4
Mouzieys-Panens (81) 250 E6
Mouzieys-Teulet (81) 271 F3
Mouzillon (44) 123 K5
Mouzon (08) 23 G5
Mouzon (16) 197 J1
Moval (90) 139 H1
Moyaux (14) 34 B5
Moydans (05) 258 B1
Moye (74) 190 D6
Moyemont (88) 94 E3
Moyen (54) 94 E1
Moyencourt (80) 19 G4
Moyencourt-lès-Poix (80) 17 J3
Moyenmoutier (88) 95 H3
Moyenneville (60) 38 C1
Moyenneville (62) 10 E4
Moyenneville (80) 9 F5
Moyenvic (57) 66 E3
Moyeuvre-Grande (57) 27 F5
Moyeuvre-Petite (57) 27 F5
Moyon (50) 31 H5
Moyrazès (12) 252 A3
Moyvillers (60) 38 C2
Mozac (63) 185 F6
Mozé-sur-Louet (49) 125 G5
Muchedent (76) 16 A3
Mudaison (34) 274 D6
Muel (35) 78 B4
Muespach (68) 97 C5
Muespach-le-Haut (68) 97 D5
Mugron (40) 264 E4
Muhlbach-sur-Bruche (67) . . . 70 B4
Muhlbach-sur-Munster (68) . . . 119 K1
Muides-sur-Loire (41) 129 G1
Muidorge (60) 37 H1
Muids (27) 35 K4
Muille-Villette (80) 19 H4
Muirancourt (60) 19 H5
Muizon (51) 40 D4
les Mujouls (06) 280 C2
la Mulatière (69) 206 A2
Mulcent (78) 57 H3
Mulcey (57) 67 F3
Mulhausen (67) 69 J5
Mulhouse (68) 97 C2
Mulsanne (72) 106 E4
Mulsans (41) 129 F1
Mun (65) 285 K4
Munchhausen (67) 25 D2
Munchhouse (68) 97 D1
Muncq-Nieurlet (62) 3 F4
Mundolsheim (67) 25 A6
Muneville-le-Bingard (50) 30 D3
Muneville-sur-Mer (50) 30 D5
le Mung (17) 177 H6
Munster (57) 67 H2
Munster (68) 96 A4
Muntzenheim (68) 96 D3
Munwiller (68) 96 C6
Mur-de-Barrez (12) 235 K2
Mûr-de-Bretagne (22) 76 D4
Mur-de-Sologne (41) 129 H4
Muracciole (2B) 321 F2
Murasson (12) 272 A4
Murat (03) 168 A6
Murat (15) 218 C5
Murat-le-Quaire (63) 201 K4
Murat-sur-Vèbre (81) 272 B5
Murato (2B) 319 G2
la Muraz (74) 191 G2
Murbach (68) 96 A6
la Mure (38) 242 B1
la Mure-Argens (04) 260 C5
Mureaumont (60) 17 G5
les Mureaux (78) 58 A2
Mureils (26) 222 C3
Mûres (74) 208 C1
Muret (31) 288 A2
Muret-et-Crouttes (02) 39 K4
Muret-le-Château (12) 252 B1
la Murette (38) 207 H6
Murianette (38) 224 B3
Murinais (38) 223 H4
Murles (34) 274 A5
Murlin (58) 150 E1
Muro (2B) 318 C4
Murol (63) 202 C4
Murols (12) 235 J3
Muron (17) 177 G4
Murs (36) 146 E5
Murs (84) 277 F1
Mûrs-Érigné (49) 125 G4
Murs-et-Gélignieux (01) 207 J3
Murtin-et-Bogny (08) 22 B3
Murvaux (55) 43 G2
Murviel-lès-Béziers (34) 291 K3
Murviel-lès-Montpellier (34) . . . 274 A6
Murville (54) 26 D4
Murzo (2A) 320 C4
Mus (30) 275 F4
Muscourt (02) 40 C3
Musculdy (64) 283 G5
Musièges (74) 190 D4

Musigny (21) 153 H1
Mussey-sur-Marne (52) 92 B3
Mussidan (24) 213 G5
Mussig (67) 71 C5
Mussy-la-Fosse (21) 134 E3
Mussy-sous-Dun (71) 187 H2
Mussy-sur-Seine (10) 115 F3
Mutigny (51) 41 F6
Mutigny (39) 137 F5
Mutrécy (14) 32 D6
Muttersholtz (67) 71 C5
Mutzenhouse (67) 70 D1
Mutzig (67) 70 C4
le Muy (83) 298 E1
Muzeray (55) 26 B5
Muzillac (56) 121 J1
Muzy (27) 57 F4
Myans (73) 208 C4
Myennes (58) 132 A4
Myon (25) 156 B3

N

Nabas (64) 283 H3
Nabinaud (16) 213 F2
Nabirat (24) 233 G3
Nabringhen (62) 2 C5
Nachamps (17) 177 J4
Nadaillac (24) 215 H5
Nadaillac-de-Rouge (46) 233 H2
Nades (03) 184 E3
Nadillac (46) 233 J6
Nagel-Séez-Mesnil (27) 56 D2
Nages (81) 272 A5
Nages-et-Solorgues (30) 275 F4
Nahuja (66) 313 H5
Nailhac (24) 214 E5
Naillat (23) 182 B2
Nailloux (31) 288 D4
Nailly (89) 88 C6
Naintré (86) 163 G1
Nainville-les-Roches (91) 87 F2
Naisey-les-Granges (25) 138 C6
Naives-en-Blois (55) 64 C5
Naives-Rosières (55) 64 B4
Naix-aux-Forges (55) 64 D6
Naizin (56) 101 F1
Najac (12) 251 F4
Nalliers (85) 160 B4
Nalliers (86) 164 K3
Nalzen (09) 308 A3
Nambsheim (68) 96 E5
Nampcel (60) 39 G1
Nampcelles-la-Cour (02) 21 G3
Nampont (80) 9 F2
Namps-Maisnil (80) 17 J3
Nampteuil-sous-Muret (02) . . . 39 K3
Nampty (80) 18 A3
Nan-sous-Thil (21) 134 D5
Nanc-lès-Saint-Amour (39) . . . 172 E5
Nançay (18) 130 D5
Nance (39) 172 E1
Nances (73) 208 A4
Nanclars (16) 196 E1
Nançois-le-Grand (55) 64 D5
Nançois-sur-Ornain (55) 64 C5
Nancras (17) 194 D2
Nancray (25) 138 B6
Nancray-sur-Rimarde (45) . . . 110 E2
Nancuise (39) 173 G4
Nancy (54) 66 A5
Nancy-sur-Cluses (74) 191 K3
Nandax (42) 187 F3
Nandy (77) 87 G1
Nangeville (45) 86 E5
Nangis (77) 88 A1
Nangy (74) 191 G2
Nannay (58) 132 C5
Nans (25) 138 D3
les Nans (39) 156 B6
Nans-les-Pins (83) 297 G3
Nans-sous-Sainte-Anne (25) . . . 156 B3
Nant (12) 273 F1
Nant-le-Grand (55) 64 B5
Nant-le-Petit (55) 64 B5
Nanteau-sur-Essonne (77) . . . 87 F4
Nanteau-sur-Lunain (77) 87 J3
Nanterre (92) 58 D3
Nantes (44) 123 G4
Nantes-en-Ratier (38) 224 B6
Nanteuil (79) 162 A5
Nanteuil-Auriac-de-Bourzac (24) . . . 213 G3
Nanteuil-en-Vallée (16) 179 H5
Nanteuil-la-Forêt (51) 40 E6
Nanteuil-la-Fosse (02) 39 K3
Nanteuil-le-Haudouin (60) . . . 38 D6
Nanteuil-lès-Meaux (77) 59 K2
Nanteuil-Notre-Dame (02) . . . 39 K5
Nanteuil-sur-Aisne (08) 41 H1
Nanteuil-sur-Marne (77) 60 C2
Nantey (39) 172 E5
Nantheuil (24) 214 C1
Nanthiat (24) 214 D1
Nantiat (87) 181 G5
Nantillé (17) 178 A6
Nantillois (55) 43 F3
Nantilly (70) 137 F3
Nantoin (38) 207 F6
Nantois (55) 64 C6
Nanton (71) 171 J2

Nantouillet (77) 59 H2
Nantoux (21) 153 K3
Nantua (01) 190 A2
Naours (80) 10 A6
Narbéfontaine (57) 45 J5
Narbonne (11) 291 H6
Narcastet (64) 284 D5
Narcy (52) 92 A1
Narcy (58) 150 D1
Nargis (45) 111 J1
Narnhac (15) 236 B1
Narp (64) 283 J3
Narrosse (40) 264 B4
Nasbinals (48) 236 D4
Nassandres (27) 34 E6
Nassiet (40) 264 C6
Nassigny (03) 167 H4
Nastringues (24) 230 E2
Nattages (01) 207 K2
Natzwiller (67) 70 B5
Naucelle (12) 251 K5
Naucelles (15) 235 H1
Naujac-sur-Mer (33) 210 C2
Naujan-et-Postiac (33) 230 B3
Nauroy (02) 19 K1
Naussac (12) 234 E6
Naussac (48) 238 B4
Naussannes (24) 232 A3
Nauvay (72) 83 F5
Nauviale (12) 235 H6
Navacelles (30) 255 J5
Navailles-Angos (64) 284 D3
Navarrenx (64) 283 J4
Naveil (41) 108 C5
Navenne (70) 138 B1
Naves (03) 185 F3
Naves (19) 216 B2
Naves (59) 11 K4
Navès (81) 289 K1
Nâves-Parmelan (74) 191 G5
Navilly (71) 154 D2
Nay (50) 30 E2
Nay (64) 284 E5
Nayemont-les-Fosses (88) . . . 95 J4
le Nayrac (12) 235 K5
Nazelles-Négron (37) 128 B4
Néac (33) 230 B1
Néant-sur-Yvel (56) 101 K1
Neau (53) 81 H6
Neaufles-Auvergny (27) 55 K3
Neaufles-Saint-Martin (27) . . . 36 D4
Neauphe-sous-Essai (61) 82 E1
Neauphe-sur-Dive (61) 54 D3
Neauphle-le-Château (78) . . . 58 A4
Neauphle-le-Vieux (78) 57 K4
Neauphlette (78) 57 G2
Neaux (42) 187 G5
Nébian (34) 273 H6
Nébias (11) 308 D4
Nébing (57) 67 G2
Nébouzat (63) 202 B3
Nécy (61) 54 B3
Nedde (87) 200 A3
Nédon (62) 5 H1
Nédonchel (62) 5 H5
Neewiller-près-Lauterbourg (67) . . . 25 D2
Neffes (05) 242 E6
Neffiès (34) 292 B1
Néfiach (66) 309 K6
Négrepelisse (82) 250 A6
Négreville (50) 28 D4
Négrondes (24) 214 B2
Néhou (50) 28 D5
Nelling (57) 67 G1
Nemours (77) 87 H5
Nempont-Saint-Firmin (62) . . . 9 F2
Nénigan (31) 286 E3
Néons-sur-Creuse (36) 164 B1
Néoules (83) 297 K3
Néoux (23) 183 H6
Nepvant (55) 23 H6
Nérac (47) 247 J5
Nerbis (40) 264 E4
Nercillac (16) 196 A2
Néré (17) 178 C5
Néret (36) 166 C3
Nérigean (33) 230 A2
Nérignac (86) 180 C1
Néris-les-Bains (03) 184 B1
Nernier (74) 174 D5
Néron (28) 85 G1
Néronde (42) 204 E1
Néronde-sur-Dore (63) 203 H2
Nérondes (18) 150 A4
Ners (30) 274 E1
Nersac (16) 196 C4
Nerville-la-Forêt (95) 37 J6
Néry (60) 38 D4
Neschers (63) 202 E4
Nescus (09) 307 H2
Nesle (80) 19 G4
Nesle-et-Massoult (21) 114 E5
Nesle-Hodeng (76) 16 D4
Nesle-la-Reposte (51) 61 F6
Nesle-le-Repons (51) 61 H1
Nesle-l'Hôpital (80) 17 F2
Nesle-Normandeuse (76) 17 F2
Nesles (62) 4 B4
Nesles-la-Montagne (02) 60 E1
Nesles-la-Vallée (95) 37 H6

383

Neslette (80) 17 F1
Nesmy (85) 159 J2
Nesploy (45) 110 E3
Nespouls (19) 215 J5
Nessa (2B) 318 D3
Nestier (65) 305 G1
Nettancourt (55) 63 J3
Neublans-Abergement (39) . . 155 F4
Neubois (67) 71 A5
le Neubourg (27) 35 G5
Neuchâtel-Urtière (25) 139 G4
Neuf-Berquin (59) 6 A4
Neuf-Brisach (68) 96 D4
Neuf-Église (63) 184 D4
Neuf-Marché (76) 36 D2
Neuf-Mesnil (59) 13 G3
Neufbosc (76) 16 C5
le Neufbourg (50) 52 D5
Neufchâteau (88) 93 G3
Neufchâtel-en-Bray (76) . . . 16 D4
Neufchâtel-en-Saosnois (72) . 82 E3
Neufchâtel-Hardelot (62) . . . 4 B4
Neufchâtel-sur-Aisne (02) . . 41 F2
Neufchef (57) 27 F5
Neufchelles (60) 39 G6
Neuffons (33) 230 D4
Neuffontaines (58) 133 H5
Neufgrange (57) 68 D3
Neuflieux (02) 19 J5
Neuflize (08) 41 H2
Neufmaison (08) 22 B3
Neufmaisons (54) 95 G2
Neufmanil (08) 22 D3
Neufmesnil (50) 28 D6
Neufmoulin (80) 9 G5
Neufmoulins (57) 67 H4
Neufmoutiers-en-Brie (77) . . 59 J4
le Neufour (55) 42 E5
Neufvillage (57) 67 F1
Neufvy-sur-Aronde (60) . . . 38 C1
Neugartheim-Ittlenheim (67) . 70 D2
Neuhaeusel (67) 25 D3
Neuil (37) 145 J1
Neuilh (65) 304 C1
Neuillac (17) 195 J5
Neuillay-les-Bois (36) 165 G1
Neuillé (49) 126 B5
Neuillé-le-Lierre (37) 128 A3
Neuillé-Pont-Pierre (37) . . . 127 H2
Neuilly (27) 57 F2
Neuilly (58) 151 H1
Neuilly (89) 112 E4
Neuilly-en-Donjon (03) . . . 169 K6
Neuilly-en-Dun (18) 150 A6
Neuilly-en-Sancerre (18) . . . 131 H6
Neuilly-en-Thelle (60) 37 J5
Neuilly-en-Vexin (95) 37 G5
Neuilly-la-Forêt (14) 31 H1
Neuilly-le-Bisson (61) 82 E2
Neuilly-le-Brignon (37) . . . 146 B4
Neuilly-le-Dien (80) 9 J3
Neuilly-le-Réal (03) 169 F5
Neuilly-le-Vendin (53) 81 K2
Neuilly-lès-Dijon (21) 136 B6
Neuilly-l'Évêque (52) 116 E3
Neuilly-l'Hôpital (80) 9 G4
Neuilly-Plaisance (93) 59 G3
Neuilly-Saint-Front (02) . . . 39 H5
Neuilly-sous-Clermont (60) . 38 A3
Neuilly-sur-Eure (61) 84 B2
Neuilly-sur-Marne (93) . . . 59 G3
Neuilly-sur-Seine (92) 58 D3
Neuilly-sur-Suize (52) 116 B2
Neulette (62) 9 K1
Neulise (42) 187 G6
Neulles (17) 195 J5
Neulliac (56) 76 D5
Neung-sur-Beuvron (41) . . . 129 K3
Neunkirchen-lès-Bouzonville (57) . 45 J2
Neure (03) 168 B1
Neurey-en-Vaux (70) 118 B5
Neurey-lès-la-Demie (70) . . 138 B2
Neussargues-Moissac (15) . . 218 D4
Neuve-Chapelle (62) 6 B5
Neuve-Église (67) 71 A4
la Neuve-Grange (27) 36 C3
la Neuve-Lyre (27) 55 K3
Neuve-Maison (02) 21 G1
Neuvecelle (74) 175 G5
Neuvéglise (15) 236 D1
Neuvelle-lès-Cromary (70) . . 138 A4
Neuvelle-lès-la-Charité (70) . 137 K2
la Neuvelle-lès-Lure (70) . . 118 E5
la Neuvelle-lès-Scey (70) . . 117 J6
Neuvelle-lès-Voisey (52) . . . 117 H4
Neuves-Maisons (54) 65 K6
la Neuville-devant-
    Lépanges (88) 95 F5
la Neuville-sous-Châtenois (88) . 93 H4
la Neuveville-sous-Châtenois (88) . 93 F5
la Neuveville-sous-Montfort (88) . 93 K5
Neuvic (19) 217 F1
Neuvic (24) 213 H4
Neuvic-Entier (87) 199 J3
Neuvicq (17) 212 B3
Neuvicq-le-Château (17) . . . 196 B1
Neuvillalais (72) 82 C6
Neuville (19) 216 B5
la Neuville (59) 6 D6
Neuville (63) 203 G2
la Neuville-à-Maire (08) . . . 22 E5
la Neuville-au-Bois (80) . . . 17 G1
Neuville-au-Cornet (62) . . . 10 B2

Neuville-au-Plain (50) 29 F5
la Neuville-au-Pont (51) 42 D5
la Neuville-aux-Bois (45) 110 B2
la Neuville-aux-Bois (51) 63 J2
la Neuville-aux-Joûtes (08) 21 J1
la Neuville-aux-Larris (51) 40 D5
la Neuville-Bosc (60) 37 G5
la Neuville-Bosmont (02) 21 H4
la Neuville-Bourjonval (62) 11 H5
la Neuville-Chant-d'Oisel (76) . . . 35 K3
la Neuville-Coppegueule (80) . . . 17 F2
la Neuville-d'Aumont (60) 37 H3
Neuville-Day (08) 42 B1
la Neuville-du-Bosc (27) 35 F5
Neuville-en-Avesnois (59) 12 D4
la Neuville-en-Beaumont (50) . . . 28 C6
la Neuville-en-Beine (02) 19 J5
la Neuville-en-Ferrain (59) 6 E3
la Neuville-en-Hez (60) 37 K2
la Neuville-en-Tourne-à-Fuy (08) . 41 J3
Neuville-en-Verdunois (55) 64 C2
la Neuville-Ferrières (76) 16 D4
la Neuville-Garnier (60) 37 G3
la Neuville-Housset (02) 20 E3
la Neuville-lès-Bray (80) 18 E1
Neuville-les-Dames (01) 188 E2
la Neuville-lès-Dorengt (02) 20 D1
la Neuville-lès-Decize (58) 168 L1
Neuville-lès-Loeuilly (80) 17 K3
Neuville-lès-This (08) 22 C3
Neuville-lès-Vaucouleurs (55) . . . 65 F6
la Neuville-lès-Wasigny (08) 21 K5
Neuville-lez-Beaulieu (08) 21 K2
Neuville-près-Sées (61) 54 E6
la Neuville-Saint-Amand (02) . . . 20 A3
la Neuville-Saint-Pierre (60) 37 J1
la Neuville-Saint-Rémy (59) 11 J4
la Neuville-Saint-Vaast (62) 10 E2
la Neuville-Sire-Bernard (80) . . . 18 C4
Neuville-sous-Montreuil (62) 4 C6
Neuville-sur-Ailette (02) 40 C1
Neuville-sur-Ain (01). 189 H3
Neuville-sur-Authou (27) 34 D5
Neuville-sur-Brenne (37) 128 A2
Neuville-sur-Escaut (59) 12 B2
la Neuville-sur-Essonne (45) 86 E6
Neuville-sur-Margival (02) 39 K2
Neuville-sur-Oise (95) 58 B1
Neuville-sur-Ornain (55) 63 J3
la Neuville-sur-Oudeuil (60) 17 J6
la Neuville-sur-Ressons (60) 19 F6
Neuville-sur-Saône (69) 188 C6
Neuville-sur-Sarthe (72) 106 E1
Neuville-sur-Seine (10) 114 E2
Neuville-sur-Touques (61) 55 F3
Neuville-sur-Vannes (10) 89 J5
la Neuville-Vault (60) 37 F1
Neuville-Vitasse (62) 11 F3
Neuviller-la-Roche (67) 70 A5
Neuviller-lès-Badonviller (54) . . . 95 H1
Neuviller-sur-Moselle (54) 94 B1
Neuvillers-sur-Fave (88) 95 J4
Neuvillette (02) 20 B2
Neuvillette (80) 10 A4
Neuvillette-en-Charnie (72) 106 A1
Neuvilley (39) 155 H4
Neuvilly (59) 12 D4
Neuvilly-en-Argonne (55) 42 E5
Neuvireuil (62) 11 G2
Neuvizy (08) 22 B5
Neuvy (03) 168 E3
Neuvy (41) 129 H2
Neuvy (51) 61 F5
Neuvy-au-Houlme (61) 54 A4
Neuvy-Bouin (79) 161 H2
Neuvy-Deux-Clochers (18) 131 H6
Neuvy-en-Beauce (28) 86 A5
Neuvy-en-Champagne (72) 106 B1
Neuvy-en-Dunois (28) 85 G6
Neuvy-en-Mauges (49) 124 D6
Neuvy-en-Sullias (45) 110 D5
Neuvy-Grandchamp (71) 170 A3
Neuvy-le-Barrois (18) 150 C5
Neuvy-le-Roi (37) 127 H2
Neuvy-Pailloux (36) 148 B5
Neuvy-Saint-Sépulchre (36) 165 K3
Neuvy-Sautour (89) 113 J2
Neuvy-sur-Barangeon (18) 130 D6
Neuvy-sur-Loire (58) 131 K3
Neuwiller (68) 97 C6
Neuwiller-lès-Saverne (67) 69 G6
Névache (05) 225 K5
Nevers (58) 150 E4
Névez (29) 99 F4
Néville (76) 15 G3
Néville-sur-Mer (50) 29 F2
Nevoy (45) 111 G6
Nevy-lès-Dole (39) 155 G3
Nevy-sur-Seille (39) 173 G1
Nexon (87) 198 D3
Ney (39) 173 K1
Neydens (74) 191 F3
les Neyrolles (01) 190 A2
Neyron (01) 206 B1
Nézel (78) 57 K2
Nézignan-l'Évêque (34) 292 C4
Niafles (53) 104 C4
Niaux (09) 307 J5
Nibas (80) 8 E5
Nibelle (45) 110 E3

Nibles (04) 259 G3
Nice (06) 281 G4
Nicey (21) 114 D4
Nicey-sur-Aire (55) 64 C3
Nicole (47) 247 A3
Nicorps (50) 30 E4
Niderhoff (57) 67 J5
Niderviller (57) 67 K4
Niederbronn-les-Bains (67) 69 J4
Niederbruck (68) 119 J4
Niederentzen (68) 96 C5
Niederhaslach (67) 70 B4
Niederhausbergen (67) 25 A6
Niederhergheim (68) 96 C5
Niederlauterbach (67) 25 D2
Niedermodern (67) 69 J5
Niedermorschwihr (68) 96 B4
Niedernai (67) 70 D5
Niederroedern (67) 25 D2
Niederschaeffolsheim (67) 25 A4
Niedersoultzbach (67) 69 H6
Niedersteinbach (67) 69 K3
Niederstinzel (57) 67 J2
Niedervisse (57) 45 J4
Nielles-lès-Ardres (62) 2 E5
Nielles-lès-Bléquin (62) 2 E6
Nielles-lès-Calais (62) 2 C3
Nieppe (59) 6 B3
Niergnies (59) 11 K4
Nieudan (15) 217 F6
Nieuil (16) 179 K6
Nieuil-l'Espoir (86) 163 F4
Nieul (87) 181 G6
Nieul-le-Dolent (85) 159 H3
Nieul-le-Virouil (17) 195 F2
Nieul-lès-Saintes (17) 195 F2
Nieul-sur-l'Autise (85) 161 F5
Nieul-sur-Mer (17) 176 D2
Nieulle-sur-Seudre (17) 194 C2
Nieurlet (59) 3 G4
Niévroz (01) 206 C1
Niffer (68) 97 D3
Niherne (36) 147 J6
Nijon (52) 93 F5
Nilvange (57) 27 F4
Nîmes (30) 275 G3
Ninville (52) 116 D1
Niort (79) 161 H6
Niort-de-Sault (11) 308 C5
Niozelles (04) 278 C1
Nissan-lez-Enserune (34) 291 K4
Nistos (65) 305 G2
Nitry (89) 133 K1
Nitting (57) 67 J5
Nivelle (59) 7 H6
Nivillac (56) 102 A5
Nivillers (60) 37 H2
Nivolas-Vermelle (38) 207 F4
Nivollet-Montgriffon (01) 189 J4
Nixéville-Blercourt (55) 43 G5
le Nizan (33) 246 C1
Nizan-Gesse (31) 286 D5
Nizas (32) 287 H2
Nizas (34) 292 C2
Nizerolles (03) 186 A4
Nizy-le-Comte (02) 21 H6
Noailhac (12) 235 G6
Noailhac (19) 215 K5
Noailhac (81) 290 B1
Noaillac (33) 230 C6
Noaillan (33) 229 K6
Noailles (19) 215 K5
Noailles (60) 37 J3
Noailles (81) 270 C1
Noailly (42) 186 E3
Noalhac (48) 236 E3
Noalhat (63) 185 J6
Noards (27) 34 C4
Nocario (2B) 319 H4
Nocé (61) 83 J4
Noceta (2B) 321 G1
Nochize (71) 170 C5
la Nocle-Maulaix (58) 169 J1
Nod-sur-Seine (21) 115 F5
Nods (25) 156 E2
Noé (31) 288 A4
Noé (89) 88 E6
la Noë-Blanche (35) 103 F2
Noë-les-Mallets (10) 115 F1
la Noë-Poulain (27) 34 C4
Noël-Cerneux (25) 157 H1
Noëllet (49) 104 B6
les Noës (42) 186 C4
les Noës-près-Troyes (10) 90 A4
Nœux-lès-Auxi (62) 9 K3
Nœux-les-Mines (62) 6 A6
Nogaret (31) 289 G2
Nogaro (32) 266 B4
Nogent (52) 116 D2
Nogent-en-Othe (10) 113 J1
Nogent-l'Abbesse (51) 41 G4
Nogent-l'Artaud (02) 60 D2
Nogent-le-Bernard (72) 83 G5
Nogent-le-Phaye (28) 85 H3
Nogent-le-Roi (28) 57 G6
Nogent-le-Rotrou (28) 84 A4
Nogent-le-Sec (27) 56 C2
Nogent-lès-Montbard (21) 134 C2
Nogent-sur-Aube (10) 90 D2
Nogent-sur-Eure (28) 85 F3
Nogent-sur-Loir (72) 127 F1
Nogent-sur-Marne (94) 59 F4

Nogent-sur-Oise (60) 38 A4
Nogent-sur-Seine (10) 89 F2
Nogent-sur-Vernisson (45) 111 J5
Nogentel (02) 60 E1
Nogna (39) 173 H6
Noguères (64) 284 A3
Nohanent (63) 202 D2
Nohant-en-Goût (18) 149 J3
Nohant-en-Graçay (18) 148 B2
Nohant-Vic (36) 166 B3
Nohèdes (66) 314 A4
Nohic (82) 269 G3
Noidan (21) 134 E5
Noidans-le-Ferroux (70) 137 K2
Noidans-lès-Vesoul (70) 138 A1
Noidant-Chatenoy (52) 116 D5
Noidant-le-Rocheux (52) 116 C4
Noilhan (32) 287 G1
Nointel (60) 38 A3
Nointel (95) 37 J6
Nointot (76) 14 E5
Noircourt (02) 21 H4
Noirefontaine (25) 139 H4
Noirémont (60) 18 A6
Noirétable (42) 204 A1
Noirlieu (51) 63 H2
Noirmoutier-en-l'Île (85) 140 B3
Noiron (70) 137 G4
Noiron-sous-Gevrey (21) 154 C1
Noiron-sur-Bèze (21) 136 D3
Noiron-sur-Seine (21) 114 C3
Noironte (25) 137 J3
Noirval (08) 42 C1
Noiseau (94) 59 G4
Noisiel (77) 59 H4
Noisseville (57) 45 G5
Noisy-le-Grand (93) 59 G4
Noisy-le-Roi (78) 58 B4
Noisy-le-Sec (93) 59 F3
Noisy-Rudignon (77) 88 A4
Noisy-sur-École (77) 87 G4
Noisy-sur-Oise (95) 37 K6
Noizay (37) 128 C3
Nojals-et-Clotte (24) 232 A4
Nojeon-en-Vexin (27) 36 C3
Nolay (21) 153 H2
Nolay (58) 151 F2
Nolléval (76) 36 B1
Nollieux (42) 204 C1
Nomain (59) 7 F6
Nomdieu (47) 248 A6
Nomécourt (52) 92 A3
Nomeny (54) 66 A2
Nomexy (88) 94 C4
Nommay (25) 139 H2
Nompatelize (88) 95 H3
Nonac (16) 196 D6
Nonancourt (27) 56 C2
Nonant (14) 32 H4
Nonant-le-Pin (61) 54 E5
Nonards (19) 216 B6
Nonaville (16) 196 C5
Noncourt-sur-le-Rongeant (52) . . 92 C3
Nonette (63) 203 F6
Nonglard (74) 190 E5
Nonhigny (54) 67 H6
Nonières (07) 239 J1
Nonsard-Lamarche (55) 65 G3
Nontron (24) 197 K5
Nonville (77) 87 J5
Nonville (88) 117 K1
Nonvilliers-Grandhoux (28) 84 D3
Nonza (2B) 317 C1
Nonzeville (88) 95 F4
Noordpeene (59) 3 H4
Nordausques (62) 2 E4
Nordheim (67) 70 D2
Nordhouse (67) 71 C4
Noreuil (62) 11 G4
Norges-la-Ville (21) 136 A4
Normandel (61) 55 K6
Normanville (27) 35 J6
Normanville (76) 15 F4
Normier (21) 134 E5
Norolles (14) 33 K5
Noron-la-Poterie (14) 32 A4
Noron-l'Abbaye (14) 54 A3
Noroy (60) 38 B2
Noroy-le-Bourg (70) 138 C2
Noroy-sur-Ourcq (02) 39 H5
Norrent-Fontes (62) 5 H5
Norrey-en-Auge (14) 54 C2
Norrois (51) 63 G5
Norroy (88) 93 J5
Norroy-le-Sec (54) 26 C5
Norroy-le-Veneur (57) 27 G6
Norroy-lès-Pont-à-Mousson (54) . 65 J2
Nort-Leulinghem (62) 2 E4
Nort-sur-Erdre (44) 123 H1
Nortkerque (62) 2 D3
Norville (76) 34 D1
la Norville (91) 86 D1
Nossage-et-Bénévent (05) 258 D2
Nossoncourt (88) 95 F2
Nostang (56) 100 B4
Noth (23) 182 A2
Nothalten (67) 70 D5
Notre-Dame-d'Aliermont (76) . . . 16 B2
Notre-Dame-d'Allençon (49) 125 H5
Notre-Dame-de-Bellecombe (73) . 191 K6
Notre-Dame-de-Bliquetuit (76) . . 34 E1
Notre-Dame-de-Boisset (42) 187 F5

Notre-Dame-de-Bondeville (76) . . . 35 H1
Notre-Dame-de-Cenilly (50) 31 F5
Notre-Dame-de-Commiers (38) . . . 224 A5
Notre-Dame-de-Courson (14) 55 F1
Notre-Dame-de-Gravenchon (76) . . 34 D1
Notre-Dame-de-la-Rouvière (30) . . 254 D6
Notre-Dame-de-l'Isle (27) 36 B5
Notre-Dame-de-Livaye (14) 33 H6
Notre-Dame-de-Livoye (50) 52 A3
Notre-Dame-de-Londres (34) 274 B3
Notre-Dame-de-l'Osier (38) 223 H2
Notre-Dame-de-Mésage (38) 224 A5
Notre-Dame-de-Monts (85) 140 C5
Notre-Dame-de-Riez (85) 140 E6
Notre-Dame-de-Sanilhac (24) 214 A4
Notre-Dame-de-Vaux (38) 224 B5
Notre-Dame-d'Elle (50) 31 J4
Notre-Dame-d'Épine (27) 34 D5
Notre-Dame-des-Landes (44) 123 G2
Notre-Dame-des-Millières (73) . . . 209 F3
Notre-Dame-d'Estrées (14) 33 H5
Notre-Dame-d'Oé (37) 127 J4
Notre-Dame-du-Bec (76) 14 B5
Notre-Dame-du-Cruet (73) 209 F6
Notre-Dame-du-Hamel (27) 55 H3
Notre-Dame-du-Parc (76) 16 A4
Notre-Dame-du-Pé (72) 105 J6
Notre-Dame-du-Pré (73) 209 J4
Notre-Dame-du-Rocher (61) 53 J4
Notre-Dame-du-Touchet (50) 52 D6
Nottonville (28) 109 G1
la Nouaille (23) 200 D1
Nouaillé-Maupertuis (86) 163 F4
Nouainville (50) 28 C2
Nouan-le-Fuzelier (41) 130 B3
Nouans (72) 82 E5
Nouans-les-Fontaines (37) 147 F2
Nouart (08) . . . . 42 E1.
Nouâtre (37) 145 J3
la Nouaye (35) 78 D3
la Noue (51) 61 G5
Noueilles (31) 288 C3
Nougaroulet (32) 267 K5
Nouhant (23) 183 J1
Nouic (87) 180 D4
Nouilhan (65) 285 H3
les Nouillers (17) 177 J5
Nouillonpont (55) 26 C4
Nouilly (57) 45 F5
Noulens (32) 266 D3
Nourard-le-Franc (60) 37 K1
Nourray (41) 108 C6
Nousse (40) 264 D4
Nousseviller-lès-Bitche (57) 69 G2
Nousseviller-Saint-Nabor (57) . . . 68 C2
Nousty (64) 284 E4
Nouvelle-Église (62) 2 D3
Nouvion (80) 9 F4
le Nouvion-en-Thiérache (02) . . . 13 F4
Nouvion-et-Catillon (02) 20 B4
Nouvion-le-Comte (02) 20 B4
Nouvion-le-Vineux (02) 40 B1
Nouvion-sur-Meuse (08) 22 D4
Nouvoitou (35) 79 H5
Nouvron-Vingré (02) 39 H2
Nouzerines (23) 166 C6
Nouzerolles (23) 165 J6
Nouziers (23) 166 B5
Nouzilly (37) 127 J3
Nouzonville (08) 22 D3
Novacelles (63) 203 H6
Novalaise (73) 208 A4
Novale (2B) 319 J5
Novéant-sur-Moselle (57) 44 E6
Novel (74) 175 J5
Novella (2B) 318 E2
Noves (13) 276 C2
Noviant-aux-Prés (54) 65 H3
Novillard (90) 139 J1
Novillars (25) 138 B5
Novillers (60) 37 J4
Novion-Porcien (08) 22 A5
Novy-Chevrières (08) 22 A6
Noyal (22) 77 J1
Noyal-Châtillon-sur-Seiche (35) . . 79 G5
Noyal-Muzillac (56) 101 J6
Noyal-Pontivy (56) 76 E6
Noyal-sous-Bazouges (35) 51 G6
Noyal-sur-Brutz (44) 103 K3
Noyal-sur-Vilaine (35) 79 H4
Noyales (02) 20 C2
Noyalo (56) 101 G6
Noyant (49) 126 D3
Noyant-d'Allier (03) 168 C5
Noyant-de-Touraine (37) 145 J2
Noyant-et-Aconin (02) 39 J3
Noyant-la-Gravoyère (49) 104 C6
Noyant-la-Plaine (49) 125 J6
Noyarey (38) 223 K2
Noyelles (62) 10 C3
Noyelles-en-Chaussée (80) 9 H4
Noyelles-Godault (62) 11 G1
Noyelles-lès-Humières (62) 9 K2
Noyelles-lès-Seclin (59) 6 D5
Noyelles-lès-Vermelles (62) 6 B6
Noyelles-sous-Bellonne (62) 11 H4
Noyelles-sous-Lens (62) 11 F1
Noyelles-sur-Escaut (59) 11 J4
Noyelles-sur-Mer (80) 9 F4
Noyelles-sur-Sambre (59) 13 F4
Noyelles-sur-Selle (59) 12 C3
Noyellette (62) 10 D2

Noyen-sur-Sarthe (72) . . . 106 B4
Noyen-sur-Seine (77) . . . 88 E3
le Noyer (05) . . . 242 D3
le Noyer (18) . . . 131 H5
le Noyer (73) . . . 208 C2
le Noyer-en-Ouche (27) . . . 55 K1
Noyers (27) . . . 36 D4
Noyers (45) . . . 111 G4
Noyers (52) . . . 116 E1
Noyers (89) . . . 114 A6
Noyers-Auzécourt (55) . . . 63 J3
Noyers-Bocage (14) . . . 32 C5
Noyers-Pont-Maugis (08) . . . 23 F4
Noyers-Saint-Martin (60) . . . 18 A6
Noyers-sur-Cher (41) . . . 129 F6
Noyers-sur-Jabron (04) . . . 258 E4
Noyon (60) . . . 19 H6
Nozay (10) . . . 90 B2
Nozay (44) . . . 103 G5
Nozay (91) . . . 58 D5
Nozeroy (39) . . . 156 C6
Nozières (07) . . . 221 H5
Nozières (18) . . . 167 F1
Nuaillé (49) . . . 143 F2
Nuaillé-d'Aunis (17) . . . 177 F1
Nuaillé-sur-Boutonne (17) . . . 178 A4
Nuars (58) . . . 133 H5
Nubécourt (55) . . . 64 B1
Nucourt (95) . . . 36 E5
Nueil-sous-Faye (86) . . . 145 G4
Nueil-sur-Argent (79) . . . 143 H4
Nueil-sur-Layon (49) . . . 143 K2
Nuelles (69) . . . 205 J1
Nuillé-le-Jalais (72) . . . 107 F3
Nuillé-sur-Vicoin (53) . . . 104 E2
Nuisement-sur-Coole (51) . . . 62 C3
Nuits (89) . . . 114 C6
Nuits-Saint-Georges (21) . . . 154 B2
Nullemont (76) . . . 16 E3
Nully-Trémilly (52) . . . 91 H3
Nuncq-Hautecôte (62) . . . 10 A3
Nuret-le-Ferron (36) . . . 165 F2
Nurieux-Volognat (01) . . . 189 K2
Nurlu (80) . . . 11 H6
Nuzéjouls (46) . . . 233 G6
Nyer (66) . . . 314 A4
Nyoiseau (49) . . . 104 D6
Nyons (26) . . . 257 H2

O

Obenheim (67) . . . 71 D4
Oberbronn (67) . . . 69 J4
Oberbruck (68) . . . 119 J4
Oberdorf (68) . . . 97 C5
Oberdorf-Spachbach (67) . . . 25 A2
Oberdorff (57) . . . 45 J3
Oberentzen (68) . . . 96 C5
Obergailbach (57) . . . 68 E2
Oberhaslach (67) . . . 70 B4
Oberhausbergen (67) . . . 71 D1
Oberhergheim (68) . . . 96 C5
Oberhoffen-lès-Wissembourg (67) . . . 25 B1
Oberhoffen-sur-Moder (67) . . . 25 B6
Oberlarg (68) . . . 97 B6
Oberlauterbach (67) . . . 25 D2
Obermodern-Zutzendorf (67) . . . 69 J4
Obermorschwihr (68) . . . 96 B5
Obermorschwiller (68) . . . 97 C4
Obernai (67) . . . 70 D5
Oberroedern (67) . . . 25 C4
Obersaasheim (68) . . . 96 E5
Oberschaeffolsheim (67) . . . 70 E3
Obersoultzbach (67) . . . 69 H6
Obersteinbach (67) . . . 69 K3
Oberstinzel (57) . . . 67 J3
Obervisse (57) . . . 45 J4
Obies (59) . . . 13 F3
Objat (19) . . . 215 H3
Oblinghem (62) . . . 5 K5
Obrechies (59) . . . 13 H3
Obreck (57) . . . 66 C2
Obsonville (77) . . . 87 G6
Obterre (36) . . . 146 D3
Obtrée (21) . . . 115 F3
Ocana (2A) . . . 320 D5
Occagnes (61) . . . 54 B4
Occey (52) . . . 136 C1
Occhiatana (2B) . . . 318 D2
Occoches (80) . . . 10 A4
Ochancourt (80) . . . 8 E5
Oches (08) . . . 42 D1
Ochey (54) . . . 65 J6
Ochtezeele (59) . . . 3 H4
Ocquerre (77) . . . 60 B1
Ocqueville (76) . . . 15 G3
Octeville (50) . . . 28 C4
Octeville-l'Avenel (50) . . . 29 F3
Octeville-sur-Mer (76) . . . 14 A6
Octon (34) . . . 273 F6
Odars (31) . . . 288 D2
Odenas (69) . . . 188 A3
Oderen (68) . . . 119 J3
Odomez (59) . . . 7 J6
Odos (65) . . . 285 H5
Odratzheim (67) . . . 70 D3
Oëlleville (88) . . . 93 K3
Oermingen (67) . . . 68 D2
Oeting (57) . . . 68 C2
Oeuf-en-Ternois (62) . . . 9 K2

Oeuilly (02) . . . 40 C2
Oeuilly (51) . . . 40 D6
Oeyregave (40) . . . 283 F1
Oeyreluy (40) . . . 264 A5
Offekerque (62) . . . 2 E2
Offemont (90) . . . 119 H6
Offendorf (67) . . . 25 D4
Offignies (80) . . . 17 G3
Offlanges (39) . . . 137 F6
Offoy (60) . . . 17 J4
Offoy (80) . . . 19 H3
Offranville (76) . . . 15 K2
Offrethun (62) . . . 2 B4
Offroicourt (88) . . . 93 K4
Offwiller (67) . . . 69 J5
Ogenne-Camptort (64) . . . 283 K4
Oger (51) . . . 62 A2
Ogeu-les-Bains (64) . . . 284 B6
Ogéviller (54) . . . 67 F6
Ogliastro (2B) . . . 317 C4
Ognes (02) . . . 19 K5
Ognes (51) . . . 61 K5
Ognes (60) . . . 38 E6
Ognéville (54) . . . 93 K2
Ognolles (60) . . . 19 G4
Ognon (60) . . . 38 C4
Ogy (57) . . . 45 G5
Ohain (59) . . . 13 J6
Oherville (76) . . . 15 F4
Ohis (02) . . . 21 G1
Ohlungen (67) . . . 69 K6
Ohnenheim (67) . . . 71 C6
l'Oie (85) . . . 142 C6
Oigney (70) . . . 117 H5
Oignies (62) . . . 6 D6
Oigny (21) . . . 135 H2
Oigny (41) . . . 108 B2
Oigny-en-Valois (02) . . . 39 G5
Oingt (69) . . . 188 A5
Oinville-Saint-Liphard (28) . . . 86 A5
Oinville-sous-Auneau (28) . . . 85 J3
Oinville-sur-Montcient (78) . . . 57 K1
Oiron (79) . . . 144 C3
Oiry (51) . . . 62 A1
Oiselay-et-Grachaux (70) . . . 137 J4
Oisemont (80) . . . 17 F1
Oisilly (21) . . . 136 D4
Oison (45) . . . 110 B1
Oisseau (53) . . . 81 F3
Oisseau-le-Petit (72) . . . 82 D4
Oissel (76) . . . 35 H3
Oissery (77) . . . 59 J1
Oissy (80) . . . 17 J2
Oisy (02) . . . 12 E6
Oisy (58) . . . 133 F4
Oisy (59) . . . 12 C2
Oisy-le-Verger (62) . . . 11 H3
Oizé (72) . . . 106 D5
Oizon (18) . . . 131 G4
Olargues (34) . . . 291 G1
Olby (63) . . . 202 B2
Olcani (2B) . . . 317 C4
Oléac-Debat (65) . . . 285 J4
Oléac-Dessus (65) . . . 285 J6
Olemps (12) . . . 252 B3
Olendon (14) . . . 54 B2
Oletta (2B) . . . 317 D6
Olette (66) . . . 314 A4
Olivese (2A) . . . 321 F6
Olivet (45) . . . 110 A4
Olivet (53) . . . 80 D6
Olizy (51) . . . 40 C5
Olizy-Primat (08) . . . 42 C3
Olizy-sur-Chiers (55) . . . 23 H6
Ollainville (88) . . . 93 H4
Ollainville (91) . . . 86 D1
Ollans (25) . . . 138 C3
Ollé (28) . . . 84 E3
Olley (54) . . . 44 B5
Ollezy (02) . . . 19 J4
les Ollières (74) . . . 191 F4
Ollières (83) . . . 297 H1
les Ollières-sur-Eyrieux (07) . . . 239 K2
Olliergues (63) . . . 203 J3
Ollioules (83) . . . 297 H6
Olloix (63) . . . 202 D4
les Olmes (69) . . . 187 K6
Olmet (63) . . . 203 J3
Olmet-et-Villecun (34) . . . 273 F5
Olmeta-di-Capocorso (2B) . . . 317 D4
Olmeta-di-Tuda (2B) . . . 317 D6
Olmi-Cappella (2B) . . . 318 D3
Olmiccia (2A) . . . 323 F2
Olmo (2B) . . . 319 H3
Olonne-sur-Mer (85) . . . 158 E3
Olonzac (34) . . . 291 F5
Oloron-Sainte-Marie (64) . . . 284 A5
Ols-et-Rinhodes (12) . . . 251 F1
Oltingue (67) . . . 97 D5
Olwisheim (67) . . . 70 E2
Omblèze (26) . . . 241 F1
Omécourt (60) . . . 17 G5
Omelmont (54) . . . 94 A1
les Omergues (04) . . . 258 C4
Omerville (95) . . . 36 D6
Omessa (2B) . . . 319 F5
Omet (33) . . . 230 A4
Omex (65) . . . 304 B1
Omey (51) . . . 62 E3

Omicourt (08) . . . 22 E5
Omiécourt (80) . . . 19 H3
Omissy (02) . . . 20 A2
Omméel (61) . . . 54 D4
Ommeray (57) . . . 67 F3
Ommoy (61) . . . 54 C3
Omont (08) . . . 22 D5
Omonville (76) . . . 15 K3
Omonville-la-Petite (50) . . . 28 A1
Omonville-la-Rogue (50) . . . 28 B1
Omps (15) . . . 235 F2
Oms (66) . . . 314 E4
Onans (25) . . . 139 F2
Onard (40) . . . 264 D3
Onay (70) . . . 137 G4
Oncieu (01) . . . 189 J5
Oncourt (88) . . . 94 D3
Oncy-sur-École (91) . . . 87 F4
Ondefontaine (14) . . . 53 G1
Ondes (31) . . . 269 H4
Ondres (40) . . . 262 B6
Ondreville-sur-Essonne (45) . . . 87 F6
Onesse-et-Laharie (40) . . . 244 E6
Onet-le-Château (12) . . . 252 B2
Oneux (80) . . . 9 H4
Ongles (04) . . . 258 D6
Onglières (39) . . . 156 B6
Onjon (10) . . . 90 C3
Onlay (58) . . . 152 B4
Onnaing (59) . . . 12 D1
Onnion (74) . . . 191 J2
Onoz (39) . . . 173 H4
Ons-en-Bray (60) . . . 37 F2
Ontex (73) . . . 208 A2
Onville (54) . . . 65 J1
Onzain (41) . . . 128 D3
Oô (31) . . . 305 G5
Oost-Cappel (59) . . . 3 K3
Opio (06) . . . 280 D4
Opoul-Périllos (66) . . . 310 B4
Oppède (84) . . . 277 F3
Oppedette (04) . . . 277 K2
Oppenans (70) . . . 138 D1
Oppy (62) . . . 11 F2
Optevoz (38) . . . 207 F2
Oraàs (64) . . . 283 G2
Oradour (15) . . . 236 C1
Oradour (16) . . . 178 E6
Oradour-Fanais (16) . . . 180 C3
Oradour-Saint-Genest (87) . . . 181 F2
Oradour-sur-Glane (87) . . . 180 E6
Oradour-sur-Vayres (87) . . . 198 B2
Orain (21) . . . 136 E1
Orainville (02) . . . 41 F1
Oraison (04) . . . 278 C2
Orange (84) . . . 256 E5
Orbagna (39) . . . 173 F3
Orbais-l'Abbaye (51) . . . 61 H2
Orban (81) . . . 270 D3
Orbec (14) . . . 55 G1
Orbeil (63) . . . 203 F5
Orbessan (32) . . . 286 D2
Orbey (68) . . . 96 A3
Orbigny (37) . . . 147 F1
Orbigny-au-Mont (52) . . . 116 E4
Orbigny-au-Val (52) . . . 116 E4
l'Orbrie (85) . . . 160 E4
Orçay (41) . . . 130 C6
Orcemont (78) . . . 85 K1
Orcenais (18) . . . 167 F2
Orcet (63) . . . 202 E3
Orcevaux (52) . . . 116 C5
Orchaise (41) . . . 128 C2
Orchamps (39) . . . 155 J1
Orchamps-Vennes (25) . . . 157 G1
Orches (86) . . . 145 G5
Orchies (59) . . . 7 F6
Orcier (74) . . . 175 F6
Orcières (05) . . . 243 G5
Orcinas (26) . . . 241 F5
Orcines (63) . . . 202 C2
Orcival (63) . . . 202 B3
Orconte (51) . . . 63 G5
Ordan-Larroque (32) . . . 267 G3
Ordiarp (64) . . . 283 G5
Ordizan (65) . . . 304 D1
Ordonnac (33) . . . 210 E2
Ordonnaz (01) . . . 189 K6
Ore (31) . . . 305 J3
Orègue (64) . . . 283 F2
Oreilla (66) . . . 314 A4
Orelle (73) . . . 225 J2
Oresmaux (80) . . . 18 A3
Organ (65) . . . 286 B4
Orgeans-Blanchefontaine (25) . . . 139 G5
Orgedeuil (16) . . . 197 H3
Orgeix (09) . . . 308 B6
Orgelet (39) . . . 173 G3
Orgères (35) . . . 79 G5
Orgères (61) . . . 55 F4
Orgères-en-Beauce (28) . . . 109 J1
Orgerus (78) . . . 57 H4
Orges (52) . . . 115 J1
Orgeux (21) . . . 136 B5
Orgeval (02) . . . 40 C1
Orgeval (78) . . . 58 B3
Orgibet (09) . . . 306 B3
Orglandes (50) . . . 28 E5
Orgnac-l'Aven (07) . . . 256 A3
Orgnac-sur-Vézère (19) . . . 215 H2
Orgon (13) . . . 276 D4
Orgueil (82) . . . 269 G2

Oricourt (70) . . . 138 D1
Orieux (65) . . . 285 K5
Orignac (65) . . . 285 J6
Origne (33) . . . 229 H6
Origné (53) . . . 105 F3
Orignolles (17) . . . 212 A3
Origny (21) . . . 115 G6
Origny-en-Thiérache (02) . . . 21 G3
Origny-le-Butin (61) . . . 83 G4
Origny-le-Roux (61) . . . 83 G4
Origny-le-Sec (10) . . . 89 H2
Origny-Sainte-Benoite (02) . . . 20 B2
Orin (64) . . . 283 K5
Orincles (65) . . . 285 H6
Oriocourt (57) . . . 66 C2
Oriol-en-Royans (26) . . . 223 G5
Oriolles (16) . . . 212 C1
Orion (64) . . . 283 H2
Orival (16) . . . 212 D2
Orival (76) . . . 35 G3
Orléans (45) . . . 110 A4
Orléat (63) . . . 203 G1
Orleix (65) . . . 285 H4
Orliac (24) . . . 232 D4
Orliac-de-Bar (19) . . . 216 B1
Orliaguet (24) . . . 233 G1
Orliénas (69) . . . 205 K3
Orlu (09) . . . 308 B6
Orlu (28) . . . 86 A4
Orly (94) . . . 58 E5
Orly-sur-Morin (77) . . . 60 C3
Ormancey (52) . . . 116 B3
Ormenans (70) . . . 138 B3
Ormersviller (57) . . . 69 F2
Ormes (10) . . . 90 B1
Ormes (27) . . . 56 B1
Ormes (45) . . . 109 K3
Ormes (51) . . . 40 E4
Ormes (71) . . . 172 A2
les Ormes (86) . . . 145 K4
les Ormes (89) . . . 112 D5
Ormes-et-Ville (54) . . . 94 B2
les Ormes-sur-Voulzie (77) . . . 88 C3
Ormesson (77) . . . 87 H5
Ormesson-sur-Marne (94) . . . 59 G4
Ormoiche (70) . . . 118 C4
Ormoy (28) . . . 57 G6
Ormoy (70) . . . 117 K3
Ormoy (89) . . . 113 G3
Ormoy (91) . . . 87 F1
Ormoy-la-Rivière (91) . . . 86 C3
Ormoy-le-Davien (60) . . . 39 F5
Ormoy-lès-Sexfontaines (52) . . . 92 A5
Ormoy-Villers (60) . . . 38 C5
Ornacieux (38) . . . 206 E6
Ornaisons (11) . . . 291 G6
Ornans (25) . . . 156 D2
Ornes (55) . . . 26 A6
Ornex (01) . . . 190 E1
Ornézan (32) . . . 286 D2
Orniac (46) . . . 233 K6
Ornolac-Ussat-les-Bains (09) . . . 307 J5
Ornon (38) . . . 224 D5
Orny (57) . . . 45 F6
Oroër (60) . . . 37 H1
Oroix (65) . . . 285 G6
Oron (57) . . . 66 D2
Oroux (79) . . . 162 B2
Orphin (78) . . . 85 K1
Orpierre (05) . . . 258 D2
Orquevaux (52) . . . 92 A4
les Orres (05) . . . 243 K5
Orret (21) . . . 135 G2
Orriule (64) . . . 283 H2
Orrouer (28) . . . 84 E3
Orrouy (60) . . . 38 E4
Orry-la-Ville (60) . . . 38 B6
Ors (59) . . . 12 E5
Orsan (30) . . . 256 C5
Orsanco (64) . . . 283 F4
Orsans (11) . . . 289 H6
Orsans (25) . . . 138 D5
Orsay (91) . . . 58 D5
Orschwihr (68) . . . 96 B6
Orschwiller (67) . . . 71 C6
Orsennes (36) . . . 165 J5
Orsinval (59) . . . 12 E3
Orsonnette (63) . . . 203 F6
Orsonville (78) . . . 85 K2
Ortaffa (66) . . . 315 H3
Ortale (2B) . . . 319 J5
Orthevielle (40) . . . 262 E6
Orthez (64) . . . 283 J1
Orthoux-Sérignac-Quilhan (30) . . . 274 D3
Ortillon (10) . . . 90 C2
Ortiporio (2B) . . . 319 H4
Orto (2A) . . . 320 D2
Oroncourt (88) . . . 94 D3
Orus (09) . . . 307 H5
Orval (18) . . . 167 G2
Orval (50) . . . 30 D4
Orvault (44) . . . 123 G4
Orvaux (27) . . . 56 C2
Orve (25) . . . 139 F4
Orveau (91) . . . 86 E3
Orveau-Bellesauve (45) . . . 86 E5
Orville (21) . . . 136 C4
Orville (36) . . . 148 A2
Orville (45) . . . 87 F5
Orville (61) . . . 55 F3

Orville (62) . . . 10 B5
Orvillers-Sorel (60) . . . 18 E6
Orvilliers (78) . . . 57 H3
Orvilliers-Saint-Julien (10) . . . 89 J3
Orx (40) . . . 262 C5
Os-Marsillon (64) . . . 284 A3
Osani (2A) . . . 316 C4
Osches (55) . . . 43 G6
Osenbach (68) . . . 96 B5
Oslon (71) . . . 154 B6
Osly-Courtil (02) . . . 39 H2
Osmanville (14) . . . 29 H6
Osmery (18) . . . 149 K5
Osmets (65) . . . 285 K4
Osmoy (18) . . . 149 H3
Osmoy (78) . . . 57 J3
Osmoy-Saint-Valery (76) . . . 16 C3
Osne-le-Val (52) . . . 92 B2
Osnes (08) . . . 23 H4
Osny (95) . . . 58 B1
Ossages (40) . . . 264 C6
Ossas-Suhare (64) . . . 283 H6
Osse (25) . . . 138 B5
Ossé (35) . . . 79 J5
Osse-en-Aspe (64) . . . 303 F2
Osséja (66) . . . 313 H5
Osselle (25) . . . 156 A1
Ossen (65) . . . 304 B1
Ossenx (64) . . . 283 J3
Osserain-Rivareyte (64) . . . 283 G3
Ossès (64) . . . 282 D4
Ossey-les-Trois-Maisons (10) . . . 89 H3
Ossun (65) . . . 285 G5
Ossun-ez-Angles (65) . . . 304 C1
Ostabat-Asme (64) . . . 283 F4
Ostel (02) . . . 40 B2
Ostheim (68) . . . 96 C3
Osthoffen (67) . . . 70 D3
Osthouse (67) . . . 70 E5
Ostreville (62) . . . 10 B1
Ostricourt (59) . . . 6 D6
Ostwald (67) . . . 71 D1
Ota (2A) . . . 316 E4
Othe (54) . . . 26 A3
Othis (77) . . . 38 C6
Ottange (57) . . . 27 F3
Ottersthal (67) . . . 70 B1
Otterswiller (67) . . . 70 B1
Ottmarsheim (68) . . . 97 D2
Ottonville (57) . . . 45 J4
Ottrott (67) . . . 70 C5
Ottwiller (67) . . . 69 F5
Ouagne (58) . . . 133 F4
Ouainville (76) . . . 15 F3
Ouanne (89) . . . 132 E1
Ouarville (28) . . . 85 J4
les Oubeaux (14) . . . 31 H1
Ouchamps (41) . . . 128 E4
Ouches (42) . . . 186 E5
Oucques (41) . . . 108 E5
Oudalle (76) . . . 34 A1
Oudan (58) . . . 132 E5
Oudeuil (60) . . . 17 J6
Oudezeele (59) . . . 3 J4
Oudincourt (52) . . . 92 A5
l'Oudon (14) . . . 54 C2
Oudon (44) . . . 123 K2
Oudrenne (57) . . . 27 J4
Oudry (71) . . . 170 C3
Oueilloux (65) . . . 285 J6
Ouerre (28) . . . 57 G5
Ouessant (29) . . . 72 A1
Ouffières (14) . . . 53 H1
Ouge (70) . . . 117 G5
Ouges (21) . . . 136 B6
Ougney (39) . . . 137 G6
Ougney-Douvot (25) . . . 138 C5
Ougny (58) . . . 151 K3
Ouhans (25) . . . 156 E3
Ouides (43) . . . 238 A1
Ouillon (64) . . . 284 E4
Ouilly-du-Houley (14) . . . 34 A5
Ouilly-le-Tesson (14) . . . 54 A1
Ouilly-le-Vicomte (14) . . . 33 K5
Ouistreham (14) . . . 33 F3
Oulches (36) . . . 164 E3
Oulches-la-Vallée-Foulon (02) . . . 40 C2
Oulchy-la-Ville (02) . . . 39 J5
Oulchy-le-Château (02) . . . 39 J5
Oulins (28) . . . 57 G3
Oulles (38) . . . 224 D5
Oulmes (85) . . . 161 F5
Oulon (58) . . . 151 G1
Ounans (39) . . . 155 J3
Oupia (34) . . . 291 F4
Our (39) . . . 155 J2
Ourcel-Maison (60) . . . 17 K6
Ourches (26) . . . 240 D2
Ourches-sur-Meuse (55) . . . 65 G5
Ourde (65) . . . 305 H3
Ourdis-Cotdoussan (65) . . . 304 C2
Ourdon (65) . . . 304 B2
Ourouër (58) . . . 151 F3
Ourouer-les-Bourdelins (18) . . . 150 A5
Ouroux (69) . . . 188 A2
Ouroux-en-Morvan (58) . . . 152 B1
Ouroux-sous-le-Bois-
  Sainte-Marie (71) . . . 170 E6
Ouroux-sur-Saône (71) . . . 172 A1
Oursbelille (65) . . . 285 H4
Ourton (62) . . . 5 J6

Ourville-en-Caux (76) . . . 15 F4
Ousse-Suzan (40) . . . 264 E1
Oussières (39) . . . 155 H4
Ousson-sur-Loire (45) . . . 131 J2
Oussoy-en-Gâtinais (45) . . . 111 H4
Oust (09) . . . 306 E4
Oust-Marest (80) . . . 8 C6
Ousté (65) . . . 304 B1
Outarville (45) . . . 86 B6
Outines (51) . . . 91 G1
Outreau (62) . . . 2 A5
Outrebois (80) . . . 10 A4
Outremécourt (52) . . . 93 G5
Outrepont (51) . . . 63 G4
Outriaz (01) . . . 189 K3
Ouvans (25) . . . 138 E5
Ouve-Wirquin (62) . . . 3 F6
Ouveillan (11) . . . 291 H4
Ouville (50) . . . 30 E4
Ouville-la-Bien-Tournée (14) . . . 54 C1
Ouville-la-Rivière (76) . . . 15 J2
Ouville-l'Abbaye (76) . . . 15 H4
Ouvrouer-les-Champs (45) . . . 110 C5
Ouzilly (86) . . . 163 F1
Ouzouer-des-Champs (45) . . . 111 H4
Ouzouer-le-Doyen (41) . . . 108 E3
Ouzouer-le-Marché (41) . . . 109 G4
Ouzouer-sous-Bellegarde (45) . . . 111 F3
Ouzouer-sur-Loire (45) . . . 111 F6
Ouzouer-sur-Trézée (45) . . . 131 J1
Ouzous (65) . . . 304 A2
Ovanches (70) . . . 137 J1
Ovillers-la-Boisselle (80) . . . 10 E6
Oxelaëre (59) . . . 3 J4
Oyé (71) . . . 170 D6
Oye-et-Pallet (25) . . . 156 E5
Oye-Plage (62) . . . 2 B2
Oyes (51) . . . 61 H4
Oyeu (38) . . . 207 H6
Oyonnax (01) . . . 190 A1
Oyré (86) . . . 145 K5
Oyrières (70) . . . 137 F2
Oysonville (28) . . . 86 A3
Oytier-Saint-Oblas (38) . . . 206 C4
Oz (38) . . . 224 D3
Ozan (01) . . . 172 A5
Oze (05) . . . 242 B6
Ozenay (71) . . . 171 K3
Ozenx-Montestrucq (64) . . . 283 J2
Ozerailles (54) . . . 26 D6
Ozeville (50) . . . 29 F4
Ozières (52) . . . 92 E6
Ozillac (17) . . . 195 J6
Ozoir-la-Ferrière (77) . . . 59 H4
Ozoir-le-Breuil (28) . . . 109 G2
Ozolles (71) . . . 170 E6
Ozon (07) . . . 222 B4
Ozon (65) . . . 285 K6
Ozouer-le-Voulgis (77) . . . 59 J6
Ozourt (40) . . . 264 C5

P

Paars (02) . . . 40 B3
Pabu (22) . . . 48 C5
la Pacaudière (42) . . . 186 D3
Pacé (35) . . . 79 F4
Pacé (61) . . . 82 C3
Pact (38) . . . 222 D1
Pacy-sur-Armançon (89) . . . 114 B5
Pacy-sur-Eure (27) . . . 57 F1
Padern (11) . . . 309 K4
Padiès (81) . . . 271 G1
Padirac (46) . . . 234 A2
Padoux (88) . . . 94 E4
Pageas (87) . . . 198 C3
Pagney (39) . . . 137 G6
Pagney-derrière-Barine (54) . . . 65 H5
Pagnoz (39) . . . 155 K4
Pagny-la-Blanche-Côte (55) . . . 93 G1
Pagny-la-Ville (21) . . . 154 D3
Pagny-le-Château (21) . . . 154 D3
Pagny-lès-Goin (57) . . . 66 A1
Pagny-sur-Meuse (55) . . . 65 G5
Pagny-sur-Moselle (54) . . . 65 J1
Pagolle (64) . . . 283 G5
Pailhac (65) . . . 305 F3
Pailharès (07) . . . 221 H5
Pailherols (15) . . . 236 A1
Pailhès (09) . . . 307 G1
Pailhès (34) . . . 291 K3
Paillart (60) . . . 18 B5
Paillé (17) . . . 178 B4
Paillencourt (59) . . . 11 K3
Paillet (33) . . . 229 K4
Pailloles (47) . . . 248 B1
le Pailly (52) . . . 116 D5
Pailly (89) . . . 88 D4
Paimbœuf (44) . . . 122 C4
Paimpol (22) . . . 48 D2
Paimpont (35) . . . 78 B5
Painblanc (21) . . . 153 J2
Pair-et-Grandrupt (88) . . . 95 J4
Paissy (02) . . . 40 C2
Paisy-Cosdon (10) . . . 89 H5
Paizay-le-Chapt (79) . . . 178 D3
Paizay-le-Sec (86) . . . 163 K3
Paizay-le-Tort (79) . . . 178 D2
Paizay-Naudouin-Embourie (16) . . . 178 E4
Pajay (38) . . . 222 E1

Paladru (38) . . . 207 H5
Palairac (11) . . . 309 K3
le Palais (56) . . . 120 B4
le Palais-sur-Vienne (87) . . . 199 F1
Palaiseau (91) . . . 58 D5
Palaiseul (52) . . . 116 D5
Palaja (11) . . . 290 B6
Palaminy (31) . . . 287 H5
Palante (70) . . . 119 F6
Palantine (25) . . . 156 B2
Palasca (2B) . . . 318 E2
Palau-de-Cerdagne (66) . . . 313 H5
Palau-del-Vidre (66) . . . 315 H3
Palavas-les-Flots (34) . . . 293 H1
Palazinges (19) . . . 216 A4
Paley (77) . . . 87 K5
Palhers (48) . . . 237 G6
Palinges (71) . . . 170 D3
Palis (10) . . . 89 H5
Palise (25) . . . 138 A4
Palisse (19) . . . 217 F1
Palladuc (63) . . . 186 A6
Pallanne (32) . . . 285 K2
Palleau (71) . . . 154 C4
Pallegney (88) . . . 94 D4
le Pallet (44) . . . 123 J5
Palleville (81) . . . 289 H2
Pallud (73) . . . 209 G2
Palluel (62) . . . 11 H3
Palluaud (16) . . . 213 H1
Pallud (73) . . . 209 G2
Palluel (62) . . . 11 H3
Pamfou (77) . . . 87 K3
Pamiers (09) . . . 307 J1
Pampelonne (81) . . . 251 J5
Pamplie (79) . . . 161 H3
Pamproux (79) . . . 162 B5
Panassac (32) . . . 286 C3
Panazol (87) . . . 199 F1
Pancé (35) . . . 103 G1
Pancey (52) . . . 92 C2
Pancheraccia (2B) . . . 321 H1
Pancy-Courtecon (02) . . . 40 B1
Pandrignes (19) . . . 216 B3
Pange (57) . . . 45 G5
Panges (21) . . . 135 J5
Panilleuse (27) . . . 36 B5
Panissage (38) . . . 207 H5
Panissières (42) . . . 205 F2
Panjas (32) . . . 266 B3
Pannecé (44) . . . 124 A3
Pannecières (45) . . . 86 C5
Pannes (45) . . . 111 H2
Pannes (54) . . . 65 G2
Pannessières (39) . . . 173 G1
Panon (72) . . . 83 F4
Panossas (38) . . . 206 E3
la Panouse (48) . . . 237 K4
Pantin (93) . . . 59 F3
Panzoult (37) . . . 145 H2
Papleux (02) . . . 13 G6
Paradou (13) . . . 276 B4
Parassy (18) . . . 149 H1
Paray-Douaville (78) . . . 86 A3
Paray-le-Frésil (03) . . . 169 H2
Paray-le-Monial (71) . . . 170 C5
Paray-sous-Briailles (03) . . . 185 H1
Paray-Vieille-Poste (91) . . . 58 E4
Parbayse (64) . . . 284 B4
Parc-d'Anxtot (76) . . . 14 D6
Parçay-les-Pins (49) . . . 126 D4
Parçay-Meslay (37) . . . 127 J4
Parçay-sur-Vienne (37) . . . 145 H2
Parcé (35) . . . 80 B4
Parcé-sur-Sarthe (72) . . . 106 A4
Parcey (39) . . . 155 G3
Parcieux (01) . . . 188 C6
Parcoul (24) . . . 212 D3
le Parcq (62) . . . 9 J2
Parcy-et-Tigny (02) . . . 39 J4
Pardailhan (34) . . . 291 G2
Pardaillan (47) . . . 231 F4
Pardies (64) . . . 284 A3
Pardies-Piétat (64) . . . 284 D5
Pardines (63) . . . 202 E5
Paréac (65) . . . 304 C1
Pareid (55) . . . 44 B5
Parempuyre (33) . . . 211 G5
Parennes (72) . . . 106 A1
Parent (63) . . . 202 E4
Parentignat (63) . . . 203 F5
Parentis-en-Born (40) . . . 244 E2
Parenty (62) . . . 4 C5
Parey-Saint-Césaire (54) . . . 93 K1
Parey-sous-Montfort (88) . . . 93 J5
Parfondeval (02) . . . 21 H4
Parfondeval (61) . . . 83 H2
Parfondru (02) . . . 40 C2
Parfondrupt (55) . . . 44 B5
Parfouru-sur-Odon (14) . . . 32 C6
Pargnan (02) . . . 40 C2
Pargny (80) . . . 19 G3
Pargny-Filain (02) . . . 40 A1

Pargny-la-Dhuys (02) . . . 61 F2
Pargny-les-Bois (02) . . . 20 D4
Pargny-lès-Reims (51) . . . 40 E4
Pargny-sous-Mureau (88) . . . 93 F3
Pargny-sur-Saulx (51) . . . 63 H4
Pargues (10) . . . 114 C2
Parignargues (30) . . . 275 F3
Parigné (35) . . . 80 B2
Parigné-le-Pôlin (72) . . . 106 D4
Parigné-l'Évêque (72) . . . 107 F3
Parigné-sur-Braye (53) . . . 81 J3
Parigny (42) . . . 187 F5
Parigny (50) . . . 52 C6
Parigny-la-Rose (58) . . . 133 F5
Parigny-les-Vaux (58) . . . 150 D3
Paris (75) . . . 58 E3
Paris-l'Hôpital (71) . . . 153 K2
Parisot (81) . . . 270 A4
Parisot (82) . . . 250 E4
Parlan (15) . . . 234 E2
Parleboscq (40) . . . 266 C2
Parly (89) . . . 112 E6
Parmain (95) . . . 37 J6
Parmilieu (38) . . . 189 H6
Parnac (36) . . . 165 F5
Parnac (46) . . . 249 J1
Parnans (26) . . . 222 E4
Parnay (18) . . . 149 J6
Parnay (49) . . . 126 C6
Parné-sur-Roc (53) . . . 105 F2
Parnes (60) . . . 36 D5
Parnoy-en-Bassigny (52) . . . 117 F2
les Paroches (55) . . . 64 E2
Paron (89) . . . 88 D6
Paroy (25) . . . 156 A3
Paroy (77) . . . 88 C2
Paroy-sur-Saulx (52) . . . 92 C2
Paroy-sur-Tholon (89) . . . 112 E3
Parpeçay (36) . . . 147 K1
Parpeville (02) . . . 20 C3
Parranquet (47) . . . 232 B4
Parroy (54) . . . 66 C5
Pars-lès-Chavanges (10) . . . 90 E2
Pars-lès-Romilly (10) . . . 89 H2
Parsac (23) . . . 183 G2
Parthenay (79) . . . 161 K2
Parthenay-de-Bretagne (35) . . . 78 E3
Partinello (2A) . . . 316 B3
Parux (54) . . . 67 H6
Parves (01) . . . 207 K2
Parville (27) . . . 56 C1
Parvillers-le-Quesnoy (80) . . . 18 E4
Parzac (16) . . . 179 J5
le Pas (53) . . . 81 F3
Pas-de-Jeu (79) . . . 144 D4
Pas-en-Artois (62) . . . 10 C4
le Pas-Saint-l'Homer (61) . . . 84 B2
Pasilly (89) . . . 114 B6
Paslières (63) . . . 185 K6
Pasly (02) . . . 39 J2
Pasques (21) . . . 135 J5
le Pasquier (39) . . . 156 A6
Passa (66) . . . 315 G3
le Passage (38) . . . 207 H4
le Passage (47) . . . 248 B4
Passais (61) . . . 81 F1
Passavant (25) . . . 138 D5
Passavant-en-Argonne (51) . . . 63 K1
Passavant-la-Rochère (70) . . . 117 K2
Passavant-sur-Layon (49) . . . 143 K2
Passel (60) . . . 19 G6
Passenans (39) . . . 155 H6
Passins (38) . . . 207 G3
Passirac (16) . . . 212 C1
Passonfontaine (25) . . . 157 F2
Passy (71) . . . 171 G4
Passy (74) . . . 192 B5
Passy (89) . . . 112 D1
Passy-en-Valois (02) . . . 39 H5
Passy-Grigny (51) . . . 40 C5
Passy-sur-Marne (02) . . . 61 F1
Passy-sur-Seine (77) . . . 88 E3
Pastricciola (2A) . . . 320 D2
Patay (45) . . . 109 J2
Patornay (39) . . . 173 H3
Patrimonio (2B) . . . 320 E6
Pau (64) . . . 284 D4
Paucourt (45) . . . 111 J2
Paudy (36) . . . 148 C3
Pauilhac (32) . . . 267 J3
Pauillac (33) . . . 211 F3
Paule (22) . . . 75 K3
Paulhac (15) . . . 218 C6
Paulhac (31) . . . 269 H4
Paulhac (43) . . . 219 G2
Paulhac-en-Margeride (48) . . . 237 H1
Paulhaguet (43) . . . 219 J3
Paulhan (34) . . . 292 C1
Paulhe (12) . . . 253 G5
Paulhenc (15) . . . 236 B2
Paulhiac (47) . . . 232 B6
Pauligne (11) . . . 308 E1
Paulin (24) . . . 215 G6
Paulinet (81) . . . 271 G3
Paulmy (37) . . . 146 B4
Paulnay (36) . . . 146 E6
Paulx (44) . . . 141 G3
Paunat (24) . . . 232 B1
Paussac-et-Saint-Vivien (24) . . . 213 J1
Pautaines-Augeville (52) . . . 92 C4
Pauvres (08) . . . 41 K2
Pavant (02) . . . 60 D2

Pavezin (42) . . . 205 K6
Pavie (32) . . . 267 H6
le Pavillon-Sainte-Julie (10) . . . 89 K4
les Pavillons-sous-Bois (93) . . . 59 G3
Pavilly (76) . . . 15 J6
Payns (10) . . . 89 K3
Payra-sur-l'Hers (11) . . . 289 G5
Payrac (46) . . . 233 H3
Payré (86) . . . 162 D6
Payrignac (46) . . . 233 G3
Payrin-Augmontel (81) . . . 290 B2
Payros-Cazautets (40) . . . 265 H6
Payroux (86) . . . 179 K2
Payssous (31) . . . 305 J2
Payzac (07) . . . 255 H1
Payzac (24) . . . 215 F1
Pazayac (24) . . . 215 G6
Paziols (11) . . . 310 A4
Pazy (58) . . . 151 J1
le Péage-de-Roussillon (38) . . . 222 B1
Péas (51) . . . 61 H5
Peaugres (07) . . . 222 A2
Péaule (56) . . . 101 K6
Péault (85) . . . 159 K4
Pébées (32) . . . 287 H2
Pébrac (43) . . . 219 J5
Pech (09) . . . 307 K5
Pech-Luna (11) . . . 289 F5
Péchabou (31) . . . 288 C2
Pécharic-et-le-Py (11) . . . 289 F6
Péchaudier (81) . . . 289 G1
Pechbonnieu (31) . . . 269 G3
Pechbusque (31) . . . 288 C1
le Pêchereau (36) . . . 165 G3
Pécorade (40) . . . 265 J3
le Pecq (78) . . . 58 C3
Pecquencourt (59) . . . 11 J1
Pecqueuse (91) . . . 58 B6
Pécy (77) . . . 60 B6
Pédernec (22) . . . 48 B4
Pégairolles-de-Buèges (34) . . . 273 J4
Pégairolles-de-l'Escalette (34) . . . 273 G4
Pégomas (06) . . . 280 D5
le Pègue (26) . . . 257 G1
Péguilhan (31) . . . 286 E4
Peigney (52) . . . 116 D4
Peillac (56) . . . 102 A3
Peille (06) . . . 281 J2
Peillon (06) . . . 281 H3
Peillonnex (74) . . . 191 H2
Peipin (04) . . . 259 G5
Peisey-Nancroix (73) . . . 193 A4
Pel-et-Der (10) . . . 90 E3
Pélissanne (13) . . . 277 F5
Pellafol (38) . . . 242 C2
Pelleautier (05) . . . 242 E6
Pellefigue (32) . . . 287 F2
Pellegrue (33) . . . 230 D3
le Pellerin (44) . . . 122 E4
la Pellerine (49) . . . 126 D4
la Pellerine (53) . . . 80 C4
Pellevoisin (36) . . . 147 H4
Pellouailles-les-Vignes (49) . . . 125 H3
Pelonne (26) . . . 258 A2
Pelouse (48) . . . 237 K6
Pelousey (25) . . . 137 J5
Peltre (57) . . . 45 F6
Pélussin (42) . . . 205 K6
Pelves (62) . . . 11 G3
Pelvoux (05) . . . 243 J1
Penchard (77) . . . 59 H2
Pencran (29) . . . 46 C6
Pendé (80) . . . 8 E4
Pénestin (56) . . . 121 G2
Penguily (22) . . . 77 J2
Penin (62) . . . 10 D3
Penly (76) . . . 16 B1
Penmarch (29) . . . 73 B6
Pennautier (11) . . . 290 A5
la Penne (06) . . . 280 D1
Penne (81) . . . 250 C6
Penne-d'Agenais (47) . . . 248 D2
la Penne-sur-Huveaune (13) . . . 296 E4
la Penne-sur-l'Ouvèze (26) . . . 257 J3
Pennedepie (14) . . . 33 K2
Pennes-le-Sec (26) . . . 241 G4
les Pennes-Mirabeau (13) . . . 296 D3
Pennesières (70) . . . 138 A3
Penol (38) . . . 206 E6
Pensol (87) . . . 198 A4
Penta-Acquatella (2B) . . . 319 H4
Penta-di-Casinca (2B) . . . 319 J3
Penvénan (22) . . . 48 B2
Péone (06) . . . 261 F4
Pépieux (11) . . . 290 E4
Pérassay (36) . . . 166 C5
Peray (72) . . . 83 F5
Perceneige (89) . . . 88 E4
Percey (89) . . . 113 J3
Percey-le-Grand (70) . . . 136 D1
le Perchay (95) . . . 37 F6
la Perche (18) . . . 167 G3
Perchède (32) . . . 266 A4
Percy (38) . . . 242 A2
Percy (50) . . . 31 G6
Percy-en-Auge (14) . . . 33 G6
Perdreauville (78) . . . 57 H2
Péré (17) . . . 177 G3

Péré (65) . . . 285 K6
Péreille (09) . . . 308 A3
Perelli (2B) . . . 319 H5
Pérenchies (59) . . . 6 D4
Péret (34) . . . 292 C1
Péret-Bel-Air (19) . . . 200 C6
Péreuil (16) . . . 196 C5
Péreyres (07) . . . 239 F3
Pergain-Taillac (32) . . . 248 B6
Peri (2A) . . . 320 D4
le Périer (38) . . . 224 D6
Périers (50) . . . 30 E2
Périers-en-Auge (14) . . . 33 G4
Périers-sur-le-Dan (14) . . . 32 E4
Pérignac (16) . . . 196 D6
Pérignac (17) . . . 195 H3
Pérignat-sur-Allier (63) . . . 202 E3
Périgné (79) . . . 178 C2
Périgneux (42) . . . 204 E6
Périgny (03) . . . 185 K2
Périgny (14) . . . 53 G2
Périgny (17) . . . 176 E2
Périgny (41) . . . 108 D6
Périgny (94) . . . 59 G5
Périgny-la-Rose (10) . . . 89 G1
Périgueux (24) . . . 214 A3
Périssac (33) . . . 211 K5
Perles (02) . . . 40 B3
Perles-et-Castelet (09) . . . 308 A6
Pern (46) . . . 249 K3
Pernand-Vergelesses (21) . . . 154 A3
Pernant (02) . . . 39 H3
Pernay (37) . . . 127 G3
la Pernelle (50) . . . 29 F2
Pernes (62) . . . 5 H5
Pernes-lès-Boulogne (62) . . . 2 B5
Pernes-les-Fontaines (84) . . . 276 D1
Pernois (80) . . . 9 K6
Pero-Casevecchie (2B) . . . 319 J4
Pérols (34) . . . 293 H1
Pérols-sur-Vézère (19) . . . 200 C4
Péron (01) . . . 190 D2
Péronnas (01) . . . 189 G2
Péronne (71) . . . 171 J5
Péronne (80) . . . 19 G1
Péronne-en-Mélantois (59) . . . 6 E5
Péronville (28) . . . 109 H2
Pérouges (01) . . . 189 G6
la Pérouille (36) . . . 165 G2
Péroy-les-Gombries (60) . . . 38 E5
Perpezac-le-Blanc (19) . . . 215 G3
Perpezac-le-Noir (19) . . . 215 J2
Perpezat (63) . . . 202 A3
Perpignan (66) . . . 310 C5
les Perques (50) . . . 28 C5
Perquie (40) . . . 265 J2
Perrancey-les-Vieux-Moulins (52) . . . 116 C4
le Perray-en-Yvelines (78) . . . 57 K5
Perrecy-les-Forges (71) . . . 170 D5
le Perréon (69) . . . 188 A4
Perret (22) . . . 76 C4
Perreuil (71) . . . 153 H6
Perreux (42) . . . 187 F4
Perreux (89) . . . 112 C4
le Perreux-sur-Marne (94) . . . 59 F4
Perrex (01) . . . 188 D1
Perrier (63) . . . 202 E5
le Perrier (85) . . . 140 D5
Perrières (14) . . . 54 B2
Perriers-en-Beauficel (50) . . . 52 D4
Perriers-la-Campagne (27) . . . 34 E5
Perriers-sur-Andelle (27) . . . 36 A2
Perrignier (74) . . . 175 F6
Perrigny (39) . . . 173 G2
Perrigny (89) . . . 113 F5
Perrigny-lès-Dijon (21) . . . 136 A6
Perrigny-sur-Armançon (89) . . . 134 C1
Perrigny-sur-l'Ognon (21) . . . 136 C5
Perrigny-sur-Loire (71) . . . 169 K4
Perrogney-les-Fontaines (52) . . . 116 B5
le Perron (81) . . . 31 K4
Perros-Guirec (22) . . . 48 B1
Perrou (61) . . . 81 H1
Perrouse (70) . . . 138 A4
Perroy (58) . . . 132 C4
Perruel (27) . . . 36 A2
Perrusse (52) . . . 116 E1
Perrusson (37) . . . 146 D2
Pers (15) . . . 235 F2
Pers (79) . . . 179 F2
Pers-en-Gâtinais (45) . . . 111 K1
Pers-Jussy (74) . . . 191 G3
Persac (86) . . . 163 G6
Persan (95) . . . 37 J5
Persquen (56) . . . 76 B6
Perthes (08) . . . 41 H1
Perthes (52) . . . 63 H6
Perthes (77) . . . 87 H3
Perthes-lès-Brienne (10) . . . 91 F3
Pertheville-Ners (14) . . . 54 B3
le Perthus (66) . . . 315 G5
le Pertre (35) . . . 104 C2
le Pertuis (43) . . . 220 D5
Pertuis (84) . . . 277 J5
la Péruse (16) . . . 180 A6
Pervenchères (61) . . . 83 G5
Perville (82) . . . 248 E5

Pescadoires (46) . . . 232 E6	Peyrouse (65) . . . 304 A1	Pierrepont (14) . . . 53 K3	Pithon (02) . . . 19 J4	Plémet (22) . . . 77 H4	
Pescadoires (63) . . . 203 H1	Peyrouzet (31) . . . 287 F5	Pierrepont (54) . . . 26 C4	Pîtres (27) . . . 35 J3	Plémy (22) . . . 77 H2	
le Pescher (19) . . . 216 A5	Peyruis (04) . . . 259 F6	Pierrepont-sur-Avre (80) . . . 18 D4	Pittefaux (62) . . . 2 B5	Plénée-Jugon (22) . . . 77 K2	
Péseux (25) . . . 139 G5	Peyrun (65) . . . 285 J4	Pierrepont-sur-l'Arentèle (88) . . . 95 F4	Pizay (01) . . . 189 F6	Pléneuf-Val-André (22) . . . 49 J5	
Peseux (39) . . . 155 F3	Peyrus (26) . . . 240 E1	Pierrerue (04) . . . 278 C1	Pizieux (72) . . . 83 F4	Plénise (39) . . . 156 C5	
Peslières (63) . . . 203 H6	Peyrusse (15) . . . 218 D3	Pierrerue (34) . . . 291 H3	le Pizou (24) . . . 212 D5	Plénisette (39) . . . 156 C6	
Pesmes (70) . . . 137 F5	Peyrusse-Grande (32) . . . 266 E6	Pierres (14) . . . 53 H3	le Pla (09) . . . 308 D6	Plerguer (35) . . . 50 E5	
Pessac (33) . . . 229 G2	Peyrusse-le-Roc (12) . . . 251 H1	Pierres (28) . . . 85 H1	Plabennec (29) . . . 46 A5	Plérin (22) . . . 49 G5	
Pessac-sur-Dordogne (33) . . . 230 D2	Peyrusse-Massas (32) . . . 267 H4	Pierreval (76) . . . 16 B6	Placé (53) . . . 80 E5	Plerneuf (22) . . . 49 F6	
Pessan (32) . . . 267 J6	Peyrusse-Vieille (32) . . . 266 D6	Pierreville (50) . . . 28 B4	les Places (27) . . . 34 B5	Plescop (56) . . . 101 F4	
Pessans (25) . . . 156 A2	Peyssies (31) . . . 287 J4	Pierreville (54) . . . 94 A1	Placey (25) . . . 137 J6	Plesder (35) . . . 50 E6	
Pessat-Villeneuve (63) . . . 185 F6	Peyzac-le-Moustier (24) . . . 214 D6	Pierrevillers (57) . . . 27 H5	Plachy-Buyon (80) . . . 18 A3	Plésidy (22) . . . 76 C1	
la Pesse (39) . . . 173 H6	Peyzieux-sur-Saône (01) . . . 188 C3	Pierric (44) . . . 103 F4	Placy (14) . . . 53 J1	Pleslin-Trigavou (22) . . . 50 D4	
Pessines (17) . . . 195 F2	Pézarches (77) . . . 60 A5	Pierry (51) . . . 61 K1	Placy-Montaigu (50) . . . 31 J4	Plesnois (57) . . . 44 E4	
Pessoulens (32) . . . 268 B3	Pezé-le-Robert (72) . . . 82 B6	Pietra-di-Verde (2B) . . . 319 H6	le Plagnal (07) . . . 238 C4	Plesnoy (52) . . . 116 E4	
Petersbach (67) . . . 69 F5	Pézenas (34) . . . 292 C4	Pietracorbara (2B) . . . 317 D3	Plagne (01) . . . 190 B2	Plessala (22) . . . 77 H3	
le Petit-Abergement (01) . . . 190 A4	Pézènes-les-Mines (34) . . . 292 A1	Pietralba (2B) . . . 319 F3	Plagne (31) . . . 287 H6	Plessé (44) . . . 102 D3	
Petit-Auverné (44) . . . 103 K5	Pezens (11) . . . 290 A5	Pietraserena (2B) . . . 321 H1	Plagnole (31) . . . 287 H3	le Plessier-Huleu (02) . . . 39 J4	
Petit-Bersac (24) . . . 213 F2	Pézilla-de-Conflent (66) . . . 309 H6	Pietricaggio (2B) . . . 319 H5	Plaigne (11) . . . 289 F6	le Plessier-Rozainvillers (80) . . . 18 D4	
le Petit-Bornand-les-Glières (74) . . . 191 H4	Pézilla-la-Rivière (66) . . . 310 E5	Pietrosella (2A) . . . 320 C5	Plailly (60) . . . 38 B6	le Plessier-sur-Bulles (60) . . . 37 K1	
le Petit-Celland (50) . . . 52 B5	Pezou (41) . . . 108 D4	Pietroso (2B) . . . 321 G2	Plaimbois-du-Miroir (25) . . . 139 G6	le Plessier-sur-Saint-Just (60) . . . 38 A1	
Petit-Couronne (76) . . . 35 H2	Pezuls (24) . . . 232 B1	Piets-Plasence-Moustrou (64) . . . 284 B1	Plaimbois-Vennes (25) . . . 139 F6	le Plessis-aux-Bois (77) . . . 59 J2	
Petit-Croix (90) . . . 139 J1	Pézy (28) . . . 85 H4	Pieusse (11) . . . 308 E1	Plaimpied-Givaudins (18) . . . 149 H4	Plessis-Barbuise (10) . . . 89 G1	
Petit-Failly (54) . . . 26 A3	Pfaffenheim (68) . . . 96 B5	les Pieux (50) . . . 28 B4	la Plaine (49) . . . 143 H2	le Plessis-Belleville (60) . . . 38 D6	
Petit-Fayt (59) . . . 13 F5	Pfaffenhoffen (67) . . . 69 J6	Piève (2B) . . . 319 H5	Plaine (67) . . . 95 K2	le Plessis-Bouchard (95) . . . 58 D2	
le Petit-Fougeray (35) . . . 103 G1	Pfalzweyer (67) . . . 69 F6	Piffonds (89) . . . 112 C2	Plaine-de-Walsch (57) . . . 67 K4	le Plessis-Brion (60) . . . 38 E1	
Petit-Landau (68) . . . 97 E2	Pfastatt (68) . . . 97 B2	Pigna (2B) . . . 318 C3	Plaine-Haute (22) . . . 77 H3	le Plessis-de-Roye (60) . . . 19 G2	
Petit-Mars (44) . . . 123 H2	Pfetterhouse (68) . . . 97 A5	Pignan (34) . . . 293 F1	la Plaine-sur-Mer (44) . . . 122 A5	le Plessis-Dorin (41) . . . 108 A1	
le Petit-Mercey (39) . . . 155 J1	Pfettisheim (67) . . . 70 E2	Pignans (83) . . . 298 A3	Plainemont (70) . . . 118 B4	le Plessis-Feu-Aussoux (77) . . . 60 B5	
Petit-Mesnil (10) . . . 91 H4	Pfulgriesheim (67) . . . 70 E2	Pignicourt (02) . . . 41 F2	Plaines-Saint-Lange (10) . . . 114 C5	le Plessis-Gassot (95) . . . 59 F1	
Petit-Noir (39) . . . 155 F4	Phaffans (90) . . . 119 J6	Pignols (63) . . . 203 H5	Plainfaing (88) . . . 95 J5	le Plessis-Grammoire (49) . . . 125 H3	
Petit-Palais-et-Cornemps (33) . . . 212 C6	Phalempin (59) . . . 6 D5	Pigny (18) . . . 149 H2	Plainoiseau (39) . . . 173 G1	le Plessis-Grimoult (14) . . . 53 G2	
le Petit-Pressigny (37) . . . 146 C5	Phalsbourg (57) . . . 70 A1	Pihem (62) . . . 3 G6	les Plains-et-Grands-Essarts (25) . . . 139 J5	le Plessis-Grohan (27) . . . 56 D2	
le Petit-Quevilly (76) . . . 35 H2	Philippsbourg (57) . . . 69 J4	Pihen-lès-Guînes (62) . . . 2 C3	Plaintel (22) . . . 77 F1	le Plessis-Hébert (27) . . . 57 F2	
Petit-Réderching (57) . . . 69 F3	Philondenx (40) . . . 265 H6	Pila-Canale (2A) . . . 322 D1	Plainval (60) . . . 38 A1	le Plessis-Lastelle (50) . . . 30 E1	
Petit-Tenquin (57) . . . 67 G4	Phlin (54) . . . 66 B2	Pillac (16) . . . 213 F2	Plainville (27) . . . 34 C6	le Plessis-l'Échelle (41) . . . 109 F5	
Petit-Verly (02) . . . 20 C1	Pia (66) . . . 310 C6	Pillemoine (39) . . . 173 K1	Plainville (60) . . . 18 C5	le Plessis-l'Évêque (77) . . . 59 J1	
la Petite-Boissière (79) . . . 143 G5	Piacé (72) . . . 82 D5	les Pilles (26) . . . 257 J2	Plaisance (12) . . . 271 J2	le Plessis-Luzarches (95) . . . 38 A6	
Petite-Chaux (25) . . . 174 C1	le Pian-Médoc (33) . . . 211 G6	Pillon (55) . . . 26 B4	Plaisance (24) . . . 231 J4	le Plessis-Macé (49) . . . 125 F2	
Petite-Forêt (59) . . . 12 C1	le Pian-sur-Garonne (33) . . . 230 A5	Pimbo (40) . . . 265 H6	Plaisance (32) . . . 266 C6	le Plessis-Pâté (91) . . . 86 E2	
la Petite-Fosse (88) . . . 95 J3	Piana (2A) . . . 316 C5	Pimelles (89) . . . 114 C5	Plaisance (86) . . . 164 A6	le Plessis-Patte-d'Oie (60) . . . 19 H4	
la Petite-Marche (03) . . . 184 A2	Pianello (2B) . . . 319 H6	Pimorin (39) . . . 173 H4	Plaisance-du-Touch (31) . . . 288 A1	le Plessis-Placy (77) . . . 60 A1	
la Petite-Pierre (67) . . . 69 E4	Piano (2B) . . . 319 H5	Pimprez (60) . . . 39 F1	Plaisia (39) . . . 173 G3	le Plessis-Robinson (92) . . . 58 D4	
la Petite-Raon (88) . . . 95 J2	Pianotolli-Caldarello (2A) . . . 323 F5	le Pin (03) . . . 170 A5	Plaisians (26) . . . 257 K4	Plessis-Saint-Benoist (91) . . . 86 B3	
Petite-Rosselle (57) . . . 68 B1	les Piards (39) . . . 173 J4	le Pin (14) . . . 34 A4	Plaisir (78) . . . 58 A4	Plessis-Saint-Jean (89) . . . 88 D4	
la Petite-Verrière (71) . . . 152 D3	la Piarre (05) . . . 242 A6	le Pin (17) . . . 212 A2	Plaissan (34) . . . 292 D1	le Plessis-Sainte-Opportune (27) . . . 35 F6	
Petitefontaine (90) . . . 119 K5	Piazzali (2B) . . . 319 J5	le Pin (30) . . . 256 B6	Plaizac (16) . . . 196 B2	le Plessis-Trévise (94) . . . 59 G4	
les Petites-Armoises (08) . . . 42 C1	Piazzole (2B) . . . 319 H5	le Pin (38) . . . 207 H5	le Plan (31) . . . 287 J6	Plessix-Balisson (22) . . . 50 C4	
les Petites-Loges (51) . . . 41 G5	Piblange (57) . . . 27 K5	le Pin (39) . . . 173 G1	Plan (38) . . . 223 H2	Plestan (22) . . . 77 K1	
Petitmagny (90) . . . 119 J5	Pibrac (31) . . . 269 F6	le Pin (44) . . . 124 B1	Plan-d'Aups-Sainte-Baume (83) . . . 297 G3	Plestin-les-Grèves (22) . . . 47 J3	
Petitmont (54) . . . 67 H6	Picarreau (39) . . . 155 K6	le Pin (70) . . . 137 J5	Plan-de-Baix (26) . . . 241 F2	Pleubian (22) . . . 48 D1	
Petiville (14) . . . 33 G4	Picauville (50) . . . 28 E5	le Pin (77) . . . 59 H3	Plan-de-Cuques (13) . . . 296 D3	Pleucadeuc (56) . . . 101 K4	
Petiville (76) . . . 34 D1	Pichanges (21) . . . 136 B3	le Pin (79) . . . 143 G5	Plan-de-la-Tour (83) . . . 298 E3	Pleudaniel (22) . . . 48 D2	
Petosse (85) . . . 160 C4	Picherande (63) . . . 202 A6	le Pin (82) . . . 268 C1	Plan-d'Orgon (13) . . . 276 D3	Pleudihen-sur-Rance (22) . . . 50 D5	
Petreto-Bicchisano (2A) . . . 322 E1	Picquigny (80) . . . 17 K1	le Pin-au-Haras (61) . . . 54 D1	Planaise (73) . . . 208 D5	Pleugriffet (56) . . . 101 G1	
Pettoncourt (57) . . . 66 C3	Pie-d'Orezza (2B) . . . 319 H5	Pin-Balma (31) . . . 269 H6	Planay (21) . . . 114 C6	Pleugueneuc (35) . . . 50 E6	
Pettonville (54) . . . 95 F1	Pied-de-Borne (48) . . . 255 H2	le Pin-en-Mauges (49) . . . 124 D6	Planay (73) . . . 209 K5	Pleumartin (86) . . . 163 H5	
Peujard (33) . . . 211 J5	Piedicorte-di-Gaggio (2B) . . . 321 H1	le Pin-la-Garenne (61) . . . 83 H1	la Planche (44) . . . 141 K3	Pleumeleuc (35) . . . 78 E3	
Peumérit (29) . . . 73 E4	Piedicroce (2B) . . . 319 H5	le Pin-Murelet (31) . . . 287 H3	Plancher-Bas (70) . . . 119 G5	Pleumeur-Bodou (22) . . . 47 K2	
Peumerit-Quintin (22) . . . 76 B2	Piedigriggio (2B) . . . 319 H5	Pinas (65) . . . 305 G1	Plancher-les-Mines (70) . . . 119 G5	Pleumeur-Gautier (22) . . . 48 C2	
Peuton (53) . . . 104 E4	Piedipartino (2B) . . . 319 H5	Pinay (42) . . . 187 F6	Plancherine (73) . . . 209 F2	Pleure (39) . . . 155 G4	
Peuvillers (55) . . . 43 H2	Piégon (26) . . . 257 H3	Pincé (72) . . . 105 J5	les Planches-en-Montagne (39) . . . 174 A2	Pleurs (51) . . . 61 J5	
Peux-et-Couffouleux (12) . . . 272 B4	Piégros-la-Clastre (26) . . . 240 E2	Pindères (47) . . . 247 F3	les Planches-près-Arbois (39) . . . 155 K5	Pleurtuit (35) . . . 50 D4	
Pévange (57) . . . 66 C2	Piégut (04) . . . 243 F6	Pindray (86) . . . 163 K4	Planchez (71) . . . 152 C2	Pleuven (29) . . . 98 D2	
Pévy (51) . . . 40 D3	Piégut-Pluviers (24) . . . 197 K4	les Pineaux (85) . . . 160 A2	Plancoët (22) . . . 50 B4	Pleuvezain (88) . . . 93 J3	
Pexiora (11) . . . 289 H5	Piencourt (27) . . . 34 B5	Pinel-Hauterive (47) . . . 248 B1	Plancy-l'Abbaye (10) . . . 89 K1	Pleuville (16) . . . 179 K4	
Pexonne (54) . . . 95 H1	Piennes (54) . . . 26 D5	Pinet (34) . . . 292 D3	la Planée (25) . . . 156 E5	Pléven (22) . . . 50 A5	
Pey (40) . . . 262 D5	Piennes-Onvillers (80) . . . 18 E4	Pineuilh (33) . . . 231 F2	Planès (66) . . . 313 J4	Plévin (22) . . . 75 J3	
Peymeinade (06) . . . 280 C5	Pierlas (06) . . . 261 H5	Piney (10) . . . 90 D4	Planèzes (66) . . . 309 J5	Pleyben (29) . . . 74 D4	
Peynier (13) . . . 297 F2	la Pierre (38) . . . 224 C4	Pino (2B) . . . 317 C2	Planfoy (42) . . . 221 H1	Pleyber-Christ (29) . . . 47 F5	
Peypin (13) . . . 296 E3	Pierre-Bénite (69) . . . 206 A4	Pinols (43) . . . 219 H5	Planguenoual (22) . . . 49 H6	Pliboux (79) . . . 179 G2	
Peypin-d'Aigues (84) . . . 277 K3	Pierre-Buffière (87) . . . 199 G3	Pinon (02) . . . 39 K1	Planioles (46) . . . 234 D5	Plichancourt (51) . . . 63 G4	
Peyrabout (23) . . . 182 D4	Pierre-Châtel (38) . . . 224 B6	les Pins (16) . . . 197 G1	le Planois (71) . . . 155 F6	Plieux (32) . . . 267 K2	
le Peyrat (09) . . . 308 B3	Pierre-de-Bresse (71) . . . 154 C4	Pins-Justaret (31) . . . 288 B2	le Planquay (27) . . . 34 B6	Plivot (51) . . . 62 A1	
Peyrat-de-Bellac (87) . . . 181 F3	Pierre-la-Treiche (54) . . . 65 J5	Pinsac (46) . . . 233 J2	Planquery (14) . . . 31 K5	Plobannalec (29) . . . 98 B3	
Peyrat-la-Nonière (23) . . . 183 H4	Pierre-Levée (77) . . . 60 B3	Pinsaguel (31) . . . 288 B2	Planques (62) . . . 5 F6	Plobsheim (67) . . . 71 D2	
Peyrat-le-Château (87) . . . 200 A1	Pierre-Morains (51) . . . 62 A4	Pinsot (38) . . . 224 E1	Planrupt (52) . . . 91 H2	Ploemel (56) . . . 100 C5	
la Peyratte (79) . . . 162 A4	Pierre-Percée (54) . . . 95 H1	Pintac (65) . . . 285 G4	les Plans (30) . . . 255 J3	Ploemeur (56) . . . 99 K5	
Peyraube (65) . . . 285 K5	Pierre-Perthuis (89) . . . 133 J4	Pinterville (27) . . . 35 J5	les Plans (34) . . . 273 F4	Ploërdut (56) . . . 76 B5	
Peyraud (07) . . . 222 B2	Pierreclos (71) . . . 171 H6	Pintheville (55) . . . 44 A5	le Plantay (01) . . . 189 F4	Ploeren (56) . . . 100 E5	
Peyre (40) . . . 265 G6	Pierrecourt (70) . . . 137 F1	les Pinthières (28) . . . 57 H5	les Plantiers (30) . . . 254 D5	Ploërmel (56) . . . 101 K2	
Peyrecave (32) . . . 268 A1	Pierrecourt (76) . . . 17 F2	Piobetta (2B) . . . 319 H5	le Plantis (61) . . . 83 F1	Ploeuc-sur-Lié (22) . . . 77 G2	
Peyrefitte-du-Razès (11) . . . 308 C2	Pierrefeu (06) . . . 280 E2	Pioggiola (2B) . . . 318 D3	Planty (10) . . . 89 G5	Ploéven (29) . . . 74 C4	
Peyrefitte-sur-l'Hers (11) . . . 289 H6	Pierrefeu-du-Var (83) . . . 298 A4	Piolenc (84) . . . 256 D4	Planzolles (07) . . . 255 H1	Ploëzal (22) . . . 48 C3	
Peyregoux (81) . . . 270 E5	Pierrefiche (12) . . . 253 F1	Pionnat (23) . . . 182 D3	Plappeville (57) . . . 44 E5	Plogastel-Saint-Germain (29) . . . 74 B6	
Peyrehorade (40) . . . 264 A6	Pierrefiche (48) . . . 238 C1	Pionsat (63) . . . 184 B3	Plasne (39) . . . 155 J6	Plogoff (29) . . . 73 B5	
Peyreleau (12) . . . 253 H5	Pierrefiques (76) . . . 14 B4	Pioussay (79) . . . 179 F4	Plasnes (27) . . . 34 D5	Plogonnec (29) . . . 74 C5	
Peyrelevade (19) . . . 200 D3	Pierrefitte (19) . . . 199 J6	Pipriac (35) . . . 102 D2	Plassac (17) . . . 195 G5	Ploisy (02) . . . 39 J3	
Peyrelongue-Abos (64) . . . 285 F2	Pierrefitte (23) . . . 183 G3	Piquecos (82) . . . 249 G4	Plassac (33) . . . 211 G4	Plomb (50) . . . 52 A4	
Peyremale (30) . . . 255 G3	Pierrefitte (79) . . . 144 A5	Pirajoux (01) . . . 172 D5	Plassac-Rouffiac (16) . . . 196 D5	Plombières-les-Bains (88) . . . 118 D2	
Peyrens (11) . . . 289 H4	Pierrefitte (88) . . . 94 B6	Piré-sur-Seiche (35) . . . 79 J5	Plassay (17) . . . 195 F1	Plombières-lès-Dijon (21) . . . 135 K5	
Peyrestortes (66) . . . 310 E5	Pierrefitte-en-Auge (14) . . . 33 K4	Pirey (25) . . . 137 K5	Plats (07) . . . 222 B5	Plomelin (29) . . . 98 C2	
Peyret-Saint-André (65) . . . 286 C4	Pierrefitte-en-Beauvaisis (60) . . . 37 G1	Piriac-sur-Mer (44) . . . 121 F5	Plaudren (56) . . . 101 G4	Plomeur (29) . . . 73 E6	
Peyriac-de-Mer (11) . . . 310 C1	Pierrefitte-en-Cinglais (14) . . . 53 J2	Pirmil (72) . . . 106 B3	Plauzat (63) . . . 202 D4	Plomion (02) . . . 21 G3	
Peyriac-Minervois (11) . . . 290 D4	Pierrefitte-ès-Bois (45) . . . 131 H3	Pirou (50) . . . 30 D2	Plavilla (11) . . . 289 G6	Plomodiern (29) . . . 74 C3	
Peyriat (01) . . . 189 K2	Pierrefitte-Nestalas (65) . . . 304 B3	Pis (32) . . . 267 K4	Plazac (24) . . . 214 D5	Plonéis (29) . . . 74 B5	
Peyrière (47) . . . 231 G5	Pierrefitte-sur-Aire (55) . . . 64 C2	Pisany (17) . . . 194 E2	Pleaux (15) . . . 217 F4	Plonéour-Lanvern (29) . . . 98 B2	
Peyrieu (01) . . . 207 J3	Pierrefitte-sur-Loire (03) . . . 169 K4	Piscop (95) . . . 58 E1	Pléboulle (22) . . . 50 A3	Plonévez-du-Faou (29) . . . 75 G3	
Peyrignac (24) . . . 215 F4	Pierrefitte-sur-Sauldre (41) . . . 130 C3	Piseux (27) . . . 56 B4	Pléchâtel (35) . . . 103 F1	Plonévez-Porzay (29) . . . 74 C4	
Peyriguère (65) . . . 285 K5	Pierrefitte-sur-Seine (93) . . . 58 E2	Pisieu (38) . . . 222 B1	Plédéliac (22) . . . 77 K1	Plorec-sur-Arguenon (22) . . . 50 A5	
Peyrilhac (87) . . . 181 F5	Pierrefonds (60) . . . 39 F3	Pisseleu (60) . . . 37 J1	Plédran (22) . . . 77 H1	Plou (18) . . . 148 E4	
Peyrillac-et-Millac (24) . . . 233 H2	Pierrefontaine-lès-Blamont (25) . . . 139 H4	Pisseloup (52) . . . 117 G4	Pléguien (22) . . . 48 E4	Plouagat (22) . . . 48 E5	
Peyrilles (46) . . . 233 H5	Pierrefontaine-les-Varans (25) . . . 139 F6	la Pisseure (70) . . . 118 C4	Pléhédel (22) . . . 48 E3	Plouaret (22) . . . 47 K4	
Peyrins (26) . . . 222 D4	Pierrefort (15) . . . 236 B1	Pissos (40) . . . 245 H3	Pleine-Fougères (35) . . . 51 H5	Plouarzel (29) . . . 72 B3	
Peyrissac (19) . . . 199 K5	Pierregot (80) . . . 10 B6	Pissotte (85) . . . 160 C4	Pleine-Selve (02) . . . 20 C3	Plouasne (22) . . . 78 D2	
Peyrissas (31) . . . 287 G4	Pierrelatte (26) . . . 256 D1	Pissy (80) . . . 17 K2	Pleine-Selve (33) . . . 211 H1	Plouay (56) . . . 100 A1	
Peyrole (81) . . . 270 D4	Pierrelaye (95) . . . 58 C1	Pissy-Pôville (76) . . . 15 K5	Plélan-le-Grand (35) . . . 78 C5	Ploubalay (22) . . . 50 C4	
Peyroles (30) . . . 254 E6	Pierrelongue (26) . . . 257 J3	Pisy (89) . . . 134 B2	Plélan-le-Petit (22) . . . 50 B5	Ploubazlanec (22) . . . 48 E3	
Peyrolles (11) . . . 309 G1	Pierremande (02) . . . 19 K6	Pitgam (59) . . . 3 H3	Plélauff (22) . . . 76 B4	Ploubezre (22) . . . 48 A3	
Peyrolles-en-Provence (13) . . . 277 K5	Pierremont (62) . . . 10 A1	Pithiviers (45) . . . 86 D5	Plélo (22) . . . 48 E5	Ploudalmézeau (29) . . . 72 C2	
Peyroules (04) . . . 280 A3	Pierremont-sur-Amance (52) . . . 117 G5	Pithiviers-le-Vieil (45) . . . 110 D1		Ploudaniel (29) . . . 46 B6	
	Pierrepont (02) . . . 20 E5			Ploudiry (29) . . . 46 D6	

387

Plouëc-du-Trieux (22)...... 48 C4
Plouédern (29)...... 46 C5
Plouégat-Guérand (29)...... 47 H4
Plouégat-Moysan (29)...... 47 J5
Plouénan (29)...... 46 E4
Plouër-sur-Rance (22)...... 50 D4
Plouescat (29)...... 46 D3
Plouézec (22)...... 48 C3
Plouézoch (29)...... 47 G4
Ploufragan (22)...... 49 F6
Plougar (29)...... 46 D4
Plougasnou (29)...... 47 G3
Plougastel-Daoulas (29)...... 72 E5
Plougonvelin (29)...... 72 B5
Plougonven (29)...... 47 H5
Plougonver (22)...... 48 A6
Plougoulm (29)...... 46 E3
Plougoumelen (56)...... 100 E5
Plougourvest (29)...... 46 D4
Plougras (22)...... 47 J6
Plougrescant (22)...... 48 C1
Plouguenast (22)...... 77 G3
Plouguerneau (29)...... 46 A4
Plouguernével (22)...... 76 B3
Plouguiel (22)...... 48 C2
Plouguin (29)...... 72 C2
Plouha (22)...... 48 E4
Plouharnel (56)...... 100 C6
Plouhinec (29)...... 73 D3
Plouhinec (56)...... 100 B4
Plouider (22)...... 46 C4
Plouigneau (29)...... 47 H5
Plouisy (22)...... 48 C5
Ploulec'h (22)...... 47 K3
Ploumagoar (22)...... 48 C5
Ploumilliau (22)...... 47 K3
Ploumoguer (29)...... 72 B4
Plounéour-Ménez (29)...... 47 F6
Plounéour-Trez (29)...... 46 C3
Plounérin (22)...... 47 J5
Plounéventer (29)...... 46 C5
Plounévez-Lochrist (29)...... 46 C4
Plounévez-Moëdec (22)...... 47 K5
Plounévez-Quintin (22)...... 76 B3
Plounévézel (29)...... 75 J2
Plourac'h (22)...... 75 J1
Plouray (56)...... 76 A4
Plourhan (22)...... 49 F4
Plourin (29)...... 72 B3
Plourin-lès-Morlaix (29)...... 47 G5
Plourivo (22)...... 48 D3
Plouvain (62)...... 11 G2
Plouvara (22)...... 48 E6
Plouvien (29)...... 46 A5
Plouvorn (29)...... 46 E4
Plouyé (29)...... 75 G2
Plouzané (29)...... 72 C4
Plouzélambre (22)...... 47 J4
Plouzévédé (29)...... 46 D4
Plovan (29)...... 73 E5
Ployart-et-Vaurseine (02)...... 40 C1
le Ployron (60)...... 18 D6
Plozévet (29)...... 73 D4
Pludual (22)...... 48 E4
Pluduno (22)...... 50 B4
Plufur (22)...... 47 J4
Pluguffan (29)...... 74 C6
Pluherlin (56)...... 101 K5
Plumaudan (22)...... 78 C1
Plumaugat (22)...... 78 B2
Plumelec (56)...... 101 G3
Pluméliau (56)...... 100 D1
Plumelin (56)...... 100 E2
Plumergat (56)...... 100 E4
Plumetot (14)...... 32 E3
Plumieux (22)...... 77 H5
Plumont (39)...... 155 J2
Pluneret (56)...... 100 D5
Plurien (22)...... 49 K5
Plusquellec (22)...... 75 K1
Plussulien (22)...... 76 D3
Pluvault (21)...... 154 E1
Pluvet (21)...... 154 E1
Pluvigner (56)...... 100 D3
Pluzunet (22)...... 48 A4
Pocancy (51)...... 62 B2
Pocé-les-Bois (35)...... 80 A6
Pocé-sur-Cisse (37)...... 128 D4
Podensac (33)...... 229 K4
le Poët (05)...... 259 F3
le Poët-Célard (26)...... 240 E6
le Poët-en-Percip (26)...... 258 A3
le Poët-Laval (26)...... 240 D6
le Poët-Sigillat (26)...... 257 K2
Poeuilly (80)...... 19 J2
Poey-de-Lescar (64)...... 284 C3
Poey-d'Oloron (64)...... 283 K5
Poëzat (03)...... 185 G4
Poggio-di-Nazza (2B)...... 321 H3
Poggio-di-Venaco (2B)...... 319 F6
Poggio-d'Oletta (2B)...... 317 D6
Poggio-Marinaccio (2B)...... 319 H4
Poggio-Mezzana (2B)...... 319 J4
Poggiolo (2A)...... 320 D2
Pogny (51)...... 62 B3
Poids-de-Fiole (39)...... 173 G3
Poigny (77)...... 88 D2
Poigny-la-Forêt (78)...... 57 J4
Poil (58)...... 152 D5
Poilcourt-Sydney (08)...... 41 F2
Poilhes (34)...... 291 J4
Poillé-sur-Vègre (72)...... 105 K3

Poilley (35)...... 80 A2
Poilley (50)...... 52 A4
Poilly (51)...... 40 D4
Poilly-lez-Gien (45)...... 131 G1
Poilly-sur-Serein (89)...... 113 K5
Poilly-sur-Tholon (89)...... 112 E4
Poinçon-lès-Larrey (21)...... 114 E4
le Poinçonnet (36)...... 165 J1
Poincy (77)...... 60 A2
Poinsenot (52)...... 115 K6
Poinson-lès-Fayl (52)...... 117 F5
Poinson-lès-Grancey (52)...... 115 K6
Poinson-lès-Nogent (52)...... 116 D2
Pointel (61)...... 53 K5
Pointis-de-Rivière (31)...... 305 J1
Pointis-Inard (31)...... 306 A1
Pointre (39)...... 137 F6
Pointvillers (25)...... 156 A2
Poinville (28)...... 86 A4
le Poiré-sur-Velluire (85)...... 160 D5
le Poiré-sur-Vie (85)...... 141 J6
Poiroux (85)...... 159 G3
Poisat (38)...... 224 B3
Poiseul (52)...... 116 E3
Poiseul-la-Grange (21)...... 135 J2
Poiseul-la-Ville-et-Laperrière (21)...... 135 G2
Poiseul-lès-Saulx (21)...... 135 K2
Poiseux (58)...... 150 E2
Poisieux (18)...... 148 D3
le Poislay (41)...... 108 C2
Poisson (71)...... 170 C6
Poissons (52)...... 92 B3
Poissy (78)...... 58 B2
Poisvilliers (28)...... 85 G2
Poisy (74)...... 190 E5
la Poitevinière (49)...... 124 D6
Poitiers (86)...... 163 F3
Poivres (10)...... 62 C5
Poix (51)...... 63 F2
Poix-de-Picardie (80)...... 17 H3
Poix-du-Nord (59)...... 12 E4
Poix-Terron (08)...... 22 C5
le Poizat (01)...... 190 B2
Polaincourt-et-Clairefontaine (70)...... 118 A3
Polastron (31)...... 287 G4
Polastron (32)...... 287 F1
Poleymieux-au-Mont-d'Or (69)...... 188 C6
Poliénas (38)...... 223 H4
Polignac (17)...... 212 A2
Polignac (43)...... 220 C5
Poligné (35)...... 103 F1
Poligny (05)...... 242 E3
Poligny (10)...... 90 D6
Poligny (39)...... 155 J5
Poligny (77)...... 87 J6
Polincove (62)...... 2 E4
Polisot (10)...... 114 D2
Polisy (10)...... 114 D2
Pollestres (66)...... 315 G3
Polliat (01)...... 189 F1
Pollieu (01)...... 207 K1
Pollionnay (69)...... 205 J2
Polminhac (15)...... 235 J1
Polveroso (2B)...... 319 H4
Pomacle (51)...... 41 G3
la Pomarède (11)...... 289 G3
Pomarède (46)...... 232 E6
Pomarez (40)...... 264 D5
Pomas (11)...... 309 F1
Pomayrols (12)...... 253 G1
Pomerol (33)...... 230 B1
Pomérols (34)...... 292 D3
Pomeys (69)...... 205 G3
Pommard (21)...... 153 K3
Pommera (62)...... 10 B4
la Pommeraie-sur-Sèvre (85)...... 143 F5
la Pommeraye (14)...... 53 J2
la Pommeraye (49)...... 124 D4
Pommeret (22)...... 77 H1
Pommereuil (59)...... 12 D5
Pommereux (76)...... 16 E5
Pommeréval (76)...... 16 B4
Pommerieux (53)...... 104 D4
Pommérieux (57)...... 66 A1
Pommerit-Jaudy (22)...... 48 B3
Pommerit-le-Vicomte (22)...... 48 D4
Pommerol (26)...... 258 A1
Pommeuse (77)...... 60 A4
Pommevic (82)...... 248 E6
Pommier (62)...... 10 D4
Pommier-de-Beaurepaire (38)...... 206 D6
Pommiers (02)...... 39 H2
Pommiers (30)...... 273 J2
Pommiers (36)...... 165 H4
Pommiers (42)...... 204 D1
Pommiers (69)...... 188 B5
Pommiers-la-Placette (38)...... 223 K1
Pommiers-Moulons (17)...... 211 K1
Pomoy (70)...... 118 D6
Pompéjac (33)...... 246 C2
Pompertuzat (31)...... 288 C2
Pompey (54)...... 66 A4
Pompiac (32)...... 287 H2
le Pompidou (48)...... 254 C4
Pompierre (88)...... 93 G5
Pompierre-sur-Doubs (25)...... 138 E3
Pompignac (33)...... 229 J2
Pompignan (30)...... 274 B3
Pompignan (82)...... 269 F4
Pompogne (47)...... 247 F4

Pomponne (77)...... 59 H3
Pomport (24)...... 231 H5
Pomps (64)...... 284 B2
Pomy (11)...... 308 D2
Poncé-sur-le-Loir (72)...... 107 J6
Poncey-lès-Athée (21)...... 136 D6
Poncey-sur-l'Ignon (21)...... 135 H3
le Ponchel (62)...... 9 J3
Ponches-Estruval (80)...... 9 G2
Ponchon (60)...... 37 J3
Poncin (01)...... 189 J3
Poncins (42)...... 204 E2
Pondaurat (33)...... 230 C6
le Pondy (18)...... 149 J6
Ponet-et-Saint-Auban (26)...... 241 G2
Ponlat-Taillebourg (31)...... 305 H1
Pons (17)...... 195 H4
Ponsampère (32)...... 286 A2
Ponsan-Soubiran (32)...... 286 A3
Ponsas (26)...... 222 B4
Ponson-Debat-Pouts (64)...... 285 G4
Ponson-Dessus (64)...... 285 G4
Ponsonnas (38)...... 242 B1
Pont (21)...... 154 E1
Pont-à-Marcq (59)...... 6 E5
Pont-à-Mousson (54)...... 65 K2
Pont-à-Vendin (62)...... 6 C6
Pont-Arcy (02)...... 40 B2
Pont-Audemer (27)...... 34 C3
Pont-Authou (27)...... 34 E4
Pont-Aven (29)...... 99 G3
Pont-Bellanger (14)...... 31 J5
le Pont-Chrétien-Chabenet (36)...... 165 G3
Pont-Croix (29)...... 73 D3
Pont-d'Ain (01)...... 189 H4
Pont-de-Barret (26)...... 240 D5
le Pont-de-Beauvoisin (38)...... 207 J4
le Pont-de-Beauvoisin (73)...... 207 J4
Pont-de-Buis-lès-Quimerch (29)...... 74 D2
Pont-de-Chéruy (38)...... 206 E2
le Pont-de-Claix (38)...... 224 A4
Pont-de-Labeaume (07)...... 239 G4
Pont-de-Larn (81)...... 290 B2
le Pont-de-l'Isère (26)...... 222 C6
Pont-de-Metz (80)...... 18 A2
le Pont-de-Montvert (48)...... 254 D2
le Pont-de-Planches (70)...... 137 J2
Pont-de-Poitte (39)...... 173 H3
Pont-de-Roide (25)...... 139 H4
Pont-de-Ruan (37)...... 127 H6
Pont-de-Salars (12)...... 252 D4
Pont-de-Vaux (01)...... 172 A5
Pont-de-Veyle (01)...... 188 D1
Pont-d'Héry (39)...... 156 A5
Pont-d'Ouilly (14)...... 53 J2
Pont-du-Bois (70)...... 118 A2
Pont-du-Casse (47)...... 248 C4
Pont-du-Château (63)...... 202 E2
Pont-du-Navoy (39)...... 173 J1
Pont-en-Royans (38)...... 223 G5
Pont-et-Massène (21)...... 134 D3
Pont-Évêque (38)...... 206 B5
Pont-Farcy (14)...... 31 H5
Pont-Hébert (50)...... 31 H3
Pont-la-Ville (52)...... 115 J1
Pont-l'Abbé (29)...... 98 B3
Pont-l'Abbé-d'Arnoult (17)...... 194 E1
Pont-lès-Bonfays (88)...... 94 A6
Pont-les-Moulins (25)...... 138 D5
Pont-l'Évêque (14)...... 33 K3
Pont-l'Évêque (60)...... 19 H6
Pont-Melvez (22)...... 48 B6
Pont-Noyelles (80)...... 18 C1
Pont-Péan (35)...... 79 F5
Pont-Remy (80)...... 9 G4
Pont-Saint-Esprit (30)...... 256 C4
Pont-Saint-Mard (02)...... 39 J1
Pont-Saint-Martin (44)...... 123 G5
Pont-Saint-Pierre (27)...... 35 K3
Pont-Saint-Vincent (54)...... 65 K6
Pont-Sainte-Marie (10)...... 90 B4
Pont-Sainte-Maxence (60)...... 38 C4
Pont-Salomon (43)...... 221 F2
Pont-Scorff (56)...... 99 K4
Pont-sur-l'Ognon (70)...... 138 D2
Pont-sur-Madon (88)...... 94 A3
Pont-sur-Meuse (55)...... 64 E4
Pont-sur-Sambre (59)...... 13 G3
Pont-sur-Seine (10)...... 89 G2
Pont-sur-Vanne (89)...... 88 E4
Pont-sur-Yonne (89)...... 88 C5
Pont-Trambouze (69)...... 187 H4
Pontacq (64)...... 285 F5
Pontailler-sur-Saône (21)...... 136 E5
Pontaix (26)...... 241 G3
Pontamafrey-Montpascal (73)...... 225 G1
Pontarion (23)...... 182 D5
Pontarlier (25)...... 157 F4
Pontarmé (60)...... 38 B5
Pontaubault (50)...... 51 K3
Pontaubert (89)...... 133 J3
Pontault-Combault (77)...... 59 G4
Pontaumur (63)...... 201 K1
Pontavert (02)...... 40 D2
Pontcarré (77)...... 59 H4
Pontcey (70)...... 137 K1
Pontchardon (61)...... 55 F7
Pontcharra (38)...... 208 C5
Pontcharra-sur-Turdine (69)...... 187 K6
Pontcharraud (23)...... 201 F1
Pontchâteau (44)...... 122 B1

Pontcirq (46)...... 233 F6
Pontécoulant (14)...... 53 G3
Ponteilla (66)...... 315 G3
Ponteils-et-Brésis (30)...... 255 F2
Pontenx-les-Forges (40)...... 244 D3
le Pontet (73)...... 208 D2
le Pontet (84)...... 276 C1
les Pontets (25)...... 174 C1
Pontevès (83)...... 278 E6
Ponteyraud (24)...... 213 F3
Pontfaverger-Moronvilliers (51)...... 41 H3
Pontgibaud (63)...... 202 B1
Pontgouin (28)...... 84 D2
Ponthévrard (78)...... 86 A1
Ponthion (51)...... 63 G4
Ponthoile (80)...... 9 F3
le Ponthou (29)...... 47 J5
Ponthoux (39)...... 173 J5
Pontiacq-Viellepinte (64)...... 285 G3
Pontigné (49)...... 126 B2
Pontigny (89)...... 113 H4
Pontis (04)...... 243 H6
Pontivy (56)...... 76 E5
Pontlevoy (41)...... 128 E5
Pontmain (53)...... 80 C2
Pontoise (95)...... 58 C1
Pontoise-lès-Noyon (60)...... 19 H6
Pontonx-sur-l'Adour (40)...... 264 C3
Pontorson (50)...... 51 J4
Pontours (24)...... 232 A2
Pontoux (71)...... 154 D4
Pontoy (57)...... 45 G6
Pontpierre (57)...... 45 K6
Pontpoint (60)...... 38 C4
Pontrieux (22)...... 48 C3
Pontru (02)...... 19 K2
Pontruet (02)...... 19 K2
Ponts (50)...... 51 K3
les Ponts-de-Cé (49)...... 125 G4
Ponts-et-Marais (76)...... 8 C6
Pontvallain (72)...... 106 D6
Popian (34)...... 273 J6
Popolasca (2B)...... 319 F4
Porcaro (56)...... 78 B6
Porcelette (57)...... 45 K4
Porchères (33)...... 212 D5
la Porcherie (87)...... 199 H4
Porcheux (60)...... 37 F3
Porcheville (78)...... 57 K2
Porcieu-Amblagnieu (38)...... 207 G1
Pordic (22)...... 49 F5
le Porge (33)...... 228 C2
Pornic (44)...... 122 B5
Pornichet (44)...... 121 K5
Porquéricourt (60)...... 19 G6
Porri (2B)...... 319 J4
Porspoder (29)...... 72 B3
Port (01)...... 189 K2
le Port (09)...... 307 F4
Port-Brillet (53)...... 104 E3
Port-de-Bouc (13)...... 295 J5
Port-de-Lanne (40)...... 262 E6
Port-de-Piles (86)...... 145 K4
Port-d'Envaux (17)...... 195 F1
Port-des-Barques (17)...... 176 E5
Port-en-Bessin-Huppain (14)...... 32 A3
Port-la-Nouvelle (11)...... 310 D2
Port-Launay (29)...... 74 D3
Port-le-Grand (80)...... 9 F4
Port-Lesney (39)...... 155 K3
Port-Louis (56)...... 99 K5
le Port-Marly (78)...... 58 C3
Port-Mort (27)...... 36 A5
Port-Saint-Louis-du-Rhône (13)...... 295 G5
Port-Saint-Père (44)...... 122 E4
Port-Sainte-Foy-et-Ponchapt (24)...... 231 F2
Port-Sainte-Marie (47)...... 247 K4
Port-sur-Saône (70)...... 117 K6
Port-sur-Seille (54)...... 66 A2
Port-Vendres (66)...... 315 J4
Port-Villez (78)...... 57 G1
la Porta (2B)...... 319 H4
Porta (66)...... 313 F4
Portbail (50)...... 28 C6
Porte-Joie (27)...... 35 K4
Porté-Puymorens (66)...... 313 F4
le Portel (62)...... 2 A5
Portel-des-Corbières (11)...... 310 C2
Portes (30)...... 255 G3
les Portes-en-Ré (17)...... 176 A1
Portes-en-Valdaine (26)...... 240 C6
Portes-lès-Valence (26)...... 240 C1
Portet (64)...... 265 K6
Portet-d'Aspet (31)...... 306 A4
Portet-de-Luchon (31)...... 305 G5
Portet-sur-Garonne (31)...... 288 B2
Portets (33)...... 229 J4
Portieux (88)...... 94 C3
Portiragnes (34)...... 292 B4
Porto-Vecchio (2A)...... 323 H3
Ports (37)...... 145 J3
Posanges (21)...... 135 F4
Poses (27)...... 35 K3
la Possonnière (49)...... 125 F4
la Postolle (89)...... 88 E5
Postroff (57)...... 67 J2
Potangis (51)...... 89 G1
Potelières (30)...... 255 J4
Potelle (59)...... 12 E3
la Poterie-au-Perche (61)...... 55 K6

la Poterie-Cap-d'Antifer (76)...... 14 B4
la Poterie-Mathieu (27)...... 34 C4
Pothières (21)...... 115 F3
Potigny (14)...... 54 A2
Potte (80)...... 19 G3
Pouan-les-Vallées (10)...... 90 A1
Pouançay (86)...... 144 C2
Pouancé (49)...... 104 A5
Pouant (86)...... 145 F3
Poubeau (31)...... 305 G5
Poucharramet (31)...... 287 J3
Poudenas (47)...... 247 H6
Poudenx (40)...... 265 F6
Poudis (81)...... 289 H2
Poueyferré (65)...... 285 F6
la Pouëze (49)...... 124 C2
Pouffonds (79)...... 178 D2
la Pouge (23)...... 182 E5
le Pouget (34)...... 273 J6
Pougnadoresse (30)...... 256 B6
Pougne-Hérisson (79)...... 161 H2
Pougny (01)...... 190 D2
Pougny (58)...... 132 A5
Pougues-les-Eaux (58)...... 150 D3
Pougy (10)...... 90 D3
Pouillac (17)...... 212 A1
Pouillat (01)...... 173 F6
Pouillé (41)...... 128 E5
Pouillé (85)...... 160 C4
Pouillé (86)...... 163 H4
Pouillé-les-Côteaux (44)...... 124 C3
Pouillenay (21)...... 134 E3
Pouilley-Français (25)...... 137 J6
Pouilley-les-Vignes (25)...... 137 K6
Pouillon (40)...... 264 B6
Pouillon (51)...... 40 E3
Pouilloux (71)...... 170 E3
Pouilly (57)...... 45 F6
Pouilly (60)...... 37 G4
Pouilly-en-Auxois (21)...... 135 F6
Pouilly-le-Monial (69)...... 188 A5
Pouilly-lès-Feurs (42)...... 204 E1
Pouilly-les-Nonains (42)...... 186 E6
Pouilly-sous-Charlieu (42)...... 187 F3
Pouilly-sur-Loire (58)...... 132 A6
Pouilly-sur-Meuse (55)...... 23 G6
Pouilly-sur-Saône (21)...... 154 D3
Pouilly-sur-Serre (02)...... 20 C4
Pouilly-sur-Vingeanne (21)...... 136 E2
le Poujol-sur-Orb (34)...... 291 J1
Poujols (34)...... 273 G4
Poulaines (36)...... 147 K2
Poulainville (80)...... 18 B1
Poulan-Pouzols (81)...... 270 D3
Poulangy (52)...... 116 C2
Pouldergat (29)...... 73 E3
Pouldouran (22)...... 48 C2
Pouldreuzic (29)...... 73 E4
Poule-les-Écharmeaux (69)...... 187 J3
Pouliacq (64)...... 284 C1
les Poulières (88)...... 95 G5
Pouligney-Lusans (25)...... 138 C5
Pouligny-Notre-Dame (36)...... 166 B5
Pouligny-Saint-Martin (36)...... 166 B4
Pouligny-Saint-Pierre (36)...... 164 C2
le Pouliguen (44)...... 121 J5
Poullan-sur-Mer (29)...... 73 D2
Poullaouen (29)...... 75 H2
Poullignac (16)...... 196 C6
Poulx (30)...... 275 H2
Poumarous (65)...... 285 J6
Poupas (82)...... 268 A2
Poupry (28)...... 109 K1
Pouques-Lormes (58)...... 133 J5
Pourcharesses (48)...... 255 F1
Pourchères (07)...... 239 J3
Pourcieux (83)...... 297 G2
Pourcy (51)...... 40 E5
Pourlans (71)...... 154 E4
Pournoy-la-Chétive (57)...... 45 F6
Pournoy-la-Grasse (57)...... 45 F6
Pourrain (89)...... 112 E6
Pourrières (83)...... 297 G1
Poursac (16)...... 179 H5
Poursay-Garnaud (17)...... 178 A5
Poursiugues-Boucoue (64)...... 284 D1
Pouru-aux-Bois (08)...... 23 G4
Pouru-Saint-Remy (08)...... 23 G4
Poussan (34)...... 292 E2
Poussanges (23)...... 200 E1
Poussay (88)...... 94 A4
Pousseaux (58)...... 133 J4
Poussignac (47)...... 247 F2
Poussy-la-Campagne (14)...... 33 F4
Pousthomy (12)...... 271 J3
le Pout (33)...... 229 K2
Pouvrai (61)...... 83 H5
Pouxeux (88)...... 94 E6
Pouy (65)...... 286 C5
Pouy-de-Touges (31)...... 287 H3
Pouy-Loubrin (32)...... 286 D2
Pouy-Roquelaure (32)...... 267 H1
Pouy-sur-Vannes (10)...... 89 G4
Pouyastruc (65)...... 285 J5
Pouydesseaux (40)...... 265 J1
Pouydraguin (32)...... 266 C5
Pouylebon (32)...... 285 K1
Pouzac (65)...... 304 D1
Pouzauges (85)...... 143 F6
Pouzay (37)...... 145 J3
Pouze (31)...... 288 C3
Pouzilhac (30)...... 256 C6

le Pouzin (07) 240 B3
Pouzol (63) 184 E4
Pouzolles (34) 292 A2
Pouzols (34) 273 J6
Pouzols-Minervois (11) 291 G5
Pouzy-Mésangy (03) 168 B2
Poyanne (40) 264 D4
Poyans (70) 136 E3
Poyartin (40) 264 D5
Poyols (26) 241 H5
Pozières (80) 10 E6
le Pradal (34) 272 E6
les Pradeaux (63) 203 F5
Pradelle (26) 241 H6
Pradelles (43) 238 C3
Pradelles (59) 3 K5
Pradelles-Cabardès (11) 290 C6
Pradelles-en-Val (11) 290 C6
Pradère-les-Bourguets (31) 268 C4
Prades (07) 239 G5
Prades (09) 308 B5
Prades (43) 219 K6
Prades (66) 314 C3
Prades (81) 270 C6
Prades-d'Aubrac (12) 236 C6
Prades-le-Lez (34) 274 B5
Prades-Salars (12) 252 D4
Prades-sur-Vernazobre (34) 291 H3
le Pradet (83) 297 K6
Pradettes (09) 308 A3
Pradières (09) 307 J3
Pradiers (15) 218 C3
Pradinas (12) 251 J3
Pradines (19) 200 B5
Pradines (42) 187 G5
Pradines (46) 249 K1
Pradons (07) 255 K1
Prads-Haute-Bléone (04) 260 B3
Prahecq (79) 178 B1
Prailles (79) 161 K6
Pralognan-la-Vanoise (73) 193 A6
Prâlon (21) 135 H5
Pralong (42) 204 D3
Pranles (07) 239 K3
Pranzac (16) 197 G3
Praslay (52) 116 B6
Praslin (10) 114 C2
Prasville (28) 85 J5
Prat (22) 48 B3
Prat-Bonrepaux (09) 306 C2
Prato-di-Giovellina (2B) 319 F4
Prats-de-Carlux (24) 233 G1
Prats-de-Mollo-la-Preste (66) 314 C6
Prats-de-Sournia (66) 309 H6
Prats-du-Périgord (24) 232 D4
Pratviel (81) 270 B6
Pratz (39) 173 J5
Prauthoy (52) 116 C6
Pray (41) 128 C1
Praye (54) 94 A2
Prayols (09) 307 J3
Prayssac (46) 249 H1
Prayssas (47) 248 C2
Praz-sur-Arly (74) 191 K6
le Pré-d'Auge (14) 33 J5
Pré-en-Pail (53) 82 A2
Pré-Saint-Évroult (28) 85 G6
le Pré-Saint-Gervais (93) 59 F3
Pré-Saint-Martin (28) 85 G6
Préaux (07) 222 A4
les Préaux (27) 34 C3
Préaux (36) 147 F3
Préaux (53) 105 H3
Préaux (76) 35 J1
Préaux-Bocage (14) 32 C6
Préaux-du-Perche (61) 83 J4
Préaux-Saint-Sébastien (14) 55 F2
Prébois (38) 242 A2
Précey (50) 51 K4
Préchac (32) 267 G4
Préchac (33) 246 B2
Préchac (65) 304 B2
Préchac-sur-Adour (32) 266 B6
Préchacq-Josbaig (64) 283 K4
Préchacq-les-Bains (40) 264 C4
Préchacq-Navarrenx (64) 283 K4
Précieux (42) 204 D4
Précigné (72) 105 J5
Précilhon (64) 284 A5
Précorbin (50) 31 J4
Précy (18) 150 B3
Précy-le-Sec (89) 133 J2
Précy-Notre-Dame (10) 90 E3
Précy-Saint-Martin (10) 90 E3
Précy-sous-Thil (21) 134 D4
Précy-sur-Marne (77) 59 J2
Précy-sur-Oise (60) 37 K5
Précy-sur-Vrin (89) 112 D3
Prédefin (62) 5 G6
Préfailles (44) 122 A4
Préfontaines (45) 111 H1
Préglibert (89) 133 H1
Préguillac (17) 195 G3
Préhy (89) 113 H6
Preignac (33) 229 K5
Preignan (32) 267 G5
Preigney (70) 117 H5
Preixan (11) 290 A6
Prémanon (39) 174 A4
Premeaux-Prissey (21) 154 A2
Prémery (58) 151 F2
Prémesques (59) 6 C4

Prémeyzel (01) 207 J2
Prémian (34) 291 G2
Premières (21) 136 C6
Prémierfait (10) 90 A2
Prémilhat (03) 183 K1
Prémillieu (01) 189 K6
Prémont (02) 12 C6
Prémontré (02) 20 B6
Prendeignes (46) 234 E4
Préneron (32) 266 E4
la Prénessaye (22) 77 H4
Prenois (21) 135 J4
Prénouvellon (41) 109 G3
Prénovel (39) 173 J3
Prény (54) 65 J1
Préporché (58) 152 A5
Prépotin (61) 55 H6
les Prés (26) 241 K6
Présailles (43) 238 D1
Préseau (59) 12 D2
Présentevillers (25) 139 G2
Préserville (31) 288 D2
Présilly (39) 173 G3
Présilly (74) 190 E3
Presle (73) 208 D5
Presles (14) 53 F3
Presles (38) 223 H4
Presles (95) 37 J6
Presles-en-Brie (77) 59 J5
Presles-et-Boves (02) 40 A2
Presles-et-Thierny (02) 40 B1
Presly (18) 130 E5
Presnoy (45) 111 G3
Pressac (86) 180 A3
Pressagny-l'Orgueilleux (27) 36 B6
Pressiat (01) 172 E6
Pressignac (16) 198 A1
Pressignac-Vicq (24) 232 A1
Pressigny (52) 117 G5
Pressigny (79) 162 B3
Pressigny-les-Pins (45) 111 J4
Pressins (38) 207 J4
Pressy (62) 5 H6
Pressy-sous-Dondin (71) 171 G4
la Prétière (25) 139 F3
Pretin (39) 156 A4
Prétot-Sainte-Suzanne (50) 28 E6
Prétot-Vicquemare (76) 15 H4
Prêtreville (14) 33 K6
Préty (71) 172 A3
Pretz-en-Argonne (55) 64 A2
Preuilly (18) 148 E3
Preuilly-la-Ville (36) 164 B2
Preuilly-sur-Claise (37) 146 C5
Preures (62) 4 D5
Preuschdorf (67) 25 A2
Preuseville (76) 16 D2
Preutin-Higny (54) 26 D4
Preux-au-Bois (59) 12 E4
Preux-au-Sart (59) 12 E3
Préval (72) 83 J5
Prévelles (72) 83 G6
Prévenchères (48) 238 C6
Préveranges (18) 166 D5
Prévessin-Moëns (01) 190 E1
Prévillers (60) 17 J5
Prévinquières (12) 251 H2
Prévocourt (57) 66 C2
Prey (27) 56 D2
Prey (88) 95 F5
Preyssac-d'Excideuil (24) 214 E2
Prez (08) 21 K3
Prez-sous-Lafauche (52) 92 E4
Priaires (79) 177 J3
Priay (01) 189 H4
Priez (02) 39 H6
Prignac (17) 195 J1
Prignac-en-Médoc (33) 210 E1
Prignac-et-Marcamps (33) 211 J3
Prigonrieux (24) 231 H2
Primarette (38) 206 C6
Primelin (29) 73 B3
Primelles (18) 148 E5
Prin-Deyrançon (79) 177 J2
Prinçay (86) 145 F4
Princé (35) 80 C5
Pringy (51) 62 E4
Pringy (74) 191 F5
Pringy (77) 87 G2
Prinquiau (44) 122 C2
Prinsuéjols (48) 237 F4
Printzheim (67) 69 H6
Prisces (02) 21 F3
Prisches (59) 13 F5
Prissac (36) 164 E4
Prissé (71) 171 J6
Prissé-la-Charrière (79) 178 A3
Privas (07) 239 K3
Privezac (12) 251 J2
Prix-lès-Mézières (08) 22 D3
Priziac (56) 75 K5
Prizy (71) 170 D6
la Proiselière-et-Langle (70) 118 E4
Proissans (24) 233 H1
Proisy (02) 20 E2
Proix (02) 20 C2
Projan (32) 265 K6
Promilhanes (46) 250 D2
Prompsat (63) 185 F5
Prondines (63) 201 K2
Pronleroy (60) 38 B1

Pronville (62) 11 G4
Propiac (26) 257 J3
Propières (69) 187 J2
Propriano (2A) 322 D2
Prosnes (51) 41 H5
Prouilly (51) 40 D3
Proupiary (31) 287 F6
Proussy (14) 53 H3
Prouvais (02) 40 E1
Prouville (80) 9 J4
Prouvy (59) 12 C2
Prouzel (80) 18 A3
Provenchère (25) 139 F5
Provenchère (70) 118 A5
Provenchères-lès-Darney (88) 93 J6
Provenchères-sur-Fave (88) 95 K3
Provency (89) 133 K3
Proverville (10) 91 G5
Proveysieux (38) 224 A2
Proville (59) 11 J4
Provin (59) 6 C5
Provins (77) 88 D1
Proviseux-et-Plesnoy (02) 40 E1
Proyart (80) 18 E2
Prudemanche (28) 56 D6
Prudhomat (46) 234 B1
Prugnanes (66) 309 G5
Prugny (10) 89 K5
Pruillé (49) 125 F2
Pruillé-le-Chétif (72) 106 D3
Pruillé-l'Éguillé (72) 107 G5
Pruines (12) 235 J6
Prunay (51) 41 G5
Prunay-Belleville (10) 89 H4
Prunay-Cassereau (41) 128 A1
Prunay-en-Yvelines (78) 85 K2
Prunay-le-Gillon (28) 85 H4
Prunay-le-Temple (78) 57 J3
Prunay-sur-Essonne (91) 86 E4
Prunelli-di-Casacconi (2B) 319 H3
Prunelli-di-Fiumorbo (2B) 321 H4
Prunet (07) 239 G5
Prunet (15) 235 H4
Prunet (31) 288 E1
Prunet-et-Belpuig (66) 314 E4
Prunières (05) 243 K1
Prunières (38) 242 B1
Prunières (48) 237 G2
Pruniers (36) 166 C1
Pruniers-en-Sologne (41) 129 H5
Pruno (2B) 319 J4
Prunoy (89) 112 C4
Prusly-sur-Ource (21) 115 G4
Prusy (10) 114 A3
Pruzilly (71) 188 B1
Puberg (67) 69 F5
Publier (74) 175 G5
Publy (39) 173 G2
Puceul (44) 103 G6
le Puch (09) 308 D6
Puch-d'Agenais (47) 247 H3
Puchay (27) 36 C3
Puchevillers (80) 10 B6
le Puech (34) 273 G5
Puéchabon (34) 273 J4
Puéchoursi (81) 289 G2
Puechredon (30) 274 D2
Puellemontier (52) 91 G2
Puessans (25) 138 C3
Puget (84) 277 G4
Puget-Rostang (06) 261 G6
Puget-sur-Argens (83) 299 G1
Puget-Théniers (06) 280 C1
Puget-Ville (83) 298 A4
Pugey (25) 156 B1
Pugieu (01) 207 J1
Puginier (11) 289 G3
Pugnac (33) 211 J4
Pugny (79) 161 G5
Pugny-Chatenod (73) 208 B2
Puichéric (11) 290 E5
le Puid (88) 95 J2
Puihardy (79) 161 J4
Puilacher (34) 292 D4
Puilaurens (11) 309 F5
Puilboreau (17) 176 D2
Puilly-et-Charbeaux (08) 23 J5
Puimichel (04) 278 D1
Puimisson (34) 292 A3
Puimoisson (04) 278 E2
la Puisaye (28) 84 B1
Puiseaux (45) 87 F6
Puiselet-le-Marais (91) 86 D3
Puisenval (76) 16 D2
le Puiset (28) 85 K6
le Puiset-Doré (49) 124 B6
Puiseux (08) 22 B5
Puiseux (28) 57 F6
Puiseux-en-Bray (60) 36 E2
Puiseux-en-France (95) 59 F1
Puiseux-en-Retz (02) 39 G4
Puiseux-le-Hauberger (60) 37 J5
Puiseux-Pontoise (95) 58 B1
Puisieulx (51) 41 F5
Puisieux (62) 11 F4
Puisieux (77) 59 K1
Puisieux-et-Clanlieu (02) 20 D2
Puissalicon (34) 292 A4
Puisseguin (33) 230 C1
Puisserguier (34) 291 J3
Puits (21) 114 E6
Puits-et-Nuisement (10) 90 E5

Puits-la-Vallée (60) 17 K6
Puivert (11) 308 D3
Pujaudran (32) 287 J1
Pujaut (30) 276 B1
Pujo (65) 285 H3
Pujo-le-Plan (40) 265 J3
les Pujols (09) 307 K1
Pujols (33) 230 C2
Pujols (47) 248 C2
Pujols-sur-Ciron (33) 229 K5
le Puley (71) 171 G2
Puligny-Montrachet (21) 153 K4
Pullay (27) 56 A5
Pulligny (54) 94 A1
Pulney (54) 93 K3
Pulnoy (54) 66 B5
Pulvérières (63) 184 D6
Pulversheim (68) 97 B1
Punchy (80) 19 F3
Punerot (88) 93 H2
Puntous (65) 286 B4
Pupillin (39) 155 K5
Pure (08) 23 H4
Purgerot (70) 117 K5
Pusey (70) 118 A6
Pusignan (69) 206 D2
Pussay (91) 86 B4
Pussigny (37) 145 J3
Pusy-et-Épenoux (70) 118 B6
Putanges-Pont-Écrepin (61) 54 A4
Puteaux (92) 58 D2
Putot-en-Auge (14) 33 G4
Putot-en-Bessin (14) 32 C4
Puttelange-aux-Lacs (57) 68 C3
Puttelange-lès-Thionville (57) 27 H2
Puttigny (57) 66 D3
Puxe (54) 44 B5
Puxieux (54) 44 C6
le Puy (25) 138 C2
le Puy (33) 230 D4
Puy-d'Arnac (19) 216 B6
Puy-de-Serre (85) 161 F3
Puy-du-Lac (17) 177 H5
le Puy-en-Velay (43) 220 C5
Puy-Guillaume (63) 185 K5
Puy-Malsignat (23) 183 G4
le Puy-Notre-Dame (49) 144 B2
Puy-Saint-André (05) 243 K1
Puy-Saint-Eusèbe (05) 243 H5
Puy-Saint-Gulmier (63) 201 J2
Puy-Saint-Martin (26) 240 D4
Puy-Saint-Pierre (05) 225 K6
Puy-Saint-Vincent (05) 243 J1
le Puy-Sainte-Réparade (13) 277 H5
Puy-Sanières (05) 243 J5
Puybarban (33) 230 C5
Puybegon (81) 270 B4
Puybrun (46) 234 B1
Puycalvel (81) 270 D5
Puycasquier (32) 267 K4
Puycelci (81) 269 K1
Puycornet (82) 249 J5
Puydaniel (31) 288 B4
Puydarrieux (65) 286 A4
la Puye (86) 163 K2
Puygaillard-de-Lomagne (82) 268 D2
Puygaillard-de-Quercy (82) 269 J1
Puygiron (26) 240 C6
Puygouzon (81) 270 E3
Puygros (73) 208 C4
Puyjourdes (46) 250 E2
Puylagarde (82) 250 E3
Puylaroque (82) 250 B4
Puylaurens (81) 289 H1
Puylausic (32) 287 G2
Puyloubier (13) 297 F1
Puymangou (24) 212 D3
Puymaurin (31) 286 E3
Puyméras (84) 257 H3
Puymiclan (47) 231 G6
Puymirol (47) 248 D5
Puymoyen (16) 196 E4
Puynormand (33) 212 D6
Puyol-Cazalet (40) 265 H6
Puyôo (64) 283 H1
Puyravault (17) 177 G5
Puyravault (85) 160 B5
Puyréaux (16) 179 G6
Puyrenier (24) 197 H5
Puyrolland (17) 177 J4
Puységur (32) 267 J4
Puysségur (31) 268 C4
Puysserampion (47) 231 G5
Puyvalador (66) 313 J3
Puyvert (84) 277 G4
Puzeaux (80) 19 F3
Puzieux (57) 66 C2
Puzieux (88) 94 A3
Py (66) 314 B4
la Pyle (27) 35 F5
Pys (80) 10 E5

Q

Quaëdypre (59) 3 J3
Quaix-en-Chartreuse (38) 224 A2
Quantilly (18) 149 H1
Quarante (34) 291 H4
Quarouble (59) 12 E1

Quarré-les-Tombes (89) 134 A5
la Quarte (70) 117 G5
le Quartier (63) 184 C3
Quasquara (2A) 320 E5
Quatre-Champs (08) 42 C1
les Quatre-Routes-du-Lot (46) 215 K6
Quatremare (27) 35 H5
Quatzenheim (67) 70 D3
Québriac (35) 79 F1
Quédillac (35) 78 C2
Queige (73) 209 G2
Quelaines-Saint-Gault (53) 104 E3
Quelmes (62) 3 F5
Quelneuc (56) 102 C2
Quéménéven (29) 74 D3
Quemigny-Poisot (21) 135 H5
Quemigny-sur-Seine (21) 135 G1
Quemper-Guézennec (22) 48 D3
Quemperven (22) 48 B3
Quend (80) 8 E2
Quenne (89) 113 G5
Quenoche (70) 138 A3
Quenza (2A) 323 F1
Quercamps (62) 2 E5
Quercitello (2B) 319 H4
Quérénaing (59) 12 D3
Quérigut (09) 308 D4
Quernes (62) 5 H4
Querqueville (50) 28 C2
Querré (49) 105 G4
Querrien (29) 99 J2
Querrieu (80) 18 C1
Quers (70) 118 D5
Quesmy (60) 19 H5
le Quesne (80) 17 G4
le Quesnel (80) 18 D3
le Quesnel-Aubry (60) 37 K1
le Quesnoy (59) 12 E4
le Quesnoy-en-Artois (62) 9 J2
Quesnoy-le-Montant (80) 8 E3
Quesnoy-sur-Airaines (80) 17 H1
Quesnoy-sur-Deûle (59) 6 D3
Quesques (62) 2 D5
Quessigny (27) 56 E2
Quessoy (22) 77 H1
Questembert (56) 101 J3
Questrecques (62) 2 B6
Quet-en-Beaumont (38) 242 C2
Quetigny (21) 136 B5
Quettehou (50) 29 F3
Quettetot (50) 28 C4
Quetteville (14) 34 A3
Quettreville-sur-Sienne (50) 30 D5
Queudes (51) 61 H6
la Queue-en-Brie (94) 59 F4
la Queue-les-Yvelines (78) 57 J4
Queuille (83) 184 C5
Quevauvillers (80) 17 J3
Quéven (56) 99 K4
Quévert (22) 50 C5
Quevillon (76) 35 G2
Quévilloncourt (54) 93 K2
Quévreville-la-Poterie (76) 35 J3
Queyrac (33) 210 D1
Queyrières (43) 220 E5
Queyssac (24) 231 J1
Queyssac-les-Vignes (19) 216 B6
Quézac (15) 235 F3
Quézac (48) 254 B2
Quiberon (56) 120 C2
Quiberville (76) 15 J2
Quibou (50) 31 G4
Quié (09) 307 J4
Quiers (77) 88 A1
Quiers-sur-Bézonde (45) 111 F3
Quiéry-la-Motte (62) 11 G2
Quierzy (02) 19 J6
Quiestède (62) 3 G5
Quiévelon (59) 13 J3
Quiévrechain (59) 12 E1
Quiévrecourt (76) 16 E2
Quiévy (59) 12 C4
Quilen (62) 4 D5
Quillan (11) 308 E3
Quillebeuf-sur-Seine (27) 34 C1
le Quillio (22) 76 E3
Quilly (08) 42 A2
Quilly (44) 102 D6
Quily (56) 101 J2
Quimper (29) 74 D6
Quimperlé (29) 99 J3
Quincampoix (76) 35 J1
Quincampoix-Fleuzy (60) 17 G4
Quincerot (21) 134 D2
Quincerot (89) 114 B3
Quincey (21) 154 B2
Quincey (70) 138 B1
Quincié-en-Beaujolais (69) 188 A3
Quincieu (38) 223 H2
Quincieux (69) 188 C6
Quincy (18) 148 E2
Quincy-Basse (02) 39 J1
Quincy-Landzécourt (55) 43 G1
Quincy-le-Vicomte (21) 134 C2
Quincy-sous-le-Mont (02) 40 A3
Quincy-sous-Sénart (91) 59 G6
Quincy-Voisins (77) 59 K3
Quinéville (50) 29 F4
Quingey (25) 156 A2

Quinquempoix (60) 18 C6
Quins (12) 251 K4
Quinsac (24) 197 K6
Quinsac (33) 229 H3
Quinson (04) 278 E4
Quinssaines (03) 183 K1
Quint-Fonsegrives (31) 288 C1
Quintal (74) 191 F6
la Quinte (72) 106 C2
Quintenas (07) 222 A3
Quintenic (22) 49 K6
Quintigny (39) 173 F1
Quintillan (11) 309 K3
Quintin (22) 76 E1
le Quiou (22) 78 D1
Quirbajou (11) 308 E5
Quiry-le-Sec (80) 18 B5
Quissac (30) 274 D2
Quissac (46) 234 A5
Quistinic (56) 100 C2
Quittebeuf (27) 35 G6
Quivières (80) 19 H3
Quoeux-Haut-Maînil (62) 9 J2

R

Rabastens (81) 269 K4
Rabastens-de-Bigorre (65) 285 J3
Rabat-les-Trois-Seigneurs (09) 307 H4
la Rabatelière (85) 142 B5
Rablay-sur-Layon (49) 125 G5
Rabodanges (61) 53 K4
Rabou (05) 242 D5
Rabouillet (66) 309 G6
Racécourt (88) 94 B4
Rachecourt-sur-Marne (52) 92 A1
Rachecourt-Suzémont (52) 91 K2
Râches (59) 11 J1
Racines (10) 113 J2
la Racineuse (71) 154 D5
Racquinghem (62) 3 H6
Racrange (57) 67 F2
Raddon-et-Chapendu (70) 118 D4
Radenac (56) 101 G1
Radepont (27) 36 A3
Radinghem (62) 5 F5
Radinghem-en-Weppes (59) 6 C4
Radon (61) 82 D2
Radonvilliers (10) 90 E4
Raedersdorf (68) 97 C6
Raedersheim (68) 96 B6
Raffetot (76) 14 E5
Rageade (15) 219 G5
Rahart (41) 108 C4
Rahay (72) 108 A3
Rahling (57) 69 F4
Rahon (25) 139 F4
Rahon (39) 155 G3
Rai (61) 55 H5
Raids (50) 31 F2
Raillencourt-Sainte-Olle (59) 11 J4
Railleu (66) 313 K3
Raillicourt (08) 22 C5
Raillimont (02) 21 H4
Raimbeaucourt (59) 11 H1
Rainans (39) 155 G1
Raincheval (80) 10 B5
Raincourt (70) 117 J4
le Raincy (93) 59 G3
Rainfreville (76) 15 J3
Rainneville (80) 18 B1
Rainsars (59) 13 H5
Rainville (88) 93 H3
Rainvillers (60) 37 G2
les Rairies (49) 126 A1
Raismes (59) 12 C1
Raissac (09) 308 A3
Raissac-d'Aude (11) 291 G5
Raissac-sur-Lampy (11) 289 K5
Raival (55) 64 C3
Raix (16) 179 F5
Raizeux (78) 57 J6
Ramasse (01) 189 H2
Ramatuelle (83) 299 F4
Rambaud (05) 243 F5
Rambervillers (88) 95 F3
Rambluzin-et-Benoite-Vaux (55) 64 C1
Rambouillet (78) 57 K6
Rambucourt (55) 65 G3
Ramburelles (80) 17 F1
Rambures (80) 17 F1
Ramecourt (62) 10 A2
Ramecourt (88) 94 A4
Ramerupt (10) 90 C2
Ramicourt (02) 20 A1
Ramillies (59) 11 K4
Rammersmatt (68) 119 K4
Ramonchamp (88) 119 G3
Ramonville-Saint-Agne (31) 288 C1
Ramoulu (45) 86 E6
Ramous (64) 283 H1
Ramousies (59) 13 H5
Ramouzens (32) 266 D3
Rampan (50) 31 H3
Rampieux (24) 232 B4
Rampillon (77) 88 B1
Rampoux (46) 233 G5
Rancé (01) 188 D5
Rancenay (25) 156 B1
Rancennes (08) 24 C1
Rances (10) 91 F2
Ranchal (69) 187 J3
Ranchot (39) 155 J1
Ranchy (14) 32 A4
Rancogne (16) 197 G3
Rancon (87) 181 G3
Rançonnières (52) 117 F3
Rancourt (80) 11 G6
Rancourt (88) 94 A5
Rancourt-sur-Ornain (55) 63 J3
Rancy (71) 172 B3
Randan (63) 185 H5
Randens (73) 209 F4
Randevillers (25) 138 E5
Randonnai (61) 55 J6
Rânes (61) 54 A6
Rang (25) 139 F3
Rang-du-Fliers (62) 8 E1
Rangecourt (52) 116 E2
Rangen (67) 70 C2
Ranguevaux (57) 27 F5
Rannée (35) 104 A3
Ranrupt (67) 70 A6
Rans (39) 155 J1
Ransart (62) 10 E4
Ranspach (68) 119 J3
Ranspach-le-Bas (68) 97 D4
Ranspach-le-Haut (68) 97 D4
Rantechaux (25) 157 F1
Rantigny (60) 38 A3
Ranton (86) 144 D3
Rantzwiller (68) 97 C3
Ranville (14) 33 F4
Ranville-Breuillaud (16) 178 D6
Ranzevelle (70) 117 K3
Ranzières (55) 64 D1
Raon-aux-Bois (88) 118 E1
Raon-lès-Leau (54) 95 K1
Raon-l'Étape (88) 95 G2
Raon-sur-Plaine (88) 95 K1
Rapaggio (2B) 319 H5
Rapale (2B) 319 G2
Rapey (88) 94 B4
Rapilly (14) 53 K3
Rapsécourt (51) 63 H1
Raray (60) 38 D4
Rarécourt (55) 43 F6
Rasiguères (66) 309 J5
Raslay (86) 144 D2
Rasteau (84) 257 G4
Ratenelle (71) 172 B4
Ratières (26) 222 D3
Ratte (71) 172 D2
Ratzwiller (67) 69 F4
Raucoules (43) 221 G3
Raucourt (54) 66 A2
Raucourt-au-Bois (59) 12 E3
Raucourt-et-Flaba (08) 23 F5
Raulhac (15) 235 K1
Rauret (43) 238 B2
Rauville-la-Bigot (50) 28 C4
Rauville-la-Place (50) 28 D5
Rauwiller (67) 67 K3
Rauzan (33) 230 B3
Raveau (58) 150 D1
Ravel (63) 203 G2
Ravenel (60) 38 B1
Ravenoville (50) 29 F5
Raves (88) 95 J4
Ravières (89) 114 C6
Ravigny (53) 82 B3
Raville (57) 45 J5
Raville-sur-Sânon (54) 66 D5
Ravilloles (39) 173 J5
la Ravoire (73) 208 C4
Ray-sur-Saône (70) 137 H2
Raye-sur-Authie (62) 9 H2
Rayet (47) 232 A4
Raymond (18) 149 K4
Raynans (25) 139 G2
Rayol-Canadel-sur-Mer (83) 298 D5
Rayssac (81) 271 G4
Razac-de-Saussignac (24) 231 F2
Razac-d'Eymet (24) 231 H4
Razac-sur-l'Isle (24) 213 K4
Raze (70) 137 K1
Razecueillé (31) 305 K3
Razengues (32) 268 C6
Razès (87) 181 H4
Razimet (47) 247 H2
Razines (37) 145 G4
Réal (66) 313 J3
Réalcamp (76) 16 E2
Réallon (05) 243 H4
Réalmont (81) 270 E4
Réalville (82) 250 A6
Réans (32) 266 C3
Réau (77) 87 H1
Réaumont (38) 223 J1
Réaumur (85) 160 E1
Réaup-Lisse (47) 247 H6
Réauville (26) 256 E1
Réaux (17) 195 J5
Rebais (77) 60 C3
Rebecques (62) 3 G6
Rébénacq (64) 284 C6
Rebergues (62) 2 D5
Rebets (76) 36 A1
Rebeuville (88) 93 G4
Rebigue (31) 288 C2
Rebourguil (12) 272 A3
Reboursin (36) 148 B2
Rebréchien (45) 110 B3
Rebreuve-Ranchicourt (62) 10 C1
Rebreuve-sur-Canche (62) 10 B3
Rebreuviette (62) 10 B3
Recanoz (39) 155 G6
Recey-sur-Ource (21) 115 J5
Réchésy (90) 97 A5
Réchicourt-la-Petite (54) 66 E4
Réchicourt-le-Château (57) 67 G5
Récicourt (55) 43 F5
Réclainville (28) 85 J4
Reclesne (71) 152 E3
Reclinghem (62) 5 F5
Réclonville (54) 67 F6
Recloses (77) 87 H4
Recologne (25) 137 J5
Recologne (70) 137 H2
Recologne-lès-Rioz (70) 137 K3
Recoubeau-Jansac (26) 241 H4
Recoules-d'Aubrac (48) 236 D4
Recoules-de-Fumas (48) 237 G5
Recoules-Prévinquières (12) 253 F3
Récourt (62) 11 H3
Récourt-le-Creux (55) 64 D1
Recouvrance (90) 139 J1
le Recoux (48) 253 H3
Recques-sur-Course (62) 4 C5
Recques-sur-Hem (62) 2 E4
Recquignies (59) 13 H3
le Reculey (14) 31 K6
Reculfoz (25) 174 C1
Recurt (65) 286 B5
Recy (51) 62 C2
Rédange (57) 26 E2
Rédené (29) 99 J3
Redessan (30) 275 J3
Réding (57) 67 K4
Redon (35) 102 C4
la Redorte (11) 290 E5
Redortiers (04) 258 C5
Réez-Fosse-Martin (60) 38 E6
Reffannes (79) 162 A3
Reffroy (55) 64 D6
Reffuveille (50) 52 C5
Régades (31) 305 K2
Régat (09) 308 B3
Regnauville (62) 9 H2
Regnévelle (88) 117 J2
Regnéville-sur-Mer (50) 30 D4
Regnéville-sur-Meuse (55) 43 H4
Regney (88) 94 C4
Régnié-Durette (69) 188 A3
Regnière-Ecluse (80) 9 F3
Regniowez (08) 22 A1
Regny (02) 20 B3
Régny (42) 187 G5
la Regrippière (44) 142 C1
Réguiny (56) 101 F1
Réguisheim (68) 96 C6
Régusse (83) 279 F5
Rehaincourt (88) 94 D3
Rehainviller (54) 66 D6
Rehaupal (88) 95 G6
Reherrey (54) 95 G1
Réhon (54) 26 C2
Reichsfeld (67) 70 C6
Reichshoffen (67) 69 K4
Reichstett (67) 25 A6
Reignac (16) 196 A6
Reignac (33) 211 H3
Reignac-sur-Indre (37) 146 C1
Reignat (63) 203 F2
Reigneville-Bocage (50) 28 E5
Reignier (74) 191 G2
Reigny (18) 166 E3
Reilhac (15) 217 H6
Reilhac (46) 234 A4
Reilhaguet (46) 233 J3
Reilhanette (26) 258 A4
Reillanne (04) 278 A2
Reillon (54) 67 F6
Reilly (60) 36 E4
Reims (51) 41 F4
Reims-la-Brûlée (51) 63 G5
Reinhardsmunster (67) 70 B2
Reiningue (68) 97 B2
Reipertswiller (67) 69 H4
Reithouse (39) 173 G3
Réjaumont (32) 267 H3
Réjaumont (65) 286 B6
Rejet-de-Beaulieu (59) 12 E6
Relanges (88) 93 K6
Relans (39) 155 G6
le Relecq-Kerhuon (29) 46 A6
Relevant (01) 188 D3
Rely (62) 5 H5
Remaisnil (80) 10 A4
Rémalard (61) 83 K3
Remaucourt (02) 20 A2
Remaucourt (08) 21 J5
la Remaudière (44) 123 K4
Remaugies (80) 18 E5
Remauville (77) 87 J6
Rembercourt-Sommaisne (55) 64 B2
Rembercourt-sur-Mad (54) 65 H1
Rémécourt (60) 38 B2
Rémelfang (57) 45 J3
Rémelfing (57) 68 D3
Rémeling (57) 27 K3
Remennecourt (55) 63 J4
Remenoville (54) 94 D2
Rémérangles (60) 37 J2
Réméréville (54) 66 C4
Rémering (57) 45 K3
Rémering-lès-Puttelange (57) 68 C3
Remicourt (51) 63 J2
Remicourt (88) 93 K4
Remiencourt (80) 18 B3
Remies (02) 20 C4
Remigny (02) 20 A4
Remigny (71) 153 K5
Rémilly (57) 45 H6
Rémilly (58) 152 A6
Remilly-Aillicourt (08) 23 F4
Remilly-en-Montagne (21) 135 H6
Remilly-les-Pothées (08) 22 B3
Remilly-sur-Lozon (50) 31 F2
Remilly-sur-Tille (21) 136 C5
Remilly-Wirquin (62) 3 F6
Réminiac (56) 102 A1
Remiremont (88) 118 E2
Remoiville (55) 43 H1
Remollon (05) 243 F6
Remomeix (88) 95 J4
Remoncourt (54) 67 F5
Remoncourt (88) 93 K5
Rémondans-Vaivre (25) 139 G4
Remoray-Boujeons (25) 156 E6
Remouillé (44) 123 J6
Remoulins (30) 275 J2
Removille (88) 93 H3
Rempnat (87) 200 B3
la Remuée (76) 14 D6
Remungol (56) 100 E2
Rémuzat (26) 257 K1
Remy (60) 38 C2
Rémy (62) 11 G3
Renac (35) 102 D3
Renage (38) 223 J1
Renaison (42) 186 D4
Renansart (02) 20 B4
Renaucourt (70) 137 H1
la Renaudie (63) 203 K2
la Renaudière (49) 142 D2
Renauvoid (88) 94 C6
Renay (41) 108 D5
Renazé (53) 104 C5
Rencurel (38) 223 A4
René (72) 82 E5
Renédale (25) 156 E3
Renescure (59) 3 H5
Renève (21) 136 E4
Réning (57) 67 G1
Rennemoulin (78) 58 B4
Rennepont (52) 91 J6
Rennes (35) 79 G4
Rennes-en-Grenouilles (53) 81 H2
Rennes-le-Château (11) 309 F3
Rennes-les-Bains (11) 309 F3
Rennes-sur-Loue (25) 156 A3
Renneval (02) 21 G4
Renneville (08) 21 H5
Renneville (27) 35 K2
Renneville (31) 288 E3
Renno (2A) 320 C1
le Renouard (61) 54 D2
Rentières (63) 218 E1
Renty (62) 4 E5
Renung (40) 265 J4
Renwez (08) 22 C2
la Réole (33) 230 C5
la Réorthe (85) 160 B2
Réotier (05) 243 K3
Repaix (54) 67 G5
la Répara-Auriples (26) 240 D4
Réparsac (16) 196 A2
Repel (88) 93 J3
Repentigny (14) 33 H4
Replonges (01) 171 K6
le Reposoir (74) 191 K4
les Repôts (39) 172 E2
Reppe (90) 119 K6
Requeil (72) 106 D5
Réquista (12) 271 H1
Résenlieu (61) 55 F4
la Résie-Saint-Martin (70) 137 F5
Résigny (02) 21 J4
Resson (55) 64 B4
Ressons-l'Abbaye (60) 37 H4
Ressons-le-Long (02) 39 G2
Ressons-sur-Matz (60) 19 F6
les Ressuintes (28) 84 B1
Restigné (37) 126 E6
Restinclières (34) 274 D5
le Retail (79) 161 H3
Rétaud (17) 195 F3
Reterre (23) 183 K4
Rethel (08) 41 J1
Retheuil (02) 39 F3
Rethondes (60) 39 F2
Rethonvillers (80) 19 G4
Réthoville (50) 29 F2
Retiers (35) 103 J1
Retjons (40) 246 C5
Retonfey (57) 45 G5
Rétonval (76) 16 E3
Retournac (43) 220 D3
Retschwiller (67) 25 B2
Rettel (57) 27 J3
Rety (62) 2 C4
Retzwiller (68) 97 A4
Reugney (25) 156 D3
Reugny (03) 167 H5
Reugny (37) 128 A3
Reuil (51) 40 D6
Reuil-en-Brie (77) 60 C2
Reuil-sur-Brêche (60) 37 J1
Reuilly (27) 35 J6
Reuilly (36) 148 D3
Reuilly-Sauvigny (02) 61 F1
Reulle-Vergy (21) 154 A1
Reumont (59) 12 C5
la Réunion (47) 247 G3
Reutenbourg (67) 70 C2
Reuves (51) 61 J4
Reuville (76) 15 H4
Reux (14) 33 J4
Réveillon (51) 60 E5
Réveillon (61) 83 H2
Revel (31) 289 H2
Revel (38) 224 C3
Revel-Tourdan (38) 222 D1
Revelles (80) 17 K2
Revens (30) 253 J6
Reventin-Vaugris (38) 206 A5
Revercourt (28) 56 C5
Revest-des-Brousses (04) 278 A1
Revest-du-Bion (04) 258 C5
le Revest-les-Eaux (83) 297 J5
Revest-les-Roches (06) 281 F1
Revest-Saint-Martin (04) 258 E6
Reviers (14) 32 D3
Revigny (39) 173 G2
Revigny-sur-Ornain (55) 63 K3
Réville (50) 29 G3
Réville-aux-Bois (55) 43 H2
Révillon (02) 40 C3
Revin (08) 22 C1
Revonnas (01) 189 H2
Rexingen (67) 67 K2
Rexpoëde (59) 3 J3
Reyersviller (57) 69 G3
Reygade (19) 216 C6
Reynel (52) 92 C4
Reynès (66) 314 E5
Reyniès (82) 269 G2
Reyrevignes (46) 234 C5
Reyrieux (01) 188 C5
Reyssouze (01) 172 A5
Reyvroz (74) 175 G6
Rezay (18) 166 D2
Rezé (44) 123 G4
Rézentières (15) 218 E4
Rezonville (57) 44 D5
Rezza (2A) 320 D2
Rhèges (10) 90 A1
le Rheu (35) 79 F4
Rhinau (67) 71 D4
Rhodes (57) 67 H4
Rhodon (41) 108 E6
Rhuis (60) 38 C3
Ri (61) 54 B4
Ria-Sirach (66) 314 B3
Riaillé (44) 103 K6
le Rialet (81) 290 C1
Rians (18) 149 J1
Rians (83) 278 B6
Riantec (56) 100 A4
Riaucourt (52) 92 B6
Riaville (55) 44 A5
Ribagnac (24) 231 H3
Ribarrouy (64) 284 E1
Ribaute (11) 309 K1
Ribaute-les-Tavernes (30) 274 D1
le Ribay (53) 81 J3
Ribeaucourt (55) 92 C1
Ribeaucourt (80) 9 J5
Ribeauville (02) 12 D6
Ribeauvillé (68) 71 A6
Ribécourt-Dreslincourt (60) 38 E1
Ribécourt-la-Tour (59) 11 J5
Ribemont (02) 20 B3
Ribemont-sur-Ancre (80) 18 D1
Ribennes (48) 237 H5
Ribérac (24) 213 G3
Ribes (07) 239 F6
Ribeyret (05) 258 B1
Ribiers (05) 259 F3
Ribouisse (11) 289 G6
Riboux (83) 297 G4
la Ricamarie (42) 221 G1
Ricarville (76) 15 F5
Ricarville-du-Val (76) 16 B3
Ricaud (11) 289 G4
Ricaud (65) 285 K6
les Riceys (10) 114 D3
la Richardais (35) 50 D3
Richardménil (54) 66 A6
Richarville (91) 86 B2
la Riche (37) 127 J4
Riche (57) 66 E2
Richebourg (52) 116 A2
Richebourg (62) 6 B5
Richebourg (78) 57 H4
Richecourt (55) 65 G2
Richelieu (37) 145 G3
Richeling (57) 68 C4
Richemont (57) 27 G5
Richemont (76) 16 E3
Richerenches (84) 257 F2
Richeval (57) 67 H5
Richeville (27) 36 C4
Richtolsheim (67) 71 C5
Richwiller (68) 97 B2
Ricourt (32) 285 J2
Ricquebourg (60) 19 F6

Riec-sur-Belon (29) 99 G3
Riedisheim (68) 97 C2
Riedseltz (67) 25 C1
Riedwihr (68) 96 D3
Riel-les-Eaux (21) 115 G3
Riencourt (80) 17 J1
Riencourt-lès-Bapaume (62) . . . 11 F5
Riencourt-lès-Cagnicourt (62) . . 11 G4
Riervescemont (90) 119 H5
Riespach (68) 97 C5
Rieucazé (31) 305 K1
Rieucros (09) 308 A1
Rieulay (59) 11 K1
Rieumajou (31) 289 F3
Rieumes (31) 287 J3
Rieupeyroux (12) 251 H3
Rieussec (34) 291 F3
Rieutort-de-Randon (48) 237 J5
Rieux (31) 287 K5
Rieux (51) 61 F3
Rieux (56) 102 B5
Rieux (60) 38 B4
Rieux (76) 16 E1
Rieux-de-Pelleport (09) 307 J2
Rieux-en-Cambrésis (59) 12 D4
Rieux-en-Val (11) 309 H1
Rieux-Minervois (11) 290 D5
Riez (04) 278 C3
Rigarda (66) 314 D3
Rigaud (06) 261 G6
Rignac (12) 251 J2
Rignac (46) 234 A3
Rigney (25) 138 B4
Rignieux-le-Franc (01) 189 G5
Rignosot (25) 138 B4
Rignovelle (70) 118 E5
Rigny (70) 137 G3
Rigny-la-Nonneuse (10) 89 G3
Rigny-la-Salle (55) 65 G6
Rigny-le-Ferron (10) 89 G6
Rigny-Saint-Martin (55) 65 G6
Rigny-sur-Arroux (71) 170 B4
Rigny-Ussé (37) 126 E6
Riguepeu (32) 267 F5
Rilhac-Lastours (87) 198 D3
Rilhac-Rancon (87) 181 H6
Rilhac-Treignac (19) 199 K5
Rilhac-Xaintrie (19) 217 F4
Rillans (25) 138 D3
Rillé (37) 126 E4
Rillieux-la-Pape (69) 206 B1
Rilly-la-Montagne (51) 41 F5
Rilly-Sainte-Syre (10) 89 K3
Rilly-sur-Aisne (08) 42 A1
Rilly-sur-Loire (41) 128 C4
Rilly-sur-Vienne (37) 145 J3
Rimaucourt (52) 92 C5
Rimbach-près-Guebwiller (68) . . 96 A6
Rimbach-près-Masevaux (68) . . 119 J4
Rimbachzell (68) 96 A6
Rimbez-et-Baudiets (40) 247 F6
Rimboval (62) 4 E6
Rimeize (48) 237 G3
Rimling (57) 69 F3
Rimogne (08) 22 B2
Rimon-et-Savel (26) 241 G4
Rimondeix (23) 183 F2
Rimons (33) 230 D4
Rimont (09) 307 F2
Rimou (35) 51 H6
Rimplas (06) 261 J5
Rimsdorf (67) 67 K1
Ringeldorf (67) 69 J6
Ringendorf (67) 69 J6
Rinxent (62) 2 B4
Riocaud (33) 231 F3
Riolas (31) 287 G4
Riols (34) 291 F2
le Riols (81) 250 E5
Riom (63) 185 F6
Riom-ès-Montagnes (15) 217 K2
Rioms (26) 258 B3
Rion-des-Landes (40) 264 C2
Rions (33) 229 K4
Riorges (42) 186 E4
Riotord (43) 221 H3
Rioux (17) 195 F3
Rioux-Martin (16) 212 D3
Rioz (70) 138 A3
Riquewihr (68) 96 B3
Ris (63) 185 K5
Ris (65) 305 F4
Ris-Orangis (91) 59 F6
Riscle (32) 266 B5
Risoul (05) 227 A4
Ristolas (05) 227 D2
Rittershoffen (67) 25 C3
Ritzing (57) 27 K3
Riupeyrous (64) 284 E3
Rivarennes (36) 165 F3
Rivarennes (37) 127 F6
Rivas (42) 204 E4
Rive-de-Gier (42) 205 J5
Rivecourt (60) 38 D3
Rivedoux-Plage (17) 176 C2
Rivehaute (64) 283 H3
Rivel (11) 308 C3
Riventosa (2B) 321 F1
Rivèrenert (09) 306 E3
Riverie (69) 205 J4
Rivery (80) 18 B2
les Rives (34) 273 F3

Rives (38) 223 J1
Rives (47) 232 A5
Rivesaltes (66) 310 B5
la Rivière (33) 229 K1
Rivière (37) 145 G2
la Rivière (38) 223 J2
Rivière (62) 10 E3
la Rivière-de-Corps (10) 90 A5
la Rivière-Drugeon (25) 156 D5
la Rivière-Enverse (74) 192 A3
Rivière-les-Fosses (52) 136 C1
la Rivière-Saas-et-Gourby (40) . 262 E5
la Rivière-Saint-Sauveur (14) . . . 34 A2
Rivière-sur-Tarn (12) 253 H5
Rivières (16) 197 G2
Rivières (30) 255 J4
Rivières (81) 270 C2
Rivières-Henruel (51) 63 F6
Rivières-le-Bois (52) 116 B1
Riville (76) 14 E4
Rivolet (69) 188 A5
Rix (39) 156 C6
Rix (58) 133 F4
Rixheim (68) 97 C2
la Rixouse (39) 173 K4
Rizaucourt-Buchey (52) 91 J5
Roaillan (33) 230 A6
Roaix (84) 257 G4
Roanne (42) 187 F4
Roannes-Saint-Mary (15) 235 H2
Robécourt (88) 93 G6
Robecq (62) 5 K4
Robersart (59) 12 E4
Robert-Espagne (55) 63 K4
Robert-Magny-Laneuville-
   à-Rémy (52) 91 J2
Robertot (76) 15 G4
Roberval (60) 38 C4
Robiac-Rochessadoule (30) . . . 255 H3
la Robine-sur-Galabre (04) 259 J4
Robion (84) 276 E3
le Roc (46) 233 H2
le Roc-Saint-André (56) 101 J3
Rocamadour (46) 233 K3
Rocbaron (83) 298 A4
Rocé (41) 108 D5
Roche (38) 206 E4
Roche (42) 204 B4
la Roche-Bernard (56) 121 K2
la Roche-Blanche (44) 124 B3
la Roche-Blanche (63) 202 D3
la Roche-Canillac (19) 216 C3
la Roche-Chalais (24) 212 D4
Roche-Charles-la-Mayrand (63) . 202 C6
la Roche-Clermault (37) 145 F2
Roche-d'Agoux (63) 184 A4
la Roche-de-Glun (26) 222 C5
la Roche-de-Rame (05) 243 K2
la Roche-Derrien (22) 48 B3
la Roche-des-Arnauds (05) 242 D5
la Roche-en-Brenil (21) 134 C5
la Roche-en-Régnier (43) 220 C3
Roche-et-Raucourt (70) 137 G1
la Roche-Guyon (95) 36 C6
Roche-la-Molière (42) 205 F6
la Roche-l'Abeille (87) 198 E4
Roche-le-Peyroux (19) 217 G1
Roche-lès-Clerval (25) 138 E4
Roche-lez-Beaupré (25) 138 B5
la Roche-Mabile (61) 82 B2
la Roche-Maurice (29) 46 C5
la Roche-Morey (70) 117 G6
la Roche-Noire (63) 202 E3
la Roche-Posay (86) 146 B6
la Roche-Rigault (86) 145 F4
Roche-Saint-Secret-Béconne (26) . 257 G1
la Roche-sur-Foron (74) 191 H3
la Roche-sur-Grane (26) 240 D4
la Roche-sur-le-Buis (26) 257 K3
Roche-sur-Linotte-et-
   Sorans-les-Cordiers (70) 138 B3
la Roche-sur-Yon (85) 159 H1
la Roche-Vanneau (21) 135 F3
la Roche-Vineuse (71) 171 J6
Rochebaudin (26) 240 E5
la Rochebeaucourt-et-
   Argentine (24) 197 G5
Rochebrune (05) 243 F6
Rochebrune (26) 257 J2
Rochechinard (26) 223 F5
Rochechouart (87) 198 A1
Rochecolombe (07) 239 J4
Rochecorbon (37) 127 K4
Rochefort (17) 177 F5
Rochefort (21) 115 H6
Rochefort (73) 207 K4
Rochefort-du-Gard (30) 276 A1
Rochefort-en-Terre (56) 101 K5
Rochefort-en-Valdaine (26) . . . 240 C6
Rochefort-en-Yvelines (78) 86 B1
Rochefort-Montagne (63) 202 A3
Rochefort-Samson (26) 222 E6
Rochefort-sur-la-Côte (52) 92 B5
Rochefort-sur-Loire (49) 125 F5
Rochefort-sur-Nenon (39) 155 H2
la Rochefoucauld (16) 197 G2
Rochefourchat (26) 241 G5
la Rochegiron (04) 258 D5
Rochegude (26) 256 E4
Rochegude (30) 255 J4
Rochejean (25) 156 E6
la Rochelle (17) 176 D2

la Rochelle (70) 117 G5
la Rochelle-Normande (50) 51 J2
Rochemaure (07) 240 A5
la Rochénard (79) 177 J2
Rochepaule (07) 221 H5
la Rochepot (21) 153 J4
Rocher (07) 239 G5
le Rochereau (86) 162 D1
Roches (23) 182 E1
Roches (41) 109 F5
Roches-Bettaincourt (52) 92 C4
les Roches-de-Condrieu (38) . . . 206 A6
Roches-lès-Blamont (25) 139 H3
Roches-Prémarie-Andillé (86) . . 163 F4
Roches-sur-Marne (52) 63 K6
Rocheservière (85) 141 H4
Rochessauve (07) 239 K4
Rochesson (88) 119 G1
Rochetaillée (52) 116 B4
Rochetaillée-sur-Saône (69) . . . 206 A1
Rochetoirin (38) 207 G4
Rochetrejoux (85) 142 D6
la Rochette (04) 280 C1
la Rochette (05) 243 F4
la Rochette (07) 239 F1
la Rochette (16) 197 F1
la Rochette (73) 208 D5
la Rochette (77) 87 H2
la Rochette-du-Buis (26) 258 A3
Rocheville (50) 28 D4
Rochonvillers (57) 27 F3
Rochy-Condé (60) 37 H2
Rocles (03) 168 B5
Rocles (07) 239 F5
Rocles (48) 238 B4
Roclincourt (62) 10 E2
Rocourt (88) 117 G1
Rocourt-Saint-Martin (02) 39 K5
Rocquancourt (14) 32 E6
la Rocque (14) 53 G3
Rocquefort (76) 15 G5
Rocquemont (60) 38 D4
Rocquemont (76) 16 B5
Rocquencourt (60) 18 C5
Rocquencourt (78) 58 C4
Rocques (14) 33 K5
Rocquigny (02) 13 H6
Rocquigny (08) 21 J4
Rocquigny (62) 11 G5
Rocroi (08) 22 B1
Rodalbe (57) 67 F2
Rodelinghem (62) 2 D4
Rodelle (12) 252 C1
Rodemack (57) 27 H3
Roderen (68) 119 K4
Rodern (68) 71 A6
Rodès (66) 314 D2
Rodez (12) 252 B3
Rodilhan (30) 275 H3
Rodome (11) 308 D5
la Roë (53) 104 B3
Roëllecourt (62) 10 B2
Roeschwoog (67) 25 D3
Roeulx (59) 11 K2
Roeux (62) 11 F2
Roézé-sur-Sarthe (72) 106 C4
Roffey (89) 113 K4
Roffiac (15) 218 D5
Rogécourt (02) 20 B5
Rogerville (76) 34 A1
Rogéville (54) 65 J3
Roggenhouse (68) 96 D6
Rogliano (2B) 317 D2
Rogna (39) 173 J6
Rognac (13) 296 B2
Rognaix (73) 209 G3
Rognes (13) 277 H5
Rognon (25) 138 C3
Rognonas (13) 276 B2
Rogny (02) 20 E3
Rogny-les-Sept-Écluses (89) . . . 111 K6
Rogues (30) 273 J3
Rogy (80) 18 A4
Rohaire (28) 56 A6
Rohan (56) 77 F6
Rohr (67) 70 D2
Rohrbach-lès-Bitche (57) 69 F3
Rohrwiller (67) 25 B4
Roiffé (86) 144 D2
Roiffieux (07) 221 K3
Roiglise (80) 19 F4
Roilly (21) 134 D4
Roinville (28) 85 J3
Roinville (91) 86 B2
Roinvilliers (91) 86 D4
Roisel (80) 19 J1
les Roises (55) 93 F2
Roisey (42) 221 K1
Roissard (38) 223 H4
Roissy-en-Brie (77) 59 H4
Roissy-en-France (95) 59 G5
Roiville (61) 55 F3
Roizy (08) 41 G2
Rolampont (52) 116 C3
Rolbing (57) 69 G2
Rollainville (88) 93 G3
Rollancourt (62) 9 J1
Rolleboise (78) 57 H1
Rolleville (76) 14 B5
Rollot (80) 18 E6
Rom (79) 179 G1

Romagnat (63) 202 D3
la Romagne (08) 21 K4
Romagne (33) 230 B3
Romagné (35) 80 A3
la Romagne (49) 142 D2
Romagne (86) 179 H1
Romagne-sous-les-Côtes (55) . . . 26 A5
Romagne-sous-Montfaucon (55) . 42 E3
Romagnieu (38) 207 H3
Romagny (50) 52 D6
Romagny (68) 139 K1
Romagny-sous-Rougemont (90) . 119 J5
Romain (25) 138 D3
Romain (39) 137 H5
Romain (51) 40 C3
Romain (54) 94 C1
Romain-aux-Bois (88) 117 G1
Romain-sur-Meuse (52) 92 E6
Romainville (93) 59 F3
Roman (27) 56 C3
Romanèche-Thorins (71) 188 B2
Romange (39) 155 H1
Romans (01) 188 E3
Romans (79) 161 K6
Romans-sur-Isère (26) 222 D5
Romanswiller (67) 70 C2
Romazières (17) 178 D5
Romazy (35) 79 J1
Rombach-le-Franc (68) 96 B1
Rombas (57) 27 G5
Rombies-et-Marchipont (59) . . . 12 E2
Rombly (62) 5 H4
Romegoux (17) 177 G6
Romelfing (57) 67 J3
Romenay (71) 172 B4
Romeny-sur-Marne (02) 60 D2
Romeries (59) 12 D4
Romery (02) 20 E2
Romery (51) 40 E6
Romescamps (60) 17 G4
Romestaing (47) 247 F2
Romeyer (26) 241 H2
la Romieu (32) 267 H1
Romigny (51) 40 C5
Romiguières (34) 273 F4
Romillé (35) 78 E3
Romilly (41) 108 C3
Romilly-la-Puthenaye (27) 56 A1
Romilly-sur-Aigre (28) 108 C2
Romilly-sur-Andelle (27) 35 K3
Romilly-sur-Seine (10) 89 H2
Romont (88) 94 E3
Romorantin-Lanthenay (41) . . . 129 J5
Rompon (07) 240 A3
Rônai (61) 54 B4
Roncenay (10) 90 A6
le Roncenay-Authenay (27) 56 C3
Roncey (50) 31 F5
Ronchamp (70) 119 F5
Ronchaux (25) 156 A2
Ronchères (02) 40 B5
Ronchères (89) 132 C1
Roncherolles-en-Bray (76) 16 D5
Roncherolles-sur-le-Vivier (76) . . 35 J1
Ronchin (59) 6 E4
Ronchois (76) 16 E4
Roncourt (57) 27 F6
Roncq (59) 6 E2
la Ronde (17) 160 D6
la Ronde-Haye (50) 30 E3
Rondefontaine (25) 156 D6
Ronel (81) 270 E4
Ronfeugerai (61) 53 H4
Rongères (03) 185 J1
Ronnet (03) 184 B2
Ronno (69) 187 J5
Ronquerolles (95) 37 J5
Ronsenac (16) 197 F5
Ronssoy (80) 19 J1
Rontalon (69) 205 J3
Rontignon (64) 284 D4
Ronvaux (55) 43 K5
Roost-Warendin (59) 11 H1
Roppe (90) 119 J6
Roppenheim (67) 25 D3
Roppentzwiller (68) 97 C5
Roppeviller (57) 69 H2
la Roque-Alric (84) 257 G5
la Roque-Baignard (14) 33 J5
la Roque-d'Anthéron (13) 277 G4
la Roque-Esclapon (83) 280 A4
la Roque-Gageac (24) 232 E2
la Roque-Sainte-Marguerite (12) . . 253 J5
la Roque-sur-Cèze (30) 256 B4
la Roque-sur-Pernes (84) 276 E1
Roquebillière (06) 311 A3
Roquebrun (34) 291 J2
Roquebrune (32) 267 F5
Roquebrune (33) 230 D5
Roquebrune-Cap-Martin (06) . . 281 J3
Roquebrune-sur-Argens (83) . . 299 F2
la Roquebrussanne (83) 297 J3
Roquecor (82) 248 E3
Roquecourbe (81) 271 F6
Roquecourbe-Minervois (11) . . . 290 E5
Roquedur (30) 273 K2
Roquefère (11) 290 B3
Roquefeuil (11) 308 C5
Roquefixade (09) 307 K3
Roquefort (32) 267 J4
Roquefort (40) 246 B6
Roquefort (47) 248 B5

Roquefort-de-Sault (11) 308 E6
Roquefort-des-Corbières (11) . . . 310 C3
Roquefort-la-Bédoule (13) 296 E4
Roquefort-les-Cascades (09) . . 307 K3
Roquefort-les-Pins (06) 280 E4
Roquefort-sur-Garonne (31) . . . 287 G6
Roquefort-sur-Soulzon (12) . . . 272 C2
Roquelaure (32) 267 H5
Roquelaure-Saint-Aubin (32) . . 268 C5
Roquemaure (30) 256 E6
Roquemaure (81) 269 J4
Roquepine (32) 267 G2
Roqueredonde (34) 273 F4
Roques (31) 288 B2
Roques (32) 267 F3
Roquesérière (31) 269 J5
Roquessels (34) 292 A1
Roquesteron (06) 280 E2
Roquestéron-Grasse (06) 280 E2
Roquetaillade (11) 308 E2
Roquetoire (62) 3 H6
la Roquette (27) 36 A4
la Roquette-sur-Siagne (06) . . . 280 D5
la Roquette-sur-Var (06) 281 F2
Roquettes (31) 288 B2
Roquevaire (13) 296 E3
Roquevidal (81) 270 B6
Roquiague (64) 283 H5
la Roquille (33) 231 F3
Rorbach-lès-Dieuze (57) 67 G3
Rorschwihr (68) 71 A6
Rosans (05) 258 B2
Rosay (39) 173 F3
Rosay (76) 16 B4
Rosay (78) 57 J3
Rosay-sur-Lieure (27) 36 B3
Rosazia (2A) 320 C2
Rosbruck (57) 68 B2
Roscanvel (29) 72 C5
Roscoff (29) 47 F2
Rosel (14) 32 D4
Rosenau (68) 97 E3
Rosenwiller (67) 70 C4
Roset-Fluans (25) 155 K1
Rosey (70) 137 K2
Rosey (71) 171 H1
Rosheim (67) 70 C4
la Rosière (70) 119 F3
Rosières (07) 255 J1
Rosières (43) 220 D4
Rosières (60) 38 C5
Rosières (81) 270 E1
Rosières-aux-Salines (54) 66 C6
Rosières-en-Haye (54) 65 J3
Rosières-en-Santerre (80) 18 E3
Rosières-près-Troyes (10) 90 B5
Rosières-sur-Barbèche (25) . . . 139 G5
Rosières-sur-Mance (70) 117 H4
Rosiers-de-Juillac (19) 215 G2
Rosiers-d'Égletons (19) 216 D1
les Rosiers-sur-Loire (49) 125 K5
Rosis (34) 272 D5
Rosnay (36) 164 D2
Rosnay (51) 40 D4
Rosnay (85) 159 J3
Rosnay-l'Hôpital (10) 90 E2
Rosnoën (29) 74 C2
Rosny-sous-Bois (93) 59 F3
Rosny-sur-Seine (78) 57 H2
Rosoy (60) 38 B3
Rosoy-en-Multien (60) 39 F6
Rosoy-le-Vieil (45) 112 A1
Rospez (22) 48 A3
Rospigliani (2B) 321 G1
Rosporden (29) 75 F4
Rosselange (57) 27 F5
Rossfeld (67) 70 E6
Rossillon (01) 207 J1
Rosteig (67) 69 G5
Rostrenen (22) 76 A3
Rosult (59) 7 G6
Rotalier (39) 173 F3
Rotangy (60) 17 J6
Rothau (67) 70 A5
Rothbach (67) 69 H5
Rotherens (73) 208 D5
la Rothière (10) 91 F4
Rothois (60) 17 H6
Rothonay (39) 173 G3
les Rotours (61) 54 A4
Rots (14) 32 D4
Rott (67) 25 B1
Rottelsheim (67) 25 A4
Rottier (26) 241 H6
Rou-Marson (49) 126 A6
Rouairoux (81) 290 D2
Rouans (44) 122 D4
la Rouaudière (53) 104 A4
Roubaix (59) 6 E3
Roubia (11) 291 F4
Roubion (06) 261 H5
Roucamps (14) 53 C1
Roucourt (59) 11 J2
Roucy (02) 40 D3
Roudouallec (56) 75 G4
Rouécourt (52) 92 A4
Rouède (31) 306 B2
Rouellé (61) 53 F6
Rouelles (52) 116 A5
Rouen (76) 35 H2
Rouessé-Fontaine (72) 82 D4

Roussé-Vassé (72)............ 82 A6
Rouet (34)............ 274 B4
Rouez (72)............ 82 B6
Rouffach (68)............ 96 B5
Rouffange (39)............ 137 G6
Rouffiac (15)............ 216 E6
Rouffiac (16)............ 212 E2
Rouffiac (17)............ 195 H3
Rouffiac (81)............ 270 D3
Rouffiac-d'Aude (11)............ 309 F1
Rouffiac-des-Corbières (11)...... 309 J4
Rouffiac-Tolosan (31)............ 269 H5
Rouffignac (17)............ 211 J1
Rouffignac-de-Sigoulès (24)...... 231 H3
Rouffignac-Saint-Cernin-
de-Reilhac (24)............ 214 D5
Rouffigny (50)............ 52 A3
Rouffilhac (46)............ 233 H3
Rouffy (51)............ 62 B2
Rougé (44)............ 103 J3
la Rouge (61)............ 83 J5
Rouge-Perriers (27)............ 35 F5
Rougefay (62)............ 9 K3
Rougegoutte (90)............ 119 H5
Rougemont (21)............ 134 C1
Rougemont (25)............ 138 D3
Rougemont-le-Château (90)...... 119 J5
Rougemontiers (27)............ 34 E3
Rougemontot (25)............ 138 C4
Rougeou (41)............ 129 G5
Rougeries (02)............ 20 E3
les Rouges-Eaux (88)...... 95 G4
le Rouget (15)............ 235 F2
Rougeux (52)............ 117 F4
Rougiers (83)............ 297 H3
Rougnac (16)............ 197 G5
Rougnat (23)............ 183 K4
Rougon (04)............ 279 H3
Rouhe (25)............ 156 B2
Rouhling (57)............ 68 C2
Rouillac (16)............ 196 C2
Rouillac (22)............ 77 K3
Rouillé (86)............ 162 C5
Rouillon (72)............ 106 D2
Rouilly (77)............ 88 D1
Rouilly-Sacey (10)............ 90 C4
Rouilly-Saint-Loup (10)............ 90 B5
Roujan (34)............ 292 B2
Roulans (25)............ 138 C5
le Roulier (88)............ 95 F5
Roullée (72)............ 83 F2
Roullens (11)............ 290 A6
Roullet-Saint-Estèphe (16)...... 196 D4
Roullours (14)............ 52 E3
Roumagne (47)............ 231 G5
Roumare (76)............ 35 G1
Roumazières-Loubert (16)...... 180 A6
Roumégoux (15)............ 235 F2
Roumégoux (81)............ 271 F4
Roumengoux (09)............ 308 B3
Roumens (31)............ 289 G2
Roumoules (04)............ 279 F3
Rountzenheim (67)............ 25 C4
Roupeldange (57)............ 27 K6
Rouperroux (61)............ 82 B1
Rouperroux-le-Coquet (72)...... 83 G5
Roupy (02)............ 19 J3
la Rouquette (12)............ 251 F3
Roure (06)............ 261 H5
le Rouret (06)............ 280 E4
Rousies (59)............ 13 H3
Roussac (87)............ 181 G4
Roussas (26)............ 256 E1
Roussay (49)............ 142 D2
Roussayrolles (81)............ 250 D6
Rousseloy (60)............ 37 K4
Roussennac (12)............ 251 J1
Roussent (62)............ 9 F2
les Rousses (39)............ 174 B4
Rousses (48)............ 254 B4
Rousset (05)............ 243 G6
Rousset (13)............ 297 F1
le Rousset (71)............ 171 F4
Rousset-les-Vignes (26)...... 257 G1
la Roussière (27)............ 55 H2
Roussieux (26)............ 258 B2
Roussillon (38)............ 222 B1
Roussillon (84)............ 277 G2
Roussillon-en-Morvan (71)...... 152 D3
Roussines (17)............ 197 J2
Roussines (36)............ 165 F5
Rousson (30)............ 255 H5
Rousson (89)............ 112 D1
Roussy-le-Village (57)............ 27 G3
Routelle (25)............ 156 A1
Routes (76)............ 15 G4
Routier (11)............ 308 D1
Routot (27)............ 34 E2
Rouvenac (11)............ 308 E3
Rouves (54)............ 66 A2
la Rouvière (30)............ 275 F2
Rouvignies (59)............ 12 C2
Rouville (60)............ 38 E5
Rouville (76)............ 14 E5
Rouvillers (60)............ 38 C2
Rouvray (21)............ 134 B4
Rouvray (27)............ 57 F1
Rouvray (89)............ 113 H4
Rouvray-Catillon (76)............ 16 D6
Rouvray-Saint-Denis (28)...... 86 A5
Rouvray-Saint-Florentin (28)..... 85 H5
Rouvray-Sainte-Croix (45)...... 109 J2

Rouvrel (80)............ 18 C3
Rouvres (14)............ 54 B1
Rouvres (28)............ 57 G4
Rouvres (77)............ 59 H1
Rouvres-en-Multien (60)...... 39 F6
Rouvres-en-Plaine (21)...... 136 B6
Rouvres-en-Woëvre (55)...... 26 C6
Rouvres-en-Xaintois (88)...... 93 K4
Rouvres-la-Chétive (88)...... 93 G4
Rouvres-les-Bois (36)............ 147 K3
Rouvres-les-Vignes (10)...... 91 H5
Rouvres-Saint-Jean (45)...... 86 D4
Rouvres-sous-Meilly (21)...... 153 H1
Rouvres-sur-Aube (52)...... 115 H4
Rouvrois-sur-Meuse (55)...... 64 E2
Rouvrois-sur-Othain (55)...... 26 B4
Rouvroy (02)............ 20 A2
Rouvroy (62)............ 11 G1
Rouvroy-en-Santerre (80)...... 18 E3
Rouvroy-les-Merles (60)...... 18 B5
Rouvroy-Ripont (51)............ 42 B4
Rouvroy-sur-Audry (08)...... 22 B3
Rouvroy-sur-Marne (52)...... 92 B4
Rouvroy-sur-Serre (02)...... 21 J4
le Roux (07)............ 238 E4
Rouxeville (50)............ 31 J3
la Rouxière (44)............ 124 B3
Rouxmesnil-Bouteilles (76)...... 15 K2
Rouy (58)............ 151 H3
Rouy-le-Grand (80)............ 19 G3
Rouy-le-Petit (80)............ 19 G3
Rouzède (16)............ 197 H3
Rouziers (15)............ 235 F3
Rouziers-de-Touraine (37)...... 127 J3
le Rove (13)............ 296 B3
Roville-aux-Chênes (88)...... 94 C3
Roville-devant-Bayon (54)...... 94 B2
Rovon (38)............ 223 H3
Roy-Boissy (60)............ 17 H6
Royan (17)............ 194 C3
Royas (38)............ 206 D5
Royat (63)............ 202 D2
Royaucourt (60)............ 18 D5
Royaucourt-et-Chailvet (02)...... 40 A1
Royaumeix (54)............ 65 H4
Roybon (38)............ 223 F2
Roye (70)............ 118 E6
Roye (80)............ 19 F4
Roye-sur-Matz (60)............ 19 F6
Royer (71)............ 171 J3
Royère-de-Vassivière (23)...... 200 B1
Royères (87)............ 199 G1
Roynac (26)............ 240 D4
Royon (62)............ 4 E6
Royville (76)............ 15 J3
Roz-Landrieux (35)............ 51 F4
Roz-sur-Couesnon (35)...... 51 H4
Rozay-en-Brie (77)............ 60 A6
le Rozel (50)............ 28 A4
Rozelieures (54)............ 94 D2
Rozérieulles (57)............ 44 E5
Rozerotte (88)............ 93 K5
Rozès (32)............ 267 G4
Rozet-Saint-Albin (02)...... 39 J5
le Rozier (48)............ 253 H5
Rozier-Côtes-d'Aurec (42)...... 220 E1
Rozier-en-Donzy (42)...... 205 F1
Rozières-en-Beauce (45)...... 109 J3
Rozières-sur-Crise (02)...... 39 J3
Rozières-sur-Mouzon (88)...... 93 G6
Roziers-Saint-Georges (87)...... 199 H2
Rozoy-Bellevalle (02)...... 60 E3
Rozoy-sur-Serre (02)...... 21 H4
Ruages (58)............ 133 H5
Ruan (45)............ 110 A1
Ruan-sur-Egvonne (41)...... 108 D2
Ruaudin (72)............ 106 E3
Rubécourt-et-Lamécourt (08)...... 23 F4
Rubelles (77)............ 87 H1
Rubempré (80)............ 10 B6
Rubercy (14)............ 31 K1
Rubescourt (80)............ 18 D5
Rubigny (08)............ 21 J4
Rubrouck (59)............ 3 H4
Ruca (22)............ 50 A4
Ruch (33)............ 230 C3
Rucqueville (14)............ 32 C4
Rudeau-Ladosse (24)...... 197 H5
Rudelle (46)............ 234 C4
Rue (80)............ 8 E3
la Rue-Saint-Pierre (60)...... 37 J2
la Rue-Saint-Pierre (76)...... 16 B6
Ruederbach (68)............ 97 B5
Rueil-la-Gadelière (28)...... 56 B5
Rueil-Malmaison (92)...... 58 D3
Ruelisheim (68)............ 97 C1
Ruelle-sur-Touvre (16)...... 196 E3
les Rues-des-Vignes (59)...... 11 K5
Ruesnes (59)............ 12 D3
Rueyres (46)............ 234 B3
Ruffec (16)............ 179 G4
Ruffec (36)............ 164 D3
Ruffey-le-Château (25)...... 137 H5
Ruffey-lès-Beaune (21)...... 154 B3
Ruffey-lès-Echirey (21)...... 136 B4
Ruffey-sur-Seille (39)...... 173 F1
Ruffiac (56)............ 102 A2
Ruffieu (01)............ 190 A4
Ruffieux (73)............ 190 C6
Ruffigné (44)............ 103 H3
Rugles (27)............ 55 K4

Rugney (88)............ 94 B3
Rugny (89)............ 114 B4
Ruhans (70)............ 138 B3
Ruillé-en-Champagne (72)...... 106 B2
Ruillé-Froid-Fonds (53)...... 105 F3
Ruillé-le-Gravelais (53)...... 104 D1
Ruillé-sur-Loir (72)............ 107 H6
Ruisseauville (62)............ 5 F6
Ruitz (62)............ 5 K6
Rullac-Saint-Cirq (12)...... 252 A5
Rully (14)............ 53 F3
Rully (60)............ 38 D4
Rully (71)............ 153 K5
Rumaucourt (62)............ 11 H3
Rumegies (59)............ 7 G6
Rumersheim-le-Haut (68)...... 97 D1
Rumesnil (14)............ 33 H5
Rumigny (08)............ 21 J3
Rumigny (80)............ 18 A3
Rumilly (62)............ 4 E5
Rumilly (74)............ 190 D6
Rumilly-en-Cambrésis (59)...... 11 J5
Rumilly-lès-Vaudes (10)...... 114 C1
Ruminghem (62)............ 3 F4
Rumont (55)............ 64 C3
Rumont (77)............ 87 F5
Runan (22)............ 48 C3
Rungis (94)............ 58 E5
Ruoms (07)............ 255 K1
Rupéreux (77)............ 60 D6
Ruppes (88)............ 93 G2
Rupt (52)............ 92 B3
Rupt-aux-Nonains (55)...... 64 A5
Rupt-devant-Saint-Mihiel (55)...... 64 D3
Rupt-en-Woëvre (55)...... 43 J6
Rupt-sur-Moselle (88)...... 119 F3
Rupt-sur-Othain (55)...... 26 A4
Rupt-sur-Saône (70)...... 137 J1
Rurange-lès-Thionville (57)...... 27 H5
Rurey (25)............ 156 B2
Rusio (2B)............ 319 G5
Russ (67)............ 70 B4
Russange (57)............ 26 E3
le Russey (25)............ 157 J1
Russy (14)............ 32 A3
Russy-Bémont (60)............ 39 F4
Rustenhart (68)............ 96 D5
Rustiques (11)............ 290 C5
Rustrel (84)............ 277 J2
Rustroff (57)............ 27 J3
Rutali (2B)............ 319 H2
Ruvigny (10)............ 90 C5
Ruy (38)............ 207 F4
Ruyaulcourt (62)............ 11 H5
Ruynes-en-Margeride (15)...... 219 F6
Ry (76)............ 36 A1
Rye (39)............ 155 G5
Ryes (14)............ 32 C3

S

Saâcy-sur-Marne (77)...... 60 C2
Saales (67)............ 95 K3
Saâne-Saint-Just (76)...... 15 J3
Saasenheim (67)............ 71 D5
Sabadel-Latronquière (46)...... 234 D4
Sabadel-Lauzès (46)...... 233 K6
Sabaillan (32)............ 287 F2
Sabalos (65)............ 285 J4
Sabarat (09)............ 307 G1
Sabarros (65)............ 286 B5
Sabazan (32)............ 266 C5
Sablé-sur-Sarthe (72)...... 105 J4
les Sables-d'Olonne (85)...... 158 E3
Sablet (84)............ 257 G3
Sablières (07)............ 238 E6
Sablonceaux (17)............ 194 D2
Sablonnières (77)............ 60 D3
Sablons (33)............ 212 B5
Sablons (38)............ 222 B2
Sabonnères (31)............ 287 H2
la Sabotterie (08)............ 22 C4
Sabran (30)............ 256 B5
Sabres (40)............ 245 H5
Saccourvielle (31)............ 305 H6
Sacé (53)............ 81 F6
Sacey (50)............ 51 J5
Saché (37)............ 127 H6
Sachin (62)............ 5 H6
Sachy (08)............ 23 G4
Saciergues-Saint-Martin (36)...... 165 F4
Saclas (91)............ 86 C4
Saclay (91)............ 58 C5
Saconin-et-Breuil (02)...... 39 H3
Sacoué (65)............ 305 H2
le Sacq (27)............ 56 C3
Sacquenay (21)............ 136 D2
Sacquenville (27)............ 35 H6
Sacy (51)............ 40 E5
Sacy (89)............ 133 J1
Sacy-le-Grand (60)............ 38 B3
Sacy-le-Petit (60)............ 38 B3
Sadeillan (32)............ 286 A3
Sadillac (24)............ 231 H3
Sadirac (33)............ 229 J3
Sadournin (65)............ 286 B4
Sadroc (19)............ 215 J2
Saessolsheim (67)............ 70 D2
Saffais (54)............ 66 C6
Saffloz (39)............ 173 J2

Saffré (44)............ 103 G6
Saffres (21)............ 135 G5
Sagelat (24)............ 232 D2
Sagnat (23)............ 182 B1
Sagnes-et-Goudoulet (07)...... 239 F3
Sagonne (18)............ 150 A6
Sagy (71)............ 172 D3
Sagy (95)............ 58 A1
Sahorre (66)............ 314 B4
Sahune (26)............ 257 J1
Sahurs (76)............ 35 G3
Sai (61)............ 54 C5
Saignes (15)............ 217 H2
Saignes (46)............ 234 B3
Saigneville (80)............ 9 F4
Saignon (84)............ 277 H2
Saiguède (31)............ 287 J1
Sail-les-Bains (42)...... 186 C2
Sail-sous-Couzan (42)...... 204 C3
Sailhan (65)............ 305 F6
Saillac (19)............ 215 K5
Saillac (46)............ 250 D3
Saillagouse (66)............ 313 H5
Saillans (26)............ 241 F4
Saillans (33)............ 212 A6
Saillant (63)............ 204 B6
Saillat-sur-Vienne (87)...... 180 C6
Saillenard (71)............ 172 E1
Sailly (08)............ 23 H5
Sailly (52)............ 92 C3
Sailly (71)............ 171 G4
Sailly (78)............ 57 K1
Sailly-Achâtel (57)............ 66 B2
Sailly-au-Bois (62)............ 10 D5
Sailly-en-Ostrevent (62)...... 11 G3
Sailly-Flibeaucourt (80)...... 9 F4
Sailly-Labourse (62)...... 6 A6
Sailly-Laurette (80)...... 18 D2
Sailly-le-Sec (80)............ 18 D1
Sailly-lez-Cambrai (59)...... 11 J4
Sailly-lez-Lannoy (59)...... 7 F4
Sailly-Saillisel (80)............ 11 G6
Sailly-sur-la-Lys (62)...... 6 B4
Sain-Bel (69)............ 205 J1
Saincaize-Meauce (58)...... 150 D5
Sainghin-en-Mélantois (59)...... 6 E5
Sainghin-en-Weppes (59)...... 6 C5
Sainneville (76)............ 14 C6
Sainpuits (89)............ 132 D3
Sains (35)............ 51 H4
Sains-du-Nord (59)............ 13 H5
Sains-en-Amiénois (80)...... 18 B3
Sains-en-Gohelle (62)...... 6 A6
Sains-lès-Fressin (62)...... 4 E6
Sains-lès-Marquion (62)...... 11 H4
Sains-lès-Pernes (62)...... 5 H6
Sains-Morainvillers (60)...... 18 C4
Sains-Richaumont (02)...... 20 D3
le Saint (56)............ 75 J5
Saint-Abit (64)............ 284 D5
Saint-Abraham (56)............ 101 J3
Saint-Acheul (80)............ 9 K4
Saint-Adjutory (16)............ 197 H2
Saint-Adrien (22)............ 48 C6
Saint-Affrique (12)............ 272 B2
Saint-Affrique-les-Montagnes (81)...... 289 K1
Saint-Agathon (22)............ 48 D5
Saint-Agnan (02)............ 61 G1
Saint-Agnan (58)............ 134 B5
Saint-Agnan (71)............ 169 K4
Saint-Agnan (81)............ 269 K5
Saint-Agnan (89)............ 88 B5
Saint-Agnan-de-Cernières (27)...... 55 H3
Saint-Agnan-en-Vercors (26)...... 223 H6
Saint-Agnan-le-Malherbe (14)...... 32 C6
Saint-Agnan-sur-Erre (61)...... 83 K4
Saint-Agnan-sur-Sarthe (61)...... 55 G6
Saint-Agnant (17)............ 177 F6
Saint-Agnant-de-Versillat (23)...... 181 K1
Saint-Agnant-près-Crocq (23)...... 201 F2
Saint-Agne (24)............ 231 K2
Saint-Agnet (40)............ 265 J6
Saint-Agoulin (63)............ 185 F4
Saint-Agrève (07)............ 221 H6
Saint-Aignan (08)............ 22 E5
Saint-Aignan (33)............ 212 A6
Saint-Aignan (41)............ 129 F6
Saint-Aignan (56)............ 76 D4
Saint-Aignan (72)............ 83 F5
Saint-Aignan (82)............ 268 D1
Saint-Aignan-de-Couptrain (53)...... 81 K2
Saint-Aignan-de-Cramesnil (14)...... 33 F6
Saint-Aignan-des-Gués (45)...... 110 E5
Saint-Aignan-des-Noyers (18)...... 167 K1
Saint-Aignan-Grandlieu (44)...... 123 F5
Saint-Aignan-le-Jaillard (45)...... 111 F6
Saint-Aignan-sur-Roë (53)...... 104 B4
Saint-Aignan-sur-Ry (76)...... 36 A1
Saint-Aigny (36)............ 164 C2
Saint-Aigulin (17)............ 212 D4
Saint-Ail (54)............ 44 D4
Saint-Albain (71)............ 171 K5
Saint-Alban (01)............ 189 J3
Saint-Alban (22)............ 49 J3
Saint-Alban (31)............ 269 G5
Saint-Alban-Auriolles (07)...... 255 J1
Saint-Alban-d'Ay (07)...... 221 K3
Saint-Alban-de-Montbel (73)...... 208 A4
Saint-Alban-de-Roche (38)...... 206 E4
Saint-Alban-des-Hurtières (73)...... 209 F5

Saint-Alban-des-Villards (73)...... 225 F1
Saint-Alban-du-Rhône (38)...... 206 A6
Saint-Alban-en-Montagne (07)...... 238 C4
Saint-Alban-les-Eaux (42)...... 186 D5
Saint-Alban-Leysse (73)...... 208 C4
Saint-Albin-de-Vaulserre (38)...... 207 K5
Saint-Alexandre (30)............ 256 C4
Saint-Algis (02)............ 20 E2
Saint-Allouestre (56)...... 101 G2
Saint-Alpinien (23)............ 183 G5
Saint-Alyre-d'Arlanc (63)...... 219 K1
Saint-Alyre-ès-Montagne (63)...... 218 D1
Saint-Amadou (09)............ 307 K1
Saint-Amancet (81)............ 289 J2
Saint-Amand (23)............ 183 G5
Saint-Amand (50)............ 31 J4
Saint-Amand (62)............ 10 C4
Saint-Amand-de-Belvès (24)...... 232 D3
Saint-Amand-de-Coly (24)...... 215 F5
Saint-Amand-de-Vergt (24)...... 214 A6
Saint-Amand-des-
Hautes-Terres (27)...... 35 G4
Saint-Amand-en-Puisaye (58)...... 132 B3
Saint-Amand-Jartoudeix (23)...... 182 B6
Saint-Amand-le-Petit (87)...... 200 A4
Saint-Amand-les-Eaux (59)...... 7 H6
Saint-Amand-Longpré (41)...... 128 B1
Saint-Amand-Magnazeix (87)...... 181 J3
Saint-Amand-Montrond (18)...... 167 G2
Saint-Amand-sur-Fion (51)...... 63 F4
Saint-Amand-sur-Ornain (55)...... 64 D6
Saint-Amand-sur-Sèvre (79)...... 143 F5
Saint-Amandin (15)............ 218 A2
Saint-Amans (09)............ 288 C6
Saint-Amans (11)............ 289 G5
Saint-Amans (48)............ 237 H4
Saint-Amans-de-Pellagal (82)...... 249 G4
Saint-Amans-des-Cots (12)...... 235 K4
Saint-Amans-du-Pech (82)...... 248 E3
Saint-Amans-Soult (81)...... 290 C2
Saint-Amans-Valtoret (81)...... 290 C2
Saint-Amant (16)............ 212 E1
Saint-Amant-de-Boixe (16)...... 196 E1
Saint-Amant-de-Bonnieure (16)...... 197 F1
Saint-Amant-de-Nouère (16)...... 196 C2
Saint-Amant-Roche-Savine (63)...... 203 J4
Saint-Amant-Tallende (63)...... 202 D3
Saint-Amarin (68)............ 119 K3
Saint-Ambreuil (71)............ 171 K2
Saint-Ambroix (18)............ 148 D5
Saint-Ambroix (30)............ 255 H4
Saint-Amé (88)............ 119 F1
Saint-Amour (39)............ 172 E5
Saint-Amour-Bellevue (71)...... 188 B1
Saint-Andelain (58)............ 132 A6
Saint-Andéol (26)............ 241 G2
Saint-Andéol (38)............ 223 J6
Saint-Andéol-de-Berg (07)...... 239 J6
Saint-Andéol-de-Clerguemort (48)...... 255 F3
Saint-Andéol-de-Fourchades (07)...... 239 G2
Saint-Andéol-de-Vals (07)...... 239 H4
Saint-Andéol-le-Château (69)...... 205 K4
Saint-Andeux (21)............ 134 B4
Saint-Andiol (13)............ 276 C3
Saint-André (06)............ 281 G3
Saint-André (31)............ 287 F5
Saint-André (32)............ 287 F1
Saint-André (66)............ 315 H4
Saint-André (73)............ 225 K2
Saint-André (81)............ 271 H2
Saint-André-Capcèze (48)...... 255 F2
Saint-André-d'Allas (24)...... 232 E2
Saint-André-d'Apchon (42)...... 186 D4
Saint-André-de-Bâgé (01)...... 188 D1
Saint-André-de-Boëge (74)...... 191 H2
Saint-André-de-Bohon (50)...... 31 F2
Saint-André-de-Briouze (61)...... 53 K5
Saint-André-de-Buèges (34)...... 273 K3
Saint-André-de-Chalencon (43)...... 220 D2
Saint-André-de-Corcy (01)...... 188 D5
Saint-André-de-Cruzières (07)...... 255 J3
Saint-André-de-Cubzac (33)...... 211 J4
Saint-André-de-Double (24)...... 213 G4
Saint-André-de-la-Marche (49)...... 142 D2
Saint-André-de-Lancize (48)...... 254 E4
Saint-André-de-l'Épine (50)...... 31 J3
Saint-André-de-l'Eure (27)...... 56 E3
Saint-André-de-Lidon (17)...... 195 F4
Saint-André-de-Majencoules (30)...... 273 K1
Saint-André-de-Messei (61)...... 53 H5
Saint-André-de-Najac (12)...... 251 G5
Saint-André-de-Roquelongue (11)...... 310 B1
Saint-André-de-Roquepertuis (30)...... 256 A4
Saint-André-de-Rosans (05)...... 258 B2
Saint-André-de-Sangonis (34)...... 273 H6
Saint-André-de-Seignanx (40)...... 262 C4
Saint-André-de-Valborgne (30)...... 254 C5
Saint-André-de-Vézines (12)...... 253 J5
Saint-André-d'Embrun (05)...... 243 K4
Saint-André-des-Eaux (22)...... 78 D1
Saint-André-des-Eaux (44)...... 121 K4
Saint-André-d'Hébertot (14)...... 34 A3
Saint-André-d'Huiriat (01)...... 188 D2
Saint-André-d'Olérargues (30)...... 256 B5
Saint-André-du-Bois (33)...... 230 B5
Saint-André-en-Barrois (55)...... 64 B1
Saint-André-en-Bresse (71)...... 172 B2
Saint-André-en-Morvan (58)...... 133 J4
Saint-André-en-Royans (38)...... 223 G4
Saint-André-en-Terre-Plaine (89)...... 134 B3
Saint-André-en-Vivarais (07)...... 221 H4

Saint-André-et-Appelles (33) 230 E2
Saint-André-Farivillers (60) 18 A6
Saint-André-Goule-d'Oie (85) 142 B5
Saint-André-la-Côte (69) 205 J3
Saint-André-Lachamp (07) 239 F6
Saint-André-le-Bouchoux (01) 188 E3
Saint-André-le-Coq (63) 185 H5
Saint-André-le-Désert (71) 171 G4
Saint-André-le-Gaz (38) 207 H4
Saint-André-le-Puy (42) 205 F3
Saint-André-les-Alpes (04) 279 J1
Saint-André-les-Vergers (10) 90 A5
Saint-André-lez-Lille (59) 6 D4
Saint-André-sur-Cailly (76) 16 E3
Saint-André-sur-Orne (14) 32 E5
Saint-André-sur-Sèvre (79) 143 G6
Saint-André-sur-Vieux-Jonc (01) . . 189 F5
Saint-André-Treize-Voies (85) 141 K4
Saint-Androny (33) 211 G3
Saint-Ange-et-Torçay (28) 56 D6
Saint-Ange-le-Viel (77) 87 K5
Saint-Angeau (16) 197 F1
Saint-Angel (03) 167 J6
Saint-Angel (19) 200 E5
Saint-Angel (63) 184 D5
Saint-Anthème (63) 204 B5
Saint-Anthot (21) 135 G5
Saint-Antoine (15) 235 G3
Saint-Antoine (25) 157 F6
Saint-Antoine (32) 268 A1
Saint-Antoine (38) 211 J5
Saint-Antoine-Cumond (24) 213 F2
Saint-Antoine-d'Auberoche (24) . . . 214 C4
Saint-Antoine-de-Breuilh (24) 230 E2
Saint-Antoine-de-Ficalba (47) 248 C3
Saint-Antoine-du-Queyret (33) . . . 230 D3
Saint-Antoine-du-Rocher (37) 127 H3
Saint-Antoine-la-Forêt (76) 14 E6
Saint-Antoine-l'Abbaye (38) 223 F4
Saint-Antoine-sur-l'Isle (33) 212 D5
Saint-Antonin (06) 280 D1
Saint-Antonin (32) 268 A5
Saint-Antonin-de-Lacalm (81) 271 F4
Saint-Antonin-de-Sommaire (27) . . 55 J4
Saint-Antonin-du-Var (83) 298 D1
Saint-Antonin-Noble-Val (82) 250 D5
Saint-Antonin-sur-Bayon (13) 296 E1
Saint-Aoustrille (36) 148 C5
Saint-Août (36) 166 B1
Saint-Apollinaire (05) 243 H5
Saint-Apollinaire (21) 136 B5
Saint-Apollinaire-de-Rias (07) 239 K1
Saint-Appolinaire (69) 187 J5
Saint-Appolinard (38) 223 F3
Saint-Appolinard (42) 221 K1
Saint-Aquilin (24) 213 J3
Saint-Aquilin-de-Corbion (61) 55 H6
Saint-Aquilin-de-Pacy (27) 57 F1
Saint-Araille (31) 287 H4
Saint-Arailles (32) 267 F6
Saint-Arcons-d'Allier (43) 219 J5
Saint-Arcons-de-Barges (43) 238 C2
Saint-Arey (38) 242 B1
Saint-Armel (35) 79 G5
Saint-Armel (56) 101 F6
Saint-Armou (64) 284 D3
Saint-Arnac (66) 309 H5
Saint-Arnoult (14) 33 J3
Saint-Arnoult (41) 108 A6
Saint-Arnoult (60) 17 G5
Saint-Arnoult (76) 15 F6
Saint-Arnoult-des-Bois (28) 84 E2
Saint-Arnoult-en-Yvelines (78) 86 A1
Saint-Arroman (32) 286 C2
Saint-Arroman (65) 305 F2
Saint-Arroumex (82) 268 C1
Saint-Astier (24) 213 J4
Saint-Astier (47) 231 F3
Saint-Auban (06) 280 B2
Saint-Auban-d'Oze (05) 242 C6
Saint-Auban-sur-l'Ouvèze (26) . . . 258 A3
Saint-Aubert (59) 12 C4
Saint-Aubert-sur-Orne (61) 53 K4
Saint-Aubin (02) 39 H1
Saint-Aubin (10) 89 F2
Saint-Aubin (21) 153 J4
Saint-Aubin (36) 148 D6
Saint-Aubin (39) 155 F3
Saint-Aubin (40) 264 E4
Saint-Aubin (47) 248 E1
Saint-Aubin (59) 13 G4
Saint-Aubin (62) 4 B6
Saint-Aubin (91) 58 C5
Saint-Aubin-Celloville (76) 35 J3
Saint-Aubin-Château-Neuf (89) . . . 112 D5
Saint-Aubin-d'Appenai (61) 83 F1
Saint-Aubin-d'Arquenay (14) 33 F4
Saint-Aubin-d'Aubigné (35) 79 G2
Saint-Aubin-de-Blaye (33) 211 H2
Saint-Aubin-de-Bonneval (61) 55 G2
Saint-Aubin-de-Branne (33) 230 B2
Saint-Aubin-de-Cadelech (24) 231 H4
Saint-Aubin-de-Courteraie (61) . . . 55 G6
Saint-Aubin-de-Crétot (76) 15 F6
Saint-Aubin-de-Lanquais (24) 231 J3
Saint-Aubin-de-Locquenay (72) . . . 82 C5
Saint-Aubin-de-Luigné (49) 125 F5
Saint-Aubin-de-Médoc (33) 229 F1
Saint-Aubin-de-Nabirat (24) 233 F4
Saint-Aubin-de-Scellon (27) 34 C5
Saint-Aubin-de-Terregatte (50) . . . 52 A6
Saint-Aubin-d'Écrosville (27) 35 G5

Saint-Aubin-des-Bois (14) 52 C3
Saint-Aubin-des-Bois (28) 85 F2
Saint-Aubin-des-Châteaux (44) . . . 103 H3
Saint-Aubin-des-Chaumes (58) . . . 133 H4
Saint-Aubin-des-Coudrais (72) 83 H6
Saint-Aubin-des-Grois (61) 83 J4
Saint-Aubin-des-Hayes (27) 55 J1
Saint-Aubin-des-Landes (35) 79 K4
Saint-Aubin-des-Ormeaux (85) . . . 142 D3
Saint-Aubin-des-Préaux (50) 51 J1
Saint-Aubin-du-Cormier (35) 79 J2
Saint-Aubin-du-Désert (53) 82 A4
Saint-Aubin-du-Pavail (35) 79 J5
Saint-Aubin-du-Perron (50) 30 E3
Saint-Aubin-du-Plain (79) 143 J4
Saint-Aubin-du-Thenney (27) 55 H1
Saint-Aubin-en-Bray (60) 37 F2
Saint-Aubin-en-Charollais (71) . . . 170 D4
Saint-Aubin-Épinay (76) 35 J2
Saint-Aubin-Fosse-Louvain (53) . . . 80 E2
Saint-Aubin-la-Plaine (85) 160 B4
Saint-Aubin-le-Cauf (76) 16 A4
Saint-Aubin-le-Cloud (79) 161 J2
Saint-Aubin-le-Dépeint (37) 127 F1
Saint-Aubin-le-Guichard (27) 55 J1
Saint-Aubin-le-Monial (03) 168 B4
Saint-Aubin-le-Vertueux (27) 55 J1
Saint-Aubin-lès-Elbeuf (76) 35 H3
Saint-Aubin-les-Forges (58) 150 E2
Saint-Aubin-Montenoy (80) 17 J2
Saint-Aubin-Rivière (80) 17 G2
Saint-Aubin-Routot (76) 14 C6
Saint-Aubin-sous-Erquery (60) 38 A2
Saint-Aubin-sur-Aire (55) 64 D5
Saint-Aubin-sur-Gaillon (27) 36 A5
Saint-Aubin-sur-Loire (71) 169 J3
Saint-Aubin-sur-Mer (14) 32 E3
Saint-Aubin-sur-Mer (76) 15 H2
Saint-Aubin-sur-Quillebeuf (27) . . . 34 C1
Saint-Aubin-sur-Scie (76) 15 K2
Saint-Aubin-sur-Yonne (89) 112 E3
Saint-Augustin (17) 194 B3
Saint-Augustin (19) 200 B6
Saint-Augustin (77) 60 B4
Saint-Augustin-des-Bois (49) 124 E3
Saint-Aulaire (19) 215 G3
Saint-Aulais-la-Chapelle (16) 196 C6
Saint-Aulaye (24) 212 E3
Saint-Aunès (34) 274 C6
Saint-Aunix-Lengros (32) 266 C6
Saint-Aupre (38) 207 K6
Saint-Austremoine (43) 219 G4
Saint-Auvent (87) 198 C1
Saint-Avaugourd-des-Landes (85) . . 159 H4
Saint-Avé (56) 101 F5
Saint-Aventin (31) 305 H5
Saint-Avertin (37) 127 J3
Saint-Avit (16) 212 D3
Saint-Avit (26) 222 D3
Saint-Avit (40) 265 H4
Saint-Avit (41) 108 B1
Saint-Avit (47) 231 F5
Saint-Avit (63) 201 H1
Saint-Avit (81) 289 J2
Saint-Avit-de-Soulège (33) 230 E2
Saint-Avit-de-Tardes (23) 183 H6
Saint-Avit-de-Vialard (24) 232 B1
Saint-Avit-Frandat (32) 267 J1
Saint-Avit-le-Pauvre (23) 183 F5
Saint-Avit-les-Guespières (28) 84 E5
Saint-Avit-Rivière (24) 232 C3
Saint-Avit-Saint-Nazaire (33) 231 F1
Saint-Avit-Sénieur (24) 232 B3
Saint-Avold (57) 68 A3
Saint-Avre (73) 225 G1
Saint-Ay (45) 109 J4
Saint-Aybert (59) 7 K6
Saint-Babel (63) 203 F4
Saint-Baldoph (73) 208 C4
Saint-Bandry (02) 39 H3
Saint-Baraing (39) 155 G3
Saint-Barbant (87) 180 D3
Saint-Bard (23) 183 J6
Saint-Bardoux (26) 222 D4
Saint-Barnabé (22) 77 G5
Saint-Barthélemy (38) 222 E1
Saint-Barthélemy (40) 282 D1
Saint-Barthélemy (50) 52 D5
Saint-Barthélemy (56) 100 D2
Saint-Barthélemy (70) 119 F5
Saint-Barthélemy (77) 60 E4
Saint-Barthélemy-d'Agenais (47) . . 231 G6
Saint-Barthélemy-d'Anjou (49) . . . 125 H3
Saint-Barthélemy-de-
   Bellegarde (24) 213 F5
Saint-Barthélemy-de-Bussière (24) . 198 A4
Saint-Barthélemy-de-
   Séchilienne (38) 224 B5
Saint-Barthélemy-de-Vals (26) . . . 222 C3
Saint-Barthélemy-Grozon (07) . . . 221 K6
Saint-Barthélemy-le-Meil (07) 239 J1
Saint-Barthélemy-le-Plain (07) . . . 222 B5
Saint-Barthélemy-Lestra (42) 205 F2
Saint-Basile (07) 221 K6
Saint-Baslemont (88) 93 H6
Saint-Baudel (18) 148 E6
Saint-Baudelle (53) 81 G4
Saint-Baudille-de-la-Tour (38) 207 F1
Saint-Baudille-et-Pipet (38) 242 B2
Saint-Bauld (37) 146 B1
Saint-Baussant (54) 65 H2
Saint-Bauzeil (09) 307 H1

Saint-Bauzély (30) 275 F2
Saint-Bauzile (07) 240 A4
Saint-Bauzile (48) 254 B1
Saint-Bauzille-de-la-Sylve (34) . . . 273 J6
Saint-Bauzille-de-Montmel (34) . . . 274 C4
Saint-Bauzille-de-Putois (34) 274 A3
Saint-Bazile (87) 198 A2
Saint-Bazile-de-la-Roche (19) 216 C4
Saint-Bazile-de-Meyssac (19) 216 A5
Saint-Béat (31) 305 J3
Saint-Beaulize (12) 272 E3
Saint-Beauzeil (82) 248 E3
Saint-Beauzély (12) 253 F5
Saint-Beauzile (81) 270 A1
Saint-Beauzire (43) 219 F2
Saint-Beauzire (63) 202 E1
Saint-Bénézet (30) 274 E1
Saint-Bénigne (01) 172 A5
Saint-Benin (59) 12 D5
Saint-Benin-d'Azy (58) 151 G4
Saint-Benin-des-Bois (58) 151 G2
Saint-Benoist-sur-Mer (85) 159 H5
Saint-Benoist-sur-Vanne (10) 89 H5
Saint-Benoît (01) 207 J2
Saint-Benoît (04) 260 E6
Saint-Benoît (11) 308 D2
Saint-Benoît (86) 163 F3
Saint-Benoît-de-Carmaux (81) . . . 270 D1
Saint-Benoît-des-Ombres (27) 34 D4
Saint-Benoît-des-Ondes (35) 50 E3
Saint-Benoît-d'Hébertot (14) 34 A3
Saint-Benoît-du-Sault (36) 165 F5
Saint-Benoît-en-Diois (26) 241 G4
Saint-Benoît-la-Chipotte (88) 95 G3
Saint-Benoît-la-Forêt (37) 145 G1
Saint-Benoît-sur-Loire (45) 110 E5
Saint-Benoît-sur-Seine (10) 90 A4
Saint-Bérain (43) 219 K5
Saint-Berain-sous-Sanvignes (71) . 170 D2
Saint-Bérain-sur-Dheune (71) 153 J6
Saint-Bernard (01) 188 B5
Saint-Bernard (21) 154 C1
Saint-Bernard (38) 224 C1
Saint-Bernard (68) 97 B3
Saint-Béron (73) 207 K5
Saint-Berthevin (53) 104 E1
Saint-Berthevin-la-Tannière (53) . . . 80 D3
Saint-Bertrand-de-
   Comminges (31) 305 H2
Saint-Biez-en-Belin (72) 106 E5
Saint-Bihy (22) 76 E2
Saint-Blaise (06) 281 G2
Saint-Blaise (74) 190 E3
Saint-Blaise-du-Buis (38) 223 J1
Saint-Blaise-la-Roche (67) 70 A6
Saint-Blancard (32) 286 D4
Saint-Blimont (80) 8 D5
Saint-Blin (52) 92 D5
Saint-Boès (64) 283 J1
Saint-Bohaire (41) 128 E1
Saint-Boil (71) 171 H2
Saint-Boingt (54) 94 D2
Saint-Bois (01) 207 J2
Saint-Bomer (28) 84 A6
Saint-Bômer-les-Forges (61) 53 G6
Saint-Bon (51) 61 F6
Saint-Bon-Tarentaise (73) 209 J5
Saint-Bonnet (16) 196 B5
Saint-Bonnet-Avalouze (19) 216 B3
Saint-Bonnet-Briance (87) 199 H3
Saint-Bonnet-de-Bellac (87) 180 E3
Saint-Bonnet-de-Chavagne (38) . . . 223 F4
Saint-Bonnet-de-Chirac (48) 237 G6
Saint-Bonnet-de-Condat (15) 218 B2
Saint-Bonnet-de-Cray (71) 187 F2
Saint-Bonnet-de-Four (03) 184 D1
Saint-Bonnet-de-Joux (71) 171 F4
Saint-Bonnet-de-Montauroux (48) . 238 A2
Saint-Bonnet-de-Mure (69) 206 C3
Saint-Bonnet-de-Rochefort (03) . . 185 F3
Saint-Bonnet-de-Salendrinque (30) . 274 B1
Saint-Bonnet-de-Salers (15) 217 H4
Saint-Bonnet-de-Valclérieux (26) . . 222 E3
Saint-Bonnet-de-Vieille-Vigne (71) . 170 D4
Saint-Bonnet-des-Bruyères (69) . . 187 J1
Saint-Bonnet-des-Quarts (42) 186 C3
Saint-Bonnet-du-Gard (30) 275 J2
Saint-Bonnet-Elvert (19) 216 C4
Saint-Bonnet-en-Bresse (71) 154 D5
Saint-Bonnet-en-Champsaur (05) . 242 E3
Saint-Bonnet-la-Rivière (19) 215 G2
Saint-Bonnet-le-Bourg (63) 203 J6
Saint-Bonnet-le-Chastel (63) 203 J6
Saint-Bonnet-le-Château (42) 204 D6
Saint-Bonnet-le-Courreau (42) . . . 204 B3
Saint-Bonnet-le-Froid (43) 221 H4
Saint-Bonnet-le-Troncy (69) 187 J4
Saint-Bonnet-l'Enfantier (19) 215 J2
Saint-Bonnet-lès-Allier (63) 202 E2
Saint-Bonnet-les-Oules (42) 205 F5
Saint-Bonnet-les-
   Tours-de-Merle (19) 216 D5
Saint-Bonnet-près-Bort (19) 201 G5
Saint-Bonnet-près-Orcival (63) . . . 202 B3
Saint-Bonnet-près-Riom (63) 185 F6
Saint-Bonnet-sur-Gironde (17) . . . 211 G1
Saint-Bonnet-Tronçais (03) 167 J2
Saint-Bonnot (58) 151 F1
Saint-Bouize (18) 131 K6
Saint-Brancher (89) 134 A4
Saint-Branchs (37) 146 B1
Saint-Brandan (22) 77 F2

Saint-Brès (30) 255 H3
Saint-Brès (32) 267 K4
Saint-Brès (34) 274 D5
Saint-Bresson (30) 273 K2
Saint-Bresson (70) 118 D3
Saint-Bressou (46) 234 D4
Saint-Brevin-les-Pins (44) 122 B3
Saint-Briac-sur-Mer (35) 50 C1
Saint-Brice (16) 195 K3
Saint-Brice (33) 230 B4
Saint-Brice (50) 52 A5
Saint-Brice (53) 105 H4
Saint-Brice (61) 81 G1
Saint-Brice (77) 88 D1
Saint-Brice-Courcelles (51) 40 E4
Saint-Brice-de-Landelles (50) 80 B1
Saint-Brice-en-Coglès (35) 51 K6
Saint-Brice-sous-Forêt (95) 58 E2
Saint-Brice-sous-Rânes (61) 54 A5
Saint-Brice-sur-Vienne (87) 180 E6
Saint-Brieuc (22) 49 G6
Saint-Brieuc-de-Mauron (56) 77 K6
Saint-Brieuc-des-Iffs (35) 78 E2
Saint-Bris-des-Bois (17) 195 H2
Saint-Bris-le-Vineux (89) 113 G5
Saint-Brisson (58) 134 B6
Saint-Brisson-sur-Loire (45) 131 H1
Saint-Broing (21) 137 G3
Saint-Broing-les-Moines (21) 115 J6
Saint-Broing-le-Bois (52) 116 E6
Saint-Broing-les-Fosses (52) 116 C6
Saint-Broladre (35) 51 G4
Saint-Bueil (38) 207 K5
Saint-Calais (72) 107 K4
Saint-Calais-du-Désert (53) 81 K2
Saint-Calez-en-Saosnois (72) 83 F4
Saint-Cannat (13) 277 G6
Saint-Caprais (03) 167 J4
Saint-Caprais (18) 149 F4
Saint-Caprais (32) 268 A6
Saint-Caprais (46) 232 E5
Saint-Caprais-de-Blaye (33) 211 H2
Saint-Caprais-de-Bordeaux (33) . . 229 J3
Saint-Caprais-de-Lerm (47) 248 C4
Saint-Capraise-de-Lalinde (24) . . . 231 K2
Saint-Capraise-d'Eymet (24) 231 H4
Saint-Caradec (22) 77 F4
Saint-Caradec-Trégomel (56) 76 A4
Saint-Carné (22) 50 C6
Saint-Carreuc (22) 77 G2
Saint-Cassien (24) 232 B4
Saint-Cassien (38) 223 J1
Saint-Cassin (73) 208 B4
Saint-Cast-le-Guildo (22) 50 B3
Saint-Castin (64) 284 D3
Saint-Célerin (72) 107 G1
Saint-Céneré (53) 105 G1
Saint-Cénéri-le-Gérei (61) 82 B3
Saint-Céols (18) 149 J1
Saint-Céré (46) 234 C2
Saint-Cergues (74) 191 H1
Saint-Cernin (15) 217 H5
Saint-Cernin (46) 233 J5
Saint-Cernin-de-Labarde (24) 231 J3
Saint-Cernin-de-Larche (19) 215 H5
Saint-Cernin-de-l'Herm (24) 232 C5
Saint-Césaire (17) 195 H2
Saint-Césaire-de-Gauzignan (30) . . 275 F1
Saint-Cézaire-sur-Siagne (06) 280 C5
Saint-Cézert (31) 268 E4
Saint-Chabrais (23) 183 G3
Saint-Chaffrey (05) 225 K6
Saint-Chamant (15) 217 H5
Saint-Chamant (19) 216 C4
Saint-Chamarand (46) 233 H4
Saint-Chamas (13) 295 J3
Saint-Chamassy (24) 232 C2
Saint-Chamond (42) 205 H5
Saint-Champ (01) 207 K1
Saint-Chaptes (30) 275 F1
Saint-Charles-de-Percy (14) 53 F2
Saint-Charles-la-Forêt (53) 105 G3
Saint-Chartier (36) 166 B2
Saint-Chef (38) 207 F3
Saint-Chels (46) 234 B6
Saint-Chély-d'Apcher (48) 237 G3
Saint-Chély-d'Aubrac (12) 236 C5
Saint-Chéron (51) 63 F6
Saint-Chéron (91) 86 C1
Saint-Chinian (34) 291 H3
Saint-Christ-Briost (80) 19 G2
Saint-Christaud (31) 287 J6
Saint-Christaud (32) 285 K1
Saint-Christo-en-Jarez (42) 205 H5
Saint-Christol (07) 239 H2
Saint-Christol (34) 274 E5
Saint-Christol (84) 258 B6
Saint-Christol-de-Rodières (30) . . . 256 D3
Saint-Christol-lès-Alès (30) 255 H5
Saint-Christoly-de-Blaye (33) 211 H4
Saint-Christoly-Médoc (33) 210 E1
Saint-Christophe (03) 186 A3
Saint-Christophe (16) 180 D5
Saint-Christophe (17) 177 F2
Saint-Christophe (23) 182 D4
Saint-Christophe (28) 109 F1
Saint-Christophe (69) 187 K1
Saint-Christophe (73) 208 A5
Saint-Christophe (81) 251 G5
Saint-Christophe (86) 145 G5
Saint-Christophe-à-Berry (02) 39 G2
Saint-Christophe-d'Allier (43) 238 A1

Saint-Christophe-de-Chaulieu (61) . 52 E4
Saint-Christophe-de-Double (33) . . 212 D5
Saint-Christophe-de-Valains (35) . . 79 J1
Saint-Christophe-des-Bardes (33) . 230 B1
Saint-Christophe-des-Bois (35) . . . 80 A5
Saint-Christophe-Dodinicourt (10) . . 90 E3
Saint-Christophe-du-Bois (49) . . . 142 E3
Saint-Christophe-du-Foc (50) 28 B2
Saint-Christophe-du-Jambet (72) . . 82 D5
Saint-Christophe-du-Ligneron (85) . 141 G5
Saint-Christophe-du-Luat (53) 81 H6
Saint-Christophe-en-Bazelle (36) . . 148 A1
Saint-Christophe-en-Boucherie (36) 166 C2
Saint-Christophe-en-Brionnais (71) . 187 F1
Saint-Christophe-
   en-Champagne (72) 106 A3
Saint-Christophe-en-Oisans (38) . . 225 F6
Saint-Christophe-et-le-Laris (26) . . 222 E3
Saint-Christophe-la-Couperie (49) . 124 A3
Saint-Christophe-le-Chaudry (18) . 167 F3
Saint-Christophe-le-Jajolet (61) . . . 54 C5
Saint-Christophe-sur-Avre (27) . . . 56 A5
Saint-Christophe-sur-Condé (27) . . 34 D4
Saint-Christophe-sur-Dolaison (43) . 220 B6
Saint-Christophe-sur-Guiers (38) . . 208 A4
Saint-Christophe-sur-le-Nais (37) . 127 G2
Saint-Christophe-sur-Roc (79) . . . 161 G3
Saint-Christophe-Vallon (12) 251 K1
Saint-Cibard (33) 230 C1
Saint-Cierge-la-Serre (07) 240 A3
Saint-Cierge-sous-le-Cheylard (07) . 239 H1
Saint-Ciergues (52) 116 C4
Saint-Ciers-Champagne (17) 195 K6
Saint-Ciers-d'Abzac (33) 212 A5
Saint-Ciers-de-Canesse (33) 211 G4
Saint-Ciers-du-Taillon (17) 195 G6
Saint-Ciers-sur-Bonnieure (16) . . . 197 F1
Saint-Ciers-sur-Gironde (33) 211 H2
Saint-Cirgue (81) 271 G2
Saint-Cirgues (43) 219 H4
Saint-Cirgues (46) 234 E4
Saint-Cirgues-de-Jordanne (15) . . 217 J6
Saint-Cirgues-de-Malbert (15) . . . 217 H5
Saint-Cirgues-de-Prades (07) 239 G5
Saint-Cirgues-en-Montagne (07) . . 238 E3
Saint-Cirgues-la-Loutre (19) 216 E5
Saint-Cirgues-sur-Couze (63) 202 D5
Saint-Cirice (82) 248 D6
Saint-Cirq (24) 232 C3
Saint-Cirq (82) 250 B5
Saint-Cirq-Lapopie (46) 250 C1
Saint-Cirq-Madelon (46) 233 G3
Saint-Cirq-Souillaguet (46) 233 H4
Saint-Civran (36) 165 F4
Saint-Clair (07) 222 A2
Saint-Clair (46) 233 H4
Saint-Clair (82) 248 E5
Saint-Clair (86) 144 D5
Saint-Clair-d'Arcey (27) 34 D6
Saint-Clair-de-Halouze (61) 53 G5
Saint-Clair-de-la-Tour (38) 207 H4
Saint-Clair-du-Rhône (38) 206 A6
Saint-Clair-sur-Epte (95) 36 D5
Saint-Clair-sur-Galaure (38) 222 E2
Saint-Clair-sur-l'Elle (50) 31 H2
Saint-Clair-sur-les-Monts (76) 15 G5
Saint-Clar (32) 267 K3
Saint-Clar-de-Rivière (31) 287 K2
Saint-Claud (16) 179 K6
Saint-Claude (39) 173 K5
Saint-Claude-de-Diray (41) 129 F2
Saint-Clément (02) 21 H3
Saint-Clément (03) 186 B4
Saint-Clément (07) 221 G6
Saint-Clément (15) 217 K6
Saint-Clément (19) 216 A2
Saint-Clément (30) 274 D3
Saint-Clément (54) 94 E1
Saint-Clément (89) 88 D2
Saint-Clément-à-Arnes (08) 41 J3
Saint-Clément-de-la-Place (49) . . . 124 E2
Saint-Clément-de-Rivière (34) 274 B5
Saint-Clément-de-Valorgue (63) . . 204 B5
Saint-Clément-de-Vers (69) 187 J2
Saint-Clément-des-Baleines (17) . . 158 B5
Saint-Clément-des-Levées (49) . . . 125 A5
Saint-Clément-les-Places (69) 205 G2
Saint-Clément-Rancoudray (50) . . . 52 E5
Saint-Clément-sur-Durance (05) . . 243 K4
Saint-Clément-sur-Guye (71) 171 G4
Saint-Clément-sur-Valsonne (69) . . 187 J6
Saint-Clémentin (79) 143 J4
Saint-Clet (22) 48 D4
Saint-Cloud (92) 58 D4
Saint-Cloud-en-Dunois (28) 109 G2
Saint-Colomb-de-Lauzun (47) 231 H5
Saint-Colomban (44) 141 H3
Saint-Colomban-des-Villards (73) . . 225 F1
Saint-Côme (33) 246 D1
Saint-Côme-de-Fresné (14) 32 C3
Saint-Côme-d'Olt (12) 236 B6
Saint-Côme-du-Mont (50) 29 F6
Saint-Côme-et-Maruéjols (30) 275 F3
Saint-Congard (56) 101 K4
Saint-Connan (22) 76 D1
Saint-Connec (22) 76 E4
Saint-Constant (15) 235 F4
Saint-Contest (14) 32 D4
Saint-Corneille (72) 107 F2
Saint-Cornier-des-Landes (61) 53 F5

393

Saint-Cosme (68). . . . 119 K5
Saint-Cosme-en-Vairais (72). . . 83 G5
Saint-Couat-d'Aude (11). . . . 290 E6
Saint-Couat-du-Razès (11). . . 308 D2
Saint-Coulitz (29). . . . 74 D3
Saint-Coulomb (35). . . . 50 E3
Saint-Coutant (16). . . . 179 K5
Saint-Coutant (79). . . . 178 E2
Saint-Coutant-le-Grand (17). . . 177 H5
Saint-Créac (32). . . . 268 A2
Saint-Créac (65). . . . 304 B1
Saint-Crépin (05). . . . 243 K3
Saint-Crépin (17). . . . 177 H4
Saint-Crépin-aux-Bois (60). . . 39 F2
Saint-Crépin-d'Auberoche (24). . 214 C4
Saint-Crépin-de-Richemont (24). . 197 J6
Saint-Crépin-et-Carlucet (24). . 215 F6
Saint-Crépin-Ibouvillers (60). . 37 G4
Saint-Crespin (76). . . . 15 K3
Saint-Crespin-sur-Moine (49). . 142 C2
Saint-Cricq (32). . . . 268 C5
Saint-Cricq-Chalosse (40). . . 264 E5
Saint-Cricq-du-Gave (40). . . 283 G1
Saint-Cricq-Villeneuve (40). . . 265 J2
Saint-Cybardeaux (16). . . . 196 C2
Saint-Cybranet (24). . . . 232 E3
Saint-Cyprien (19). . . . 215 G3
Saint-Cyprien (24). . . . 232 D2
Saint-Cyprien (42). . . . 204 E5
Saint-Cyprien (46). . . . 249 J3
Saint-Cyprien (66). . . . 315 H3
Saint-Cyprien-sur-Dourdou (12). . 235 H6
Saint-Cyr (07). . . . 222 A2
Saint-Cyr (50). . . . 28 E4
Saint-Cyr (71). . . . 171 K2
Saint-Cyr (86). . . . 163 G1
Saint-Cyr (87). . . . 198 C2
Saint-Cyr-au-Mont-d'Or (69). . 206 A1
Saint-Cyr-de-Favières (42). . . 187 F5
Saint-Cyr-de-Salerne (27). . . 34 D5
Saint-Cyr-de-Valorges (42). . . 187 H6
Saint-Cyr-des-Gâts (85). . . . 160 D3
Saint-Cyr-du-Bailleul (50). . . 80 E1
Saint-Cyr-du-Doret (17). . . . 177 G1
Saint-Cyr-du-Gault (41). . . . 128 B2
Saint-Cyr-du-Ronceray (14). . . 55 F1
Saint-Cyr-en-Arthies (95). . . 57 J1
Saint-Cyr-en-Bourg (49). . . . 144 C1
Saint-Cyr-en-Pail (53). . . . 82 A3
Saint-Cyr-en-Talmondais (85). . 159 J4
Saint-Cyr-en-Val (45). . . . 110 B5
Saint-Cyr-la-Campagne (27). . . 35 H4
Saint-Cyr-la-Lande (79). . . . 144 C3
Saint-Cyr-la-Rivière (91). . . . 86 C4
Saint-Cyr-la-Roche (19). . . . 215 H3
Saint-Cyr-la-Rosière (61). . . 83 J4
Saint-Cyr-le-Chatoux (69). . . 187 K4
Saint-Cyr-le-Gravelais (53). . . 104 C2
Saint-Cyr-l'École (78). . . . 58 B4
Saint-Cyr-les-Champagnes (24). . 215 G1
Saint-Cyr-les-Colons (89). . . 113 H6
Saint-Cyr-les-Vignes (42). . . 205 F3
Saint-Cyr-Montmalin (39). . . 155 J4
Saint-Cyr-sous-Dourdan (91). . 86 B1
Saint-Cyr-sur-le-Rhône (69). . 206 B5
Saint-Cyr-sur-Loire (37). . . . 127 J4
Saint-Cyr-sur-Menthon (01). . 188 D1
Saint-Cyr-sur-Mer (83). . . . 297 G5
Saint-Cyr-sur-Morin (77). . . 60 C3
Saint-Cyran-du-Jambot (36). . 146 E3
Saint-Dalmas-le-Selvage (06). . 261 F2
Saint-Daunès (46). . . . 249 H3
Saint-Denis (11). . . . 289 K4
Saint-Denis (30). . . . 275 J4
Saint-Denis (89). . . . 88 D5
Saint-Denis (93). . . . 58 E2
Saint-Denis-Catus (46). . . . 233 G6
Saint-Denis-Combarnazat (63). . 185 H5
Saint-Denis-d'Aclon (76). . . 15 J2
Saint-Denis-d'Anjou (53). . . 105 H5
Saint-Denis-d'Augerons (27). . 55 G2
Saint-Denis-d'Authou (28). . . 84 B4
Saint-Denis-de-Cabanne (42). . 187 G2
Saint-Denis-de-Gastines (53). . 80 E4
Saint-Denis-de-Jouhet (36). . . 166 A4
Saint-Denis-de-l'Hôtel (45). . . 110 C4
Saint-Denis-de-Mailloc (14). . 34 A6
Saint-Denis-de-Méré (14). . . 53 H3
Saint-Denis-de-Palin (18). . . 149 H5
Saint-Denis-de-Pile (33). . . 212 B6
Saint-Denis-de-Vaux (71). . . 153 J6
Saint-Denis-de-Villenette (61). . 81 H1
Saint-Denis-des-Coudrais (72). . 83 G6
Saint-Denis-des-Monts (27). . . 35 H4
Saint-Denis-des-Murs (87). . . 199 H2
Saint-Denis-des-Puits (28). . . 84 D3
Saint-Denis-d'Oléron (17). . . 176 B4
Saint-Denis-d'Orques (72). . . 105 K2
Saint-Denis-du-Béhélan (27). . 56 B3
Saint-Denis-du-Maine (53). . . 105 H3
Saint-Denis-du-Payré (85). . . 159 K5
Saint-Denis-du-Pin (17). . . . 177 K5
Saint-Denis-en-Bugey (01). . . 189 H5
Saint-Denis-en-Margeride (48). . 237 J3
Saint-Denis-en-Val (45). . . . 110 A4
Saint-Denis-la-Chevasse (85). . 142 A5
Saint-Denis-le-Ferment (27). . 36 D3
Saint-Denis-le-Gast (50). . . . 31 F5
Saint-Denis-le-Thiboult (76). . 36 A2
Saint-Denis-le-Vêtu (50). . . . 30 E5
Saint-Denis-lès-Bourg (01). . . 189 G2
Saint-Denis-lès-Martel (46). . . 233 K1

Saint-Denis-les-Ponts (28). . . 108 E2
Saint-Denis-lès-Rebais (77). . . 60 C4
Saint-Denis-Maisoncelles (14). . 31 K5
Saint-Denis-sur-Coise (42). . . 205 G4
Saint-Denis-sur-Huisne (61). . . 83 H2
Saint-Denis-sur-Loire (41). . . 129 F2
Saint-Denis-sur-Ouanne (89). . 112 C5
Saint-Denis-sur-Sarthon (61). . 82 B2
Saint-Denis-sur-Scie (76). . . 15 K4
Saint-Deniscourt (60). . . . 17 G5
Saint-Denoeux (62). . . . 4
Saint-Denoual (22). . . . 49 K6
Saint-Derrien (29). . . . 46 D4
Saint-Désert (71). . . . 171 H1
Saint-Désir (14). . . . 33 K5
Saint-Désirat (07). . . . 222 B2
Saint-Désiré (03). . . . 167 F4
Saint-Dézéry (30). . . . 275 F1
Saint-Didier (21). . . . 134 C5
Saint-Didier (35). . . . 79 K4
Saint-Didier (39). . . . 173 F1
Saint-Didier (58). . . . 133 G5
Saint-Didier (84). . . . 276 E1
Saint-Didier-au-Mont-d'Or (69). . 206 A1
Saint-Didier-d'Allier (43). . . 220 A6
Saint-Didier-d'Aussiat (01). . . 172 B6
Saint-Didier-de-Bizonnes (38). . 207 H5
Saint-Didier-de-Formans (01). . 188 C5
Saint-Didier-de-la-Tour (38). . 207 H4
Saint-Didier-des-Bois (27). . . 35 H4
Saint-Didier-en-Bresse (71). . . 154 C5
Saint-Didier-en-Brionnais (71). . 170 C6
Saint-Didier-en-Donjon (03). . 169 K6
Saint-Didier-en-Velay (43). . . 221 G2
Saint-Didier-la-Forêt (03). . . 185 H2
Saint-Didier-sous-Aubenas (07). . 239 H5
Saint-Didier-sous-Écouves (61). . 82 C1
Saint-Didier-sous-Riverie (69). . 205 J4
Saint-Didier-sur-Arroux (71). . 152 D6
Saint-Didier-sur-Beaujeu (69). . 187 K3
Saint-Didier-sur-Chalaronne (01). . 188 C4
Saint-Didier-sur-Doulon (43). . 219 J2
Saint-Didier-sur-Rochefort (42). . 204 A2
Saint-Dié (88). . . . 95 J4
Saint-Dier-d'Auvergne (63). . . 203 H3
Saint-Diéry (63). . . . 202 C5
Saint-Dionizy (30). . . . 275 F4
Saint-Disdier (05). . . . 242 C3
Saint-Divy (29). . . . 46 B6
Saint-Dizant-du-Bois (17). . . 195 G6
Saint-Dizant-du-Gua (17). . . 195 F6
Saint-Dizier (52). . . . 63 J6
Saint-Dizier-en-Diois (26). . . 241 J6
Saint-Dizier-la-Tour (23). . . 183 G3
Saint-Dizier-les-Domaines (23). . 182 E1
Saint-Dizier-l'Évêque (90). . . 139 J2
Saint-Dizier-Leyrenne (23). . . 182 B4
Saint-Dolay (56). . . . 102 B5
Saint-Domet (23). . . . 183 H4
Saint-Domineuc (35). . . . 78 E1
Saint-Donan (22). . . . 49 F6
Saint-Donat (63). . . . 201 K6
Saint-Donat-sur-l'Herbasse (26). . 222 D4
Saint-Dos (64). . . . 283 G2
Saint-Doulchard (18). . . . 149 G2
Saint-Drézéry (34). . . . 274 D5
Saint-Dyé-sur-Loire (41). . . 129 G1
Saint-Ebremond-de-Bonfossé (50). . 31 G4
Saint-Edmond (71). . . . 187 G2
Saint-Égrève (38). . . . 224 A2
Saint-Elier (27). . . . 56 B2
Saint-Éliph (28). . . . 84 C3
Saint-Élix (32). . . . 286 E2
Saint-Élix-le-Château (31). . . 287 J5
Saint-Élix-Séglan (31). . . . 287 F6
Saint-Élix-Theux (32). . . . 286 B3
Saint-Ellier-du-Maine (53). . . 80 C1
Saint-Ellier-les-Bois (61). . . 82 B2
Saint-Éloi (01). . . . 189 F5
Saint-Éloi (23). . . . 182 C4
Saint-Éloi (58). . . . 150 E4
Saint-Éloi-de-Fourques (27). . . 35 F4
Saint-Éloy (29). . . . 74 D1
Saint-Éloy-d'Allier (03). . . . 166 E4
Saint-Éloy-de-Gy (18). . . . 149 G2
Saint-Éloy-la-Glacière (63). . . 203 J5
Saint-Éloy-les-Mines (63). . . 184 D4
Saint-Éloy-les-Tuileries (19). . . 199 F6
Saint-Éman (28). . . . 84 D4
Saint-Émiland (71). . . . 153 G5
Saint-Émilion (33). . . . 230 B1
Saint-Ennemond (03). . . . 169 F2
Saint-Épain (37). . . . 145 J2
Saint-Epvre (57). . . . 66 C1
Saint-Erblon (35). . . . 79 G5
Saint-Erblon (53). . . . 104 B5
Saint-Erme-Outre-
et-Ramecourt (02). . . . 40 D1
Saint-Escobille (91). . . . 86 B3
Saint-Esteben (64). . . . 282 E3
Saint-Estèphe (24). . . . 197 K4
Saint-Estèphe (33). . . . 211 F2
Saint-Estève (66). . . . 310 B6
Saint-Estève-Janson (13). . . . 277 H5
Saint-Étienne (42). . . . 205 G6
Saint-Étienne-à-Arnes (08). . . 41 K3
Saint-Étienne-au-Mont (62). . . 2 A6
Saint-Étienne-au-Temple (51). . 62 D1
Saint-Étienne-aux-Clos (19). . . 201 H5
Saint-Étienne-Cantalès (15). . . 235 F1
Saint-Étienne-d'Albagnan (34). . 291 G1
Saint-Étienne-de-Baïgorry (64). . 263 E4

Saint-Étienne-de-Boulogne (07). . 239 J4
Saint-Étienne-de-Brillouet (85). . 160 C3
Saint-Étienne-de-Carlat (15). . 235 J1
Saint-Étienne-de-Chigny (37). . 127 G5
Saint-Étienne-de-Chomeil (15). . 217 K2
Saint-Étienne-de-Crossey (38). . 207 J4
Saint-Étienne-de-Fontbellon (07). . 239 J2
Saint-Étienne-de-Fougères (47). . 248 B2
Saint-Étienne-de-Fursac (23). . 181 K3
Saint-Étienne-de-Gourgas (34). . 273 J2
Saint-Étienne-de-Lisse (33). . . 230 C1
Saint-Étienne-de-l'Olm (30). . . 255 H6
Saint-Étienne-de-Lugdarès (07). . 238 D4
Saint-Étienne-de-Maurs (15). . . 235 F4
Saint-Étienne-de-Mer-Morte (44). . 141 G4
Saint-Étienne-de-Puycorbier (24). . 213 G5
Saint-Étienne-de-Saint-Geoirs (38). . 223 G1
Saint-Étienne-de-Serre (07). . . 239 J2
Saint-Étienne-de-Tinée (06). . . 261 F3
Saint-Étienne-de-Tulmont (82). . 269 H1
Saint-Étienne-de-Valoux (07). . 222 B3
Saint-Étienne-de-Vicq (03). . . 185 K3
Saint-Étienne-de-Villeréal (47). . 232 A5
Saint-Étienne-des-Champs (63). . 201 J1
Saint-Étienne-des-Guérets (41). . 128 J2
Saint-Étienne-des-Oullières (69). . 188 A4
Saint-Étienne-des-Sorts (30). . . 256 D4
Saint-Étienne-d'Orthe (40). . . 262 E6
Saint-Étienne-du-Bois (01). . . 189 G1
Saint-Étienne-du-Bois (85). . . 141 H5
Saint-Étienne-du-Grès (13). . . 276 A4
Saint-Étienne-du-Gué-de-l'Isle (22). . 77 G3
Saint-Étienne-du-Rouvray (76). . 35 H3
Saint-Étienne-du-Valdonnez (48). . 254 B1
Saint-Étienne-du-Vauvray (27). . 35 J4
Saint-Étienne-du-Vigan (43). . . 238 B3
Saint-Étienne-en-Bresse (71). . 172 B1
Saint-Étienne-en-Coglès (35). . 51 K6
Saint-Étienne-en-Dévoluy (05). . 242 C4
Saint-Étienne-Estréchoux (34). . 272 D5
Saint-Étienne-la-Cigogne (79). . 178 A3
Saint-Étienne-la-Geneste (19). . 201 F6
Saint-Étienne-la-Thillaye (14). . 33 J3
Saint-Étienne-la-Varenne (69). . 188 A4
Saint-Étienne-l'Allier (27). . . 34 D5
Saint-Étienne-Lardeyrol (43). . 220 D5
Saint-Étienne-le-Laus (05). . . 243 F6
Saint-Étienne-le-Molard (42). . 204 D2
Saint-Étienne-les-Orgues (04). . 258 E6
Saint-Étienne-lès-Remiremont (88). . 119 F1
Saint-Étienne-Roilaye (60). . . 39 F3
Saint-Étienne-sous-Bailleul (27). . 36 A6
Saint-Étienne-sous-Barbuise (10). . 90 D1
Saint-Étienne-sur-Blesle (43). . 218 E2
Saint-Étienne-sur-Chalaronne (01). . 188 C4
Saint-Étienne-sur-Reyssouze (01). . 172 B5
Saint-Étienne-sur-Suippe (51). . 41 F2
Saint-Étienne-sur-Usson (63). . 203 G5
Saint-Étienne-Vallée-
Française (48). . . . 254 E5
Saint-Eugène (02). . . . 61 F1
Saint-Eugène (17). . . . 195 K5
Saint-Eugène (71). . . . 170 C1
Saint-Eulien (51). . . . 63 H3
Saint-Euphraise-et-Clairizet (51). . 40 D5
Saint-Euphrône (21). . . . 134 E3
Saint-Eusèbe (71). . . . 171 F1
Saint-Eusèbe (74). . . . 190 D5
Saint-Eusèbe-en-Champsaur (05). . 242 E3
Saint-Eustache (74). . . . 208 D1
Saint-Eustache-la-Forêt (76). . . 14 D6
Saint-Eutrope (16). . . . 196 D6
Saint-Eutrope-de-Born (47). . . 231 K5
Saint-Évarzec (29). . . . 98 D2
Saint-Evroult-de-Montfort (61). . 55 F4
Saint-Evroult-Notre-
Dame-du-Bois (61). . . . 55 G4
Saint-Exupéry (33). . . . 230 B5
Saint-Exupéry-les-Roches (19). . 201 H5
Saint-Fargeau (89). . . . 132 B1
Saint-Fargeau-Ponthierry (77). . 87 G2
Saint-Fargeol (03). . . . 184 A3
Saint-Faust (64). . . . 284 C4
Saint-Félicien (07). . . . 221 K5
Saint-Féliu-d'Amont (66). . . 310 A6
Saint-Féliu-d'Avall (66). . . 315 F2
Saint-Félix (03). . . . 185 K2
Saint-Félix (16). . . . 212 D1
Saint-Félix (17). . . . 177 J3
Saint-Félix (46). . . . 234 E5
Saint-Félix (60). . . . 37 J3
Saint-Félix (74). . . . 208 C1
Saint-Félix-de-Bourdeilles (24). . 197 J5
Saint-Félix-de-Foncaude (33). . 230 C4
Saint-Félix-de-l'Héras (34). . . 273 F3
Saint-Félix-de-Lodez (34). . . 273 H5
Saint-Félix-de-Lunel (12). . . 235 J6
Saint-Félix-de-Pallières (30). . . 274 C1
Saint-Félix-de-Reillac-
et-Mortemart (24). . . . 214 C6
Saint-Félix-de-Rieutord (09). . . 307 J2
Saint-Félix-de-Sorgues (12). . . 272 C5
Saint-Félix-de-Tournegat (09). . 307 K1
Saint-Félix-de-Villadeix (24). . . 231 K1
Saint-Félix-Lauragais (31). . . 289 G3
Saint-Fergeux (08). . . . 21 J6
Saint-Ferjeux (70). . . . 138 C2
Saint-Ferme (33). . . . 230 D4
Saint-Ferréol (31). . . . 286 E4
Saint-Ferréol (74). . . . 209 F1

Saint-Ferréol-d'Auroure (43). . . 221 F1
Saint-Ferréol-des-Côtes (63). . 203 K5
Saint-Ferréol-Trente-Pas (26). . 257 J1
Saint-Ferriol (11). . . . 308 E4
Saint-Fiacre (22). . . . 48 D3
Saint-Fiacre (77). . . . 60 A3
Saint-Fiacre-sur-Maine (44). . . 123 H5
Saint-Fiel (23). . . . 182 D2
Saint-Firmin (05). . . . 242 D2
Saint-Firmin (54). . . . 94 A2
Saint-Firmin (58). . . . 151 G3
Saint-Firmin (71). . . . 153 G6
Saint-Firmin-des-Bois (45). . . 111 K3
Saint-Firmin-des-Prés (41). . . 108 C5
Saint-Firmin-sur-Loire (45). . . 131 H4
Saint-Flavy (10). . . . 89 H3
Saint-Florent (2B). . . . 317 D5
Saint-Florent (45). . . . 131 F1
Saint-Florent-des-Bois (85). . . 159 J2
Saint-Florent-sur-Auzonnet (30). . 255 H4
Saint-Florent-sur-Cher (18). . . 149 G4
Saint-Florentin (36). . . . 148 B3
Saint-Florentin (89). . . . 113 H3
Saint-Floret (63). . . . 202 D5
Saint-Floris (62). . . . 5 K4
Saint-Flour (15). . . . 218 D4
Saint-Flour (63). . . . 203 H3
Saint-Flour-de-Mercoire (48). . . 238 B4
Saint-Flovier (37). . . . 146 D4
Saint-Floxel (50). . . . 29 F4
Saint-Folquin (62). . . . 3 F2
Saint-Fons (69). . . . 206 B4
Saint-Forgeot (71). . . . 153 F4
Saint-Forget (78). . . . 58 B5
Saint-Forgeux (69). . . . 205 G1
Saint-Forgeux-Lespinasse (42). . 186 D3
Saint-Fort (53). . . . 105 F4
Saint-Fort-sur-Gironde (17). . . 195 G5
Saint-Fort-sur-le-Né (16). . . . 195 K4
Saint-Fortunat-sur-Eyrieux (07). . 240 A2
Saint-Fraigne (16). . . . 178 E5
Saint-Fraimbault (61). . . . 81 F2
Saint-Fraimbault-de-Prières (53). . 81 G4
Saint-Frajou (31). . . . 287 F4
Saint-Franc (73). . . . 207 K5
Saint-Franchy (58). . . . 151 G2
Saint-François-de-Sales (73). . . 208 C2
Saint-François-Lacroix (57). . . 27 K4
Saint-François-Longchamp (73). . 209 F6
Saint-Frégant (29). . . . 46 B4
Saint-Fréjoux (19). . . . 201 G5
Saint-Frézal-d'Albuges (48). . . 238 B6
Saint-Frézal-de-Ventalon (48). . 254 E4
Saint-Frichoux (11). . . . 290 D5
Saint-Frion (23). . . . 200 E1
Saint-Fromond (50). . . . 31 H2
Saint-Front (16). . . . 179 H2
Saint-Front (43). . . . 220 E6
Saint-Front-d'Alemps (24). . . 214 B2
Saint-Front-de-Pradoux (24). . . 213 G5
Saint-Front-la-Rivière (24). . . 197 K6
Saint-Front-sur-Lémance (47). . 232 C3
Saint-Front-sur-Nizonne (24). . 197 J5
Saint-Froult (17). . . . 176 E5
Saint-Fulgent (85). . . . 142 B5
Saint-Fulgent-des-Ormes (61). . 83 H3
Saint-Fuscien (80). . . . 18 B3
Saint-Gabriel-Brécy (14). . . 32 C3
Saint-Gal (48). . . . 237 H5
Saint-Gal-sur-Sioule (63). . . 184 C3
Saint-Galmier (42). . . . 205 F4
Saint-Gand (70). . . . 137 J2
Saint-Ganton (35). . . . 102 E3
Saint-Gatien-des-Bois (14). . . 33 K3
Saint-Gaudens (31). . . . 305 K1
Saint-Gaudent (86). . . . 179 H3
Saint-Gaudéric (11). . . . 308 A1
Saint-Gaultier (36). . . . 165 F3
Saint-Gauzens (81). . . . 270 B4
Saint-Gein (40). . . . 265 J4
Saint-Gelais (79). . . . 161 H5
Saint-Gelven (22). . . . 76 C2
Saint-Gély-du-Fesc (34). . . 274 B5
Saint-Génard (79). . . . 178 D2
Saint-Gence (87). . . . 181 F6
Saint-Généroux (79). . . . 144 A3
Saint-Genès-Champanelle (63). . 202 C3
Saint-Genès-Champespe (63). . . 218 A1
Saint-Genès-de-Blaye (33). . . 211 G3
Saint-Genès-de-Castillon (33). . 230 C1
Saint-Genès-de-Fronsac (33). . 211 K5
Saint-Genès-de-Lombaud (33). . 229 K3
Saint-Genès-du-Retz (63). . . 185 G4
Saint-Genès-la-Tourette (63). . 203 H5
Saint-Genest (03). . . . 184 A2
Saint-Genest (88). . . . 94 E3
Saint-Genest-d'Ambière (86). . . 145 J3
Saint-Genest-de-Beauzon (07). . 255 H1
Saint-Genest-de-Contest (81). . 270 E4
Saint-Genest-Lachamp (07). . . 239 H2
Saint-Genest-Lerpt (42). . . . 205 F6
Saint-Genest-Malifaux (42). . . 221 H1
Saint-Genest-sur-Roselle (87). . 199 G3
Saint-Geneys-près-
Saint-Paulien (43). . . . 220 B4
Saint-Gengoulph (02). . . . 39 J6
Saint-Gengoux-de-Scissé (71). . 171 H4
Saint-Gengoux-le-National (71). . 171 H3
Saint-Geniès (24). . . . 215 G3
Saint-Geniès-Bellevue (31). . . 269 G5
Saint-Geniès-de-Comolas (30). . 256 D6

Saint-Geniès-de-Fontedit (34). . 291 K2
Saint-Geniès-de-Malgoirès (30). . 275 F2
Saint-Geniès-de-Varensal (34). . 272 C5
Saint-Geniès-des-Mourgues (34). . 274 D5
Saint-Geniez (04). . . . 259 G3
Saint-Geniez-d'Olt (12). . . . 253 F1
Saint-Geniez-ô-Merle (19). . . 216 D5
Saint-Genis (05). . . . 258 D1
Saint-Genis-de-Saintonge (17). . 195 G5
Saint-Génis-des-Fontaines (66). . 315 H3
Saint-Génis-d'Hiersac (16). . . 196 C2
Saint-Genis-du-Bois (33). . . 230 B4
Saint-Genis-l'Argentière (69). . 205 H3
Saint-Genis-Laval (69). . . . 206 A3
Saint-Genis-les-Ollières (69). . 205 H2
Saint-Genis-Pouilly (01). . . 190 E1
Saint-Genis-sur-Menthon (01). . 188 E1
Saint-Genix-sur-Guiers (73). . . 207 J4
Saint-Genou (36). . . . 147 G5
Saint-Genouph (37). . . . 127 H5
Saint-Geoire-en-Valdaine (38). . 207 J5
Saint-Geoirs (38). . . . 223 G1
Saint-Georges (15). . . . 218 H6
Saint-Georges (16). . . . 179 H5
Saint-Georges (32). . . . 268 B5
Saint-Georges (47). . . . 248 K1
Saint-Georges (57). . . . 67 H5
Saint-Georges (62). . . . 9 J2
Saint-Georges (82). . . . 250 C4
Saint-Georges-Antignac (17). . 195 H5
Saint-Georges-Armont (25). . . 139 F4
Saint-Georges-Blancaneix (24). . 231 G1
Saint-Georges-Buttavent (53). . 81 F4
Saint-Georges-d'Annebecq (61). . 53 K6
Saint-Georges-d'Aunay (14). . . 53 G2
Saint-Georges-d'Aurac (43). . . 219 J4
Saint-Georges-de-Baroille (42). . 204 D1
Saint-Georges-de-Bohon (50). . 31 F1
Saint-Georges-de-Chesné (35). . 80 A4
Saint-Georges-de-Commiers (38). . 224 A5
Saint-Georges-de-Didonne (17). . 194 C3
Saint-Georges-de-Gréhaigne (35). . 51 H4
Saint-Georges-de-la-Couée (72). . 107 H5
Saint-Georges-de-la-Rivière (50). . 28 B4
Saint-Georges-de-Lévéjac (48). . 253 J3
Saint-Georges-de-Livoye (50). . 52 B4
Saint-Georges-de-
Longuepierre (17). . . . 178 B4
Saint-Georges-de-Luzençon (12). . 253 F6
Saint-Georges-de-Mons (63). . . 184 C6
Saint-Georges-de-Montaigu (85). . 142 A4
Saint-Georges-de-Montclard (24). . 231 K1
Saint-Georges-de-Noisné (79). . 161 K4
Saint-Georges-de-Pointindoux (85). . 159 G2
Saint-Georges-de-Poisieux (18). . 167 G2
Saint-Georges-de-
Reintembault (35). . . . 80 A1
Saint-Georges-de-Reneins (69). . 188 B4
Saint-Georges-de-Rex (79). . . 177 J1
Saint-Georges-de-Rouelley (50). . 53 F6
Saint-Georges-d'Elle (50). . . 31 J3
Saint-Georges-des-Agoûts (17). . 211 G1
Saint-Georges-des-Coteaux (17). . 195 G2
Saint-Georges-des-Gardes (49). . 143 G1
Saint-Georges-des-
Groseillers (61). . . . 53 H4
Saint-Georges-des-Hurtières (73). . 209 F5
Saint-Georges-des-Sept-Voies (49). . 125 J5
Saint-Georges-d'Espéranche (38). . 206 D4
Saint-Georges-d'Oléron (17). . 176 B4
Saint-Georges-d'Orques (34). . 274 B6
Saint-Georges-du-Bois (17). . . 177 H3
Saint-Georges-du-Bois (49). . . 125 K3
Saint-Georges-du-Bois (72). . . 106 D3
Saint-Georges-du-Mesnil (27). . 34 C4
Saint-Georges-du-Rosay (72). . 83 G6
Saint-Georges-du-Vièvre (27). . 34 D4
Saint-Georges-en-Auge (14). . . 54 D1
Saint-Georges-en-Couzan (42). . 204 B3
Saint-Georges-Haute-Ville (42). . 204 D5
Saint-Georges-la-Pouge (23). . 182 E5
Saint-Georges-Lagricol (43). . . 220 C2
Saint-Georges-le-Fléchard (53). . 105 F2
Saint-Georges-le-Gaultier (72). . 82 B4
Saint-Georges-lès-
Baillargeaux (86). . . . 163 F2
Saint-Georges-les-Bains (07). . 240 B2
Saint-Georges-les-Landes (87). . 164 G6
Saint-Georges-Montcocq (50). . 31 H3
Saint-Georges-Motel (27). . . 57 F4
Saint-Georges-Nigremont (23). . 201 F1
Saint-Georges-sur-Allier (63). . 202 D4
Saint-Georges-sur-Arnon (36). . 148 D4
Saint-Georges-sur-Baulche (89). . 113 F6
Saint-Georges-sur-Cher (41). . 128 C5
Saint-Georges-sur-Erve (53). . 81 K6
Saint-Georges-sur-Eure (28). . 85 F3
Saint-Georges-sur-Fontaine (76). . 16 A6
Saint-Georges-sur-la-Prée (18). . 148 C1
Saint-Georges-sur-l'Aa (59). . . 3 J2
Saint-Georges-sur-Layon (49). . 143 K1
Saint-Georges-sur-Loire (49). . 124 E4
Saint-Georges-sur-Moulon (18). . 149 G1
Saint-Georges-sur-Renon (01). . 188 E3
Saint-Geours-d'Auribat (40). . . 264 D4
Saint-Geours-de-Maremne (40). . 262 D5
Saint-Gérand (56). . . . 76 E5
Saint-Gérand-de-Vaux (03). . . 169 F6
Saint-Gérand-le-Puy (03). . . 185 K2
Saint-Géraud (47). . . . 230 E5
Saint-Géraud-de-Corps (24). . . 213 F6
Saint-Géréon (44). . . . 124 A4

Saint-Germain (07)............239 H6
Saint-Germain (10)............90 A5
Saint-Germain (54)............94 C2
Saint-Germain (70)............118 E5
Saint-Germain (86)............164 A3
Saint-Germain-au-Mont-d'Or (69)...188 C6
Saint-Germain-Beaupré (23)......182 A1
Saint-Germain-Chassenay (58)....169 F1
Saint-Germain-d'Anxure (53)....81 F5
Saint-Germain-d'Arcé (72).....126 E1
Saint-Germain-d'Aunay (61)....55 G2
Saint-Germain-de-Belvès (24)...232 D3
Saint-Germain-de-Calberte (48)..254 E4
Saint-Germain-de-Clairefeuille (61)...54 E5
Saint-Germain-de-Confolens (16)...180 B4
Saint-Germain-de-Coulamer (53)..82 A5
Saint-Germain-de-Fresney (27)...56 E2
Saint-Germain-de-Grave (33)....230 A5
Saint-Germain-de-Joux (01).....190 B2
Saint-Germain-de-la-Coudre (61)...83 H5
Saint-Germain-de-la-Grange (78)..58 A4
Saint-Germain-de-la-Rivière (33)..211 K6
Saint-Germain-de-Livet (14).....33 K6
Saint-Germain-de-Longue-Chaume (79).....161 J1
Saint-Germain-de-Lusignan (17)..195 H6
Saint-Germain-de-Marencennes (17)....177 G3
Saint-Germain-de-Martigny (61)..83 G1
Saint-Germain-de-Modéon (21)...134 B5
Saint-Germain-de-Montbron (16)..197 G4
Saint-Germain-de-Montgommery (14).....54 E2
Saint-Germain-de-Pasquier (27)..35 G4
Saint-Germain-de-Prinçay (85)..160 C1
Saint-Germain-de-Salles (03)...185 G3
Saint-Germain-de-Tallevende-la-Lande-Vaumont (14)......52 E4
Saint-Germain-de-Tournebut (50)..28 E4
Saint-Germain-de-Varreville (50)..29 G5
Saint-Germain-de-Vibrac (17)...195 K6
Saint-Germain-d'Ectot (14).....32 B5
Saint-Germain-d'Elle (50)......31 J3
Saint-Germain-des-Angles (27)...35 J6
Saint-Germain-des-Bois (18)....149 H5
Saint-Germain-des-Bois (58)....133 F5
Saint-Germain-des-Champs (89)..133 K4
Saint-Germain-des-Essourts (76)..16 B6
Saint-Germain-des-Fossés (03)..185 J2
Saint-Germain-des-Grois (61)...84 A3
Saint-Germain-des-Prés (24)....214 D2
Saint-Germain-des-Prés (45)....111 K3
Saint-Germain-des-Prés (49)....124 D4
Saint-Germain-des-Prés (81)....289 J1
Saint-Germain-des-Vaux (50)....28 A1
Saint-Germain-d'Esteuil (33)...210 E2
Saint-Germain-d'Étables (76)...16 A2
Saint-Germain-du-Bel-Air (46)..233 H5
Saint-Germain-du-Bois (71).....172 D1
Saint-Germain-du-Corbéis (61)..82 C3
Saint-Germain-du-Crioult (14)..53 G3
Saint-Germain-du-Pert (14).....29 H6
Saint-Germain-du-Pinel (35)....104 B2
Saint-Germain-du-Plain (71)....172 A1
Saint-Germain-du-Puch (33).....229 K2
Saint-Germain-du-Puy (18).....149 H3
Saint-Germain-du-Salembre (24)..213 H4
Saint-Germain-du-Seudre (17)...195 F5
Saint-Germain-du-Teil (48)....253 H1
Saint-Germain-en-Brionnais (71)..170 D6
Saint-Germain-en-Coglès (35)...80 A3
Saint-Germain-en-Laye (78).....58 C3
Saint-Germain-en-Montagne (39)..156 B6
Saint-Germain-et-Mons (24)....231 J2
Saint-Germain-la-Blanche-Herbe (14)......32 D5
Saint-Germain-la-Campagne (27)..55 G1
Saint-Germain-la-Chambotte (73)..208 B1
Saint-Germain-la-Montagne (42)..187 H2
Saint-Germain-la-Poterie (60)..37 G2
Saint-Germain-la-Ville (51)....62 E3
Saint-Germain-l'Aiguiller (85)..160 D1
Saint-Germain-Langot (14).....53 K2
Saint-Germain-Laprade (43)....220 D5
Saint-Germain-Laval (42)......204 C1
Saint-Germain-Laval (77)......88 A3
Saint-Germain-Lavolps (19)....200 E4
Saint-Germain-Laxis (77)......87 H1
Saint-Germain-le-Châtelet (90)..119 J5
Saint-Germain-le-Fouilloux (53)..80 E6
Saint-Germain-le-Gaillard (28)..84 E3
Saint-Germain-le-Gaillard (50)..28 B4
Saint-Germain-le-Guillaume (53)..80 E5
Saint-Germain-le-Rocheux (21)..115 G6
Saint-Germain-le-Vasson (14)..53 K1
Saint-Germain-le-Vieux (61)...55 F6
Saint-Germain-Lembron (63)....202 E6
Saint-Germain-lès-Arlay (39)...155 H6
Saint-Germain-lès-Arpajon (91)..86 D1
Saint-Germain-lès-Belles (87)..199 H4
Saint-Germain-lès-Buxy (71)...171 J1
Saint-Germain-lès-Corbeil (91)..59 F6
Saint-Germain-lès-Paroisses (01)..207 J1
Saint-Germain-lès-Senailly (21)..134 D2
Saint-Germain-les-Vergnes (19)..215 K2
Saint-Germain-Lespinasse (42)..186 D3
Saint-Germain-l'Herm (63).....203 H6
Saint-Germain-près-Herment (63)..201 H3
Saint-Germain-Source-Seine (21)..135 H3
Saint-Germain-sous-Cailly (76)..16 A6
Saint-Germain-sous-Doue (77)...60 C3
Saint-Germain-sur-Avre (27)....56 E4

Saint-Germain-sur-Ay (50).....30 C1
Saint-Germain-sur-Bresle (80)..17 F3
Saint-Germain-sur-Eaulne (76)..16 D3
Saint-Germain-sur-École (77)...87 G2
Saint-Germain-sur-Ille (35)....79 G2
Saint-Germain-sur-l'Arbresle (69)..205 J1
Saint-Germain-sur-Meuse (55)...65 F5
Saint-Germain-sur-Moine (49)...142 C2
Saint-Germain-sur-Morin (77)...59 K3
Saint-Germain-sur-Renon (01)...188 E3
Saint-Germain-sur-Rhône (74)...190 C3
Saint-Germain-sur-Sarthe (72)..82 D5
Saint-Germain-sur-Vienne (37)..144 E1
Saint-Germain-Village (27).....34 C3
Saint-Germainmont (08)........41 G1
Saint-Germé (32)..............266 A5
Saint-Germer-de-Fly (60)......36 E2
Saint-Germier (31)............288 E2
Saint-Germier (32)............268 B5
Saint-Germier (79)............162 B4
Saint-Germier (81)............270 E5
Saint-Géron (43)..............219 G2
Saint-Gérons (15).............235 F1
Saint-Gervais (30)............256 C4
Saint-Gervais (33)............211 J5
Saint-Gervais (38)............223 J4
Saint-Gervais (85)............140 D4
Saint-Gervais-d'Auvergne (63)..184 C4
Saint-Gervais-de-Vic (72).....107 K4
Saint-Gervais-des-Sablons (61)..54 D3
Saint-Gervais-du-Perron (61)...82 D1
Saint-Gervais-en-Belin (72)...106 E4
Saint-Gervais-en-Vallière (71)..154 B4
Saint-Gervais-les-Bains (74)...192 B5
Saint-Gervais-les-Trois-Clochers (86).....145 H5
Saint-Gervais-sous-Meymont (63)..203 J3
Saint-Gervais-sur-Couches (71)..153 H4
Saint-Gervais-sur-Mare (34)...272 D6
Saint-Gervais-sur-Roubion (26)..240 C5
Saint-Gervasy (30)............275 H3
Saint-Gervazy (63)............219 F1
Saint-Géry (24)...............213 G6
Saint-Géry (46)...............250 B1
Saint-Geyrac (24).............214 C5
Saint-Gibrien (51)............62 C2
Saint-Gildas (22).............76 E1
Saint-Gildas-de-Rhuys (56)....120 C2
Saint-Gildas-des-Bois (44)....102 C6
Saint-Gilles (30).............275 H5
Saint-Gilles (35).............78 E3
Saint-Gilles (36).............165 F4
Saint-Gilles (50).............31 G3
Saint-Gilles (51).............40 B4
Saint-Gilles (71).............153 J5
Saint-Gilles-Croix-de-Vie (85)..158 D1
Saint-Gilles-de-Crétot (76)...15 F6
Saint-Gilles-de-la-Neuville (76)..14 D6
Saint-Gilles-des-Marais (61)...53 F6
Saint-Gilles-du-Mené (22).....77 J3
Saint-Gilles-les-Bois (22)....48 D4
Saint-Gilles-les-Forêts (87)...199 K4
Saint-Gilles-Pligeaux (22)....76 D2
Saint-Gilles-Vieux-Marché (22)..76 E3
Saint-Gineis-en-Coiron (07)...239 J5
Saint-Gingolph (74)...........175 J4
Saint-Girod (73)..............208 C1
Saint-Girons (09).............306 D3
Saint-Girons (64).............264 D6
Saint-Girons-d'Aiguevives (33)..211 H4
Saint-Gladie-Arrive-Munein (64)..283 H3
Saint-Glen (22)...............77 J2
Saint-Goazec (29).............75 G4
Saint-Gobain (02).............20 A5
Saint-Gobert (02).............20 E3
Saint-Goin (64)...............283 K5
Saint-Gondon (45)............131 G1
Saint-Gondran (35)...........78 E2
Saint-Gonlay (35)............78 C4
Saint-Gonnery (56)...........77 F5
Saint-Gor (40)...............246 C6
Saint-Gorgon (56)............102 A4
Saint-Gorgon (88)............95 F3
Saint-Gorgon-Main (25).......156 E3
Saint-Gouéno (22)............77 H3
Saint-Gourgon (41)...........128 B1
Saint-Gourson (16)...........179 H5
Saint-Goussaud (23)..........182 A4
Saint-Gratien (80)...........18 C1
Saint-Gratien (95)...........58 D2
Saint-Gratien-Savigny (58)...151 J5
Saint-Gravé (56).............102 A3
Saint-Grégoire (35)..........79 G4
Saint-Grégoire (81)..........271 F2
Saint-Grégoire-d'Ardennes (17)..195 H5
Saint-Grégoire-du-Vièvre (27)..34 D4
Saint-Griède (32)............266 B4
Saint-Groux (16).............179 G6
Saint-Guen (22)..............76 E4
Saint-Guilhem-le-Désert (34)..273 J5
Saint-Guillaume (38).........223 K6
Saint-Guinoux (35)...........50 E4
Saint-Guiraud (34)...........273 H5
Saint-Guyomard (56)..........101 H4
Saint-Haon (43)..............238 B2
Saint-Haon-le-Châtel (42)....186 D4
Saint-Haon-le-Vieux (42).....186 D4
Saint-Héand (42).............205 G5
Saint-Hélen (22).............50 D5

Saint-Hélier (21).............135 G4
Saint-Hellier (76)...........16 A4
Saint-Herblain (44)..........123 F4
Saint-Herblon (44)...........124 B4
Saint-Hérent (63)............202 E6
Saint-Hernin (29)............75 H3
Saint-Hervé (22).............77 F3
Saint-Hilaire (03)...........168 B4
Saint-Hilaire (11)...........309 F1
Saint-Hilaire (25)...........138 C4
Saint-Hilaire (31)...........288 A3
Saint-Hilaire (38)...........224 C1
Saint-Hilaire (43)...........219 H1
Saint-Hilaire (46)...........234 E3
Saint-Hilaire (63)...........184 A4
Saint-Hilaire (91)...........86 C3
Saint-Hilaire-au-Temple (51)..62 D1
Saint-Hilaire-Bonneval (87)...199 G3
Saint-Hilaire-Cottes (62).....5 H5
Saint-Hilaire-Cusson-la-Valmitte (42)....220 D1
Saint-Hilaire-de-Beauvoir (34)..274 D4
Saint-Hilaire-de-Brens (38)...207 F3
Saint-Hilaire-de-Brethmas (30)..255 H6
Saint-Hilaire-de-Briouze (61)..53 K5
Saint-Hilaire-de-Chaléons (44)..122 D5
Saint-Hilaire-de-Clisson (44)..123 J6
Saint-Hilaire-de-Court (18)...148 D1
Saint-Hilaire-de-Gondilly (18)..150 B3
Saint-Hilaire-de-la-Côte (38)..207 F6
Saint-Hilaire-de-la-Noaille (33)..230 D5
Saint-Hilaire-de-Lavit (48)...254 E4
Saint-Hilaire-de-Loulay (85)..142 A3
Saint-Hilaire-de-Lusignan (47)..248 A4
Saint-Hilaire-de-Riez (85)....140 E6
Saint-Hilaire-de-Villefranche (17)..177 K6
Saint-Hilaire-de-Voust (85)...161 F3
Saint-Hilaire-des-Landes (35)..79 K1
Saint-Hilaire-des-Loges (85)..161 F4
Saint-Hilaire-d'Estissac (24)..213 J6
Saint-Hilaire-d'Ozilhan (30)..275 K1
Saint-Hilaire-du-Bois (17)....195 H6
Saint-Hilaire-du-Bois (33)....230 C4
Saint-Hilaire-du-Harcouët (50)..52 C6
Saint-Hilaire-du-Maine (53)...80 D5
Saint-Hilaire-du-Rosier (38)..223 F4
Saint-Hilaire-en-Lignières (18)..166 D1
Saint-Hilaire-en-Morvan (58)..152 B3
Saint-Hilaire-en-Woëvre (55)..44 B6
Saint-Hilaire-Foissac (19)....216 E2
Saint-Hilaire-Fontaine (58)...169 H1
Saint-Hilaire-la-Croix (63)...184 E4
Saint-Hilaire-la-Forêt (85)...159 G4
Saint-Hilaire-la-Gérard (61)..54 D6
Saint-Hilaire-la-Gravelle (41)..108 D4
Saint-Hilaire-la-Palud (79)...177 H1
Saint-Hilaire-la-Plaine (23)..182 E3
Saint-Hilaire-la-Treille (87)..181 H2
Saint-Hilaire-le-Château (23)..182 D5
Saint-Hilaire-le-Châtel (61)..83 H1
Saint-Hilaire-le-Grand (51)...41 K5
Saint-Hilaire-le-Lierru (72)..107 H1
Saint-Hilaire-le-Petit (51)...41 J4
Saint-Hilaire-le-Vouhis (85)..160 B1
Saint-Hilaire-les-Andrésis (45)..112 B2
Saint-Hilaire-les-Courbes (19)..200 A4
Saint-Hilaire-les-Monges (63)..201 J1
Saint-Hilaire-les-Places (87)..198 E4
Saint-Hilaire-lez-Cambrai (59)..12 C4
Saint-Hilaire-Luc (19).......217 F1
Saint-Hilaire-Petitville (50)..31 G1
Saint-Hilaire-Peyroux (19)....215 K3
Saint-Hilaire-sous-Charlieu (42)..187 G3
Saint-Hilaire-sous-Romilly (10)..89 G2
Saint-Hilaire-sur-Benaize (36)..164 C3
Saint-Hilaire-sur-Erre (61)...83 H4
Saint-Hilaire-sur-Helpe (59)..13 G4
Saint-Hilaire-sur-Puiseaux (45)..111 H4
Saint-Hilaire-sur-Risle (61)..55 H5
Saint-Hilaire-sur-Yerre (28)..108 E2
Saint-Hilaire-Taurieux (19)...216 B5
Saint-Hilarion (78)..........57 J6
Saint-Hilliers (77)..........60 D6
Saint-Hippolyte (12).........235 K4
Saint-Hippolyte (15).........218 A3
Saint-Hippolyte (17).........177 F5
Saint-Hippolyte (25).........139 H4
Saint-Hippolyte (33).........230 B2
Saint-Hippolyte (37).........146 E3
Saint-Hippolyte (66).........310 C5
Saint-Hippolyte (68).........71 A6
Saint-Hippolyte-de-Caton (30)..255 J6
Saint-Hippolyte-de-Montaigu (30)..275 J1
Saint-Hippolyte-du-Fort (30)..274 C2
Saint-Hippolyte-le-Graveyron (84)..257 H5
Saint-Honoré (38)............224 B6
Saint-Honoré (76)............16 A3
Saint-Honoré-les-Bains (58)..152 A5
Saint-Hostien (43)...........220 D5
Saint-Hubert (57)............27 J6
Saint-Huruge (71)............171 G3
Saint-Hymer (14).............33 K4
Saint-Hymetière (39).........173 G6
Saint-Igeaux (22)............76 C3
Saint-Igest (12).............251 G2
Saint-Ignan (31).............286 D6
Saint-Ignat (63).............185 H6
Saint-Igny-de-Roche (71).....187 H2
Saint-Igny-de-Vers (69)......187 J2
Saint-Illide (15)............217 G5
Saint-Illiers-la-Ville (78)..57 G2

Saint-Illiers-le-Bois (78)....57 G2
Saint-Ilpize (43)............219 H3
Saint-Imoges (51)............40 E6
Saint-Inglevert (62).........2 B1
Saint-Ismier (38)............224 B2
Saint-Izaire (12)............271 K2
Saint-Jacques (04)...........279 H1
Saint-Jacques-d'Aliermont (76)..16 B2
Saint-Jacques-d'Ambur (63)...184 C6
Saint-Jacques-d'Atticieux (07)..221 K1
Saint-Jacques-de-la-Lande (35)..79 F5
Saint-Jacques-de-Néhou (50)...28 C5
Saint-Jacques-des-Arrêts (69)..188 A1
Saint-Jacques-des-Blats (15)..218 A5
Saint-Jacques-des-Guérets (41)..107 K5
Saint-Jacques-en-Valgodemard (05)....242 E2
Saint-Jacut-de-la-Mer (22)...50 B3
Saint-Jacut-du-Mené (22).....77 J3
Saint-Jacut-les-Pins (56)....102 A3
Saint-Jal (19)...............215 K1
Saint-James (50).............51 K5
Saint-Jammes (64)............284 E3
Saint-Jans-Cappel (59).......6 A2
Saint-Jean (31)..............269 H5
Saint-Jean-aux-Amognes (58)..151 F4
Saint-Jean-aux-Bois (08).....21 K4
Saint-Jean-aux-Bois (60).....38 E3
Saint-Jean-Bonnefonds (42)...205 G6
Saint-Jean-Brévelay (56).....101 G3
Saint-Jean-Cap-Ferrat (06)...281 H4
Saint-Jean-Chambre (07)......239 J1
Saint-Jean-d'Aigues-Vives (09)..308 B3
Saint-Jean-d'Alcapiès (12)...272 C2
Saint-Jean-d'Angély (17).....177 K5
Saint-Jean-d'Angle (17)......194 D1
Saint-Jean-d'Ardières (69)...188 B3
Saint-Jean-d'Arves (73)......225 G2
Saint-Jean-d'Arvey (73)......208 C4
Saint-Jean-d'Assé (72).......82 D6
Saint-Jean-d'Ataux (24)......213 H4
Saint-Jean-d'Aubrigoux (43)..220 B1
Saint-Jean-d'Aulps (74)......192 A1
Saint-Jean-d'Avelanne (38)...207 K5
Saint-Jean-de-Barrou (11)....310 B3
Saint-Jean-de-Bassel (57)....67 H3
Saint-Jean-de-Beauregard (91)..58 C6
Saint-Jean-de-Belleville (73)..209 H5
Saint-Jean-de-Beugné (85)....160 B3
Saint-Jean-de-Blaignac (33)..230 B2
Saint-Jean-de-Boeuf (21).....153 K1
Saint-Jean-de-Boiseau (44)...123 F4
Saint-Jean-de-Bonneval (10)..90 A6
Saint-Jean-de-Bournay (38)...206 D5
Saint-Jean-de-Braye (45).....110 B4
Saint-Jean-de-Buèges (34)....273 K3
Saint-Jean-de-Ceyrargues (30)..255 J6
Saint-Jean-de-Chevelu (73)...208 A2
Saint-Jean-de-Côle (24)......198 B6
Saint-Jean-de-Cornies (34)...274 D4
Saint-Jean-de-Couz (73)......208 A5
Saint-Jean-de-Crieulon (30)..274 D2
Saint-Jean-de-Cuculles (34)..274 B4
Saint-Jean-de-Daye (50)......31 H2
Saint-Jean-de-Duras (47).....231 F4
Saint-Jean-de-Folleville (76)..14 E6
Saint-Jean-de-Fos (34).......273 J5
Saint-Jean-de-Gonville (01)..190 D1
Saint-Jean-de-la-Blaquière (34)..273 H5
Saint-Jean-de-la-Croix (49)..125 G4
Saint-Jean-de-la-Forêt (61)..83 J4
Saint-Jean-de-la-Haize (50)..51 K2
Saint-Jean-de-la-Léqueraye (27)..34 C4
Saint-Jean-de-la-Motte (72)..106 C6
Saint-Jean-de-la-Neuville (76)..14 D6
Saint-Jean-de-la-Porte (73)..208 D4
Saint-Jean-de-la-Rivière (50)..28 B5
Saint-Jean-de-la-Ruelle (45)..110 A4
Saint-Jean-de-Laur (46)......250 E2
Saint-Jean-de-Lier (40)......264 D3
Saint-Jean-de-Linières (49)..125 F3
Saint-Jean-de-Liversay (17)..177 G1
Saint-Jean-de-Livet (14).....33 K6
Saint-Jean-de-Losne (21).....154 E2
Saint-Jean-de-Luz (64).......263 B1
Saint-Jean-de-Marcel (81)....251 J6
Saint-Jean-de-Marsacq (40)...262 D5
Saint-Jean-de-Maruéjols-et-Avéjan (30)...255 J4
Saint-Jean-de-Maurienne (73)..225 G2
Saint-Jean-de-Minervois (34)..291 G3
Saint-Jean-de-Moirans (38)...223 J1
Saint-Jean-de-Monts (85).....140 D5
Saint-Jean-de-Muzols (07)....222 B5
Saint-Jean-de-Nay (43).......220 A5
Saint-Jean-de-Niost (01).....206 E1
Saint-Jean-de-Paracol (11)...308 D3
Saint-Jean-de-Rebervilliers (28)..84 E1
Saint-Jean-de-Rives (81).....270 A5
Saint-Jean-de-Sauves (86)....144 E5
Saint-Jean-de-Savigny (50)...31 J2
Saint-Jean-de-Serres (30)....274 D1
Saint-Jean-de-Sixt (74)......191 J5
Saint-Jean-de-Soudain (38)...207 G4
Saint-Jean-de-Tholome (74)...191 H3
Saint-Jean-de-Thouars (79)...144 B4
Saint-Jean-de-Thurac (47)....248 C5
Saint-Jean-de-Thurigneux (01)..188 D5
Saint-Jean-de-Touslas (69)...205 J4
Saint-Jean-de-Trézy (71).....153 H6

Saint-Jean-de-Valériscle (30)..255 H4
Saint-Jean-de-Vals (81)......271 F5
Saint-Jean-de-Vaulx (38).....224 B5
Saint-Jean-de-Vaux (71)......153 J6
Saint-Jean-de-Védas (34).....293 G1
Saint-Jean-de-Verges (09)....307 J2
Saint-Jean-Delnous (12)......271 H1
Saint-Jean-des-Baisants (50)..31 J3
Saint-Jean-des-Bois (61).....53 F5
Saint-Jean-des-Champs (50)...51 J1
Saint-Jean-des-Échelles (72)..107 J1
Saint-Jean-des-Essartiers (14)..31 K4
Saint-Jean-des-Mauvrets (49)..125 H4
Saint-Jean-des-Ollières (63)..203 G4
Saint-Jean-des-Vignes (69)...188 B6
Saint-Jean-d'Estissac (24)...213 J5
Saint-Jean-d'Étreux (39).....172 E5
Saint-Jean-devant-Possesse (51)..63 H3
Saint-Jean-d'Eyraud (24).....213 H6
Saint-Jean-d'Hérans (38).....242 B1
Saint-Jean-d'Heurs (63)......203 G1
Saint-Jean-d'Illac (33)......229 F2
Saint-Jean-d'Ormont (88).....95 J3
Saint-Jean-du-Bouzet (82)....268 B4
Saint-Jean-du-Bruel (12).....273 G1
Saint-Jean-du-Cardonnay (76)..35 H1
Saint-Jean-du-Castillonnais (09)..306 D3
Saint-Jean-du-Corail (50)....52 D6
Saint-Jean-du-Corail-des-Bois (50)..52 B4
Saint-Jean-du-Doigt (29).....47 G3
Saint-Jean-du-Falga (09).....307 J1
Saint-Jean-du-Gard (30)......254 E6
Saint-Jean-du-Pin (30).......255 G5
Saint-Jean-du-Thenney (27)...55 G1
Saint-Jean-en-Royans (26)....223 G5
Saint-Jean-en-Val (63).......203 F5
Saint-Jean-et-Saint-Paul (12)..272 C2
Saint-Jean-Froidmentel (41)..108 D3
Saint-Jean-Kerdaniel (22)....48 D5
Saint-Jean-Kourtzerode (57)..70 A1
Saint-Jean-la-Bussière (69)..187 H5
Saint-Jean-la-Fouillouse (48)..238 A4
Saint-Jean-la-Poterie (56)...102 B4
Saint-Jean-la-Vêtre (42).....204 B4
Saint-Jean-Lachalm (43)......238 A1
Saint-Jean-Lagineste (46)....234 B2
Saint-Jean-Lasseille (66)....315 G3
Saint-Jean-le-Blanc (14).....53 G2
Saint-Jean-le-Blanc (45).....110 A4
Saint-Jean-le-Centenier (07)..239 J5
Saint-Jean-le-Comtal (32)....286 C1
Saint-Jean-le-Thomas (50)....51 J2
Saint-Jean-le-Vieux (01).....189 H4
Saint-Jean-le-Vieux (38).....224 C3
Saint-Jean-le-Vieux (64).....282 E5
Saint-Jean-lès-Buzy (55).....44 B5
Saint-Jean-lès-Deux-Jumeaux (77)..60 A2
Saint-Jean-lès-Longuyon (54)..26 A3
Saint-Jean-Lespinasse (46)...234 B2
Saint-Jean-Lherm (31)........269 J5
Saint-Jean-Ligoure (87)......199 G3
Saint-Jean-Mirabel (46)......234 E5
Saint-Jean-Pied-de-Port (64)..282 D5
Saint-Jean-Pierre-Fixte (28)..84 A5
Saint-Jean-Pla-de-Corts (66)..315 F4
Saint-Jean-Poudge (64).......284 E1
Saint-Jean-Poutge (32).......267 G5
Saint-Jean-Rohrbach (57).....68 B4
Saint-Jean-Roure (07)........239 H1
Saint-Jean-Saint-Germain (37)..146 E3
Saint-Jean-Saint-Gervais (63)..219 G1
Saint-Jean-Saint-Maurice-sur-Loire (42)..186 E5
Saint-Jean-Saint-Nicolas (05)..243 G4
Saint-Jean-Soleymieux (42)...204 C5
Saint-Jean-sur-Couesnon (35)..79 K2
Saint-Jean-sur-Erve (53).....105 J2
Saint-Jean-sur-Mayenne (53)..81 F6
Saint-Jean-sur-Moivre (51)...63 F3
Saint-Jean-sur-Reyssouze (01)..172 E3
Saint-Jean-sur-Tourbe (51)...42 B5
Saint-Jean-sur-Veyle (01)....188 D1
Saint-Jean-sur-Vilaine (35)..79 K4
Saint-Jean-Trolimon (29).....98 B3
Saint-Jeannet (04)...........278 E1
Saint-Jeannet (06)...........281 F3
Saint-Jeanvrin (18)..........166 D3
Saint-Jeoire (74)............191 J2
Saint-Jeoire-Prieuré (73)....208 C4
Saint-Jeure-d'Andaure (07)...221 H5
Saint-Jeure-d'Ay (07)........222 A4
Saint-Jeures (43)............221 F5
Saint-Joachim (44)...........122 A2
Saint-Jodard (42)............187 F6
Saint-Joire (55).............64 D6
Saint-Jores (50).............30 E1
Saint-Jorioz (74)............191 F6
Saint-Jory (31)..............269 G5
Saint-Jory-de-Chalais (24)...198 B5
Saint-Jory-las-Bloux (24)....214 C1
Saint-Joseph (42)............205 J4
Saint-Joseph (50)............28 D3
Saint-Joseph-de-Rivière (38)..207 K6
Saint-Joseph-des-Bancs (07)..239 H3
Saint-Josse (62).............4 B6
Saint-Jouan-de-l'Isle (22)...78 D4
Saint-Jouan-des-Guérets (35)..50 D4
Saint-Jouin (14).............33 H4
Saint-Jouin-Bruneval (76)....14 B5
Saint-Jouin-de-Blavou (61)...83 G3

396

Saint-Jouin-de-Marnes (79) 144 C5
Saint-Jouin-de-Milly (79) 161 F1
Saint-Jouvent (87) 181 G5
Saint-Juan (25) 138 D5
Saint-Judoce (22) 78 D1
Saint-Juéry (12) 271 K2
Saint-Juéry (48) 236 E2
Saint-Juéry (81) 270 E2
Saint-Juire-Champgillon (85) 160 B3
Saint-Julia (31) 289 G2
Saint-Julia-de-Bec (11) 309 H6
Saint-Julien (21) 136 B4
Saint-Julien (22) 77 F1
Saint-Julien (31) 287 J5
Saint-Julien (34) 291 H1
Saint-Julien (39) 173 F5
Saint-Julien (69) 188 A4
Saint-Julien (83) 278 C4
Saint-Julien (88) 117 J2
Saint-Julien-aux-Bois (19) 216 E4
Saint-Julien-Beychevelle (33) 211 F3
Saint-Julien-Boutières (07) 221 G6
Saint-Julien-Chapteuil (43) 220 E5
Saint-Julien-d'Ance (43) 220 C2
Saint-Julien-d'Armagnac (40) 266 A1
Saint-Julien-d'Arpaon (48) 254 C3
Saint-Julien-d'Asse (04) 278 E2
Saint-Julien-de-Bourdeilles (24) . . . 213 J1
Saint-Julien-de-Briola (11) 289 G6
Saint-Julien-de-Cassagnas (30) . . . 255 H4
Saint-Julien-de-Chédon (41) 128 D5
Saint-Julien-de-Civry (71) 170 D6
Saint-Julien-de-Concelles (44) 123 J3
Saint-Julien-de-Coppel (63) 203 F3
Saint-Julien-de-Crempse (24) 231 J1
Saint-Julien-de-Gras-Capou (09) . . . 308 D2
Saint-Julien-de-Jonzy (71) 187 F2
Saint-Julien-de-la-Liègue (27) . . . 35 K6
Saint-Julien-de-la-Nef (30) 273 K2
Saint-Julien-de-Lampon (24) 233 G2
Saint-Julien-de-l'Escap (17) 177 K5
Saint-Julien-de-l'Herms (38) 206 D6
Saint-Julien-de-Mailloc (14) 34 A6
Saint-Julien-de-Peyrolas (30) 256 B3
Saint-Julien-de-Raz (38) 223 K1
Saint-Julien-de-Toursac (15) 235 F3
Saint-Julien-de-Vouvantes (44) . . . 124 A1
Saint-Julien-des-Chazes (43) 219 K5
Saint-Julien-des-Landes (85) 159 F2
Saint-Julien-des-Points (48) 255 F4
Saint-Julien-d'Eymet (24) 231 H3
Saint-Julien-d'Oddes (42) 204 C1
Saint-Julien-du-Gua (07) 239 H3
Saint-Julien-du-Pinet (43) 220 D4
Saint-Julien-du-Puy (81) 270 D4
Saint-Julien-du-Sault (89) 112 D2
Saint-Julien-du-Serre (07) 239 H4
Saint-Julien-du-Terroux (53) 81 J2
Saint-Julien-du-Tournel (48) 254 C1
Saint-Julien-du-Verdon (04) 279 K1
Saint-Julien-en-Beauchêne (05) . . . 242 A4
Saint-Julien-en-Born (40) 244 C6
Saint-Julien-en-Champsaur (05) . . . 243 F4
Saint-Julien-en-Genevois (74) . . . 190 E2
Saint-Julien-en-Quint (26) 241 G2
Saint-Julien-en-Saint-Alban (07) . . 240 A3
Saint-Julien-en-Vercors (26) 223 H5
Saint-Julien-Gaulène (81) 271 G1
Saint-Julien-la-Geneste (63) 184 B4
Saint-Julien-la-Genête (23) 183 K3
Saint-Julien-la-Vêtre (42) 204 A1
Saint-Julien-Labrousse (07) 239 J1
Saint-Julien-l'Ars (86) 163 G3
Saint-Julien-le-Châtel (23) 183 H3
Saint-Julien-le-Faucon (14) 33 J6
Saint-Julien-le-Pèlerin (19) 216 E6
Saint-Julien-le-Petit (87) 199 K1
Saint-Julien-le-Roux (07) 240 A2
Saint-Julien-le-Vendômois (19) . . . 199 F6
Saint-Julien-lès-Gorze (54) 65 H1
Saint-Julien-lès-Metz (57) 45 F5
Saint-Julien-lès-Montbéliard (25) . . 139 G2
Saint-Julien-les-Rosiers (30) 255 H5
Saint-Julien-lès-Russey (25) 139 G6
Saint-Julien-les-Villas (10) 90 B5
Saint-Julien-Maumont (19) 216 A6
Saint-Julien-Molhesabate (43) 221 H3
Saint-Julien-Molin-Molette (42) . . . 221 K2
Saint-Julien-Mont-Denis (73) 225 H2
Saint-Julien-près-Bort (19) 217 H1
Saint-Julien-Puy-Lavèze (63) 201 K3
Saint-Julien-sous-les-Côtes (55) . . 65 F3
Saint-Julien-sur-Bibost (69) 205 H1
Saint-Julien-sur-Calonne (14) 33 K3
Saint-Julien-sur-Cher (41) 129 J6
Saint-Julien-sur-Dheune (71) 153 H6
Saint-Julien-sur-Reyssouze (01) . . . 172 C5
Saint-Julien-sur-Sarthe (61) 83 F2
Saint-Julien-sur-Veyle (01) 188 D2
Saint-Julien-Vocance (07) 221 J3
Saint-Junien (87) 180 D6
Saint-Junien-la-Bregère (23) 182 C6
Saint-Junien-les-Combes (87) 181 F4
Saint-Jure (57) 66 A2
Saint-Jurs (04) 279 F2
Saint-Just (01) 189 G2
Saint-Just (07) 256 C3
Saint-Just (15) 237 F2
Saint-Just (18) 149 H4
Saint-Just (24) 213 J2
Saint-Just (27) 36 B6
Saint-Just (34) 274 E5

Saint-Just (35) 102 D3
Saint-Just (63) 204 A6
Saint-Just-Chaleyssin (38) 206 C4
Saint-Just-d'Avray (69) 187 J5
Saint-Just-de-Claix (38) 223 G5
Saint-Just-en-Bas (42) 204 B2
Saint-Just-en-Brie (77) 88 B1
Saint-Just-en-Chaussée (60) 38 A1
Saint-Just-en-Chevalet (42) 186 C6
Saint-Just-et-le-Bézu (11) 309 F4
Saint-Just-et-Vacquières (30) 255 J5
Saint-Just-Ibarre (64) 283 F5
Saint-Just-la-Pendue (42) 187 G6
Saint-Just-le-Martel (87) 199 G1
Saint-Just-Luzac (17) 194 C1
Saint-Just-Malmont (43) 221 G1
Saint-Just-près-Brioude (43) 219 G3
Saint-Just-Saint-Rambert (42) 204 E5
Saint-Just-Sauvage (51) 89 H1
Saint-Just-sur-Dive (49) 144 C1
Saint-Just-sur-Viaur (12) 251 K5
Saint-Justin (32) 285 J2
Saint-Justin (40) 265 K1
Saint-Juvat (22) 78 D1
Saint-Juvin (08) 42 D3
Saint-Lactencin (36) 147 H5
Saint-Lager (69) 188 B3
Saint-Lager-Bressac (07) 240 A4
Saint-Lamain (39) 155 H6
Saint-Lambert (14) 53 H4
Saint-Lambert (78) 58 B5
Saint-Lambert-du-Lattay (49) 125 F5
Saint-Lambert-et-
   Mont-de-Jeux (08) 42 A1
Saint-Lambert-la-Potherie (49) . . . 125 F3
Saint-Lambert-sur-Dive (61) 54 D4
Saint-Langis-lès-Mortagne (61) . . . 83 H2
Saint-Lanne (65) 266 B6
Saint-Laon (86) 144 D4
Saint-Lary (09) 306 D1
Saint-Lary (32) 267 H5
Saint-Lary-Boujean (31) 286 E5
Saint-Lary-Soulan (65) 304 E4
Saint-Lattier (38) 223 F4
Saint-Launeuc (22) 77 K4
Saint-Laure (63) 185 H6
Saint-Laurent (08) 22 D3
Saint-Laurent (18) 148 E1
Saint-Laurent (22) 48 A5
Saint-Laurent (23) 182 E3
Saint-Laurent (31) 287 F4
Saint-Laurent (47) 247 K4
Saint-Laurent (58) 132 A5
Saint-Laurent (74) 191 H3
Saint-Laurent-Blangy (62) 11 F2
Saint-Laurent-Bretagne (64) 284 E3
Saint-Laurent-Chabreuges (43) 219 G2
Saint-Laurent-d'Agny (69) 205 K3
Saint-Laurent-d'Aigouze (30) 275 F6
Saint-Laurent-d'Andenay (71) 171 F1
Saint-Laurent-d'Arce (33) 211 J5
Saint-Laurent-de-Belzagot (16) . . . 212 E1
Saint-Laurent-de-Brèvedent (76) . . . 14 C6
Saint-Laurent-de-Carnols (30) 256 B4
Saint-Laurent-de-Cerdans (66) 314 E6
Saint-Laurent-de-Céris (16) 179 K5
Saint-Laurent-de-Chamousset (69) . . 205 G2
Saint-Laurent-de-Cognac (16) 195 J3
Saint-Laurent-de-Condel (14) 53 J1
Saint-Laurent-de-Cuves (50) 52 C4
Saint-Laurent-de-Gosse (40) 282 D1
Saint-Laurent-de-Jourdes (86) 163 H5
Saint-Laurent-de-la-Barrière (17) . . 177 H4
Saint-Laurent-de-
   la-Cabrerisse (11) 309 K1
Saint-Laurent-de-la-Plaine (49) . . . 124 E5
Saint-Laurent-de-la-Prée (17) 176 E4
Saint-Laurent-de-la-Salanque (66) . . 310 C5
Saint-Laurent-de-la-Salle (85) . . . 160 C3
Saint-Laurent-de-Lévézou (12) 253 F4
Saint-Laurent-de-Lin (37) 126 E3
Saint-Laurent-de-Mure (69) 206 C3
Saint-Laurent-de-Muret (48) 237 F5
Saint-Laurent-de-Neste (65) 305 G1
Saint-Laurent-de-Terregatte (50) . . 52 A6
Saint-Laurent-de-Trèves (48) 254 C4
Saint-Laurent-de-Vaux (69) 205 J2
Saint-Laurent-de-Veyrès (48) 236 E3
Saint-Laurent-des-Arbres (30) 256 D6
Saint-Laurent-des-Autels (49) 124 A5
Saint-Laurent-des-Bois (27) 56 E3
Saint-Laurent-des-Bois (41) 109 F5
Saint-Laurent-des-Combes (16) 212 D1
Saint-Laurent-des-Combes (33) 230 B1
Saint-Laurent-des-Hommes (24) 213 F5
Saint-Laurent-des-Mortiers (53) . . . 105 G5
Saint-Laurent-des-Vignes (24) 231 H2
Saint-Laurent-d'Oingt (69) 187 K5
Saint-Laurent-d'Olt (12) 253 G4
Saint-Laurent-d'Onay (26) 222 E3
Saint-Laurent-du-Bois (33) 230 B4
Saint-Laurent-du-Cros (05) 242 E4
Saint-Laurent-du-Mont (14) 33 H5
Saint-Laurent-du-Mottay (49) 124 C5
Saint-Laurent-du-Pape (07) 240 B2
Saint-Laurent-du-Plan (33) 230 B5
Saint-Laurent-du-Pont (38) 207 K6
Saint-Laurent-du-Tencement (27) . . . 55 J5
Saint-Laurent-du-Var (06) 281 G4
Saint-Laurent-du-Verdon (04) 278 E4
Saint-Laurent-en-Beaumont (38) . . . 242 C1

Saint-Laurent-en-Brionnais (71) . . . 187 G1
Saint-Laurent-en-Caux (76) 15 H4
Saint-Laurent-en-Gâtines (37) 127 K2
Saint-Laurent-en-Grandvaux (39) . . . 174 A3
Saint-Laurent-en-Royans (26) 223 G5
Saint-Laurent-la-Conche (42) 204 E3
Saint-Laurent-la-Gâtine (28) 57 G5
Saint-Laurent-la-Roche (39) 173 F5
Saint-Laurent-la-Vallée (24) 232 E3
Saint-Laurent-la-Vernède (30) 256 A5
Saint-Laurent-le-Minier (30) 273 K2
Saint-Laurent-les-Bains (07) 238 D5
Saint-Laurent-les-Églises (87) . . . 181 K5
Saint-Laurent-les-Tours (46) 234 C2
Saint-Laurent-Lolmie (46) 249 H3
Saint-Laurent-Médoc (33) 210 E4
Saint-Laurent-Nouan (41) 109 H6
Saint-Laurent-Rochefort (42) 204 B2
Saint-Laurent-sous-Coiron (07) . . . 239 J5
Saint-Laurent-sur-Gorre (87) 198 C2
Saint-Laurent-sur-Manoire (24) . . . 214 B4
Saint-Laurent-sur-Mer (14) 29 K6
Saint-Laurent-sur-Othain (55) 26 A4
Saint-Laurent-sur-Oust (56) 101 K4
Saint-Laurent-sur-Saône (01) 188 C1
Saint-Laurent-sur-Sèvre (85) 142 A4
Saint-Laurs (79) 161 G4
Saint-Léger (06) 261 F6
Saint-Léger (16) 196 D6
Saint-Léger (17) 195 H3
Saint-Léger (47) 247 J3
Saint-Léger (53) 105 H1
Saint-Léger (62) 11 F4
Saint-Léger (73) 209 F5
Saint-Léger (77) 60 D4
Saint-Léger-aux-Bois (60) 39 F1
Saint-Léger-aux-Bois (76) 16 E3
Saint-Léger-Bridereix (23) 182 A1
Saint-Léger-de-Balson (33) 246 A1
Saint-Léger-de-Fougeret (58) 152 B3
Saint-Léger-de-la-Martinière (79) . . 178 D2
Saint-Léger-de-Montbrillais (86) . . 144 D3
Saint-Léger-de-Montbrun (79) 144 C4
Saint-Léger-de-Peyre (48) 237 G5
Saint-Léger-de-Rôtes (27) 34 D6
Saint-Léger-des-Aubées (28) 85 J3
Saint-Léger-des-Bois (49) 125 F3
Saint-Léger-des-Prés (35) 51 G6
Saint-Léger-des-Vignes (58) 151 G6
Saint-Léger-du-Bois (71) 153 G3
Saint-Léger-du-Bourg-Denis (76) . . . 35 J2
Saint-Léger-du-Gennetey (27) 34 E4
Saint-Léger-du-Malzieu (48) 237 G2
Saint-Léger-du-Ventoux (84) 257 J4
Saint-Léger-Dubosq (14) 33 H4
Saint-Léger-en-Bray (60) 37 G2
Saint-Léger-en-Yvelines (78) 57 J5
Saint-Léger-la-Montagne (87) 181 J4
Saint-Léger-le-Guérétois (23) 182 C3
Saint-Léger-le-Petit (18) 150 C2
Saint-Léger-lès-Authie (80) 10 C5
Saint-Léger-lès-Domart (80) 9 H4
Saint-Léger-lès-Mélèzes (05) 243 F4
Saint-Léger-lès-Paray (71) 170 C4
Saint-Léger-les-Vignes (44) 123 F5
Saint-Léger-Magnazeix (87) 181 H1
Saint-Léger-près-Troyes (10) 90 B5
Saint-Léger-sous-Beuvray (71) 152 D5
Saint-Léger-sous-Brienne (10) 90 E3
Saint-Léger-sous-Cholet (49) 142 E2
Saint-Léger-sous-la-Bussière (71) . . 187 K1
Saint-Léger-sous-Margerie (10) . . . 90 E2
Saint-Léger-sur-Bresle (80) 17 F2
Saint-Léger-sur-Dheune (71) 153 J5
Saint-Léger-sur-Roanne (42) 186 E4
Saint-Léger-sur-Sarthe (61) 83 F2
Saint-Léger-sur-Vouzance (03) 170 A5
Saint-Léger-Triey (21) 136 D5
Saint-Léger-Vauban (89) 134 A4
Saint-Léomer (86) 164 B5
Saint-Léon (03) 169 H5
Saint-Léon (31) 288 D2
Saint-Léon (33) 230 A3
Saint-Léon (47) 247 H3
Saint-Léon-d'Issigeac (24) 231 K4
Saint-Léon-sur-l'Isle (24) 213 J4
Saint-Léon-sur-Vézère (24) 214 E6
Saint-Léonard (32) 267 K3
Saint-Léonard (51) 41 F4
Saint-Léonard (62) 2 A6
Saint-Léonard (76) 14 D4
Saint-Léonard (88) 95 J5
Saint-Léonard-de-Noblat (87) 199 H1
Saint-Léonard-des-Bois (72) 82 B4
Saint-Léonard-des-Parcs (61) 55 F6
Saint-Léonard-en-Beauce (41) 109 F5
Saint-Léons (12) 253 F4
Saint-Léopardin-d'Augy (03) 168 C2
Saint-Léry (56) 78 A4
Saint-Leu-d'Esserent (60) 38 A5
Saint-Leu-la-Forêt (95) 58 D1
Saint-Lézer (65) 285 H3
Saint-Lézin (49) 124 E6
Saint-Lieux-Lafenasse (81) 270 E4
Saint-Lieux-lès-Lavaur (81) 270 A4
Saint-Lin (79) 161 K4
Saint-Lions (04) 260 A6
Saint-Lizier (09) 306 D2
Saint-Lizier-du-Planté (32) 287 G3
Saint-Lô (50) 31 H3
Saint-Lô-d'Ourville (50) 28 C6
Saint-Lon-les-Mines (40) 262 E5

Saint-Longis (72) 83 F4
Saint-Lormel (22) 50 B4
Saint-Lothain (39) 155 J5
Saint-Loube (32) 287 H3
Saint-Loubert (33) 230 B5
Saint-Loubès (33) 229 J1
Saint-Loubouer (40) 265 H5
Saint-Louet-sur-Seulles (14) 32 B6
Saint-Louet-sur-Vire (50) 31 J5
Saint-Louis (57) 70 A2
Saint-Louis (68) 97 J3
Saint-Louis-de-Montferrand (33) . . . 211 H6
Saint-Louis-et-Parahou (11) 309 F4
Saint-Louis-lès-Bitche (57) 69 G4
Saint-Loup (03) 168 C6
Saint-Loup (17) 177 J4
Saint-Loup (23) 183 H3
Saint-Loup (39) 154 E3
Saint-Loup (41) 129 K6
Saint-Loup (50) 52 A5
Saint-Loup (51) 61 J5
Saint-Loup (58) 132 A4
Saint-Loup (69) 187 K6
Saint-Loup (82) 248 D6
Saint-Loup-Cammas (31) 269 H5
Saint-Loup-Champagne (08) 41 G1
Saint-Loup-de-Buffigny (10) 89 G3
Saint-Loup-de-Fribois (14) 33 H6
Saint-Loup-de-Gonois (45) 111 K2
Saint-Loup-de-la-Salle (71) 154 B4
Saint-Loup-de-Naud (77) 88 C2
Saint-Loup-de-Varennes (71) 171 K1
Saint-Loup-des-Chaumes (18) 149 G6
Saint-Loup-des-Vignes (45) 111 F2
Saint-Loup-d'Ordon (89) 112 C2
Saint-Loup-du-Dorat (53) 105 J4
Saint-Loup-du-Gast (53) 81 G3
Saint-Loup-en-Comminges (31) 286 C5
Saint-Loup-Hors (14) 32 B4
Saint-Loup-Lamairé (79) 144 B6
Saint-Loup-Nantouard (70) 137 G4
Saint-Loup-sur-Aujon (52) 116 A4
Saint-Loup-sur-Semouse (70) 118 C3
Saint-Loup-Terrier (08) 22 C6
Saint-Loyer-des-Champs (61) 54 C5
Saint-Lubin-de-Cravant (28) 56 C5
Saint-Lubin-de-la-Haye (28) 57 H4
Saint-Lubin-des-Joncherets (28) . . . 56 D4
Saint-Lubin-en-Vergonnois (41) . . . 128 D2
Saint-Luc (27) 56 E2
Saint-Lucien (28) 57 H6
Saint-Lumier-en-Champagne (51) . . . 63 F4
Saint-Lumier-la-Populeuse (51) . . . 63 H5
Saint-Lumine-de-Clisson (44) 123 J6
Saint-Lumine-de-Coutais (44) 123 F6
Saint-Lunaire (35) 50 C3
Saint-Luperce (28) 84 E3
Saint-Lupicin (39) 173 J5
Saint-Lupien (10) 89 H4
Saint-Lyé (10) 90 A4
Saint-Lyé-la-Forêt (45) 110 B2
Saint-Lyphard (44) 121 K3
Saint-Lys (31) 287 J2
Saint-Macaire (33) 230 A5
Saint-Macaire-du-Bois (49) 144 A2
Saint-Macaire-en-Mauges (49) 142 D2
Saint-Maclou (27) 34 B3
Saint-Maclou-de-Folleville (76) . . . 15 K4
Saint-Maclou-la-Brière (76) 14 E5
Saint-Macoux (86) 179 H3
Saint-Maden (22) 78 C1
Saint-Magne (33) 229 G6
Saint-Magne-de-Castillon (33) 230 C2
Saint-Maigner (63) 184 B4
Saint-Maigrin (17) 195 K6
Saint-Maime (04) 278 D2
Saint-Maime-de-Péreyrol (24) 213 K6
Saint-Maixant (23) 183 G5
Saint-Maixant (33) 230 A5
Saint-Maixent (72) 107 J1
Saint-Maixent-de-Beugné (79) 161 F4
Saint-Maixent-l'École (79) 161 K5
Saint-Maixent-sur-Vie (85) 141 F6
Saint-Maixme-Hauterive (28) 84 D1
Saint-Malo (35) 50 D3
Saint-Malo-de-Beignon (56) 78 B6
Saint-Malo-de-Guersac (44) 122 B2
Saint-Malo-de-la-Lande (50) 30 D4
Saint-Malo-de-Phily (35) 103 F1
Saint-Malo-des-
   Trois-Fontaines (56) 101 J1
Saint-Malô-du-Bois (85) 142 E4
Saint-Malo-en-Donziois (58) 132 D6
Saint-Malon-sur-Mel (35) 78 C4
Saint-Mamert (69) 188 A1
Saint-Mamert-du-Gard (30) 275 F3
Saint-Mamet (31) 305 H5
Saint-Mamet-la-Salvetat (15) 235 G2
Saint-Mammès (77) 87 J4
Saint-Mandé (94) 59 F4
Saint-Mandé-sur-Brédoire (17) 178 B4
Saint-Mandrier-sur-Mer (83) 300 C5
Saint-Manvieu-Bocage (14) 52 D3
Saint-Manvieu-Norrey (14) 32 D5
Saint-Marc (15) 237 F1
Saint-Marc-à-Frongier (23) 183 F6
Saint-Marc-à-Loubaud (23) 200 C1
Saint-Marc-du-Cor (41) 108 D3
Saint-Marc-Jaumegarde (13) 296 E1
Saint-Marc-la-Lande (79) 161 G2
Saint-Marc-le-Blanc (35) 79 J1

Saint-Marc-sur-Couesnon (35) 79 K2
Saint-Marc-sur-Seine (21) 115 G6
Saint-Marcan (35) 51 G4
Saint-Marceau (08) 22 D4
Saint-Marceau (72) 82 D5
Saint-Marcel (01) 188 E5
Saint-Marcel (08) 22 B3
Saint-Marcel (27) 36 B4
Saint-Marcel (36) 165 G3
Saint-Marcel (54) 44 D5
Saint-Marcel (56) 101 J3
Saint-Marcel (70) 117 H4
Saint-Marcel (71) 154 B4
Saint-Marcel (73) 209 H4
Saint-Marcel-Bel-Accueil (38) 206 E3
Saint-Marcel-Campes (81) 251 F6
Saint-Marcel-d'Ardèche (07) 256 C3
Saint-Marcel-de-Careiret (30) 256 B5
Saint-Marcel-de-Félines (42) 187 G6
Saint-Marcel-du-Périgord (24) 232 A1
Saint-Marcel-d'Urfé (42) 186 D6
Saint-Marcel-en-Marcillat (03) . . . 184 A3
Saint-Marcel-en-Murat (03) 184 E1
Saint-Marcel-l'Éclairé (69) 187 J6
Saint-Marcel-lès-Annonay (07) 221 K2
Saint-Marcel-lès-Sauzet (26) 240 B5
Saint-Marcel-lès-Valence (26) 222 D6
Saint-Marcel-Paulel (31) 269 J6
Saint-Marcel-sur-Aude (11) 291 H5
Saint-Marcelin-de-Cray (71) 171 G3
Saint-Marcellin (38) 223 G4
Saint-Marcellin-en-Forez (42) 204 E5
Saint-Marcellin-lès-Vaison (84) . . . 257 H4
Saint-Marcet (31) 286 E6
Saint-Marcory (24) 232 C4
Saint-Marcouf (14) 31 J1
Saint-Marcouf (50) 29 F4
Saint-Mard (02) 40 B2
Saint-Mard (17) 177 H3
Saint-Mard (54) 94 B1
Saint-Mard (77) 59 H1
Saint-Mard (80) 19 F4
Saint-Mard-de-Réno (61) 83 J2
Saint-Mard-de-Vaux (71) 153 J6
Saint-Mard-lès-Rouffy (51) 62 B2
Saint-Mard-sur-Auve (51) 63 G1
Saint-Mard-sur-le-Mont (51) 63 H2
Saint-Mards (76) 15 J3
Saint-Mards-de-Blacarville (27) . . . 34 C2
Saint-Mards-de-Fresne (27) 34 C6
Saint-Mards-en-Othe (10) 89 J4
Saint-Marien (23) 166 D5
Saint-Mariens (33) 211 J4
Saint-Mars-de-Coutais (44) 122 E5
Saint-Mars-de-Locquenay (72) 107 G3
Saint-Mars-d'Égrenne (61) 81 F1
Saint-Mars-d'Outillé (72) 107 F4
Saint-Mars-du-Désert (44) 123 J2
Saint-Mars-du-Désert (53) 82 A4
Saint-Mars-la-Brière (72) 107 F2
Saint-Mars-la-Jaille (44) 124 A2
Saint-Mars-la-Réorthe (85) 142 E5
Saint-Mars-sous-Ballon (72) 82 E6
Saint-Mars-sur-Colmont (53) 81 F3
Saint-Mars-sur-la-Futaie (53) 80 C2
Saint-Mars-Vieux-Maisons (77) 60 D5
Saint-Marsal (66) 314 E4
Saint-Martial (07) 239 G2
Saint-Martial (15) 236 D2
Saint-Martial (16) 212 D1
Saint-Martial (17) 178 A4
Saint-Martial (30) 274 A1
Saint-Martial (33) 230 A1
Saint-Martial-d'Albarède (24) 214 D2
Saint-Martial-d'Artenset (24) 213 F5
Saint-Martial-de-Gimel (19) 216 C3
Saint-Martial-de-Mirambeau (17) . . . 211 H1
Saint-Martial-de-Nabirat (24) 233 F3
Saint-Martial-de-Valette (24) 197 J5
Saint-Martial-de-Vitaterne (17) . . . 195 J5
Saint-Martial-Entraygues (19) 216 D4
Saint-Martial-le-Mont (23) 183 F4
Saint-Martial-le-Vieux (23) 201 F3
Saint-Martial-sur-Isop (87) 180 D3
Saint-Martial-Viveyrol (24) 213 G1
Saint-Martin (32) 286 A2
Saint-Martin (54) 67 G6
Saint-Martin (56) 102 A3
Saint-Martin (65) 285 H6
Saint-Martin (66) 309 H5
Saint-Martin (67) 70 B6
Saint-Martin (83) 278 C6
Saint-Martin-au-Bosc (76) 17 F3
Saint-Martin-au-Laërt (62) 3 G5
Saint-Martin-aux-Arbres (76) 15 H5
Saint-Martin-aux-Bois (60) 38 B1
Saint-Martin-aux-Buneaux (76) 14 E3
Saint-Martin-aux-Champs (51) 62 E4
Saint-Martin-aux-Chartrains (14) . . 33 K3
Saint-Martin-Belle-Roche (71) 171 K5
Saint-Martin-Bellevue (74) 191 F5
Saint-Martin-Boulogne (62) 2 A5
Saint-Martin-Cantalès (15) 217 G5
Saint-Martin-Château (23) 200 A1
Saint-Martin-Choquel (62) 2 D6
Saint-Martin-Curton (47) 247 F3
Saint-Martin-d'Abbat (45) 110 D4
Saint-Martin-d'Ablois (51) 61 J1
Saint-Martin-d'Août (26) 222 D3
Saint-Martin-d'Arberoue (64) 282 E3
Saint-Martin-d'Arc (73) 225 H2

Saint-Martin-d'Arcé (49) 126 B2
Saint-Martin-d'Ardèche (07) 256 B3
Saint-Martin-d'Armagnac (32) 266 B5
Saint-Martin-d'Arrossa (64) 282 D4
Saint-Martin-d'Ary (17) 212 B2
Saint-Martin-d'Aubigny (50) 31 F2
Saint-Martin-d'Audouville (50) . . . 29 F4
Saint-Martin-d'Auxigny (18) 149 G1
Saint-Martin-d'Auxy (71) 171 G1
Saint-Martin-de-Bavel (01) 190 B6
Saint-Martin-de-Beauville (47) . . . 248 D4
Saint-Martin-de-Belleville (73) . . . 209 H6
Saint-Martin-de-Bernegoue (79) . . . 178 B2
Saint-Martin-de-Bienfaite-la-Cressonnière (14) . . 55 F1
Saint-Martin-de-Blagny (14) 31 J2
Saint-Martin-de-Bonfossé (50) . . . 31 G4
Saint-Martin-de-Boscherville (76) . . . 35 G2
Saint-Martin-de-Bossenay (10) . . . 89 H3
Saint-Martin-de-Boubaux (48) 255 F4
Saint-Martin-de-Bréthencourt (78) . . . 86 A2
Saint-Martin-de-Brômes (04) 278 D3
Saint-Martin-de-Caralp (09) 307 H3
Saint-Martin-de-Castillon (84) 277 J3
Saint-Martin-de-Cenilly (50) 31 F5
Saint-Martin-de-Clelles (38) 241 K2
Saint-Martin-de-Commune (71) . . . 153 H5
Saint-Martin-de-Connée (53) 82 A5
Saint-Martin-de-Coux (17) 212 C4
Saint-Martin-de-Crau (13) 276 B5
Saint-Martin-de-Fontenay (14) 32 E5
Saint-Martin-de-Fraigneau (85) . . . 160 E5
Saint-Martin-de-Fressengeas (24) . . . 198 B6
Saint-Martin-de-Fugères (43) 238 C1
Saint-Martin-de-Goyne (32) 267 H1
Saint-Martin-de-Gurson (24) 212 E6
Saint-Martin-de-Hinx (40) 262 D6
Saint-Martin-de-Juillers (17) 178 B5
Saint-Martin-de-Jussac (87) 180 E6
Saint-Martin-de-la-Brasque (84) . . . 277 J4
Saint-Martin-de-la-Cluze (38) 224 A6
Saint-Martin-de-la-Lieue (14) 33 K6
Saint-Martin-de-la-Mer (21) 134 C4
Saint-Martin-de-la-Place (49) 126 A5
Saint-Martin-de-la-Porte (73) 225 H2
Saint-Martin-de-Lamps (36) 147 J4
Saint-Martin-de-Landelles (50) . . . 80 B1
Saint-Martin-de-Lansuscle (48) . . . 254 D4
Saint-Martin-de-l'Arçon (34) 291 H1
Saint-Martin-de-Laye (33) 212 A4
Saint-Martin-de-Lenne (12) 253 F2
Saint-Martin-de-Lerm (33) 230 C4
Saint-Martin-de-Lixy (71) 187 G2
Saint-Martin-de-Londres (34) 274 A4
Saint-Martin-de-Mâcon (79) 144 C3
Saint-Martin-de-Mailloc (14) 34 A4
Saint-Martin-de-Mieux (14) 54 A3
Saint-Martin-de-Nigelles (28) 85 H1
Saint-Martin-de-Queyrières (05) . . . 243 H1
Saint-Martin-de-Ré (17) 176 B2
Saint-Martin-de-Ribérac (24) 213 G3
Saint-Martin-de-Saint-Maixent (79) . . . 161 K5
Saint-Martin-de-Salencey (71) . . . 171 G4
Saint-Martin-de-Sallen (14) 53 H2
Saint-Martin-de-Sanzay (79) 144 B2
Saint-Martin-de-Seignanx (40) . . . 262 B6
Saint-Martin-de-Sescas (33) 230 B5
Saint-Martin-de-Valamas (07) 239 H1
Saint-Martin-de-Valgalgues (30) . . . 255 G5
Saint-Martin-de-Varreville (50) . . . 29 G5
Saint-Martin-de-Vaulserre (38) . . . 207 K5
Saint-Martin-de-Vers (46) 233 J5
Saint-Martin-de-Villeréal (47) 232 B5
Saint-Martin-de-Villeregian (11) . . . 308 E1
Saint-Martin-d'Ecublei (61) 55 J4
Saint-Martin-d'Entraunes (06) . . . 260 E4
Saint-Martin-des-Besaces (14) . . . 31 K5
Saint-Martin-des-Bois (41) 107 K6
Saint-Martin-des-Champs (18) . . . 150 B2
Saint-Martin-des-Champs (29) . . . 47 G4
Saint-Martin-des-Champs (50) . . . 51 K3
Saint-Martin-des-Champs (77) . . . 60 D4
Saint-Martin-des-Champs (78) . . . 57 J3
Saint-Martin-des-Champs (89) . . . 132 B1
Saint-Martin-des-Combes (24) . . . 213 H6
Saint-Martin-des-Entrées (14) . . . 32 B3
Saint-Martin-des-Fontaines (85) . . . 160 D3
Saint-Martin-des-Lais (03) 169 H2
Saint-Martin-des-Landes (61) 82 B1
Saint-Martin-des-Monts (72) 107 H1
Saint-Martin-des-Noyers (85) 160 A1
Saint-Martin-des-Olmes (63) 204 A5
Saint-Martin-des-Pézerits (61) . . . 55 G6
Saint-Martin-des-Plains (63) 203 F5
Saint-Martin-des-Prés (22) 76 E3
Saint-Martin-des-Puits (11) 309 J2
Saint-Martin-des-Tilleuls (85) 142 D3
Saint-Martin-d'Estréaux (42) 186 C2
Saint-Martin-d'Hardinghem (62) . . . 5 F4
Saint-Martin-d'Hères (38) 224 B3
Saint-Martin-d'Heuille (58) 150 E3
Saint-Martin-d'Ollières (63) 203 G6
Saint-Martin-Don (14) 31 J6
Saint-Martin-d'Oney (40) 265 F2
Saint-Martin-d'Ordon (89) 112 C2
Saint-Martin-d'Oydes (09) 288 C6
Saint-Martin-du-Bec (76) 14 B5
Saint-Martin-du-Bois (33) 212 A5
Saint-Martin-du-Bois (49) 104 E6
Saint-Martin-du-Boschet (77) 60 E5
Saint-Martin-du-Clocher (16) 179 G4
Saint-Martin-du-Fouilloux (49) . . . 125 F4

Saint-Martin-du-Fouilloux (79) . . . 162 A3
Saint-Martin-du-Frêne (01) 189 K3
Saint-Martin-du-Lac (71) 186 E2
Saint-Martin-du-Limet (53) 104 C4
Saint-Martin-du-Manoir (76) 14 B6
Saint-Martin-du-Mesnil-Oury (14) . . . 54 D1
Saint-Martin-du-Mont (01) 189 H1
Saint-Martin-du-Mont (21) 135 H4
Saint-Martin-du-Mont (71) 172 D2
Saint-Martin-du-Puy (33) 230 C4
Saint-Martin-du-Puy (58) 133 K5
Saint-Martin-du-Tartre (71) 171 G2
Saint-Martin-du-Tertre (89) 88 D6
Saint-Martin-du-Tertre (95) 37 K6
Saint-Martin-du-Tilleul (27) 34 C6
Saint-Martin-du-Var (06) 281 K3
Saint-Martin-du-Vieux-Bellême (61) . . . 83 H3
Saint-Martin-du-Vivier (76) 35 J1
Saint-Martin-d'Uriage (38) 224 B3
Saint-Martin-en-Bière (77) 87 G3
Saint-Martin-en-Bresse (71) 154 C6
Saint-Martin-en-Campagne (76) . . . 16 B3
Saint-Martin-en-Gâtinois (71) 154 C4
Saint-Martin-en-Haut (69) 205 H4
Saint-Martin-en-Vercors (26) 223 H5
Saint-Martin-Gimois (32) 287 F2
Saint-Martin-la-Campagne (27) . . . 56 C1
Saint-Martin-la-Garenne (78) 57 J1
Saint-Martin-la-Méanne (19) 216 D4
Saint-Martin-la-Patrouille (71) . . . 171 G3
Saint-Martin-la-Plaine (42) 205 J5
Saint-Martin-la-Sauveté (42) 204 B1
Saint-Martin-Labouval (46) 250 D1
Saint-Martin-Lacaussade (33) . . . 211 G4
Saint-Martin-Laguépie (81) 251 F5
Saint-Martin-l'Aiguillon (61) 54 A1
Saint-Martin-Lalande (11) 289 H4
Saint-Martin-l'Ars (86) 180 A2
Saint-Martin-Lars-en-Sainte-Hermine (85) . . . 160 C3
Saint-Martin-l'Astier (24) 213 G5
Saint-Martin-le-Beau (37) 128 A5
Saint-Martin-le-Bouillant (50) . . . 52 B4
Saint-Martin-le-Châtel (01) 189 F1
Saint-Martin-le-Colonel (26) . . . 223 G6
Saint-Martin-le-Gaillard (76) 16 C1
Saint-Martin-le-Gréard (50) 28 C3
Saint-Martin-le-Hébert (50) 28 C4
Saint-Martin-le-Mault (87) 164 D6
Saint-Martin-le-Noeud (60) 37 G2
Saint-Martin-le-Pin (24) 197 J5
Saint-Martin-le-Redon (46) 232 D6
Saint-Martin-le-Vieil (11) 289 J4
Saint-Martin-le-Vieux (87) 198 D2
Saint-Martin-le-Vinoux (38) 224 A3
Saint-Martin-les-Eaux (04) 278 B2
Saint-Martin-lès-Langres (52) . . . 116 C4
Saint-Martin-lès-Melle (79) 178 D2
Saint-Martin-Lestra (42) 205 F3
Saint-Martin-l'Heureux (51) 41 J4
Saint-Martin-l'Hortier (76) 16 C4
Saint-Martin-Longueau (60) 38 C3
Saint-Martin-Lys (11) 308 E5
Saint-Martin-Osmonville (76) . . . 16 B5
Saint-Martin-Petit (47) 230 D5
Saint-Martin-Rivière (02) 12 D6
Saint-Martin-Saint-Firmin (27) . . . 34 C4
Saint-Martin-Sainte-Catherine (23) . . . 182 A5
Saint-Martin-Sepert (19) 199 H6
Saint-Martin-sous-Montaigu (71) . . . 153 K6
Saint-Martin-sous-Vigouroux (15) . . . 236 B1
Saint-Martin-sur-Armançon (89) . . . 114 D4
Saint-Martin-sur-Cojeul (62) . . . 11 F3
Saint-Martin-sur-Écaillon (59) . . . 12 D3
Saint-Martin-sur-Lavezon (07) . . . 240 A4
Saint-Martin-sur-le-Pré (51) 62 D2
Saint-Martin-sur-Nohain (58) . . . 132 A5
Saint-Martin-sur-Ocre (45) 131 H1
Saint-Martin-sur-Ocre (89) 112 D5
Saint-Martin-sur-Ouanne (89) . . . 112 B5
Saint-Martin-Terressus (87) 181 J6
Saint-Martin-Valmeroux (15) . . . 217 H4
Saint-Martin-Vésubie (06) 261 K5
Saint-Martinien (03) 183 K1
Saint-Martory (31) 287 G6
Saint-Mary (16) 197 G1
Saint-Mary-le-Plain (15) 218 E4
Saint-Masmes (51) 41 H3
Saint-Mathieu (87) 198 A3
Saint-Mathieu-de-Tréviers (34) . . . 274 B4
Saint-Mathurin (85) 159 F3
Saint-Mathurin-sur-Loire (49) . . . 125 J4
Saint-Matré (46) 249 G2
Saint-Maudan (22) 77 F5
Saint-Maudez (22) 50 B5
Saint-Maugan (35) 78 C4
Saint-Maulvis (80) 17 G2
Saint-Maur (18) 166 E3
Saint-Maur (32) 286 A2
Saint-Maur (36) 147 K6
Saint-Maur (39) 173 G2
Saint-Maur (60) 17 H5
Saint-Maur-des-Bois (50) 52 B3
Saint-Maur-des-Fossés (94) . . . 59 F4
Saint-Maur-sur-le-Loir (28) . . . 109 F1
Saint-Maurice (52) 116 D4
Saint-Maurice (58) 151 H2
Saint-Maurice (63) 202 E3
Saint-Maurice (67) 71 C4
Saint-Maurice (94) 59 F4

Saint-Maurice-aux-Forges (54) 95 G1
Saint-Maurice-aux-Riches-Hommes (89) . . . 89 F4
Saint-Maurice-Colombier (25) . . . 139 F3
Saint-Maurice-Crillat (39) 173 J3
Saint-Maurice-d'Ardèche (07) . . . 239 H6
Saint-Maurice-de-Beynost (01) . . . 206 C1
Saint-Maurice-de-Cazevieille (30) . . . 275 F1
Saint-Maurice-de-Gourdans (01) . . . 206 E1
Saint-Maurice-de-Lestapel (47) . . . 231 J5
Saint-Maurice-de-Lignon (43) . . . 220 E3
Saint-Maurice-de-Rémens (01) . . . 189 G5
Saint-Maurice-de-Rotherens (73) . . . 207 K3
Saint-Maurice-de-Satonnay (71) . . . 171 J5
Saint-Maurice-de-Tavernole (17) . . . 195 J5
Saint-Maurice-de-Ventalon (48) . . . 254 E3
Saint-Maurice-des-Champs (71) . . . 171 G2
Saint-Maurice-des-Lions (16) 180 B5
Saint-Maurice-des-Noues (85) . . . 160 E3
Saint-Maurice-d'Ételan (76) 34 D1
Saint-Maurice-d'Ibie (07) 239 J6
Saint-Maurice-du-Désert (61) . . . 53 J6
Saint-Maurice-en-Chalencon (07) . . . 239 K2
Saint-Maurice-en-Cotentin (50) . . . 28 C5
Saint-Maurice-en-Gourgois (42) . . . 221 F1
Saint-Maurice-en-Quercy (46) . . . 234 C3
Saint-Maurice-en-Rivière (71) . . . 154 C5
Saint-Maurice-en-Trièves (38) . . . 242 A3
Saint-Maurice-en-Valgodemard (05) . . . 242 E2
Saint-Maurice-la-Clouère (86) . . . 163 F6
Saint-Maurice-la-Fougereuse (79) . . . 143 J3
Saint-Maurice-la-Souterraine (23) . . . 181 J2
Saint-Maurice-le-Girard (85) . . . 160 E2
Saint-Maurice-le-Vieil (89) 112 E5
Saint-Maurice-les-Brousses (87) . . . 198 E3
Saint-Maurice-lès-Charencey (61) . . . 55 K6
Saint-Maurice-lès-Châteauneuf (71) . . . 187 G2
Saint-Maurice-lès-Couches (71) . . . 153 H5
Saint-Maurice-l'Exil (38) 222 B1
Saint-Maurice-Montcouronne (91) . . . 86 C1
Saint-Maurice-Navacelles (34) . . . 273 J3
Saint-Maurice-près-Crocq (23) . . . 201 F1
Saint-Maurice-près-Pionsat (63) . . . 184 A4
Saint-Maurice-Saint-Germain (28) . . . 84 C2
Saint-Maurice-sous-les-Côtes (55) . . . 65 F1
Saint-Maurice-sur-Adour (40) . . . 265 H4
Saint-Maurice-sur-Aveyron (45) . . . 112 A5
Saint-Maurice-sur-Eygues (26) . . . 257 G3
Saint-Maurice-sur-Fessard (45) . . . 111 H3
Saint-Maurice-sur-Huisne (61) . . . 83 J3
Saint-Maurice-sur-Mortagne (88) . . . 94 E3
Saint-Maurice-sur-Moselle (88) . . . 119 H3
Saint-Maurice-sur-Vingeanne (21) . . . 136 D2
Saint-Maurice-Thizouaille (89) . . . 112 E5
Saint-Maurin (47) 248 E4
Saint-Max (54) 66 A5
Saint-Maxent (80) 9 F6
Saint-Maximin (30) 275 H1
Saint-Maximin (38) 208 C6
Saint-Maximin (60) 38 A5
Saint-Maximin-la-Sainte-Baume (83) . . . 297 H2
Saint-Maxire (79) 161 H5
Saint-May (26) 257 K1
Saint-Mayeux (22) 76 D3
Saint-Méard (87) 199 H3
Saint-Méard-de-Drône (24) 213 H3
Saint-Méard-de-Gurçon (24) 230 E1
Saint-Médard (16) 196 B5
Saint-Médard (17) 195 J6
Saint-Médard (31) 306 A1
Saint-Médard (32) 286 B2
Saint-Médard (36) 147 F4
Saint-Médard (46) 233 G6
Saint-Médard (57) 66 E3
Saint-Médard (64) 284 A1
Saint-Médard (79) 178 C2
Saint-Médard-d'Aunis (17) 177 F2
Saint-Médard-de-Guizières (33) . . . 212 C5
Saint-Médard-de-Mussidan (24) . . . 213 G5
Saint-Médard-de-Presque (46) . . . 234 B2
Saint-Médard-d'Excideuil (24) . . . 214 D2
Saint-Médard-d'Eyrans (33) 229 H3
Saint-Médard-en-Forez (42) 205 F4
Saint-Médard-en-Jalles (33) 229 F1
Saint-Médard-la-Rochette (23) . . . 183 H3
Saint-Médard-Nicourby (46) 234 D3
Saint-Médard-sur-Ille (35) 79 G2
Saint-Méen (29) 46 C4
Saint-Méen-le-Grand (35) 78 B3
Saint-Méloir-des-Bois (22) 50 B5
Saint-Méloir-des-Ondes (35) 50 E3
Saint-Même-le-Tenu (44) 122 E6
Saint-Même-les-Carrières (16) . . . 196 B3
Saint-Memmie (51) 62 D2
Saint-Menge (88) 93 J4
Saint-Menges (08) 23 F3
Saint-Menoux (03) 168 C3
Saint-Merd-de-Lapleau (19) 216 E3
Saint-Merd-la-Breuille (23) 201 G2
Saint-Merd-les-Oussines (19) . . . 200 C4
Saint-Méry (77) 87 J1
Saint-Meslin-du-Bosc (27) 35 F5
Saint-Mesmes (77) 59 H2
Saint-Mesmin (10) 89 K3
Saint-Mesmin (21) 135 G5
Saint-Mesmin (24) 215 F1

Saint-Mesmin (85) 143 G6
Saint-Mexant (19) 215 K2
Saint-Mézard (32) 267 H1
Saint-M'Hervé (35) 80 B5
Saint-M'Hervon (35) 78 C2
Saint-Micaud (71) 171 G2
Saint-Michel (02) 21 H1
Saint-Michel (09) 307 H1
Saint-Michel (16) 196 D3
Saint-Michel (31) 287 H6
Saint-Michel (32) 286 B3
Saint-Michel (34) 273 G3
Saint-Michel (45) 110 E2
Saint-Michel (64) 282 E6
Saint-Michel (82) 268 B1
Saint-Michel-Chef-Chef (44) 122 B4
Saint-Michel-d'Aurance (07) 239 H1
Saint-Michel-de-Bannières (46) . . . 216 A6
Saint-Michel-de-Boulogne (07) . . . 239 H4
Saint-Michel-de-Castelnau (33) . . . 246 E3
Saint-Michel-de-Chabrillanoux (07) . . . 239 K2
Saint-Michel-de-Chaillol (05) . . . 243 F3
Saint-Michel-de-Chavaignes (72) . . . 107 H2
Saint-Michel-de-Dèze (48) 255 F4
Saint-Michel-de-Double (24) 213 F5
Saint-Michel-de-Feins (53) 105 G5
Saint-Michel-de-Fronsac (33) 230 A1
Saint-Michel-de-la-Pierre (50) . . . 30 E3
Saint-Michel-de-la-Roë (53) 104 B4
Saint-Michel-de-Lanès (11) 289 F4
Saint-Michel-de-Lapujade (33) . . . 230 D5
Saint-Michel-de-Livet (14) 54 D1
Saint-Michel-de-Llotes (66) 314 E2
Saint-Michel-de-Maurienne (73) . . . 225 J2
Saint-Michel-de-Montaigne (24) . . . 230 D2
Saint-Michel-de-Montjoie (50) . . . 52 C4
Saint-Michel-de-Plélan (22) 50 B5
Saint-Michel-de-Rieufret (33) 229 J5
Saint-Michel-des-Saint-Geoirs (38) . . . 223 G2
Saint-Michel-des-Andaines (61) . . . 81 J1
Saint-Michel-en-Beaumont (38) . . . 242 C1
Saint-Michel-en-Brenne (36) 146 E6
Saint-Michel-en-Grève (22) 47 J3
Saint-Michel-en-l'Herm (85) 159 K5
Saint-Michel-Escalus (40) 262 D5
Saint-Michel-et-Chanveaux (49) . . . 104 B6
Saint-Michel-Labadié (81) 271 G1
Saint-Michel-les-Portes (38) 241 K1
Saint-Michel-l'Observatoire (04) . . . 278 A2
Saint-Michel-Loubéjou (46) 234 B2
Saint-Michel-Mont-Mercure (85) . . . 142 E5
Saint-Michel-sous-Bois (62) 4 D5
Saint-Michel-sur-Loire (37) 127 F5
Saint-Michel-sur-Meurthe (88) . . . 95 H3
Saint-Michel-sur-Orge (91) 58 E6
Saint-Michel-sur-Rhône (42) 205 K6
Saint-Michel-sur-Savasse (26) . . . 222 E4
Saint-Michel-sur-Ternoise (62) . . . 10 B2
Saint-Michel-Tuboeuf (61) 55 J5
Saint-Mihiel (55) 64 E2
Saint-Mitre-les-Remparts (13) . . . 295 J4
Saint-Molf (44) 121 J3
Saint-Momelin (59) 3 G4
Saint-Mont (32) 266 A5
Saint-Montant (07) 256 C1
Saint-Moré (89) 133 J2
Saint-Moreil (23) 199 K1
Saint-Morel (08) 42 B3
Saint-Morillon (33) 229 H4
Saint-Mury-Monteymond (38) . . . 224 C2
Saint-Myon (63) 185 F5
Saint-Nabor (67) 70 C5
Saint-Nabord (88) 118 E1
Saint-Nabord-sur-Aube (10) 90 C2
Saint-Nauphary (82) 269 G2
Saint-Nazaire (30) 256 C4
Saint-Nazaire (44) 122 A4
Saint-Nazaire (66) 315 H2
Saint-Nazaire-d'Aude (11) 291 G5
Saint-Nazaire-de-Ladarez (34) . . . 291 J2
Saint-Nazaire-de-Pézan (34) 274 E6
Saint-Nazaire-de-Valentane (82) . . . 249 F4
Saint-Nazaire-des-Gardies (30) . . . 274 D1
Saint-Nazaire-en-Royans (26) . . . 223 F5
Saint-Nazaire-le-Désert (26) 241 G5
Saint-Nazaire-les-Eymes (38) . . . 224 B2
Saint-Nazaire-sur-Charente (17) . . . 176 E5
Saint-Nectaire (63) 202 C4
Saint-Nexans (24) 231 J2
Saint-Nic (29) 74 B3
Saint-Nicodème (22) 76 A2
Saint-Nicolas (62) 10 E2
Saint-Nicolas-aux-Bois (02) 20 B6
Saint-Nicolas-d'Aliermont (76) . . . 16 B2
Saint-Nicolas-d'Attez (27) 56 B4
Saint-Nicolas-de-Bliquetuit (76) . . . 34 E1
Saint-Nicolas-de-Bourgueil (37) . . . 126 D6
Saint-Nicolas-de-la-Balerme (47) . . . 248 D5
Saint-Nicolas-de-la-Grave (82) . . . 249 F6
Saint-Nicolas-de-la-Haie (76) . . . 15 F6
Saint-Nicolas-de-la-Taille (76) . . . 34 C1
Saint-Nicolas-de-Macherin (38) . . . 207 J6
Saint-Nicolas-de-Pierrepont (50) . . . 28 D4
Saint-Nicolas-de-Port (54) 66 B5
Saint-Nicolas-de-Redon (44) 102 C4

Saint-Nicolas-de-Sommaire (61) . . . 55 J4
Saint-Nicolas-des-Biefs (03) 186 C4
Saint-Nicolas-des-Bois (50) 52 B4
Saint-Nicolas-des-Bois (61) 82 C2
Saint-Nicolas-des-Laitiers (61) . . . 55 G3
Saint-Nicolas-des-Motets (37) . . . 128 C2
Saint-Nicolas-du-Bosc (27) 35 F5
Saint-Nicolas-du-Pélem (22) 76 C2
Saint-Nicolas-du-Tertre (56) 102 A2
Saint-Nicolas-la-Chapelle (10) . . . 89 F2
Saint-Nicolas-la-Chapelle (73) . . . 191 K6
Saint-Nicolas-lès-Cîteaux (21) . . . 154 C2
Saint-Nizier-d'Azergues (69) 187 J4
Saint-Nizier-de-Fornas (42) 220 E1
Saint-Nizier-du-Moucherotte (38) . . . 223 K3
Saint-Nizier-le-Bouchoux (01) . . . 172 C4
Saint-Nizier-le-Désert (01) 189 F4
Saint-Nizier-sous-Charlieu (42) . . . 187 F3
Saint-Nizier-sur-Arroux (71) 152 D6
Saint-Nolff (56) 101 G5
Saint-Nom-la-Bretèche (78) 58 B3
Saint-Offenge-Dessous (73) 208 C2
Saint-Offenge-Dessus (73) 208 C2
Saint-Omer (14) 53 J2
Saint-Omer (62) 3 G5
Saint-Omer-Capelle (62) 3 F3
Saint-Omer-en-Chaussée (60) . . . 17 J6
Saint-Ondras (38) 207 H5
Saint-Onen-la-Chapelle (35) 78 B3
Saint-Oradoux-de-Chirouze (23) . . . 201 F2
Saint-Oradoux-près-Crocq (23) . . . 201 G1
Saint-Orens (32) 268 B5
Saint-Orens-de-Gameville (31) . . . 288 C1
Saint-Orens-Pouy-Petit (32) 267 G2
Saint-Ost (32) 286 B3
Saint-Ouen (17) 178 D6
Saint-Ouen (41) 108 C5
Saint-Ouen (80) 9 J6
Saint-Ouen (93) 58 E3
Saint-Ouen-d'Attez (27) 56 B4
Saint-Ouen-d'Aunis (17) 176 E1
Saint-Ouen-de-la-Cour (61) 83 H3
Saint-Ouen-de-Mimbré (72) 82 C5
Saint-Ouen-de-Pontcheuil (27) . . . 35 G2
Saint-Ouen-de-Sécherouvre (61) . . . 83 G1
Saint-Ouen-de-Thouberville (27) . . . 35 F3
Saint-Ouen-des-Alleux (35) 79 J1
Saint-Ouen-des-Besaces (14) . . . 31 K4
Saint-Ouen-des-Champs (27) . . . 34 C2
Saint-Ouën-des-Toits (53) 80 D6
Saint-Ouën-des-Vallons (53) 81 G6
Saint-Ouen-Domprot (51) 62 D6
Saint-Ouen-du-Breuil (76) 15 J5
Saint-Ouen-du-Mesnil-Oger (14) . . . 33 G5
Saint-Ouen-du-Tilleul (27) 35 G4
Saint-Ouen-en-Belin (72) 106 C5
Saint-Ouen-en-Brie (77) 87 K1
Saint-Ouen-en-Champagne (72) . . . 106 A3
Saint-Ouen-l'Aumône (95) 58 C1
Saint-Ouen-le-Brisoult (61) 81 K2
Saint-Ouen-le-Houx (14) 54 E2
Saint-Ouen-le-Mauger (76) 15 J3
Saint-Ouen-le-Pin (14) 33 J5
Saint-Ouen-lès-Parey (88) 93 G5
Saint-Ouen-les-Vignes (37) 128 B4
Saint-Ouen-Marchefroy (28) 57 G3
Saint-Ouen-sous-Bailly (76) 16 B2
Saint-Ouen-sur-Gartempe (87) . . . 181 F3
Saint-Ouen-sur-Iton (61) 55 J5
Saint-Ouen-sur-Loire (58) 151 F5
Saint-Ouen-sur-Maire (61) 54 A5
Saint-Ouen-sur-Morin (77) 60 C3
Saint-Oulph (10) 89 J2
Saint-Ours (63) 202 B1
Saint-Ours (73) 208 C1
Saint-Outrille (18) 148 B2
Saint-Ovin (50) 52 A5
Saint-Oyen (73) 209 H4
Saint-Pabu (29) 72 C2
Saint-Paër (76) 35 F1
Saint-Pair (14) 33 F5
Saint-Pair-sur-Mer (50) 51 H1
Saint-Pal-de-Chalencon (43) 220 C1
Saint-Pal-de-Mons (43) 221 F3
Saint-Pal-de-Senouire (43) 219 K3
Saint-Palais (03) 166 E5
Saint-Palais (18) 149 G1
Saint-Palais (33) 211 H2
Saint-Palais (64) 283 G3
Saint-Palais-de-Négrignac (17) . . . 212 B2
Saint-Palais-de-Phiolin (17) 195 G5
Saint-Palais-du-Né (16) 195 K4
Saint-Palais-sur-Mer (17) 194 B3
Saint-Pancrace (24) 197 K6
Saint-Pancrace (73) 225 G2
Saint-Pancrasse (38) 224 C2
Saint-Pancré (54) 26 B2
Saint-Pandelon (40) 264 B5
Saint-Pantaléon (46) 249 G4
Saint-Pantaléon (84) 277 F2
Saint-Pantaléon-de-Lapleau (19) . . . 217 F2
Saint-Pantaléon-de-Larche (19) . . . 215 H4
Saint-Pantaléon-les-Vignes (26) . . . 257 G2
Saint-Pantaly-d'Ans (24) 214 D3
Saint-Pantaly-d'Excideuil (24) . . . 214 D2
Saint-Papoul (11) 289 H4
Saint-Pardon-de-Conques (33) . . . 230 B5
Saint-Pardoult (17) 178 A4
Saint-Pardoux (79) 161 J2
Saint-Pardoux (87) 181 H4

Saint-Pardoux-Corbier (19). 199 G6
Saint-Pardoux-d'Arnet (23). 201 F1
Saint-Pardoux-de-Drône (24). 213 H3
Saint-Pardoux-du-Breuil (47). 247 H1
Saint-Pardoux-et-Vielvic (24). . . . 232 D3
Saint-Pardoux-Isaac (47). 231 G5
Saint-Pardoux-la-Croisille (19). . . . 216 D3
Saint-Pardoux-la-Rivière (24). . . . 197 K5
Saint-Pardoux-le-Neuf (19). 201 F4
Saint-Pardoux-le-Neuf (23). 183 G6
Saint-Pardoux-le-Vieux (19). 201 F4
Saint-Pardoux-les-Cards (23). 183 F4
Saint-Pardoux-l'Ortigier (19). 215 J2
Saint-Pardoux-Morterolles (23). . . 182 C6
Saint-Pargoire (34). 292 D1
Saint-Parize-en-Viry (58). 168 K1
Saint-Parize-le-Châtel (58). 150 E6
Saint-Parres-aux-Tertres (10). . . . 90 B4
Saint-Parres-lès-Vaudes (10). 90 C6
Saint-Parthem (12). 235 G5
Saint-Pastour (47). 248 B1
Saint-Pastous (65). 304 B2
Saint-Paterne (72). 82 D3
Saint-Paterne-Racan (37). 127 G2
Saint-Pathus (77). 59 J1
Saint-Patrice (37). 126 E6
Saint-Patrice-de-Claids (50). 30 E2
Saint-Patrice-du-Désert (61). 81 K1
Saint-Paul (06). 281 F4
Saint-Paul (19). 216 C3
Saint-Paul (33). 211 H4
Saint-Paul (60). 37 G2
Saint-Paul (61). 53 G4
Saint-Paul (65). 305 G1
Saint-Paul (73). 208 A3
Saint-Paul (87). 199 G2
Saint-Paul (88). 93 H4
Saint-Paul-aux-Bois (02). 19 K6
Saint-Paul-Cap-de-Joux (81). 270 C6
Saint-Paul-de-Baïse (32). 267 F4
Saint-Paul-de-Fenouillet (66). . . . 309 H5
Saint-Paul-de-Fourques (27). 35 F4
Saint-Paul-de-Jarrat (09). 307 J3
Saint-Paul-de-Loubressac (46). . . . 250 A3
Saint-Paul-de-Salers (15). 217 J4
Saint-Paul-de-Serre (24). 213 K5
Saint-Paul-de-Tartas (43). 238 C3
Saint-Paul-de-Varax (01). 189 F3
Saint-Paul-de-Varces (38). 223 K4
Saint-Paul-de-Vern (46). 234 C2
Saint-Paul-de-Vézelin (42). 187 F6
Saint-Paul-des-Landes (15). 235 G1
Saint-Paul-d'Espis (82). 249 F5
Saint-Paul-d'Izeaux (38). 223 H1
Saint-Paul-d'Oueil (31). 305 H4
Saint-Paul-du-Bois (49). 143 J2
Saint-Paul-du-Vernay (14). 32 A4
Saint-Paul-d'Uzore (42). 204 D3
Saint-Paul-en-Born (40). 244 D4
Saint-Paul-en-Chablais (74). 175 G5
Saint-Paul-en-Cornillon (42). 221 F1
Saint-Paul-en-Forêt (83). 280 B6
Saint-Paul-en-Gâtine (79). 161 F2
Saint-Paul-en-Jarez (42). 205 J5
Saint-Paul-en-Pareds (85). 142 D5
Saint-Paul-et-Valmalle (34). 273 K6
Saint-Paul-la-Coste (30). 255 F5
Saint-Paul-la-Roche (24). 198 C6
Saint-Paul-le-Froid (48). 237 J3
Saint-Paul-le-Gaultier (72). 82 B4
Saint-Paul-le-Jeune (07). 255 H4
Saint-Paul-lès-Dax (40). 264 B4
Saint-Paul-lès-Durance (13). 278 A5
Saint-Paul-lès-Fonts (30). 256 C6
Saint-Paul-lès-Monestier (38). . . . 223 K6
Saint-Paul-lès-Romans (26). 222 E5
Saint-Paul-Lizonne (24). 213 G2
Saint-Paul-Mont-Penit (85). 141 H5
Saint-Paul-sur-Isère (73). 209 G3
Saint-Paul-sur-Save (31). 268 E5
Saint-Paul-sur-Ubaye (04). 227 B5
Saint-Paul-Trois-Châteaux (26). . . 256 D2
Saint-Paulet (11). 289 G3
Saint-Paulet-de-Caisson (30). . . . 256 C3
Saint-Paulien (43). 220 D4
Saint-Pavace (72). 106 D2
Saint-Pé-d'Ardet (31). 305 J2
Saint-Pé-de-Bigorre (65). 304 A1
Saint-Pé-de-Léren (64). 283 G1
Saint-Pé-Delbosc (31). 286 E5
Saint-Pé-Saint-Simon (47). 266 D1
Saint-Pée-sur-Nivelle (64). 263 D2
Saint-Pellerin (28). 108 D2
Saint-Pellerin (50). 31 G1
Saint-Péran (35). 78 C5
Saint-Péravy-la-Colombe (45). . . . 109 J3
Saint-Péray (07). 222 C6
Saint-Perdon (40). 265 F2
Saint-Perdoux (24). 231 J3
Saint-Perdoux (46). 234 D4
Saint-Père (35). 50 E4
Saint-Père (58). 132 A4
Saint-Père (89). 133 J4
Saint-Père-en-Retz (44). 122 C4
Saint-Père-sur-Loire (45). 110 E6
Saint-Péreuse (58). 152 A3
Saint-Pern (35). 78 D2
Saint-Perreux (56). 102 B4
Saint-Péver (22). 48 D6
Saint-Pey-d'Armens (33). 230 B2
Saint-Pey-de-Castets (33). 230 C2
Saint-Phal (10). 114 A1

Saint-Philbert-de-Bouaine (85). . . . 141 J3
Saint-Philbert-de-Grand-Lieu (44). . 123 F6
Saint-Philbert-des-Champs (14). . . 34 A4
Saint-Philbert-du-Peuple (49). . . . 126 B4
Saint-Philbert-en-Mauges (49). . . . 142 D1
Saint-Philbert-sur-Boissey (27). . . 34 E4
Saint-Philbert-sur-Orne (61). 53 J3
Saint-Philbert-sur-Risle (27). 34 D3
Saint-Philibert (21). 154 C1
Saint-Philibert (56). 100 D6
Saint-Philippe-d'Aiguille (33). . . . 230 C1
Saint-Philippe-du-Seignal (33). . . . 231 F2
Saint-Piat (28). 85 H2
Saint-Pierre (04). 280 D1
Saint-Pierre (15). 217 H1
Saint-Pierre (31). 269 G5
Saint-Pierre (39). 173 K3
Saint-Pierre (51). 62 C2
Saint-Pierre (67). 70 D6
Saint-Pierre-à-Arnes (08). 41 J3
Saint-Pierre-Aigle (02). 39 H3
Saint-Pierre-Avez (05). 258 E3
Saint-Pierre-Azif (14). 33 H3
Saint-Pierre-Bellevue (23). 182 D6
Saint-Pierre-Bénouville (76). 15 H4
Saint-Pierre-Bois (67). 70 C6
Saint-Pierre-Brouck (59). 3 F3
Saint-Pierre-Canivet (14). 54 A2
Saint-Pierre-Chérignat (23). 182 A5
Saint-Pierre-Colamine (63). 202 C5
Saint-Pierre-d'Albigny (73). 208 D4
Saint-Pierre-d'Allevard (38). 208 D6
Saint-Pierre-d'Alvey (73). 207 K3
Saint-Pierre-d'Amilly (17). 177 H2
Saint-Pierre-d'Argençon (05). . . . 242 A6
Saint-Pierre-d'Arthéglise (50). . . . 28 C5
Saint-Pierre-d'Aubézies (32). 266 D6
Saint-Pierre-d'Aurillac (33). 230 B5
Saint-Pierre-d'Autils (27). 36 B6
Saint-Pierre-de-Bailleul (27). 36 A6
Saint-Pierre-de-Bat (33). 230 A4
Saint-Pierre-de-Belleville (73). . . . 209 F5
Saint-Pierre-de-Boeuf (42). 222 A1
Saint-Pierre-de-Bressieux (38). . . . 223 G2
Saint-Pierre-de-Buzet (47). 247 H4
Saint-Pierre-de-Cernières (27). . . . 55 H2
Saint-Pierre-de-Chandieu (69). . . . 206 C3
Saint-Pierre-de-Chartreuse (38). . . 224 B1
Saint-Pierre-de-Chérennes (38). . . 223 G4
Saint-Pierre-de-Chevillé (72). . . . 127 G1
Saint-Pierre-de-Chignac (24). . . . 214 B4
Saint-Pierre-de-Clairac (47). 248 D5
Saint-Pierre-de-Côle (24). 214 B1
Saint-Pierre-de-Colombier (07). . . 239 G4
Saint-Pierre-de-Cormeilles (27). . . 34 B4
Saint-Pierre-de-Coutances (50). . . 30 E4
Saint-Pierre-de-Curtille (73). 208 A1
Saint-Pierre-de-Frugie (24). 198 C4
Saint-Pierre-de-Fursac (23). 181 K3
Saint-Pierre-de-Genebroz (73). . . . 207 K5
Saint-Pierre-de-Jards (36). 148 C3
Saint-Pierre-de-Juillers (17). 178 B5
Saint-Pierre-de-la-Fage (34). 273 H4
Saint-Pierre-de-Lages (31). 288 D1
Saint-Pierre-de-Lamps (36). 147 H4
Saint-Pierre-de-l'Île (17). 178 A4
Saint-Pierre-de-Maillé (86). 164 A2
Saint-Pierre-de-Mailloc (14). 34 A6
Saint-Pierre-de-Manneville (76). . . 35 G2
Saint-Pierre-de-Méaroz (38). 242 B1
Saint-Pierre-de-Mésage (38). 224 B5
Saint-Pierre-de-Mézoargues (13). . 275 K3
Saint-Pierre-de-Mons (33). 230 A5
Saint-Pierre-de-Nogaret (48). 253 H1
Saint-Pierre-de-Plesguen (35). . . . 50 E5
Saint-Pierre-de-Rivière (09). 307 H3
Saint-Pierre-de-Salerne (27). 34 D5
Saint-Pierre-de-Semilly (50). 31 J3
Saint-Pierre-de-Soucy (73). 208 D5
Saint-Pierre-de-Trivisy (81). 271 G4
Saint-Pierre-de-Varengeville (76). . 35 G1
Saint-Pierre-de-Varennes (71). . . . 153 H5
Saint-Pierre-de-Vassols (84). 257 H5
Saint-Pierre-dels-Forcats (66). . . . 313 J4
Saint-Pierre-d'Entremont (38). . . . 208 B6
Saint-Pierre-d'Entremont (61). . . . 53 G4
Saint-Pierre-d'Entremont (73). . . . 208 B6
Saint-Pierre-des-Bois (72). 106 A3
Saint-Pierre-des-Champs (11). . . . 309 J2
Saint-Pierre-des-Corps (37). 127 J4
Saint-Pierre-des-Échaubrognes (79). 143 G3
Saint-Pierre-des-Fleurs (27). 35 G4
Saint-Pierre-des-Ifs (14). 33 J4
Saint-Pierre-des-Ifs (27). 34 D4
Saint-Pierre-des-Jonquières (76). . 16 D2
Saint-Pierre-des-Landes (53). 80 C4
Saint-Pierre-des-Loges (61). 55 G5
Saint-Pierre-des-Nids (53). 82 B3
Saint-Pierre-des-Ormes (72). 83 G4
Saint-Pierre-des-Tripiers (48). . . . 253 J4
Saint-Pierre-d'Exideuil (86). 179 H3
Saint-Pierre-d'Eyraud (24). 231 G2
Saint-Pierre-d'Irube (64). 282 B1
Saint-Pierre-d'Oléron (17). 176 B5
Saint-Pierre-du-Bosguérard (27). . 35 F4
Saint-Pierre-du-Bû (14). 54 A3
Saint-Pierre-du-Champ (43). 220 C3
Saint-Pierre-du-Chemin (85). 161 F1
Saint-Pierre-du-Fresne (14). 53 F1
Saint-Pierre-du-Jonquet (14). . . . 33 G5
Saint-Pierre-du-Lorouër (72). 107 H5

Saint-Pierre-du-Mesnil (27). 55 H2
Saint-Pierre-du-Mont (14). 29 J6
Saint-Pierre-du-Mont (40). 265 G2
Saint-Pierre-du-Mont (58). 133 F5
Saint-Pierre-du-Palais (17). 212 B4
Saint-Pierre-du-Perray (91). 87 F1
Saint-Pierre-du-Regard (61). 53 H3
Saint-Pierre-du-Val (27). 34 B2
Saint-Pierre-du-Vauvray (27). 35 J4
Saint-Pierre-Église (50). 28 E2
Saint-Pierre-en-Faucigny (74). . . . 191 H3
Saint-Pierre-en-Port (76). 14 E3
Saint-Pierre-en-Val (76). 8 C6
Saint-Pierre-en-Vaux (21). 153 H2
Saint-Pierre-es-Champs (60). 36 D2
Saint-Pierre-Eynac (43). 220 D5
Saint-Pierre-la-Bourlhonne (63). . . 203 H3
Saint-Pierre-la-Bruyère (61). 83 K4
Saint-Pierre-la-Garenne (27). 36 A5
Saint-Pierre-la-Noaille (42). 187 F2
Saint-Pierre-la-Palud (69). 205 J1
Saint-Pierre-la-Rivière (61). 54 B1
Saint-Pierre-la-Roche (07). 239 K4
Saint-Pierre-la-Vieille (14). 53 H2
Saint-Pierre-Lafeuille (46). 233 H6
Saint-Pierre-Langers (50). 51 J1
Saint-Pierre-Laval (03). 186 C2
Saint-Pierre-Lavis (76). 15 F5
Saint-Pierre-le-Bost (23). 166 E6
Saint-Pierre-le-Chastel (63). 202 B2
Saint-Pierre-le-Moûtier (58). 168 C1
Saint-Pierre-le-Vieux (48). 237 G2
Saint-Pierre-le-Vieux (71). 187 K1
Saint-Pierre-le-Vieux (76). 15 H2
Saint-Pierre-le-Vieux (85). 160 E5
Saint-Pierre-le-Viger (76). 15 H3
Saint-Pierre-lès-Bitry (60). 39 G2
Saint-Pierre-lès-Bois (18). 166 E2
Saint-Pierre-lès-Elbeuf (76). 35 H4
Saint-Pierre-les-Étieux (18). 167 H1
Saint-Pierre-lès-Franqueville (02). . 20 E3
Saint-Pierre-lès-Nemours (77). . . . 87 H5
Saint-Pierre-Montlimart (49). 124 C5
Saint-Pierre-Roche (63). 202 A3
Saint-Pierre-Saint-Jean (07). 255 H1
Saint-Pierre-sur-Dives (14). 54 C1
Saint-Pierre-sur-Doux (07). 221 H4
Saint-Pierre-sur-Dropt (47). 230 E4
Saint-Pierre-sur-Erve (53). 105 J2
Saint-Pierre-sur-Orthe (53). 82 A5
Saint-Pierre-sur-Vence (08). 22 C4
Saint-Pierre-Tarentaine (14). 53 F2
Saint-Pierre-Toirac (46). 234 C6
Saint-Pierremont (02). 21 F4
Saint-Pierremont (08). 42 D1
Saint-Pierremont (88). 94 E2
Saint-Pierreville (55). 26 C4
Saint-Plaisir (03). 168 B3
Saint-Plancard (31). 286 C6
Saint-Planchers (50). 51 J1
Saint-Plantaire (36). 165 J5
Saint-Point (71). 171 H6
Saint-Point-Lac (25). 156 E5
Saint-Pois (50). 52 C4
Saint-Poix (53). 104 C3
Saint-Pol-de-Léon (29). 47 F3
Saint-Pol-sur-Mer (59). 3 H1
Saint-Pol-sur-Ternoise (62). 10 B1
Saint-Polgues (42). 186 E6
Saint-Polycarpe (11). 309 F2
Saint-Pompain (79). 161 F5
Saint-Pompont (24). 232 E4
Saint-Poncy (15). 219 F4
Saint-Pons (04). 260 C1
Saint-Pons (07). 239 K5
Saint-Pons-de-Mauchiens (34). . . 292 D2
Saint-Pons-de-Thomières (34). . . 291 F5
Saint-Pons-la-Calm (30). 256 B5
Saint-Pont (03). 185 H3
Saint-Porchaire (17). 194 E1
Saint-Porquier (82). 268 E1
Saint-Pôtan (22). 50 A4
Saint-Pouange (10). 90 A5
Saint-Pourçain-sur-Besbre (03). . . 169 H5
Saint-Pourçain-sur-Sioule (03). . . 185 H1
Saint-Prancher (88). 93 H1
Saint-Préjet-Armandon (43). 219 J3
Saint-Préjet-d'Allier (43). 237 K1
Saint-Prest (28). 85 H2
Saint-Preuil (16). 196 A4
Saint-Priest (07). 239 J4
Saint-Priest (23). 183 H4
Saint-Priest (69). 206 B3
Saint-Priest-Bramefant (63). 185 J4
Saint-Priest-d'Andelot (03). 185 G4
Saint-Priest-de-Gimel (19). 216 C2
Saint-Priest-des-Champs (63). . . . 184 C5
Saint-Priest-en-Jarez (42). 205 G5
Saint-Priest-en-Murat (03). 168 A4
Saint-Priest-la-Feuille (23). 181 K2
Saint-Priest-la-Marche (18). 166 D5
Saint-Priest-la-Plaine (23). 182 B2
Saint-Priest-la-Prugne (42). 186 B5
Saint-Priest-la-Roche (42). 187 F6
Saint-Priest-la-Vêtre (43). 204 A1
Saint-Priest-les-Fougères (24). . . . 198 C5
Saint-Priest-Ligoure (87). 199 F3
Saint-Priest-Palus (23). 182 B6
Saint-Priest-sous-Aixe (87). 198 D1

Saint-Priest-Taurion (87). 181 J6
Saint-Prim (38). 206 A6
Saint-Privat (07). 239 H5
Saint-Privat (19). 216 E4
Saint-Privat (34). 273 H4
Saint-Privat-d'Allier (43). 220 A6
Saint-Privat-de-Champclos (30). . . 255 K3
Saint-Privat-de-Vallongue (48). . . 254 E3
Saint-Privat-des-Prés (24). 213 F3
Saint-Privat-des-Vieux (30). 255 H5
Saint-Privat-du-Dragon (43). 219 H4
Saint-Privat-du-Fau (48). 237 G1
Saint-Privat-la-Montagne (57). . . . 27 F6
Saint-Privé (71). 171 G1
Saint-Privé (89). 132 A1
Saint-Prix (03). 186 A2
Saint-Prix (07). 239 J1
Saint-Prix (71). 152 C4
Saint-Prix (95). 58 D1
Saint-Prix-lès-Arnay (21). 153 G2
Saint-Projet (46). 233 H3
Saint-Projet (82). 250 D3
Saint-Projet-de-Salers (15). 217 J5
Saint-Projet-Saint-Constant (16). . 197 G2
Saint-Pryvé-Saint-Mesmin (45). . . 109 K4
Saint-Puy (32). 267 G3
Saint-Python (59). 12 C4
Saint-Quantin-de-Rançanne (17). . 195 G5
Saint-Quay-Perros (22). 48 A2
Saint-Quay-Portrieux (22). 49 F4
Saint-Quentin (02). 19 K2
Saint-Quentin-au-Bosc (76). 16 C1
Saint-Quentin-de-Baron (33). . . . 230 A2
Saint-Quentin-de-Blavou (61). . . . 83 A2
Saint-Quentin-de-Caplong (33). . . 230 E3
Saint-Quentin-de-Chalais (16). . . 212 D2
Saint-Quentin-des-Isles (27). 55 H1
Saint-Quentin-des-Prés (60). 36 E1
Saint-Quentin-du-Dropt (47). 231 J4
Saint-Quentin-en-Mauges (49). . . 124 D5
Saint-Quentin-en-Tourmont (80). . 8 E2
Saint-Quentin-Fallavier (38). 206 D3
Saint-Quentin-la-Chabanne (23). . 200 E1
Saint-Quentin-la-Motte-
    Croix-au-Bailly (80). 8 C5
Saint-Quentin-la-Poterie (30). . . . 256 A6
Saint-Quentin-la-Tour (09). 308 B2
Saint-Quentin-le-Petit (08). 21 H2
Saint-Quentin-le-Verger (51). 61 H6
Saint-Quentin-les-Anges (53). . . . 104 D5
Saint-Quentin-lès-
    Beaurepaire (49). 126 B1
Saint-Quentin-les-
    Chardonnets (61). 53 F4
Saint-Quentin-les-Marais (51). . . . 63 G3
Saint-Quentin-sur-Charente (16). . 197 K1
Saint-Quentin-sur-Coole (51). . . . 62 D3
Saint-Quentin-sur-Indrois (37). . . 146 D1
Saint-Quentin-sur-Isère (38). 223 J2
Saint-Quentin-sur-le-Homme (50). . 52 A5
Saint-Quentin-sur-Nohain (58). . . 132 B5
Saint-Quentin-sur-
    Sauxillanges (63). 203 G5
Saint-Quintin-sur-Sioule (63). . . . 185 F4
Saint-Quirc (09). 288 C5
Saint-Quirin (57). 67 J5
Saint-Rabier (24). 214 E4
Saint-Racho (71). 187 H1
Saint-Rambert-d'Albon (26). 222 B5
Saint-Rambert-en-Bugey (01). . . . 189 J5
Saint-Raphaël (24). 214 E2
Saint-Raphaël (83). 299 G2
Saint-Régis-du-Coin (42). 221 H2
Saint-Règle (37). 128 C2
Saint-Remèze (07). 256 B2
Saint-Remimont (54). 94 B1
Saint-Remimont (88). 93 J5
Saint-Rémy (01). 189 F2
Saint-Rémy (12). 251 G2
Saint-Rémy (14). 53 H2
Saint-Rémy (21). 134 D1
Saint-Rémy (24). 230 E1
Saint-Remy (70). 118 A4
Saint-Rémy (71). 171 J1
Saint-Rémy (79). 161 G5
Saint-Rémy (88). 95 G3
Saint-Rémy-au-Bois (62). 9 F3
Saint-Rémy-aux-Bois (54). 94 C2
Saint-Rémy-Blanzy (02). 39 J4
Saint-Rémy-Boscrocourt (76). . . . 8 C6
Saint-Remy-Chaussée (59). 13 G4
Saint-Rémy-de-Blot (63). 184 D4
Saint-Rémy-de-Chargnat (63). . . . 203 F5
Saint-Rémy-de-Chaudes-
    Aigues (15). 236 D3
Saint-Rémy-de-Maurienne (73). . . 209 F6
Saint-Rémy-de-Provence (13). . . . 276 B4
Saint-Rémy-de-Sillé (72). 82 B6
Saint-Rémy-des-Landes (50). 28 C6
Saint-Rémy-des-Monts (72). 83 G4
Saint-Remy-du-Nord (59). 13 G3
Saint-Rémy-du-Plain (35). 79 H1
Saint-Rémy-du-Val (72). 82 E4
Saint-Remy-en-Bouzemont-
    Saint-Genest-et-Isson (51). . . 63 G6
Saint-Remy-en-l'Eau (60). 38 A1
Saint-Rémy-en-Mauges (49). 124 B5
Saint-Rémy-en-Rollat (03). 185 J3
Saint-Rémy-la-Calonne (55). 43 K6
Saint-Rémy-la-Vanne (77). 60 C4

Saint-Rémy-la-Varenne (49). 125 J4
Saint-Rémy-le-Petit (08). 41 H2
Saint-Rémy-lès-Chevreuse (78). . . 58 C2
Saint-Rémy-l'Honoré (78). 58 A5
Saint-Remy-sous-Barbuise (10). . . 90 B2
Saint-Remy-sous-Broyes (51). . . . 61 H5
Saint-Rémy-sur-Avre (28). 56 E5
Saint-Remy-sur-Bussy (51). 42 A4
Saint-Rémy-sur-Creuse (86). 146 A4
Saint-Rémy-sur-Durolle (63). 186 A6
Saint-Renan (29). 72 C4
Saint-Restitut (26). 256 E3
Saint-Révérend (85). 158 E1
Saint-Révérien (58). 151 H1
Saint-Rieul (22). 77 K1
Saint-Rigomer-des-Bois (72). 82 D3
Saint-Rimay (41). 108 B6
Saint-Riquier (80). 9 H5
Saint-Riquier-en-Rivière (76). 16 B2
Saint-Riquier-ès-Plains (76). 15 F3
Saint-Rirand (42). 186 C4
Saint-Rivoal (29). 74 E1
Saint-Robert (19). 215 G3
Saint-Robert (47). 248 D4
Saint-Roch (37). 127 H4
Saint-Roch-sur-Égrenne (61). 81 F1
Saint-Rogatien (17). 176 E2
Saint-Romain (16). 212 E2
Saint-Romain (21). 153 J3
Saint-Romain (63). 204 B5
Saint-Romain (86). 179 J2
Saint-Romain-au-Mont-d'Or (69). . 206 A1
Saint-Romain-d'Ay (07). 222 A4
Saint-Romain-de-Benet (17). 194 E2
Saint-Romain-de-Colbosc (76). . . . 14 D6
Saint-Romain-de-Jalionas (38). . . 206 E2
Saint-Romain-de-Lerps (07). 222 B6
Saint-Romain-de-Monpazier (24). . 232 B4
Saint-Romain-de-Popey (69). 205 H1
Saint-Romain-de-Surieu (38). . . . 222 C6
Saint-Romain-d'Urfé (42). 186 C6
Saint-Romain-en-Gal (69). 206 B5
Saint-Romain-en-Gier (69). 205 K4
Saint-Romain-en-Jarez (42). 205 H4
Saint-Romain-en-Viennois (84). . . 257 H3
Saint-Romain-et-
    Saint-Clément (24). 198 B6
Saint-Romain-la-Motte (42). 186 E4
Saint-Romain-la-Virvée (33). 211 J6
Saint-Romain-Lachalm (43). 221 G2
Saint-Romain-le-Noble (47). 248 D5
Saint-Romain-le-Preux (89). 112 D3
Saint-Romain-le-Puy (42). 204 D5
Saint-Romain-les-Atheux (42). . . . 221 G1
Saint-Romain-sous-Gourdon (71). . 170 E3
Saint-Romain-sous-Versigny (71). . 170 C2
Saint-Romain-sur-Cher (41). 129 F5
Saint-Romain-sur-Gironde (17). . . 194 D5
Saint-Roman (26). 241 H4
Saint-Roman-de-Codières (30). . . . 274 A1
Saint-Roman-de-Malegarde (84). . 257 F3
Saint-Romans (38). 223 G4
Saint-Romans-des-Champs (79). . . 178 B2
Saint-Romans-lès-Melle (79). 178 D2
Saint-Rome (31). 288 E3
Saint-Rome-de-Cernon (12). 272 C1
Saint-Rome-de-Dolan (48). 253 H4
Saint-Rome-de-Tarn (12). 272 B1
Saint-Romphaire (50). 31 H4
Saint-Rustice (31). 269 F4
Saint-Saëns (76). 16 B5
Saint-Saire (76). 16 D4
Saint-Salvadou (12). 251 G4
Saint-Salvadour (19). 216 B1
Saint-Salvi-de-Carcavès (81). . . . 271 J4
Saint-Salvy (47). 247 K3
Saint-Salvy-de-la-Balme (81). . . . 271 G6
Saint-Samson (14). 33 G5
Saint-Samson (53). 82 A2
Saint-Samson-de-Bonfossé (50). . . 31 G4
Saint-Samson-de-la-Roque (27). . . 34 B2
Saint-Samson-la-Poterie (60). . . . 17 F6
Saint-Samson-sur-Rance (22). . . . 50 D5
Saint-Sandoux (63). 202 D4
Saint-Santin (12). 235 F5
Saint-Santin-Cantalès (15). 217 F6
Saint-Santin-de-Maurs (15). 235 F5
Saint-Sardos (47). 248 A3
Saint-Sardos (82). 268 D2
Saint-Satur (18). 131 K5
Saint-Saturnin (15). 218 B3
Saint-Saturnin (16). 196 D3
Saint-Saturnin (18). 166 D4
Saint-Saturnin (48). 253 H2
Saint-Saturnin (51). 61 K6
Saint-Saturnin (63). 202 D3
Saint-Saturnin (72). 106 D2
Saint-Saturnin-de-Lenne (12). . . . 253 F2
Saint-Saturnin-de-Lucian (34). . . . 273 H5
Saint-Saturnin-du-Bois (17). 177 J3
Saint-Saturnin-du-Limet (53). . . . 104 B4
Saint-Saturnin-lès-Apt (84). 277 H1
Saint-Saturnin-lès-Avignon (84). . . 276 C1
Saint-Saturnin-sur-Loire (49). . . . 125 H4
Saint-Saud-Lacoussière (24). 198 A5
Saint-Sauflieu (80). 18 A3
Saint-Saulge (58). 151 H2
Saint-Saulve (59). 12 D1
Saint-Saury (15). 234 E2
Saint-Sauvant (17). 195 H2
Saint-Sauvant (86). 162 C6
Saint-Sauves-d'Auvergne (63). . . . 201 K4

Saint-Sauveur (05) 243 J5
Saint-Sauveur (21) 136 E4
Saint-Sauveur (24) 231 J2
Saint-Sauveur (29) 46 E6
Saint-Sauveur (31) 269 G4
Saint-Sauveur (33) 210 E3
Saint-Sauveur (38) 223 G4
Saint-Sauveur (54) 67 J6
Saint-Sauveur (60) 38 D3
Saint-Sauveur (70) 118 D4
Saint-Sauveur (80) 18 A1
Saint-Sauveur (86) 145 K6
Saint-Sauveur-Camprieu (30) 254 A6
Saint-Sauveur-d'Aunis (17) 177 G2
Saint-Sauveur-de-Carrouges (61) . . 82 B1
Saint-Sauveur-de-Cruzières (07) . . . 255 J3
Saint-Sauveur-de-Flée (49) 104 E5
Saint-Sauveur-de-Ginestoux (48) . . 237 K4
Saint-Sauveur-de-Landemont (49) . 123 K3
Saint-Sauveur-de-Meilhan (47) . . . 247 F1
Saint-Sauveur-de-Montagut (07). . . 239 K2
Saint-Sauveur-de-Peyre (48) 237 G4
Saint-Sauveur-de-Pierrepont (50) . . 28 C6
Saint-Sauveur-de-
    Puynormand (33) 212 C6
Saint-Sauveur-d'Émalleville (76) . . . 14 C5
Saint-Sauveur-des-Landes (35) . . . 79 K1
Saint-Sauveur-en-Diois (26) 241 F4
Saint-Sauveur-en-Puisaye (89) 132 C2
Saint-Sauveur-en-Rue (42) 221 J2
Saint-Sauveur-Gouvernet (26) 257 K2
Saint-Sauveur-la-Pommeraye (50) . 51 J1
Saint-Sauveur-la-Sagne (63) 219 K1
Saint-Sauveur-la-Vallée (46) 233 J5
Saint-Sauveur-Lalande (24) 213 F6
Saint-Sauveur-le-Vicomte (50) 28 D5
Saint-Sauveur-Lendelin (50) 30 E3
Saint-Sauveur-lès-Bray (77) 88 C3
Saint-Sauveur-Marville (28) 84 E1
Saint-Sauveur-sur-École (77) 87 G2
Saint-Sauveur-sur-Tinée (06) 261 H5
Saint-Savier (03) 166 H1
Saint-Sauvy (32) 268 A5
Saint-Savin (33) 211 J4
Saint-Savin (38) 207 F4
Saint-Savin (65) 304 A2
Saint-Savin (86) 164 A3
Saint-Savinien (17) 177 H6
Saint-Saviol (86) 179 H3
Saint-Savournin (13) 296 E2
Saint-Sébastien (23) 165 G6
Saint-Sébastien (38) 242 B1
Saint-Sébastien-d'Aigrefeuille (30) . 255 G6
Saint-Sébastien-de-Morsent (27) . . 56 C1
Saint-Sébastien-de-Raids (50) 30 E2
Saint-Sébastien-sur-Loire (44) 123 H4
Saint-Secondin (86) 163 G6
Saint-Ségal (29) 74 D3
Saint-Séglin (35) 102 H1
Saint-Seine (58) 169 K1
Saint-Seine-en-Bâche (21) 155 F2
Saint-Seine-l'Abbaye (21) 135 H4
Saint-Seine-sur-Vingeanne (21) . . . 136 E2
Saint-Selve (33) 229 H4
Saint-Senier-de-Beuvron (50) 52 A6
Saint-Senier-sous-Avranches (50) . . 51 K3
Saint-Senoch (37) 146 C3
Saint-Senoux (35) 103 H1
Saint-Sériès (34) 274 E4
Saint-Sernin (07) 239 H5
Saint-Sernin (11) 289 F5
Saint-Sernin (47) 231 H4
Saint-Sernin-du-Bois (71) 153 G6
Saint-Sernin-du-Plain (71) 153 H6
Saint-Sernin-lès-Lavaur (81) 289 H1
Saint-Sernin-sur-Rance (12) 271 J3
Saint-Sérotin (89) 88 C5
Saint-Servais (22) 76 A1
Saint-Servais (29) 46 D5
Saint-Servant (56) 101 J2
Saint-Setiers (19) 200 D3
Saint-Seurin-de-Bourg (33) 211 H5
Saint-Seurin-de-Cadourne (33) . . . 211 F2
Saint-Seurin-de-Cursac (33) 211 G3
Saint-Seurin-de-Palenne (17) 195 H3
Saint-Seurin-de-Prats (24) 230 D2
Saint-Seurin-sur-l'Isle (33) 212 D5
Saint-Sève (33) 230 C2
Saint-Sever (40) 265 G4
Saint-Sever-Calvados (14) 52 C3
Saint-Sever-de-Rustan (65) 285 K3
Saint-Sever-de-Saintonge (17) . . . 195 H3
Saint-Sever-du-Moustier (12) 271 K4
Saint-Séverin (13) 213 F2
Saint-Séverin-d'Estissac (24) 213 H5
Saint-Séverin-sur-Boutonne (17) . . 178 A3
Saint-Siffret (30) 275 H1
Saint-Sigismond (45) 109 J3
Saint-Sigismond (49) 124 C3
Saint-Sigismond (74) 192 A3
Saint-Sigismond (85) 160 E6
Saint-Sigismond-de-Clermont (17) . 195 H6
Saint-Silvain-Bas-le-Roc (23) 183 G1
Saint-Silvain-Bellegarde (23) 183 H5
Saint-Silvain-Montaigut (23) 182 C3
Saint-Silvain-sous-Toulx (23) 183 G2
Saint-Siméon (27) 34 C4
Saint-Siméon (61) 81 F2
Saint-Siméon (77) 60 C4
Saint-Siméon-de-Bressieux (38) . . 223 F1
Saint-Simeux (16) 196 C3
Saint-Simon (02) 19 J4

Saint-Simon (15) 235 J1
Saint-Simon (16) 196 B3
Saint-Simon (46) 234 B4
Saint-Simon-de-Bordes (17) 195 H6
Saint-Simon-de-Pellouaille (17) . . . 195 F3
Saint-Sixt (74) 191 H3
Saint-Sixte (42) 204 C2
Saint-Sixte (47) 248 F5
Saint-Solve (19) 215 H2
Saint-Sorlin (69) 205 J4
Saint-Sorlin-d'Arves (73) 225 F2
Saint-Sorlin-de-Conac (17) 211 G1
Saint-Sorlin-de-Morestel (38) 207 H3
Saint-Sorlin-de-Vienne (38) 206 B5
Saint-Sorlin-en-Bugey (01) 189 H6
Saint-Sorlin-en-Valloire (26) 222 C2
Saint-Sornin (03) 168 B5
Saint-Sornin (16) 197 G3
Saint-Sornin (17) 194 C1
Saint-Sornin-la-Marche (87) 180 E2
Saint-Sornin-Lavolps (19) 215 H1
Saint-Sornin-Leulac (87) 181 H2
Saint-Soulan (32) 287 F2
Saint-Souplet (59) 12 D5
Saint-Souplet-sur-Py (51) 41 H4
Saint-Soupplets (77) 59 J1
Saint-Sozy (46) 233 J2
Saint-Stail (88) 95 K3
Saint-Suliac (35) 50 D1
Saint-Sulpice (01) 172 B6
Saint-Sulpice (41) 128 C2
Saint-Sulpice (46) 234 B6
Saint-Sulpice (49) 125 H4
Saint-Sulpice (53) 105 H3
Saint-Sulpice (58) 151 F3
Saint-Sulpice (60) 37 H3
Saint-Sulpice (63) 201 J4
Saint-Sulpice (70) 138 D2
Saint-Sulpice (73) 208 A4
Saint-Sulpice (81) 269 K4
Saint-Sulpice-d'Arnoult (17) 194 E1
Saint-Sulpice-de-Cognac (16) 195 J2
Saint-Sulpice-de-Faleyrens (33) . . . 230 B1
Saint-Sulpice-de-Favières (91) 86 D2
Saint-Sulpice-de-Grimbouville (27) . 34 B2
Saint-Sulpice-de-Guilleragues (33) . 230 D5
Saint-Sulpice-de-Mareuil (24) 197 H6
Saint-Sulpice-de-Pommiers (33) . . 230 B4
Saint-Sulpice-de-Roumagnac (24) . 213 H3
Saint-Sulpice-de-Royan (17) 194 C3
Saint-Sulpice-de-Ruffec (16) 179 H5
Saint-Sulpice-des-Landes (35) . . . 103 G3
Saint-Sulpice-des-Landes (44) . . . 124 A2
Saint-Sulpice-des-Rivoires (38) . . . 207 J5
Saint-Sulpice-d'Excideuil (24) 214 D1
Saint-Sulpice-en-Pareds (85) 160 D2
Saint-Sulpice-et-Cameyrac (33) . . . 229 J1
Saint-Sulpice-la-Forêt (35) 79 H3
Saint-Sulpice-Laurière (87) 181 K4
Saint-Sulpice-le-Dunois (23) 182 C2
Saint-Sulpice-le-Guérétois (23) . . . 182 C2
Saint-Sulpice-le-Verdon (85) 141 K4
Saint-Sulpice-les-Bois (19) 200 D3
Saint-Sulpice-les-Champs (23) . . . 182 E5
Saint-Sulpice-les-Feuilles (87) 181 J1
Saint-Sulpice-sur-Lèze (31) 288 A4
Saint-Sulpice-sur-Risle (61) 55 J4
Saint-Supplet (54) 26 C4
Saint-Sylvain (14) 33 F6
Saint-Sylvain (19) 216 C4
Saint-Sylvain (76) 15 F2
Saint-Sylvain-d'Anjou (49) 125 H3
Saint-Sylvestre (07) 222 B6
Saint-Sylvestre (74) 190 E6
Saint-Sylvestre (87) 181 J5
Saint-Sylvestre-Cappel (59) 3 J1
Saint-Sylvestre-de-Cormeilles (27) . 34 B4
Saint-Sylvestre-Pragoulin (63) . . . 185 J4
Saint-Sylvestre-sur-Lot (47) 248 D2
Saint-Symphorien (18) 149 F6
Saint-Symphorien (27) 34 C3
Saint-Symphorien (33) 246 A1
Saint-Symphorien (48) 237 K2
Saint-Symphorien (72) 106 B1
Saint-Symphorien (79) 161 F4
Saint-Symphorien-d'Ancelles (71). . 188 B2
Saint-Symphorien-de-Lay (42) . . . 187 G5
Saint-Symphorien-de-Mahun (07) . . 221 J4
Saint-Symphorien-
    de-Marmagne (71) 153 F6
Saint-Symphorien-
    de-Thénières (12) 236 A4
Saint-Symphorien-des-Bois (71) . . . 170 D6
Saint-Symphorien-
    des-Bruyères (61) 55 H4
Saint-Symphorien-des-Monts (50) . 80 D1
Saint-Symphorien-d'Ozon (69) . . . 206 B3
Saint-Symphorien-le-Château (28) . 85 J2
Saint-Symphorien-le-Valois (50) . . 30 D1
Saint-Symphorien-
    sous-Chomérac (07) 240 A3
Saint-Symphorien-sur-Coise (69) . . 205 G3
Saint-Symphorien-sur-Couze (87). . 181 G4
Saint-Symphorien-sur-Saône (21) . . 154 E2
Saint-Thégonnec (29) 47 F5
Saint-Thélo (22) 77 F4
Saint-Théodorit (30) 274 E2
Saint-Théoffrey (38) 224 B5
Saint-Thibaud-de-Couz (73) 208 A5
Saint-Thibault (10) 90 B6
Saint-Thibault (21) 135 F5
Saint-Thibault (60) 17 G4

Saint-Thibault-des-Vignes (77) . . . 59 H3
Saint-Thibaut (02) 40 B3
Saint-Thibéry (34) 292 C3
Saint-Thiébaud (39) 156 A3
Saint-Thiébault (52) 93 F5
Saint-Thierry (51) 40 E3
Saint-Thois (29) 75 F4
Saint-Thomas (02) 40 D1
Saint-Thomas (31) 287 H2
Saint-Thomas-de-Conac (17) 195 F6
Saint-Thomas-de-Courceriers (53) . 81 K5
Saint-Thomas-en-Argonne (51) . . . 42 D5
Saint-Thomas-en-Royans (26) . . . 223 G5
Saint-Thomas-la-Garde (42) 204 D4
Saint-Thomé (07) 239 K6
Saint-Thonan (29) 46 B3
Saint-Thual (35) 78 E1
Saint-Thurial (35) 78 D5
Saint-Thuriau (56) 76 E6
Saint-Thurien (27) 34 C2
Saint-Thurien (29) 99 H2
Saint-Thurin (42) 204 B1
Saint-Tricat (62) 2 C3
Saint-Trimoël (22) 77 J2
Saint-Trinit (84) 258 B5
Saint-Trivier-de-Courtes (01) 172 B4
Saint-Trivier-sur-Moignans (01). . . . 188 D4
Saint-Trojan (33) 211 H4
Saint-Trojan-les-Bains (17) 176 C6
Saint-Tropez (83) 299 F4
Saint-Tugdual (56) 76 A5
Saint-Ulphace (72) 83 K6
Saint-Ulrich (68) 97 A4
Saint-Uniac (35) 78 D3
Saint-Urbain (29) 46 C6
Saint-Urbain (85) 140 D4
Saint-Urbain-Maconcourt (52) 92 D3
Saint-Urcisse (47) 248 D5
Saint-Urcisse (81) 269 J2
Saint-Urcize (15) 236 D4
Saint-Usage (10) 115 G1
Saint-Usage (21) 154 E2
Saint-Usuge (71) 172 D2
Saint-Utin (51) 90 E1
Saint-Uze (26) 222 C3
Saint-Vaast-de-Longmont (60) . . . 38 D4
Saint-Vaast-d'Équiqueville (76) . . . 16 B3
Saint-Vaast-Dieppedalle (76) 15 G3
Saint-Vaast-du-Val (76) 15 J4
Saint-Vaast-en-Auge (14) 33 H4
Saint-Vaast-en-Cambrésis (59) . . . 12 C4
Saint-Vaast-en-Chaussée (80) 18 A1
Saint-Vaast-la-Hougue (50) 29 G3
Saint-Vaast-lès-Mello (60) 37 K4
Saint-Vaast-sur-Seulles (14) 32 B5
Saint-Vaize (17) 195 G1
Saint-Valbert (70) 118 D4
Saint-Valentin (36) 148 B4
Saint-Valérien (85) 160 C3
Saint-Valérien (89) 88 B6
Saint-Valery (60) 17 F4
Saint-Valéry-en-Caux (76) 15 G2
Saint-Valery-sur-Somme (80) 8 E4
Saint-Vallerin (71) 171 H2
Saint-Vallier (16) 212 C2
Saint-Vallier (26) 222 B3
Saint-Vallier (71) 170 E2
Saint-Vallier (88) 94 C4
Saint-Vallier-de-Thiey (06) 280 C6
Saint-Vallier-sur-Marne (52) 116 D4
Saint-Varent (79) 144 B5
Saint-Vaury (23) 182 C2
Saint-Venant (62) 5 K4
Saint-Vénérand (43) 238 A2
Saint-Vérain (58) 132 B3
Saint-Vérand (38) 223 G3
Saint-Vérand (69) 187 K6
Saint-Vérand (71) 188 B1
Saint-Vert (43) 219 J1
Saint-Viance (19) 215 H3
Saint-Viâtre (41) 130 A3
Saint-Viaud (44) 122 C3
Saint-Victeur (72) 82 C4
Saint-Victor (03) 167 H6
Saint-Victor (07) 222 A4
Saint-Victor (15) 217 G6
Saint-Victor (24) 213 H2
Saint-Victor-de-Buthon (28) 84 B3
Saint-Victor-de-Cessieu (38) 207 H4
Saint-Victor-de-Chrétienville (27) . . 34 C6
Saint-Victor-de-Malcap (30) 255 J4
Saint-Victor-de-Morestel (38) 207 H2
Saint-Victor-de-Réno (61) 83 J2
Saint-Victor-d'Épine (27) 34 D5
Saint-Victor-des-Oules (30) 256 B6
Saint-Victor-en-Marche (23) 182 C3
Saint-Victor-et-Melvieu (12) 272 B1
Saint-Victor-la-Coste (30) 256 C6
Saint-Victor-la-Rivière (63) 202 B5
Saint-Victor-l'Abbaye (76) 16 A4
Saint-Victor-Malescours (43) 221 G2
Saint-Victor-Montvianeix (63) 186 A6
Saint-Victor-Rouzaud (09) 307 H1
Saint-Victor-sur-Arlanc (43) 220 B2
Saint-Victor-sur-Avre (27) 56 A5
Saint-Victor-sur-Ouche (21) 135 H6
Saint-Victor-sur-Rhins (42) 187 H5
Saint-Victoret (13) 296 B2
Saint-Victour (19) 201 G6
Saint-Victurnien (87) 180 E6
Saint-Vidal (43) 220 B5

Saint-Vigor (27) 35 K6
Saint-Vigor-des-Mézerets (14) . . . 53 G2
Saint-Vigor-des-Monts (50) 31 H6
Saint-Vigor-d'Ymonville (76) 34 B1
Saint-Vigor-le-Grand (14) 32 B3
Saint-Vincent (31) 289 F3
Saint-Vincent (43) 220 C4
Saint-Vincent (63) 202 B5
Saint-Vincent (64) 285 F6
Saint-Vincent (82) 250 A5
Saint-Vincent-Bragny (71) 170 C4
Saint-Vincent-Cramesnil (76) 34 B1
Saint-Vincent-de-
    Barbeyrargues (34) 274 C5
Saint-Vincent-de-Barrès (07) 240 A4
Saint-Vincent-de-Boisset (42) 187 F5
Saint-Vincent-de-Connezac (24) . . 213 H4
Saint-Vincent-de-Cosse (24) 232 E2
Saint-Vincent-de-Durfort (07) 239 K2
Saint-Vincent-de-Lamontjoie (47) . 248 A6
Saint-Vincent-de-Mercuze (38) . . . 208 C6
Saint-Vincent-de-Paul (33) 211 J6
Saint-Vincent-de-Paul (40) 264 B4
Saint-Vincent-de-Pertignas (33) . . 230 B2
Saint-Vincent-de-Reins (69) 187 J4
Saint-Vincent-de-Salers (15) 217 J3
Saint-Vincent-de-Tyrosse (40) . . . 262 C5
Saint-Vincent-des-Bois (27) 57 F1
Saint-Vincent-des-Landes (44) . . . 103 H4
Saint-Vincent-des-Prés (71) 171 G4
Saint-Vincent-des-Prés (72) 83 F4
Saint-Vincent-d'Olargues (34) 291 G1
Saint-Vincent-du-Boulay (27) 34 C6
Saint-Vincent-du-Lorouër (72) . . . 107 G5
Saint-Vincent-du-Pendit (46) 234 C2
Saint-Vincent-en-Bresse (71) 172 B2
Saint-Vincent-Jalmoutiers (24) . . . 213 F3
Saint-Vincent-la-Châtre (79) 178 E2
Saint-Vincent-la-
    Commanderie (26) 222 E6
Saint-Vincent-le-Paluel (24) 233 F2
Saint-Vincent-les-Forts (04) 243 H6
Saint-Vincent-Lespinasse (82) . . . 248 E5
Saint-Vincent-Rive-d'Olt (46) 249 J1
Saint-Vincent-Sterlanges (85) 160 B1
Saint-Vincent-sur-Graon (85) 159 J3
Saint-Vincent-sur-Jabron (04) 258 D4
Saint-Vincent-sur-Jard (85) 159 G5
Saint-Vincent-sur-l'Isle (24) 214 C3
Saint-Vincent-sur-Oust (56) 102 B3
Saint-Vit (25) 155 K1
Saint-Vital (73) 209 F3
Saint-Vite (47) 248 E1
Saint-Vitte (18) 167 G4
Saint-Vitte-sur-Briance (87) 199 H4
Saint-Vivien (17) 176 E3
Saint-Vivien (24) 230 E1
Saint-Vivien-de-Blaye (33) 211 H4
Saint-Vivien-de-Médoc (33) 194 C6
Saint-Vivien-de-Monségur (33) . . . 230 E5
Saint-Voir (03) 169 G5
Saint-Vougay (29) 46 D4
Saint-Vrain (51) 63 H5
Saint-Vrain (91) 86 E2
Saint-Vran (22) 77 J4
Saint-Vulbas (01) 207 F1
Saint-Waast (59) 13 F2
Saint-Witz (95) 38 B6
Saint-Xandre (17) 176 E2
Saint-Yaguen (40) 264 E2
Saint-Yan (71) 170 B5
Saint-Ybard (19) 199 H6
Saint-Ybars (09) 288 B3
Saint-Yon (91) 86 D1
Saint-Yorre (03) 185 J4
Saint-Yrieix-la-Montagne (23) 182 E6
Saint-Yrieix-la-Perche (87) 198 E5
Saint-Yrieix-le-Déjalat (19) 200 C6
Saint-Yrieix-les-Bois (23) 182 D4
Saint-Yrieix-sous-Aixe (87) 198 D1
Saint-Ythaire (71) 171 G3
Saint-Yvoine (63) 202 E4
Saint-Yvy (63) 74 E6
Saint-Yzan-de-Soudiac (33) 211 J4
Saint-Yzans-de-Médoc (33) 211 F1
Saint-Zacharie (83) 297 F3
Sainte-Adresse (76) 33 J1
Sainte-Agathe (63) 203 J1
Sainte-Agathe-d'Aliermont (76) . . . 16 C3
Sainte-Agathe-en-Donzy (42) 205 F1
Sainte-Agathe-la-Bouteresse (42) . 204 D2
Sainte-Agnès (06) 281 J2
Sainte-Agnès (38) 224 C2
Sainte-Agnès (39) 173 F2
Sainte-Alauzie (46) 249 J3
Sainte-Alvère (24) 232 B1
Sainte-Anastasie (15) 218 D4
Sainte-Anastasie (30) 275 D4
Sainte-Anastasie-sur-Issole (83) . . 298 A3
Sainte-Anne (32) 268 C4
Sainte-Anne (41) 108 C6
Sainte-Anne-d'Auray (56) 100 D4
Sainte-Anne-Saint-Priest (87) 199 K3
Sainte-Anne-sur-Brivet (44) 102 C6
Sainte-Anne-sur-Gervonde (38) . . . 206 E5
Sainte-Anne-sur-Vilaine (35) 102 E3
Sainte-Aulde (77) 60 C2
Sainte-Aurence-Cazaux (32) 286 B3
Sainte-Austreberthe (62) 9 J2

Sainte-Austreberthe (76) 15 J5
Sainte-Barbe (57) 45 G4
Sainte-Barbe (88) 95 F2
Sainte-Barbe-sur-Gaillon (27) 35 K5
Sainte-Bazeille (47) 230 D6
Sainte-Beuve-en-Rivière (76) 16 D3
Sainte-Blandine (38) 207 G4
Sainte-Blandine (79) 178 C1
Sainte-Brigitte (56) 76 C4
Sainte-Camelle (11) 289 F5
Sainte-Catherine (62) 10 E2
Sainte-Catherine (63) 203 H6
Sainte-Catherine (69) 205 H4
Sainte-Catherine-de-Fierbois (37). . 145 K2
Sainte-Cécile (36) 147 K1
Sainte-Cécile (50) 52 B3
Sainte-Cécile (71) 171 H5
Sainte-Cécile (85) 142 C6
Sainte-Cécile-d'Andorge (30) 255 F4
Sainte-Cécile-du-Cayrou (81) 270 A1
Sainte-Cécile-les-Vignes (84) 257 F4
Sainte-Céronne-lès-Mortagne (61) . 83 H1
Sainte-Cérotte (72) 107 J4
Sainte-Christie (32) 267 J4
Sainte-Christie-d'Armagnac (32). . . 266 C4
Sainte-Christine (49) 124 D5
Sainte-Christine (63) 184 C4
Sainte-Colombe (05) 258 D3
Sainte-Colombe (16) 197 F1
Sainte-Colombe (17) 212 A2
Sainte-Colombe (21) 134 E4
Sainte-Colombe (25) 156 E4
Sainte-Colombe (33) 230 C1
Sainte-Colombe (35) 103 J1
Sainte-Colombe (40) 265 G5
Sainte-Colombe (46) 234 D4
Sainte-Colombe (50) 28 D5
Sainte-Colombe (69) 206 B5
Sainte-Colombe (76) 15 G3
Sainte-Colombe (77) 88 D2
Sainte-Colombe (89) 134 A2
Sainte-Colombe-de-Duras (47) . . . 230 E4
Sainte-Colombe-de-
    la-Commanderie (66) 315 F3
Sainte-Colombe-de-Peyre (48) . . . 237 F4
Sainte-Colombe-de-
    Villeneuve (47) 248 C2
Sainte-Colombe-des-Bois (58) . . . 132 C2
Sainte-Colombe-en-Bruilhois (47) . 248 A5
Sainte-Colombe-
    la-Commanderie (27) 35 G6
Sainte-Colombe-près-Vernon (27) . 36 A6
Sainte-Colombe-sur-Gand (42) . . . 187 H6
Sainte-Colombe-sur-Guette (11) . . 308 C3
Sainte-Colombe-sur-l'Hers (11) . . . 308 C3
Sainte-Colombe-sur-Loing (89) . . . 132 D2
Sainte-Colombe-sur-Seine (21) . . . 115 F4
Sainte-Colome (64) 303 H1
Sainte-Consorce (69) 205 K2
Sainte-Croix (01) 188 E6
Sainte-Croix (02) 40 C1
Sainte-Croix (12) 251 F2
Sainte-Croix (24) 232 B3
Sainte-Croix (26) 241 G3
Sainte-Croix (46) 249 H3
Sainte-Croix (71) 172 D3
Sainte-Croix (81) 270 D2
Sainte-Croix-à-Lauze (04) 277 K2
Sainte-Croix-aux-Mines (68) 96 A2
Sainte-Croix-de-Caderle (30) 254 E6
Sainte-Croix-de-Mareuil (24) 197 G6
Sainte-Croix-de-Quintillargues (34) . 274 C4
Sainte-Croix-de-Verdon (04) 279 F4
Sainte-Croix-du-Mont (33) 230 A5
Sainte-Croix-en-Jarez (42) 205 J5
Sainte-Croix-en-Plaine (68) 96 C5
Sainte-Croix-Grand-Tonne (14) . . . 32 C4
Sainte-Croix-Hague (50) 28 B2
Sainte-Croix-sur-Aizier (27) 34 D2
Sainte-Croix-sur-Buchy (76) 16 C6
Sainte-Croix-sur-Mer (14) 32 D3
Sainte-Croix-sur-Orne (61) 53 K4
Sainte-Croix-Vallée-Française (48) . 254 D5
Sainte-Croix-Volvestre (09) 306 D1
Sainte-Dode (32) 286 A3
Sainte-Eanne (79) 162 A5
Sainte-Engrâce (64) 302 C2
Sainte-Énimie (48) 254 B3
Sainte-Eugénie-de-Villeneuve (43). . 219 K4
Sainte-Eulalie (07) 239 G2
Sainte-Eulalie (11) 289 K5
Sainte-Eulalie (15) 217 G4
Sainte-Eulalie (33) 229 J1
Sainte-Eulalie (48) 237 H3
Sainte-Eulalie-d'Ans (24) 214 D3
Sainte-Eulalie-de-Cernon (12) 272 E2
Sainte-Eulalie-d'Eymet (24) 231 G4
Sainte-Eulalie-d'Olt (12) 253 F1
Sainte-Eulalie-en-Born (40) 244 D3
Sainte-Eulalie-en-Royans (26) . . . 223 G5
Sainte-Euphémie (01) 188 C5
Sainte-Euphémie-sur-Ouvèze (26) . 258 A3
Sainte-Eusoye (60) 18 A6
Sainte-Fauste (36) 148 B6
Sainte-Féréole (19) 215 J3
Sainte-Feyre (23) 182 D3
Sainte-Feyre-la-Montagne (23) . . . 183 G6
Sainte-Flaive-des-Loups (85) 159 G2
Sainte-Florence (33) 230 C2
Sainte-Florence (85) 142 C6
Sainte-Florine (43) 219 G1
Sainte-Foi (09) 308 B1

Sainte-Fortunade (19) 216 B3
Sainte-Foy (40) 265 K2
Sainte-Foy (71) 187 F1
Sainte-Foy (76) 16 A3
Sainte-Foy (85) 159 F3
Sainte-Foy-d'Aigrefeuille (31) 288 D1
Sainte-Foy-de-Belvès (24) 232 D3
Sainte-Foy-de-Longas (24) 232 A1
Sainte-Foy-de-Montgommery (14) . . 54 E2
Sainte-Foy-de-Peyrolières (31) 287 J2
Sainte-Foy-la-Grande (33) 231 F2
Sainte-Foy-la-Longue (33) 230 B5
Sainte-Foy-l'Argentière (69) 205 H3
Sainte-Foy-lès-Lyon (69) 206 A2
Sainte-Foy-Saint-Sulpice (42) 204 D2
Sainte-Foy-Tarentaise (73) 193 B3
Sainte-Gauburge-
   Sainte-Colombe (61) 55 G5
Sainte-Gemme (17) 194 D1
Sainte-Gemme (32) 268 A4
Sainte-Gemme (33) 230 D5
Sainte-Gemme (36) 147 G6
Sainte-Gemme (51) 40 B5
Sainte-Gemme (79) 144 A5
Sainte-Gemme (81) 251 H6
Sainte-Gemme-en-Sancerrois (18) . 131 J5
Sainte-Gemme-la-Plaine (85) 160 B4
Sainte-Gemme-Martaillac (47) . . . 247 G2
Sainte-Gemme-Moronval (28) 57 F5
Sainte-Gemmes (41) 108 E5
Sainte-Gemmes-d'Andigné (49) . . . 104 D6
Sainte-Gemmes-le-Robert (53) 81 J6
Sainte-Gemmes-sur-Loire (49) . . . 125 G4
Sainte-Geneviève (02) 21 H4
Sainte-Geneviève (50) 29 F2
Sainte-Geneviève (54) 65 K2
Sainte-Geneviève (60) 37 J4
Sainte-Geneviève (76) 16 C5
Sainte-Geneviève-des-Bois (45) . . . 111 J5
Sainte-Geneviève-des-Bois (91) . . . 58 E6
Sainte-Geneviève-lès-Gasny (27) . . 36 C6
Sainte-Geneviève-
   sur-Argence (12) 236 B3
Sainte-Hélène (33) 210 E6
Sainte-Hélène (48) 237 K6
Sainte-Hélène (56) 100 B4
Sainte-Hélène (71) 171 H1
Sainte-Hélène (88) 95 F4
Sainte-Hélène-Bondeville (76) 14 D3
Sainte-Hélène-du-Lac (73) 208 D5
Sainte-Hélène-sur-Isère (73) 209 F3
Sainte-Hermine (85) 160 B3
Sainte-Honorine-de-Ducy (14) 32 A5
Sainte-Honorine-des-Pertes (14) . . 32 A2
Sainte-Honorine-du-Fay (14) 32 D6
Sainte-Honorine-
   la-Chardonne (61) 53 H3
Sainte-Honorine-la-Guillaume (61) . 53 J4
Sainte-Innocence (24) 231 H3
Sainte-Jalle (26) 257 J2
Sainte-Jamme-sur-Sarthe (72) . . . 106 D1
Sainte-Julie (01) 189 G6
Sainte-Juliette (82) 249 H3
Sainte-Juliette-sur-Viaur (12) 252 B4
Sainte-Léocadie (66) 313 H5
Sainte-Lheurine (17) 195 J5
Sainte-Livrade (31) 268 D6
Sainte-Livrade-sur-Lot (47) 248 B2
Sainte-Lizaigne (36) 148 D4
Sainte-Luce (38) 242 C1
Sainte-Luce-sur-Loire (44) 123 H3
Sainte-Lucie-de-Tallano (2A) 323 F2
Sainte-Lunaise (18) 149 G5
Sainte-Magnance (89) 134 B4
Sainte-Marguerite (43) 219 K3
Sainte-Marguerite (88) 95 J4
Sainte-Marguerite-
   de-Carrouges (61) 82 B1
Sainte-Marguerite-de-l'Autel (27) . . 56 A3
Sainte-Marguerite-de-Viette (14) . . 54 D1
Sainte-Marguerite-d'Elle (14) 31 J2
Sainte-Marguerite-des-Loges (14) . 54 E1
Sainte-Marguerite-en-Ouche (27) . . 55 J1
Sainte-Marguerite-Lafigère (07) . . 255 F1
Sainte-Marguerite-sur-Duclair (76) . 35 F1
Sainte-Marguerite-sur-Fauville (76) . 15 F4
Sainte-Marguerite-sur-Mer (76) . . . 15 J2
Sainte-Marie (05) 258 B1
Sainte-Marie (08) 42 B2
Sainte-Marie (15) 236 C2
Sainte-Marie (25) 139 G2
Sainte-Marie (32) 268 B5
Sainte-Marie (35) 102 C3
Sainte-Marie (58) 151 G2
Sainte-Marie (65) 305 J3
Sainte-Marie (66) 310 D6
Sainte-Marie-à-Py (51) 41 K4
Sainte-Marie-au-Bosc (76) 14 B4
Sainte-Marie-aux-Chênes (57) 27 F6
Sainte-Marie-aux-Mines (68) 96 A2
Sainte-Marie-Cappel (59) 3 J4
Sainte-Marie-d'Alloix (38) 208 C6
Sainte-Marie-d'Alvey (73) 207 K4
Sainte-Marie-de-Chignac (24) 214 B4
Sainte-Marie-de-Cuines (73) 225 G1
Sainte-Marie-de-Gosse (40) 262 D6
Sainte-Marie-de-Ré (17) 176 C2
Sainte-Marie-de-Vatimesnil (27) . . . 36 C4
Sainte-Marie-de-Vaux (87) 198 D1
Sainte-Marie-des-Champs (76) 15 G5
Sainte-Marie-du-Bois (50) 80 E1
Sainte-Marie-du-Bois (53) 81 H2

Sainte-Marie-du-
   Lac-Nuisement (51) 63 H6
Sainte-Marie-du-Mont (38) 208 C6
Sainte-Marie-du-Mont (50) 29 G6
Sainte-Marie-en-Chanois (70) 118 E4
Sainte-Marie-en-Chaux (70) 118 C4
Sainte-Marie-Kerque (62) 3 F3
Sainte-Marie-la-Blanche (21) 154 B4
Sainte-Marie-la-Robert (61) 54 B6
Sainte-Marie-Lapanouze (19) 201 F6
Sainte-Marie-Laumont (14) 31 J6
Sainte-Marie-Outre-l'Eau (14) 31 H5
Sainte-Marie-sur-Ouche (21) 135 J6
Sainte-Marthe (27) 56 A2
Sainte-Marthe (47) 247 G2
Sainte-Maure (10) 90 A4
Sainte-Maure-de-Peyriac (47) 266 D1
Sainte-Maure-de-Touraine (37) . . . 145 K2
Sainte-Maxime (83) 299 F3
Sainte-Même (17) 178 A6
Sainte-Menehould (51) 42 D6
Sainte-Mère (32) 267 J1
Sainte-Mère-Église (50) 29 F5
Sainte-Mesme (78) 86 A2
Sainte-Mondane (24) 233 G2
Sainte-Montaine (18) 130 E3
Sainte-Nathalène (24) 233 F1
Sainte-Néomaye (79) 161 K6
Sainte-Olive (01) 188 D4
Sainte-Opportune (61) 53 J4
Sainte-Opportune-du-Bosc (27) . . . 35 F5
Sainte-Opportune-la-Mare (27) . . . 34 C2
Sainte-Orse (24) 214 E3
Sainte-Osmane (72) 107 H4
Sainte-Ouenne (79) 161 H5
Sainte-Pallaye (89) 133 H1
Sainte-Paule (69) 187 K5
Sainte-Pazanne (44) 122 E5
Sainte-Pexine (85) 160 A3
Sainte-Pience (50) 52 A4
Sainte-Pôle (54) 95 G1
Sainte-Preuve (02) 21 F5
Sainte-Radegonde (12) 252 C3
Sainte-Radegonde (17) 177 G6
Sainte-Radegonde (24) 231 K4
Sainte-Radegonde (32) 267 H3
Sainte-Radegonde (33) 230 D2
Sainte-Radegonde (71) 170 B2
Sainte-Radegonde (79) 144 B4
Sainte-Radegonde (86) 163 J2
Sainte-Radegonde-
   des-Noyers (85) 160 B5
Sainte-Ramée (17) 195 F6
Sainte-Reine (70) 137 H3
Sainte-Reine (73) 208 D3
Sainte-Reine-de-Bretagne (44) . . . 122 A1
Sainte-Ruffine (57) 44 E5
Sainte-Sabine (21) 153 J1
Sainte-Sabine-Born (24) 232 A4
Sainte-Sabine-sur-Longève (72) . . 106 D1
Sainte-Savine (10) 90 A5
Sainte-Scolasse-sur-Sarthe (61) . . . 83 G1
Sainte-Segrée (80) 17 H4
Sainte-Sève (29) 47 F5
Sainte-Sévère (16) 196 A2
Sainte-Sévère-sur-Indre (36) 166 C4
Sainte-Sigolène (43) 221 F3
Sainte-Solange (18) 149 J2
Sainte-Soline (79) 179 F1
Sainte-Souline (16) 212 D1
Sainte-Soulle (17) 176 E2
Sainte-Suzanne (09) 288 B5
Sainte-Suzanne (25) 139 H2
Sainte-Suzanne (53) 105 J1
Sainte-Suzanne-sur-Vire (50) 31 H4
Sainte-Terre (33) 230 B2
Sainte-Thérence (03) 184 A2
Sainte-Thorette (18) 148 E3
Sainte-Trephine (22) 76 C3
Sainte-Trie (24) 215 F2
Sainte-Tulle (04) 278 B3
Sainte-Valière (11) 291 G5
Sainte-Vaubourg (08) 42 A1
Sainte-Verge (79) 144 B3
Sainte-Vertu (89) 113 K6
Sainteny (50) 31 F2
Saintes (17) 195 G2
Saintes-Maries-de-la-Mer (13) . . . 294 C5
Saintines (60) 38 D3
Saintry-sur-Seine (91) 87 F1
Saints (77) 60 B5
Saints (89) 132 D2
Saints-Geosmes (52) 116 D4
Sainville (28) 86 A3
Saires (86) 145 F5
Saires-la-Verrerie (61) 53 H5
Saissac (11) 289 K4
Saisseval (80) 17 K2
Saisy (71) 153 H4
Saivres (79) 161 K5
le Saix (05) 242 C6
Saïx (81) 289 K1
Saix (86) 144 D2
Saizenay (39) 156 A4
Saizerais (54) 65 K3
Saizy (58) 133 H5
Sajas (31) 287 H3
Salagnac (24) 215 F2
Salagnon (38) 207 F3
Salaise-sur-Sanne (38) 222 B1
Salans (39) 155 K1
Salasc (34) 273 G6

Salaunes (33) 210 E6
Salavas (07) 255 K2
Salavre (01) 172 K2
Salazac (30) 256 B4
Salbris (41) 130 B4
les Salces (48) 237 F6
Saléchan (65) 305 J3
Saleich (31) 306 B2
Saleignes (17) 178 D4
Saleilles (66) 315 H2
les Salelles (07) 255 G1
les Salelles (48) 253 J1
Salency (60) 19 H6
Salenthal (67) 70 B2
Saléon (05) 258 A2
Salérans (05) 258 D3
Salerm (31) 287 F4
Salernes (83) 279 G6
Salers (15) 217 J4
Sales (74) 190 D6
Salescheles (59) 12 D4
la Salette-Fallavaux (38) 242 D1
Salettes (26) 240 D5
Salettes (43) 238 D2
Saleux (80) 18 A2
Salice (2A) 320 D3
Saliceto (2B) 319 G4
Saliès (81) 270 D3
Salies-de-Béarn (64) 283 H2
Salies-du-Salat (31) 306 B1
Salignac (04) 259 G4
Salignac (33) 211 K5
Salignac-de-Mirambeau (17) 211 J1
Salignac-Eyvigues (24) 215 G6
Salignac-sur-Charente (17) 195 J4
Saligney (39) 137 G6
Saligny (85) 141 K5
Saligny (89) 88 E6
Saligny-le-Vif (18) 150 A3
Saligny-sur-Roudon (03) 169 J5
Saligos (65) 304 B3
Salindres (30) 255 H5
Salinelles (30) 274 D4
Salins (15) 217 H4
Salins (77) 88 B3
Salins-les-Bains (39) 156 A4
Salins-les-Thermes (73) 209 H5
Salives (21) 135 K1
Sallagriffon (06) 280 D2
Sallanches (74) 192 A5
Sallaumines (62) 11 F1
la Salle (71) 171 K5
la Salle (88) 95 G3
la Salle-de-Vihiers (49) 143 H1
la Salle-en-Beaumont (38) 242 C1
la Salle-et-Chapelle-Aubry (49) . . . 124 C6
la Salle-Prunet (48) 254 C3
Salleboeuf (33) 229 J2
Sallèdes (63) 203 F3
Sallèles-Cabardès (11) 290 C4
Sallèles-d'Aude (11) 291 H5
la Salle les Alpes (05) 225 K6
Sallen (14) 31 K3
Sallenelles (14) 33 F4
Sallenôves (74) 190 E4
Sallertaine (85) 140 E5
Salles (33) 228 E5
les Salles (42) 204 A1
Salles (47) 232 B6
Salles (65) 304 A2
Salles (79) 162 A5
Salles (81) 251 F6
Salles-Adour (65) 285 H6
Salles-Arbuissonnas-
   en-Beaujolais (69) 188 A4
Salles-Courbatiès (12) 251 G1
Salles-Curan (12) 252 D5
Salles-d'Angles (16) 195 K4
Salles-d'Armagnac (32) 266 B3
Salles-d'Aude (11) 291 K5
Salles-de-Barbezieux (16) 196 B6
Salles-de-Belvès (24) 232 D4
les Salles-de-Castillon (33) 230 D1
Salles-de-Villefagnan (16) 179 G5
les Salles-du-Gardon (30) 255 G6
Salles-et-Pratviel (31) 305 H4
Salles-la-Source (12) 252 B2
Salles-Lavalette (16) 213 F1
les Salles-Lavauguyon (87) 197 K2
Salles-Mongiscard (64) 283 J1
Salles-sous-Bois (26) 257 F1
Salles-sur-Garonne (31) 287 J5
Salles-sur-l'Hers (11) 289 F4
Salles-sur-Mer (17) 176 E3
les Salles-sur-Verdon (83) 279 F3
Sallespisse (64) 283 K1
Salmagne (55) 64 C4
Salmaise (21) 135 G3
Salmbach (67) 25 D2
Salmiech (12) 252 B5
Salomé (59) 6 C5
Salon (10) 62 A6
Salon (24) 214 B6
Salon-de-Provence (13) 276 E5
Salon-la-Tour (19) 199 H5
Salonnes (57) 66 D3
Salornay-sur-Guye (71) 171 G4
Salouël (80) 18 A2
Salperwick (62) 3 G5
Salsein (09) 306 C3
Salses-le-Château (66) 310 C4
Salsigne (11) 290 B4

Salt-en-Donzy (42) 205 F2
Salvagnac (81) 269 K2
Salvagnac-Cajarc (12) 250 E1
la Salvetat-Belmontet (82) 269 H2
la Salvetat-Lauragais (31) 289 F1
la Salvetat-Peyralès (12) 251 H4
la Salvetat-Saint-Gilles (31) 288 A1
la Salvetat-sur-Agout (34) 271 K6
Salvezines (11) 309 F5
Salviac (46) 233 F4
Salvizinet (42) 205 F2
Salza (11) 309 H3
Salzuit (43) 219 J3
Samadet (40) 265 G6
Saman (31) 286 E5
Samaran (32) 286 C3
Samatan (32) 287 F4
Samazan (47) 247 G1
Sambin (41) 128 E4
Sambourg (89) 114 A5
Saméon (59) 7 G6
Samer (62) 2 B1
Samerey (21) 155 F2
Sames (64) 282 E1
Sammarçolles (86) 144 E3
Sammeron (77) 60 B2
Samoëns (74) 192 B3
Samognat (01) 189 K1
Samogneux (55) 43 H4
Samois-sur-Seine (77) 87 J3
Samonac (33) 211 H5
Samoreau (77) 87 J3
Samouillan (31) 287 G5
Samoussy (02) 20 E6
Sampans (39) 155 G2
Sampigny (55) 64 D3
Sampigny-lès-Maranges (71) 153 J5
Sampolo (2A) 321 F5
Sampzon (07) 255 K1
Samson (25) 156 A2
Samsons-Lion (64) 285 F2
Samuran (31) 305 H2
San-Damiano (2B) 319 H4
San-Gavino-d'Ampugnani (2B) . . . 319 J4
San-Gavino-di-Carbini (2A) 323 G2
San-Gavino-di-Fiumorbo (2B) 321 H4
San-Gavino-di-Tenda (2B) 317 C6
San-Giovanni-di-Moriani (2B) 319 J5
San-Giuliano (2B) 319 J5
San-Lorenzo (2B) 319 G5
San-Martino-di-Lota (2B) 317 E6
San-Nicolao (2B) 319 K5
Sana (31) 287 H5
Sanary-sur-Mer (83) 297 H6
Sancé (71) 171 K6
Sancergues (18) 150 B2
Sancerre (18) 131 K5
Sancey-le-Grand (25) 139 F3
Sancey-le-Long (25) 139 F3
Sancheville (28) 85 H6
Sanchey (88) 94 C5
Sancoins (18) 150 B6
Sancourt (27) 36 D3
Sancourt (59) 11 J3
Sancourt (80) 19 H3
Sancy (54) 26 E4
Sancy (77) 60 A3
Sancy-les-Cheminots (02) 39 K2
Sancy-lès-Provins (77) 60 E5
Sand (67) 70 E6
Sandarville (28) 85 F4
Sandaucourt (88) 93 H4
Sandillon (45) 110 B5
Sandouville (76) 34 A1
Sandrans (01) 188 E4
Sangatte (62) 2 C2
Sanghen (62) 2 D5
Sanguinet (40) 228 C6
Sanilhac (07) 239 G6
Sanilhac-Sagriès (30) 275 H2
Sannat (23) 183 J3
Sannerville (14) 33 F4
Sannes (84) 277 J4
Sannois (95) 58 D2
Sanous (65) 285 G3
Sanry-lès-Vigy (57) 27 H6
Sanry-sur-Nied (57) 45 G6
Sans-Vallois (88) 94 A6
Sansa (66) 313 K3
Sansac-de-Marmiesse (15) 235 G2
Sansac-Veinazès (15) 235 H3
Sansais (79) 177 K1
Sansan (32) 286 D1
Sanssac-l'Église (43) 220 B5
Sanssat (03) 185 J2
Santa-Lucia-di-Mercurio (2B) 319 G5
Santa-Lucia-di-Moriani (2B) 319 K4
Santa-Maria-di-Lota (2B) 317 D4
Santa-Maria-Figaniella (2A) 322 E2
Santa-Maria-Poggio (2B) 319 J5
Santa-Maria-Siché (2B) 317 D5
Santa-Reparata-di-Balagna (2B) . . 318 C2
Santa-Reparata-di-Moriani (2B) . . . 319 J5
Sant'Andréa-di-Bozio (2B) 319 H6
Sant'Andréa-di-Cotone (2B) 319 J5
Sant'Andréa-d'Orcino (2A) 320 C4
Santans (39) 155 G2
Sant'Antonino (2B) 318 C2
Santeau (45) 110 C1
Santec (29) 46 E3
Santenay (21) 153 J5
Santenay (41) 128 C2

Santeny (94) 59 G5
Santes (59) 6 D4
Santeuil (28) 85 J4
Santeuil (95) 37 F6
Santigny (89) 134 B2
Santilly (28) 110 A1
Santilly (71) 171 H3
Santo-Pietro-di-Tenda (2B) 317 C6
Santo-Pietro-di-Venaco (2B) 321 F1
Santoche (25) 138 E3
Santosse (21) 153 J3
Santranges (18) 131 J3
Sanvignes-les-Mines (71) 170 D2
Sanxay (86) 162 B4
Sanzay (79) 143 J4
Saon (14) 31 K1
Saône (25) 138 B6
Saonnet (14) 31 K1
Saorge (06) 311 D3
Saosnes (72) 82 E4
Saou (26) 240 C4
le Sap (61) 55 F3
le Sap-André (61) 55 G4
Sapignicourt (51) 63 H6
Sapignies (62) 11 F5
Sapogne-et-Feuchères (08) 22 D4
Sapogne-sur-Marche (08) 23 J5
Sapois (39) 156 B6
Sapois (88) 119 G1
Saponay (02) 40 A5
Saponcourt (70) 117 K4
le Sappey (74) 191 F3
le Sappey-en-Chartreuse (38) . . . 224 B2
Saramon (32) 286 E1
Saran (45) 110 A3
Saraz (25) 156 B3
Sarbazan (40) 265 J1
Sarcé (72) 106 E6
Sarceaux (61) 54 C5
Sarcelles (95) 58 E2
Sarcenas (38) 224 B2
Sarcey (52) 116 C2
Sarcey (69) 187 K6
Sarcos (32) 286 D3
Sarcus (60) 17 G4
Sarcy (51) 40 D5
Sardan (30) 274 D3
Sardent (23) 182 D4
Sardieu (38) 223 F1
Sardon (63) 185 G5
Sardy-lès-Épiry (58) 151 K1
Sare (64) 263 C2
Sargé-lès-le-Mans (72) 106 E2
Sargé-sur-Braye (41) 108 A4
Sari-d'Orcino (2A) 320 C3
Sari-Solenzara (2A) 321 J6
Sariac-Magnoac (65) 286 C4
Sarlabous (65) 304 E1
Sarlande (24) 198 D6
Sarlat-la-Canéda (24) 233 F2
Sarliac-sur-l'Isle (24) 214 C3
Sarniguet (65) 285 H4
Sarnois (60) 17 H5
Saron-sur-Aube (51) 89 H1
Sarp (65) 305 H2
Sarpourenx (64) 283 K2
Sarragachies (32) 266 B5
Sarrageois (25) 174 C1
Sarraguzan (32) 286 A3
Sarralbe (57) 68 D4
Sarraltroff (57) 67 J3
Sarran (19) 216 C1
Sarrance (64) 303 F1
Sarrancolin (65) 305 F3
Sarrant (32) 268 A2
Sarras (07) 222 B3
Sarrazac (24) 198 C6
Sarrazac (46) 215 J5
Sarraziet (40) 265 G5
Sarre-Union (67) 67 J1
Sarrebourg (57) 67 J4
Sarreguemines (57) 68 D2
Sarreinsming (57) 68 D3
Sarremezan (31) 286 D5
Sarrewerden (67) 67 J1
Sarrey (52) 116 D2
Sarriac-Bigorre (65) 285 J3
Sarrians (84) 257 G6
Sarrigné (49) 125 J3
Sarrogna (39) 173 G4
Sarrola-Carcopino (2A) 320 C4
Sarron (40) 265 J6
Sarrouilles (65) 285 H5
Sarroux (19) 217 H1
Sarry (51) 62 D2
Sarry (71) 187 F1
Sarry (89) 134 B1
le Sars (62) 10 E5
Sars-et-Rosières (59) 7 G6
Sars-le-Bois (62) 10 B3
Sars-Poteries (59) 13 H4
Sartène (2A) 322 E3
Sartes (88) 93 G5
Sartilly (50) 51 J2
Sarton (62) 10 B5
Sartrouville (78) 58 C2
Sarzay (36) 166 A3
Sarzeau (56) 121 F1
Sasnières (41) 108 B6

400

Sassangy (71) 171 H1
Sassay (41) 129 F5
Sassegnies (59) 13 F4
Sassenage (38) 224 A3
Sassenay (71) 154 B6
Sassetot-le-Malgardé (76) 15 H3
Sassetot-le-Mauconduit (76) . . . 14 E3
Sasseville (76) 15 F3
Sassey (27) 56 E1
Sassey-sur-Meuse (55) 43 F2
Sassierges-Saint-Germain (36) . . 166 A1
Sassis (65) 304 B4
Sassy (14) 54 B1
Sathonay-Camp (69) 206 B1
Sathonay-Village (69) 206 B1
Satillieu (07) 221 H4
Satolas-et-Bonce (38) 206 D3
Saturargues (34) 274 E5
Saubens (31) 288 C4
Saubion (40) 262 C5
Saubole (64) 285 F4
Saubrigues (40) 262 C5
Saubusse (40) 262 E5
Saucats (33) 229 G4
Saucède (64) 283 K4
la Saucelle (28) 56 C6
Sauchay (76) 16 A1
Sauchy-Cauchy (62) 11 H3
Sauchy-Lestrée (62) 11 H3
Sauclières (12) 273 G2
Saudemont (62) 11 H3
Saudoy (51) 61 H5
Saudron (52) 92 C2
Saudrupt (55) 64 A5
Saugeot (39) 173 J2
Saugnac-et-Cambran (40) 264 B5
Saugnacq-et-Muret (40) 245 G1
Saugon (33) 211 J3
Saugues (43) 237 J1
Sauguis-Saint-Étienne (64) . . . 283 H6
Saugy (18) 148 D4
Saujac (12) 250 E4
Saujon (17) 194 D3
la Saulce (05) 259 G1
Saulce-sur-Rhône (26) 240 B4
Saulces-Champenoises (08) 41 K1
Saulces-Monclin (08) 22 B6
Saulcet (03) 185 G1
Saulchery (02) 60 D2
le Saulchoy (60) 17 K5
Saulchoy (62) 9 G2
Saulchoy-sous-Poix (80) 17 H4
Saulcy (10) 91 H5
le Saulcy (88) 95 J2
Saulcy-sur-Meurthe (88) 95 J4
Saules (25) 156 D1
Saules (71) 171 H2
Saulgé (86) 164 A6
Saulgé-l'Hôpital (49) 125 J6
Saulges (53) 105 J3
Saulgond (16) 180 C5
Sauliac-sur-Célé (46) 234 A6
Saulieu (21) 134 C6
Saulles (52) 116 E6
Saulmory-et-Villefranche (55) . . 43 F1
Saulnay (36) 147 F5
Saulnes (54) 26 A2
Saulnières (28) 56 E6
Saulnières (35) 103 G1
Saulnot (70) 139 F1
Saulny (57) 44 E5
Saulon-la-Chapelle (21) 154 C1
Saulon-la-Rue (21) 136 A6
la Saulsotte (10) 89 F2
Sault (84) 258 A5
Sault-Brénaz (01) 189 J6
Sault-de-Navailles (64) 283 K1
Sault-lès-Rethel (08) 41 J1
Sault-Saint-Remy (08) 41 G2
Saultain (59) 12 D2
Saulty (62) 10 C4
Saulvaux (55) 64 D5
Saulx (70) 118 C6
Saulx-le-Duc (21) 136 A2
Saulx-lès-Champlon (55) 44 A6
Saulx-les-Chartreux (91) 58 D5
Saulx-Marchais (78) 57 K4
Saulxerotte (54) 93 J2
Saulxures (67) 95 K2
Saulxures-lès-Bulgnéville (88) . . 93 H5
Saulxures-lès-Nancy (54) 66 B5
Saulxures-lès-Vannes (54) 93 H1
Saulxures-sur-Moselotte (88) . . . 119 G2
Saulzais-le-Potier (18) 167 G3
Saulzet (03) 185 G3
Saulzet-le-Froid (63) 202 B4
Saulzoir (59) 12 C3
Saumane (04) 258 D5
Saumane (30) 254 D5
Saumane-de-Vaucluse (84) 276 E2
Sauméjan (47) 247 F4
Saumeray (28) 84 E5
Saumont (47) 247 K5
Saumont-la-Poterie (76) 16 E6
Saumos (33) 210 D6
Saumur (49) 126 B6
Saunay (37) 128 B2
la Saunière (23) 182 D3
Saunières (71) 154 C5
Sauqueville (76) 15 K2
Saurais (79) 162 A4
Saurat (09) 307 H4

Sauret-Besserve (63) 184 C5
Saurier (63) 202 C5
Sausheim (68) 97 C2
Saussan (34) 293 F1
Saussay (28) 57 F3
Saussay (76) 15 J5
Saussay-la-Campagne (27) 36 A3
la Saussaye (27) 35 G4
Saussemesnil (50) 28 E3
Saussenac (81) 271 F1
Saussens (31) 288 E1
Sausses (04) 260 E6
Sausset-les-Pins (13) 295 K6
Sausseuzemare-en-Caux (76) . . . 14 C4
Saussey (21) 153 H3
Saussey (50) 30 E4
Saussignac (24) 231 G3
Saussines (34) 274 D4
Saussy (21) 135 K3
Sautel (09) 308 A3
Sauternes (33) 229 K6
Sauteyrargues (34) 274 C3
Sauto (66) 313 J4
Sautron (44) 123 F3
la Sauvagère (61) 53 J6
les Sauvages (69) 187 H6
Sauvagnac (16) 197 J2
Sauvagnas (47) 248 C4
Sauvagnat (63) 201 J2
Sauvagnat-Sainte-Marthe (63) . . 202 E4
Sauvagney (25) 137 J5
Sauvagnon (64) 284 C3
Sauvagny (03) 167 K5
Sauvain (42) 204 B3
Sauvat (15) 217 H2
Sauve (30) 274 C2
la Sauve (33) 229 K3
Sauvelade (64) 283 K3
Sauverny (01) 174 B6
Sauvessanges (63) 220 C1
la Sauvetat (32) 267 H3
la Sauvetat (63) 202 E4
la Sauvetat-de-Savères (47) . . . 248 D4
la Sauvetat-du-Dropt (47) 231 G4
la Sauvetat-sur-Lède (47) 248 C1
Sauveterre (30) 276 B1
Sauveterre (32) 287 F2
Sauveterre (65) 285 H2
Sauveterre (81) 290 D2
Sauveterre (82) 249 J4
Sauveterre-de-Béarn (64) 283 H3
Sauveterre-de-Comminges (31) . . 305 J2
Sauveterre-de-Guyenne (33) . . . 230 C4
Sauveterre-de-Rouergue (12) . . . 251 J4
Sauveterre-la-Lémance (47) . . . 232 D5
Sauveterre-Saint-Denis (47) . . . 248 C5
Sauviac (32) 286 B3
Sauviac (33) 246 D2
Sauvian (34) 292 A4
Sauviat (63) 203 H3
Sauviat-sur-Vige (87) 182 A6
Sauvignac (16) 212 C2
Sauvigney-lès-Gray (70) 137 H3
Sauvigney-lès-Pesmes (70) 137 F5
Sauvigny (55) 93 G2
Sauvigny-le-Beuréal (89) 134 B3
Sauvigny-le-Bois (89) 133 K3
Sauvigny-les-Bois (58) 151 F4
Sauville (08) 22 E6
Sauville (88) 93 G6
Sauvillers-Mongival (80) 18 C4
Sauvimont (32) 287 G2
Sauvoy (55) 65 F6
Saux (46) 249 G3
Saux-et-Pomarède (31) 286 E6
Sauxillanges (63) 203 G5
Sauze (06) 261 F5
Sauzé-Vaussais (79) 179 F3
Sauzelles (36) 164 B6
Sauzet (26) 240 B5
Sauzet (30) 275 F2
Sauzet (46) 249 H2
la Sauzière-Saint-Jean (81) . . . 269 J2
Sauzon (56) 120 A3
Savarthès (31) 306 A1
Savas (07) 222 A2
Savas-Mépin (38) 206 D5
Savasse (26) 240 B5
Savenay (44) 122 D2
Savenès (82) 268 E3
Savennes (23) 182 D4
Savennes (63) 201 H4
Savennières (49) 125 F4
Saverdun (09) 288 D5
Savères (31) 287 J3
Saverne (67) 70 B1
Saveuse (80) 18 A2
Savianges (71) 171 G2
Savières (10) 89 K3
Savigna (39) 173 G4
Savignac (12) 251 F3
Savignac (33) 230 B6
Savignac-de-Duras (47) 230 E4
Savignac-de-l'Isle (33) 212 A6
Savignac-de-Miremont (24) 214 D6
Savignac-de-Nontron (24) 197 K5
Savignac-Lédrier (24) 215 F1
Savignac-les-Églises (24) 214 C2
Savignac-les-Ormeaux (09) 308 A1
Savignac-Mona (32) 287 H2
Savignac-sur-Leyze (47) 248 D1

Savignargues (30) 274 E2
Savigné (86) 179 H3
Savigné-l'Évêque (72) 107 F2
Savigné-sous-le-Lude (72) 126 C1
Savigné-sur-Lathan (37) 127 F4
Savigneux (01) 188 C4
Savigneux (42) 204 D4
Savignies (60) 37 F1
Savigny (50) 31 F4
Savigny (52) 117 G1
Savigny (69) 205 H1
Savigny (74) 190 D3
Savigny (88) 94 B3
Savigny-en-Revermont (71) 172 E2
Savigny-en-Sancerre (18) 131 J4
Savigny-en-Septaine (18) 149 J3
Savigny-en-Terre-Plaine (89) . . 134 B3
Savigny-en-Véron (37) 144 E1
Savigny-le-Sec (21) 136 A4
Savigny-le-Temple (77) 87 G1
Savigny-le-Vieux (50) 80 C1
Savigny-lès-Beaune (21) 154 A3
Savigny-Lévescault (86) 163 G4
Savigny-Poil-Fol (58) 169 K1
Savigny-sous-Faye (86) 145 G5
Savigny-sous-Mâlain (21) 135 H5
Savigny-sur-Aisne (08) 42 B3
Savigny-sur-Ardres (51) 40 C4
Savigny-sur-Braye (41) 107 K4
Savigny-sur-Clairis (89) 112 B3
Savigny-sur-Grosne (71) 171 H3
Savigny-sur-Orge (91) 58 E6
Savigny-sur-Seille (71) 172 B2
Savilly (21) 152 E2
Savines-le-Lac (05) 243 H5
Savins (77) 88 C2
Savoillan (84) 258 A4
Savoisy (21) 114 E6
Savolles (21) 136 C4
Savonnières (37) 127 H5
Savonnières-devant-Bar (55) . . . 64 B4
Savonnières-en-Perthois (55) . . 64 A6
Savouges (21) 154 C1
Savournon (05) 258 E1
Savoyeux (70) 137 H2
Savy (02) 19 J3
Savy-Berlette (62) 10 E3
Saxel (74) 191 H1
Saxi-Bourdon (58) 151 H3
Saxon-Sion (54) 93 K2
Sayat (63) 202 D1
Saze (30) 276 A2
Sazeray (36) 166 C5
Sazeret (03) 168 A6
Sazilly (37) 145 G2
Sazos (65) 304 B4
Scaër (29) 75 G6
Scata (2B) 319 H4
Sceau-Saint-Angel (24) 197 K5
Sceautres (07) 239 K5
Sceaux (89) 134 A3
Sceaux (92) 58 E4
Sceaux-d'Anjou (49) 125 G1
Sceaux-du-Gâtinais (45) 111 J3
Sceaux-sur-Huisne (72) 107 H1
Scey-Maisières (25) 156 C2
Scey-sur-Saône-et-Saint-Albin (70) . . . 117 K3
Schaeffersheim (67) 70 E5
Schaffhouse-près-Seltz (67) . . . 25 D2
Schaffhouse-sur-Zorn (67) 70 D1
Schalbach (57) 67 K3
Schalkendorf (67) 69 J6
Scharrachbergheim-Irmstett (67) . 70 D3
Scheibenhard (67) 25 D1
Scherlenheim (67) 70 D1
Scherwiller (67) 70 D6
Schillersdorf (67) 69 H5
Schiltigheim (67) 25 A6
Schirmeck (67) 70 A5
Schirrhein (67) 25 B4
Schirrhoffen (67) 25 B4
Schleithal (67) 25 D1
Schlierbach (68) 97 D3
Schmittviller (57) 68 E4
Schneckenbusch (57) 67 J4
Schnersheim (67) 70 D2
Schoenau (67) 71 D5
Schoenbourg (67) 69 F6
Schoeneck (57) 68 C1
Schoenenbourg (67) 25 B2
Schopperten (67) 67 J1
Schorbach (57) 69 G3
Schweighouse-sur-Moder (67) . . . 25 A4
Schweighouse-Thann (68) 97 A2
Schwenheim (67) 70 C2
Schwerdorff (57) 45 J2
Schweyen (57) 69 G2
Schwindratzheim (67) 70 D1
Schwoben (68) 97 C4
Schwobsheim (67) 71 C5
Sciecq (79) 161 H5
Scientrier (74) 191 H3
Scieurac-et-Flourès (32) 285 J1
Sciez (74) 174 E6
Scillé (79) 161 G3
Scionzier (74) 191 K3
Scolca (2B) 319 H4
Scorbé-Clairvaux (86) 145 H6
Scrignac (29) 47 H6
Scrupt (51) 63 H5
Scy-Chazelles (57) 44 E5
Scye (70) 118 A6

Séailles (32) 266 D4
la Séauve-sur-Semène (43) 221 F2
Sébazac-Concourès (12) 252 B2
Sébécourt (27) 56 A2
Sébeville (50) 29 F5
Seboncourt (02) 20 B1
Sebourg (59) 12 C2
Sébrazac (12) 235 K6
Séby (64) 284 C2
Secenans (70) 139 F2
Séchault (08) 42 B4
Secheras (07) 222 B4
Séchilienne (38) 224 B5
Séchin (25) 138 C4
Secondigné-sur-Belle (79) 178 C2
Secondigny (79) 161 H3
Secqueville-en-Bessin (14) . . . 32 C4
Sedan (08) 23 F4
Sédeilhac (31) 286 C6
Séderon (26) 258 B4
Sedze-Maubecq (64) 285 F3
Sedzère (64) 285 F4
Seebach (67) 25 C2
Sées (61) 54 E6
Séez (73) 193 A3
Ségalas (47) 231 J5
Ségalas (65) 285 H3
la Ségalassière (15) 235 F2
Séglien (56) 76 C5
Ségny (01) 174 B6
Segonzac (16) 196 A4
Segonzac (19) 215 F2
Segonzac (24) 213 H3
Ségos (32) 265 K6
Ségoufielle (32) 268 D6
Segré (49) 104 D6
Ségreville (31) 288 E2
Ségrie (72) 82 C6
Ségrie-Fontaine (61) 53 J3
Segrois (21) 154 A1
Ségry (36) 148 D5
la Séguinière (49) 142 E2
Ségur (12) 252 E3
le Ségur (81) 251 G6
Ségur-le-Château (19) 199 F6
Ségur-les-Villas (15) 218 B3
Ségura (09) 307 K2
Séguret (84) 257 G4
Ségus (65) 304 B1
Seich (65) 305 G2
Seichamps (54) 66 B4
Seichebrières (45) 110 D3
Seicheprey (54) 65 G3
Seiches-sur-le-Loir (49) 125 J2
Seignalens (11) 308 C1
Seigné (17) 178 C5
Seignelay (89) 113 G4
Seigneulles (55) 64 B3
Seignosse (40) 262 C4
Seigny (21) 134 E2
Seigy (41) 129 F6
Seilh (31) 269 F5
Seilhac (19) 216 A1
Seilhan (31) 305 H2
Seillac (41) 128 C3
Seillans (83) 280 A5
Seillonnaz (01) 207 H1
Seillons-Source-d'Argens (83) . . 297 H1
Seine-Port (77) 87 G1
Seingbouse (57) 68 B3
Seissan (32) 286 D2
Seix (09) 306 E4
le Sel-de-Bretagne (35) 103 G1
Selaincourt (54) 93 J1
Selens (02) 39 H1
Sélestat (67) 71 B5
Séligné (79) 178 C3
Séligney (39) 155 H4
la Selle-Craonnaise (53) 104 C4
la Selle-en-Coglès (35) 51 K6
la Selle-en-Hermoy (45) 111 K3
la Selle-en-Luitré (35) 80 B4
la Selle-Guerchaise (35) 104 B3
la Selle-la-Forge (61) 53 H4
la Selle-sur-le-Bied (45) 111 K2
Selles (27) 34 C3
Selles (51) 41 H3
Selles (62) 2 D6
Selles (70) 118 A2
Selles-Saint-Denis (41) 130 A5
Selles-sur-Cher (41) 129 G6
Selles-sur-Nahon (36) 147 H4
Sellières (39) 155 H5
Selommes (41) 108 D6
Seloncourt (25) 139 H3
Selongey (21) 136 B2
Selonnet (04) 259 K1
Seltz (67) 25 D3

Séméac (65) 285 H5
Séméacq-Blachon (64) 285 F2
Sémécourt (57) 27 G6
Sémelay (58) 152 A6
Semens (33) 230 A5
Sementron (89) 132 E2
Séméries (59) 13 H5
Semerville (41) 109 F3
Semezanges (21) 154 A1
Sémézies-Cachan (32) 286 E2
Semide (08) 42 A3
Semillac (17) 195 G6
Semilly (52) 92 E5
Semmadon (70) 117 J5
Semoine (10) 62 B5
Semond (21) 115 G6
Semondans (25) 139 G2
Semons (38) 206 C6
Semousies (59) 13 H4
Semoussac (17) 195 G6
Semoutiers-Montsaon (52) 116 A2
Semoy (45) 110 A4
Sempesserre (32) 267 J1
Sempigny (60) 19 H6
Sempy (62) 4 D6
Semur-en-Auxois (21) 134 D3
Semur-en-Brionnais (71) 187 F1
Semur-en-Vallon (72) 107 J2
Semussac (17) 194 D4
Semuy (08) 42 B1
le Sen (40) 246 A5
Sénac (65) 285 J3
Senaide (88) 117 H2
Sénaillac-Latronquière (46) . . . 234 B5
Sénaillac-Lauzès (46) 233 K5
Senailly (21) 134 D2
Senan (89) 112 E4
Senantes (28) 57 H6
Senantes (60) 36 E1
Sénarens (31) 287 G4
Senargent-Mignafans (70) 138 E1
Senarpont (80) 17 F2
Sénas (13) 276 E4
Senaud (39) 172 E5
Senaux (81) 271 J4
Sencenac-Puy-de-Fourches (24) . . 213 K2
Senconac (09) 307 K5
Sendets (33) 246 E1
Séné (56) 101 F6
Sénéchas (30) 255 G3
Sénergues (12) 235 J5
Sénestis (47) 247 H2
Séneujols (43) 220 B6
Senez (04) 279 H1
Sénezergues (15) 235 H4
Sengouagnet (31) 305 K2
Séniergues (46) 233 J4
Senillé (86) 163 H1
Seninghem (62) 2 E5
Senlecques (62) 2 D5
Senlis (60) 38 B5
Senlis (62) 5 F5
Senlis-le-Sec (80) 10 D5
Senlisse (78) 58 B6
Sennecey-le-Grand (71) 171 K2
Sennecey-lès-Dijon (21) 136 B5
Sennely (45) 130 C1
Sennevières (37) 146 E2
Senneville-sur-Fécamp (76) . . . 14 D3
Sennevoy-le-Bas (89) 114 D5
Sennevoy-le-Haut (89) 114 D5
Senon (55) 26 C5
Senonches (28) 84 C1
Senoncourt (70) 118 A4
Senoncourt-les-Maujouy (55) . . . 43 H6
Senones (88) 95 J2
Senonges (88) 93 K6
Senonnes (53) 104 A5
Senots (60) 37 G4
Senouillac (81) 270 C2
Sénoville (50) 28 B5
Senozan (71) 171 K5
Sens (89) 88 D6
Sens-Beaujeu (18) 131 H5
Sens-de-Bretagne (35) 79 H1
Sens-sur-Seille (71) 172 D1
Sentein (09) 306 B4
Sentelie (80) 17 J4
Sentenac-de-Sérou (09) 307 G3
Sentenac-d'Oust (09) 306 D4
Sentheim (68) 119 K6
Sentilly (61) 54 B4
la Sentinelle (59) 12 C2
Sentous (65) 286 A5
Senuc (08) 42 C3
Senven-Léhart (22) 76 D1
Sépeaux (89) 112 D3
Sepmeries (59) 12 D3
Sepmes (37) 145 K3
Seppois-le-Bas (68) 97 A5
Seppois-le-Haut (68) 97 B5
Sept-Forges (61) 81 H2
Sept-Frères (14) 31 H6
Sept-Meules (76) 16 C1
Sept-Saulx (51) 41 H4
Sept-Sorts (77) 60 B2
Sept-Vents (14) 31 K4
Septème (38) 206 C4
Septèmes-les-Vallons (13) 296 C3
Septeuil (78) 57 J3
Septfonds (82) 250 B5

Septfontaines (25) 156 D3
Septmoncel (39) 173 K5
Septmonts (02) 39 J3
Septsarges (55) 43 F3
Septvaux (02) 20 B6
Sepvigny (55) 93 F1
Sepvret (79) 178 E1
Sepx (31) 287 F6
Sequedin (59) 6 D4
Sequehart (02) 20 A1
le Sequestre (81) 270 D2
Serain (02) 12 B6
Seraincourt (08) 21 J5
Seraincourt (95) 58 A1
Sérandon (19) 217 G1
Séranon (06) 280 B3
Serans (60) 36 E5
Serans (61) 54 B5
Seranville (54) 94 D2
Séranvillers-Forenville (59) 11 K5
Seraucourt-le-Grand (02) 19 K3
Seraumont (88) 93 F2
Serazereux (28) 85 F1
Serbannes (03) 185 H4
Serbonnes (89) 88 C4
Serches (02) 39 J4
Sercoeur (88) 94 E4
Sercus (59) 3 J5
Sercy (71) 171 H3
Serdinya (66) 314 B3
Sère (32) 286 D3
Sère-en-Lavedan (65) 304 A2
Sère-Lanso (65) 304 B1
Sère-Rustaing (65) 285 K5
Serécourt (88) 117 H1
Séreilhac (87) 198 D2
Serémange-Erzange (57) 27 G5
Sérempuy (32) 268 A4
Sérénac (81) 271 F2
Sérent (56) 101 J3
Sérévillers (60) 18 C5
Serez (27) 57 F2
Sérézin-de-la-Tour (38) 207 F4
Sérézin-du-Rhône (69) 206 A3
Sergeac (24) 214 E6
Sergenaux (39) 155 H5
Sergenon (39) 155 G4
Sergines (89) 88 D4
Sergy (01) 190 D1
Sergy (02) 40 B5
Séricourt (62) 10 A3
Sériers (15) 218 D6
Sérifontaine (60) 36 E3
Sérignac (46) 249 G2
Sérignac (82) 268 C2
Sérignac-Péboudou (47) 231 J3
Sérignac-sur-Garonne (47) 248 A4
Sérignan (34) 292 A5
Sérignan-du-Comtat (84) 256 E4
Sérigné (85) 160 D4
Sérigny (61) 83 H4
Sérigny (86) 145 G5
Sérilhac (19) 216 A4
Seringes-et-Nesles (02) 40 A5
Séris (41) 109 G6
Serley (71) 154 E4
Sermages (58) 152 A3
Sermaise (49) 125 K3
Sermaise (91) 86 C2
Sermaises (45) 86 D5
Sermaize (60) 19 G5
Sermaize-les-Bains (51) 63 J4
Sermamagny (90) 119 H5
Sermange (39) 155 J1
Sermano (2B) 319 G6
Sermentizon (63) 203 H2
Sermérieu (38) 207 G3
Sermersheim (67) 70 D6
Sermesse (71) 154 C5
Sermiers (51) 40 E5
Sermizelles (89) 133 J3
Sermoise (02) 39 K3
Sermoise-sur-Loire (58) 150 E4
Sermoyer (01) 172 A4
Sermur (23) 183 J5
Sernhac (30) 275 J2
Serocourt (88) 117 J1
Séron (64) 285 F4
Serpaize (38) 206 B4
la Serpent (11) 308 E3
Serques (62) 3 F4
Serqueux (52) 117 G3
Serqueux (76) 16 D5
Serquigny (27) 34 E6
Serra-di-Ferro (2A) 322 C4
Serra-di-Fiumorbo (2B) 321 H4
Serra-di-Scopamène (2A) 323 F1
Serralongue (66) 314 D6
Serraval (74) 209 F1
la Serre (12) 271 K3
la Serre-Bussière-Vieille (23) 183 H4
Serre-les-Moulières (39) 137 G6
Serre-les-Sapins (25) 137 K6
Serre-Nerpol (38) 223 H2
Serres (05) 258 D1
Serres (11) 309 H3
Serres (54) 66 D5
Serres-Castet (64) 284 D3
Serres-et-Montguyard (24) 231 H4
Serres-Gaston (40) 265 G5
Serres-Morlaàs (64) 284 E4
Serres-Sainte-Marie (64) 284 B2

Serres-sur-Arget (09) 307 H3
Serreslous-et-Arribans (40) 265 K5
Serriera (2A) 316 D4
Serrières (07) 222 B2
Serrières (71) 188 B1
Serrières-de-Briord (01) 207 G1
Serrières-en-Chautagne (73) 190 C6
Serrières-sur-Ain (01) 189 J2
Serrigny (89) 113 K5
Serrigny-en-Bresse (71) 154 D6
Serris (77) 59 J4
Serrouville (54) 26 E4
Serruelles (18) 149 G5
Sers (16) 197 F4
Sers (65) 304 C4
Servais (02) 20 A5
Servance (70) 119 F4
Servanches (24) 212 E4
Servant (63) 184 D3
Servas (01) 189 F3
Servas (30) 255 H5
Servaville-Salmonville (76) 35 K1
Serverette (48) 237 H4
Serves-sur-Rhône (26) 222 B4
Servian (34) 292 B3
Servières (48) 237 H5
Servières-le-Château (19) 216 D4
Serviers-et-Labaume (30) 255 K6
Serviès (81) 270 C6
Serviès-en-Val (11) 309 H1
Servignat (01) 172 B5
Servigney (70) 118 C5
Servigny (50) 30 D3
Servigny-lès-Raville (57) 45 H5
Servigny-lès-Sainte-Barbe (57) 45 G5
Serville (28) 57 G4
Servilly (03) 186 A1
Servin (25) 138 C5
Servins (62) 10 D1
Servon (50) 51 J4
Servon (77) 59 G5
Servon-Melzicourt (51) 42 C4
Servon-sur-Vilaine (35) 79 J4
Servoz (74) 192 B5
Sery (08) 21 K5
Sery (89) 133 H2
Sillegny (57) 66 A1
Séry-lès-Mézières (02) 20 B3
Séry-Magneval (60) 38 E4
Serzy-et-Prin (51) 40 C4
Sessenheim (67) 25 C4
Sète (34) 293 F3
Setques (62) 3 F5
Seugy (95) 37 K6
Seuil (08) 41 J1
Seuil-d'Argonne (55) 63 K1
Seuillet (03) 185 J2
Seuilly (37) 145 F2
Seur (41) 128 C3
le Seure (17) 195 J1
Seurre (21) 154 D3
Seux (80) 17 K2
Seuzey (55) 64 E1
Sevelinges (42) 187 H3
Sevenans (90) 139 H1
Sévérac (44) 102 C5
Sévérac-le-Château (12) 253 G3
Sévérac-l'Église (12) 252 E2
Seveux (70) 137 H2
Sévignac (22) 78 A1
Sévignacq (64) 284 E2
Sévignacq-Meyracq (64) 284 C6
Sévigny (61) 54 C4
Sévigny-la-Forêt (08) 22 B2
Sévigny-Waleppe (08) 21 H5
Sévis (76) 16 A4
Sevrai (61) 54 B5
Sevran (93) 59 G2
Sèvres (92) 58 D4
Sèvres-Anxaumont (86) 163 G3
Sevrey (71) 171 K1
Sévrier (74) 191 F6
Sévry (18) 150 A2
Sewen (68) 119 J4
Sexcles (19) 216 D5
Sexey-aux-Forges (54) 65 K6
Sexey-les-Bois (54) 65 J4
Sexfontaines (52) 92 A5
Seychalles (63) 203 F2
Seyches (47) 231 F6
Seyne (04) 260 A2
la Seyne-sur-Mer (83) 297 H6
Seynes (30) 255 J5
Seynod (74) 191 F5
Seyre (31) 288 E4
Seyresse (40) 264 B5
Seyssel (01) 190 C5
Seyssel (74) 190 C5
Seysses (31) 288 A2
Seysses-Savès (32) 287 H2
Seyssinet-Pariset (38) 224 A3
Seyssins (38) 224 A3
Seyssuel (38) 206 B4
Seythenex (74) 209 F2
Seytroux (74) 192 A1
Sézanne (51) 61 H5
Siarrouy (65) 285 H4
Siaugues-Sainte-Marie (43) 219 K5
Sibiril (29) 46 E3
Sibiville (62) 10 A2
Siccieu-Saint-Julien-
et-Carisieu (38) 207 F2

Sichamps (58) 151 F2
Sickert (68) 119 J4
Sideville (50) 28 C3
Sidiailles (18) 166 E4
Siecq (17) 196 A1
Siegen (67) 25 D2
les Sièges (89) 89 F6
Sierck-les-Bains (57) 27 J3
Sierentz (68) 97 D3
Siersthal (57) 69 G3
Sierville (76) 15 K6
Siest (40) 262 E5
Sieurac (81) 270 D4
Sieuras (09) 288 A6
Siévoz (38) 242 C1
Siewiller (67) 69 F6
Sigale (06) 280 D2
Sigalens (33) 246 E1
Sigean (11) 310 C2
Sigloy (45) 110 D5
Signac (31) 305 J3
Signes (83) 297 H5
Signéville (52) 92 C5
Signy-l'Abbaye (08) 22 A4
Signy-le-Petit (08) 21 J2
Signy-Montlibert (08) 23 J5
Signy-Signets (77) 60 B2
Sigogne (16) 196 B2
Sigolsheim (68) 96 B3
Sigonce (04) 278 C1
Sigottier (05) 258 D1
Sigoulès (24) 231 H3
Sigournais (85) 160 C5
Sigoyer (04) 259 F2
Sigoyer (05) 242 D6
Siguer (09) 307 H5
Sigy (77) 88 C2
Sigy-en-Bray (76) 16 D6
Sigy-le-Châtel (71) 171 J3
Silfiac (56) 76 C4
Silhac (07) 239 K1
Sillans (38) 223 H1
Sillans-la-Cascade (83) 279 F6
Sillars (86) 163 K5
Sillas (33) 246 E2
Sillé-le-Guillaume (72) 82 B6
Sillé-le-Philippe (72) 107 F1
Sillegny (57) 66 A1
Sillery (51) 41 G5
Silley-Amancey (25) 156 D3
Silley-Bléfond (25) 138 C5
Sillingy (74) 190 E5
Silly-en-Gouffern (61) 54 D4
Silly-en-Saulnois (57) 66 B1
Silly-la-Poterie (02) 39 G5
Silly-le-Long (60) 38 D6
Silly-sur-Nied (57) 45 G5
Silly-Tillard (60) 37 H3
Silmont (55) 64 B4
Siltzheim (67) 68 D3
Silvacane (2B) 319 H4
Silvarouvres (52) 115 H2
Simacourbe (64) 285 F2
Simandre (71) 172 A2
Simandre-sur-Suran (01) 189 J2
Simandres (69) 206 B4
Simard (71) 172 C1
Simencourt (62) 10 D3
Simeyrols (24) 233 G1
Simiane-Collongue (13) 296 D2
Simiane-la-Rotonde (04) 277 J1
Simorre (32) 286 E2
Simplé (53) 104 E4
Sin-le-Noble (59) 11 H2
Sinard (38) 224 A6
Sinceny (02) 19 K6
Sincey-lès-Rouvray (21) 134 B4
Sindères (40) 245 F6
Singles (63) 201 H5
Singleyrac (24) 231 H3
Singly (08) 22 D5
Singrist (67) 70 C2
Sinsat (09) 307 J5
Sinzos (65) 285 J5
Sion (32) 266 C4
Sion-les-Mines (44) 103 G3
Sioniac (19) 216 B6
Sionne (88) 93 F3
Sionviller (54) 66 D5
Siorac-de-Ribérac (24) 213 G3
Siorac-en-Périgord (24) 232 D2
Siouville-Hague (50) 28 A3
Sirac (32) 268 B5
Siracourt (62) 10 A2
Siradan (65) 305 H3
Siran (15) 234 E1
Siran (34) 290 E4
Sireix (65) 304 A2
Sireuil (16) 196 C4
Sirod (39) 174 A1
Siros (64) 284 B3
Sisco (2B) 317 D3
Sissonne (02) 21 F6
Sissy (02) 20 B3
Sistels (82) 248 D6
Sisteron (04) 259 F4
Sivergues (84) 277 H3
Sivignon (71) 171 F5
Sivry (54) 66 A3
Sivry-Ante (51) 63 H1
Sivry-Courtry (77) 87 J2
Sivry-la-Perche (55) 43 G5

Sivry-sur-Meuse (55) 43 G3
Six-Fours-les-Plages (83) 297 H6
Sixt-Fer-à-Cheval (74) 192 B3
Sixt-sur-Aff (35) 102 C2
Sizun (29) 46 D6
Smarves (86) 163 F4
Smermesnil (76) 16 D2
Soccia (2A) 320 D2
Sochaux (25) 139 H2
Socourt (88) 94 B3
Socx (59) 3 H1
Sode (31) 305 H5
Soeurdres (49) 105 G6
Sognolles-en-Montois (77) 88 C2
Sogny-aux-Moulins (51) 62 D3
Sogny-en-l'Angle (51) 63 H4
Soignolles (14) 54 A1
Soignolles-en-Brie (77) 59 H6
Soindres (78) 57 J2
Soing-Cubry-Charentenay (70) 137 J2
Soings-en-Sologne (41) 129 G4
Soirans (21) 154 E1
Soissons (02) 39 J2
Soissons-sur-Nacey (21) 136 E6
Soisy-Bouy (77) 88 D2
Soisy-sous-Montmorency (95) 58 E2
Soisy-sur-École (91) 87 F2
Soisy-sur-Seine (91) 59 F6
Soize (02) 21 H4
Soizé (28) 84 A6
Soizy-aux-Bois (51) 61 H4
Solaize (69) 206 A3
Solaro (2B) 321 H5
Solbach (67) 70 A5
Soleilhas (04) 280 A2
Solemont (25) 139 G4
Solente (60) 19 G4
le Soler (66) 315 F2
Solérieux (26) 256 E2
Solers (77) 59 H6
Solesmes (59) 12 D4
Solesmes (72) 105 K4
Soleymieu (38) 207 F3
Soleymieux (42) 204 C5
Solférino (40) 245 F5
Solgne (57) 66 B1
Soliers (14) 32 E5
Solignac (87) 199 F2
Solignac-sous-Roche (43) 220 D3
Solignac-sur-Loire (43) 220 C6
Solignat (63) 202 E5
Soligny-la-Trappe (61) 55 H2
Soligny-les-Étangs (10) 89 F3
Sollacaro (2A) 322 D2
Sollières-Sardières (73) 226 E2
Solliès-Pont (83) 297 K5
Solliès-Toucas (83) 297 K5
Solliès-Ville (83) 297 K5
Sologny (71) 171 H6
Solomiac (32) 268 B4
Solre-le-Château (59) 13 J4
Solrinnes (59) 13 J3
Solterre (45) 111 J4
Solutré-Pouilly (71) 188 B1
Somain (59) 11 K2
Sombacour (25) 156 E4
Sombernon (21) 135 H5
Sombrin (62) 10 C3
Sombrun (65) 285 G2
Somloire (49) 143 H3
Sommaing (59) 12 D3
Sommancourt (52) 91 K2
Sommant (71) 152 E3
Sommauthe (08) 42 D1
Somme-Bionne (51) 42 E4
Somme-Suippe (51) 42 A6
Somme-Tourbe (51) 42 B6
Somme-Vesle (51) 63 F2
Somme-Yèvre (51) 63 H2
Sommecaise (89) 112 D5
Sommedieue (55) 43 J6
Sommeilles (55) 63 J2
Sommelans (02) 39 J6
Sommelonne (55) 63 K5
Sommepy-Tahure (51) 42 A4
Sommerance (08) 42 E1
Sommerécourt (52) 93 F5
Sommereux (60) 17 H5
Sommeron (02) 21 F3
Sommervieu (14) 32 B3
Sommerviller (54) 66 C5
Sommery (76) 16 D5
Sommesnil (76) 15 F4
Sommesous (51) 62 C5
la Sommette (25) 138 E6
Sommette-Eaucourt (02) 19 J4
Sommeval (10) 89 K6
Sommevoire (52) 91 J3
Sommières (30) 274 E4
Sommières-du-Clain (86) 179 J1
Sompt (79) 178 D3
Sompuis (51) 62 D5
Somsois (51) 90 E1
Son (08) 21 K6
Sonac (12) 234 B4
Sonchamp (78) 86 A1
Soncourt (88) 93 J3
Soncourt-sur-Marne (52) 92 A5
Sondernach (68) 119 K2
Sondersdorf (68) 97 C6
la Sône (38) 223 G4
Songeons (60) 17 G6

Songeson (39) 173 J2
Songieu (01) 190 B5
Songy (51) 62 E4
Sonnac (12) 234 E6
Sonnac (17) 195 K1
Sonnac-sur-l'Hers (11) 308 C2
Sonnay (38) 222 C1
Sonnaz (73) 208 B3
Sonneville (16) 196 B1
Sons-et-Ronchères (02) 20 D3
Sonthonnax-la-Montagne (01) 189 K1
Sonzay (37) 127 G3
Soorts-Hossegor (40) 262 B5
Soppe-le-Bas (68) 119 K5
Soppe-le-Haut (68) 119 K5
Sor (09) 306 C3
Sorans-lès-Breurey (70) 138 A4
Sorbais (02) 21 F2
Sorbets (32) 266 B4
Sorbets (40) 265 J5
Sorbey (55) 26 B4
Sorbey (57) 45 G6
Sorbier (03) 169 H6
Sorbiers (05) 258 C2
Sorbiers (42) 205 G5
Sorbo-Ocagnano (2B) 319 J3
Sorbollano (2A) 323 F1
Sorbon (08) 21 K6
Sorbs (34) 273 G3
Sorcy-Bauthémont (08) 22 B6
Sorcy-Saint-Martin (55) 65 F5
Sorde-l'Abbaye (40) 283 F1
Sore (40) 245 K3
Soréac (65) 285 J4
Sorède (66) 315 H4
Sorel (80) 11 H6
Sorel-en-Vimeu (80) 9 G6
Sorel-Moussel (28) 57 F4
Sorèze (81) 289 J2
Sorgeat (09) 308 B6
Sorges (24) 214 C2
Sorgues (84) 276 C1
Sorigny (37) 127 J6
les Sorinières (44) 123 G5
Sorio (2B) 319 G2
Sormery (89) 113 H1
Sormonne (08) 22 B3
Sornac (19) 200 E3
Sornay (70) 137 G5
Sornay (71) 172 C2
Sornéville (54) 66 C4
Sorquainville (76) 14 E4
Sorrus (62) 4 B6
Sort-en-Chalosse (40) 264 C5
Sortosville (50) 28 E4
Sortosville-en-Beaumont (50) 28 B5
Sos (47) 247 G6
Sospel (06) 281 J1
Sossais (86) 145 G5
Sost (65) 305 H3
Sotta (2A) 323 G4
Sottevast (50) 28 D4
Sotteville (50) 28 B3
Sotteville-lès-Rouen (76) 35 H2
Sotteville-sous-le-Val (76) 35 J3
Sotteville-sur-Mer (76) 15 H2
Soturac (46) 249 F1
Sotzeling (57) 66 E2
Souain-Perthes-lès-Hurlus (51) 41 K5
Soual (81) 289 J1
Souancé-au-Perche (28) 84 A5
Souanyas (66) 314 A4
Souastre (62) 10 D4
Soubès (34) 273 G4
Soubise (17) 176 E5
Soublecause (65) 285 G1
Soubran (17) 211 H1
Soubrebost (23) 182 D5
Soucé (53) 81 G2
Soucelles (49) 125 H2
la Souche (07) 239 F5
Souchez (62) 10 E1
Soucht (57) 69 G4
Soucia (39) 173 J3
Soucieu-en-Jarrest (69) 205 K3
Soucirac (46) 233 J4
Souclin (01) 189 J6
Soucy (02) 39 G3
Soucy (89) 88 D5
Soudaine-Lavinadière (19) 199 K5
Soudan (44) 103 K3
Soudan (79) 162 A5
Soudat (24) 197 J4
Soudé (51) 62 D5
Soudeilles (19) 200 D6
Soudorgues (30) 254 E6
Soudron (51) 62 C3
Soueich (31) 305 K2
Soueix-Rogalle (09) 306 E4
Souel (81) 270 C1
Soues (65) 285 H5
Soues (80) 17 J1
Souesmes (41) 130 C4
Souffelweyersheim (67) 25 A4
Soufflenheim (67) 25 C3
Souffrignac (16) 197 H4
Sougé (36) 147 H4
Sougé (41) 107 J5
Sougé-le-Ganelon (72) 82 C4
Sougéal (35) 51 H5
Sougères-en-Puisaye (89) 132 D2

402

Sougraigne (11) 309 G4
Sougy (45) 109 K2
Sougy-sur-Loire (58) 151 G6
les Souhesmes-Rampont (55) 43 G6
Souhey (21) 134 E3
le Souich (62) 10 B3
Souilhanels (11) 289 G4
Souilhe (11) 289 G3
Souillac (46) 233 H1
Souillé (72) 106 D1
Souilly (55) 64 C1
Soula (09) 307 K3
Soulac-sur-Mer (33) 194 B5
Soulages (15) 219 G5
Soulages-Bonneval (12) 236 B4
Soulaines-Dhuys (10) 91 H3
Soulaines-sur-Aubance (49) 125 G2
Soulaire-et-Bourg (49) 125 G2
Soulaires (28) 85 H2
Soulan (09) 306 E3
Soulanges (51) 63 F4
Soulangis (18) 149 H1
Soulangy (14) 54 A2
Soulatgé (11) 309 H4
Soulaucourt-sur-Mouzon (52) 93 G5
Soulaures (24) 232 C4
Soulce-Cernay (25) 139 H4
Soulgé-sur-Ouette (53) 105 G1
le Soulié (34) 290 E1
Soulières (51) 61 K3
Soulignac (33) 230 A4
Souligné-Flacé (72) 106 C3
Souligné-sous-Ballon (72) 106 C1
Soulignonne (17) 194 E1
Souligny (10) 90 A6
Soulitré (72) 107 G2
Soullans (85) 140 E5
Soulles (50) 31 G4
Soulom (65) 304 B3
Soulomès (46) 233 J5
Soulosse-sous-Saint-Élophe (88) . . 93 G3
Soultz-Haut-Rhin (68) 96 B6
Soultz-les-Bains (67) 70 D3
Soultz-sous-Forêts (67) 25 B2
Soultzbach-les-Bains (68) 96 A4
Soultzeren (68) 119 K1
Soultzmatt (68) 96 B5
Soulvache (44) 103 H4
Soumaintrain (89) 113 J2
Soumans (23) 183 H1
Soumensac (47) 231 G4
Souméras (17) 211 J2
Soumont (34) 273 G5
Soumont-Saint-Quentin (14) 54 A2
Soumoulou (64) 284 E4
Soupex (11) 289 G3
Soupir (02) 40 B2
Souppes-sur-Loing (77) 87 J6
Souprosse (40) 264 E3
Souraïde (64) 263 D2
Sourans (25) 139 F3
Sourcieux-les-Mines (69) 205 J1
le Sourd (02) 20 E2
Sourdeval (50) 52 D4
Sourdeval-les-Bois (50) 31 H6
Sourdon (80) 18 B4
Sourdun (77) 88 E2
le Sourn (56) 76 D6
Sournia (66) 309 H6
Sourniac (15) 217 G2
Sourribes (04) 259 G4
Sourzac (24) 213 H5
Sous-Parsat (23) 182 E4
Sousceyrac (46) 234 D2
Sousmoulins (17) 211 K2
Souspierre (26) 240 D6
Soussac (33) 230 D3
Soussans (33) 211 G5
Soussey-sur-Brionne (21) 135 F5
Soustelle (30) 255 G5
Soustons (40) 262 C4
Souternon (42) 186 E6
la Souterraine (23) 181 K2
Soutiers (79) 161 K3
Souvans (39) 155 H3
Souvignargues (30) 274 E3
Souvigné (16) 179 F5
Souvigné (37) 127 F3
Souvigné (79) 161 K6
Souvigné-sur-Même (72) 83 J5
Souvigné-sur-Sarthe (72) 105 J4
Souvigny (03) 168 D4
Souvigny-de-Touraine (37) 128 C1
Souvigny-en-Sologne (41) 130 C1
Souyeaux (65) 285 J5
Souzay-Champigny (49) 126 B6
Souzy (69) 205 G3
Souzy-la-Briche (91) 86 C2
Soveria (2B) 319 F5
Soyans (26) 240 D4
Soyaux (16) 196 E3
Soye (25) 138 E3
Soye-en-Septaine (18) 149 H3
Soyécourt (80) 19 F2
Soyers (52) 117 G4
Soyons (07) 240 C1
Sparsbach (67) 69 G5
Spay (72) 106 D3
Spechbach-le-Bas (68) 97 B3

Spechbach-le-Haut (68) 97 B3
Speloncato (2B) 318 C3
Spéracèdes (06) 280 C5
Spézet (29) 75 G4
Spicheren (57) 68 C2
Spincourt (55) 26 C5
Sponville (54) 44 C6
Spoy (10) 91 G5
Spoy (21) 136 C3
Spycker (59) 3 G2
Squiffiec (22) 48 C4
Staffelfelden (68) 97 B1
Stains (93) 58 E2
Stainville (55) 64 B6
Staple (59) 3 J5
Stattmatten (67) 25 C4
Stazzona (2B) 319 H5
Steenbecque (59) 3 J6
Steene (59) 3 H2
Steenvoorde (59) 3 K4
Steenwerck (59) 6 B3
Steige (67) 70 A6
Steinbach (68) 97 A1
Steinbourg (67) 70 C1
Steinbrunn-le-Bas (68) 97 C3
Steinbrunn-le-Haut (68) 97 C3
Steinseltz (67) 25 B1
Steinsoultz (68) 97 C5
Stenay (55) 43 F1
Sternenberg (68) 97 A3
Stetten (68) 97 D4
Stigny (89) 114 C5
Still (67) 70 C4
Stiring-Wendel (57) 68 C1
Stonne (08) 23 F6
Storckensohn (68) 119 J3
Stosswihr (68) 119 K1
Stotzheim (67) 70 D6
Strasbourg (67) 71 D1
Strazeele (59) 3 K5
Strenquels (46) 215 K6
Strueth (68) 97 A4
Struth (67) 69 F5
Stuckange (57) 27 H4
Stundwiller (67) 25 C2
Sturzelbronn (57) 69 J3
Stutzheim-Offenheim (67) 70 E2
Suarce (90) 139 K1
Suaux (16) 197 H1
le Subdray (18) 149 F4
Sublaines (37) 128 B6
Subles (14) 32 A4
Subligny (18) 131 J4
Subligny (50) 51 K2
Subligny (89) 88 C6
Suc-et-Sentenac (09) 307 G5
Succieu (38) 207 F5
Sucé-sur-Erdre (44) 123 H2
Sucy-en-Brie (94) 59 G4
Suèvres (41) 129 F3
Sugères (63) 203 G4
Sugny (08) 42 B3
Suhescun (64) 282 E4
Suilly-la-Tour (58) 132 B5
Suin (71) 171 F5
Suippes (51) 41 K5
Suisse (57) 66 E1
Suizy-le-Franc (51) 61 H2
Sulignat (01) 188 D2
Sully (14) 32 A3
Sully (60) 17 G6
Sully (71) 153 G5
Sully-la-Chapelle (45) 110 D3
Sully-sur-Loire (45) 110 E6
Sulniac (56) 101 H5
Sumène (30) 274 A1
Sundhoffen (68) 96 C5
Sundhouse (67) 71 C5
Supt (39) 156 B5
Surat (63) 185 G6
Surba (09) 307 H4
Surbourg (67) 25 B3
Surcamps (80) 9 J5
Surdoux (87) 199 J4
Suré (61) 83 G4
Suresnes (92) 58 D3
Surfonds (72) 107 G3
Surfontaine (02) 20 B4
Surgères (17) 177 H3
Surgy (58) 133 F3
Suriauville (88) 93 H6
Surin (79) 161 H4
Surin (86) 179 J4
Suris (16) 197 J1
Surjoux (01) 190 E4
Surmont (25) 139 F5
Surques (62) 2 D5
Surrain (14) 29 K5
Surtainville (50) 28 B4
Surtauville (27) 35 H5
Survie (61) 54 E3
Surville (14) 33 K3
Surville (27) 35 H5
Surville (50) 30 C1
Survilliers (95) 38 B6
Sury (08) 22 C4
Sury-aux-Bois (45) 110 E3
Sury-en-Vaux (18) 131 K3
Sury-ès-Bois (18) 131 H4
Sury-le-Comtal (42) 204 E5
Sury-près-Léré (18) 131 K3
Surzur (56) 101 G6

Sus (64) 283 J4
Sus-Saint-Léger (62) 10 B3
Susmiou (64) 283 J4
Sussac (87) 199 J3
Sussargues (34) 274 D5
Sussat (03) 185 F3
Sussey (21) 153 F1
Susville (38) 224 B6
Sutrieu (01) 190 A5
Suzan (09) 307 G2
Suzanne (08) 22 C6
Suzanne (80) 19 F1
Suzannecourt (52) 92 B2
Suzay (27) 36 B3
Suze (26) 240 E3
Suze-la-Rousse (26) 256 E3
la Suze-sur-Sarthe (72) 106 C4
Suzette (84) 257 G5
Suzoy (60) 19 G6
Suzy (02) 20 B6
Sy (08) 22 E6
Syam (39) 174 A1
Sylvains-les-Moulins (27) 56 C3
Sylvanès (12) 272 C3
le Syndicat (88) 119 F1

T

Tabaille-Usquain (64) 283 H3
Tabanac (33) 229 J3
la Table (73) 208 E5
le Tablier (85) 159 J3
Tabre (09) 308 B3
la Tâche (16) 179 J6
Tachoires (32) 286 D2
Tacoignières (78) 57 J4
Taconnay (58) 133 F6
Taden (22) 50 D5
Tadousse-Ussau (64) 284 E1
Taglio-Isolaccio (2B) 319 J4
la Tagnière (71) 152 E6
Tagnon (08) 41 H2
Tagolsheim (68) 97 B3
Tagsdorf (68) 97 C4
Tailhac (43) 219 H5
Taillades (84) 276 E3
le Taillan-Médoc (33) 229 G1
Taillancourt (55) 93 G1
Taillant (17) 177 J6
Taillebois (61) 53 J4
Taillebourg (17) 195 G1
Taillebourg (47) 247 H1
Taillecavat (33) 230 E4
Taillecourt (25) 139 H2
la Taillée (85) 160 C5
Taillefontaine (02) 39 F3
Taillepied (50) 28 D5
Taillet (66) 314 E4
Taillette (08) 22 B1
Taillis (35) 80 A5
Tailly (21) 154 A4
Tailly (80) 17 H1
Tain-l'Hermitage (26) 222 B6
Taingy (89) 132 E2
Taintrux (88) 95 H4
Taisnières-en-Thiérache (59) 13 F4
Taisnières-sur-Hon (59) 13 G2
Taissy (51) 41 F4
Taïx (81) 270 D1
Taizé (71) 171 H4
Taizé (79) 144 A4
Taizé-Aizie (16) 179 H1
Taizy (08) 21 J6
Tajan (65) 286 B6
Talairan (11) 309 K2
Talais (33) 194 C5
Talange (57) 27 G4
Talant (21) 136 A5
Talasani (2B) 319 J4
la Talaudière (42) 205 G5
Talazac (65) 285 H4
Talcy (41) 109 F6
Talcy (89) 134 B2
Talence (33) 229 G2
Talencieux (07) 222 B3
Talensac (35) 78 D4
Talissieu (01) 190 B6
Talizat (15) 218 D4
Tallans (25) 138 C3
Tallard (05) 242 E6
Tallenay (25) 138 A5
Tallende (63) 202 D3
Taller (40) 264 B2
Talloires (74) 191 G6
Tallone (2B) 321 J1
le Tallud (79) 161 J2
Tallud-Sainte-Gemme (85) 160 D1
Talmas (80) 10 A6
Talmay (21) 136 E5
Talmont-Saint-Hilaire (85) 159 F4
Talmont-sur-Gironde (17) 194 D4
Talmontiers (60) 36 D2
Talon (58) 133 G5
Talus-Saint-Prix (51) 61 H4
Taluyers (69) 205 K3
Tamerville (50) 28 E4
Tamnay-en-Bazois (58) 151 K3
Tamniès (24) 214 E6
Tanavelle (15) 218 D6

Tanay (21) 136 C4
Tancarville (76) 34 C1
Tancoigné (49) 143 K1
Tancon (71) 187 G2
Tanconville (54) 67 H5
Tancrou (77) 60 B2
Tancua (39) 174 A3
Tangry (62) 5 H6
Taninges (74) 191 K3
Tanis (50) 51 J4
Tanlay (89) 114 B4
Tannay (08) 22 E6
Tannay (58) 133 G5
Tanneron (83) 280 C5
Tannerre-en-Puisaye (89) 112 C6
Tannières (02) 40 A4
Tannois (55) 64 B5
Tanques (61) 54 B5
Tantonville (54) 94 A2
le Tanu (50) 51 K1
Tanus (81) 251 J6
Tanville (61) 82 C1
Tanzac (17) 195 G4
Taponas (69) 188 B3
Taponnat-Fleurignac (16) 197 G2
Tarabel (31) 288 E2
Taradeau (83) 298 D1
Tarare (69) 187 J6
Tarascon (13) 275 K3
Tarascon-sur-Ariège (09) 307 J4
Tarasteix (65) 285 G4
Tarbes (65) 285 H5
Tarcenay (25) 156 C1
Tardes (23) 183 H3
Tardets-Sorholus (64) 283 H6
la Tardière (85) 160 E2
Tardinghen (62) 2 A3
Tarentaise (42) 221 J1
Tarerach (66) 309 H6
Targassonne (66) 313 H4
Target (03) 185 F1
Targon (33) 230 A3
Tarnac (19) 200 C3
Tarnès (33) 211 K6
Tarnos (40) 262 B6
Taron-Sadirac-Viellenave (64) 284 E1
Tarquimpol (57) 67 F3
Tarrano (2B) 319 H5
Tarsac (32) 266 A5
Tarsacq (64) 284 B3
Tarsul (21) 135 K2
Tart-l'Abbaye (21) 154 E1
Tart-le-Bas (21) 154 E1
Tart-le-Haut (21) 154 D1
Tartaras (42) 205 J4
Tartas (40) 264 D3
Tartécourt (70) 117 K4
Tartiers (02) 39 H2
Tartigny (60) 18 B5
Tartonne (04) 260 A5
le Tartre (71) 172 E1
le Tartre-Gaudran (78) 57 H5
Tarzy (08) 21 K2
Tasque (32) 266 C6
Tassé (72) 106 A4
Tassenières (39) 155 G4
Tassillé (72) 106 B2
Tassin-la-Demi-Lune (69) 206 A2
Tasso (2A) 321 F5
Tatinghem (62) 3 F5
le Tâtre (16) 196 A6
Taugon (17) 160 D6
Taulé (29) 47 F4
Taulignan (26) 257 F1
Taulis (66) 314 E4
Taupont (56) 101 J1
Tauriac (33) 211 H5
Tauriac (46) 234 B1
Tauriac (81) 269 J3
Tauriac-de-Camarès (12) 272 D4
Tauriac-de-Naucelle (12) 251 J5
Tauriers (07) 239 G6
Taurignan-Castet (09) 306 D2
Taurignan-Vieux (09) 306 D2
Taurinya (66) 314 C3
Taurize (11) 309 H1
Taussac (12) 235 K2
Taussac-la-Billière (34) 272 D6
Tautavel (66) 310 A5
Tauves (63) 201 J5
Tauxières-Mutry (51) 41 F6
Tauxigny (37) 146 B1
Tavaco (2A) 320 D4
Tavant (37) 145 H2
Tavaux (39) 155 F3
Tavaux-et-Pontséricourt (02) 21 F4
Tavel (30) 276 A1
Tavera (2A) 320 E3
Tavernay (71) 152 E3
Tavernes (83) 278 A6
Taverny (95) 58 D1
Tavers (45) 109 H6
Tavey (70) 139 G1
Taxat-Senat (03) 185 F2
Taxenne (39) 137 G6
Tayac (33) 212 D6
Taybosc (32) 267 K4
Tayrac (12) 251 H4
Tayrac (47) 248 D4
Tazilly (58) 170 A1
le Tech (66) 314 D5

Técou (81) 270 C3
le Teich (33) 228 C4
Teigny (58) 133 H5
le Teil (07) 240 A6
Teilhède (63) 185 F5
Teilhet (09) 308 A1
Teilhet (63) 184 C4
Teillay (35) 103 H2
Teillé (44) 123 K1
Teillé (72) 82 E6
Teillet (81) 271 G3
Teillet-Argenty (03) 183 K2
le Teilleul (50) 80 E1
Teillots (24) 215 F3
Teissières-de-Cornet (15) 217 G6
Teissières-lès-Bouliès (15) 235 J2
Telgruc-sur-Mer (29) 72 K6
Tellancourt (54) 26 B2
Tellecey (21) 136 C5
Tellières-le-Plessis (61) 55 G6
Teloché (72) 106 E4
le Temple (33) 228 D1
le Temple (41) 108 B3
le Temple-de-Bretagne (44) 122 E2
Temple-Laguyon (24) 214 E3
le Temple-sur-Lot (47) 248 A2
Templemars (59) 6 D5
Templeuve (59) 6 E5
Templeux-la-Fosse (80) 19 H1
Templeux-le-Guérard (80) 19 J1
Tenay (01) 189 K5
Tence (43) 221 F4
Tencin (38) 224 C1
Tende (06) 311 D2
Tendon (88) 95 F6
Tendron (18) 150 A4
Tendu (36) 165 H2
Teneur (62) 5 G6
Tennie (72) 106 B1
Tenteling (57) 68 C2
Tercé (86) 163 H4
Tercillat (23) 166 C5
Tercis-les-Bains (40) 264 A5
Terdeghem (59) 3 J4
Tergnier (02) 20 A5
Terjat (03) 184 A2
Termes (08) 42 C3
Termes (11) 309 J2
Termes (48) 237 F4
Termes-d'Armagnac (32) 266 B5
Termignon (73) 226 B1
Terminiers (28) 109 J2
Ternand (69) 187 K5
Ternant (17) 177 J5
Ternant (21) 154 A1
Ternant (58) 169 K1
Ternant-les-Eaux (63) 202 D6
Ternas (62) 10 B2
Ternat (52) 116 B3
Ternay (41) 107 K6
Ternay (69) 206 A4
Ternay (86) 144 C3
les Ternes (15) 218 D6
Ternuay-Melay-et-Saint-Hilaire (70) . 119 F4
Terny-Sorny (02) 39 J2
Terramesnil (80) 10 B5
la Terrasse (38) 224 C1
la Terrasse-sur-Dorlay (42) 205 J6
Terrasson-Lavilledieu (24) 215 G4
Terrats (66) 315 F3
Terraube (32) 267 H2
Terre-Clapier (81) 271 F4
Terre-Natale (52) 117 F3
Terrebasse (31) 287 G5
Terrefondrée (21) 115 J3
Terrehault (72) 83 G6
les Terres-de-Chaux (25) 139 G4
la Terrisse (12) 236 B3
Terroles (11) 309 G3
Terron-sur-Aisne (08) 42 B1
Terrou (46) 234 D3
Tersanne (26) 222 B3
Tersannes (87) 181 F1
Terssac (81) 270 D2
le Tertre-Saint-Denis (78) 57 H2
Tertry (80) 19 H2
Terville (57) 27 G4
Tessancourt-sur-Aubette (78) 58 A1
Tessé-Froulay (61) 81 J2
Tessé-la-Madeleine (61) 81 J1
Tessel (14) 32 C5
Tesson (17) 195 G3
Tessonnière (79) 144 B6
la Tessoualle (49) 143 F3
Tessy-sur-Vire (50) 31 H5
la Teste-de-Buch (33) 228 B4
Tétaigne (08) 23 G4
Téteghem (59) 3 J2
Téterchen (57) 45 J3
Téthieu (40) 264 C4
Teuillac (33) 211 H4
Teulat (81) 269 K6
Teurthéville-Bocage (50) 28 E3
Teurthéville-Hague (50) 28 B3
Teyjat (24) 197 J4
Teyran (34) 274 C5
Teyssières (26) 257 H1
Teyssieu (46) 234 C1
Teyssode (81) 270 C6
Thaas (51) 61 J6
Thaims (17) 194 E3

Thairé (17) 176 E3
Thaix (58) 151 K6
Thal-Drulingen (67) 67 K2
Thal-Marmoutier (67) 70 K2
Thalamy (19) 201 H5
Thann (68) 97 A2
Thannenkirch (68) 96 B2
Thanvillé (67) 71 A4
Thaon (14) 32 D4
Thaon-les-Vosges (88) 94 D4
Tharaux (30) 255 K6
Tharoiseau (89) 133 J4
Tharot (89) 133 J3
Thaumiers (18) 149 K6
Thauron (23) 182 C5
Thauvenay (18) 131 K6
Thèbe (65) 305 H3
Théding (57) 68 C2
Thédirac (46) 233 G5
Thégra (46) 234 A2
Théhillac (56) 102 B5
le Theil (03) 168 C6
le Theil (15) 28 E3
le Theil (61) 83 J5
le Theil-Bocage (14) 53 F4
le Theil-de-Bretagne (35) 103 J1
le Theil-en-Auge (14) 34 A3
le Theil-Nolent (27) 34 C5
Theil-Rabier (16) 179 F4
Theil-sur-Vanne (89) 88 E6
Theillay (41) 130 B6
Theillement (27) 35 F4
Theix (56) 101 G5
Theizé (69) 188 A5
Thel (69) 187 H3
Théligny (72) 83 K6
Thélis-la-Combe (42) 221 J2
Thélod (54) 93 K1
Thelonne (08) 23 F5
Thélus (62) 11 F2
Théméricourt (95) 37 F6
Thémines (46) 234 B3
Théminettes (46) 234 B4
Thénac (17) 195 G3
Thénac (24) 231 G3
Thenailles (02) 21 F3
Thenay (36) 165 F3
Thenay (41) 128 E5
Thenelles (02) 20 B3
Thénésol (73) 209 G2
Theneuil (37) 145 H2
Theneuille (03) 167 K3
Thénezay (79) 162 B1
Thénioux (18) 130 A6
Thenissey (21) 135 G3
Thénisy (77) 88 C2
Thennelières (10) 90 B5
Thennes (80) 18 C4
Thenon (24) 214 D4
Thénorgues (08) 42 D2
Théoule-sur-Mer (06) 280 D6
Therdonne (60) 37 H2
Thérines (60) 17 H5
Thermes-Magnoac (65) 286 D4
Thérondels (12) 236 B2
Thérouanne (62) 3 G6
Thérouldeville (76) 14 E4
Thervay (39) 137 G6
Thésée (41) 128 E5
Thésy (39) 156 B4
Theuley (70) 137 H1
Théus (05) 243 F6
Theuville (28) 85 H4
Theuville (95) 37 G5
Theuville-aux-Maillots (76) 14 E3
Thevet-Saint-Julien (36) 166 C3
Théville (50) 28 E2
Thevray (27) 55 K2
They-sous-Montfort (88) 93 J5
They-sous-Vaudemont (54) 93 K3
Theys (38) 224 D1
Théza (66) 315 H3
Thézac (17) 194 E3
Thézac (47) 249 F2
Thézan-des-Corbières (11) 310 A1
Thézan-lès-Béziers (34) 291 K3
Thèze (04) 259 F2
Thèze (64) 284 D2
Thézey-Saint-Martin (54) 66 B2
Théziers (30) 275 K2
Thézillieu (01) 190 A6
Thézy-Glimont (80) 18 C3
Thiais (94) 58 E5
Thiancourt (90) 139 K2
Thianges (58) 151 H5
Thiant (59) 12 C2
Thiat (87) 180 E1
Thiaucourt-Regniéville (54) 65 H2
Thiaville-sur-Meurthe (54) 95 G2
Thiberville (27) 34 B5
Thibie (51) 62 C2
Thibivillers (60) 37 F4
Thibouville (27) 35 F5
Thicourt (57) 66 D1
Thiébauménil (54) 66 E6
Thiéblemont-Farémont (51) 63 G5
Thiébouhans (25) 139 H5
Thieffrain (10) 90 E6
Thieffrans (70) 138 C2
Thiéfosse (88) 119 G2
Thiel-sur-Acolin (03) 169 G4
Thiembronne (62) 4 E4

Thiénans (70) 138 C3
Thiennes (59) 3 J6
Thiepval (80) 10 E6
Thiergeville (76) 14 E4
Thiernu (02) 20 E3
Thiers (63) 203 H1
Thiers-sur-Thève (60) 38 B5
Thierville (27) 34 E4
Thierville-sur-Meuse (55) 43 H5
Thiéry (06) 261 H6
Thiescourt (60) 19 G6
Thiétreville (76) 14 E4
le Thieulin (28) 84 D3
Thieulloy-la-Ville (80) 17 H4
Thieulloy-l'Abbaye (80) 17 H3
Thieuloy-Saint-Antoine (60) 17 H5
la Thieuloye (62) 10 B1
Thieux (60) 18 B6
Thieux (77) 59 H1
Thiéville (14) 54 C1
Thièvres (62) 10 C5
Thièvres (80) 10 C5
Thiézac (15) 217 K6
Thignonville (45) 86 C5
Thil (01) 206 C1
Thil (10) 91 H4
le Thil (27) 36 C3
Thil (31) 268 C5
Thil (51) 40 E3
Thil (54) 26 A3
Thil-Manneville (76) 15 J2
le Thil-Riberpré (76) 16 E5
Thil-sur-Arroux (71) 152 D6
Thilay (08) 22 D2
le Thillay (95) 59 F2
Thilleux (52) 91 H3
les Thilliers-en-Vexin (27) 36 C4
Thillois (51) 40 E4
Thillombois (55) 64 D2
Thillot (55) 65 F1
le Thillot (88) 119 G3
Thilouze (37) 145 J1
Thimert-Gâtelles (28) 84 E1
Thimonville (57) 66 C1
Thimory (45) 111 G4
Thin-le-Moutier (08) 22 B4
Thiolières (63) 203 K4
Thionne (03) 169 G5
Thionville (57) 27 G4
Thiouville (76) 15 F4
Thiraucourt (88) 93 K4
Thiré (85) 160 C3
Thiron Gardais (28) 84 C2
This (08) 22 C3
Thise (25) 138 A5
Thivars (28) 85 G4
Thivencelle (59) 7 K6
Thiverny (60) 38 A4
Thiverval-Grignon (78) 58 A3
Thivet (52) 116 C2
Thiviers (24) 198 B6
Thiville (28) 109 F2
Thizay (36) 148 C5
Thizay (37) 144 E1
Thizy (69) 187 H4
Thizy (89) 134 B2
Thoard (04) 259 H4
Thodure (38) 222 E2
Thoigné (72) 82 E5
Thoiras (30) 255 F6
Thoiré-sous-Contensor (72) 82 E4
Thoiré-sur-Dinan (72) 107 G6
Thoires (21) 115 G3
Thoirette (39) 189 K1
Thoiria (39) 173 H3
Thoiry (01) 190 D1
Thoiry (73) 208 C4
Thoiry (78) 57 K3
Thoissey (01) 188 C2
Thoisy-la-Berchère (21) 134 D6
Thoisy-le-Désert (21) 135 F6
Thoix (80) 17 J4
Thol-lès-Millières (52) 92 E6
Thollet (86) 164 C5
Thollon-les-Mémises (74) 175 H5
le Tholonet (13) 296 D1
le Tholy (88) 95 G6
Thomer-la-Sôgne (27) 56 D3
Thomery (77) 87 J3
Thônac (24) 214 E6
Thônes (74) 191 H5
Thonnance-lès-Joinville (52) 92 B2
Thonnance-les-Moulins (52) 92 C3
Thonne-la-Long (55) 23 K5
Thonne-le-Thil (55) 23 J5
Thonne-les-Près (55) 23 K6
Thonnelle (55) 23 K6
Thonon-les-Bains (74) 175 F5
Thonville (57) 66 D1
le Thor (84) 276 D2
Thorailles (45) 111 K2
Thoraise (25) 156 A1
Thorame-Basse (04) 260 B5
Thorame-Haute (04) 260 C6
Thoras (43) 237 J2
Thoré-la-Rochette (41) 108 B5
Thorée-les-Pins (72) 106 C4
Thorens-Glières (74) 191 G4
Thorey (89) 114 B4

Thorey-en-Plaine (21) 154 D1
Thorey-Lyautey (54) 93 K2
Thorey-sous-Charny (21) 134 E5
Thorey-sur-Ouche (21) 153 J2
Thorigné (79) 178 C1
Thorigné-d'Anjou (49) 125 F1
Thorigné-en-Charnie (53) 105 J2
Thorigné-Fouillard (35) 79 H4
Thorigné-sur-Dué (72) 107 H2
Thorigny (79) 177 K2
Thorigny (85) 159 K2
Thorigny-sur-Marne (77) 59 H3
Thorigny-sur-Oreuse (89) 88 E5
le Thoronet (83) 298 C2
Thorrenc (07) 222 B3
Thors (10) 91 H4
Thors (17) 195 K1
Thory (80) 18 C4
Thory (89) 133 K2
le Thou (17) 177 F3
Thou (18) 131 H4
Thou (45) 131 K2
Thouarcé (49) 125 G6
Thouaré-sur-Loire (44) 123 H3
Thouars (79) 144 B4
Thouars-sur-Arize (09) 287 K6
Thouars-sur-Garonne (47) 247 J4
Thouarsais-Bouildroux (85) 160 D2
le Thoult-Trosnay (51) 61 H3
le Thour (08) 21 H6
le Thoureil (49) 125 K4
Thourie (35) 103 H2
Thouron (87) 181 G5
Thourotte (60) 38 E1
Thoury (41) 129 H2
Thoury-Férottes (77) 88 A3
Thoux (32) 268 C5
Thuboeuf (53) 81 J2
le Thuel (02) 21 H5
Thuès-Entre-Valls (66) 313 K4
Thueyts (07) 239 F4
Thugny-Trugny (08) 41 J1
la Thuile (73) 208 D4
les Thuiles (04) 260 C1
Thuillières (88) 93 K6
Thuir (66) 315 F3
le Thuit (27) 36 A4
le Thuit-Anger (27) 35 G4
Thuit-Hébert (27) 35 F3
le Thuit-Signol (27) 35 G4
le Thuit-Simer (27) 35 G4
Thulay (25) 139 H3
Thumeréville (54) 26 D6
Thumeries (59) 6 D6
Thun-l'Évêque (59) 11 K3
Thun-Saint-Amand (59) 7 H6
Thun-Saint-Martin (59) 11 K3
Thurageau (86) 162 E1
Thuré (86) 145 H6
Thuret (63) 185 G5
Thurey (71) 172 C1
Thurey-le-Mont (25) 138 B4
Thurins (69) 205 J3
Thury (21) 153 H3
Thury (89) 132 D2
Thury-en-Valois (60) 39 F5
Thury-Harcourt (14) 53 J1
Thury-sous-Clermont (60) 37 K3
Thusy (74) 190 D5
Thuy (65) 285 K5
Thyez (74) 191 K3
Tibiran-Jaunac (65) 305 H2
Ticheville (61) 55 F3
Tichey (21) 154 E3
le Tiercent (35) 79 J1
Tiercé (49) 125 H1
Tiercelet (54) 26 E3
Tierceville (14) 32 C3
Tieste-Uragnoux (32) 285 H1
la Tieule (48) 253 H2
Tiffauges (85) 142 C2
Tigeaux (77) 59 K4
Tigery (91) 59 G6
Tignac (09) 308 A6
Tigné (49) 143 K1
Tignécourt (88) 117 J1
Tignes (73) 193 C5
le Tignet (06) 280 C5
Tignieu-Jameyzieu (38) 206 E2
Tigny-Noyelle (62) 9 F2
Tigy (45) 110 D5
Til-Châtel (21) 136 B3
Tilh (40) 264 D6
Tilhouse (65) 304 E1
Tillac (32) 285 K2
Tillay-le-Péneux (28) 109 J1
Tillé (60) 37 H2
Tillenay (21) 155 F1
le Tilleul (76) 14 B4
le Tilleul-Dame-Agnès (27) 56 B1
le Tilleul-Lambert (27) 35 G6
le Tilleul-Othon (27) 35 F6
Tilleux (88) 93 G4
Tillières (49) 142 C1
Tillières-sur-Avre (27) 56 C5
Tilloloy (80) 19 F6
Tillou (79) 178 D3
Tilloy-et-Bellay (51) 63 F1
Tilloy-Floriville (80) 8 E6

Tilloy-lès-Conty (80) 17 K4
Tilloy-lès-Hermaville (62) 10 C2
Tilloy-lès-Mofflaines (62) 11 F3
Tilloy-lez-Cambrai (59) 11 J4
Tilloy-lez-Marchiennes (59) 11 K1
Tilly (27) 36 B5
Tilly (36) 164 D5
Tilly (78) 57 H3
Tilly-Capelle (62) 5 G6
Tilly-la-Campagne (14) 32 E6
Tilly-sur-Meuse (55) 64 D1
Tilly-sur-Seulles (14) 32 B5
Tilques (62) 3 F5
Tincey-et-Pontrebeau (70) 137 H1
Tinchebray (61) 53 F4
Tincourt-Boucly (80) 19 H1
Tincques (62) 10 C2
Tincry (57) 66 C2
Tingry (62) 4 B4
Tinqueux (51) 40 E4
Tinténiac (35) 78 E1
Tintry (71) 153 G4
Tintury (58) 151 J4
Tiranges (43) 220 D2
Tirent-Pontéjac (32) 287 F1
Tirepied (50) 52 A5
le Titre (80) 9 F4
Tivernon (45) 110 A1
Tiviers (15) 218 E5
Tizac-de-Curton (33) 230 A2
Tizac-de-Lapouyade (33) 212 A5
Tocane-Saint-Apre (24) 213 J3
Tocqueville (27) 34 D2
Tocqueville (50) 29 F2
Tocqueville-en-Caux (76) 15 H3
Tocqueville-les-Murs (76) 14 E5
Tocqueville-sur-Eu (76) 8 B6
Toeufles (80) 9 F5
Toges (08) 42 C2
Togny-aux-Boeufs (51) 62 E3
Tolla (2A) 320 E4
Tollaincourt (88) 117 G1
Tollent (62) 9 H3
Tollevast (50) 28 C3
la Tombe (77) 88 B4
Tombeboeuf (47) 231 H6
Tomblaine (54) 66 B5
Tomino (2B) 317 D2
les Tonils (26) 241 F5
Tonnac (81) 250 E6
Tonnay-Boutonne (17) 177 H5
Tonnay-Charente (17) 177 F5
Tonneins (47) 247 J2
Tonnerre (89) 114 A4
Tonneville (50) 28 C2
Tonnoy (54) 94 B1
Tonquédec (22) 48 B5
Torcé (35) 104 A1
Torcé-en-Vallée (72) 107 F1
Torcé-Viviers-en-Charnie (53) 105 K1
Torcenay (52) 116 E4
Torchamp (61) 81 F1
Torchefelon (38) 207 G5
Torcheville (57) 67 G2
Torcieu (01) 189 J5
Torcy (62) 4 E6
Torcy (71) 153 G6
Torcy (77) 59 H3
Torcy-en-Valois (02) 39 J6
Torcy-et-Pouligny (21) 134 C3
Torcy-le-Grand (10) 90 B2
Torcy-le-Grand (76) 16 A3
Torcy-le-Petit (10) 90 C2
Torcy-le-Petit (76) 16 A3
Tordères (66) 315 F4
Tordouet (14) 55 F1
Torfou (49) 142 C3
Torfou (91) 86 D2
Torigni-sur-Vire (50) 31 J4
Tornac (30) 274 D1
Tornay (52) 117 F6
le Torp-Mesnil (76) 15 H4
Torpes (25) 156 A1
Torpes (71) 155 F5
le Torpt (27) 34 B3
le Torquesne (14) 33 K4
Torreilles (66) 310 D5
Torsac (16) 196 E4
Torsiac (43) 219 F2
Tortebesse (63) 201 J3
Tortefontaine (62) 9 H2
Tortequesne (62) 11 H3
Torteron (18) 150 C3
Torteval-Quesnay (14) 32 A5
Tortezais (03) 167 K5
Tortisambert (14) 54 D2
Torvilliers (10) 89 K5
Torxé (17) 177 J5
Tosny (27) 36 A5
Tosse (40) 262 C4
Tossiat (01) 189 H3
Tostat (65) 285 H4
Tostes (27) 35 H4
Totainville (88) 93 J4
Tôtes (76) 15 K4
Touchay (18) 166 D2
la Touche (26) 240 C6
les Touches (44) 123 J1
les Touches-de-Périgny (17) 178 C6
Toucy (89) 112 D2
Toudon (06) 281 F1

Touët-de-l'Escarène (06) 281 H2
Touët-sur-Var (06) 280 D1
Touffailles (82) 249 F4
Toufflers (59) 7 F4
Touffréville (14) 33 F5
Touffreville (27) 36 B3
Touffreville-la-Cable (76) 15 F6
Touffreville-la-Corbeline (76) 15 G6
Touffreville-sur-Eu (76) 8 B6
Touget (32) 268 B5
Touille (31) 306 B1
Touillon (21) 134 E1
Touillon-et-Loutelet (25) 157 F5
Toujouse (32) 266 C3
Toul (54) 65 H5
Toulaud (07) 240 B1
Toulenne (33) 230 A5
Touligny (08) 22 C4
Toulis-et-Attencourt (02) 20 E4
Toulon (83) 297 J6
Toulon-sur-Allier (03) 168 E4
Toulon-sur-Arroux (71) 170 C2
Toulonjac (12) 251 F2
Toulouges (66) 315 G2
Toulouse (31) 269 G6
Toulouse-le-Château (39) 155 H5
Toulouzette (40) 264 E4
Toulx-Sainte-Croix (23) 183 G1
Touques (14) 33 J3
le Touquet-Paris-Plage (62) 4 A5
Touquettes (61) 55 G4
Touquin (77) 60 B4
la Tour (06) 261 J6
la Tour (74) 191 J2
la Tour-Blanche (24) 213 H1
la Tour-d'Aigues (84) 277 J4
la Tour-d'Auvergne (63) 201 K5
Tour-de-Faure (46) 250 C1
la Tour-de-Salvagny (69) 205 K1
la Tour-de-Scay (25) 138 C4
la Tour-du-Crieu (09) 307 J1
le Tour-du-Meix (39) 173 H3
le Tour-du-Parc (56) 121 G2
la Tour-du-Pin (38) 207 G4
Tour-en-Bessin (14) 32 A3
la Tour-en-Jarez (42) 205 G5
Tour-en-Sologne (41) 129 G3
la Tour-Saint-Gelin (37) 145 H3
la Tour-sur-Orb (34) 272 E6
Tourailles (41) 128 D1
les Tourailles (61) 53 J4
Tourbes (34) 292 B2
Tourcelles-Chaumont (08) 42 A2
Tourch (29) 75 F6
Tourcoing (59) 6 E3
Tourdun (32) 285 J1
la Tourette (42) 204 D6
la Tourette-Cabardès (11) 290 B3
Tourette-du-Château (06) 281 F1
Tourgéville (14) 33 J3
la Tourlandry (49) 143 G1
Tourlaville (50) 28 D2
Tourliac (47) 232 B4
Tourly (60) 37 F4
Tourmignies (59) 6 E6
Tourmont (39) 155 J5
Tournai-sur-Dive (61) 54 D4
Tournan (32) 286 E3
Tournan-en-Brie (77) 59 J5
Tournans (25) 138 C3
Tournavaux (08) 22 D2
Tournay (65) 285 K6
Tournay-sur-Odon (14) 32 C6
le Tourne (33) 229 J3
Tournebu (14) 53 K2
Tournecoupe (32) 268 A3
Tournedos-Bois-Hubert (27) 35 G6
Tournedos-sur-Seine (27) 35 K4
Tournefeuille (31) 288 A1
Tournehem-sur-la-Hem (62) 2 E4
Tournemire (12) 272 D2
Tournemire (15) 217 H5
Tournes (08) 22 C3
le Tourneur (14) 31 K5
Tournières (14) 31 J2
Tournissan (11) 309 K1
Tournoisis (45) 109 H3
Tournon (73) 209 F3
Tournon-d'Agenais (47) 249 F2
Tournon-Saint-Martin (36) 164 B1
Tournon-Saint-Pierre (37) 164 B1
Tournon-sur-Rhône (07) 222 B5
Tournous-Darré (65) 286 A4
Tournous-Devant (65) 286 B5
Tournus (71) 171 K3
Tourny (27) 36 C5
Tourouvre (61) 83 J1
Tourouzelle (11) 291 F5
Tourreilles (11) 308 E2
les Tourreilles (31) 305 H1
Tourrenquets (32) 267 J4
Tourrette-Levens (06) 281 G3
les Tourrettes (26) 240 B4
Tourrettes (83) 280 B5
Tourrettes-sur-Loup (06) 280 D4
Tourriers (16) 196 E1
Tours (37) 127 J4
Tours-en-Savoie (73) 209 G3
Tours-en-Vimeu (80) 8 E6
Tours-sur-Marne (51) 62 B1

Tours-sur-Meymont (63) 203 J3
Tourtenay (79) 144 C3
Tourteron (08) 22 C6
Tourtoirac (24) 214 D2
Tourtour (83) 279 G6
Tourtouse (09) 306 D1
Tourtrès (47) 231 H6
Tourtrol (09) 308 A2
Tourves (83) 297 J2
Tourville-en-Auge (14) 33 K3
Tourville-la-Campagne (27) 35 G4
Tourville-la-Chapelle (76) 16 B1
Tourville-la-Rivière (76) 35 H3
Tourville-les-Ifs (76) 14 D4
Tourville-sur-Arques (76) 15 K2
Tourville-sur-Odon (14) 32 D5
Tourville-sur-Pont-Audemer (27) . . . 34 D4
Tourville-sur-Sienne (50) 30 D4
Toury (28) 86 A6
Toury-Lurcy (58) 169 F1
Toury-sur-Jour (58) 168 D1
Tourzel-Ronzières (63) 202 D5
Toussaint (76) 14 D4
Toussieu (69) 206 C3
Toussieux (01) 188 C5
Tousson (77) 87 F4
Toussus-le-Noble (78) 58 C5
Toutainville (27) 34 C3
Toutenant (71) 154 D5
Toutencourt (80) 10 C6
Toutens (31) 288 E2
Toutlemonde (49) 143 F3
Toutry (21) 134 B3
Touvérac (16) 212 B1
le Touvet (38) 224 C1
Touville (27) 34 E3
Touvois (44) 141 G4
Touvre (16) 197 F3
Touzac (16) 196 B4
Touzac (46) 249 G1
Tox (2B) 319 J6
Toy-Viam (19) 200 B4
Tracy-Bocage (14) 32 B6
Tracy-le-Mont (60) 39 F1
Tracy-le-Val (60) 39 F1
Tracy-sur-Loire (58) 131 K5
Tracy-sur-Mer (14) 32 B3
Trades (69) 187 K1
Traenheim (67) 70 C3
Tragny (57) 66 C1
Traînel (10) 88 E3
Traînou (45) 110 C3
le Trait (76) 35 F1
Traitiéfontaine (70) 138 A4
Traize (73) 207 K3
Tralaigues (63) 184 A6
Tralonca (2B) 319 F5
Tramain (22) 77 K2
Tramayes (71) 188 A1
Trambly (71) 171 G6
Tramecourt (62) 5 F6
Tramery (51) 40 D4
Tramezaïgues (65) 304 E5
Tramolé (38) 207 F5
Tramont-Émy (54) 93 J3
Tramont-Lassus (54) 93 J3
Tramont-Saint-André (54) 93 J3
Tramoyes (01) 188 D6
Trampot (88) 92 D3
la Tranche-sur-Mer (85) 159 H5
la Tranclière (01) 189 G3
Trancrainville (28) 85 K5
Trangé (72) 106 D2
le Tranger (36) 147 F4
Trannes (10) 91 F4
Tranqueville-Graux (88) 93 H2
Trans (53) 81 K5
Trans-en-Provence (83) 298 D1
Trans-la-Forêt (35) 51 H5
Trans-sur-Erdre (44) 123 J1
le Translay (80) 17 F1
le Transloy (62) 11 F5
Tranzault (36) 165 K3
Trappes (78) 58 B4
Trassanel (11) 290 C4
Traubach-le-Bas (68) 97 A3
Traubach-le-Haut (68) 97 A3
Trausse (11) 290 D4
Travaillan (84) 257 F4
Traversères (32) 286 D1
Traves (70) 137 K1
le Travet (81) 271 F4
Trayes (79) 161 H2
Tréal (56) 102 A2
Tréauville (50) 28 B3
Trébabu (29) 72 B4
Treban (03) 168 D5
Tréban (81) 251 K6
Trébas (81) 271 H2
Trébédan (22) 50 B6
Trèbes (11) 290 C5
Trébeurden (22) 47 J2
Trébons (65) 304 D1
Trébons-de-Luchon (31) 305 H5
Trébons-sur-la-Grasse (31) 288 E2
Trébrivan (22) 75 K2
Trébry (22) 77 J2
Tréclun (21) 154 E1
Trécon (51) 62 A3
Trédaniel (22) 77 H2
Trédarzec (22) 48 C3

Trédias (22) 78 B1
Trédion (56) 101 H3
Trédrez-Locquémeau (22) 47 J3
Tréduder (22) 47 J4
Trefcon (02) 19 J2
Treffendel (35) 78 D5
Treffiagat (29) 98 B3
Treffieux (44) 103 H5
Trefflléan (56) 101 G5
Treffort (38) 242 A1
Treffort-Cuisiat (01) 189 H1
Treffrin (22) 75 J2
Tréflaouénan (29) 46 D4
Tréflévénez (29) 46 D6
Tréflez (29) 46 C3
Tréfols (51) 61 F4
Tréfumel (22) 78 D1
Trégarantec (29) 46 C4
Trégarvan (29) 74 C2
Trégastel (22) 47 K2
Tréglamus (22) 48 B5
Tréglonou (29) 72 D2
Trégomeur (22) 49 F5
Trégon (22) 50 B4
Trégonneau (22) 48 C4
Trégourez (29) 75 F2
Trégrom (22) 48 A4
Tréguennec (29) 73 E5
Trégueux (22) 49 G6
Tréguidel (22) 48 E5
Tréguier (22) 48 C2
Trégunc (29) 99 F3
Tréhet (41) 107 H6
Tréhorenteuc (56) 78 A5
le Tréhou (29) 74 D1
Treignac (19) 200 A5
Treignat (03) 166 E6
Treigny (89) 132 C3
Treilles (11) 310 C3
Treilles-en-Gâtinais (45) 111 H2
Treillières (44) 123 G2
Treix (52) 92 B6
Treize-Septiers (85) 142 B3
Treize-Vents (85) 143 F4
Tréjouls (82) 249 H4
Trélans (48) 253 G1
Trélazé (49) 125 H3
Trélévern (22) 48 B2
Trelins (42) 204 E3
Trélissac (24) 214 B3
Trélivan (22) 50 C6
Trelly (50) 30 E5
Trélon (59) 13 J5
Trélou-sur-Marne (02) 40 B6
Trémaouézan (29) 46 C5
Trémargat (22) 76 B2
Trémauville (76) 14 E5
la Tremblade (17) 194 B1
Tremblay (35) 51 J6
le Tremblay (49) 104 C6
Tremblay-en-France (93) 59 G2
Tremblay-les-Villages (28) 85 F1
le Tremblay-Omonville (27) 35 G6
le Tremblay-sur-Mauldre (78) 58 A4
Tremblecourt (54) 65 J3
le Tremblois (70) 137 F4
Tremblois-lès-Carignan (08) 23 J4
Tremblois-lès-Rocroi (08) 22 B2
Trémeheuc (35) 51 G6
Trémel (22) 47 J4
Tréméloir (22) 49 F5
Trémentines (49) 143 F2
Tréméoc (29) 98 C2
Tréméreuc (22) 50 D4
Trémery (57) 27 H5
Trémeur (22) 78 B1
Tréméven (22) 48 E4
Tréméven (29) 99 J3
Tréminis (38) 242 B3
Trémoins (70) 139 G1
Trémolat (24) 232 D2
Trémons (47) 248 E2
Trémont (49) 143 J1
Trémont (61) 82 E1
Trémont-sur-Saulx (55) 63 K4
Trémonzey (88) 118 B2
Trémorel (22) 78 A3
Trémouille (15) 218 A1
Trémouille-Saint-Loup (63) 201 H6
Trémouilles (12) 252 C4
Trémoulet (09) 288 E6
Trémuson (22) 49 F6
Trenal (39) 173 F2
Trensacq (40) 245 H4
Trentels (47) 248 E1
Tréogan (22) 75 J4
Tréogat (29) 73 E4
Tréon (28) 56 E6
Tréouergat (29) 72 C3
Trépail (51) 41 G6
le Tréport (76) 8 C5
Trépot (25) 156 D1
Tréprel (14) 53 K3
Trept (38) 207 F3
Trésauvaux (55) 43 K6
Tresboeuf (35) 103 H1
Trescault (62) 11 H5
Treschenu-Creyers (26) 241 J3
Trescléoux (05) 258 D2
Tresilley (70) 137 K3
Treslon (51) 40 D4
Tresnay (58) 168 D2

Trespoux-Rassiels (46) 249 K2
Tresques (30) 256 C5
Tressan (34) 292 D1
Tressandans (25) 138 C2
Tressange (57) 27 F4
Tressé (35) 50 E5
Tresserre (66) 315 G4
Tresserve (73) 208 A3
Tresses (33) 229 J2
Tressignaux (22) 48 E4
Tresson (72) 107 H4
Treteau (03) 169 G6
la Trétoire (77) 60 D3
Trets (13) 297 F2
Treux (80) 18 D1
Treuzy-Levelay (77) 87 J3
Trévé (22) 77 F4
Trévenans (90) 139 H1
Tréveneuc (22) 49 F4
Tréveray (55) 64 D6
Trévérec (22) 48 D4
Trévérien (35) 78 E1
Trèves (30) 253 K6
Trèves (69) 205 K5
Trévien (81) 251 G6
Trévières (14) 31 K1
Trévignin (73) 208 B2
Trévillach (66) 309 H6
Tréville (11) 289 G3
Trévillers (25) 139 L6
Trévilly (89) 134 B3
Trévol (03) 168 E3
Trévou-Tréguignec (22) 48 B2
Trévoux (01) 188 C5
le Trévoux (29) 99 H3
Trézelles (03) 186 A1
Trézény (22) 48 B2
Tréziers (11) 308 C2
Trézilidé (29) 46 D4
Trézioux (63) 203 H3
Triac-Lautrait (16) 196 B3
le Triadou (34) 274 B4
Triaize (85) 160 A5
Tribehou (50) 31 G2
Trichey (89) 114 B3
Tricot (60) 18 D6
Trie-Château (60) 36 E4
Trie-la-Ville (60) 36 E4
Trie-sur-Baïse (65) 286 A4
Triel-sur-Seine (78) 58 B2
Triembach-au-Val (67) 70 B6
Trieux (54) 26 E5
Trigance (83) 279 J3
Trignac (44) 122 A2
Trigny (51) 40 D3
Triguères (45) 112 A3
Trilbardou (77) 59 J2
Trilla (66) 309 H6
Trilport (77) 60 A2
Trimbach (67) 25 C2
Trimer (35) 78 E1
la Trimouille (86) 164 C5
Trinay (45) 110 A2
la Trinitat (15) 236 C3
la Trinité (06) 281 H3
la Trinité (27) 56 E2
la Trinité (50) 52 B4
la Trinité (73) 208 D5
la Trinité-de-Réville (27) 55 H2
la Trinité-de-Thouberville (27) 35 F3
la Trinité-des-Laitiers (61) 55 G4
la Trinité-du-Mont (76) 14 E6
la Trinité-Porhoët (56) 77 H5
la Trinité-sur-Mer (56) 100 C6
la Trinité-Surzur (56) 101 H6
Triors (26) 222 E4
le Trioulou (15) 235 F4
Tripleville (41) 109 G3
Triquerville (76) 34 D1
Triqueville (27) 34 B3
Trith-Saint-Léger (59) 12 C2
Trivy (71) 171 F5
Trizac (15) 217 J3
Trizay (17) 177 F6
Trizay-Coutretot-Saint-Serge (28) 84 A3
Trizay-lès-Bonneval (28) 84 E6
Troarn (14) 33 F5
Troche (19) 215 H1
Trochères (21) 136 D5
Trocy-en-Multien (77) 60 A1
Troësnes (02) 39 H5
Troguéry (22) 48 C3
Trogues (37) 145 J2
les Trois-Domaines (55) 64 C2
Trois-Fonds (23) 183 G2
Trois-Fontaines-l'Abbaye (51) 63 J5
Trois-Monts (14) 32 D6
les Trois-Moutiers (86) 144 D3
Trois-Palis (16) 196 D3
les Trois-Pierres (76) 14 D6
Trois-Puits (51) 41 F5
Trois-Vèvres (58) 151 G5
Trois-Villes (64) 283 H6
Troisfontaines (57) 67 K5
Troisfontaines-la-Ville (52) 91 K1
Troisgots (50) 31 H4
Troissereux (60) 37 G1
Troissy (51) 40 C6
Troisvaux (62) 10 B1

Troisvilles (59) 12 C5
Tromarey (70) 137 G5
Tromborn (57) 45 J3
Troncens (32) 285 J2
la Tronche (38) 224 A3
le Tronchet (35) 51 F5
le Tronchet (72) 82 D6
Tronchoy (89) 113 K4
Tronchy (71) 172 B1
le Troncq (27) 35 G5
Trondes (54) 65 G5
Tronget (03) 168 C5
le Tronquay (14) 32 A4
le Tronquay (27) 36 B2
Tronsanges (58) 150 D2
Tronville (54) 44 C6
Tronville-en-Barrois (55) 64 C5
Troo (41) 107 K5
Trosly-Breuil (60) 39 F2
Trosly-Loire (02) 39 H1
Trouans (10) 62 C6
Troubat (65) 305 H3
Trouhans (21) 154 E1
Trouhaut (21) 135 H4
Trouillas (66) 315 F3
Trouley-Labarthe (65) 285 K4
Troussencourt (60) 18 A5
Troussey (55) 65 G5
Troussures (60) 37 G2
Trouvans (25) 138 D3
Trouville (76) 15 F6
Trouville-la-Haule (27) 34 D2
Trouville-sur-Mer (14) 33 J2
Trouy (18) 149 G4
Troye-d'Ariège (09) 308 B2
Troyes (10) 90 B4
Troyon (55) 64 D1
Trucy (02) 40 B1
Trucy-l'Orgueilleux (58) 132 E4
Trucy-sur-Yonne (89) 133 H2
le Truel (12) 272 A1
Trugny (21) 154 D4
Truinas (26) 240 E5
Trumilly (60) 38 D4
Trun (61) 54 C3
Trungy (14) 32 B4
Truttemer-le-Grand (14) 52 E4
Truttemer-le-Petit (14) 52 E4
Truyes (37) 128 A6
Tubersent (62) 4 B5
Tuchan (11) 310 A4
Tucquegnieux (54) 26 E5
Tudeils (19) 216 B5
Tudelle (32) 266 E5
Tuffé (72) 107 H1
Tugéras-Saint-Maurice (17) 211 K1
Tugny-et-Pont (02) 19 J3
la Tuilière (42) 186 C5
Tulette (26) 257 F3
Tulle (19) 216 B3
Tullins (38) 223 J2
Tully (80) 8 D5
Tupigny (02) 20 C1
Tupin-et-Semons (69) 206 A5
la Turballe (44) 121 H4
la Turbie (06) 281 J3
Turcey (21) 135 H4
Turckheim (68) 96 B4
Turenne (19) 215 J5
Turgon (16) 179 J5
Turgy (10) 114 A2
Turny (89) 113 H2
Turquant (49) 144 D1
Turquestein-Blancrupt (57) 67 K6
Turqueville (50) 29 F5
Turretot (76) 14 B5
Turriers (04) 259 H1
Tursac (24) 214 D6
Tusson (16) 179 F5
Tuzaguet (65) 305 G1
le Tuzan (33) 245 K1
Tuzie (16) 179 G5

U

Uberach (67) 69 J5
Ubexy (88) 94 B3
Ubraye (04) 280 A1
Ucciani (2A) 320 E3
Ucel (07) 239 H5
Uchacq-et-Parentis (40) 265 G2
Uchaud (30) 275 F4
Uchaux (84) 256 E4
Uchentein (09) 306 C4
Uchizy (71) 171 K4
Uchon (71) 152 E6
Uckange (57) 27 G5
Ueberstrass (68) 97 A5
Uffheim (68) 97 D3
Uffholtz (68) 97 A1
Ugine (73) 209 G1
Uglas (65) 286 B6
Ugnouas (65) 285 H4
Ugny (54) 26 C3
Ugny-le-Gay (02) 19 J5
Ugny-l'Équipée (80) 19 H3
Ugny-sur-Meuse (55) 65 G6

Uhart-Cize (64) 282 D5
Uhart-Mixe (64) 283 G4
Uhlwiller (67) 69 K6
Uhrwiller (67) 69 J5
Ulcot (79) 143 K3
les Ulis (91) 58 C6
Ully-Saint-Georges (60) 37 J4
les Ulmes (49) 144 B1
Umpeau (28) 85 J2
Unac (09) 308 A5
Uncey-le-Franc (21) 135 F5
Unchair (51) 40 C4
Ungersheim (68) 96 B6
Unias (42) 204 E4
Unienville (10) 91 F4
Unieux (42) 221 F1
l'Union (31) 269 H6
Unverre (28) 84 C6
Unzent (09) 288 C6
Upaix (05) 259 F2
Upie (26) 240 D2
Ur (66) 313 G5
Urau (31) 306 D2
Urbalacone (2A) 320 D6
Urbanya (66) 314 A3
Urbeis (67) 96 A1
Urbès (68) 119 J3
Urbise (42) 186 D2
Urçay (03) 167 H3
Urcel (02) 40 A1
Urcerey (90) 139 H1
Urciers (36) 166 C4
Urcuit (64) 282 D1
Urcy (21) 135 J6
Urdens (32) 267 K3
Urdès (64) 284 C3
Urdos (64) 303 F4
Urepel (64) 263 D5
Urgons (40) 265 H5
Urgosse (32) 266 B4
Uriménil (88) 94 D6
Urmatt (67) 70 B4
Urost (64) 285 F4
Urou-et-Crennes (61) 54 C4
Urrugne (64) 263 B2
Urs (09) 307 K5
Urschenheim (68) 96 D4
Urt (64) 282 D1
Urtaca (2B) 319 F2
Urtière (25) 139 J5
Uruffe (54) 93 G1
Urval (24) 232 C2
Urville (10) 91 G6
Urville (14) 53 K1
Urville (50) 28 E5
Urville (88) 93 G5
Urville-Nacqueville (50) 28 B2
Urvillers (02) 20 A3
Ury (77) 87 G4
Urzy (58) 150 E3
Us (95) 37 F6
Usclades-et-Rieutord (07) 239 F3
Usclas-d'Hérault (34) 292 C2
Usclas-du-Bosc (34) 273 G5
Usinens (74) 190 C4
Ussac (19) 215 J3
Ussat (09) 307 J5
Usseau (17) 177 K2
Usseau (86) 145 J5
Ussel (15) 218 C5
Ussel (19) 201 F5
Ussel (46) 233 J5
Ussel-d'Allier (03) 185 G2
Usson (63) 203 F5
Usson-du-Poitou (86) 180 A1
Usson-en-Forez (42) 220 C1
Ussy (14) 53 K2
Ussy-sur-Marne (77) 60 B2
Ustaritz (64) 263 D1
Ustou (09) 306 E5
Utelle (06) 281 G1
Uttenheim (67) 70 E5
Uttenhoffen (67) 69 K5
Uttwiller (67) 69 H6
Uvernet-Fours (04) 260 C1
Uxeau (71) 170 B2
Uxegney (88) 94 C5
Uxelles (39) 173 J2
Uxem (59) 3 J1
Uz (65) 304 A2
Uza (40) 244 C6
Uzan (64) 284 B2
Uzay-le-Venon (18) 149 H6
Uzech (46) 233 H5
Uzein (64) 284 C1
Uzel (22) 77 F3
Uzelle (25) 138 D3
Uzemain (88) 118 C1
Uzer (07) 239 G6
Uzer (65) 304 D1
Uzerche (19) 199 J6
Uzès (30) 275 H1
Uzeste (33) 246 C1
Uzos (64) 284 D4

V

Vaas (72) 127 F1
Vabre (81) 271 G5
Vabre-Tizac (12) 251 H4

406

Vabres (15) . . . 219 F5
Vabres (30) . . . 274 C1
Vabres-l'Abbaye (12) . . . 272 B2
Vacherauville (55) . . . 43 H4
Vachères (04) . . . 277 K2
Vachères-en-Quint (26) . . . 241 G4
Vacheresse (74) . . . 175 H5
la Vacheresse-et-la-Rouillie (88) . . . 93 H6
la Vacherie (27) . . . 35 J4
Vacognes-Neuilly (14) . . . 32 C6
la Vacquerie (14) . . . 31 K4
la Vacquerie-et-Saint-Martin-de-Castries (34) . . . 273 H4
Vacquerie-le-Boucq (62) . . . 9 K3
Vacqueriette-Erquières (62) . . . 9 J2
Vacqueville (54) . . . 95 G1
Vacqueyras (84) . . . 257 G5
Vacquières (34) . . . 274 C3
Vacquiers (31) . . . 269 H4
Vadans (39) . . . 155 J4
Vadans (70) . . . 137 F5
Vadelaincourt (55) . . . 43 G6
Vadenay (51) . . . 41 J6
Vadencourt (02) . . . 20 C1
Vadencourt (80) . . . 10 C6
Vadonville (55) . . . 64 E4
Vagnas (07) . . . 255 K2
Vagney (88) . . . 119 G2
Vahl-Ebersing (57) . . . 68 A3
Vahl-lès-Bénestroff (57) . . . 67 G2
Vahl-lès-Faulquemont (57) . . . 45 K6
Vaiges (53) . . . 105 H2
Vaihauquès (34) . . . 274 A5
Vaihourles (12) . . . 250 E3
Vaillac (46) . . . 233 J4
Vaillant (52) . . . 116 B6
Vailly (10) . . . 90 B4
Vailly (74) . . . 175 G6
Vailly-sur-Aisne (02) . . . 40 A2
Vailly-sur-Sauldre (18) . . . 131 H4
Vains (50) . . . 51 K3
Vairé (85) . . . 158 E2
Vaire-Arcier (25) . . . 138 B5
Vaire-le-Petit (25) . . . 138 B5
Vaire-sous-Corbie (80) . . . 18 D2
Vaires-sur-Marne (77) . . . 59 H3
Vaison-la-Romaine (84) . . . 257 G4
Vaïssac (82) . . . 269 J1
Vaite (70) . . . 137 G1
la Vaivre (70) . . . 118 C3
Vaivre-et-Montoille (70) . . . 138 A1
le Val (83) . . . 297 K2
le Val-d'Ajol (88) . . . 118 E3
Val-d'Auzon (10) . . . 90 D3
le Val-David (27) . . . 56 E2
Val-de-Bride (57) . . . 67 F3
Val-de-Chalvagne (04) . . . 280 C1
Val-de-Fier (74) . . . 190 D5
le Val-de-Gouhenans (70) . . . 138 E1
le Val-de-Guéblange (57) . . . 67 H1
Val-de-la-Haye (76) . . . 35 G2
Val-de-Mercy (89) . . . 133 G1
Val-de-Meuse (52) . . . 116 E2
Val-de-Reuil (27) . . . 35 J4
Val-de-Roulans (25) . . . 138 C4
Val-de-Saâne (76) . . . 15 J4
Val-de-Vesle (51) . . . 41 G5
Val-de-Vière (51) . . . 63 G4
Val-d'Épy (39) . . . 172 E5
Val-des-Marais (51) . . . 61 K3
Val-des-Prés (05) . . . 226 A6
le Val-d'Esnoms (52) . . . 116 C6
Val-d'Isère (73) . . . 193 C5
Val-d'Izé (35) . . . 79 K3
Val-d'Ornain (55) . . . 64 A4
Val-d'Orvin (10) . . . 89 G4
Val-et-Châtillon (54) . . . 67 H6
Val-Maravel (26) . . . 241 K5
le Val-Saint-Éloi (70) . . . 118 B5
le Val-Saint-Germain (91) . . . 86 B1
le Val-Saint-Père (50) . . . 51 K3
Val-Suzon (21) . . . 135 J4
Valady (12) . . . 251 K1
Valailles (27) . . . 34 D6
Valaire (41) . . . 128 E4
Valanjou (49) . . . 125 G6
Valaurie (26) . . . 256 E1
Valavoire (04) . . . 259 H3
Valay (70) . . . 137 G5
Valbeleix (63) . . . 202 C6
Valbelle (04) . . . 259 F4
Valbois (55) . . . 65 F2
Valbonnais (38) . . . 242 C1
Valbonne (06) . . . 280 E5
Valcabrère (31) . . . 305 H2
Valcanville (50) . . . 29 F2
Valcebollère (66) . . . 313 H6
Valcivières (63) . . . 204 A4
Valcourt (52) . . . 63 J6
Valdahon (25) . . . 156 E1
Valdampierre (60) . . . 37 G4
Valdeblore (06) . . . 261 J5
le Valdécie (50) . . . 28 C5
Valderiès (81) . . . 270 E1
Valderoure (06) . . . 280 B3
Valdieu-Lutran (68) . . . 119 H4
Valdivienne (86) . . . 163 H4
Valdoie (90) . . . 119 H6
Valdrôme (26) . . . 241 K6
Valdurenque (81) . . . 290 A1
Valeille (42) . . . 205 F3

Valeilles (82) . . . 248 E2
Valeins (01) . . . 188 C3
Valempoulières (39) . . . 156 A5
Valençay (36) . . . 147 J2
Valence (16) . . . 179 H6
Valence (26) . . . 240 C1
Valence (82) . . . 248 E6
Valence-d'Albigeois (81) . . . 271 G1
Valence-en-Brie (77) . . . 87 K3
Valence-sur-Baïse (32) . . . 267 F3
Valenciennes (59) . . . 12 D2
Valencin (38) . . . 206 C4
Valencogne (38) . . . 207 H5
Valennes (72) . . . 107 K3
Valensole (04) . . . 278 D3
Valentigney (25) . . . 139 H3
Valentine (31) . . . 305 J1
Valenton (94) . . . 59 F5
Valergues (34) . . . 274 D5
Valernes (04) . . . 259 G3
Valescourt (60) . . . 38 A1
Valette (15) . . . 217 K3
la Valette (38) . . . 224 C6
la Valette-du-Var (83) . . . 297 J6
Valeuil (24) . . . 213 K2
Valeyrac (33) . . . 194 D6
Valezan (73) . . . 209 K3
Valff (67) . . . 70 D5
Valfin-sur-Valouse (39) . . . 173 F5
Valflaunès (34) . . . 274 B4
Valfleury (42) . . . 205 H5
Valframbert (61) . . . 82 D2
Valfroicourt (88) . . . 94 A5
Valgorge (07) . . . 238 E5
Valhey (54) . . . 66 D5
Valhuon (62) . . . 10 B1
Valiergues (19) . . . 201 F6
Valignat (03) . . . 185 F3
Valigny (03) . . . 167 K2
Valines (80) . . . 8 E5
Valjouffrey (38) . . . 242 D1
Valjouze (15) . . . 218 D4
la Valla (42) . . . 204 B2
la Valla-en-Gier (42) . . . 205 H6
Vallabrègues (30) . . . 275 K3
Vallabrix (30) . . . 256 B6
Vallan (89) . . . 113 F6
Vallangoujard (95) . . . 37 H6
Vallans (79) . . . 177 K2
Vallant-Saint-Georges (10) . . . 89 K2
Vallauris (06) . . . 280 E5
Valle-d'Alesani (2B) . . . 319 J5
Valle-di-Campoloro (2B) . . . 319 J5
Valle-di-Mezzana (2A) . . . 320 C4
Valle-di-Rostino (2B) . . . 319 G4
Valle-d'Orezza (2B) . . . 319 H5
Vallecalle (2B) . . . 317 D6
la Vallée (17) . . . 177 G6
la Vallée-au-Blé (02) . . . 20 E2
la Vallée-Mulâtre (02) . . . 12 D6
Vallègue (31) . . . 289 F3
Valleiry (74) . . . 190 D3
Vallenay (18) . . . 149 G6
Vallentigny (10) . . . 91 F3
Vallerange (57) . . . 67 F1
Vallérargues (30) . . . 255 K5
Valleraugue (30) . . . 254 C6
Vallères (37) . . . 127 G5
Valleret (52) . . . 91 K2
Vallereuil (24) . . . 213 J5
Vallerois-le-Bois (70) . . . 138 C2
Vallerois-Lorioz (70) . . . 138 B2
Valleroy (25) . . . 138 B4
Valleroy (52) . . . 117 G6
Valleroy (54) . . . 26 E6
Valleroy-aux-Saules (88) . . . 94 A5
Valleroy-le-Sec (88) . . . 93 K5
Vallery (89) . . . 88 B5
Vallesvilles (31) . . . 288 D1
Vallet (44) . . . 123 K5
Valletot (27) . . . 34 D3
Vallica (2B) . . . 318 E3
Vallière (23) . . . 182 E6
Vallières (10) . . . 114 A3
Vallières (74) . . . 190 D5
Vallières-les-Grandes (41) . . . 128 D4
Valliguières (30) . . . 275 J1
Valliquerville (76) . . . 15 F5
Valloire (73) . . . 225 H3
Vallois (54) . . . 94 E2
les Vallois (88) . . . 94 A6
Vallon-en-Sully (03) . . . 167 H4
Vallon-Pont-d'Arc (07) . . . 256 A2
Vallon-sur-Gée (72) . . . 106 B3
Vallorcine (74) . . . 192 D3
Vallouise (05) . . . 243 J1
Valmanya (66) . . . 314 D4
Valmascle (34) . . . 273 F6
Valmeinier (73) . . . 225 J3
Valmestroff (57) . . . 27 H4
Valmigère (11) . . . 309 G3
Valmondois (95) . . . 37 H6
Valmont (57) . . . 68 A3
Valmont (76) . . . 14 E4
Valmunster (57) . . . 45 J3
Valmy (51) . . . 42 C6
Valognes (50) . . . 28 E4
Valojoulx (24) . . . 214 E6
Valonne (25) . . . 139 G4
Valoreille (25) . . . 139 G5
Valouse (26) . . . 257 J1
Valprionde (46) . . . 249 G3

Valprivas (43) . . . 220 D2
Valpuiseaux (91) . . . 86 E3
Valras-Plage (34) . . . 292 B5
Valréas (84) . . . 257 G2
Valros (34) . . . 292 B3
Valroufié (46) . . . 233 H6
Vals (09) . . . 308 A1
Vals-des-Tilles (52) . . . 116 A6
Vals-le-Chastel (43) . . . 219 J2
Vals-les-Bains (07) . . . 239 H4
Vals-près-le-Puy (43) . . . 220 C5
Valsemé (14) . . . 33 J4
Valserres (05) . . . 243 F6
Valsonne (69) . . . 187 J5
le Valtin (88) . . . 95 J6
Valuéjols (15) . . . 218 C5
Valvignères (07) . . . 239 K6
Valz-sous-Châteauneuf (63) . . . 218 G6
Valzergues (12) . . . 251 H1
Vanault-le-Châtel (51) . . . 63 G3
Vanault-les-Dames (51) . . . 63 H3
Vançais (79) . . . 179 F1
Vancé (72) . . . 107 J5
la Vancelle (67) . . . 96 B1
Vanclans (25) . . . 157 F2
Vandeins (01) . . . 188 E2
Vandelainville (54) . . . 65 J1
Vandelans (70) . . . 138 B4
Vandeléville (54) . . . 93 J2
Vandélicourt (60) . . . 38 D1
Vandenesse (58) . . . 151 K5
Vandenesse-en-Auxois (21) . . . 153 H1
Vandeuil (51) . . . 40 D4
Vandières (51) . . . 40 C6
Vandières (54) . . . 65 J1
Vandoeuvre-lès-Nancy (54) . . . 66 A5
Vandoncourt (25) . . . 139 J3
Vandré (17) . . . 177 H4
Vandrimare (27) . . . 36 A3
Vandy (08) . . . 42 B2
Vanlay (10) . . . 114 A2
Vannaire (21) . . . 115 F4
Vanne (70) . . . 137 H1
le Vanneau (79) . . . 177 J1
Vannecourt (57) . . . 66 D2
Vannecrocq (27) . . . 34 B3
Vannes (56) . . . 101 F5
Vannes-le-Châtel (54) . . . 93 K1
Vannes-sur-Cosson (45) . . . 110 D6
Vannoz (39) . . . 156 B6
Vanosc (07) . . . 221 J3
les Vans (07) . . . 255 H2
Vantoux (57) . . . 45 F5
Vantoux-et-Longevelle (70) . . . 137 J3
Vanves (92) . . . 58 E4
Vanvey (21) . . . 115 H4
Vanville (77) . . . 88 B1
Vanxains (24) . . . 213 G3
Vany (57) . . . 45 F5
Vanzac (17) . . . 212 A1
Vanzay (79) . . . 179 F2
Vanzy (74) . . . 190 D4
Vaour (81) . . . 250 D6
Varacieux (38) . . . 223 G3
Varades (44) . . . 124 C4
Varages (83) . . . 278 D6
Varaignes (24) . . . 197 H4
Varaire (46) . . . 250 C3
Varaize (17) . . . 178 A5
Varambon (01) . . . 189 H4
Varanges (21) . . . 136 C6
Varangéville (54) . . . 66 B5
Varaville (14) . . . 33 G4
Varces-Allières-et-Risset (38) . . . 224 A4
Vareilles (23) . . . 181 K1
Vareilles (71) . . . 187 G1
Vareilles (89) . . . 89 F6
Varen (82) . . . 250 E5
Varengeville-sur-Mer (76) . . . 15 J2
Varenguebec (50) . . . 28 D6
la Varenne (49) . . . 123 J3
Varenne-l'Arconce (71) . . . 170 C6
Varenne-Saint-Germain (71) . . . 170 B5
Varennes (24) . . . 231 K2
Varennes (31) . . . 288 E2
Varennes (37) . . . 146 C3
Varennes (80) . . . 10 C6
Varennes (82) . . . 269 H3
Varennes (86) . . . 162 D1
Varennes (89) . . . 113 J4
Varennes-Changy (45) . . . 111 H4
Varennes-en-Argonne (55) . . . 42 E4
Varennes-Jarcy (91) . . . 59 G6
Varennes-le-Grand (71) . . . 171 K1
Varennes-lès-Mâcon (71) . . . 188 C1
Varennes-lès-Narcy (58) . . . 150 D1
Varennes-Saint-Honorat (43) . . . 219 K4
Varennes-Saint-Sauveur (71) . . . 172 D4
Varennes-sous-Dun (71) . . . 187 H1
Varennes-sur-Allier (03) . . . 185 J1
Varennes-sur-Fouzon (36) . . . 147 J1
Varennes-sur-Loire (49) . . . 126 C6
Varennes-sur-Morge (63) . . . 185 G6
Varennes-sur-Seine (77) . . . 87 K4
Varennes-sur-Tèche (03) . . . 186 A1
Varennes-sur-Usson (63) . . . 203 F5
Varennes-Vauzelles (58) . . . 150 D4
Vares (47) . . . 247 J1
Varesnes (60) . . . 19 H6
Varessia (39) . . . 173 G3
Varetz (19) . . . 215 H3
Varilhes (09) . . . 307 J2

Varinfroy (60) . . . 39 F6
Variscourt (02) . . . 40 E2
Varize (28) . . . 109 G1
Varize (57) . . . 45 H5
Varmonzey (88) . . . 94 B4
Varogne (70) . . . 118 B5
Varois-et-Chaignot (21) . . . 136 B5
Varouville (50) . . . 29 F2
Varrains (37) . . . 144 C1
Varreddes (77) . . . 59 K2
Vars (05) . . . 227 A4
Vars (16) . . . 196 D2
Vars (70) . . . 137 F2
Vars-sur-Roseix (19) . . . 215 G3
Varsberg (57) . . . 45 K4
Varzay (17) . . . 195 F2
Varzy (58) . . . 132 E5
Vascœuil (27) . . . 36 A2
Vasles (79) . . . 162 B3
Vasperviller (57) . . . 67 J5
Vassel (63) . . . 203 F2
Vasselay (18) . . . 149 G2
Vasselin (38) . . . 207 G3
Vassens (02) . . . 39 G1
Vasseny (02) . . . 40 A3
Vassieux-en-Vercors (26) . . . 241 H1
Vassimont-et-Chapelaine (51) . . . 62 B4
Vassincourt (55) . . . 63 K4
Vassogne (02) . . . 40 C2
Vassonville (76) . . . 15 K4
Vassy (14) . . . 53 G3
Vassy (89) . . . 134 C2
le Vast (50) . . . 29 F2
Vasteville (50) . . . 28 B3
les Vastres (43) . . . 221 F6
Vatan (36) . . . 148 B3
Vathiménil (54) . . . 94 E1
Vatierville (76) . . . 16 D3
Vatimont (57) . . . 66 D1
Vatry (51) . . . 62 C4
Vattetot-sous-Beaumont (76) . . . 14 D5
Vattetot-sur-Mer (76) . . . 14 C4
Vatteville (27) . . . 35 K4
Vatteville-la-Rue (76) . . . 34 E1
Vaubadon (14) . . . 31 K2
Vauban (71) . . . 187 G1
Vaubecourt (55) . . . 64 A2
Vaubexy (88) . . . 94 B4
Vaucelles (14) . . . 32 A3
Vaucelles-et-Beffecourt (02) . . . 20 C6
Vauchamps (25) . . . 138 C5
Vauchamps (51) . . . 61 G3
Vauchassis (10) . . . 89 K5
Vauchelles (60) . . . 19 G6
Vauchelles-lès-Authie (80) . . . 10 C5
Vauchelles-lès-Domart (80) . . . 9 J5
Vauchelles-lès-Quesnoy (80) . . . 9 G5
Vauchignon (21) . . . 153 J4
Vauchonvilliers (10) . . . 91 F5
Vauchoux (70) . . . 117 K6
Vauchrétien (49) . . . 125 H5
Vauciennes (51) . . . 61 J1
Vauciennes (60) . . . 39 F4
Vauclaix (58) . . . 152 A1
Vauclerc (51) . . . 63 G5
Vaucluse (25) . . . 139 G5
Vauclusotte (25) . . . 139 G5
Vaucogne (10) . . . 90 D2
Vauconcourt-Nervezain (70) . . . 117 H6
Vaucouleurs (55) . . . 65 F6
Vaucourt (54) . . . 67 F5
Vaucourtois (77) . . . 60 A3
Vaucresson (92) . . . 58 C4
Vaudancourt (60) . . . 36 E4
Vaudebarrier (71) . . . 170 E5
Vaudelnay (49) . . . 144 B2
Vaudeloges (14) . . . 54 C2
Vaudemanges (51) . . . 41 G6
Vaudémont (54) . . . 93 K2
Vaudes (10) . . . 90 C6
Vaudesincourt (51) . . . 41 J4
Vaudesson (02) . . . 40 A1
Vaudeurs (89) . . . 113 F1
Vaudevant (07) . . . 221 K4
Vaudeville (54) . . . 94 B2
Vaudéville (88) . . . 94 E5
Vaudeville-le-Haut (55) . . . 93 F2
Vaudherland (95) . . . 59 F2
Vaudigny (54) . . . 94 B2
le Vaudioux (39) . . . 173 K1
Vaudoncourt (55) . . . 26 C5
Vaudoncourt (88) . . . 93 H5
le Vaudoué (77) . . . 87 G4
Vaudoy-en-Brie (77) . . . 60 B5
Vaudreching (57) . . . 45 J3
Vaudrecourt (52) . . . 93 F5
Vaudrémont (52) . . . 115 J1
le Vaudreuil (27) . . . 35 J4
Vaudreuille (31) . . . 289 H3
Vaudreville (50) . . . 29 F4
Vaudrey (39) . . . 155 H3
Vaudricourt (62) . . . 5 K6
Vaudricourt (80) . . . 8 D5
Vaudrimesnil (50) . . . 30 E3
Vaudringhem (62) . . . 2 E6
Vaudrivillers (25) . . . 138 D5
Vaudry (14) . . . 52 E3
Vaufrey (25) . . . 139 J4
Vaugines (84) . . . 277 H4

Vaugneray (69) . . . 205 J2
Vaugrigneuse (91) . . . 86 C1
Vauhallan (91) . . . 58 D5
Vaujany (38) . . . 224 E3
Vaujours (93) . . . 59 G2
Vaulandry (49) . . . 126 B2
le Vaulmier (15) . . . 217 J4
Vaulnaveys-le-Bas (38) . . . 224 B4
Vaulnaveys-le-Haut (38) . . . 224 B4
Vaulry (87) . . . 181 F4
Vault-de-Lugny (89) . . . 133 J3
Vaulx (62) . . . 9 J3
Vaulx (74) . . . 190 E5
Vaulx-en-Velin (69) . . . 206 C1
Vaulx-Milieu (38) . . . 206 E4
Vaulx-Vraucourt (62) . . . 11 G4
le Vaumain (60) . . . 37 F3
Vaumas (03) . . . 169 H5
Vaumeilh (04) . . . 259 F3
Vaumoise (60) . . . 39 F4
Vaumort (89) . . . 112 E1
Vaunac (24) . . . 214 B1
Vaunaveys-la-Rochette (26) . . . 240 D3
Vaunoise (61) . . . 83 G4
la Vaupalière (76) . . . 35 G1
Vaupillon (28) . . . 84 B3
Vaupoisson (10) . . . 90 C2
Vauquois (55) . . . 42 E4
Vauréal (95) . . . 58 A1
Vaureilles (12) . . . 251 H1
le Vauroux (60) . . . 37 F3
Vausseroux (79) . . . 162 A3
Vautebis (79) . . . 162 A4
Vauthiermont (90) . . . 119 K5
Vautorte (53) . . . 80 E4
Vauvenargues (13) . . . 277 K6
Vauvert (30) . . . 275 G5
Vauville (14) . . . 33 J3
Vauville (50) . . . 28 A2
Vauvillers (70) . . . 118 A3
Vauvillers (80) . . . 18 E2
Vaux (03) . . . 167 H5
Vaux (31) . . . 289 F2
Vaux (57) . . . 44 E5
Vaux (86) . . . 179 H1
Vaux-Andigny (02) . . . 12 D6
Vaux-Champagne (08) . . . 41 K2
Vaux-devant-Damloup (55) . . . 26 A6
Vaux-en-Amiénois (80) . . . 18 A1
Vaux-en-Beaujolais (69) . . . 188 A4
Vaux-en-Bugey (01) . . . 189 H5
Vaux-en-Dieulet (08) . . . 42 E1
Vaux-en-Pré (71) . . . 171 G2
Vaux-en-Vermandois (02) . . . 19 J3
Vaux-et-Chantegrue (25) . . . 156 E5
Vaux-Lavalette (16) . . . 196 E6
Vaux-le-Moncelot (70) . . . 137 J3
Vaux-le-Pénil (77) . . . 87 H2
Vaux-lès-Mouron (08) . . . 42 C3
Vaux-lès-Mouzon (08) . . . 23 G5
Vaux-lès-Palameix (55) . . . 64 E1
Vaux-lès-Prés (25) . . . 137 J6
Vaux-lès-Rubigny (08) . . . 21 J4
Vaux-lès-Saint-Claude (39) . . . 173 J5
Vaux-Marquenneville (80) . . . 17 G1
Vaux-Montreuil (08) . . . 22 B6
Vaux-Rouillac (16) . . . 196 B2
Vaux-Saules (21) . . . 135 J3
Vaux-sous-Aubigny (52) . . . 136 C1
Vaux-sur-Aure (14) . . . 32 B3
Vaux-sur-Blaise (52) . . . 91 K2
Vaux-sur-Eure (27) . . . 57 F1
Vaux-sur-Lunain (77) . . . 88 A4
Vaux-sur-Mer (17) . . . 194 C3
Vaux-sur-Poligny (39) . . . 155 J5
Vaux-sur-Saint-Urbain (52) . . . 92 B3
Vaux-sur-Seine (78) . . . 58 B1
Vaux-sur-Seulles (14) . . . 32 B4
Vaux-sur-Somme (80) . . . 18 D1
Vaux-sur-Vienne (86) . . . 145 J5
Vaux-Villaine (08) . . . 22 B3
Vauxaillon (02) . . . 39 K1
Vauxbons (52) . . . 116 B4
Vauxbuin (02) . . . 39 J3
Vauxcéré (02) . . . 40 B3
Vauxrenard (69) . . . 188 A2
Vauxrezis (02) . . . 39 J2
Vauxtin (02) . . . 40 B3
Vavincourt (55) . . . 64 B3
Vavray-le-Grand (51) . . . 63 G4
Vavray-le-Petit (51) . . . 63 G4
Vaxainville (54) . . . 95 G1
Vaxoncourt (88) . . . 94 D4
Vaxy (57) . . . 66 D2
Vay (44) . . . 103 F5
Vaychis (09) . . . 308 A4
Vaylats (46) . . . 250 C3
Vayrac (46) . . . 234 A1
Vayres (33) . . . 229 K1
Vayres (87) . . . 198 A2
Vayres-sur-Essonne (91) . . . 86 E3
Vazeilles-Limandre (43) . . . 220 A4
Vazeilles-près-Saugues (43) . . . 237 K1
Vazerac (82) . . . 249 J5
Veauce (03) . . . 184 E3
Veauche (42) . . . 205 F4
Veauchette (42) . . . 205 F4
Veaugues (18) . . . 131 H4
Veaunes (26) . . . 222 C5
Veauville-lès-Baons (76) . . . 15 G5
Veauville-lès-Quelles (76) . . . 15 G4
Vèbre (09) . . . 307 K5

Vebret (15) 217 J2
Vebron (48) 254 B4
Veckersviller (57) 67 K2
Veckring (57) 27 J4
Vecoux (88) 119 F2
Vecquemont (80) 18 C2
Vecqueville (52) 92 B2
Vedène (84) 276 C1
Védrines-Saint-Loup (15) 219 G5
Végennes (19) 216 B4
Vého (54) 67 F6
Veigné (37) 127 J6
Veigy-Foncenex (74) 174 D6
Veilhes (81) 270 A6
Veilleins (41) 129 H4
Veilly (21) 153 H2
Veix (19) 200 A5
Velaine-en-Haye (54) 65 J5
Velaine-sous-Amance (54) 66 B4
Velaines (55) 64 C5
Velanne (38) 207 J5
Velars-sur-Ouche (21) 135 K5
Velaux (13) 296 B1
Velennes (60) 37 H1
Velennes (80) 17 J3
Velesmes-Echevanne (70) 137 G4
Velesmes-Essarts (25) 156 A1
Velet (70) 137 F4
Vélieux (34) 291 F3
Vélines (24) 230 E2
Vélizy-Villacoublay (78) 58 D4
Velle-le-Châtel (70) 138 A1
Velle-sur-Moselle (54) 94 B1
Vellèches (86) 145 J4
Vellechevreux-et-Courbenans (70) 138 E2
Velleclaire (70) 137 J3
Vellefaux (70) 138 B2
Vellefrey-et-Vellefrange (70) 137 H3
Vellefrie (70) 118 B6
Velleguindry-et-Levrecey (70) 138 A2
Velleminfroy (70) 118 C6
Vellemoz (70) 137 H3
Velleron (84) 276 D1
Vellerot-lès-Belvoir (25) 139 F4
Vellerot-lès-Vercel (25) 138 E6
Velles (36) 165 H2
Velles (52) 117 G4
Vellescot (70) 139 K1
Vellevans (25) 138 E5
Vellexon-Queutrey-et-Vaudey (70) 137 H2
Velloreille-lès-Choye (70) 137 H4
Velogny (21) 134 E2
Velone-Orneto (2B) 319 J4
Velorcey (70) 118 B5
Velosnes (55) 26 A2
Velotte-et-Tatignécourt (88) 94 A4
Vélu (62) 11 G5
Velving (57) 45 J3
Vélye (51) 62 B3
Velzic (15) 217 J6
Vémars (95) 59 G1
Venables (27) 35 K5
Venaco (2B) 321 F1
Venansault (85) 159 H1
Venanson (06) 261 K5
Venarey-les-Laumes (21) 134 E2
Venarsal (19) 215 K3
Venas (03) 167 J5
Venasque (84) 276 E1
Vence (06) 281 F3
Vendargues (34) 274 C5
Vendat (03) 185 H3
Vendays-Montalivet (33) 210 C1
Vendegies-au-Bois (59) 12 D4
Vendegies-sur-Ecaillon (59) 12 D3
Vendel (35) 79 K2
la Vendelée (50) 30 E3
Vendelles (02) 19 J2
Vendémian (34) 292 D1
Vendenesse-lès-Charolles (71) . . . 170 E5
Vendenesse-sur-Arroux (71) . . . 170 B3
Vendenheim (67) 25 A6
Vendes (14) 32 C5
Vendeuil (02) 20 A4
Vendeuil-Caply (60) 18 A5
Vendeuvre (14) 54 B1
Vendeuvre-du-Poitou (86) 162 E1
Vendeuvre-sur-Barse (10) 90 E5
Vendeville (59) 6 E5
Vendhuile (02) 11 J6
Vendières (02) 60 E3
Vendin-le-Vieil (62) 6 C6
Vendin-lès-Béthune (62) 5 K5
Vendine (31) 289 F1
Vendoeuvres (36) 147 G6
Vendoire (24) 197 F6
Vendôme (41) 108 C5
Vendranges (42) 187 F5
Vendrennes (85) 142 C5
Vendres (34) 292 A5
Vendresse (08) 22 D5
Vendresse-Beaulne (02) 40 B2
Vendrest (77) 60 B1
la Vendue-Mignot (10) 90 B6
Vénéjan (30) 256 C4
Venelles (13) 277 J6
Vénérand (17) 195 H1
Venère (70) 137 G4
Vénérieu (38) 207 F3
Vénérolles (02) 12 E6
Venerque (31) 288 B3

Vénès (81) 270 E5
Venesmes (18) 149 F6
Vénestanville (76) 15 H3
Venette (60) 38 D2
Veneux-les-Sablons (77) 87 J4
Veney (54) 95 G2
Vengeons (50) 52 D4
Venise (25) 138 A4
Venisey (70) 117 K4
Vénissieux (69) 206 B3
Venizel (02) 39 K3
Venizy (89) 113 H2
Vennans (25) 138 C5
Vennecy (45) 110 B3
Vennes (25) 157 G1
Vennezey (54) 94 D2
Venon (27) 35 H5
Venon (38) 224 B3
Vénosc (38) 224 E5
Venouse (89) 113 H4
Venoy (89) 113 G5
Vensac (33) 194 C6
Vensat (63) 185 G4
Ventabren (13) 296 B1
Ventavon (05) 259 F2
Ventelay (51) 40 D3
Ventenac (09) 307 K2
Ventenac-Cabardès (11) 290 A5
Ventenac-en-Minervois (11) 291 G5
Venterol (04) 259 H1
Venterol (26) 257 H2
les Ventes (27) 56 C2
les Ventes-de-Bourse (61) 82 E2
Ventes-Saint-Rémy (76) 16 B4
Venteuges (43) 219 J6
Venteuil (51) 40 D6
Venthon (73) 209 G2
Ventiseri (2B) 321 H4
Ventouse (16) 179 H6
Ventron (88) 119 H2
la Ventrouze (61) 55 J6
Venzolasca (2B) 319 J3
Ver (50) 30 E6
Ver-lès-Chartres (28) 85 G4
Ver-sur-Launette (60) 38 C6
Ver-sur-Mer (14) 32 C4
Vérac (33) 211 K6
Véranne (42) 221 K1
Vérargues (34) 274 E5
Véraza (11) 309 F3
Verberie (60) 38 D3
Verbiesles (52) 116 B1
Vercel-Villedieu-le-Camp (25) . . . 138 D6
Verchain-Maugré (59) 12 C3
Verchaix (74) 192 A3
Vercheny (26) 241 G3
les Verchers-sur-Layon (49) 144 A1
Verchin (62) 5 F6
Verchocq (62) 4 E5
Vercia (39) 173 F3
Verclause (26) 258 A2
Vercoiran (26) 257 K3
Vercourt (80) 9 F2
Verdaches (04) 259 K3
Verdalle (54) 289 K2
Verdelais (33) 230 A5
Verdelot (77) 60 E3
Verdenal (54) 67 G6
Verderel-lès-Sauqueuse (60) 37 H1
Verderonne (60) 38 B3
Verdes (41) 109 F3
Verdèse (2B) 319 H4
Verdets (64) 284 A5
le Verdier (81) 270 B1
la Verdière (83) 278 D5
Verdigny (18) 131 J3
Verdille (16) 178 D6
Verdilly (02) 39 K6
Verdon (24) 231 K2
Verdon (51) 61 G2
le Verdon-sur-Mer (33) 194 C4
Verdonnet (21) 114 D6
Verdun (09) 307 K6
Verdun (55) 43 H5
Verdun-en-Lauragais (11) 289 J4
Verdun-sur-Garonne (82) 268 C3
Verdun-sur-le-Doubs (71) 154 C5
Vereaux (18) 150 B5
Verel-de-Montbel (73) 207 K4
Verel-Pragondran (73) 208 B3
Véretz (37) 127 K5
Vereux (70) 137 G2
Verfeil (31) 269 J6
Verfeil (82) 250 E5
Verfeuil (30) 256 A5
Vergaville (57) 67 F3
Vergéal (35) 104 A2
la Vergenne (70) 138 E1
le Verger (35) 78 D4
Vergeroux (17) 177 F5
Verges (39) 173 H2
Vergetot (76) 14 C5
Vergezac (43) 220 A5
Vergèze (30) 275 F4
Vergheas (63) 184 A4
Vergies (80) 17 G5
Vergigny (89) 113 H3
Vergisson (71) 188 B1
Vergné (17) 177 K3
la Vergne (17) 177 K5
Vergoignan (32) 265 K4
Vergoncey (50) 51 K4

Vergongheon (43) 219 G1
Vergonnes (49) 104 B5
Vergons (04) 279 K1
Vergranne (25) 138 D3
Vergt (24) 214 A5
Vergt-de-Biron (24) 232 B5
le Verguier (02) 19 J1
Véria (39) 173 F4
Vérignon (83) 279 G5
Vérin (42) 205 K6
Vérines (17) 177 F2
Vérissey (71) 172 C1
Verjon (01) 172 E6
Verjux (71) 154 B5
Verlans (70) 139 G1
Verlhac-Tescou (82) 269 H2
Verlin (89) 112 D2
Verlincthun (62) 4 C1
Verlinghem (59) 6 D3
Verlus (32) 265 K6
Vermand (02) 19 J2
Vermandovillers (80) 19 F2
Vermelles (62) 6 B6
Vermenton (89) 133 H1
le Vermont (88) 95 J2
Vern-d'Anjou (49) 124 E1
Vern-sur-Seiche (35) 79 G5
Vernais (18) 167 J1
Vernaison (69) 206 A3
Vernajoul (09) 307 J3
Vernancourt (51) 63 H3
Vernantes (49) 126 C4
Vernantois (39) 173 G2
la Vernarède (30) 255 G3
Vernas (38) 207 F1
Vernassal (43) 220 A4
Vernaux (09) 307 K5
Vernay (69) 187 K3
la Vernaz (74) 175 G6
Verne (25) 138 D4
Vernègues (13) 277 F5
Verneiges (23) 183 H2
le Verneil (73) 208 B5
Verneil-le-Chétif (72) 106 E6
Verneix (03) 167 H6
la Vernelle (36) 129 K4
le Vernet (03) 185 J3
le Vernet (04) 260 A3
le Vernet (09) 288 D6
le Vernet (31) 288 B3
le Vernet (43) 220 A5
Vernet-la-Varenne (63) 203 G6
Vernet-les-Bains (66) 314 B4
le Vernet-Sainte-Marguerite (63) . . . 202 C4
Verneugheol (63) 201 H2
Verneuil (16) 197 K2
Verneuil (18) 149 J6
Verneuil (51) 40 B6
Verneuil (58) 151 H5
Verneuil-en-Bourbonnais (03) 168 D6
Verneuil-en-Halatte (60) 38 B4
Verneuil-Grand (55) 23 K6
Verneuil-le-Château (37) 145 H3
Verneuil-l'Étang (77) 59 J6
Verneuil-Moustiers (87) 164 C6
Verneuil-Petit (55) 23 K6
Verneuil-sous-Coucy (02) 20 A6
Verneuil-sur-Avre (27) 56 B5
Verneuil-sur-Igneraie (36) 166 B2
Verneuil-sur-Indre (37) 146 D3
Verneuil-sur-Seine (78) 58 B2
Verneuil-sur-Serre (02) 20 D5
Verneuil-sur-Vienne (87) 198 D1
Verneusses (27) 55 G3
Vernie (72) 82 C6
Vernierfontaine (25) 156 E2
Vernines (63) 202 B3
Verniolle (09) 307 J1
Vernioz (38) 206 B6
Vernix (50) 52 B4
Vernoil (49) 126 C4
le Vernois (39) 173 G1
Vernois-lès-Belvoir (25) 139 F4
Vernois-lès-Vesvres (21) 136 B1
Vernois-sur-Mance (70) 117 H4
Vernols (15) 218 C3
Vernon (07) 239 F6
Vernon (27) 36 B6
Vernon (86) 163 G5
Vernonvilliers (10) 91 G4
Vernosc-lès-Annonay (07) 222 A3
Vernot (21) 135 K3
la Vernotte (70) 137 J2
Vernou-en-Sologne (41) 129 J3
Vernou-la-Celle-sur-Seine (77) . . . 87 K4
Vernou-sur-Brenne (37) 128 A4
Vernouillet (28) 57 F5
Vernouillet (78) 58 B2
Vernoux (01) 172 C4
Vernoux-en-Gâtine (79) 161 G2
Vernoux-en-Vivarais (07) 239 K1
Vernoux-sur-Boutonne (79) 178 C2
le Vernoy (25) 139 G1
Vernoy (89) 112 C1
Vernusse (03) 184 E1
Verny (57) 66 A1
Vero (2A) 320 D3
Véron (89) 112 D1
Véronne (26) 241 F3
Véronnes (21) 136 C2

Verosvres (71) 171 F5
Verpel (08) 42 D2
la Verpillière (38) 206 D3
Verpillières (80) 19 F5
Verpillières-sur-Ource (10) 115 F2
Verquières (13) 276 C3
Verquin (62) 6 A6
Verrens-Arvey (73) 209 F3
Verreries-de-Moussans (34) 290 E3
Verrey-sous-Drée (21) 135 H5
Verrey-sous-Salmaise (21) 135 G4
Verricourt (10) 90 D3
Verrie (49) 126 A6
la Verrie (85) 142 D4
la Verrière (78) 58 B5
Verrières (08) 42 C1
Verrières (10) 90 B5
Verrières (12) 253 G4
Verrières (16) 195 K4
Verrières (51) 42 D6
Verrières (61) 83 K3
Verrières (63) 202 C4
Verrières (86) 163 H5
Verrières-de-Joux (25) 157 G4
Verrières-du-Grosbois (25) 138 C6
Verrières-en-Forez (42) 204 C4
Verrières-le-Buisson (91) 58 D5
Verrue (86) 144 E5
Verruyes (79) 161 J4
Vers (46) 250 B1
Vers (71) 171 K3
Vers (74) 190 E3
Vers-en-Montagne (39) 156 B5
Vers-Pont-du-Gard (30) 275 J1
Vers-sous-Sellières (39) 155 H5
Vers-sur-Méouge (26) 258 C4
Vers-sur-Selles (80) 18 A2
Versailles (78) 58 C4
Versailleux (01) 189 F5
Versainville (14) 54 B2
la Versanne (42) 221 J2
Versaugues (71) 170 B6
Verseilles-le-Bas (52) 116 C5
Verseilles-le-Haut (52) 116 C5
Versigny (02) 20 B5
Versigny (60) 38 D5
Versols-et-Lapeyre (12) 272 C3
Verson (14) 32 D5
Versonnex (01) 174 B6
Versonnex (74) 190 D5
le Versoud (38) 224 C3
Vert (40) 245 K5
Vert (78) 57 J2
le Vert (79) 178 B3
Vert-en-Drouais (28) 56 E5
Vert-le-Grand (91) 86 E1
Vert-le-Petit (91) 86 E1
Vert-Saint-Denis (77) 87 H1
Vert-Toulon (51) 61 K3
Vertain (59) 12 D3
Vertaizon (63) 203 F2
Vertamboz (39) 173 H2
Vertault (21) 114 D4
Verteillac (24) 213 G1
Verteuil-d'Agenais (47) 247 K1
Verteuil-sur-Charente (16) 179 G5
Verthemex (73) 208 A3
Vertheuil (33) 210 E2
Vertolaye (63) 203 K3
Verton (62) 8 E1
Vertou (44) 123 H5
Vertrieu (38) 189 H6
Vertus (51) 62 A3
Vervant (16) 196 D1
Vervant (17) 178 A5
Vervezelle (88) 95 G5
Vervins (02) 21 F2
Véry (55) 42 E4
Verzé (71) 171 J6
Verzeille (11) 309 F1
Verzenay (51) 41 G5
Verzy (51) 41 G5
Vesaignes-sous-Lafauche (52) . . . 92 D4
Vesaignes-sur-Marne (52) 116 C2
Vesancy (01) 174 B5
Vesc (26) 241 F6
Vescemont (90) 119 H5
Vescheim (57) 69 F6
Vescles (39) 173 G5
Vescours (01) 172 B4
Vescovato (2B) 319 J3
Vesdun (18) 167 F4
Vésigneul-sur-Marne (51) 62 E3
Vésines (01) 171 K6
le Vésinet (78) 58 C3
Vesles-et-Caumont (02) 20 E5
Veslud (02) 20 E6
Vesly (27) 36 D4
Vesly (50) 30 D1
Vesoul (70) 138 B1
la Vespière (14) 55 G1
Vesseaux (07) 239 H4
Vessey (50) 51 J5
Vestric-et-Candiac (30) 275 F4
Vesvres (21) 135 F4
Vesvres-sous-Chalancey (52) 116 B6
Vétheuil (95) 57 J1
Vétraz-Monthoux (74) 191 G2
Vétrigne (90) 119 J6
Veuil (36) 147 J2
Veuilly-la-Poterie (02) 39 H6
Veules-les-Roses (76) 15 H2

Veulettes-sur-Mer (76) 15 F2
le Veurdre (03) 168 B1
Veurey-Voroize (38) 223 K2
la Veuve (51) 62 D1
Veuves (41) 128 C4
Veuvey-sur-Ouche (21) 153 J1
Veuxhaulles-sur-Aube (21) 115 H3
Vevy (39) 173 H2
Vexaincourt (88) 95 J1
le Vey (14) 53 J2
Veynes (05) 242 C5
Veyrac (87) 181 F6
Veyras (07) 239 J3
Veyre-Monton (63) 202 E3
Veyreau (12) 253 J5
Veyrier-du-Lac (74) 191 F6
Veyrières (15) 217 G2
Veyrières (19) 201 G6
Veyrignac (24) 233 G2
Veyrines-de-Domme (24) 232 E3
Veyrines-de-Vergt (24) 214 A6
Veyrins-Thuellin (38) 207 H3
les Veys (50) 29 G6
Veyssilieu (38) 206 E3
Vez (60) 39 F4
Vézac (15) 235 J2
Vézac (24) 232 E2
Vézannes (89) 113 J4
Vézaponin (02) 39 H2
Vèze (15) 218 D3
la Vèze (25) 138 A6
Vézelay (89) 133 H4
Vézelise (54) 93 K2
Vézelois (90) 139 J1
Vezels-Roussy (15) 235 J3
Vézénobres (30) 255 H6
Vézeronce-Curtin (38) 207 G3
Vezet (70) 137 J2
Vézézoux (43) 219 G1
le Vézier (51) 60 E4
Vézières (86) 144 E2
Vézillon (27) 36 A4
Vézilly (02) 40 C5
Vezin-le-Coquet (35) 79 F4
Vézinnes (89) 113 K4
Vezins (49) 143 G2
Vézins-de-Lévézou (12) 253 F4
Vezot (72) 83 F4
Vezzani (2B) 321 G2
Viabon (28) 85 J6
Viala-du-Pas-de-Jaux (12) 272 D2
Viala-du-Tarn (12) 252 E6
Vialas (48) 254 E3
Vialer (64) 285 F1
Viam (19) 200 B4
Viane (81) 271 J5
Vianges (21) 153 F2
Vianne (47) 247 J4
Viâpres-le-Petit (10) 90 A1
Viarmes (95) 37 K6
Vias (34) 292 C4
Viazac (46) 234 E5
le Vibal (12) 252 D3
Vibersviller (57) 67 H2
Vibeuf (76) 15 H4
Vibrac (16) 196 C3
Vibrac (17) 211 K1
Vibraye (72) 107 K2
Vic-de-Chassenay (21) 134 D3
Vic-des-Prés (21) 153 J2
Vic-en-Bigorre (65) 285 H3
Vic-Fezensac (32) 267 F4
Vic-la-Gardiole (34) 293 G2
Vic-le-Comte (63) 202 E4
Vic-le-Fesq (30) 274 E3
Vic-sous-Thil (21) 134 D5
Vic-sur-Aisne (02) 39 G2
Vic-sur-Cère (15) 217 K6
Vic-sur-Seille (57) 66 D3
Vicdessos (09) 307 H5
le Vicel (50) 29 F2
Vichel (63) 202 E6
Vichel-Nanteuil (02) 39 J5
Vichères (28) 84 B5
Vicherey (88) 93 J3
Vichy (03) 185 J3
Vico (2A) 316 E5
la Vicogne (80) 10 A6
la Vicomté-sur-Rance (22) 50 D4
Vicq (03) 185 F3
Vicq (52) 117 F3
Vicq (59) 12 D1
Vicq (78) 57 K4
Vicq-d'Auribat (40) 264 D3
Vicq-Exemplet (36) 166 C3
Vicq-sur-Breuilh (87) 199 G4
Vicq-sur-Gartempe (86) 164 A1
Vicq-sur-Nahon (36) 147 J2
Vicques (14) 54 B2
Victot-Pontfol (14) 33 H5
Vidai (61) 83 F2
Vidaillac (46) 250 D3
Vidaillat (23) 182 D5
Vidauban (83) 298 D2
Videcosville (50) 29 F3
Videix (87) 197 K2
Vidou (65) 286 A4
Vidouville (50) 31 K3
Vidouze (65) 285 G2
Viefvillers (60) 17 K5
le Vieil-Baugé (49) 126 A3

le Vieil-Dampierre (51) 63 J1
le Vieil-Evreux (27) 56 E1
Vieil-Hesdin (62) 9 J2
Vieil-Moutier (62) 2 D6
Vieille-Brioude (43) 219 H3
Vieille-Chapelle (62) 6 A4
Vieille-Église (62) 2 E3
Vieille-Église-en-Yvelines (78) . . 58 A6
la Vieille-Loye (39) 155 H3
la Vieille-Lyre (27) 55 K2
Vieille-Toulouse (31) 288 B2
Vieilles-Maisons-sur-Joudry (45) . . 111 F4
Vieillespesse (15) 218 E4
Vieillevie (15) 235 H5
Vieillevigne (31) 288 E3
Vieillevigne (44) 141 K3
Vieilley (25) 138 A5
Vieilmoulin (21) 135 G5
Viel-Arcy (02) 40 B2
Viel-Saint-Remy (08) 22 B5
Viella (32) 266 A6
Viella (65) 304 B4
Vielle-Adour (65) 285 H6
Vielle-Aure (65) 305 F4
Vielle-Louron (65) 305 F4
Vielle-Saint-Girons (40) 262 D1
Vielle-Soubiran (40) 246 D6
Vielle-Tursan (40) 265 H5
Viellenave-d'Arthez (64) 284 B3
Viellenave-de-Navarrenx (64) . . 283 J3
Viellességure (64) 283 K3
Vielmanay (58) 132 C6
Vielmur-sur-Agout (81) 270 D6
Vielprat (43) 238 D2
Viels-Maisons (02) 60 E3
Vielverge (21) 136 E6
Viennay (79) 161 K2
Vienne (38) 206 B5
Vienne-en-Arthies (95) 57 J1
Vienne-en-Bessin (14) 32 C3
Vienne-en-Val (45) 110 C5
Vienne-la-Ville (51) 42 D5
Vienne-le-Château (51) 42 D5
Viens (84) 277 K2
Vienville (88) 95 H5
Vier-Bordes (65) 304 B2
Viersat (23) 183 J1
Vierville (28) 86 A4
Vierville (50) 29 G6
Vierville-sur-Mer (14) 29 K6
Vierzon (18) 148 D1
Vierzy (02) 39 J4
Viesly (59) 12 C4
Viessoix (14) 53 F3
Viéthorey (25) 138 D3
Vieu (01) 190 B6
Vieu-d'Izenave (01) 189 K3
Vieure (03) 168 A4
Vieussan (34) 291 H1
Vieuvicq (28) 84 D5
Vieuvy (53) 80 E2
Vieux (14) 32 D6
Vieux (81) 270 B1
Vieux-Berquin (59) 3 K6
Vieux-Boucau-les-Bains (40) . . 262 B3
Vieux-Bourg (14) 34 A3
le Vieux-Bourg (22) 76 E1
le Vieux-Cérier (16) 179 K5
Vieux-Champagne (77) 88 C1
Vieux-Charmont (25) 139 H2
Vieux-Château (21) 134 B3
Vieux-Condé (59) 7 J6
Vieux-Ferrette (68) 97 C5
Vieux-Fumé (14) 33 G6
Vieux-lès-Asfeld (08) 41 F1
Vieux-Lixheim (57) 67 K3
Vieux-Manoir (76) 16 B6
le Vieux-Marché (22) 47 K4
Vieux-Mareuil (24) 197 H6
Vieux-Mesnil (59) 13 G3
Vieux-Moulin (60) 38 E2
Vieux-Moulin (88) 95 J2
Vieux-Pont (14) 54 D1
Vieux-Pont (61) 54 B6
Vieux-Port (27) 34 D2
Vieux-Reng (59) 13 H2
Vieux-Rouen-sur-Bresle (76) . . 17 F3
la Vieux-Rue (76) 35 K1
Vieux-Ruffec (16) 179 J5
Vieux-Thann (68) 97 A2
Vieux-Viel (35) 51 H5
Vieux-Villez (27) 35 K5
Vieux-Vy-sur-Couesnon (35) . . 79 J1
Vieuzos (65) 286 B5
Viévigne (21) 136 C4
Viéville (52) 92 B5
Viéville-en-Haye (54) 65 H2
Viévy (21) 153 G3
Vievy-le-Rayé (41) 108 E4
Viey (65) 304 B4
Vif (38) 224 A5
Viffort (02) 60 E2
le Vigan (30) 273 J1
le Vigan (46) 233 H3
le Vigean (15) 217 G3
le Vigeant (86) 180 B2
le Vigen (87) 199 F2
Vigeois (19) 215 J1
Viger (65) 304 B1
Vigeville (23) 183 F3
Viggianello (2A) 322 E2
Viglain (45) 110 E6

Vignacourt (80) 9 K6
Vignale (2B) 319 H3
Vignats (14) 54 B3
le Vignau (40) 265 J4
Vignaux (31) 268 D5
les Vigneaux (05) 243 J1
Vignec (65) 304 E4
Vignely (77) 59 J2
Vignemont (60) 38 D1
les Vignes (48) 253 J4
Vignes (64) 284 C1
Vignes (89) 134 B3
Vignes-la-Côte (52) 92 C5
Vigneul-sous-Montmédy (55) . . 23 J1
Vigneulles (54) 66 C6
Vigneulles-lès-Hattonchâtel (55) . . 65 F1
Vigneux-Hocquet (02) 21 G4
Vigneux-sur-Seine (91) 59 F5
Vignevieille (11) 309 H2
Vignieu (38) 207 G3
Vignoc (35) 79 F2
Vignol (58) 133 H5
Vignoles (21) 154 A3
Vignolles (16) 196 B5
Vignols (19) 215 H2
Vignonet (33) 230 B2
Vignory (52) 92 A5
Vignot (55) 65 F4
Vignoux-sous-les-Aix (18) 149 H1
Vignoux-sur-Barangeon (18) . . 148 E1
Vigny (57) 66 B1
Vigny (95) 37 F6
Vigoulant (36) 166 C5
Vigoulet-Auzil (31) 288 C2
Vigoux (36) 165 G4
Vigueron (82) 268 C3
Vigy (57) 27 J6
Vihiers (49) 143 J2
Vijon (36) 166 C5
Vilcey-sur-Trey (54) 65 J2
Vildé-Guingalan (22) 50 C5
le Vilhain (03) 167 K4
Vilhonneur (16) 197 G3
Villabé (91) 87 F1
Villabon (18) 149 K3
Villac (24) 215 F4
Villacerf (10) 90 A3
Villacourt (54) 94 C2
Villadin (10) 89 H4
Villafans (70) 138 E1
Village-Neuf (68) 97 E4
Villaines-en-Duesmois (21) . . 135 F1
Villaines-la-Carelle (72) 83 F3
Villaines-la-Gonais (72) 107 H1
Villaines-la-Juhel (53) 81 K4
Villaines-les-Prévôtes (21) 134 D2
Villaines-les-Rochers (37) 145 J1
Villaines-sous-Bois (95) 37 K6
Villaines-sous-Lucé (72) 107 G4
Villaines-sous-Malicorne (72) . . 106 B5
Villainville (76) 14 C5
Villalet (27) 56 C2
Villalier (11) 290 B5
Villamblain (45) 109 G3
Villamblard (24) 213 J5
Villamée (35) 80 A2
Villampuy (28) 109 G2
Villandraut (33) 246 B1
Villandry (37) 127 G5
Villanière (11) 290 B4
Villanova (2A) 320 A5
Villapourçon (58) 152 B4
Villar-d'Arène (05) 225 G5
Villar-en-Val (11) 309 H1
Villar-Loubière (05) 243 F2
Villar-Saint-Anselme (11) 309 F2
Villar-Saint-Pancrace (05) 227 A1
Villard (23) 182 B1
Villard (74) 191 J1
Villard-Bonnot (38) 224 C2
Villard-de-Lans (38) 223 J4
Villard-d'Héry (73) 208 D4
Villard-Léger (73) 208 E4
Villard-Notre-Dame (38) 224 D5
Villard-Reculas (38) 224 D4
Villard-Reymond (38) 224 D5
Villard-Saint-Christophe (38) . . 224 B6
Villard-Saint-Sauveur (39) 173 K5
Villard-Sallet (73) 208 D5
Villard-sur-Bienne (39) 173 K4
Villard-sur-Doron (73) 209 H2
Villardebelle (11) 309 G2
Villardonnel (11) 290 A4
Villards-d'Héria (39) 173 H5
les Villards-sur-Thônes (74) . . 191 H5
Villarembert (73) 225 G2
Villargent (70) 138 E2
Villargoix (21) 134 D6
Villargondran (73) 225 H2
Villariès (31) 269 H4
Villarlurin (73) 209 H5
Villarodin-Bourget (73) 226 A3
Villaroger (73) 193 B3
Villaroux (73) 208 D5
Villars (24) 198 A6
Villars (28) 85 G5
Villars (42) 205 F6
le Villars (71) 172 A4
Villars (84) 277 H2
Villars-Colmars (04) 260 C4
Villars-en-Azois (52) 115 H2

Villars-en-Pons (17) 195 G4
Villars-et-Villenotte (21) 134 E3
Villars-Fontaine (21) 154 A2
Villars-le-Pautel (70) 117 J3
Villars-le-Sec (90) 139 K3
Villars-lès-Blamont (25) 139 J4
Villars-les-Bois (17) 195 J1
Villars-les-Dombes (01) 188 E4
Villars-Saint-Georges (25) 155 K2
Villars-Santenoge (52) 115 K5
Villars-sous-Dampjoux (25) . . 139 G4
Villars-sous-Écot (25) 139 G3
Villars-sur-Var (06) 280 E1
Villarzel-Cabardès (11) 290 C5
Villarzel-du-Razès (11) 308 E1
Villasavary (11) 289 H5
Villate (31) 288 E3
Villaudric (31) 269 G3
Villautou (11) 289 H1
Villavard (41) 108 A6
Villaz (74) 191 F5
Ville (60) 19 G6
Villé (67) 70 B6
Ville-au-Montois (54) 26 D4
Ville-au-Val (54) 65 K3
la Ville-aux-Bois (10) 91 G3
la Ville-aux-Bois-lès-Dizy (02) . . 21 G5
la Ville-aux-Bois-lès-Pontavert (02) . . 40 D2
la Ville-aux-Clercs (41) 108 C4
la Ville-aux-Dames (37) 127 K4
Ville-d'Avray (92) 58 D4
Ville-devant-Belrain (55) 64 C3
Ville-devant-Chaumont (55) . . 43 J3
Ville-di-Paraso (2B) 318 D3
Ville-di-Pietrabugno (2B) 317 D5
la Ville-Dieu-du-Temple (82) . . 268 E1
Ville-Dommange (51) 40 E5
la Ville-du-Bois (91) 58 D6
Ville-du-Pont (25) 157 G3
Ville-en-Blaisois (52) 91 K3
Ville-en-Sallaz (74) 191 J2
Ville-en-Selve (51) 41 F4
Ville-en-Tardenois (51) 40 D5
Ville-en-Vermois (54) 66 B6
Ville-en-Woëvre (55) 44 A5
la Ville-ès-Nonais (35) 50 E4
Ville-Houdlémont (54) 26 B2
Ville-la-Grand (74) 191 G1
Ville-Langy (58) 151 H4
Ville-le-Marclet (80) 9 J6
Ville-Saint-Jacques (77) 87 K4
Ville-Savoye (02) 40 B4
Ville-sous-Anjou (38) 222 C1
Ville-sous-la-Ferté (10) 115 H1
la Ville-sous-Orbais (51) 61 G2
Ville-sur-Ancre (80) 18 D1
Ville-sur-Arce (10) 114 E1
Ville-sur-Cousances (55) 43 F6
Ville-sur-Illon (88) 94 B5
Ville-sur-Jarnioux (69) 188 A5
Ville-sur-Lumes (08) 22 D3
Ville-sur-Retourne (08) 41 J2
Ville-sur-Saulx (55) 64 A5
Ville-sur-Terre (10) 91 H4
Ville-sur-Tourbe (51) 42 C5
Ville-sur-Yron (54) 44 C5
Villeau (28) 85 H5
Villebadin (61) 54 D4
Villebarou (41) 128 E2
Villebaudon (50) 31 G5
Villebazy (11) 309 F2
Villebéon (77) 88 A6
Villebernier (49) 126 B6
Villeberny (21) 135 G4
Villebichot (21) 154 C2
Villeblevin (89) 88 B4
Villebois (01) 189 J6
Villebois-Lavalette (16) 197 F5
Villebois-les-Pins (26) 258 C2
Villebon (28) 84 D3
Villebon-sur-Yvette (91) 58 D5
Villebougis (89) 88 C6
Villebourg (37) 127 H1
Villebout (41) 108 D3
Villebramar (47) 231 H6
Villebret (03) 184 B4
Villebrumier (82) 269 G2
Villecelin (18) 148 E6
Villecerf (77) 87 K4
Villecey-sur-Mad (54) 65 J1
Villechantria (39) 173 F5
Villechauve (41) 128 B1
Villechenève (69) 205 G1
Villechétif (10) 90 B4
Villechétive (89) 113 F1
Villechien (50) 52 D6
Villecien (89) 112 D3
Villécloye (55) 23 K6
Villecomtal (12) 235 J6
Villecomtal-sur-Arros (32) 285 J3
Villecomte (21) 136 A3
Villeconin (91) 86 C2
Villecourt (80) 19 H3
Villecresnes (94) 59 G5
Villecroze (83) 279 G6
Villedaigne (11) 291 G5
Villedieu (15) 218 D6
la Villedieu (17) 178 B4
Villedieu (21) 114 D2
la Villedieu (23) 200 B2
les Villedieu (25) 156 E6
la Villedieu (48) 237 J4

Villedieu (84) 257 G3
la Villedieu-du-Clain (86) 163 F5
la Villedieu-en-Fontenette (70) . . 118 B5
Villedieu-la-Blouère (49) 142 D1
Villedieu-le-Château (41) 107 A5
Villedieu-lès-Bailleul (61) 54 C4
Villedieu-les-Poêles (50) 52 B3
Villedieu-sur-Indre (36) 147 J6
Villedômain (37) 147 F3
Villedômer (37) 128 A3
Villedoux (17) 176 E1
Villedubert (11) 290 C5
Villefagnan (16) 179 F4
Villefargeau (89) 113 F5
Villefavard (87) 181 G3
Villeferry (21) 135 F4
Villefloure (11) 309 G1
Villefollet (79) 178 C3
Villefontaine (38) 206 D4
Villefort (11) 308 C3
Villefort (48) 255 F1
Villefranche (32) 286 E3
Villefranche (89) 112 C3
Villefranche-d'Albigeois (81) . . 271 F3
Villefranche-d'Allier (03) 167 K6
Villefranche-de-Conflent (66) . . 314 B3
Villefranche-de-Lauragais (31) . . 288 E3
Villefranche-de-Lonchat (24) . . 212 D6
Villefranche-de-Panat (12) 252 C6
Villefranche-de-Rouergue (12) . . 251 F3
Villefranche-du-Périgord (24) . . 232 D5
Villefranche-du-Queyran (47) . . 247 H3
Villefranche-le-Château (26) . . 258 B4
Villefranche-sur-Cher (41) 129 J5
Villefranche-sur-Mer (06) 281 H4
Villefranche-sur-Saône (69) 188 B5
Villefrancoeur (41) 128 D1
Villefranque (64) 263 D1
Villefranque (65) 285 G2
Villegailhenc (11) 290 B5
Villegats (16) 179 G5
Villegats (27) 57 G2
Villegaudin (71) 154 D6
Villegenon (18) 131 G4
Villegongis (36) 147 J5
Villegouge (33) 211 K6
Villegouin (36) 147 G4
Villegusien-le-Lac (52) 116 D6
Villeherviers (41) 129 K5
Villejésus (16) 179 F6
Villejoubert (16) 196 E1
Villejuif (94) 58 E4
Villejust (91) 58 D6
Villelaure (84) 277 H4
Villeloin-Coulangé (37) 147 F2
Villelongue (65) 304 B3
Villelongue-d'Aude (11) 308 D2
Villelongue-de-la-Salanque (66) . . 310 C6
Villelongue-dels-Monts (66) . . 315 G6
Villeloup (10) 89 J4
Villemade (82) 249 J6
Villemagne (11) 289 J4
Villemagne-l'Argentière (34) . . 272 E6
Villemain (79) 178 D4
Villemandeur (45) 111 H3
Villemanoche (89) 88 C5
Villemardy (41) 108 D6
Villemaréchal (77) 87 K5
Villemareuil (77) 60 A3
Villematier (31) 269 H3
Villemaur-sur-Vanne (10) 89 H5
Villembits (65) 286 A4
Villembray (60) 37 F1
Villemer (77) 87 J5
Villemer (89) 113 F4
Villemereuil (10) 90 B6
Villemeux-sur-Eure (28) 57 G6
Villemoirieu (38) 206 E2
Villemoiron-en-Othe (10) 89 J6
Villemoisan (49) 124 D3
Villemoisson-sur-Orge (91) . . 58 E6
Villemolaque (66) 315 G6
Villemomble (93) 59 G3
Villemontais (42) 186 D5
Villemontoire (02) 39 J4
Villemorien (10) 114 D1
Villemorin (17) 178 B4
Villemort (86) 164 B4
Villemotier (01) 172 E6
Villemoustaussou (11) 290 B5
Villemoyenne (10) 90 C6
Villemur (65) 286 C5
Villemur-sur-Tarn (31) 269 H3
Villemurlin (45) 130 E1
Villemus (04) 278 A2
Villenauxe-la-Grande (10) 89 F1
Villenauxe-la-Petite (77) 88 D3
Villenave (40) 264 D1
Villenave-de-Rions (33) 229 K4
Villenave-d'Ornon (33) 229 H3
Villenave-près-Béarn (65) 285 F3
Villenave-près-Marsac (65) . . 285 H4
Villenavotte (89) 88 D5
Villeneuve (01) 188 D1
Villeneuve (04) 278 A4
Villeneuve (09) 306 C3
Villeneuve (12) 251 F2
la Villeneuve (23) 183 J6
Villeneuve (33) 211 G4

Villeneuve (63) 202 E6
la Villeneuve (71) 154 D4
la Villeneuve-au-Châtelot (10) . . 89 G1
la Villeneuve-au-Chemin (10) . . 113 J1
la Villeneuve-Bellenoye-
et-la-Maize (70) 118 C6
Villeneuve-d'Allier (43) 219 H3
Villeneuve-d'Amont (25) 156 C3
Villeneuve-d'Ascq (59) 6 E4
Villeneuve-d'Aval (39) 155 H4
Villeneuve-de-Berg (07) 239 J6
Villeneuve-de-Duras (47) 231 F3
Villeneuve-de-la-Raho (66) . . 315 H3
Villeneuve-de-Marc (38) 206 D5
Villeneuve-de-Marsan (40) 265 J2
Villeneuve-de-Rivière (31) 305 J1
Villeneuve-d'Entraunes (06) . . 260 E4
Villeneuve-d'Olmes (09) 308 A4
Villeneuve-du-Latou (09) 288 B6
Villeneuve-du-Paréage (09) . . 288 D6
la Villeneuve-en-Chevrie (78) . . 57 G1
Villeneuve-en-Montagne (71) . . 171 G1
Villeneuve-Frouville (41) 108 E5
Villeneuve-la-Comptal (11) . . 289 G5
Villeneuve-la-Comtesse (17) . . 177 K3
Villeneuve-la-Dondagre (89) . . 112 C1
Villeneuve-la-Garenne (92) . . 58 E2
Villeneuve-la-Guyard (89) 88 B4
Villeneuve-la-Lionne (51) 60 E4
Villeneuve-la-Rivière (66) 310 B6
Villeneuve-l'Archevêque (89) . . 89 F5
Villeneuve-le-Comte (77) 59 J4
Villeneuve-le-Roi (94) 59 F5
Villeneuve-Lécussan (31) 286 C6
Villeneuve-lès-Avignon (30) . . 276 B1
Villeneuve-lès-Béziers (34) 292 A4
Villeneuve-lès-Bordes (77) 88 B2
Villeneuve-lès-Bouloc (31) 269 G4
Villeneuve-lès-Cerfs (63) 185 H5
la Villeneuve-lès-Charleville (51) . . . 61 H4
Villeneuve-lès-Charnod (39) . . 173 F6
la Villeneuve-lès-Convers (21) . . 135 F2
Villeneuve-lès-Corbières (11) . . 310 A3
Villeneuve-lès-Genêts (89) 112 B6
Villeneuve-lès-Lavaur (81) 270 A6
Villeneuve-lès-Maguelone (34) . . 293 G1
Villeneuve-lès-Montréal (11) . . 289 G6
Villeneuve-les-Sablons (60) 37 G4
Villeneuve-Loubet (06) 281 F4
Villeneuve-Minervois (11) 290 C4
Villeneuve-Renneville-
Chevigny (51) 62 A2
Villeneuve-Saint-Denis (77) 59 J4
Villeneuve-Saint-Georges (94) . . 59 F5
Villeneuve-Saint-Germain (02) . . 39 J3
Villeneuve-Saint-Nicolas (28) . . 85 H5
Villeneuve-Saint-Salves (89) . . 113 G4
Villeneuve-Saint-Vistre-
et-Villevotte (51) 61 H6
Villeneuve-sous-Charigny (21) . . 134 E4
Villeneuve-sous-Dammartin (77) . . 59 H1
Villeneuve-sous-Pymont (39) . . 173 G1
la Villeneuve-sous-Thury (60) . . 39 G5
Villeneuve-sur-Allier (03) 168 D2
Villeneuve-sur-Auvers (91) 86 D2
Villeneuve-sur-Bellot (77) 60 D3
Villeneuve-sur-Cher (18) 148 E3
Villeneuve-sur-Conie (45) 109 H2
Villeneuve-sur-Fère (02) 40 A5
Villeneuve-sur-Lot (47) 248 C2
Villeneuve-sur-Verberie (60) . . 38 C4
Villeneuve-sur-Vère (81) 270 C1
Villeneuve-sur-Yonne (89) 112 D2
Villeneuve-Tolosane (31) 288 A2
Villeneuvette (34) 273 G6
Villennes-sur-Seine (78) 58 B2
Villenouvelle (31) 288 E3
Villenoy (77) 59 K2
Villentrois (36) 147 H1
Villeny (41) 129 J2
Villepail (53) 81 K3
Villeparisis (77) 59 G2
Villeparois (70) 118 B6
Villeperdrix (26) 257 J1
Villeperdue (37) 145 K1
Villeperrot (89) 88 C5
Villepinte (11) 289 J5
Villepinte (93) 59 G2
Villeporcher (41) 128 B1
Villepot (44) 103 K3
Villepreux (78) 58 B4
Villequier (76) 34 E1
Villequier-Aumont (02) 19 K5
Villequiers (18) 150 A3
Viller (57) 66 E1
Villerable (41) 108 C6
Villerbon (41) 129 F1
Villeréal (47) 232 A5
Villereau (45) 110 B2
Villereau (59) 12 E3
Villerest (42) 186 E5
Villeret (02) 19 J1
Villeret (10) 91 F2
Villereversure (01) 189 H2
Villermain (41) 109 G4
Villeromain (41) 108 D6
Villeron (95) 59 G1
Villerouge-Termenès (11) 309 J2
Villeroy (77) 59 J2
Villeroy (80) 17 F1
Villeroy (89) 88 C6

Villeroy-sur-Méholle (55) 64 E6
Villers (42) 187 G3
Villers (88) 94 A4
Villers-Agron-Aiguizy (02) 40 C5
Villers-Allerand (51) 41 F5
Villers-au-Bois (62) 10 D2
Villers-au-Flos (62) 11 G5
Villers-au-Tertre (59) 11 J2
Villers-aux-Bois (51) 61 K2
Villers-aux-Érables (80) 18 D3
Villers-aux-Nœuds (51) 40 E5
Villers-aux-Vents (55) 63 K3
Villers-Bocage (14) 32 B6
Villers-Bocage (80) 10 A6
Villers-Bouton (70) 137 K3
Villers-Bretonneux (80) 18 D2
Villers-Brûlin (62) 10 C2
Villers-Buzon (25) 137 J6
Villers-Campsart (80) 17 G2
Villers-Canivet (14) 54 A2
Villers-Carbonnel (80) 19 G2
Villers-Cernay (08) 23 G4
Villers-Châtel (62) 10 D1
Villers-Chemin-et-Mont-lès-Etrelles (70) 137 J3
Villers-Chief (25) 138 E6
Villers-Cotterêts (02) 39 G4
Villers-devant-Dun (55) 43 F2
Villers-devant-le-Thour (08) 41 F1
Villers-devant-Mouzon (08) 23 G5
Villers-Écalles (76) 15 J6
Villers-en-Argonne (51) 63 J1
Villers-en-Arthies (95) 36 D6
Villers-en-Cauchies (59) 12 C3
Villers-en-Haye (54) 65 J3
Villers-en-Ouche (61) 55 G3
Villers-en-Prayères (02) 40 B2
Villers-en-Vexin (27) 36 C4
Villers-Farlay (39) 155 K3
Villers-Faucon (80) 19 J1
Villers-Franqueux (51) 40 E3
Villers-Grélot (25) 138 C4
Villers-Guislain (59) 11 J6
Villers-Hélon (02) 39 H4
Villers-la-Chèvre (54) 26 C2
Villers-la-Combe (25) 138 E6
Villers-la-Faye (21) 154 A2
Villers-la-Montagne (54) 26 D3
Villers-la-Ville (70) 138 E2
Villers-le-Château (51) 62 C2
Villers-le-Lac (25) 157 H2
Villers-le-Rond (54) 26 A3
Villers-le-Sec (02) 20 C3
Villers-le-Sec (51) 63 H4
Villers-le-Sec (55) 64 C6
Villers-le-Sec (70) 138 B1
Villers-le-Tilleul (08) 22 D5
Villers-le-Tourneur (08) 22 B5
Villers-les-Bois (39) 155 H4
Villers-lès-Cagnicourt (62) 11 G3
Villers-lès-Guise (02) 20 D1
Villers-lès-Luxeuil (70) 118 C5
Villers-lès-Mangiennes (55) 26 A4
Villers-lès-Moivrons (54) 66 B3
Villers-lès-Nancy (54) 66 A5
Villers-les-Ormes (36) 147 K5
Villers-les-Pots (21) 155 F1
Villers-lès-Roye (80) 18 E4
Villers-l'Hôpital (62) 9 K3
Villers-Marmery (51) 41 G5
Villers-Outréaux (59) 11 K6
Villers-Pater (70) 138 B3
Villers-Patras (21) 115 F3
Villers-Plouich (59) 11 J5
Villers-Pol (59) 12 C5
Villers-Robert (39) 155 G4
Villers-Rotin (21) 155 F1
Villers-Saint-Barthélemy (60) 37 F2
Villers-Saint-Christophe (02) 19 J3
Villers-Saint-Frambourg (60) 38 C4
Villers-Saint-Genest (60) 38 E6
Villers-Saint-Martin (25) 138 A4
Villers-Saint-Paul (60) 38 A4
Villers-Saint-Sépulcre (60) 37 J3
Villers-Semeuse (08) 22 D3
Villers-Sir-Simon (62) 10 C2
Villers-Sire-Nicole (59) 13 H2
Villers-sous-Ailly (80) 9 H5
Villers-sous-Chalamont (25) 156 C4
Villers-sous-Châtillon (51) 40 D6
Villers-sous-Foucarmont (76) 16 E2
Villers-sous-Montrond (25) 156 C1
Villers-sous-Pareid (55) 44 B5
Villers-sous-Prény (54) 65 J2
Villers-sous-Saint-Leu (60) 37 K5
Villers-Stoncourt (57) 45 H6
Villers-sur-Auchy (60) 36 E1
Villers-sur-Authie (80) 9 F2
Villers-sur-Bar (08) 40 A5
Villers-sur-Bonnières (60) 17 H6
Villers-sur-Coudun (60) 38 D1
Villers-sur-Fère (02) 40 A5
Villers-sur-le-Mont (08) 22 C4
Villers-sur-le-Roule (27) 36 A5
Villers-sur-Mer (14) 33 H3
Villers-sur-Meuse (55) 64 D1
Villers-sur-Nied (57) 66 D2
Villers-sur-Port (70) 118 A6
Villers-sur-Saulnot (70) 139 F2
Villers-sur-Trie (60) 36 E3
Villers-Tournelle (80) 18 C5
Villers-Vaudey (70) 117 H6

Villers-Vermont (60) 17 F6
Villers-Vicomte (60) 18 A5
Villerserine (39) 155 J5
Villersexel (70) 138 D2
Villerupt (54) 26 E3
Villerville (14) 33 J2
Villery (10) 90 A6
Villes (01) 190 C3
Villes-sur-Auzon (84) 257 J6
Villeselve (60) 19 J4
Villeséque (46) 249 J2
Villeséque-des-Corbières (11) 310 B2
Villeséquelande (11) 289 K5
Villesiscle (11) 289 J5
Villespassans (34) 291 G4
Villespy (11) 289 J4
Villetaneuse (93) 58 E2
la Villetelle (23) 183 H6
Villetelle (34) 274 E4
Villethierry (89) 88 B5
Villeton (47) 247 H2
Villetoureix (24) 213 G2
Villetritouls (11) 309 H1
Villetrun (41) 108 D3
Villette (54) 26 B3
Villette (78) 57 J2
Villette-d'Anthon (38) 206 D1
Villette-de-Vienne (38) 206 A4
Villette-lès-Arbois (39) 155 K4
Villette-lès-Dole (39) 155 G3
Villette-sur-Ain (01) 189 G5
Villette-sur-Aube (10) 90 B2
Villettes (27) 35 H5
les Villettes (43) 221 F3
Villeurbanne (69) 206 B2
Villevallier (89) 112 D2
Villevaudé (77) 59 H3
Villevenard (51) 61 J4
Villevêque (49) 125 H2
Villeveyrac (34) 292 D4
Villevieille (30) 274 E4
Villevieux (39) 173 F1
Villevocance (07) 221 K3
Villevoques (45) 111 H2
Villexanton (41) 109 F6
Villexavier (17) 211 J3
le Villey (39) 155 G5
Villey-le-Sec (54) 65 J5
Villey-Saint-Étienne (54) 65 J4
Villey-sur-Tille (21) 136 B2
Villez-sous-Bailleul (27) 36 A6
Villez-sur-le-Neubourg (27) 35 F5
Villié-Morgon (69) 188 B3
Villiers (36) 146 E5
Villiers (86) 162 D2
Villiers-Adam (95) 58 D1
Villiers-au-Bouin (37) 126 E2
Villiers-aux-Corneilles (51) 89 H1
Villiers-Charlemagne (53) 105 F3
Villiers-Couture (17) 178 D5
Villiers-en-Bière (77) 87 G2
Villiers-en-Bois (79) 178 A3
Villiers-en-Désœuvre (27) 57 G2
Villiers-en-Lieu (52) 63 J5
Villiers-en-Morvan (21) 152 E2
Villiers-en-Plaine (79) 161 G5
Villiers-Fossard (50) 31 H3
Villiers-Herbisse (10) 62 B6
Villiers-le-Bâcle (91) 58 C5
Villiers-le-Bel (95) 58 E1
Villiers-le-Bois (10) 114 C3
Villiers-le-Duc (21) 115 H5
Villiers-le-Mahieu (78) 57 J3
Villiers-le-Morhier (28) 57 H6
Villiers-le-Pré (50) 51 K5
Villiers-le-Roux (16) 179 F4
Villiers-le-Sec (14) 32 C3
Villiers-le-Sec (52) 116 A1
Villiers-le-Sec (58) 132 E5
Villiers-le-Sec (95) 58 E1
Villiers-lès-Aprey (52) 116 C5
Villiers-les-Hauts (89) 114 B6
Villiers-Louis (89) 88 E6
Villiers-Saint-Benoît (89) 112 C5
Villiers-Saint-Denis (02) 60 D2
Villiers-Saint-Fréderic (78) 58 A4
Villiers-Saint-Georges (77) 60 E6
Villiers-Saint-Orien (28) 109 G1
Villiers-sous-Grez (77) 87 H4
Villiers-sous-Mortagne (61) 83 H2
Villiers-sous-Praslin (10) 114 C2
Villiers-sur-Chizé (79) 178 B3
Villiers-sur-Loir (41) 108 B5
Villiers-sur-Marne (94) 59 G4
Villiers-sur-Morin (77) 59 K3
Villiers-sur-Orge (91) 58 E6
Villiers-sur-Seine (77) 88 E3
Villiers-sur-Suize (52) 116 B3
Villiers-sur-Tholon (89) 112 E4
Villiers-sur-Yonne (58) 133 G4
Villiers-Vineux (89) 113 J3
Villiersfaux (41) 108 B6
Villieu-Loyes-Mollon (01) 189 G5
Villing (57) 45 K3
Villognon (16) 179 F6
Villon (89) 114 C4
Villoncourt (88) 94 E4
Villons-les-Buissons (14) 32 D4
Villorceau (45) 109 H5
Villosanges (63) 184 B6

Villotran (60) 37 G3
Villotte (88) 117 H1
Villotte-devant-Louppy (55) 64 A3
Villotte-Saint-Seine (21) 135 H4
Villotte-sur-Aire (55) 64 C3
Villotte-sur-Ource (21) 115 G3
Villouxel (88) 93 F4
Villy (08) 23 H5
Villy (89) 113 H4
Villy-Bocage (14) 32 B6
Villy-en-Auxois (21) 135 H5
Villy-en-Trodes (10) 90 D6
Villy-le-Bois (10) 90 B6
Villy-le-Bouveret (74) 191 F4
Villy-le-Maréchal (10) 90 B6
Villy-le-Moutier (21) 154 B3
Villy-le-Pelloux (74) 191 F4
Villy-lez-Falaise (14) 54 B3
Villy-sur-Yères (76) 16 D1
Vilory (70) 118 B5
Vilosnes-Haraumont (55) 43 G3
Vilsberg (57) 70 A1
Vimarcé (53) 82 A6
Vimenet (12) 253 F2
Viménil (88) 95 F3
Vimines (73) 208 B4
Vimont (14) 33 F5
Vimory (45) 111 H3
Vimoutiers (61) 54 E2
Vimpelles (77) 88 C3
Vimy (62) 11 F2
Vinantes (77) 59 J1
Vinassan (11) 291 J6
Vinax (17) 178 C4
Vinay (38) 223 H3
Vinay (51) 61 J1
Vinça (66) 314 D3
Vincelles (39) 173 F3
Vincelles (51) 40 B6
Vincelles (71) 172 D2
Vincelles (89) 113 G6
Vincelottes (89) 113 G6
Vincennes (94) 59 F4
Vincent (39) 155 G6
Vincey (88) 94 C3
Vincly (62) 5 F5
Vincy-Manœuvre (77) 39 F6
Vincy-Reuil-et-Magny (02) 21 H4
Vindecy (71) 170 B6
Vindefontaine (50) 28 E6
Vindelle (16) 196 D2
Vindey (51) 61 H5
Vindrac-Alayrac (81) 250 E6
Vinets (10) 90 C2
Vineuil (36) 147 K5
Vineuil (41) 129 F2
Vineuil-Saint-Firmin (60) 38 B5
la Vineuse (71) 171 G4
Vinezac (07) 239 G6
Vingrau (66) 310 A4
Vingt-Hanaps (61) 82 D2
Vinnemerville (76) 14 E3
Vinneuf (89) 88 C4
Vinon (18) 131 K6
Vinon-sur-Verdon (83) 278 B4
Vins-sur-Caramy (83) 298 A2
Vinsobres (26) 257 G2
le Vintrou (81) 290 D2
Vinzelles (63) 185 J6
Vinzelles (71) 188 B1
Vinzier (74) 175 J5
Vinzieux (07) 222 A2
Viocourt (88) 93 H4
Viodos-Abense-de-Bas (64) 283 H5
Violaines (62) 6 B5
Violay (42) 205 F1
Violès (84) 257 F5
Violot (52) 116 E5
Viols-en-Laval (34) 274 A4
Viols-le-Fort (34) 274 A4
Vioménil (88) 94 B4
Vion (07) 222 B4
Vion (72) 105 K5
Vions (73) 208 A1
Vionville (57) 44 D5
Viozan (32) 286 B3
Viplaix (03) 167 F5
Vira (09) 308 D1
Vira (66) 309 G5
Virac (81) 270 D1
Virandeville (50) 28 B3
Virargues (15) 218 C4
Virazeil (47) 231 F6
Viré (71) 171 K5
Viré-en-Champagne (72) 105 J3
Vire-sur-Lot (46) 249 G1
Vireaux (89) 114 A5
Virecourt (54) 94 C2
Virelade (33) 229 J4
Vireux-Molhain (08) 24 C2
Vireux-Wallerand (08) 24 C2
Virey (50) 52 B6
Virey-le-Grand (71) 154 A4
Virey-sous-Bar (10) 114 D1
Virginy (51) 42 C5
Viriat (01) 189 G1
Viricelles (42) 205 G3
Virieu (38) 207 H5
Virieu-le-Grand (01) 190 A6
Virieu-le-Petit (01) 190 B5

Virigneux (42) 205 F3
Virignin (01) 207 K2
Viriville (38) 223 F2
Virlet (63) 184 B3
Virming (57) 67 H1
Viroflay (78) 58 C4
Virollet (17) 195 F4
Vironchaux (80) 9 G2
Vironvay (27) 35 J5
Virsac (33) 211 J5
Virson (17) 177 F3
Virville (76) 14 D5
Viry (39) 173 J6
Viry (71) 170 E4
Viry (74) 190 E3
Viry-Châtillon (91) 58 E6
Viry-Noureuil (02) 19 K5
Vis-en-Artois (62) 11 G3
Visan (84) 257 F3
Viscomtat (63) 203 K1
Viscos (65) 304 B3
Visker (65) 285 H6
Vismes (80) 8 E6
Visoncourt (70) 118 C5
Vissac-Auteyrac (43) 219 K4
Vissec (30) 273 H3
Visseiche (35) 79 K6
Viterbe (81) 270 B5
Viterne (54) 65 K6
Vitot (27) 35 G5
Vitrac (15) 235 G3
Vitrac (24) 233 F2
Vitrac (63) 184 D5
Vitrac-en-Viadène (12) 236 B3
Vitrac-Saint-Vincent (16) 197 H2
Vitrac-sur-Montane (19) 216 C1
Vitrai-sous-Laigle (61) 55 J5
Vitray (03) 167 H3
Vitray-en-Beauce (28) 85 F5
Vitreux (39) 137 G6
Vitrey (54) 93 K2
Vitrey-sur-Mance (70) 117 H4
Vitrimont (54) 66 D6
Vitrolles (05) 259 F1
Vitrolles (13) 296 B2
Vitrolles-en-Lubéron (84) 277 K3
Vitry-aux-Loges (45) 110 D5
Vitry-en-Artois (62) 11 G2
Vitry-en-Charollais (71) 170 B5
Vitry-en-Montagne (52) 116 A4
Vitry-en-Perthois (51) 63 F4
Vitry-la-Ville (51) 62 E3
Vitry-Laché (58) 151 H1
Vitry-le-Croisé (10) 91 F6
Vitry-le-François (51) 63 F5
Vitry-lès-Cluny (71) 171 G4
Vitry-lès-Nogent (52) 116 D2
Vitry-sur-Loire (71) 169 J2
Vitry-sur-Orne (57) 27 G5
Vitry-sur-Seine (94) 58 E4
Vittarville (55) 43 H2
Vitteaux (21) 135 F4
Vittefleur (76) 15 F3
Vittel (88) 93 J5
Vittersbourg (57) 67 H1
Vittoncourt (57) 45 H6
Vittonville (54) 65 K1
Vitz-sur-Authie (80) 9 J3
Viuz-en-Sallaz (74) 191 H2
Viuz-la-Chiésaz (74) 208 C1
Vivaise (02) 20 C1
Vivario (2B) 321 F2
Vivans (42) 186 D2
Vivey (52) 116 A6
le Vivier (66) 309 H5
Vivier-au-Court (08) 22 D3
le Vivier-sur-Mer (35) 51 F4
Vivières (02) 39 G4
Viviers (07) 256 D1
Viviers (57) 66 C2
Viviers (89) 113 K5
Viviers-du-Lac (73) 208 B3
Viviers-le-Gras (88) 93 J6
Viviers-lès-Lavaur (81) 270 A6
Viviers-lès-Montagnes (81) 289 K1
Viviers-lès-Offroicourt (88) 93 K4
Viviers-sur-Artaut (10) 114 E1
Viviers-sur-Chiers (54) 26 D2
Viviès (09) 308 A2
Viviez (12) 235 F6
Viville (16) 196 B5
Vivonne (86) 162 E6
Vivy (49) 126 B5
Vix (21) 115 F4
Vix (85) 160 D5
Vizille (38) 224 B4
Vizos (65) 304 B3
Vocance (07) 222 A3
Vodable (63) 202 D5
Voegtlinshoffen (68) 96 B5
Voelfling-lès-Bouzonville (57) 45 K3
Voellerdingen (67) 67 K1
Voeuil-et-Giget (16) 196 E4
Vogelgrun (68) 96 E5
Voglans (73) 208 B3

Vogüé (07) 239 H6
Voharies (02) 20 E3
Void-Vacon (55) 65 F5
Voigny (10) 91 H5
Voilemont (51) 63 H1
Voillans (25) 138 D4
Voillecomte (52) 91 J2
Voimhaut (57) 45 H6
Voinémont (54) 94 A1
Voingt (63) 201 H2
Voinsles (77) 60 A5
Voipreux (51) 62 A3
Voires (25) 156 D2
Voiron (38) 223 K1
Voiscreville (27) 34 E4
Voise (28) 85 J3
Voisenon (77) 87 H4
Voisey (52) 117 H3
Voisines (52) 116 B4
Voisines (89) 88 E5
Voisins-le-Bretonneux (78) 58 B5
Voissant (38) 207 K5
Voissay (17) 177 J5
Voiteur (39) 155 H6
la Voivre (70) 118 C4
la Voivre (88) 95 H3
les Voivres (88) 118 C1
Voivres-lès-le-Mans (72) 106 C3
Volckerinckhove (59) 3 G4
Volesvres (71) 170 C4
Volgelsheim (68) 96 E4
Volgré (89) 112 D4
Volksberg (67) 69 F4
Vollore-Montagne (63) 203 J2
Vollore-Ville (63) 203 J2
Volmerange-les-Boulay (57) 27 K6
Volmerange-les-Mines (57) 27 F3
Volmunster (57) 69 G2
Volnay (21) 153 K3
Volnay (72) 107 G3
Volon (70) 137 G1
Volonne (04) 259 G5
Volpajola (2B) 319 H3
Volstroff (57) 27 H5
Volvent (26) 241 H5
Volvic (63) 202 C1
Volx (04) 278 C2
Voméecourt (88) 94 E4
Voméecourt-sur-Madon (88) 94 A3
Voncourt (52) 117 G6
Voncq (08) 42 B1
Vonges (21) 136 E5
Vongnes (01) 207 K1
Vonnas (01) 188 E2
Voray-sur-l'Ognon (70) 137 K5
Voreppe (38) 223 K2
Vorey (43) 220 C3
Vorges (02) 40 B1
Vorges-les-Pins (25) 156 A1
Vorly (18) 149 H4
Vornay (18) 149 J4
Vosbles (39) 173 G6
Vosne-Romanée (21) 154 B1
Vosnon (10) 113 J1
Vou (37) 146 B3
Vouarces (51) 89 J1
Voudenay (21) 153 F2
Voué (10) 90 B3
Vouécourt (52) 92 B5
Vougécourt (70) 117 K3
Vougeot (21) 154 B1
Vougrey (10) 114 C1
Vougy (42) 187 F3
Vougy (74) 191 J3
Vouharte (16) 196 D1
Vouhé (17) 177 G2
Vouhé (79) 161 K3
Vouhenans (70) 118 E6
Vouillé (79) 161 J6
Vouillé (86) 162 D2
Vouillé-les-Marais (85) 160 C5
Vouillers (51) 63 H5
Vouillon (36) 148 C6
Vouilly (14) 31 H1
Voujeaucourt (25) 139 F2
Voulaines-les-Templiers (21) 115 H5
Voulangis (77) 59 K3
Voulême (79) 179 H3
Voulgézac (16) 196 D5
Voulon (86) 162 E6
Voulpaix (02) 20 E2
la Voulte-sur-Rhône (07) 240 B2
Voultegon (79) 143 J4
Voulton (77) 60 D6
Voulx (77) 88 A5
Vouneuil-sous-Biard (86) 162 E3
Vouneuil-sur-Vienne (86) 163 H1
Vourey (38) 223 J1
Vourles (69) 206 A3
Voussac (03) 185 F1
Voutenay-sur-Cure (89) 133 J2
Voutezac (19) 215 H2
Vouthon (16) 197 H3
Vouthon-Bas (55) 93 F2
Vouthon-Haut (55) 93 F2
Voutré (53) 81 K6
Vouvant (85) 160 E3
Vouvray (37) 127 K4
Vouvray-sur-Huisne (72) 107 H1
Vouvray-sur-Loir (72) 107 G6
Vouxey (88) 93 H3
Vouzailles (86) 162 C1